W9-AXQ-644

Bank
Management
Second Edition

Bank Management

Second Edition

Timothy W. Koch
University of South Carolina

The Dryden Press
A Harcourt Brace Jovanovich College Publisher

Fort Worth   Philadelphia   San Diego
New York   Orlando   Austin   San Antonio
Toronto   Montreal   London   Sydney   Tokyo

Acquisitions Editor: Ann Heath
Developmental Editor: Millicent Treloar
Project Editor: Susan Jansen
Art and Design Manager: Alan Wendt
Production Manager: Barb Bahnsen
Permissions Editor: Doris Milligan
Director of Editing, Design, and Production: Jane Perkins

Text Designer: C.J. Petlick
Copy Editor: Alison Shurtz
Indexer: Leoni McVey
Compositor: Dryden Desktop/Karen Schroeder
Text Type: 8/10 Times Roman

Library of Congress Cataloging-in-Publication Data

Koch, Timothy W.
Bank management/Timothy W. Koch.—2nd ed.
   p. cm.
Includes bibliographical references and index.
ISBN 0-03-032694-X
1. Bank management. I. Title.
HG1615.K625 1991
332.1'068—dc20   91-12587

Printed in the United States of America
123-016-987654321
Copyright © 1992, 1988 by The Dryden Press.

Address orders:
The Dryden Press
Orlando, Florida 32887

Address editorial correspondence:
The Dryden Press
301 Commerce Street, Suite 3700
Fort Worth, TX 76102

The Dryden Press
Harcourt Brace Jovanovich
Cover source: © Bill Farnsworth.

To my parents, Lowell and Marilyn

The Dryden Press Series in Finance

Preface

Commercial banks operate in a rapidly changing regulatory and economic environment. The government agencies that supervise and regulate banks are gradually eliminating distinctions between commercial banks and other financial institutions, while allowing nontraditional financial firms, such as Sears, General Electric, and General Motors, to offer competitive banking services. This increased competition often coincides with severe economic difficulties caused by problems in energy, real estate, and agriculture. As competitive pressures have increased, however, so have opportunities to offer new products, compete in expanded geographic markets, and consolidate operations. Bank managers must be prepared to take advantage of these opportunities.

The purpose of this book is to apply traditional finance concepts to the management of commercial banks. It emphasizes decision making and specific problem-solving techniques. The basic format is to introduce a problem, discuss the relevant financial concepts, provide an analytical framework, and then apply the decision tools using sample data. Thus there is considerable emphasis on data analysis and interpretation. Early chapters provide background information to facilitate learning.

Upon completion of this book, the reader should understand the issues confronting bank managers today, be familiar with the fundamental financial models, and be able to examine the risk and return impacts of various credit, investment, operational, and funding decisions. The text forces the student to recognize the trade-offs involved in making financial decisions and to develop a logical thought process in arriving at reasonable conclusions.

The concept of bank asset and liability management serves as the unifying theme for the book. While asset and liability management initially focused on monitoring interest rate risk, most banks now use an asset and liability management committee to develop and implement comprehensive strategies involving credit quality, liquidity planning, capital planning, expense control, generating fee income, and tax planning. This book addresses each of these topics separately and then integrates them in a unified framework by demonstrating how decisions in each area affect other decisions by altering the overall risk and return profile of a bank.

The book is designed for use in upper division undergraduate or graduate banking courses at universities. As prerequisites, students should have completed course work in elementary accounting and money and banking and be familiar with basic interest rate concepts. The book can also be used for broad-based instructional purposes in bank training departments. For someone new to banking, the text provides an overview of the bank as a firm, describes the range of bank activities, and demonstrates how bank managers make decisions. For practitioners, it clarifies how decisions in one area affect performance and opportunities in other areas and thus provides a comprehensive view of managing the entire bank.

SPECIAL FEATURES

The second edition builds on the topics and features of the first edition. There are 28 chapters, including 19 from the first edition. The 9 new chapters are:

1. Chapter 1, which provides an overview of key banking issues through an acquirer's examination of a problem bank whose management has put the bank up for sale;

2. Chapter 5, which introduces strategic planning, budgeting, and marketing in banks;

3. Chapters 6 and 7, which provide basic background information on the pricing of securities and determinants of interest rates. These chapters describe fundamental interest rate concepts and demonstrate why interest rates vary over time and differ between securities;

4. Chapter 10, which introduces the fundamentals of options on financial futures and demonstrates how banks can use options to help manage interest rate risk;

5. Chapters 17 and 18 distinguish between taxable investment alternatives, such as money market instruments, agencies, and mortgage-backed securities, and tax-exempt alternatives, such as bank qualified municipals and loans to ESOPs;

6. Chapter 25, which introduces traditional off-balance sheet activities and demonstrates their impact on bank risk and return; and

7. Chapter 28, which documents recent consolidation in banking via mergers and acquisitions, and examines alternative procedures for valuing banking organizations.

In addition, the chapter on bank cost of funds is extended to include a discussion of strategies bank managers employ to control noninterest expense.

This edition includes numerous topics that are not covered or receive only limited attention in competing textbooks. Several are listed below.

Chapters 8 through 10 provide a comprehensive treatment of interest rate risk analysis. Included are a detailed discussion of GAP and duration gap models to measure interest rate risk, and how managers can use interest rate swaps, financial futures, and options on financial futures to manage interest rate risk.

Chapter 15 introduces the concept of liquidity risk and demonstrates how liquidity GAP models can be used to monitor and manage liquidity risk.

Chapter 17 describes the growing importance of taxable securities in bank investment portfolios and concentrates on the features of alternative securities: mortgage-backed pass throughs and collateralized mortgage obligations (CMOs). The importance of prepayments on valuation is discussed in detail.

Chapter 18 summarizes the impact of the Tax Reform Act of 1986 in altering bank municipal investments. The chapter demonstrates why banks still buy qualified municipals and how to determine and compare effective yields from such tax-advantaged investments.

Bank regulators now require cash flow estimates for a bank to justify extending credit to businesses and individuals. Chapter 21 develops a framework for analyzing a commercial firm's historical cash flow from operations and projecting debt service capabilities by converting traditional financial statements to a cash basis. Chapter 22 extends the analysis to studying relevant cash flows for consumer loans.

Each chapter concludes with a series of discussion questions and problems that apply the decision models introduced in the chapter to sample data. In addition, issues raised in Chapter 1 for a problem bank are reviewed and clarified at the end of selected chapters. Six comprehensive cases that include a description of the problem, financial information, and specific questions and assignments appear at the end of the text. Six additional cases appear in the *Instructor's Manual*. The cases cover bank performance analysis, interest rate risk analysis, liquidity planning, investment strategies and tax planning, and credit analysis.

ORGANIZATION OF THE BOOK

The book is divided into six parts. Each part consists of four to five chapters covering related issues and responsibilities. The chapters begin with a brief overview of the chapter content and an example of a current banking issue or problem.

Part One provides an overview of commercial bank management. Chapter 1 introduces key issues facing bank managers in the current environment by describing the difficulties faced by a problem bank. Later chapters provide greater detail on those issues. Chapter 2 covers the organizational structure of commercial banks and savings and loan associations, the regulatory and legislative environment, and the operational features of bank holding companies. Chapter 3 describes four fundamental forces of change—regulation, financial innovation, securitization, and globalization—that affect competitive trends between banks and nonbank competitors such as Sears and Merrill Lynch. Basic bank financial statements are introduced in Chapter 4, along with a procedure for analyzing the trade-off between profitability and risk in banking. Chapter 5 introduces strategic planning, budgeting, and marketing efforts at banks.

Part Two introduces asset and liability management strategies and decision models for managing interest rate risk. Chapters 6 and 7 provide basic background information on interest rates and security pricing. Decision models based on funding GAP and duration gap analysis are developed and applied in Chapter 8. Chapters 9 and 10 then demonstrate how banks can use financial futures and options on futures to hedge interest rate risk.

Part Three focuses on capital, cash assets, and bank liabilities. Chapters 11 and 12 describe the features of bank liabilities and regulatory capital requirements. A procedure for estimating a bank's weighted marginal cost of funds and a description of internal transfer pricing schemes are introduced in Chapter 13. In each case the features are related to asset allocation decisions and a bank's overall risk profile. The last part of Chapter 13 examines approaches to managing noninterest expense. Chapters 14 and 15 develop planning models for estimating and meeting legal reserve requirements, temporary cash deficiencies, and longer-term liquidity needs.

Part Four documents the role of investment securities in asset and liability management decisions. Chapter 16 introduces the role of securities and investment policy guidelines. Chapters 17 and 18 describe specific features of various taxable and tax-sheltered investments, with special emphasis on prepayment risk and the impact of tax planning. Various investment strategies related to determining the optimal size of a bank's tax-exempt portfolio, swapping securities, and selling bonds with put options are described in Chapter 19.

Part Five covers credit analysis principles and applications. Separate chapters apply the principles to working capital loans, term commercial loans, and consumer loans. Considerable emphasis is placed on interpreting financial statements and generating cash flow estimates to determine repayment prospects from financial data. Related chapters cover problem loans and a framework for analyzing customer account profitability.

Part Six introduces four special topics: off-balance sheet activities, international banking, trust banking, and mergers and acquisitions. Off-balance sheet activities are an attractive source of revenues given capital constraints. International banking is especially important because financial institutions throughout the world are entering into joint ventures and conducting increased business outside domestic boundaries. Trust banking documents recent efforts to extend personal banking services to a broader range of customers under relationship banking strategies. Trust services are combined with brokerage and personal financial services to help banks better compete with other institutions. Finally, mergers and acquisitions are an integral part of the industry's consolidation. The subsequent discussion summarizes the issues involved in analyzing the costs and benefits of specific transactions.

SUPPLEMENTARY MATERIALS

An *Instructor's Manual and Test Bank* and Lotus 1-2-3® template with applications are available from The Dryden Press to assist those who use the book.

Instructor's Manual and Test Bank

A comprehensive *Instructor's Manual and Test Bank* accompanies the text. It provides teaching objectives and outlines of the chapter material, answers to end-of-chapter questions and problems, detailed solutions to all cases, and test questions. To avoid repetition, the manual includes additional cases that can be substituted for those in the text.

Lotus 1-2-3® Template

A Lotus 1-2-3® template is available for those who want to use microcomputers to perform and extend the data analysis presented in the text. The template provides the basic decision models and data for key problems and cases in the text. With the template, instructors and/or students can use the models and financial data to conduct "what if" balance sheet and income statement projections regarding bank performance or specific credit requests. This sensitivity analysis allows the user to quickly examine a range of outcomes rather than simple static "solutions." The template also covers topics including duration analysis, risk-based capital, and customer profitability analysis.

ACKNOWLEDGMENTS

The first edition was written when I taught at Texas Tech University and served as director of the Texas Tech School of Banking. I could not have written it without the opportunities provided by both responsibilities. As director of the Banking School, I had regular contact with bankers throughout the Southwest who introduced me to various bank decision models and typical data analysis. Banking and finance students at Texas Tech then critiqued my interpretations in the classroom. Both contributions were invaluable. This revision has benefited from continued discussions with banking professionals throughout the Carolinas and students at the University of South Carolina.

I especially want to thank those bankers and other individuals who assisted in the project: Frank Adams, Susan Bies, Richard Brock, Jimmy Campbell, Steve Christenson, Suzette Deno, Gayle Earls, Charles Funk, Grant Henderson, Raleigh Hortenstine III, Ira Kawaller, Nancy McDonnell, Scott Obenshain, Don Powell, William Rudolph, George Sell, Jennifer Thomas, and Kirk Thomas. In addition to providing case materials and related documentation, they patiently answered my numerous questions. Several academic friends—Linda Allen, Charles Haley, Scott Hein, Gordon Karels, Nelson Lacey, Scott MacDonald, James McNulty, Sandra Planisek, J.T. Rose, Robert Schweitzer, Richard Stolz, and Ernie Swift—also offered suggestions on parts of the manuscript. Sandra Planisek wrote most of the end-of-chapter questions. Scott MacDonald is responsible for programming the Lotus 1-2-3® template.

I appreciate the guidance and assistance of Ann Heath, finance editor for The Dryden Press, Susan Jansen, project editor, and Alan Wendt, art manager. It was a pleasure to work with them and the entire Dryden staff in seeing this project through.

Finally, I want to thank my family for their constant support during the writing process. I dedicate this book to my parents, Lowell and Marilyn Koch, whose support and encouragement have always been evident and appreciated.

Timothy W. Koch
Columbia, South Carolina
August 1991

About the Author

Timothy W. Koch is Professor of Finance and holds the South Carolina Bankers Association Chair of Banking at the University of South Carolina. He received a B.A. degree in mathematics from Wartburg College and Ph.D. in economics from Purdue University. He has also taught at Baylor University and Texas Tech University and served as Director of the Texas Tech School of Banking. In addition to college teaching, Professor Koch teaches at several banking schools throughout the United States including the Stonier Graduate School, the Graduate School of Banking of the South, the National and Graduate Schools of Bank Investments and Financial Management, and the South Carolina Bankers School.

Professor Koch's professional research and writing focuses on bank management, financial futures, fixed-income securities, and public finance, and he has published extensively in a wide range of academic and professional journals. He also serves as a contributing editor to the *Bank Asset/Liability Management Report* and writes curriculum materials for the American Bankers Association's *General Banking* program offered at state-sponsored banking schools.

Contents

Chapter 12

Managing Capital Risk   *385*

Chapter 13

Measuring the Cost of Funds and Controlling Noninterest Expense   *419*

Chapter 14

Why Hold Cash Assets?   *451*

Cases

Chapter 1

Issues in Bank Management

"Banks must be able and willing to change—or they will disappear."

The financial management of commercial banks involves selecting the portfolio and mix of products and services offered to balance expected returns with assumed risk, within the objective of maximizing shareholder value. The greater the assumed risk is, the greater the expected return will be.

During the past decade, the competitive position of banks has deteriorated. Traditionally, they were the only firms to offer checking accounts and they dominated the market for commercial and consumer loans. Today, less regulated nonbank firms offer competing products and services that take profitable business away from banks. Rather than borrow from banks, corporations issue debt directly to investors. Individuals purchase money market funds that offer the same transactions features and pay higher yields. The impact has been extraordinary. The following data on the assets of financial institutions demonstrate that commercial banks' share of U.S. financial assets dropped from over 34 percent in 1960 to just 26 percent in 1990. Other depository institutions, including savings banks and credit unions, experienced a similar decline. Money market mutual funds, pension and retirement funds, and mortgage pools were the big gainers.

	1960	1990
Commercial Banks	34.2%	26.1%
Insurance Companies	21.8	14.5
Other Depository Institutions	17.0	12.9
Pension and Retirement Funds	8.8	15.9
Mutual and Money Market Funds	2.6	8.4
Government Sponsored Agencies and Mortgage Pools	1.7	10.8
Other	13.9	11.4
	100.0%	100.0%

The recent problems of banks reflect a combination of regulatory constraints, perverse incentives of deposit insurance, and mismanagement of the risk and return trade-off. Banks are restricted in the types of business they can enter. For example, they cannot sell a broad range of insurance products or offer investment banking services, such as brokerage and securities underwriting. They are limited in the types of loans they can make and closely monitored in reporting problem loans. One fundamental advantage they have had is federal deposit insurance in which individual accounts are insured up to $100,000. If a bank fails, the government pays off insured depositors up to this amount so deposit holders are not at risk. Deposit insurance allows banks to borrow at low, subsidized rates and speculate by buying risky assets. If the assets are uncollectible through default, the government and not the bank's managers lose. With regulatory asset restrictions, many banks have speculated on real estate—and lost large amounts. Not surprisingly, earnings have suffered and many banks are aggressively seeking merger partners.

C‌hapter 1 outlines the types of problems that many bank managers face in the current banking environment. It describes a situation in which a problem bank is actively searching for a merger partner. The objective is to demonstrate the types of decisions that managers make and the general interrelationship between investment, lending, funding, and operations activities. After reading the entire text, the student should be able to reread this chapter and make specific policy recommendations to improve the bank's risk and return profile.

SMQ INVESTMENTS

As the elevator reached the fourth floor executive offices, C. William Hampton III imagined what he would discover during the next few days. His employer, SMQ Investments, was considering the purchase of First Financial Bank, the fifth largest depository institution in Florida and one known to be suffering serious problems. C.W. had come to Jacksonville, First Financial's headquarters, to conduct a preliminary review of the firm's condition. If completed, this would be SMQ's third acquisition of a financial institution. During the previous two years, SMQ had purchased a large commercial bank and a medium-sized savings and loan in Atlanta. C.W. thought it somewhat peculiar that senior management was suddenly interested in buying banks after years of meticulously avoiding anything that could not produce a 20 percent annualized rate of return on investment. Perhaps the changing banking environment offered better opportunities than other alternatives.

Ralph Treadway, First Financial's president, met C.W. at the elevator and escorted him to the boardroom where the bank's Board of Directors had gathered. After brief introductions, Mr. Treadway reminded the Board that they had invited SMQ to analyze the bank's recent performance and financial condition in order to determine whether it might like to submit a bid. He explained that all officers and directors were to provide SMQ with whatever information was requested and to answer all questions. With that, he opened the floor for discussion.

C.W. was startled when everyone immediately turned to him. They must be eager to sell, he mused, so he quickly went on the offensive. SMQ was a highly capitalized, privately held investment company that specialized in turnaround situations. The firm typically purchased problem companies at distressed prices, brought in new management, restructured by cutting costs and refocusing product lines, and eventually sold its interest once profitability was restored. While it had only a limited track history in acquiring banks, SMQ thought that First Financial represented a profitable turnaround opportunity. The group had examined the bank's balance sheet and income statement data, but frankly had little confidence in aggregate figures that could easily hide problems. C.W. said he planned to visit with each of the directors and senior officers about the major issues currently facing the bank, and to return later with a team of analysts that would review the bank's files. With that statement, he requested copies of First Financial's strategic plan and summaries of the bank's credit policy, investment policy, and general operating policy. He planned to keep a record of the perceived problems that each individual identified, and later to compare the list with the conclusions from SMQ's own detailed analysis of internal records.

DISCUSSIONS WITH BANK OFFICERS

In order to get a broad overview of the bank's situation, C.W. sat down first with Ralph Treadway. As president, Treadway was the chief operating officer who managed the bank's day-to-day activities. The senior loan officer, investment officer, funds management officer, and the bank's comptroller all reported directly to him. This group also served as the asset and liability management committee that met each week to review the bank's performance and develop strategies. Treadway's father, who was the largest stockholder in First Financial, served as Chairman of the Board of Directors as well as chief executive officer (CEO), but had no day-to-day responsibilities.

Treadway immediately offered his views of the bank's problems. Foremost was bad real estate loans. First Financial had a long history of lending to real estate developers, but in recent years had extended too much credit to two firms that failed. Changes in the tax laws that made real estate less attractive to investors and the national recession were largely to blame for the failures. Defaults on commercial loans had forced the bank to report losses for the past two years, and the bank wasn't likely to report positive net income for at least two more years. Because of the losses, First Financial's capital had fallen below the minimum permitted by bank regulators, and many depositors had withdrawn their funds. First Financial was subsequently borrowing a significant amount from the Federal Reserve Bank. The Fed was in turn strongly encouraging the bank to find a buyer, such as SMQ.

The Board of Directors had fired the loan officer who handled the major real estate accounts. Treadway felt that the current management team was not responsible for past problems and was capable of turning the bank around. Unfortunately, the losses had prevented First Financial from pursuing several new lines of business, such as writing new types of insurance, securities underwriting, and developing a mergers and acquisitions group. Regulators had recently approved a variety of new services for banks, and Treadway felt that these ventures would eventually allow the bank to diversify its risk.

C.W. asked whether the bank had violated any regulatory guidelines or was under any directives that restricted its operations. Treadway admitted that the regulators had found several violations at the most recent exam, but said the bank was now in compliance with all regulations. Each line officer would provide specific details. C.W. also asked about the bank's strategic plan and policy statements. He was surprised that a bank with almost $1 billion in assets could summarize its policies and objectives in four brief pages. Treadway brushed aside the question, stating that the Board believed in action and not formal documents. The strategic plan and policy statement were only prepared because the regulators demanded it.

Credit Issues

C.W. introduced himself to Mark Logue, the bank's senior loan officer who smiled because he had been expecting Hampton. Logue briefly mentioned that he had been hired six months before to clean up the bank's loan portfolio. He could be especially candid because his reputation and job security were not on the line. Logue needed no prompting to disclose his findings.

First Financial had $600 million in loans on its books; $500 million was to commercial borrowers—mostly in real estate, and $100 million was to individuals. While the bank had few problems with individuals not paying, the real estate loans were a mess. Roughly 15 percent of the commercial loans were nonperforming, which meant that these borrowers were not making timely interest and principal payments. In virtually all of these cases, there was no chance that the bank would ever receive any interest. The bank would be fortunate to collect even 50 cents on each dollar of principal. The problems arose largely because the bank had concentrated its portfolio in real estate holdings along the Atlantic Ocean controlled by two developers, both of whom were currently in bankruptcy. The officer who originally handled the accounts had continued to lend funds even after the firms' problems were known because each new loan generated fees. The parties involved also believed that the real estate market would eventually improve so that the properties could be sold and everyone repaid. According to current appraisals, however, the property was valued at less than two-thirds of what First Financial held in outstanding loans.

When asked about the bank's loan policy, Logue pulled out a folder that contained a list of problem loans. The bank had no effective loan policy so that junior officers had no formal guidelines documenting acceptable loan criteria or credit approval procedures. The senior loan officer signed off on all loans and the Board of Directors rubber-stamped his decisions. There was no discussion of loan standards, types of loans to be avoided, or credit approval criteria, and thus no mention of potential risks. All commercial loans were priced on a floating rate basis at a mark-up over some index, and the senior officer determined the size of the mark-up. The bank had a reputation for price cutting, and most commercial loans were priced at less than 1.5 percent above the respective index. The policy statement made no mention of loan maturity.

The bank's loan review policy was also weak. Logue pointed out several sample loans from the file that were renewed even though the borrower had not paid all the interest previously owed or any principal. The loans were reviewed only by the senior loan officer and the rate charged was occasionally lowered. Other loans were to tenants of the two developers' shopping malls. The bank had obtained little historical financial information on the tenants and the files contained virtually no documentation other than the loan agreement. Thus the bank's ability to collect on underlying collateral was questionable.

First Financial was also facing several serious regulatory and legal problems. Bank regulators limit how much a bank can lend to any single borrower. The purpose is to force management to diversify and reduce the risk of failure in case of loan defaults. In violation of regulatory policy, the bank had loaned each of the two problem developers far more than the allowed amounts. The officer in charge had incorrectly argued that there were no violations because the loans were to separate subsidiaries of the parent firms and thus not subject to the limitation.

On the consumer side, regulators had determined that the bank was ignoring its commitment under the Community Reinvestment Act (CRA). This Act stipulated that the bank should fund a certain amount of loans to borrowers within its primary trade area, determined primarily by where it obtained its deposits. The bank had problems because most of its individual loans were to people outside Jacksonville, while most of its depositors lived in the Jacksonville area. The bank had similarly failed to keep and provide information on the income level, racial make-up, and gender of its mortgage loan applicants in violation of federal regulations.

In addition, two borrowers had filed legal suits against First Financial claiming that the bank had inappropriately forced them out of business when it tried to collect on its loans. In one case, the bank had taken possession of collateral that it later sold to offset its losses on an unpaid loan. In the other, the bank had put two of its officers on the Board of a failing firm. The suit charged that the officers dictated operating policy to the firm's Board and these policies subsequently drove the firm into bankruptcy. The bank's liability in the suits was a combined $45 million, plus the bank was not collecting any interest or principal on the loans.

C.W. grimaced at the description, but was not surprised. Many banks had difficulty understanding the broad range of federal and state regulations and did not employ a knowledgeable compliance officer who could adequately monitor performance. Lender liability suits had also become increasingly common since the late 1980s as borrowers looked for any means to share their losses with lenders. In many instances the courts sided with borrowers and banks had been forced to pay significant damages. Most importantly, C.W. had little confidence that many of the bank's loans would meet SMQ's rigorous credit standards for quality.

Investments and Funding Issues

Joan Nystrom and Michael Peek headed up the bank's investments and funds management areas, respectively. Both looked somewhat stressed when C.W. stopped by, but they seemed eager to hear about SMQ's plans for the bank if acquired. The tone of their questions and comments left a clear impression that a sale was inevitable.

Michael described his last few month's activity as "searching for liquidity." Because of its commercial lending focus, First Financial had a small consumer deposit base. The bank had always borrowed large amounts in the money market. This created serious problems, however, in the current environment. As the bank's problems were publicized by the state and national press, foreign and U.S. corporate depositors increasingly refused to renew their deposits when they matured. Individuals similarly moved their balances to other institutions even though First Financial aggressively advertised that customer deposits were federally insured. Initially Michael had been able to replace the lost deposits with new funds obtained through brokers. More recently, he was buying funds by paying up to one percent more than the prevailing market rate on large certificates of deposit. During the past three months the bank had been forced to borrow emergency funds from the Federal Reserve Bank.

C.W. expressed his surprise at the deposit composition because he knew that First Financial operated several branches throughout northern Florida. Peek replied that while the branches did exist, they generated little business. The bank did not advertise any consumer products, so customers largely ignored the bank's services and branch locations. Other institutions operated far more aggressive branches in similar locales and seemed to cater to individuals. First Financial's branches were overstaffed and underutilized.

From an earnings viewpoint, the investment portfolio was supplying the bank with most of its revenues. The investment portfolio consisted of Treasury bills and bonds, bonds issued by federal housing agencies, collateralized mortgage obligations (CMOs), and municipal bonds. Municipal bonds represented a particular sore spot because they paid tax-exempt interest, which the bank did not need because it had paid no taxes during the past two years of losses. While taxable bond interest would improve the bank's revenue stream, First Financial could not sell its holdings of municipals without taking large capital losses that would wipe out the bank's remaining capital. In addition, the bank was unable to trade securities when profitable opportunities arose because many of the securities were pledged as collateral against bank borrowing. Most of the bank's Treasury securities, for example, were pledged against the bank's repo borrowings and loans from the Federal Reserve Bank. This meant that they could not be sold from the portfolio unless another security was substituted and thus could not be used for liquidity if depositors withdrew funds.

From a longer term perspective, Nystrom was concerned about investment directives she was receiving from the Board of Directors. Several members had strongly pushed her to buy some of the new types of mortgage-backed securities, such as CMOs. Their rationale was that CMOs paid higher rates than Treasury securities and the bank needed all the interest income it could get. She and the Board were not familiar with the riskiness of CMOs or other hybrid securities that vendors were always trying to sell the bank. In addition, the Board had recommended that she buy long-term securities because they paid the highest rates. Joan knew that these long-term bonds were riskier than short-term bonds. If interest rates were to increase, the bank would be locked in to below-market yields. But this was consistent with the bank's recent history. Most of the bank's interest-paying liabilities had short maturities, while its earning assets had longer maturities, on average. When interest rates fell the bank's profits improved because interest expense fell more than interest income. When interest rates rose, however, profits declined because interest expense increased more than interest income. In short, the bank had problems trying to take advantage of general interest rate changes and would lose again if interest rates rose.

C.W. laughed to himself. One thing First Financial did not do well was manage risk. SMQ would have little trouble improving on that. The difficulty was in determining what value could be realized from the bank's existing assets, core deposit base, and overall franchise.

Operations Issues

First Financial's operations department had been largely ignored until four years ago. At that time, the bank had purchased a smaller bank in St. Augustine and the acquisition had caused nothing but problems. Each bank had its own computer system. After the acquisition, a team from First Financial tried to convert the other bank's item processing to First Financial's system. Unfortunately, when they first attempted to merge the systems they lost a substantial portion of customer deposit information. They didn't even have a written record of customer balances, but had to rely on depositors for account information. In addition to the deposit uncertainty, customers were unhappy with the communications problems, statement errors, and technological mix-ups that necessarily followed. Because of its other problems, management had not focused enough on these operational difficulties and the bank still suffered from a public perception that the Keystone Cops were running the show.

When C.W. visited the comptroller and operations personnel, he quickly learned that employee morale was low. Management had first responded to its losses in the past two years by laying off operations staffers, who were among the lowest-paid employees. The remaining personnel felt that they were still putting out fires and were totally unappreciated. They also knew that any sale of the bank likely meant that many would lose their jobs.

DISCUSSIONS WITH THE BOARD OF DIRECTORS

Hampton was curious about the directors' role in the bank's problems over the past years. In a well-run bank the directors are typically stockholders who recognize that they represent not only stockholders but also bank customers, employees, and the community in general. They are expected to provide input to management based on their own business experience and judgment. Their focus should be on establishing broad-based bank policy and long-range planning. They should not waste time on day-to-day banking activity or small details. The best directors are often independent business people who are not cronies of the bank's CEO or president.

The following day C.W. met with the eight Board members who were not bank employees. As they gathered in the meeting room, Hampton noted that they were all men and appeared to be well over 50 years old. He asked everyone to introduce himself and summarize his business experience. All eight represented families that were original investors in the bank and each had served on the Board for at least four years. They were senior officers in their own businesses, and conducted their own corporate and personal banking business with First Financial. C.W. proceeded to ask questions regarding how Board meetings were conducted, what information Board members were provided, and what their primary responsibilities were.

Board Meetings

The Board met monthly over lunch to share information on developments in Jacksonville and listen to reports on the bank's performance from bank officers. They were deluged with reports and financial information that they received after lunch, just prior to the official meeting. They subsequently had little time to analyze the reports or formulate questions. The normal procedure was for an officer to discuss activity in his or her area, covering loans, investments and deposit funding, then Treadway would summarize trends and implications. While reference was made to the written reports, Treadway paid detailed attention only to the bank's income statement. The Board members' primary responsibility was to contact prospective customers in order to bring new business to the bank. Fully one-half of every meeting was spent by the directors describing what new business contacts were made. They were rarely asked to vote on policy issues, but rather rubber-stamped subcommittee reports or Treadway's recommendations without much discussion. At no time did they get directly involved in developing a long-range strategic plan for the bank.

Board Membership

The Board members had known each other for many years and appeared to be personal friends. Four members were from prominent families in Florida who had extensive business contacts throughout Florida and the southeast. There was a general unwillingness to criticize each other and the bank because they conducted their own business with each other. Two members, in fact, had a partnership interest with Treadway in several real estate ventures. The Board's composition clearly discouraged confrontation and open debate because members did not want to antagonize one another and thereby damage their own businesses or social standing.

Organization of the Board

First Financial's Board was structured around its executive, loan, audit, and compensation committees. The executive committee, comprised of Ralph Treadway, his father, and three outside Board members controlled by Treadway, served as a senior policy board. This committee met informally between Board meetings, but never made any specific policy recommendations. There was some discussion that Ralph Treadway used the committee to convince his father to approve certain policies that might be questioned in open Board meetings.

The loan committee met monthly to review loans made by bank officers and thereby monitor loan quality. The bank's senior credit officer chaired the committee, which was comprised of four outside directors representing different businesses around Jacksonville. One of the committee members continually borrowed large amounts from the bank, but always made his loan payments on time. The committee largely served to identify sources of new borrowers. It rarely addressed how the terms of each loan were set or how accept or reject decisions were made, but did formally approve all new loans over $100,000 at the end of each meeting.

First Financial's audit committee was chaired by its comptroller, a CPA. This committee periodically verified that the bank's records were accurate, that all loan documentation was in place, and that loan quality was acceptable. It also coordinated its work with the annual audit by the bank's outside auditor. Unfortunately, the comptroller had little influence with Treadway. When the internal auditor identified potential problems or discrepancies, the comptroller reported them to Treadway, but the report was simply filed and never acted upon.

The bank's compensation committee handled personnel policy. In general, the committee evaluated total personnel costs including salaries, fringe benefits, and training expenses. Committee members made recommendations regarding issues ranging from the choice of medical insurance to whether employees should be offered stock options, company cars, or country club memberships. The intent was to establish and implement a consistent compensation program that allowed the bank to compete for and retain quality employees. During the past two years, however, the focus had been on cutting staff and reducing payroll expense. With the recent losses, bank officers had lost many of their perks and salaries were essentially frozen.

Advent of Recent Problems

Outside Board members first became fully aware of First Financial's problems after the national bank examiners conducted an unannounced examination of the bank 30 months ago. At that time, the bank was required to increase its provisions for loan losses by 300 percent and restate earnings for the prior year. The regulators also determined that First Financial had violated numerous regulatory requirements, and the Board was asked to sign a cease and desist order admitting error and agreeing to correct all inappropriate activity. The bank increased its loan loss provisions the following year when loan quality continued to deteriorate.

With the losses, First Financial's qualifying capital fell below the minimum allowed by regulators. Each Board member was subsequently asked to buy more bank stock. Albeit somewhat late, the Board initiated a close review of the bank's performance, conducted by an independent consulting group. They were shocked at the depth of the bank's problems and claimed not to know how the bank had gotten in trouble. They were also confused and annoyed at their potential personal liability resulting from the legal suits filed by the two bankrupt credit customers. With the continued deterioration in First Financial's condition, a majority of the Board was committed to finding a buyer, preferably a local one. None of the directors blamed Treadway for the bank's conditions, at least not publicly.

ASSESSMENT OF PROBLEMS AND OPPORTUNITIES

As he boarded the flight home, C.W. contemplated the nature of his report to SMQ's acquisition group. He felt that while First Financial faced serious near-term problems, its long-term potential was excellent. The world of banking was rapidly changing. The best way for SMQ to make money was to buy the right assets at the right price in the right situation. Depending on the results of a careful review of the bank's financial condition, C.W. was going to recommend that SMQ pursue the acquisition. He identified the following factors that needed to be included in the final analysis.

The General Banking Environment

Competition. Many firms offer the same financial products and services. Commercial banks must compete with savings and loans, credit unions, finance companies, money market mutual funds, insurance companies, and investment banks for business. Distinctions between firms are quickly fading as regulation changes to allow all firms to offer similar products anywhere in the United States. Many banking organizations are trying to enter the Florida market because of its population base, international importance, and business potential. Other bidders are no doubt also interested in First Financial.

Regulation. Federal and state bank regulation constantly changes to address changes in the banking environment. Three trends are evident:

1. Regulators have removed most restrictions on what interest rates banks can charge on loans and pay on customer deposits.
2. Most U.S. banks can purchase banks, savings and loans, and other related firms located outside their home state; foreign banks can also buy U.S. financial institutions. National interstate branching is likely in the near future.
3. Regulators still limit the range of products and services banks can offer, but the list of new products and services is expanding rapidly. Through bank subsidiaries, First Financial could eventually offer new insurance, credit card, and real estate products. It could also underwrite securities, offer discount brokerage services, operate a travel agency, and form a mergers and acquisitions group.

International Trends. Financial markets and institutions are becoming increasingly international in scope. Geographic boundaries no longer constrain market activity as U.S. firms compete directly with foreign firms as well as other domestic firms. U.S. banks make loans to and accept deposits from foreign as well as U.S.

customers. Foreign banks compete directly with U.S. banks for customers. Many firms are entering into partnerships with foreign firms to gain an entry to foreign markets.

Problems with First Financial's Current Financial Condition

First Financial's management clearly ignored fundamental risk versus return considerations. In general, the bank suffered because it did no planning and did not attempt to maximize shareholder value. Senior management and the Board of Directors had no feel for how the bank was performing and whether it was earning an acceptable return for the risks it was taking. An abbreviated list of problems would include the regulatory violations, real estate losses and nonperforming loans, low existing capital with limited sources of additional capital, liquidity problems caused by lost consumer deposits and Treasury securities that could not be sold because they were pledged as collateral, a large debt owed to the Federal Reserve Bank, and the lack of any interest rate risk management strategy. The Board of Directors appeared to be controlled by Ralph Treadway and reeked of cronyism. Potential losses from the lender liability suits were also substantial. The bank had assumed too much risk, as indicated below.

Credit Risk Assessment

1. No formal loan policy
2. Violations of limits on loan amount to a single borrower and Community Reinvestment Act requirements
3. Concentration of loans in real estate to two borrowers
4. Poor loan documentation
5. Focus on loan fees rather than creditworthiness
6. No formal loan pricing procedure
7. No effective loan review

Liquidity Risk Assessment

1. Small base of stable consumer deposits
2. Heavy reliance on borrowing from the Federal Reserve Bank; the likely near-term substitute is expensive borrowed funds in the money market
3. Municipal bonds are not liquid because they earn below market rates
4. Most Treasury securities cannot be sold because they are used as collateral against bank borrowing
5. Limited bank capital makes it expensive to compete for borrowed funds
6. Marketability of CMOs is unknown

Interest Rate Risk Assessment

1. Assets are generally long-term and thus repriced infrequently

2. Liabilities are generally short-term and thus repriced more frequently
3. Profits will vary sharply with increases or decreases in interest rates
4. Market value of bank stock will vary sharply as interest rates and profits vary
5. Price volatility and income stream of CMOs is not known

Operational Risk Assessment

1. Noninterest expense is uncontrolled
2. Inefficient use of branches
3. Insufficient number of technically qualified personnel
4. Low personnel morale

Capital Risk Assessment

1. Existing capital is deficient—it does not meet the regulatory minimums
2. Loan quality is unknown, and potential losses may reduce capital still more

Potential Opportunities

The acquisition of First Financial would allow SMQ to enter the Florida market quickly with a major presence. Jacksonville is an attractive home base because it is a port city and thus exhibits significant growth opportunities for international business. SMQ's Atlanta banks have developed several attractive consumer products and services that could be readily marketed in Jacksonville. SMQ needs to accumulate additional loan and deposit volume to lower unit operating costs across its existing banks.

SMQ's management also recognizes that federal regulators will continue to expand the range of products and services banks can offer. The plan is to eventually focus on noncredit services that offer much greater returns relative to the potential risk. Florida is an attractive market because of its large retirement population with above-average wealth and subsequent need for money management services.

SUMMARY

In recent years changes in regulation have allowed banks to compete in many different markets and to offer many new products and services. The financial management of banks involves selecting the portfolio and mix of products and services to balance expected returns with the assumed risks, within the objective of maximizing shareholder value. There is a fundamental trade-off between risk and return.

C.W. Hampton's evaluation of First Financial Bank reveals many of the issues that managers face, even when a bank is in strong financial condition. Managers must determine how to earn a reasonable return while they control the bank's credit, liquidity, capital, operations, and interest rate risk within acceptable targets. First Financial's performance demonstrates many of the areas in which critical decisions are made, and the importance of understanding economic trends, competitive conditions, and changes in regulation. The remainder of this book addresses these issues.

Questions

1. As C.W. prepares for his trip to Florida he reviews a typical bank balance sheet. What types of assets does a bank own and what types of liabilities fund them?

2. SMQ's policy has been to invest in projects yielding at least a 20 percent return on investment. What factors has C.W. been sent to investigate? How might these cause SMQ to revise the 20 percent rule?

3. What are some of the techniques used by investment companies such as SMQ to turn around problem firms? What would appear to work here?

4. Draw an organizational chart for this bank and name the key people. What are the functions of each of the major divisions? What are the main problems of each division?

5. Who serves on First Financial's asset and liability management committee and what is its function?

6. Explain how a slump in the real estate market drove First Financial to seek a buyer.

7. Explain how ignoring the principle of diversification exacerbated First Financial's problems.

8. What function should a loan policy statement serve? What topics should it discuss?

9. What argument could you, as a citizen, make in favor of the Community Reinvestment Act?

10. Banks are financial intermediaries that bring together savers and borrowers. One view of this function is that banks are information managers. This bank seems to have neglected to collect some critical information. What are some of these variables and why should the bank have collected each? In other words, who is interested in each type of information and what is the penalty for not collecting it?

11. Explain how unfavorable publicity about a bank can lead to liquidity problems.

12. When consumer deposits are inadequate to meet a bank's liquidity needs, what alternative sources of liquidity are available?

13. In corporate finance there is an argument that to create value a corporation must be able to perform a function that a stockholder cannot perform for himself. How does this relate to First Financial? Whose investment portfolio is the primary profit generator for the bank?

14. What is the relation between the bank's investment management and its funding management?

15. What are the duties of a well-run bank's board of directors? If SMQ bought First Financial, would it be able to change the structure and members of the board of directors? How might SMQ want to change it to prevent a repeat of current problems?

16. Give one reason for and one reason against a bank making loans to the members of its Board of Directors?

17. C.W. is sitting on the plane considering First Financial. He realizes that the bank has many problems, some of which can be resolved quickly while some will take longer. Make a list of First Financial's top three problems and indicate how quickly they can be resolved.

18. Some problems can be conquered more cheaply than others. Rate First Financial's problems by the expense involved in their resolution.

19. A basic premise of finance is that a corporation should be run for the benefit of its stockholders. Banks are accountable to their stockholders, but they are also accountable to other constituencies. Why are banks unique in having many masters, and who are some of these other groups?

20. Assume that SMQ acquires First Financial. Discuss the costs and benefits of keeping Ralph Treadway on the senior management team. Discuss the costs and benefits of immediately firing Ralph Treadway.

Part I

Overview

Chapter 2

Bank Organization and Regulation

Should commercial banks be allowed to open branches anywhere in the United States? How might restrictions affect operating strategies?

If banks can underwrite corporate securities outside the United States, why are they not allowed to do the same domestically? Is securities underwriting a good business for banks to enter?

Can a commercial bank be too large to fail?

Should banks be allowed to sell a full range of insurance products and own real estate for investment purposes? What risks and return opportunities would this provide for banks?

Should the government eliminate differences between commercial banks, credit unions, and investment banks?

Should Sears, Roebuck & Co., General Motors, Merrill Lynch, Household Finance, General Electric, Beneficial Insurance, and AT&T own commercial banks? Should banks be allowed to own other financial institutions? How would cross ownership affect banks' operating strategies and overall risk-return profile?

Government agencies that regulate commercial banks have had to address each of the above issues as part of their continuing evaluation of bank performance. The answers affect the organizational structure of banks as well as the markets in which they compete with other firms. Clearly, barriers that once separated banking from other activities are quickly disappearing. This creates opportunities for well-managed banks and related firms, but also puts pressure on management to perform. Managers must make decisions regarding a broad range of new issues that formerly did not affect the industry, and the decisions are increasingly complex because of changes in the economic environment, competitive pressures, and regulation.

This book focuses on commercial bank management. Because regulatory differences are slowly disappearing among commercial banks, savings and loans, and credit unions, the concepts and decision models apply generally to any depository institution. Thus while the term *bank* serves as an abbreviation for commercial bank, the analysis encompasses the behavior of other depository institutions. The purpose of this book is to introduce and apply financial concepts to the fundamental decisions that bank managers make. It is applications-oriented, with ample reference to data and examples. Upon completing the book, the reader should understand how basic decisions are made and how decisions in one functional area of management affect decisions in other areas.

Chapter 2 provides an overview of the banking environment by focusing on the organizational structure of the banking industry and individual banking institutions, and describing the regulatory climate in which banks operate. It initially documents how individual banks are organized to take maximum advantage of opportunities. It then summarizes what products and services banks can offer, where banks can conduct business, and what pricing restrictions apply. The final discussion introduces important regulatory issues that are currently unresolved. The material provides a useful framework for the decision analysis that follows in later chapters.

STRUCTURE OF THE BANKING INDUSTRY

For many years commercial banks were viewed as a special type of financial organization. They were the only firms allowed to issue demand deposits and thus dominated the payments system throughout the United States. Interest-bearing checking accounts did not exist except at credit unions. Because of this status, authorities closely regulated bank operations to control deposit growth and to ensure the safety of customer deposits. Among other restrictions, government regulators required cash reserves against deposits, specified maximum interest rates banks could pay on deposits, set minimum capital requirements, and placed limits on the size of loans to borrowers. In addition to regulatory constraints, federal banking law further limited bank operations to activities closely related to banking and, in conjunction with state laws, prohibited interstate branching.

Since 1980 commercial banks and other depository institutions have offered a range of products and services that is quite similar. Savings and loan associations, mutual savings banks, and credit unions, for example, now have the authority to offer interest-bearing transactions accounts, just like commercial banks. These firms can also make commercial loans, issue credit cards, and establish trust departments. Just as significantly, the distinction between these depository institutions and other financial services firms is gradually fading. Numerous large brokerage houses, insurance companies, finance companies, and retailers now offer transactions accounts and loans that compete directly with products offered by depository institutions. Many of these firms actually own commercial banks and thrift institutions.[1]

Commercial banks play an important role in facilitating economic growth. On a macroeconomic level, they represent the primary conduit of Federal Reserve monetary policy. Bank deposits represent the most liquid form of money (M1) such that Federal Reserve efforts to control the nation's money supply and level of aggregate economic activity do so by changing the availability of credit at banks. On a microeconomic level, commercial banks still represent the primary source of credit to most small businesses and many individuals. A community's vitality typically reflects the strength of its major financial institutions and the innovative character of its business leaders.

While the economic role of commercial banks has varied little over time, the nature of commercial banks and competing financial institutions is constantly changing. Depository institutions, brokerage firms, insurance companies, and general retail stores now offer products and services traditionally associated only with commercial banks. Commercial banks, in turn, offer a variety of insurance, real estate, and investment banking services they were once denied. They are not full-service institutions, however, though they are evolving to it. The term *bank* today refers as much to the range of services traditionally offered by depository institutions as to a specific type of institution.

Exhibit 2.1 documents changes in the number of institutions and total assets controlled by commercial banks, savings banks, and credit unions from 1970 through 1989. During the two decades, commercial banks' share of assets remained relatively constant around 65 percent. Credit unions increased their share from just over 2 percent to 4 percent in 1989 at the expense of thrifts. Note the sharp drop in number of competing institutions of all types. The data for commercial banks and thrifts reflect consolidation through failures and mergers and acquisitions. Credit unions, in contrast, have fallen with consolidations and a limited number of failures. Exhibit 2.2 demonstrates the high rate of bank failures since 1980 and the volume of deposits affected. The data actually understate the true number of failures because regulators often arranged mergers rather than simply close failed banks. The sharp increase in failures coincides with economic problems throughout various sectors of the U.S. economy ranging from agriculture to energy to real estate. As regional economies faltered, problem loans grew at banks and thrifts that overextended themselves and subsequent losses forced closings.

Unit versus Branch Banking

Commercial banks are classified either as unit banks, with all operations housed in a single office, or branch banks, with multiple offices. State law determines the extent to which commercial banks can branch. The McFadden Act of 1927 and later amendments allow national banks to establish branches only to the degree that states permit state banks to branch. The trend has been to expand branching opportunities. In 1961, 16 states prohibited branches, 15 states allowed them in a limited geographic area,

---

[1]Savings and loan associations and mutual savings banks are designated as thrift institutions.

**Exhibit 2.1 Number and Total Assets of Various Depository
Institutions (Billions of Dollars)**

A. Change, 1970–1989

	1970	1980	1989	Annual Growth Rate in Assets 1980–1989
Commercial Banks				
Number	13,550	14,163	12,410	
Total assets	$517.4	$1,484.6	$3,231.1	9.03%
Thrift Institutions[a]				
Number	5,669	4,594	3,011	
Total assets	$249.5	$783.6	$1,516.5	7.61%
Credit Unions				
Number	23,819	21,930	15,205	
Total assets	$17.6	$67.3	$199.7	12.85%

B. Size Distribution By Total Assets, 1988

	Commercial Banks		Thrift Institutions		Credit Unions	
	No.	% of Assets	No.	% of Assets	No.	% of Assets
<$25 million	4,168	1.8	301	0.3	12,437	28.4
$25–$49.9 million	3,430	3.6	493	1.3	732	14.4
$50–$99.9 million	2,861	5.9	668	3.5	390	15.5
$100–$499.9 million	2,471	14.4	1,064	17.2	304	30.2
≥$500 million	701	74.3	423	77.7	15	11.5
Total	13,631	100.0%	2,949	100.0%	13,878	100.0%

[a]Savings and loan associations and mutual savings banks.

Sources: Flow of Funds Accounts, Board of Governors of the Federal Reserve System; Savings & Loan Fact Book, U.S. League of Savings & Loan Associations; Credit Union Report, Credit Union National Association

such as the city or county where the main office was located, and 19 states permitted statewide branching. At year-end 1990, only 3 states prohibited branches, 23 specified limited branches, and 24 allowed unlimited statewide branches. Exhibit 2.3 indicates which states fall into each category. Unit banks are roughly equal in number to banks with branches, but most of the resources are controlled by branch banking organizations.

States originally limited branches to help retain deposits in local communities and to provide local bank ownership and management. The fear was that large branch banks in metropolitan areas would take deposits out of rural areas to lend in the bigger cities. Branching restrictions presumably increased credit availability in rural areas, especially for small businesses and farmers. They also prevented a few large banks from gaining too much market power, in which case they could charge higher interest rates and provide second-rate services. Most experts have analyzed the arguments against branches and concluded that they are generally unsupported.[2]

---

[2]See Evanoff and Fortier, 1986.

Exhibit 2.2 Bank Failures

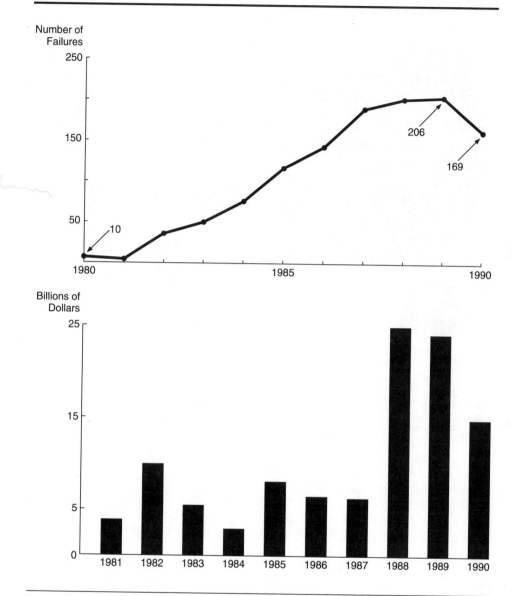

Source: Federal Deposit Insurance Corp.

As might be expected, unit banking states had large numbers of small banks. Banks were smaller, on average, because they operated in limited geographic markets and were less able to attract deposits. Even the largest banks suffered because they were

Exhibit 2.3 Branching Provisions Throughout the United States: 1990

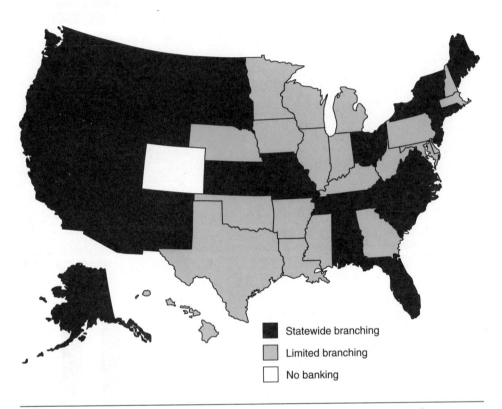

Statewide branching

Limited branching

No banking

Source: Federal Reserve Board of Governors.

unable to adequately enlarge their consumer deposit base, and their operating costs were artificially high. Consider the situation in Texas, which converted from unit banking to limited branching in 1987. In 1981 there were over 1800 distinct commercial banks in the state. Each bank had its own Board of Directors, a complete staff of officers, and separate documents and technology for conducting business. Clearly, expenses were higher than if each independent bank was instead operated as a branch. Risk was also greater because individual banks were less diversified and more prone to problems if depositors withdrew their funds en masse.

It is entirely predictable that states with the highest bank failure rates historically restricted branching. Branching generally reduces the number of competitors, lowers expenses, allows greater asset diversification, and expands each bank's consumer deposit base, reducing the likelihood of a run on deposits. Each of these factors decreases the chances of failure. In 1987 the Texas legislature authorized limited branching. One immediate response was that many holding companies (discussed in the next section) consolidated their operations by converting banks into branches. The number of in-state banks soon dropped to approximately 1200.

Bank Holding Companies

Any organization that owns controlling interest in one or more commercial banks is a bank holding company. Control is defined as ownership or indirect control via the power to vote more than 25 percent of the voting shares in a bank. The Federal Reserve examines ownership or control of less than 25 percent on a case-by-case basis to determine whether effective control exists. One-bank holding companies (OBHCs) control only one bank and typically arise when the owners of an existing bank exchange their shares for stock in the holding company. The holding company then acquires the original bank stock. Multibank holding companies (MBHCs) control at least two commercial banks.

The primary motivation behind forming bank holding companies is to circumvent restrictions regarding branching and the products and services banks can offer. Under current regulation, holding companies can acquire nonbank subsidiaries that offer products and services closely related to banking. This presumably limits speculation and thus overall risk. Large organizations generally form OBHCs because they want to control a bank and thus be able to provide traditional banking services, but more importantly want to combine the bank's capabilities with their financial activities in order to better compete nationwide. Sears is effectively a OBHC through its ownership of Sears Savings Bank. Large insurance and finance companies have similarly used this vehicle. In 1990 AT&T took the concept one step further by offering bank credit card services but avoiding regulation as a OBHC (see Contemporary Issues: AT&T's Universal Card).

Small OBHCs are often formed because the owners can realize tax benefits and gain better access to funds via the capital markets. MBHCs offer the same interstate opportunities as OBHCs, and also allow their owners to expand their banking business within a state. Thus a MBHC typically acquires banks in the major geographic markets within its home state. Such structure provides some of the advantages of branching, such as a more diversified asset base and broader funding base, but retains the cost disadvantages of operating distinct bank offices rather than branches. As might be expected, bank holding companies are especially prevalent in unit banking and limited branching states with over 5,000 OBHCs and 1,000 MBHCs at the end of 1990.

Regulation clearly affects the organizational form of commercial banks. As branching restrictions are removed within states, MBHCs convert subsidiary banks to branches. The same will eventually occur nationwide. Later sections describe interstate branching restrictions in greater detail. Consider now, however, the impact of a (currently hypothetical) federal law that allows unrestricted nationwide branching. There would be no need for MBHCs.

The specific organizational form, permissible activities, and stream of cash flows between a holding company and its subsidiaries are described in the following sections. Subsequent sections document regulatory restrictions regarding bank products offered, geographic markets served, and pricing.

AT&T'S Universal Card

In 1990 AT&T entered the bank credit card business in a big way. From scratch, it developed a bank credit card base that numbered 7.5 million accounts by early 1991, enough to rank it seventh among the top ten card issuers. AT&T, however, is neither a bank nor a bank holding company and thus avoids regulation by banking regulators. It can thus conduct business anywhere management chooses and bank regulators cannot restrict its business activity in nonbanking areas.

AT&T accomplished this through an ingenious arrangement with Universal Bank, a bank subsidiary of Synovus Financial Corp. AT&T advertises a Visa and MasterCard that allow customers to charge long-distance telephone calls as well as make normal credit card purchases. The cards are formally issued by Universal Bank, hence the Master-Card or Visa logo. By agreement, another subsidiary processes all transactions and bills the credit card holders. Universal Bank then sells the credit card receivables to AT&T. The cards are attractive for several reasons. With the Visa and MasterCard logo, customers can use cards anywhere other bank cards qualify. In addition, AT&T discounts telephone calls authorized with the card by 10 percent, offers 90-day insurance coverage of purchases, and does not charge an annual fee for use of the card, as many banks do.

ORGANIZATIONAL FORM

C.W. Hampton's interviews with officers of First Financial Bank, summarized in Chapter 1, revealed numerous problems facing the firm. Several of the most obvious ones pertained to Ralph Treadway's role as president and his relationship with members of the bank's Board of Directors and other bank officers. To fully comprehend the implications, it is necessary to understand how banks are organized and the responsibilities of various players.

Independent Banks

The term *independent bank* normally refers to a bank that is not controlled by a multibank holding company or any other outside interest. While such a bank is often part of a one-bank holding company and may operate branches, it is typically linked closely with a single community in which the bank is located. In fact, many bankers consider *community bank* to be synonymous with independent bank.

Consider an independent bank that is not part of a holding company. Its general organizational form will follow the outline of Exhibit 2.4. The general structure typically consists of five levels of responsibility and reporting. At the bottom of the chart are the line personnel, who have primary responsibility in customer contact and handling back room operations such as check processing and teller services. Their role is extremely important because most depositors and loan customers deal with these individuals. They largely project the bank's image and serve to market bank services.

Most independent banks then separate activities into at least the four or five functional areas listed above the line personnel. A senior credit officer is responsible for implementing a bank's credit policy. At many small banks, the president and chief

Exhibit 2.4 Organizational Structure of an Independent Bank

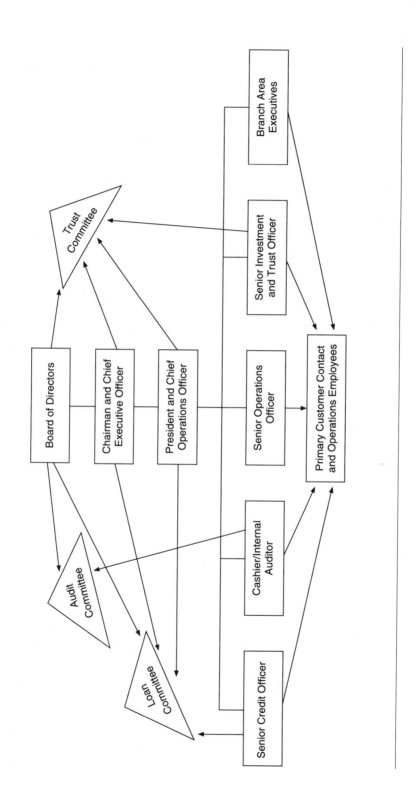

executive officer (CEO) also manage loan portfolios because they deal directly with borrowers. A bank's cashier or chief financial officer is responsible for financial management responsibilities in the areas of budgeting, accounting, and recordkeeping. This individual verifies that financial information conforms to regulatory guidelines and is conveyed correctly to stockholders and regulators. Each bank should also have an internal auditor who monitors financial reporting.

The senior operations officer is responsible for back room operations involving data processing, lock box services, and check processing. An independent bank may also have a senior investment officer who buys and sells securities for the investment portfolio and also handles trust business if the bank has a trust department. At small banks, the president or CEO may handle these responsibilities. Finally, a bank with branches will typically designate a branch area executive. One individual may be responsible for all branches, or the branches may be segmented by city, county, or other area such that several individuals serve as branch executives and report directly to the president. If the bank is large enough, it may also separate the human resources function and delegate it to a senior officer who reports to the president.

The next tier of responsibility consists of the bank's chief operations officer, who often carries the title of president. He or she often makes loans, reviews key loan and investment decisions made by others, and handles much of the bank's marketing effort. Senior officers in each of the functional areas normally report to this individual, who then conveys the information to the CEO. At most independent banks, the CEO focuses on public relations activities, overall strategic planning, and works closely with members of the Board of Directors. Occasionally, the CEO will not give up day-to-day operating decision-making and thus either claims both the CEO and president titles or names a president who has limited duties. At the top is the bank's Board of Directors, which oversees the entire operation of the bank.

Outside members of the Board of Directors are generally key business leaders in the community and thus often significant bank customers and even bank stockholders. Inside members consist of the bank's CEO, president, and senior lending officer. The primary role of directors is to represent and serve stockholders, who are the owners of the bank. A secondary role is to represent customers and employees. Directors use their expertise to oversee the broad direction of the bank, solve problems, and make decisions regarding bank policy. Their role is not to manage the bank by getting involved in day-to-day operations or the detail of each specific pricing, investment, or credit decision. Because the Board is ultimately responsible for the bank's performance, most banks establish directors' committees that set policy guidelines in the major functional areas and regularly monitor performance. Many banks have gotten into difficulty because directors have blindly followed the dictates of senior management instead of setting policy and monitoring performance.

The independent bank in Exhibit 2.4 has directors' committees. A loan committee oversees the lending function to ensure loan quality and verify that regulatory guidelines are met. This committee must typically approve all loans over some base amount and thus serves as a final review board. Because business leaders are familiar with the community and are experts in their own line of business, they should bring experience and keen judgment to the evaluation process. By law, any bank with a trust department must have a directors' trust committee. As indicated in Chapter 27, trust departments handle estates, guardianships, and related services under legal trust agreements. A trust committee monitors the legal aspects of the trust business and whether trust business contributes to the bank's overall profitability. A third committee is the audit committee. Note that this is the only committee in which inside directors do not directly participate. This reflects the monitoring role inherent in an audit. The committee selects the bank's auditors, reviews the audit report, and makes recommendations to management. All these activities should be independent of the bank's operating officers. Finally, the directors may have a representative on the bank's asset and liability management committee.

First Financial Bank's difficulties, described in Chapter 1, demonstrate the problems that can arise when a bank's officers and members of the Board of Directors do not fulfill their responsibilities. First, Ralph Treadway effectively ran the bank independently of the CEO, his retired father, and the Board of Directors, who rubber-stamped his actions. Treadway stated that the bank had a strategic plan and brief policy statements only to satisfy bank regulators. It is hard to imagine that the officers paid much attention to the guidelines, as evidenced by past loan problems, regulatory violations, and legal suits. Second, the Board of Directors is ultimately responsible for seeing that regulations are met and management has a long-term strategic plan that outlines firm objectives. First Financial clearly had no direction. The branch system was underutilized; the recent merger created check processing errors that were resolved poorly; and lending activity was out of control. If Board members had done their job, they would have known of the violations and asset problems well in advance of an examination. The fact that the internal auditor reported directly to Treadway indicates that controls were effectively ignored. Finally, it is generally inappropriate for a bank's president to be in partnership with Board members. Is it possible that First Financial made loans to the partnership? If so, how objectively might these loans be viewed?

Bank Holding Companies

A bank holding company is essentially a shell organization that owns and manages subsidiary firms. The holding company obtains financing from stockholders and creditors and uses the proceeds to buy stock in other companies, make loans, and purchase securities. The holding company is labeled the parent organization and the operating entities are the subsidiaries. If the parent owns at least 80 percent of a subsidiary's stock, it files a consolidated tax return.

Like commercial banks, bank holding companies are heavily regulated by states and the federal government. State laws determine the extent to which holding companies can operate in a state. All states permit OBHCs. In 1990 only Mississippi prohibited MBHCs entirely. Six states restricted MBHCs' geographic scope and twelve others limited the percentage of statewide deposits that a single MBHC could control. The Bank Holding Company Act stipulates that the Board of Governors of the Federal Reserve System must approve all holding company formations and acquisitions. Approval is normally granted unless there is evidence that the acquisition will substantially lessen competition in the local banking market.

**Exhibit 2.5 Nonbank Activities for Bank Holding Companies
under Section 4(c)8 of Regulation Y, November 1984**

Activities Permitted by Regulation	Activities Permitted by Order	Activities Denied by the Board	Activities Permitted by Order Since 1984
1. Extensions of credit[b], mortgage banking, finance companies (consumer, sales, and commercial), credit cards, factoring	1. Issuance and sale of travelers checks[b,f]	1. Insurance premium funding (combined sales of mutual funds and insurance)	1. Financial feasibility studies, valuation services, utility rate testimony, credit ratings
2. Industrial bank, Morris Plan banks, industrial loan company	2. Buying and selling gold and silver bullion and silver coin[b,d]	2. Underwriting life insurance not related to credit extensions	2. Tax preparation for individuals
3. Servicing loans and other extensions of credit[b]	3. Issuing money orders and general-purpose variable denominated payment instruments[a,b,d]	3. Sale of level-term credit life	3. Real estate consulting services, personal property appraisals
4. Trust company[b]	4. Futures commission merchant to cover gold and silver bullion and coins[a,b]	4. Real estate brokerage (residential)	4. Credit card loss reporting services, merchant voice transaction verification
5. Investment or financial advising[b]	5. Armored car	
6. Full-payout leasing of personal or real property[b]	5. Underwriting certain federal, state, and municipal securities[a,b]	6. Land development	5. Employee benefits consulting
7. Investments in community welfare projects[b]		7. Real estate syndication	6. Municipal securities brokers' broker
8. Providing bookkeeping or data processing services[b]	6. Check verification[a,b,d]	8. General management consulting	7. Student loan servicing
	7. Financial advice to consumers[a,b]	9. Property management	8. Consumer financial consulting
9. Acting as insurance agent or broker primarily in connection with credit extensions[b]	8. Issuance of small denomination debt instruments[a]	10. Computer output microfilm services	9. Futures and options advisory services
	9. Arranging for equity financing of real estate	11. Underwriting mortgage guaranty insurance[c]	10. Operation of collection agency
10. Underwriting credit life, accident, and health insurance	10. Acting as futures commissions merchant	12. Operating a savings and loan association[a,e]	
11. Providing courier services[b]	11. Discount brokerage	13. Operating a travel agency[a,b]	
		14. Underwriting property and casualty insurance[a]	*(continued)*

Nonbank Activities Permitted Bank Holding Companies. The Federal Reserve Board similarly regulates nonbank activities that are "closely related to banking" in which holding companies may acquire subsidiaries. Restrictions came about for three reasons. First, it was feared that large financial conglomerates would control the financial system because they would have a competitive advantage. Second, there was concern that banks would require customers to buy nonbank services in order to obtain loans. Third, some critics simply did not believe that bank holding companies should engage in businesses that were not allowed banks because these businesses were less regulated and thus relatively risky.

Under amendments to the Bank Holding Company Act of 1956, the Federal Reserve allows banks to offer the services listed in Exhibit 2.5 anywhere in the United

Exhibit 2.5 *(Continued)*

Activities Permitted by Regulation	Activities Permitted by Order	Activities Denied by the Board	Activities Permitted by Order Since 1984
12. Management consulting to all depository institutions	12. Operating a distressed savings and loan association	15. Underwriting home loan life mortgage insurance[a]	
13. Sale at retail of money orders with a face value of not more than $1000, travelers checks, and savings bond[a,b,g]	13. Operating an Article XII Investment Company	16. Investment note issue with transactional characteristics	
14. Performing appraisals of real estate[a]	14. Executing foreign banking unsolicited purchases and sales of securities	17. Real estate advisory services	
15. Issuance and sale of travelers checks	15. Engaging in commercial banking activities abroad through a limited purpose Delaware bank		
16. Arranging commercial real estate equity financing	16. Performing appraisal of real estate and real estate advisor and real estate brokerage on nonresidential properties		
17. Securities brokerage	17. Operating a Pool Reserve Plan for loss reverses of banks for loans to small businesses		
18. Underwriting and dealing in government obligations and money market instruments	18. Operating a thrift institution in Rhode Island		
19. Foreign exchange advisory and transactional services	19. Operating a guarantee savings bank in New Hampshire		
20. Futures commission merchant	20. Offering informational advice and transactional services for foreign exchange services		
21. Options on financial futures			
22. Advice on options on bullion and foreign exchange			

[a] Added to list since January 1, 1975.

[b] Activities permissible to national banks.

[c] Board orders found these activities closely related to banking but denied proposed acquisitions as part of its "go slow" policy.

[d] To be decided on a case-by-case basis.

[e] Operating a thrift institution has been permitted by order in Rhode Island, Ohio, New Hampshire, and California.

[f] Subsequently permitted by regulation.

[g] The amount subsequently was changed to $10,000.

Source: Federal Reserve Board.

**Exhibit 2.6 Nonbank Assets Held by Bank Holding
Companies, by Type of Activity, 1988**

Activity[1]	Total Assets in Activity (Millions of Dollars)	Percentage of Aggregate Nonbank Assets in Activity	Number of Bank Holding Companies Engaged in Activity	Growth in Assets, 1987–1988 (Percent)	Percentage of Assets Held by Top Five Firms Engaged in Activity[2]
Commercial finance	$ 37,128.3	17.7%	58	8.99%	63.6%
Securities brokerage	32,320.9	15.4	83	53.99	86.1
Mortgage banking	27,470.8	13.1	110	–6.69	75.1
Consumer finance	24,043.7	11.5	51	–4.38	63.7
Other depository institutions	19,697.2	9.4	14	–8.70	95.0
Leasing	9,156.7	4.4	96	6.40	51.5
Data processing	1,838.0	.8	88	–9.42	68.9
Insurance underwriting	1,678.4	.8	111	–4.41	62.1
Small business investment company	650.6	.3	26	9.31	79.8
Insurance agency	340.0	.2	75	–28.51	61.2
Other nonbank	55,524.7	26.5	183	–2.35	71.0
Aggregated nonbank assets	209,849.3	—	—	—	—

[1] As specified on FR-Y11AS form.

[2] Because the financial data reported on the FR-Y11AS are consolidated within the eleven categories, the percentage of assets held by the top five firms engaged in the activity refers to the consolidated nonbank subsidiaries for each bank holding company rather than to a single subsidiary.

Source: Liang and Savage, *Federal Reserve Bulletin*, Board of Governors of the Federal Reserve System, May 1990.

States. Most of these activities relate to the extension of specific types of loans, underwriting and brokerage services, consulting services, general management services, and data processing. The largest bank holding companies must report to the Federal Reserve annually regarding the performance of their nonbank subsidiaries. They classify each subsidiary into one of 11 categories based on its primary activity. Exhibit 2.6 provides a breakdown of the volume of business in these nonbank activities in 1988. While most assets are concentrated in credit services, leasing, and securities brokerage, a large number of holding companies engage in insurance underwriting and operate insurance agencies. Under current law, however, banks can underwrite only credit life insurance, provide financial guarantees on securities offerings, and sell annuities.[3] Banks consequently offer only limited competition to full service insurance companies.

As indicated in Exhibit 2.5, banks are expressly denied some activities. Of these, banks would most like to compete in full-scale securities underwriting, sell a broad range of insurance products, and invest in real estate for their own account. Banks

[3] Some states permit state-chartered banks to underwrite additional types of insurance and banks in smaller communities can sell additional types of insurance.

have long been able to underwrite federal debt securities and certain types of municipal bonds. Since passage of the Glass–Steagall Act in 1933, they have been prevented from underwriting corporate debt and equity. In 1989 the Federal Reserve authorized several banks to underwrite corporate debt, and in 1990 it authorized two banks to underwrite corporate stock. There are strict limitations on how much revenue can be generated from underwriting corporate securities, so banks have done little corporate business. But the door has been opened. As noted above, insurance activities are similarly severely restricted. Many bankers believe that insurance products dovetail nicely with other financial services and see insurance business as a convenient outlet for diversifying bank activities to reduce overall risk.

It is fundamentally inequitable that nonbank financial institutions can offer commercial banking services, ranging from transactions accounts to commercial and consumer loans, in addition to their own basic services, yet banks are precluded from offering services in their primary line of business. Full-line insurance companies and investment banks own commercial banks but banks cannot own full-line insurance companies and full-service brokerage houses. Commercial banks are constantly pushing regulators to expand the list of nonbank activities allowed them.

Organizational Structure of Bank Holding Companies. Exhibit 2.7 outlines the simple organizational structures of a OBHC and a MBHC. Consider first the OBHC. At the top is the Board of Directors for the parent organization that owns controlling interest in the subsidiaries. This Board operates much like the Board for an independent bank, except that its responsibilities now extend to all lines of business in which the entire organization is involved. In a OBHC the subsidiary bank normally operates like an independent bank. The only difference is that business decisions must now be reconciled with the objectives and decisions associated with the nonbank subsidiaries. Bank officers are represented on the Board, as are officers of the nonbank subsidiaries. In general, nonbank firms have fewer senior officers than do banks.

The MBHC structure differs slightly. The substantive difference is that the parent corporation owns more than one commercial bank subsidiary. This generally enables the banking organization to compete in more geographic markets. Even within this structure, operating styles may vary. Some MBHCs operate as closely knit units with the management of each subsidiary bank reporting daily to key personnel at either the lead bank or the parent company. In this case the subsidiaries are effectively branches. Important decisions must be approved by authorities outside the local community so that local bank officers have only limited autonomy. Local bank loan officers, for example, might have to get all loans over $100,000 approved by a regional holding company credit officer located in a different community who oversees all lending decisions. This has the advantage of guaranteeing uniformity in loan decisions. It also has disadvantages related to the perception that local authorities have limited powers. Decisions are too often delayed and consequently relayed to customers too late. Not surprisingly, well-run community banks emphasize their local autonomy and community focus.

Exhibit 2.7 Organizational Structure of Bank Holding Companies

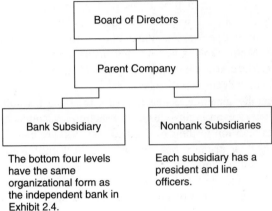

A. One–Bank Holding Company

Board of Directors

Parent Company

Bank Subsidiary   Nonbank Subsidiaries

The bottom four levels have the same organizational form as the independent bank in Exhibit 2.4.

Each subsidiary has a president and line officers.

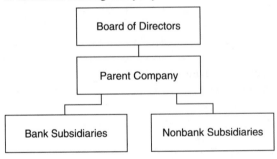

B. Multibank Holding Company

Board of Directors

Parent Company

Bank Subsidiaries   Nonbank Subsidiaries

Other MBHCs allow managers of subsidiary banks to retain key decision-making authority and to operate quasi-independently as long as performance is strong. It is more difficult for these firms to realize economies of scale—they are unable to run a single marketing and advertising program, for example—and thus some of the benefits of size are lost. The advantage, however, is that such banks typically retain close ties to their communities and realize the associated benefits.

Holding Company Financial Statements and Cash Flows. MBHC expansion enables banks to diversify their operations by competing in different geographic and product markets. Diversification reduces the risk of failure by stabilizing earnings. The parent company typically coordinates the operating strategies for the entire organization and provides services for which it charges fees. It assists bank subsidiaries in asset and

Exhibit 2.8   Multibank Holding Company Balance Sheet: Parent Company Only (Millions of Dollars)

Assets	
Cash and due from subsidiary banks	$ 10
Short-term investments	390
Commercial loans	50
Receivables from subsidiaries	725
Investments in subsidiaries	1,250
Other assets	75
Total assets	$2,500
Liabilities and Stockholders' Equity	
Commercial paper and federal funds purchased	$1,250
Long-term debentures	150
Accrued expenses and dividends payable	50
Total liabilities	$1,450
Stockholders equity	1,050
Total Liabilities and Stockholders' Equity	$2,500

liability management, loan review, data processing, and business development and may provide debt and equity funding. It also provides strategic planning, project analysis, and financing for nonbank subsidiaries.

While the consolidated financial statements of a holding company and its subsidiaries reflect aggregate performance, it is useful to analyze the parent company's statements alone. Exhibits 2.8 and 2.9 present the balance sheet and income statement for a MBHC with wholly-owned bank and nonbank subsidiaries. The parent owns four basic types of assets: cash and money market investments, loan participations, receivables from subsidiaries, and equity (stock) in the subsidiaries. Cash and short-term interest-bearing investments are held for transactions purposes, liquidity, and yield. The parent company purchases loans from a bank subsidiary when a credit exceeds the maximum legal loan size permitted a single member bank. These loan participations may be distributed to other banks in the holding company or kept by the parent. Finally, the parent advances funds to subsidiaries through the purchase of notes and receivables or equity. The equity investment represents the value of subsidiary stock at the time of purchase. These assets are financed by short-term debt, long-term debt, and bank holding company stockholders.

The parent's net income is derived from fees, interest income, and dividends from equity in subsidiaries in excess of operating expenses and interest paid on holding company debt. In Exhibit 2.9, the bulk of the parent's $210 million operating income comes from dividends of bank subsidiaries and interest on receivables from nonbank subsidiaries. Interest on debt, in turn, accounts for 87 percent of operating expenses. The parent pays no income tax because 80 percent of the dividends from subsidiaries is exempt. Taxable income from the remaining 20 percent and interest income is far

Exhibit 2.9 Multibank Holding Company Income Statement: Parent Company Only (Millions of Dollars)

Operating Income	
Dividends from subsidiaries	$ 95
Interest on loans	8
Interest on receivables from subsidiaries	100
Other income	7
Total operating income	$210
Operating Expenses	
Interest expense	
Commercial paper and federal funds	$125
Long-term debentures	15
Total interest expense	$140
Salaries and benefits	15
Expenses paid to subsidiaries	4
Charges paid by subsidiaries	(5)
Other expenses	10
Total operating expenses	$164
Income before Taxes and Equity in Undistributed Income of Subsidiaries	$ 40
Applicable income tax benefit	10
Income before Equity in Undistributed Income of Subsidiaries	56
Equity in undistributed income of subsidiaries	100
Net Income	$156

less than deductible expenses. Under Internal Revenue Service provisions, each subsidiary actually pays taxes quarterly on its taxable income. With a consolidated tax return, however, the parent company can use taxable income from its subsidiaries to offset its "loss." Thus the parent reports a noncash tax benefit of $10 million representing the reclamation of tax overpayments by subsidiaries. The final item before net income represents the holding company's claim to $100 million in subsidiary income that was not paid out as dividends.

Financial Services Holding Company

An increasingly common form of organization is the financial services holding company in which a bank holding company and a thrift holding company are owned by a parent company, as indicated in Exhibit 2.10. Each of these holding companies owns subsidiaries, while the parent financial services holding company also owns other subsidiaries directly. The structure is similar to that of a bank holding company's relationship to its subsidiaries but there is one more layer of management and thus control. As commercial banks consolidate with other financial institutions, both domes-

Exhibit 2.10 Organizational Structure of Financial Services Companies

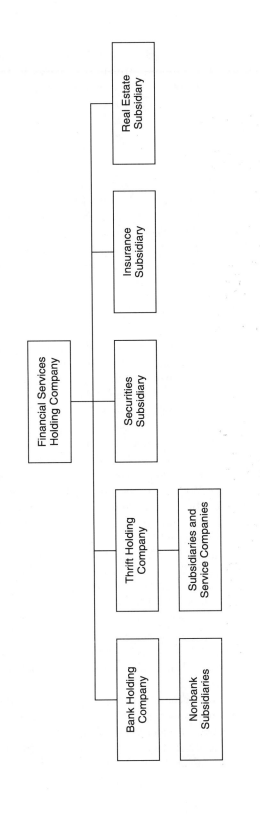

tically and abroad, this type of organization will become more prevalent. Alternatively, we may see nonfinancial companies affiliate with banks in this type of structure, as indicated by the 1991 Treasury regulatory reform proposal (see Contemporary Issues: 1991 Treasury Regulatory Reform Proposal).

BANK REGULATION

Commercial banks are the most heavily regulated financial institutions in the United States. This largely reflects the historical role of banks in the payments system and in providing credit to individuals and businesses. Prior to the establishment of the Federal Reserve System in 1913, private banks operated free of close government scrutiny. The frequency of abuses and the large number of failed banks during the Depression forced the federal government to redesign its regulatory framework to encompass supervision and deposit insurance.

Reasons for Regulation

There are four fundamental objectives of bank regulation. The first is to ensure the safety and soundness of banks and financial instruments. The purpose is to maintain domestic and international confidence, protect depositors and ultimately taxpayers, and maintain financial stability. This goal is generally accomplished by limiting risk taking at individual institutions, by limiting entry and exit, and by the federal government's willingness to act as a lender of last resort. Recent difficulties with federal deposit insurance and the large number of failed banks and thrifts demonstrates that risk-taking among depository institutions got out of hand, and U.S. taxpayers will bear the brunt of the cost. Second, the Federal Reserve System uses regulation to provide monetary stability. This is evidenced by efforts to control the growth in the nation's money supply and maintain the efficient operation of the payments system.

The third objective is to provide an efficient and competitive financial system. Regulation should prevent the undue concentration of banking resources, which would be anticompetitive, yet allow firms to alter their product mix and delivery systems to meet economic and market needs. This goal is generally accomplished by restricting mergers and acquisitions that reduce the number and market power of competing institutions. Finally, regulation should protect consumers from abuses by credit granting institutions. Historically, some individuals found it difficult to obtain loans for reasons not related to their financial condition. Thus regulations now stipulate that borrowers should have equal credit opportunities regardless of their race, gender, age, geographic location, and so forth. Lenders must also disclose why a borrower is denied a loan.

It is also important to recognize that there are certain things regulation cannot achieve. For example, it does not prevent bank failures. It cannot eliminate risk in the economic environment or in a bank's normal operations. It does not guarantee that bankers will make sound management decisions or act ethically. Regulation simply serves as a guideline for sound operating policies.

1991 Treasury Regulatory Reform Proposal

In 1991 the Treasury department proposed dramatic changes to the financial structure of U.S. depository institutions. One of the most controversial was a recommendation that well-capitalized commercial banks be allowed to formally affiliate with securities firms, mutual funds, and insurance companies under a financial services holding company format. Specifically, commercial firms would be permitted to own financial services holding companies. These holding companies in turn could engage in a broad range of securities underwriting and insurance activities that were previously denied banks.

The presumed result would be the creation of large, well-diversified financial and nonfinancial conglomerates that could offer a wide range of financial services. There were two important caveats. First, only banks that have substantial amounts of capital qualify. Such banks presumably exhibit a lower risk of failure than poorly capitalized banks. Second, financial and nonfinancial activities would be closely monitored to prohibit anticompetitive restraints among the subsidiaries. Regulators would have the power to prohibit specific affiliate transactions and increased disclosure where appropriate. If passed, these firms would be better positioned to compete globally. The potential cost is that the firms may take on too much risk leading to expensive failures, or that intracompany activities may be anticompetitive. Regardless, it seems likely that such firms will soon exist in the United States.

Three separate federal agencies, along with each state's banking department, issue and enforce regulations related to a wide variety of activities. The federal agencies are the Federal Reserve, the Federal Deposit Insurance Corporation (FDIC), and the Office of the Comptroller of the Currency (OCC). Most regulations can be classified in one of three basic categories linked to the reasons for regulation introduced earlier: 1) supervision, examination, deposit insurance, chartering activity, and product restrictions, which are associated with safety and soundness; 2) branching, mergers and acquisitions, and pricing, which are related to an efficient and competitive financial system; and 3) regulations related to consumer protection. The different regulatory groups' responsibilities overlap, but the agencies generally coordinate policies and decisions. Exhibit 2.11 summarizes the division of responsibilities.

Safety and Soundness

Supervision and Examination. Regulators periodically examine individual banks and provide supervisory directives that request changes in operating policies. Exhibit 2.11 lists the various examiners and their areas of concern. The purpose is to guarantee the safety and soundness of the banking system by identifying problems before a bank's financial condition deteriorates to the point where it fails and the FDIC has to pay off insured depositors. The OCC and FDIC assess the overall quality of a bank's condition according to the CAMEL system. The letters in CAMEL refer to capital adequacy, asset quality, management quality, earnings quality, and liquidity, respectively. Regulators assign ratings from 1 (best) to 5 (worst) for each category and an overall rating for all features combined.

Exhibit 2.11 Depository Institutions and Their Regulators[a]

	Safety & Soundness		
Commercial Banks	**Supervision and Examination**	**Deposit Insurance**	**Chartering & Licensing**
National	Comptroller	FDIC	OCC
State member	Federal Reserve and state authority	FDIC	State authority
Insured state nonmember	FDIC and state authority	FDIC	State authority
Noninsured state nonmember	State authority	State insurance or none	State authority
Bank holding companies	Federal reserve	Not applicable	Federal Reserve and state authority

Examiners spend most of their efforts appraising asset quality and management.[4] The asset quality rating generally indicates the relative volume of problem loans. Examiners review the terms and documentation on loans, particularly those with past-due payments, to determine the magnitude of likely loan losses. If repayment prospects are poor, regulators may force a bank to recognize the loss and build up loan-loss reserves in support of future losses. Management quality is assessed in terms of senior officers' awareness and control of a bank's policies and performance. Examiners carefully review bank policy statements regarding loans, investments, capital, and general budgeting to determine whether the bank is well run. Think back to the management quality evidenced by Ralph Treadway and First Financial's Board of Directors in Chapter 1. The lack of concern over policy statements and regulatory guidelines should have been an indicator of future problems. Capital adequacy, earnings strength, and liquidity are determined by formulas based on the composition and size of various bank balance sheet accounts. These facets of risk are addressed in detail in subsequent chapters.

When an examination is completed, the regulatory staff makes a series of policy recommendations that address problems it has discovered. The recommendations may be informal advisories, a *memorandum of understanding*, or a *cease and desist order*. A memorandum of understanding is a formal regulatory document that identifies specific violations and prescribes corrective action. A cease and desist order is a legal document that orders a firm to stop an unfair practice under full penalty of law. In the case of First Financial, the regulators would likely have issued a memorandum of understanding that required the bank to get into compliance with legal lending limits to single borrowers and meet community reinvestment standards within a set period of time. Only the cease and desist order has legal standing, but each type of recommendation notifies a bank if its house is not in order.

---

[4]Cocheo, 1986, analyzes the steps in the typical examination process of a community bank and describes the basic questions and problems that arise.

Exhibit 2.11 *(Continued)*

Efficiency & Competitiveness

Branching	Mergers & Acquisitions	Pricing New Products	Consumer Protection
Comptroller	Comptroller	Federal Reserve and state authority	Federal Reserve
Federal Reserve and state authority	Federal Reserve and state authority	Federal Reserve and state authority	Federal Reserve and state authority
FDIC and state authority	FDIC and state authority	Federal Reserve and state authority	Federal Reserve, FDIC, and state authority
State authority	State authority	Federal Reserve and state authority	Federal Reserve and state authority
Federal Reserve and state authority	Federal Reserve and state authority	Not applicable	Not applicable

[a]OCC indicates Office of the Comptroller of the Currency; FDIC indicates Federal Deposit Insurance Corp.

Federal Deposit Insurance. Regulators attempt to maintain public confidence in banks and the financial system through federal deposit insurance. For many years there were two funds: the FDIC fund for commercial banks and the Federal Savings and Loan Insurance fund (FSLIC) for savings and loans. With the large number of thrift failures, the FSLIC fund went bankrupt during the late 1980s. The FDIC currently insures customer deposits up to $100,000 per account. In order to maintain different funding schemes, there are two insurance funds under the FDIC with the Bank Insurance Fund (BIF) for banks and the Savings Association Insurance Fund (SAIF) for savings and loans. In 1989 insured banks and thrifts paid a fee equal to 12 cents per $100 dollars of domestic deposits for the coverage. By 1991 those same institutions paid 23 cents per $100 in deposits.[5] During 1991 the pace of failures continued such that the FDIC chairman announced that the FDIC fund needed a cash infusion of $25–40 billion to cover anticipated payouts—that is, the fund was insolvent. Future payments will likely come from higher deposit insurance assessments and general taxpayer financing directly through the Treasury.

Deposit insurance is becoming increasingly important as the number of problem banks and bank failures rises. Following World War II, bank failures were negligible, given the heavy regulation of banking activities and strict policies regarding who could open and operate a bank. However, the number of bank and thrift failures rose from under 50 in 1982 to over 500 in 1990. When a bank or thrift fails, the government pays insured depositors the full amount of their account balances. Customers with uninsured deposits bear the risk that they will not recover the full value of their account

---

[5]Congress passed the Financial Institutions Reform, Recovery and Enforcement Act of 1989 largely to address problems in the thrift industry. Specific provisions of the Act are discussed later in the chapter. Two insurance funds were established to maintain the appearance that banks were distinguishable from savings and loans. Initially, thrifts paid higher premiums than banks. In actuality, both funds were deficient and premiums have continually increased to where both types of firms pay the same rate. Deposit insurance works because the federal government stands behind it with its full faith, credit, and taxing authority.

balances. Historically, regulators have not allowed the very largest institutions to fail, so that uninsured depositors received, in effect, 100 percent deposit insurance. Regulators implicitly assume that large bank failures would seriously undermine public confidence in financial institutions and markets, so they generally prop up large banks with federal aid or find a merger partner. The OCC and state banking authorities officially designate banks as insolvent, but the Federal Reserve and FDIC assist in closings. Frequently, the Federal Reserve System (FRS) extends credit to a problem bank until an ownership transfer occurs. The FDIC's liquidation staff handles the disposition of a failed bank's assets and liabilities. These and other problems with deposit insurance are described in Chapter 11.

The Federal Reserve also serves as the federal government's lender of last resort. When a bank loses funding sources, the FRS may make a loan through its discount window to support operations until a solution appears. When Continental Illinois experienced difficulties in 1984, for example, the Federal Reserve loaned it over $4 billion until it effectively nationalized the bank. The same occurred with the Bank of New England in late 1990. The Federal Reserve's crisis management, however, is not limited to direct bank assistance. In recent years, it has intervened in disputes related to the collapse of silver prices due to the Hunt family's attempt to corner the silver market, junk bond financing of leveraged buyouts, the failure of securities dealers in repurchase agreements, the failures of privately insured thrift institutions in Ohio and Maryland, and the funding crisis faced by the Farm Credit System. In most cases, the firm in crisis requests back-up financing from the FRS if the crisis worsens. In other cases, market participants simply need expert advice. As lender of last resort, the Federal Reserve has the resources and clout to advise management and prevent serious financial problems.

New Charters. Groups interested in starting a commercial bank have the option of requesting a new charter from the Office of the Comptroller of the Currency or from the appropriate state banking authority. The source of the charter determines how the bank is regulated. Banks chartered by the OCC retain the word "national" in their names and are extensively regulated by three federal agencies: the OCC, Federal Reserve System, and FDIC. In addition to granting charters, the OCC conducts periodic examinations of national banks, evaluates merger applications when the resulting firm is a national bank, and authorizes branches where applicable. All national banks are members of the FRS and must purchase FDIC insurance.

State-chartered banks have the option of joining the FRS and purchasing FDIC insurance. All state banks that choose Federal Reserve membership must obtain deposit insurance. The FRS sets reserve requirements, approves proposed mergers and new branches, and examines state member banks. It also makes loans to banks, establishes consumer regulations, authorizes the formation of bank holding companies, and approves all holding company activities and acquisitions, regardless of how a bank was chartered. Insured state banks that choose not to join the FRS are regulated predominantly by the FDIC, while noninsured nonmembers are regulated by state banking authorities.

Exhibit 2.12 Federal Reserve Bank Regulations

Regulation	Subject
A. Safety and Soundness	
F	Financial information disclosed to stockholders
L	Interlocking directorates among banking organizations
O	Loans to "insiders" including directors, officers, and shareholders
R	Interlocking relationships between commercial banks and securities firms
B. Efficiency and Competitiveness	
K	International banking activities
Q	Interest rate ceilings on deposit liabilities
C. Consumer Protection	
AA	Deceptive practices
B	Equal credit opportunity
BB	Community reinvestment
C	Home mortgage disclosure
E	Electronic funds transfers
M	Consumer leasing
S	Privacy
Z	Truth-in-lending practices

Product Restrictions. The Federal Reserve also regulates specific activities of banks and bank holding companies as indicated in Exhibit 2.12. In the area of safety and soundness, regulations take the form of restricting interlocking relationships among directors of banks and between banks and securities firms to ensure independence, and restricting the terms of loans to insiders, such as directors, bank officers and shareholders.

Efficient and Competitive Financial System

Regulators have spent considerable effort in recent years analyzing and modifying regulations regarding where banks can compete, what prices they can charge, and what products and services they can offer.

Branching. As discussed previously, branching provisions are largely dictated by state branching laws. There is no federal provision for branching out of state. If federal legislation is passed allowing nationwide branching, the entire structure of banking organizations will change. Branches would allow firms to better diversify assets, expand the deposit base, and control expenses.

Mergers and Acquisitions. Regulators closely monitor bank expansion through mergers and acquisitions. The intent is to protect consumers from undue concentration of banking resources and to provide for the efficient delivery of services. Research generally shows that economies of scale in banking are reached at a relatively small firm size.[6] Large size is not justified strictly on the basis of lower unit production costs. Too many resources under one firm's control, however, may adversely affect pricing and credit availability. National banks are approved by the OCC, state member banks by the Federal Reserve, state nonmember, insured banks by the FDIC, and uninsured nonmembers by the appropriate state authority.

Historically, regulators applied strict criteria when evaluating potential anticompetitive effects. They would define the geographic market in which the acquired firm operated, determine the number of direct competitors, and calculate concentration measures that indicated the degree of control by the combined firm versus all competitors. Because commercial banks were viewed as the only direct competitors, bank mergers and acquisitions were frequently denied if the acquiring firm already had a presence in the market. In the current environment, however, the criteria are much more flexible. Other depository institutions and nonbank financial institutions are included as competitors. The relevant geographic market now includes a much broader area, which typically lowers the degree of concentration and makes it easier to approve an acquisition.[7] Regulators seem to agree that expansion via merger and acquisition is necessary to improve the safety and soundness of the nation's banking system. It is also easier to regulate a smaller number of distinct firms.

Interstate Banking. State law has historically determined whether banks can buy other banks outside their home state. For many years most banks conducted banking business exclusively in the state where the head office was located. A few bank holding companies ventured out of state to buy banks, but these transactions were generally small. Acquisitions stopped in 1956 when the Douglas amendment to the McFadden Act restricted bank holding companies from buying controlling interest in banks located outside the home state. This presented problems during the early stages of the 1980s' bank and thrift failures, as there were no buyers for large problem institutions. A provision of the Garn-St Germain Act subsequently allowed interstate takeovers of failed or failing institutions, but the number of transactions was small until the late 1980s. The pace of interstate activity quickened during the mid-1980s when many states authorized some form of interstate banking. This typically resulted from fear that in-state banks would be put at a competitive disadvantage to large out-of-state institutions. Other provisions regarding interstate banking are described in the following sections.

---

[6]Benston, 1982, summarizes recent studies and conducts comprehensive tests for U.S. commercial banks. He concludes that unit costs are lowest, on average, for banks with $50 million in total assets. Later studies related to economies of scope involving the joint production of products and services indicate that the most efficient institution is larger.

[7]When evaluating anticompetitive effects during the 1980s, the Federal Reserve used the Herfindahl-Hirschmann Index (HHI) to measure market concentration. The HHI is computed by identifying the appropriate market, then summing the squares of each competitor's market share. For example, three competing firms with market shares of 50%, 30%, and 20% would produce an index of 3800 (2500+900+400). To be guaranteed approval, the HHI after a merger or acquisition must be no greater than 1800 and/or cause the HHI to increase by no more than 200. Since 1990, regulators have been much more lenient in approving transactions that violate this standard.

Exhibit 2.13 Grandfathered Bank Holding Companies with Subsidiaries in More Than One State

Bank Holding Company	Home State	No. of States	Grandfathered Subsidiary Locations
Domestic			
First Interstate Bancorp, Inc.	CA	13	AZ, CA, CO, ID, MT, NM, OR, NV, WA, WY, UT, OK, TX
Norwest Corp.	MN	7	IA, MN, MT, NE, ND, SO, WI
First Bank System	MN	5	MN, MT, ND, SD, WI
First American Bancshares Corp.	DC	5	DC, MD, NY, TN, VA
Bremer Financial Corp.	MN	3	MN, ND, WI
General Bancshares Corp.	MO	3	IL, MO, TN
First Security Corp.	UT	3	ID, WY, UT
North Carolina National Bank Corp.	NC	2	FL, NC
Northern Trust Corp.	IL	2	FL, IL
Foreign			
Bank of Montreal	NY	2	CA, NY
Canadian Imperial Bank of Commerce	NY	2	CA, NY
Bank of Tokyo Ltd.	NY	2	CA, NY
Sumitomo Bank Ltd.	CA	2	CA, HI
Barclays Bank Ltd.	NY	2	CA, NY
Royal Bank of Canada	NY	2	NY, PR
Banco Central, S.A.	NY	2	NY, PR

Source: Federal Reserve Board of Governors.

Grandfather Clauses. Prior to the passage of the Douglas amendment, 16 bank holding companies owned affiliate banks outside their home states (Exhibit 2.13). These banks can continue all interstate operations initiated before interstate restrictions. Seven of the holding companies are foreign-based, and nine have their main offices in the United States. Several of these organizations, such as Norwest, NCNB, and First Interstate Bancorp, have aggressively expanded into other states through normal channels via the purchase of failed and healthy institutions.

Takeovers of Failing Institutions. Federal regulations permit financial institutions to acquire failed firms in other states. When a firm fails, regulators solicit bids from interested parties and select the best bid, determined by the type, location, and offering price of the acquiring firm. Both commercial banks and savings and loans can submit bids. Intrastate bidders of the same type, however, generally have the advantage. Once in a state, a firm can expand by buying other sound institutions in that state as permitted by law.

Public attention focused on this provision after several large bank holding companies acquired failed banks and thrifts during the early 1980s. In June 1983 Bank-America Corp. in California purchased Seafirst Corp. in Washington. Chase Manhattan Bank in New York purchased several privately insured savings and loans in Ohio in

1985. At year-end 1986 New York's Citicorp had acquired several failed savings and loans, allowing it to enter the California, Illinois, Florida, Maryland, and Nevada markets. In 1986 First Interstate entered Oklahoma by purchasing the state's second largest bank when it was ordered closed. In Texas, Chemical Bank purchased Texas Commerce, NCNB purchased First Republic Bancorp., and Bank One acquired 20 of MCorp's largest banks. State residents are often torn by the transactions because the acquirer brings necessary capital, but is viewed as having outside management that is not familiar with or sensitive to in-state needs.

State Authorization. Recent efforts to extend interstate banking have focused on convincing state legislatures to permit reciprocal agreements. Before 1980 no states allowed interstate acquisitions. By the end of 1990, only Hawaii, Montana, and North Dakota did not allow some form of interstate banking. Most allowed out-of-state banks and thrifts to acquire in-state firms or open new banks. Only Kansas differentiated, allowing interstate activity with thrifts but not banks.

There are many reasons for this drastic change. Some states saw an opportunity to increase capital availability in-state simply by opening their doors. These states include those that are geographically isolated, such as Alaska, as well as those with severe economic problems, such as Oklahoma and Texas. Other states used regional interstate compacts to allow their in-state banks to grow large enough to compete with banks in other states. Exhibit 2.14 documents the status of various states in terms of four classifications: nationwide entry, regional reciprocal pacts, regional reciprocal pacts with a trigger date for nationwide banking, and regional nonreciprocal pacts.[8]

Nationwide banking agreements are structured so that acquiring banks or bank holding companies can be from any state. Some states allow such acquisitions only if the acquirer's state also permits out-of-state banks the same opportunity. In this case, the agreement is labeled a nationwide reciprocal pact. Nationwide arrangements provide for the greatest number of potential competitors, the greatest number of merger and acquisition partners, and the broadest geographic representation. This has become the most popular form of interstate banking agreement, as indicated in Exhibit 2.14.

Regional reciprocal pacts are generally an alternative to nationwide banking. By limiting the number of bidders to firms in a subset of states, a state encourages in-state banks to merge with banks in similar geographic regions. States with regional compacts include those in the Northeast and Southeast. Because New York and California banks are typically excluded, regional banking organizations can grow in size until they are better able to compete nationally with the largest money center banks. Regional pacts prevent local banks from being immediately purchased by money center banks. Limiting the number of bidders, however, may be counterproductive if many large banks in a state are in distress; there simply may not be enough interested regional buyers to acquire failing banks. A regional nonreciprocal pact is more flexible because it does not require other states to allow the same opportunities to in-state banks.

---

[8]In June 1985 the U.S. Supreme Court ruled that state legislatures could establish regional banking agreements that excluded banks from other states.

Exhibit 2.14 The Status of Interstate Banking Agreements in 1990

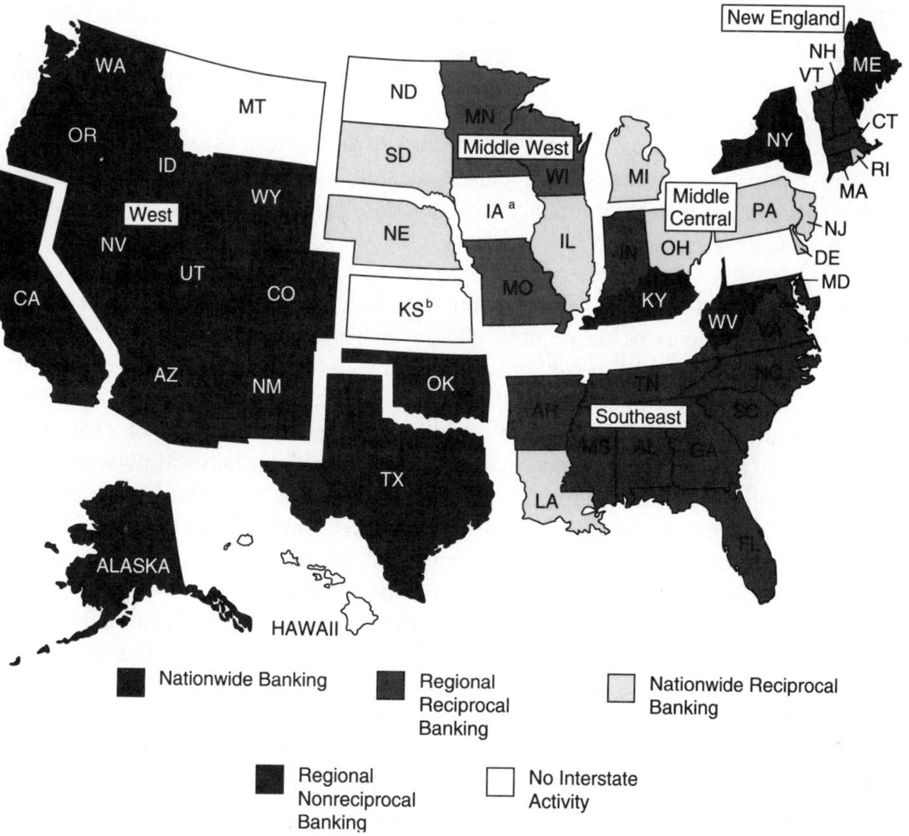

a) Iowa allows only Norwest to buy Iowa banks under the grandfather clause.

b) Kansas allows interstate activity only for thrift institutions.

Source: "Trigger Dates: A Look at Laws Granting Interstate Powers to Banks," *American Banker*, March 28, 1991.

The attraction of regional pacts is that in-state banks retain a regional identity. Another advantage is that large regional banks have traditionally emphasized middle-market lending rather than lending to multinational corporations or foreign governments, which many money center banks deal with. Credit availability to middle-market borrowers should thus be maintained.

Nonbank Banks. Even without explicit interstate banking authority, commercial banks can conduct business nationwide through holding company subsidiaries. Most large banking organizations have established Edge Act corporations, loan production offices, and consumer banks outside their home states. Edge Act corporations provide a full range of banking services but, by law, deal only in international transactions. There are two types of Edge corporations, banks and investment companies. Banking Edges operate as commercial banks, accepting deposits and making loans to firms with international business. Investment Edges engage strictly in activities outside the United States that are permitted under federal regulation. Loan production offices make commercial loans but do not accept deposits. Consumer banks accept deposits but make only consumer loans. Federal Reserve approval of these firms allowed large bank holding companies to form an interstate banking network throughout the nation. Federal legislation restricted this activity in 1987 so that geographic expansion in this form has slowed.

Pricing. Prior to 1980 legislation limited the rates banks could pay on certain types of deposits and the rates they could charge on certain types of loans. The Federal Reserve wanted to control money growth, and banks were the sole supplier of demand deposits, the primary component of the money supply. Banks were essentially guaranteed a positive spread between the yield on assets and the interest cost of most liabilities and the system of banks was safe. There was also a national policy of making housing available and affordable to as many families as possible. Thus savings and loans were allowed to pay slightly higher regulated rates on interest-bearing deposits than banks as long as they invested a significant portion of their assets in mortgages or other housing-related investments. While these price controls did not necessarily make the financial system more efficient, they did channel resources in desired areas. Banks competed with other banks primarily in terms of service and the range of noncredit products.

Interest rate ceilings were phased out beginning in 1980. Today, banks can compete without restriction on most interest rates they pay on deposits or charge on loans. This provides for a more efficient allocation of resources, but puts a greater burden on bank managers to assess and manage risk.

Consumer Protection

State legislatures and the Federal Reserve have implemented numerous laws and regulations to protect the rights of individuals who try to borrow. The purposes are wide-ranging, varying from restricting deceptive advertising or trade practices to prohibiting discrimination. Exhibit 2.12 lists the broad areas in which the Federal Reserve has established consumer regulations. Equal credit opportunity, for example, makes it illegal for any lender to discriminate against a borrower on the basis of race, sex, marital status, religion, age, or national origin. It establishes guidelines for structuring loan applications and specifies how information can be used in making credit decisions. Community reinvestment prohibits *redlining*, in which lenders as a matter of policy do not lend in certain geographic markets. Chapter 22 summarizes the key federal regulations as they pertain to consumer borrowing.

TRENDS IN FEDERAL LEGISLATION AND REGULATION

The focus of federal legislation and regulation from 1970 through 1986 was to define and ultimately expand the product and geographic markets served by depository institutions and to increase competition. Subsequent problems with failed savings and loans and commercial banks raised concerns that only a few large organizations will survive because all financial institutions will eventually have the same powers and large firms will drive small firms out of business. Key legislative and regulatory changes addressed these basic issues: What is a bank? Where can banks conduct business? What products can banks offer and what interest rates may be charged or paid? Significant regulatory developments are identified in the following section, with particular attention paid to the Depository Institutions Deregulation and Monetary Control Act of 1980 (DIDMCA) and the Garn–St Germain Depository Institutions Act of 1982 (GSG). Both are credited with accelerating changes in the current banking environment that worsened the thrift and banking crisis causing failures and the depletion of deposit insurance funds.

Key Legislation: 1956 to 1986

Ever since the collapse of banks in the 1930s—almost 4,000 institutions failed in 1933—federal and state governments have closely regulated the activities of commercial banks. In addition to providing deposit insurance and periodic examinations, the regulations specify where banks can locate offices, what products they can offer, and what interest rates they can charge and pay. Only recently have many restrictions been removed. The trend appears to be toward greater competition and market determination of prices and services and toward allowing institutions to fail. Exhibit 2.15 briefly summarizes important legislation and regulatory actions that have altered fundamental competitive opportunities for banks.

Legislation from 1956 to 1970 focused on limiting bank geographic and product expansion and restricting interest rate competition on deposits. To achieve this, regulators needed a formal designation of what constitutes a bank. The operational definition through the early 1980s was that a commercial bank both accepted demand deposits and made commercial loans. Not surprisingly, this led to the development of limited-service banks that offered only deposit services or only credit services, but avoided regulation as banks because they did not do both. Banks were generally restricted to operating within very narrow geographic markets, until they created limited-service banks that could locate anywhere.

Banks versus Nonbank Banks. While many firms would like to offer banking services, some do not want to be regulated as commercial banks or bank holding companies. This is especially true for insurance companies, brokerage firms, and general retailers whose banking services supplement their primary line of business. Banking regulation provides this opportunity.

In 1956 Congress passed the Bank Holding Company Act. Its fundamental intent was to enable government regulators to control the concentration of resources by large

Exhibit 2.15 Key Regulations and Legislation on Banking Expansion: 1956–1986

A. What is a Bank?

Bank Holding Company Act (1956)

Applies to bank holding companies that control at least two commercial banks. Gave Federal Reserve System authority to approve formation of bank holding companies, bank acquisitions, allowable nonbank activities, plus responsibility to examine bank holding companies.

Amendment to Bank Holding Company Act (1966)

Defines bank as any institution that accepts deposits payable on demand.

Amendment to Bank Holding Company Act (1970)

Defines bank as any institution that both accepts deposits that depositor has right to withdraw on demand and engages in business of making commercial loans.

Garn–St Germain Depository Institutions Act (1982)

Allows thrifts to offer commercial demand deposit accounts and make commercial loans. Specifically excludes any institution insured by Federal Savings and Loan Insurance Corp. or chartered by Federal Home Loan Bank Board from definition of bank.

March 1983

Comptroller of Currency declares moratorium on new national charters for limited-service (nonbank) banks.

January 1984

Federal Reserve System broadens definition of making commercial loans to include purchase of commercial paper, certificates of deposit, and bankers' acceptances; includes interest-bearing checking accounts in definition of demand deposits. Restricted limited-service banks from investing in corporate securities or offering negotiable orders of withdrawal accounts.

January 1986

U.S. Supreme Court rules Federal Reserve acted outside its statutory authority in its 1984 definition of banks. Limited-service banks are legal entities.

B. Where Can Banks Conduct Business?

Edge Act (Amendment to the Federal Reserve Act) (1919)

Authorizes commercial banks to open Edge Act subsidiaries outside their home state to offer international banking services.

McFadden Act (1927) and Amendment (1933)

Authorizes national banks to establish branch facilities to same extent state law allows state banks to branch.

Douglas Amendment to Bank Holding Company Act (1956)

Prohibits bank holding company from owning banks in more than one state.

(continued)

banking organizations and to ensure that banks engaged in activities closely related to banking. Under the Act and later amendments, the Federal Reserve System must approve all bank holding company formations and acquisitions of banks and nonbanks. The Federal Reserve also rules on what activities bank holding companies can and cannot engage in.

Exhibit 2.15 *(Continued)*

International Banking Act (1978)

Requires foreign banks to conform to same branching and interstate restrictions as domestic banks.

December 1981

Federal Reserve authorizes U.S. banks to establish international banking facilities in U.S. that are exempt from selected regulations.

1982–present

State legislatures authorize interstate banking compacts.

November 1986

Federal Reserve approves Sumitomo Ltd.'s plan to acquire ownership interest in Goldman, Sachs & Co.

C. What Products Can Banks Offer? What Interest Rates Can Banks Charge and Pay?

Glass-Steagall Act (1933)

Prohibits banks from underwriting or acting as brokers for corporate and municipal revenue securities. Banks allowed to underwrite and deal in federal securities, certificates of deposit, municipal general obligation securities. Investment banks with these powers prohibited from offering demand deposits.

Regulation Q (1933)

Prohibits banks from paying interest on demand deposits and limits rates banks can pay on other deposits.

Federal Reserve Regulations Pursuant to Bank Holding Company Act

Specifies nonbank activities bank holding companies can and cannot engage in. Recently authorized discount brokerage, futures and options services, expanded insurance powers.

Depository Institutions Deregulation and Monetary Control Act (1980)

Phases out Regulation Q, certain usury ceilings. Authorizes new deposit and asset products.

Garn–St Germain Depository Institutions Act (1982)

Authorizes new asset and deposit products.

March 1986

Depository Institutions Deregulation Committee removes last interest rate ceilings on all but commercial demand deposits.

Competitive Equality Banking Act (1987)

Restricted the types of products and growth of grandfathered nonbank banks.

Financial Institutions Reform, Recovery, and Enforcement Act (1989)

Savings and loans were forced to divest their junk bond investments by July 1994. Savings and loans were required to hold no less than 70% of their assets in mortgage-related investments.

In 1980 Gulf & Western acquired a bank and sold its commercial loan portfolio, creating the first limited-service bank. Other institutions of various types quickly followed suit including Prudential-Bache, Merrill Lynch, Sears, Fidelity Mutual Funds, and Beneficial Finance. Large commercial banking organizations similarly located limited-service banks outside their home states in order to expand their presence nationwide.

Small commercial banks protested that limited-service banks were simply a means for firms in any line of business to engage in most banking activities but avoid regulation as banks. In 1983 the Federal Reserve System agreed and attempted to restrict limited-service banks by redefining commercial loans to include the purchase of commercial paper, certificates of deposit, and bankers acceptances. It also included interest-bearing checking accounts in its definition of demand deposits. Limited-service banks could no longer offer interest-bearing transactions accounts, and those that sold off their commercial loans could no longer invest in corporate securities unless they chose to register as bank holding companies. In 1986 the U.S. Supreme Court ruled that the Federal Reserve's definition exceeded its authority and thus nonbank banks were legal. Federal legislation in 1987, however, prohibited new nonbank banks from being chartered, so that competition now comes only from grandfathered (already existing) firms.

Finally, the Glass–Steagall Act of 1933 explicitly distinguished between commerce and banking in determining what products different firms could offer. One focus of current legislation is to expand the range of products that banks can offer. Today's remaining prohibitions still do not allow most banks to underwrite corporate securities and municipal revenue bonds. Curiously, banks can underwrite all types of securities, including stocks, outside the United States. Large firms such as Citicorp, Bankers Trust, and J.P. Morgan generate a substantial share of their net income from these international activities. Part C of Exhibit 2.15 summarizes trends in the regulation of allowable products and interest rates at banks.

The Depository Institutions Deregulation and Monetary Control Act

DIDMCA was the culmination of long-standing efforts to change the structure of the financial services industry. While specific reforms had been debated since 1961, the economic environment in the late 1970s magnified financial institutions' operating problems and forced legislation. Rates depository institutions could pay on most deposits were fixed by Regulation Q. From 1976 through 1979, the monthly inflation rate, as measured by the consumer price index, increased from under 5 percent (annually) to over 15 percent. Money market interest rates similarly rose from around 6 percent to over 14 percent. During the same period, the prime rate changed 65 times, considerably more often than in previous years.

This period coincided with the extraordinary growth of money market mutual funds. These funds simply sell shares to individuals, usually at a fixed unit price, and use the proceeds to buy money market instruments such as Treasury bills, bank certificates of deposit, and commercial paper. None of these instruments were subject to Regulation Q ceilings so that shareholders would effectively receive money market rates less a small service charge. Money market mutual funds would even provide transactions privileges by allowing individuals to write checks as long as the minimum amount was several hundred dollars. Many individuals effectively substituted these shares for bank deposits.

Market participants subsequently altered their behavior. Savers earning fixed and relatively low interest rates on deposits subject to Regulation Q withdrew their funds and invested in alternative instruments paying market rates. Commercial banks that were required by FRS membership to hold large amounts of nonearning reserves withdrew from the system because the opportunity cost grew prohibitive. Usury ceilings limited the rates lenders could charge and many home buyers, farmers, and small businesses could not obtain credit. As a result, banks and thrifts saw their cost of funds rise yet could not raise asset yields to keep pace. Savings and loans holding long-term mortgages at below-market rates experienced a severe profit and cash flow squeeze. Under this pressure, Congress approved DIDMCA and dramatically altered the long-term operating environment of financial institutions.

The stated goals of DIDMCA were to improve Federal Reserve monetary control, to allow institutions to pay market rates on deposits, and to expand the range of services offered. The intent was to gradually equalize treatment of different types of depository firms and increase competition. The most significant components of DIDMCA are summarized in Exhibit 2.16.

In October 1979 the Federal Reserve announced that it would examine the monetary aggregates more closely in the future as intermediate targets of monetary policy. Implicitly, less attention would be paid to short-term interest rates. DIDMCA made control of money growth easier. Prior to 1980, nonmember commercial banks were subject to reserve requirements set by states. Savings and loan associations' reserves were set by thrift regulators. Only member banks had to hold reserves according to Federal Reserve guidelines. DIDMCA extended reserve requirements to all institutions offering transactions accounts and provided that the amount would be equal for similar sized firms after a phase-in period. For most institutions, reserve requirement ratios were lowered. In return, all firms gained access to the discount window and the Federal Reserve began to charge for services that it used to provide free.

Most importantly, the Act provided for the removal of interest rate ceilings. One set of regulations mandated that the Depository Institutions Deregulation Committee, made up of the chief officers of the four main regulatory agencies, phase out rate ceilings on time and savings deposits by 1986. Another set superseded state usury ceilings on loans for residential real property and business and agriculture loans over $25,000. The message was that borrowers and lenders should get accustomed to paying and charging market rates.[9] Coincidentally, FDIC insurance coverage was raised to $100,000 from $40,000 per account at all types of institutions. While this was done in part to adjust for inflation, it granted a significant competitive advantage to banks and thrifts in attracting new deposits. Increased insurance made bank deposits safer than money market mutual funds and helped banks recoup some of their lost deposits. Contemporary Issues: The Long-Term Effect of $100,000 Deposit Insurance summarizes the thought that went into the decision to increase deposit insurance, which played a critical role in subsequent thrift failures.

---

[9]Rate ceilings on all bank liabilities except demand deposits were removed in March 1986, after which the Depository Institutions Deregulation Committee was terminated.

Exhibit 2.16 Key Provisions of the Depository Institutions Deregulation and Monetary Control Act of 1980

Improvement of Monetary Control
- Extends reserve requirements set by Federal Reserve to all federally insured depository institutions.
- Imposes new reserve requirements on transactions accounts and nonpersonal time deposits offered by banks and thrift institutions that are not Federal Reserve members. Over time all firms of equal size will be subject to same percentage requirements.
- Allows all depository institutions that offer transactions accounts to borrow at Federal Reserve discount window.

Pricing of Federal Reserve Services
- Federal Reserve must explicitly price services provided financial institutions based on cost of providing services.
- All services are available to member and nonmember institutions.

Interest Rate Ceilings and Deposit Insurance
- Gives Depository Institutions Deregulation Committee responsibility to phase out interest rate ceilings on deposits at financial institutions. Overrides state limits on deposit rates.
- Overrides state usury ceilings on loans for residential property unless reimposed by state legislatures.
- Raises ceiling rates on business and agriculture loans to 5 percent over discount rate.
- Increases federal deposit insurance to $100,000 at all federally insured institutions.

New Powers for Banks and Thrift Institutions
- Authorizes depository institutions to offer negotiable orders of withdrawal accounts.
- Authorizes credit unions to issue share drafts.
- Allows new investment for thrifts:
  Up to 20% of assets in consumer loans, commercial paper, corporate debt securities.
  Up to 5% of assets in education, community development, unsecured construction loans.
- Allows shares of open-end investment companies to satisfy liquidity requirements.
- Authorizes thrifts to issue credit cards and provide trust services.
- Allows qualifying thrifts to issue mutual capital certificates that constitute net worth.

Finally, DIDMCA granted new powers to depository institutions. First, all institutions could legally offer interest-bearing transactions accounts; banks and thrifts could offer negotiable orders of withdrawal (NOWs); and credit unions could offer share drafts.[10] Second, thrift institutions were authorized to invest additional assets in consumer loans and corporate securities. These assets could presumably be repriced more frequently and thus would reduce thrifts' exposure to increases in the cost of funds. The Act further authorized thrifts to offer credit card and trust services like those at commercial banks. Finally, thrifts were allowed to issue mutual capital certificates, which were acquired by federal regulators and included in thrifts' capital base. In essence, the regulators provided liquidity to capital-deficient firms with limited access to borrowed funds.

---

[10]New England firms were allowed to offer these accounts in the mid-1970s. Prior to 1980, other institutions circumvented Regulation Q restrictions by creating new accounts such as automatic transfers from savings. See Chapter 11.

The Garn–St Germain Depository Institutions Act of 1982

GSG continued the deregulation process. Thrifts were having difficulty competing for deposits and earning high enough yields on assets to be profitable. In many cases their cost of funds exceeded asset yields because they were paying market rates on deposits, but the bulk of assets still carried below market mortgage rates. Rising interest rates raised interest expense more than interest income grew. Key provisions, listed in Exhibit 2.17, expanded deposit sources of funds, granted new asset powers, and provided for emergency takeovers of failing institutions.

GSG authorized three new sources of funds. The first, the money market deposit account (MMDA), was created to stop the flow of funds to unregulated money market mutual funds. Initially, there was no limit on the rate that banks could pay on balances in excess of $2,500. Depositors could write up to three checks per month with an additional three telephone transfers allowed, and the first $100,000 was federally insured. The Depository Institutions Deregulation Committee later authorized Super NOW accounts, which had the same basic features as MMDAs except that the number of transactions was unlimited. By 1986 all minimum balance requirements and rate ceilings on MMDAs and Super NOWs had been eliminated. The second new source was that all government units were permitted to hold NOW accounts. Previously, only individuals and nonprofit, nongovernment organizations could open accounts. Third, federal savings and loans could accept demand deposits from qualifying business loan customers.

Most of the expanded asset powers were designed to benefit thrifts. GSG authorized them to make commercial loans, to enforce due-on-sale clauses in mortgage contracts, and to convert to stock associations. The first two provisions enabled savings and loans to increase the interest sensitivity of asset holdings and enter new markets. Conversion to stock ownership from mutual organizations increased each firm's ability to raise capital. Commercial banks were allowed to increase loan limits for individual borrowers to 15 percent of bank capital and surplus for unsecured credits and 25 percent for secured credits.

The last set of provisions allowed mergers and acquisitions of problem financial institutions across state lines. According to GSG, federal regulators can arrange the acquisition of a failed firm by any type of insured institution, regardless of location. Qualified investors include commercial banks, bank holding companies, insured savings and loans, and other companies.

Both DIDMCA and GSG had their greatest impact on the incentives for risk-taking to managers of banks and thrifts. Consider the manager of a small thrift that found itself locked in to a portfolio of fixed-rate mortgages that yielded less than what the firm was paying on its liabilities. Its interest expense would change with changes in market interest rates, while its interest income would remain relatively constant. As rates increased, the firm would lose. Federal deposit insurance provided a strategy to offset such problems. Why not package deposits into $100,000 units that carried full deposit insurance, and sell the deposits to individuals and businesses throughout the country? Any firm could easily sell such units through brokers who simply called potential investors and offered to pay a premium over the prevailing deposit rate.

CONTEMPORARY ISSUES

The Long-Term Effect of $100,000 Deposit Insurance

Prior to DIDMCA, federal deposit insurance amounted to $40,000 per account. Due at least in part to the efforts of the U.S. League of Savings Institutions, the savings and loan association lobbying arm, and the Chairman of the House Banking Committee, Fernand St Germain, Congress raised coverage to $100,000 with little debate. The effect, however, was monumental and immediate.

Brokerage houses quickly negotiated deals with aggressive thrifts and banks to sell certificates of deposit in $100,000 blocks to interested investors anywhere in the world. Because the principal was fully federally insured, an investor did not have to worry about the issuer defaulting. Ultimately, the U.S. Treasury, and thus taxpayers, would pay. To attract funds, a bank or thrift needed only to pay a rate that was slightly above the prevailing market rate. Unfortunately, there were no controls on the banks and thrifts regarding how to invest the funds. As later performance revealed, many of these institutions speculated on real estate or simply frittered the money away. Thrift managers were essentially playing with the government's (taxpayers') money. Estimates of the cost of thrift failures alone reach as high as $500 billion.

Buyers of the deposits would not be at risk because the federal government would pay off the claim if the thrift failed. The thrift in turn would take the proceeds from these *brokered deposits* and invest in higher yielding, and riskier, assets than mortgages. If the assets paid the promised returns, they could pay the new depositors and use the profits to offset losses on the old mortgages.

This is what many thrift managers did. Deposit insurance essentially allowed them to borrow at the government's (taxpayers') risk, yet speculate with the proceeds to reap personal gains. If the thrift failed, managers lost only their jobs and any small equity they might own in the thrift. The temptation was so great, however, that numerous thrift managers fraudulently used thrift resources for personal benefit and ultimately went to jail when the thrift failed and the true operating condition of the firm became known.

The Tax Reform Act of 1986

For many years the public perceived that banks did not pay their fair share of taxes. Large banks, especially those with publicly traded stock, often used tax-sheltered investments, including municipal bond interest, accelerated depreciation allowances obtained through subsidiary activities, and foreign and investment tax credits to reduce their reported tax liabilities close to zero. While Congress passed the Tax Reform Act of 1986 to restructure the entire federal income tax code, many provisions dramatically altered the tax treatment of commercial banks. The intent, at least in part, was to eliminate the perceived tax shelters available to banks.

Several of the Act's major changes are briefly summarized as follows. The major benefit is that the corporate income tax rate was lowered to 34 percent. The new law

Exhibit 2.17 Key Provisions of the Garn–St Germain
Depository Institutions Act of 1982

New Sources of Deposit Funds
- Authorizes depository institutions to issue money market deposit account to any customer with:
  Minimum balance of $2,500
  No minimum maturity
  No interest rate ceiling
  Limit of six transactions per month with three by check
  Federal insurance
- Allows federal, state, local governments to open negotiable orders of withdrawal accounts.
- Allows federally chartered savings and loans to issue demand deposits to firms and individuals they have business loan relationships with.

Expanded Powers
- Authorizes thrifts to make commercial loans and overdraft loans.
- Preempts state restrictions against due-on-sale clauses in mortgage contracts.
- Increases legal lending limit for any single customer as percentage of commercial bank capital and surplus.
- Permits thrifts to switch between state and federal charters, between mutual and stock form of organization, between savings and loan and savings bank charters.

Emergency Regulatory Powers
- Allows regulatory agencies to arrange mergers and acquisitions for problem institutions across geographic and institutional barriers.
- Allows regulators to make loans to problem firms or acquiring firm.
- Allows regulators to guarantee assets and liabilities of problem institution.
- Allows regulators to issue net worth certificates to problem institutions.

also forced banks to restructure the composition of assets. The provisions generally took effect in 1987.

Deductions for Bad Debts. From 1969 to 1986 banks were allowed to set up loan-loss reserves as a percentage of their loan portfolio and deduct allocations to the loss reserve from income. Banks with loan growth could generally take deductions in excess of actual loan-loss experience, with the difference representing a tax shelter. The Tax Reform Act retains the reserve system for banks with $400 million or less in total assets. All other banks can now deduct only what they actually charge off during a year.

Carrying Costs for Municipal Bonds. At the end of 1985 banks owned 35 percent of all municipal bonds outstanding. Interest on municipals is exempt from federal income taxes. For many years banks could deduct all of the financing costs of buying municipals. With the Tax Reform Act, banks can deduct only 80 percent of their borrowing costs associated with buying municipals issued for essential public purposes, if the municipality issues less than $10 million in securities per year. Banks lose the entire interest deduction on financing costs for new purchases of all other municipal securities.

Tax Credits. Many bank holding companies own subsidiaries involved in leasing and other capital-intensive activities. The Tax Reform Act eliminated the investment tax credit which arose when depreciable assets were purchased. Leasing subsidiaries do not now generate tax credits, and accelerated depreciation deductions have been reduced. The Act also disallowed foreign tax credits over an 8-year phase-out period.

Individual Retirement Accounts. Banks have successfully marketed certificates of deposit to customers for individual retirement accounts. These accounts are long-term, stable deposits because the owner can defer income from taxes until it is withdrawn. The Act makes these accounts less attractive by eliminating the tax deduction for contributions to an account for high-income individuals who are covered by existing retirement plans.

Alternative Minimum Tax. Corporations must now calculate their federal income tax in two ways. First, they calculate their tax liability under the regular income tax as revised. Second, they calculate alternative minimum tax income and apply a flat 20 percent tax rate. They pay the greater of the two tax liabilities. Alternative minimum tax income equals regular taxable income plus preference items, including excess accelerated depreciation claimed, a portion of tax-exempt municipal interest, and excess loss reserve deductions. Many banks will pay the alternative minimum tax, which essentially guarantees they will pay at least a basic amount of taxes.

Competitive Equality Banking Act of 1987

During 1987 Congress passed the Competitive Equality Banking Act of 1987. The legislation served two main purposes. First, it formally legitimized the rights of existing nonbank banks. At the time of passage, there was concern that firms such as Sears, Roebuck, & Co. and American Express were able to operate limited-service banks in direct competition with commercial banks, yet avoided regulation as banks or bank holding companies. The Act placed restrictions on the type of products and growth of these grandfathered firms. It also prohibited new ones from being chartered.

Second, the Act offered several provisions to assist in the handling of problem thrift institutions. Prior to the Act, many savings and loans were operating at a loss and depleting their capital. The Federal Savings and Loans Insurance Corporation (FSLIC), the federal agency that insured thrifts, found that its reserves were depleted from large payouts to depositors at thrift closings, so that the fund was technically insolvent. The Act authorized the issuance of $10.8 billion in securities with the proceeds to be used to assist in thrift closings. Healthy savings and loans were assessed an added charge to their normal deposit insurance fee to help pay interest on the bonds. In addition, the regulator of thrifts, the Federal Home Loan Bank Board, was required to use supervisory forbearance and not close thrifts that did not meet the minimum net worth requirements imposed by regulation. Thrifts were perceived to be only temporarily unsafe and were to be given time to work out their problems. As the later crisis indicates, forbearance aggravated the problems faced today by increasing the ultimate cost of the thrift bailout.

The Financial Institutions Reform, Recovery and Enforcement Act of 1989 (FIRREA)

On August 9, 1989, President Bush signed FIRREA into law. The stated purpose of the legislation was to provide for the efficient handling of problem savings and loan associations. In short, the FSLIC was insolvent and there was widespread concern that thrift institutions were fundamentally unsafe. FIRREA addressed these problems by:

- improving the financial condition of the deposit insurance funds
- changing the regulatory structure of the savings and loan industry
- raising capital requirements and restricting investment activities of savings and loans
- strengthening the enforcement powers of regulators

Specific provisions included the following.

Changing Regulatory Structure. FIRREA replaced the Federal Home Loan Bank Board, which had historically regulated savings and loans, with the Office of Thrift Supervision (OTS), a division of the U.S. Treasury. The OTS is charged with conducting routine examinations of all federal and state-chartered savings institutions, and will supervise their business conduct.

FIRREA similarly eliminated the FSLIC and replaced it with two deposit insurance funds operated by the FDIC. The Savings Associations Insurance Fund (SAIF) is for savings institutions, while the Bank Insurance Fund (BIF) is for commercial banks. The law mandated different assessments for deposit insurance premiums between the two funds, which were later increased by Congress.

Improving the Condition of the Insurance Funds. The legislation created a Resolution Trust Corp. (RTC) and a Resolution Funding Corp. (RefCorp) to assist in the closing of failed thrift institutions. RefCorp issues bonds authorized by Congress, while the RTC, under FDIC supervision, manages firms placed into receivership and disposes of assets obtained by the government in closing failed thrifts.

Raising Capital and Restricting Investment Powers. To reduce the risk associated with operating a savings institution, FIRREA mandated that the OTS set minimum capital standards that are not less stringent than those required of national banks. Such standards effectively limit how much debt compared to equity a savings institution must have in its financial structure. Replacing debt with equity lowers financial risk.

The Act also forced thrifts to divest of all *junk bonds* in their portfolios by July 1, 1994. Junk bonds are high-yield bonds that carry a rating lower than either Baa or BBB, or are nonrated. Such bonds are perceived to exhibit substantial default risk because the borrower is likely to not repay the full amount of principal and interest owed. Prior to FIRREA, many savings and loans owned large amounts of junk bonds that were deemed to be too risky for their portfolios. The Act further restricted how much savings and loans could lend to any single borrower, which in some cases was less than outstanding loans and loan commitments.

Finally, FIRREA forced savings and loans to meet a *qualified thrift lender (QTL)* test to continue to be treated as a savings institution. The simple requirement was that no less than 70 percent of the firm's portfolio assets must be held in mortgage-related investments. Qualifying investments include single- and multiple-family mortgages, mortgage-backed securities, and loans for construction, home improvement, manufactured housing, and home equity loans. This feature is somewhat curious as it forces thrifts to concentrate their assets in a smaller set of investments, and thus reduce diversification, while these assets earn risk-adjusted returns that are relatively low compared with other alternatives. It does, however, force thrift managers to concentrate business efforts in areas where historically they have demonstrated some expertise. The QTL test will likely accelerate consolidation within the thrift industry.

Strengthening the Enforcement Powers of Regulators. FIRREA specifically authorizes penalties for firms that violate the law or regulations, or misstate financial information. Regulators can more readily issue cease and desist orders that restrict thrift activities and opportunities, and even remove individuals from certain management positions.

Many analysts believe that FIRREA represents the death-knell for thrift institutions as a separate industry. Meeting the QTL test will reduce profitability over time, especially if capital requirements are increased. Firms will have to shrink in size, rather than grow, and will thus have limited opportunities to pay shareholders a reasonable return. Ultimately, thrifts will merge with other financial services companies to obtain additional capital and thereby offer a broader range of services.

CURRENT UNRESOLVED REGULATORY ISSUES

Bank regulation evolves in response to economic and competitive conditions. At any time, managers of banks express concern regarding limitations on their allowable activities and unfavorable competitive conditions, while regulators try to respond by identifying the appropriate rules to guide behavior and achieve the objectives presented earlier. At the start of the 1990s, many issues were under debate regarding the future structure and operating environment of financial services institutions. Key facets of the debate are identified below, with the topics discussed in greater detail throughout the book.

Capital Adequacy

During the 1980s, bank and thrift failures soared. The U.S. economy experienced what is referred to as a rolling recession, in which different geographic markets suffered significant economic problems. Consider, for example, the farm crisis in the Midwest, problems with the steel industry in the Mideast, the energy problems in the Southwest, and real estate problems throughout the country. Financial institution failures correspondingly increased, reflecting both economic problems and general mismanagement.

Effective in 1992, banks and thrifts will be subject to minimum capital requirements that are designed to reduce the overall risk of the banking industry. Conceptually, these requirements stipulate the minimum amount of stockholders' equity and maximum amount of debt banks can use to finance their assets. The greater the equity, the lower the risk. The 1992 standards base the minimum equity on the general riskiness of bank assets. The current debate focuses on how much capital is enough. Regulators would like to increase the minimum requirement because it reduces the likelihood of failure. Bankers, in contrast, argue that it is expensive and difficult to obtain additional equity, and high requirements restrict their competitiveness.

Too Big To Fail

Historically, regulators have not allowed the largest commercial banks to fail. Early in 1991, for example, the Bank of New England, with $22 billion in assets, failed and all depositors were fully protected. When large banks have gotten into trouble, regulators have arranged mergers or acquisitions and effectively protected depositors who held balances in excess of $100,000. Thus federal deposit insurance was extended to all depositors regardless of their balances. In contrast, small banks are routinely allowed to fail and uninsured depositors lose a portion of their uninsured balance. One month before Bank of New England's failure, Freedom National Bank in Harlem, with $98 million in assets, failed. Here uninsured depositors were promised 50 cents per dollar of uninsured deposits. Isn't this discriminatory? Why are large banks not allowed to fail?

Deposit Insurance Reform

The structure of deposit insurance during the 1980s clearly contributed to the high rate of failures and the huge cost of the thrift bailout. The debate concerns the appropriate structure, purpose, and cost of deposit insurance. If it is truly insurance, shouldn't premiums paid by banks reflect their risk and thus probability of failure? At present, all banks pay the same flat rate insurance premium based on the size of domestic deposits. In order to reduce the incentive for bank managers to take excessive risks caused by deposit insurance, shouldn't coverage be reduced from $100,000 per account? If the regulators will not allow the largest banks to fail, shouldn't insurance premiums be based on foreign deposits as well as domestic deposits?

Market Value versus Book Value Accounting

As an incentive to reduce risk-taking and provide clearer information to both investors and regulators, many analysts contend that banks should be forced to report assets and liabilities at market values on their balance sheets, and report the change in market values—whether realized or not—on their income statements. Thus if interest rates rise, the market value of assets will decline as will the market value of liabilities. The market value of bank equity, which equals the difference between the market value of assets and liabilities, will either rise or fall depending on the size of the comparative changes in value. The advantage is that the market value of equity provides a better picture of a firm's true financial condition. The disadvantage is that market value accounting will add considerable volatility to financial statements, and thus indicate substantial banking risk, and that it is extremely difficult to accurately measure the market value of many individual balance sheet items.

New Powers

Banks are continually pressing for additional investment powers and the opportunity to enter new lines of business. Many banks, for example, would like to offer full lines of insurance products. Others would like to engage in broad-based investment banking activities, such as underwriting all types of securities and arranging mergers and acquisitions.

SUMMARY

According to regulatory definition, a commercial bank is a firm that both accepts demand deposits and makes commercial loans. The Comptroller of the Currency and state banking departments approve new bank charters and, along with the Federal Reserve and FDIC, regulate and examine qualifying banks. Many banks operate as unit banks with only one office, while others are part of branch banking systems. Both unit and branch banks may be part of a bank holding company, which owns controlling interest in subsidiary banks. Through holding companies, many banking organizations engage in activities closely related to banking, such as leasing, data processing, investment banking, and mortgage banking. State legislative rulings permit banks in all but three states to acquire banks in other states so that interstate banking is now a significant part of commercial banking.

Commercial banks compete with other banks and depository institutions. These institutions can offer identical deposit products and invest in the same assets, as well as possess additional real estate investment powers. Banks also compete with limited-service banks, or nonbank banks, that operate as part of nationwide financial service companies. This chapter describes the organizational structure of the commercial banking industry and the legislation and regulation that guide operating policies. Early restrictions regarding branching encouraged the formation of holding companies and the development of nonbank banks as a means of circumventing branching restrictions. The impact of interest deregulation and increased deposit insurance was to encourage risk-taking by banks and thrifts, so that many firms failed during the 1980s and early 1990s. Congress approved legislation (FIRREA) in 1989 that substantially restructured the thrift industry by redefining acceptable business activities. The current regulatory trend is to remove differences in opportunities now available to different types of financial services companies, and thus expand the number of competitors in most product areas.

FIRST FINANCIAL REVISITED

Most of First Financial's problems can be characterized by an inattention to internal controls regarding bank operating policies and the lack of concern over regulatory guidelines. The bank had no effective loan or investment policy. Ralph Treadway ran the bank as a one man show. He made the critical decisions and largely kept the Board of Directors uninformed. The Board in turn abdicated its responsibilities by not protecting the interests of shareholders who appeared to be poised to lose their investment in the bank. Ultimately, the Board's inattention will cost employees jobs and perhaps the community local ownership.

A list of regulatory violations includes:

1. Loans in excess of legal lending limits

2. Community Reinvestment Act violations

3. Little or no loan documentation supporting loans

4. Treadway's business interest with member of the Board is a potential violation if favorable terms were available. It also appears to be unethical.

5. Bank policy statements were incomplete.

6. Bank is operating with too little capital.

Whoever takes over management of First Financial will have to focus on risk management. Regulators are also likely to restrict future activities until management demonstrates that the bank is in compliance with all regulations. If you were in charge of SMQ, would you keep Treadway and the existing group of officers as managers? Would you keep the current Board of Directors? What are the costs and benefits of making changes?

Questions

Structure of the Industry

1. Regulations have limited bank branching. Why? What has been the unpleasant result of these restrictions?

2. How does a one-bank holding company differ from a bank? How does a multibank holding company differ from a one-bank holding company?

3. What motivated the creation of bank holding companies?

4. Describe the five levels of management typically found in an independent bank. In which of these levels would a finance graduate typically start his or her professional career? Which level do you think is the most important in the bank and why?

5. How do the duties of the bank's chief operations officer differ from those of the chief executive officer?

6. What are the duties of the outside members of the Board of Directors and to whom are they responsible?

7. Which of the following activities can a bank holding company become involved in?
   a) Offer bank management classes for the managers of any bank
   b) Offer discount brokerage services
   c) Run an armored car service
   d) Underwrite municipal securities
   e) Underwrite corporate stock issues
   f) Offer tax preparation services
   g) Perform real estate appraisals
   h) Act as a real estate broker
   i) Offer financial advice to customers
   j) Run a courier service

8. What is the major source of income and the major expense for a bank holding company?

9. Is a bank holding company an economically viable independent institution? Could it continue a profitable existence if its subsidiaries were all closed?

10. What are the basic assets and liabilities of a multibank holding company?

Regulation

11. Bank regulators have four objectives. What are they?

12. What are the four main bank regulatory agencies? What are the three categories of regulations? Devise a simpler improved regulatory structure.

13. Which regulatory agency (or agencies) focus on:
    a. soundness of the system
    b. competitiveness of the system
    c. protection of customers

14. What does the acronym CAMEL represent? Which of these are the most important based on the amount of time examiners spend on them? Do you think this is an appropriate focus?

15. If a regulatory examination discloses problems, what does the regulator do?

16. Has deposit insurance kept banks from failing? Has it kept depositors from losing money in failures? Should it do either or both of these things?

17. What does it mean to be "the lender of last resort"? Which regulatory agency serves this role?

18. Bank regulators control charters, mergers, and branches to protect consumers from what?

19. How do regional reciprocal interstate banking agreements differ from full nation-wide agreements? What is the motivation underlying a regional reciprocal compact? Who determines which kind of agreement applies to a bank?

20. Will small community banks be able to compete successfully with large commercial banks after total interstate banking? Will small community banks be able to compete successfully with firms such as Sears and Merrill Lynch or companies like General Electric and General Motors which offer financial services?

21. What is a nonbank bank? Why are banks interested in them? Why are nonbanking firms interested in them?

22. A fundamental responsibility of bank loan officers is to segregate good loan applications from bad. What criteria is a bank prohibited from using in determining acceptable loan applications? What criteria does this leave for segregating the two groups?

Trends

23. Since the 1950s federal legislation has loosened control in some types of regulation while strengthening control in others. Of the three main regulatory areas (soundness, competition, consumer protection) which has been most loosened and which has been most tightened?

24. What was the motivation for the DIDMCA? Has it proved successful?

25. Besides removing interest rate ceilings, what two major areas of banking did the DIDMCA change?

26. What was the motivation for the Garn–St Germain Act? What did it change?

27. How did the Tax Reform Act of 1986 affect banking?

28. What were the two purposes of the Competitive Equality Banking Act of 1987?

29. What was the main purpose of FIRREA?

References

Barth, James, Philip Bartholomew and Michael Bradley. "Determinants of Thrift Institutions Resolution Costs." *Journal of Finance* (July 1990)

Barth, James, George Benston, and Philip Wiest. "The Financial Institutions Reform, Recovery and Enforcement Act of 1989: Description, Effects and Implications." *Issues in Bank Regulation* (Winter 1990).

Becketti, Sean. "The Truth About Junk Bonds." *Economic Review* (Federal Reserve Bank of Kansas City, July/August 1990).

Benston, George. "Scale Economies in Banking: A Restructuring and Reassessment." *Journal of Money, Credit and Banking* (November 1982).

"Big Bank CEOs Look at the Present and Future." *American Banker* (March 15, 1984).

Brady, Nicholas. "Global Competition: A Catalyst for Restructuring U.S. Financial Services." *Issues in Bank Regulation* (Summer 1990).

Bush, Vanessa, and Katherine Morall. "FIRREA Slows Deregulation and Closes the Gap Between Commercial Banks and Savings Institutions." *Savings Institutions* (October 1989).

Carron, Andrew. *The Plight of the Thrift Industry*. Washington, D.C.: The Brookings Institute, 1982.

Cocheo, Steve. Anatomy of an Examination." *ABA Banking Journal* (February 1986).

"The Depository Institutions Deregulation and Monetary Control Act of 1980." *Economic Perspectives* (Federal Reserve Bank of Chicago, September–October, 1980).

Evanoff, Douglas, and Diana Fortier. "The Impact of Geographic Expansion in Banking: Some Axioms to Grind." *Economic Perspectives* (Federal Reserve Bank of Chicago, May–June 1986).

The Federal Guide. Chicago: United States League of Savings Associations, 1985.

Fraust, Bart. "Crossing State Lines: How Some Did It." *American Banker* (April 3, 1984).

Frieder, Larry. "Toward Nationwide Banks." *Economic Perspectives* (Federal Reserve Bank of Chicago, special issue 1986).

"The Garn–St Germain Depository Institutions Act of 1982." *Economic Perspectives* (Federal Reserve Bank of Chicago, March–April, 1983).

Golembe, Carter H., and David S. Holland. *Federal Regulation of Banking: 1983–84*. Washington, D.C.: Golembe Associates Inc., 1983.

Kane, Edward. *The S&L Insurance Mess: How Did It Happen?* The Urban Institute Press, Washington, DC, 1989.

Kane, Edward. "Principal-Agent Problems in S&L Salvage." *Journal of Finance* (July 1990).

Liang, Nellie, and Donald Savage. "The Nonbank Activities of Bank Holding Companies." *Federal Reserve Bulletin* (Board of Governors of the Federal Reserve System, May 1990).

Molay, Paul. "Trigger Dates: A Look at Laws Granting Interstate Powers to Banks." *American Banker*, March 28, 1991.

"New Directions in Interstate Banking." *Economic Review* (Federal Reserve Bank of Atlanta, special issue, January 1985).

The Savings and Loan Sourcebook. Chicago: United States League of Savings Associations, 1988.

Statistics on Banking. Washington, D.C.: Federal Deposit Insurance Corporation, 1990.

Wright, Don. *The Effective Bank Director*. Reston, Va.: Reston Publishing Co., Inc., 1985.

Chapter 3

Banking Trends and Competition

Increased competition is quickly changing the nature of commercial banking. Firms as different as Sears, Merrill Lynch, Ford Motor, Charles Schwab, Prudential-Bache, and Fidelity Mutual Funds offer interest-bearing checking accounts, mutual funds, and credit cards in addition to their primary products. Consumers have more choices now than ever before when purchasing financial services.

The good news is that commercial banks are gaining greater flexibility in diversifying their asset base and competing with nonbank banks and diversified financial companies. The bad news is that many banks, especially small ones, are still suffering through earnings problems attributable to past energy, real estate, and agriculture loan problems. They operate at a cost disadvantage to larger financial services providers and are finding it increasingly difficult to compete.

Chapter 3 examines recent competitive trends affecting the banking industry, as manifested by the greater number of suppliers and greater variety of products and services offered. The chapter identifies four fundamental forces of change—deregulation, financial innovation, securitization, and globalization—that will continue to affect the structure of banking. It demonstrates how these forces, in turn, will continue to accelerate three basic trends—increased competition, greater consolidation, and increased capital requirements—in the restructuring of worldwide financial institutions and markets. As part of the analysis, the chapter compares profitability between different types of financial services companies. As an example, it describes the structure and performance of Sears as a financial conglomerate and major bank competitor.

To the casual observer, events of the 1980s involving financial institutions might seem unrelated: the federal government bails out Continental Illinois; NCNB, Chemical Bank, and Banc One acquire the three largest Texas banks; Drexel Burnham

65

files for bankruptcy resulting from its junk bond activities; Mexico renegotiates its debt payments to U.S. banks; savings and loans collapse in large numbers; investment banks help finance hostile corporate acquisitions with junk bonds; and stock market volatility increases with dramatic intraday swings in market indexes. All of these incidents, however, are interrelated. After three decades of relative calm, financial markets and institutions are undergoing a structural change that will permanently alter competitive relationships.

This structural change is frequently attributed to deregulation of the financial services industry. In fact, it is a natural response to increased competition between depository institutions and nondepository financial firms, and between like competitors across world markets. Competition is marked by four fundamental forces that transform the structure of markets and institutions: deregulation and reregulation, financial innovation, securitization, and globalization. The latter factors actually represent responses to deregulation and reregulation. These combined forces have altered corporate balance sheets by inducing firms to compete in new product and geographic markets and to use new financial instruments to facilitate transactions and adjust their risk profiles. While consumers have benefited from these changes, the long-term trend for financial institutions entails consolidation and realignment of corporate objectives as firms attempt to develop a market niche. Firms can expect regulators to closely monitor changes in risk and continually increase capital requirements.

This chapter examines recent trends in the structure of banking markets and financial instruments. It begins by describing the nature and impact of the four forces of change. It then demonstrates how these forces enhance three general trends toward increased competition, greater consolidation, and increased capital requirements. Greater competition is reflected in the markets for bank deposits, loans, and new products or services in the form of price pressure and the types of providers competing. Greater consolidation arises as firms fail or merge. Increased capital requirements demonstrate that regulators intend to better control banking risk compared with the banking environment of the 1980s.

The basic theme is that increased competition, brought about by continued deregulation, has encouraged banks to assume increased portfolio risks in order to earn acceptable returns. As bank regulators have tried to reduce overall risk by raising capital requirements, banks have moved assets off their balance sheets and tried to replace interest income with fee income. In these efforts banks attempt to be more like insurance brokers, realtors, and investment bankers, competing with a broader range of firms in more product markets. As capital becomes increasingly costly or impossible to obtain, individual firms are forced to merge to continue operations.

THE FUNDAMENTAL FORCES OF CHANGE

Historically, commercial banks have been the most heavily regulated companies in the United States, and thus among the safest and most conservative businesses. Regulations took many forms, including maximum interest rates that could be paid on deposits or charged on loans, minimum capital-to-asset ratios, minimum legal reserve requirements, limited geographic markets for full-service banking, constraints on the type of investments permitted, and restrictions on the range of products and services offered. While regulations limited opportunities and risks, they virtually guaranteed a profit if management did not perpetrate fraud.

Since World War II banks and other market participants have consistently restructured their operations to circumvent regulation and meet perceived customer needs. In response, regulators or lawmakers would step in to impose new restrictions, which market participants would again circumvent. This process of regulation, market response, and imposition of new regulations (reregulation) is the *regulatory dialectic*.[1] One aspect of regulatory response is financial innovation. Securitization and globalization are extensions of this response in the development of new products and international competition. The fear is that the four forces have influenced financial markets and institutions so rapidly that the aggregate risk of the U.S. financial system has increased.

Deregulation and Reregulation

Commercial bank regulatory agencies have always tried to control the individuals and activities associated with financial intermediation. Their fundamental purpose is to protect the public's resources and confidence in the financial system. Banking is a public trust that, if left to industry whims, might assume too much risk, ultimately leading to extensive losses and widespread lack of confidence in the soundness and integrity underlying financial intermediation. Regulations specify who is allowed to manage a bank, where banks are permitted to locate, and what products and services banks are allowed to offer, as well as specific portfolio constraints.

Deregulation is the process of eliminating existing regulations, such as the elimination of Regulation Q interest rate ceilings imposed on time and demand deposits offered by depository institutions. Deregulation is often confused with reregulation, which is the process of implementing new restrictions or modifying existing controls. Reregulation arises in response to market participants' efforts to circumvent existing regulations.

The Federal Reserve membership issue during the 1970s serves as an excellent example of the regulator-bank relationship. Banks that are members of the FRS hold required reserves in the form of nonearning cash assets equal to a percentage of qualifying liabilities. These reserves represent a tax because banks do not earn interest on the assets. During the 1970s this tax rose dramatically as short-term market interest rates increased. Banks that were not FRS members were required to hold fewer reserves and could typically hold interest-bearing securities to meet requirements. As such, their lost interest income was much smaller. To circumvent regulation, many member banks gave up FRS membership rather than absorb the loss. The FRS and Congress worried about losing control of the money supply and passed the Depository Institutions Deregulation and Monetary Control Act, which allowed interest-bearing checking accounts but forced all financial institutions that offered them to be FRS

---

[1]A discussion of the regulatory dialectic can be found in Kane, 1977 and 1981.

members and hold reserves set by the FRS. This reregulation was an attempt to reimpose regulatory control over all depository institutions.

Efforts at deregulation and reregulation generally address either pricing issues, allowable geographic market penetration, or the ability to offer new products and services. Recent pricing regulations have focused on removing price controls on allowable interest rates paid depositors and allowable rates charged borrowers (usury ceilings). Regulations addressing geographic markets have generally expanded the locations where competing firms can conduct business. Finally, the various regulatory agencies are quickly expanding banks' product choices on a case-by-case basis as banks apply for permission to offer new products such as insurance, brokerage services, and securities underwriting. Recent changes have thus produced greater price competition, a greater number of competitors offering banking services, a broadening of the types of services provided banking customers, and expanded opportunities across geographic markets. Greater competition has, in turn, lowered aggregate returns as firms attempt to establish a permanent market presence.

Financial Innovation

Financial innovation is the catalyst behind the evolving financial services industry and the restructuring of financial markets. It represents the systematic process of change. Innovations take the form of new securities and financial markets, new products and services, new organizational forms, and new delivery systems. Financial institutions change the characteristics of financial instruments traded by the public and create new financial markets, which provide liquidity. Bank managers change the composition of their banks' balance sheets by altering the mix of products or services offered and by competing in extended geographic markets. Financial institutions form holding companies, acquire subsidiaries, and merge with other entities. Finally, institutions may modify the means by which they offer products and services. Recent trends incorporate technological advances in the development of cash management accounts, including the use of automatic teller machines, home banking via microcomputer, and shared national and international electronic funds transfer systems.

Innovations have many causes. Firms may need to stop the loss of deposits, enter new geographic or product markets, deliver services with cheaper and better technology, increase their capital base, alter their tax position, reduce their risk profile, or cut operating costs. In virtually every case, the intent is to improve the firm's competitive position.

Eisenbeis documents the relationship between regulation, financial innovation, and reregulation for Regulation Q avoidance.[2] Exhibit 3.1 summarizes various financial innovations associated with pricing deposits and new markets and financial instruments. Some are a response to burdensome regulation, while others represent the normal process of change. Financial innovation related to Regulation Q evolved as depository institutions tried to slow disintermediation, in which depositors withdrew funds from fixed-rate accounts at banks and reinvested the funds in instruments paying

---

[2]See Eisenbeis, 1985.

Exhibit 3.1 Regulation and Financial Innovation: Deposit Rate Ceilings and New Instruments

A. Regulation Q and Interest Rate Ceilings on Time and Savings Deposits

Date   **Financial Innovation**

1961   Citicorp issues negotiable certificates of deposit (CDs).
1966   Development and growth of Eurodollar market.
1969   Bank holding companies issue commercial paper. Banks issue short-term paper as early as 1964.
1972   Negotiable orders of withdrawal (NOW) accounts permitted in Massachusetts.
1973   Citicorp issues variable-rate CDs with minimum denominations of $1,000.
1973   Development of money market mutual funds paying fluctuating market rates without fixed maturities and early withdrawal penalties.
1973   Merrill Lynch offers Cash Management Account.
1978   Depository institutions allowed to offer 6-month money market time deposits with rates tied to 26-week Treasury bill auction rate.
1980   DIDMCA authorizes interest-bearing transactions accounts nationally (NOWs, automatic transfers from savings, share drafts).
1981   Commercial banks offer "sweep accounts" that automatically transfer deposit balances to money market mutual fund.
1982   Garn-St Germain authorizes money market deposit accounts.
1983   Garn-St Germain authorizes Super NOW accounts.
1985   Minimum balances on money market deposit accounts reduced to $1,000.
1986 $1,000 minimum balance on transactions accounts removed. Interest rate ceilings on savings accounts and all time deposits eliminated.
1987   Interest payments on CDs tied to stock market, gold prices, oil prices, college tuition increases.
1988   Bank offerings of tax deferred annuities take off.

B. New Instruments and Markets

Date   **Financial Innovation**

1961   Negotiable CDs.
1963   Eurodollars.
1970   Government National Mortgage Association pass-through certificate created.
1971   Third-party insurance as security for municipal bonds.
1972   NOWs in Massachusetts
1972   Currency futures developed and traded on Chicago Mercantile Exchange.
1973   Money market mutual funds.
1973   Listed stock options begin trading on Chicago Board Options Exchange.
1976   Treasury bill futures begin trading on Chicago Mercantile Exchange.
1978   Treasury bond futures begin trading on Chicago Board of Trade.
1978   Development of 1-year Treasury bill futures.
1981   Development of CD futures on Chicago Board of Trade.
1981   Interest rate swaps.
1981   Floating-rate notes and Eurobonds.
1983   Development of Eurodollar futures.
1983   Development of options on Treasury bond futures.
1983   Development of options on Eurodollar futures.
1983   Collateralized mortgage obligations first issued.
1984   Extensive use of junk bonds to finance leveraged buyouts.
1985   Securitized car loans, leases, credit card receivables.
1987   Mutual funds for bank-qualified municipal bonds.
1988   Buyers assurance plans for bank credit card purchases.
1989   Insurance on credit card purchases.
1990   AT&T Universal credit card.

market rates of interest. In most cases, banks developed new vehicles to compete with Treasury bills or other instruments such as money market mutual funds and cash management accounts offered through brokerage houses.

Federal regulators typically responded by imposing marginal reserve requirements against the new instrument, raising the interest rate ceiling, then authorizing another new deposit instrument. Regulation Q was voided in 1986 for all deposits when interest rate ceilings on savings accounts were eliminated. Under the Glass-Steagall Act, banks still cannot pay interest on commercial demand deposits. More recent innovations with securities take the form of new futures, options, and options-on-futures contracts, or the development of markets for a wide range of securitized assets. Exhibit 3.1 lists just a few of the new financial futures and options contracts which speculators and hedgers use to conduct business. Banks use financial futures to hedge interest rate risk in their portfolios. They can be used to offset mismatches in maturities of assets and liabilities, to price fixed-rate loans, or to create synthetic deposits. Several large banks also earn fee income and commissions by serving as futures merchants and advisors. The development of futures and options has led to more active trading in many of the securities banks issue, trade, or buy for their own accounts.

Financial institutions have also successfully circumvented restrictions against geographic expansion (Exhibit 3.2). Bank holding companies established out-of-state loan production offices, Edge Act corporations, and nonbank subsidiaries and entered into shared facility arrangements with electronic funds transfer systems. More recently, they established reciprocal banking pacts with other states that encourage interstate mergers and acquisitions.[3] Of course, innovations are not restricted to banks. Major retailers such as J. C. Penney, Kroger, and Sears acquired banks, savings and loans, insurance companies, and real estate companies, enabling them to offer banking products. They operate offices nationwide without regulatory interference. Investment banks have similarly linked up with consumer banks to provide a vehicle for offering credit card and transactions services nationally.

Innovation in delivery systems normally takes the form of new technological developments to facilitate funds transfers. During the 1980s banks popularized automatic teller machines and point-of-sale terminals in retail outlets. More recent innovations include the development of the smart card and home banking networks. While customer acceptance has been slow, these systems are gradually gaining favor.

Securitization

During the early 1980s deregulation and financial innovation increased the risk of commercial bank operations. Borrowing costs increased as depositors converted low-rate savings accounts and demand deposits into deposits bearing market rates. Deposit balances also became less stable because customers were increasingly rate sensitive,

---

[3]Chapter 2 provides a detailed summary of interstate banking arrangements in place during 1990. In 1991 the U.S. Treasury proposed unrestricted nationwide branching, which will likely be approved in the near future.

Exhibit 3.2 Financial Innovation: Geographic and Product Expansion and New Delivery Systems

A. Geographic and Product Expansion

- Commercial banks formed multibank holding companies to circumvent state restrictions against branching.
- Commercial banks formed bank holding companies to increase range of products and services, enabling diversification of operations. Nonbank subsidiaries conducted business without geographic restrictions. Independent banks formed service corporations.
- Commercial banks established loan production offices and Edge Act corporations to offer credit and international trade services nationally.
- State legislatures passed laws providing for interstate banking activities through regional pacts or nationwide activity.
- Commercial banks formed joint ventures as "reverse holding companies," which offered services, such as data processing, a single firm could not offer economically alone.
- Financial institutions other than commercial banks acquired nonbank banks, enabling them to offer a subset of banking services without being regulated under the Bank Holding Company Act. Nonbank banks can conduct business without geographic restrictions.
- Firms formed financial conglomerates to expand range of financial services. Mergers and acquisitions typically include brokerage house, insurance company, finance company, and retailer.
- Commercial banks formed subsidiaries to offer discount brokerage services and sell mutual funds.
- State legislators removed restrictions on out-of-state banks buying in-state banks.
- J. P. Morgan and Bankers Trust were allowed to underwrite corporate securities.

B. New Delivery Systems

- Commercial banks set up automatic teller machines (ATMs) to provide convenient banking services.
- Financial institutions link ATMs into networks with shared facilities.
- Commercial banks establish point-of-sale systems in retail outlets.
- Commercial banks provide home banking services that allow customers to pay bills, transfer funds, and review statements via microcomputers.
- Financial institutions develop smart cards that contain a computer chip with customer's password or identification number, allowing instantaneous authorization.
- New York banks develop clearing system for electronic payments related to international trade, called CHIPS.
- Commercial banks develop telecommunications system, designated SWIFT, which processes electronic messages between institutions.
- Banks contract with nonbank vendors like IBM and EDS to handle item (check) processing.
- Banks use image processing for storing and reading financial documents.
- Banks merge bank office item processing operations.

moving their balances to firms paying the highest rates. With banks, savings and loans, credit unions, and mutual funds competing for the same deposits, depositors could easily find high-rate alternatives. Because loans offer the highest gross yields, many banks tried to compensate for declining interest margins by increasing loan-to-asset ratios. The average riskiness of loans outstanding increased and loan yields subsequently fell relative to borrowing costs as lending institutions competed for a decreasing pool of quality credits. In many cases, this eventually led to greater loan losses and long-term earnings problems.

High loan growth also raises bank capital requirements. Regulators consider most loans to be risky assets and require banks to add to loss reserves and their capital base as the amount of loans increases. Higher provisions for loan losses reduce reported net income. Because equity capital is more expensive than debt, higher capital requirements, in turn, increase the marginal cost of financing operations.

One competitive response to asset quality problems and earnings pressure has been to substitute fee income for interest income by offering more fee-based services. Banks also lower their capital requirements and reduce credit risk by selling assets and servicing the payments between borrower and lender, rather than holding the same assets to earn interest. This process of converting assets into marketable securities is called *securitization*. A bank originates assets, typically loans, combines them in pools with similar features, and sells pass-through certificates, which are secured by the interest and principal payments on the original assets. Residential mortgages and mortgage-backed pass-through certificates served as the prototype. The originating bank collects interest and principal payments on the loans, which it passes through to certificate holders minus a servicing fee. If the bank sells the certificates without recourse, regulators permit it to take the original assets off its books.[4] The bank does not have to allocate loan-loss reserves against the assets, and its capital requirements decline proportionately. Securitization also eliminates interest-rate risk associated with financing the underlying assets. In essence, the bank serves as an investment banker generating fee income from servicing the loans without assuming additional credit risk.

The objectives behind securitization include:

- to free capital for other uses
- to improve return on equity (ROE) via servicing income
- to diversify credit risk
- to obtain new sources of liquidity
- to reduce interest rate risk.

The process itself is costly because a bank must pay underwriting expenses and fees for credit enhancement guarantees. Such credit enhancements normally involve a letter of credit that guarantees the investor in the underlying securities that obligated payments will be made. For this guarantee, a bank will pay approximately 50 basis points (0.50%).

The increased securitizaton of financial assets is one of the dominant financial trends of the 1980s. Banks, in particular, are eager to securitize and sell a broader base of loan receivables. This makes them loan originators as much as lenders with full credit risk. Since 1985 banks have successfully securitized commercial loans, residential mortgages, automobile loans, computer leases, Small Business Association guaranteed loans, mobile home loans, and credit card receivables. Most of these arrangements

---

[4]Banks that issue securities backed by their assets are legally classified as investment companies. If they are not exempted, they are regulated by the Securities Exchange Commission (SEC) according to the Investment Company Act of 1940. The SEC requires that banks guarantee securities before it grants an exemption. This inconsistency with bank regulatory treatment effectively restricts banks to private rather than public placement for the securities. See Brenner, 1986b.

Securitizing Credit Card Loans[a]

On April 10, 1986, Banc One announced that it had entered into an agreement with Salomon Brothers Inc. to sell a portion of its credit card receivables to investors via collateralized certificates. The deal was unique because investors had recourse in case of default, but Banc One retained no liability and no third-party insurance was provided. The innovation involved establishing a loss reserve fund.

Banc One created a pool of credit card receivables carrying an effective yield of 19 percent. Salomon Brothers privately placed $50 million of pass-through certificates backed by interest and principal payments on the credit card receivables. The certificates, labeled certificates for amortizing revolving debts or CARDs, carried a fixed rate of 8.35 percent and a stated maturity of five years. A portion of the difference between interest and principal payments on the receivables and payments to investors was allocated to a reserve fund. In case of defaults, proceeds were taken from the reserve to pay investors.

The reserve effectively constituted insurance and made the certificates attractive to investors. Because of the reserve, bank regulators authorized the sale and Banc One could remove the credit card loans from its books. In this instance, Banc One set the size of the reserve equal to 200 percent of its historical loss experience on credit card loans and agreed to service the loans. It retained a 30 percent interest in the pool, which essentially represented servicing income, plus kept any reserve funds in excess of actual defaults.

---

[a]Brenner, Lynn, "Credit Card Deal May Be Model for Securitization," *American Banker* (April 14, 1986), describes the basic features of the transaction.

---

are facilitated by an investment bank and involve a letter of credit guarantee from a foreign bank or insurance company, which retains some recourse with the originating bank. Banc One's credit card sale (see Contemporary Issues: Securitizing Credit Card Loans) is one example that did not involve such a guarantee.

Not all assets can be securitized. Loans that best qualify exhibit standard features regarding maturity, size, pricing, collateral, and use of proceeds. They typically generate predictable losses over time. Residential mortgages have been the most popular because they are similar regardless of the geographic area where they originate. Commercial loans, in contrast, represent negotiated contracts and thus exhibit substantially different characteristics. Diversity increases the difficulty of pooling loans and attracting investors who do not want to investigate the features of each loan in the pool. Commercial loan losses are also highly variable. To securitize commercial loans, banks must facilitate the process by accumulating less risky credits and standardizing the loan features. Exhibit 3.3 indicates that credit card receivables and automobile paper dominated the non-mortgage asset-backed issues at banks in 1990.

Securitization enhances competition for the underlying assets. With standardized features, such as those on government-guaranteed mortgages, borrowers can easily compare prices and select the least costly alternative. Securitization also changes the composition of bank balance sheets because not all assets can be securitized. Highly

Exhibit 3.3 Asset-Backed Issues

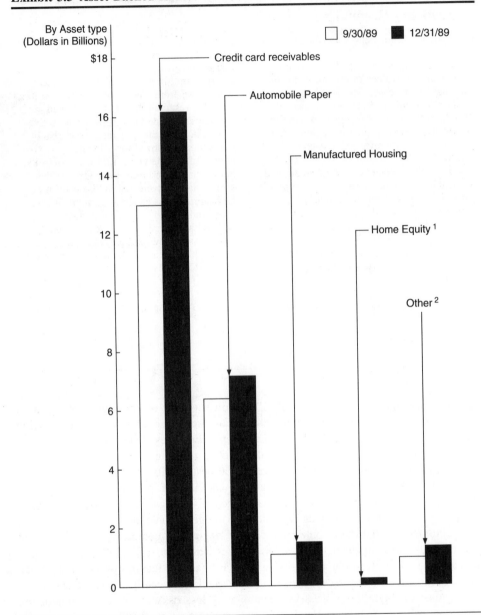

By Asset type
(Dollars in Billions)

□ 9/30/89   ■ 12/31/89

Credit card receivables

Automobile Paper

Manufactured Housing

Home Equity [1]

Other [2]

[1] No data available for 9/30/89.

[2] Equipment leases, boat loans, nonperforming loans.

Source:—"A Small Bank Tries Its Hand at Securities," *American Banker* (January 25, 1990).

risky loans to small businesses, for example, are designed to meet the specific needs of a single firm. Because they do not have identical features, it is difficult to determine the credit quality of an entire pool of loans and to use them as collateral against security issues. Banks will keep these loans in their portfolios. Credit card receivables and automobile loans, however, offer a sharp contrast. Terms are fairly standard and losses are predictable. The effect is that the credit quality of loans kept on the bank's books is declining.

Globalization

Financial markets and institutions are becoming increasingly international in scope. U.S. corporations, for example, can borrow from domestic or foreign institutions. They can issue securities denominated in U.S. dollars or foreign currencies of the countries in which they do business. Foreign corporations have the same alternatives. Investors increasingly view securities issued in different countries as comparable alternatives. Large firms thus participate in both domestic and foreign markets such that interest rates on domestic instruments closely track foreign interest rates.

Globalization is the gradual evolution of markets and institutions so that geographic boundaries do not restrict financial transactions. One country's economic policies affect the economies of other countries. Funds flow freely between countries because of efficient money and capital markets and currency exchange. The establishment of the European Community in 1992 represents a prime example. Under a formal agreement, 12 industrialized nations in Western Europe have eliminated most trade restrictions, standardized basic product designs, reduced taxes and fees, and linked monetary control in order to facilitate trade.[5] The intent is to have a common currency and fully integrated market that operates as one without borders. This should sharply lower inflation rates and enhance export opportunities for these countries.

Globalization requires that businesses, individuals, and governments recognize that events throughout the world influence their domestic performance. They should be aware of foreign competition and foreign opportunities when developing market strategies. Chapter 25 analyzes the nature of international transactions in detail, including the impact of both U.S. firms abroad and foreign firms in the United States.

Most large money center banks have the capability and expertise to help customers obtain capital in any currency in the form of either debt or equity. A multitude of firms have offices all over the world and provide services in all geographic markets. Four Japanese banks, for example, serve as primary securities dealers in activities with the U.S. Federal Reserve. Five of the best known U.S. investment banks, Shearson Lehman, Goldman Sachs, Paine Webber, Blackstone, and Wasserstein, are at least 12.5 percent owned by foreign investors. Borrowers look less at where the supplier of a good or service is located and more at the quality and price of the good or service. Clearly, only the largest firms can successfully compete worldwide. Globalization in

---

[5]The 12 nations include Belgium, Denmark, France, Germany, Greece, Ireland, Italy, Luxembourg, the Netherlands, Portugal, Spain and the United Kingdom.

financial services implies that the top layer of firms will consist of a few, very large consolidated organizations.

INCREASED COMPETITION

The McFadden Act of 1927 and the Glass-Steagall Act of 1933 determined the framework within which financial institutions operated for the next 50 years. The McFadden Act ensured that banks would be sheltered from unbridled competition with other banks by extending state restrictions on geographic expansion to national banks. The Glass-Steagall Act forbade banks from underwriting equities and other corporate securities, thereby separating banking from commerce. Commercial banking meant deposit-taking and lending. Investment banks emerged to underwrite and distribute securities.

The commercial banking industry was quite stable. Individuals who wanted to start a new bank found it difficult to get a charter from either federal or state regulators. The FRS, in turn, limited interest rates that banks could pay depositors, effectively subsidizing banks by mandating low-cost sources of funds. Because depositors had few substitutes unless they held more than $100,000, bank deposits grew systematically with economic conditions. Regulations also specified maximum rates that banks could charge on certain types of loans. Such usury ceilings were intended to protect customers from price gouging and essentially passed through a portion of the value of low cost bank deposits to bank borrowers.

Competition for Deposits

The free ride of a guaranteed spread between asset yields and liability costs abruptly ended during the late 1970s. The primary catalyst was high inflation due in part to foreign control of the oil market and the doubling of oil prices. While ceiling rates on bank deposits limited interest to 5.25 percent on savings accounts and nothing on checking accounts, 8 to 12 percent inflation rates guaranteed that consumers lost purchasing power. Consumers had two choices: save less and spend more or find higher-yielding investments. In 1973 several investment banks created money market mutual funds (MMMFs), which accepted deposits from individuals and invested the proceeds in Treasury bills, large certificates of deposit (CDs), and other securities that paid market yields.[6] Not surprisingly, the attractiveness and growth of MMMFs tracked the spread between money market interest rates and Regulation Q ceilings. Exhibit 3.4 shows the growth in MMMFs during the 1980s. Without competing instruments, MMMFs increased from $10.4 billion in 1978 to almost $189 billion in 1981. During this interval, three-month Treasury bill rates exceeded the ceiling rate on bank savings

---

[6]Technically, money market mutual funds sell shares to individuals. The funds generally buy insured CDs or Treasury securities and transfer the income to shareholders, minus a management fee. Most funds allow shareholders to write checks against their balance or transfer funds to other investments. The shares exhibit little default risk but are not directly federally insured.

Exhibit 3.4 MMDA versus MMMF Growth

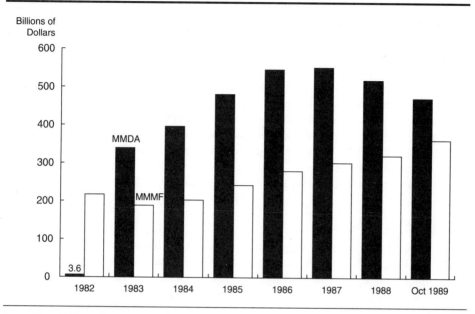

Source: From Linda Aguilar, "Still Toe-to-Toe:—Banks and Nonbanks at the End of the '80s," *Economic Perspectives* (Federal Reserve Bank of Chicago, January/February 1990).

accounts by as much as 9 percent. After 1981 the growth slowed to where MMMFs totaled $350 billion at the end of 1989.

MMMF growth came largely at the expense of banks and thrifts as depositors simply shifted to mutual fund shares. Banks argued vigorously for a "level playing field"—equivalent regulation that would allow them to compete—such as Congress declaring MMMFs illegal or forcing them to hold reserves against shares. In a practical sense, once depositors realized they could earn market rates on transactions or savings balances, Congress dared not deny them the opportunity. Instead, it passed legislation enabling banks and thrifts to offer similar accounts including money market deposit accounts (MMDAs) and Super NOWs. Exhibit 3.4 shows the enormous success of MMDAs after their introduction in 1982 as they grew from just $3.6 billion outstanding to over $500 billion outstanding in 1987. In subsequent years outstanding MMDAs declined as Congress eliminated interest rate ceilings and minimum denominations for deposits. Customers could then earn market rates on all time deposits, so there was less incentive to shift to MMDAs. Bank liability rate deregulation was thus complete.

In today's environment deposit competition takes many forms. First, institutions are virtually unconstrained in the terms they can offer. Thus customers can negotiate any minimum denomination, market interest rate, and maturity. Firms must, however, make the same deposit terms available to all qualifying customers. The range of deposit products has therefore become much broader. Second, a wide variety of firms accept time deposits and offer checking accounts. Merrill Lynch, for example, offers a cash management account for high-balance customers to use as part of their investment activity.[7] Individuals can have proceeds from all financial transactions automatically invested at market rates until they make new investment decisions. They can also write checks against outstanding balances.

American Express and Sears similarly offer their credit card customers the opportunity to invest in small time deposits that pay competitive rates. For high-balance depositors, foreign banks and branches of large U.S. banks offer Eurodollar deposits that pay higher rates than domestic certificates of deposits. Finally, deposit services are typically priced to encourage customers to conduct the bulk of their banking business with one firm. Thus yields increase and service charges decline as a customer's balance increases. Firms often make other services, such as travel discounts and life insurance, available in a package with deposit accounts.

Competition for Loans

As bank funding costs rose, competition for loans put downward pressure on loan yields and interest spreads. Prime corporate borrowers have always had the option to issue commercial paper or long-term bonds rather than borrow from banks. The growth in MMMFs accelerated the development and growth of the commercial paper market and improved investment banks' ties with nonfinancial corporations. Investment banks continued to underwrite commercial paper issues and use money market fund assets to purchase the paper. Because the Glass-Steagall Act prevented commercial banks from underwriting commercial paper, banks lost corporate borrowers, who now bypassed them by issuing commercial paper at lower cost.

The development of the junk bond market extended this loan competition to medium-sized companies representing lower-quality borrowers. Junk bonds are corporate securities that are unrated or rated Ba and lower and thus are not investment grade. Historically, firms with debt ratings below Baa were precluded from issuing significant amounts of new debt and had to rely instead on bank loans. During the early 1980s several investment banks, particularly Drexel Burnham Lambert Inc., convinced investors that many Ba and lower rated bonds were sound investments. Historical default rates were so low that the 3.5 to 5 percent yield premium offered on the bonds more than compensated for default risk. Investment banks were soon able to help companies that could not issue prime-grade commercial paper sell junk bonds in the new issue market. These bonds had several advantages over bank loans, including access to larger amounts of funds, longer-term financing, and fewer restrictive covenants. In many cases, the interest costs were well below loan rates quoted by a bank. New issue junk bonds effectively served as substitutes for commercial loans.

In 1989 the junk bond market started a long decline as the federal government charged Drexel and its junk bond specialist, Michael Milken, with a series of securities

---

[7]Since 1986 Merrill Lynch has offered small- to medium-sized businesses a working capital management account modeled after its cash management account for individuals. The business account provides a $2 million credit line, check writing capabilities, and a variety of pension, insurance, and investment services. The credit line and ancillary services are designed as substitutes for traditional working capital loans at banks.

law violations. At that time, Drexel provided much of the secondary market support for junk bonds that investors wanted to trade. With Drexel's bankruptcy filing in 1990, the secondary market shrunk and junk bond prices collapsed. Firms planning to place new junk bond issues with investors were generally unable to obtain financing. These firms slowly turned to banks, although bank financing terms were quite different from junk bond terms.

These developments permanently altered the commercial banking industry. The growth in junk bonds reduced the pool of good-quality loans and lowered risk-adjusted yield spreads over bank borrowing costs. Banks generally responded either by increasing the riskiness of their loan portfolios or by trying to move into investment banking and other service areas that generate fee income. Banks choosing the first path sacrificed long-term profitability and solvency for short-term gains. They maintained yield spreads temporarily, but increased default risk on the loans ultimately eroded earnings through higher loan charge-offs. Most banks seeking greater fee income have had limited options. They would like to provide a full range of securities underwriting services, sell new types of insurance, and offer other products without the inherent credit risk of loans. This would allow them to diversify their asset base and revenue stream and lower the risk of failure. Regulation, however, has been slow in opening many of these activities.

Today, different sized banks generally pursue different strategies. Small- to medium-sized banks continue to concentrate on loans but seek to strengthen the customer relationship by offering personal service. They now measure their costs better and price loans and deposits to cover their costs plus meet profit targets. The best evidence is that most banks now calculate their cost of funds and price loans using their own index rather than a money-center bank's prime rate. These same banks have generally rediscovered the consumer loan. Historically, consumer loan rates have far exceeded default rates and the cost of financing so that their net profits have exceeded that with commercial loans. A further advantage with retail customers is that consumer deposits are much less rate-sensitive than large certificates of deposit and other borrowed funds. The biggest losers are low-balance depositors who have seen service charges double to cover the bank's costs of providing transactions services.

The largest banks, in contrast, are looking to move assets off the balance sheet. Regulatory capital requirements and the new corporate debt substitutes make the remaining loans too expensive and too risky, given the available yield spreads. Total commercial loans at the five largest U.S. commercial banks have remained constant at 1982 levels while the same firms have dramatically increased off-balance sheet activity. Meanwhile, their noninterest income as a percentage of total assets increased to an average of 1.45 percent at year-end 1989 from under 1.3 percent in 1985.

This trend is not without risk. Because they cannot underwrite and distribute securities domestically, large banks have emphasized international underwriting efforts and entered the financial guarantee and commitment business. These guarantees take the form of loan commitments, standby letters of credit, and commitments related to interest rate swaps, currency exchange, leases, and insurance on securities. Guarantees generate excellent fee income and do not require large capital support. However, because guarantees do not appear explicitly on published financial statements, banks

Exhibit 3.5 Large Banks' Off-Balance Sheet Commitments, Year-end 1985 (Billions of Dollars)

Type of Liability	Citicorp	Bank-America	Chase Manhattan	Manufacturers Hanover	Morgan Guaranty
Loan commitments	$ 34.4	$ 49.1	$ 27.9	$ 23.8	$ 24.4
Standby letters of credit	15.9	13.2	11.5	11.1	9.0
Other		2.2	2.6	1.8	0.7
Municipal bond insurance	29.1				
Interest rate swaps					
Notional amount	36.4	7.0	10.0	22.6	21.6
Estimated risk	NS	NS	0.270	NS	1.2
Commitments related to:					
Futures, options, money market instruments	38.3	5.6	3.6	8.6	6.7
Foreign currency sales or purchases	167.5	101.8	80.9	46.0	65.7
Leases	1.2	1.9	1.4	1,0	0.8
Collateral	13.3			3.6	7.1
Total off-balance sheet commitments	$336.1	$180.8	$137.9	$118.5	$136.0
Total assets	$173.6	$118.5	$ 87.7	$ 76.5	$ 69.4
Total shareholders equity	$ 7.8	$ 4.5	$ 3.8	$ 3.5	$ 4.4

NS indicates not significant.

Standby letters of credit do not include letters either secured by marketable securities or participated out to other institutions.

Source: *American Banker*, March 21, 1986.

continue to assume the risk that they might need to make good on a defaulted obligation. Exhibit 3.5 lists the off-balance sheet commitments of the five largest U.S. bank holding companies in the mid-1980s. In each case, total commitments equal at least 150 percent of total assets and are much greater than total shareholder equity. Later chapters describe specific features of each activity.

Competition for Other Bank Services

Banks and their affiliates offer many products and services in addition to deposits and loans. A partial list includes trust services, discount brokerage, data processing, securities underwriting, real estate appraisal, credit life insurance, and personal financial consulting. Not surprisingly, there are strong competitors in these markets as well, many of whom have established well-defined market niches. In their search for nontraditional sources of income and diversification, many banks would like to expand the list even further. They see the ideal structure as a one-stop financial conglomerate that offers a full range of deposit, credit, insurance, investment, and consulting services. In essence, current distinctions between financial firms would be eliminated.

Commercial banks find these services attractive because traditional suppliers have often earned higher returns than banks. Exhibit 3.6 documents the comparative average performance for seven types of firms from 1980 to 1988.[8] In terms of overall profitability measured by return on equity (ROE), commercial banks ranked above only savings and loans. Their volatility of returns measured by the standard deviation of ROE, however, was relatively low, indicating that other firms typically experienced wider swings in annual returns. The asset-to-equity ratio signifies the impact of financial leverage. The greater this ratio, the more debt there is in the capital structure of the underlying firms. Again, commercial banks ranked above only savings and loans, suggesting that other firms were better capitalized. Finally, banks realized the lowest rates of growth in financial assets, albeit from a larger base.

The 1980s represented a period of intense competition during which nonbank competitors aggressively entered traditional banking business lines. Commercial banks suddenly found themselves competing with nonbank banks, finance companies, and high-growth thrifts for loans and deposits. Once-loyal customers moved their funds for better terms. Unfortunately, the increased competition coincided for many banks with loan problems in energy, real estate, and agriculture, which made it even more difficult to maintain quality assets and market share. The bank competitors described in the following sections engage in activities that many banks would like to pursue and demonstrate the degree of competition faced by banks.

Investment Banking. Commercial banks consider investment banking attractive because most investment banks already offer many banking services to prime commercial customers and individuals with high net worth and sell a wide range of products not available through banks. They can compete in any geographic market without the heavy regulation of the FRS, FDIC, and OCC. They earn extraordinarily high fees for certain types of transactions and can put their own capital at risk in selected investments. They are often aligned with other financial conglomerates, such as Shearson Lehman Brothers and American Express, which allows them to diversify their operations.

The Securities Exchange Commission, which regulates investment banks, classifies firms in terms of their primary trading activity and head office location. Two categories of firms dominate the investment banking industry. *National full-line firms*, such as Merrill Lynch and Dean Witter, offer a complete set of services, including an extensive network of branch offices located throughout the United States to handle retail business. Large *investment banking firms*, such as Salomon Brothers and First Boston, do not have extensive branch networks and instead focus on large-scale trading, underwriting, and mergers and acquisitions. The two types of firms manage most underwriting syndicates. The top six investment banking houses manage the bulk of new issue investment-grade securities and thus are referred to as special bracket firms.[9]

---

[8]Chapter 4 examines profitability measures for banks and provides sample calculations. For purposes of this exhibit, note that return on equity indicates aggregate average profitability while assets-to-equity indicates financial leverage.

[9]The special bracket firms are currently Salomon Brothers, First Boston, Goldman Sachs, Morgan Stanley, Merrill Lynch, and Shearson Lehman Brothers.

Exhibit 3.6 Profitability and Asset Growth Measures for Various Types of U.S. Financial Firms: Means for 1980–1988

Type of Firm	ROE[a]	Standard Deviation ROE[a]	Assets-to-Equity	Average Annual Asset Growth[b]
Life/health insurance	16.5%	5.2%	14.3×	11.9%
Securities firms	16.1	7.3	15.8	16.2
Finance companies	13.6	3.5	14.5	11.7
Mortgage banks	13.5	5.0	8.2	9.8
Credit unions	15.6	2.9	15.8	13.8
Savings and loans[c]	3.5	10.7	23.3	10.2
Commercial banks	10.4	3.4	16.6	8.4

[a] ROE = Return on stockholders' equity

[b] Data for 1980–1988

[c] Solvent firms under generally accepted accounting principles.

Source: Barth, James, and James Freund, "The Evolving Financial Services Sector 1970–1988," The Office of Thrift Supervision, September 1989.

Even though just 20 firms qualify as national full-line or large investment banks, they control over two-thirds of all assets held by all investment banks.

Investment banking encompasses three broad functions: underwriting public offerings of new securities, trading existing securities, and advising and financing mergers and acquisitions. Issuers of large blocks of securities typically use investment banks as underwriters. An underwriter buys the new securities from the issuer at an agreed-upon price and redistributes them to investors. As temporary owner of the securities, an underwriter acts as a dealer in assuming the risk that it can resell the securities at higher prices. The differential between the final sale price and the negotiated purchase price represents its profit. For this reason, an underwriter normally presells the issue by obtaining commitments from investors.[10] Because risk increases with issue size, investment banks frequently form underwriting syndicates, or groups of investment banks, to diversify the risk and increase the number of selling firms. While commercial banks have long been able to underwrite general obligation municipal bonds and U.S. government securities, they have been allowed to underwrite corporate debt only recently. Thus their aggregate market presence is small and investment banks dominate the new issue market for most securities.

Data for firms with the largest underwriting volume in the first three months of 1991 appear in Exhibit 3.7. Merrill Lynch and Goldman Sachs underwrote over one-third of all new U.S. issues. Altogether, the top ten investment banks were responsible for over 88 percent of new issue volume. The top ten underwriters of global debt and equity offerings, in contrast, handled approximately 69 percent of new issues.

---

[10] Original issuers let investment banks either bid competitively for the right to underwrite a new issue or negotiate directly with a single firm to handle the entire issue. Underwriters contact final investors prior to submitting a bid to assess market demand and determine a market price.

Exhibit 3.7 Leading Underwriters, January–March, 1991

	Amount (In millions)	Market Share	Total Fees (In millions)
Top Underwriters of U.S. Debt and Equity (Manager)			
Merrill Lynch	$ 21,594.5	20.7%	$104.4
Goldman Sachs	13,533.6	13.0	120.1
First Boston	11,299.4	10.8	55.0
Morgan Stanley	9,293.7	8.9	47.0
Lehman Brothers	9,185.8	8.8	51.1
Kidder Peabody	8,715.3	8.3	11.6
Salomon Brothers	7,678.9	7.3	44.4
Bear Stearns	4,987.9	4.8	
Prudential Securities	3,917.6	3.7	
Donaldson Lufkin	2,002.8	1.9	
Subtotals	$ 92,209.3	88.2%	
Industry Totals	$104,502.5	100.0%	
Top Global Underwriters of Debt and Equity (Manager)			
Merrill Lynch	$ 27,295.4	15.8%	
Morgan Stanley	16,063.3	9.3	
Goldman Sachs	16,027.8	9.3	
First Boston	14,978.4	8.7	
Lehman Brothers	9,975.0	5.8	
Kidder Peabody	8,964.3	5.2	
Salomon Brothers	8,555.3	5.0	
Banque Paribas	6,407.2	3.7	
Nomura Securities	6,280.3	3.6	
Bear Stearns	4,987.9	2.9	
Subtotals	$119,535.1	69.3%	
Industry Total	$172,569.4	100.0%	

Source:: *The Wall Street Journal*, March 29, 1991.

Merrill Lynch again dominated with almost 16 percent of the market. Note that the largest firms earn substantial fee income for their underwriting efforts.

Investment banks also serve as brokers or dealers in secondary market transactions. Through trading departments they make markets in previously issued securities by executing trades for selected customers or for their own account. Many trades, especially those involving retail customers, are simply brokered, i.e., the trader matches prospective buyers and sellers. The investment bank assumes no inventory risk and earns a straight commission on the exchange. Traders may also act as dealers, setting bid and ask prices for every security traded. The bid indicates the price at which the firm agrees to buy securities, and the ask indicates the sales price. Dealers incur inventory risk and adjust the size of the bid-ask spread to vary the size of their inventory. If necessary, a dealer may hedge inventory risk by trading futures and options.

The third function, facilitating corporate mergers and acquisitions, represents the quickest route for investment banks to generate speculative profits. This activity is spurred by corporate takeover specialists and junk bond financing. Target companies are those with stock market values far below the value of corporate assets. Acquiring firms issue large volumes of junk bond debt and use the proceeds to buy controlling interest in a target company's stock. They then sell some of the acquired firm's assets to refund the initial debt or to generate cash flow that covers the debt service. Companies pursuing these leveraged buyouts often earn extraordinary profits when the market value of the underlying stocks later increases.

Investment banks aggressively court merger and acquisition business. Many banks can raise takeover funds quickly for acquiring firms through junk bond trading relationships. Investment banks, however, invest their own capital in acquired companies. Rather than rely on fee income, they pursue speculative profits that may occur if the target firm's stock increases in price after acquisition. Merger and acquisition activity has restructured corporate finance. Because it is no longer difficult to initiate a hostile takeover, many corporations have actively enhanced their balance sheets, repurchased outstanding stock, or even entrenched current management in recognition that they may be a target.

Captive Automobile Finance Companies. The three largest U.S. automobile manufacturers, like other companies, are aggressively expanding in the financial services industry as part of their long-term strategic plans. The captive finance companies of General Motors, Ford Motor, and Chrysler have long provided financing for automobile buyers. At the end of 1989, they held over $110 billion in installment loans. They also provide dealer financing for inventories, capital improvements, and lease programs. Profitability of these groups compares favorably with that of commercial banks. Part of the success is due to operations beyond automobile finance. General Motors Acceptance Corp. owns two mortgage-servicing companies and ranks as the second largest mortgage servicer in the United States; Ford Motor Credit owns First Nationwide Savings, the nation's eighth largest savings and loan, and Associates Corp., a highly profitable finance company; and Chrysler Financial Corp. owns an equipment leasing firm, a factoring company, and a consumer finance company. Exhibit 3.8 compares the market shares of various consumer loans for different types of lenders between 1982 and 1987.

The apparent strategy is to seek economies of scale by applying expertise in automobile financing to other comparable financial enterprises. Cars and homes are the two most prominent consumer purchases. During 1989 individuals bought an estimated 12 million cars from the big three domestic manufacturers, 30 percent of which were financed through the captive finance subsidiaries. In both automobile and home financing, most individuals make monthly payments and lenders qualify borrowers using the same type of criteria. The mortgage market's continuous loan demand presumably helps offset the cycles in automobile sales.

Other Finance Companies. General purpose finance companies cover the spectrum of lending activities. Most specialize in lending to individuals for durable goods purchases. They traditionally emphasize automobile loans, home improvement loans, and second mortgage loans which are secured by real estate. Others specialize in

Exhibit 3.8 Market Share of Various Consumer Loans by Sector: 1982–1987

	1–4 Family Mortgage Loans		Auto Loans		Revolving Credit		Other Consumer Loans	
	1982	1987	1982	1987	1982	1987	1982	1987
Commercial banks	15.9	27.0	45.2	40.6	54.6	62.0	38.4	39.9
Finance companies	n.a.	1.8	37.5	36.7	n.a.	n.a.	30.9	22.5
Savings institutions	41.7	27.3	n.a.	6.4	n.a.	8.3	9.4	17.9
Credit unions	n.a.	n.a.	17.3	16.3	n.a.	4.2	18.8	16.6
Retailers	n.a.	n.a.	n.a.	n.a.	39.3	23.2	2.5	3.1
Life insurance co.'s	1.5	0.6	n.a.	n.a.	n.a.	n.a.	n.a.	n.a.
Other	40.9	43.3	n.a.	n.a.	6.1	2.3	n.a.	n.a.

n.a. = not available.

Source: Board of Governors of the Federal Reserve System. From Linda Aguilar, "Still Toe-to-Toe:—Banks and Nonbanks at the End of the '80s," *Economic Perspectives* (Federal Reserve Bank of Chicago, January/February 1990).

lending to businesses, either directly or through factoring a firm's accounts receivable, or in equipment leasing. Finance companies fund their investments by issuing commercial paper and long-term bonds and by borrowing directly from banks. Historically, their loans have been to relatively high credit risks. Even though their default experience exceeds that of banks, finance companies have generally earned greater returns because they price their loans at a premium, which compensates for the greater charge-offs. As shown in Exhibit 3.6, finance companies reported substantially greater profitability ratios than commercial banks throughout most of the 1980s.

CAPITAL REQUIREMENTS

The regulatory agencies have long required commercial banks to operate with minimum amounts of capital. Historically, they have specified capital requirements in terms of balance sheet ratios that mandate minimum amounts of capital as a fraction of total assets. The intent is to limit risk-taking. In 1985, the regulators agreed that every bank should hold capital to at least 6 percent of assets. Effective in 1992, banks must meet higher capital standards in which required capital is tied to the riskiness of bank assets.[11]

In general, bank regulators appear to want to continually increase minimum capital requirements. With the widespread savings and loan failures and deficiencies in deposit insurance funds, bank stockholders will be expected to assume more risk. Increased capital reduces risk to the insurance funds because more assets can default before a bank fails.

---

[11]Chapter 11 describes bank capital requirements in detail and examines the implications for bank management.

The ramifications of greater capital requirements are enormous. First, equity is more expensive than debt because interest payments are tax deductible to the bank while dividends on stock are not. It is thus costly to issue new stock. Second, few banks have ready access to the equity market and most banks therefore find it extremely difficult to add capital externally. Small banks' stocks are simply not broadly traded. Banks that need capital must rely either on retaining earnings or finding a merger partner. Thus the final impact is that increased capital requirements lead to consolidation. Capital-rich firms have market power to purchase capital-deficient firms relatively inexpensively. From the regulators' perspective, higher capital has two attractive features: overall risk in banking is lowered and fewer distinct firms exist that must be regulated.

INCREASED CONSOLIDATION

The dominant trend regarding the structure of financial institutions is toward consolidation. Consider, for example, authorization of the Resolution Trust Corporation to arrange the closings of failed thrifts and their sale to solvent institutions. With the asset quality problems of Texas banks, the regulators authorized acquisitions by out-of-state banks including Chemical Bank, Bank One, First Interstate, and NCNB. Interstate and national banking pacts and cross-industry acquisitions have the same consolidating effect on healthy banks and nonbank financial institutions. The catalysts are obvious. Technological advances allow firms to compete for customers electronically without branch facilities on every street corner. Increased capital requirement restrict growth and make it difficult to compete as a small entity. The net effect will be fewer and increasingly larger firms.

Most large banks have been positioning themselves to be acquirers rather than acquirees. They have laid off employees, cut other operating expenses, and sold subsidiaries to streamline operations. Many issued stock when the market was favorable. Others have tried to shrink assets and focus on specific customers, such as consumers, to improve profitability and reduce risk.

Consolidation will affect all types of financial firms, both foreign and domestic, and not just banks. Many firms are entering joint ventures and thus combining resources. Exhibit 3.9 demonstrates that Japanese firms had significant investments in 7 of the largest U.S. investment banks in 1990. Such partnerships provide capital to expand operations and allow shared expertise to improve a firm's competitive position.

SEARS, ROEBUCK & CO.:
A RETAIL AND FINANCIAL CONGLOMERATE

Increased competition among financial institutions has led to the development and growth of diversified financial services companies and nationwide commercial banking organizations. Community bank managers express concern that they do not possess the same resources or opportunities as financial giants and may be priced out of business.

Exhibit 3.9 The Major Investments from Japan

U.S. Investment Banking Firm	Japanese Investor	Investment	
		Amount (Millions)	Percent of Equity
Shearson Lehman	Nippon Life	$508.0	13.0%
Goldman Sachs	Sumitomo Bank	500.0	12.5
PaineWebber	Yasuda Mutual Life	300.0	20.0
Blackstone	Nikko Securities	100.0	20.0
Wasserstein	Nomura Securities	100.0	20.0
Wolfersonn	Fuji Bank	52.5	0.0[a]
Mitsui Bank	Carlyle Group	25.0	0.0[b]

[a]Each owns 50% of a joint venture

[b]Mitsui committed at least $25 million to a Carlyle fund\

Data: *Business Week*

Source: From "Japan's Waiting Game on Wall Street." *Business Week* (February 19, 1990).

Many analysts, however, contend that community banks have inherent advantages, ranging from a record of long-term personal service to better knowledge of customer needs because of local ownership and control. Employees of companies affiliated with financial conglomerates are often only order-takers because local officials do not make important decisions. Community banks should prosper in this environment.

Whether a community bank survives or disappears depends largely on management's ability to establish a strong market position in product areas where the bank has competitive advantages and continue to serve customer needs. In some instances, a community bank may act as a franchise of larger networks to provide services it cannot offer alone at competitive prices. Innovation in the delivery and pricing of banking services, however, has become widely accepted and expected, to the point where competition is now much more intense than it was during the past decade. Many customers choose an institution on the basis of the range of services offered and the potential for one-stop shopping. This has given rise to the term *financial services shopping center*, a diversified financial firm with a nationwide delivery system for broad-based financial products.

American Banker conducted a nationwide survey in 1986 asking consumers to select an institution where they would shop for basic financial services, assuming equal safety and convenience.[12] Respondents could choose from among their primary local institution and Sears, Merrill Lynch, American Express, Prudential, and Fidelity Investments. The results are summarized in Exhibit 3.10. Consumers overwhelmingly preferred local institutions for checking and savings accounts, installment loans, mort-

---

[12]Gross, 1986, summarizes the results of the 1986 survey and compares responses to those from prior years. Comparisons generally indicated that consumers, especially younger respondents, were more willing to use financial conglomerates in 1986 over previous years.

Exhibit 3.10 The Financial Services Shopping Center of the Future

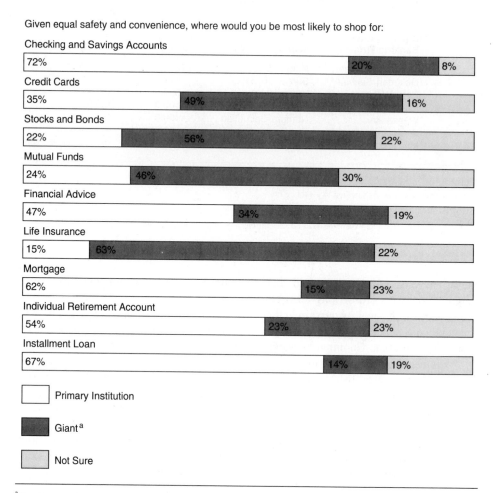

Given equal safety and convenience, where would you be most likely to shop for:

Checking and Savings Accounts

| 72% | 20% | 8% |

Credit Cards

| 35% | 49% | 16% |

Stocks and Bonds

| 22% | 56% | 22% |

Mutual Funds

| 24% | 46% | 30% |

Financial Advice

| 47% | 34% | 19% |

Life Insurance

| 15% | 63% | 22% |

Mortgage

| 62% | 15% | 23% |

Individual Retirement Account

| 54% | 23% | 23% |

Installment Loan

| 67% | 14% | 19% |

☐ Primary Institution

■ Giant[a]

▨ Not Sure

[a]The giants are Sears, Roebuck & Co., Merrill Lynch & Co., American Express Co., Prudential Insurance Co., and Fidelity Investments.

Source: Gross, Laura. "Diversified Financial Giants Gaining Approval, *American Banker* (September 24, 1986).

gages, retirement accounts, and general financial advice. They preferred the five financial conglomerates over local banks to provide stocks and bonds, life insurance, credit cards, and mutual funds.

Interestingly, the survey suggests that both banks and diversified financial service companies are perceived as credible suppliers of services they were once prohibited from offering. Banks would like to offer mutual funds, insurance products, and stock and bond underwriting, while the financial giants would like to be your banker.

Ominously for banks, individuals aged 18 to 34 were the least likely to prefer local financial institutions, indicating that future growth will be highly contested.

In the same survey, 20 percent of the respondents rated Sears, Roebuck & Co. as the best company in meeting customer needs among the major financial conglomerates, including BankAmerica and Citicorp. In subsequent years, Sears' profit performance has weakened, but its market penetration in financial services has grown.

Sears, once the largest retailer in the United States, now relies on nonretailing activities for the bulk of its earnings. In 1990 Sears' merchandising unit, for which the company is best known, generated only $257 million in profit from $32 billion in sales. At this level Sears ranks behind Wal-Mart and Kmart Corporation in sales and earnings. The fundamental problems have been increased competition for discounters and an industry-high level of expenses. Today, Sears operates a nationwide network of financial companies, which gives it a major presence in the financial services industry. Sears was one of the first nontraditional financial institutions to articulate and implement a strategic plan to expand into banking, real estate, insurance, and investment banking. By 1990 financial activities contributed 72 percent of the company's net income. Sears' corporate structure and long-range strategic plan are similar to those of other large, diversified financial services companies.

Sears has long possessed one of the most respected names in U.S. retailing. It operates retail stores in all 50 states and has a nationwide customer base exceeding 40 million families. In 1931 Sears acquired Allstate Insurance Co., which is now the second-largest property-casualty insurer in the country. It later purchased Dean Witter Reynolds, a large retail brokerage, and Coldwell Banker Real Estate and operates a stand-alone credit services business. Sears' long-range plan is simple: it intends to diversify into financial services, which it will market to its retail customer base. Management expects that individuals, presented with a comprehensive list of financial products, will choose to shop for these at Sears' affiliates.

Business Groups

In 1990 Sears segmented its operations into four business groups: Sears Merchandise, Allstate Insurance, Dean Witter Financial Services, and Coldwell Banker Real Estate. Exhibit 3.11 summarizes the basic business activity and distribution channels within each group and compares each group's contribution to the corporation's assets, revenues, and net income in 1990. The merchandise group operates almost 800 retail stores, which represent Sears' core business. In addition to general merchandise, the group manages over 200 specialty stores that sell computer products, surplus items, or paint and hardware. Much of the group's earnings derive from its revolving credit operations through Sears Acceptance Corp. Over 70 million Sears credit cards (excluding Discover cards) were outstanding in 1990, with 33 million active accounts.

The entire merchandise group earned $257 million in 1990, less than 30 percent of total corporate net income. Total sales grew but fell short of sales at competitors Wal-Mart and Kmart. This represents a sharp reversal from the mid-1980s when the group earned over $650 million annually and dominated other retailers. In response, the merchandise unit has undergone several restructurings. The first major change was

Exhibit 3.11 Sears, Roebuck & Co.'s Operations; (1989–1992)

	Merchandise Group	Allstate Insurance	Dean Witter Financial	Coldwell Banker
Business Activity	Merchandising Specialty retailing: surplus, computers, paint, hardware Revolving credit International	Property-casualty insurance Life and health insurance Mature Outlook (mail-order discounter)	Retail brokerage Mutual funds Discover card Underwriting and trading securities Sears Payment Systems	Residential mortgage Residential and commercial real estate brokerage Real estate development
Distribution Channels	Sears Acceptance Corp. Sears Specialty Merchandising 799 retail stores 2,361 catalog sales locations 226 specialty stores 160 other outlets 317,000 Employed	1,130 Sears stores 3,630 neighborhood offices 2,770 independent agencies selling Allstate products 1 direct marketing Sears Savings Bank in Calif.	Sears Mortgage Corp Greenwood Trust Co. in Delaware Hurley State Bank in S.D. 308 Dean Witter branch offices 375 institutional sales and training offices Discover card with $11.6 billion in receivables; 37.8 million cardholders; 1.24 million outlets	16 residential real estate offices 179 commercial real estate offices 48 properties in Homart Development Co. Mortgage production exceeded 34.5 billion

	Merchandise Group	Allstate Insurance	Dean Witter Financial	Coldwell Banker	Totals[a]
Total Assets	$25,539	$39,950	$21,690	$7,852	$96,253
Total Revenue	$31,986	$18,199	$ 4,607	$1,377	$55,972
Net Income	$ 257	$ 701	$ 233	$ 26	$ 902

[a]Totals net out amounts for corporate operations and intergroup transactions.

Source: Byrne, Harlan. "New Life at Sears." *Baron's*, January 27, 1986 with updates.

to introduce specialty stores that concentrated on selling name brand clothing and furniture items. Customers, however, still generally preferred smaller specialty shops. A second move toward one-price shopping involved lowering day-to-day prices across the board to make Sears' products more price competitive with those of discounters. Unfortunately, Sears' prices in many cases were still above competitors'. Each change was accompanied by a round of cost-cutting by laying off employees and eliminating jobs. The long-term strategy appears to be one of cutting expenses until its "everyday low price" concept is attractive because prices are low enough.

In 1981 Sears acquired Dean Witter Reynolds and Coldwell Banker Real Estate, which it lumped with Allstate Insurance to form the Sears Financial Network. The network concept involved opening financial centers in Sears' retail outlets that housed representatives of each unit. The goal was to offer one-stop financial shopping for consumer services including insurance, mortgages, mutual fund shares, and related brokerage services.

Allstate's revenues exceeded $18 billion in 1990, primarily from its property-casualty insurance business, where it is a major provider of automobile and home-owner's insurance. Allstate has moved into life and health insurance and formed Mature Outlook, a mail-order discounter that markets goods and services to older individuals. Allstate also owns Sears Savings Bank, the second largest savings and loan in the United States, from which it offers mortgage and deposit services and manages real estate. Allstate regularly contributes a major share of Sears' net income, even when its insurance underwriting declines, because it holds extensive investments in fixed-income securities and common stocks. Allstate's net income in 1990 totaled $701 million, almost three times the earnings at the merchandise group.

Dean Witter Financial Services group is a financial conglomerate in itself, with its two banking operations and Sears Home Mortgage Corp. in addition to its brokerage units. Dean Witter employs over 7,000 brokers who handle securities transactions ranging from selling mutual fund shares to brokering stocks and bonds. It focuses almost exclusively on individual customers, unlike many investment banks. In 1990 it earned $233 million, its highest ever, while the securities industry reported a loss. Dean Witter serves as a link with other Sears affiliates by selling annuities and bond funds managed by Allstate. Sears also owns Greenwood Trust Co., a Delaware-based consumer bank, and a similar bank in South Dakota.[13]

Greenwood Trust issues Sears' Discover Card, the medium through which Sears hopes individuals will conduct most of their financial business. Discover was initially test-marketed as a general credit card in competition with VISA, MasterCard, and American Express in five states, then introduced nationally in January 1986. Customers use the card to charge purchases from retail outlets, obtain cash advances, withdraw funds from savings accounts at Greenwood Trust or Sears Savings Bank, transfer funds between securities offered through Dean Witter, make mortgage payments, pay insurance, and buy securities. Much like Merrill Lynch's Cash Management Account or Schwab's All in One Account, Discover cardholders can access many services and receive confirmation on one comprehensive monthly statement. The Discover card, then, is the mechanism for providing convenient full-service banking to Sears' customers and fills a critical role in the company's strategic plan.

Sears' investment in Discover entails considerable risk because the bank credit card market is already saturated, with many individuals holding MasterCard, VISA, American Express, and other multipurpose cards. Sears, in fact, lost money on Discover for several years, but it now generates a profit. In an effort to attract customers, it offers new cardholders free annual membership and a refund equal to 1 percent of their retail charge card purchases. Members also receive coupons for use in Sears stores. Other sales establishments that accept the card pay fees below those on other bank cards for Sears to process the charge.

---

[13]The nonbank bank does not make commercial loans. Thus Sears avoids regulation as a commercial bank under the Bank Holding Company Act.

In 1986 Sears consolidated its mortgage activities into Sears Mortgage Corp., combining the operations of Allstate's mortgage business and Sears Savings Bank. During 1990 Sears serviced approximately 250,000 mortgage loans valued at $13 billion. It will continue to service mortgages originated largely by its Coldwell Banker subsidiary.

The final business group is Coldwell Banker Real Estate, which offers realty services that generate fees plus mortgages that can be pooled and resold by Dean Witter in the secondary market. As a mortgage banker, Coldwell Banker originates both residential and commercial mortgages and generates income from mortgage servicing. Coldwell Banker, Sears Mortgage Corp., and Dean Witter combine to take mortgages from origination to the portfolios of institutional investors, collecting fees along the way. Coldwell Banker originates the mortgages through its realty offices, then sells them to Sears Mortgage Corp., which services the loans after they are packaged and sold to investors through Dean Witter. The real estate group also includes Homart Development Co., which develops shopping centers and related properties. Coldwell Banker's earnings have been stable but contribute only a small fraction of Sears' total net income. In 1990, for example, net income totaled just $26 million.

Management Strategies

Sears long-term strategy is to diversify through linking consumer financial services. The Discover credit card is the critical link between its financial services and its merchandise trade unit. For many years, Sears has been the world's largest general merchandise retailer, yet it faces intense competition from discounters and specialty stores. Historically, Sears stores have catered to middle-class homeowners by offering a broad range of standard merchandise from appliances to clothing. Over time this class of consumers has shrunk in size and increasingly shifted to discount stores or tried to upgrade purchases to status items offered by special merchandisers. In 1987 Sears established a special merchandising unit to compete with specialty stores. In 1990 it moved to "everyday low pricing" to better compete with discount stores. This was necessary, as was its aggressive cost-cutting campaign, because Sears' prices were above those elsewhere.

Sears hopes to use its well-known name and marketing strength to sell financial services to its current customer base. It will focus on consumer banking rather than commercial banking, thus concentrating on retail business. Demographic trends that harm merchandise sales should help Dean Witter brokerage activities and Allstate Insurance products. Coldwell Banker's fortunes change with the housing market. Linking these diverse activities is the Discover credit card, which gives customers the opportunity to combine purchases of many different products into one transactions medium. Marketing efforts can be extremely cost-effective by targeting cardholders throughout the country simultaneously in national promotions. Diversification means that earnings should stabilize and growth can be achieved in a variety of different product areas.

Exhibit 3.12 The Battleground: How Nonbanks Currently Compete with Banks

	Branch Deposit Taking	Credit Cards	Auto Lending	Securities Underwriting	Commercial Finance	Mortgage Banking
Typical banking company	X	X	X		X	X
American Express		X		X		
AT&T		X			X	
Ford Motor	X	X	X		X	X
General Electric		X		X	X	X
General Motors			X			X
Household International	X	X	X			X
Sears, Roebuck		X	X	X	X	X

Source: Zuckerman, "As Washington Dithers, Nonbanks Advance," *American Banker* (March 15, 1991).

Competitive Responses

Small banks view Sears as an example of unequal regulation gone bad. Sears operates in all 50 states, unlike independent banks that conduct business in a much smaller trade area. Through its affiliates, Sears offers savings accounts, mortgages, and credit cards, which compete directly with bank products. It also provides insurance, real estate, and brokerage services not available at banks. With its sophisticated communications and data processing network, Sears can process transactions at lower unit costs, a long-term competitive advantage that could force small banks to reassess their product base, customer base, and delivery system.[14]

While large bank holding companies and related financial services companies also recognize the competitive inequities, they are interested in forming the same types of networks. This inclination explains the extensive merger and acquisition activity across industry segments. Financial conglomerates such as Citicorp, General Electric, and American Express similarly expect to compete aggressively in most facets of consumer and commercial banking. Their preference is to continue the deregulation process along geographic and product lines. Exhibit 3.12 documents the range of services offered by several of the large, better-known nonbank financial services providers. The point is that these firms currently offer many of the same products as banks. Do they have cost and regulatory advantages? It seems so.

SUMMARY

Differences between depository institutions are quickly disappearing. Banks now compete with savings and loans, credit unions, and affiliates of nationwide financial

---

[14]Sears offered a legislative proposal to Congress to approve family banks, which would concentrate on deposit and loan services for individuals and small businesses. Firms would be allowed to form chains of such banks nationally as long as the banks directed most of their loans to borrowers within the home state. Community bankers were outraged, claiming that Sears' description of a family bank already existed as the traditional small, independent bank.

conglomerates in providing basic banking services. Increased competition has arisen from deregulation, financial innovation, securitization, and globalization of financial institutions and markets. Deregulation is the removal of regulations that limit financial institutions' activities. Financial innovation is the continual development of new products and change in market structure to circumvent regulation and meet customer needs. Securitization is the process of converting assets to marketable securities. From a bank's perspective, securitization moves assets off the balance sheet and substitutes fee income for interest income. Finally, globalization involves the de facto elimination of geographic barriers to trade and financial market activity.

Consumers and businesses benefit from lower interest rates and increased capital availability. Market participants can choose from a larger number of suppliers, which places a premium on customer service. To remain competitive, banks should identify the products with which they have a market advantage and provide personal service that distinguishes them from their competitors.

Questions

1. Banking is in a state of change caused by changes in the banking environment. What are some of these changes? What factors are causing them?

2. Change is always good for some participants and bad for others. Which types of banks can profit from current changes and which cannot? Why?

3. Which of the four forces of change do you feel has had the most dramatic effect on banking in the past five years? Which will have in the next five years?

4. Explain two instances in which banks have successfully circumvented regulatory restrictions. Which of these resulted in reregulation?

5. Explain the significance of using the terms *deregulation* and *reregulation* together. What benefits have been generated by this process?

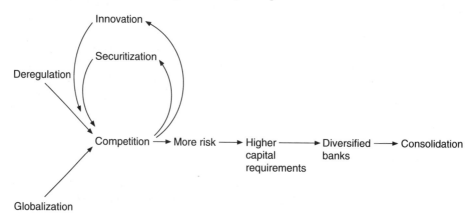

6. The factors involved in the changing banking field are highly interrelated. In the organizational scheme shown above, consolidation of the banking industry is the

ultimate effect of a series of causes. Some banking writers contend the ultimate effect is not consolidation, but globalization. Redraw the diagram, using the same phrases, to show a line leading to globalization.

7. Our free capitalistic system has long supported regulation of the banking industry. What makes banking so unique that it needs government regulation when other industries do not?

8. Critics of government bank regulation contend that it works as well as communism in supporting inferior management. What arguments would support this view?

9. Some contend that the government plays a game of catch-up in reregulation. The game is initiated by bankers, who respond to their economic environment with new and often creative products to circumvent existing regulation. Regulators try to catch up by eliminating or rewriting old rules to reflect the new reality. Meanwhile, bankers are circumventing regulation in different areas, creating more new work for regulators. Explain how offering interest on checking accounts provides an anecdote to support this view of banker-regulator relations.

10. Securitization results largely from deregulation. Explain why deregulation induces banks to move assets off their balance sheets.

11. What impact is securitization likely to have on the quality of bank assets?

12. Give one advantage and one disadvantage for banks in securitizing:
mortgages
credit card loans
small business loans

13. A local bank has launched a major advertising campaign to announce that it has become "globalized." As a student customer of this bank, will globalization have any impact on your banking?

14. Globalization results in more efficient financial markets. Give two reasons that bankers might justifiably fear globalization. Is it different for community banks versus money-center banks?

15. Explain how the growth in commercial paper and junk bonds has affected commercial lending at banks.

16. In what areas do captive automobile finance companies compete with banks? What advantages and disadvantages do the automobile finance companies have?

17. Describe the basic services provided by investment banks. Why are large commercial banks eager to offer investment banking services?

18. Does a small local bank or a large regional bank seem to dominate the financial markets of your town? What advantages does the dominant institution exploit? What advantage could the suboptimal bank develop to offer stiffer competition?

19. What are the arguments for increasing bank capital requirements? In what ways will depositors, equity owners, and society benefit from increased capital? In what ways will they be disadvantaged?

20. What arguments support the view that the Sears Financial Network is competing unfairly with banks.

21. Suppose you are the president of a commercial bank in a university town. The town has four banks, two savings and loans, and a Sears Financial Network operation, none of which currently operates on campus. You feel the campus, with 15,000 students, could profitably support one ATM. Develop the arguments you might use to convince the campus administration that they should allow you exclusive rights to operate an ATM in the student center. Design an advertising campaign to initiate student use of the new machine.

Activities

1. Which banks in your area seem to have best adapted to change? How are you deciding? Would you rather work for a totally modern bank where your colleagues would be well-informed and adaptable, or for a laggard bank with substantial room for improvement where your best ideas might either be adopted to great benefit or ignored?

2. How many banks were there in your home town five years ago? How many are there now? Why has the number changed? (Try checking an old phone book or the chamber of commerce.)

3. What are the current branching laws in your state? Do any out-of-state banks operate in your city? Any foreign banks? Identify the strengths and weaknesses of each.

References

Aguilar, Linda. "Still Toe-to-Toe: Banks and Nonbanks at the End of the '80s." *Economic Perspectives* (Federal Reserve Bank of Chicago, January/February 1990).

Bianco, Anthony. "Playing with Fire." *Business Week* (September 16, 1985).

Brenner, Lynn. "Credit Card Deal May Be Model for Securitization." *American Banker* (April 14, 1986).

Brenner, Lynn. "Turning Assets into Securities is Knotty Problem, Panel Says." *American Banker* (May 2, 1986).

Brewer, Elijah, Diana Fortier, and Christine Pavel. "Bank Risk from Nonbank Activities." *Economic Perspectives* (Federal Reserve Bank of Chicago, July/August 1988).

Byrne, Harlan. "New Life at Sears." *Barron's* (January 27, 1986).

Davis, Richard. "The Recent Performance of the Commercial Banking Industry." *Quarterly Review* (Federal Reserve Bank of New York, Summer 1986).

Eisenbeis, Robert. "Inflation and Regulation: The Effects on Financial Institutions and Structure." Chapter 3 in *Handbook for Banking Strategy,* edited by Richard Aspinwall and Robert Eisenbeis. New York: John Wiley & Sons, 1985.

Garsson, Robert. "Auto Makers Veer Into Financial Services Traffic." *American Banker* (December 26, 1985).

Gross, Laura. "Diversified Financial Giants Gaining Consumer Approval." *American Banker* (September 24, 1986).

Kane, Edward. "Good Intentions and Unintended Evil: The Case Against Selective Credit Allocation." *Journal of Money Credit and Banking* (February 1977).

Kane, Edward. "Accelerating Inflation, Technological Innovation, and the Decreasing Effectiveness of Banking Regulation." *Journal of Finance* (May 1981).

Miller, Merton. "Financial Innovation: The Last Twenty Years and the Next." *Journal of Financial and Quantitative Analysis* (December 1986).

Nathans, Leah, and William Glasgall. "Japan's Waiting Game on Wall Street." *Business Week* (February 19, 1990).

Orr, Bill. "International Debt Problem Clarified." *ABA Banking Journal* (May 1986).

Pavel, Christine. "Securitization." *Economic Perspectives* (Federal Reserve Bank of Chicago, July–August 1986).

Pavel, Christine, and John McElvaney, "Globalization in the Financial Services Industry." *Economic Perspectives* (Federal Reserve Bank of Chicago, May/June 1990).

Pozdena, Randall. "Securitization and Banking." *Weekly Letter* (Federal Reserve Bank of San Francisco, July 4, 1986).

Rogowski, Robert. "The Role of Commercial Banks in a Securitized World." *The Bankers Magazine* (July–August 1988).

Zuckerman, Sam. "As Washington Dithers, Nonbanks Advance." *American Banker* (March 15, 1991).

Analyzing Bank Performa

Early in 1990 Boston-based Bank of New England Corp. announced that it would post a $1.2 billion loss for the fourth quarter of 1989. It simultaneously announced that it would sell $6 billion in assets including commercial loans, home mortgages, home equity loans, credit card receivables, automobile loans, and a leasing subsidiary. The loss resulted primarily from problems with the bank's real estate loans. Asset sales were necessary because the bank could not adequately borrow in the capital markets and was being forced to pay premium rates on its short-term deposits to prevent large-scale withdrawals. The objective was to increase the bank's equity capital and strengthen its financial position. Bank of New England eventually failed, and the remnants were sold in 1991.

Many banking organizations have experienced similar problems with loan losses. Bank of New England's quarterly loss, for example, ranked as just the sixth largest from 1987 to 1989. Frequently, the earnings declines have surprised stockholders and analysts, who could not accurately detect the increase in risk or problem loans from regular financial statements. With the increased complexity of bank operations, it has become much more difficult to evaluate bank performance from published figures. Net income can be manipulated by management to disguise fundamental problems. Furthermore, no two analysts agree on how to measure risk.

This chapter presents a procedure for analyzing bank performance using periodic balance sheet and income statement data. It describes the components of financial statements, provides a framework for comparing the trade-off between bank profitability and risk, and compares the performance of small community banks with that of large money center banking organizations.

om 1984 to 1990, 1,090 commercial banks failed throughout the United States. The failures were largely concentrated in the Southwest and Farm Belt as almost 450 banks failed in Texas, Oklahoma, and Louisiana and approximately 275 failed in Colorado, Kansas, Missouri, Iowa, and Minnesota. Many other banks avoided closing only because of federal aid, or were placed on the regulators' problem bank list indicating severe operating difficulties. Can an objective observer identify problem institutions before they fail? Is it possible to distinguish between strong and weak banks on the basis of reported earnings and balance sheet figures? How should risk be measured? How can the trade-off between risk and profitability be evaluated? These and other questions have become increasingly important as banks face greater competition from nontraditional competitors and regulators demonstrate a willingness to close banks.

Many observers attribute recent failures to deregulation and economic conditions. Deregulation did encourage banks to increase the size of their loan portfolios, which, in turn, produced greater loan losses when regional economic conditions deteriorated and agriculture, energy, and real estate problems appeared. Deregulation also changed the way bankers view branch offices and personnel by forcing them to cut operating expenses. Most firms realize, however, that the competitive environment has changed since the 1960s. To maintain or improve their earnings performance, they must reduce operating costs, offer new products at favorable prices, or assume greater risk in their asset portfolios. Strong banks consistently report operating earnings without extraordinary changes in their risk profile. Weak banks often report excellent earnings for a few years, but generally assume too much risk in their operations which eventually produces losses.

This chapter explains how to evaluate commercial bank performance. The analysis begins by introducing bank financial statements. A return on equity framework is then used to describe the trade-offs between profitability and risk and provide measures that differentiate between high- and low-performance banks. The analytical framework is applied to Valley National Corporation's data, then used to compare the characteristics of different-sized banks. The chapter also describes the CAMEL system used by federal supervisors to rate banks. Finally, because banks often disguise adverse changes in their performance from year to year, special attention is paid to financial statement manipulation.

COMMERCIAL BANK FINANCIAL STATEMENTS

Like other financial intermediaries, commercial banks facilitate the flow of funds from surplus spending units (savers) to deficit spending units (borrowers). Their financial characteristics largely reflect government-imposed operating restrictions and peculiar features of the specific markets served. Three characteristics stand out. First, because their function is primarily financial, most banks own few fixed assets. They have few fixed costs, and thus low operating leverage. Second, many bank liabilities are payable on demand or carry short-term maturities so depositors can renegotiate deposit rates as market interest rates change. Interest expense thus changes with short-run changes in market interest rates. This creates serious asset allocation and pricing problems. Third, banks operate with less equity capital than do nonfinancial companies, which increases financial leverage and the volatility of earnings. Each characteristic presents special problems and risks to the bank manager.

The Balance Sheet

A bank's balance sheet presents financial information comparing what a bank owns with what it owes and the ownership interest of stockholders. Assets indicate what the bank owns; liabilities represent what the bank owes; and equity refers to the owners' interest such that:

$$\text{Assets} = \text{Liabilities} + \text{Equity}. \qquad (4.1)$$

Balance sheet figures are calculated at a particular point in time and thus represent stock values. Regulators require that banks report balance sheet and income statement data quarterly, so figures are available publicly at the end of March, June, September, and December each year.

Balance sheets for two banking organizations are shown in Exhibit 4.1. The first represents the consolidated statement for Valley National Corporation, a large multibank holding company, and its subsidiaries. Valley National Corp. owns 100 percent of the stock in several commercial banks and nonbank subsidiaries with domestic and foreign offices. For reporting purposes, consolidation nets out all intracompany transactions. In 1988 Valley National controlled almost $11 billion in assets, with approximately 7 percent in cash, 20 percent in securities, and 70 percent in loans. The second balance sheet is for Community State Bank, a $100 million independent bank located outside a metropolitan area. The bank owns no subsidiaries and holds almost 37 percent of its assets in cash and securities and 60 percent in net loans. These statements are representative of the differences in balance sheet composition for large versus small banks, and indicate significant performance differences for 1988.

Bank Assets. Bank assets fall into one of four general categories: cash and due from banks, investment securities, loans, and other assets. **Cash and due from banks** consists of vault cash, deposits held at Federal Reserve Banks, deposits held at other financial institutions, and cash items in the process of collection. Vault cash is coin and currency that the bank holds to meet customer withdrawals. Deposits held at Federal Reserve or other banks are demand balances used to meet legal reserve requirements, assist in check clearing and wire transfers, or effect the purchase and sale of Treasury securities. The amount of required reserve deposits is set by regulation as a fraction of qualifying bank deposit liabilities. Balances are held at other financial institutions, called correspondent banks, primarily to purchase services. The amount is determined by the volume and cost of services provided such that income from investing the deposits at least covers the cost of the services provided by the correspondent bank. The largest component of cash assets, cash items in the process of collection, represents checks written against other institutions and presented to the bank for payment for which credit has not been given. To verify that actual balances support

Exhibit 4.1 Balance Sheet Information for Valley National Corporation and Community State Bank

	1988 Average Balances (Dollars in Thousands)[a]			
Assets	Valley National Corporation	Percent of Total	Community State Bank	Percent of Total
Cash and due from banks	$ 744,000	6.8%	$ 4,000	4.0%
Investments:				
Time deposits at banks	218,000	2.0	1,500	1.5
Federal funds sold & RPs	408,000	3.7	4,100	4.1
U.S. government securities	777,000	7.1	10,600	10.6
Federal agency securities	129,000	1.2	6,400	6.4
State and municipal securities	605,000	5.5	9,400	9.4
Other securities	52,000	0.4	800	0.8
Total investments	$ 2,189,000	19.9%	$ 32,800	32.8%
Loans:				
Business	$ 2,418,000	22.0%	$ 30,800	30.8%
Real estate	2,182,000	19.9	11,600	11.6
Consumer	2,792,000	25.4	18,100	18.1
International	128,000	1.1		
Leases	182,000	1.7	500	0.5
Total loans & leases	$ 7,702,000	70.1%	$ 61,000	61.0%
Less reserve for loan losses	192,000	1.7	1,400	1.4
Net loans	$ 7,510,000	68.4%	$ 59,600	59.6%
Other assets	539,000	4.9	3,600	3.6
Total Assets[b]	$10,982,000	100.0%	$100,000	100.0%
Liabilities and Equity				
Demand deposits (non-interest bearing)	$ 1,756,000	16.0%	$ 10,700	10.7%
Interest-bearing checking	805,000	7.3	14,300	14.3
Regular savings	528,000	4.8	6,200	6.2
Money market savings	2,274,000	20.7	11,900	11.9
Consumer time deposits (<$10,000)	2,668,000	24.5	40,200	40.2
CDs ≥$100,000	1,331,000	12.1	7,100	7.1
Total interest-bearing deposits	$ 7,626,000	69.4%	$ 79,700	79.7%
Federal funds purchased and RPs	341,000	3.1		
Commercial paper	195,000	1.8		
Other short-term borrowings	33,000	0.3	300	0.3
Long-term debt	308,000	2.8	1,000	1.0
Total interest-bearing funds	$ 8,503,000	77.4%	$ 81,000	81.0%
Other liabilities	128,000	1.2	500	0.5
Total liabilities	$10,387,000	94.6%	$ 92,200	92.2%
Common stock	$ 50,000	0.5%	$ 2,000	2.0%
Surplus	120,000	1.1	1,000	1.0
Retained earnings	428,000	3.9	4,800	4.8
Other equity accounts	(3,000)	–0.1		
Total stockholders' equity	$ 595,000	5.4%	$ 7,800	7.8%
Total liabilities and equity	$10,982,000	100.0%	$100,000	100.0%

[a] RPs indicates repurchase agreements; CDs certificates of deposit.

[b] Earning assets equals $9,699,000(VNC); $92,400 (CSB).

each check, the bank delays credit until the check clears or a reasonable time elapses. The volume of net deferred credit is commonly called *float.*

Investment securities consist of assets held to earn interest and help meet liquidity needs. Banks typically own a large amount of short-term securities that can easily be sold to obtain cash, but pay less interest than that available on longer-term securities. These short-term investments include time deposits due from other banks, federal funds sold, securities purchased under agreement to resell (repurchase agreements or RPs), Treasury bills, and municipal tax warrants. They have maturities ranging from overnight to 1 year and carry returns that vary quickly with changes in money market conditions. They are extremely liquid as they can easily be sold at a price close to that initially paid by the bank.

Long-term investment securities consist of Treasury notes and bonds that generate taxable or tax-exempt interest. Treasury securities and obligations of federal agencies such as the Farm Credit Association comprise the bulk of taxable investments. Banks also purchase mortgage-backed securities, commercial paper, and small amounts of foreign and corporate bonds. Most of these carry fixed-rate interest payments, with maturities up to 20 years. Until 1983 banks owned more state and municipal securities than any other investor group. These government securities are classified as *general obligation* or *revenue bonds* and pay interest that is exempt from federal income taxes. Recent changes in bank tax rules, however, have made most municipal securities unattractive to banks.[1] Banks cannot generally purchase corporate stock as an investment. They can own stock under two conditions; if it is acquired as collateral on a loan, and as members of the Federal Reserve System they own stock in the Federal Reserve Bank.

Many large banks also operate as security dealers that maintain an inventory of securities for resale and underwrite municipal issues. The inventory is comprised mainly of Treasury obligations, which are listed as trading account securities on the balance sheet. The bank earns interest on this inventory but operates to make a profit on the difference between the purchase and sale price of the securities. It subsequently bears the risk that the market value of its inventory might decrease.

Loans are commercial banks' major asset and generate the greatest amount of income. They also exhibit the highest default risk and are relatively illiquid. A bank negotiates loan terms with each borrower that vary with the use of proceeds, source of repayment, and type of collateral. Maturities range from call loans payable on demand to residential mortgages amortized over 30 years. The interest rate may be fixed over the life of the loan or vary with changes in market interest rates. Similarly, the loan principal may be repaid periodically or as a lump sum.

Exhibit 4.1 groups loans into four categories according to the use of proceeds. Business loans appear in many forms but typically finance working capital needs, equipment purchases, and plant expansions. This category also includes credit extended to other financial institutions, security brokers and dealers, and farmers. Real estate loans consist either of property loans secured by first mortgages or interim construction

---

[1]As noted in Chapter 2, the Tax Reform Act of 1986 eliminated bank deductions for borrowing costs associated with financing the purchase of most municipal bonds. The impact of this tax change is described in Chapter 18.

loans. Consumer loans are credit extended to individuals both directly and indirectly through the purchase of retail paper. Loans made for the purchase of credit card items and durable goods comprise the greatest volume of consumer credit. International loans are essentially business loans made to foreign enterprises or loans guaranteed by foreign governments. Many large U.S. banks substantially increased their international lending throughout the 1970s and early 1980s, eventually to find that many borrowers could not service the debt. International loans carry significant risks beyond normal business default risk.

Two adjustments are made to obtain a net loan figure. First, many banks own assets that are leased to customers. The dollar amount of outstanding leases is included in gross loans because lease financing is an alternative to direct loans. Second, gross loans are reduced by the dollar magnitude of a bank's loan-loss reserve, which exists in recognition that some loans will not be repaid. The reserve's maximum size is determined by tax law but increases with the growth in gross loans and decreases with net loan charge-offs. A bank is permitted a tax deduction for net additions to the loss reserve, denoted as the provision for loan losses on the income statement.[2]

Other assets are residual assets of relatively small magnitudes, including the depreciated value of bank premises and equipment, interest receivable, prepaid expenses, other real estate owned, and customers' liability to the bank under acceptances. An asset is listed separately when it becomes significantly large. For many problem banks, other real estate owned is substantial because it normally represents property taken as collateral against a loan that was unpaid. As indicated earlier, commercial banks own relatively few fixed assets. They operate with low fixed costs relative to nonfinancial firms and exhibit low operating leverage.

Bank Liabilities and Stockholders' Equity. Bank funding sources are classified according to the type of debt instrument and equity component. The characteristics of various debt instruments differ in terms of check-writing capabilities, interest paid, maturity, whether they carry FDIC insurance, and whether they can be traded in the secondary market. Historically, banks were limited in what interest rates they could pay on different types of deposits. Since 1986 all interest rate restrictions have been eliminated, except for the prohibition of interest on corporate demand deposits. Banks can now compete for deposits by offering unrestricted interest rates on virtually all of their liabilities. The components of equity also have different characteristics and arise under varied circumstances such as the issuance of stock, net income not paid out as dividends, and Treasury stock or related transactions.

Demand deposits are transactions accounts held by individuals, partnerships, corporations, and governments that pay no interest. Prior to the Depository Institutions Act of 1980, they served as the only legal transactions account nationally that could be offered by depository institutions. Businesses now own the bulk of existing demand deposits because they are not allowed to own an interest-bearing transactions account at a bank.

---

[2]The reported provision for loan losses is normally less than the actual tax deduction allowed by the Internal Revenue Service and claimed by the bank. Chapter 23 discusses this in detail.

Two types of interest-bearing accounts constitute **interest/checking deposits** at banks.[3] **Negotiable orders of withdrawal (NOWs)** and **Super NOWs** pay interest set by each bank without federal restrictions. Banks often require minimum balances before a depositor earns interest, impose service charges, and may limit the number of free checks a customer can write each month, but these terms vary among institutions. NOWs are available only to noncommercial customers. **Money market deposit accounts (MMDAs)** similarly pay market rates, but a customer is limited to no more than six checks or automatic transfers each month. This restriction exempts banks from holding required reserves against MMDAs as they are technically savings accounts. Thus banks can pay higher rates of interest on MMDAs versus NOWs for the same effective cost.

Savings and time deposits represent the bulk of interest-bearing liabilities at banks. Passbook savings deposits are small-denomination accounts that have no set maturity and no check-writing capabilities. Two general time deposit categories exist with a $100,000 denomination separating the groups. Time deposits in excess of $100,000, labeled jumbo **certificates of deposit (CDs)**, are negotiable with a well-established secondary market. The most common maturities are 1 month, 3 months, and 6 months, with $1 million the typical size. Most CDs are sold to nonfinancial corporations, local government units, and other financial institutions. The features of smaller time deposits under $100,000 are not as standardized. Banks and customers negotiate the maturity, interest rate, and dollar magnitude of each deposit. The only stipulation is that small time deposits carry early withdrawal penalties whereby banks reduce the effective interest paid if a depositor withdraws funds prior to the stated maturity date. Most banks market standardized instruments so that customers are not confused.

Most banks closely monitor changes in their core deposits. As the name suggests, **core deposits** are all deposits that are relatively stable in that they are not withdrawn over short periods of time. They are thus not highly rate-sensitive and represent a more permanent funding base than purchased liabilities. Banks usually estimate the dollar amount of core deposits as the sum of demand deposits, NOWs, Super NOWS, MMDAs, savings deposits, and small time deposits.

Deposits in foreign offices refers to the same types of dollar-denominated demand and time deposits discussed above except that the balances are issued by a bank subsidiary (owned by the bank holding company) located outside the United States. The average foreign deposit balance is generally quite large. Nonfinancial corporations engaged in international trade and government units own most of these deposits.

Large banks also rely on other rate-sensitive borrowings that can be used to acquire funds quickly; **federal funds purchased** and **RPs** are the most popular source. These immediately available funds are traded in multiples of $1 million overnight or with extended maturities. Reputable banks need only offer a small premium over the current market rate to acquire funds. Large banks also issue commercial paper through

---

[3]Prior to 1983, banks and S&Ls could not pay market interest rates on most deposits under $100,000. Limits were gradually removed through 1986, when only demand deposits were restructured. Calem, 1985, describes the evolution of the current environment.

their holding companies and borrow Eurodollars. Commercial paper represents unsecured corporate promissory notes, while Eurodollars are dollar-denominated deposits borrowed by institutions located outside the United States.

Liabilities that are highly rate-sensitive do not represent a stable source of funding, particularly when a bank gets into trouble. They are normally issued in denominations above the amount that is federally insured so the depositor bears some risk of default. Thus if a bank reports problems or a competitor offers a higher rate, customers are quite willing to move their deposits. Jumbo CDs, federal funds purchased, securities sold under agreement to repurchase, and Eurodollar liabilities are subsequently referred to as *purchased liabilities, volatile deposits,* or *hot money.*

Subordinated notes and debentures consist of notes and bonds with maturities in excess of one year. Most meet requirements as bank capital. Unlike deposits, the debt is not federally insured and claims of bondholders are subordinated to claims of depositors. Thus when a bank fails, depositors are paid before subordinated debt holders. Other liabilities include acceptances outstanding, taxes and dividends payable, trade credit, and other miscellaneous claims.

Stockholders' equity is the ownership interest in the bank. Common and preferred stock are listed at their par values, while the surplus account represents the amount of proceeds received by the bank in excess of par when it issued the stock. Retained earnings represents the bank's cumulative net income since the firm started operation, minus all dividends paid to stockholders. Other equity is small and usually reflects capital reserves. The book value of equity equals the difference between the book value of assets and aggregate liabilities. A detailed discussion of each component of stockholders' equity and associated regulatory requirements appears in Chapter 11.

The Income Statement

A bank's income statement reflects the financial nature of banking, as interest on loans and investments comprises the bulk of revenue. Interest payments on borrowings similarly represent the primary expense. The format thus starts with interest income, then subtracts interest expense to produce net interest income. The next step is to subtract provisions for loan losses, which represent management's estimate of potential lost revenue from bad loans. The next two categories are noninterest income and noninterest expense. While banks constantly try to increase their noninterest income and reduce noninterest expense, the latter usually exceeds the former such that the difference is labeled the bank's **burden.** Subtracting income taxes and any accounting adjustments produces net income. Formally, if we define

II = total interest income
IE = total interest expense
PL = provisions for loan losses
OI = noninterest income
OE = noninterest expense
T = taxes (includes accounting adjustments),

then NII = (II – IE) equals net interest income before provisions, and (OE – OI) equals burden. Conceptually, a bank's net income (NI) can thus be viewed as having four contributing factors: net interest income, provisions for loan losses, burden, and taxes,

$$NI = NII - PL - Burden - T. \qquad (4.2)$$

Income statements for the two banking organizations described earlier are presented in Exhibit 4.2. Not surprisingly, the two groups' net income differs substantially, reflecting their diverse portfolios. Net income for Valley National equaled $67.316 million, while Community Bank's was $1.750 million. The contribution of each of the four components in thousands of dollars is summarized below.

	Valley National Corp.	**Community State Bank**
NII	$440,241	$3,894
– PL	– 87,000	– 524
– Burden	– 269,647	– 1,105
– T	– 16,278	– 515
= NI	$ 67,316	$1,750

Interest income is the sum of interest and fees earned on all of a bank's assets, including loans, deposits held at other institutions, municipal and taxable securities, and trading account securities. It also includes rental receipts from lease financing. All income is taxable except for the interest on state and municipal securities, which is exempt from federal income taxes. For comparative purposes, tax-exempt interest can be converted to a taxable equivalent amount by dividing tax-exempt interest by one minus the bank's marginal income tax rate.

$$Taxable\,equivalent\,municipal\,interest = \frac{Municipal\,interest}{1 - bank\,tax\,rate}$$

Tax equivalent interest for the two banks equals $65,785 and $1,102, respectively, with a 34 percent tax rate. **Interest expense** is the sum of interest paid on all interest-bearing liabilities, including transactions, time and savings deposits, short-term purchased liabilities, and long-term debt. Gross interest income minus gross interest expense is labeled **net interest income.** This figure is important because its variation over time indicates how well management is controlling interest rate risk.

Provision for loan losses is a deduction from income representing a bank's periodic allocation to its loan loss reserve on the balance sheet. Conceptually, management is allocating a portion of income to a reserve to protect against potential loan losses. It is a noncash expense but indicates management's perception of the quality of the bank's loans. It is subtracted from net interest income in recognition that some of the reported interest income overstates what will actually be received when some of the loans go into default. While management determines the size of the provision and thus what is reported to stockholders, Internal Revenue Service (IRS) rules specify the maximum allowable tax deduction, which normally exceeds what is reported to shareholders.[4]

---

[4] The amount of provisions reported is highly subjective and can be easily manipulated by management to alter earnings.

Exhibit 4.2 Income Statements for Valley National Corporation and Community State Bank (Dollars in Thousands)[a]

	Valley National Corp.	Percent of Operating Income[b]	Community State Bank	Percent of Operating Income[b]
Interest Income				
Interest and fees on loans	$828,690	72.2%	$6,945	58.4%
Interest on time deposits at banks	17,470	1.5	118	
Interest on federal funds sold & RPs	31,765	2.8	308	2.6
Interest on U.S. government securities	54,405	4.7	840	7.0
Interest on federal agency securities	11,077	1.0	591	5.0
Interest on state & municipal[c] securities	43,418	3.8	727	6.1
Interest on other securities	3,685	0.3	71	0.6
Total interest income	$990,510	86.3%	$9,600	80.7%
Interest Expense				
Interest on checking	$ 36,000	3.1%	$ 732	6.1%
Interest on regular savings	25,400	2.2	329	2.8
Interest on money market savings	120,200	10.5	716	6.0
Interest on consumer time deposits	202,000	17.6	3,275	27.5
Interest on CDs ≥$100,000	91,671	8.0	546	4.6
Interest on deposits	$475,271	41.4%	$5,598	47.0%
Interest on federal funds purchased & RPs	24,800	2.2		
Interest on commercial paper	15,300	1.3		
Interest on other short-term borrowings	3,298	0.3	18	0.1
Interest on long-term debt	31,600	2.8	90	0.8
Total interest expense	$550,269	48.0%	$5,706	47.9%
Net interest income	$440,241	38.3%	$3,894	32.7%
Provision for loan losses	87,000	7.5	524	4.4
Net Interest Income after Provisions	$353,241	30.8%	$3,370	28.3%
Noninterest Income				
Service charges on deposits	$ 63,291	5.5%	$1,322	11.1%
Trust income	25,055	2.2	215	1.8
Credit card fees	16,321	1.4		
Securities gains	782	0.1	87	0.7
Other income	51,429	4.5	676	5.7
Total noninterest income	$156,878	13.7%	$2,300	19.3%
Noninterest Expense				
Salaries & employee benefits	$235,143	20.5%	$1,760	14.8%
Occupancy expense	35,242	3.1	283	2.3
Furniture & equipment expense	43,335	3.8	364	3.1
Other operating expense	112,805	9.8	998	8.4
Total noninterest expense	$426,525	37.2%	$3,405	28.6%
Income before taxes & accounting adjustments	$ 83,594	7.3%	$2,265	19.0%
Applicable income taxes	21,263	1.8	515	4.3
Effect of change in accounting principle	4,985	0.4		
Net income	$ 67,316	5.9%	$1,750	14.7%

[a]RPs indicates repurchase agreements; CDs certificates of deposit.

[b]Total operating income: $1,147,388 (VNC); $11,900 (CSB).

[c]Tax-equivalent municipal interest: $65,785 (VNC); $1,102 (CSB).

Noninterest income is becoming increasingly important because of pricing pressure on net interest income. Fees and service charges typically generate the bulk of noninterest income. Banks impose charges on checking account activity, safety-deposit boxes, and many other transactions. Securitization has increased fee income because banks earn servicing fees for handling the underlying payments on securitized assets. Trust income reflects what a bank earns from operating a trust department. Investment securities gains (or losses) arise when a bank sells securities at prices above (or below) the cost to the bank. All such profits are reported and taxed as ordinary income. In March 1983 the Securities and Exchange Commission (SEC) mandated that banks treat investment securities gains and losses as operating income or losses. Previously, banks displayed securities profits after net operating income and thus reported two bottom line earnings figures, one for net operating income before investment gains or losses and another for net income after gains or losses. Securities gains were viewed as extraordinary income even though all profits were taxed as ordinary income.

Other income combines all miscellaneous revenues such as that from the sale of real assets, the sale of a subsidiary, and other extraordinary items. It is important that analysts distinguish between extraordinary items and normal operating income and expenses. Extraordinary items are nonrecurring and thus affect the income statement only in the period in which they appear. As such, reported net income may overstate true operating income.

Noninterest expense is composed primarily of salaries and fringe benefits paid to bank employees, occupancy expense from rent and depreciation on equipment and premises, and other operating expenses, including utilities and deposit insurance premiums. Noninterest expense far exceeds noninterest income at most banks. Reducing this burden will improve profitability.

Income before income taxes equals net interest income plus noninterest income minus noninterest expense and provision for loan losses. It represents the bank's operating profit before taxes. **Net income** is the operating profit less all federal, state, and local income taxes, plus or minus any accounting adjustments. The reported income tax figure equals estimated taxes to be paid over time, not actual tax payments. Accounting adjustments generally represent a restatement of earnings resulting from a change in accounting treatment of certain transactions. Total operating income equals interest income plus noninterest income and is comparable to net sales for a nonfinancial firm. Total operating expense similarly equals the sum of interest expense and noninterest expense comparable to cost of goods sold plus operating expenses.

THE RELATIONSHIP BETWEEN THE BALANCE SHEET AND INCOME STATEMENT

A bank's balance sheet and income statement are interrelated. The composition of assets and liabilities and the relationships between different interest rates determine net interest income. The mix of deposits between consumer and commercial customers affects the choice of assets and thus the magnitude of noninterest expense. The ownership of nonbank subsidiaries increases fee income, but often raises noninterest expenses. The following analysis emphasizes these interrelationships.

Let

A_i = Dollar magnitude of the ith asset
L_j = Dollar magnitude of the jth liability
NW = Dollar magnitude of stockholders' equity
r_i = Average pretax yield on the ith asset
c_j = Average interest cost of the jth liability

where n equals the number of assets and m equals the number of liabilities. The balance sheet identity (4.1) can be restated as:

$$\sum_{i=1}^{n} A_i = \sum_{j=1}^{m} L_j + NW \qquad (4.3)$$

while net interest income can be represented as:

$$NII = \sum_{i=1}^{n} r_i A_i - \sum_{j=1}^{m} c_j L_j \qquad (4.4)$$

Interest earned on each asset equals the product of the average yield (r_i) and the average dollar investment (A_i). Thus $\sum_{i=1}^{n} r_i A_i$ equals total interest income. Similarly, interest paid on each liability equals the product of the average interest cost (c_j) and the average dollar funding (L_j) from that source, so that $\sum_{j=1}^{m} c_j L_j$ equals total interest expense. Net interest income (NII) equals the difference between interest earned and interest paid.

This restatement of NII indicates what factors can cause net interest income to change over time or differ between institutions. First, net interest income changes when the composition or volume of assets and liabilities changes. In terms of (4.4), as portfolio composition changes the respective A's and L's change in magnitude. This alters net interest income because each A or L is multiplied by a different interest rate. Second, even if portfolio composition is unchanged, average asset yields and interest costs may rise or fall due to changing interest rates and lengthening or shortening of maturities on the underlying instruments.

Analysts, for example, generally distinguish between retail and wholesale banks based on their target customers. Each type of bank has a fundamentally different balance sheet composition reflecting the preferences of its customers. **Retail banks** are those that focus on individual consumer banking relationships. Thus individual demand, savings, and time deposits comprise most of the liabilities while consumer loans dominate the loan portfolio. **Wholesale banks** deal primarily with commercial customers so that they typically operate with fewer consumer deposits, more purchased liabilities, and hold proportionately more business loans. This difference in portfolio composition, in turn, produces different yields on earning assets (r_i) and costs of liabilities (c_j).

Noninterest income, expenses, and loan-loss provisions indirectly reflect the same balance sheet composition. The greater is the size of a bank's loan portfolio, the greater is operating overhead and provision for loan losses. Likewise, banks that emphasize consumer loans operate with more overhead. They often invest in extensive branch systems and equipment to attract consumer deposits and handle small, multiple-payment consumer loans. Bank holding companies with nonbank subsidiaries generate more fee income.

A bank's net income thus varies with the magnitudes of assets and liabilities and the associated cash flows:

$$NI = \sum_{i=1}^{n} r_i A_i - \sum_{j=1}^{m} c_j L_j - PL - Burden - T. \tag{4.5}$$

Net income in excess of dividend payments to shareholders increases retained earnings and thus total equity.

BANKING RISKS AND RETURNS: THE PROFITABILITY, LIQUIDITY, AND SOLVENCY TRADE-OFF

The fundamental objective of bank management, as with other firms, is to maximize shareholders' wealth. This goal is typically interpreted to mean maximizing the market value of a firm's common stock. Wealth maximization, in turn, requires that managers evaluate the present value of cash flows under uncertainty with larger, near-term cash flows preferred when evaluated on a risk-adjusted basis.

In terms of Equation 4.5, profit maximization appears to suggest that the bank manager simply invest in assets that generate the highest gross yields and keep costs down. But profit maximization differs from wealth maximization. To obtain higher yields, a bank must either take on increased risk or lower operating costs. Greater risk manifests itself in greater volatility of net income and market value of a bank's stockholders' equity. Wealth maximization requires that the manager evaluate and balance the trade-off between the opportunity for higher returns, the probability of not realizing those returns, and the possibility that the bank might fail.

There are five fundamental risks in banking:

1. Credit risk
2. Liquidity risk
3. Interest rate risk
4. Operational risk
5. Capital or solvency risk

Each risk is associated with the possibility that expected net returns on assets will not be realized. The following analysis focuses on specific aspects of each type of risk.

Credit Risk

Whenever a bank acquires an earning asset, it assumes the risk that the borrower will default, that is, not repay the principal and interest on a timely basis. Credit risk is the potential variation in net income and market value of equity resulting from this nonpayment or delayed payment. Different types of assets have different default probabilities. Loans typically exhibit the greatest credit risk. Changes in general economic conditions and a firm's operating environment alter the cash flow available for debt service. These conditions are difficult to predict. Similarly, an individual's ability to repay debts varies with changes in employment and personal net worth. For this reason, banks perform a credit analysis on each loan request to assess a borrower's capacity to repay. Bank investment securities generally exhibit less credit risk because the borrowers are predominantly federal, state, and local government units. Banks are also generally restricted to investment grade securities, those rated Baa or higher, which exhibit less risk. There have, however, been significant municipal bond defaults, such as the 1983 default of the Washington Public Power Supply System on $2.25 billion in bonds to finance nuclear power plants.

Liquidity Risk

Liquidity risk is the variation in net income and market value of equity caused by a bank's difficulty in obtaining cash at reasonable cost from either the sale of assets or new borrowings. Liquidity risk is greatest when a bank cannot anticipate new loan demand or deposit withdrawals and does not have access to new sources of cash. Liquidity is generally discussed in terms of assets with reference to an owner's ability to convert the asset to cash with minimal loss from price depreciation. Most banks hold some assets that can be readily sold near par to meet liquidity needs. Bank liabilities are also liquid in the sense that debt can easily be issued to obtain cash at a reasonable cost. Thus when banks need cash they can either sell assets or increase borrowing. Banks continuously monitor potential cash outflows, funds needs, and their ability to meet these payment obligations.

Interest Rate Risk

Traditional analysis compares the sensitivity of interest income to changes in asset yields with the sensitivity of interest expense to changes in interest costs of liabilities. The purpose is to determine how much net interest income will vary with movements in market interest rates. Less familiar, comprehensive portfolio analysis compares the duration of assets with the duration of liabilities to assess the impact of rate changes on net interest income and the value of stockholders' equity. Duration is an elasticity measure that indicates the relative price sensitivity of different securities.[5]

Interest rate risk refers to the potential variability in a bank's net interest income and market value of equity due to changes in the level of market interest rates. It

---

[5]Chapter 6 formally defines duration measures and demonstrates their application to risk analysis and management.

encompasses the total portfolio composition, focusing on mismatched asset and liability maturities and durations as well as potential changes in interest rates. For example, the removal of rate ceilings forced banks to pay market rates on an increased portion of their liabilities. This increased the sensitivity of interest expense to changes in interest rates and, in turn, increased the likelihood of lower net interest income and firm value with rising rates. Monitoring interest rate risk is a fundamental result of the asset and liability management analysis introduced in Chapter 8.

Operational Risk

There are many causes of earnings variability in a bank's operating policies. Some banks are relatively inefficient in controlling direct costs and employee processing errors. Banks must also absorb losses due to employee and customer theft. Operating risk refers to the possibility that operating expenses might vary significantly from what is expected, producing a decline in net income and firm value. A bank's operating risk is thus closely related to its Burden, number of divisions or subsidiaries, and number of employees.

Capital or Solvency Risk

A bank that assumes too much risk can become insolvent and fail. Operationally, a failed bank's cash inflows from debt service payments, new borrowings, and asset sales are insufficient to meet mandatory cash outflows due to operating expenses, deposit withdrawals, and maturing debt obligations. A cash flow deficiency is caused by the market's evaluation that the market value of bank equity is negative. High credit risk typically manifests itself through significant loan charge-offs. High interest rate risk manifests itself through mismatched maturities and durations between assets and liabilities. High operating risk appears with costs being out of control. Banks operating with high risk are expected to have greater capital than banks with low risk. When creditors and shareholders perceive that a bank has high risk, they demand a premium on bank debt and bid share prices lower. This creates liquidity problems by increasing the cost of borrowing and potentially creating a run on the bank. Banks ultimately fail because they cannot independently generate cash to meet deposit withdrawals and operate with insufficient capital to absorb losses if they were forced to liquidate assets. The market value of liabilities exceeds the market value of assets.

Capital risk represents the possibility that a bank may become insolvent. A firm is technically insolvent when it has negative net worth or stockholders' equity. The economic net worth of a firm is the difference between the market value of its assets and liabilities. Thus capital risk refers to the potential decrease in net asset values before economic worth is zero. A bank with equity capital equal to 10 percent of assets can withstand a greater percentage decline in asset value than a bank with capital equal to only 6 percent of assets.

Capital risk is closely associated with financial leverage, which refers to the use of debt and preferred stock paying fixed rates as part of a firm's capital structure.

High amounts of fixed-rate sources of funds increase the expected volatility of a firm's income because interest payments are mandatory. If a bank were funded entirely from common equity, it would pay dividends, but these payments would be discretionary. Omitting dividends does not produce a default. Firms with high capital risk—evidenced by low capital-to-asset ratios—exhibit high levels of financial leverage, have a higher cost of capital, and normally experience greater periodic fluctuations in earnings.

MAXIMIZING THE MARKET VALUE OF BANK EQUITY

A bank manager's role is to make and implement decisions that increase the value of shareholders' wealth.[6] Firm value is, in turn, closely tied to the underlying portfolio risk and return profile. The greater is perceived risk relative to expected returns, the lower is perceived value, as shareholders discount anticipated cash flows to a greater degree. The lower is perceived risk, the lower is the discount rate, but the lower also are expected cash flows. Banks with actively traded common stock can look to quoted share prices and cumulative market value as measures of firm value. Share prices are determined by return prospects versus risk characteristics and capture the market's perception of historical and anticipated performance. Performance can also be measured via financial ratios using accounting information.

Given the objective of maximizing the market value of bank equity, managers pursue strategies in several policy areas including:

1. Asset management (composition and volume)
2. Liability management (composition and volume)
3. Management of off-balance sheet activities
4. Interest rate spread management
5. Credit risk management
6. Liquidity management
7. Management of the Burden
8. Tax management

Each area of strategic decisions is closely tied with a bank's profitability as measured in (4.5). The primary responsibilities are to acquire assets through appropriate financing and to control the Burden while maintaining an acceptable risk profile. Bank regulators attempt to help managers keep their firm operating by regulating allowable activities.

Bank regulation is largely designed to limit risk-taking by commercial banks. Banks cannot engage in activities not closely associated with banking (Exhibit 2.5), buy common stock as an investment, or buy noninvestment-grade bonds without documentation. Similarly, regulators limit the size of a loan to any single borrower to reduce the concentration of bank resources. To assess bank risk, regulators routinely

---

[6]An extensive literature suggests that bank managers may pursue goals other than wealth maximization, such as market share and expense preference. Heggestad, 1979, summarizes key concepts and empirical results.

examine the quality of assets, mismatched maturities of assets and liabilities, and internal operating controls. If they determine that a bank has assumed too much risk, they require additional equity financing.

THE RETURN ON EQUITY MODEL

In 1972 David Cole introduced a procedure for evaluating bank performance via ratio analysis.[7] This procedure, summarized in Exhibit 4.3, enables an analyst to evaluate the source and magnitude of bank profits relative to selected risks taken. This section employs the **return on equity model** to analyze bank profitability and identifies specific measures of credit risk, liquidity risk, interest rate risk, operational risk, and capital risk. The ratios are used to assess the performance of the two banking organizations introduced earlier. Contemporary Issues: Financial Ratios provides useful guidelines on constructing and interpreting ratios.

Profitability Analysis

If you cornered a group of bank presidents and asked them to summarize performance for the past year, most would quote either their bank's return on equity or return on assets. If these measures were higher than those of peers, they would drop the phrase "high performance bank" into the conversation. Of course, for a firm to report higher returns it must either take on more risk, price assets and liabilities better, or realize cost advantages compared to peers. The following analysis starts with these aggregate profit measures, then decomposes return on assets into component ratios to determine why banks' performance varies.

Aggregate bank profitability is typically measured and compared in terms of return on equity (ROE) and return on assets (ROA). The ROE model simply relates ROE to ROA and financial leverage, then decomposes ROA into its contributing elements. By definition,

$$ROE = \frac{Net\,income}{Total\,equity}$$

ROE equals net income divided by total equity and thus measures the percentage return on each dollar of stockholders' equity.[8] The higher the return the better, as banks can add more to retained earnings and pay more in dividends when profits are higher. ROA equals net income divided by total assets and thus measures net income per dollar of average assets owned during the period. ROE is linked to ROA by the equity multiplier (EM) which equals total assets divided by total equity, such that

[7]The following discussion is based on the duPont system of financial analysis and adaptations by Cole, 1972. A more meaningful definition of return on equity is the ratio of net income minus preferred stock dividends to common stockholders' equity.

[8]Balance sheet figures should always be averaged for use with income statement figures. This reduces any distortion caused by unused transactions around reporting dates. All balance sheet values in the following discussion are assumed to be average figures.

Exhibit 4.3 The Decomposition of Return on Assets: The Nature of Bank Profits

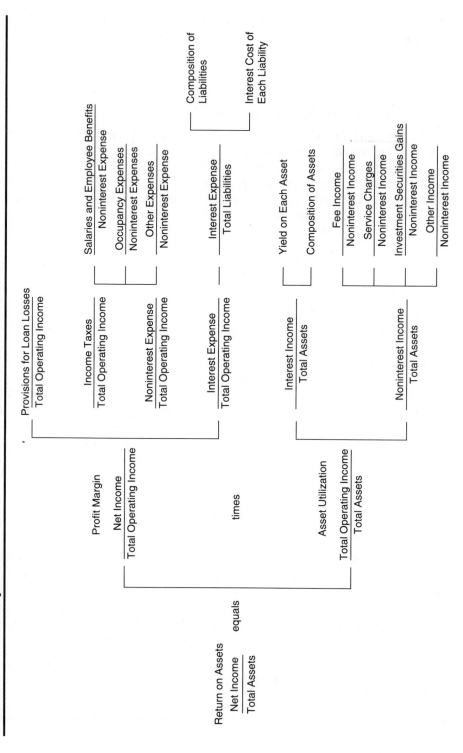

Financial Ratios

The interpretation of historical financial data typically begins with ratio analysis. To be meaningful, ratios must be calculated consistently and compared with benchmark figures. Ratios are constructed by dividing one balance sheet or income statement item by another. The value of any ratio depends on the magnitude of both the numerator and denominator and will change when either changes.

Several rules apply when constructing ratios. First, remember that balance sheet items are stock figures measuring value at a point in time, while income statement items are flow figures measuring value over time, such as 1 year. When constructing ratios combining balance sheet and income statement figures, average balance sheet data should be used. For example, suppose that only year-end balance sheet figures for 1990 and 1991 are available, along with 1991 income statement figures. Return on equity in 1991 would be calculated as the ratio of 1991 net income to one-half the sum of year-end 1990 and 1991 total equity. It would be better to use quarterly average balance sheet figures, with daily averages the best. Second, a single ratio by itself is generally meaningless. Calculate ratios over different intervals to discern interesting changes. Determine whether the changes are due to factors affecting the numerator or denominator. This typically requires comparing trends in two related ratios. Third, compare ratios with similar figures from a control group at the same point in time. The control group represents average performance for a comparable firm.

Accounting data may not reflect accepted accounting procedures and may be manipulated. Important data, such as the volume of a bank's outstanding loan commitments, may be omitted, which biases the figures. Footnotes to financial statements generally provide sources and an explanation for many calculations.

$$\text{ROE} = \frac{\text{Net income}}{\text{Total assets}} \times \frac{\text{Total assets}}{\text{Total equity}} \qquad (4.6)$$

$$= \text{ROA} \times \text{EM}$$

A bank's equity multiplier compares assets with equity such that large values indicate a large amount of debt financing relative to equity. EM thus measures financial leverage and represents both a profit and risk measure. Consider two competing banks that each hold $100 million in assets with identical composition. Asset quality is thus the same. One bank is financed with $90 million in debt and $10 million in common equity, while the other bank is financed with $95 million in debt and just $5 million in common equity. In this example EM equals 10 for the first bank and 20 for the second bank.

$$\text{EM} = \$100/\$10 = 10 \times \text{ for the bank with } \$10 \text{ million in equity;}$$
$$\text{EM} = \$100/\$5 \ = 20 \times \text{ for the bank with } \$5 \text{ million in equity.}$$

EM affects a bank's profits because it has a multiplier impact on ROA to determine a bank's ROE. In the above example, if both banks earned one percent on assets, the first bank would report an ROE of 10 percent, while the second bank's ROE would equal 20 percent. Financial leverage works to the bank's advantage when earnings are positive as the second bank provides shareholders a return that is twice that of its competitor. But there are two sides to leverage, as it also accentuates the negative impact of losses. If each bank reported an ROA equal to negative one percent, the second bank's ROE would equal −20 percent, or twice the loss of the first bank. Relation (4.6) suggests that higher ROE targets can be obtained either by increasing ROA or increasing financial leverage.

EM represents a risk measure because it reflects how many assets can go into default before a bank becomes insolvent. Consider the ratio of total equity to total assets, or 1/EM. This ratio equals 10 percent for the first bank in the example, and 5 percent for the second bank. Although the two banks hold identical assets, the first is in a less risky position because twice as many of its assets can default compared to the second bank, before they are insolvent. Thus a high EM raises ROE when net income is positive, but also indicates high capital risk, as discussed later.

Profit Margin and Asset Utilization

ROA can be decomposed into the product of a bank's profit margin (PM) and asset utilization (AU). PM measures net income per dollar of total operating income while AU represents the gross yield on assets. Here total operating income equals interest income plus noninterest income:

$$PM = \frac{\text{Net income}}{\text{Total operating income}}$$

$$AU = \frac{\text{Total operating income}}{\text{Total assets}}$$

such that

$$ROA = PM \times AU \tag{4.7}$$

The decomposition of PM appears at the top of Exhibit 4.3. Because net income equals total operating income minus expenses and taxes, PM measures a bank's ability to control expenses and reduce taxes. The greater is PM, the more efficient a bank is in reducing expenses or taxes. Suppose, for example, that two banks generate the same total operating income, but one reports net income that is twice as large as the other's so that its PM is twice as large. To produce this difference, the bank with the greater PM must have reported either lower expenses or lower taxes or both. Four additional ratios isolate the impact of specific types of expenses and taxes:

$$\text{Interest expense ratio} = \frac{\text{Interest expense}}{\text{Total operating income}}$$

$$\text{Noninterest expense ratio} = \frac{\text{Noninterest expense}}{\text{Total operating income}}$$

$$\text{Provision for loan loss ratio} = \frac{\text{Provisions for loan losses}}{\text{Total operating income}}$$

$$\text{Tax ratio} = \frac{\text{Income taxes}}{\text{Total operating income}}$$

The sum of these ratios and profit margin equals one. All other factors being equal, the lower each ratio is, the more profitable a bank is. The value of each measure compared with similar ratios of peer banks reveals whether specific types of expenses or taxes contribute to significant differences in performance. When the ratios differ, an analyst should examine additional ratios that reflect why and where differences arise.

Interest expense and noninterest expense should be further examined by source. Interest expense may vary between banks for three reasons; rate, composition, or volume effects.

Rate effects suggest that the interest cost per liability—c_i from Equation (4.4) which indicates the average cost of financing assets—may differ between banks. Differences arise in part because banks pay different risk premiums depending on how the market perceives their asset quality and overall risk. The greater the risk, the higher the cost of liabilities. Banks also time their borrowings differently relative to the interest rate cycle. If they borrow when rates are low, their interest costs will fall below those of banks that issue new debt when rates are higher. Finally, banks use different maturities of deposits and debt that pay different rates depending on the yield curve. Typically, longer-term deposits pay higher rates than short-term deposits.

Composition effects suggest that the mix of liabilities may differ. Banks with substantial amounts of demand deposits pay less in interest because these deposits are non-interest-bearing. A bank that relies on CDs and federal funds purchased will thus pay higher average rates than a bank with a larger base of lower-cost demand and small time deposits. This is one advantage of core deposits over purchased liabilities.

Volume effects recognize that a bank may operate with different amounts of debt and equity and thus pay interest on a different amount of liabilities. A bank's relative amount of debt is revealed by its equity multiplier. When EM is high, interest expense may be high reflecting proportionately high amounts of debt financing. When EM is low, interest expense is normally low.

Noninterest expense can be similarly decomposed. Measures of salaries and benefits, occupancy expense, and other operating expenses as a percentage of total noninterest expense indicate where cost efficiencies are being realized, or where a bank has a comparative disadvantage. Similar ratios are often constructed comparing these expenses to average assets to allow comparisons among different-sized banks. Noninterest expense may vary between banks depending on the composition of liabilities. Banks with large amounts of transactions deposits, for example, exhibit greater relative overhead costs.

The decomposition of AU appears at the bottom of Exhibit 4.3. Initially, total operating income is segmented into interest income and noninterest income relative to the bank's assets.

$$AU = \frac{\text{Interest income}}{\text{Total assets}} + \frac{\text{Noninterest income}}{\text{Total assets}}$$

This indicates how much of a bank's gross yield on assets results from interest income and noninterest income. Interest income may differ between banks for the same three reasons discussed with interest expense: rate, composition, and volume effects. An examination of pretax (gross) yields per asset, r_i from Equation (4.4) allows the bank to compare realized returns with those of peer banks. Differences may reflect different maturities, the timing of purchases relative to the interest rate cycle, or a different composition of holdings within each asset category. For example, a bank that invests heavily in new construction loans should earn higher gross yields on loans than a bank that lends primarily to Fortune 500 companies because construction loans are riskier. Differences in investment security yields, in turn, typically reflect differences in average maturities with higher yields on longer term securities. Finally, a review of a bank's **earnings base** compares the proportionate investment in earning assets to total assets and thus indicates whether one bank has more or less assets earning interest than peers.

Noninterest income should be decomposed into its contributing sources. Examining the proportion of noninterest income contributed by fees, service charges, securities gains, and other income relative to total assets or total noninterest income identifies which component contributes the most to AU. It also identifies whether other income, which can be biased by nonrecurring extraordinary items, is substantial. When a bank reports nonrecurring income, an analyst should subtract the amount from noninterest income before calculating the performance ratios. This purges extraordinary income so that a truer picture of operating performance appears. In summary form:

$$ROE = PM \times AU \times EM \tag{4.8}$$

Several other aggregate profitability measures are commonly cited. These include net interest margin (NIM), spread, earnings base, and noninterest efficiency ratios:

$$NIM = \frac{\text{Net interest income}}{\text{Earning assets}}$$

$$Spread = \frac{\text{Interest income}}{\text{Earning assets}} - \frac{\text{Interest expense}}{\text{Interest bearing liabilities}}$$

$$\text{Earnings base} = \frac{\text{Earning assets}}{\text{Total assets}}$$

$$\text{Noninterest efficiency} = \frac{\text{Noninterest income}}{\text{Noninterest expense}}$$

Earning assets include all assets that generate explicit interest income or lease receipts. It is typically measured by subtracting all nonearning assets, such as cash and due from banks, premises, and other assets from total assets. NIM is a summary measure of net interest returns on income-producing assets. Spread, which equals the average yield on earning assets minus the average cost of interest-bearing liabilities, is a measure of the rate spread or funding differential. These two measures are extremely important in evaluating a bank's ability to manage interest rate risk. As interest rates change, so will a bank's interest income and interest expense. NIM and spread indicate whether a bank has positioned its assets and liabilities to take advantage of rate changes, that is, whether it has profited or lost when interest rates rose or fell.

The earnings base indicates what proportion of the bank's total assets generates explicit income. The greater the earnings base, the greater is AU. Historically, this ratio has taken a value well below one. Noninterest efficiency measures the fraction of noninterest expense covered by fees, service charges, securities gains, and other income. It is closely linked with the measurement of burden, as the lower the ratio falls, the more noninterest expense exceeds noninterest income. Banks measure the success of recent efforts to supplement earnings from increasing fees by this ratio. The greater is each ratio, the more profitable the bank, all other factors being equal. Profitability measures for the two hypothetical banking organizations are shown in Exhibit 4.4.

Risk Measures

A bank's profitability should vary directly with the riskiness of its portfolio and operations. While some risks can be sought out or avoided, others are inherent in the prevailing economic environment and specific markets served. Banks in agriculture or energy-related areas, for example, typically lend to businesses involved in these cyclical industries. Even though management can control the credit evaluation procedure, returns to the bank vary with returns to its customers.

Using historical accounting data, it is possible to examine potential sources of risk assumed in achieving the returns indicated by the ROE model.[9] Exhibit 4.5 lists selected risk measures categorized under the risk types introduced earlier. These data do not typically appear in general balance sheets and income statements but must be obtained from footnotes to the financial statements or 10-K reports.

Credit risk is associated with the quality of assets and the likelihood of default. Credit risk measures focus predominantly on loan experience because loans exhibit the highest default rates. Most ratios examine either net loan losses or classified loans. Gross loan losses (charge-offs) equal the dollar value of loans actually written off as uncollectible during the period. Recoveries refer to dollar amount of loans initially charged-off that is repaid. Net charge-offs equals the difference between recoveries and gross charge-offs. Classified or nonperforming loans are those in which borrowers are experiencing some repayment problems. Nonaccrual loans are not currently accruing interest. Past-due loans represent loans for which contracted interest and principal payments have not been made within 90 days after the due date. Because some loans, such as speculative construction loans, are riskier than others, an analyst should examine the composition of a bank's loan portfolio and the magnitude of classified loans relative to net loans. Finally, banks with high loan growth often assume greater risk, as credit analysis and review procedures are less rigorous. In many instances the loans perform for a while, but losses eventually rise.

Ideally, it would useful to examine the credit files of a bank to assess the quality of specific loans. While this information is provided regulators, it is not available to

---

[9]Risk is traditionally measured by the standard deviation or coefficient of variation of returns. The following discussion identifies sources of potential variation in returns. Sources of returns risk are evidenced by simple ratios that reflect portfolio allocations or income streams that differ from industry averages.

Exhibit 4.4 Profitability Measures for Valley National Corporation and Community State Bank[a]

Ratio	Valley National Corp.	Peer Group[b]	Community State Bank	Peer Bank[b]
ROE = Net income/Total equity	11.31%	16.26%	22.43%	12.67%
ROA = Net income/Total assets	0.61	0.94	1.75	1.04
EM = Total assets/Total equity	18.46×	17.30×	12.82×	12.18×
PM = Net income/Total operating income	5.87	9.34	14.71	10.88
AU = Total operating income/Total assets	10.45	10.06	11.90	9.56
PM Components				
Interest expense/Total operating income	47.96	53.78	47.95	53.03
Noninterest expense/Total operating income	37.17	29.52	28.61	27.09
Provision for loan losses/Total operating income	7.58	3.98	4.40	3.35
Taxes/Total operating income	1.42[c]	3.38	4.33	5.65
Liabilities: Percentage of Total Assets				
Demand deposits	15.99	14.16	10.70	10.51
Interest-bearing checking	7.33	3.87	14.30	11.52
Regular savings	4.80	4.13	6.20	6.90
Money market savings	20.71	9.88	11.90	11.61
Time deposits <100,000	24.48	8.29	40.20	37.68
Core deposits	73.31	40.33	83.30	78.22
CDs ≥ $100,000	12.12	10.79	7.10	9.85
Foreign deposits		17.51		
Federal funds & RPs	3.10	11.62		0.25
Commercial paper & other ST borrowings	2.08	5.63	0.30	0.15
Long-term dept	2.80	3.96	1.00	1.00
Other liabilities	1.17	4.38	0.50	1.00
Total liabilities	95.58	94.22	92.20	91.79
Stockholders' equity	5.42	5.78	7.80	8.21
Average Interest Cost of Liabilities				
Interest-bearing checking	4.47	4.77	5.12	5.06
Regular savings	4.81	5.48	5.31	5.22
Money market savings	5.29	5.65	6.02	5.56
Time deposits <$100,000	7.51	7.28	8.15	7.04
CDs ≥$100,000	6.89	7.65	7.69	6.98
Federal funds purchased & RPs	7.27	7.49		6.32
Commercial paper & ST borrowings	8.16	7.46	6.00	6.65
Long-term debt	10.26	8.65	9.00	8.56
Percentage of Noninterest Expense				
Salaries and employee benefits	55.13	49.16	51.69	50.00
Occupancy and furniture expense	18.42	16.84	19.00	13.28
Other operating expense	26.45	34.00	29.31	36.72
Percentage of Total Assets				
Interest expense	5.01	5.41	5.71	5.07
Provisions for loan losses	0.79	0.40	0.52	0.32
Noninterest expense	3.88	2.97	3.41	2.56
Salaries & employee benefits	2.14	1.46	1.76	1.28
Occupancy and furniture expense	0.72	0.50	0.65	0.34

Exhibit 4.4 *(Continued)*

Ratio	Valley National Corp.	Peer Group[b]	Community State Bank	Peer Bank[b]
AU Components				
Interest income/Total assets	9.02%	8.49%	10.00%	9.07%
Noninterest income/Total assets	1.43	1.57	2.60	0.49
Percentage of Total Assets				
Cash and due from banks	6.77	6.43	4.00	3.96
Time deposits at banks	1.99	6.26	1.50	2.27
Federal funds sold & RPs	3.72	3.40	4.10	4.92
U.S. government & agency securities	8.25	6.47	17.00	27.04
State & municipal securities	5.51	2.84	9.40	7.50
Other securities	0.47	3.30	0.80	3.47
Total loans and leases	70.13	63.46	61.00	46.89
Business loans	22.02	23.84	30.80	17.56
Real estate loans	19.87	15.50	11.60	20.49
Consumer loans	25.42	7.49	18.10	8.84
Leases	1.66	2.48		0.20
International	1.17	14.15		
Loss reserve	1.75	2.08	1.40	0.78
Other assets	4.91	8.72	3.60	4.53
Average Gross Yields on Assets				
Time deposits at banks	8.01	8.05	7.87	7.93
Federal funds sold & RPs	7.79	7.45	7.51	7.56
U.S. government & agency securities	7.23	7.85	8.42	8.08
State and municipal securities	7.18	6.95	7.73	7.45
Total loans	10.76	9.95	11.90	10.87
Percentage of Noninterest Income				
Service charges	40.34	39.88	57.48	51.56
Securities gains	0.50	1.03	3.78	2.04
All other income	59.16	59.09	38.74	46.40
EB = Earning assets/Total assets	88.32	89.10	92.40	91.51
Noninterest income/Noninterest expense	36.78	52.86	67.55	19.14
Burden/Total assets	−2.46	−1.40	−1.11	−2.06
NIM[d] = Net interest income (te)/Earning assets	4.77	3.46	4.62	4.30
Spread (te)	3.97	2.91	3.75	3.34

[a]RPs indicates repurchase agreements; CDs certificates of deposit; ST short-term.

[b]Peer group data are from the Uniform Bank Performance Report for insured banks with total assets in excess of $10 billion for VNC, and total assets between $50 million and $100 million for CSB.

[c]Taxes include the accounting adjustment for Valley National Corp.

[d]Tax-equivalent basis; VNC: $\dfrac{(440,241 - 43,418) + 65,785}{9,699,000}$; CSB: $\dfrac{(3,894 - 727) + 1,102}{92,400}$

the public. Regulators, in fact, assign each bank a rating for asset quality as part of the CAMEL rating system. There has been some discussion of publishing these ratings, a policy that analysts desire but bankers fear.

Exhibit 4.5 Risk Measures for Valley National Corporation and Community State Bank

Ratio	Valley National Corp.	Peer Group[a]	Community State Bank	Peer Group[a]
Credit Risk				
Net charge-offs/Total loans	1.34%	1.14%	0.92%	0.76%
Loss reserve/Total loans	2.49	3.12	2.30	1.70
Provision for loan losses/Total loans	1.13	0.61	0.86	0.68
Nonaccrual loans/Total loans	4.63	2.69	0.85	0.81
Past due loans[b]/Total loans	0.85	0.30	0.71	0.58
Annual loan growth rate	0.59	5.37	9.06	6.48
Liquidity risk				
Total equity/Total assets	5.42	5.78	7.80	8.21
Core deposits/Total assets	73.31	40.33	83.30	78.22
Purchased liabilities/Total assets	17.23	45.55	7.40	10.25
Securities maturing ≤1 year/Total assets	5.27	2.05	8.94	11.54
Securities: Market value/Book value	99.09	97.79	98.13	98.81
Interest Rate Risk				
(Assets –Liabilities)/Earning assets				
Repriced within 3 months	−19.24		−10.55	
Repriced within 1 year	−20.03		− 6.10	
Capital Risk				
Total equity/Total assets	5.42	5.78	7.80	8.21
Primary capital/Total assets	6.70	7.33	9.39	9.96
Cash dividends/Net income	42.22	37.04	32.75	44.12
Operational Risk				
Total assets[c]/Number of employees	$ 1,510	$ 2,800	$ 1,923	$ 2,150
Salaries & benefits/Number of employees	$32,322	$39,020	$34,510	$25,400
Occupancy & furniture expense/ Noninterest expense	18.42%	16.84%	19.00%	13.28%

[a]Peer group data are from the Uniform Bank Performance Report.

[b]More than 90 days past due.

[c]In thousands of dollars.

Liquidity risk encompasses the risk that a bank cannot meet payment obligations in a timely, cost-effective manner. Risk measures indicate both the bank's ability to borrow funds and its liquid assets near maturity or available for sale. The equity-to-asset ratio and purchased liability-to-asset ratio represent the bank's equity base and borrowing capacity in the money markets. Purchased liabilities are those with denominations in excess of $100,000. If two banks hold similar assets, the one with the greater equity and lower financial leverage can take on more debt with less chance of becoming insolvent. A bank that relies less on jumbo CDs, federal funds, RPs, Eurodollars, and commercial paper can issue greater amounts of new debt in this form.

In both instances, the cost of borrowing is lower than that for a bank with the opposite profile.

Core deposits are deposits considered to be stable and not highly interest rate-sensitive. Thus a bank will retain most of these deposits even when interest rates paid by competitors increase relative to the bank's own rates. Core deposits include demand deposits, NOW accounts, MMDAs, and small time deposits that the bank expects to remain on deposit over various business cycle stages. The greater are core deposits, the lower are potential new funding requirements. Purchased liquidity is also related to asset quality. The lower are high risk assets relative to equity, the greater is the bank's borrowing capacity and the lower are its borrowing costs.

Banks purchase short-term securities for yield and marketability. Federal funds sold, RPs, and unpledged investment securities that mature within one year are the most liquid assets. **Pledging requirements** stipulate that banks pledge either Treasury or municipal securities as collateral against deposit liabilities such as Treasury deposits, municipal deposits, and borrowings from Federal Reserve banks. These securities are often held by a third-party trustee and cannot be sold without a release. Cash assets are held to meet customer withdrawals and legal reserve requirements or to purchase services from other financial institutions. Banks attempt to minimize cash holdings because they do not earn interest. Balances held at banks for clearing purposes can decline temporarily but must be replenished to meet reserves or pay for correspondent services. Cash items in the process of collection vary with the volume of checks handled and cannot be manipulated by the bank. Cash assets as a group are thus illiquid because a bank cannot reduce its holdings for any length of time. Liquid assets therefore consist of unpledged, marketable short-term securities plus federal funds sold and securities purchased under agreement to resell.

Loans provide liquidity in two ways. First, cash inflows from periodic interest and principal payments can be used to meet cash outflows. Second, some loans are highly marketable and can be sold to other institutions. It is difficult to assess loan liquidity, however, from general balance sheet information. Finally, long-term investments are less liquid because they carry greater risk of price depreciation. The market-to-book value of securities provides evidence of the unrealized depreciation in the bank's portfolio. Banks are more willing to sell any security that currently trades at a price above book value because, at worst, they can report a securities gain.

Interest rate risk is represented by the sensitivity of cash flows to changes in the level of interest rates. An asset or liability is rate-sensitive if it can be repriced within a certain time period. Repricing involves a change in the cash flow associated with an item. For example, an asset can be repriced if it matures or if its interest rate changes automatically each period. The net interest sensitivity position between assets and liabilities is approximated by comparing assets and liabilities that can be repriced over similar time frames. The funding difference is measured by the dollar difference between rate-sensitive assets and rate-sensitive liabilities for 30 days, 30 to 90 days, and so forth. Exhibit 4.5 relates the difference in rate-sensitive assets and rate-sensitive liabilities to earning assets for 30-day and 1-year intervals. If this measure is positive, the bank will likely realize a decrease in net interest income if the level of short-term interest rates falls. If the measure is negative, the bank's net interest income will likely

ecline in rates, but decrease with rising rates. The larger the absolute
o, the greater the risk. A detailed discussion of interest rate risk,
e funding difference between rate-sensitive assets and liabilities and
appears in Chapter 8.

risk refers to the cost efficiency of the bank's activities. The
ed represent expense control or productivity. Typical ratios focus
r employee or total personnel expense per employee. There is no
to estimate the likelihood of fraud or other contingencies from

is the risk that a bank might become insolvent. In this situation the
value of bank assets falls below the market value of bank liabilities. If such a
bank were to liquidate its assets, it would not be able to pay all creditors, and thus
would be bankrupt. Capital risk is closely tied to asset quality and a bank's overall
risk profile; the more risk taken, the greater the amount of capital required. Appropriate
risk measures include all the risk measures discussed earlier as well as ratios measuring
the fraction of assets financed by stockholders' equity and regulatory capital. Importantly, a bank's dividend policy affects its capital risk by influencing retained earnings.

EVALUATING BANK PERFORMANCE: AN APPLICATION

The following discussion analyzes the financial data of Valley National Corporation
(VNC) introduced in Exhibits 4.1 and 4.2. It examines the data for 1988 relative to
peer banks plus summarizes trends from 1985 to 1987. Profitability is characterized
according to the ROE model and is contrasted with the firm's risk position in the five
categories noted. Supplemental data are provided for clarification.

VNC offers a variety of financial services through several commercial bank and
nonbank subsidiaries. The principal subsidiary is a large commercial bank headquartered in Arizona, with limited foreign branches. The nonbank subsidiaries are
engaged in consumer finance, leasing, commercial finance, and data processing activities. Consolidated balance sheet and income statement data are provided in Exhibits
4.1 and 4.2. Total assets for VNC averaged just under $11 billion in 1988.

VNC's Profitability and Risk Versus Peers in 1988

Profitability ratios are provided in Exhibit 4.4. Comparative figures for other U.S.
banks with more than $10 billion in assets according to the Uniform Bank Performance
Report appear as peer bank averages.[10] VNC's ROE for 1988 was 11.31 percent, well
below that of peers. This was generated by an ROA of 0.61 percent and an equity

---

[10]Peer group figures are provided by the regulatory agencies and many private consulting companies. A
commonly cited resource is the Uniform Bank Performance Report which provides a standardized presentation
of individual bank balance sheet and income statement data and key financial ratios, along with peer bank
figures for all banks of the same size and average data within each state. Individuals can purchase these data
for a nominal fee by writing the Federal Financial Institutions Examination Council, UBPR, Department 4320,
Chicago, Illinois, 60673.

multiplier of 18.46. Not only did VNC's ROA fall short of peers, it also used more debt financing so that its equity multiplier was higher. Without the additional leverage VNC's ROE would have been even lower relative to peers. Thus VNC appears to have been a low-performance bank in 1988. It reported lower aggregate profits and more financial leverage, indicating greater risk.

The ROA is generated by a profit margin of 5.87 percent and an asset utilization of 10.45 percent such that:

$$0.61\% = 5.87\% \times 10.45\%$$

The profit margin indicates that VNC was far less efficient than its peers in controlling expenses. However, asset utilization indicates that its gross yield on assets was 39 basis points above that for peers, which partially offset the lower profit margin.[11] The remaining ratios clarify these results. VNC paid a lower percentage of its operating income in taxes and had significantly lower interest expense, while its noninterest expense and provisions for loan losses were substantially higher. Lower interest expense reflects VNC's greater core deposit base and the low interest cost of deposits relative to purchased funds. VNC also paid lower average rates on every type of liability except commercial paper and long-term debt. Thus rate and composition effects outweighed VNC's greater reliance on debt. Taxes were low because VNC sheltered a high fraction (64 percent) of its net income with tax-exempt interest from state and municipal bonds. Noninterest expense was well above average because of VNC's large investment in branch bank facilities and high salaries and benefits. Occupancy expense similarly exceeded that for comparable banks. These facilities and employees assist in obtaining low-cost deposits and essentially substitute for a greater reliance on purchased funds. VNC effectively trades interest expense for noninterest expense.

VNC's provision for loan losses relative to operating income is almost double that of peer banks. Management recognizes that the bank is exposed to large losses from problem loans and thus reported interest income overstates what actually will be earned after charge-offs. If VNC could reduce this to the norm, its profit margin would equal that of peers and its ROE would exceed peers'.

VNC's greater asset utilization was due to higher interest income. Relative to total assets, interest income was 56 basis points above average, largely because VNC invested almost 7 percent more of its assets in loans, and its gross loan yield was 81 basis points above that of peers'. This yield difference can in turn be attributed to the heavy concentration in high-rate consumer and real estate loans relative to peer banks. The risk is that when a bank invests more in loans it often experiences greater loan losses. These rate and composition effects outweighed the volume effect, where VNC had considerably fewer earning assets than peers. High-interest income and low interest expense were responsible for an NIM 131 basis points above average.

As a percentage of assets, noninterest income was less than that of comparable banks. The data reveal that service charges were above peers' as was other income, but securities gains were below peers' relative to operating income. VNC did not

---

[11]One percent equals 100 basis points.

supplement its income to the same extent as other banks by selling securities, either because it did not have securities to sell or it did not want to sacrifice future earnings. VNC's Burden relative to total assets was more than 1 percent less than peers, indicating that the bank performed well below average in generating noninterest income to cover its noninterest expense.

The component analysis of net income summarizes profitability differences between VNC and peers. The following figures divide each component by total assets. As indicated, VNC reported net interest income that was 0.93 percent higher. Its provision for loan losses was 0.39 percent higher, however, and its Burden 1.06 percent lower, which reduced profitability well below peers'. Lower taxes did not reduce the difference greatly, and VNC earned 0.33 percent less on assets than peers.

		Percentage of Assets		
		VNC	**Peers**	**Difference**
	NII	4.01%	3.08%	0.93%
−	PL	− .79%	− .40%	− .39%
	−Burden	−2.46%	−1.40%	−1.06%
−	T	− .15%	− .34%	+ .19%
	NI	0.61%	0.94%	−0.33%

VNC's lower relative returns suggest that it was either taking below-average risk or that it had assumed too much risk in prior periods and was paying the price. Selected risk measures for 1988 appear in Exhibit 4.5. The bank's credit risk appears to exceed peers' risk according to virtually every measure. In particular, loan charge-offs and provisions far exceed peers', while the loss reserve was lower than average. Nonaccrual and past due loans were similarly well above peer averages. This is not surprising, given that VNC charged higher rates on its loans to compensate for the greater default risk. The only factor suggesting lower risk is that VNC's loan portfolio grew at a slower rate. Loan growth rates in prior periods were quite high, however. Given this higher credit risk, it is troublesome that VNC's equity base was below average relative to peers.

VNC's liquidity risk measures provide mixed signals. Its core deposits are much greater and its purchased liabilities are lower, indicating that the bank has a large, stable consumer deposit base. If necessary, it can presumably borrow additional funds in the money markets at a reasonable cost. Unfortunately, the bank's low equity base indicates that it may have to pay a premium on borrowings, especially with its greater credit risk. VNC also holds proportionately more securities maturing within 1 year, which suggests that securities can readily be sold to obtain funds if needed. Because the bank's securities have depreciated less than peers' and are priced close to cost, VNC would have to absorb little in securities losses if the securities were sold. Of course, data are not provided on how many or which of the securities are pledged as collateral and cannot be sold.

The bank's interest rate risk position is indicated by the difference between rate-sensitive assets and liabilities. Peer data are not available for comparative purposes. Because rate-sensitive assets are a smaller fraction of total assets than rate-sensitive liabilities, VNC has positioned itself so that net interest income will rise if short-term interest rates fall. If rates rise, borrowing costs will likely rise faster than asset returns, and net interest income will decline. Interest rate risk appears to be substantial because the difference is a large fraction (–20 percent) of total assets. Total interest rate risk, however, cannot be determined without more detailed rate-sensitivity data and measures of duration.

As indicated by the credit risk ratios, VNC has more problem loans than peers and thus more risk assets. The bank should reasonably be expected to have more equity capital. Both capital ratios reveal the opposite—VNC has less equity and primary (regulatory) capital than peers. One source of capital is retained earnings. One might thus expect VNC to pay less in dividends, but at least in 1988 the bank paid out a higher fraction of its net income in dividends. Capital risk is clearly greater for VNC than for peers.

VNC's operational risk is somewhat difficult to assess. Its branch operations require a greater investment in facilities, producing high personnel, occupancy, and overhead expenses. To some extent this compensates for lower interest expense. The bank employed far more people than peers did relative to its asset base, however, which suggests a lower productivity level. Salaries and benefits per employee were also below average.

VNC's performance reflects the long-term trade-off between return and risk. ROE and ROA were below average because of higher loan losses and greater noninterest expense. The loan losses likely reflect prior credit activities which had a negative impact on earnings in 1988. VNC has more nonaccrual and past-due loans and has experienced higher charge-offs. Even though it has greater credit risk, the bank has less equity and thus more capital risk also. While it operates with more low-cost, less rate-sensitive core deposits, it may lose these if its asset quality continues to deteriorate. Above average liquid sources of funds appear to be available, however, so liquidity risk is low for the near term. In terms of interest rate risk, VNC will likely gain if rates decline, but will lose net interest income if rates rise. Operationally, VNC employs more people per dollar of assets and appears to operate much less efficiently than peers.

VNC's Profitability versus Risk: 1985–1987

Valley National Corporation's 1988 performance can be better understood by examining trends in the performance ratios for the three prior years. Exhibit 4.6 presents key profitability and risk ratios. Most noticeably, the bank reported a $44 million loss in 1987. This followed two years of strong profits and high loan growth. The loss appears to have resulted from bad loans, as the bank's net interest margin was only 17 basis points below the figure for 1986. VNC raised its provisions for loan losses sharply, which produced a greater loss reserve even after accounting for charge-offs that exceeded the previous two years combined. Nonaccrual and past due loans (nonperforming) rose substantially as well over the three years. The bank also saw its noninterest expense rise sharply in each year. In

Exhibit 4.6   Historical Performance Measures for Valley National Corporation (Percentages Unless Otherwise Noted)

	1987	1986	1985
Profitability Ratios			
Net income (loss)	–$44 million	$89 million	$84 million
Return on equity	–6.59%	14.44%	14.98%
Return on assets	–0.41	0.84	0.87
Total assets/Total equity	16.8×	17.1×	17.3×
Net interest margin (te)[a]	4.74	4.91	5.33
Credit Risk			
Net charge-offs/Total loans	2.02	1.03	0.61
Loss reserve/Total loans	2.46	1.39	1.18
Nonperforming assets/Total loans	3.42	2.95	2.72
Loan growth rate	4.09	9.11	20.01
Capital Risk			
Total equity/Total assets	5.96	5.84	5.78
Primary capital/Total assets (adj.)	7.32	6.71	6.53
Dividends/Net income	0.00	31.7	31.0
Operational Efficiency			
Noninterest expense/Total assets	4.09	3.94	3.81
Total assets[b]/Number of employees	$1,352	$1,310	$1,203

[a]Tax-equivalent.

[b]In thousands of dollars.

response, VNC issued stock in 1987 and paid no dividends to strengthen its equity base and reduce its leverage.

These trends are reflected in the 1988 figures. The impact of problem loans persists for several years as management typically understates the amount of losses. Thus charge-offs and provisions remain high and serve to lower profits long after losses are initially recognized. The high dividend payment in 1988 represents a response to not paying dividends the prior year. VNC's noninterest expense as a fraction of total assets actually declined in 1988 relative to prior years, indicating management's efforts to control costs.

CAMEL RATINGS

Federal and state regulators regularly assess the general financial condition of each bank and specific risks faced via on-site examinations and periodic reports. Federal regulators rate banks according to the Uniform Financial Institutions Rating system which encompasses five general categories of performance under the label CAMEL. Each letter refers to a specific category, including

C = capital adequacy,
A = asset quality,
M = management quality,
E = earnings, and
L = liquidity.

The regulators numerically rate each bank in each category, ranging from the highest or best rating (1) to the worst or lowest rating (5). They also assign a composite rating for the bank's overall operation. A composite rating of 1 or 2 indicates a fundamentally sound bank, A ranking of 3 indicates that the bank shows some underlying weakness that should be corrected. A rating of 4 or 5 indicates a problem bank with some near-term potential for failure. Exhibit 4.7 shows the increase in problem commercial and savings banks, those with 4 and 5 ratings, from 1984 through 1990.

PERFORMANCE CHARACTERISTICS OF DIFFERENT-SIZED BANKS

Commercial banks of different sizes exhibit sharply different operating characteristics. Some differences reflect government regulation; others are associated with variances in the markets served. Prior to the mid-1980s, small banks generated higher ROAs, on average, and generally assumed less risk. This has changed with increased competition, expansion into new product and geographic markets, and more recent economic events. This section examines differences in the risk-return performance of different-sized banks. Contemporary Issues: All Banks Are Not Created Equal indicates that there are clear advantages to size.

Consider the distinction between wholesale and retail banks. Wholesale banks focus their credit efforts on commercial customers and purchase substantial funds from large corporate and government depositors. Retail banks, in contrast, obtain considerably more of their deposits from individuals and emphasize consumer, agriculture, and mortgage loans. Within each category, there are significant differences in the types of loans and funding sources. For example, the largest U.S. money center banks compete in more product and geographic markets than other large, regional banks. Smaller banks' performance typically reflects local economic conditions, which differ dramatically across geographic regions. Recognizing these difficulties, it is still useful to compare aggregate performance by size.

Summary profitability and risk measures for all U.S. banks in 1990 appear in Exhibit 4.8. The banks are divided into six groups by total assets. The final column indicates general trends in each ratio going from the smallest banks, with less than $25 million in assets, to the largest banks, with assets greater than $10 billion. As indicated by the final column, almost every ratio exhibits a consistent relationship with size. ROE, for example, increases with size through $300 million, then decreases such that the largest banks report the lowest return. Many of the smallest banks reported losses in 1988, which lowered the average ROE for banks under $25 million. ROA similarly

**Exhibit 4.7 Number of Commercial and Savings Banks
on FDIC's "Problem List" 1984–1990**

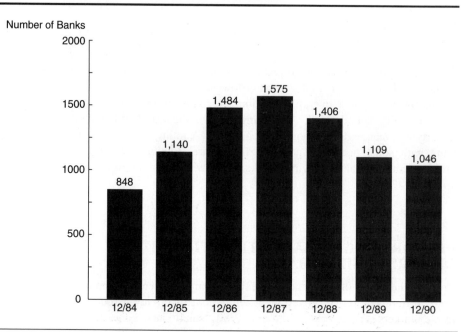

Number of Banks

Source: *The FDIC Quarterly Banking Profile*, Fourth Quarter, 1990.

increases up to banks with $100 to $300 million in assets, then declines slightly. This can be attributed to profit margins rising then falling for the same groups of banks, as asset utilization was roughly the same for all size categories. The equity multiplier increases with size because larger banks operate with less equity and more debt. Regulation effectively mandates the equity multiplier relationship, as regulators generally require more equity at smaller banks to compensate for less asset diversification and more limited borrowing options.[12] Percentage equity requirements were equalized in 1985 and raised effective in 1992, but small banks have a greater equity cushion.

The direct relationship between size and PM demonstrates the difficulty small banks have in controlling expenses. Remember that AU is roughly constant, suggesting that interest and noninterest income are comparable across size categories relative to assets. Small banks' interest expense is typically lower because of their greater core deposits and lesser reliance on purchased liabilities. Not surprisingly, NIM is higher. Still, both provisions for loan losses and noninterest expense are generally higher for small banks, offsetting the benefit of a higher NIM. Note that the negative values for burden become smaller with size, indicating that large banks generate more noninterest income relative to noninterest expense.

---

[12]The regulatory rationale for this discriminatory treatment is discussed in Chapter 11.

All Banks Are Not Created Equal

In the early 1980s, bank regulators relaxed restrictions against mergers and acquisitions among banking organizations. State legislatures similarly expanded interstate banking opportunities. Not surprisingly, many bank holding companies quickly agreed to consolidate or decided to acquire smaller firms. The interesting question is: Why do banks seek high growth? Are large banks more efficient? Are they more likely to survive in a deregulated environment?

Evidence on economies of scale in banking suggests that unit operating costs generally decline until a bank reaches $50 million to $75 million in assets. Unit operating costs of billion-dollar banks increase with additional growth. The largest banks thus do not appear to be the most efficient.

One rationale underlying growth relates to survival and regulatory policy regarding bank failure. Some banks merge so that their combined size makes them a very expensive acquisition. They essentially choose their own partners rather than be gobbled up by some unknown entity. Federal regulators have also demonstrated a general willingness to let small banks fail while guaranteeing the viability of large organizations. For example, after the bailout of Continental Illinois in 1984, the Comptroller of the Currency, C.T. Conover, indicated that regulators would not let the 11 largest banks in the United States fail. Such government-arranged mergers and loans indicate that large bank liabilities are essentially contingent obligations of the government. Banks must continue to grow until they reach the minimum size necessary to receive the government guarantee. Another strong motive is that senior officers of the largest banking groups generally receive the highest salaries and greatest level of executive perks.

The risk ratios at the bottom of Exhibit 4.8 reveal several other systematic differences. In particular, larger banks typically invest more in loans, and in 1990 reported the highest net charge-offs. Banks with less than $300 million in assets operate with greater core deposits and thus a more stable funding base, especially compared with the largest banks. The largest banks, however, have a reputation advantage nationally and internationally and consequently have far greater access to purchased liabilities in the money and capital markets. Finally, larger banks employ far fewer people per dollar of assets.

Comparative Performance: Valley National Corp. versus Community State Bank

Performance differences between banks indicate differences in management philosophy as well as differences in the markets served. Large banks often rely more on commercial business, while small banks focus more on consumers. In recent years, however, even the largest money center banks have aggressively pursued consumer loans and deposits because individuals appear to be more loyal or at least not as interest-sensitive as businesses. Consider the profitability and risk measures for Valley National Corporation and Community State Bank (CSB) in Exhibits 4.4 and 4.5. VNC was a low-performance bank and CSB a high-performance bank, but the two banks illustrate general differences in small versus large banks.

Exhibit 4.8 Summary Profitability and Risk Measures for Different-Sized Banks, 1990 (Percentages unless Otherwise Noted)

Performance Measure	Assets in Millions of Dollars						Trend with Greater Size
	≤25	25–100	100–300	300–1,000	1,000–10,000	≥10,000	
Profitability							
Return on equity	9.42%	12.06%	12.89%	12.74%	10.44%	10.40%	↑ then ↓
Return on assets	0.81	1.04	1.09	0.94	0.66	0.49	↑ then ↓
Equity multiplier	11.6×	11.6×	11.8×	13.6×	15.8×	21.2×	↑
Profit margin	7.88	8.78	10.48	8.65	6.26	4.47	↑ then ↓
Asset utilization	10.28	11.85	10.40	10.87	10.54	10.96	none
Net interest margin(te)[a]	4.74	4.84	4.65	4.55	4.30	3.52	↓
Earnings base	92.03	93.33	93.73	91.91	91.33	89.10	↑ then ↓
Burden/Total assets	−2.77	−2.72	−2.52	−2.23	−2.04	−1.66	↑
Risk							
Loan/Assets	52.53	56.99	62.75	65.93	63.91	62.94	↑
Net charge-offs/ Loans	0.55	0.32	0.42	0.61	0.90	1.67	↓ then ↑
Core deposits/Assets	83.31	81.15	79.58	73.90	68.16	52.00	↓
Equity/Assets	8.62	8.62	8.47	7.35	6.33	4.72	↓
Assets[b]/Number of employees	$1.48	$1.73	$1.86	$2.04	$2.21	$2.57	↑
Number of banks	6,404	5,899	2,043	620	325	47	

[a]Tax-equivalent.

[b]In millions of dollars.

There are many reasons for the higher ROA at Community State Bank. In general terms, the bank's profit margin and asset utilization are both substantially higher. Profit margin is high because CSB reports lower provisions for loan losses and lower noninterest expense. Even though it has 10 percent more core deposits, its interest expense is comparable because it pays higher rates to retain the deposits. VNC uses its branch system to attract and retain deposits.

The higher asset utilization indicates that the small bank earned a higher gross yield on assets. In this case, the CSB earned more interest income and noninterest income per dollar of assets. There are three reasons for the higher interest income. First, the earnings base at the small bank exceeded that at VNC by over 4 percent. Thus more assets earned interest. Second, CSB invested proportionately more in U.S. government and agency securities and municipal bonds that generated yields 1.19 percent and 0.55 percent higher than VNC's assets did. This was presumably achieved by holding longer maturity instruments. Finally, even though the small bank held less in loans, it earned 1.14 percent more on each dollar invested. This largely offset the reduced investment. The primary factor, however, is CSB's noninterest income, which contributes 2.6 percent to the bank's AU, or 1.17 percent more than at Valley National Corp. CSB apparently prices its deposit accounts aggressively, as service charges account for over 57 percent of noninterest income. The bank also sold more securities at a gain, but this is a nonrecurring transaction that CSB might not be able to repeat with other securities, depending on how interest rates move. The bank's Burden is far less than that of Valley National.

The small bank also appears to have taken on less risk. Lower credit risk is evidenced by lower nonperforming loans and loan losses as a fraction of net loans. Its equity base was also a higher proportion of assets so capital risk is less. Similarly, both its core deposits and its liquid assets were a smaller fraction of assets, suggesting lower overall liquidity risk. Unfortunately, these ratios do not adequately measure risk for different-sized banks. Small banks are less able to diversify credits and frequently lend heavily within a specific industry and geographic market. If economic conditions deteriorate, loan losses can erase any interest earnings. Small banks also do not have the same access to purchased funds, as borrowings are restricted to creditors who understand the bank's reputation and performance. Thus small banks must rely more on liquid assets to meet payment obligations.

In terms of interest rate risk, small banks often own proportionately more fixed-rate assets than larger banks. They purchase longer-maturity securities and make fewer variable-rate loans. This is partially balanced by a higher proportion of core deposits that are not as rate-sensitive as purchased liabilities. The liability mix is gradually changing with the shift from demand deposits to MMDAs, small time deposits, and large CDs. Small banks generally cannot borrow in the money markets with the same ease and low cost as large banks and also cannot easily alter the magnitude of rate-sensitive assets to adjust the GAP. In this example, both banks had more rate-sensitive liabilities than assets and thus were positioned to gain if rates fell. CSB's net difference equaled a lower fraction of earning assets, signifying less proportionate interest rate risk.

In summary, Community State Bank was a high-performance bank while Valley National Corporation was a low-performance bank in 1988. Key differences appear in the small bank's ability to better control noninterest expense and asset quality. The small bank also generated considerable income from service charges that went directly to net income. The small bank's risk profile was also much better because it had ample liquidity and a stronger equity base.

Comparative Performance of Small Banks

Numerous performance characteristics seem to persist over time. In a study of small banks, Sherrill Shaffer compared profit and risk ratios for different-sized banks with less than $500 million in assets from 1984 to 1988. Exhibit 4.9 presents comparative ratios for ROE, ROA, net charge-offs, and failed banks. Note the consistent performance rankings. The largest banks reported the highest ROEs in each year and the highest ROAs after 1986. The smallest banks, in turn, reported the highest fraction of loan charge-offs and had the greatest percentage of banks fail in each year.

Exhibit 4.9 Comparative Ratios for ROE, ROA, Net Charge-Offs, and Failed Banks

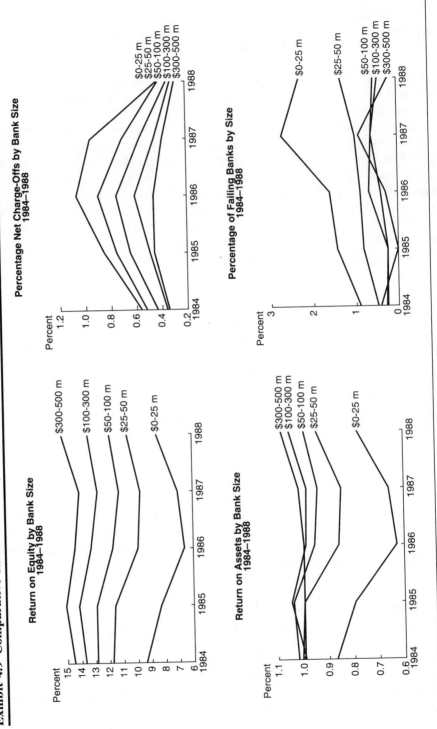

Source: FDIC *Statistics on Banking*, Table RT-1, various years (1988 figures from Call Report tapes).

To a large degree, the performance of the smallest banks is the weakest because they have suffered most from increased competition. While banking markets used to be relatively isolated local markets, increasingly sophisticated customers and the availability of new technologies enable customers to move their banking business from local banks to national firms. Unless small banks can sharply lower their operating costs, they will continue to experience profit pressures as competition increases.

FINANCIAL STATEMENT MANIPULATION

The usefulness of bank financial statements depends on the quality and consistency of the data. Ideally, banks would use the same accounting rules in each period and isolate the effects of nonrecurring events. This would make comparisons over time and between banks simple. Unfortunately, banks have wide discretion in reporting certain items and often use extraordinary transactions to disguise unfavorable events or trends. Analysts should delete the impact of any unusual changes to make valid comparisons.

Banks use numerous techniques to manipulate their financial statements, such as including nonrecurring extraordinary transactions, discretionary interpretation of reporting requirements, and accounting changes that mask true operating performance. The net effect is to distort the magnitude of period-ending balance sheet figures, net income, and related ratios. In most cases, banks do not violate federal regulations or generally accepted accounting principles. Often the reporting techniques are mandated but make interpretation more difficult.

Many banks have long engaged in window dressing, or increasing period-ending assets or deposits. Some banks want to be the largest or fastest-growing bank in their market because customers like to associate with bigness. One technique used to increase total assets is to encourage large business customers to borrow from the bank temporarily rather than issue commercial paper. The bank finances the loans in the federal funds market. Another involves inducing institutions to which the bank provides correspondent services to increase their deposit balances at the bank. Some large banks similarly solicit short-term deposits from overseas. None of these transactions materially alters earnings, but all give a false impression of true size.

In some instances, banks engage in transactions that substantially improve their perceived operating performance. Some banks eliminate borrowing from Federal Reserve Banks because of the perception that such borrowing indicates weakness, paying off Federal Reserve loans just prior to the reporting date. The biggest reporting problems arise when banks attempt to offset declines in reported net income or improve credit quality measures. They might sell nonconventional assets for one-time profits or understate problem loans. In many cases, banks have temporarily sold loan participations just before reporting periods to reduce loan exposures. Transactions and reporting requirements involving preferred stock, non-performing loans, securities transactions, and nonrecurring asset sales complicate the evaluation process.

Preferred Stock

Many large banking organizations have recently issued preferred stock to help meet equity capital requirements imposed by regulators. Preferred stock does not pay interest but instead pays dividends out of earnings available for common stockholders. Banks that use preferred stock overstate their NIM and other profitability measures relative to actual fixed charges. Operating performance is best compared by netting preferred dividends from income when computing profit measures.

Consider the income statements and profitability measures for the $1.5 billion bank listed in Exhibit 4.10. The two columns of data summarize the bank's performance with alternative financing. The first column assumes that the bank finances $10 million of earning assets with long-term debt issued at 11 percent. The second column summarizes performance when the bank issues 500,000 shares of $20 par value perpetual preferred stock. A contractual annual dividend of $2.40 per share yields 12 percent to preferred stockholders. The magnitude and composition of assets is assumed to be identical in both cases.

If the bank issues debt, its net interest income is $60.9 million, with a NIM of 4.87 percent. Net income is just under $9.5 million, producing an ROA of 0.63 percent and an ROE of 12.38 percent. Earnings per share of common stock equals $3.14, with 3 million shares outstanding. The preferred stock issue substantially alters these profitability measures. First, interest expense is $1.1 million less without the debt, so that net interest income equals $62 million and NIM equals 4.96 percent. Net income and ROA similarly increase to $10 million and 0.67 percent, respectively. However, common stockholders are actually worse off with the preferred issue. ROE, net of preferred dividends, actually drops 80 basis points to 11.58 percent, while net earnings per common share decline to $2.93. Issues of preferred stock clearly distort changes in NIM and ROA over time.

Nonperforming Loans

Loans are designated as nonperforming when they are placed on nonaccrual status or when the terms are substantially altered in a restructuring. Nonaccrual means that banks deduct all interest on the loans that was recorded but not actually collected. Banks have traditionally stopped accruing interest when debt payments were more than 90 days past due. However, the interpretation of when loans qualified as past due varied widely. Many banks did not place loans on nonaccrual if they were brought under 90 days past due by the end of the reporting period. This permitted borrowers to make late partial payments and the banks to report all interest as accrued, even when it was not collected. On occasion, banks would lend the borrower the funds that were used to make the late payment.

The impact of this practice on financial statements is twofold. First, nonperforming loans are understated on the balance sheet, so that credit risk is actually higher than it appears. Second, interest accrued but not collected increases net interest income, thus overstating NIM, ROA, and ROE.

Exhibit 4.10 Impact of Preferred Stock on Reported Earnings (Thousands of Dollars)

Data Items	Debt	Preferred Stock
Interest income	$146,000	$146,000
Interest expense	85,100	84,000
Net interest income	60,900	62,000
Noninterest income	40,000	40,000
Noninterest expense	90,000	90,000
Income before taxes	10,900	12,000
Taxes	1,494	2,000
Net income	9,406	10,000
Cash dividends on preferred stock		1,200
Net income available for common equity	9,406	8,800
Total assets	$1,500 million	$1,500 million
Earning assets	1,250 million	1,250 million
Total equity (net of preferred stock)	76 million	76 million
Return on assets	0.63%	0.67%
Net interest margin	4.87%	4.96%
Return on equity (net of preferred dividends)	12.38%	11.58%
Earnings per share (net of preferred dividends)	$3.14	$2.93

In response to foreign loan problems at large banks in 1983 and 1984, federal regulators formally tightened the accounting rules for nonperforming loans. On July 1, 1984, loans were put on nonaccrual as soon as any repayment went beyond 90 days past due. Interest could not be recorded until the bank received an actual payment or the loan was made current.

A related factor that distorts financial reports is the bank's provisions for loan losses and reserves against losses. For tax purposes, the maximum size of the reserve and the allowable deduction for losses is set by IRS regulations. However, management uses discretion in determining how much it should report as provisions for loan losses in financial statements. During some periods banks have minimized the provision, understating the reported reserve for losses and overstating earnings. Severe loan problems in the early 1980s forced many banks to report large provisions for losses to compensate for prior understatements.

Securities Gains and Losses

Prior to 1983 banks reported gains and losses on securities transactions after net income from operations. The rationale was that securities transactions were not a normal part of bank operations and could easily be manipulated to alter net income. Traditional ROA calculations used net operating income and thus excluded any impact of securities sales and purchases.

In 1983 the SEC required banks to include securities gains and losses in net operating income. It is now possible for a bank to offset a potential decline in other earnings with securities gains, thereby distorting historical operating performance.

Comparisons of net income must distinguish figures from before and after 1983. Securities results in 1983 were generally strong relative to 1982 because many banks sold securities at substantial discounts in 1982. Lower interest rates in 1983 enabled banks to report large gains. Citicorp, for example, reported a net gain of $11 million in 1983 after losses of $46 million and $42 million the previous two years. Declining interest rates through 1989 enabled many banks to sell securities at gains that offset substantial declines in net interest income and increased loan losses.

Nonrecurring Sales of Assets

Banks can often bolster earnings with one-time sales of assets. Most sales involve real estate, subsidiaries, lease assets, or hidden assets that banks have acquired through debt restructuring and foreclosures. Typically, many foreclosed assets are listed at little value on the bank's books but may generate large gains if the problem customer's performance improves. The Lockheed Corp.'s debt restructuring is a good example. In the early 1970s, Lockheed ran into financial difficulty and restructured its loan commitments from creditors. As part of the agreement, many large banks acquired Lockheed common stock. By the early 1980s the value of the stock had soared so that banks sold their shares for substantial profits. Manufacturer's Hanover, Bankers Trust, J.P. Morgan, and Irving Bank each reported large gains in 1983 from the sale of these securities.

In 1983 Mercantile Texas Corp. reported a similar $7.2 million pretax gain from the sale of $90 million in credit card receivables to Southwest Bancshares Inc. Interestingly, the two bank holding companies had agreed to merge that same year. While the merger was not formally approved until 1984, Mercantile effectively sold its receivables to itself and reported the profit to shareholders. Shareholders actually lost with the transaction, though, because Mercantile had to pay taxes on the gain. By 1989 the merged bank holding, renamed MCorp, had failed and was sold to Banc One which used MCorp to enter the Texas market.

In 1987 BankAmerica sold its Charles Schwab discount brokerage subsidiary for $230 million and the right to share in 15 percent of the increase in Schwab's value when it went public. This price represented a pretax gain of more than $175 million. The buyer was Charles Schwab, the firm's namesake, who paid a bargain basement price because BankAmerica was having difficulty raising capital. In today's environment the most popular assets for sale are credit cards and mortgage banking subsidiaries because they fetch top dollar.

CHARACTERISTICS OF HIGH-PERFORMANCE AND FAILED BANKS

Bank managers continuously monitor their own banks' performance in line with the risk-return analysis described earlier, and compare figures with their closest competitors. As such, they should be keenly aware of the strategies that differentiate strong from weak firms. What are the characteristics of high performance banks and failed banks?

High-Performance Banks

Even though aggregate bank profitability rises and falls with economic conditions, a subset of banks appears to outperform the competition year after year by earning above-average profits. The existence of persistent high performers might seem to contradict the risk-return model unless the banks systematically take above-average risks, or exhibit some market power in controlling prices. Most studies, however, have concluded that there is little, if any, pricing collusion in banking. This leaves excess risk-taking to explain differences in performance.

Benton Gup and John Walter conducted a nationwide study of banks with less than $100 million in assets to identify the characteristics of high-performance banks from 1982 to 1987.[13] High-performance banks were defined as those that generated ROAs of at least 1.5 percent in each year. Exhibit 4.11 summarizes the results of their ratio analysis. In general, high-performance banks benefitted primarily from better interest and noninterest expense control while limiting credit and capital risk. Specifically, high performers operated with more demand deposits and more capital, suggesting that volume and composition effects reduced the interest cost of liabilities. While aggregate noninterest expense was lower, they had fewer employees who were better paid. Thus the banks' asset-to-employee ratios were higher indicating a more efficient operation. High-performance banks similarly invested proportionately more in earning assets and owned more securities and fewer loans. Securities holdings were, in turn, heavily concentrated in state and local government obligations that earned tax-exempt interest.

These results are inconsistent with excessive overall risk-taking. In fact, high-performance small banks reported lower equity multipliers, smaller loan portfolios, fewer loan charge-offs and less provision for loan losses, and greater operating efficiency. The figures also suggest that high performers have greater borrowing capacity at lower rates and more securities to sell, if necessary, for liquidity. The only adverse risk feature is that the banks hold more long-maturity securities, indicating that interest rate risk might be greater.

The essential conclusion is that high-performance banks manage their risk positions better than other banks do. Over this time interval, they benefitted from low-cost liabilities attributable to retail deposits, and avoided problem loans. Theory suggests that increased competition will erode these above-average profits as firms compete for the same customers.

Failed Banks

The recent rate and breadth of bank failures across geographic markets and different-sized firms is unprecedented since the Depression years. While the existence of federal deposit insurance has prevented wide-scale runs and failures, recent history suggests that bank failures follow patterns of regional economic difficulties. Agriculture problems in the Midwest and energy problems in the Southwest during the 1980s were

---

[13]See Gup and Walters, 1989.

Exhibit 4.11 Significant Differences Between High-Performance Small Banks and All Small Banks

Area of Difference	High-Performance Small Banks vs. All Small Banks
Interest Income/Total Assets	Higher
High-performance small banks produced significantly more interest income relative to assets than the average for small banks while bearing less credit risk.	
Loans/Total Assets	Lower
The high-performance, small banks had a significantly lower ratio of loans to total assets than the average small bank, meaning that they bore less credit risk since loans generally are more risky than the other major category of assets held by banks—securities.	
Securities/Total Assets	Higher
Higher ratio at high-performance banks indicating lower credit risk.	
Municipal Securities/Total Securities	Higher
High-performance banks had more income to shelter so they made greater use of the tax advantage of municipals.	
Earning Assets/Total Assets	Higher
Interest Expense/Total Assets	Lower
High-performance banks funded themselves at lower cost by emphasizing a traditional liability structure and a conservative capital structure.	
Demand Deposit/Total Liabilities	Higher
High-performance banks made greater use of the most traditional of funding sources.	
Interest Expense/Interest-Bearing Liabilities	Lower
High-performance banks made greater use of low-cost retail deposits to gather funds.	
Capital/Total Assets	Higher
High-performance banks had a stronger or more conservative capital structure.	
Noninterest Expense/Total Assets	Lower
High-performance banks held these expenses to a lower level indicating a more efficient use of resources.	

followed by a large number of failures among both large and small banks. Real estate problems during the early 1990s has produced the same result.

Why do some banks fail and not others when they compete in the same markets? A surprisingly small number of failures are attributed to fraud. In most cases, failures arise from poorly diversified asset holdings and problem loans within a concentrated industry. The credit analysis is deficient and failed banks'

Exhibit 4.11 *(Continued)*

Area of Difference	High-Performance Small Banks vs. All Small Banks
Assets/Employees High-performance banks required fewer employees per million dollars in assets.	Higher
Salaries/Employees High-performance banks' employees were better paid.	Higher
Loan Loss Provisions/Total Assets High-performance banks limited their lending and only lent to high-quality borrowers—restraining their credit risk.	Lower
Loan Charge-Offs/Total Loans Lending to high-quality borrowers meant fewer loan charge-offs at high-performance banks.	Lower
Nonperforming Loans/Total Loans Lending to high-quality borrowers meant high-performance banks carried fewer bad loans on their books.	Lower

Factors Not Showing Significant Differences Between High-Performance Small Banks and All Small Banks.

Location in a Metropolitan Area

Bank Holding Company Affiliation

Loan Income/Total Loans

Securities Income/Total Securities

Loan Portfolio Composition

Loan Maturity

Noninterest Income/Total Assets
High-performance small banks placed no more emphasis on these less traditional sources of income than the average small bank.

Fee Income/Total Assets

Gains or Losses on Securities/Total Assets

Source: Gup, Benton and John Walters. *Economic Review*, November/December 1989.

capital is insufficient to protect against insolvency. Often a failed bank exhibits strong loan growth 3 to 5 years before the problems arise. In today's banking environment, the market appears to focus on a bank's credit risk profile when discounting or rewarding performance.

SUMMARY

This chapter introduces financial statements of commercial banks and presents a procedure for analyzing bank profitability and risks using historical data. The procedure involves decomposing aggregate profit ratios into their components to help identify key factors that influence performance. It then identifies financial ratios for credit risk, liquidity risk, interest rate risk, solvency risk, and operational risk to demonstrate the trade-off between risks and returns. Sample data are provided for a large MBHC and a smaller community bank. The chapter presents a summary analysis of the holding company's performance and compares the performance of two different-sized banking groups. The final sections describe how banks may manipulate financial data to alter summary profit and risk measures and draw comparisons between high-performance and failed banks.

Questions

Financial Statement

1. Categorize bank assets into three large groupings and indicate what percentage each would make in a typical large bank and in a typical small bank. Report these to the nearest 5%.

2. Categorize the right side of a bank's balance sheet into three broad groupings and indicate what percentage each would make in a typical large bank and in a typical small bank. Report these to the nearest 5%.

3. Using Valley National Corp. in Exhibit 4.1 as a typical large bank with typical account names, which accounts would be impacted by the following transactions? Indicate at least two accounts affected by each transaction.
   a. Joan DeVries opens a money market account with $10,000. The funds are loaned to a nearby bank for 3 days.
   b. The bank buys a kidney dialysis machine with money from last year's profits. The machine is leased to a local hospital.
   c. Just as a local developer is paying off his construction loan of $1 million, a newly graduated student receives approval for a home mortgage.
   d. The bank hires a brokerage firm to sell its CDs to the public. The bank will use the funds to retire its 20-year bonds 3 years early.
   e. The bank decides it needs to keep more cash on hand to fill its very successful ATM. It will use the money a local resident just used to pay on his car loan.
   f. The bank hires an investment banker to sell shares of its stock to the public. In the meantime the bank is throwing out some furniture that is old, worn, and fully depreciated. It is also buying a large block of local municipal bonds.
   g. A bank's recent advertising campaign has increased the number and size of checking accounts of local residents. The bank has also approved a loan application by a local business that wants to expand its operations.

4. Indicate whether the following items would be classified on a bank income statement as: net interest income, burden, or provisions for loan losses:

a. Customers pay for their safety deposit boxes.

b. Payment is made for employee health benefits.

c. Interest payments are made on jumbo CDs.

d. Loans likely to have 5% default rates have been accepted by the loan committee.

e. Treasury securities formerly bought under a repo are resold.

f. Payment is received on municipal bonds in the bank's investment portfolio.

g. Payment is collected from bank customers who bounced checks last month.

h. The bank pays for a shipment of computer paper for the back room.

5. Construct a bank balance sheet in proper order using the following items. What major category must be added to the right side of the balance sheet to make it complete?

Mortgages of the bank's customers

Subordinated debentures of the bank

Federal funds sold

T-bills bought under a provision to resell

Demand deposits

NOW accounts

Cash in the vault

The bank's time deposits held at Citicorp

Jumbo CDs issued with the help of a broker

Consumer loans

Leases to bank customers

Property seized as collateral for loans in default

The bank's furniture

Business loans written

Municipal securities the bank has purchased

Reserve for loan losses

6. Arrange the following items into an income statement. Label and calculate the bottom line.

Dividends paid to bank stockholders of $1 per share on 2,000 shares.

Interest paid on time deposits of $35,000

Interest paid on jumbo CDs of $82,000

Interest paid on bonds of $23,000

Interest received on government securities of $105,000

Interest received on tax-free municipals of $40,000

Fees received on mortgage originations of $2,000

Service fees received of $13,000

Fees paid for correspondent bank services of $1,000

Depreciation on fixed assets of $500

Employee salaries and benefits paid of $12,000

IRS-allowed deduction for loan losses of $3,000

Purchase of a new building for $600,000

Taxes of 20% paid

7. Classify the following items as belonging to a bank income statement or a bank balance sheet.

   Reserve for loan losses   Retained earnings
   Provision for loan losses   Depreciation
   Leases   Surplus
   Lease payments   Demand deposits
   Lease receipts   Cash and due from banks
   Federal funds purchased   Credit card fees
   Dividends paid   Salaries and employee benefits

8. How does the asset and liability composition of wholesale banks differ from retail banks? How do their interest income and expenses differ?

Return on Equity Model

9. Define each of the following components of the return on equity model and discuss their relationship:
   Return on equity (ROE)
   Return on assets (ROA)
   Equity multiplier (EM)
   Profit margin (PM)
   Asset utilization (AU)

10. What is the advantage of using the decomposition of return analysis?

11. Give a typical range of values for these ratios:
    ROE
    ROA
    Equity multiplier
    Profit margin

12. Bank L operates with an equity-to-asset ratio of 5 percent while Bank S operates at 8 percent. Calculate the equity multiplier for each bank and the corresponding return on equity if each bank earns 1.3 percent on assets. Suppose, instead, both banks report an ROA of 0.9 percent. What does this suggest about financial leverage?

13. Define net interest margin and spread. What do the two measures try to say about a bank? How do they differ?

14. Upscale Bank (UB) has a 30 percent dividend payout ratio and a 20 percent tax rate.

Balance Sheet for UB
(In Millions)

Assets			Liabilities		
Cash and due from banks	$ 40		Demand deposits (no interest)	$ 75	
Investments	300		Time deposits	200	
Federal funds	0		Federal funds	200	
Loans	150		Common equity	25	
Premises	10		Total liabilities	$500	
Total assets	$500				

Income statement

Interest income	$98
Interest expense	68
Provision for loan losses	3
Noninterest income	2
Noninterest expense	20

Calculate as many of the ratios of Exhibit 4.3 as possible with this limited data. Using Exhibit 4.8, discuss what this bank is doing well and poorly.

15. Evaluate the performance of Community State Bank relative to peer banks using the data in Exhibits 4.1, 4.2, 4.4, and 4.5.
   a. Conduct a return on equity decomposition analysis.
   b. Identify strengths and weaknesses in the bank's performance.
   c. What is the bank's Burden?
   d. Compare the bank's risk with its peers.
   e. Will the bank be happy to hear of a sudden increase in interest rates?
   f. What recommendations would you make to improve the bank's risk and return profile?

16. Give three possible explanations for a bank having a higher ratio of interest expense to total liabilities than its peers.

17. Explain why each trend in Exhibit 4.9 persists. Use the data in Exhibit 4.8 for justifications.

18. Regulators use the CAMEL system to analyze banks. What does CAMEL stand for?

19. What are the five primary sources of risk facing bank managers? Suggest two ratios to measure each type of risk and explain how to interpret the values.

20. Categorize the following types of bank deposits based on how quickly their interest rates will be reset. Use the following three categories: not interest-rate sensitive, readjusts in less than a year, readjusts in more than a year.
   Demand deposits
   NOW accounts
   MMDAs
   Passbook savings
   Time deposits
   Jumbo CDs
   Federal funds purchased

Repurchase agreements
Eurodollar liabilities
Subordinated debentures

21. Each of the following transactions would change a bank's risk. For each, indicate which risk or risks would increase or decrease. Consider the following risks: credit risk, liquidity risk, interest rate risk, and operational risk.

    a. A 4-year student loan is financed with a 4-year CD.

    b. A line of credit (with withdrawals available on demand) has been made available to a local firm. It has been funded with a 5-year CD.

    c. The bank has decided to offer customers its own MasterCard even though the returns are low and the processing costs, default rates, and employee errors are high.

    d. Today's newspaper reports that a competing bank has an employee who embezzled over $1 million last year.

    e. The bank has historically written mortgages funded by 6-month CDs. It has just instituted a plan to securitize a majority of its mortgages.

    f. Interest rates have fallen drastically and huge numbers of bank customers are paying off their mortgages.

22. Rank the following assets from lowest to highest liquidity risk.
    Standardized government-insured mortgages
    Treasury bills
    One-payment 5-year business loans
    Installment-payment 5-year business loans
    One-payment 1-year business loans
    Check-sorting equipment
    Pledged securities
    Municipal bonds

23. Rank the following assets from lowest to highest credit risk.
    Student loans
    Corporate loan to a Fortune 500 company
    Corporate loan to small midwest company
    Lease to a small midwest corporation
    Business loans to a local partnership collateralized with work-in-progress inventory
    Business loans to a local partnership collateralized with accounts receivable
    Municipal bonds
    One-payment 5-year construction loan
    Installment-payment 5-year construction loan

Comparison of Banks

24. What ratios on common-sized financial statements would indicate a small bank versus a big bank?

25. What ROA level has been used to define a high-performance small bank?

26. What clues on a common-sized balance sheet would indicate a high-performance bank?

27. Many theories have been postulated for the recent flood of bank failures. What seems to be the number one cause of failure? Besides moving to a different part of the country, what can a bank do to thwart failure?

Manipulation of Data

28. What three methods can banks use to manipulate their financial statements? Why do they do this?

29. From a window-dressing point of view, what are the advantages of issuing preferred stock? Are there any real economic advantages?

30. If a borrower falls behind in loan payments, the bank might lend him more money to make the payments. What are the advantages of this policy to the bank managers? stockholders? What are the risks? When do you think this risk and return trade-off is warranted?

31. This quarter your bank has experienced an unexpected drop in net income, a drop that you think is a one-time fluke. It is still a month before the quarterly financial statements must be assembled. What can you do to hide the income drop from stockholders?

Activities

1. Find a recent article discussing the profitability or risk of a bank. Answer the following questions.
What made this bank newsworthy?
Was this news announced by the bank or discovered by a reporter?
Was it a one-time phenomenon or a recurring event?
Was it good or bad news? Do you think this is typical?
Did the stock price go up or down in response to the news?

2. Collect the financial statements of a local bank. Perform a risk and return analysis, compare the bank with peers, and discuss the bank's strengths and weaknesses. Do these strengths and weaknesses seem to fit the local economy?

Problems

I. Profitability ratios for 1991 are provided in Table 1 for Broadway National Bank with $500 million in assets and its peer banks. Use this information to explain whether this bank was a high or low performance bank. Discuss specifically 1) financial leverage, 2) expense control, and 3) the contribution of interest income and noninterest income to overall bank profitability. List three areas that management should focus on to improve performance.

II. A manager can use basic balance sheet and income statement data to analyze a bank's past performance and evaluate future prospects through pro forma analysis. Using specific assumptions about interest rates and targeted portfolio composition,

Table 1 Performance Data for Broadway National Bank (BNB) versus Peer Banks in 1991

	BNB	Peer Banks
Return on equity	13.9%	13.7%
Return on assets	0.94	1.05
Equity multiplier	14.8×	13.0×
Profit Margin	8.5	9.6
Asset utilization	11.06	10.94
Interest income/Total assets	9.31	9.35
Noninterest income/Total assets	1.75	1.59
Interest expense/Operating income	49.6	47.7
Noninterest expense/Operating income	32.3	33.0
Provision for loan losses/Operating income	6.4	6.5
Taxes/Operating income	3.2	3.2
Service charges/Noninterest income	35.2	38.8
Fees/Noninterest income	39.8	45.4
Securities gains/Noninterest income	12.1	2.7
Other income/Noninterest income	12.9	13.1
Net interest margin	4.54	4.88
Earning assets/Total assets	84.3	84.6

a manager can project what the bank's financial statements will look like several periods into the future. These projections provide information regarding the bank's risk and return profile resulting from each scenario of future events.

Suppose that you are the chief financial officer for Valley National Corporation whose financial data for the past year are provided in Exhibits 4.1 and 4.2. Exhibits 4.4 and 4.5 provide summary profitability and risk measures, respectively. Senior management has indicated that the bank must increase its net interest margin in order to improve profitability and build its capital base. One means to achieve this is by implementing the policies listed under Scenario A. Assume that all funds allocations are immediately made for the full year and are in addition to last year's outstanding balances and net income.

Scenario A Projections

1. Time deposits over $100,000 increase by 35.5%.

2. Cash and due from banks increases by 12.31% of total deposits.

3. Business loans increase by 13%.

4. Real estate loans increase by 41.5%.

5. Consumer loans increase by 12%.

6. Treasury securities (other investment securities) increase by 25%.

7. Federal funds represent the plug figure.

8. Nominal interest rates average the values indicated in parentheses:

    a.   Time deposits over $100,000: (8.6%)

    b. Federal funds rate: (8.1%)

    c. Treasury securities: (8.3%)

    d. Business loans: (12.1%)

    e. Real estate loans: (13.0%)

    f. Consumer loans: (14.4%)

9. Noninterest income will increase by 9.4%; noninterest expense will rise by 5.5%; provisions for loan losses will increase by 5.6%; net loan charge-offs will equal $200,000 so that loan loss reserves increase by 9.9%.

10. Taxes equal 35% of income before taxes; dividends equal 30% of net income.

11. All other balance sheet and income statement values are unchanged.

Questions: Scenario A

1. Using the projections, construct an income statement for the next year and determine the source of the estimated increase in retained earnings. Determine the amount of funds that will be invested in consumer loans.

2. Calculate the projected values for the bank's return on equity, return on assets, profit margin, asset utilization, and net interest margin.

3. Calculate the basic credit risk, liquidity risk, and interest rate risk measures from Exhibit 4.5 using the projected figures for the year.

4. Evaluate the differences in the bank's risk and return profile under Scenario A versus last year's position. What problems appear?

Suppose instead that management decides to pursue a more conservative strategy and invest a portion of newly available funds in marketable securities. Answer the same four questions listed previously assuming that the bank pursues the policies listed under Scenario B. Then explain why the two scenarios produce sharply different outcomes.

Scenario B Projections

1. Time deposits over $100,000 increase by 35.5%.

2. Cash and due from banks increases by 12.31% of total deposits.

3. Business loans decrease by 3%.

4. Federal funds represent the plug figure.

5. State and municipal securities increase by 20%.

6. Treasury securities (6-month maturity) increase by 65%.

7. Nominal interest rates average the values indicated in parentheses:

    a. Time deposits over $100,000: (8.6%)

    b. Federal funds rate: (8.1%)

    c. Treasury securities: (8.3%)

    d. Business loans: (12.1%)

    e. State and municipal securities: (7.0%)

Table 2 Management Discussion of Operations
(Dollars in Millions Except per Share Amounts)

	1990	1989	1988	1987	1986	1985
Statement of Income						
Net Interest Income	$423	$450	$442	$423	$418	$419
Provision for Credit Losses	89	348	87	240	98	59
Noninterest Income	183	174	155	146	186	125
Operating Expense	510	499	427	438	417	368
Accounting Change*	—	—	5	—	18	—
Net Income (Loss)	8	(149)	67	(44)	89	84
Per Share Data						
Net Income (Loss)	$ 0.38	$ (7.55)	$ 3.41	$ (2.25)	$ 4.55	$ 4.26
Dividends Paid (Cash)	—	1.08	1.44	1.44	1.35	1.23
Shareholders' Equity (Book Value)	22.82	22.60	31.29	29.40	33.09	29.83
Year-end Market Price	10.88	12.88	24.50	26.88	38.63	41.25
Key Performance Ratios						
Return on Average Assets	0.07%	**	.61%	**	.84%	.87%
Return on Average Equity	1.65	**	11.31	**	14.44	14.98
Primary Capital Ratio (Tier 1: 1990)	6.51	6.88%	6.67	6.74%	6.50	6.21
Total Capital Ratio (Tier 2: 1990)	7.34	8.19	8.33	8.48	8.29	7.22
Dividends (Year-end Annual Rate) As a Percent of Net Income	—	**	42.23	**	31.65	30.99
Price/Earnings Ratio (Year-end)	28.63	**	7.18	**	8.49	9.68
Net Interest Margin—Taxable Equivalent (T.E.)	4.86	4.91	4.71	4.75	4.91	5.34

8. Noninterest income will increase by 8.7%; noninterest expense will rise by 5.4%; provisions for loan losses will be unchanged; net loan charge-offs will equal $100,000 so that loan loss reserves increase by 4%.

9. Taxes will equal 35% of income before taxes; dividends will equal 30% of net income. Everything else is unchanged from last year's figures.

III. Analysis of Valley National Corporation: 1989–1990

The profitability and risk trade-off at Valley National Corp. (VNC) received considerable attention in Chapter 4. Table 2 provides additional data for 1989 and 1990 related to selected profit and risk figures. Use this information to determine whether your analysis and the text's discussion accurately evaluated the bank's risk and return profile at the end of 1988. Specifically, answer the following questions.

1. What happened to net income after 1988? What seems to be the primary cause of its decline?

2. Has VNC controlled its noninterest expense?

	1990	1989	1988	1987	1986	1985
Asset Quality						
Allowance for Credit Losses to:						
Total Loans	3.30%	4.07%	2.29%	2.46%	1.39%	1.18%
Nonaccrual Loans	71.19	75.54	50.11	80.13	63.74	56.11
Nonperforming Assets as a Percent of Total Loans and Other Real Estate Owned	7.19	7.20	5.70	3.69	2.61	2.50
Net Charge-offs as a Percent of Loans	2.51	3.02	1.34	2.02	1.03	.61
Efficiency						
Operating Expense as a Percent of:						
Average Assets	4.98%	4.66%	3.88%	4.09%	3.94%	3.81%
Net Revenue (te)	80.85	77.31	68.59	72.75	64.32	63.52
Average Balances						
Loans	$ 6,776	$ 7,596	$ 7,702	$ 7,657	$ 7,356	$6,742
Investment Securities	1,605	1,484	1,551	1,583	1,655	1,414
Interest-earning Assets	9,209	9,612	9,911	9,602	9,422	8,504
Assets	10,240	10,716	10,982	10,698	10,584	9,650
Deposits:						
Interest-bearing	7,559	7,421	7,626	7,357	7,080	6,385
Noninterest-bearing	1,634	1,697	1,756	1,817	1,791	1,667
Total	9,193	9,118	9,382	9,174	8,871	8,052
Interest-bearing Funds	8,028	8,330	8,503	8,104	7,958	7,140
Liabilities	9,785	10,151	10,387	10,060	9,965	9,092
Shareholders' Equity	455	565	595	638	619	558

*Accounting Change explanations—1988 adoption of SFAS No. 96—Income Taxes; 1986 adoption of SFAS Nos. 87 and 88 on pension accounting; te = taxable equivalent.

**Not meaningful

Source: Annual Reports.

3. Why are provisions for loan losses so volatile? Consider the psychology of management in determining when to declare loan losses and the appropriate magnitude. Remember that provisions for loan losses is a noncash expense and somewhat subjectively determined by management. Can it be used to manipulate or disguise true operating results?

4. Assess overall asset quality at VNC. What are the prospects for future loan losses? Make a forecast of provisions for loan losses and net income for 1991. Review VNC's annual report to assess your forecast.

5. What has happened to the bank's asset growth? Why?

6. Describe the bank's dividend policy after 1986. Can VNC justify paying dividends? Why or why not?

7. Examine the bank's stock price from 1985 through 1990. Explain the source of the trend. Would you buy stock in VNC?

References

Calem, Paul. "The New Bank Deposit Markets: Goodbye to Regulation Q." *Business Review* (Federal Reserve Bank of Philadelphia, November–December 1985).

Cates, David. "Are Small Banks Still Profitable?" *ABA Banking Journal* (April 1986).

Cates, David. "Bank Shareholder Value: Strategies for the '90s." *Bank Managment* (February 1991).

Clair, Robert. "Financial Strategies of Top-Performance Banks in the Eleventh District." *Economic Review* (January 1987).

Cole, David W. "A Return-on-Equity Model for Banks." *The Bankers Magazine* (Summer 1972).

Crews, Joseph M. "Monitoring Bank Risks: New Requirements Yield Useful Ratios." *Magazine of Bank Administration* (October 1986).

Danker, Deborah J., and Mary M. McLaughlin. "Profitability of U.S. Chartered Insured Commercial Banks in 1985." *Federal Reserve Bulletin* (September 1986).

Federal Deposit Insurance Corporation. *FDIC Quarterly Banking Profile.* Washington, D.C.: Office of Research and Statistics, Fourth Quarter 1990.

Fortier, Diana, and Dave Phillis. "Bank and Thrift Performance Since DIDMCA." *Economic Perspectives* (Federal Reserve Bank of Chicago, September–October 1985).

Garea, Raymond, and Gail Triner. "What's the Secret of Profitable Retail Banking?" *ABA Banking Journal* (April 1986).

Gup, Benton, and John Walters. "Top Performing Small Banks: Making Money the Old-Fashioned Way." *Economic Review* (Federal Reserve Bank of Richmond, November/December 1989).

Hector, Gary. *Breaking the Bank: The Decline of BankAmerica.* Little Brown, 1988.

Lowe, William and Christopher Svare, "Restructuring Intensifies." *Bank Management* (January 1991).

Mester, Loretta. "Owners versus Managers: Who Controls the Bank?" *Business Review* (Federal Reserve Bank of Philadelphia, May/June 1989).

Shaffer, Sherrill. "Challenges to Small Banks' Survival." *Business Review* (Federal Reserve Bank of Philadelphia, September/October 1989).

Sheshunoff, Alex. "Banks Climb Back in the Saddle." *ABA Banking Journal* (July 1989).

Wall, Larry. "Why Are Some Banks More Profitable Than Others?" *Journal of Bank Research* (Winter 1985).

Wolfson, Martin, and Mary McLaughlin. "Recent Developments in the Profitability and Lending Practices of Commercial Banks." *Federal Reserve Bulletin* (July 1989).

Chapter 5

Bank Strategic Planning, Budgeting, and Marketing

The business world is replete with stories of firms that successfully develop, implement, and adapt strategies that astound the marketplace. Even though the cost of taking a family of four to one of the Disney theme parks for one day is well over $150, the crowds are as big as ever, profits are strong, and the firm continues to expand. American Express recognizes that it is selling a lifestyle of convenience, prestige, and luxury. How else can it convince customers to pay $300 annually for a platinum credit card? Who would have guessed that Federal Express could make money by providing guaranteed overnight delivery? Of course, some firms do not understand the marketplace and fail to adapt as times change. Pullman Motor Cars, once the dominant manufacturer of railroad cars, failed because its managers did not adapt when the passenger railroad business deteriorated. For many years Sears refused to accept any credit cards other than its own from customers wishing to purchase merchandise on credit. Even though the policy inconvenienced customers and cost Sears business, management believed other cards would not add sufficient business to justify the cost. Eventually management adapted by providing immediate approval of applicants wanting to receive a Sears credit card.

To be successful, bank managers must have a vision of where the firm should be headed. This requires planning. To be effective, such planning should be part of a formal, ongoing process that critically examines the nature and future of the business. Such a process is labeled strategic planning and involves four fundamental steps:

1. Evaluating historical performance

2. Setting objectives

3. *Developing action plans*

4. *Comparing actual with planned performance.*

This chapter introduces the planning process. It builds on bank performance analysis by linking a bank's current financial condition to the setting of short-term and long-term goals and developing strategies to achieve the goals. The chapter also addresses budgeting and marketing issues, which are closely tied to the planning function.

WHY PLAN?

Why should managers plan? The answer is simple. Bankers who plan improve the odds that their firm will be a winner in the increasingly competitive financial services industry. When interest rates were closely regulated, asset choices were limited, and banks were allowed to compete only in selected geographic and product markets, planning consisted primarily of developing and implementing the annual budget. In today's competitive environment, pricing issues are critical, as banks can pay market-determined rates on virtually all liabilities and can invest in a wide range of assets. Technological change is rapidly altering how financial services are delivered, and banks compete with nondepository institutions for traditional banking products as well as nontraditional underwriting, insurance, real estate, and investment products. Aggressive competition and rapid change necessitate an ongoing awareness of the prevailing environment and opportunities. Planning allows management to reduce risk and take advantage of opportunities as they arise.

Consider the four strategic planning steps introduced earlier. On what basis do managers make decisions if they do not understand their bank's current financial and operating condition? How can managers set objectives if they have no idea what type of firm the bank should be? Action plans, in turn, necessarily follow from specific goals and strategies. Finally, managers should systematically perform audits of actual versus planned performance to assess whether goals are being met, and if not, how plans should be modified to ensure success.

THE STRATEGIC PLANNING PROCESS

Traditionally, bank managers viewed the business plan as a necessary evil; something put together for the regulators and dusted off at each periodic examination. It was often reactive rather than proactive—managers would only review and revise their plans after specific problems arose. Part of the problem was that bank regulators also reacted to rather than anticipated change. For example, banks responded to difficulties in maintaining net interest margin when interest rate volatility increased by incorporating specific interest rate risk targets in their plans. Credit problems similarly produced risk and pricing guidelines for the loan portfolio. In today's environment, regulators require formal and specific business plans. A good business plan serves as a guide for management to evaluate the bank's current situation and design strategies for the future. When problems arise, such a plan will contain the assessment procedure and controls necessary to reduce the impact on performance.

A good plan is thus a road map to the future. It indicates where a bank is headed. It documents specific financial objectives against which the bank's actual performance can be compared. It identifies specific financial, marketing, and operating strategies and the action plans appropriate to achieve objectives. Strategic plans thus incorporate traditional profit plans and marketing plans in one document.

Strategic planning is the process through which managers formulate the bank's mission, establish goals and objectives, assess strengths and weaknesses of the bank's current operating and financial condition, identify opportunities and threats, and design strategies to achieve desired objectives. The business plan is the output of the process. Importantly, strategic planning is much more than preparing an annual budget or forecasting the bank's balance sheet and income statement over the next few years. It integrates external factors with internal factors in determining where management wants to lead the bank. In the planning process, managers determine what risks to take. In this regard, planners are risk managers. As described in Chapter 4, bank managers balance credit risk, interest rate risk, solvency risk, liquidity risk, and operational risk with potential returns available from various strategies. The appropriate time frame for planning is thus well beyond one year.

The planning process used by each bank will differ depending on the each firm's organizational structure and size. The basic format, however, is outlined in Exhibit 5.1. A strategic plan has six essential parts:

1. Mission statement
2. Financial objectives
3. Situation analysis
4. Analysis of strengths, weaknesses, opportunities, and threats (SWOT)
5. Action plans
6. Goals and timetables

The first three parts address the bank's current condition. The analysis of strengths, weaknesses, opportunities, and threats (SWOT analysis) indicates what the bank *could* be like in the future. It makes managers aware of problem areas and of strengths that can be emphasized. The final two parts require that managers determine *what* the bank wants to be like in the future and specify *how* and *when* to accomplish it. At this time, precise performance targets are identified and the time frame to achieve each is specified. Most plans look forward at least 5 years, although there are no strict requirements. Once a plan is in place, management conducts regular audits to monitor performance and modify the plan where appropriate.

Exhibit 5.1 The Strategic Planning Process

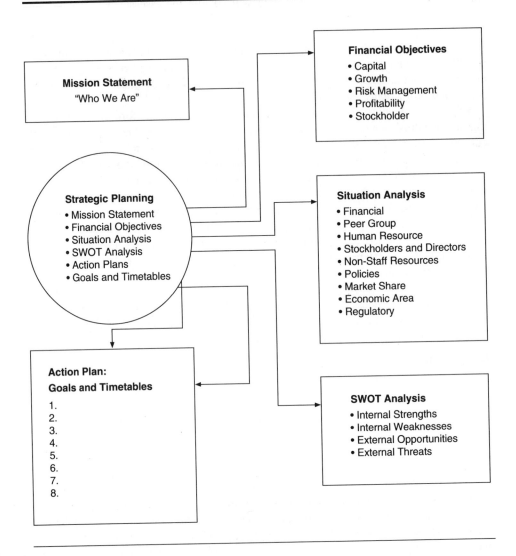

Mission Statement

A bank's mission statement answers the questions "What is the Bank?" or "Who are We?" As a general rule, a bank's mission statement should include the following essential points.[1]

---

[1]These items were identified in a presentation to bankers attending the Graduate School of Banking of the South in 1990.

1. State precisely the business that the bank is in; describe businesses that the bank does not want to be in.

2. Describe what makes the bank different from the competition.

3. Establish clearly the bank's key values that must be adhered to by all employees.

4. Indicate the values reflected in the bank's corporate culture and realistically expressed by senior management.

5. Provide guidelines that allow for flexibility in response to internal and external change.

6. Demonstrate an understanding of market opportunities and how the bank will respond.

7. Affirm the bank's profit orientation.

Before a bank can determine where it is headed, it must have a vision regarding its mission. This vision articulates priorities and key values in serving customers. It identifies target markets and the bank's desired position in those markets. A mission statement should not consist of broad generalities or precise financial forecasts, but should rather focus on the items listed above. Furthermore, a bank's Board of Directors and senior management must be responsible for articulating the vision. Without their support and involvement, the planning process will not get off the ground.

Exhibit 5.2 offers a general classification for commercial banks based on the type of orientation reflected in their revenue and cost structure. There are six categories ranked from highest average profitability, fee-based banks, to lowest average profitability, money center banks, in 1988. The various market features indicate the balance sheet and income statement features that distinguished performance. Fee-based firms performed the best because they did not assume the same amounts of credit risk as other firms, yet generated better net income from high fee income. At the other extreme, money center banks were the lowest performers because they assumed considerable credit risk and reported the greatest charge-offs.

Financial Objectives

Goals and objectives serve two purposes. They allow a bank to allocate funds, labor, computer time, and other resources in an objective manner; and they allow for the communication of organizational intent throughout a bank by relating each employee's job to overall bank objectives. In practice, goals and objectives are best established after management understands the environment and strengths, weaknesses, opportunities, and threats a bank faces. Setting goals and objectives thus involves a two-step process. The first step entails defining broad goals in line with a bank's mission statement. The second step involves refining these broad-based goals after the situation analysis is completed and supplementing them with specific numerical objectives and standards.

Managers typically specify different goals over different time intervals. **Short-term goals** are those that can normally be attained during 1 year. Such goals are often the highest priority because they ensure the viability of continued operations. Goals

Exhibit 5.2 Average Profitability Rankings and Market Features of Different Types of Commercial Banks

Firm Type: 1988 Bank	Market Feature
1. Fee-based	a. Information & data processing services, trust, brokerage activities
	b. Fee income/TA[a] is high
	c. Interest expense/TA is low
	d. Noninterest income/TA is high
2. Commercial finance	a. Middle market loans to commercial & real estate firms
	b. Interest income/TA is high
	c. Interest expense/TA is high—heavy reliance on borrowed funds
	d. Net charge-offs/TA is low
3. Consumers' intermediators	a. Consumer loans/TA is high
	b. Consumer deposits/TA is high
	c. Interest income/TA is high
	d. Interest expense/TA is low—so *NIM is high*
4. Low-cost funding	a. Demand deposits/TA is high
	b. Interest expense/TA is low
	c. Securities/TA is high; low risk C&I loans
	d. Interest income/TA is low
5. Undifferentiated	a. All ratios below average.
6. Money center	a. High charge-offs.

[a]TA = total assets.

Categories: First Manhattan Consulting Group.

for holding satisfactory liquid assets to meet potential cash deficiencies or changing the pricing of transactions accounts to increase core deposits are two examples. In most banks, the annual budgeting effort is closely linked to short-term goal setting. **Intermediate-term goals** are typically targeted for a 1 to 3 year horizon. Such goals might include changes in a bank's capital structure to obtain more equity, shifts in the loan portfolio to variable rate mortgages from fixed rate mortgages, and a move to increased reliance on consumer rather than commercial deposit funding. Finally, **long-term goals** are those that extend beyond three years. Such goals often focus on new markets to be served and new products to be offered, or address permanent changes in portfolio composition and capital structure.

Strategic planning requires attention to financial objectives over each time horizon. Long-range financial goals are generally grouped in the following categories:

- Earnings: measured by return on equity, return on assets, and net interest margin,

- Risk Management: controllable versus noncontrollable credit, interest rate, liquidity, operational, exchange rate, and political risks are identified and acceptable ranges for performance measures are specified,

- Capital: measured by a bank's qualifying capital as a fraction of assets; with risk-based capital standards, capital adequacy is measured as core capital (stockholders' equity) and total regulatory capital as a fraction of risk assets.

- Growth: measured by the percentage increase in deposits, loans, and total assets; also broken down by market share in target product markets,

- Dividends: measured in absolute dollar payout and as a percentage of net income,

- Regulatory compliance: indicated by performance at compliance exams, and

- Community Service: measured by portfolio composition and employee involvement in the community.

Simply articulating goals forces management to recognize several important factors. First, there is an obvious trade-off between certain goals. High dividend payments slow capital accumulation and reduce growth opportunities unless external financing is available. The greater is bank capital, the more difficult it is to meet return on equity targets. Second, the use of specific goals enables a better accounting of performance and assists in rewarding those who achieve objectives. Finally, individuals within the bank should be assigned responsibility to implement goals and monitor performance. Employee performance often improves when all employees are aware of overall bank objectives, specifically if individual compensation is tied to firm performance.

Situation Analysis

Before managers can make decisions, they need to understand their bank's current financial condition. This "situation audit" involves evaluating historical performance using internal balance sheet and income statement data, and relating this performance to external factors that influence activities. External factors include demographic trends, such as regional income, population, and employment growth, regulatory trends, the economic environment, and expectations of stockholders and bank customers. The internal analysis typically follows the return on equity decomposition introduced in Chapter 4.

In order to conduct the analysis, management should develop an information base in each of the following areas.

Financial Condition. The analysis consists of evaluating the bank's profit position in terms of the ROE model, then evaluating the bank's risk profile. Key performance ratios should be calculated over different years so that management can identify important trends. The same ratios should be compared with those of peer banks to determine where differences exist and whether the differences affect overall profitability and risk. Using this framework, management gets a good sense of whether the bank performs above or below average, and why.

Products and Services Offered. Each bank should develop a list or inventory of all products and services offered. The list should indicate the name of the specific product or service, the associated target market, the current pricing policy, the current market share, and which department and individuals within the bank are responsible for the item. Such a list should then be compared with competitors' offerings to identify key differences.

Customer Base and Trade Area. Managers cannot know what business the bank is in without understanding who the bank's customers are. A situation audit should examine the characteristics of the bank's current deposit and loan customers in detail by collecting data on customer income, education, employment, age, and area of residence. With this information, managers can better assess potential growth and target products that appeal to existing customers.

Human Resources. Every bank should develop a human resource inventory. Such a list identifies key management and staff personnel within each department. Alongside, it should itemize the specific skills and areas of interest and responsibility of each individual. Such a list will reveal the range and depth of lending operations, marketing, clerical, and administrative skills available. When implementing new strategies or replacing personnel, management can select individuals knowing their specific skills and existing responsibilities.

Economic, Industry, and Regulatory Environment. Economic and regulatory factors influence the environment in which banks compete. They determine growth opportunities and areas where significant risks will likely arise. Industry factors include pricing and marketing efforts of a bank's direct competitors in its existing trade area, as well as comparable efforts from regional and national competitors. Basic economic data needs consist of information regarding demographic trends, household formation patterns, local housing activity, the growth in regional per-capita income, employment growth and composition by industry, and information on retail sales. An industry assessment should focus on comparative deposit and loan growth, profitability, capitalization, and market penetration. Regulatory influences can only be subjectively forecast, but management should be aware of the areas of regulatory interest.

Analysis of Strengths, Weaknesses, Opportunities, and Threats

Once an information base is generated, management analyzes the bank's strategic strengths, weaknesses, opportunities, and threats (SWOT). This analysis forces managers to critically appraise the quality of specific individuals' skills, firm products, marketing policies, and the bank's past operating performance. It serves as the basis for designing new strategies that emphasize strengths, overcome weaknesses, take advantage of opportunities, or counter threats.

Strengths. Strengths consist of areas within the bank that provide an inherent advantage over competitors. They may arise from bank image, the characteristics of bank personnel, the bank's financial soundness, product line, or quality of facilities. Implicitly, management can take advantage of these perceived strengths in their marketing plans as well as by reassigning product responsibilities and developing new products.

Weaknesses. Weaknesses consist of areas within the bank that need significant improvement or restructuring. In many instances, this information can only be obtained by customer survey. Weak areas may be the opposite side of the factors listed under strengths. Bank image may be poor due to continued customer problems with monthly checking account statements or long waiting lines at teller windows. A bank may not offer the range of products desired within the community. Again, management must determine how to overcome these weaknesses which may involve product, personnel, and marketing changes.

Opportunities. Managers should make a prioritized list of external opportunities that will potentially provide a competitive advantage to the bank. A common example is cross-selling opportunities to existing customers. Another is growth and market penetration available from new bank or nonbank subsidiaries acquired by a bank holding company. In each instance, cost estimates should be attached to help assess feasibility.

Threats. Managers should also make a prioritized list of all external threats confronting the bank. Such threats typically come in the form of regulatory restrictions, competitive products available from other providers, a competitor's marketing strategy, poor relations with the media, and dramatic changes in local economic conditions. Each threat essentially represents a lost opportunity in the form of customer attrition.

After completion of the SWOT analysis, management should refine the bank's goals and objectives by specifying precise numerical targets and performance measures encompassing all time frames. Typically, strategies take advantage of bank strengths and minimize the impact of weaknesses. In line with the new targets, managers now identify specific strategies that will achieve the desired objectives. Financial strategies address asset and liability volume, mix, and maturity, capital structure, pricing policies, and overall credit policy. Marketing strategies similarly address product and service mix, the trade area in which products will be marketed, and the optimal delivery systems.

Action Plans

As part of designing strategies, management identifies specific tactics and action plans that should help the bank achieve its targets. Regardless of individual decisions made, an action plan must be customer driven; it must enhance the long-run profitability of the bank; and it should not increase bank risk beyond acceptable levels and thereby endanger the bank's capital. At this stage, management conducts "what-if" analysis by simulating possible outcomes from alternative strategies and actions.

Actions plans may be both broad and specific. A plan may specify, for example, that a bank will look more to the investment portfolio for yield and balancing interest rate risk. Precise action plans might then focus on implementing a contracyclical investment strategy whereby the bank lengthens the maturities of bonds purchased when loan demand is high, and shortens bond maturities when loan demand is low. To reduce interest rate risk, a bank might similarly choose to increase floating rate commercial loans at the expense of fixed rate loans. The results from simulating balance sheet and income statement outcomes then reveal the trade-offs between alternative strategies and plans.

Goals and Timetables

After selecting specific action plans, management must establish a realistic timetable for each objective. This ensures that employees who are responsible for implementing the strategies and actions understand their importance and concentrate their efforts accordingly. It also provides a meaningful way to evaluate results. In many instances, certain plans cannot be implemented before other plans are in place. Examples include efforts to enter new markets. Initially, promotional spots and specific product advertising introduce a product. Then line managers implement cross-selling strategies to improve market share.

Once action plans are underway, key employees are responsible for regularly monitoring performance to determine whether the bank is progressing toward its objectives. If not, the bank has time to alter its tactics or change direction. It should thus be emphasized that strategic plans are not static. They should be constantly revised depending on customer acceptance and market conditions. Banks that win will be those that adapt best.

BUDGETING AND CONTROL

Historically, many banks used the annual budgeting process as their strategic planning vehicle. Budgeting generally consists of determining target revenues and expenses by component and by department. Managers periodically compare actual performance against planned performance. Where deviations exist, individuals responsible must justify the differences and modify behavior if necessary. By nature, then, a budget controls activity, particularly on the expense side.

The problems with using a budget as a strategic plan should be obvious. First, budgets look forward only 1 year. Too much attention is paid to short-term decisions and problem solving rather than to long-term strategies. Second, without a detailed analysis of the bank's current situation, it is difficult to allocate resources to take advantage of strengths and minimize the impact of weaknesses. Strategies and action plans are thus based on incomplete information and funds are potentially misallocated. Third, many banks base annual budgets on the prior year's expenses. Revisions consist of adjusting each expense category by the expected inflation rate. There is little justification for this approach, unless the prior year's budget meets this year's objectives. But management will not know whether this is the case unless it has formalized its goals and strategies.

Still, budgeting is an integral part of the strategic planning process. Annual budgeting requires that managers review every major expense category and justify specific expenditures. It is thus relatively easy to identify the source of rising expenses and conduct a cost-benefit analysis. It also imposes a measure of control by requiring managers to explain significant deviations in expenditures from the plan. Budgeting also represents an initial step in obtaining a profit plan. Such a plan essentially serves as a forecast of the bank's earnings for the period, and can be used to evaluate actual profitability.

The Operating Budget

An operating budget represents expected revenues and expenses during the coming year. In most banks, the controller's department is responsible for coordinating the formulation of the annual budget. Each department's management prepares preliminary budget needs and requests that are then evaluated by senior management. Requests should, in turn, reflect the financial objectives of the bank's strategic plan. Not surprisingly, funding requests often exceed the level of expenses targeted by senior management. Department managers then must revise their requests by prioritizing needs. The process continues until an aggregate budget conforms to the bank's strategic objectives. As the year progresses, the controller prepares monthly summaries of actual versus planned operating results so that senior management can determine where and why differences exist, and take corrective action if appropriate.

Strategic planning has a significant impact on a bank's operating budget. If management targets a new loan or deposit market, for example, it must allocate staff and supporting resources to generate new business. Unless the anticipated expenses represent an addition to the existing budget, resources will have to be taken from other departments or expense categories. Branch closings and sales require a similar real-location of personnel and resources. It is not difficult to see why turf battles arise throughout the planning and budgeting process.

The Profit Planning Process

Budgeting is actually part of a bank's overall profit planning process, as indicated in Exhibit 5.3. In the first stage, each department prepares a detailed report of actual costs and personnel resources. This information may be supplied by the bank's cost accountants, or can be estimated from Federal Reserve Functional Cost Analysis data. The departments then use this information in conjunction with the bank's strategies and action plans and projected pricing policies to generate a budget. The next step is to forecast growth in each asset and liability item which, combined with an economic forecast, can be used to project an income statement for the upcoming year. Such forecasting entails considerable "what-if" analysis by incorporating high and low interest rate environments as well as strong or weak loan demand and deposit growth.

Once departmental plans are available, senior management consolidates them to obtain an overall profit plan. The separate plans clearly reveal how department managers view their own groups' performance during the year. At this stage, the chief executive officer and other senior officers review each group's proposed plan and suggest changes. Changes normally reflect inconsistencies between departments or

Exhibit 5.3 The Profit Planning Process

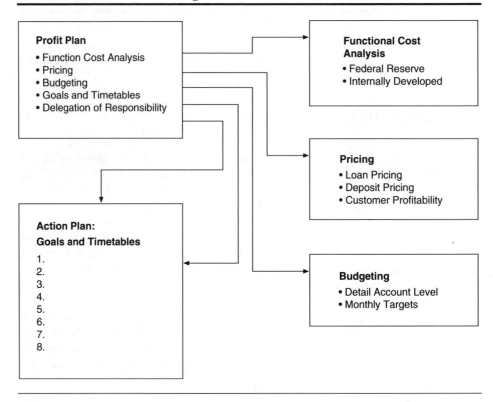

with the bank's strategic objectives. For example, a bank may have insufficient capital to support the targeted growth in loans. This raises the issue as to whether an external common stock offering should be considered or whether growth should be curtailed. After the reviews and refinements are completed, the bank adopts a formal profit plan that reflects its financial objectives and overall action plans.

This leads to the final step in profit planning: setting a timetable for implementing the plan and delegating responsibility. The controller is again generally responsible for data generation, while department managers submit monthly reports of actual performance. This establishes a chain of reporting by which senior management can monitor performance and identify deviations from the plan.

Control

Control represents the auditing function. It consists of comparing actual performance with planned or budgeted performance, identifying significant deviations, and suggesting managerial actions. Control systems vary according to the size of bank and nature of operations. Yet good control programs share the following features.

1. Standards are established that represent desired performance. Most banks, for example, will specify minimum acceptable market shares for key products and deposits. There are also a wide range of internal operating targets in terms of employee turnover, cross-selling of services, and unit costs for processing loans.

2. Actual bank performance is compared with the standard.

3. Differences between actual performance and standards are used by management as signals for corrective action whenever the actual performance is below standard. Revised action plans are subsequently put in place.

4. Standards are examined periodically for possible revision. Standards are imposed on previously unmeasured activities as new products are offered.

MARKETING BANK SERVICES

Marketing is an integral part of the strategic planning process. It represents a fundamental philosophy of banking in which management recognizes that the bank should be market-driven, and thus adopts strategies that focus on meeting consumer needs. Coincident with a profit plan, banks should have a marketing plan. Mary Ann Pezzullo has, in fact, outlined a model for the marketing process that closely parallels the strategic planning process. Exhibit 5.4 documents the steps in marketing planning as conducting a situation analysis, setting objectives, selecting target markets, designing a marketing strategy, implementing the plan, and conducting a post-audit.

Marketing Basics

Successful marketing efforts exhibit three basic features: they are customer-focused; they achieve customer satisfaction that is profitable to the bank; and they involve the entire organization.

Customer Orientation. When asked, many bankers describe the nature of the banking business in terms of the products and services offered. They focus on the types of deposits and loans available. In fact, however, products and services are merely a means for a bank to meet customer needs. Consider, for example, different products that have declined in popularity because improved products replaced them. Can anyone remember passenger trains, or hair rollers, or wooden baseball bats? Customer needs change, and a bank's ability to meet those needs must also change.

Bank customer surveys typically reveal four basic wants: faster service, convenient business hours, feeling wanted, and the prompt and fair resolution of problems. Who wants to wait in long lines? Most banks recognize that customers have little patience and try to increase their teller staff or open all drive-up teller windows at peak times. Several banks have offered customers a small cash payment if they wait in a line beyond some minimum amount of time. Banks have similarly modified the design of automatic teller machines to allow customers to handle all transactions from their cars

Exhibit 5.4 Model for the Strategic Marketing Management Process

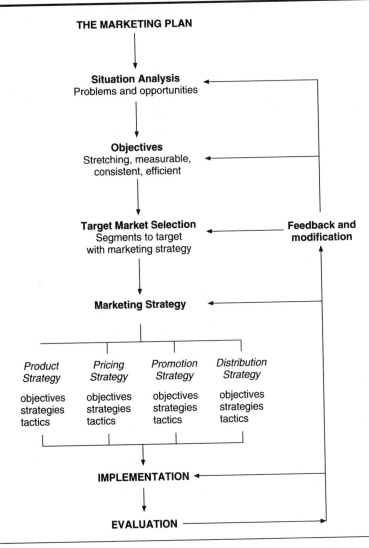

Source: Mary Ann Pezzullo, *Marketing for Bankers*, 1988.

rather than be required to walk up to the window. People want to handle their banking business at times convenient to them, and not necessarily when the bank is normally open. People also like to be recognized and treated as important. They thus want to conduct business with people they know or those who are respectful. Finally, many customers complain that banks do not handle their problems quickly or accurately. They are made to feel at fault, regardless of where the blame actually lies. A customer-focused bank recognizes these wants and takes steps to accommodate its customers.

With increased competition in the financial services industry, banks that pay special attention to their customers will operate at a real competitive advantage. A 1990 *Business Week* article, titled "King Customer," suggested seven strategies to ensure that a firm would be customer-focused. They are:

1. Make sure the commitment to being customer-driven starts at the top—by edict and example.

2. Get customer participation at the design stage to limit the need for adjustments later.

3. Give employees at the front lines and on the factory floor more authority to solve problems on the spot.

4. Collect customer satisfaction ratings and give them substantial weight in employee performance reviews and incentive plans.

5. Talk to your competitors' customers as well as your own—and find out why they do business elsewhere.

6. Make it easy for customers to reach you with complaints or questions.

7. Hire your customers. What better way to boost service than to employ someone from the other side?

Long-Term Profitability. Without customers, banks would have no revenues. Marketing is directed at protecting and expanding this stream of revenue. It does so by keeping existing customers, broadening their banking relationships by cross-selling services, and attracting new customers. Again, without a customer orientation, other institutions will entice customers away by offering the relationship they desire.

It is important to recognize that all customers are not equal, however. They generally fit into one of three categories: key customers, normal customers, and problem customers. Key customers are the most profitable. They purchase the highest volume of services and maintain the largest deposit balances. Bankers often refer to the 80/20 rule, in which 80 percent of deposit dollars are generated by just 20 percent of all customers. Most of a bank's customers consist of normal customers. They maintain average account activity and slowly progress through the financial life cycle from wealth creators (transactions oriented) to wealth preservers (savings oriented). The smallest group is problem customers, who cause the majority of problems. They are slow to pay on loans, often overdraw their transactions accounts, and are chronic complainers. Which customers do you suppose receive the greatest attention at most banks? Who should?

Organizational Commitment. Marketing is the responsibility of every bank employee. Whether at work or in their leisure time, every employee who comes into contact with a potential or existing customer is marketing the bank. Banks thus have a responsibility to train employees in terms of how to interact with the public. This focus starts with senior management and the Board of Directors, and is equally important for tellers and other line personnel.

The Marketing Plan

As indicated in Exhibit 5.4, marketing planning evolves from a bank's strategic plan, particularly the situation analysis and formation of objectives. During these stages, management identifies the bank's strengths, weaknesses, opportunities, and threats and targets new and existing market segments. Small businesses might need special forms of working capital financing. Elderly customers might need new savings products or financial planning services. The target segment determines what services will be offered and to whom.

When developing a marketing strategy, firms normally focus on the marketing mix. These factors define the total relationship between a bank and a particular customer and include

1. Product or service features

2. Price

3. Promotion

4. Physical distribution, and

5. Human delivery.

While these factors are generally self-explanatory, the last three merit special attention. The basic element of a product is the benefit that a customer expects to realize: transactions convenience from a checking account, for example. Pricing, of course, influences the quantity demanded and relative profitability to the bank. Promotion refers to the types of activities employed by a bank to communicate with customers regarding a product or service. Advertising, which is paid communication, and publicity, which is free communication, both attempt to increase the demand for the underlying service. Physical distribution refers to the process by which a bank delivers the product or service to the consumer. This may be a credit card, an automatic teller machine, a drive-up window, a teller or loan officer at a branch office, or a home video system. Human delivery or personal selling represents direct contact between bank employees and customers. Most banking products are delivered in this manner. The current trend is for banks to employ customer contact specialists. Such individuals aggressively sell bank services and provide direct customer service. Here selling involves identifying customer problems and solving them. M. Ray Grubbs uses the concept of core values to identify whether a bank is serious about providing quality sales and customer service. Exhibit 5.5 lists nine core values and provides an example of each. In his view, it is the responsibility of bank managers to establish such values as responsiveness, accessibility, credibility, courtesy, competency, understanding of customers, accuracy, reliability, and communication, and to see that employees use them to deliver services.

The final stages in a marketing plan involve implementation and evaluation. As with each component of a strategic plan, managers put certain individuals in charge of

Exhibit 5.5 The Core Value of Quality Service

Core Value	Example
1. Responsiveness	Have transaction slips mailed on time.
2. Accessibiity	Answer the phone by the fourth ring.
3. Credibility	Do not promise more than you can deliver.
4. Courtesy	Be friendly, even in the face of inaccurate or embarrassing situations
5. Competency	Know your products.
6. Understanding Customers	Take time to learn customer needs.
7. Accuracy	Be accurate with the customer's money.
8. Reliability	Give good service every time and across organizational units.
9. Communication	Be able to explain different services to different customers in language they can understand.

implementing specific strategies and hold them accountable for performance. Assigning responsibility accelerates the planning process.

A good strategic plan thus combines marketing strategies and action plans with profit planning and risk analysis. Each type of strategy should be coordinated to achieve common goals. Each contributes to profitability by targeting markets and eliminating duplicate or conflicting efforts.

SUMMARY

Regulators require banks to plan for their future. This entails coordinating risk analysis with profit planning and marketing in a comprehensive business plan. Strategic planning involves four fundamental issues: evaluating historical performance, setting objectives, developing specific action plans, and comparing actual with planned performance. There are six parts to a strategic plan, including the mission statement, statement of financial objectives, situation analysis, analysis of strengths, weaknesses, opportunities, and threats, the schedule of action plans, and a timetable for meeting objectives.

The planning process forces management to determine what business the bank is in, and to identify the best and worst features of its operating situation. After assessing the bank's current situation, managers design strategies and action plans that will help achieve specific objectives. Such strategies and actions must be customer-focused, they must enhance long-term profitability, and they must maintain the bank's risk profile within acceptable limits.

Questions

Strategic Planning Questions

1. There are six essential parts to a good strategic plan: the mission statement, financial objectives, situation analysis, SWOT, action plans, and goals and timetables. What is the purpose of each part? In what order are the parts created?

2. The following events will have repercussions on one or more of the parts of a bank's strategic plan. Which part will be affected and how could the bank respond?

    a. A foreign bank is preparing to open an office across the street from the bank's principal branch.

    b. A bank employee has been discovered stealing office supplies.

    c. The bank's ATMs have been broken 75 percent more days this past month than for the same period last year.

    d. At the local Senior Support's annual banquet the bank was recognized for its outstanding assistance to local senior citizens.

    e. Research indicates that savings by the 18- to 25-year old population has increased by 25 percent over the past year.

    f. Recently customers have faced long lines at both the teller and the ATM.

    g. The bank recently advertised a limited-time offer of free safety deposit box rental. Not one customer requested the free service.

3. In which of the six parts of the strategic plan would you most likely find the following statements?

    a. The bank will increase deposits by 10 percent each of the next 3 years.

    b. Congress is expected to repeal the Glass-Steagall Act in 2 years.

    c. The bank is a retail bank specializing in the young adult market. Young adults are heavy users of check-writing deposit accounts and home loans.

    d. The bank operates an extremely efficient computer system with outstanding staff.

    e. The bank has and will continue to pay a dividend of 2 dollars per share.

    f. The population in this area is expected to grow at 5 percent per year for the next 5 years. The bank anticipates attracting 5 percent more deposits and consumer loans from this growing market.

    g. The bank will locate a new branch at the corner of Main and Division streets. Ground breaking will occur in January and construction will be completed by September. The office will begin operation by Thanksgiving.

    h. The bank stresses commitment to the local community.

Budgeting Questions

4. Explain the functions of the operating budget and the profit plan. How do they differ?

5. What are the problems of using a budget as a planning tool?

6. Suppose you are the chief financial officer for River Bottom Corporation, whose financial data for the past year are provided below. This is a multibank holding company comparable in size with Valley National Bank and its peers shown in Exhibits 4.4 and 4.5. Senior management has indicated that the bank must increase its net interest margin in order to improve profitability and build its capital base. The policies in Exhibit A have been proposed to achieve these goals.

Assume that all Treasury securities mature in more than 1 year, business and consumer loans mature within 1 year, 10 percent of real estate loans mature within 1 year, and 20 percent of all time deposits mature within 1 year. Demand deposits are never repriced. Carry all calculations to two decimals.

River Bottom Corp.
Balance Sheet
(In Millions of Dollars)

Assets		Liabilities	
Cash	$ 7	Demand deposits	$16
Investments:		Time deposits	57
Federal funds sold	6	Federal funds bought	5
Treasury securities	14	Bonds (mature 2010)	6
		Common stock and surplus	4
Loans		Retained earnings	7
Business	22		
Real estate	20		
Consumer	26		
Total Assets	$95	Total liabilities and equity	$95

River Bottom Corp.
Income Statement
(In Millions of Dollars)

Interest income:	
From investments	$1.40
From loans	7.40
Interest expense:	
On time deposits	4.00
On federal funds	0.10
On bonds	0.90
Net interest income	3.80
Provisions for loan losses	0.80
Noninterest income:	
Fees	1.40
Noninterest expense:	
Salaries and benefits (800 employees)	3.70
Income before tax	0.70
Tax	0.25
Net income	0.45
Dividends	0.14
Retained earnings	0.31

Exhibit A

Cash increases by 12%.
Federal funds sold are zero.
Treasury securities increase by 25%.
Business loans increase by 23%.
Real estate loans increase by 42%.
Consumer loans increase by 20%.
Time deposits increase by 35%.
Forecast average interest rates:
Time deposits: 8.6%
Federal funds: 8.1%
Treasury securities: 8.3%
Business loans: 12.2%
Real estate loans: 13.0%
Consumer loans: 14.4%
Bonds: 15%
Taxes equal 35% of income before taxes.
Dividends equal 30% of net income.
All values not specifically mentioned are unchanged from last year.

---

a. Construct a pro forma balance sheet for next year. Be sure to adjust the retained earnings account to reflect this past year's profits.

b. How much in federal funds will this bank need to purchase to balance its books?

c. Management views the proposed changes as very risky. What risky policy do these changes represent?

d. Construct a pro forma income statement to see if it is likely that this risk will generate increased returns.

e. Management has either forecast no change in loan losses or has forgotten to consider this account. With the other assumptions of Exhibit A, do you think no change is realistic? Are you thinking about actual loan losses or the provision for loan loss account?

f. Calculate the current and projected ROE, ROA, profit margin, asset utilization, and net interest margin.

g. Calculate one measure each of credit risk, liquidity risk, and interest rate risk. For interest rate risk consider the assets and liabilities maturing in less than 1 year.

h. Has the bank increased its risk? What problems will the bank face under this plan? is the additional return adequate?

i. What additional information must be added to this report to generate a compete profit plan?

7. After evaluating the first projection, management decides to consider a more conservative strategy and invest heavily in marketable securities. Exhibit B details the more conservative plan.

Exhibit B

Cash increases 12%.
Business loans decrease by 3%.
Real estate and consumer loans do not change from last year.
Municipal securities of $10 are purchased. They mature in 3 years and pay a taxable equivalent return of 12%.
Treasury securities increase by 65%.
Demand deposits and time deposits do not change from last year.
Noninterest income will increase by 8.7%.
Noninterest expense will rise by 5.4%.

a. Calculate a pro forma balance sheet. Will this bank be buying or selling federal funds?

b. Calculate a pro forma income statement.

c. What is the nominal (contract) interest rate on the municipals?

d. Calculate ROE, ROA, profit margin, asset utilization, and net interest margin for plan B.

e. Calculate risk measures in each key category and interpret differences with A.

f. Explain why the two scenarios of Exhibit A and B produce different outcomes. Which plan would you recommend?

Marketing Questions

8. What four basic wants of customers should the bank marketing plan address?

9. Who in the bank is responsible for marketing the bank's products?

10. How could a bank determine if a customer is a key, normal, or problem customer? Is it right to offer each group different services at different prices? Whether you think it is right or not, what could the bank offer to key customers to encourage their continued relationship?

11. The bank has decided to emphasize three of the nine core values presented in Exhibit 5.5. Which three do you think are most important?

References

Austin, Douglas, and Thomas Scampini. "Long-Term Strategic Planning." *The Bankers Magazine* (January–February 1984).

Board of Governors of the Federal Reserve System. *Functional Cost Analysis.* Washington, D.C. (annual publication).

Booker, Irene, and Robert Rogowski. "Long-Term Bank Management." *Bankers Magazine* (May/June 1987).

Donnelly, James, et al. *Marketing Financial Services: A Strategic Vision.* Homewood, Ill.: Dow Jones-Irwin, 1985.

Aspenwall, Richard, and Robert Eisenbeis, editors. *Handbook for Banking Strategy.* New York: John Wiley & Sons, 1985.

Hart, N. Berne. "Strategic Planning: Responsibility of the CEO." *The Magazine of Bank Administration* (March 1984).

Humphrey, David. "Cost Dispersion and the Measurement of Economies in Banking." *Economic Review* (Federal Reserve Bank of Richmond, May/June 1987).

Kauss, James. "A Guide to Strategic Planning for Banks." *Bank Administration* (August 1987).

"King Customer." *Business Week* (March 12, 1990).

Kolari, James, and Asghar Zardkoohi. *Bank Costs, Structure and Performance.* Lexington, Mass.: D.C. Heath & Company, 1987.

Mester, Loretta. "Efficient Production of Financial Services: Scale and Scope Economies." *Business Review* (Federal Reserve Bank of Philadelphia, January/February 1987).

Pezzullo, Mary Ann. *Marketing For Bankers.* Washington, D.C.: American Bankers Association, 1988.

Reidenbach, Eric, and M. Ray Grubbs. *Developing New Banking Products.* Englewood Cliffs, N.J.: Prentice-Hall, 1987.

Weisler, James. "Planning for Success: Back to Basics." *The Magazine of Bank Administration* (July 1986).

White, William. *Strategic Planning for Bankers.* Washington, D.C.: American Bankers Association, 1984.

Part II

Asset and Liability Management

Chapter 6

Pricing Securities

Suppose you have $1 million to invest for 1 year. The interest rate quoted on every 1-year fixed-income security you consider is 8 percent. If the security pays simple interest, interest income for the year will equal $80,000. If the security pays interest compounded continuously, interest income will total $83,290, or $3,290 more. If the rate is quoted on a money market basis assuming a 360-day year, interest income will equal $81,111. The point is, interest rates that appear to be equal are not necessarily equal. The same percentage quote may produce a different return depending on the frequency of compounding and whether the quote assumes a 360-day or 365-day year.

Of course, interest rates are important to both borrowers and investors. Regulations assist consumer borrowers by requiring banks to quote financing charges at an annual percentage rate that adjusts for these computational differences, and thus enable a direct comparison of alternative borrowing costs. Security investors, in contrast, must fend for themselves and decipher how alternative rate quotes affect the investment's true yield.

This chapter examines three basic issues. First, it introduces the mathematics of interest rates for fixed-income bonds and demonstrates the impact of compounding. Second, it describes the relationship between the interest rate on a security and the security's market price. The concept of duration is used to measure relative price sensitivity to interest rate changes, which can then be compared between securities. Finally, it explains how specific interest rates on different money market and capital market instruments are quoted. Particular attention is paid to differences between money market, bond equivalent, and effective interest rate calculations. Subsequent chapters will refer to these interest rate calculations and incorporate them in various applications.

THE MATHEMATICS OF INTEREST RATES

Just as there are many different types of securities, interest rates are calculated and reported differently. Depending on the characteristics of the security and pricing conventions of securities traders, interest may be simple or compound; interest rates may be quoted on a discount basis or interest-bearing basis; and the assumed number of days in a year for reporting purposes may be 360 or 365. It is virtually impossible to compare quoted rates without a precise understanding of these differences in calculations.

Future Value and Present Value: Single Payment

The mathematics of interest rates are based on the simple recognition that cash in your possession today is worth more than the same amount of cash to be received at some time in the future. For example, are you better off with $50,000 in your hands today or a contract to receive $50,000 in 6 months? Obviously, if you had the cash today, you could invest it for 6 months and it would be worth more than $50,000 at the end of that time. Clearly, the difference in value depends on the interest rate that characterizes your opportunity cost or investment opportunities. This concept, or more precisely that of future value and present value, provides the framework for interest rate calculations.

Suppose that at the beginning of a year, an individual purchases a security for $1,000. The seller of the security, in turn, promises to pay the individual $1,080 exactly 1 year later. In this scenario, $1,000 represents the present value (PV) of the security, $1,080 represents the future value after one year (FV1), and $80 is interest. Expressing the $80 relative to the initial investment as a rate of interest (i),

$$i = \$80/\$1,000 = .08.$$

Alternatively,

$$\$1,000\,(1 + i) = \$1,080,$$

or

$$i = \$1,080/\$1,000 - 1$$
$$= .08.$$

In general, with a single payment (FV1) after one year that includes both interest and the initial investment, the following relationship applies:

$$PV(1 + i) = FV1. \tag{6.1}$$

Suppose that the same individual decides to buy another 1-year security at the end of the first year, and the seller agrees to pay 8 percent on the entire $1,080 invested. Note that the individual is effectively earning interest on the initial $1,000 plus the first year's $80 in interest, so that $1,080 now represents the present value at the beginning of the second year. Substituting $1,080 for PV and .08 for i in equation (6.1) reveals that the future value after the second year (FV2) equals $1,166.40.[1]

---

[1] The numbers in the notations FV1 and FV2 refer to the number of periods from the present until the cash flow arises. This example assumes that interest is earned on interest (compounding), and that interest is compounded annually.

$$\$1,080\,(1+.08)=\$1,164.40=FV2.$$

Combining this with equation (6.1) produces

$$\$1,000\,(1+.08)(1+.08)=\$1,164.40=FV2, \text{ or} \qquad (6.2)$$
$$PV(1+i)^2=FV2.$$

Alternatively, if the future value and present value are known, we can calculate the fixed annual interest rate as:

$$i=[FV2/PV]^{1/2}-1 \qquad (6.3)$$

Using data from the previous example,

$$i=[\$1,164.40/\$1,000]^{1/2}-1=.08.$$

When an amount is invested for several periods and interest is earned on both the initial investment plus periodic interest (compound interest), the following general relationship holds:

$$PV(1+i)^n=FVn \qquad (6.4)$$

where n represents the number of years until the future value is determined. Equation (6.4) can be viewed from several vantage points. There are four variables. As long as three are known, we can solve for the fourth. Thus if we know the initial present value, the periodic interest rate, and the number of years that interest applies, we can solve for the future value as in (6.4). If we know everything except the interest rate, we can use equation (6.5) to solve for i.

$$i=\left[\frac{FVn}{PV}\right]^{1/n}-1. \qquad (6.5)$$

For example, the future value of $1,000 invested for 6 years at 8 percent per year with annual compounding (FV6) is $1,586.87.

$$\$1,000\,(1.08)=\$1,586.87$$

Suppose, instead, that we know that with $1,000 invested today for 6 years, the initial investment plus accumulated interest will be worth $1,700 in 6 years. What is the annual interest rate realized? Clearly, the rate must exceed 8 percent because the future value is greater than the $1,586.87 realized above. Using (6.5), we know that

$$i=\left[\frac{\$1,700}{\$1,000}\right]^{1/6}-1=.0925.$$

In many instances, investors and borrowers are more interested in determining the present value of some future cash payment or receipt. Investors often forecast future cash flows from an asset and want to know their value in today's dollars, that is, how much to pay. Equation (6.4) provides the calculation for the present value of a single future cash flow received after n periods when we solve for PV.

$$PV = \frac{FVn}{(1+i)^n} \tag{6.6}$$

In this case, the future value is said to be discounted back to a present value equivalent. Suppose that you have a choice between receiving an immediate $30,000 cash payment or $37,500 in 2 years. Which would you choose? Assuming you aren't in desperate need of cash today, the answer can be obtained by comparing the present value of $37,500 to $30,000. If your opportunity cost of money is 8 percent, i.e., your investment alternatives yield 8 percent, the present value of the future cash flow is $32,150.

$$PV = \frac{\$37,500}{(1.08)^2} = \$32,150.$$

Intuitively, you would need to invest $32,150 today at 8 percent to accumulate $37,500 in 2 years. Alternatively, the future cash flow is worth $2,150 more than the immediate cash payment offered.

Future Value and Present Value: Multiple Payments

Future value and present value analysis is only slightly more complicated when more than one cash flow is involved. All that changes is that the future or present value of each cash flow is computed separately, with the cumulative value determined as the sum of the computations for each cash flow.

Suppose, for example, that an individual makes a $1,000 deposit in a bank earning 8 percent annually at the beginning of each of the next 2 years. What is the cumulative future value of both deposits after the second year? The first deposit earns 2 years of interest, while the second deposit earns just 1 year of interest. The future value of both deposits after 2 years is:

$$
\begin{aligned}
\text{FV of first deposit} &= \$1,000\,(1.08)^2 &= \$1,164.40 \\
\text{FV of second deposit} &= \$1,000\,(1.08) &= \underline{\$1,080.00} \\
\text{Cumulative future value} & & \$2,244.40
\end{aligned}
$$

In general, setting CFn equal to the periodic cash flow in period n and assuming that all cash flows are invested at the beginning of each year at the fixed rate i, the cumulative future value of a series of cash flows (CFVn) after n periods can be expressed as:

$$CFVn = CF1(1+i)^n + CF2(1+i)^{n-1} + CF3(1+i)^{n-2} + \ldots + CFn(1+i) \tag{6.7}$$

This type of calculation is often used when trying to determine how much needs to be invested periodically to fund a future expenditure, such as payments for a child's college education.

The present value concept is more typically applied to a series of future cash flows. Investors may know the promised payments on a bond, or they forecast the expected cash flows from buying a business. The present value of a series of cash flows equals the sum of the present value of the individual cash flows. Using the above notation and assumptions, the present value of a series of n cash flows can be expressed as:

$$PV = \frac{CF1}{(1+i)} + \frac{CF2}{(1+i)^2} + \frac{CF3}{(1+t)^3} + \dots + \frac{CFn}{(1+i)^n} \qquad \textbf{(6.8)}$$

or, using summation notation

$$PV = \sum_{t=1}^{n} \frac{CFt}{(1+i)^t}$$

Intuitively, each future cash flow is discounted back to its present value equivalent, and the respective present values are added. Note that (6.8) assumes the same discount rate (i) applies to each cash flow.

For example, how much would you pay for a security that pays $90 at the end of each of the next 3 years plus another $1,000 at the end of the third year if the relevant interest rate is 10 percent? Using equation (6.8),

$$PV = \frac{\$90}{(1.1)} + \frac{\$90}{(1.1)^2} + \frac{\$1,090}{(1.1)^3} = \$975.13.$$

Again, if the present value, futures values, and number of periods are known, we can solve equation (6.8) for i to determine the relevant discount rate. For fixed-income securities, this discount rate is the market rate of interest.

Simple versus Compound Interest

In practice, the amount of interest paid on a security is determined in many different ways. One difference is that interest may be computed as *simple interest* or *compound interest*. Simple interest is interest that is paid only on the initial principal invested. Bank commercial loans, for example, normally quote simple interest payments. In contrast, compound interest is interest paid on outstanding principal plus any interest that has been earned, but not paid out. Most bank deposits pay compound interest.

Simple interest equals the outstanding principal amount times the periodic interest rate times the number of periods. With the previous notation,

$$\text{simple interest} = PV(i)n \qquad \textbf{(6.9)}$$

In this case, the interest rate i is the periodic rate while n refers to the number of periods. Thus if n equals one year and i equals 12 percent per annum, simple interest on $1,000 equals

$$\text{simple interest} = \$1,000\,(.12)1 = \$120.$$

Suppose that interest on the above contract is paid monthly. What is the monthly simple interest payment?

$$\text{monthly simple interest} = \$1,000\,(.12/12)1 = \$10.$$

The example following equation (6.5) demonstrated that $1,000 invested for six years at 8 percent assuming annual interest compounding produced a future value of $1,586.87. This assumed that interest was earned annually on the previous years' cumulative interest. Suppose that interest is 8 percent simple interest. What will the future value of principal plus interest equal?

$$\text{simple interest} = \$1,000 \,(.08)\, 6 = \$480$$
$$\text{original principal} = \$1,000$$
$$\text{future value} = \$1,480$$

Obviously, the actual interest varies dramatically depending on whether simple or compound interest applies.

As indicated, compound interest assumes that interest is paid on principal and interest. Each of the equations (6.1) through (6.8) uses annual interest rates and assumes annual compounding.

Compounding Frequency

Interest may be compounded over a variety of intervals. In many cases, it is compounded over periods much less than a year, such as daily or monthly. Fortunately, the same formulas apply with a small adjustment. The adjustment consists of converting the annual interest rate to a periodic interest rate that coincides with the compounding interval, and letting the number of periods equal n times the number of compounding periods in a year (m). Specifically, letting m equal the number of compounding periods in one year,

$$\text{PV} \,(1 + i/m)^{nm} = \text{Future Value} \tag{6.10}$$

and

$$\text{PV} = \frac{\text{FVn}}{(1 + i/m)^{nm}} \tag{6.11}$$

If compounding occurs daily, m equals 365 and the periodic rate equals the annual rate divided by 365. If compounding occurs monthly, m equals 12 and the periodic rate equals i divided by 12. The product of n times m equals the total number of compounding periods. Exhibit 6.1 demonstrates the impact of different intrayear compounding intervals on future value and present value in line with equations (6.10) and (6.11). As indicated, the future value after 1 year is greatest when compounding frequency is the highest. This is an intuitive result because more frequent compounding means that interest is applied to previous interest more frequently. In a similar vein, the present value of a fixed amount is the lowest when compounding frequency is highest. Again, the more interest that can be earned, the lower the initial value required to invest and return the same future value.

Exhibit 6.1 also demonstrates the impact of different effective interest rates. An effective interest rate, in contrast to a nominal or contract rate of interest, incorporates the effect of compounding and thus allows a comparison of yields. Assuming com-

Exhibit 6.1 The Effect of Compounding on Future Value and Present Value

A. What is the future value after 1 year of $1,000 invested at an 8% annual nominal rate?

Compounding Interval	Number of Compounding Intervals in 1 Year (m)	Future Value (FV1)[a]	Effective Interest Rate
Year	1	$1080.00	8.00%
Semiannual	2	1081.60	8.16
Quarter	4	1082.43	8.24
Month	12	1083.00	8.30
Day	365	1083.21	8.32
Continuous	[b]	1083.29	8.33

B. What is the present value of $1,000 received at the end of 1 year with compounding at 8%?

Compounding Interval	Number of Compounding Intervals in 1 year (m)	Present Value (PV)[a]	Effective Interest Rate[a]
Year	1	$925.93	8.00%
Semiannual	2	924.56	8.16
Quarter	4	923.85	8.24
Month	12	923.36	8.30
Day	365	923.18	8.32
Continuous	[b]	923.16	8.33

[a]Most financial calculators can easily generate the required calculations

[b]Continuous compounding assumes that compounding occurs over such short intervals that it is instantaneous, or that m in equations 6.10 and 6.11 approaches infinity. Mathematically, continuous compounding is based on Euler's e such that

$\text{limit}\left(1+\dfrac{1}{m}\right)^{m} = e^{i}$ as z approaches infinity, where e = 2.71828. Thus equations 6.10 and 6.11 produce $FVn = PVe^{in}$, and

$PV = \dfrac{FVn}{e^{in}}$.

pounding frequency of at least once a year, the effective annual interest rate, i*, can be calculated from (6.12).[2]

$$i^{*} = (1 + i/m)^{m} - 1. \qquad (6.12)$$

THE RELATIONSHIP BETWEEN INTEREST RATES AND BOND PRICES

As indicated earlier, present value and future value are linked via precise mathematical relationships (6.4) and (6.8). This suggests that there are systematic relationships between PV, future cash flows, i, and n. In fact, much research has attempted to characterize the exact influence of each variable on the pricing relationships. The following analysis focuses on the relationship between bond prices and their associated market interest rates, and how this relationship changes as the magnitude and timing of

[2]With continuous compounding $i^{*} = e^{i} - 1$.

Exhibit 6.2 Price and Yield Relationships for Bonds that are Equivalent Except for the Feature Analyzed

Relationship	Impact
1. Market interest rates and bond prices vary inversely.	1. Bond prices fall as interest rates rise, and rise as interest rates fall.
2. For a specific absolute change in interest rates, the proportionate incease in bond prices when rates fall exceeds the proprotionate decrease in bond prices when rates rise. The proportionate difference increases with maturity and is larger the lower a bond's periodic interest payment.	2. For the identical absolute change in interest rates, a bond holder will realize a greater capital gain when rates decline than capital loss when rates increase.
3. Long-term bonds change proportionately more in price than short-term bonds for a given change in interest rates from the same base level.	3. Investors can realize greater capital gains and capital losses on long-term securities than on short-term securities when interest rates change by the same amount.
4. Low-coupon bonds change proportionately more in price than high-coupon bonds for a given change in interest rates from the same base level.	4. Low-coupon bonds exhibit greater relative price volatility than do high-coupon bonds.

future cash flows vary.[3] Exhibit 6.2 summarizes the features of four systematic price relationships.

Bond Prices and Interest Rates Vary Inversely

Market interest rates and prices on fixed-income securities vary coincidentally and are inversely related.[4] Prices decline when interest rates rise and prices rise when interest rates decline. The sensitivity of the price move to the change in interest rates is determined by the size and timing of the cash flows on the underlying security. For coupon bonds, the periodic cash flows consist of interest payments and par value at maturity. The appropriate pricing relationship is characterized by equation (6.8). Only now, the price of a security equals the present value and the interest rate equals the yield to maturity.

Consider a bond that makes fixed semiannual interest payments of $470 and matures in exactly 3 years, at which time the investor receives $10,000 in principal. If the current market interest rate equals 9.4 percent per annum (4.7 percent semiannually), the prevailing price of the bond equals $10,000 as determined below.

---

[3]The following discussion is based on Burton Malkeil (1962) and Fabozzi and Fabozzi (1989).

[4]Securities that carry floating rates or variable rates pay interest that changes as market rates change. Such instruments consequently trade close to par. The following price/yield relationships apply only to fixed-income securities.

$$\text{Price} = \sum_{t=1}^{6} \frac{\$470}{(1.047)^t} + \frac{\$10,000}{(1.047)^6} = \$10,000.$$

At 9.4 percent, this bond sells at par or face value.

Now suppose that the corporate issuer of the bonds announces unexpectedly poor earnings and forecasts a declining capacity to service its debt in the future. Owners of the bonds subsequently rush to sell their holdings. What should happen to the market interest rate and price of the bond? If the announcement was truly unexpected, then the perceived riskiness of the security has increased. Holders recognize that there is a greater probability that the promised cash flows may not materialize. Therefore, they discount the expected cash flows at a higher rate. This means that investors now require a larger default risk premium, reflected by a higher market interest rate, to entice them to buy the bond. If the annual rate increased to 10 percent, the price of the bond would fall to $9,847.72. With a price below par, this bond becomes a discount bond.

$$\text{Price} = \sum_{t=1}^{6} \frac{\$470}{(1.05)^t} + \frac{\$10,000}{(1.05)^6} = \$9,847.72.$$

Thus a bond's price and market interest rate vary inversely when market rates rise. If, instead, the market interest rate immediately fell to 8.8 percent, the bond's price would rise to $10,155.24. In this scenario, the bond becomes a premium bond because its price exceeds par.

$$\text{Price} = \sum_{t=1}^{6} \frac{\$470}{(1.044)^t} + \frac{\$10,000}{(1.044)^6} = \$10,155.24.$$

Exhibit 6.3 plots the relationship between the price and market interest rate on this bond. As indicated, higher bond prices are associated with lower market interest rates, and vice versa.

The ratio of the annualized periodic interest payment to a bond's par value is labeled the coupon rate. In the previous example, the coupon rate equaled 9.4 percent ($2 \times \$470/\$10,000$). The following schedule describes the general relationship between yield to maturity, coupon rate, and bond price.

Type of Bond	Yield to Maturity vs Coupon Rate
Par Bond	Yield to maturity = coupon rate
Discount Bond	Yield to maturity > coupon rate
Premium Bond	Yield to maturity < coupon rate

Bond Prices Change Asymmetrically to Rising and Falling Rates

For a given absolute change in interest rates, the percentage increase in a bond's price will exceed the percentage decrease. Consider the price-to-yield relationship in Exhibit 6.3. When the bond is priced at par, the market rate equals 9.4 percent. If the market yield suddenly increases by 60 basis points to 10 percent, the price falls by $152.28, or 1.52 percent. If the market yield suddenly decreases by the same 60 basis points to 8.8 percent, the price rises by $155.24, or 1.55 percent. While the proportionate

Exhibit 6.3 Relationship Between Price and Interest Rate on a 3-year $10,000 par bond that pays $470 in Semiannual Interest

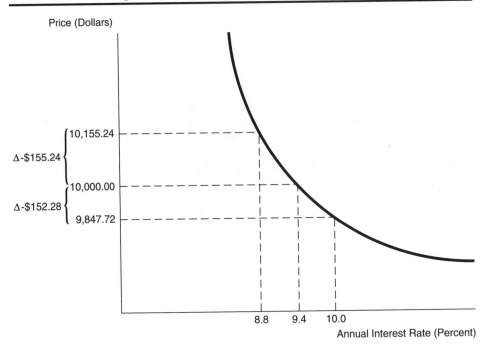

difference may seem small, it increases with maturity and is larger for bonds with lower periodic interest payments. The dollar difference will also increase with greater par value.

This asymmetric price relationship is due to the convex shape of the curve in Exhibit 6.3, which reflects a difference in bond duration at different interest rate levels. The duration concept and applications are discussed later in the chapter. The primary implication is that for the same change in interest rates, holders of bonds will realize a greater capital gain when rates fall than capital loss when rates rise.

Maturity Influences Bond Price Sensitivity

Short-term and long-term bonds exhibit different price volatility. For bonds that pay the same coupon interest rate, long-term bonds change proportionately more in price than short-term bonds for a given change in rates. Exhibit 6.4 contrasts the price-yield relationship for a 9.4 percent coupon bond with 6 years to maturity to that of the 3-year bond with the same coupon discussed earlier. Note than the only difference between the two bonds is final maturity and thus the number of interim cash flows prior to maturity. When both market rates equal 9.4 percent, both bonds are priced at par. The

Exhibit 6.4 The Effect of Maturity on the Relationship Between Price and Interest Rate on Fixed-Income Bonds

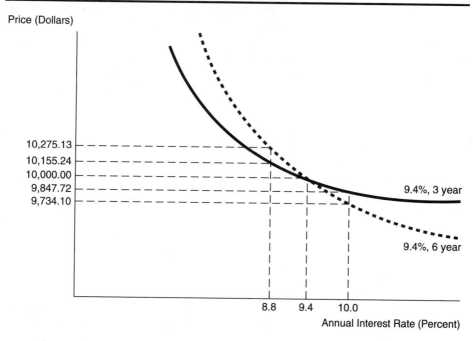

following calculations indicate the price of the 6-year bond when the market rate rises to 10 percent and falls to 8.8 percent, respectively.

$$\text{Price} = \sum_{t=1}^{12} \frac{\$470}{(1.05)^t} + \frac{\$10,000}{(1.05)^{12}} = \$9,734.10$$

$$\text{Price} = \sum_{t=1}^{12} \frac{\$470}{(1.044)^t} + \frac{\$10,000}{(1.044)^{12}} = \$10,275.13$$

As indicated in Exhibit 6.4, when rates increase by 60 basis points on both bonds, the price of the 6-year bond falls lower than the price of the 3-year bond. The proportionate price declines are 2.66 percent and 1.52 percent, respectively. When rates decline by 60 basis points, the 6-year bond increases 2.75 percent in price while the 3-year bond's price increases by 1.55 percent.

The rationale for the different price sensitivity has to do with the basic present value equation (6.8). The buyer of a 6-year bond contracts to receive fixed interest payments for twice as many periods as the buyer of a 3-year bond. When priced at par, the coupon and market rate equal 9.4 percent. If market rates increase, buyers of newly issued par bonds will receive periodic interest at a higher market (and coupon) rate. Holders of "old" discount bonds now receive below-market interest payments. With the 6-year bond these below-market payments will persist for twice as long as with the 3-year bond. Thus the price of the 6-year bond declines more than the price of the 3-year bond. The opposite holds when interest rates fall. The holder of a 6-year bond receives above market interest payments which are locked in for twice as long as for the 3-year bond. Thus the price of a 6-year bond will rise above the price of a 3-year bond.

Suppose that an investor owned a similar 9.4 percent coupon bond with 9 years to maturity. If the market rate changes from 9.4 percent to 10 percent, its price drops from $10,000 to $9,649.29.

$$\text{Price} = \sum_{t=1}^{18} \frac{\$470}{(1.05)^t} + \frac{\$10,000}{(1.05)^{18}} = \$9,649.29$$

Not surprisingly, this is well below the price of the 6-year bond at 10 percent. The following schedule compares the percentage price changes for the 3, 6, and 9-year bonds when interest rates rise from 9.4 percent to 10 percent.

	Price Change		
	3-Year	**6-Year**	**9-Year**
Percentage Change	−1.52%	−2.66%	−3.51%
Difference		−1.14%	−0.85%

Note that the rate of change in the percentage price decline falls from 1.14 percent to 0.85 percent as maturity lengthens. This relationship holds in general; as maturity lengthens the rate of change in the percentage price change declines. You should verify this for the 9-year bond in the case where its rate falls to 8.8 percent.

The Size of Coupon Influences Bond Price Sensitivity

High-coupon and low-coupon bonds exhibit different price volatility. Suppose that two bonds are priced to yield the same rate to final maturity. For a given change in market rate, the bond with the lower coupon will change more in price than the bond with the higher coupon. This is demonstrated in Exhibit 6.5, which plots the price and yield relationship for two otherwise identical 3-year maturity instruments: a zero coupon bond and the 9.4 percent coupon bond introduced earlier. As the market rate falls below 9.4 percent, the price of the zero coupon bond rises by proportionately more than the price of the coupon bond. At 8.8 percent, the price of the zero coupon bond rises by 1.7 percent while the price of the 9.4 percent bond rises by just 1.55 percent. The same comparative relationship appears when the market rate rises to 10 percent. Again, this difference rises with maturity and may be quite substantial with large-denomination securities.

DURATION AND PRICE VOLATILITY

The previous discussion of bond price volatility focuses on the relationship between a security's market rate of interest, periodic interest payment, and final maturity. The

Exhibit 6.5 The Relationship Between Price and
Interest Rate on Fixed-Income Bonds

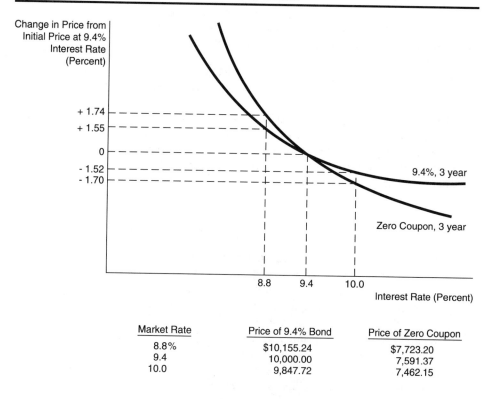

Market Rate	Price of 9.4% Bond	Price of Zero Coupon
8.8%	$10,155.24	$7,723.20
9.4	10,000.00	7,591.37
10.0	9,847.72	7,462.15

price rules, in fact, indicate that volatility changes systematically as each of these factors changes. Most financial economists look to **duration** as a comprehensive measure of these same volatility relationships. Simply focusing on interest rate changes ignores the size of interest payments and length of time until each payment is received. Because maturity simply identifies how much time elapses until final payment, it ignores all information about the timing and magnitude of interim payments. The size of coupon, in turn, provides no information as to the rate at which interim cash flows can be reinvested or even how many cash flows are promised.

Duration as an Elasticity Measure

Duration is a measure of effective maturity that incorporates the timing and size of a security's cash flows. It captures the combined impact of market rate, the size of interim payments, and maturity on a security's price volatility. Conceptually, duration is most easily understood as a measure of interest elasticity in determining the market value of a security. Thus, if a security's duration is known, an investor can readily estimate the size of a change in value (or price) for different magnitudes of interest rate changes.[5]

Recall that the price elasticity of demand for a good or service indicates how much quantity demanded will change when the price changes. In general,

$$\text{price elasticity of demand} = -\frac{\%\text{ change in quantity demanded}}{\%\text{ change in price}}$$

Because quantity demanded varies inversely with price changes, the minus sign converts the relative percentage changes to a positive measure. Thus, if a bank raises its charge for usage of an automatic teller machine (ATM) from 50 cents to 75 cents per item, and the number of monthly ATM transactions drops from 100,000 to 70,000, the price elasticity of demand is estimated at 0.6.

$$\text{price elasticity of demand} = -\frac{-30,000/100,000}{\$0.25/\$0.50} = \frac{.3}{.5} = 0.6$$

This elasticity measure indicates that a proportionate change in price coincides with a smaller proportionate change in quantity demanded. If the elasticity remained constant at higher prices, the bank could estimate that a price increase to $1 per item (25 percent) would lower usage to 59,500 (–15 percent) items monthly.

A security's duration can similarly be interpreted as an elasticity measure. Instead of the relationship between quantity demanded and price, however, duration provides information about the change in market value as a result of interest rate changes. Letting P equal the price of a security and i equal the prevailing market interest rate on the security, duration can be approximated by the following expression.

$$\text{Duration} \cong -\left[\frac{\dfrac{\Delta P}{P}}{\dfrac{\Delta i}{(1+i)}}\right] \tag{6.13}$$

Consider the 3-year zero coupon bond from Exhibit 6.5 that pays $10,000 at maturity. At an annual market rate of 9.4%, this bond's price equals $7,591, assuming semiannual compounding. As demonstrated later, this bond has a duration of exactly 3 years, or six semiannual periods. An analyst can use (6.13) to estimate the change in price of this bond when the market rate changes. Restating the expression,

$$\Delta P = -\text{ Duration } [\Delta i/(1+i)]\, P \tag{6.14}$$

Suppose the market rate rises immediately from 4.7 percent to 5 percent semiannually. Using semiannual data, the estimated change in price equals -$130.50, or 1.72 percent of the price.

---

[5]The following discussion uses Macaulay's measure of duration which is introduced formally later in the chapter.

$$\Delta P = -6[.003/1.047]\$7,591$$
$$= -\$130.50$$

Exhibit 6.5 demonstrates that the actual price change equals –$129.22.

Measuring Duration

Duration is measured in units of time, and represents a security's effective maturity. More precisely, it is a weighted average of the time until expected cash flows from a security will be received, relative to the current price of the security. The weights are the present values of each cash flow. Early cash flows thus carry a greater weight than later cash flows, and the greater the cash flow the greater the weight and contribution to the duration estimate.

The following examples use Macaulay's duration, which was first introduced in 1938. While this duration measure has been modified to improve its applicability, it serves as a useful first approximation. Chapter 8, which addresses interest rate risk management issues, summarizes criticisms of Macaulay's duration and offers extensions.

Consider the 9.4 percent, 3-year bond with a face value of $10,000. The duration of this security, assuming that it is currently priced at par, is not called prior to maturity, and all interest and principal payments are made as scheduled, is 5.36 semiannual periods. This calculation is demonstrated in Exhibit 6.6. Note that each cash flow is converted to its present value by discounting at the prevailing market rate of 4.7 percent. Each present value is then multiplied by the units of time until the cash flow arises, with the sum then divided by the prevailing price.

Using general notation, Macaulay's duration (D) appears as:

$$D = \frac{\displaystyle\sum_{t=1}^{k} \frac{CF_t(t)}{(1+i)^t}}{\displaystyle\sum_{t=1}^{k} \frac{CF_t}{(1+i)^t}} \tag{6.15}$$

where

CFt = dollar value of the cash flow at time t
  t = the number of periods of time until the cash flow payment
  i = the yield to maturity of the security generating the cash flow
  k = the number of cash flows.

As described earlier, the numerator equals the present value of each cash flow times the number of periods until the cash flow arises. The denominator is simply the price of the instrument. A basic contribution of duration is that it accounts for differences between securities in time until interim cash flows are received. Large, near-term cash flows receive the greatest weight and thus shorten estimated duration.

Consider, for example, the coupon bond and zero coupon bond described in Exhibit 6.5. With the zero coupon security there are no interim cash flows. The only

Exhibit 6.6 A Sample Duration Calculation

A. Time Line Characterizing Cash Flows

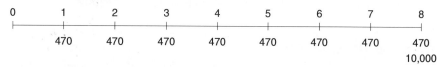

B. Estimated Macaulay's Duration

$$\text{Duration} = \frac{\dfrac{470[1]}{(1.047)} + \dfrac{470[2]}{(1.047)^2} + \dfrac{470[3]}{(1.047)^3} + \dfrac{470[4]}{(1.047)^4} + \dfrac{470[5]}{(1.047)^5} + \dfrac{10,470[6]}{(1.047)^6}}{10,000}$$

$$= \frac{448.91[1] + 428.8[2] + 409.5[3] + 391.1[4] + 373.6[5] + 7,948[6]}{10,000}$$

$$= \frac{53,656.6}{10,000}$$

$$= 5.36 \text{ semiannual periods (or 2.68 years)}$$

payment is \$10,000 after 3 years. Using (6.15), its estimated duration is six semiannual periods.

$$\text{Duration of 3-year zero} = \frac{[\$10,000/1.047]^6}{\$10,000/1.047} = 6$$

Yet, the 3-year coupon bond's duration is just 5.36 semiannual periods because there are interim cash flows. Its effective maturity is shorter because an investor receives cash payments prior to final maturity. In general, the duration of a zero coupon security equals its final maturity. The duration of any security with interim cash flows will be less than its final maturity.

Comparative Price Sensitivity

The duration concept is useful because it enables market participants to estimate the relative price volatility of different securities. The greater a security's duration, the greater is its price sensitivity. This is reflected in relationship (6.14) and the following extensions.

$$\frac{\Delta P}{P} \cong -\text{Duration}\left[\frac{\Delta i}{1+i}\right] \tag{6.16}$$

$$\frac{\Delta P/P}{\Delta i/i} = -\text{Duration}\left[\frac{i}{1+i}\right] \tag{6.17}$$

Relationship (6.17) characterizes the formal elasticity relationship between interest rates and bond prices. These relationships are quite intuitive. For example, two par bonds may carry the same market rate of interest, but have different maturities and durations. The two bonds in Exhibit 6.4 are both priced at par when market rates equal 9.4 percent. According to the above formulas, the bond with the longest duration will exhibit the greatest price volatility.

This relationship is demonstrated in Exhibit 6.7 for these two coupon bonds and two zero coupon bonds. All of the bonds are assumed to carry an annual yield of 9.4 percent, but have different prices and durations depending on maturity and whether interim interest payments are made. Thus the two zero coupon bonds have durations of 6 and 12 semiannual periods, and trade at discount prices well below the $10,000 face value common to all four bonds. As implied above, the durations of the coupon bonds are slightly less than final maturity.

Suppose that market yields on all four bonds suddenly increase to 10 percent, or 5 percent semiannually. The comparative absolute change in price, percentage change in price, and initial elasticities are provided at the bottom of the Exhibit. Consider the two zero coupon bonds. With the same absolute and percentage change in market rates, the longer duration 6-year bond exhibits the greater price decline both in absolute and percentage terms. This is consistent with its greater interest rate elasticity of 0.5387 versus 0.2693. Consider now the two coupon bonds. Not surprisingly, the same relative price sensitivity appears. With the rate increase, the bond with duration of 9.45 semiannual periods falls more than $117 in price from the $10,000 base compared with the shorter duration bond. This is again consistent with its higher interest rate elasticity.

Exhibit 6.7 thus reveals that there is a direct relationship between duration and relative price sensitivity. The greater is duration, the greater is a security's percentage change in price and interest rate elasticity when securities carry the same initial yields. When securities carry different yields, they can similarly be ranked by relative interest rate elasticities and durations.

MONEY MARKET YIELDS

Unfortunately, while the general pricing relationships introduced above are straightforward, practical applications are complicated by the fact that interest rates on different securities are measured and quoted in different terms. This is particularly true of yields on money market instruments such as Treasury bills, federal funds, CDs, repurchase agreements, Eurodollars, bankers acceptances, and commercial paper, which have initial maturities of less than 1 year. Some of these instruments trade on a discount basis, while others are interest-bearing. Some yields are quoted assuming a 360-day year, while others assume a 365-day year. The following discussion extends the analysis of interest rate mathematics to money market instruments and provides procedures that allow a comparison of effective annual yields.

Exhibit 6.7 Comparative Price Sensitivity Indicated by Duration

	Type of Bond			
	3-Yr Zero	**6-Yr Zero**	**3-Yr Coupon**	**6-Yr Coupon**
Initial market rate (annual)	9.40%	9.40%	9.40%	9.40%
Initial market rate (semiannual)	4.70%	4.70%	4.70%	4.70%
Maturity value	$10,000	$10,000	$10,000	$10,000
Initial price	$7,591.37	$5,762.89	$10,000	$10,000
Duration: semiannual periods	6.00	12.00	5.36	9.45
Rate Increases to 10% (5% Semiannually)				
Estimated ΔP	−$130.14	−$198.15	−$153.58	−$270.77
Estimated $\dfrac{\Delta P}{P}$	−1.71%	−3.44%	−1.54%	−2.71%
Initial elasticity	0.2693	0.5387	0.2406	0.4242

Formulas

$$\Delta P = -\text{Duration}\,[\Delta i/(1+i)]P$$

$$\frac{\Delta P}{P} = -\text{Duration}\,[\Delta i/(1+i)]$$

$$\frac{\Delta P/P}{\Delta i/i} = -\text{Duration}\,[i/(1+i)]$$

Interest-Bearing Loans With Maturities of 1 Year or Less

Many short-term consumer and commercial loans have maturities less than 1 year in which the borrower makes periodic interest payments and repays the principal at maturity. The effective annual rate of interest depends on the term of the loan and the compounding frequency. If the loan has exactly 1 year to maturity, equation (6.12) characterizes the effective annual yield. Thus a 1-year loan that requires monthly interest payments at 12 percent annually (one percent monthly), carries an effective yield of 12.68 percent.

$$i^* = (1.01)^{12} - 1 = 0.1268$$

Suppose, instead, that the same loan was made for just 90 days at an annualized stated rate of 12 percent. With this short maturity, there is more than one compounding period in a year. The modified form of (6.12) assumes a 365-day year and calculates the number of compounding periods as 365 divided by the number of days in the contract holding period (h), which is 90 in this example. In general,

$$i^* = \left[1 + \frac{i}{(365/h)}\right]^{365/h} - 1 \tag{6.18}$$

This 90-day loan thus has 365/90 compounding periods in a year, and the effective annual yield is 12.55 percent.

$$i^* = \left[1 + \frac{.12}{(365/90)} \right]^{365/90} - 1 = 0.1255$$

360-Day versus 365-Day Yields

The effective annual yield on a security must reflect the true yield to an investor who holds the underlying instrument for a full year, that is, for 365 days in all but leap years. Some money market rates are, in fact, reported on the basis of an assumed 360-day year. While interest is actually earned for all 365 days in a year, the full amount of interest implied by the reported rate is earned in just 360 days. Thus, $1,000 invested for one year at 8 percent under the 360-day method pays $80 in interest after 360 days, rather than after 365 days. Because the investor gets the same interest 5 days earlier, the principal and interest can be invested for 5 additional days' interest. An investor therefore earns a higher effective rate of interest under the 360-day method.

It is easy to convert a 360-day rate to a 365-day rate, and vice versa. This is done according to the following formula:

$$i_{365} = i_{360}\,(365/360)$$

where

$$i_{365} = 365\text{-day rate, and}$$
$$i_{360} = 360\text{-day rate.}$$

The 360-day rate is simply multiplied by a factor of 365/360. Effective annual yields, in turn, must reflect both 365 days of interest and compounding frequency. Converting a 360-day yield to an effective annual yield thus involves two steps. First, the yield is converted to a 365-day yield. Second, the 365-day yield is used for i in equations (6.12) and (6.18).

For example, a 1 year investment that carries an 8 percent nominal rate quoted on a 360-day basis generates an effective annual yield of 8.11 percent.

$$i_{365} = .08(365/360)$$
$$= .0811.$$

This rate would be used in all formulas to compute effective yields.

Discount Yields

Some money market instruments, such as Treasury bills, repurchase agreements, commercial paper, and bankers acceptances are pure discount instruments. This means that the purchase price is always less than the par value at maturity. The difference between the purchase price and par value equals the periodic interest. Yields on discount instruments are calculated and quoted on a discount basis assuming a 360-day year, and thus are not comparable to yields on interest-bearing instruments.

The pricing equation for discount instruments used by professional traders is:

$$i_{dr} = \left[\frac{Pf - Po}{Pf} \right] \frac{(360)}{h} \qquad \textbf{(6.19)}$$

where

i_{dr} = discount rate,
Po = initial price of the instrument,
Pf = final price of the instrument at maturity or sale, and
h = number of days in holding period.

There are several peculiar features to this discount rate. First, the amount of interest earned is divided by the final price or maturity value, and not by the initial amount invested to obtain a percentage return. Second, as noted above, it assumes a 360-day year. The discount rate thus understates the effective annual rate. In order to obtain an effective yield, the formula must be modified to reflect a 365-day year and to account for the fact that returns are normally computed by dividing interest received by the amount invested. These problems can be addressed by calculating a bond equivalent rate (i_{be}) according to (6.20).

$$i_{be} = \left[\frac{Pf - Po}{Po} \right] \frac{(365)}{h} \qquad (6.20)$$

Consider, for example, a $1 million par value Treasury bill with exactly 182 days to maturity, priced at $965,400. The discount rate on the bill is 7.02 percent.

$$i_{dr} = \left[\frac{\$1,000,000 - \$964,500}{\$1,000,000} \right] \frac{(360)}{182}$$

$$= .0702$$

The bond equivalent rate, in turn, equals 7.38 percent.

$$i_{be} = \left[\frac{\$1,000,000 - \$964,500}{\$964,500} \right] \frac{(365)}{182}$$

$$= .0738$$

To obtain an effective annual rate, compounding must be incorporated by applying equation (6.18). Implicitly, an investor is assumed to reinvest the proceeds at the same periodic rate for the remainder of the 365 days in a year. Here the effective annual rate equals 7.52 percent.

$$i^* = \left(1 + \frac{.0738}{(365/182)} \right)^{365/182} - 1$$

$$= .0752$$

Yields on repurchase agreements, commercial paper, and bankers acceptances are also quoted on a discount basis. For comparison with non-discount instruments, their yields must be converted in the same manner as those of Treasury bills in a two-step process. The 360-day yield is converted to a 365-day bond equivalent yield, then compounding is taken into account via equation (6.18).

Yields on Single-Payment Interest-Bearing Securities

Some money market instruments, such as large, negotiable certificates of deposit (CDs), Eurodollars, and federal funds, pay interest that is calculated against the par value of the security and make a single payment of both interest and principal at maturity. The nominal interest rate is quoted as a percentage of par and assumes a 360-day year. Thus, the nominal rate again understates the effective annual rate.

Consider a 182-day CD with a par value of $1,000,000 and quoted yield of 7.02 percent, the same quoted rate as the Treasury bill. The actual amount of interest paid after 182 days equals

$$(.0702)(182/360)\$1,000,000, \text{ or } \$3549.$$

The 365-day yield equals

$$i_{365} = .0702 (365/360) = .0718.$$

Finally, the effective annual rate equals

$$i^* = \left[1 + \frac{.0718}{(365/182)}\right]^{365/182} - 1 = .0731.$$

A careful reader will note that both the 365-day yield and the effective annual rate on the CD are below the corresponding bond equivalent yield and effective annual rate on the Treasury bill with the same maturity and a 7.02 percent discount rate. This demonstrates the difference between discount and interest-bearing instruments. In particular, the discount rate is calculated as a return on par value, not on initial investment as with interest-bearing instruments. Thus a discount rate understates both the 365-day rate and effective rate by a greater percentage.

Exhibit 6.8 summarizes the conventions for interest rate quotations in the money market and identifies specific instruments that are priced under each convention. The essential point is that investors must be aware of how yields are quoted and calculated before they compare percentages.

SUMMARY

Interest rates play an important role in facilitating the flow of funds between lenders and borrowers. Borrowers prefer low rates that will lower interest expense, while lenders prefer high rates that will enhance interest income. This chapter provides an overview of the mathematics of interest rates to assist in comparing quoted rates between securities and presents concepts that are useful in evaluating the price sensitivity of fixed-income securities.

There are several key conclusions. First, fixed-income securities are priced according to the mathematics of present value and future value. The effective price and yield in turn depends on the frequency of compounding. The greater is the compounding frequency, the greater is the amount of interest. Second, prices and yields on fixed-income securities exhibit well-defined relationships. When interest rates change, prices

Exhibit 6.8 Summary of Money Market Yield Quotations and Calculations

A. Simple Interest Rate i_s:

$$i_s = \frac{Pf - Po}{Po}$$

B. Discount Rate i_{dr}:

$$i_{dr} = \left[\frac{Pf - Po}{Pf}\right]\frac{360}{h}$$

C. Money Market 360-Day Rate i_{360}:

$$i_{360} = \left[\frac{Pf - Po}{Po}\right]\frac{360}{h}$$

D. Bond Equivalent 365-Day Rate i_{365}:

$$i_{365} = \left[\frac{Pf - Po}{Po}\right]\frac{365}{h}$$

E. Effective Annual Interest Rate i^*:

$$i* = \left[1 + \frac{i}{(365/h)}\right]^{365/h}$$

Definitions

Pf = Final value

Po = Initial value

h = Number of days in holding period

Discount Yield Quotes: Treasury bills
Repurchase agreements
Commercial paper
Bankers acceptances

Interest-Bearing, Single Payment: Negotiable CDs
Federal funds

---

move in the opposite direction. The proportionate price move is relatively greater when rates fall compared to when rates rise. Similarly, the proportionate magnitude of the price move typically increases with maturity and decreases with the size of the coupon payment. This is largely revealed by a security's duration because the greater is duration, the greater is the proportionate price change for a given change in interest rates. Thus longer-duration securities exhibit greater price volatility. Finally, rates on specific money market securities differ because some are quoted on a 360-day versus a 365-day basis and some are discount rates versus bond-equivalent rates. The primary point is that borrowers and lenders must carefully examine the contract terms of specific securities to understand the effective cost or yield.

Questions

The Math

1. If you invest $300 today in a security paying 12% compounded quarterly, how much will the investment be worth 7 years from today?

2. If you invest $200 in an investment today, how much will it be worth 6 years from today? The investment pays 8% compounded monthly.

3. What is the effective annual interest rate of 20% compounded quarterly and 20% compounded daily?

4. What would the loan payments be for a $15,000 loan at 12% compounded monthly? The loan will be repaid in 24 monthly payments.

5. How much would you be willing to pay today for an investment which will return $1,800 to you 12 years from today if your required rate of return is 9.5%?

6. Six years ago you placed $250 in a savings account which is now worth $1,040.28. When you put the funds into the account you were told it would pay 24% interest. You expected to find the account worth $908.80 at the end of the 6 years. You looked at several accounts before you invested whose interest compounded annually, semiannually, monthly, and daily. What compounding did you think this account used, and what did it end up being?

7. If you invest $46,000 today at 8% compounded annually but after 3 years the interest rate increases to 10% compounded semiannually, what is the investment worth 7 years from today?

8. Suppose a customer's house increased in value over 5 years from $100,000 to $200,000. What was the annual growth rate of the property value during this 5-year interval?

9. Three local banks pay different interest rates on time deposits. Rank the three banks from highest to lowest investor return.

    Bank 1: 8.2% per year compounded annually.
    Bank 2: 8.0% per year compounded quarterly.
    Bank 3: 7.9% per year compounded daily.

10. You want to buy a new car, but you know that the most you can afford for payments is $215 per month. You want 48-month financing, and you can arrange such a loan at 12% compounded monthly. You have nothing to trade and no down payment. The most expensive car you can purchase is: 1) an old junker for $3,000, 2) an Alliance for $6,000, 3) a Chevette for $7,000, 4) a Toyota for $8,000 or 5) a Mazda for $10,000?

Bond Pricing

11. Consider a 9% coupon U.S. government note that has a $1,000 face value and matures 10 years from today. This note pays interest semiannually. The current market interest rate on the bond is 8%. Would you expect this bond to be a

premium, discount, or par value bond? Calculate the actual price of this bond using the present value formula.

12. How much would you be willing to pay in 1992 for the following corporate bond if you require a return of 10%? Would you buy the bond?

	Current Yield	Closing Price
ABC8s95	8.16	98

13. Judi Williams purchased a 12%-coupon corporate bond that matured in 20 years and paid interest semiannually. She paid $1,300 and 6 months later, immediately following an interest payment, she sold the bond. At the time of sale, the market interest rate on bonds of this type was 10%. What was Judi's selling price? What was Judi's rate of return for the 6 months of bond ownership? What is this return on an annual basis? Did the market interest rate on this bond increase or decrease during the 6 months Judi owned it?

14. What is the duration of a bond with a par value of $1,000, a coupon rate of 8% compounded semiannually, and a maturity of 2 years? Assume the required rate of return is 6% compounded semiannually?

15. Guess the duration on the following investment. Would it be less than 2 years, between 2 and 3 years, between 3 and 4 years, or greater than 4 years? Using a discount rate of 10%, calculate the duration.

Years from now	1	2	3	4
Cash flow	$0	$1,000	$5,000	$2,000

16. In each of the following financial situations, fill in the blank with high, low, or zero duration, as appropriate.
    a) If you were considering buying a bond and you expected interest rates to increase, you would prefer a bond with a _____ .
    b) Relative to a bond with a high coupon rate, a bond with a low coupon rate would have a _____ .
    c) A bond with a short maturity has a _____ compared to one with a long maturity.
    d) A 1-year corporate bond with a 5% coupon rate has a _____ relative to a 1-year T-bill.

17. One author says that duration is the weighted average life of a financial instrument. A different author says duration is a measure of elasticity. Which author is correct?

18. Suppose that a bond selling at par has a duration of 2 years. If interest rates increase from 6% to 7%, the value of the bond will fall from $1,000 to _____ .

19. If interest rates fall from 6% to 5%, the price of the bond in the above problem will increase. Will the change in the bond price be smaller or larger than in the above problem? How does this conclusion lead to the further conclusion that duration is only an approximation to elasticity?

Money Market Yields

20. Which money market instruments are typically quoted on a discount basis?

21. What is the bond equivalent yield of a 180-day, $20,000 face value Treasury bill whose discount rate is 9.5%?

22. On which money market instruments are rates calculated based on par rather than on purchase price?

23. You would like to purchase a Treasury bill that has a $10,000 face value and 270 days to maturity. The current price of the Treasury bill is $9,400. What is the discount rate on this security? What is its bond equivalent yield?

Activity Projects

1. Rates for most popular financial instruments can be found in the *Wall Street Journal*. Collect the rates for the following securities. This information can be found on the front of the section "Money and Investing" and in the inside column "Credit Markets."
3-month T-bill
1-10 yr Treasury
10+ yr Treasury
3-month CD
3-month Eurodollar deposit
Federal funds
DJ 20 Bond Index
10 yr tax-exempts (A)
Rank them from highest to lowest. Why might the rates differ between securities?

2. Locate the first AT&T bond maturing in the next century as reported in *The Wall Street Journal*. What is its coupon rate, its maturity, and its pattern of payments? At the rate of return earned most recently on the DJ 20 Bond Index, what price would you be willing to pay for this bond? Comparing this price with its closing price, is the bond earning more or less than the DJ Index? If you were going to buy a bond, would you choose this one? What factors would you consider in picking the one for your portfolio?

References

Benesh, Gary, and Stephen Celec. "A Simplified Approach for Calculating Bond Duration." *Financial Review* (November 1984).

Bierwag, G.. *Duration Analysis: Managing Interest Rate Risk*. Boston, Mass.: Ballinger Press, 1987.

Bierwag, G., George Kaufman, and Alden Toevs. "Duration: Its Development and Use in Bond Portfolio Management." *Financial Analysts Journal* (July/August 1983).

Bierwag, G., George Kaufman, and Cynthia Latta. "Duration Models: A Taxonomy." *Journal of Portfolio Management* (Fall 1988).

Chua, Jess. "A Closed-Form Formula for Calculating Bond Duration." *Financial Analysts Journal* (May–June 1984).

Fabozzi, Frank, and T. Dessa Fabozzi. *Bond Markets, Analysis and Strategies.* Englewood Cliffs, N.J.: Prentice Hall, 1989.

Liebowitz, Martin, William Kraoker, and Ardavan Nozari. "Spread Duration: A New Tool for Bond Portfolio Management." *Journal of Portfolio Management* (Spring 1990).

Macaulay, Frederick. *Some Theoretical Problems Suggested by the Movements of Interest Rates, Bond Yields, and Stock Prices in the U.S. since 1856.* New York: National Bureau of Economic Research, 1938.

Moser, James, and James Lindley. "A Simple Formula for Duration: An Extension." *Financial Review* (November 1989).

Rosenberg, Joel. "The Joys of Duration." *The Bankers Magazine* (March–April 1986).

Stigum, Marcia, in collaboration with John Mann. *Money Market Calculations: Yields, Break-evens, and Arbitrage.* Homewood, Ill: Dow Jones-Irwin, 1981.

Yawitz, Jess. "The Relative Importance of Duration and Yield Volatility on Bond Price Volatility." *Journal of Money, Credit, and Banking* (February 1977).

Chapter 7

The Determinants
of Interest Rates

Many individuals and businesses pay close attention to movements in interest rates. Retirees living off their investments in interest-bearing securities often prefer high rates because this increases their spendable income. Borrowers, such as first-time home-buyers and small businesses financing inventories, prefer low rates because this lowers their periodic interest payments. Others may look to changes in interest rates as a signal of where the economy is headed, either in terms of aggregate growth or its impact on their specific business and investment interests.

The financial press and television networks offer regular analyses that forecast whether interest rates are likely to rise or fall and how changes will affect consumers and businesses. Unfortunately, different experts arrive at fundamentally different inter-pretations, and thus the information provided is often contradictory. There is a well-known saying that if you lined up all economists end-to-end, they still wouldn't reach a conclusion. But that is the beauty of financial markets and financial analysis. If everyone knew what was going to happen, there would be no interest rate risk. There would be little need for specialized investment strategies and the volume of market activity would be likely to drop sharply.

This chapter addresses two fundamental issues: Why do interest rates rise and fall? and Why do interest rates differ between securities? To see the importance of the first issue, consider two commonly cited views regarding the level of interest rates. One states that the Chairman of the U.S. Federal Reserve System can no longer influence interest rates as in prior periods because activity in foreign financial markets now drives U.S. interest rates. To know whether rates will increase or decrease we need only examine what the Japanese and German governments are doing with their domestic rates, and whether foreign investors are more or less likely to invest in U.S.

securities. Another view states that the best predictor of economic conditions is the relationship between short-term and long-term interest rates.[1] In particular, within 12 to 18 months after short-term rates rise above long-term rates, the U.S. economy is likely to slide into a recession.

The importance of the second issue is demonstrated by recent events in the junk bond market.[2] During the 1980s, junk bonds grew in volume and popularity. They carried relatively high promised yields and were often used to assist in the financing of corporate acquisitions of other firms. Numerous savings and loans and several insurance companies purchased large amounts of junk bonds for their investment portfolios, and many brokerages aggressively marketed junk bonds because they offered the highest returns. In 1989, liquidity in the junk bond market collapsed. Junk bond owners could only sell their securities at huge losses. Why the sudden change in return? The answer has to do with why promised yields on junk bonds were higher than yields on other investment vehicles.

This chapter introduces the basic determinants of interest rates and the various factors that influence the pricing of securities. It specifically addresses the impact of inflation and inflation expectations, the business cycle, foreign financial market activity, and a security's default risk, marketability and liquidity, tax treatment, maturity, call and put provisions, and whether it is convertible into common stock.

WHY DO INTEREST RATES RISE AND FALL?

Economists have expended much effort trying to identify factors that determine the level of interest rates. The explanations, or models, can be categorized under the general labels *liquidity preference theory* or *loanable funds theory*. Liquidity preference theory focuses on the supply of and demand for liquid assets, particularly money. The model explains movements in a single interest rate which is an average of the rates on short-term securities. The loanable funds theory focuses on the supply of and demand for aggregate loanable funds throughout the economy. This model analyzes factors that affect borrowers and lenders in all financial markets. It is concerned with the flow of funds between institutions and markets, and explains movements in both short-term and long-term securities. While both theories explain interest rate movements, the loanable funds framework, which is examined below, emphasizes the role and activity of different institutions in different markets.

---

[1]The relationship between yields on securities that differ only in terms of maturity can be characterized by a diagram called a yield curve. Whether short-term rates are above or below long-term rates determines the shape of the yield curve. Yield curves are discussed in detail later in the chapter.

[2]Junk bonds are bonds that are either nonrated or carry a rating below investment grade (the four highest classes). The perceived credit quality is typically lower than average.

LOANABLE FUNDS THEORY

The loanable funds framework divides market participants into four categories: consumers, businesses, governments, and foreign participants. Within each category, units represent borrowers and lenders. The phrase "loanable funds" refers to the credit needs of all borrowers and the associated sources of financing provided by all lenders. Borrowing takes the form of issuing debt securities, while lending takes the form of saving, new money creation by the government, and the dishoarding of money. When all debt markets are aggregated, the theory posits that the risk-free rate of interest is determined by the interaction of the demand for and supply of all loanable funds.

Supply of and Demand for Loanable Funds

The generalized loanable funds framework is readily characterized by supply and demand analysis. The demand for loanable funds represents the behavior of borrowers and thus evidences the supply of all debt instruments. It is determined by the credit needs of all individuals, businesses, government units, and foreign participants relative to various rates of interest. The supply of loanable funds represents the behavior of lenders and thus the demand for owning debt instruments. It is derived from saving, money creation through the banking system, and the dishoarding of money.

Exhibit 7.1 illustrates this general loanable funds framework. The risk-free rate appears on the vertical axis, while the dollar volume of loanable funds appears on the horizontal axis. The demand for loanable funds (DF) slopes downward to the right, indicating that borrowers demand greater amounts of loanable funds at lower interest rates. The supply of loanable funds (SF) slopes upward to the right indicating that more funds will be forthcoming from lenders at higher interest rates. The intersection of the two curves determines the equilibrium interest rate and volume of loans.

Factors Affecting the Supply of Loanable Funds. Lenders want to own interest-bearing securities for a variety of reasons. Individuals might have excess income relative to what they spend on consumption goods, or they may simply need to reinvest their stock of wealth. In addition, they may simply choose to reduce their holdings of money and substitute earning assets. The primary catalyst is the expected rate of return on loanable funds relative to expected returns on alternative investments. Equally important, however, is the relative degree of risk associated with different investments. It is not enough for a security to offer a higher yield if the likelihood of receiving the interest is extremely low. Finally, individuals buy securities as part of financial plans for future expenditures including anticipated education, health, and retirement outlays. The supply of loanable funds by individuals thus varies with expected returns, the expected variablility in returns (as a measure of risk), future spending needs, and their total wealth.

Nonfinancial businesses often have excess cash that they invest temporarily before they use the proceeds for operating or capital expenses. This cash arises due to a mismatch in the timing of cash flows and planned operating and real expenditures. The

Exhibit 7.1 Loanable Funds Framework

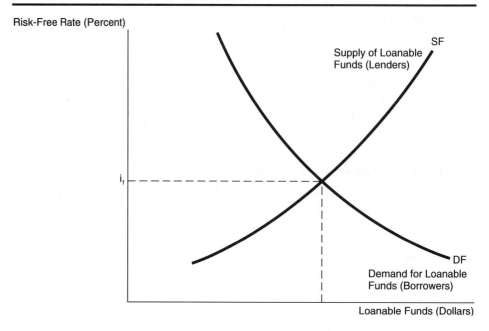

Risk-Free Rate (Percent)

SF

Supply of Loanable
Funds (Lenders)

i_f

DF
Demand for Loanable
Funds (Borrowers)

Loanable Funds (Dollars)

primary determinant of this supply of funds is the expected risk-adjusted return on loanable funds relative to the return on real assets.

Government units affect the supply of loanable funds in two ways. First, some units, particularly state and local governments, invest excess cash in securities to provide additional revenue until the funds are needed elsewhere. Second, the federal government, through the Federal Reserve System, expands and contracts the growth rate in the banking system's reserves, thereby influencing the availability of credit and growth in the money supply. A growing money supply and increased credit increase national income and the amount of funds available for consumption and saving.

Finally, foreign investors view U.S. securities as alternatives to their own domestic securities, and purchase those with the most attractive risk and return features. This emphasizes the important fact that market participants evaluate alternative investments from a global perspective. If expected risk-adjusted yields are higher in the United States than in other countries, capital will flow into the United States as investors from throughout the world seek out the highest net returns. During the 1980s, the foreign sector supplied a significant amount of loanable funds to U.S. money and capital markets.

Factors Affecting the Demand for Loanable Funds. Many factors induce borrowers to issue interest-bearing securities. They primarily reflect the specific need of the borrower for funds, and the availability and terms associated with alternative sources of funds. Individuals borrow largely to finance the purchase of housing and durable goods, such as furniture, appliances, automobiles, and recreational vehicles. They take on more debt when economic conditions are good and are perceived to improve. They also borrow more when the cost of borrowing is perceived to be low relative to the utility of the asset being financed or its rate of appreciation. Nonprice terms are also important, particularly when the underlying asset is an automobile. Here consumers tend to focus on the size of the downpayment and the monthly payment rather than on the rate alone.

Businesses borrow to finance working capital needs and capital expenditures. Working capital needs consist of accounts receivable or inventory financing and typically arise because a firm is growing and does not have alternative sources of short-term credit. Similarly, firms typically use the bond markets to obtain financing for profitable capital investments in new physical plants or equipment. The magnitude of their funds needs reflects, in part, their internally generated cash flow from operations. If internal cash flow is strong, they will need to borrow less than if their cash flow is weak.

Governments are always significant borrowers. State and local government units regularly issue debt to finance temporary imbalances in operating revenues versus expenses, and have regular capital needs for schools, roads, water treatment facilities, and so forth. While many of these units run surpluses, most regularly issue long-term bonds for necessary capital improvements. The federal government, in contrast, has operated at a substantial budget deficit during the past two decades, in which revenues have fallen as much as $250 billion below outlays in a single year. The U.S. Treasury must continually finance the deficit by issuing additional securities to cover the deficiency. Still, the budget reflects only part of the government's demand for loanable funds as off-budget expenditures require substantial borrowing as well. Federal expenditures are not sensitive to interest rates as the funds will be spent regardless of the interest cost.

Foreign participants are also important borrowers in U.S. markets. Much as investors view all securities as potential substitutes, borrowers look for the cheapest sources of funds globally. U.S. corporations can issue securities denominated in yen, sterling, and deutschemarks, just as foreign borrowers can issue securities denominated in U.S. dollars. Most foreign borrowing in the United States with dollar-denominated instruments arises from the needs of foreign businesses.

Changes in Supply and Demand for Loanable Funds

According to the Loanable Funds Theory, the level of interest rates is determined as the market clearing rate, i_f, in Exhibit 7.1. The level of rates will thus rise when the demand for loanable funds increases relative to the supply of loanable funds at the prevailing rate. The level of rates will fall when the demand for loanable funds decreases relative to the supply of loanable funds. Both outcomes may result from changes in either the supply of or demand for loanable funds, or both.

The key issue is to determine what can cause a change in supply and demand. Examine the curves DF and SF from Exhibit 7.1. Any change in the risk-free rate represents a movement along DF and SF. Thus changes in i_f coincide with changes in quantity demanded or quantity supplied read off the horizontal axis, and do not cause the curves to shift. The diagram assumes that all other factors that potentially influence DF and SF are held constant as i_f changes. Factors that cause a change in supply and demand were described previously. Any factor that affects the supply of loanable funds will induce a diagrammatic shift in SF. Any factor that affects the demand for loanable funds will induce a shift in DF.

Consider the situation in which states and local governments must increase their capital expenditures on roads and utilities to help remedy the decaying infrastructure of U.S. cities. Any growth in these outlays will be financed by issuing long-term bonds independent of the prevailing interest rate. In a loanable funds framework, the impact can be characterized by a shift outward and to the right of DF. Holding all other factors constant, this increase in borrowing will raise the equilibrium interest rate from i_f' to i_f''. The impact on rates and the quantity of loanable funds is represented by a shift from DF_1 to DF_2 in the top panel of Exhibit 7.2.

Suppose, instead, that the shock to current conditions is that Japanese investors restrain from buying U.S. interest-bearing securities. The catalyst may be an increase in expected risk-adjusted yields on Japanese securities, or a need for funds due to a decline in the Tokyo stock market. Given their substantial investment in prior periods, this represents a decrease in the supply of loanable funds from SF_1 to SF_2 in the bottom panel of Exhibit 7.2. With fewer investors, the existing securities can only be sold at higher interest rates, unless borrowers withdraw from the market or other investors replace the Japanese.

These examples demonstrate the application of loanable funds analysis. The framework can be used to forecast or explain broad trends in interest rates by documenting the change in the demand for loanable funds relative to the supply of loanable funds. This requires a careful review of the financial and real activities of all market participants and all financial markets. The analysis is often refined to examine the behavior of specific governments or financial institutions and supply and demand activity for specific instruments. Such historical data are provided via the **Flow of Funds Accounts** by the Board of Governors of the Federal Reserve System.[3]

THE RELATIONSHIP BETWEEN INFLATION AND THE LEVEL OF INTEREST RATES

Analysts routinely attribute changes in interest rates to changes in inflation or expected inflation.[4] There is a direct relationship, as higher interest rates are associated with

---

[3]The Appendix to Chapter 7 presents sample data from the Flow of Funds Accounts for commercial bank financial activity and all participants in the market for residential mortgages.

[4]Inflation is defined as a continuous increase in prices. The U.S. government measures inflation by a variety of price indexes that track the average price of different representative market baskets of goods and services. The Consumer Price Index (CPI), Producer Price Index (PPI), and GNP deflator are commonly cited and signify average prices for goods and services sold at retail, at all stages of production, and for all final goods and services, respectively.

Exhibit 7.2 Changes in the Level of Interest Rates

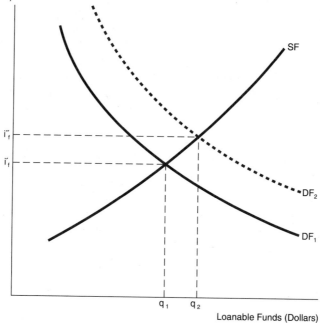

A. Increased Borrowing by State and Local Government

Risk-Free Rate (Percent)

SF

i''_f

i'_f

DF$_2$

DF$_1$

q_1 q_2

Loanable Funds (Dollars)

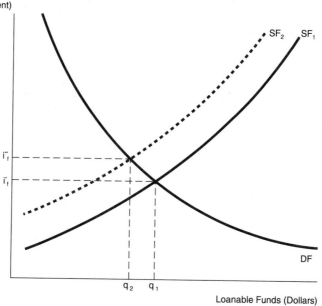

B. Japanese Investors Reduce Their Investment for U.S. Securities

Risk-Free Rate (Percent)

SF$_2$ SF$_1$

i''_f

i'_f

DF

q_2 q_1

Loanable Funds (Dollars)

greater inflation and with an increase in expected inflation. Rates decline with lower inflation expectations. This is intuitively appealing. If it costs more to buy goods, an investor who buys a financial asset rather than real goods and services should earn a higher interest rate to compensate for the greater opportunity cost of foregone consumption. It can also be demonstrated in a loanable funds framework. If expected inflation increases, lenders will lend less at prevailing interest rates because expected yields net of inflation will fall. Borrowers, in contrast, will borrow more to take advantage of low interest rates, expecting to make interest payments with depreciated dollars. In terms of Exhibit 7.1, the demand for loanable funds increases and the supply of loanable funds decreases such that the market clearing rate rises.

The Fisher Relation

In 1896 Irving Fisher published an article that presented an equilibrium interest rate relationship with expected inflation. In the absence of taxes, the equilibrium condition decomposed the nominal market interest rate (i) into an expected real interest rate component (r), an expected inflation premium (pe), and the cross-product between the real rate and expected inflation premium.

$$(i + i) = (1 + r)(1 + pe), \text{ or}$$

$$i = r + pe + rpe \tag{7.1}$$

Equation (7.1), or its modified form (7.2), are commonly labeled the Fisher Relation.[5]

$$i = r + pe \tag{7.2}$$

Conceptually, the expected real rate represents the required return to investors to compensate them at the margin for postponing consumption. This rate is determined before the fact (ex ante), which means before the actual inflation rate is known. The inflation premium represents the return required to compensate investors for the loss of purchasing power due to rising prices during the interval the security is outstanding.

It is important to recognize that the Fisher Relation is theoretical and thus actual data may not support it. Rational investors will demand a positive return for postponing consumption such that r is greater than zero. Consider the case where the ex ante real rate is constant. Then, changes in expected inflation determine changes in the level of nominal rates. Panel A of Exhibit 7.3 demonstrates a one-to-one relationship. In this panel, the real rate is constant at 3 percent and the nominal rate rises and falls by the same amount as the change in expected inflation. For example, as expected inflation changes from 2 to 5 percent, the market rate changes from 5 to 8 percent. With a constant real rate, the Fisher Relation implies that market interest rates will change in the same direction and by the same amount as expected inflation. This is noted in the last two columns of data.

---

[5]The cross-product term is often dropped because it is small in magnitude relative to r and pe.

**Exhibit 7.3 The Real Rate, Expected Inflation, and
Nominal Interest Rates (Percentages)**

A. Fisher Relation: $i = r + pe$

Period	Ex Ante Real Rate	Expected Inflation Rate	Market Rate	Δi	Δpe
1	3	−1	2		
2	3	0	3	1	1
3	3	2	5	2	2
4	3	5	8	3	3
5	3	7	10	2	2

B. Mundell-Tobin: r varies inversely with pe: $i = r + pe$

1	3.60	−1	2.60		
2	3.25	0	3.25	0.65	1
3	3.00	2	5.00	1.75	2
4	2.60	5	7.60	2.60	3
5	2.50	7	9.50	1.90	2

C. Fisher Relation with Taxes: $i = ra/(1-t) + pe/(1-t)$; $t = 20\%$

Period	ra	ra/(1−t)	pe	pe/(1−t)	i	Δi	Δpe
1	3	3.75	−1	−1.25	2.50		
2	3	3.75	0	0	3.75	1.25	1
3	3	3.75	2	2.50	6.25	2.50	2
4	3	3.75	5	6.25	10.00	3.75	3
5	3	3.75	7	8.75	12.50	2.50	2

Mundell-Tobin. The Fisher Relation has evoked much debate among economists. Two of the earliest criticisms were offered by Robert Mundell and James Tobin, who argued that changes in expected inflation alter the ex ante real rate in the opposite direction.[6] If expected inflation increases, r decreases and vice versa. The rationale underlying this inverse relationship is that increased inflation lowers the value of an individual's real wealth. In order to raise real wealth to its previous level, individuals must save more of their income. But increased saving lowers required returns for postponing consumption, such that the ex ante real rate declines. Lowered inflation expectations produce the opposite result as real wealth rises and saving falls.

If r varies inversely with pe, any change in market rates will be less than one-to-one with changes in expected inflation. To see this, examine panel B of Exhibit 7.3. As expected inflation increases from 2 to 5 percent, the ex ante real rate declines from 3 to 2.6 percent. Thus, while expected inflation increases by 3 percent, the market rate rises by just 2.6 percent from 5 percent to 7.6 percent. The Mundell and Tobin arguments suggest that the ex ante real rate is not constant, and market rates consequently change in the same direction as expected inflation, but the change is less than one-to-one. This is again revealed in the last two columns of data.

---

[6]See Mundell (1963) and Tobin (1965).

Darby-Feldstein. Michael Darby and Martin Feldstein extended the debate over the Fisher Relation by incorporating income tax effects.[7] Both authors argued that lenders are concerned primarily with expected after-tax real rates, and not r in equation (7.2). Designating ra as the ex ante after-tax real rate and t as the marginal tax rate of the marginal lender,

$$ra = i(1 - t) - pe \qquad (7.3)$$

Solving for i,

$$i = ra/(1 - t) + [1/(1 - t)]pe \qquad (7.4)$$

the after-tax version of the Fisher Relation appears as equation (7.4).

The primary difference between equations (7.2) and (7.4) has to do with the tax factor multiplying the expected inflation premium. If the marginal tax rate is positive and less than one, this tax factor $[1/(1 - t)]$ will be greater than one. The implication is that market interest rates change by more than the change in expected inflation. Panel C of Exhibit 7.3, for example, uses a 20 percent marginal tax rate so that the tax factor equals 1.25, and assumes a constant ex ante real rate of 3 percent. As expected inflation changes, market rates change in the same direction, but the relationship is greater than one-to-one. Thus the increase in expected inflation from 2 percent to 5 percent coincides with an increase in market rates from 6.25 percent to 10 percent.

The belief that interest rates should change by more than expected inflation is highly intuitive given the U.S. tax system. Most loans are specified in current dollars. With inflation, taxes are imposed on nominal interest income and thus will also rise with price increases. For investors to remain at least as well off as before inflation, interest rates must increase more than inflation to provide the additional receipts necessary to pay the incremental income taxes and keep the ex ante real rate constant.

Actual Inflation and Market Interest Rates

The three theories introduced above propose three different relationships between market interest rates and expected inflation, but ignore actual inflation. Unfortunately, it is difficult to test the theories empirically because it is difficult to accurately measure expected inflation and the ex ante real rate is not known. In addition, actual inflation may not accurately track expected inflation.

Ex Post Real Rates. The ex post real rate (r^*) is determined after the actual inflation rate is known. It is calculated by subtracting the actual inflation rate (p) from the observed market rate over the same time period.

$$r^* = i - p \qquad (7.5)$$

Because actual inflation may be above or below market interest rates, the ex post real rate can be either positive or negative. Exhibit 7.4 demonstrates this by plotting

---

[7] See Darby (1975) and Feldstein (1976).

Exhibit 7.4 Relationship Between Market Rate and Annual Inflation Rate; Ex-Post Real Rate

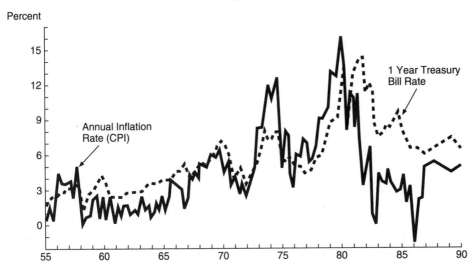

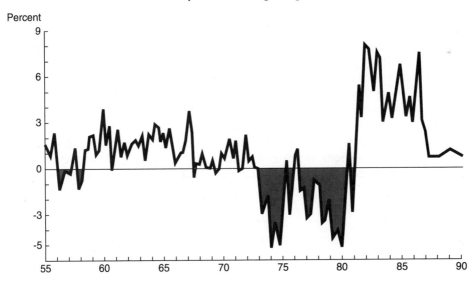

the market rate on 1-year Treasury bills versus the actual annual inflation rate measured by the CPI, and the corresponding ex post real rate. Note that (7.5) does not recognize the impact of taxes. If taxes were taken into account, the after-tax ex post real rate would equal the after-tax market rate less the inflation rate, and would be more negative than r* in Exhibit 7.4.[8]

As indicated in Exhibit 7.4, the relationship between actual interest rates and inflation has not been stable. During the 1970s inflation consistently exceeded the 1-year T-bill rate so that the ex post real rate was negative. In 1974 and 1979, r* fell as low as −5 percent. After inflation dropped during the 1980s, r* increased sharply because the level of interest rates did not drop coincidentally. The 1-year T-bill rate systematically exceeded the inflation rate, at times by as much as 8 percent. During the 1970s, investors lost considerable purchasing power while borrowers were able to repay their debts with cheap funds. During the 1980s this reversed, with borrowers paying extremely high real rates to lenders during the first 5 years, even though the level of interest rates fell. Real rates returned to more normal levels after 1986.

In terms of the three theories, these results may be due to a variety of phenomena. If actual inflation was correctly anticipated, the data suggest that ex ante real rates are not constant and may, in fact, be negative. It seems more likely, however, that actual inflation does not closely track expected inflation. If this is the case, ex post real rates would be negative when market participants underestimate actual inflation, and positive when participants overestimate actual inflation. Implicitly, from 1973 through 1980 actual inflation exceeded expected inflation, while expected inflation exceeded actual inflation from 1982 through 1989. The difficulty with this argument is that it suggests participants did not revise their expectations for long periods of time during these intervals.

While there is some evidence that price expectations are formed over long periods and thus change only with lengthy lags, it also seems plausible that there was a structural shift in the Fisher Relation during the past two decades. Specifically, some economists have argued that changes in Federal Reserve monetary policy and U.S. federal budget policy have altered the inflation–interest rate relationship. Monetary policy has presumably accentuated the volatility of interest rates. Federal budget deficits have similarly altered long-term inflation forecasts and the volatility of rates because the large deficits increase the anticipated borrowing requirements of the Treasury. Market interest rates presumably incorporate a volatility premium to capture this uncertainty.

Inspection of the top of Exhibit 7.4 reveals that there is still a broad-based direct relationship between the level of interest rates and actual inflation. Interest rates generally rise and fall together with inflation, even though the rates of change now may vary substantially.

---

[8] In terms of the above notation, the after-tax ex post real rate equals i(1-t) - p.

INTEREST RATES AND THE BUSINESS CYCLE

Most analysts agree that the level of interest rates and economic growth vary coincidentally over time. Interest rates tend to rise when total spending rises and fall when total spending falls. Trends in aggregate economic activity are typically evaluated in terms of the percentage change in real gross national product (GNP).[9] GNP rises when consumers increase spending, housing starts rise, businesses accumulate inventory and increase capital expenditures, and net exports increase. In general, interest rates also rise as borrowers compete for loans to finance this spending. GNP declines when the economy contracts. As consumers and businesses reduce spending, the investment in housing slows, net exports decline, and total spending similarly declines. Interest rates typically decrease at the same time.

Historically, the real economy, measured by the percentage change in GNP, has evidenced a cyclical pattern as indicated in Exhibit 7.5. The market interest rate is on the vertical axis and time is on the horizontal axis. Concentrate for the moment only on the solid line. The line begins at the middle of the expansion phase of the cycle. During the expansion, consumers are spending more and businesses are borrowing to accumulate inventory and finance capital expenditures. This puts upward pressure on prices because production often lags behind the demand for goods and services. Interest rates rise because the demand for loanable funds increases more than the supply of loanable funds.

At peak growth in GNP, loan demand is still high because spending is high. Consumers, however, stabilize or slow their spending and business investment follows. In an effort to slow inflation, the Federal Reserve typically restricts credit availability by slowing the growth in the banking system's reserves. This puts upward pressure on interest rates because the supply of loanable funds is shrinking while the demand for loanable funds is still relatively strong. This leads to a contractionary phase. During the contraction, consumer spending declines, businesses contract their inventories and postpone capital expenditures, and loan demand drops. Inflation typically slows. During the latter stage of the contraction, the Federal Reserve accelerates reserves growth in an effort to stimulate spending and reduce unemployment, and interest rates decline. Finally, the percentage change in GNP bottoms out at the trough, along with the level of interest rates. The cycle then repeats itself.

Obviously, the pattern is a simplistic representation of reality. It appears, for example, that the length of an expansion equals the length of a contraction. In reality, expansionary periods are typically much longer than contractionary periods. For example, the U.S. recession which began in 1981, lasted under 2 years, with many previous recessions lasting around 12 months. Starting in 1982, the United States experienced the longest expansionary period since World War II. During most of this period, interest rates continued to decline. Most analysts attribute this to a sharp

---

[9]This section presents a very simplified version of the macroeconomy. In actuality, the relationships are much more complex, given the nature of government intervention and international relationships. The purpose here is to provide a general flavor of interest rate relationships and spending behavior. GNP equals the dollar sum of consumption expenditures, government spending, investment expenditures, and net exports. Real gross national product equals gross national product in current dollars divided by the GNP deflator.

Exhibit 7.5 Interest Rates over the Business Cycle
with Constant Inflation Expectations

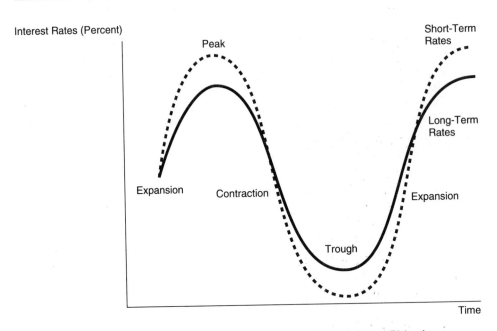

- **Expansion**: Increasing Consumer Spending, Inventory Accumulation, and Rising Loan Demand; Federal Reserve Begins to Slow Money Growth.
- **Peak**: Monetary Restraint, High Loan Demand, Little Liquidity.
- **Contraction**: Falling Consumer Spending, Inventory Contraction, Falling Loan Demand; Federal Reserve Accelerates Money Growth.
- **Trough**: Monetary Ease, Limited Loan Demand, Excess Liquidity.

reduction in inflation and inflation expectations, which is unusual for an expansion. This decline in rates was reversed in 1989 but does not alter the fact that in general interest rates have varied directly with rates of economic growth over long periods of U.S. economic activity. The expansionary period ended in late 1990 as the economy moved into recession which was again short-lived.

WHY DO INTEREST RATES DIFFER BETWEEN SECURITIES?

The loanable funds framework focuses on a single, risk-free rate of interest. Obviously, there are many different securities with different features and varying degrees of risk. Various debt instruments mature at different intervals, pay interest that may or may not be subject to income taxes, have call or put option features, and may even be convertible into common stock. Not surprisingly, securities with different features typically carry different market rates of interest. Exhibit 7.6 plots yields on a variety of short-term and long-term securities from 1988 to 1991 and illustrates that all interest rates are not the same. The following analysis examines specific aspects of default risk, marketability, tax treatment, the existence of call or put options, convertibility, and maturity on interest rates. The fundamental premise is that these characteristics have value to investors and borrowers and thus are explicitly priced in the marketplace. A market-determined interest rate reflects this valuation in equilibrium.

DEFAULT RISK

The pricing of fixed-income securities in Chapter 6 assumed that the size and exact timing of each cash flow in the present value calculation are known with certainty. A bond's price equals the sum of the present values of all cash flows. More precisely, a security represents nothing more than a promise to pay the contractual interest and principal at a prespecified time. Clearly, such a promise may not be kept. Default risk on debt instruments is the probability or likelihood that a borrower will not make the contractual interest and principal payments as promised. When this occurs, an investor either receives a lower payment than that promised or receives full payment at a later date. In either case, the realized value of the actual cash flows will be less than that promised so the investor is worse off.

When there is a real possibility that the borrower will not make the promised payments, investors will demand a higher interest rate. The greater the actual or perceived likelihood of default, the higher will be the market interest rate. A basic issue in pricing securities is thus, how much of an increase in rate is required to compensate investors for default losses.

Default Risk Premiums

Not all bonds exhibit the same default risk. The U.S. Treasury, for example, can readily issue new debt to pay existing security holders because of the government's commitment and power to raise taxes or print money to raise funds. Treasury securities are thus default-risk-free. Other borrowers, such as corporations in cyclical industries or those close to bankruptcy, have less predictable cash flows and investors recognize a real possibility that the firms might default. In fact, all borrowers other than the Treasury exhibit default risk that is greater than that for Treasury securities because no guarantee is as strong as the federal government's.

Analysts compare interest rates between securities by means of default risk premiums. Such premiums are calculated as the effective annual interest rate on a taxable security with default risk minus the effective market interest rate on a Treasury

Exhibit 7.6 Yields on Long-Term Bonds

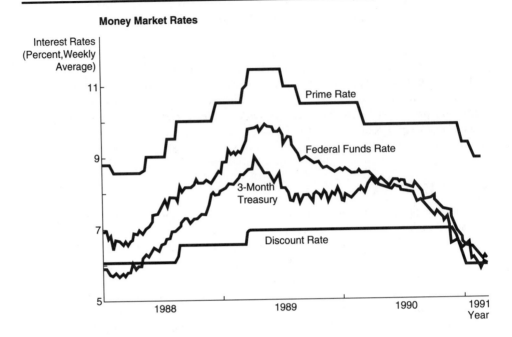

Money Market Rates

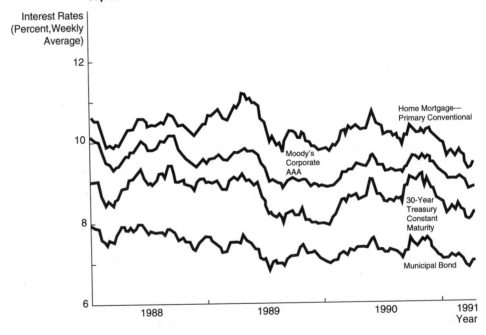

Capital Market Rates

Source: *Economic Trends*, Federal Reserve Board of Cleveland.

Exhibit 7.7 Default Risk Premiums on Selected Securities

Market Interest Rates on Securities with Different Maturities, January 1989

Type of Security	Maturity				
	3-Month	6-Month	1 Year	5 Years	10 Years
U.S. Treasury	8.30%	8.35%	9.01%	9.09%	9.01%
FNMA	8.94	9.02	9.18	9.32	9.25
Commercial paper: prime grade	8.95	9.00			
CDs (≥ $100,000)	8.66	8.88	9.15		
Corporate bonds (Aaa/AAA)			9.21	9.57	9.98
Corporate bonds (Baa/BB)			9.42	10.14	10.65
Municipal bonds (Aaa/AAA)			6.30	6.90	7.40
Municipal bonds (Baa/BBB)			6.67	7.45	8.05
Junk Bonds					13.00%+

Default-Risk Premiums

Type of Security	3 Month	6 Month	1 Year	5 Years	10 Years
FNMA	0.64%	0.67	0.17	0.23	0.24
Commercial paper	0.65	0.65			
CDs (≥$100,000)	0.36	0.53	0.14		
Corporate bonds (Aaa/AAA)			0.20	0.48	0.97
Corporate bonds (Baa/BBB)			0.41	1.05	1.64

security of the same maturity or duration.[10] Formally, if we let

i_t = interest rate on a Treasury with n periods to maturity,
i_r = interest rate on a taxable security subject to default risk
     with n periods to maturity, and
drp = default risk premium,

then

$$drp = i_r - i_t \qquad\qquad (7.6)$$

The risk premium will always be positive because risky securities offer higher yields than comparable maturity Treasury securities. Because i_r and i_t are market-determined, drp represents the expected default loss measured as the incremental yield required on a risky security to compensate for expected losses. Exhibit 7.7 compares default risk premiums for different types of securities in January 1989. Two conclusions stand out. First, securities with the same maturity often display different default risk premiums. Second, default risk premiums increase with maturity. The latter occurs because the longer investors must wait for a return of principal, the greater the likelihood of loss.

---

[10]Some securities pay interest that is not subject to federal income taxes. Yields on these securities cannot be directly compared with yields on taxable securities. Tax effects and default premiums on tax-exempt securities are addressed later in the chapter.

Exhibit 7.8   Rating Classifications

Municipal Bonds

Standard & Poor's[a]	Moody's[a]	Description
Investment Grade		
AAA	Aaa	Highest quality
AA	Aa	High quality, slightly more risk than top rating
A	A-1, A	Upper-medium grade, possible future impairment
BBB	Baa	Medium grade, lacks outstanding investment characteristics
Noninvestment Grade		
BB	Ba	Some speculative characteristics
B	B	Highly speculative, small assurance of interest and principal payments
CCC	Caa	Low quality, probable default
CC	Ca	Low quality, poor prospect of attaining investment standing
C, D	C	Lowest quality, in default

Municipal Notes and Commercial Paper

Standard & Poor's Commercial Paper	Moody's		Description
	Commercial Paper	Notes	
A-1 +	P-1	MIG 1	Highest quality
A-1	P-1	MIG 2	High quality
A-2	P-2	MIG 3	Strong degree of safety
A-3	P-3	MIG 4	Satisfactory degree of safety

[a]Standard & Poors ratings within each category may also be assigned relative rankings within each class denoted by a plus, representing highest quality, or a minus, representing lowest quality. Moody's attaches a numerical value from 1 to 3 with a similar interpretation.

Bond Ratings

To accurately assess default risk, investors must analyze an issuer's ability to service debt under adverse economic conditions. This involves a careful review of the issuer's financial condition as well as specific features of each security, which can be quite costly and time-consuming. Several private firms provide this service by evaluating a security's default risk and assigning a credit rating. The rating agencies charge borrowers a one-time fee prior to the release of the rating. The borrower's objective is to obtain a rating that enhances investor interest and thereby lowers the interest rate by enough to cover the fee paid the rating agencies. Investors review these ratings and require higher promised returns from lower quality (higher default probability) securities.

Exhibit 7.8 summarizes the various ratings provided by Moody's and Standard & Poor's for bonds, short-term municipal notes, and commercial paper, ranked from highest to lowest quality. Bonds that receive ratings from Aaa (AAA) to Baa (BBB) are labeled investment grade bonds. Bonds rated Ba (BB) and lower or nonrated bonds are labeled *junk bonds*. The rating agencies periodically review an issuer's financial condition and may assign a new rating that is either better or worse. When a rating is upgraded, market participants react favorably and bid the market rate lower. If a security is downgraded, the market rate rises to reflect a higher default risk premium.

MARKETABILITY AND LIQUIDITY

All assets can be converted to cash if the holder has enough time to find a buyer and negotiate terms. In many cases it is easy to sell an asset at a predictable price because there are many buyers who know the asset's characteristics and the cost of effecting the sale is low. Treasury bills and bonds meet this description. In other cases it is difficult to sell an asset because buyers know little about it. A 2-acre parcel of mountain property located near a ski resort might qualify here. A buyer must determine where the land is located, if it is accessible, whether utilities are available, what similar property has sold for, and what the broker's fee is before knowing what a fair market price might be. Arriving at this price may be costly and often takes considerable time.

Marketability Effects

Marketability refers to the rapidity and ease with which an asset can be converted to cash. Liquidity extends the marketability concept to encompass the fact that the sale should occur with minimal unanticipated loss to the owner. Highly marketable and liquid assets, such as Treasury securities, trade frequently in well-established secondary markets so that buyers and sellers can readily estimate the precise sales price. In general, an asset's liquidity is closely tied to its maturity or duration.

For interest-bearing securities, marketability and liquidity depend on the issuer's reputation, the size of issue, trading volume, the source of cash flow to service the debt, whether payments are government guaranteed, and whether there are any complicated covenants that lenders have difficulty understanding. The most marketable securities are generally large issues from well-known borrowers with standardized features and no unusual covenants. It also helps if the securities carry a government guarantee and provide for debt service from a predictable cash source. Liquidity is linked to maturity and duration, which determine the relative price-sensitivity of an asset to changes in interest rates. As indicated in Chapter 6, longer maturity and duration bonds vary more in price than shorter-term and duration bonds for a given change in interest rates. Thus when other factors are held constant, investors prefer shorter-term instruments because they take less price risk.

Liquidity Premiums

Investors generally prefer liquid assets over illiquid assets because they can readily sell them at predictable prices with low transactions costs. The market interest rate on a security reflects its relative liquidity, with highly liquid assets carrying the lowest rates. In general, Treasury securities are the most liquid, followed by U.S. government agency securities and highly rated corporate and municipal securities. Borrowers can enhance liquidity in several ways. First, if they obtain an investment grade rating, more participants are willing to trade their securities. Second, borrowers can purchase bond insurance, which automatically enhances the rating to the highest grade by reducing default risk. Third, they can improve liquidity by creating a secondary market in the specific type of debt.

In the early 1960s, for example, Citicorp (then City Bank) originated the jumbo CD market by agreeing to buy outstanding issues prior to maturity. Throughout the 1980s, Drexel Burnham Lambert captured the bulk of the junk bond business by making a secondary market for outstanding issues that holders needed to liquidate. Investors were more willing to buy junk securities because Drexel provided an implied guarantee that it would buy securities back or find another buyer at market prices. During much of the 1980s this system worked well and the junk bond market flourished as volume grew from $18 billion to over $160 billion in outstandings in 1989. At the end of 1989, however, Drexel pleaded guilty to a variety of securities violations and the firm ultimately went bankrupt. The firm's principal investment banker, Michael Milken, pleaded guilty to securities fraud in early 1990. With Drexel's failure the secondary market collapsed and junk bond owners saw their inventories quickly decline by 20 to 25 percent in value, on average, and more for individual securities of bankrupt firms.

INCOME TAX EFFECTS

To this point we have discussed interest rates in terms of pretax yields. Clearly, the realized return from buying a security depends on whether an investor pays taxes on any of the proceeds. Tax payments reduce spendable cash receipts so that after-tax yields are less than promised pretax yields.

The impact of federal income taxes is readily demonstrated with the present value analysis of Chapter 6.[11] Suppose you purchased a 3-year Aaa-rated corporate bond for $10,000 that pays $850 in interest at the end of each year and returns $10,000 at maturity. Your marginal tax rate is 28 percent. Because you bought the bond at par, taxes apply only against the periodic interest. Your after-tax interest income thus equals $612 annually for an effective after tax yield (i*) of 6.12 percent.

$$10,000 = \frac{850\,(1-.28)}{(1+i^*)} + \frac{850\,(1-.28)}{(1+i^*)^2} + \frac{850\,(1-.28)}{1+i^*)^3} + \frac{10,000}{(1+i^*)^3}$$

$$10,000 = \frac{612}{(1+i^*)} + \frac{612}{(1+i^*)^2} + \frac{10,612}{(1+i^*)^3}$$

Solving for i^* produces $i^* = .0612$.

In general, the after-tax yield for a bond purchased at par and held to maturity equals the pretax yield times 1 minus the investor's applicable marginal tax rate (t).

---

[11]Some states and local governments also levy income taxes, which increases the effective marginal tax rate on income. State and local taxes are ignored in the following analysis.

$$i^* = i(1 - t) \qquad\qquad (7.7)$$

In the previous example, i^* equals $.085(1 - .28)$ or 6.12 percent.

The tax treatment of bonds purchased at a discount or premium is slightly more complex. When an investor buys a bond for less than par value (a discount bond), a portion of the return consists of price appreciation. As time elapses the bond's price approaches par value even with no change in the level of interest rates. When pricing the bond, the difference between par value and the discount price is amortized over the remaining life of the bond. This represents income and investors must pay taxes on the realized price appreciation at maturity or sale. With premium bonds the price decreases to par value so that amortization represents a loss and thus serves to reduce taxable income.[12]

Municipal Securities

Municipal securities are debt obligations issued by state and local governments and their political subdivisions, such as school districts or water treatment facilities. Most municipals pay interest that is exempt from federal income taxes, so investors are willing to accept pretax yields that are lower than those on taxable securities of comparable maturity and risk.[13] Consider an Aaa-rated, 3-year municipal that is priced at $10,000 par and is otherwise comparable to the 3-year corporate yielding 8.5 percent, except that interest is tax-exempt. Suppose the municipal pays $700 a year in interest. Its pretax yield (im) equals 7 percent, which is the same as its after-tax yield.

An investor who pays taxes at the 28 percent rate will prefer the municipal over the previous corporate bond because the after-tax yield is 0.88 (7.00 − 6.12) percent higher. This explains why the municipal rates in Exhibit 7.7 are less than the pretax yields on all taxable securities of the same maturity. Muncipal rates are already tax-adjusted.

The tax treatment of tax-exempt discount and premium municipal bonds parallels that of taxable bonds. Specifically, any price appreciation is taxable, while premium bonds generate tax losses if they are sold or mature at prices below cost. Interest income is still tax-exempt, however.

State and Local Taxes

Many state and local goverments impose taxes that apply to income from securities, much like the federal income tax. There are subtle differences, however. First, states and localities that have an income tax specifically exempt interest on Treasury securities. Second, states and localities selectively exempt municipal interest from taxes.

---

[12]This discussion applies to bonds that trade at prices other than par due to interest rate changes. In the case where bonds are originally issued at a discount, taxes apply annually to amortized income regardless of whether the bondholder receives any cash.

[13]Municipals issued for private purposes in which the proceeds are effectively used by corporations pay interest that is taxable, and thus are labeled taxable municipals.

Most states exempt interest for all bonds issued within the state, but tax interest on bonds issued outside the state. The purpose is to increase the demand for in-state municipals and thereby lower in-state borrowing costs relative to other municipals. Investors must be aware of both federal and state/local income taxes before buying any security. Brokerage houses recognize the impact of state taxes by structuring municipal bond funds that buy securities from a single state and thus cater to investors from those states.

Municipal Default Risk

Due to the federal income tax exemption, pretax yields on municipals are not directly comparable with pretax yields on taxable securities. This alters the definition of a municipal default risk premium. A review of Exhibit 7.7, for example, reveals that the risky municipal yield minus the risk-free Treasury yield in each maturity group is always negative. This contradicts the intuitive notion that municipals are riskier than Treasuries.

One alternative might be to compare tax-equivalent yields on municipals with pretax taxable yields. A tax-equivalent muncipal yield is defined as the pretax yield that a security would offer to provide an investor the same after-tax yield available on the municipal. It is calculated by dividing the municipal rate by 1 minus the investor's marginal tax rate.

$$\text{tax–equivalent muncipal yield} = \frac{i_m}{(1 - t)}$$

An investor in the 28 percent tax bracket would thus find that the 5-year municipal paying 6.9 percent in Exhibit 7.7 yields 9.58 percent on a tax-equivalent basis. The effective default risk premium equivalent to equation (7.6) equals 0.49 percent (.0958 − .0909). The obvious problem is that this risk premium varies with the investor's tax rate. An investor in the 15 percent tax bracket, for example, would compare an 8.12 percent tax-equivalent yield to a higher Treasury yield, and the imputed risk premium would be negative.

Another alternative is to redefine the municipal default risk premium solely in terms of municipal rates. In contrast to equation (7.6), define the municipal default risk premium (drpm) as

$$\text{drpm} = \text{interest rate on risky municipal} - \text{interest rate on Aaa–rated municipal} \quad \textbf{(7.8)}$$

Using the data from Exhibit 7.7, risk premiums on the Baa-rated municipals equal 0.37 percent, 0.55 percent, and 0.65 percent for 1-year, 5-year, and 10-year securities, respectively. Because Aaa-rated municipals are risky, drpm measures the incremental expected default loss on a lower-rated municipal relative to the highest grade municipal.

CONVERTIBILITY

Some corporations issue securities that are hybrids of debt and common stock. Such securities, labeled **convertible bonds**, make fixed coupon payments like straight bonds but carry the additional provision that holders may convert the bonds to common stock at a predetermined price. The convertible owner essentially has an option which changes in value with the market's perception of the underlying corporation's financial condition. Once a bond is converted to stock, however, the transaction cannot be reversed.

Because the conversion feature has value, investors are willing to accept a yield below that offered on straight debt. The yield exceeds the dividend yield on the firm's common stock and the prespecified conversion price exceeds the prevailing value of a share of stock. For example, in 1986 Wherehouse Entertainment, Inc., issued $50 million in convertible bonds paying 6.25 percent annual interest, with the option to convert each $1,000 face-value bond into 36 shares of the firm's stock. At that time, Wherehouse paid 11 percent coupon interest on its straight bonds. The conversion value of each bond in terms of stock equaled $27.50, which represented a 26 percent premium over the $22 stock price at the time of issue. This means that an investor would convert the bond to stock if Wherehouse's stock price increased above $27.50. With convertibles, an investor earns a relatively low corporate bond yield, but might gain if the stock price rises high enough.

Convertibles are riskier than straight bonds because the claims of owners are subordinated to the claims of straight debtholders. In case of default, bond holders are paid before holders of convertibles. Part of the lower interest yield thus represents a higher default risk premium. At the same time, convertibles are not as risky as common stock.

TERM TO FINAL MATURITY

Final maturity is important because it determines how long an investor must wait before the security issuer makes the last promised interest and principal payment. This length of time affects a security's liquidity risk, default risk, and interest rate risk and thus significantly influences its pricing. In general, the longer is maturity, the greater are these risks.

Yield Curves

A yield curve is a diagram that compares the market yields on securities that differ only in terms of maturity. Default risk, tax treatment, marketability and all other features must be identical across securities in order to isolate the effects of maturity. The general relationship is also referred to as the **term structure of interest rates**. The visual representation provides a concise picture of how maturity influences interest rates. Examples of yield curves for Treasury securities as of April 1989 and April 1990 appear in Exhibit 7.9. Notice that in April 1989 Treasury yields rose from the 3-month maturity through 2 years, then fell continuously through 30 years. In contrast, yields

Exhibit 7.9 Alternative Shapes of the Treasury Yield Curve

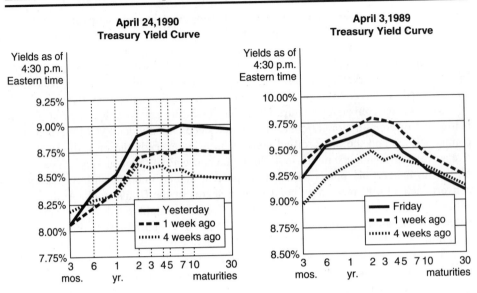

April 24,1990
Treasury Yield Curve

April 3,1989
Treasury Yield Curve

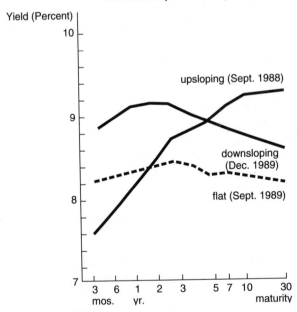

General Shape of Yield Curves

in April 1990 rose sharply through 2 years from a lower initial level, increased slightly from 2 to 7 years, then leveled off at 9 percent. The three general shapes that yield curves take appear at the bottom of Exhibit 7.9. Why the different shapes? The **unbiased** following analysis explains the shape of the yield curve in terms of three theories, the **expectations theory**, the **liquidity premium theory**, and the **market segmentation theory**.

The following discussion focuses on maturity effects for Treasury securities because all Treasuries exhibit no default risk, are highly liquid, and are subject to the same tax treatment. There are problems, however, even with this comparison. To obtain a "pure" term structure, one must compare option-free, zero coupon securities. The Treasury securities used to construct the yield curves in Exhibit 7.9 carry different coupon rates and some are callable prior to maturity. Still, these data are the best available.

Unbiased Expectations Theory

There are two forms of expectations theories. The **unbiased expectations theory** focuses on the behavior of investors and attributes the relationship between yields on different maturity securities entirely to differences in expectations regarding future interest rates. The liquidity premium theory incorporates the impact of liquidity differences for different securities with varying expectations.

Suppose you have $100,000 to invest for a 2-year period. In order to minimize default risk, you have decided to restrict your purchase to Treasury securities. With your 2-year time horizon, you are considering the following options and will choose the one that maximizes expected yield over 2 years.

- Option I: Invest in a 1-year Treasury. When it matures, invest in another 1-year Treasury.

- Option II: Invest in a 2-year Treasury.

A call to your broker reveals that a 1-year Treasury currently yields 8.4 percent, while a 2-year Treasury yields 9.0 percent. At first glance, it might appear that option II is better because the 2-year security pays 60 basis points (0.60 percent) more than the 1-year security. The appropriate comparison, however, is not that simple because it ignores the second year of the holding period. The key factor is that you do not know what a 1-year Treasury will yield 1 year from today. If the yield is high enough, two consecutive 1-year securities might yield cumulatively more in total interest than the 2-year security.

The following information, ignoring compounding, summarizes your decision. The only uncertain factor is the unknown yield 1 year from today.

Expected Interest

	Option I	Option II
Year 1	$8,400	$ 9,000
Year 2	?	$ 9,000
Total		$18,000

If the only objective is to maximize interest income, you will be indifferent if the total interest from option I equals $18,000, the total available from option II. In this case, interest on a 1-year Treasury purchased exactly 1 year from the present would have to equal $9,600. Your decision is thus based on a straightforward rate comparison. If the rate on a 1-year Treasury acquired 1 year from today

(i) equals 9.6%, then you will be indifferent between option I and option II,

(ii) exceeds 9.6%, then you will buy two consecutive 1-year securities (option I),

(iii) is less than 9.6%, then you will buy the 2-year security (option II).

The unbiased expectations theory attaches considerable importance to the implied interest rate at which investors are indifferent between securities with different maturities. According to this theory, the interest rate that equates the return on a series of short-term securities with the return on a long-term security through the same final maturity reflects the market's consensus forecast of what the future interest rate will equal. In the previous example, the consensus forecast of what a 1-year Treasury will yield 1 year from the present is 9.6 percent, ignoring compounding. Whenever market participants change their consensus expectations, yields on different maturity securities change to reflect the new expectation. Formally,

> **Unbiased Expectations Theory:** Long-term interest rates are an average of current and expected short-term interest rates. The expected short-term interest rate is the market's unbiased forecast of future interest rates.

Applying this to the previous data, the 2-year yield (9.0 percent) is a simple average of the current 1-year yield (8.4 percent) plus the expected 1-year yield, 1 year from the present (9.6 percent). The 9.6 percent implied rate represents the consensus forecast of the 1-year Treasury rate in 1 year.

$$9.0\% = (8.4\% + 9.6\%)/2$$

The theory applies to securities of all maturities. It implicitly assumes that investors are willing to substitute across maturities on the basis of yield differentials. Thus if 15-year yields rise above that consistent with expectations, investors will substitute 15-year bonds for whatever bonds they hold in their portfolios. Such trades are also presumably costless.

The unbiased expectations theory is normally formulated in terms of compound interest rates. Long-term interest rates are a geometric average of current and expected short-term interest rates. Using the above data, the implied rate that would make investors indifferent between options I and II, denoted by f, can be computed as:

$$(1.09)(1.09) = (1.084)(1 + f)$$

$$f = \frac{(1.09)(1.09)}{(1.084)} - 1$$

$$= .09603$$

With compounding, this rate slightly exceeds the 9.6 percent computed earlier.

Forward Rates

Conceptually, a forward rate is a rate quoted today on a forward loan that originates at some future period. The 1-year Treasury security to be issued 1 year from today in the above example is such a forward loan. As in the example, forward rates can be extracted from actual yields on securities traded in the cash market. Mathematically, one need only solve a relationship that characterizes equal compound returns on two alternative investment options. Relationship (7.9) expresses the current yield (at time t) on a 2-period security ($_t i_2$) in terms of the current yield on a 1-period security ($_t i_1$) and a 1-period forward rate (f_1), 1 period from the present ($_{t+1} f_1$).

$$(1 + _t i_2)(1 + _t i_2) = (1 + _t i_1)(1 + _{t+1} f_1) \qquad (7.9)$$

Because $_t i_1$ and $_t i_2$ are readily available from the current yield curve, it is easy to solve for the forward rate.

In general, any long term interest rate can be expressed in terms of relationship (7.10).

$$(1 + _t i_n)^n = (1 + _t i_1)(1 + _{t+1} f_1)(1 + _{t+2} f_1) \dots (1 + _{t+n-1} f_1) \qquad (7.10)$$

where

$_t i_n$ = market rate on an n-period security at time t,

$_t i_1$ = market rate on a 1-period security at time t,

$_{t+1} f_1$ = 1-period forward rate on a security to be delivered 1 year from the present (t + 1),

$_{t+2} f_1$ = 1-period forward on a security to be delivered 2 years from the present (t + 2),

.

.

.

$_{t+n-1} f_1$ = 1-period forward rate on a security to be delivered 1 year from the present (t + n − 1).

With this notation, all market interest rates are represented by the letter i. The prefix refers to the time at which the yield is quoted, with t representing the present. The letter n refers to the number of periods remaining until final maturity. All interest rates denoted by the letter f are forward rates. The suffix refers to the maturity of the underlying security.

Suppose a 3-year Treasury is currently priced to yield 9.5 percent. Combining this with the 1-year and 2-year yields discussed earlier, we can use (7.10) to obtain a series of 1-year forward rates implied by the yield data. Specifically, if $_t i_3$ equals .095, $_t i_2$ equals .090, and $_t i_1$ equals .084, then applying (7.9) produces $_{t+1} f_1$ = .09603. Applying (7.10) yields

$$(1.095)^3 = (1.084)(1.09603)(1 + _{t+2} f_1), \text{ or}$$

$$_{t+2}f_1 = \frac{(1.095)^3}{(1.084)(1.09603)} - 1$$

$$= .1051$$

The unbiased expectations theory states that forward rates obtained from observed market interest rates equal the unbiased forecast for a security of that maturity at each respective future period. Alternatively, these expectations determine why otherwise comparable securities with different maturities carry different rates. Why, for example, do the three Treasury yields increase as maturity lengthens? According to the unbiased expectations theory, the consensus forecast is that short-term interest rates will increase in the near future. The 2-year Treasury rate exceeds the 1-year Treasury rate because the 1-year rate forward rate, one year from today ($_{t+1}f_1$) exceeds the current 1-year Treasury rate. The same holds for the 2 and 3-year Treasury yields.

The shapes of the yield curves in Exhibit 7.9 similarly reflect different expectations regarding interest rates and thus reveal different forward rates. In April 1989, the consensus forecast was that rates would increase through 2 years, then decline. Thus the yield curve rose through the shorter maturities, then systematically fell. In April 1990, the consensus forecast was that rates would rise sharply, then remain relatively constant. Thus short-term rates continuously increased and long-term rates remained roughly constant.

In general, yield curves can take any shape. When long-term rates continuously rise above short-term rates, the yield curve is said to be normal or upsloping. The bottom panel in Exhibit 7.9 indicates that the yield curve took this shape in September 1988. When long-term rates fall below short-term rates, the yield curve is said to be inverted or downsloping. Normal yield curves can be generally characterized as consistent with expectations of rising interest rates, while inverted or downsloping yield curves are consistent with expectations of declining interest rates. Occasionally, the yield curve is flat as rates are approximately equal at all maturities. The bottom panel of Exhibit 7.9 demonstrates that this was the case in September 1989. As indicated, the yield curve took a variety of different shapes in 1988 and 1989.

Liquidity Premium Theory

The unbiased expectations theory assumes that securities which differ only in terms of maturity are perfect substitutes. Investors presumably shift between maturities on the basis of promised yields. In fact, the earlier discussion of liquidity recognizes that there is a built-in preference for short-term securities by investors because there is less price risk. If the expected return on a series of short-term securities equals the expected return on a long-term security, investors will prefer the short-term securities. The **liquidity premium theory** extends the unbiased expectations theory by incorporating investor expectations of price risk in establishing market rates. Expectations still determine the fundamental shape of the yield curve. However, when expected returns are the same on long-term versus the series of short-term securities, borrowers must pay investors a risk premium to induce them to buy the long-term securities. This premium is in addition to the rate expected to prevail in the future. Because price risk increases with maturity, the risk premium also increases with maturity.

Liquidity Premium Theory: Long-term rates are an average of current rates, expected short-term rates, and liquidity premiums. The forward rate equals the expected rate plus a liquidity premium.

This theory suggests that the forward rate can be decomposed into two parts; the expected future short-term rate and the liquidity premium. Letting

$_{t+1}e_1$ = expected interest rate on a 1-period security, 1 year from the present, and
$_{t+1}p_1$ = liquidity premium component of a 1-period forward rate, 1 year from the present,

$$_{t+1}f_1 = {}_{t+1}e_1 + {}_{t+1}p_1. \qquad (7.11)$$

Unfortunately, neither the expected short-term rate nor the liquidity premium is directly observable from market information. We can only draw inferences from observed yields and calculated forward rates. Assume that market interest rates reflect the tenets of the liquidity premium theory. Several implications seem apparent. First, even if the consensus forecast is for short-term rates to remain constant, the yield curve will be continuously upsloping. This results from the notion that liquidity premiums are positive and increase with maturity. Longer-term rates will therefore remain above short-term rates. Second, the normal shape of the yield curve is upsloping because liquidity premiums impart an upward bias to long-term rates compared with short-term rates. Third, liquidity differences between very-long-term securities should disappear. This explains, in part, why yield curves tend to flatten out at long maturities, as there is no differential price risk. Finally, when the yield curve is inverted, short-term rates are expected to decline sharply because the rate decrease must offset rising liquidity premiums.

The Impact of Changing Expectations The Treasury yield curve has taken a variety of shapes at different times. It is often upsloping, occasionally flat, and periodically inverts for short periods. Because it shows the relationship between interest rates and maturity at a given point in time, the yield curve will shift or change shape whenever expectations change. Consider the original example with the Treasury securities yielding 8.4 percent, 9.0 percent, and 9.5 percent, and suppose that all investors, fearing a recession, suddenly lower their expectations regarding future interest rates. Believing that 1-year rates, 1 year from the present will be less than 9.603 percent, investors will purchase 2-year securities to maximize their return. This increased demand for 2-year securities relative to the available supply lowers the 2-year yield, while the reduced demand for 1-year securities raises the 1-year yield. The impact is that short-term rates rise, long-term rates decline and the yield curve flattens out. Depending on the degree of the change in expected rates, the yield curve could remain upsloping, go flat, or become inverted.

Suppose, instead, that all investors suddenly expect rates to be much higher than 9.603 percent in 1 year. The relative demand for 1-year Treasuries increases while the demand for 2-year Treasuries decreases. Short-term rates would thereby fall while long-term rates would rise and the yield curve would increase in slope. The essential point is that if the basic shape of the yield curve is determined by expectations, long-term rates will change immediately relative to short-term rates to reflect changing expectations.

Market Segmentation Theory

Market segmentation theory is based on the premise that investors and borrowers do not view securities with different maturities as perfect substitutes. Market participants tend to concentrate their transactions within specific maturity ranges, regardless of interest rates on securities outside the preferred maturities. Interest rates are thus determined by distinct supply and demand conditions within each maturity group, and changes in interest rates do not induce any substitution between different maturity securities. Hence the term "market segmentation."

There are many reasons why borrowers and lenders may restrict transactions to a specific maturity. First, they may be required to use certain maturity instruments because of government regulation. An example is state governments which, by law, must operate with balanced operating budgets. They issue short-term debt to finance temporary imbalances between operating revenues and expenses, and long-term debt to finance capital expenditures. They cannot issue long-term debt to finance operating expenses. Second, participants may limit maturities as part of a general policy to reduce risk in their business.

Commercial banks, for example, normally concentrate their investments in securities with maturities under 10 years because most of their liabilities are relatively short-term. This allows them to approximately match the maturities of their assets with the maturities of their liabilities in order to reduce the risk of losses when interest rates change. Life insurance companies similarly buy long-term securities because they can actuarily predict claim payments over long periods of time. Long-term securities offer attractive yields and can be timed to mature at intervals that coincide, on average, with expected claims. Third, participants may lack the expertise to switch maturities with any frequency, or may simply be unwilling to take advantage of opportunities because they are not profit maximizers. The U.S. Treasury falls into this last group as it refuses, as a matter of policy, to adjust the maturity of outstanding Treasury debt to take advantage of the prevailing yield curve.

Maturity restrictions resulting from government regulation create what can be referred to as *strong form market segmentation.* Borrowers and lenders have rigid legal restrictions that prohibit maturity substitution. Limitations resulting from other motives produce *weak form market segmentation.* Implicitly, participants can be induced to shift between maturities if interest premiums are sufficiently large.

> **Market Segmentation Theory**: Interest rates on securities with different maturities are determined by distinct supply and demand conditions within each maturity. Borrowers and lenders concentrate their transactions within preferred maturities and cannot be induced to substitute between maturities by small yield changes.

Exhibit 7.10 demonstrates the impact of market segmentation on the yield curve. The analysis assumes that the maturity spectrum is divided into one short-term security and one long-term security. The diagrams display aggregate borrower and lender activity within each maturity group and are drawn to equivalent scale. The top panel outlines conditions that produce a normal, or upsloping, yield curve. At each interest rate, the amount of funds that lenders are willing to lend relative to the prospective borrowing requested is greater for short-term securities than for long-term securities. Thus, at a market rate of 10 percent, the short-term market is in equilibrium while lenders in the long-term market are not willing to lend all the funds that long-term borrowers want. The greater relative demand pressure for short-term securities pushes short-term rates below long-term rates and the yield curve is upsloping.

The bottom panel outlines conditions for an inverted, or downsloping, yield curve. The previous borrower and lender relationships are essentially reversed. At each interest rate, the amount of funds borrowers request relative to the amount lenders are willing to commit is far greater for short-term securities than for long-term securities. Thus, short-term rates exceed long-term rates and the yield curve slopes downward.

The Yield Curve and the Business Cycle

Many analysts track changes in the Treasury yield curve for information about where the economy is headed with regard to the business cycle. Changes in the shape of the yield curve presumably reflect changing expectations concerning where interest rates are headed, and certain patterns are associated with different stages of the business cycle. Exhibit 7.5 indicates the normal relationship between the shape of the yield curve and economic conditions. Note that the dashed line characterizes the movement in short-term rates while the solid line characterizes the pattern in long-term rates. During the early stages of the expansion, unemployment and inflation are relatively low and businesses operate with some excess capacity. The Federal Reserve typically provides lenders with sufficient reserves to make new loans in order to stimulate growth. This keeps short-term rates low relative to long-term rates as noted by the dashed line below the solid line at the trough and immediately following. Thus the yield curve slopes upward. As consumers spend and businesses expand production, aggregate income rises. This raises borrowing requirements and interest rates move higher. Eventually inflation starts to accelerate so that long-term rates increase, reflecting greater inflation expectations. At the peak, loan demand is high, inflation is high and rising, and the Federal Reserve acts to reduce the growth in loanable funds. This policy puts upward pressure on short-term rates and stabilizes or decreases inflation expectations, thereby moving long-term rates lower. The yield curve thus inverts. Eventually, high rates deter consumer and business spending so that GNP declines, unemployment increases, and inflation eases. The level of interest rates moves lower with short-term rates falling farther than long-term rates, and the yield curve is again upsloping.

The implication of Exhibit 7.5 is that the shape of the Treasury yield curve indicates where the U.S. economy is in terms of the business cycle. In particular, after the yield curve inverts, an economic slowdown typically follows. Exhibit 7.11 com-

Exhibit 7.10 Market Segmentation and the Slope of the Yield Curve

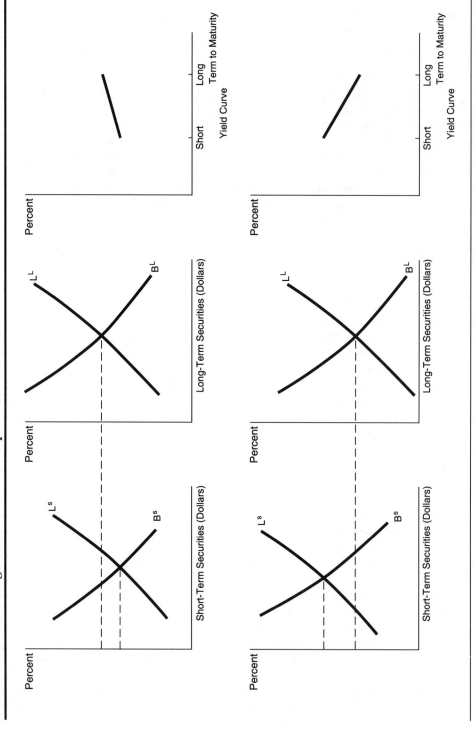

Exhibit 7.11 Relationship Between the Yield Curve and Recessions

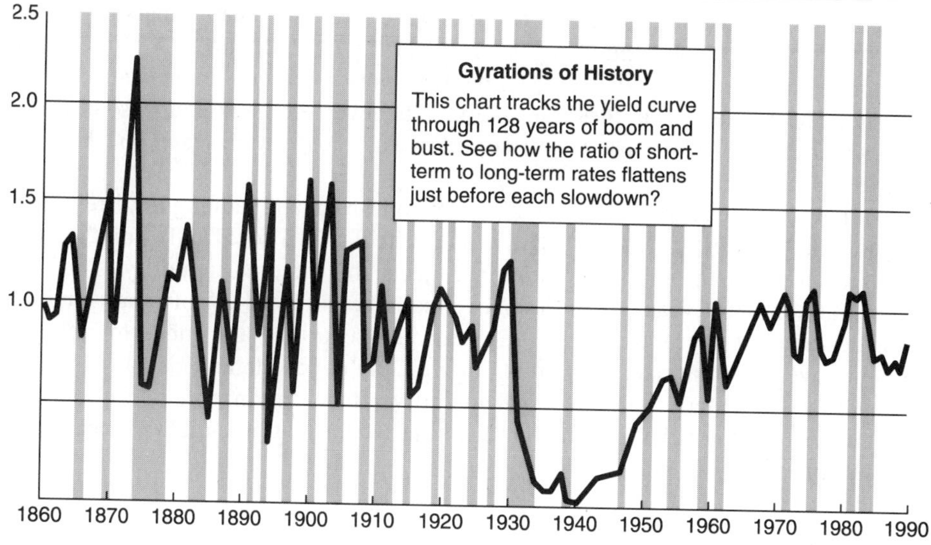
Gyrations of History
This chart tracks the yield curve through 128 years of boom and bust. See how the ratio of short-term to long-term rates flattens just before each slowdown?
2.5
2.0
1.5
1.0
1860
1870
1880
1890
1900
1910
1920
1930
1940
1950
1960
1970
1980
1990

Source: Taken from "Dangerous Shapes," *Forbes*, January 23, 1989, by Jack Willoughby.

pares the relationship between short-term and long-term interest rates and economic growth. The solid line measures the ratio of short-term to long-term rates. When it exceeds 1 the yield curve is inverted. The shaded areas signify periods in which the U.S. economy was in recession. In all but one instance, the shift to an inverted yield curve preceded a recession by 12 to 18 months. The relationship has been remarkably robust.

TERM TO REPRICING VARIABLE RATE AND FLOATING RATE SECURITIES

Some loan contracts call for the repayment of principal to be deferred, but loan interest reset at periodic intervals prior to final maturity or principal payment. Suppose, for instance, that a depositor wants to deposit $1 million in a bank for 1 year, but expects interest rates to increase well above current rates later in the year. A bank would like the certainty of funds remaining on deposit for the year, which provides greater investment flexibility. The two parties might agree to structure the deposit as a CD with a 1-year maturity, but with the interest rate set every 3 months at the prevailing 3-month CD rate. The depositor is protected against rate increases because the earning rate will rise when CD rates rise, while the bank has use of the funds for the full year.

A security is classified as **variable rate** if the applicable market interest rate is reset at predetermined intervals. The CD in the previous example is a variable rate CD. A security is classified as **floating rate** if the applicable market interest rate is tied to some index and changes whenever the index changes. A prime-based loan priced at the bank's current prime rate plus 1 percent represents such a contract. The prime rate is the base index. Whenever the bank changes its prime rate, which normally occurs at varied intervals, the contract rate on the loan changes coincidentally.

Variable rate securities are priced in terms of the time remaining until repricing and not final maturity. Conceptually, a lender locks in a yield only for the time until repricing, so the term to repricing reflects the effective maturity. Thus the market rate on the 1-year CD in the above example is priced off of other 3-month securities and not 1-year securities. Floating rate securities are priced to reflect a premium over the base rate. This premium typically covers default risk and the cost of handling the underlying loan. Final maturity affects the market rate because it may influence default risk or other costs to the lender that potentially appear prior to maturity.

CALL AND PUT PROVISIONS

Many securities contain provisions that alter the effective maturity of a security. Two special option features that are often attached to bonds have this impact. One common option, a **call provision**, enables the issuer of a security to call an outstanding bond for repayment at a predetermined price prior to final maturity. The call feature has value because it protects a borrower in the event that interest rates decline after the securities are originally issued. A significant decrease in rates enables a borrower to issue new debt at lower rates and use the proceeds to prepay old debt that carries higher rates. Investors are hurt because they must forego high rates on the old debt as prepayment forces them to reinvest the proceeds at lower rates.

A call option has value to a borrower and is priced accordingly. In order to induce investors to purchase callable securities, borrowers typically stipulate that the securities must be called at a premium over par value. Thus a bond with a $10,000 par value might be callable at 107 percent of par. This means that the issuer would have to pay an investor $10,700 to buy back the bond regardless of whether the bond's actual price were lower. In many cases issuers defer for several years the initial date at which a security might be callable. A bond with a 20-year maturity might not be callable for the first 5 years. The premium that must be paid at call usually decreases the farther out a bond is called. The justification for a call premium is that if interest rates fall enough to make calling a bond attractive to the issuer, the market price would be well above the call price if the bond were noncallable. The premium represents a sharing of the increase in value. In practice, the market price will not rise above the call price because such a bond will likely be called eventually.

Investors demand higher interest rates on callable bonds compared with noncall-able bonds. This compensates investors for the risk that they might lose the above-

---

Put Bonds and Corporate Buyouts

The corporate merger and acquisition craze that swept U.S. firms and financial markets throughout the 1980s created a market for another type of put bond whose intent was to protect bondholders from adverse price moves resulting from a buyout. In the typical buyout, one firm purchases the stock of another firm and finances the transaction primarily with new debt. The combined firm's financial leverage (debt divided by equity) increases sharply, and thus the credit risk of outstanding debt tends to deteriorate. The rating agencies often respond by lowering quality ratings and bondholders find their claims subordinated even more. In many instances, bondholders have seen the value of

their holdings drop by 10 to 20 percent in a matter of days after a buyout is announced. Krohlberg, Kravis & Robert's acquisition of R.J. Reynold in 1988, for example, saw bondholders lose 22 percent of the value of their securities in 2 days.

Bond investors reacted to these events by filing lawsuits claiming a violation of fiduciary responsibilities and generally refusing to purchase additional debt from buyout candidates without some form of protection. A popular option is now to attach a put feature to a bond which specifies that a bond is puttable back to the issuer at par if certain adverse conditions appear as a result of a buyout proposal.

---

market interest if rates drop, and thus the incremental yield serves as the price of the call option. The longer the deferment period, the lower the yield that an issuer must pay. Market participants generally assume that a callable bond will be called, and price the security to the first call date rather than to final maturity. The market rate is termed the yield to first call.

Another type of option that is becoming increasingly common is the put option. A **put option** gives the lender the right to put, or sell, a security back to the issuer at a predetermined price prior to final maturity. This option has value to an investor because the predetermined price is typically at least par, and the investor can sell the security without a loss if interest rates rise. Without a put option, an investor would have to sell the security at a loss or hold it to maturity to receive and reinvest the principal. If interest rates fall, an investor can simply hold on to the security, which now pays a higher-than-market rate, and can be sold at a premium in the secondary market. A put option is costly to an issuer because it eliminates the potential for interest rate savings from locking in low rates when borrowing occurs at rate troughs. Contemporary Issues: Put Bonds and Corporate Buyouts demonstrates that put bonds are increasingly attractive due to problems bondholders experienced with recent corporate buyouts.

As with any option, a put feature is priced accordingly. Conceptually, a put option is priced much like a variable rate loan because the put decision is effective at predetermined intervals. A 20-year bond, for example, might be puttable at each 1-year anniversary of the issue date for the first 10 years, after which the put option elapses. If at the anniversary date rates are above the rate on the security, an investor will put the bond back to the issuer, who then agrees to pay a market rate rather than return principal to the investor. If the investor demands a return of principal, the issuer will find another investor to buy the security. Thus a put bond effectively changes yield at each put period according to prevailing rates when rates rise. Put yields remain constant at each put period when rates fall.

Again, the importance of final maturity is reduced when a put feature is attached to a security. The interest rate on a put instrument is normally linked to the rate on a similar security without a put option. The link is that the length of time between put anniversary dates coincides with the maturity of the related security. Thus a bond that is puttable at 1-year intervals is priced at a slight premium over the prevailing 1-year rate.

SUMMARY

Many factors influence interest rates. This chapter introduces a loanable funds framework that uses supply and demand analysis to characterize movements in the level of interest rates. Rates fall when the supply of loanable funds increases relative to the demand for loanable funds and rise when the opposite occurs. The level of interest rates also varies directly with changes in inflation expectations and exhibits a pattern over the business cycle, rising during expansionary periods and falling during contractionary periods.

This chapter also examines specific factors that affect the pricing of individual interest-bearing securities. It describes the impact of default risk, liquidity, tax treatment, convertibility, maturity, and the existence of call and put options and explains differences in security yields in terms of these factors. Interest rates are generally higher the greater the default risk, the less liquid the security, and when call provisions exist. Interest rates are lower when default risk is low, the security is highly liquid, interest is tax-exempt, the security is convertible into common stock, and the security contains a put option. Maturity is important because yields reflect expectations of future interest rates, premiums for limited liquidity and price risk, and the fact that certain market participants do not view different maturity securities as substitutes. The fundamental point is that the market prices specific features of each security in terms of their value to either borrowers or lenders.

Questions

Loanable Funds Theory

1. What does the loanable funds theory attempt to explain? Graphically, what is plotted on the vertical axis and what on the horizontal?

2. Indicate which of the following would be a portion of the supply of loanable funds (SF) and which would be a portion of the demand (DF) for loanable funds.
   a. A student puts enough spending money in his savings account for the semester.
   b. A local retailer deposits funds in a demand deposit account overnight.
   c. The same local retailer borrows enough money to pave its parking lot.

  d. You take out a mortgage to finance your first home.

  e. Your university deposits the tuition payments for the semester into an interest-bearing account.

  f. A major corporation issues bonds to finance a new factory.

  g. You take a cash advance on your credit card.

  h. The government needs billions of dollars to rescue the savings and loan industry.

  i. A new sports arena in town has been financed with revenue bonds.

  j. Honda takes excess cash from its Ohio plant and buys Treasury bills.

3. Indicate whether the following changes in the interest rate are caused by a shift in the loanable funds demand curve (DF) or a shift in the supply curve (SF). Draw a graph to show each effect.

  a. A major business expansion in the economy is driving up interest rates.

  b. A reduction in global tensions is reducing spending by the military and interest rates are falling.

  c. Yuppies are saving substantially more money and interest rates are falling.

  d. Massive numbers of foreign investors bid for Treasury bills in large volume at the last auction resulting in the lowest rate in 2 years.

  e. Falling world lumber prices have made homes more affordable and consumers are rushing to take advantage of this. The result is tight financing at record interest rates.

  f. Businesses have overbuilt their inventory levels and no longer need to borrow money for expansion, so interest rates have fallen.

  g. State and local governments borrow heavily to finance the decaying roads and bridges throught the United States.

Interest Rates and Inflation

4. According to the Fisher Relation, what causes nominal market interest rates to be volatile? How long does it take before participants change inflation expectation?

5. You believe the real rate is a constant 4% and you believe the Fisher Relation. If you believe inflation will be 6% in this upcoming year and 10% in the following year, what minimal rate of interest would entice you to lend money for a year? Would you accept a higher rate? What minimal rate would you demand to lend money for 2 years? Why?

6. The major argument surrounding the Fisher Relation deals with the relationship between the real rate and expected inflation. What would each of these discussants claim that relationship to be and what is the implication of each position? Fisher, Mundell-Tobin, and Darby-Feldstein. Is there a difference between the ex ante and ex post real rate relationship?

7. The Fisher Relation is based upon expectations of inflation and not actual inflation. Why? How often do the two differ? Can ex ante real rates be negative? Can ex post real rates be negative?

Rates and the Business Cycle

8. The business cycle is usually measured with what variables? How do these measures of the economy vary with the level of interest rates?

9. Explain how the loanable funds theory would explain rising interest rates during the expansion phase of the business cycle. Would the supply and/or the demand curve be shifting?

Rates and Securities' Features

10. Which one from each of the following pairs is likely to have higher default risk? Explain your reasoning.
    a. a 90-day loan or a 2-year loan to the same company
    b. a loan requiring periodic payments or a loan with all principal and interest due at the end
    c. a loan to a company rated AA by S&P or one rated A-1 by Moody's
    d. a loan to a student to buy a car or a loan to the same student to pay tuition

11. Explain the difference between marketability and liquidity. Give an example of an asset that is marketable but not necessarily liquid.

12. If you were going to invent a security that you wanted to assure would not be very marketable, what features would you give it? Can you think of a security that approximates this?

13. Your university has decided to issue tax-exempt revenue bonds to finance the building of a new dorm. What interest rate will it have to pay if taxable bonds of comparable risk are paying 11% and the marginal tax rate is 28%?

14. If the highest marginal individual tax rate is 28% and the highest corporate rate is 34%, which group will get the greatest benefit from holding municipal securities as investments?

15. Why might a firm that is raising funds choose to issue convertible bonds rather than regular bonds? Under what economic conditions would convertibles be most advantageous?

Yield Curves and Maturity

You note the following yield curve in the *Wall Street Journal.*

Maturity	Yield
6 months	4.7%
1 Year	5.3%
2 years	5.8%
3 years	5.6%
4 years	4.2%

16. What is the 1-year forward rate for the period beginning 1 year from today?

17. If you believe the unbiased expectations theory, what does this mean? How does this interpretation change if you believe the liquidity premium theory? the market segmentation theory?

18. What is the 1-year forward rate for the period beginning 2 years from today?

19. What do investors expect inflation to do over the next several years if the real rate remains constant at 3 percent?

20. Some researchers believe that all three theories—unbiased expectations, liquidity premium, and market segmentation—are correct. All three are continually on the minds of investors, but depending on the current economic conditions one may seem more important than the other two. What economic climate might make investors particularly sensitive to liquidity premiums?

21. Drawing on all of these theories, give two possible explanations for a downsloping yield curve.

22. What would be considered the repricing maturity of the following investments:
   a. a 10-year corporate bond with a 5% coupon rate
   b. a variable rate mortgage with the rate reset quarterly to the cost of funds of the S&L
   c. a floating rate small business loan tied to prime
   d. a 5-year callable bond with an 8% coupon rate, call deferred for 1 year
   e. a bond that is puttable at 1-year intervals

Summary

23. Although of considerably longer maturity, an individual's mortgage usually carries a lower interest rate than his or her car loan. Why?

24. Which of the factors discussed in this chapter might explain why your mortgage rate is 500 basis points higher than your next door neighbor's?

25. This chapter has introduced an abundant list of factors to explain different and changing interest rates. Describe six of these factors.

Activity Projects

1. Using Treasury bond and note rates from the *Wall Street Journal*, fill in the following table to generate a yield curve.

Matures	Yield
6 months	
1 year	
2 years	
3 years	
5 years	
15 years	

   a. Based on this data, what will be the 1-year risk-free rate starting 1 year from today if you believe the unbiased expectations theory?
   b. If you believe the liquidity premium theory, do you expect the risk-free rate 1 year from today to be higher or lower than the number computed above?

2. When was the last time the yield curve was inverted? Did a recession follow in the time interval suggested by Exhibit 7.11? If not enough time has lapsed, is a recession due?

3. Discover your local and state tax rules on Treasury securities and in-state municipal bond interest. Explain how these taxes should affect municipal bonds rates in your state. Should they be higher or lower than rates on comparable municipals issued in other states?

References

Altman, Edward. "How 1989 Changed the Hierarchy of Fixed Income Security Performance." *Financial Analysts Journal* (May–June 1990).

Becketti, Sean. "The Truth About Junk Bonds." *Economic Review* (Federal Reserve Bank of Kansas City, July/August 1990).

Carrington, Samantha, and Robert Crouch. "Interest Rate Differentials on Short-Term Securities and Rational Expectations of Inflation." *Journal of Banking and Finance* (September 1987).

Darby, Michael. "The Financial and Tax Effects of Monetary Policy on Interest Rates." *Economic Inquiry* (June 1975).

Dwyer, Gerald, and R. W. Hafer. "Interest Rates and Economic Announcements." *Review* (Federal Reserve Bank of St. Louis, March/April 1989).

Englander, Steven, and Gary Stone. "Inflation Expectations Surveys as Predictors of Inflation and Behavior in Financial and Labor Markets." *Quarterly Review* (Federal Reserve Bank of New York, Autumn 1989).

Fama, Eugene. "Short-Term Interest Rates as Predictors of Inflation." *American Economic Review* (June 1975).

Fama, Eugene, and Robert Bliss. "The Information in Long Maturity Forward Rates." *American Economic Review* (September 1987).

Feldstein, Martin. "Inflation, Income Taxes and the Rate of Interest: A Theoretical Analysis." *American Economic Review* (December 1976).

Fisher, Irving. "Appreciation and Interest." *Publications of the American Economic Association* (August 1896).

Fisher, Irving. *The Theory of Interest.* New York: Macmillan, 1930.

Garfinkel, Michelle. "What is an 'Acceptable' Rate of Inflation?—A Review of the Issues." *Review* (Federal Reserve Bank of St. Louis, July/August 1989).

Hafer, R. W., and Scott Hein. "Comparing Futures and Survey Forecasts of Near-Term Treasury Bill Rates." *Review* (Federal Reserve Bank of St. Louis, May/June 1989).

Hakkio, Craig. "Interest Rates and Exchange Rates—What is the Relationship?" *Economic Review* (Federal Reserve Bank of Kansas City, November 1986).

Humphrey, Thomas. "The Early History of the Real/Nominal Interest Rate Relationship." *Economic Review* (Federal Reserve Bank of Richmond, May/June 1983).

Kool, Clemens, and John Tatom. "International Linkages in the Term Structure of Interst Rates." *Review* (Federal Reserve Bank of St. Louis, July/August 1988).

Laurent, Robert. "Testing the 'Spread.'" *Economic Perspectives* (Federal Reserve Bank of Chicago, July/August 1989).

Malkiel, Burton. *The Term Structure of Interest Rates: Theory, Empirical Evidence, and Applications.* Silver Burdett, 1970.

McCulloch, Huston. "The Monotonicity of the Term Premium." *Journal of Financial Economics* (March 1987).

Mundell, Robert. "Inflation and Real Interest." *Journal of Political Economy* (June 1963).

Santoni, G. J., and Courtenay Stone. "Navigating Through the Interest Rate Morass: Some Basis Principles." *Economic Review* (Federal Reserve Bank of St. Louis, March 1981).

Tobin, James. "Money and Economic Growth." *Econometrica* (October 1965).

Wigmore, Barrie. "The Decline in Credit Quality of New-Issue Junk Bonds." *Financial Analysts Journal* (September–October 1990).

Wood, John. "Are Yield Curves Normally Upward Sloping? The Term Structure of Interest Rates, 1862–1982." *Economic Perspectives* (Federal Reserve Bank of Chicago, July/August 1983).

APPENDIX TO CHAPTER 7

A. Flow-of-Funds for U.S. Chartered Commercial Banks

U.S.-Chartered Commercial Banks	Annual Flows, $ Billions							
	1983	1984	1985	1986	1987	1988	1989	1990
1 Gross saving	−.5	−2.5	.2	2.2	1.4	1.3	1.5	2.9
2 Fixed nonres. investment	8.8	14.3	15.6	17.6	19.6	24.7	27.8	30.0
3 Net acq.of financial assets	130.3	165.3	191.4	175.8	90.3	127.1	159.7	99.0
4 Total bank credit	133.9	166.2	183.4	163.8	97.0	129.0	155.3	90.9
5 U.S. govt. securities	44.2	1.3	4.6	42.4	24.8	19.8	34.0	54.4
6 Treasury issues	43.5	2.5	7.5	5.9	−3.1	−9.4	−20.3	1.7
7 Agency issues	.7	−1.2	−2.9	36.5	27.9	29.3	54.2	52.8
8 Tax-exempt obligations	3.8	12.6	57.2	−28.4	−29.1	−22.7	−17.8	−16.4
9 Corporate bonds	3.6	3.2	2.3	18.4	20.7	12.3	2.3	1.0
10 Total loans	82.3	149.1	119.3	131.5	80.6	119.6	136.9	51.8
11 Mortgages	29.4	44.1	49.4	67.0	80.7	69.1	85.4	64.1
12 Consumer credit	22.7	45.2	37.5	24.8	16.5	33.1	22.5	4.1
13 Bank loans n.e.c.	27.1	55.7	28.4	46.4	−14.6	19.2	25.3	−12.4
14 Open-market paper	1.1	−.6	−2.8	−.7	1.1	−1.4	−.5	1.4
15 Security credit	2.0	4.7	6.8	−5.9	−3.2	−.4	4.2	−5.4
16 Cust. liab. on acceptances	4.6	−2.8	−11.1	−7.3	−1.0	−3.1	−5.2	−4.1
17 Vault cash & res. at F.R.	−3.9	2.5	5.7	17.3	−6.8	.3	−2.5	6.3
18 Miscellaneous assets	−4.3	−.5	13.4	1.9	1.1	.8	12.0	5.9
19 Net increase in liabilities	146.2	178.5	198.9	178.2	92.9	165.1	149.0	115.4
20 Checkable deposits	15.6	30.2	51.8	93.2	−19.1	15.8	−3.5	21.5
21 U.S. government	−5.3	4.0	10.3	1.7	−5.8	7.3	−3.4	5.3
22 Foreign	1.4	2.8	.1	2.7	−1.5	−.6	−.3	−.4
23 Private domestic	19.5	23.4	41.4	88.8	−11.8	9.1	.2	16.6
24 Small time & sugs. deposits	130.8	74.6	80.3	71.6	27.4	73.1	96.5	121.7
25 Large time deposits	−38.7	33.9	10.8	−6.6	37.7	35.2	24.0	−20.5
26 Fed. funds & security RPs	11.3	1.9	26.8	10.8	11.9	16.3	35.5	−33.3
27 Net interbank liabilities	6.9	4.8	8.0	−4.8	20.3	.6	−22.3	15.9
28 Federal Reserve float	−1.2	−.7	.1	.3	−.5	.5	−.2	1.5

	U.S.-Chartered Commercial Banks	Annual Flows, $ Billions							
		1983	1984	1985	1986	1987	1988	1989	1990
29	Borrowing at F.R. banks	.2	2.7	−.5	−1.5	2.3	−1.6	−1.7	−.3
30	To domestic banking	−.1	4.6	−1.7	−.9	1.4	−.6	−14.7	−6.9
31	To foreign banks	7.9	−1.8	10.1	−2.7	17.1	2.4	−5.8	21.7
32	Acceptance liabilities	3.0	−3.6	−10.9	−8.7	−1.0	−3.3	−5.3	−4.4
33	Corporate equities	.8	1.1	1.4	1.4	1.6	1.7	1.7	1.3
34	Corporate bonds	−.2	3.6	4.5	2.2	.7	−.3	2.8	4.2
35	Profit taxes payable	−.1	*	.1	*	.1	.2	.2	−.2
36	Miscellaneous liabilities	16.9	32.0	26.0	19.1	13.6	25.7	19.4	9.2
37	Inv. by dom. affiliates	15.5	18.9	15.6	16.7	19.8	21.3	8.6	8.6
38	Other	1.4	13.1	10.3	2.4	−6.2	4.4	10.8	.6
39	Discrepancy	6.6	−3.6	−7.9	−13.0	−15.6	14.5	−37.0	−10.7
40	Memo: Credit mkt. funds adv.	136.5	158.7	165.6	162.5	99.2	126.4	146.0	92.2

B. Financial Flows in the Market for 1–4 Family Mortgages

		1983	1984	1985	1986	1987	1988	1989	1990
1	Net borrowing	120.4	136.7	156.8	218.7	234.9	231.0	218.0	214.4
2	Households	116.4	134.7	153.3	214.9	233.0	230.8	221.6	217.0
3	Nonfarm noncorp. business	4.0	2.0	3.8	1.9	.9	.1	−1.8	−1.3
4	Nonfin. corporate business	*	*	−.3	1.9	.9	.1	−1.8	−1.3
5	Net change in assets	120.4	136.7	156.8	218.7	234.9	231.0	218.0	214.4
6	Households	−.1	4.9	3.8	33.9	7.6	25.1	15.1	17.1
7	Nonfarm noncorp. business	1.6	3.3	.6	2.2	.5	.5	.5	.5
8	State and local governments	5.2	5.4	5.9	3.9	1.2	2.5	6.5	3.1
9	U.S. government	.7	.6	.9	−.7	−3.3	.3	.2	16.3
10	Spons. credit agencies	9.4	11.2	11.7	−3.4	.1	9.7	9.0	2.8
11	Mortgage pools	65.2	43.4	78.6	134.3	137.8	69.7	120.2	145.3
12	Commercial banking	8.7	12.9	17.3	20.0	37.4	38.0	51.0	59.3
13	Savings institutions	30.0	50.9	33.7	13.5	55.5	80.0	3.4	−54.5
14	Savings and loan assn.	22.1	45.4	26.1	.5	32.9	56.8	−4.7	−53.2
15	Mutual savings banks	5.1	3.3	4.4	6.1	12.0	15.0	.6	−5.5
16	Credit unions	2.8	2.2	3.2	6.9	10.5	8.2	7.6	4.2
17	Insurance	−2.8	−.7	−2.1	*	−.7	2.0	−1.6	−.2
18	Life insurance companies	−1.4	−1.2	−1.7	.4	.4	2.1	−1.5	.6
19	Private pension funds	−1.4	.6	−.3	.2	−1.4	*	.6	−1.0
20	St. & loc. gvt. rtr. funds	*	−.1	−.1	−.6	.3	−.1	−.7	.2
21	Finance companies	2.7	4.6	6.5	14.9	−1.2	3.2	13.7	24.8
22	REITs	*	*	.1	*	*	*	*	*

Chapter 8

Managing Interest Rate Risk

Periodically, managers of financial institutions "bet the bank" by speculating on interest rate movements. They typically lengthen the maturity of assets by buying long-term securities in anticipation of declining interest rates. If rates subsequently decline, the bank can either sell the securities at a gain or it has locked in above-market yields. Of course, if rates rise, the bank can only sell the securities at a loss and may even end up funding the securities at a negative spread with liabilities that pay higher rates.

Late in 1987 First Bank System Inc. of Minneapolis reported an unrealized loss of $640 million on $8 billion in bonds that it owned. Earlier, in January of 1987 the bond portfolio had an $81 million gain. Clearly, the sharp increase in interest rates during the year eroded the value of the bonds. This loss reflected aggressive risk-taking by the bank's senior management. During 1986 when rates fell, First Bank System realized almost $400 million in securities gains by selling bonds prior to maturity after their prices increased. These gains not only covered the bank's $385 million in loan losses, but allowed the bank to report record profits. Anticipating a further decline in rates, the bank lengthened security maturities to an average 14 years plus increased the overall size of the bond portfolio. At the margin, securities were financed with shorter-term liabilities.

As rates rose in 1987, the bank hedged its position so that future unanticipated rate increases would not drive the bond values lower. Unfortunately, the annual cost of hedging the bonds reached $35 million, or over 50 percent of the bank's expected profits. Management subsequently decided to sell almost $5 billion of its bonds and reported a quarterly loss exceeding $400 million. At least it no longer had to pay the hedging costs.

Why did First Bank System's management gamble on interest rates? The gamble eventually cost the president and CEO their jobs as both resigned under duress. The bank's stock traded at $37 a share early in 1987 but fell below $18 by the end of 1989 *so long-term investors also lost. Should banks speculate on future interest rate movements? Should they consciously mismatch asset and liability maturities? Should they hedge against the risk of loss when interest rates move adversely?*

This chapter examines the management of a bank's interest rate risk position. Interest rate risk refers to the volatility in net interest income and the value of the bank attributable to changes in the level of interest rates. A bank that takes substantial risk will see its net interest margin and market value of stockholders' equity vary widely when rates increase or decrease. A bank that assumes little interest rate risk will observe little change in its performance due to rate changes.

The analysis initially introduces measures of interest rate risk. In doing so, it distinguishes between GAP and duration models. Gap models focus on net interest income as the target measure of bank performance, while duration models primarily target the market value of bank equity. Each model is introduced along with examples that clarify how changes in interest rates and other factors affect the respective target performance measures. The analysis then compares the objectives, strengths, and weaknesses of each model.

Throughout the 1970s banks viewed credit and liquidity risks as the major constraints on profitability. Subsequent events, however, focused attention on interest rate risk. In October 1979 the Federal Reserve announced that monetary policy would focus more on controlling monetary aggregates and less on stabilizing interest rates. Regulatory directives in the early 1980s largely eliminated restrictions against interest rates paid on bank liabilities. The effect was to increase interest rate volatility and bank funding costs. Exhibit 8.1 documents the movement of selected interest rates from 1965 to 1990. Rate volatility for both short- and long-term instruments increased in late 1979. The monthly standard deviation for the federal funds rate rose from 2.13 percent for the 33 months prior to the October policy shift to 3.10 percent in the following 27 months. It then returned to historical stability after 1981. Similar patterns appeared for 3-month Treasury bills, certificates of deposit (CDs), and 10-year Treasury bonds.

Recent changes in the economic and regulatory environment have further eliminated the guaranteed spread between bank asset yields and funding costs. Interest rate fluctuations alter the value of a bank unless management implements strategies to reduce the impact. Interest rate risk management is extremely important because no one can consistently forecast interest rates accurately. Today, most banks use an asset and liability management committee (ALCO) to regularly assess interest rate risk. ALCO policies additionally address capital requirements, the contribution of noninterest income to cover overhead and the bank's tax position, and also monitor liquidity sources.

MANAGING INTEREST RATE RISK

Unexpected changes in interest rates can significantly alter a bank's profitability and market value of equity. Interest rate risk encompasses this volatility. Depending on the

Exhibit 8.1 Interest Rates 1965–1990

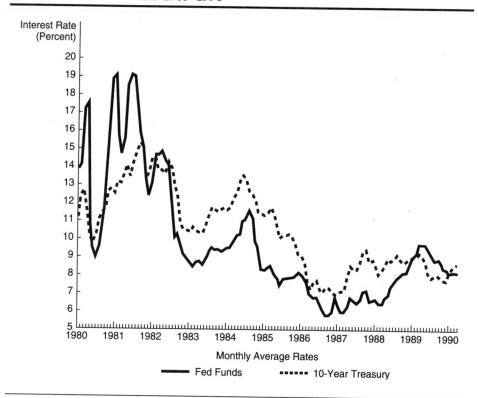

Source: Federal Reserve Bank of St. Louis

cash flow characteristics of a bank's assets and liabilities, interest rate changes may raise or lower net interest income and the market value of assets and liabilities. Many banks and thrifts, for example, suffered serious cash flow problems from 1980 to 1982 as a result of reduced net interest margins (NIMs) and were short of funds even though they experienced few loan losses. Not surprisingly, the market values of the firms fell to where many were economically insolvent.

Consider a traditional bank or thrift institution that makes 30-year, fixed-rate mortgage loans, and finances these loans primarily with 3-month to 1-year deposits. The initial spread between the yields on the mortgages and cost of deposits presumably reflects both the cost of doing business and the expected change in rates over the investment horizon. If all interest rates increase above that expected, interest expense on deposits will rise more than interest income on assets such that net interest income and the value of the firm decline. If interest rates fall below that expected, the difference between interest income and interest expense will widen and the value of the firm will increase.

Efforts at managing interest rate risk force a bank to establish specific financial goals for net interest income and the market value of stockholders' equity, measure its risk exposure, and formulate strategies to attain the goals. These goals and strategies presumably reflect management's view of actions that will lead to maximizing the value of the bank. Most banks use either a GAP model, duration model, or combination of the two. While the two models are complementary, they differ in objective, risk measurement, and strategic recommendations.

The following sections describe the application of each planning model and examine their strengths and weaknesses. Important terminology is summarized in Exhibit 8.2.

GAP ANALYSIS: MANAGING NET INTEREST INCOME AND NEAR-TERM CASH FLOWS

GAP models focus on managing net interest income in the short run. The objective is typically to stabilize expected net interest income or improve it. Interest rate risk is measured by calculating GAPs over different time intervals based on aggregate balance sheet data at a fixed point in time. These GAP values are then examined to infer how much net interest income will change if rates change. There are four basic steps to GAP analysis.

1. Management selects a time frame for determining how rate-sensitive assets and liabilities are.

2. Assets and liabilities are grouped into time "buckets" according to maturity or the time until the first possible repricing. The principal portion of an asset or liability that can be repriced is classified as rate-sensitive.

3. The GAP then equals the dollar difference between rate-sensitive assets (RSAs) and rate-sensitive liabilities (RSLs) for each time interval.

4. Management interprets GAP information directly and via sensitivity analysis.

Formally,

$$GAP = RSAs - RSLs$$

where rate-sensitive assets and liabilities are those allocated within each time bucket. This information is used either to hedge net interest income against changing interest rates or to speculatively alter the size of the GAP in an attempt to raise net interest income. Hedging involves reducing the volatility of net interest income either by directly adjusting the dollar amounts of rate-sensitive assets and liabilities, or by taking an off-balance-sheet position such as with forwards, futures, and option contracts and interest rate swaps.[1] Directly altering the size of GAP to take advantage of perceived

---

[1]The use of forwards, futures, options, and interest rate swaps is explained and demonstrated in Chapters 9 and 10.

Exhibit 8.2 Important Terminology

ALCO: Acronym for asset and liability management committee.

ALM: Acronym for asset and liability management.

Base rate: Any interest rate used as an index to price loans or deposits; quoted interest rates are typically set at some mark-up, such as 0.25% or 1%, over the base rate and thus change whenever the base rate changes.

Cost of funds: Interest expense divided by the dollar volume of interest-bearing liabilities.

Duration: A measure of the approximate price sensitivity of an asset or portfolio to a change in interest rates.

Earning ratio: The dollar volume of a bank's earning assets divided by the dollar volume of total assets.

Floating rate: Assets or liabilities that carry rates tied to the prime rate or other base rates. The instrument is repriced whenever the base rate changes.

GAP: The dollar volume of rate-sensitive assets minus the dollar volume of rate-sensitive liabilities.

GAP ratio: The dollar volume of rate-sensitive assets divided by the dollar volume of rate-sensitive liabilities.

Hedging: Taking a position or implementing a transaction to reduce overall risk associated with an existing position.

Net interest margin (NIM): Tax-equivalent net interest income divided by earning assets.

Net overhead: Noninterest expense minus noninterest income.

Nonrate gap: Noninterest-bearing liabilities plus equity minus nonearning assets as a ratio of earning assets.

Rate-sensitive assets (RSAs): The dollar value of assets that either mature or can be repriced within a selected time period, such as 90 days.

Rate-sensitive liabilities (RSLs): The dollar value of liabilities that either mature or can be repriced within a selected time period, such as 90 days.

Speculation: Taking a position or implementing a transaction that increases risk in hopes of earning above average returns.

Spread: Yield rate minus the cost of funds.

Variable rate: Assets or liabilities that are automatically repriced at regular intervals.

Yield rate: Tax-equivalent interest income divided by the dollar volume of earning assets.

---

rate changes is speculative because it assumes that management can forecast interest rates better than the market can.

What Determines Rate Sensitivity?

The first two steps in GAP analysis require the classification of assets and liabilities as rate-sensitive or fixed-rate, within specific time intervals. Management typically selects a variety of time buckets that provide useful information, as outlined in subsequent sections. The important issue, however, is to determine what constitutes rate sensitivity.

Consider a 3-month time frame. What assets and liabilities listed on a bank's balance sheet can be repriced within 3 months? Obviously, any instrument that matures can be repriced because the bank can reinvest the proceeds or must reset the deposit rate at prevailing yields. Thus any investment security or deposit that matures within 3 months—federal funds sold, 1-month T-bills, NOW accounts—is rate-sensitive. Similarly, any principal payment on a loan is rate-sensitive if management expects to

receive it within the time interval. This includes final principal payments as well as interim principal payments, such as the principal component of the regular monthly payment on a mortgage or car loan. In addition, some assets and deposit liabilities pay rates that vary with some index. These instruments are repriced whenever the index changes. In this example, if management knows that the index will contractually change within 3 months, the underlying asset or liability is rate-sensitive. Such is the case with a variable rate commercial loan that reprices every 3 months based on changes in the 3-month CD rate as an index.

Some loans and deposits carry rates tied to indexes for which the bank has no control or definite knowledge of when the index will change. For example, a commercial loan priced at 1 percent over some other bank's prime rate carries a floating rate, but may or may not be repriced with any frequency. The loan is rate-sensitive in the sense that its yield can change at any time, but its effective rate-sensitivity depends on how frequently the index changes. These floating rate instruments are normally counted as rate-sensitive, but can dramatically alter effective GAP measures if the underlying indexes do not change within the respective time intervals.

Factors Affecting Net Interest Income

Many factors affect net interest income. These include changes in the level of interest rates, in the relationship between bank yield rates and interest costs, in the volume of assets and liabilities outstanding, and in the composition of assets and liabilities. Some factors are at least partially controllable, while others are not. Asset and liability management examines the impact of all factors on net interest income. The following analysis documents circumstances in which income rises and falls by comparing income at a hypothetical bank before and after each influence.

Consider a bank with the general balance sheet accounts listed in Exhibit 8.3. The RSAs and RSLs either mature or can be repriced within a set time interval. For ease of example, the classification in Exhibit 8.3 assumes a 1-year time horizon. Thus the RSAs and RSLs either mature within 1 year, represent variable-rate contracts that are automatically repriced within 1 year, or carry floating-rate yields. The RSAs include short-term securities, federal funds sold, expected principal payments on loans, and the outstanding principal on all variable-rate and floating-rate loans. The RSLs include jumbo CDs maturing within 1 year, federal funds purchased, negotiable orders of withdrawal, and money market deposit accounts. The critical feature is that cash flows associated with rate-sensitive contracts vary with changes in interest rates. Fixed-rate assets and liabilities carry rates that are constant throughout the time interval. Cash flows do not change unless there is a default. Nonearning assets generate no explicit income, and nonpaying liabilities pay no interest.

Average yield rates (r_i from Chapter 4) and interest costs (c_j from Chapter 4) appear beside each account. If these balance sheet and interest rate figures reflect average performance during the year, the bank's tax-equivalent net interest income is expected to equal $40.90 per $1,000 in assets. Selected performance measures are listed at the bottom of the exhibit. These figures represent benchmark estimates. During the year, the level of interest rates normally changes from that initially projected, as do the

Exhibit 8.3 Expected Balance Sheet Composition and Average Interest Rates For a Hypothetical Bank[a]

	Assets	Average Yield Rates	Liabilities	Interest Costs
Rate-sensitive	$ 500	12%	$ 600	9%
Fixed-rate	350	15	220	8
Nonearning/Nonpaying	150		100	
Total			$ 920	
			Equity	
			$ 80	
Total	$1,000		$1,000	

Net interest income $= 0.12(\$500) + 0.15(\$350) - 0.09(\$600) - 0.08(\$220)$
$= \$112.50 - \$71.60$
$= \$40.90$
Net interest margin $= \$40.90/\$850 = 4.81\%$
GAP $=$ RSAs $-$ RSLs $= \$500 - \$600 = -\$100$

---

[a]RSAs indicates rate-sensitive assets RSLs rate-sensitive liabilities. The assumed time frame for classifying RSAs and RSLs is 1 year. Yield rates computed on a tax-equivalent basis.

composition and volume of assets and liabilities. Many banks focus on the GAP when managing net interest income over the near term. This bank's 1-year GAP equals −$100. The sign and magnitude of GAP provide information regarding interest rate risk.

Changes in the Level of Interest Rates

Fluctuating interest rates can raise, lower, or not affect a bank's net interest income, depending on portfolio mix, rate sensitivity, and GAP value. A negative GAP indicates that the bank has more RSLs than RSAs. When interest rates rise during the time interval, the bank pays higher rates on all repriceable liabilities and earns higher yields on all repriceable assets. If all rates rise by equal amounts at the same time, interest expense rises more than interest income because more liabilities are repriced. The spread between the bank's average yield on earning assets and average cost of interest-bearing liabilities declines. Net interest income thus declines. When interest rates fall during the interval, more liabilities than assets are repriced at the lower rates, the average spread widens, and net interest income increases.

A positive GAP indicates that a bank has more RSAs than RSLs. When short-term rates rise, interest income increases more than interest expense because more assets are repriced. The spread and net interest income similarly increase. Decreases in short-term rates have the opposite effect. Interest income falls more than interest expense such that the bank's spread and net interest income fall. If the bank has a zero GAP, RSAs equal RSLs and equal interest rate changes do not alter net interest income because changes in interest income equal changes in interest expense. These relationships are summarized as follows:

Gap Summary

Gap	Change in Interest Rates	Change in Interest Income		Change in Interest Expense	Change in Net Interest Income
Positive	Increase	Increase	>	Increase	Increase
Positive	Decrease	Decrease	>	Decrease	Decrease
Negative	Increase	Increase	<	Increase	Decrease
Negative	Decrease	Decrease	<	Decrease	Increase
Zero	Increase	Increase	=	Increase	None
Zero	Decrease	Decrease	=	Decrease	None

Panel A of Exhibit 8.4 shows the relationship between rising rates and a negative GAP for the hypothetical bank. All short-term rates are assumed to increase by an average of 1 percent during the year, with the bank's portfolio composition and size unchanged. With the rate increase, interest income rises by $5 to $117.50, but interest expense rises by $6 to $77.60 so that net interest income declines by $1 relative to that initially projected in Exhibit 8.3. NIM subsequently falls by 12 basis points.

Suppose instead that short-term rates decrease by 1 percent relative to the base case. The average yield rate on rate-sensitive assets declines to 11 percent, while the interest cost of rate-sensitive liabilities declines to 8 percent. Interest income falls by $5 while interest expense falls by $6 so that net interest income rises by $1. This occurs because the bank now pays lower rates on a greater amount of liabilities ($600) than it has assets ($500) that are now earning lower yields. NIM also widens.

The change in net interest income arises because the amount of rate-sensitive assets differs from the amount of rate-sensitive liabilities. The larger the difference, the greater is the impact. If the two were equal, the change in interest income would be matched by the change in interest expense so that net interest income would be unchanged. Whether net interest income rises or falls, in turn, depends on whether the GAP is positive or negative relative to the change in level of interest rates.

Specifically, if the 1-year GAP is set at any positive value, net interest income will increase when short-term rates rise, and will decrease when short-term rates fall. Suppose, for example, that the above bank's initial position consists of $650 in rate-sensitive assets and $200 in fixed-rate assets with all other factors the same. The 1-year GAP equals $50. At the rates listed, interest income is expected to equal $108 while interest expense is still $71.6, producing $36.4 in net interest income. If short-term rates rise by 1 percent, interest income rises by $6.5 while interest expense rises by just $6. With a positive GAP, net interest income now increases by $0.5. It declines when rates fall.[2] In this context, the sign and size of GAP provide information regarding a bank's interest rate risk position.

---

[2] The reader should verify that interest income changes by the same amount as interest expense in these examples when the GAP equals zero.

Changes in the Relationship Between Short-Term Asset Yields and Liability Costs

Net interest income may similarly differ from that expected if the spread between asset yields and interest costs changes. Asset yields may vary relative to interest costs because of an unexpected shift in the yield curve (unequal changes in the level of different interest rates), an increase or decrease in risk premiums, and nonsynchronous changes in indexes on floating-rate assets and liabilities. If, for instance, liabilities are short-term and assets are long-term, the spread will narrow when the yield curve inverts and will widen when the yield curve increases in slope. Similarly, asset yields may be tied to base rates that change monthly while liability costs change weekly with money market rates. Panel B of Exhibit 8.4 examines the impact of a 1-percent decrease in the spread on rate-sensitive assets and liabilities for the year. With the portfolio composition unchanged, net interest income declines to $34.40. Of course, net interest income increases whenever the spread increases.

Changes in Volume

Net interest income varies directly with changes in the volume of earning assets and interest-bearing liabilities, regardless of the level of interest rates. Consider Panel C in Exhibit 8.4, in which the bank doubles in size. The portfolio composition and interest rates are unchanged. Net interest income doubles because the bank earns the same spread on a higher volume of assets. NIM is unchanged and equals the same proportion of total assets, even though GAP doubles to −$200. Growth leads to an increase in the dollar volume of earnings but does not alter profitability measures. A bank that alternatively contracts in size experiences a decrease in net interest income.

Changes in Portfolio Composition

Any variation in portfolio mix potentially alters net interest income. Bank managers may attempt to increase asset rate sensitivity by pricing more loans on a floating-rate basis or shortening maturities of investment securities. They may try to decrease liability rate sensitivity by substituting longer-term CDs for overnight federal funds purchased. These transactions change both the GAP and the bank's interest rate risk position. They also change net interest income from that initially expected. Panel D of Exhibit 8.4 summarizes the impact of a $40 shift of fixed-rate assets to RSAs and a corresponding $40 shift from RSLs to fixed-rate liabilities. In this case, the level of rates is unchanged and net interest income falls by $.80 from the initial estimate of $40.90. This decline is caused by a decline in the average yield on earning assets relative to the interest cost of liabilities. In addition to changing expected net interest income, this change in composition alters the GAP to −$20 and thus changes the bank's interest rate risk profile.

There is no fixed relationship between changes in portfolio mix and net interest income. The impact varies with the relationships between rate-sensitive and fixed-rate

Exhibit 8.4 Factors Affecting Net Interest Income[a]

A. *1% Increase in Level of All Short-Term Rates*

	Assets	Yield Rates	Liabilities	Interest Costs
Rate-sensitive	$ 500	13%	$ 600	10%
Fixed-rate	350	15	220	8
Nonearning/nonpaying	150		100	
			Equity	
			80	
Total	$1,000		$1,000	

Net interest income = 0.13($500) + 0.15($350) − 0.1($600) − 0.08($220)
$$= \$117.50 - \$77.60$$
$$= \$39.90$$
Net interest margin = $39.90/$850 = 4.69%
GAP = $500 − $600 = −$100

B. *1% Decrease in Spread Between Asset Yields and Interest Costs*

	Assets	Yield Rates	Liabilities	Interest Costs
Rate-sensitive	$ 500	12.5%	$ 600	10.5%
Fixed-rate	350	15	220	8
Nonearning/nonpaying	150		100	
			Equity	
			80	
Total	$1,000		$1,000	

Net interest income = 0.125($500) + 0.15($350) − 0.105($600) − 0.08($220)
$$= \$115.00 - \$80.60$$
$$= \$34.40$$
Net interest margin = $34.40/$850 = 4.05%
GAP = $500 − $600 = −$100

---

[a]RSA indicates rate-sensitive asstes; RSLs, rate-sensitive liabilities.

yields and between interest costs and the magnitude of the funds shifts. If, for example, the change in mix were reversed in the above case, net interest income would increase. Net interest income would also rise if the $40 shift in liabilities were the only change in portfolio composition. In many cases, banks change mix as part of initiatives to offset anticipated adverse changes in net interest margin. This is true of recent efforts to shift into consumer loans. Consumer loan yields are typically lowered slowly when other interest rates decline. Commercial loan rates move much more closely with general interest rate movements. In a declining rate environment, this type of portfolio change improves spread and stabilizes NIM.

Changes in the magnitudes of nonearning assets and nonpaying liabilities also influence net interest income and NIM. If a bank can reduce its nonearning assets, net interest income increases automatically, with the magnitude determined by how the funds are invested. For example, net interest income rises by $6.50 (.13($50) − 0) with

C. Proportionate Doubling in Size

	Assets	Yield Rates	Liabilities	Interest Costs
Rate-sensitive	$1,000	12%	$1,200	9%
Fixed-rate	700	15	440	8
Nonearning/nonpaying	300		200	
			Equity	
			160	
Total	$2,000		$2,000	

Net interest income = 0.12($1,000) + 0.15($700) − 0.09($1,200) − 0.08($440)
= $81.80
Net interest margin = $81.80/$1,700 = 4.81%
GAP = $1,000 − $1,200 = −$200

D. Increase in RSAs and Decrease in RSLs

	Assets	Yield Rates	Liabilities	Interest Costs
Rate-sensitive	$ 540	12%	$ 560	9%
Fixed-rate	310	15	260	8
Nonearning/nonpaying	150		100	
			Equity	
			80	
Total	$1,000		$1,000	

Net interest income = 0.12($540) + 0.15($310) − 0.09($560) − 0.08($260)
= $40.10
Net interest margin = $40.10/$850 = 4.72%
GAP = $540 − $560 = −$20

a $50 shift to RSAs. A $50 shift to fixed-rate assets increases net interest income by $7.50 (.15($50) − 0). In both cases, NIM and spread rise because the bank's funding costs are unchanged with higher interest income.

This view of GAP and net interest income is simplistic. Obviously, asset yields and interest costs do not change coincidentally or by equal amounts. Even within distinct time intervals, assets and liabilities are repriced at varied intervals, producing cash flows that may differ substantially from those implied by the GAP. For example, if all RSAs from Exhibit 8.3 matured in 1 month while all RSLs matured in 6 months, projected cash flows would reflect interest rate and portfolio changes occurring 5 months apart.

Managers should calculate the GAP over relatively short periods for its optimum use. Unfortunately, this may create problems with floating-rate loans when interpreting GAP figures. The frequency of changes in base rates or indexes cannot be accurately forecast because management does not know when market interest rates will change.

In 1980 the New York prime rate, a popular base rate for commercial loans, changed 52 times. In 1983 it changed only three times. Prime-based loans were considerably more rate sensitive in 1980. GAP figures do not directly reflect this historical frequency of base rate changes.

Asset and liability management requires that a bank continuously monitor interest rate, portfolio mix, and volume effects. The next section introduces a procedure to evaluate a bank's interest rate risk position according to GAPs constructed using different time buckets. Data for Security Bank, a $100 million organization, are used to demonstrate the planning requirements.

Rate Sensitivity Reports

Many managers monitor their bank's risk position and potential changes in net interest income using a framework like that in Exhibit 8.5. This report classifies Security Bank's assets and liabilities as rate-sensitive in selected time buckets through 1 year. Each column of data reflects the dollar volume of repriceable items within a distinct time period. For example, of the $9.5 million in Treasury and agency securities owned, $700,000 can be repriced in 8 to 30 days, $3.6 million is repriceable in 31 to 90 days, and so forth. The bank's MMDAs and Super NOWs carry rates that may change weekly. All balances thus appear in the nearest-term time bucket. The figures listed by row alongside total assets and total liabilities and equity indicate aggregate rate-sensitive items in each time period. All floating-rate loans tied to a base rate are designated as rate-sensitive from 8 to 30 days out. This classification reflects Security Bank's experience in changing base rates monthly on average during the past year.

Periodic GAPs across the different time buckets indicate the timing of potential income effects from interest rate changes. Cumulative GAPs, in contrast, measure aggregate interest rate risk over the entire period examined. A periodic GAP for each separate interval is listed near the bottom of the exhibit. RSLs actually exceed RSAs in each interval through 1 year, except for the 8- to 30-day period that includes floating-rate loans among RSAs. The cumulative GAP measures the sum of the periodic GAPs through the longest time frame considered. Thus the cumulative GAP at 31 to 90 days of −$15 million equals the sum of the periodic GAPs for 1 to 7 days (−$16 million), 8 to 30 days ($9 million), and 31 to 90 days (−$8 million). Cumulative GAP figures are the most important because they directly measure a bank's net interest sensitivity through the last day of the time bucket by comparing how many assets and liabilities reprice through that last day.

Note that each period's cumulative GAP is negative. Security Bank has positioned itself to gain if short-term rates fall over the next year. Specifically, if short-term rates decrease uniformly during the year, the bank's net interest income would increase unless offset by changes in portfolio mix or bank size. If short-term rates rise, net interest income would decline. Furthermore, the size of the GAP indicates that the bank's performance may vary substantially over the next 6 months as the cumulative GAP is −$22 million, which is more than 25 percent of earning assets.

The rate sensitivity report provides a view of a bank's interest rate risk profile at a point in time. It can also be used to evaluate the impact of past changes in interest

Exhibit 8.5 Rate Sensitivity Analysis for Security Bank, June 30, 1992 (Millions of Dollars)

	Time Frame for Rate Sensitivity							
	1-7 Days	8-30 Days	31-90 Days	91-180 Days	181-365 Days	Over 1 Year	Non Rate Sensitive	Total
Assets								
U.S. Treasury and agency securities		$ 0.7	$ 3.6	$ 1.2	$ 0.3	$ 3.7		$ 9.5
Money market investments			1.2	1.8				3.0
Municipal securities			0.7	1.0	2.2	7.6		11.5
Federal funds sold and repurchase agreements	$ 5.0							5.0
Commercial loans[a]	1.0	13.8	2.9	4.7	4.6	15.5		42.5
Installment loans	0.3	0.5	1.6	1.3	1.9	8.2		13.8
Earning assets								$ 85.3
Cash and due from banks							$ 9.0	9.0
Other assets							5.7	5.7
Nonearning assets								$ 14.7
Total assets	$ 6.3	$15.0	$10.0	$10.0	$ 9.0	$35.0	$14.7	$100.0
Liabilities and Equity								
Money market deposit accounts	$17.3							17.3
Super NOW accounts	2.2							2.2
CDs under $100,000	0.9	$ 2.0	$ 5.1	$ 6.9	$ 1.8	$ 2.9		19.6
CDs over $100,000	1.9	4.0	12.9	10.1	1.2			30.1
Federal funds purchased and repurchase agreements								
NOW accounts					7.4			7.4
Savings accounts						1.9		1.9
Market-rate liabilities								$ 78.5
Demand deposits							13.5	13.5
Other liabilities							1.0	1.0
Equity							7.0	7.0
Nonpaying liabilities and equity							21.5	$ 21.5
Total liabilities and equity	$22.3	$ 6.0	$18.0	$17.0	$10.4	$ 4.8	$21.5	$100.0
Periodic GAP	−$16.0	$ 9.0	−$8.0	−$7.0	−$1.4	$30.2		
Cumulative GAP	−16.0	−7.0	−15.0	−22.0	−23.4	6.8		

[a]Floating-rate loans total $10 million and are classified as repriceable in 8 to 30 days. There is no guarantee that base rates will change in this time period.

rates, asset volume, and portfolio mix or net interest income and to project the impact of future changes. Many banks include a net income analysis in their annual reports to stockholders that allocates portions of actual changes in net interest income to either rate, volume, or composition effects. The purpose is to attribute changes in net interest income to sources that are controllable, such as volume and composition effects, and to uncontrollable sources such as changing interest rates.

Exhibit 8.6 demonstrates these calculations under the label "performance variance analysis" for Security Bank from May to June.[3] The analysis distinguishes between effects produced by the controllable flow of funds among bank assets and liabilities and uncontrollable interest rate changes between two points in time. Exhibit 8.7 provides a framework for forecasting changes in net interest income due to flow-of-funds and interest rate effects. Bank managers follow this break-even analysis procedure to verify the accuracy of their forecasting techniques.

Performance Variance Analysis

Performance variance analysis examines differences in historical balance sheet values per account category, average asset yield rates, liability cost rates, and their corresponding impacts on net interest income. It effectively attributes changes in net interest income between two periods to either interest rate, volume, or composition changes. Interest rate effects are uncontrollable, while other effects reflect conscious management decisions. Thus an analyst can determine what portion of volatility in net interest income can be attributed to management discretion. Exhibit 8.6 presents a 30-day variance analysis for Security Bank. Balance sheet and interest rate figures are averages for both months. The bank's funding GAP through May was negative through 1 year. Interest income and expense are calculated over a 30-day time horizon.[4]

Consider the composition and volume effects indicated by balance sheet variances. Between May and June, Security Bank liquidated $1 million of U.S. government and money market securities and added $1 million in federal funds sold and $500,000 in commercial loans. The net effect was to increase the volume of earning assets by $500,000. The bank financed this growth out of earnings and new MMDAs. The CD transactions offset each other as the bank replaced $1 million of small CDs with $1 million of large CDs. As indicated under the average interest rate variances, the bank earned an average of 12.95 percent on the earning assets that changed and paid an average of 9.97 percent on the liabilities. Independent of rate changes, the composition and volume effects combined would have increased net interest income by $1,225 for June (.0298 × $0.5 × 30/365).

The effect of rate changes was quite different. Average interest rates rose during the month by different magnitudes across instruments. The data suggest that money market rates increased by 10 to 25 basis points (0.10% − 0.25%), while the bank's base loan rate was unchanged. Given Security Bank's negative GAP, the increase in rates reduced overall net interest income because composition and volume effects were small relative to the indicated rate-induced changes in interest income and interest expense.

---

[3]The use of the term *variance* in this analysis differs from the traditional finance usage as a statistical measure of risk. It refers to differences from prior period values.

[4]All interest rates are annualized and quoted on an interest bearing basis assuming a 365-day year. For example, interest expense for MMDAs in June equals (.0935)($17,300,000)(30/365), or $132,949.

**Exhibit 8.6 Performance Variance Analysis for Security Bank:
May vs. June, 30-day Horizon (Millions of Dollars)**

Balance Sheet Composition Variances[a]	May	June	Difference
Earning Assets			
U.S. Treasury and agency securities	$10.0	$ 9.5	$–0.5
Money market investments	3.5	3.0	–0.5
Muncipals	11.5	11.5	0.0
Federal funds sold and RPs	4.0	5.0	1.0
Commercial loans	42.0	42.5	0.5
Installment loans	13.8	13.8	0.0
Total volume effect	$84.8	$ 85.3	$0.5
Liabilities and Equity			
MMDAs	$16.9	$ 17.3	$0.4
Super NOWs	2.2	2.2	0.0
CDs under $100,000	20.6	19.6	–1.0
CDs over $100,000	29.1	30.1	1.0
NOWs and savings	9.3	9.3	0.0
Demand deposits and other	14.5	14.5	0.0
Equity	6.9	7.0	0.1
Total volume effect	$99.5	$100.0	$0.5

Average Interest Rate Variances	May	June	Difference
Assets:			
U.S. Treasury and agency securities	9.15%	9.25%	0.10%
Money market investments	9.65	9.70	0.05
Federal funds sold and RPs	9.90	10.05	0.15
Commercial loans	15.05	15.07	0.02
Weighted Average	12.95		
Liabilities:			
MMDAs	9.25	9.35	0.10
Super NOWs	8.00	8.10	0.10
CDs under $100,000	10.00	10.05	0.05
CDs over $100,000	10.35	10.60	0.25
Weighted Average	9.97%		
Spread	2.98		

[a]RPs indicates repurchase agreements; MMDAs, money market deposit accounts; NOWs, negotiable orders of withdrawal; and CDs, certificates of deposit.

Consider the 30-day interest income and expense variances. The increase in interest income of $8,816 during the 30 days represents the combined rate, volume, and mix effects. With the negative GAP, interest expense increased by $11,920, or $3,104 more than interest income. Thus net interest income fell from May to June so that the net interest rate effect totaled –$4,329 ($3,104 = –$4,329 + $1,255) after adjustment for the volume and mix effects. Higher interest expense resulted from the 10-basis-point rise in rates paid on MMDAs and the substitution of higher-cost large CDs paying 10.6 percent for small CDs paying only 10 percent. The

Exhibit 8.6 *(Continued)*

Interest Income and Expense Variances (30-Day Difference)[b]

	Difference in Actual Dollars
Interest Income	
U.S. Treasury and agency securities	−$2,979
Money market investments	−3,842
Federal funds sold and RPs	8,753
Commercial loans	6,884
Total change	$ 8,816
Interest Expense	
MMDAs	$ 4,463
Super NOWs	179
CDs under $100,000	−7,414
CDs over $100,000	14,692
Total change	$11,920
Net Interest Income Change	−$3,104

Interest Spread on Variant Items[c]

$$\text{May: Spread} = \frac{\$655,057}{\$59,500,000} \times \frac{365}{30} - \frac{\$559,818}{\$68,800,000} \times \frac{365}{30}$$

$$= 13.39\% - 9.90\%$$

$$= 3.49\%$$

$$\text{June: Spread} = \frac{\$663,863}{\$60,000,000} \times \frac{365}{30} - \frac{\$571,738}{\$69,200,000} \times \frac{365}{30}$$

$$= 13.46\% - 10.05\%$$

$$= 3.41\%$$

---

[b] Each difference is measured by subtracting May's value of the income or expense from the value in June. For example, the income variance for federal funds sold and RPs is calculated as: ($5 million)(.1005)(30/365) − ($4 million)(.099)(30/365).

[c] Variant items include assets and liabilities with a nonzero balance sheet change or nonzero rate changes. The spread is calculated as the monthly average interest yield on variant assets minus the monthly average interest cost of variant liabilities.

---

change in spread on variant items summarizes these influences. While portfolio composition, volume, and rate changes from May to June combined to raise average asset yields by 7 basis points from 13.39 percent to 13.46 percent, average interest costs rose by 15 basis points from 9.90 percent to 10.05 percent so that the spread fell by 8 basis points.

Forecasting Changes in Net Interest Income

Bank managers often use a framework like that in Exhibit 8.7 to verify the accuracy of their forecasts concerning rate effects, and to help position the bank under adverse conditions. Estimates of GAP influences on future earnings follow from the rate

Exhibit 8.7 Forecasted Changes in Net Interest Income for Security Bank: Calculate a Break-Even Asset Yield

	Amount ($)	Annualized Average Rate (%)
Rollover of Rate-Sensitive Assets and Liabilities: Interest Rates Unchanged		
Repriceable assets	$21,300,000	14.1%
Repriceable liabilities	28,300,000	9.5
GAP	−7,000,000	
Interest income (next 30 days)	246,847	
Interest expense (next 30 days)	220,973	
Net interest return	$ 25,874	
Forecasted Break-even Yield on Assets		
"New" interest expense on existing rate-sensitive liabilities (0.2% decline in average rates)	$ 216,321	9.3
Interest expense on $1 million of new large CDs	8,548	10.4
Target net interest spread on repriceables	25,874	
Required interest income	$ 250,743	
Break-even asset yield (annualized)[a]	$\dfrac{250{,}743}{22{,}270{,}000} \times \dfrac{365}{30} =$	13.7%

[a]Divisor equals existing repriceable assets plus investable certificate of deposit balances. In this case, investable certificate of deposit balances equal $970,000, or $1 million in new deposits less $30,000 in required reserves.

sensitivity analysis of Exhibit 8.5. Any estimate is subjective because it is based on an interest rate forecast. Still, sensitivity analysis using a variety of interest rate scenarios provides useful information for the magnitude of interest rate risk. Exhibit 8.7 focuses on repriceable assets and calculates a break-even yield required to maintain stable net interest income after rates or volume change. A bank's ALCO members then determine whether the break-even yield is attainable and realign the portfolio or change pricing accordingly.

Consider Security Bank's rate sensitivity position at the end of June. The bank has a −$7 million GAP over the next 30 days with $10 million in floating-rate loans. Management plans immediately to issue $1 million in CDs to finance new loans. Most economists project a substantial decline in interest rates. Exhibit 8.7 examines the potential impact of a general decrease in short-term rates. In this example, Security Bank's average interest cost on the $28.3 million in RSLs is assumed to fall by 20 basis points from 9.5 to 9.3 percent. The bank also issues $1 million in new CDs at 10.4 percent, of which $970,000 is investable.

During July, $21.3 million of assets and $28.3 million of liabilities can be repriced. The assets currently yield an average 14.1 percent and the liabilities pay 9.5 percent. If interest rates, volume, and mix remain unchanged, the bank expects to earn $25,874 on this net funding over the 30 days. Suppose, however, that the average rate paid on repriceable liabilities falls by 20 basis points and the bank issues $1 million in new

CDs at 10.4 percent. This anticipated drop in rates lowers expected monthly interest expense on existing liabilities to $216,321. Interest on the new CDs equals $8,548. Adding in the targeted $25,874 to hold the net interest return constant on the repriceable instruments, Security Bank needs to earn 13.7 percent on repriceable assets to maintain the same profit position.

The ease with which the bank can do this depends on how much its asset yields decline. Security Bank has some control over events because it determines the timing of changes in its base rate and can possibly postpone any decrease, depending on competitive conditions. Banks generally lower base rates with a lag relative to decreases in money market borrowing costs. If, however, pricing pressures are intense, a bank may feel compelled to lower loan rates immediately with the decline in borrowing costs.

There are three complications with this analysis. First, it is extremely difficult to forecast the direction and magnitude of interest rates, even for the near term. Management should perform sensitivity analysis to evaluate projected break-even yields under a range of best-case, worst-case, and most-likely interest rate scenarios. Second, base rate changes are highly uncertain, and corresponding income effects are unpredictable. If all short-term interest costs had increased by 30 basis points in the above example, Security Bank's break-even yield would have risen to 14.35 percent. This would be difficult to realize if the bank did not increase its base rate. Key management decisions revolve around whether and when to increase base rates and whether to shift the portfolio into higher-yielding (riskier) assets. Third, GAP measures do not accurately indicate interest rate risk because they do not recognize timing differences in cash flows for assets and liabilities within the same maturity groupings. GAP measures only approximate true interest rate risk. When the GAP equals zero, net interest income still varies because asset cash flows are not perfectly synchronized with liability cash flows. Even short maturity groupings do not permit the exact matching of cash flows.

Managing the GAP

GAP measures indicate the general interest rate risk faced by bank management. As demonstrated below, the cumulative GAP signifies how much risk an institution takes concerning interest rates.

$$\Delta NII = (GAP)(\Delta i_{exp}) \tag{8.1}$$

where

ΔNII = the expected change in net interest income,
GAP = cumulative GAP over the interval, and
Δi_{exp} = the expected permanent change in the level of interest rates.

If interest rates are expected to rise during the GAP period, a positive cumulative GAP will lead to an increase in net interest income. If rates are expected to fall, a negative GAP will lead to an increase in net interest income. The actual change in net interest income will meet expectations only if interest rates change in the direction and amount anticipated. Importantly, the GAP signifies how much risk a bank is taking. The larger is the absolute value of GAP, the greater is the change in net interest income for a given change in rates. The size of the GAP indicates the magnitude of risk assumed. If banks want to earn above-average profits via NIM, they must assume above-average risk unless they can capture some market inefficiency.

The GAP model suggests that a bank which chooses not to speculate on future interest rates can reduce interest rate risk by obtaining a zero GAP. Regardless of rate changes, net interest income does not change when the GAP is zero. The bank is fully hedged because its interest rate risk is negligible. Alternatively, a bank may choose to speculate on future interest rates and actively manage the GAP. Equation 8.1 suggests that a bank can systematically increase net interest income if it can accurately forecast rates and vary its GAP accordingly. If management expects rates to increase, it should increase the GAP. If it expects rates to decrease, it should decrease the GAP. Contemporary Issues: Wells Fargo: Intentionally Mismatched Maturities addresses which GAP value is best. Below are listed steps that banks can take to shrink GAP to zero and reduce interest rate risk.

Strategies to Shrink GAP to Zero

1. Calculate periodic GAPs over short time intervals.

2. Match fund repriceable assets with similar repriceable liabilities so that periodic GAPs approach zero.

3. Match fund long-term assets with non-interest-bearing liabilities.

4. Use off-balance-sheet transactions, such as interest rate swaps and financial futures, to construct "synthetic" securities and thus hedge.

Unfortunately, it is difficult to vary the GAP actively and consistently win. First, interest rate forecasts are frequently wrong. To change the GAP accurately and increase net interest income, management must outpredict consensus market forecasts of future interest rates. Many banks try to get around this difficulty by selectively adjusting the GAP only over short intervals, while rates are rising or falling as expected relative to the business cycle. Second, even when rate changes are predicted correctly, banks have limited flexibility in varying the GAP and must often sacrifice yield to do so. Loan customers and depositors select terms from a range of alternatives provided by the bank. Banks have only partial control over pricing and maturities.

The first difficulty can be demonstrated by an example. Suppose a bank operates with a negative GAP through 1 year. Management believes that interest rates will rise and decides to move the GAP closer to zero. At this time, the yield curve is upsloping because the consensus forecast is that interest rates will increase over time. Active GAP management requires that the bank increase its RSAs and lower its RSLs. Consider the effect of the following strategies: the bank i) shortens the maturities of its bond portfolio, and ii) reprices its CDs to attract long-term deposits relative to short-term deposits. With an upsloping yield curve, long-term interest rates exceed short-term interest rates. The bank will accept a lower yield initially when it buys short-term securities, and can only attract long-term deposits by paying a premium rate over short-term deposit rates. Both tend to reduce a bank's initial net interest margin. Importantly, the bank gains only when interest rates move favorably relative to current forward rates.[5] Specifically, the investment in short-term rather than long-term securities is advantageous only if interest rates rise above forward rates; that is, only if rates increase above the break-even yield contained in the yield curve. Long-term deposits are better than short-term deposits only in the same instance when market rates ultimately rise above forward rates. The bank loses if rates remain below forward rates. Thus by adjusting the GAP a bank is speculating that its interest rate forecast is better than the consensus.

The second difficulty is similar. Suppose, for example, that a retail bank desires to increase RSAs because it expects interest rates to increase. While the bank plans to make only variable-rate or floating-rate loans, its customers seek fixed-rate loans because they also expect rates to rise. The bank must offer a substantial inducement, such as a significantly lower variable-rate loan, to book RSAs. This would lower the interest spread and offset part of the benefit from increasing the GAP. If the bank offered only variable-rate loans, it would not be competitive and would lose considerable goodwill.

When adjusting maturities and pricing, a bank may have to make yield concessions or assume interest rate risk. Active GAP adjustments are thus highly speculative. Interestingly, when a bank successfully structures its GAP to take advantage of interest rate movements, its loan customers and depositors who have not hedged lose because they miscalculated rates.

Link between GAP and Net Interest Margin

Most ALM programs focus on the GAP or GAP ratio when evaluating interest rate risk. When the GAP is positive the GAP ratio is greater than 1. A negative GAP, in turn, is consistent with a GAP ratio less than 1.

$$\text{GAP Ratio} = \frac{\text{RSAs}}{\text{RSLs}}$$

Neither the GAP nor GAP ratio provide direct information on the potential variability in earnings when rates change. The GAP ratio is further deficient because it ignores size. Consider two banks that have $500 million in total assets. The first bank has $3 million in RSAs and $2 million in RSLs so that its GAP equals $1 million and its GAP ratio equals 1.5. The second bank has $300 million in RSAs and $200 million in RSLs. Its GAP equals $100 million yet it reports the same 1.5 GAP ratio. Clearly, the second bank assumes greater interest rate risk because its net interest income will change more when interest rates change. A better risk measure relates the absolute value of a bank's GAP to earning assets. The greater is this ratio, the greater the interest rate risk.

---

[5]Chapter 7 provides a discussion of yield curves and the role of forward rates.

Wells Fargo: Intentionally Mismatched Maturities

What GAP value is best? Some banks pursue a strategy of matching asset and liability maturities as closely as possible to reduce the GAP to zero and reduce the volatility of net interest income. Other banks aggressively vary the GAP in line with their interest rate forecast. If they expect rates to increase, they attempt to increase the GAP by repricing assets more frequently than liabilities. An expected decrease in rates coincides with efforts to lower the GAP and possibly make it negative by repricing relatively more liabilities sooner. Which strategy is better depends on whether management can accurately forecast rates and adjust the GAP accordingly.

Wells Fargo Bank in San Francisco pursues a strategy that is independent of short-term interest rate forecasts. The bank targets a negative funding GAP through at least 180 days. This action follows from a belief that liquidity premiums impart a consistent upward bias to the slope of the yield curve. Even when short-term interest rates are expected to remain constant, long-term rates will be higher because investors, on average, prefer to own more liquid short-term securities. Yields on 6-month securities may consequently rise by 30 to 75 basis points above overnight rates as a premium for investors. A negative GAP, brought about by a short-funding strategy, where short-term deposits finance longer-term assets, allows the bank to earn the liquidity premium as part of its spread.

Wells Fargo's managers recognize that they cannot forecast interest rates better than the market can. The strategy will work in the long run, regardless of the near-term shape of the yield curve, because of the 30- to 75-basis-point spread on mismatched assets and liabilities with less than 6 months to maturity. The mismatch is generally restricted to the 6-month horizon because liquidity premiums increase over this interval, then level off. Mismatches constructed with longer-term assets involve more risk but offer the same effective spread.

This ratio has the additional advantage that it can be directly linked to variations in NIM. In particular, management can determine a target value for GAP in light of specific risk objectives stated in terms of a bank's target NIM.[6]

Consider a bank with $50 million in earning assets that expects to generate a 5 percent NIM. As part of management strategy, the bank has decided it will risk changes in NIM equal to plus or minus 20 percent during the year. Thus NIM should fall between 4 and 6 percent. This risk assessment in conjunction with expected interest rates imposes policy limits on an acceptable GAP. The general relationship is:

$$\frac{\text{Target GAP}}{\text{Earning assets}} = \frac{(\text{Allowable percentage in NIM})(\text{Expected NIM})}{\text{Expected percentage change in interest rates}}$$

For example, suppose that management expected interest rates to vary up to 4 percent during the upcoming year. According to Equation (8.2), the bank's ratio of its 1-year cumulative GAP (absolute value) to earning assets should not exceed 25 percent.

---

[6]Binder and Lindquist, 1982, elaborate on this and provide a matrix that outlines potential GAP variances for different levels of NIM risk.

Target GAP/Earning assets = (20)(5)/4 = 25%

Relationship (8.2) and management's willingness to allow only a 20-percent variation in NIM sets limits on the GAP, which would be allowed to vary from −$12.5 million to $12.5 million, based on $50 million in earning assets.

Using the data from Exhibit 8.5, suppose alternatively that Security Bank's management establishes the same 20-percent variance in NIM as a risk objective but expects its NIM to equal 4.5 percent over the next year. If it expects interest rates to rise by 2 percent, it would target the GAP-to-earning-asset ratio at 45 percent. Exhibit 8.5 indicates that the bank's 1-year cumulative GAP is −$23.4 million, or 27.5 percent of earning assets. Thus management could increase its negative GAP to as much as −$38 million and remain within its target risk profile.

THE DURATION GAP: MANAGING THE MARKET VALUE OF EQUITY

In addition to GAP analysis, many banks examine duration measures for individual securities and of their entire portfolio to assess risk. Duration analysis is not as easy to understand or apply, but it provides additional information and a comprehensive view of interest rate risk. As Chapter 6 demonstrates, duration is most easily understood as a measure of relative interest elasticity for determining changes in the market value of securities. Changes in asset values relative to changes in the value of liabilities determine changes in the market value of firm equity. This section examines duration gap analysis as an alternative to and extension of GAP policies.

Duration gap (DGAP) models focus on managing net interest income or the market value of stockholders' equity, recognizing the timing of all individual cash flows. Management's goal is typically to stabilize or increase net interest income or the value of the firm.[7] Duration is an attractive measure because it is additive across securities in a portfolio. Thus aggregate bank interest rate risk is indicated by comparing the weighted duration of assets with the weighted duration of liabilities. Management can adjust this DGAP to hedge or to accept interest rate risk by speculating on future interest rate changes.

Duration analysis recognizes that interest rate risk arises when the timing of cash inflows differs from the timing of cash outflows. While traditional GAP analysis compares approximate asset and liability cash flows by structuring short-term maturity buckets, duration hedges establish asset and liability portfolios that change equally in value when interest rates change. These portfolios include all assets and liabilities. In a perfect hedge the timing and magnitude of aggregate cash flows on assets are matched with aggregate cash flows on liabilities so that the market value of equity is unchanged.

---

[7]This section focuses on the market value of equity as a target variable and follows closely the discussion in Kaufman, 1984. The use of net interest income as a target is discussed by Toevs (1983).

Chapter 6 demonstrated that duration is computed as a weighted average of the time until cash flows are received. With Macaulay's duration the weights equal the present value of each cash flow as a fraction of the security's current price and time refers to the length of time in the future until payment or receipt. Conceptually, duration measures the average life of an instrument. It equals the average time necessary to recover the initial cost. For example, a bond with 4 years until final maturity with a duration of 3.5 years indicates that an investor would recover the initial cost of the bond in 3.5 years, on average, regardless of intervening interest rate changes. If interest rates increase, for example, the decrease in market value of the bond will be just offset by higher reinvestment income from the periodic coupon interest payments, so that the promised return is still realized after 3.5 years.

There are many measures of duration. Macaulay's duration (D) appears below:

$$D = \frac{\sum\limits_{t=1}^{k} \dfrac{P_t}{(1+i)^t} }{\sum\limits_{t=1}^{k} \dfrac{P_t}{(1+i)^t}} \qquad\qquad (8.3)$$

where

CF_t = dollar value of the cash flow at time t,
   t = the number of periods until the cash flow payment,
   i = the yield to maturity of the instrument generating the cash flow, and
   k = the number of cash flows.

For single-payment (zero coupon) instruments, duration equals maturity because the weight of the only payment at maturity equals one. For multiple-payment instruments, duration is always less than maturity because some payments are received prior to maturity and these payments are weighted, with the sum of all weights equal to one.

Alternatively, duration is an approximate measure of market value interest elasticity. In this context, duration equals the percentage change in market value of a security divided by the relative change in interest rates. Relationship (6.13) is repeated below as (8.4).

$$D \cong - \left[\frac{\dfrac{\Delta V}{V}}{\dfrac{\Delta i}{(1+i)}} \right] \qquad\qquad (8.4)$$

where

V = the market value of a security, and
i = the current yield to maturity of the security.

Equation 8.4 indicates that the relationship between duration and market value is linear. Thus a security with 6-year duration is twice as sensitive to interest rate changes as a security with a 3-year duration. Equation 8.4 can also be used to approximate the change in market value of an instrument with known duration whenever interest rates vary. Duration analysis compares the change in market value of a bank's asset portfolio with the change in market value of its liabilities. Hedging policies attempt to equalize this sensitivity so that the market value of equity is unchanged when interest rates change.

A Duration Application at Banks

A bank is concerned with its total risk exposure from all assets and liabilities. When it receives cash inflows from assets prior to obligated payments on liabilities, it bears the risk that it may have to reinvest the proceeds at reduced rates. When it makes debt payments before it receives cash inflows, it bears the risk that borrowing costs will rise. Any differential in the timing of asset and liability cash flows is reflected in average durations.

Duration gap analysis requires that the bank specify a performance target, such as the market value of equity, and manage the difference between the average duration of total assets and the average duration of total liabilities. Each can be obtained by summing the products of the durations of individual securities with their respective proportionate market values. Each proportion equals the market value of the asset or liability divided by the market value of total assets or total liabilities, as appropriate. The market value of equity is not included in the calculation.

Consider the balance sheet of another hypothetical bank in Exhibit 8.8. The bank just opened for business, and all dollar amounts are market values. It owns three assets: cash, a 3-year final maturity commercial loan earning 14 percent, and a 9-year Treasury bond earning 12 percent. It pays interest on 1-year time deposits (TDs) at 9 percent and on 4-year CDs at 10 percent. Equity represents the residual between asset and liability values and equals $80, or 8 percent of assets. The analysis assumes that there will be no defaults, prepayments, or early withdrawals. All securities make equal annual interest payments with annual compounding. The duration of each account is listed beside the current market rate. The duration of cash is zero because cash doesn't change in value when interest rates change. Duration measures for the commercial loan, the 4-year CD, and the average total asset and liability durations are computed at the bottom of the exhibit. Initially, the average duration of assets exceeds the average duration of liabilities by almost 1 year. Expected net interest income, assuming no change in interest rates, is $35.20 per $1,000 of assets.[8]

Interest rate risk is evidenced by the mismatch in average durations of assets and liabilities. When interest rates change, the value of assets and liabilities will change by different amounts, and future interest income will change relative to future interest expense. Suppose all interest rates increase by 1 percent immediately after the hypothetical bank contracts for its assets and liabilities. An adjusted balance sheet at market

---

[8]This analysis uses economic income instead of accounting income. Economic interest is calculated as the product of market value of each security and its market interest rate. Economic income varies directly with accounting income in these examples, although the relationship is not linear.

Exhibit 8.8 Hypothetical Bank Balance Sheet

Assets	Market Value	Rate	Duration	Liabilities and Equity	Market Value	Rate	Duration
Cash	$ 100			Time deposit	$ 520	9%	1.00 yr.
Commercial loan	700	14%	2.65 yrs.	Certificate of deposit	400	10	3.49
Treasury bond	200	12	5.97	Total liabilities	920		2.08 yrs.
			3.05 yrs.	Equity	$ 80		
Total	$1,000				$1,000		

Duration of assets = ($700/$1,000)(2.65) + ($200/$1,000)(5.97) = 3.05 yrs.

Duration of liabilities = ($520/$920)(1) + ($400/$920)(3.49) = 2.08 yrs.

Expected economic net interest income = 0.14($700) + 0.12($200) − 0.09($520) − 0.10($400) = $35.20

DGAP = 3.05 − ($920/$1,000)(2.08) = 1.14 yrs.

Sample Duration Calculations

$$\text{Commercial loan} = \frac{\dfrac{98}{(1.14)} + \dfrac{98(2)}{(1.14)^2} + \dfrac{798(3)}{(1.14)^3}}{\$700} = .123(1) + .108(2) + .769(3) = 2.65 \text{ yrs.}$$

$$\text{Certificate of deposit} = \frac{\dfrac{40}{(1.1)} + \dfrac{40(2)}{(1.1)^2} + \dfrac{40(3)}{(1.1)^3} + \dfrac{440(4)}{(1.1)^4}}{\$400} = .09(1) + .083(2) + .075(3) + .751(4)$$
$$= 3.49 \text{ yrs.}$$

values (Exhibit 8.9) shows that with the increase in rates, the market value of assets declines by $27, liabilities decrease by $18, and the market value of equity falls by $9 to $71.

The new value of each instrument can be obtained using Equation 8.4. The value of assets falls more than the value of liabilities because the weighted duration of assets (3.05 years) exceeds the weighted duration of liabilities (2.08 years) by a substantial amount. The equity to asset ratio declines from 8 percent to 7.3 percent. In general, the percentage change in market value can be approximated by multiplying the change in interest rates by the negative of a security's duration. Expected net interest income similarly decreases because the bank will pay higher rates on liabilities relative to the higher yields it receives on reinvested cash inflows over the combined lifetime of the securities. Clearly, this bank's operating position has worsened with the increase in rates.

A decrease in rates produces opposite results. The market value of assets increases more than the market value of liabilities because of the duration mismatch. The market value of equity thus rises. Net interest income also rises, and the bank is better off.

Bank management can use duration measures to evaluate interest rate risk. The appropriate measure depends on the performance target. If a bank targets the market value of equity, it will be completely hedged when the composite duration of assets equals the product of the composite duration of liabilities and the bank's debt-to-total

Exhibit 8.9 Hypothetical Bank Balance Sheet after an Immediate Change in Interest Rates (One Percent Increase in All Rates)

Assets	Market Value	Rate	Duration	Liabilities and Equity	Market Value	Rate	Duration
Cash	$100			Time deposit	$515	10%	1.00 yr.
Commercial loan	684	15%	2.64 yrs.	Certificate of deposit	387	11	3.48
Treasury bond	189	13	5.89	Total liabilities	$902		2.06 yrs.
Total	$973		3.00 yrs.	Equity	$ 71		
					$973		

Duration of assets = .702(2.64) + .195(5.89) = 3.00 yrs.

Duration of liabilities = .57(1) + .43(3.48) = 2.06 yrs.

Expected economic net interest income = $33.10

Change in market value of: assets = –$27.00
                            liabilities = –$18.00
                            equity = –$9.00

Sample Calculations of Market Value Using Equation 4.4

Commercial loan: $\Delta V = (.01/1.14)(-2.65)(\$700) = -\$16.3$

Certificate of deposit: $\Delta V = (.01/1.10)(-3.49)(\$400) = -\$12.7$

---

asset ratio. If, instead, a bank chooses to target or hedge the ratio of equity to total assets or net interest margin, it should equate the composite duration of assets with the composite duration of liabilities.[9]

Using the market value of equity as its performance target, a bank can manage its risk position according to its DGAP:

$$DGAP = DA - uDL \tag{8.5}$$

where

DA = composite duration of assets measured by the sum of the products of each asset's duration and proportionate share of total asset market value,

DL = composite duration of liabilities measured by the sum of the products of each liability's duration and proportionate share of total liability market value, and

u = ratio of total liabilities to total assets.

When DGAP is positive, the market value of equity declines with rising interest rates and increases with falling interest rates. This is the situation faced by the hypothetical bank in Exhibit 8.8 with a duration gap of 1.14 years. When DGAP is negative, equity value increases when interest rates rise but decreases when rates fall. A bank can immunize its equity value from interest rate changes only when DGAP equals zero. The greater the absolute value of DGAP, the greater is interest rate risk. A bank that is perfectly hedged will thus operate with its asset duration slightly below its liability duration to maintain positive equity. These relationships are summarized as follows:

[9]See Kaufman, 1984, for general proofs.

DGAP Summary

DGAP	Change in Interest Rates	Change in Market Value—Assets	Change in Market Value—Liabilities	Change in Market Value—Equity
Positive	Increase	Decrease	> Decrease	Decrease
Positive	Decrease	Increase	> Increase	Increase
Negative	Increase	Decrease	< Decrease	Increase
Negative	Decrease	Increase	< Increase	Decrease
Zero	Increase	Decrease	= Decrease	None
Zero	Decrease	Increase	= Increase	None

Duration gap measures can also be used to approximate the expected change in market value of equity for a given change in interest rates. In particular, relationship (8.6) can be used to estimate the −$9 change in market value of equity from Exhibits 8.8 and 8.9 ($80 to $71). The approximate relationship is:[10]

$$\frac{\Delta\,\text{Market value of equity}}{\text{Total assets}} \cong -\text{DGAP}\left[\frac{\Delta i}{1+i}\right] \tag{8.6}$$

Applying this to the hypothetical bank, the 1 percent increase in interest rates lowered equity value by roughly 1 percent of assets, or $10 (1.14 [.01/1.122] $1,000). The actual decrease was $9. This bank's assets will change in value by 50 percent more than its liabilities for any interest rate variation, as measured by the relative durations, and equity will vary accordingly.

An Immunized Portfolio

To insulate the value of equity from rate changes, the hypothetical bank would need to either shorten its asset duration by 1.14 years or increase its liability duration by 1.24 years. The latter could be accomplished by reducing time deposits to $240 and issuing $280 in new 5-year zero coupon CDs (Exhibit 8.10). Any immediate rate change would leave equity unchanged. This is demonstrated in the bottom part of the exhibit, where all interest rates are assumed to increase by 1 percent. The market value of every rate-sensitive account declines. Equity value remains constant at $80 because the $27 decrease in market value of assets just equals the $27 decrease in market value of liabilities. There are, of course, many other alternatives to adjust the size of DGAP to zero, but each would produce the desired hedge.

Banks may choose to target variables other than the market value of equity in managing interest rate risk. Many banks, for example, are interested in stabilizing the book value of net interest income. This can be done for a 1-year time horizon, with the appropriate DGAP measure shown as follows:[11]

---

[10]Using the average yield on earning assets for i provides a reasonable approximation.

[11]Toevs, 1983, introduced this formula and discussed the implications in detail. Extensions include targeting the market value of net interest income by setting the duration of a bank's equity equal to the length of the time horizon during which the bank wishes to hedge net interest income. The duration of equity can be approximated as follows:

$$\text{Duration of equity} = \frac{(\text{Market value of assets})\text{Duration of assets} - (\text{Market value of liabilities})\text{Duration of liabilities}}{\text{Market value of equity}}$$

Exhibit 8.10 Immunized Portfolio

Bank Balance Sheet: DGAP = 0

Assets	Market Value	Rate	Duration	Liabilities and Equity	Market Value	Rate	Duration
Cash	$ 100			Time deposit	$ 240	9%	1 yr.
Commercial loan	700	14%	2.65 yrs.	4-yr. certificate of deposit	400	10	3.49
Treasury bond	200	12	5.97	5-yr. certificate of deposit[a]	280	10	5
			3.05 yrs.	Total liabilities	$ 920		3.31 yrs.
				Equity	$ 80		
Total	$1,000				$1,000		

DGAP = 3.05 − .92(3.31) = 0

1% Increase in All Rates: DGAP = 0

	Market Value	Rate	Duration		Market Value	Rate	Duration
Cash	$100			Time deposits	$238	10%	1 yr.
Commercial loan	684	15%	2.64 yrs.	4-yr. certificate of deposit	388	11%	3.48
Treasury bond	189	13	5.89	5-yr. certificate of deposit	267	11%	5
			3.00 yrs.	Total liabilities	$893		3.27 yrs.
				Equity	$ 80		
Total	$973				$973		

[a]Par value = $451.

$$DGAP^* = MVRSA(1 - DRSA) - MVRSL(1 - DRSL) \qquad (8.7)$$

where

MVRSA = cumulative market value of RSAs,
MVRSL = cumulative market value of RSLs,
    DRSA = composite duration of RSAs equal to the sum of each asset's duration and relative share of total asset market value, and
    DRSL = composite duration of RSLs equal to the sum of each liability's duration and relative share of total liability market value.

If DGAP* is positive, the bank's net interest income will decrease when interest rates decrease, and increase when rates increase. If DGAP* is negative, the relationship is reversed. Only when DGAP* equals zero is interest rate risk eliminated. The important point is that banks can use duration analysis to stabilize a number of different variables reflecting bank performance.

GAP VERSUS DURATION GAP: WHICH MODEL IS BETTER?

Both GAP and duration gap models are used by bankers in assessing interest rate risk. Each has slightly different objectives. GAP analysis focuses on the potential volatility of net interest income over distinct time intervals. Net interest income is calculated in book value terms, not market values. A bank manages the effects of volatile interest rates within each time period separately. The duration approach focuses on the potential variability of a bank's market value of equity. Duration gap is a single measure that summarizes the cumulative impact of interest rate changes on a bank's total portfolio. Thus the bank continuously manages total rate risk according to this one number. Because the models have different objectives, they address different issues.

Strengths and Weaknesses: GAP Analysis. The principal attraction of funding GAP analysis is that it is easy to understand. Periodic GAPs indicate the relevant interest rate risk over distinct maturities and clearly suggest magnitudes of portfolio changes to alter risk. GAP measures can also be easily calculated once the cash flow characteristics of each instrument are identified.

Unfortunately, the funding GAP procedure also contains numerous weaknesses. First, there are serious ex post measurement errors. For example, how rate-sensitive are loans tied to a bank's prime rate or loans that float with CD rates? When there is uncertainty over the frequency of base rate changes because the bank cannot control rate changes, GAP measures reflect any errors in allocating loans differently than actual rate changes would require. The section on Contemporary Issues: Confusing Rate-Sensitivity Profiles documents a frequent problem at banks when they evaluate rate sensitivity over the shortest time intervals. To overcome this problem, a bank should evaluate the statistical rate sensitivity of all base rates to selected market indexes.[12] Funds should be allocated to time buckets according to their effective (statistical) rate sensitivity to avoid misinterpreting risk.

Second, GAP analysis ignores the time value of money. The construction of maturity buckets does not differentiate between cash flows that arise at the beginning of the period versus those at the end. Whether a bank gains with rising or falling interest rates depends on the actual timing of repricings within each interval. Thus a bank with a zero GAP will still see net interest income change when rates change.

Third, the procedure essentially ignores the cumulative impact of interest rate changes on a bank's risk position. GAP measures should be calculated over the entire range of repricings, yet they often focus only on near-term changes in net interest income. Interest rate changes also affect the value of fixed-rate assets and liabilities and total risk beyond 1 year. These changes are ignored. Of course, it is not the objective of GAP analysis to examine changes in market values.

Finally, many banks allocate demand deposits as non-rate-sensitive liabilities. As such, GAP analysis does not recognize any rate risk associated with demand deposit flows, even though a bank typically loses deposits when short-term interest rates rise. To be effective, GAP analysis must allocate demand deposits to the appropriate time buckets depending on their actual rate sensitivity. It is extremely difficult, however, to know exactly how rate-sensitive these deposits are.

Strengths and Weaknesses: Duration Gap. The principal attraction of duration analysis is that it provides a comprehensive measure of interest rate risk for the total portfolio. The smaller the absolute value of the DGAP, the less sensitive the value of

---

[12]This procedure is called the *effective gap* approach and requires sophisticated statistical measurement.

CONTEMPORARY ISSUES

Confusing Rate-Sensitivity Profiles

Many community banks use a simple rate-sensitivity report that disguises true interest-rate risk. Much like the format in Exhibit 8.5, the first column in the report often lists data for variable-rate instruments. All of the bank's floating rate loans are included as are all liabilities, such as NOW accounts, MMDAs, and floating rate CDs that can be repriced immediately. For most banks such immediately repriceable assets are less than immediately repriceable liabilities, so that the GAP for floating rate instruments is a large negative number. This GAP figure is then combined with later periodic GAPs to produce negative cumulative GAPs through 1 year.

Problems arise as management tries to interpret these GAP figures. Typically, the perception is that net interest margin will decline when interest rates rise and increase when rates fall. The key point, however, is that floating rate instruments are repriced at different intervals. Some actually vary in yield daily. Still, most are fixed to some base rate or index and are repriced much less frequently. A commercial loan priced at the

bank's prime rate plus 1 percent, for example, is a floating rate asset because the interest charged changes whenever management changes the prime rate. This does not occur daily and may in fact not occur for several months in a stable rate environment. Another common situation is one in which banks include MMDAs in the shortest time bucket or as floating rate instruments and thus report a large negative GAP. Because they rarely change the rate paid on MMDAs, the true GAP is much less negative or even positive so that rising rates benefit the bank. All base rates exhibit different volatilities that must be recognized separately.

In order to provide useful data, managers must allocate floating rate instruments within the appropriate time frame according to an estimate of how frequently the base rate or index changes. A portion of each account balance can be allocated to different intervals so that effective GAP data characterize the estimated volume of rate sensitive assets and liabilities, regardless of what contracts imply.

---

bank equity is to interest rate changes. Unlike GAP, DGAP recognizes the time value of each cash flow, avoiding the difficulty with time buckets. Duration measures are additive, so the bank can match total assets with total liabilities rather than match individual accounts. Finally, duration analysis takes a longer-term viewpoint and provides managers with greater flexibility in adjusting rate sensitivity because they can use a wide range of instruments to balance value sensitivity.

Duration analysis has weaknesses as well. First, it is difficult to compute duration accurately. Duration measurement requires numerous subjective assumptions. Data needs are complex, requiring information on each account's interest rate, repricing schedule, possibility of principal prepayment, call and put options, early withdrawal potential, and default probability. A bank must routinely assess the probability that contracted cash flows will be received on a timely basis, and constantly monitor whether actual cash flows conform to expectations.

Second, a bank must also forecast the timing of base rate changes and the level of rates at the time of future cash flows. Conceptually, correct duration analysis requires that each future cash flow be discounted by a distinct discount rate reflecting the expected future rate at the time the cash flow arises. Where does the bank obtain these discount rates?[13] The bank must similarly estimate the true rate sensitivity of demand deposits.

Third, a bank must continuously monitor and adjust the duration of its portfolio. As Macaulay's duration equation indicates, duration changes with changes in interest rates. Thus a bank should restructure its balance sheet whenever rates change substantially, which could be daily or weekly. Furthermore, even when rates are constant, duration changes with the passage of time as t in Equation 8.3 decreases over time. The duration of assets and liabilities may "drift" at different rates and require constant rebalancing.

In summary, duration measures are highly subjective. Active management requires constant tinkering with the bank portfolio to adjust the duration gap. For many firms the costs of this activity may exceed the benefits.

SUMMARY

A bank's ALCO (asset and liability management committee) is responsible for monitoring the bank's risk and return profile. It analyzes the firm's operating condition and devises strategies for meeting firm objectives. Asset and liability management (ALM) refers to the coordination of decisions that determine how much risk a bank chooses to assume to achieve its profit targets.

Traditional ALM focuses on measuring interest rate risk and setting policies to stabilize or increase net interest income. This chapter analyzes two general measures of interest rate risk, funding GAP and duration gap. The first method separates a bank's balance sheet into assets and liabilities that can be repriced within specified time intervals. Differences in the magnitudes of these rate-sensitive instruments are labeled funding GAPs and indicate how much risk the bank assumes if interest rates change. The second method considers the entire portfolio and calculates measures of the weighted durations of all assets and liabilities. Differences in these weighted durations provide relative elasticity measures regarding how the market value of bank equity will change when interest rates change.

Financial institutions today view ALM much more comprehensively. Current ALM also considers liquidity risk, credit risk, solvency risk, and the interrelationships of decisions affecting each. This chapter summarizes only interest rate risk. Later chapters demonstrate how bank management analyzes other types of risk.

Questions

Interest Rate Risk

1. Why is interest risk a concern for bankers? Looking back over the history of interest rates (see Exhibit 7.4), when do you suspect interest rate risk grew into a major topic of concern? Why?

---

[13]The bank could derive forward rates from a yield curve. To eliminate coupon bias, forward rates should be obtained from a zero-coupon-equivalent yield curve.

2. Which bank financial statements or data would you request if you were trying to evaluate a bank's interest rate risk? What measures of bank performance suffered before banks learned to manage interest rate risk?

3. What is the name of the bank committee charged with managing interest rate risk? Why is this committee important? What, in addition to interest rate risk, does this committee often manage?

4. Successful management of interest rate risk means setting target values for net interest income, net interest margin, market value of equity, or stock price. What are the differences between these goals and which might be considered the best? Why?

5. Which would a bank's ALCO find easier to manage, a floating-rate or a variable-rate loan? Why?

6. Why is tax-equivalent rather than cash interest income used when calculating the yield rate and the net interest margin?

7. Identify the counterpart of the following terms.
   rate-sensitive assets
   cost of funds
   hedger
   GAP

GAP

8. Which measure of bank performance is managed using GAP analysis? If a bank is successfully hedging interest rate risk, how will this measure vary over time?

9. If you were hired as a consultant to establish a bank's first GAP management system, what would be the first piece of information you would request? Why should this be first?

10. What constraints must be considered when determining the length of repricing buckets?

11. What determines an asset or liability's rate sensitivity? Name one type of asset and one type of deposit that would be difficult to locate in the appropriate bucket.

12. Create a repricing table for the following firm. Interpret the GAP figures.

Investments	
Fed funds sold	$100
15-day T-bills	300
Loans	
Variable rate every 10 days, tied to T-bills	200
2-year balloon	100
7-month balloon	400
Deposits	
Checking (no interest paid)	50
NOW accounts	200
3-month CDs	750
Equity	100

Planning horizon	1–30 days	30–180 days	180–360 days	1–3 years	Not rate sensitive
RSA					
RSL					
GAP					
cumulative GAP					

a. If the bank plans to minimize interest rate risk over the 1-year planning horizon by attracting 1-year or shorter CDs, how many must it attract?

b. If the bank takes a shorter view and plans to minimize interest rate risk over the next 6 months, what might it do?

c. Which planning horizon is more appropriate and what action do you recommend?

Variables Influencing Net Interest Income

13. What are the two noncontrollable variables that influence net interest income? What are the two influential variables management can control?

14. A bank has classified its balance sheet into 1-year sensitivity buckets as follows:

Assets	Amount	Rate	Liabilities/Equity	Amount	Rate
Rate-sensitive	$2,700	10.8%	Rate-sensitive	$3,400	8.4%
Fixed-rate	1,400	9.0	Fixed-rate	650	8.0
Non-earning	400		Non-paying	450	
Total	$4,500		Total	$4,500	

a. Calculate this bank's GAP, net interest income, and net interest margin. This bank is positioned to profit if interest rates go which way?

b. Assume the total yield curve shifts upward 2% during the year and recalculate the bank's net interest income and net interest margin. Which seems to be a better indicator of the bank's interest rate risk? Why?

c. Suppose instead of the across-the-board increase in interest rates in part b interest rates increase unevenly. Calculate the bank's net interest income if all asset rates increase 2.5% and all liability rates increase only 2%. Is an uneven change more or less likely to occur than an even change? Explain a situation in which rates might change unevenly.

d. A careful ALCO will construct one forecast for asset interest rates and another for liabilities. If those forecasts indicate that the asset rate will increase substantially and the liability rate will increase only moderately, what would the ALCO of a bank with a positive GAP predict for the future of its net interest income?

15. The following bank is trying to hedge its risk exposure over the next year. Although members of the ALCO worry a great deal about interest rate risk, they do not believe they can accurately forecast interest rates so they don't try. They know that they can control net interest income by adjusting the size of the earning portion of the balance sheet relative to its total size and by switching the composition of assets and liabilities. Will both of these strategies have an impact on the bank's NIM? Will both have an impact on the value of the bank? Assume 1-year rate sensitivity buckets.

Assets	Amount	Rate	Liabilities/Equity	Amount	Rate
Rate-sensitive	$32,000	7.60%	Rate-sensitive	$20,000	7.00%
Fixed-rate	50,000	8.00	Fixed-rate	62,000	7.20
Non-earning	10,000		Non-paying	10,000	
Total	$92,000		Total	$92,000	

a. What is the bank's net interest income and net interest margin? If the bank does not hedge, it is speculating that interest rates will change in which direction?

b. What would be the bank's net interest income if it moves $3,000 of maturing liabilities into 2-year CDs? Why might this bank want to convert its rate-sensitive liabilities into long-term ones? Would this roll-over be considered hedging or speculating?

c. The bank in part a has decided to replace an antiquated branch office with an ATM and use the released funds to reduce its interest rate risk. If the replacement produces $6,000 what do you recommend they do with the money? Why?

d. If the bank in part a doubles its size by purchasing a competitor bank with an identical balance sheet, the combined bank can eliminate some duplication of equipment and one branch. The resulting balance sheet would double all account balances except non-earning assets, which would only increase to $15,000. The savings would be paid out to stockholders as one large dividend. What would be the effect of this merger on the bank's net interest income and net interest margin?

16. Complete the following table for Bank A and Bank B.

Bank A has $10 million invested in a 9-month fixed-rate loan backed by $10 million in 2-month CDs.

Bank B has $10 million invested in a 3-year fixed-rate loan backed by $10 million in 5-month CDs.

	Bucket		
	0–3 Months	3–6 Months	6 Months to 1 Year
Bank A			
GAP			
Cumulative GAP			
Bank B			
GAP			
Cumulative GAP			

a. What additional information is produced by calculating the cumulative GAP?

b. Which bank would prefer an immediate rather than a delayed drop in interest rates?

Performance Variance Analysis

17. ALCOs are concerned with managing the future performance of the bank. How does preparing and analyzing a performance variance analysis fit with this role?

18. A bank shows the following balance sheets and income statement for January and July of last year.

January 1

Earning Assets	Amount	Rate	Liabilities	Amount	Rate
Treasury securities	$ 3,000	6%	Variable-rate deposits	$ 5,000	6%
Federal funds sold	7,000	9	Short-term CDs	12,000	9
Loans	130,000	11	Long-term CDs	100,000	10
Non-earning Assets	4,000		**Equity**	24,000	

Annualized Income from:

Treasury securities	$ 180
Federal funds	630
Loans	14,300

Expense for:

Variable-rate deposits	300
Short-term CDs	1,080
Long-term CDs	10,000
Net Interest Income	$ 3,730

July 1

Earning Assets	Amount	Rate	Liabilities	Amount	Rate
Treasury securities	$ 14,000	6%	Variable-rate deposits	$ 5,000	6%
Federal funds sold	27,000	10	Short-term CDs	5,000	10
Loans	100,000	11.5	Long-term CDs	110,000	10
Non-earning Assets	3,000		**Equity**	24,000	

Annualized Income from:

Treasury securities	$ 840
Federal funds	2,700
Loans	11,500

Expense for:

Variable-rate deposits	300
Short-term CDs	500
Long-term CDs	11,000
Net Interest Income	$ 3,240

a. What would net interest income have been if only uncontrollable changes in interest rates had occurred?

b. What would it have been if only controllable factors had changed?

c. If half of the loans are rate-sensitive and the goal of the ALCO was to eliminate interest rate risk, how well did they perform?

Planning Using GAP

19. At its weekly meeting the ALCO has been handed the following information:

	Amount	Rate
1-year rate-sensitive assets	$40,000	10.2%
1-year rate-sensitive liabilities	37,000	7.4

Interest rate forecast:

Interest rates are expected to remain at their current levels for the next 9 months, then they are expected to fall 50 basis points. Half of the rate-sensitive assets are tied to prime, which will lag and only fall 40 basis points. It is possible that rates will only fall 30 basis points with prime settling 20 basis points lower. But it is just as likely that rates will fall 60 basis points and prime will also fall 60 basis points. Once this deep plunge has occurred, rates will stabilize throughout the remainder of the year.

a. Discuss a plan that would eliminate interest rate risk for this bank. What is the bank's net interest income? Assume that all interest-bearing accounts are rate-sensitive.

b. What will net interest income be if rates move to the worst possible forecast? If they move to the expected forecast?

c. Explain why the bank benefits if rates move to the most likely forecast even though that forecast is for falling rates.

20. Which of the following statements is true? Why?

a. A zero GAP indicates that net interest income will not change from year to year.

b. The best strategy is for a bank to maintain a zero GAP.

c. Banks that actively vary their GAP with the interest rate cycle must be able to forecast interest rates better than the market to generate extraordinary net interest income.

d. GAP measures beyond 1 year are not useful in understanding interest rate risk.

e. To hedge away interest rate risk is to hedge away the potential for extraordinary returns from rate movements.

21. Why might a bank desire a large negative GAP if the yield curve is dramatically upsloping?

Duration

22. A bank purchased at par a $10,000 Treasury bond with a 4-year duration paying 9% annual interest. Calculate the change in the bond's value if market interest rates fall from 9% to 8%. What would be the change in the value if the bond had an 8-year duration? If the duration doubles how much does the value change?

23. What is the principal difference between the GAP and duration gap techniques?

24. Suppose your bank owns two assets, $500 in a commercial loan with a 1.2-year duration and $500 in a Treasury bond with a 4.5-year duration. Which of the following funding schemes would most closely approximate an immunized portfolio?

	Amount	Duration in Years
Scheme A		
Small time deposit	$520	4.1
Large CD	380	1.3
Equity	100	
Scheme B		
Small time deposit	475	4.1
Zero coupon CD	325	3.0
Large CD	100	1.3
Equity	100	
Scheme C		
Small time deposit	400	4.1
Zero coupon CD	290	3.0
Large CD	260	1.3
Equity	50	

25. Calculate the duration gap of the following bank if the ALCO is targeting the bank's market value of equity.

Assets	Amount	Rate	Duration	Liabilities/Equity	Amount	Rate	Duration
Cash	$ 500			Deposits	$ 3,000	7.0%	0.3 yrs.
Treasuries	1,000	6.8%	8.2 yrs.	CDs	8,000	8.0	4.2
Loans	13,500	8.5	2.3	Equity	4,000		
Total	$15,000			Total	$15,000		

a. Estimate the change in the market value of equity if all rates decline by 1.4%. Compare the results using Equation (8.4) for each instrument versus using Equation (8.6).

b. Provide two distinct transactions that the bank could implement that will reduce its risk exposure to zero as measured by duration gap.

26. If a bank with $2 billion in assets has a duration gap of 2.56, what change in market value can it anticipate if interest rates increase from 10.00% to 12.20%?

27. What information is contained in the fact that a bank's duration gap is positive? Is it best for a bank to operate with a duration gap equal to zero?

Comparison of GAP and Duration

28. Compare the strengths and weakness of GAP versus duration gap as measures of interest rate risk. If your bank were just initiating a plan of control for interest rate risk, which of these techniques would you recommend and why?

29. Suppose your bank possesses the flexibility to manage its GAP over the interest rate cycle. What strategy should the bank pursue to maximize net interest income when the Treasury yield curve is upsloping and rates are rising? What strategy is appropriate when the yield curve is inverted? Is it important that the bank forecast rates better than those implied in the yield curve?

30. Discuss the problems that loans tied to a bank's base rate present in measuring interest rate risk where the base rate is not tied directly to a specific market interest rate.

Activities

31. Calculate your personal GAP for the time buckets of 90 days, 1 year, and more than 1 year. What problems do you have collecting the necessary information? Which of these problems would a bank also experience in collecting data?

32. Calculate the duration of one of your loans, or if necessary one of your friends' loans. Do you own any asset with approximately the same duration? If not, what asset might you acquire to meet this criteria? As an individual, would there be any advantage to having an immunized personal balance sheet?

References

Belongia, Michael, and G. J. Santoni. "Hedging Interest Rate Risk with Financial Futures: Some Basic Principles." *Review* (Federal Reserve Bank of St. Louis, October 1984).

Binder, Barrett, and Thomas Lindquist. *Asset/Liability Management and Funds Management at Commercial Banks.* Rolling Meadows, Ill.: Bank Administration Institute, 1982.

Brewer, Elijah. "Bank Gap Management and the Use of Financial Futures." *Economic Perspectives* (Federal Reserve Bank of Chicago, March–April 1985).

Dew, James K. "Which Asset-Liability Management Model?" *American Banker* (February 14, 1984).

Kaufman, George. "Measuring and Managing Interest Rate Risk: A Primer." *Economic Perspectives* (Federal Reserve Bank of Chicago, January–February 1984).

Leibowitz, Martin, Eric Sorensen, Robert Arnott, and Nicholas Hanson. "A Total Differential Approach to Equity Duration." *Financial Analysts Journal* (September/October 1989).

McNulty, James. "Measuring Interest Rate Risk: What Do We Really Know?" *Journal of Retail Banking* (Spring/Summer 1986).

McNulty, James. "Interest Rate Risk: How Much Is Too Much?" *The Bankers Magazine* (January–February 1987).

Mengle, David. "Market Value Accounting and the Bank Balance Sheet." *Contemporary Policy Issues* (April 1990).

Morris, Charles, and Gordon Sellon. "Market Value Accounting for Banks: Pros and Cons." *Economic Review* (Federal Reserve Bank of Kansas City, March/April 1991).

Nguyen, Chy, and Alan Winger. "The Rudiments of a Duration Model." *Quarterly Review 2* (Federal Home Loan Bank of Cincinnati, 1984).

Olson, Ronald, and Harold Sollenberger. "Interest Margin Variance Analysis: A Tool of Current Times." *The Magazine of Bank Administration* (May 1978).

Platt, Robert. *Controlling Interest Rate Risk: New Techniques & Applications for Money Management.* New York: John Wiley & Sons, 1986.

Rose, Sanford. "Getting Paid to Take Rate Risk." *American Banker* (February 26, 1986).

Rosenberg, Joel. "The Joys of Duration." *The Bankers Magazine* (March–April 1986).

Scheibla, Shirley. "The Untold Philadelphia Story—First Pennsylvania: No Bottom Line." *Barrons* (October 13, 1980).

Stigum, Marcia, and Rene Branch, Jr. *Managing Bank Assets and Liabilities.* Homewood, Ill.: Dow Jones-Irwin, 1983.

Toevs, Alden. "GAP Management: Managing Interest Rate Risk in Banks and Thrifts." *Economic Review* (Federal Reserve Bank of San Francisco, Spring 1983).

Toevs, Alden, and David Jacob. *Interest Rate Futures: A Comparison of Alternative Hedge Ratio Methodologies.* New York: Morgan Stanley, June 1984.

Chapter 9

Financial Futures and Interest Rate Swaps

Banking professionals constantly search for new products and opportunities to improve bank operating performance. Financial futures and interest rate swaps are two relatively new tools used by banks. While financial futures have been available since 1975, only a few commercial banks actively use them to help manage interest rate risk. Most banks use futures either to fix the interest cost of liabilities or shorten/lengthen liability maturities. Interest rate swaps, in contrast, have grown from their introduction in 1980 to an estimated volume of $650 billion outstanding in 1989. Most users swap interest rate payment streams to better match asset and liability cash flows. Commercial banks and savings and loan associations have been active in this market.

This chapter explains the mechanics of financial futures and swap transactions. It describes several applications, which show each tool's strengths and weaknesses. The financial futures applications focus on Eurodollar futures, one of the fastest-growing contracts used by financial institutions. The concepts, however, apply to all futures contracts. Chapter 10 extends the analysis to options on financial futures.

Interest rate deregulation and the growth in deposit products that pay market interest rates have increased financial institutions' awareness of interest rate risk. When interest rates change unexpectedly, banks and thrifts may find that their net interest income and market value of equity decline, threatening growth opportunities and financial soundness. Chapter 8 introduced procedures for measuring interest rate risk, including funding GAP and duration gap analysis. Associated GAP measures indicated how a bank's net interest income and market value of equity would be likely to vary with a change in the level of interest rates.

This chapter extends the earlier discussion by describing two general tools that banks can use to adjust the amount of assumed interest rate risk. The first, financial futures contracts, have been available since 1975 but have only recently gained acceptability. The second, interest rate swaps, were introduced in 1980 and are now used actively by the largest banking organizations. Both tools can be used to complement existing strategies involving matching or consciously mismatching rate-sensitive assets and liabilities and corresponding durations. The responsibility of bank managers is to manage, not totally eliminate, risk. Entering into futures or swap contracts that reduce risk also eliminates potential extraordinary returns from risk taking.

CHARACTERISTICS OF FINANCIAL FUTURES

Financial futures contracts represent a commitment between two parties—a buyer and a seller—on the price of a standardized financial asset or index at a specified time in the future. Buyers of futures contracts, referred to as *long* futures, agree to pay the underlying futures price, while sellers of futures contracts, referred to as *short* futures, agree to deliver the underlying asset as stipulated in the contract. The contracts are transferable because they are traded on organized exchanges called *futures markets.* Thus buyers and sellers can eliminate their commitments by taking the opposite position prior to contract expiration by selling and buying the futures contract, respectively.

Because futures prices fluctuate daily, buyers and sellers find that their initial position changes in value daily. When futures prices increase buyers gain at the expense of sellers, while sellers gain at the expense of buyers when prices fall. At the end of each day participants must pay any decrease in value or alternatively receive any increase in value. When the contract expires, they pay or receive the final change in value (cash settlement) or exchange the actual underlying asset (physical delivery) for cash at the initial negotiated price. The process fixes the underlying instrument's price at the time of the trade for the future date designated by the contract. The underlying financial asset may be a short-term money market instrument, a long-term bond, units of a foreign currency, precious metals, or even common stock indexes. Futures contracts are traded daily prior to the formal delivery date, with the price changing as market conditions dictate. These unique features stand out when compared with cash market transactions and forward contracts.

Cash or *spot market transactions* represent the exchange of any asset between two parties who agree on the asset's characteristics and price, in which the buyer tenders payment and takes possession of the asset when the price is set. Most transactions take this form. A *forward contract* involves two parties agreeing on an asset's characteristics and price but deferring the actual exchange until a specified future date. Forward contracts do not necessarily involve standardized assets. Both parties to the transaction must simply agree on the asset's quality and price. Because the underlying asset is not standardized, the parties deal directly with each other and there is little opportunity to walk away from the commitment prior to delivery. Finally, once the terms of a forward contract are set, the parties do not make any payments or deliveries until the specified forward transactions date. Forward contracts, however, frequently require collateral or a letter of credit to guarantee performance.

The Mechanics of Futures Trading

Futures contracts are traded on formal, organized exchanges that serve as clearinghouses. Trading occurs in an open outcry auction market. Each party to a futures transaction effectively trades with exchange members who, in turn, guarantee the performance of all participants. In practice, a buyer and seller are found for each transaction, but the exchange assumes all obligations at the end of each trading day, forcing members to settle their net positions. This procedure enables any trader to offset an initial position by taking the opposite position any time prior to the futures contract's delivery date. For example, a buyer of a Treasury-bill futures contract with delivery in 60 days can offset the position by selling the same contract 1 week later when 53 days remain to delivery. This liquidity is not found with forward contracts. It results from trading standardized assets through an exchange where each party does not have to renegotiate with the same party who initiated the contract.

Futures contracts entail cash flow obligations for buyers and sellers during the entire time the position is outstanding. At initiation of a futures position, traders must post a cash deposit or U.S. government securities as *initial margin* with the exchange member simply for initiating a transaction. In most cases, the amount is small, involving less than 5 percent of the underlying asset's value. Exchange members also require traders to meet *maintenance margin* requirements that specify the minimum amount on deposit at the end of each day. Unlike margin accounts for stocks, futures margin deposits represent a form of performance bond by which a trader guarantees that mandatory payment obligations will be met. When the margin deposits fall below the minimum, an exchange member can close out a trader's account.

As futures prices vary prior to expiration of the contract, each trader must either increase the cash deposit or can withdraw any excess deposit, depending on whether prices move unfavorably or favorably. For example, a trader who buys a futures contract agrees to pay the negotiated price at delivery.[1] If the futures price increases in the interim, the market value of the initial position also rises and the buyer can withdraw this increase in contract value. If instead the futures price falls, the value of the initial position declines and the buyer must cover this decrease in value. Formally, exchange members identify the change in value of each trader's account at the end of every day, then credit the margin accounts of those with gains and debit the margin accounts of those with losses. The market labels this daily settlement process *marking to market* and the daily change in value *variation margin*.

Every futures contract has a formal expiration date. At expiration trading stops and participants settle their final positions. Contracts may provide for either physical

---

[1] Futures contracts with cash settlement at delivery differ from contracts with physical delivery in that traders settle their positions by paying or receiving the change in value of the contract between the trade date and expiration date.

delivery of the underlying asset or cash settlement. With physical delivery, the buyer of futures (longs) will make a cash payment to a seller, while the seller supplies the physical asset. Because financial futures contracts involve securities, delivery is handled via the wire transfer of funds and securities. With cash settlement, there is no physical delivery as participants simply exchange the final change in position value after the last trading day. Less than 1 percent of financial futures contract require physical delivery at expiration because most participants offset their futures positions in advance.

An Example: 90-Day Eurodollar Time Deposit Futures

One of the fastest-growing interest rate futures contracts is the 90-day Eurodollar time deposit future. Its popularity is due to the breadth of participants who use Eurodollars and the allowance for cash settlement at delivery. Chapter 4 briefly introduced cash market Eurodollars as comparable to jumbo CDs in the domestic market. Chapter 14 describes cash market Eurodollar time deposits in detail. Later examples with futures and options on futures build on this discussion.

Eurodollar futures contracts are traded on the International Monetary Market (IMM), a division of the Chicago Mercantile Exchange.[2] The underlying asset is a Eurodollar time deposit with a 3-month maturity. Conceptually, Eurodollars are U.S. dollar-denominated deposits in banks located outside the United States. The holder cannot write checks against the account but earns interest at a rate slightly above that on domestic CDs issued by the largest U.S. banks. Eurodollar rates are quoted on an interest-bearing basis assuming a 360-day year. Each Eurodollar futures contract represents $1 million initial face value of Eurodollar deposits maturing 3 months after contract expiration. Ten separate contracts are traded at any point in time as contracts expire in March, June, September, and December, 4 years out from the current date.[3] Settlement or delivery is in the form of cash, with the price established from a survey of current Eurodollar rates.

Eurodollar futures contracts trade according to an index that equals 100 percent minus the futures interest rate expressed as a percentage. An index of 91.50, for example, indicates a futures rate of 8.5 percent and an associated interest outlay of $21,250. Each basis point change in the futures rate equals a $25 change in value of the contract $(0.0001 \times (\$1 \text{ million} \times 90/360))$. If futures rates increase, the value of the contract decreases and vice versa.

Buyers of Eurodollar futures are classified as "long" because they own a commitment regarding the final price that can be sold prior to expiration. Sellers are "short" because they may ultimately be forced to deliver or come up with cash they do not currently have. With cash settlement buyers and sellers of Eurodollar futures have simply agreed on the price at expiration. What a buyer owns is a commitment from the seller to pay cash if the price of the underlying asset rises in the interim. The seller owns a commitment from the buyer to pay cash if the asset price falls. Buyers make

---

[2]Equivalent Eurodollar futures contracts are traded on the Singapore International Monetary Exchange.

[3]The last day of trading (expiration day) is the second London business day prior to the third Wednesday in each delivery month.

a futures profit when futures rates fall (prices rise), while sellers gain when futures rates rise (prices fall). Conceptually, profits arise because buyers can offset their initial position by selling the same futures contract after prices have increased. Sellers can similarly buy the futures back at a lower price after rates rise. As indicated earlier with daily settlement, the Eurodollar futures contract changes in value daily when prices change, and participants can withdraw profits from their margin accounts prior to expiration.

Exhibit 9.1 indicates how *The Wall Street Journal* reports price quotes for 3-month Eurodollar futures traded on the International Monetary Market and selected money rates for cash market transactions. The data are for the close of business on April 11, 1991. The first column of futures information indicates the settlement month and year. Each row lists price and yield data for a distinct futures contract expiring sequentially every 3 months. The next four columns report the index price quotes for each contract during the day including the opening price, high and low price, and closing settlement price. The next column, headed "Chg," indicates the change in settlement price from the previous day. The two columns under Yield convert the settlement price to a Eurodollar futures rate as

$$100 - \text{settlement price} = \text{futures rate}$$

and again indicate the change from the previous day. The final column reports *open interest* equal to the total number of futures contracts outstanding at the end of the day.

For example, the Eurodollar futures contract expiring in March 1992 had a settlement price of 92.66 for a futures rate of 7.34 percent. The contract opened trading at 92.63, rose as high as 92.67, and fell as low as 92.60 during the day before trading stopped. The closing price was 4 basis points above the close the prior day, indicating that the futures rate fell by 4 basis points. At the close of business 57,744 contracts were outstanding.

The money rate data, in turn, indicate prevailing interest rates on cash market securities traded for physical delivery on April 11. The Eurodollar time deposit rate is reported as the London Interbank Offered Rate (LIBOR) by convention, as the market is based in London. The data, in turn, indicate that the cash 3-month Eurodollar time deposit rate equaled 6 3/16 percent on April 11.

The cash flows associated with futures trading can be demonstrated by an example. Consider a trader who at the end of April 11, 1991 buys one March 1992 3-month Eurodollar futures contract at 91.66 or 7.34 percent, posting Treasury bills as initial margin. The futures contract expires on March 17, approximately 11 months after the initial purchase, during which time the futures price and rate fluctuate daily. On April 11 the March 1992 futures rate exceeds the prevailing cash rate by 115 basis points (1.15 percent). Exhibit 9.2 shows one possible pattern of rate movements in which the futures rate initially drops below 7.34 percent, then rises continuously to 9 percent at expiration. The cash Eurodollar time deposit rate is assumed to also decline initially, then increase through expiration, at which time it equals the futures rate of 9 percent.

Because our trader is long futures, the contract increases in value when prices rise, or rates decline. He can thus withdraw cash from his margin account immediately after April 11 equal to the increase in value. Assuming the lowest futures rate reached is 7

Exhibit 9.1 Data For Three-Month Eurodollar Futures Contracts and Cash Market Money Rates

EURODOLLAR (IMM) – $1 million; pts of 100%

	Open	High	Low	Settle	Chg	Yield Settle	Chg	Open Interest
June	93.66	93.75	93.63	93.71	+ .06	6.29	– .06	269,473
Sept	93.34	93.41	93.31	93.38	+ .05	6.62	– .05	147,229
Dec	92.86	92.91	92.83	92.90	+ .05	7.10	– .05	92,638
Mr92	92.63	92.67	92.60	92.66	+ .04	7.34	– .04	57,744
June	92.27	92.31	92.25	92.30	+ .03	6.70	– .03	39,903
Sept	91.97	92.01	91.94	92.00	+ .03	8.00	– .03	33,256
Dec	91.67	91.71	91.62	91.69	+ .02	8.31	– .02	27,231
Mr93	91.60	91.64	91.57	91.62	+ .02	8.38	– .02	21,422
June	91.49	91.54	91.46	91.51	+ .02	8.49	– .02	15,813
Sept	91.39	91.44	91.37	91.41	+ .02	8.59	– .02	13,153
Dec	91.21	91.26	91.19	91.23	+ .02	8.77	– .02	9,303
Mr94	91.18	91.23	91.16	91.20	+ .02	8.80	– .02	6,160
June	91.10	91.15	91.08	91.12	+ .02	8.88	– .02	5,071
Sept	91.04	91.09	91.00	91.06	+ .02	8.94	– .02	3,668
Dec	90.93	90.98	90.91	90.95	+ .02	9.05	– .02	3,326
Mr95	90.89	90.93	90.84	90.91	+ .03	9.09	– .03	1,491

Est vol 163,974; vol Wed 84,620; open int 746,780, +8,876.

MONEY RATES

Thursday, April 11, 1991

The key U.S. and foreign annual interest rates below are a guide to general levels but don't always represent actual transactions.

PRIME RATE: 8¾%–9%. The base rate on corporate loans at large U.S. money center commercial banks.

FEDERAL FUNDS: 5 11/16% high, 5½% low, 5½% near closing bid, 5⅝% offered. Reserves traded among commercial banks for overnight use in amounts of $1 million or more. Source: Babcock Fulton Prebon (U.S.A.) Inc.

DISCOUNT RATE: 6%. The charge on loans to depository institutions by the New York Federal Reserve Bank.

CALL MONEY: 7½% to 8½%. The charge on loans to brokers on stock exchange collateral.

COMMERCIAL PAPER placed directly by General Motors Acceptance Corp.: 5.85% 30 to 59 days; 5.875% 60 to 149 days; 5.90% 150 to 270 days.

COMMERCIAL PAPER: High-grade unsecured notes sold through dealers by major corporations in multiples of $1,000: 6% 30 days; 6% 60 days; 6% 90 days.

CERTIFICATES OF DEPOSIT: 5.77% one month; 5.82% three months; 5.95% six months; 6.40% one year. Average of top rates paid by major New York banks on primary new issues of negotiable C.D.s, usually on amounts of $1 million and more. The minimum unit is $100,000. Typical rates in the secondary market: 6% one month; 6.03% three months; 6.10% six months.

BANKERS ACCEPTANCES: 5.85% 30 days; 5.93% 60 days; 5.92% 90 days; 5.87% 120 days; 5.87% 150 days; 5.87% 180 days. Negotiable, bank-backed business credit instruments typically financing an import order.

LONDON LATE EURODOLLARS: 6 1/16% – 5 15/16% one month; 6⅛% – 6% two months; 6 3/16% – 6 1/16% three months; 6¼% – 6⅛% four months; 6 5/16% – 6 3/16% five months; 6 5/16% – 6 3/16% six months.

LONDON INTERBANK OFFERED RATES (LIBOR): 6 1/16% one month; 6 3/16% three months; 6⅜% six months; 6 13/16% one year. The average of interbank offered rates for dollar deposits in the London market based on quotations at five major banks. Effective rate for contracts entered into two days from date appearing at top of this column.

FOREIGN PRIME RATES: Canada 10.75%; Germany 10.50%; Japan 8.25%; Switzerland 11.13%; Britain 12.50%. These rate indications aren't directly comparable; lending practices vary widely by location.

TREASURY BILLS: Results of the Monday, April 8, 1991, auction of short-term U.S. government bills, sold at a discount from face value in units of $10,000 to $1 million: 5.60% 13 weeks; 5.68% 26 weeks.

FEDERAL HOME LOAN MORTGAGE CORP. (Freddie Mac): Posted yields on 30-year mortgage commitments for delivery within 30 days. 9.49%, standard conventional fixed-rate mortgages; 6.50%, 2% rate capped one-year adjustable rate mortgages. Source: Telerate Systems Inc.

FEDERAL NATIONAL MORTGAGE ASSOCIATION (Fannie Mae): Posted yields on 30 year mortgage commitments for delivery within 30 days (priced at par). 9.43%, standard conventional fixed rate-mortgages; 7.25%, 6/2 rate capped one-year adjustable rate mortgages. Source: Telerate Systems Inc.

MERRILL LYNCH READY ASSETS TRUST: 5.95%. Annualized average rate of return after expenses for the past 30 days; not a forecast of future returns.

Source: *The Wall Street Journal.*

percent on June 20, 1991, the trader could earn a maximum of $850 in this example ($25 times 34 basis points). When the futures rate rises above 7.34 percent after

October 4, 1991, the contract decreases in value and the trader must make additional variation margin payments. At expiration, the futures contract is worth $4,150 less than its value on April 11, 1991 because the Eurodollar futures rate increased 166 basis points to 9 percent. If the trader held the contract to expiration, he would have settled his position by paying a total of $4,150 at the close.

The Basis

The term *basis* refers to the cash price of an asset minus the corresponding futures price for the same asset at a point in time. Typically, it applies to the cash price of a security that is being hedged. For Eurodollar futures, the basis can be calculated as the futures rate minus the cash rate. The basis is plotted at the bottom of Exhibit 9.2 for the pattern of cash and futures data discussed above. Later discussions indicate that the basis is important in determining the effectiveness of hedging interest rate risk.

The basis does not normally behave as nicely as in Exhibit 9.2. It may be positive or negative depending on whether futures rates are above or below cash rates. It further rises and falls daily as economic conditions and market sentiment change. While the basis can take any value, there are two general price relationships between futures and cash instruments. First, the basis must equal zero at expiration. Suppose it takes on some nonzero value. Just prior to expiration, any trader could buy the cheaper contract and sell the more expensive making a riskless profit. Such arbitrage drives the two prices together. Second, because futures and cash prices must be equal at expiration, the basis normally narrows as expiration approaches. If it is positive, it declines to zero. If it is negative, it increases to zero.

SPECULATION VERSUS HEDGING

Participants use futures for a variety of purposes. According to one view, futures prices represent the consensus forecast of the underlying asset's future price at contract expiration. When a trader's expectation of the correct futures price differs from the actual price, he can either buy or sell the future, depending on whether the contract is perceived to be undervalued or overvalued. Such a participant is a speculator who takes on additional risk to earn speculative profits. For example, a speculator who believed that March 1992 Eurodollar futures at 7.34 percent were undervalued (futures rates were too high) would buy the contract, anticipating a decline in futures rates and an increase in price prior to expiration. Speculators who felt the contract was overvalued (futures rates were too low) would alternatively sell futures, expecting to make a profit after futures rates increased and prices fell.

The top part of Exhibit 9.3 characterizes speculation in terms of two profit diagrams for the March 1992 Eurodollar futures data from Exhibit 9.1. The first summarizes the profits and losses from buying the futures contract at the settlement price relative to possible futures prices after the contract is purchased. Specifically, on April 11 the settlement price equals 92.66. If a speculator sells the futures contract at any higher price, he earns a profit equal to $25 times the difference in the sales price

**Exhibit 9.2 The Relationship Between Futures Rates and
Cash Rates—One Possible Pattern**

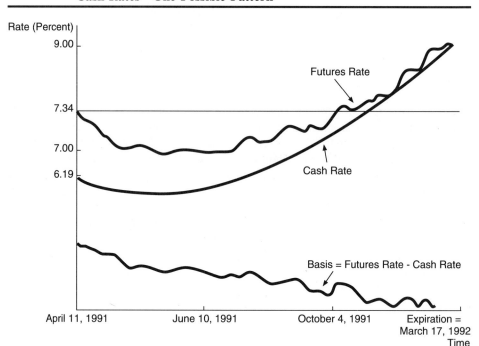

and 92.66. If the futures price declines and he sells at less than 92.66, he suffers a loss. The second diagram summarizes profits and losses for the seller of the same futures contract. Not surprisingly, the seller profits when the futures price declines and loses when the price rises.

Speculation is extremely risky. For the most part, futures rates and prices on nearby contracts are determined by arbitrage activity. Even when a speculator views a contract as overvalued or undervalued, any position taken can backfire in that a major market move could overwhelm the initial mispricing. Exhibit 9.3 demonstrates that the loss potential is virtually unlimited. Pure speculative activity with single contracts is thus relatively rare.

Hedging differs from speculation in terms of the participants' risk position prior to executing a trade and overall trade objectives. Speculators begin with no risk and take a position that increases their risk profile. Many hedgers focus on avoiding or reducing risk. They thus enter futures transactions because their normal business operations involve certain risks that they are trying to reduce. This pre-existing risk can generally be at least partially offset because futures prices tend to move directly with cash prices and thus futures rates closely track cash interest rates. Hedgers take

Exhibit 9.3 Profit Diagrams for a Speculator with March 1992 Eurodollar Futures Contracts

A. Speculation

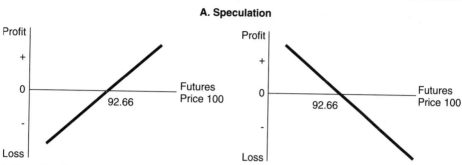

1. Buy a March 1992 Eurodollar Futures at 92.66.   2. Sell a March 1992 Eurodollar Futures at 92.66.

B. Profit Hedges

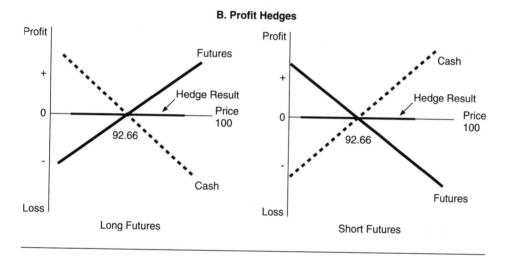

Long Futures   Short Futures

the opposite position in a futures contract relative to their cash market risk so that losses in one market are reduced by gains in the other market.

For example, a trader who loses when cash market interest rates decrease will normally gain in the futures market with a long position as futures rates also decrease (and prices rise) and the contract increases in value. This is characterized at the bottom of Exhibit 9.3. The first diagram adds to the long futures position a dashed line that indicates the profit and loss from an unhedged cash position. In this case the hedger loses when prices increase (rates decrease) and gains when prices decrease (rates increase). In a perfect hedge denoted by adding the profits and losses on both the futures and cash position, the net profit equals zero at each price, which is characterized by the bold horizontal line along the zero profit figure.

It is also argued that participants use futures because transactions costs are lower with futures than with cash assets. Futures hedges are transactions whereby participants can replicate cash market positions but lower their cost of taking a position. For example, an investor who has funds to invest for 1 year in the Treasury market on January 1 could simply buy a 1-year Treasury bill. Alternatively, he could buy a 6-month Treasury bill and two 3-month Treasury bill futures contracts that expire in June and September, respectively, expecting to take delivery at each expiration. The latter option might be attractive because the combined yield exceeded that for the 1-year bill and transactions costs are lower. Similarly, a bank might trade Eurodollar futures to limit the increase in future borrowing costs or to set a cap on a loan rate.

A Long Hedge

A long hedge is applicable for a participant who wants to reduce the cash market risk associated with a decline in interest rates. The appropriate strategy is to buy futures contracts on securities similar to those evidencing the cash market risk. If cash rates decline, futures rates will typically also decline so that the value of the futures position will likely increase. Any loss in the cash market is at least partially offset by a gain in futures. Of course, if cash market rates increase, futures rates will also increase and the futures position will show a loss. This reveals an important aspect of hedging. In this latter case the investor would have profited more from not hedging because cash rates moved in his favor. The objective, however, was risk reduction. When the risk was lowered, the expected return was also lower.

Suppose a bank anticipates investing funds that will be available in 60 days in 3-month Eurodollar time deposits. Using data for August 2, 1990, provided below, the current cash market rate equals 8 percent while the December 1990 futures rate equals 7.82 percent. Bank management is concerned that rates will decrease substantially and the bank will lose interest by not being able to lock in current rates. Ideally, if the bank had the funds in hand, it would buy Eurodollar deposits on August 2. To hedge, the bank instead buys one December Eurodollar futures contract with the expectation that potential losses in the cash market will be offset by futures market gains.

Rates: 3-month Eurodollars: August 2, 1990

Cash rate: 8%	Futures rate:	
	Sept. 90	7.90%
	Dec. 90	7.82
	Mar. 91	7.81
	June 91	7.95

Exhibit 9.4 summarizes the hedge results assuming the bank buys futures in August and sells them in October when the bank actually buys Eurodollars in the cash market. In August the cash Eurodollar rate exceeds the futures rate by 18 basis points. This difference, designated the basis, determines the risk and net performance of the hedge. In October the bank purchases $1 million in 3-month Eurodollars at 7.55 percent. As feared, cash rates fall, producing an opportunity loss of $1,125 in interest for the 3-month period. Futures rates also fall to 7.40 percent, however, so that the bank sells its contract at a higher price, earning a direct profit of $1,050. Note that the gain on the futures position is $75 less than the opportunity loss with the cash Eurodollars.

Exhibit 9.4 Long Hedge Using Eurodollar Futures

Date	Cash Market	Futures Market	Basis
8/2/90 (Initial futures position)	Bank anticipates investing $1 million in Eurodollars in 2 months; current cash rate = 8.00%	Bank buys one Dec. 1990 Eurodollar futures contract at 7.82%; price = 92.18	7.82% − 8.00% = −0.18%
10/25/90 (Close futures position)	Bank invests $1 million 3-month Eurodollars at 7.55%	Bank sells one Dec. 1987 Eurodollar futures contract at 7.40%; price = 92.60	7.40% − 7.55% = −0.15%
Net effect	Opportunity loss: 8.00% − 7.55% = 0.45%; 45 basis points worth $25 each = $1,125	Futures gain 7.82% − 7.40% = 0.42%; 42 basis points worth $25 each = $1,050	Basis change: −0.15% − (−0.18%) = 0.03%

Cumulative investment income:

$$\text{Interest at } 7.55\% = \$1,000,000(.0755)(90/360) = \$18,875$$
$$\text{Profit from futures trades} = \underline{\quad 1,050 \quad}$$
$$\text{Total} = \$19,925$$
$$\text{Effective return} = \frac{\$19,925}{\$1,000,000} \frac{(360)}{(90)} = 7.97\%$$

The bank's effective percentage return is calculated at the bottom of the exhibit. Investment income consists of $18,875 in interest and $1,050 in futures profits for a 7.97 percent return. Note finally that this net percentage return is just 3 basis points below the initial cash Eurodollar rate on August 2 that the bank hoped to lock in.

A Short Hedge

A short hedge applies to any participant who wants to reduce the risk of an increase in interest rates. The appropriate strategy is to sell futures contracts on securities similar to those evidencing the cash market risk. If cash rates increase, futures rates will generally increase so the loss in the cash position will be at least partially offset by a gain in value of futures. Again, if cash rates actually decrease, the gain in the cash market will be offset by a loss from futures.

Suppose, for example that on August 2, 1990 a bank anticipates it will need to sell a 5-month Eurodollar deposit from its investment portfolio in 50 days. The deposit yields 8.25 percent and management, expecting a sharp increase in interest rates, would like to hedge against a decline in value of the deposit at the time of sale. The cash market risk of loss is that Eurodollar time deposit rates will be higher in 50 days. To hedge, the bank should sell Eurodollar futures.

Exhibit 9.5 summarizes the hedge results assuming the bank sells December 1990 Eurodollar futures in August, and buys them back in September when it liquidates its Eurodollar investment. In August the futures rate equals 7.82 percent. When the bank actually sells the Eurodollar from its portfolio, its market rate increases to 8.37 percent even though it has a shorter maturity, while the futures rate increases to 8.09 percent.

Exhibit 9.5 Short Hedge Using Eurodollar Futures

Date	Cash Market	Futures Market	Basis
8/2/90	Bank anticipates selling $1 million Eurodollar deposit in 50 days; current cash rate = 8.25%	Bank sells one Dec. 1990 Eurodollar futures contract at 7.82%; price = 92.18	7.82% – 8.25% = –0.43%
9/25/90	Bank sells $1 million Eurodollar deposit at 8.37%	Bank buys one Dec. 1990 Eurodollar futures contract at 8.09%; price = 91.91	8.09% – 8.37% = –0.28%
Net result:	Opportunity loss: 8.37% – 8.25% = 0.12%; 12 basis points worth $25 each = $300	Futures gain: 7.82% – 8.09% (92.18 – 91.19) = 0.27%; 27 basis points worth $25 each = $675	Basis change: 0.28% – (–0.43%) = 0.15%

Effective gain = $6.75 – $300 = $375
Plus value of Eurodollar deposit at sale.

Thus the bank has an approximate opportunity loss of $300 on its cash position and a futures gain of $675 for a net profit of $375.[4] Thus the hedge allows the bank to sell the deposit and use futures profits to more than offset the decline in value of the Eurodollar deposit.

Change in the Basis

Both the long and short hedges worked in the previous examples in the sense that the futures rate moved coincidentally with the cash rate. With the long hedge, the futures rate fell by 42 basis points, or 3 basis points less than the opportunity loss in the cash market, so that futures profits did not quite offset the cash market loss. Had the cash rate increased instead of decreased, the bank would have invested its funds at a yield above 8 percent but would have realized a loss on its futures position as the contract price declined with an increase in the futures rate. With the short hedge, the futures rate increased by 27 basis points, which was 15 basis points more than the increase in cash rates. The net effect was that the futures profit exceeded the cash market loss.

The actual risk assumed by a trader in both hedges is not that the level of interest rates will move against the cash position, but that the basis might change adversely between the time the hedge is initiated and closed. The effective return from Exhibit 9.4 can also be expressed as:

$$\text{Effective return} = \text{Initial cash rate} - \text{Change in basis} \qquad \textbf{(9.1)}$$

---

[4]The calculation assumes that the deposit has exactly 90 days remaining maturity such that a basis point is worth $25. At initiation of the hedge, the deposit had at least 140 days remaining to final maturity, so each basis point was initially worth more than $25.

or 8 percent −0.3 percent.[5] The change in the basis equals the basis when the hedge is closed minus the basis when the hedge is initiated. At the time a trade is initiated, the only unknown is the change in basis. Thus a hedger still faces the risk that futures rates and cash rates will not change coincidentally. In this example, the basis increased from −18 to −15 basis points. Had the basis declined to −25 basis points, the effective return would have risen to 8.07 percent, 8.00 percent − (−0.25 percent − 0.18 percent). Had the basis increased, the effective return would have fallen below 8 percent. This is true regardless of whether the level of rates increased or decreased after August 2.

The effective cost of a short hedge is also determined by Equation 9.1. The effective risk is again that the basis might change between the time a hedge is initiated and the time it is offset. However, the short hedger benefits when the basis increases and loses when the basis decreases. This is the opposite of a hedger who takes a long position. Using the data from the example in Exhibit 9.5, the effective cost of the Eurodollar deposit sale was 8.25 percent − (−0.15 percent), or 8.10 percent. This indicates that the bank was able to sell the time deposit at a lower yield and thus greater net value.

Generally, directional movements in the basis are more predictable than movements in the level of cash market rates. Thus the risk of hedging is normally less than the risk of not hedging. While basis changes can be substantial, most factors that influence cash rates influence futures rates simultaneously. Futures rates are further tied to cash rates by arbitrage activity so that the two rates associated with most instruments move together.

Basis Risk and Cross Hedging

In a perfect hedge the profit or loss in the cash position is exactly offset by the profit or loss from the futures position. This would occur if the basis change always equaled zero. In practice, it is extremely difficult to obtain a perfect hedge and there are numerous instances when basis risk can be substantial. One such instance involves *cross hedges*. A cross hedge is one in which a participant uses a futures contract based on a security that differs from the security being hedged in the cash market. An example would be using Eurodollar futures to hedge price movements for commercial paper transactions. The risk is potentially greater for cross hedges because futures and cash interest rates may not move closely together because they are based on different underlying securities. If the basis is volatile and unpredictable, Equation 9.1 suggests that the effective return or cost from a hedge might also be volatile and unpredictable.

Basis risk can also be substantial because futures and cash rates for the same underlying security may move in opposite directions prior to expiration. In fact, the basis change is only known with certainty when the planned cash transactions being hedged coincide with futures contract expiration. In this case, the basis equals zero, and thus the basis change equals the negative of the basis at the time the hedge is initiated. Typically, however, most transactions do not coincide with futures expirations

---

[5] 8.00% − 0.03% = 7.97%. The effective return is actually higher because the bank could withdraw variation margin funds and invest the proceeds after futures prices moved favorably.

Hedging and Opportunity Losses

During the summer of 1982, senior management at Berkeley Federal Savings in Milburn, New Jersey, decided to use financial futures to hedge the firm's cost of funds. Berkeley had approximately $400 million of its deposits in 6-month savings certificates that paid rates that floated with current Treasury bill rates.

Berkeley decided to partially hedge its borrowing costs by selling $400 million in 3-month Treasury bill futures contracts. The expectation was that if cash Treasury bill rates increased and Berkeley's actual borrowing costs rose, Treasury bill futures rates would also increase so that the firm would profit by buying the futures back at lower prices. In actuality, the opposite occurred.

In August the bank president left for a short vacation. At that time, losses on the association's futures position totaled $200,000. During the next few days, Treasury bill cash and futures rates dropped

sharply. By the time the president returned 1 week later, losses had reached $1.5 million by the time the association closed out its futures position.

The hedge worked in the sense that the firm's funds cost was stabilized as cash market gains in the form of lower interest costs on the savings certificates were offset by futures contract losses. Management was dissatisfied, however, because it paid out $1.5 million in futures losses immediately and could have borrowed at lower rates even if it had not hedged at all. The president even suggested that he would have liquidated the futures position earlier to cut futures losses had he not been on vacation. Of course, it is not a hedge if a firm liquidates its position when futures rates move adversely. The fundamental point is that hedging reduces risk but also eliminates the potential to realize gains from unhedged positions. These opportunity losses represent the cost of hedging.

and changes in futures rates may differ sharply from changes in cash rates. Finally, as Contemporary Issues: Hedging and Opportunity Losses suggests, futures trades are not riskless and often produce opportunity losses.

MICROHEDGING APPLICATIONS

One of the basic decisions risk managers at banks make is whether to hedge specific individual transactions or the aggregate risk exposure of the bank. The previous examples of a long hedge and a short hedge involved individual transactions. Alternatively, management could choose to hedge aggregate risk exposure evidenced by a nonzero GAP or nonzero duration gap. *Microhedges* refer to the hedging of a transaction associated with a specific asset, liability, or commitment. *Macrohedges* involve taking futures positions to reduce aggregate portfolio interest rate risk, typically measured by a GAP or duration gap.

According to regulations, banks are restricted to using financial futures for hedging purposes. In their accounting, they must recognize futures on a micro basis by linking each futures transaction with a specific cash instrument or commitment. Yet many analysts feel that such linkages force microhedges that may increase a firm's total risk because they ignore all other portfolio components. Thus accounting requirements potentially focus attention on inappropriate risk measures. Macrohedging, in turn, is difficult to implement because of problems in accurately measuring a firm's overall interest rate risk and in monitoring hedging effectiveness. This section analyzes various microhedges, and is followed by a section on macrohedging.

Creating a Synthetic Liability with a Short Hedge

On May 12, 1992, a large money center bank agreed to finance a $1 million 6-month working capital loan to a corporate customer. Management wanted to match fund the loan by issuing 6-month Eurodollar time deposits. On May 12 the 6-month cash Eurodollar rate was 10.15 percent while the corresponding 3-month rate was 9.88 percent. Three-month Eurodollar futures rates for June 1992 and September 1992 delivery equaled 9.92 percent and 10.3 percent, respectively. Rather than issue a direct 6-month Eurodollar liability at 10.15 percent, the bank created a synthetic 6-month liability by shorting futures. The objective was to use the futures market to borrow at a lower rate than the 6-month cash Eurodollar rate. It was to be achieved by initially issuing a 3-month Eurodollar, then issuing another when the first matured. Futures would reduce the risk of rising interest rates for the second Eurodollar. The following time line indicates the rate comparison. Exhibit 9.6 outlines the steps.

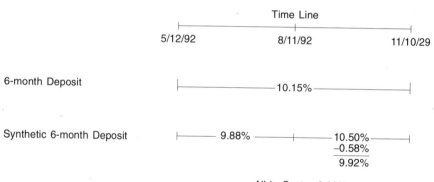

On May 12 the bank issued a $1 million, 91-day Eurodollar time deposit at 9.88 percent and simultaneously sold one June 1992 Eurodollar futures contract at 9.92 percent. The bank will sell a September 1992 Eurodollar future when the June future expires. Alternatively, the bank could sell a single September future in May. The use of both futures contracts reduces basis risk. The bank expected to roll over its 91-day Eurodollar deposit by issuing another 3-month deposit on August 11 for an effective 6-month maturity. The short hedge reduced the risk that the bank would lose if cash Eurodollar rates increased when the bank reissued its deposit.

Prior to expiration of the June 1992 futures contract on June 11, the bank rolled its hedge forward by buying one June 1992 contract and selling one September 1992 futures contract. The bank made a $200 profit on the June futures as rates rose by 8 basis points. When the first 91-day cash Eurodollar deposit matured on August 11,

Exhibit 9.6 Creating a Synthetic 6-Month Eurodollar Liability

Summary of Relevant Eurodollar Rates and Transactions

May 12 1992
3-month cash rate = 9.88%
6-month cash rate = 10.15%
June 1992 futures rate = 9.92%

June 11, 1992
Buy: June 1992 futures rate = 10.00%
Sell: September 1992 futures rate = 10.25%

August 11, 1992
3-month cash rate = 10.50%
Buy: September 1992 futures rate = 10.75%

Date	Cash Market	Futures Market
5/12/92	Bank issues $1 million, 91-day Eurodollar time deposit at 9.88%; 3-mo. interest expense = $24,975	Bank sells one June 1992 Eurodollar futures contract at 9.92%
6/11/92		Bank buys one June 1992 contract at 10%; profit = $200; bank sells 1 Sept. 1992 Eurodollar futures contract at 10.25%
8/11/92	Bank issues $1 million, 91-day Eurodollar time deposit at 10.50%; 3-mo., interest expense = $26,542 (increase in interest expense over previous period = $1,567)	Bank buys one Sept. 1992 Eurodollar futures contract at 10.75%; profit = $1,250
Net Effect:	6-mo. interest expense = $51,517	Futures profit = $1,450

$$\text{Effective 6--mo. borrowing cost} = \frac{\$51,517 - \$1,450}{\$1,000,000} \frac{(360)}{(182)} = 9.90\%$$

Interest on 6-month Eurodollar deposit issued May 12 = $51,314 at 10.15%

rates had risen substantially and the bank issued another 3-month Eurodollar deposit at 10.5 percent. It simultaneously closed out its futures position by buying one September 1992 futures contract at 10.75 percent. In this example, both cash and futures rates increased so that the $1,450 profit from futures almost completely offset the $1,567 increase in interest expense to $26,542. The effective borrowing cost thus approximately equaled the initial 3-month cash Eurodollar rate. These calculations are summarized at the bottom of Exhibit 9.6.[6]

A bank can typically benefit from this strategy when the following inequality exists:

---

[6]This example ignores the effect of transactions costs and margin requirements. Transactions costs on futures are negligible, while margin costs depend on the type of collateral and whether the bank reinvests its excess variation margin.

$$\left(1 + \text{RC3e}\,\frac{90}{360}\right)\left(1 + \left(\text{RFNe} + \hat{\beta}\right)\frac{90}{360}\right) < \left(1 + \text{RC6e}\,\frac{180}{360}\right) \qquad \textbf{(9.2)}$$

where

RC3 = 3-month cash Eurodollar deposit rate
 RF = 3-month Eurodollar futures rate on nearby contract
RC6 = 6-month cash Eurodollar deposit rate
 $\hat{\beta}$ = expected basis effect

with all interest rates expressed in decimals. Using data from the previous example and assuming the basis will be unchanged, the comparison is:

$$(1.0247)(1.0248) < (1.05075)$$

The actual benefit, of course, depends on how cash rates change relative to futures rates. In essence, the bank has substituted basis risk for the risk that cash rates will change adversely. In this example, the bank could lose if cash rates increased substantially more than futures rates increased. Briefly, the true borrowing cost rises as the basis (futures rate - cash rate) decreases, while the cost falls as the basis increases.[7]

The Mechanics of Applying a Microhedge

A bank should carefully analyze the opportunities and risks associated with hedging. The following discussion demonstrates the type of information required and procedural steps underlying successful hedging programs.[8]

Determine the Bank's Interest Rate Risk Position. To formulate the correct hedge, management must determine the bank's interest rate risk position. With a microhedge this involves examining the bank's actual and anticipated cash market position and how specific interest rate changes will affect interest income or expense. Frequently, banks then compare their rate forecast and their potential losses if these rates materialize. Selectively hedging when losses will arise if the forecast is realized is a form of speculation. The key hedging decision involves determining how much risk the bank will accept.

Forecast the Dollar Flows Expected in Cash Market Transactions. To determine how many futures contracts are necessary, management should estimate the dollar magnitude of anticipated cash flows from cash market transactions. This may equal the amount of investable funds, the size of a loan commitment, or the amount of liabilities to be issued or rolled over.

---

[7]The appropriate basis comparison is complicated by rolling the futures hedge forward. Between May 12 and August 11 cash rates increased by 0.62 percent, while futures rates effectively increased by 0.58 percent (0.08 percent + 0.50 percent). Thus the actual borrowing cost just exceeded the initial 3-month Eurodollar rate.

[8]This analysis is based on steps outlined by Kawaller, 1983.

Choose the Appropriate Futures Contract. A bank should select a hedging vehicle that reduces interest rate risk. Because changes in the basis determine hedging risk, the appropriate futures contract is usually one whose rates correlate highly with those of the cash asset or liability being hedged. Typically, the correlation is highest for like instruments, such as Treasury bill futures relative to cash Treasury bills. If a like futures instrument is unavailable, a bank can examine historical correlations for different futures contracts and choose the contract with the highest correlation coefficient. As described earlier, the use of a futures contract that is not identical to the cash instrument being hedged is referred to as a cross-hedge. It is also important to assess the liquidity of different contracts. Only when trading volume is large can a bank easily buy or sell futures at relatively stable basis levels.

Determine the Correct Number of Futures Contracts. Five factors, listed below, determine the correct number of futures contracts. This calculation, or hedge ratio, is expressed numerically as:

$$C = \frac{(A \cdot Mc)}{(F \cdot Mf)} b \qquad\qquad (9.3)$$

where

C = number of futures contracts
A = dollar value of cash flow to be hedged
F = face value of futures contract
Mc = maturity or duration of anticipated cash asset or liability
Mf = maturity or duration of futures contract
$b = \dfrac{\text{Expected rate movement on cash instrument}}{\text{Expected rate movement on futures contract}}$

If futures rates are expected to move coincidentally with cash rates, b equals 1. If futures rates are expected to exhibit larger moves relative to cash rates, b is less than 1, and vice versa.[9] Using the information from Exhibit 9.6 and assuming b equals 1 with Eurodollar cash and futures rates, the bank needed one futures contract:

$$C = \frac{\$1,000,000}{\$1,000,000} \times \frac{91\,\text{days}}{90\,\text{days}} \times 1 \cong 1$$

Determine the Appropriate Time Frame for the Hedge. Typically, a bank matches the length of a hedge with the timing of cash flows for the underlying asset or liability. For example, a bank that knows it will have funds to invest in 6 months will use a futures contract that expires in 6 or more months. If consecutive cash flows are expected, such as principal payments on a term loan, a bank will hedge by spreading different futures contracts over the term of the cash flows. This process, labeled

---

[9]In practice, the appropriate factor is determined as the slope of the regression line from running a regression of cash price changes on futures price changes using historical data.

stripping futures, consists of buying or selling equal amounts of successive futures contracts.[10]

Monitor Hedge Performance. Once a hedge is in place, management should monitor interest rate changes and the bank's cash position to verify the hedge performance. One concern is that the anticipated cash position might vary. Another is that the basis might move against the cash rate, whereby the bank loses in both the cash and futures market. If the bank's risk profile changes, it may want to lift a hedge. In practice, many participants adjust their hedge when the basis moves against them, implicitly extrapolating that the movement is permanent. In doing so, they are speculating.

MACROHEDGING APPLICATIONS

Macrohedging focuses on reducing interest rate risk associated with a bank's entire portfolio rather than with individual components or transactions. As suggested in Chapter 8, macrohedging assumes that interest rate risk is best evidenced by GAP or duration gap measures. Banks can use futures contracts to hedge this net portfolio rate sensitivity.

Hedging and the GAP

When establishing a macrohedge, a bank should initially examine its aggregate interest rate risk position. Banks using funding GAP analysis designate different time intervals and identify rate-sensitive assets and liabilities within each time frame. The dollar magnitude of rate-sensitive assets minus the dollar magnitude of rate-sensitive liabilities equals the funding GAP. In general, if the funding GAP is positive, net interest income rises when interest rates rise, and falls when interest rates fall. If the funding GAP is negative, net interest income falls when rates increase and rises when rates decrease. The funding GAP thus serves as a measure of interest rate risk.

Hedging strategies attribute different funding GAP values to specific blocks of rate-sensitive assets or rate-sensitive liabilities. With a positive GAP a bank will institute a long hedge, whereby declining interest rates should generate futures profits that offset the decline in net interest income. Banks alternatively offset a negative GAP via a short hedge, which should produce futures profits that offset increases in net interest expense.

Consider the summary rate sensitivity data in Exhibit 9.7 for the hypothetical bank from Exhibit 8.5 in Chapter 8. This bank has a negative cumulative GAP through 365 days. Each periodic GAP is also negative except for the assumed repricing of $10 million in floating-rate loans within 30 days. The near-term negative GAP can be

---

[10]If the term of the cash flows exceeds the time frame for which futures contracts are available, hedgers can "stack" contracts by loading up on the last available contract and systematically switching into new futures contracts as they become available. This involves additional risk and increases transactions costs.

Exhibit 9.7 Summary Rate-Sensitivity Data from Exhibit 8.5

Item	Time Frame for Rate Sensitivity (Days)					
	1–7	8–30	31–90	91–180	181–365	>365
Rate-sensitive assets	$ 6.3	$15.0[a]	$10.0	$10.0	$ 9.0	$35.0
Rate-sensitive liabilities	22.3	6.0	18.0	17.0	10.4	4.8
Periodic GAP	−16.0	9.0	−8.0	−7.0	−1.4	30.2
Cumulative GAP	−16.0	−7.0	−15.0	−22.0	−23.4	6.8

[a]Includes $10 million in floating-rate loans.

largely attributed to money market deposit accounts, while the later-term GAP is dominated by large CD liabilities.

$$C = \frac{\$10,000,000}{\$10,000,000} \times \frac{180 \text{ days}}{90 \text{ days}} \times 1.0 = 20$$

This assumes that the bank uses Eurodollar futures and that the expected movement between the effective interest rate on the rate-sensitive liabilities relative to the Eurodollar futures rate equals 1. The bank would likely sell 10 contracts (20 contracts/2 quarters) that expire in both September and December, liquidating the hedge by periodically buying back futures at selected intervals. This type of hedge is clearly a cross-hedge, as the cash rate is actually a combination of several rates, all different from the Eurodollar futures rate. The bank might alternatively choose Treasury bill futures if the correlation were higher because money market deposit accounts pay interest tied to cash Treasury bill rates. If interest rates did increase and the bank's net interest income declined, part of the loss should be offset by an increase in the value of the futures contracts with rising futures rates. In effect, the short hedge moves the GAP closer to zero over the time period considered.

Hedging and Duration Gap

One of the presumed advantages of duration gap analysis is that it lends itself to hedging applications. Duration gap is a single-valued measure of total interest rate risk in which a bank targets its market value of equity. Duration gap equals the weighted duration of bank assets minus the weighted duration of bank liabilities times the bank's debt-to-asset ratio. A positive gap measure indicates that aggregate assets will vary more in value relative to aggregate liabilities when interest rates change equally. If rates increase, the market value of assets falls more than the market value of liabilities, so the market value of equity declines. A bank with a negative duration gap will see its equity increase in value when rates rise.

To eliminate this risk, a bank could structure its portfolio so that the duration gap equals zero. Alternatively, it can use futures to balance the value sensitivity of the portfolio. Equation 8.6 is listed as follows:

$$\frac{\Delta \text{ Market value of equity}}{\text{Total assets}} \cong - \text{DGAP} \left[\frac{\Delta i}{1+i} \right] \tag{9.4}$$

where DGAP equals the duration gap and i equals some average interest rate for a bank's portfolio. If management wants to immunize market value of equity, it should set the bank's duration gap at zero. This can be done by using futures to create a synthetic gap that approximately equals zero. The appropriate size of a futures position can be determined by solving equation 9.5 for the market value of futures contracts (MVF), where DF is the duration of the futures contract used, DA is the weighted duration of assets, and DL is the weighted duration of liabilities:[11]

$$\frac{\text{DA(MVRSA)}}{(1+i_a)} - \frac{\text{DL(MVRSL)}}{(1+i_l)} + \frac{\text{DF} \times \text{(MVF)}}{(1+i_f)} = 0 \tag{9.5}$$

The subscripts on the interest rate measures refer to assets (a), liabilities (l), and futures (f), and all rates are assumed to change by the same amount. MVRSA and MVRSL refer to the market value of rate-sensitive assets and rate-sensitive liabilities, respectively.

As an illustration, consider the bank balance sheet data provided in Exhibit 8.8 converted to thousands. Because the bank has a positive duration gap of 1.14 years, it will see its market value of equity decline if interest rates rise. It thus needs to sell interest rate futures contracts in order to hedge its risk position. The short position indicates that the bank will make a profit if futures rates increase. This should at least partially offset any decline in the market value of equity caused by corresponding increases in cash rates. Assuming the bank uses the Eurodollar futures contract currently trading at 11 percent with a duration of 0.25 years, the target market value of futures contracts (MVF*) can be obtained from applying Equation 9.5:

$$\frac{3.05(\$900)}{1.13} - \frac{2.08(\$920)}{1.095} + \frac{0.25(\text{MVF}^*)}{1.11} = 0$$

or MVF* = −\$3,026.40. This suggests that the bank should sell three Eurodollar futures contracts. If all interest rates did increase by 1 percent, the profit on the three futures contracts would total \$7,500 (3 × 100 × \$25), or \$1,500 less than the decrease in market value of equity associated with the increase in cash rates (see Exhibit 8.9). The discrepancy derives from using interest rate averages and a discrete number of futures contracts. The concept, however, is clear. Duration gap mismatches can be hedged through the use of futures without dramatic changes in the portfolio.

Accounting Requirements and Tax Implications

Regulators generally limit banks to using futures for hedging purposes. However, if a bank has a dealer operation, it can use futures as part of its trading activities. In such accounts, gains and losses on these futures must be marked to market as they accrue,

---

[11]Because futures contracts have no fixed price or cash flow, they have no duration. Under certain assumptions, however, it can be shown that the duration of a futures contract equals the duration of the underlying deliverable instrument. See Kolb and Gay, 1982.

thereby affecting current income. Such current recognition of gains or losses clearly increases the volatility of reported earnings over short intervals. For hedging applications, futures contracts must be recognized on a micro basis by linking each contract to a specific cash instrument. Gains or losses on these contracts can be deferred and recognized as an adjustment to the reported cost of the hedged item.

To qualify as a hedge, the use of futures must meet several criteria. A bank must show that a cash transaction exposes it to interest rate risk, a futures contract must lower the bank's risk exposure, and the bank must designate the contract as a hedge. The primary difficulty involves determining whether futures reduce bank risk. Financial Accounting Standards Board statement number 80 states that this condition is met if the correlation between price changes in futures and the hedged instrument is high. Unfortunately, there are no well-defined rules for establishing what time period should be used to calculate the correlation or even what amount of correlation is high enough. If a high correlation does not prevail, a bank must immediately stop deferring futures gains and losses and account for the proceeds as current income.

The tax treatment of futures contracts has undergone a broad transition. Prior to 1981, futures profits were taxed as ordinary income or capital gains depending on the length of the trader's holding period. Tax payments were due in the year the futures position was offset. This enabled futures traders to spread contracts by taking opposite positions in different contracts, where one produced a loss and the other a gain for similar interest rate movements. At the end of the tax year, they would take the loss to reduce taxes and defer gains. In 1981, speculative traders were required to mark contract values to market at the end of the tax year and pay the obligated taxes in that year. Finally, the Tax Reform Act of 1986 eliminated the lower tax rate on long-term capital gains. Thus all futures profits are taxed as ordinary income.

INTEREST RATE SWAPS AS A RISK MANAGEMENT TOOL

Interest rate swaps originated in the Eurobond market in 1980. An interest rate swap is an agreement between two parties to exchange payments for a specific maturity on a specified principal amount. Maturities range from 6 months to 15 years, with most swaps in the 2- to 10-year range. They represent another means for firms facing mismatched assets and liabilities to reduce interest rate risk. Initially, only firms involved in the international money and capital markets used swaps, and virtually all transactions were priced in terms of the London Interbank Offered Rate (LIBOR). More recently, medium-sized U.S. firms with only domestic operations have begun using swaps and Treasury rates are used to determine the underlying payment obligations.

Swaps have several important advantages over financial futures. First, futures contracts are usually available only 2 to 4 years out. Swaps can be constructed for any term. Second, futures traders must mark their contracts to market, which exposes them to unexpected cash outflows. Swaps do not carry this risk. Third, swap documentation is quite standardized and participating firms can negotiate master agreements with partners that enhance the development of long-term business relationships. Finally, swaps are administratively cheaper because they require less monitoring. This section documents the nature of swap transactions and demonstrates how U.S. financial institutions use them as a risk management tool.

In its classic form, a *plain vanilla swap* arises when two firms face substantially different interest rate risk over the same period. One firm is a high quality borrower while the other exhibits greater perceived default risk. An interest rate swap can be structured to take advantage of the perceived credit quality differences by using the high-quality borrower's reputation to lower each firm's borrowing cost and provide the preferred type of fixed-rate or floating-rate financing.

One firm may own fixed-rate assets financed with floating-rate liabilities, which produce a persistent negative funding GAP, while another firm operates with a positive GAP because its floating-rate assets are financed by fixed-rate liabilities. The firm with a negative GAP will lose if interest rates rise, while the firm with a positive GAP gains. If rates fall, the firm with a negative GAP gains while the other loses. With an interest rate swap transaction, the two firms essentially trade interest rate payments on a portion of their portfolios. Risk can be reduced if the firm with a negative GAP makes a fixed-rate interest payment in exchange for a floating-rate interest payment. The firm with a positive GAP takes the opposite position by making floating-rate interest payments in exchange for a fixed-rate receipt. The credit quality of the high-rated borrower also enables both firms to borrow at lower rates than if they didn't swap interest payments.

This exchange is facilitated by a third party, typically a bank, acting as an intermediary (Exhibit 9.8) who arranges the swap. Its continuing role is to collect the interest payments and pay the difference to either party, depending on the contractual terms and the applicable interest rates. The intermediary may simply serve as an agent with no credit risk exposure or as a dealer, where it is a counterparty to each side of the transaction. As a dealer, the intermediary may enter into contracts without negotiating the other side of the swap. With the recent surge in swap volume, intermediaries now frequently guarantee the performance of parties to the swap. Many large commercial banks and investment banks serve as intermediaries.

The Quality Spread

The following section outlines a hypothetical swap transaction. The swap is possible because two firms facing the opposite interest rate risk exhibit different perceived credit risk. It involves a foreign bank with a positive GAP that prefers floating-rate liabilities to reduce its interest rate risk, and a U.S. savings and loan (S&L) with a negative GAP that prefers fixed-rate liabilities to reduce risk. The foreign bank is a high-quality borrower while the savings and loan is perceived to be much riskier. The two firms have the borrowing opportunities listed below, where the quality spread equals the difference in borrowing costs for each type of debt:

	Foreign Bank	**U.S. S&L**	**Quality Spread**
Floating-rate Debt (6-month)	LIBOR +0.5%	LIBOR +2.0%	1.5%
Fixed-rate Debt (5-year)	12.00	14.5	2.5
		Difference	1.0%

Exhibit 9.8 The Structure of Interest Rate Swaps

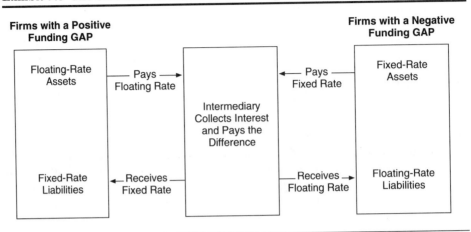

The critical factor is the difference in the quality spread between the floating-rate and fixed-rate debt. The foreign bank can issue 6-month floating-rate debt at 1.5 percent less than the S&L and fixed-rate debt at 2.5 percent less. The quality spread for fixed-rate debt is greater, reflecting a larger term premium because of the differential default risk and liquidity risk on longer-term contracts. The 1-percent difference represents a window to negotiate a swap.

An Example of a Swap Transaction

Suppose that the S&L operates with a large negative GAP caused by its reliance on short-term deposit liabilities to finance longer-term mortgage assets. It would like to substitute long-term fixed-rate debt for its short-term liabilities, but its cost of fixed-rate financing at 14.5 percent for 5-year funds is too high. If interest rates increase, the S&L will experience a significant decline in net interest income. At the same time, a foreign commercial bank operates with a positive GAP caused by fixed-rate liabilities financing floating-rate Eurodollar loans. The foreign bank has access to 5-year Eurobond financing at a much lower 12 percent rate, but prefers floating-rate debt to reduce its risk.

Assume that an intermediary bank locates both parties and arranges an interest rate swap. The swap terms are summarized in Exhibit 9.9. After negotiation, the two parties agree to exchange interest payments on $50 million for 5 years. The foreign bank has a comparative advantage with 5-year debt and thus issues $50 million in 5-year bonds at 12 percent, even though it prefers floating-rate financing. The intermediary agrees to pay the foreign bank 12 percent to cover its fixed-rate borrowing cost. The intermediary then negotiates with the S&L which agrees to make fixed-rate interest payments at 12.15 percent equal to the foreign bank's interest expense plus 15 basis points. The S&L, in turn, issues $50 million in 6-month floating-rate debt at LIBOR plus 2 percent. As part of the swap the foreign bank agrees to make floating-rate

Exhibit 9.9 Interest Rate Swap between a Savings & Loan (S&L) and Foreign Commercial Bank

Swap Terms: $50 million for 5 years

Foreign Commercial Bank (Positive GAP)

- Issues $50 million in 5-year Eurobonds at a fixed 12% rate
- Agrees to make semiannual interest payments to the intermediary at floating rate equal to 6-month London Interbank Offer Rate (LIBOR)
- Receives swap payment of 12% fixed rate from intermediary

Savings & Loan (Negative GAP)

- Issues $50 million in floating-rate debt at LIBOR + 2.0%
- Agrees to make semiannual interest payments to intermediary at fixed rate of 12.15% per year
- Receives swap payment of LIBOR from intermediary

Intermediary

- Agrees to pay foreign bank 12% fixed rate
- Agrees to pay S&L LIBOR floating rate
- Receives from foreign bank floating-rate payment at LIBOR
- Receives from S&L 12.15% fixed-rate payment
- Guarantees performance by each party to transaction
- Every 6 months it calculates obligated interest payments and remits difference to appropriate party

interest payments to the intermediary equal to the average monthly LIBOR rate during each interval. The intermediary then channels this LIBOR payment to the S&L to offset its interest on floating-rate debt. Interest payments on both the floating-rate debt and the 5-year Eurobonds are semiannual.

The effective costs of borrowing for both the foreign bank and S&L are calculated at the bottom of Exhibit 9.9. Consider first the foreign bank. Its 12-percent bond interest is effectively paid by the S&L so that its net borrowing cost equals LIBOR, the rate it pays the intermediary. The foreign bank thus obtains its preferred floating-rate financing at 50 basis points below its cost if it used the money market directly. The S&L, in turn, pays a 12.15 percent fixed rate plus LIBOR plus 2 percent on its floating-rate borrowing. The foreign bank effectively pays LIBOR to the S&L with its swap payment, which lowers the S&L's net borrowing cost to a fixed 14.15 percent (12.15 percent plus 2 percent). The S&L gets its preferred fixed-rate financing and saves 0.35 percent because it would have paid 14.5 percent if it borrowed directly in the capital market. Finally, the intermediary bank receives 12.15 percent plus LIBOR and pays 12 percent plus LIBOR, so its net return is a 0.15 percent intermediation fee. Note that the three parties have essentially split the 1 percent quality spread differential (0.50% + 0.35% + 0.15%).

The role of the intermediary is to arrange the swap terms between the parties. Typically it guarantees performance by each party, much like an exchange, and collects and remits the swapped interest payments between parties.

**Exhibit 9.10 Hypothetical Interest Payments between
Swap Partners—First 30 Months**

Time Frame	Fixed-Rate S&L Payment at 12.15%	LIBOR Average (Annual %)	Floating-Rate Bank Payment at LIBOR	Net Payment
6 months	$3,037,500	12.15%	$3,037,500	$ 0
1 year	3,037,500	10.00	2,500,000	537,500 to bank
18 months	3,037,500	11.50	2,875,000	162,500 to bank
2 years	3,037,500	12.50	3,125,000	87,500 to S&L
30 months	3,037,500	13.00	3,250,000	212,500 to S&L

The data in Exhibit 9.10 outline the pattern in semiannual interest payments at different LIBOR values. Note that the S&L's fixed-rate swap payment equals $3,037,500 every 6 months regardless of LIBOR. When LIBOR equals 12.15 percent the foreign bank's swap payment will also equal $3,037,500, so that the swap payments and receipts offset each other for both firms. For any value of LIBOR below 12.15 percent, the foreign bank receives a net cash inflow from the S&L because its swap payment is less than what it receives (at 12.15 percent) from the intermediary. If LIBOR exceeds 12.15 percent, the S&L receives a net cash inflow from the foreign bank. The final column indicates whether the bank or S&L receives the net interest payment at each assumed LIBOR value. In this example, both parties receive net interest payments because LIBOR is below and above 12 percent during different periods.

The above example assumes that both parties to a swap actually borrow by issuing debt in the money and capital markets. In practice, however, swap parties exchange only the obligated interest payments against some notional principal amount. The term "notional" indicates that the principal amount exists only to serve as a basis for calculating interest payments. Thus they never actually issue floating-rate debt or long-term bonds as part of swap agreements.

The net impact of a swap position is that a firm obligates itself to make the types of payments noted in the final column of the previous data. For the foreign bank, this indicates that it will receive a net cash inflow when LIBOR is below 12.15 percent. The swap presumably helps meet risk-reduction objectives because the bank has better matched the cash flow characteristics of its net rate-sensitive assets following from its positive GAP. When rates are low and declining, the bank loses because interest income will decline relative to interest expense. The swap payment helps offset the reduced net interest income. Alternatively, when LIBOR rises above 12.15 percent, the foreign bank's net interest income should rise but the gain will be matched with a swap payment to the intermediary. In this context, the swap constitutes a hedge. It reduces the net cash flow volatility associated with changes in net interest income due to adverse interest rate movements.

The situation is similar for the S&L. The S&L in turn, now better matches fixed-rate interest income from its mortgage portfolio with a fixed-rate interest obligation, presumably at a positive spread. When LIBOR rises above 12.15 percent the S&L

receives a swap payment. But this cash inflow presumably helps offset the decline in net interest income that follows from operating with a negative GAP in a rising-interest-rate environment. When LIBOR declines below 12.15 percent, the S&L's net interest income should increase but will be offset by a swap payment. A swap still involves some interest rate risk, however, because rates on the S&L's liabilities likely do not float with LIBOR. Therefore, changes in actual interest expense will vary differently relative to interest rate changes than do the cash flow obligations from a LIBOR-based swap agreement.

In practice, participants can enter standardized swap agreements quite easily once they have agreed to terms with an intermediary. Transactions are handled much like buying and selling Treasury securities through securities dealers. Consider the sample price quote sheet that appears as Exhibit 9.11. The prices indicate alternative interest rates that swap parties pay under different positions. The first column indicates the term of the swap agreement. All interest rates are, in turn, priced off rates on U.S. Treasury bonds at a set mark-up. The second column of data indicates the current Treasury bond rate for the term identified in each row. The swap spread signifies the mark-up, with the first figure representing the number of basis points over the Treasury yield for a party that wants to pay a floating rate and receive a fixed rate. The second figure indicates the number of basis points for a party that wants to pay the fixed rate and receive a floating rate. The final column indicates the total swap cost, which is quoted on a bond equivalent basis.

For example, a firm that wants to swap fixed-rate payments for floating-rate receipts for 3 years agrees to pay the prevailing 3-year Treasury rate of 8.36 percent plus 77 basis points, or 9.13 percent fixed rate. Depending on the agreement the firm has with the intermediary, it may also pay additional basis points to cover credit risk. The intermediary will try to reduce its risk by finding a firm that wants 3-year floating rate payments at the Treasury rate plus 66 basis points. The spread difference represents the intermediary's fee for providing the service. Intermediaries will adjust the spreads to influence behavior and control risk associated with their inventory of swaps.

Note the similarities between interest rate swaps and financial futures. A party enters an agreement which provides for cash receipts or cash payments depending on how interest rates move. Both allow managers to alter a bank's interest rate risk exposure.

There are many types of interest rate swaps other than the plain vanilla example provided here. Most swaps are similarly structured, but may use different indexes such as Treasury bill, CD, or commercial paper rates and interest payments may be monthly, quarterly, or annually. In a *basis swap* both parties pay a floating rate, but the difference is in maturities—for example, 3-month versus 1-month financing. Recently, swap agreements have been structured around the income streams from assets in order to convert cash flow streams from fixed-rate to floating-rate, or vice versa. Regardless of label, interest rate swaps are similarly structured to alter a bank's net cash flows, and thus are useful hedging tools.

Exhibit 9.11 Price Quotes for Interest Rate Swaps

Term	Treasury Rate	Spread	Cost
2 Years	8.22%	T + 49/57	8.71/8.79
3 Years	8.36	T + 66/77	9.02/9.13
4 Years	8.43	T + 70/80	9.13/9.23
5 Years	8.51	T + 73/81	9.24/9.32
6 Years	8.64	T + 76/84	9.40/9.48
7 Years	8.80	T + 80/89	9.60/9.69

The Risk with Swaps

While interest swaps are an alternative to futures, they also entail risks. The recent experience of savings and loans is an example. When interest rates increased sharply during the early 1980s, many thrifts took advantage of interest rate swaps to obtain fixed-rate financing. When mortgage rates averaged 13 to 14 percent, it seemed reasonable to fix borrowing costs at 11 percent. Unfortunately for these swap players, the level of interest rates moved dramatically lower in the mid-1980s. Had thrifts waited, they could have paid much lower rates on both fixed-rate and floating-rate debt. Thus they locked in much higher interest expense for the benefit of risk reduction. The problems were compounded as homeowners took advantage of the lower rates to refinance their mortgages. In many instances, thrifts lost their high-yielding fixed-rate assets via prepayments but kept their fixed-rate interest obligations. Selling the swap obligations to a third party prior to expiration would have produced a direct income statement loss.

Market participants have tried to reduce firm exposure to swap positions by developing a secondary market for swaps. This entails trying to standardize swap documentation to create attractive trading instruments. Straightforward plain vanilla swaps, like the one described in Exhibit 9.9, can be arranged within 1 business day and thus lend themselves to standardization. Still, each swap is a negotiated contract between two parties. When the terms are unusual, the attractiveness decreases in the secondary market. Furthermore, without guarantees or easily identifiable default risk, the liquidity of swaps diminishes.

There is some credit risk with swaps as well, but this is not as great as it originally seems. Remember that swap parties exchange only interest payments. Thus no principal is at risk. The $50 million notional principal amount in the above example never changes hands. The credit risk arises when the counterparty to a swap defaults. This is not a problem, however, if interest rates have moved against the remaining partner. Suppose in the above example that LIBOR increases dramatically, at which time the S&L fails. With LIBOR above 12.15 percent the foreign bank owes the S&L a swap payment, so the S&L's failure does not directly represent a loss to the foreign bank. It does require that the foreign bank enter a new swap agreement which may not have as favorable terms. Recent estimates of the degree of credit risk in a swap indicate that the cost ranges from 1 to 4 percent of the notional amount.[12]

---

[12]See the *Bank of England Quarterly Bulletin*, February 1987.

SUMMARY

Bank managers are paid to manage risk. In many cases, it is appropriate to reduce a bank's exposure to potentially adverse changes in interest rates. Hedging with financial futures contracts and entering into swap agreements are two methods banks can use to reduce interest rate risk. The concept underlying hedging with futures is that a bank enters into a pricing agreement whereby losses or gains on its actual cash transactions due to interest rate changes are at least partially offset by gains or losses on its futures position. Risk reduction occurs because the net loss or gain is typically less with a hedge than if no futures position is taken. The concept underlying interest rate swaps is that a bank can trade fixed interest payments or receipts for floating interest payments or receipts that better match other portfolio cash flows.

This chapter explains the mechanics of microhedging and macrohedging with Eurodollar futures. Microhedges associate futures positions with specific cash transactions. Macrohedges involve reducing interest rate risk for a bank's entire portfolio by associating futures positions with a funding GAP or duration gap. The fundamental conclusion is that managers have alternatives to alter a bank's interest rate risk position other than traditional cash transactions.

Questions

Futures

1. How does a futures contract differ from a cash contract? How does it differ from a forward contract?

2. Explain what it means to say: "Each party to a futures transaction trades with exchange members." Is this an advantage or disadvantage for the market participants? Why?

3. Some analysts compare the initial margin on a futures contract to a down payment. The exchanges vocally disagree. In what way is it like a down payment and in what way is it different? Why don't the exchanges want it to be called a down payment?

4. Explain the difference between initial margin, maintenance margin, and variation margin. Which of these varies daily? What numbers would you compare at the end of a trading day to determine if you owe money to your margin account?

5. Why is the 90-day Eurodollar time deposit futures contract so popular?

The Math

6. If the 90-day Eurodollar futures contract were for $185,000 worth of Eurodollars rather than a million dollars, 1 basis point change in the contract would not be worth $25 but rather would be worth how much? What would 1 basis point on this new contract be worth if it were for 180-days rather than 90-day Eurodollars?

7. You are speculating that interest rates will go up in the Eurodollar futures market. Should you trade long or short? Why?

8. Assume that on July 1 the current 3-month cash Eurodollar rate equals 8 percent while the September futures rate equals 7.7 percent. A bank buys September Eurodollar futures on July 1, expecting to hedge. The bank holds its position until the December expiration of the futures contract when it sells futures and buys spot 90-day Eurodollars. What is the bank's effective rate of return on the Eurodollars?

9. You went long one December '91 Eurodollar contract based on this information in the *Wall Street Journal* on September 17, 1990. (See exhibit following.)
   a. What was the spot and futures rate at that time? What was the contract's basis?
   b. A month after you entered the contract the futures rate dropped to 7.84 percent. Did you have to add to or could you withdraw from your margin account at this time? How much money?
   c. Gradually interest rates reversed and increased to 8.63 percent by December '91. At the expiration of the contract the basis was how large? How do you know that?
   d. Near expiration you went short in the futures market and long in the spot market. How much money did you make or lose in the futures market? Was it real cash or only an opportunity gain or loss? When you rolled over into the spot market what rate did you receive for the 90-day Eurodollars?
   e. To know if this trade was a hedge or a speculation you would need to know what additional information?

10. A hedge in the futures market replaces interest rate risk with what type of risk? Describe the circumstances necessary for a futures hedge to be risk-free.

Microhedges

11. A bank hedging in the futures market can practice micro- or macrohedging. What are the advantages of each?

12. Determine whether the bank should hedge long or short in the 90-day Eurodollar futures market under these circumstances: (Hint: First determine where the risk of interest rate changes comes into the problem.)
   a. The bank is expecting to receive in 30 days a huge payment on a third-world loan which has been in arrears.
   b. A major investor in the bank has notified you that when his CDs expire in 60 days he will withdraw his money from the bank. You will be forced to liquidate a substantial portion of the bank's investment portfolio to cover the withdrawal.
   c. The bank has just won a court settlement against a competitor and will receive a large settlement check in 2 weeks.
   d. The bank has decided to issue 15-year bonds to increase the bank's capital but the issue can't be ready for 6 months.

13. The bank is going to hedge in the 90-day Eurodollar futures market using the standard $1 million contract. How many contracts should the bank trade in the following circumstances?

EURODOLLAR (IMM)—$1 million; pts of 100%

	Open	High	Low	Settle	Chg	Yield Settle	Chg	Open Interest
Sept	91.88	91.88	91.87	91.87	− .03	8.13 +	.03	129,346
Dec	92.07	92.09	92.05	92.06	− .03	7.94 +	.03	239,582
Mr91	92.07	92.10	92.06	92.08	− .01	7.92 +	.01	116,259
June	91.89	91.92	91.88	91.89	− .03	8.11 +	.03	64,102
Sept	91.67	91.69	91.66	91.67	− .03	8.33 +	.03	50,577
Dec	91.40	91.42	91.38	91.40	− .03	8.60 +	.03	41,243
Mr92	91.31	91.34	91.31	91.33	− .01	8.67 +	.01	31,069
June	91.22	91.25	91.22	91.23	− .01	8.77 +	.01	23,069
Sept	91.14	91.17	91.14	91.16	− .01	8.84 +	.01	14,925
Dec	91.01	91.03	91.00	91.02	− .01	8.98 +	.01	12,094
Mr93	90.98	91.01	90.97	90.99	− .01	9.01 +	.01	10,222
June	90.89	90.92	90.88	90.90	− .01	9.10 +	.01	7,204
Sept	90.83	90.85	90.83	90.84	− .01	9.16 +	.01	4,421
Dec	90.73	90.75	90.73	90.74	− .01	9.26 +	.01	3,175
Mr94	90.70	90.72	90.70	90.72	....	9.28	....	2,739
June	90.64	90.66	90.64	90.66	....	9.34	....	1,942

MONEY RATES

Monday, September 17, 1990

The key U.S. and foreign annual interest rates below are a guide to general levels but don't always represent actual transactions.

PRIME RATE: 10%. The base rate on corporate loans at large U.S. money center commercial banks.

FEDERAL FUNDS: 8 1/16% high, 7 15/16% low, 8% near closing bid, 8% offered. Reserves traded among commercial banks for overnight use in amounts of $1 million or more. Source: Babcock Fulton Prebon (U.S.A.) Inc.

DISCOUNT RATE: 7%. The charge on loans to depository institutions by the New York Federal Reserve Bank.

CALL MONEY: 9¼%. The charge on loans to brokers on stock exchange collateral.

COMMERCIAL PAPER placed directly by General Motors Acceptance Corp.: 7.975% 30 to 44 days; 7.90% 45 to 59 days; 7.80% 60 to 89 days; 7.75% 90 to 119 days; 7.70% 120 to 149 days; 7.65% 150 to 179 days; 7.50% 180 to 270 days.

COMMERCIAL PAPER: High-grade unsecured notes sold through dealers by major corporations in multiples of $1,000: 8.05% 30 days; 7.97% 60 days; 7.90% 90 days.

CERTIFICATES OF DEPOSIT: 7.60% one month; 7.63% two months; 7.66% three months; 7.63% six months; 7.85% one year. Average of top rates paid by major New York banks on primary new issues of negotiable C.D.s, usually on amounts of $1 million and more. The minimum unit is $100,-000. Typical rates in the secondary market: 8.05% one month; 8.05% three months; 8.05% six months.

BANKERS ACCEPTANCES: 7.95% 30 days; 7.84% 60 days; 7.73% 90 days; 7.71% 120 days; 7.65% 150 days; 7.60% 180 days. Negotiable, bank-backed business credit instruments typically financing an import order.

LONDON LATE EURODOLLARS: 8 3/16% − 8 1/16% one month; 8⅛% − 8% two months; 8⅛% − 8% three months; 8⅛% − 8% four months; 8⅛% − 8% five months; 8⅛% − 8% six months.

LONDON INTERBANK OFFERED RATES (LIBOR): 8⅛% one month; 8⅛% three months; 8⅛% six months; 8¼% one year. The average of interbank offered rates for dollar deposits in the London market based on quotations at five major banks.

FOREIGN PRIME RATES: Canada 13.75%−14.25%; Germany 10.50%; Japan 7.38%; Switzerland 9.50%; Britain 15%. These rate indications aren't directly comparable; lending practices vary widely by location.

TREASURY BILLS: Results of the Monday, September 17, 1990, auction of short-term U.S. government bills, sold at a discount from face value in units of $10,000 to $1 million: 7.39%, 13 weeks; 7.30%, 26 weeks.

FEDERAL HOME LOAN MORTGAGE CORP. (Freddie Mac): Posted yields on 30-year mortgage commitments for delivery within 30 days. 10.10%, standard conventional fixed-rate mortgages; 8.25%, 2% rate capped one-year adjustable rate mortgages. Source: Telerate Systems Inc.

FEDERAL NATIONAL MORTGAGE ASSOCIATION (Fannie Mae): Posted yields on 30 year mortgage commitments for delivery within 30 days (priced at par). 10.07%, standard conventional fixed rate-mortgages; 8.40%, 6/2 rate capped one-year adjustable rate mortgages. Source: Telerate Systems Inc.

MERRILL LYNCH READY ASSETS TRUST: 7.57%. Annualized average rate of return after expenses for the past 30 days; not a forecast of future returns.

Source: *The Wall Street Journal*, September 18, 1990.

a. The bank will be rolling over $125 million of 6-month CDs in 2 months. The Eurodollar rate moves 1.25 times as much as the CD rate.

b. In 3 months the bank will be rolling over $50 million in 30-day loans. The loan rates move exactly the same as the Eurodollar rates.

c. Six months from now the bank will write $5 million in floating-rate loans tied to the Eurodollar rate.

14. A major loan of $6 million will be paid off next month. Although you know that hedgers don't worry about forecasting interest rates and you are planning to be a hedger, you can't ignore the wooly-bear index, which predicts that the current loan rates of 9 percent will plunge in the next 4 days. The 6-million-dollar loan payment will be rolled over into a 1-year fixed-rate loan at the going rates a month from now. You decide to hedge in the Eurodollar futures market.

    a. Should you go long or short? How many contracts should you trade to hedge the whole risk if the rates on your loans and Eurodollars move exactly the same? Under what circumstances might you consider hedging only a portion of the $6 million?

    b. The nearest maturing futures contract expires 2 months from now and is currently trading at a rate of 9.32 percent. If you institute a hedge now how large will the initial basis be?

    c. Time has passed and you are ready to lift your hedge because the $6 million will be rolled over tomorrow at 9.75 percent interest. During the past month you have anxiously watched interest rates steadily rise as your esteem for wooly bears steadily fell. Your broker informs you that the futures rates on Eurodollars is now 9.87 percent. As you lift the hedge, how large is the basis?

    d. How much of a profit or loss did you make on the futures trade? Was it real money or opportunity gains or losses?

    e. How much did you make or lose on the cash market? Was it real money or opportunity gains or losses?

    f. Is it easier to justify opportunity losses than real cash losses? Should it be easier?

    g. Evaluate this hedge discussing whether it was prudent to initiate at the outset, whether it succeeded at its objective, and what might have made it work better. Should banks try to forecast interest rates?

15. What is a cross-hedge? Explain why cross-hedges generally exhibit greater risk.

16. You have been assigned the task of designing a form to collect the information necessary to implement a microhedge. When any bank officer, whether working in the loan department or the deposit department, sees a potential hedging situation he or she will complete one of these forms and pass it to the ALCO for action. What information must be included on the form?

Macrohedge

17. You have now been assigned to design a form for macrohedging situations. What information must it request?

18. Would a bank with a positive duration gap that expects interest rates to increase hedge by going long or short? Would they do the same if they had a positive GAP to hedge instead? Would they do the same if they expected interest rates to decrease?

19. A bank has assets of $4,000,000 earning an average return of 9 percent and with a duration of 1.40. It has liabilities of $3,000,000 costing 7 percent with a duration

of 4.60. Eurodollar futures are trading at 10 percent. The bank wants to construct a macrohedge.

a. Should they go long or short in the futures market?

b. How many contracts should they trade?

c. If interest rates on Eurodollars futures fall to 8 percent, how much money would this bank make or lose on its futures position?

20. Regulators require that a hedge meet three conditions. What are they and why do you think regulators require them?

Swaps

21. What is an interest rate swap and what market conditions must exist to permit all swap participants to make money?

22. Discuss the relationship between efficient markets and the existence of suitable conditions for a successful swap.

23. What are the advantages and disadvantages of swaps over futures as interest rate risk management tools? What are the unique risks involved in swap contracts?

24. A regional bank holding company recently bought a $100 million package of mortgages from the RTC. The holding company will establish a new subsidiary to manage this package. This subsidiary will be financed by selling its own 90-day commercial paper. Market conditions dictate this arrangement although the management realizes the subsidiary is burdened with huge interest rate risk because the average duration of the mortgages is 7 years. The bank decides to arrange a swap for the subsidiary.

a. Does this subsidiary want to buy floating-rate payments or fixed-rate payments in the swap market?

b. The subsidiary will pay 9 percent interest on its commercial paper. This rate will vary with the Fed funds rate and be recalculated as Fed funds plus 1 percent. If forced to issue longer term bonds the subsidiary would have to pay 12 percent. A swap partner has been located. The partner can raise variable-rate funds for itself at Fed funds plus 0.4 percent and it can sell bonds at 10 percent. Does the situation exist for a successful swap?

c. Would a better swap result with a partner that could raise variable-rate funds at the Fed funds rate and sell bonds at 11 percent? Why or why not?

d. Describe one swap arrangement that would be satisfactory to the subsidiary, the swap partner described in part b of this problem, and the intermediary.

e. Are there any other possible contracts that would prove advantageous to all three parties? If so, what determines which arrangement actually results?

References

Bank of England Quarterly Bulletin. "Recent Developments in the Swap Market." February 1987.

Belongia, Michail, and G. J. Santoni. "Hedging Interest Rate Risk with Financial Futures: Some Basic Principles." *Review* (Federal Reserve Bank of St. Louis, October 1984).

Booth, James, Richard Smith, and Richard Stolz. "Use of Interest Rate Futures by Financial Institutions." *Journal of Bank Research* (Spring 1984).

Chance, Don. *An Introduction to Options and Futures*. Hinsdale, Ill.: The Dryden Press, 1989.

Drabenstott, Mark, and Anne O'Mara McDonley. "Futures Markets: A Primer for Financial Institutions." *Economic Review* (Federal Reserve Bank of Kansas City, November 1984).

Figlewski, Stephen. *Hedging with Financial Futures for Institutional Investors*. Cambridge, Mass.: Ballinger Publishing Co., 1986.

Kaufman, George. "Measuring and Managing Interest Rate Risk: A Primer." *Economic Perspectives* (Federal Reserve Bank of Chicago, January–February 1984).

Kawaller, Ira. "Liability Side Gap Management: Risks and Opportunities." *Market Perspectives* (Chicago Mercantile Exchange, August 1983).

Kawaller, Ira. "The Futures Contract Alternative." *The Bankers Magazine* (March–April 1985).

Kawaller, Ira. "Interest Rate Swaps Versus Eurodollar Strips." *Financial Analysts Journal* (September–October 1989).

Kolb, Robert, and Gerald Gay. "Bank Immunization with Interest Rate Futures." Proceedings of a Conference on Bank Structure and Competition, Federal Reserve Bank of Chicago, Chicago, Illinois, April 1982.

Kolb, Robert, and Raymond Chiang. "Duration, Immunization, and Hedging with Interest Rate Futures." *The Journal of Financial Research* (Summer 1982).

Koppenhaver, G. D. "Futures Market Regulation." *Economic Perspectives* (Federal Reserve Bank of Chicago, January–February 1987).

Koppenhaver, G. D. "Futures Options and their Use by Financial Intermediaries." *Economic Perspectives* (Federal Reserve Bank of Chicago, January–February 1986).

Kuprianov, Anatoli. "Short-Term Interest Rate Futures." *Economic Review* (Federal Reserve Bank of Richmond, September–October 1986).

Labuszewski, John, and John Nyhoff. *Trading Financial Futures*. New York: John Wiley & Sons, Inc., 1988.

Lereah, David. "The Growth of Interest Rate Swaps." *The Bankers Magazine* (May–June 1986).

Loeys, Jan. "Interest Rate Swaps: A New Tool for Managing Risk." *Business Review* (Federal Reserve Bank of Philadelphia, May–June 1985).

Northam, Malcolm. "Financial Futures and Hedging: A Regulator's View." *Magazine of Bank Administration* (September 1986).

Simons, Katerina. "Measuring Credit Risk in Interest Rate Swaps." *New England Economic Review* (Federal Reserve Bank of Boston, November/December 1989).

Smirlock, Michael. "Hedging Bank Borrowing Costs with Financial Futures." *Business Review* (Federal Reserve Bank of Philadelphia, May–June, 1986).

Whittaker, J. Gregg. "Interest Rate Swaps: Risk and Regulation." *Economic Review* (Federal Reserve Bank of Kansas City, March 1987).

Chapter 10

Use of Options
on Financial Futures

Options on financial futures contracts are a relatively new phenomenon. They provide another vehicle for financial institutions to hedge interest rate risk exposure with different features than pure futures contracts or interest rate swaps. Their primary advantage is that they retain the opportunity to profit if prices change favorably. Their primary disadvantage is that price changes must be substantial to improve on futures positions.

Options on financial instruments represent one of the most important innovations in financial markets over the past 25 years. They can be used both as investment and hedging vehicles and offer clear advantages to alternative instruments in many situations. The biggest advantage is that users must put up only a small fraction of the underlying asset's total value and this up-front cost is fixed. Conceptually, options are comparable to insurance. There is a cost to buying insurance represented by the cost of the option. If the underlying asset changes in value, the option holder may be compensated for the value adjustment.

This chapter focuses on the use of options to manage interest rate risk at banks. Special attention is paid to using options on financial futures, such as those on Eurodollar time deposits, as an alternative to either financial futures alone or interest rate swaps. Each vehicle has a different risk and return profile. The benefit of options, however, is that the downside risk measured by the potential loss on the option is limited to the up-front cash premium payment, just like with insurance.

THE NATURE OF OPTIONS ON FINANCIAL FUTURES

An option is an agreement between two parties in which one gives the other the right, but not the obligation, to buy or sell a specific asset at a set price for a specified period of time. The buyer of an option pays for the opportunity to decide whether to effect the transaction (to exercise the option). The option seller (also called the option writer) receives the initial option price. This discussion examines options in which the underlying asset is a financial futures contract.

There are two types of options, with a buyer and seller for each transaction. A *call option* gives the buyer the right to buy a fixed amount of the underlying asset at a specific strike price for a set period of time. The seller of the call option, in turn, is obligated to deliver the underlying asset to the buyer when the buyer exercises the option. A *put option* gives the buyer the right to sell a fixed amount of the underlying asset at a specific strike price for a set period of time. The seller of a put option is obligated to buy the underlying asset when the put option buyer exercises the option. In both cases the buyer of the option determines the timing of exercise.

At any point in time the market price of the underlying asset may be above, below, or equal to the option strike price. This price comparison determines the option's value. The buyer of a call option with a strike price below the current market price can exercise the option and immediately sell the underlying asset for more than the strike price. Such an option is said to be "in the money." The greater the price differential, the greater is the value of the position. Similarly, a put option is "in the money" if the underlying asset's market price is below the strike price because the buyer can acquire the asset for sale at a price below the contracted sale price. When an option holder cannot exercise the option at a favorable price compared with the strike price, the option is "out of the money." For example, a call option is out of the money when the market price of the underlying asset is below the strike price. A put option is out of the money when the market price exceeds the strike price. If the two prices are equal, the option is "at the money." Key terms are defined in Exhibit 10.1

EXAMPLES USING EURODOLLAR FEATURES

Consider the data in Exhibit 10.2 for options on 90-day Eurodollar futures (introduced in Chapter 9). The data represent settlement (closing) quotes for August 2, 1990. Eurodollar futures and options prices are quoted by subtracting the appropriate Eurodollar rate, measured in percentage points to two decimal places, from 100. Because the futures carry a face value of $1 million and have a 3-month maturity, each basis point change in price or interest rate has a $25 value.

The first column of options data lists various strike prices from lowest to highest. The coincident futures rates range from 8.50 percent (91.50) to 7.25 percent (92.75). The remaining columns of data list the prices of various options. The exhibit identifies three call options that expire in September and December of 1990, and March of 1991, respectively. The three put options expire in the same months. These option expiration dates coincide with the expiration dates on the underlying futures.

Exhibit 10.1 Key Terminology

At the money. An option where the market price of the underlying asset equals the strike price.

Call option. An option in which the buyer has the right to buy an underlying asset at a predetermined strike price for a set period of time.

Exercise an option. The buyer of an option liquidates the position by enforcing terms of the option.

Futures option. An option on a futures contract.

In the money. A call option in which the market price exceeds the strike price; a put option in which the strike price exceeds the market price.

Intrinsic value. For a call option, the greater of the difference between the market price and the strike price or zero; for a put option, the greater of the difference between the strike price and market price or zero.

Out of the money. A call option in which the strike price exceeds the market price; a put option in which the market price exceeds the strike price.

Premium. The price of an option.

Put option. An option in which the buyer has the right to sell the underlying asset at a predetermined strike price for a set period of time.

Strike price. The predetermined price at which a call option allows the buyer to buy the underlying asset; the predetermined price at which a put option allows the buyer to sell the underlying asset.

Time value. The difference between the option premium and the intrinsic value.

The September 1990 Eurodollar call option at the 91.50 strike price gives the buyer the right to purchase a September Eurodollar futures contract at 91.50, or 8.50 percent. The seller of this call option will, in turn, be required to sell a September Eurodollar futures contract when the buyer exercises the option.[1] The coincident September Eurodollar futures price on August 2, 1990 was 92.10 (7.90 percent). This option is in the money because the market price exceeds the strike price. A buyer could exercise the option (buy a September Eurodollar futures contract) at 91.50 and immediately sell a September futures at 92.10 for a gain of $1,500 (60 × $25). The September Eurodollar call option at 92.50 strike price is, in contrast, out of the money because the strike price exceeds the market price.

Each option's price, labeled the *premium,* reflects the consensus value of the position. All options have some positive value because prices could move favorably prior to expiration until the option is in the money. Analysts frequently distinguish between an option's intrinsic value and time value. *Intrinsic value* equals the dollar value of the difference between the current market price and the strike price or zero, whichever is greater. The September call option at 91.50, for example, exhibits an intrinsic value of $1,500. When the strike price is above the market price, a call option's intrinsic value is zero because the option cannot be exercised at a net gain. The *time value* of an option equals the difference between the option price and the intrinsic value. In the case of the September call at 91.50, the premium equaled $1,525 (61 × $25) so that the time value of the option totaled only $25.

---

[1]The buyer of an option pays the option price at the time of purchase but has no margin or cash flow obligation until the option is exercised or sold. The seller of an option, in contrast, immediately receives the option price as payment but must post a margin deposit with the exchange to collateralize the position. If prices move against the seller, additional margin will be required.

Exhibit 10.2 Data for Options on 90-Day Eurodollar Futures:
IMM August 2, 1990

	Option Premium[a]					
	Calls-Settle			Puts-Settle		
Strike Price	Sep-C	Dec-C	Mar-C	Sep-P	Dec-P	Mar-P
9150	0.61	0.70	0.74	0.01	0.04	0.08
9175	0.37	0.50	0.55	0.02	0.08	0.14
9200	0.16	0.32	0.39	0.06	0.14	0.21
9225	0.05	0.19	0.26	0.20	0.26	0.32
9250	0.02	0.10	0.16	0.42	0.41	. . .
9275	0.01	0.05	0.10	. . .	. . .	. . .

Est. vol. 31,703, Wed vol. 36,583 calls, 18,882 puts.
Open interest Wed: 192,718 calls, 163,473 puts.

Eurodollar Futures Prices (Rates): August 2, 1990

September 1990: 92.10
December 1990: 92.18
March 1991: 92.19

[a]Measured in basis points; each basis point is worth $25.

The magnitude of a call option's intrinsic value and premium decreases as the strike price increases. Data for the September call options indicate this pattern. At a strike price of 92.25 the intrinsic value is zero, yet the premium is $125, which equals the time value of the option. Investors pay for the possibility that this option may eventually be in the money. The time value of an option normally increases with the length of time until option expiration because the market price has a longer time to reach a profitable level and then continue to move favorably. For example, the time value of the December call at the 92.25 strike price equals $475 (19 × $25), while that for the March call at the 92.25 strike price equals $650. The time values of the December and March calls exceed that for September calls at each strike price because the option holder has an additional 3 to 6 months for prices to move further in the money.

Data for the put options reveal the same basic relationships. The put premiums increase with higher strike prices. Again, a September 1990 put option gives the buyer the right to sell September 1990 Eurodollar futures at the respective strike price. The higher the strike price, the greater is the value of the option, given a constant current value for the September Eurodollar future. The seller of the put option is obligated to buy a September 1990 Eurodollar future if the option is exercised.

Because the current September 1990 futures price is 92.10, the September put options at the three lowest strike prices are out of the money. The option holder benefits only if the market price falls below the respective strike prices, at which time the holder could buy a cheaper Eurodollar future to sell at the higher strike price. The intrinsic value of these options is zero, with the 1, 2, and 6 basis point premiums equal to the time value of the option. Notice that the patterns in time values are the same as for call options. For each strike price the time value increases from the September to the March option, and increase here with higher strike prices. The other September put options with strike prices of 92.25 or higher are in the money. The put option at 92.50, for example, has an intrinsic value of $1,000 because the holder can sell September Eurodollar futures at a price 40 basis points above the prevailing market price. Both December and March put options exhibit the same patterns, as the underlying futures prices are 92.18 and 92.19, respectively.

The Eurodollar futures contract and associated options are traded at the International Monetary Market of the Chicago Mercantile Exchange. When the underlying futures prices change, the exchange opens additional options at new exercise prices to bracket the current futures price. Option holders have three choices to offset their positions. They may exercise the option, let the option expire, or offset the option by taking the opposite position prior to expiration.[2] They will exercise the option only when it is in the money and its time value is zero. They will offset the option when the time value is positive because the option premium exceeds the intrinsic value and thus the total gain is larger. Offsetting an option involves selling the same call or put option if either was purchased initially, or buying the same option if it was previously sold. For example, the buyer of a March call at 92.00 in Exhibit 10.2 would sell (write) a March call at 92.00 to collect the premium.

PROFIT DIAGRAMS

What advantages do options on futures have over futures contracts? When is a trader better off using options? This section introduces profit diagrams that demonstrate key differences between futures and options on futures.[3] It compares the general risk reduction characteristics of various strategies.

Eurodollar Futures

Institutional traders occasionally buy and sell futures contracts to hedge positions in the cash market. Panel A of Exhibit 10.3 demonstrates when an unhedged futures position is profitable, using the data on Eurodollar futures from Exhibit 10.2. The vertical axis indicates the profit or loss equal to $25 times each basis point indicated. The horizontal axis measures the level of the futures price (F). These figures ignore transactions costs and opportunity gains or losses from margin requirements.

According to panel A, the buyer of a December 1990 Eurodollar futures contract at 92.18 gains when futures prices increase above 92.18 (futures rates fall below 7.82 percent). Sellers of futures gain when the futures price falls after the initial transaction. Buyers can lose up to the full purchase price, and sellers can lose up to the point where

---

[2]All options traded in the United States (American options) can be exercised any time prior to expiration.

[3]The discussion follows Koppenhaver, 1986, and Kuprianov, 1986.

Exhibit 10.3 Profit Diagrams for Unhedged Futures and Options on Futures Assuming Traders Take Positions Using the Data from Exhibit 10.2

A. Unhedged Futures Positions

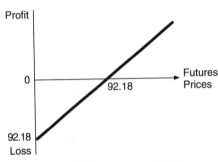

1. Buy Dec., 1990 Eurodollars at 92.18.

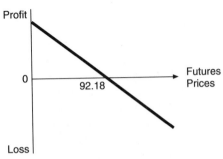

2. Sell Dec., 1990 Eurodollars at 92.18.

B. Call Options on Futures

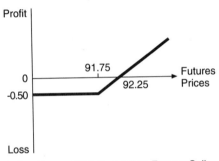

1. Buy Dec., a 1990 Eurodollars Futures Call Option, at 91.75.

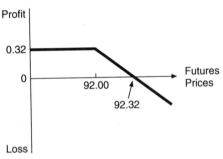

2. Sell a Dec., 1990 Eurodollars Futures Call Option, at 92.00.

C. Unhedged Put Options on Futures

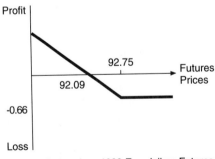

1. Buy a September, 1990 Eurodollars Futures Put Option at 92.75.

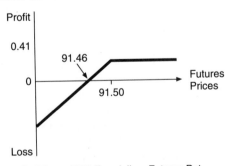

2. Sell Dec., 1990 Eurodollars Futures Put Options at 91.50.

Eurodollar rates equal zero (the futures price equals 100). In practice, futures prices have not varied that widely over the brief life of futures contracts.

Call Options on Eurodollar Futures

Panel B of Exhibit 10.3 shows the profit profile of a trader who buys or sells a December 1990 Eurodollar futures call option. The buyer of a December call at 91.75 pays a $1,250 premium (50 × $25), which represents the maximum loss if the option expires unexercised. At the time of purchase the futures price exceeds the strike price by 0.43, so the option is in the money. The buyer, however, pays 7 basis points more and thus does not earn a profit until the futures price rises above 92.25, which equals the strike price plus the 50 basis point premium.[4] In general, the buyer's profit equals the eventual futures price minus the strike price and the initial call premium. In this example, the buyer's profit increases directly with increases in December Eurodollar futures prices and is limited only if rates fall to zero. Compared with a pure long futures position, the buyer of a call option on the same futures contract faces less risk of loss if futures prices fall, yet realizes the same potential gains. If, however, the December futures price does not rise above 92.25, the call option holder loses. At any price above 92.18 the buyer of a futures contract gains. Thus large price movements are necessary before a call option increases substantially in value.

The seller of a December 1990 Eurodollar call option will gain or lose in similar fashion when futures prices move in the opposite direction. Consider the seller of a December call at 92.00 from Exhibit 10.2. The seller immediately receives $800 (32 × $25), the maximum profit. Only if the December futures price rises above 92.32 (92.00 + 0.32) will the seller lose. The seller earns the full $800 if the option is not exercised. The profit is reduced by the amount by which the eventual futures price exceeds the strike price. If the futures price at exercise of the option equals 92.20, the seller earns $300 ($800 − 20 × $25). Compared with a pure short futures position, the seller of a call option has limited profit potential but captures the time value component of the premium (14 basis points in the example). A short futures position loses if prices rise above 92.18, which is 14 basis points lower than the break-even point for the seller of a call option. Selling a call option is most valuable when interest rates are stable.

Put Options on Eurodollar Futures

The buyer of a put option gains if futures prices fall or futures rates rise. Consider the purchase of a September 1990 Eurodollar futures put option at 92.50. The buyer pays a premium of $1,050 (42 × $25) for the right to sell September futures at 92.50 when the current price equals 92.10. The option is already in the money by $1,000 such that the buyer's incremental cost is initially $50. While the buyer's potential profit is unlimited, the net gain will be positive only if the futures price falls below 92.08, or 2 basis points below its current level. The buyer's maximum loss equals the initial

---

[4]The analysis assumes that all options are held until expiration.

premium of $1,050. If the eventual futures price at expiration falls between 92.08 and 92.50, the buyer loses less than $1,050.

The purchase of a put option on financial futures is comparable to the direct short sale of a futures contract (panel A2 in Exhibit 10.3). In both cases the position is profitable when futures prices fall but generates losses when futures prices rise. The use of a put option, however, limits losses to the option premium, while a pure futures sale exhibits greater loss potential. Still, the futures position is profitable once futures prices decrease. The buyer of a put option does not gain until the futures price falls below the strike price minus the premium. Thus large price movements are necessary before a put option increases substantially in value.

Panel C2 of Exhibit 10.3 summarizes the profit potential for the seller of a December 1990 Eurodollar future put option at 91.50. This option requires the seller to buy a futures contract at 91.50 if the option is exercised. The option is currently out of the money because the market price at 92.18 exceeds the strike price. If the futures price exceeds the strike price at expiration, the seller earns the maximum profit equal to the $100 premium. If the eventual futures price is below the strike price, the option will be exercised and the seller of a put option will have to buy the futures contract at the higher strike price. If the final market price is below 91.46, the loss from liquidating the obligated futures position will exceed the 4-basis-point premium and the seller will suffer a net loss. For example, if the futures price is 91.20 at expiration, the seller of an option will have to buy futures at 91.20, and the subsequent 30-basis-point loss exceeds the 4-basis-point premium initially received, for a net loss of $650 (26 × $25).

The sale of a put option is comparable to the direct purchase of a Eurodollar futures contract (panel A1 in Exhibit 10.3). Both positions face potentially large losses if futures prices fall substantially. Futures prices would have to fall at least 40 basis points, however, before the seller of a December 1990 put option at 91.50 loses, while a long futures position loses as soon as the futures price declines. The maximum profit on the put sale is limited, however, while the long futures position is open-ended when futures prices rise.

THE USE OF OPTIONS ON FUTURES BY COMMERCIAL BANKS

Commercial banks can use financial futures options for the same hedging purposes for which they use financial futures. Managers must first identify the bank's relevant interest rate risk position. Such risk can be measured on a micro basis, focusing on a specific transaction, or a macro basis, using the bank's funding GAP or duration gap profile. The bank's interest rate risk position determines what type of risk-offsetting trade is necessary.

Profiting from Rising Interest Rates

Suppose that a bank would be adversely affected if the level of interest rates increases. This might occur because the bank has a negative GAP or a positive

Exhibit 10.4 Profit and Loss Potential on Futures and Options on Futures Positions[a]

Generate Profits If Futures Rates Rise

Transaction	Potential Profit	Potential Loss
Sell financial futures	Unlimited	Unlimited
Sell call options on futures	Limited to call premium	Unlimited
Buy put options on futures	Unlimited	Limited to put premium

Generate Profits If Futures Rates Fall

Transaction	Potential Profit	Potential Loss
Buy financial futures	Unlimited	Unlimited
Buy call options on futures	Unlimited	Limited to call premium
Sell put options on futures	Limited to put premium	Unlimited

[a]Profits and losses are limited when futures rates equal 0 percent and 100 percent.

duration gap, or simply anticipates issuing new CDs in the near term. It wishes to take a futures or options position so it can earn a profit that offsets the potential loss in the cash market.

A bank has three alternatives that should reduce the overall risk associated with rising interest rates. It can sell financial futures contracts directly, sell call options on financial futures, or buy put options on financial futures. Exhibit 10.3 indicates that each position will earn a profit if futures prices fall sufficiently and futures rates increase. Each alternative, however, exhibits different risk and return characteristics. The short futures position produces profits as soon as futures rates rise but will generate losses once futures rates decline. Selling a call option also produces profits once futures rates rise but sets a maximum profit equal to the initial call premium received. Potential losses are virtually unlimited if rates fall. The sale of a call option thus protects a bank only against relatively small interest rate changes but may generate premium income. Buying a put option produces unlimited profits once the futures price falls below the strike price net of the put premium. If rates fall, the bank loses only the put premium, so it does not have the same rate exposure as with a short futures position. These relationships are summarized in Exhibit 10.4.

Profiting from Falling Interest Rates

Banks with positive GAPs or negative duration gaps will be adversely affected if the level of interest rates declines. Their appropriate use of futures or options on futures will be to take positions that produce profits when futures rates decline. Again, a bank has three alternatives. It can buy futures directly, buy call options on futures, or sell put options on futures. Exhibit 10.4 lists the potential outcomes. While the futures position offers unlimited gains and losses that are presumably offset by changes in value of the cash position, a purchased call option offers the same approximate gain but limits the loss to the initial call premium. The sale of a put limits the gain and has unrestricted losses.

The best choice is not known at the time the trade is initiated, but several general statements apply. Futures positions produce unlimited gains or losses depending on which direction futures rates move. Thus a hedger is protected from adverse rate changes but loses the potential gains if rates move favorably. Also, buying a put or call option on futures limits the bank's potential losses if rates move adversely. This type of position has been classified as a form of insurance because the option buyer has to pay a premium for this protection. When rates move favorably, a bank can realize unlimited gains. Still, rates have to move more than with a futures position for the purchased options to be profitable. Finally, selling a call or put option limits the potential gain but leaves the bank unprotected if rates move adversely. Rates typically must vary substantially before losses appear, however. Determining the best alternative depends on how far management expects rates to change and how much risk of loss is acceptable.

USING OPTIONS ON FUTURES TO HEDGE BORROWING COSTS

The previous discussion summarizes the differences between using futures versus using options on futures to reduce the risk of interest rate changes. This section provides a numerical example that documents the mechanics of each type of hedge and characterizes the risk and return trade-off. The anticipated cash transaction being hedged is a bank's issuance of 3-month Eurodollar time deposit liabilities.

Suppose that on August 2, 1990 your bank agrees to make a $1 million commercial loan with a 1-year maturity. The loan carries a 10-percent fixed rate. The bank initially finances the loan by issuing a $1 million 3-month Eurodollar time deposit paying 8 percent. After the first 3 months, the bank expects to finance the loan by issuing a series of 3-month Eurodollar deposits timed to coincide with the maturity of the preceding deposit. The time line in Exhibit 10.5 characterizes the anticipated sequence of cash market transactions.

Because the bank chooses to finance the fixed-rate loan with a series of shorter-term deposits, it will lose if 3-month Eurodollar rates increase throughout the year. In particular, the bank has locked in a 2-percent spread for the first 3 months, but does not know what the spread will be after November 1, 1990. If the 3-month Eurodollar rate rises above 10 percent, the bank will pay more in interest than it earns on the loan.

Hedging with 3-Month Eurodollar Futures

The most direct way to reduce the risk of loss with rising interest rates is to sell Eurodollar futures. The bank anticipates issuing 3-month Eurodollar deposits in the cash market at three specific future dates; November 1, 1990, January 31, 1991, and May 1, 1991. Because the bank loses if Eurodollar rates rise from current levels, the

Exhibit 10.5 Funding a 1-Year Loan with a Series of 3-Month Eurodollar Time Deposits

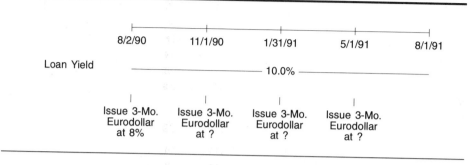

appropriate strategy is to sell futures contracts. Because the loan amount is $1 million, on August 2, 1990 the bank can sell one of each of the December 1990, March 1991, and June 1991 3-month Eurodollar futures contracts to hedge. Exhibit 10.6 summarizes the bank's initial position and reports the initial basis with each futures contract. Remember that with futures the trader assumes basis risk.

Consider the sale of the December 1990 future at 7.82 percent. The contract expires in mid-December, but the bank must offset its futures position in November because it will be issuing 3-month Eurodollars in the cash market. The bank thus assumes the risk that the basis, represented by the difference between the futures rate and the initial cash rate, will decline between August 2 and November 1. Because the futures contract expiration is 1.5 months after the offset, the basis may take on any value.

The bottom of Exhibit 10.6 summarizes the results of the hedged transactions for all dates. On November 1, the bank actually issued Eurodollars at 8.25 percent as cash rates increased. The bank simultaneously offset its December futures position by buying one contract at 8.31 percent. The net effect was a $1,225 futures profit that more than offset the $625 opportunity loss in the cash market. As such, the effective borrowing cost of the November Eurodollar was 7.76 percent. This reflects the fact that the basis actually increased to 6 basis points from −18 basis points at initiation of the hedge.

The basis follows the opposite pattern for the January 1991 transaction date. In January, cash rates decline and the bank issues Eurodollars at 7.88 percent, representing an opportunity gain over the initial 8 percent rate available in August. The March 1991 futures rate also declines from 7.81 percent in August to 7.66 percent for a loss of $375. The loss in the futures market exceeded the cash market gain, however, as the basis again decreased from −19 basis points to −22 basis points. Thus the effective borrowing cost of the January Eurodollar was 8.03 percent.

Finally, cash and futures rates increased sharply through May 1991. This produced an opportunity loss in the cash market and a futures profit. The futures profit exceeded the cash loss by $725 as the basis again increased, so that the effective borrowing cost fell to 7.71 percent.

Exhibit 10.6 Using Futures to Hedge Borrowing Costs

3-Month Eurodollar Cash and Futures Rates

August 2, 1990

3-month cash rate = 8%
December 1990 futures rate = 7.82%
March 1991 futures rate = 7.81%
June 1991 futures rate = 7.95%

Initial Basis
7.82% − 8.00% = −0.18%
7.81% − 8.00% = −0.19%
7.95% − 8.00% = −0.05%

November 1, 1990

3-month cash rate = 8.25%
December 1990 futures rate = 8.31%

January 31, 1991

3-month cash rate = 7.88%
March 1991 futures rate = 7.66%

May 1, 1991

3-month cash rate = 9.60%
June 1991 futures rate = 9.84%

Date	Cash Market	Futures Market	Basis
8/2/90	Bank issues $1 million in 3-month Eurodollars at 8%	Bank sells 1 Dec. '90 Eurodollar future at 7.82%; 1 March '91 Eurodollar futures at 7.81%; 1 June '91 Eurodollar future at 7.95%	
11/1/90	Bank issue 1 million in 3-month Eurodollars at 8.25%; Opportunity loss = 25 × $25 = $625	Bank buys 1 Dec. '90 Eurodollar future at 8.31% Profit = (8.31 − 7.82) × $25 = $1,225	0.06%
1/31/90	Bank issues $1 million in 3-month Eurodollars at 7.88%. Opportunity gain = 12 × $25 = $300	Bank buys March '91 Eurodollar future at 7.66% Loss = 15 × $25 = $375	−0.22%
5/1/91	Bank issues $1 million in 3-month Eurodollars at 9.60% Opportunity loss = 160 × $25 = $4,000	Bank buys 1 June '91 Eurodollar future at 9.84% Profit = 189 × $25 = $4,725	0.24%

Effective Cost of Borrowing

Eurodollar Issue Date	Cost = initial cash rate − Δ Basis
8/2/90	8%
11/1/90	8% − (0.06% − (−0.18%)) = 7.76%
1/31/90	8% − (−0.22% − (−0.19%)) = 8.03%
5/1/90	8% − (0.24% − (−0.05%)) = 7.71%
Average	7.88%

The net result of the hedge with Eurodollar futures is that the bank was able to borrow at a combined 7.88 percent. Thus the net interest spread on the commercial loan exceeded 2 percent during the year. On August 2, 1990 the 6-month and 1-year cash Eurodollar rates were above 8 percent, so the availability of futures not only enabled the bank to hedge its borrowing costs but even to lower them. The risk again was that the basis could have declined sharply at each repricing. In this situation, the bank's effective borrowing cost would have exceeded 8 percent, but the bank would still likely have been able to maintain a positive spread.

Hedging with Options on Eurodollar Futures

As indicated in Exhibit 10.4, a participant who wants to reduce the risk associated with rising interest rates can buy put options on financial futures. In the above example with the bank issuing a series of Eurodollars, the bank would want to buy one put option on each of the December 1990, March 1991, and June 1991 Eurodollar futures. The purchase of a put option essentially places a cap on the bank's borrowing cost. If futures rates rise above the strike price plus the premium on the option, the put will produce a profit that offsets dollar-for-dollar the increased cost of cash Eurodollars.[5] If futures rates do not change much or decline, the option may expire unexercised and the bank will have lost a portion or all of the option premium. Along with this, however, cash Eurodollar rates should remain stable or decline so that the borrowing cost does not vary substantially from current rates. In this context, buying a put option is comparable to buying insurance against rising rates. The option premium represents the cost of the insurance.

Assume that the bank decides to buy the December, March, and June put options at the 92.00 strike price. The nature of the bank's risk profile after buying the options is revealed by the profit diagrams in Exhibit 10.7. Panel A characterizes the situation with the December 1990 put option. With a strike price of 92.00 and premium of 0.14, the break-even price is 91.86. The option will thus be in the money if the December Eurodollar futures rate rises above 8 percent, and will recover its premium only after the futures rate rises above 8.14 percent. Of course, the bank will be better off if all interest rates decline sharply. In this scenario the option will be out of the money, but the cash Eurodollar rates will be very low. The bank will simply lose the option premium, or its "insurance" payment. On August 2, 1990 the December 1990 futures price (F) is 92.18 so this option is out of the money.

Panels B and C characterize the situations with the March 1991 put option and June 1991 put option, respectively. Both options are out of the money. The break-even rate with the March option is 8.21 percent, while the break-even rate with the June option is 8.32 percent. These rates effectively represent caps, or the highest possible rate that each respective borrowing cost might reach.

Exhibit 10.8 clarifies these concepts by tracking the bank's performance from buying put options on the Eurodollar futures listed above. The cash and futures rates are the same as those in the example from the previous section with Eurodollar futures. Consider the December put option hedge on November 1, 1990. At this time, the Eurodollar futures rate equaled 8.31 percent. Exhibit 10.7 demonstrates that at this rate (price = F′) the December put option is in the money. The bank is assumed to be able to sell the option for $500 (0.20 premium) which partially offsets the

[5]This assumes that Eurodollar cash and futures rates move in the same direction by the same amount.

Exhibit 10.7 Profit Diagrams for Put Options on Eurodollar Futures: August 2, 1990[a]

A. Buy: December 1990 Put Option; Strike Price = 92.00.

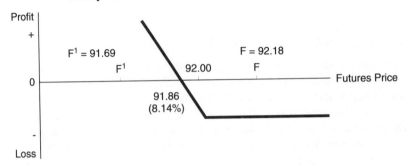

B. Buy: March 1991 Put Option is Strike Price = 92.00.

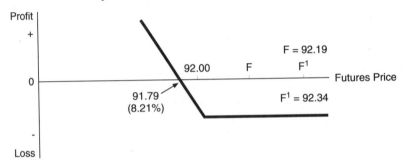

C. Buy: June 1991 Put Option; Strike Price = 92.00.

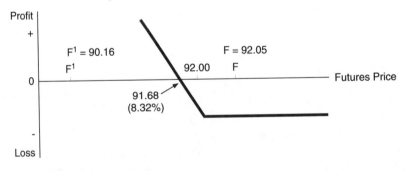

[a]F = Futures Price as of August 2, 1990.

F^1 = Price when bank offets the option.

Exhibit 10.8 Buying Put Options on Eurodollar Futures to Hedge Borrowing Costs

3-Month Eurodollar Futures Rates and Put Option Premiums for the 92.00 Strike Price

August 2, 1990

December 1990 futures rate = 7.82%
March 1991 futures rate = 7.81%
June 1991 futures rate = 7.95%

December Put at 92.00 = 0.14
March Put at 92.00 = 0.21
June Put at 92.00 = 0.32

November 1, 1990

3-month cash rate = 8.25%
December 1990 futures rate = 8.31%

January 31, 1991

3-month cash rate = 7.88%
March 1991 futures rate = 7.66%

May 1, 1991

3-month cash rate = 9.60%
June futures rate = 9.84%

Date	Cash Market	Put option
8/2/90	Bank issues $1 million in 3-month Eurodollars at 8%	Bank buys 1 Dec. '90 put on Eurodollar futures with strike = 92 for 0.14; 1 March '90 put on Eurodollar futures with strike = 92 for 0.21; 1 June '90 put on Eurodollar futures with strike = 92 for 0.32
11/1/91	Bank issues 1 million in 3-month Eurodollars at 8.25% Opportunity loss = 25 × $25 = $625	Dec. '90 Eurodollar futures rate = 8.31%; Bank sells put option for 0.20; receives $500
1/31/90	Bank issues $1 million in 3-month Eurodollars at 7.88% Opportunity gain = 12 × 25 = $300	March '91 Eurodollar futures rate = 7.66%; Put option is out of the money
5/1/91	Bank issues $1 million in 3-month Eurodollars at 9.60% Opportunity loss = 160 × $25 = $4,000	June '91 Eurodollar futures rate = 8.84%; Bank sells put option for 1.56; receives $3,900

Effective Cost of Borrowing

Eurodollar Issue Date	Cost: Initial Cash rate − Δ value of cash − Δ value of future[a]
8/2/90	8%
11/1/90	8% + 0.25% − 0.20% = 8.05%
1/31/90	8% − 0.12% = 7.88%
5/1/90	8% + 1.60% − 1.56% = 8.04%
	Average 7.99%

[a] measured in basis points; each $25 = 1 basis point. The calculation ignores the price of the option or 0.14%, 0.27%, and 0.32%, respectively.

$625 opportunity loss in the cash market. The effective borrowing cost at this repricing is thus 8.05 percent, represented by the initial 8 percent cash rate plus the 5 basis point net change in value of the cash versus option position.[6]

In January interest rates declined such that the bank realized a $300 opportunity gain in the cash market. Not surprisingly, with the decline in rates the March futures put option is out of the money. The option position therefore does not affect the bank's borrowing cost, which equals the cash rate of 7.88 percent. Finally, in May interest rates rise sharply. The cash Eurodollar issue shows a loss while the June put option is in the money. In this example, the cash market opportunity loss of $4,000 is approximately offset by the $3,900 received from the sale of the June option. The $100 net loss represents a 4-basis-point increment to the bank's borrowing cost.

Over the life of the loan and series of option hedges, the bank's effective 3-month borrowing cost ranged from 7.88 percent to 8.05 percent. The average for the year was 7.99 percent, or 11 basis points above the average in the example with straight Eurodollar futures. The difference can be attributed to the assumption that the basis generally increased at each repricing interval. This comparison also ignores the up-front cost of buying each option, which raises the effective cost of borrowing across the board.

Caps and Floors

The purchase of a put option on Eurodollar futures essentially places a cap on the bank's borrowing cost. Examine the data from Exhibits 10.7 and 10.8 for the December put option. Any futures price below 91.86 (rate above 8.14 percent) generates a profit on the option that can be used to offset the cost of higher cash market interest rates. In November, the option was in the money because the futures price was just 91.69 while the strike price was 92.00. If this represented the futures price at expiration, the bank could sell the option for 0.31, use 0.17 to reduce cash borrowing costs, and 0.14 would cover the option premium. In essence the bank capped its borrowing rate at 8 percent, for which it paid $350 (14 × $25). The same holds for the June put option in panel C. The eventual futures rate increased well above 8 percent, but the bank used the option proceeds to offset most of its cash borrowing costs and pay the 0.32 option premium.

The advantage of a put option in this scenario is that for a fixed price, the option premium, the bank can set a cap on its borrowing costs, yet it retains the possibility of benefiting from rate declines. If the bank is willing to give up some of the profit potential from declining rates, it can reduce the net cost of insurance. It can accomplish this by accepting a floor, or minimum level, for its borrowing cost. The bank might agree to do this because management does not expect rates to decline substantially and a floor would not be binding.

A bank borrower in the above example can establish a floor by selling a call option on Eurodollar futures. The seller of a call receives the option premium, but agrees to

---

[6]The analysis ignores the option price when computing the effective borrowing cost. This is consistent with the view that the option purchase represents the purchase of insurance.

sell the call option buyer the underlying Eurodollar futures at the agreed strike price upon exercise. Panel B of Exhibit 10.3 demonstrates that the call seller's maximum profit is set at the call premium, and losses arise if the futures price rises above the strike price plus option premium, which is consistent with futures rates declining. Conceptually, the bank borrower is using the call option premium to reduce the net cost of a put option premium for a cap. Any decline in futures rates should, in turn, coincide with a decline in cash rates. The floor thus exists because any opportunity gain in the cash market from borrowing at lower rates will be offset by the loss on the sold call option.

Exhibit 10.9 presents a variety of combined caps and floors using the option premium data for different strike prices from Exhibit 10.2. The transactions consist of buying a put option and selling a call option on the same Eurodollar futures contract. In each case the cap equals 100 minus the put option strike price; the floor equals 100 minus the call option strike price; and the net premium equals the put option premium minus the call option premium.

For example, a bank that is willing to accept a minimum borrowing cost of 7.50 percent and a cap of 8.00 percent (row A) can buy a December 1990 put option with a 92.00 strike price and sell a December 1990 call option with a 92.50 strike price. The net premium cost is $100. While this might appear to be low cost, remember that near-term Eurodollar futures rates are declining. One view is that futures rates signify interest rate expectations and the consensus is that short-term rates are expected to decline. Therefore, the call option premium is relatively high compared with the put option premium. As row C indicates, a borrower that wants to establish a lower floor and cap at 7.25 percent to 7.50 percent will have to pay $900, reflecting the higher cost of insurance that buys lower borrowing rates. In general, hedgers will not sell call options independent of other options or futures positions because the potential profit is limited while the loss potential is unlimited.

One of the practical difficulties in using options is that options contracts do not extend out for any length of time. In other words, there is very little liquidity for trading either puts or calls on financial futures very far out in the future. Also, only a limited number of strike prices are offered. To get around this, many of the larger commercial and investment banks offer the service of creating "synthetic" options and futures positions via **dynamic hedging**. This consists of using liquid futures and options contracts in combination and altering the combination over time to replicate the effect of longer-term options and futures. Such hedged portfolios exhibit pricing characteristics of the caps and floors described above. The mechanics of establishing dynamic hedges is quite complicated, but it is important to recognize that such innovation frequently appears to resolve a problem with existing financial contracts.[7]

---

[7]The interested reader should examine the articles by Abken (1989), Mattu (1986), and Platt (1986) for details regarding dynamic hedging.

Exhibit 10.9 Using Options on Eurodollar Futures to Establish Caps and Floors on Bank Borrowing Costs

Cap: Buy a December 1990 Put. Floor: sell a December 1990 Call.

| | **Put** | | **Call** | | | |
	Strike Price	Option Premium Price	Strike Price	Option Premium Price	Range of Borrowing Cost	Net Premium Cost
A.	92.00	0.14	92.50	0.10	7.50% – 8.00%	0.04 = $100
B.	91.75	0.08	92.75	0.05	7.25% – 8.25%	0.03 = $ 75
C.	92.50	0.41	92.75	0.05	7.25% – 7.50%	0.36 = $900
D.	92.25	0.26	92.25	0.19	7.75% – 7.75%	0.07 = $175

Profit Diagram

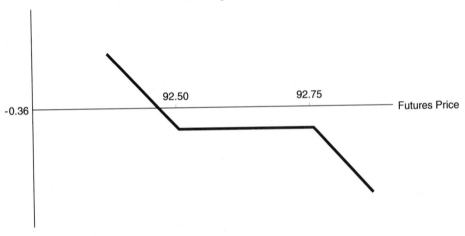

C. Cap at 7.50%; floor at 7.25%; cost = 0.36 basis points.

SUMMARY

Interest rate risk management is an increasingly complex task at financial institutions. Many banks and thrifts now use a variety of tools, such as financial futures and options on financial futures, to assist in their risk management objectives. This chapter introduces financial futures and demonstrates how banks might use futures to hedge interest rate risk. Particular emphasis is placed on 3-month Eurodollar futures, the most heavily traded contract today. Applications are provided on a micro basis in which banks identify specific portfolio transactions that involve potential losses with rising rates or falling rates, and an appropriate hedged position with futures is established to reduce the risk of loss. Macro hedges that reduce overall portfolio interest rate risk associated with a bank's duration gap are also demonstrated.

The chapter also introduces the characteristics of options on financial futures and demonstrates how options can be used to reduce interest rate risk. Specific applications focus on using put options to set cap rates on borrowing, and combining caps with floors by selling call options to set a range of borrowing costs with low up-front cost. The essential point is that these instruments can be used to help manage interest rate risk off-balance-sheet rather than by directly adjusting a bank's holdings of loans and investments and its deposit structure.

Questions

Options

1. What are the primary advantages and disadvantage of using options to hedge interest rate risk?

2. Options, swaps, and futures all manage interest rate risk. It's conceivable that one bank could be using all three techniques. What circumstances would favor each technique? Would you consider the choice of the suitable technique for the current circumstances to be a form of speculating?

3. The market value of an option differs from its immediately redeemable value. What are the names of these two values? Which would you expect to be the larger? Under what circumstances would the other be the larger? The difference between these values is called the _____ value.

4. Which of the following situations would represent a call option and which would be a put option? In each case, would you be the writer or the buyer of the option?
   a. You are buying a new home and have found one you like, but you still want to look a little more. You are afraid you might lose the first house, so you give the owners a little money in return for the guarantee that they will call you if they get another offer and you can have first chance at the house.
   b. You buy a home and finance it with a mortgage. You make certain the mortgage lets you pay off any amount at any time without a penalty.
   c. You buy a callable bond.
   d. You buy books at the bookstore with the agreement that during the first week of the semester you can return them at full value.
   e. You agree to buy your roommate's finance book at the end of the semester if he decides to sell it. In return he agrees to make your dinner for 1 full week.

Futures options on Eurodollars

5. Consider the following list of spot, futures, and futures options on 90-day Eurodollars. (See exhibit.)
   a. Which of the call options are in-the-money? Which of the put options? Are any of them at-the-money?
   b. For the first December call option listed, what is its

FUTURES OPTIONS

EURODOLLAR (IMM) $ million; pts. of 100%

Strike	Calls – Settle			Puts – Settle		
Price	Dec-c	Mar-c	Jun-c	Dec-p	Mar-p	Ju..-p
9150	0.50	0.59	0.58	0.06	0.14	0.26
9175	0.32	0.43	0.43	0.12	0.21	0.35
9200	0.18	0.29	0.30	0.23	0.31	0.47
9225	0.09	0.18	0.20	0.39	0.45	0.61
9250	0.05	0.10	0.13	0.60	....	0.78
9275	0.03	0.06	0.08	0.82	....	....

Est. vol. 30,387, Wed vol. 12,508 calls, 11,382 puts
Open interest Wed; 183,355 calls, 141,505 puts

MONEY RATES

LONDON INTERBANK OFFERED RATES (LIBOR):
8¼% one month; 8¼% three months; 8¼% six months; 8 5/
16% one year. The average of interbank offered rates for
dollar deposits in the London market based on quotations at
five major banks.

FUTURES

EURODOLLAR (IMM)–$1 million; pts of 100%

	Open	High	Low	Settle	Chg	Yield Settle	Chg	Open Interest
Dec	91.97	91.98	91.93	91.95	– .05	8.05 +	.05	246,910
Mr91	92.00	92.01	91.97	91.98	– .05	8.02 +	.05	118,179
June	91.85	91.87	91.83	91.84	– .03	8.16 +	.03	64,341
Sept	91.60	91.65	91.60	91.62	– .03	8.38 +	.03	50,088
Dec	91.35	91.38	91.35	91.36	– .02	8.64 +	.02	40,991
Mr92	91.27	91.32	91.27	91.30	....	8.70	....	31,053
June	91.17	91.22	91.17	91.20	....	8.80	....	23,261
Sept	91.10	91.14	91.10	91.13	....	8.87	....	14,659
Dec	90.96	91.00	90.96	90.99	....	9.01	....	12,416
Mr93	90.92	90.97	90.92	90.96	....	9.04	....	10,465
June	90.86	90.88	90.86	90.87	....	9.13	....	7,603
Sept	90.81	90.81	90.80	90.80	– .01	9.20 +	.01	4,920
Dec	90.70	90.71	90.68	90.69	– .02	9.31 +	.02	3,163
Mr94	90.67	90.69	90.67	90.67	– .02	9.33 +	.02	2,840
June	90.63	90.63	90.62	90.61	– .02	9.39 +	.02	2,025
Sept	90.59	90.59	90.58	90.57	– .01	9.43 +	.01	221

Est vol 94,312; vol Wed201,390; open int 633,135, –3,051.
EURODOLLAR (LIFFE)–$1 million; pts of 100%

Source: *The Wall Street Journal*, September 1990.

1. intrinsic value
2. premium
3. strike price
4. time value

c. As the call option's expiration date gets further in the future, which of these would you expect to increase in value?

   1. intrinsic value
   2. premium
   3. strike price
   4. time value

d. As the strike price on a call increases, which of these do you also expect to increase?

   1. intrinsic value
   2. premium
   3. time value

e. Would the answers to parts c and d differ if you were considering a put option instead?

f. On this trading day there were more calls traded and outstanding than puts. When do you think that is typical and why?

Hedging and Speculating

6. If you anticipate interest rates increasing, should you buy or sell futures to make a profit? Should you buy or sell calls? Should you buy or sell puts? Since all three

will generate profits, knowing what additional information would allow you to choose among the three?

7. If you go long on the December call with a strike of 9200 you hope the price will go _____. What new price must the futures achieve before you can make a profit on the option (ignore transactions fees)?

8. If you short the March put with a strike price of 9200 you hope the price will go _____. What new price must the futures achieve before you can assure a profit on the option (ignore transactions fees)?

9. If you are trying to hedge a negative duration, what trade might you make in call options? Would it offer unlimited gain potential or unlimited loss potential? What would you be forecasting about interest rates to make the option most profitable? Is it a hedge?

10. If you are trying to hedge a negative GAP, what trade might you make in put options? Would this trade offer unlimited gain potential or unlimited loss potential?

11. A bank is going to hedge a negative 3-month GAP of $5 million. It decides to trade March Eurodollar futures or futures options.
    a. If it hedges with futures and the hedge is lifted in March, at the futures expiration when rates are 9.50%, how much money will the bank gain or lose in the cash market? in the futures market? What is the net gain or loss on the total hedge?
    b. If it hedges with call options at the strike price of 9200, how much money will it gain in the options market? What is the net gain or loss?
    c. If it hedges with put options at the strike price of 9200, how much money will it gain in the options market? What is the net gain or loss?

12. Explain why buying a put option places a cap on a bank's borrowing costs. What does it cost to establish this cap? Would buying a put also establish a cap on the investment portfolio's returns?

13. Explain why selling a call option establishes a floor under a bank's borrowing costs. Since banks are always trying to reduce their costs, why would a bank ever want a floor below which its costs could not fall?

References

Abken, Peter. "Interest-Rate Caps, Collars, and Floors." *Economic Review*, Federal Reserve Bank of Atlanta (November/December 1989).

Koppenhaver, G. D. "Futures Options and Their Use by Financial Intermediaries." *Economic Perspectives*, (Federal Reserve Bank of Chicago, January–February 1986).

Kuprianov, Anatoli. "Options on Short-Term Interest Rate Futures." In *Instruments of the Money Market,* 6th ed. Richmond, Va.: Federal Reserve Bank of Richmond, 1986.

Labuszewski, John, and John Nyhoff. *Trading Options on Futures.* New York: John Wiley & Sons, Inc., 1988.

Mattu, Ravi. "Hedging Floating Rate Liabilities: Locks, Caps and Floors." Chicago Mercantile Exchange Strategy Paper, 1986.

Platt, Robert. *Controlling Interest Rate Risk: New Techniques & Applications For Money Management*. New York: John Wiley & Sons, 1986.

Spahr, Ronald, Jan Luytjes, and Donald Edwards. "The Impact of the Use of Caps as Deposit Hedges for Financial Institutions." *Issues in Bank Regulation* (Summer 1988).

Part III

Bank Capital, Cash Assets, and the Competition for Funds

Chapter 11

Managing Liabilities

Liability management plays an important role in the risk/return trade-off at commercial banks. Ever since regulators removed interest rate ceilings on liabilities and expanded the types of deposit products banks could offer, liability management decisions have dramatically influenced a bank's profitability and risk position. During the 1980s, for example, many thrift institutions used brokered deposits to finance extraordinary asset growth. In one infamous case Vernon Savings, a once-small Texas savings and loan, grew from $45 million in assets to $1.1 billion in just 3 years, financed primarily via large CDs sold through brokerages. The bank's managers, in turn, speculated on real estate to such an extent that when the thrift failed 96 percent of its loans were in default.

Liability management decisions affect profitability by determining interest expense on borrowed funds; noninterest expense associated with check handling costs, personnel costs, and fixed assets; and noninterest income from fees and deposit service charges. They affect interest rate and liquidity risk by determining the rate sensitivity of liabilities, the stability of deposits toward preventing unanticipated deposit outflows, and the ease of access to purchased funds.

With depositor confidence in the banking system damaged by the savings and loan crisis, many banks are pursuing strategies that target individual retail customers. Individuals, as a group, are generally not as interest rate sensitive as wholesale customers such as commercial firms and government units. Thus if banks can attract consumer deposits, these funds are likely to remain on the books for longer periods of time and not move readily to other banks when interest rates change modestly. The associated buzzwords in banking are building long-term customer relationships or establishing a strong core deposit base.

The first part of this chapter examines the risk-return characteristics of various bank liabilities. The second part focuses on structural influences on bank liabilities such as lifeline banking and the changing role and nature of federal deposit insurance.

THE COMPOSITION OF BANK FUNDS

There are many different types of liabilities. Some offer transactions capabilities with relatively low rates. Others offer limited check-writing capabilities but pay higher rates. Liabilities with long-term fixed maturities typically pay the highest rates. Each instrument responds differently to interest rate changes. Thus the composition and maturity or duration of each bank's liabilities are important determinants of the cost and risk associated with performance.

Prior to 1960 banks relied on standardized demand and savings deposits as their primary source of funds. Government regulators determined allowable interest rates, and virtually all banks paid the maximum. Banks could compete for funds only by differentiating the quality of service and paying implicit interest through lowering service charges or offering premiums to open accounts. The primary strategy for most retail banks centered on having a well-located home office and branches where allowed.

In 1961 Citibank, then First National City Bank, introduced the first truly marketable CD by arranging for securities dealers to make a secondary market that provided investors liquidity to trade large CDs after the initial purchase. Regulators still set maximum allowable rates on new issues, but in most periods the market rate fell below the ceiling. The evolution of other market rate instruments similarly followed from bank efforts to circumvent regulation. Whenever regulators attempted to restrict borrowing capabilities via specific liabilities, banks either developed new instruments or expanded their use of alternative liabilities.

The credit crunches of the 1960s reveal this tendency. In 1969, for example, regulators let secondary market rates on CDs rise above the maximum allowable rate on new CD issues so that banks found it difficult to roll over or obtain new CD funds. Large banks, in particular, substituted unregulated Eurodollar liabilities and commercial paper for CDs rather than reduce credit availability to loan customers.[1] Thus while all U.S. banks experienced a net CD outflow of $15.5 billion in 1969, they realized a net $7.4 billion gain in Eurodollar liabilities to foreign banks and a $4.3 billion increase in commercial paper outstanding.

When CD rates were again competitive in 1970, banks resumed their traditional financing by obtaining $23.5 billion in net new CDs and letting Eurodollars and commercial paper run off by a combined $8.3 billion. In similar fashion, large deposit runoffs to money market mutual funds in the early 1980s induced banks to create automatic transfers from savings accounts and retail repurchase agreements (RPs). Automatic transfer accounts paid passbook interest on checking accounts while retail RPs paid market rates on short-term savings certificates held by individuals.

Today, virtually all bank liabilities are free of regulatory restrictions on allowable rates, maturities, and minimum denominations. Price competition is the dominant consideration in attracting new funds. Aggressive pricing and the development of electronic funds transfer systems and home banking have reduced the importance of

---

[1] Eurodollars are dollar-denominated deposits in banks located outside the United States. Domestic banks can acquire the funds either from foreign banks or branches of U.S. banks. Most bank commercial paper is issued by multibank holding companies. Specific features of each are discussed later in the chapter.

location to the point that many individuals now purchase banking services from firms located outside their home state.

Recent Trends for Large and Small Banks

Perhaps the most difficult problem facing bank management is how to develop strategies to compete for funding sources. With no interest rate ceilings on deposits or restrictions on maturities, banks can offer any deposit product customers demand. While this freedom creates market opportunities, it also presents significant problems. First, bank customers have become much more rate-conscious. They shop around for the highest yields and typically pay less attention to long-term bank relationships. From the bank's perspective, liabilities have become more interest elastic, so that small rate changes can produce large fluctuations in outstanding balances. Second, many customers have demonstrated a strong preference for shorter-term deposits. High inflation rates in the late 1970s combined with reserves-based monetary policy to produce wide swings in interest rates and generally increase rate volatility and uncertainty. Depositors can reduce their interest rate risk by investing in short-term contracts that almost always trade close to par. The rate sensitivity of liabilities is thus greater, creating difficulties in pricing assets to manage net interest margin (NIM) and the level of interest rate risk.

Exhibit 11.1 documents recent trends in the composition of bank funds for banks in two different size groupings. Each column represents the percentage of total assets financed by the specific funds source indicated for the average bank in each size group. Examine first the 1990 versus 1986 figures for banks with assets from $3 to $10 billion. Regardless of bank size, five key differences exist. In 1990 these large banks operated with fewer demand deposits, more NOW and ATS accounts, fewer money market savings and more small time deposits, more brokered and large time deposits, and more equity capital.

The decline in demand deposits reflects the factors discussed earlier. With alternative interest-bearing transactions accounts available, individuals shifted into NOWs, Super NOWs, and money market mutual funds. MMDAs declined with the growth in small bank time deposits. They can earn higher market rates of interest on these instruments and still have transactions capabilities. Corporate depositors have similarly reduced demand balances through efficient cash management techniques, often taught by banks, that allow them to minimize nonearning deposits.

With the decline in demand balances, banks raised rates on savings and time deposits to replace lost financing. In many cases, depositors simply moved balances from low-rate to high-rate accounts at the same institution. This increased bank borrowing costs without increasing the total amount of funds acquired. At the end of 1990, core deposits comprised 60.3 percent of total assets. Conceptually, core deposits are stable deposits that customers are less likely to move when interest rates on competing investments rise. They are not as rate sensitive as large denomination purchased liabilities.

Bank reliance on nondeposit liabilities, including non-core deposits, federal funds purchased, securities sold under agreement to repurchase, borrowings from the Federal

Exhibit 11.1 The Percentage Contribution of Various Sources of Bank Funds: A Comparison of Large versus Small Banks: 1986 and 1990 (Percentage of Total Assets)

Liabilities & Stockholders Equity	Banks with Assets from $3 to $10 Billion		Banks with Assets from $10 to $25 Million	
	1988	1986	1988	1986
Demand deposits	14.6%	19.4%	13.9%	16.1%
NOW & ATS accounts[b]	6.1	4.6	11.3	8.5
MMDA Savings[b]	12.1	13.8	8.8	14.1
Other savings deposits	4.8	4.3	7.8	7.7
Non-brokered time deposits ≤ $100,000	22.7	16.7	40.2	34.0
Core deposits	60.3%	58.8%	82.0%	80.4%
Brokered deposits	1.6%	0.7%	0.0%	0.0%
Non-brokered time deposits > $100,000	8.8	9.0	8.6	8.8
Deposits in foreign offices	2.5	4.8	0.0	0.0
Other deposits	4.4	2.0	0.2	0.9
Total deposits	77.6%	75.3%	90.8%	90.1%
Federal funds purchased & RPs	10.6%	12.4%	0.0%	0.1%
Other borrowings	2.1	2.3	0.0	0.0
Volatile liabilities	31.2	31.8	9.3	9.7
Acceptances & other liabilities	3.4	3.9	1.4	1.7
Total liabilities	93.7%	92.9%	92.2%	91.9%
Subordinated notes & bonds	0.2%	0.4%	0.0%	0.0%
Common equity & preferred stock	6.1	5.7	7.8	8.1
Total	100.0%	100.0%	100.0%	100.0%

[a]Source: Uniform Bank Performance Report.

[b]NOW = Negotiable orders of withdrawal; ATS = automatic transfer from savings; MMDA = money market deposit account.

Reserve, and Eurodollars has remained relatively constant. Except for discount window borrowings, these funds all have large denominations, pay market rates, and have relatively short-term maturities. Investors are especially rate-sensitive and will move their funds if other institutions pay higher rates or if it is rumored that the borrower has financial difficulties. Such volatile liabilities accounted for 31 percent of financing for these large banks in 1990. In summary, all banks are paying market rates on a greater proportion of their liabilities, with less customer loyalty and thus greater liquidity risk. Bank capital has also increased with regulatory pressure in response to problem loans.

Data for banks with assets between $10 and $25 million reveal similar trends, but different magnitudes. In 1990 demand deposits also declined proportionately, but the net loss was less than for the larger banks. Money market deposits similarly declined proportionately. Total core deposits rose to 82 percent in 1990 because the gain in NOW and ATS accounts and non-brokered time deposits more than offset the declines in demand deposits and money market deposit accounts. Nondeposit liabilities account for only 9 percent of funding at these banks. Because deposits typically cost less than nondeposit liabilities, large banks' borrowing costs normally exceed small banks' costs. In addition, only the large banks obtained significant overseas financing, as foreign deposits totaled 2.5 percent of their assets. Finally, as indicated in Chapter 4, large banks finance proportionately fewer assets with equity capital. In 1990 common and preferred equity capital at the larger banks accounted for 6 percent of financing, or just over than three-fourths of the 7.8 percent of financing for the smaller banks.

The comparison of changes in outstanding deposits reflects key differences between retail and wholesale banks. Small banks generally obtain more deposits from individuals and partnerships, while large regional and money center banks deal with large corporate customers. The largest banks suffered a smaller deposit loss but still relied more on nondeposit liabilities to finance growth. If regulators were to allow interest payments on corporate demand deposits, all banks would be affected, but large banks would experience the greatest impact.

Small banks also have an advantage in terms of the average interest rates they pay on most liabilities. Consider the data in Exhibit 11.2. Banks with assets from $10 to $25 million not only operate with proportionately more core deposits, but paid 0.12 percent less in interest or deposits than did banks with assets from $3 to $10 billion in 1990. In fact, the smaller banks paid lower rates on all but federal funds purchased and subordinated debt, of which they have little.

CHARACTERISTICS OF SMALL-DENOMINATION LIABILITIES

The characteristics of small denomination liabilities (under $100,000) are fundamentally different from those of large-denomination liabilities. Instruments under $100,000 are normally held by individual investors and are not actively traded in the secondary market. Large-balance instruments typically carry denominations in multiples of $1 million and can be readily sold in the secondary market. Individuals traditionally had few alternatives to banks when selecting interest-bearing deposits. Today, commercial banks, savings and loans, credit unions, money market mutual funds, and insurance companies offer deposit products with similar features. All pay market interest rates. The primary advantage of banks, savings and loans, and credit unions is that deposits are insured up to $100,000 per account.

ACCOUNTS WITH TRANSACTIONS PRIVILEGES

Individuals and businesses own checking accounts for transactions purposes. Checks are attractive because they are readily accepted and provide formal verification of payment. Most banks offer four different accounts with transactions privileges: demand deposits (DDAs), negotiable orders of withdrawal (NOWs), Super NOWs, and money market deposit accounts (MMDAs). Banks differentiate between deposits in the

Exhibit 11.2 Average Annual Cost of Liabilities: A Comparison of Large versus Small Banks: 1990

Liabilities	Banks with Assets from $3 to $10 Billion 1990	Banks with Assets from $10 to $25 Million 1990
Transaction accounts	4.75%	4.99%
MMDAs	6.12	5.71
Other savings deposits	5.12	5.12
Large CDs	7.99	8.01
All the time deposits	8.03	7.78
Foreign office deposits	8.01	—
Total interest-bearing deposits	6.99%	6.87%
Federal funds & RPs	7.79%	8.26%
Other borrowed money	6.80	2.77
Subordinated notes & bonds	8.63	10.00
All interest-bearing funds	7.09	6.86

Source: Uniform Bank Performance Report.

number of checks permitted, the minimum denomination required to open an account, and the interest rate paid. All carry FDIC insurance up to $100,000 per account.

Demand deposits are non-interest-bearing checking accounts held by individuals, businesses, and government units. While explicit interest payments are prohibited, there are no regulatory restrictions on the number of checks or minimum balances. Today, commercial customers own most DDAs because, unlike individuals and governments, they cannot hold NOWs or Super NOWs. Individuals with sufficiently large balances prefer interest-bearing accounts that provide transactions privileges.

A NOW account is simply a demand deposit that pays interest. These accounts have been available nationally since 1981 and have attracted considerable funds away from DDAs since that time.[2] Only individuals and nonprofit organizations can hold NOWs. Every bank can price NOWs based on competitive conditions without restriction. Many limit the number of checks that can be written without fees and impose minimum balance requirements before paying interest. Many pay tiered interest rates that increase with the size of the deposit. The rationale is to encourage individuals to consolidate accounts. Depositors are better off if they centralize their accounts because they can earn higher yields and pay lower service charges.

In late 1982 federal regulators authorized Super NOWs and MMDAs, which also offered transactions capabilities.[3] Initially, Super NOWs were checking accounts that

[2]NOWs were introduced on an experimental basis in 1972 in New England. Murphy and Mandell, 1980, document bank performance with NOWs from 1972 to 1980 prior to nationwide authorization in 1981.

[3]Congress authorized Super NOWs on December 14, 1982, and MMDAs on January 14, 1983. Money market deposit accounts are classified as time deposits, not transaction accounts, when calculating required reserves. They are discussed here because they provide limited check-writing capabilities. Minimum balance requirements on both accounts were initially set at $2,500. This level was lowered to $1,000 in January 1985 and removed entirely in January 1986. Super NOWs are now functionally equivalent to NOWs.

paid market rates only if a depositor's average balance equaled at least $2,500. In 1986 regulators removed all minimum balance requirements so that Super NOWs now exhibit the same features as NOWs. Money market deposit accounts were introduced to provide banks an instrument competitive with money market mutual funds offered by large brokerages. They are formally time deposits with limited checking privileges. These accounts differ from NOWs in that depositors are limited to six transactions per month, of which only three can be checks. The average size of each MMDA check is thus much larger than for other transactions accounts. Banks find MMDAs especially attractive because required reserves against them are considerably below required reserves on DDAs and NOWs. Limited check processing and low reserves reduce their effective cost. Banks can therefore afford to pay higher rates to attract MMDA funds. Interestingly, banks have rarely paid rates as high as those on money market mutual funds. The primary reason is that customers are willing to accept a lower rate because of deposit insurance and the fact that they can establish personal banking relationships via their deposit business.

The ownership of bank transactions accounts is changing rapidly as institutions offer new deposit products and refine their pricing schedules. Individuals, once loyal customers, previously would not withdraw their funds unless a crisis arose. The advent of interest-bearing checking accounts, however, has increased interest rate awareness so that customers today move deposits between accounts and institutions, depending on which pays the highest rates.

Pricing strategies influence the composition of accounts via service charges, minimum balance requirements, and interest rates paid. Service charges may be imposed as flat monthly fees, per-check charges, or a combination of both. Many banks specify minimum balance requirements high enough to limit the number of small-balance accounts, for which they impose high monthly service charges. Banks often encourage customers to consolidate accounts by offering tiered interest rates that increase with deposit size and club programs that provide a range of transactions services for a fixed monthly fee. Individuals with demand deposits typically cannot meet minimum balance requirements to open a NOW account.

Functional Cost Analysis

Each year the Federal Reserve System conducts a survey called the Functional Cost Analysis Program to collect cost and income data on commercial bank operations. It then publishes average data for banks grouped by deposit size. The cost data are somewhat imprecise because banks subjectively allocate expenses to various products and services, but they are the best data publicly available for analyzing costs and provide useful comparisons between firms.

According to functional cost analysis data, demand deposits are the least expensive source of funds. Costs are still substantial, however, as most banks employ a large staff to process checks. Functional cost analysis classifies check processing activities as either home debits, transit checks, deposits, or general account maintenance. Home debits are checks drawn on a customer's account. Transit checks are drawn on other banks but deposited in the customer's account. Deposits represent checks or currency

Exhibit 11.3 Cost and Revenue Analysis of Selected Transactions Accounts: Banks with Deposits of $50 Million to $200 Million, 1989

Activity	Average Unit Cost	DDAs	Interest-Bearing Checking	Commercial DDAs	Personal Checking
***Average Month Cost/Account*[a]**					
Home debits	$.2022	$ 4.61	$ 3.60	$ 7.19	$ 4.91
Transit checks	.1117	2.37	1.15	7.36	1.05
Deposits	$.4155	1.80	1.41	3.65	1.67
Account maintenance		5.78	5.77	5.79	6.02
Operating cost		$ 14.56	$ 11.93	$ 23.99	$ 13.66
Interest expense			$ 33.46		8.69
Total cost		$ 14.56	$ 45.39	$ 23.99	$ 22.35
Average account size		$2,778.00	$7,952.00	$9,346.00	$2,639.00
Average annual percent cost		6.30%	6.85%	3.08%	10.16%
Average Monthly Revenue/Account					
Service charges and fees		$ 5.57	$ 1.86	$ 5.68	$ 5.08
Investment income[b]		17.09	53.19	62.78	17.76
Total revenue		$ 22.66	$ 55.05	$ 68.46	$ 22.84
Net earnings/month		$ 8.10	$ 9.66	$ 44.47	$ 0.49

[a]DDAs indicates demand deposit accounts interest-bearing checking includes negotiable orders of withdrawal (NOWs) and Super NOWs but excludes money market deposit accounts. Personal checking includes all DDAs, NOWs, and Super NOWs held by individuals.

[b]Assumes 10% annual earnings credit on investable deposit balances, investable balances equal ledger balances minus float and required reserves. Float is assumed to equal 10% of ledger balances for commercial DDAs and 5% elsewhere. Required reserves equal 12% of ledger balances less float.

Source: *Functional Cost Analysis*, Board of Governors of the Federal Reserve System, 1989.

directly deposited in the customer's account. Account maintenance refers to preparing and mailing a periodic statement.

Exhibit 11.3 summarizes 1989 average cost and revenue information for various transactions accounts at medium-sized banks (deposits of $50 to $200 million). Note that these data are obtained voluntarily, so there may be biases toward the features of the healthiest banks. Also, few very large institutions participate in the survey so figures are generally not available for the largest banks.

The first column indicates the average cost per item for each activity. The following two columns list monthly data for the average DDA and interest-bearing checking account for all depositors. The last two columns list similar data for specific categories by deposit owner. Examine first the operating costs. Demand deposit accounts cost $2.63 more each month to handle than interest-bearing checking accounts because of higher transactions activity. Still, they pay no interest so that the total monthly cost is almost $31 lower for the average checking account. Interest expense overstates the relative cost of interest-bearing checking accounts, however, because their average balance is more than two times larger than that of DDAs. The average percentage cost, measured as the total annual cost per account divided by the average balance, adjusts for this size discrepancy. Using average figures, DDAs cost 6.30 percent, while interest-bearing checking accounts cost 6.85 percent in 1989.

The breakdown of commercial DDAs versus individual checking accounts reveals several additional differences. First, commercial DDAs exhibit the greatest activity and operating cost. The average balance is also the greatest at $9,346, so that their 3.08 percentage cost is the lowest. Second, personal checking accounts are much smaller, on average, and the most expensive. Comparing data across all classifications, it appears that commercial DDAs cost the least, followed by interest-bearing checking accounts and personal DDAs.

Whether these accounts are profitable depends on how much a bank earns from service charges and fees and from investing deposit balances. Estimates of these average monthly revenues are listed at the bottom of Exhibit 11.3. Investment income is calculated assuming a 10-percent earnings rate on balances in excess of float and required reserves. Not surprisingly, total revenue varies directly with the average size of the deposit. Only in the case of personal checking did fee income cover at least one-half the monthly operating cost for any account. Net earnings are greatest for commercial DDAs and least for individual accounts, ranging from just $0.49 to $44.47 per account.[4]

Data for other banks show similar cost and revenue relationships across account categories. Smaller banks generally realize lower costs per account but also earn less because they handle much smaller accounts. Larger banks have the highest costs but earn more revenue because they handle larger deposits.

Exhibit 11.4 provides 1989 figures for savings deposits and money market deposit accounts (MMDAs) at medium-sized banks. For MMDAs, the average account balance is $15,613, indicating that MMDAs serve primarily as a savings vehicle with transactions protection. The annual operating cost per account is $177.94, or $14.78 monthly, comprised mainly of account maintenance. The average annual cost equaled 7.38 percent, most of which is interest expense. Still, these accounts were quite profitable in 1989, assuming a 10-percent return on investable balances.

Savings Accounts

Passbook savings accounts are one of the last remnants of a highly regulated banking environment. In March 1986 federal regulators eliminated interest ceilings on passbooks, allowing banks to pay competitive rates. Existing accounts essentially represent money market deposits that come with a passbook. Banks have not phased out these accounts because some customers prefer the security of a passbook. The accounts are relatively low cost because customers cannot write checks and do not receive monthly statements. Many banks reduce activity further by limiting the number of withdrawals and imposing substantial minimum balances. Cost and revenue data in Exhibit 11.4 suggest that passbook savings accounts cost an average of 7.33 percent in 1989.

---

[4]Carraro and Thornton, 1986, calculated similar costs associated with different transactions accounts using data for different types of depositors.

Exhibit 11.4 Cost Analysis of Selected Savings Deposits and MMDAs: Banks with Deposits of $50 Million to $200 Million, 1987

Activity	Average Unit Cost		Average Annual Cost/Account[a]	
	Regular Savings	MMDAs	Regular Savings	MMDAs
Deposits	$0.76	$0.76	$ 5.13	$ 11.43
Withdrawals/Debits	1.46	0.92	8.59	11.56
Account opening	4.62	0.20	0.81	
Account closing	2.56		0.58	
Transit checks				6.40
Interest posting	2.81	2.81	12.15	33.39
Account maintenance			19.99	115.15
Operating cost			$ 48.88	$ 177.94
Interest expense			116.75	973.82
Total annual cost			$ 165.63	$ 1,151.76
Average account size			$2,261.00	$15,613.00
Average annual percent cost			7.33%	7.38%
Fee income			$ 3.27	
Investment income[b]			205.23	$ 1,418.54
Total revenue			$ 208.50	$ 1,418.54
Annual net earnings			$ 42.87	$ 266.78

[a]Approximately 90 percent of these accounts are money market deposit accounts.

[b]Assumes 3 percent required reserves and 10 percent earnings credit.

Source: *Functional Cost Analysis*, Federal Reserve System, 1989.

Small Time Deposits

Small time deposits have denominations under $100,000, specified maturities ranging from 7 days to any longer negotiated term, and substantial interest penalties for early withdrawal. Banks can pay market rates on any account regardless of deposit size. Since 1983 bank customers have had the flexibility to negotiate maturity and rate for any size account maturing beyond 31 days. Banks can control the flow of deposits by offering only products with specific maturities and minimum balances and varying the relative rates paid according to these terms. The effective cost of small time deposits is comparable to that for MMDAs. Average interest cost is higher, but operating costs are lower.

Service Charges

For many years banks priced check-handling services below cost. While competition may have forced this procedure, it was acceptable because banks paid below-market rates on most deposits. This low interest subsidy implicitly covered losses on check handling. The popular view was that the 20 percent of bank customers with the largest deposit balances subsidized the 80 percent with lower balances.

Deregulation removed this subsidy and induced banks to modify their pricing policies. Because banks now pay market rates on deposits, they want all customers to pay at least what services cost. This has brought about relationship pricing, in which service charges decline and interest rates rise with increases in customers' deposit balances. Many banks have unbundled services and price each separately. Some charge for services once considered simple courtesies, such as check cashing and balance inquiries. For most customers, service charges and fees for banking services increased substantially during the 1980s and early 1990s.

Such pricing schemes have essentially created a caste system of banking. Large depositors receive the highest rates, pay the lowest fees, and often get free checking. They do not wait in long teller lines and receive attention from their personal banker. Small depositors earn lower rates, if any, and pay higher fees, with less personal service. Consider the pricing terms outlined in Exhibit 11.5. Unless an individual keeps a minimum of $1000 in checking balances each month, the monthly service charge equals $15, or $180 per year. Similarly, the bank pays no interest on a NOW account unless the minimum balance is $2,000. The related charges for insufficient funds checks, stop payment orders, and check-cashing for noncustomers are substantial as well. This bank also charges $3 for each balance inquiry made by a customer. The point is that this bank wants small-balance customers only if they generate substantial fee income.

CHARACTERISTICS OF LARGE-DENOMINATION LIABILITIES

In addition to small-denomination deposits, banks purchase funds in the money markets. Money center and large regional banks effect most transactions over the telephone, either directly with trading partners or through brokers. Most trades are denominated in $1 million multiples. Smaller banks generally deal directly with customers and have limited access to national and international markets. Some types of liabilities, such as jumbo CDs sold directly by a bank, are viewed as permanent sources of funds, while others are used infrequently. Banks must pay market rates on all sources and can normally attract additional funds by paying a small premium over the current quoted market rate. Because customers move their investments on the basis of small rate differentials, these funds are labeled "hot money" or volatile liabilities.

Jumbo CDs

Large, negotiable certificates of $100,000 or more are referred to as jumbo CDs. These CDs are issued primarily by the largest banks and purchased by businesses and government units. Since their introduction in the early 1960s, CDs have grown to be the most popular hot money, large-source financing used by banks.

While CDs come in many varieties, they all possess certain characteristics. First, they have a minimum maturity of 7 days. The most common maturities are 30 and 90 days, but recent issues of zero coupon CDs extend the maturity out as long as 10 years.

Exhibit 11.5 Pricing Example of Individual Transactions Accounts

Individual Transaction Account Pricing

Account Type	Minimum Balance	Monthly Service Charge
Individual DDA	$0–999	$15
	≥1,000	0
NOW	0–1,999	10
	≥ 2,000	0
	No interest is paid if the average balance falls below $1,000.	
Super NOW	0–4,999	15
	5,000–9,999	10
	≥10,000	0
	If the average balance falls below $2,500, the NOW account rate is paid.	
MMDA	0–4,999	15
	5,000–9,999	10
	≥10,000	0
	If the average balance falls below $2,500, the NOW account rate is paid.	

Selected Charges

	Item Charge
Insufficient funds	$30
Stop payment orders	30
Automatic teller machine withdrawal—off premise	1
Automatic teller machine withdrawal—on premise	0
Balance inquiry	3
Check cashing—noncustomer	15

Second, CD interest rates are quoted on the basis of a 360-day year. Except for zeros, CDs are issued at face value and traded as interest-bearing instruments. Thus trades are settled at market value of the principal plus interest accrued from the original purchase. Third, CDs are insured up to $100,000 per investor per institution. Any balances in excess of $100,000 are at risk to the purchaser. For example, investors in CDs issued by Penn Square Bank of Oklahoma City that failed in 1983 received only 65 cents on the dollar for the uninsured portion of their CDs. Jumbo CDs are thus risky instruments and are traded accordingly. When an issuing bank has financial difficulties, it must pay a stiff premium over current yields, often 2 to 3 percent, to attract funds. When traders perceive that all large banks are experiencing difficulties, as with recent foreign loans, they bid CD rates higher relative to comparable-maturity Treasury bill rates.

Banks issue jumbo CDs directly to investors or indirectly through dealers and brokers. Whenever they use an intermediary, banks pay approximately 1/8 of 1 percent or 12.5 basis points for the service. Deposits obtained in this manner are labeled **brokered deposits**. The broker places a bank's CDs with investors who demand insured deposits. The advantage is that brokers provide small banks access to purchased funds. They package CDs in $100,000 increments so that all deposits are fully insured, and market them to interested investors. In essence, the broker is selling deposit insurance because the buyer assumes only the risk that the government will not pay off insured depositors, which has never happened. Thus a bank or savings and loan might request that a broker obtain $50 million in CDs, which could be handled by dividing the $50 million into 500 fully-insured $100,000 CDs.

Not surprisingly, bank regulators argue that brokered CDs are too often abused and that there is a link between brokered deposits and failed banks. Banks and thrifts can use the funds to speculate on high-risk assets, yet if the investments deteriorate and the bank fails it is the FDIC, not the owners of the bank, that must pay insured depositors. In fact, many failed institutions grew too rapidly during the 1980s by buying funds through brokers and making speculative loans. Loan losses subsequently followed. For this reason, regulators monitor each bank's reliance on brokered deposits and have lobbied for restrictions on their use.

Large multibank holding companies have successfully marketed large-denomination CDs by agreeing to allocate a total investment among affiliate banks in $100,000 increments so that the full amount is insured. Thus a holding company with 60 subsidiary banks could place $6 million within the group with full insurance coverage. Deposit insurance again provides greater access to funding in this form. Interestingly, pension fund deposits are insured up to $100,000 per individual pensioner, amounts that reach many millions of dollars.

Uncertainty over future interest rates has induced many investors to shorten their investment horizon, making short-term CDs the most popular maturities. Many banks prefer to lengthen CD maturities, thereby reducing rate sensitivity because they currently operate with negative funding GAPs near-term. Banks have gone to extremes to attract long-term CD funds, often creating hybrid CDs that appeal to selected investors. Several of these are identified below, including Contemporary Issues: Earnings-Based CDs.

Variable-Rate CDs. Traditionally, CDs were fixed-rate contracts that were renegotiated at 1-, 3-, and 6-month maturities. Since the mid-1970s, large banks have issued variable-rate contracts for longer periods, with rates renegotiated at specified intervals. For example, a bank might issue a CD in which the depositor agrees to keep funds on deposit for 2 years. The bank prices the contract as a series of eight CDs, with the rate renegotiated every 3 months. The rate paid at each interval is equal to the average of 3-month CD rates quoted by securities dealers.[5] These variable-rate CDs appeal to investors who expect rising rates or want the added liquidity inherent in a 3-month CD over a 2-year CD.

---

[5]A newer twist, popular at smaller banks, is to give the depositor the alternative to keep the original rate or reinvest at a higher rate if rates go up. Because this option transfers all interest rate risk to the issuing bank, a customer should be willing to accept a lower initial yield.

CONTEMPORARY ISSUES

Earnings-Based CDs

Earnings-based CDs are any deposit account with interest payments that vary according to the profitability of the issuing firm's investments. These accounts have been aggressively marketed by thrift institutions in an attempt to lengthen the maturity of their liabilities. Some depositors like them because they can presumably share in the profits of a savings and loan's real estate holdings.

One of the first earnings-based CDs offered directly to depositors was marketed by Murray Savings Bank in 1984. The certificates carried 12-year maturities and guaranteed customers 10 percent simple annual interest. Murray invested the funds in income-producing commercial real estate and promised to pay depositors additional interest and an equity kicker tied to the real estate returns. The Federal Home Loan Bank Board quickly imposed restrictions on this type of contract. Firms with net worth below 3 percent of as-

sets were prohibited from issuing earnings-based CDs. Other firms could issue them as long as the total volume did not exceed 5 percent of assets.

There are obvious problems with these CDs from an investor's perspective. First, the customer has no say in what projects are financed. A savings and loan would make more money if it allocated its low-performing loans to this equity CD portfolio and kept the most profitable loans in its regular portfolio. Second, much of the return is generated from equity participations when the projects are sold. An earnings-based CD converts returns that would be tax-sheltered as capital gains under direct investment into fully taxed ordinary income. Finally, the CDs are relatively illiquid with a 12-year maturity, and there is a long waiting time until the incremental income is received.

Zero Coupon CDs. Like zero coupon bonds, zero coupon CDs are sold at a steep discount from par and appreciate to face value at maturity. They carry fixed rates and fixed maturities. For example, a bank might issue a certificate with a current price of $500,000 that pays $1 million in 6 years. The investor receives a fixed 12.24 percent annual return and knows with certainty what the value of the investment is after 6 years. The primary disadvantage is that the amortized portion of the original discount is subject to federal income taxes, even though the investor does not actually receive current income. For this reason, many banks market the zeros to individual retirement or Keogh accounts. Whenever the maturity value is below $100,000, the CD is fully insured. The attraction to issuing banks is in getting longer-term funds. In this case, the bank obtains $500,000 immediately with no corresponding cash outflow for 6 years. This deposit's effective duration is 6 years.

Immediately Available Funds

As the name suggests, immediately available funds are balances that are accepted as a means of payment within 1 business day on demand. Two types of balances are immediately available: deposit liabilities of Federal Reserve Banks and certain "collected" liabilities of commercial banks that may be transferred or withdrawn during a business day on order of account holders.[6] Through its wire transfer facilities, the

---

[6]Immediately available funds are discussed by Lucas, Jones, and Thurston, 1977. Deposit liabilities of Federal Reserve Banks to financial institutions constitute the major portion of the banking system's legal required reserves. Bank management of these balances is discussed in Chapter 14.

Federal Reserve System can electronically move deposits anywhere throughout the United States within 24 hours. Collected balances of banks are ledger balances appearing on a bank's books minus float. All checks written against such accounts, but not yet cleared, have been deducted, and the remaining balances are transferable within 1 day. Most large transactions are settled in immediately available funds, including maturing CDs, federal funds, and security repurchase agreements.

Federal Funds Purchased

The term *federal funds* is often used to refer to excess reserve balances that are traded between banks. This is grossly inaccurate, given reserves averaging as a method of computing reserves, different nonbank players in the market, and the motivation behind many trades. In some instances, nonbank participants, such as securities dealers and state governments, trade federal funds. In other cases, bank reserve balances at Federal Reserve Banks do not change ownership. The formal definition of *federal funds* is unsecured short-term loans that are settled in immediately available funds. They encompass transactions outside the arena of bank reserve trading by including any participant that holds large balances at Federal Reserve Banks or collected liabilities at depository institutions. Thus thrift institutions, foreign governments, and the U.S. Treasury can trade federal funds.

Most transactions are overnight loans, although maturities are negotiated and can extend up to several weeks. Interest rates are negotiated between trading partners and are quoted on a 360-day basis. The absence of collateral suggests that participants are well known by their trading partners as lenders accept default risk. Large transactions are denominated in multiples of $1 million and are typically handled by brokers. On the other side of the spectrum, small banks frequently buy and sell federal funds in amounts as low as $50,000. When a bank purchases federal funds, its cost of borrowing equals the interest rate plus the brokerage fee because the bank does not have to hold required reserves against this liability.

Exhibit 11.6 distinguishes between two types of federal funds transactions. T-accounts representing changes in balance sheet entries indicate the transaction effects. The first portrays First State Bank lending $1 million in deposit balances held at a Federal Reserve Bank to City National Bank. City National generates a liability, federal funds purchased, while First State books an overnight loan, federal funds sold. If the negotiated rate equals 10 percent, City National pays $277.78 in interest and the transaction reverses the next day.[7] This is the traditional reserves loan between banks where City National is short on reserves and First State holds excess reserves.

The second type of transaction documents City National borrowing $100,000 in correspondent balances that First State holds with it. Again, the borrower assumes the liability, federal funds purchased, while the lender receives an earning asset, federal funds sold. Reserve balances at both banks, however, are unaffected. Instead First State's deposit balances at City National decline. The rationale for this transaction is

---

[7]($1 million)(.10/360) = $277.78

Exhibit 11.6 Hypothetical Transactions Using Immediately Available Funds

A. City National Bank borrows $1 million in federal funds from First State Bank

City National Bank		First State Bank	
ΔASSETS	ΔLIABILITIES	ΔASSETS	ΔLIABILITIES
Deposit balances at Federal Reserve banks +$1 million	Federal funds purchased +$1 million	Deposit balances at Federal Reserve banks −$1 million Federal funds sold +$1 million	
+$1 million	+ $1 million	No change	

B. City National Bank borrows $100,000 of correspondent balances held with it by First State Bank

City National Bank		First State Bank	
ΔASSETS	ΔLIABILITIES	ΔASSETS	ΔLIABILITIES
	Demand deposits owed First State Bank −$100,000 Federal funds purchased +$100,000	Demand deposits at City National Bank −$100,000 Federal funds sold +$100,000	
	No change	No change	

that First State owns correspondent balances in excess of the amount necessary to compensate City National for services rendered. By agreement, any excess balances are rolled over into federal funds sold, thereby generating interest income. If City National did not provide this rollover, First State Bank would move its correspondent banking relationship to a bank that did. In both cases, reserves-free federal funds transactions are settled in immediately available funds.[8]

The federal funds market is important to monetary policy because the federal funds rate is a key target variable for the Federal Reserve System. Federal Reserve policies, particularly Federal Open Market Committee purchases and sales of securities, directly alter the bank reserves component of immediately available funds, increasing or decreasing the federal funds rate. Increases in bank reserves reduce borrowing pressure relative to desired lending of immediately available funds, and the federal funds rate declines over the near term. The opposite occurs with decreases in bank reserves.

---

[8]The decline in deposits owed First State Bank actually reduces City National Bank's required reserves by lowering the deposit base against which reserves are computed.

Security Repurchase Agreements

Security repurchase agreements (RPs or Repos) are short-term loans secured by government securities that are settled in immediately available funds. They are virtually identical to federal funds in function and form except they are collateralized. Technically, the loans embody a sale of securities with a simultaneous agreement to buy them back later at a fixed price plus accrued interest. The later date is normally the next day, as most RPs have 24-hour maturities. Some loans are for longer periods, with maturity and rate negotiated. While securities dealers dominate the market, any institution can trade RPs as long as it meets collateral and balance requirements.

Repo transactions can be characterized in terms of the first T-accounts of Exhibit 11.6. If City National Bank used an RP to acquire immediately available funds, the only change would be to substitute the liability, securities sold under agreement to repurchase, in place of federal funds purchased. City National has to post securities as collateral against the borrowing, but the securities do not appear as separate balance sheet entries. Whenever the collateral is U.S. government or agency securities, the funds obtained are free of reserves. First State would book the secured loan, securities purchased under agreement to resell, instead of federal funds sold. In market terminology, the lender's transaction is a reverse RP. Banks participate both as borrowers and lenders directly or as securities dealers.

In most cases, the market value of the collateral is set above the loan amount when the contract is negotiated. This difference is labeled the *margin*. If, for example, City National pledged $1.1 million of U.S. government securities against its $1 million borrowing, the margin equals $100,000. Positive margin protects the lender from potential decreases in collateral value if interest rates increase. This protection makes RPs less risky compared to unsecured federal funds transactions and thus RP rates fall below federal funds rates for similar-maturity contracts.

Such collateral proved inadequate in 1982, when two government securities dealers, Drysdale Government Securities and Lombard-Wall Inc., were forced into bankruptcy when they could not pay accrued interest owed on heavy borrowings via RPs. When the loans came due, neither firm could pay the accrued interest on the government securities they had borrowed. As a result, Chase Manhattan Bank and Manufacturers Hanover took losses from Drysdale alone equal to $285 million and $21 million, respectively. While both banks initially disclaimed liability, they eventually made good on losses their customers otherwise would have incurred because the banks arranged the RP transactions.

In 1985 E.S.M. Group Inc. similarly collapsed after suffering losses trading RPs, bringing about the failure of Home State Savings in Ohio and the closing of over 70 thrifts that faced losses from a massive run on deposits. Deposits at Home State and the thrifts were privately insured, but the insurance pool was insufficient to meet payments obligations. The closed thrifts ultimately reopened with federal deposit insurance coverage.[9]

---

[9]A series of articles from "Repurchase Agreements: Taking a Closer Look at Safety" (Federal Reserve Bank of Atlanta, September 1985) discuss the structure of the RP market and factors influencing credit and interest rate risk.

These failures increased regulatory scrutiny of the RP market and focused attention on the true legal status of a repo. In particular, creditors of Drysdale and Lombard-Wall who held RP collateral sold the securities. If, in fact, RPs are secured loans, bankruptcy law prohibits creditors from selling any assets owned by the failed firms. If RPs are separate contracts to sell and repurchase securities, creditors can liquidate the securities. Technically, the securities are the lender's because the borrower failed to repurchase them. Court rulings appear to side with the creditors, allowing them to liquidate security holdings, although the issue is still unresolved.

Eurodollar Liabilities

Most large U.S. commercial banks compete aggressively in international markets. They borrow from and extend credit to foreign-based individuals, corporations, and governments. In recent years international financial markets and multinational businesses have become increasingly sophisticated to the point where bank customers go overseas for cheaper financing and feel unfettered by national boundaries.

Transactions in short-term international markets take place in the Eurocurrency market. The term *Eurocurrency* refers to a financial claim denominated in a currency other than that of the country where the issuing institution is located. The most important Eurocurrency is the *Eurodollar,* a dollar-denominated financial claim at a bank outside the United States. The banks may be foreign-owned or foreign branches of U.S. banks. The Eurodollar market comprises both loans and deposits, each with different characteristics and participants.

Eurodollar deposits are dollar-denominated deposits in banks outside the United States. They are virtually identical to time deposits issued directly by domestic banks, except for the country of issue. In all cases, dollar deposits at U.S. banks support the creation of a Eurodollar deposit. These base deposits never physically leave the United States, only the ownership does. Maturities range from call to 5 years, and most deposits are traded in denominations of $1 million or more. Eurodollar CDs, the counterpart of domestic CDs, are the most popular Eurodollar deposit. They carry short-term maturities, typically 3 to 6 months, and can be traded in the secondary market prior to maturity. While most Eurodollar CDs pay fixed rates, floating-rate instruments are becoming increasingly popular. Eurodollar rates are quoted on an interest-bearing basis, assuming a 360-day year. Eurodollar deposit rates must be competitive with rates on comparable maturity instruments, such as federal funds and jumbo CDs.[10] Otherwise, the deposits would not attract funds away from U.S.-based instruments.

Eurodollar depositors include individuals, businesses, and governments from around the world. Many transactions, in fact, are merely interbank deposits. Exhibit 11.7 characterizes the origination of Eurodollar deposits and the eventual path to a Eurodollar loan. It summarizes activities of four groups and encompasses three stages of transactions. In the first stage, a U.S. manufacturing corporation based in New York opens a Eurodollar deposit at the Bank of England in London and effectively transfers

---

[10]Goodfriend, 1981, discusses these relationships and general Eurodollar characteristics in detail.

Exhibit 11.7 The Origin and Expansion of Eurodollar Deposits

Stage I: U.S. manufacturer opens $10 million Eurodollar account at Bank of England, London.
Stage II: Bank of England, London, opens Eurodollar account at U.S. Money Center Bank, London.
Stage III: U.S. Money Center Bank, London, extends $10 million Eurodollar loan to British corporation in London.

	U.S. Manufacturer, New York		U.S. Money Center Bank New York		U.S. Money Center Bank, London		Bank of England, London		British Corp., London	
	ΔASSETS	ΔLIABILITIES	ΔASSETS	ΔLIABILITIES	ΔASSETS	ΔLIABILITIES	ΔASSETS	ΔLIABILITIES	ΔASSETS	ΔLIABILITIES
Stage I:	Demand deposits due from MCB-NY −$10 million; Eurodollar deposit due from BE-L +$10 million			Demand deposits due to U.S. manuf.-NY −$10 million; Demand deposit due to BE-L +$10 million			Demand deposit due from MCB-NY +$10 million	Eurodollar deposit due to U.S. manuf.-NY +$10 million		
Stage II:				Demand deposit due to BE-L −$10 million; Demand deposit due to MCB-L +$10 million	Demand deposit due from MCB-NY +$10 million	Eurodollar deposit due to BE-L +$10 million	Demand deposit due from MCB-NY −$10 million; Eurodollar deposit due from MCB-L +$10 million			
Stage III:				Demand deposit due to MCB-L −$10 million; Demand deposit due to British corp. +$10 million	Demand deposit due from MCB-NY −$10 million; Eurodollar loan to British corp. +$10 million				Demand deposit due from MCB-NY +$10 million	Eurodollar loan from MCB-L +$10 million

ownership of a demand balance held at a U.S. Money Center Bank in New York. The terms of the Eurodollar deposit are negotiated as discussed above. At the end of this transaction, $10 million in Eurodollar deposits has been created. The amount of demand deposits at U.S. banks, however, is unchanged. Only the ownership has changed, from the U.S. manufacturer to the Bank of England.

During Stage II, the Bank of England redeposits the dollars with the U.S. Money Center Bank's London office. Ownership of the original demand balance at the New York bank again changes, but the deposit does not physically leave the United States. Another $10 million in Eurodollar deposits has been created with no change in total demand deposits at U.S. banks.

Stage III documents a Eurodollar loan made to a British corporation such that the foreign firm ultimately owns the original demand deposit. This intermediation among banks permits the multiple expansion of Eurodollar deposits based on a fixed demand deposit at a U.S. bank. There are no reserve requirements on Eurodollar deposits, and a bank will move the entire balance as long as it can earn a profitable spread. The base rate paid on interbank deposits (stage II) is termed the London Interbank Offer Rate (LIBOR). Additional interbank deposits are typically made at spreads of 0.125 to 0.250 percent. Thus if the initial deposit at the Bank of England paid 8 percent, the Bank of England would require at least 8.125 percent on its redeposit. The spread on a Eurodollar loan to the ultimate borrower is considerably greater.

Individual Retirement Accounts

Individual retirement accounts (IRAs) are savings plans for wage-earners and their spouses. The plans encompass many types of savings vehicles with varied maturities, interest rates, and other earnings features. Individuals can choose between different financial services companies and many different products. Commercial banks, thrift institutions, brokerage houses, and insurance companies dominate IRA investments. Investor options range from small time deposits and MMDAs at banks and savings and loans to common stocks, zero coupon Treasury securities, and shares in limited real estate partnerships offered by brokerages.

The primary attraction of IRAs is their tax benefits. Each wage-earner can invest up to $2,000 of earned income annually in an IRA. Prior to 1987, the principal contribution was tax-deductible, and any accumulated earnings in the account were tax-deferred until withdrawn. The Tax Reform Act of 1986 removed the tax-deductibility of contributions for individuals already covered by qualified pension plans if they earned enough income.[11] Funds withdrawn before age 59½ are subject to a 10 percent Internal Revenue Service penalty. Investors can change investments prior to this age but must pay another penalty if the change does not occur when the underlying savings vehicle matures. These features make IRAs an attractive source of long-term

---

[11]If a wage-earner's spouse has no earned income, a couple can contribute a combined $2,250 in two separate IRAs. Prior to January 1982, individuals covered by qualified business or government retirement plans were prohibited from opening IRAs. The Tax Reform Act of 1986 eliminated the deduction for making a contribution if couples filing jointly reported adjusted gross income of at least $40,000 ($25,000 for singles) and were covered by a pension plan. Interest income from an IRA investment remains exempt until withdrawn.

funds for commercial banks and other issuers that can be used to balance the rate sensitivity of longer-term assets. Customers opening accounts are less likely to move them as long as the bank pays competitive rates.

Commercial banks and thrifts offer IRA products related to small time deposits with fixed maturities and MMDAs. These deposits are federally insured, which appeals to many individuals. Money market deposit accounts are the most rate sensitive, as banks change rates at least every 30 days. Banks can typically induce customers to lengthen deposit maturities by paying higher rates on longer-term instruments. Small CDs carrying variable rates tied to external indexes have become increasingly popular with the greater uncertainty over future interest rate movements.

RISK CHARACTERISTICS

Banks face two fundamental problems in managing their liabilities: uncertainty over what rates they must pay to retain and attract funds and uncertainty over the likelihood that customers will withdraw their money regardless of rates. The basic fear is that they will be vulnerable to a liquidity crisis arising from unanticipated deposit withdrawals. Banks must have the capacity to borrow in financial markets to replace deposit outflows and remain solvent. Liquidity problems have grown with the increased reliance on "hot money" and brokered deposits. When a bank is perceived to have asset quality problems, customers with uninsured balances move their deposits. The problem bank must then pay substantial premiums to attract replacement funds or rely on regulatory agencies to extend emergency credit.

During the years that deposit rates were regulated and banks paid the maximum rates allowed, deposits were relatively stable and liquidity was less of a problem. Interest rate deregulation and bank competition have since increased depositors' rate awareness so that many individuals and firms move funds to institutions paying the highest rates. Customer loyalty is closely tied to deposit size and the quality of bank service. Small-balance depositors are generally more loyal than large-balance depositors, especially if they receive consistently good service. All customers are more loyal if they purchase a bundle of credit, deposit, and other services.

Liquidity risk associated with a bank's deposit base is a function of many factors, including the number of depositors, average size of accounts, location of the depositor, and specific maturity and rate characteristics of each account. These features are customer-driven, and banks cannot dictate the terms of deposit contracts. But banks can monitor potential deposit outflows if they are aware of seasonal patterns in outstanding balances and the timing of large transactions such as payroll draws on commercial accounts and maturing large-balance CDs. They can periodically contact large depositors to provide rate quotes and assess the probability of the customer reinvesting the funds.

Equally important is the interest elasticity of customer demand for each funding source. How much can market interest rates change before the bank experiences deposit outflows? If the bank raises its rates, how many new funds will it attract?[12]

---

[12]Methods for estimating interest elasticities are discussed in Chapter 15.

Ideally, a bank would like to lower its customers' rate sensitivity. It can do so by packaging deposit products with other services or privileges so that withdrawals deprive the customer of all services or by developing personal relationships with depositors. In this way management can determine the base funding level (core deposit base) below which outstanding balances never fall.

Most banks try to build a liquidity buffer into their deposit base. Small banks with limited access to national financial markets promote customer service to expand core deposits and reduce liability interest elasticity. Many large banks periodically borrow more funds than they need to guarantee access to deposit sources. Northern Trust Corp. of Chicago, for example, routinely borrows in the Eurodollar market to ensure open access if a crisis ever arises.[13] When it does not need the funds, it still borrows and simply invests in short-term loans. The amount of liquidity available to large banks via purchased funds can be approximated by comparing a bank's current borrowings to its maximum debt outstanding over the previous year.

BORROWING FROM THE FEDERAL RESERVE

Federal Reserve Banks are authorized to make loans to depository institutions to help them meet reserve requirements. Before 1980, only commercial banks that were members of the Federal Reserve System could borrow under normal circumstances. DIDMCA opened borrowing to any depository institution that offers transactions accounts subject to reserve requirements. The borrowing facility is called the *discount window*. All Federal Reserve Banks charge a fixed rate, known as the discount rate, which is formally set by the district Federal Reserve Banks and approved by the Board of Governors. In practice, the Board determines when rate changes are necessary and requests approval from district representatives.

The Federal Reserve establishes conditions and procedures for borrowing. Banks must apply and provide acceptable collateral before a loan is granted. Eligible collateral includes U.S. government securities, bankers acceptances, and qualifying short-term commercial or government paper. Frequent borrowers typically use U.S. Treasury securities already held in bookkeeping form at Federal Reserve Banks. Federal Reserve Regulation A states that borrowing is a privilege and banks should view the Federal Reserve as a lender of last resort. Banks consequently borrow to meet temporary reserve deficiencies, not to obtain permanent financing.

Discount window loans directly increase a member bank's reserve assets. Exhibit 11.8 documents a $2 million transaction. Advances are loans secured by qualifying collateral. Discounts refer to member banks temporarily selling eligible loans to the Federal Reserve. The Federal Reserve agrees to return the loan to the bank at maturity. The discount rate charged determines the interest payment in both cases and is set by the Federal Reserve in light of current economic conditions. Frequently, the discount rate is below the current federal funds rate. The Federal Reserve prohibits

---

[13]Bailey, 1984, documents several banks' strategies in dealing with potential liquidity problems.

Exhibit 11.8 Discount Window Borrowing

Member Bank		Federal Reserve Bank	
ΔASSETS	ΔLIABILITIES	ΔASSETS	ΔLIABILITIES
Deposit held at Federal Reserve bank $2 million	Borrowing from Federal Reserve bank $2 million	Discounts and advances $2 million	Deposits owed Member bank $2 million

arbitrage by not allowing banks to sell federal funds and borrow at the discount window simultaneously.

Federal Reserve policies distinguish among three types of loans. The first, short-term adjustment loans, are made to banks experiencing unexpected deposit outflows or overdrafts caused by computer problems. Large banks frequently use adjustment credit and typically borrow for 1-day periods. Small banks are also permitted to borrow under a seasonal borrowing privilege if they can demonstrate that they experience systematic and predictable deposit withdrawals or new loan demand. Banks serving agricultural or resort communities often qualify. The needs must persist for at least 8 weeks, so seasonal loans have considerably longer maturities. The final loan type, extended credit, receives the most attention but is the least prevalent. These loans are granted to banks that are experiencing more permanent deposit outflows typically associated with a run on the bank. In July 1984, for example, the Federal Reserve extended $4 billion in credit to Continental Illinois of Chicago to offset deposit losses of customers fearful that the bank was about to fail.

Each Federal Reserve Bank employs a discount officer who has the authority to accept or reject borrowing requests. If a bank borrows infrequently, the request is normally granted. The officer restricts overuse of the discount window either by a discreet telephone call to senior management indicating that the request will be denied or by raising the indirect costs of the loan. Indirect costs include delays in processing paperwork and increased uncertainty over future access to borrowings. As such, many small banks are reluctant to borrow without a crisis. Large banks with other financing alternatives use the discount window more aggressively, attempting to borrow as much as possible when the discount rate is low. Large banks thus account for the weekly fluctuations in discount window borrowing.

Exhibit 11.9 lists the relative monthly magnitudes for extended and seasonal discount window loans from 1982 to 1990. Short-term adjustment borrowing appears in Exhibit 11.10. The level of adjustment borrowing measures Federal Reserve pressure on bank reserves through open market operations. When the Federal Reserve contracts reserves, banks increase their borrowing. Changes in adjustment borrowing, which typically dominates seasonal and extended credit, are especially indicative of tight or easy money. However, extended credit rises every time the Federal Reserve assists large banks such as First National Bank in Midland (1983), Continental Illinois (1984), First Oklahoma (1985), First RepublicBank (1987 to 1988), and MCorp (1988 to 1989).

Exhibit 11.9 Borrowring at Federal Reserve Banks: Monthly, 1982–1990 (Millions of Dollars)

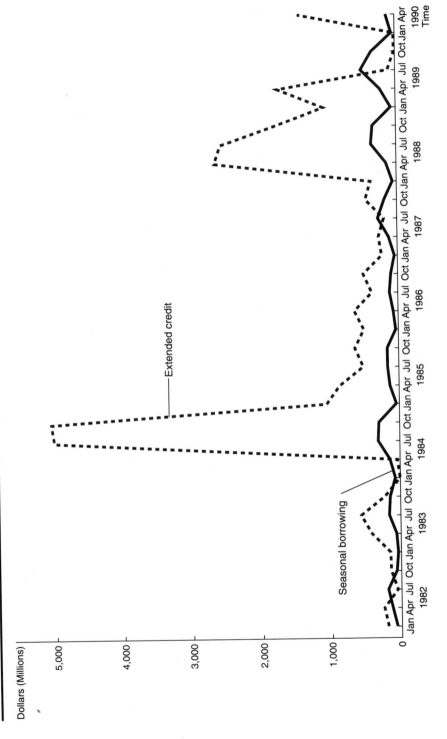

Exhibit 11.10   The Relationship between Federal Reserve Bank Adjustment Borrowing and the Spread between the Federal Funds Rate and Discount Rate

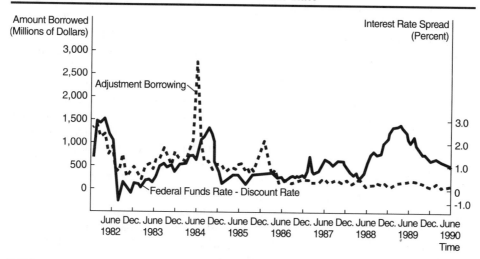

Extended credit falls as the loans are repaid after each crisis is resolved. Seasonal credit normally rises in line with loan demand at agriculture banks, during spring and summer, then declines as the loans are repaid.

Both seasonal and extended credit are relatively interest-inelastic because banks need the financing regardless of interest rate levels. Adjustment credit, in contrast, varies directly with the spread between the federal funds and discount rates. When the federal funds rate exceeds the discount rate, discount borrowing rises because it is less costly. The wider the spread, the greater is adjustment borrowing (see Exhibit 11.10). The apparent inverse relationship from April to June in 1984 reflects adjustment loans that were effectively extended credit to troubled banks. When the spread is negative, bank borrowing is negligible. This relationship leads many analysts to recommend a penalty discount rate policy, in which the Federal Reserve automatically sets the discount rate at a fixed premium over the federal funds rate. Discount window borrowing would never be less expensive than federal funds, and borrowings would be limited to crises. Historically, the Fed subsidized seasonal borrowing by charging small banks the discount rate rather than a marked rate. This will change in 1992 when the Fed will charge a rate comparable to the average federal funds rate and thereby eliminate the interest rate advantage from borrowing at the Fed on seasonal credits.

FEDERAL DEPOSIT INSURANCE

The Banking Act of 1933 established the FDIC and authorized federal insurance for bank deposits up to $2,500. The Act followed 3 years in which more than 5,000 banks failed and investors lost confidence in the country's financial system. The initial objective of insurance was to prevent liquidity crises caused by large-scale deposit withdrawals. With insurance, depositors' funds were safe, even if the bank failed. The Federal Savings and Loan Insurance Corporation (FSLIC) was established in 1934 to replicate federal assistance for savings and loan associations.[14] The insurance funds were funded via premiums paid by member banks with payouts mandated when banks failed and regulators paid insured depositors. The true backing, however, was the borrowing and taxing authority of the federal government. Until 1980, deposit insurance worked well as there were few depositor runs on federally insured banks and bank failures were negligible.

While federal deposit insurance facilitated stability in the U.S. financial system throughout its early history, it precipitated many of the problems experienced during and after the 1980s. So many savings and loans failed or were taken over by solvent firms with federal assistance in the 1980s that the FSLIC fund went bankrupt. Data on failed commercial banks in Exhibit 11.11 reveal similar problems for the FDIC fund. From 1941 through 1980 fewer than 10 banks failed per year, on average. Thus premium receipts and investment income exceeded annual payouts. During the 1980s, however, failures rose sharply, exceeding 100 in each year since 1985. This put pressure on the FDIC by slowly depleting the reserve fund. The bottom part of Exhibit 11.11 compares insurance funds losses from 1977 through 1990 with depositor losses in the years prior to the Depression.

As indicated in Chapter 2, the Financial Institution Reform, Recovery, and Enforcement Act of 1989 (FIRREA) authorized the issuance of bonds to finance the bailout of the FSLIC and provide resources to close problem thrifts. The Act also created two new insurance funds, the Savings Association Insurance Fund (SAIF) and the Bank Insurance Fund (BIF), to replace the old funds with both controlled by the FDIC. In subsequent years the FDIC raised deposit insurance premiums to keep pace with losses from closing failed institutions.

Problems with Deposit Insurance as Historically Structured

The deposit insurance funds were always viewed as providing basic insurance coverage. Yet there were three fundamental problems with the pricing of deposit insurance. First, premium levels were not sufficient to cover potential payouts. The FDIC and FSLIC were initially expected to establish reserves amounting to 5 percent of covered deposits funded by premiums. Unfortunately, actual reserves never exceeded 2 percent of insured deposits as Congress kept increasing coverage while insurance premiums remained constant. For example, the standard insurance premium was a flat 1/12 of 1 percent of insured deposits. Yet deposit insurance coverage slowly increased from

---

[14]The National Credit Union Share Insurance Fund (NCUSIF) insures credit unions.

Exhibit 11.11 Bank Closing and Deposit Insurance Losses

Years	Average Number of Closings per Year		Average Deposits in Closed Banks (Millions)
	All Banks	Insured Banks	Insured Banks
1934-1940	64.2	51.1	62.3
1941-1950	7.3	6.1	9.9
1951-1960	4.3	2.8	10.5
1961-1970	6.3	5.0	33.5
1971-1980	8.3	7.9	529.1
1981-1985	59.8	59.8	6,023.4
1986	138	138	6,471.1
1987	184	184	6,281.5
1988	200	200	37,200
1989	206	206	25,700
1990	169	169	28,500

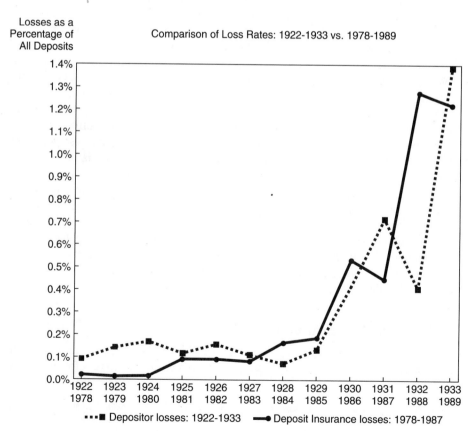

Comparison of Loss Rates: 1922-1933 vs. 1978-1989

Losses as a Percentage of All Deposits

•••■ Depositor losses: 1922-1933   ━●━ Deposit Insurance losses: 1978-1987

$15,000 per account per institution in 1966 to $20,000 in 1969, $40,000 in 1974, and $100,000 in 1980. Even then customers could obtain multiple account coverage at any single institution by carefully structuring ownership of each account. (See Contemporary Issues: The Extent of Deposit Insurance Coverage.) The high rate of failures during the 1980s and depletion of the insurance funds demonstrate that premiums were inadequate.

The second problem is that premiums were not assessed against all of a bank's insured liabilities. There were many liabilities that the federal government effectively guaranteed or for which the holders had a prior claim on bank assets that should have required insurance premiums. For example, insured deposits consisted only of domestic deposits while foreign deposits were exempt. Why? In numerous cases federal regulators arranged for buyers to take over large failing banks rather than close them, reasoning that a large bank failure would severely disrupt the smooth functioning of financial markets. This led to a *too big to fail* doctrine toward large banks. As such, any creditor, domestic or foreign, of a large bank in practice received 100 percent insurance coverage regardless of the size or type of liability. At the same time, the regulators were much more willing to let smaller banks fail and force their uninsured depositors and other creditors to take losses. If all of the larger banks' liabilities were effectively covered by federal insurance, the firm should have paid insurance premiums on all liabilities. The argument for not charging premiums against foreign deposits is that large U.S. banks would presumably be less competitive with foreign banks.

Finally, deposit insurance ignored the riskiness of a bank's operations, which represents the critical factor that lead to failure. Thus two banks with equal amounts of domestic deposits paid the same insurance premium, even though one invested heavily in risky loans and had no uninsured deposits while the other owned only U.S. government securities and just 50 percent of its deposits were fully insured. This created a *moral hazard* problem whereby bank managers had an incentive to increase risk. Suppose that a bank had a large portfolio of problem assets that was generating little revenue. Managers could use deposit insurance to access funds via brokered CDs in $100,000 blocks. Buyers of the CDs were not concerned about the quality of the underlying bank because their funds were fully insured. The bank's managers were able to use these funds to speculate on risky projects, in essence betting the bank. If the risky investments succeeded, managers could use the returns to pay the depositors and offset the lack of revenue from the problem assets. In fact, if the bank obtained enough deposits, it could make enough loans to swamp the problem assets. If the risky investments went bankrupt, the bank would fail but the deposit insurance fund would have to pay creditors.[15]

Handling Problem Institutions

Since 1980 over 800 banks and savings and loans have failed. This figure understates the true magnitude of recent difficulties, as regulators arranged mergers for many large

---

[15]This represents a classic principal/agent problem in finance. The intent of bank regulation and periodic examination is to limit bank risk-taking and reduce the incentives to abuse deposit insurance.

The Extent of Deposit Insurance Coverage

It pays to understand deposit insurance. Do you? As a test, answer the following questions. Both banks carry deposit insurance.

1. You have $100,000 in a CD at First National Bank, and another $100,000 in a CD at First State Bank. Are both deposits fully insured?

2. Your parents are concerned about their health and managing their resources if one becomes incapacitated. They own two $75,000 CDs at First National Bank jointly. Are both deposits fully insured?

3. Your grandfather has a joint account with your father for $60,000, another joint account with your sister for $50,000, and another joint account with you for $50,000, all at First State Bank. Are all deposits fully insured?

4. You own a $100,000 CD from First State Bank and your grandmother opened a trust account in your name for another $100,000. Are both accounts fully insured?

5. You own a $94,000 CD at First National Bank. At the time the bank fails, you are owed the $94,000 plus $9,000 in interest. How much will you be paid from deposit insurance?

The Rules

Account balances held by the same individual in his or her name are insured up to $100,000, including both principal and interest, per institution. The $100,000 coverage extends to total deposit balances summing across all types of accounts.

Joint accounts held by the same individuals are combined to determine insurance coverage, with $100,000 maximum coverage. It does not matter whether the underlying deposit accounts differ in form or if the individuals list their names in different orders. The insurance funds assume equal ownership among joint owners. Suppose that two parents own a $100,000 account jointly, another $90,000 jointly with a daughter, and another $90,000 jointly with a son. With equal ownership, the father and mother own $110,000 each for insurance purposes so that $10,000 is not insured for each. Each child's $30,000 balance is fully insured.

With trust accounts, each account is insured separately for each beneficiary and each owner. Thus two parents with two children can establish $400,000 in trust balances that are fully insured. Each parent sets up a $100,000 trust in his or her name for each child.

Individual retirement accounts (IRAs) and Keogh accounts are treated separately for deposit insurance purposes.

---

banks during this span and let insolvent firms continue to operate. When an insured bank fails, the FDIC has two options. Under the *payout option*, it immediately pays depositors the full amount of their insured funds. The FDIC assumes the depositors' claims and becomes a general creditor of the bank. It also serves as receiver and liquidates the failed bank's assets, from which it pays uninsured deposit holders and other creditors. Payments frequently total 60 to 80 percent of the claim and can be delayed several years because of lawsuits.

Under the *purchase and assumption option*, the FDIC negotiates a merger of the failed bank with a solvent firm. The acquiring bank assumes all deposits and other nonsubordinated liabilities. It uses these funds to purchase selected assets of the failed bank, including fixed assets, government securities, and performing loans. It also receives or pays an amount of cash, less the purchase premium, equal to the amount necessary for the acquired assets to equal the assumed liabilities. The FDIC owns all rejected assets, typically problem loans with limited repayment prospects. In this case, uninsured depositors and other creditors lose nothing. Instead, they receive claims on the new bank's assets equal to their prior claims on the failed bank. Shareholders lose the full amount of their investment under both options.

During the mid-1980s, federal regulators employed two additional procedures. The first was a *deposit transfer* in which regulators transferred all insured deposits plus a fraction less than 100 percent of uninsured deposits of a failing bank to an acquiring bank. The fraction of insured deposits that was transferred was based on the regulators' assessment of what they would collect from the failing bank's assets, and thus what the likely payout to uninsured creditors would equal. In the second, the regulators created a *bridge bank* to temporarily assume control of and manage a failed bank's assets until a buyer could be found. The expectation was twofold; that the value of the bridge bank would increase during the time of the initial closing and final takeover by a solvent bank, and that the process would allow the regulators to force uninsured creditors of bank holding companies to take losses. The latter would presumably force these creditors to carefully scrutinize their investments in problem institutions and thus impose market discipline in the pricing of bank stocks and bonds prior to failure. The bridge bank concept was used in the closing of both First RepublicBank Corp. and MCorp. in Texas during 1988 and 1989, which were eventually taken over by NCNB and Bank One, respectively. (See Contemporary Issues: Regulatory Policy Toward Large Bank Failures.)

The FDIC chooses the option that minimizes costs to the insurance fund. In virtually all cases, FDIC payouts involve small banks that, because of location or limited deposit base, are not attractive to investors. Large bank failures are normally handled via purchase and assumption. This option costs less because the acquirer pays a premium for the "going concern" value of the bank that disappears under a payout.

Criticisms of Recent Policies

When the number of failures was small, bank regulators were not concerned about deposit insurance. The large number of thrift and bank failures during the 1980s and the incredible cost of bailing out the insurance funds focused considerable attention on how regulators handle failures and how to restructure the insurance system. Different proposals to modify the insurance system are based on three fundamental criticisms of regulatory policy: (1) the insurance funds are inadequate to cover potential payouts; (2) regulators discriminate between problem banks, selectively allowing only certain firms to fail; and (3) deposit insurance encourages banks to take excessive risk at limited cost to the bank.

The insurance funds are clearly inadequate to cover possible failure costs. Because fund balances fall far short of the value of insured deposits, a deposit run on the entire banking system would generate losses greater than the combined reserve. But this scenario ignores the true purpose of insurance—to strengthen public confidence in the safety of financial institution deposits, not to provide a reserve for losses. As with the Social Security system, the term *insurance* is a misnomer, compounded by banks paying "insurance premiums." Deposit insurance premiums are essentially fees paid

Regulatory Policy Toward Large Bank Failures

In July 1988, bank regulators declared First RepublicBank Corp. of Texas insolvent and turned over management of its subsidiary banks to NCNB. In contrast to prior failures of large bank holding companies, the terms of closing wiped out the claims of all stockholders and left bondholders to fight with other creditors for the remains of the holding company. Regulators used a bridge bank to handle the closing, which fostered numerous lawsuits claiming that the rights of investors in First RepublicBank were violated.

Consider the following sequence of events.

March 17, 1988: The FDIC lent $1 billion to First RepublicBank Corp. to help meet deposit outflows. This was a 6-month loan secured by stock in each of First RepublicBank's subsidiary banks.

July 29, 1988: The FDIC announced that it would not renew the 6-month loan when it came due in September. As prearranged, the Federal Reserve advised First RepublicBank that it would refuse to lend any additional funds via the discount window and the bank would have to repay the $3.5 billion it owed. Because First Republic-Bank could not pay, the Comptroller of the Currency declared that the bank had formally failed. The FDIC then called its $1 billion loan. When First RepublicBank Corp. did not pay, the FDIC charged the amount of each

subsidiary bank's guarantee against its capital, which then made each subsidiary bank insolvent.

July 29, 1988: The FDIC created a bridge bank owned jointly with NCNB that took over and managed the failed subsidiary banks. NCNB paid approximately $200 million for 20 percent ownership with the right to buy the remaining 80 percent over the next 5 years. NCNB retained the right to put problem loans back to the FDIC so that its risk was lowered, and received enough federal tax benefits to pay for the entire bridge bank in a few years.

October 15, 1988: In a bankruptcy filing, First RepublicBank Corp. indicated that it had $3.5 billion in liabilities and just $300,000 in assets.

In March 1989 bank regulators failed several subsidiary banks of MCorp., another large Texas bank holding company. While the events followed the pattern with First RepublicBank Corp., the regulators were essentially held hostage by MCorp.'s managers. Prior to the failures, MCorp.'s problems were well known. Regulators had strongly encouraged the holding company to downstream $400 million in funds to its subsidiary banks to shore up their capital. MCorp.'s management realized that once it made the transfer the regulators would fail the firm and they would lose any leverage

---

for a government guarantee of bank deposits. When the soundness of the banking system is threatened, the Federal Reserve System uses its lending powers to prevent system-wide deposit runs. For example, the Federal Reserve extended Continental Illinois over $4 billion in credit when the bank's liquidity problems surfaced in 1984. The insurance fund would have been quickly depleted had other banks failed as well. Still, efforts to increase insurance premiums place an increasing burden on healthy banking institutions.

The second criticism is far more valid. As indicated earlier, the FDIC has the option of paying insured depositors or merging failed banks with solvent ones. A third, unofficial option is to prop up a failing firm with federal capital. In the case of a merger or capital injection, regulators effectively extend deposit insurance to all liabilities of

CONTEMPORARY ISSUES *(Continued)*

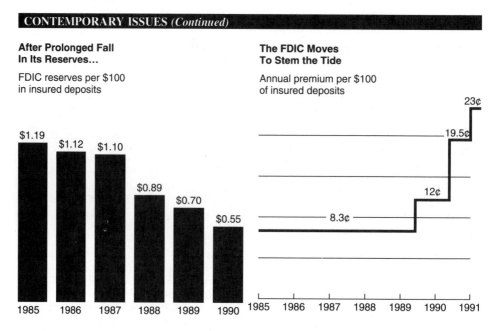

**After Prolonged Fall
In Its Reserves...**

FDIC reserves per $100
in insured deposits

**The FDIC Moves
To Stem the Tide**

Annual premium per $100
of insured deposits

they had in negotiating their own failure resolution plan. The holding company thus did not transfer the $400 million. Eventually, the regulators called loans to the holding company's lead bank and charged the losses when it could not pay to MCorp.'s subsidiaries based on their federal funds loans to the lead bank and other interbank deposits. The 20 subsidiaries with losses in excess of their capital subsequently failed and were taken over by the FDIC. Again the FDIC created a bridge bank that was soon sold to Bank One.

Issues related to this procedure for failing bank holding companies have not yet been fully resolved. Bondholders and other creditors have sued claiming that the regulators discriminated against the bank's creditors and effectively manufactured the failures of solvent subsidiary banks. As part of FIRREA, Congress in turn instituted a system of cross-guarantees whereby subsidiaries of bank holding companies must effectively guarantee the performance of all other subsidiaries.

---

a failed bank. In practice, the regulators let smaller banks fail while injecting capital into larger banks such as Continental Illinois. The FDIC claims that liquidating large banks would disrupt the worldwide financial system. The impact, however, is discriminatory in that two banks of different size with similar problems are treated differently.

The third criticism is similarly true. Deposit insurance is assessed at a flat rate and does not vary with the riskiness of the bank's assets. Insured depositors are largely insensitive to a bank's operating policies because they rely on the government for protection. The federal government thus subsidizes banks because deposit insurance allows banks to pay interest rates below those required to compensate depositors for actual default risk assumed in their investments. Clearly, banks would pay higher rates if deposit insurance were eliminated. Banks can acquire risky assets without affecting borrowing costs on insured deposits. Banks do pay higher rates to attract uninsured deposits, such as large banks that pay tiered CD rates associated with the perceived riskiness of each bank's portfolio.

In response to these criticisms, many proposals have been offered to protect the viability of the insurance funds and ensure the safety and soundness of the banking system. Among the most prominent are

1. Early intervention: Allow the regulators to close a problem institution once its capital falls below some minimum fraction of risk assets.

2. Limit immediate payouts to all large depositors in failed institutions to some fraction on the dollar, regardless of whether the payout or purchase and assumption option is used.

3. Limit insurance coverage to $100,000 per depositor, and not per insured account.

4. Lower deposit insurance coverage to $40,000 per depositor or per insured account.

5. Charge risk-adjusted insurance premiums such that banks with riskier operations pay higher deposit insurance rates.

6. Narrow bank: Only insure deposits that are used to support government-guaranteed assets or risk-free assets. All other liabilities would need to be insured privately, if at all.

7. Privatize deposit insurance. Premiums would be based on a bank's overall risk profile as determined by private insurance companies.

The motivation behind each proposal is obvious. Each proposal would presumably impose market discipline on institutional risk-taking. Early closings would force managers to monitor risks more closely and either raise new capital when they approach the minimums or hedge the bank's risk. Any limits on deposit insurance coverage or payouts at failure would force creditors to closely monitor their investments and move their balances from high-risk banks because they share in losses. Brokers currently funnel deposits in $100,000 increments throughout the country to the highest bidders. Banks and savings and loans can obtain these fully-insured funds at subsidized rates to finance whatever speculative ventures they choose. Limits on the amounts of brokered deposits would reduce the funds available for high-growth, highly speculative investments. The last three proposals suggest that the insurance system should be put on a sound financial basis by charging market-determined premiums. In fact, deposit insurance premiums have increased to 23 cents per $100 of deposits (see Contemporary Issues), but this is still insufficient given projected payouts.

The primary weakness of these proposals is that they require bank customers to perform a detailed analysis of each bank's riskiness. Particularly hurt would be smaller institutions where customers typically do not evaluate performance measures but rely on management. Deposits would likely flow to large firms that analysts rate as low risk. Risk-adjusted premiums would also raise borrowing costs for risky banks that charge higher insurance costs to depositors, making them less competitive and indirectly reducing the attractiveness of risky investments. In practice, there is no easy method to measure bank risk accurately. Current failure prediction models are only partially successful in identifying problem banks.[16] What is needed is the consistent application of regulatory review with the tools already available to the regulators.

The lack of a consistent plan to handle continued bank failures has forced regulators to control banking risk by other means and to consider other options. One alternative is to increase regulatory capital requirements. If banks are forced to operate with more equity capital, their financial risk will decrease and there will be fewer failed banks. Chapter 12 evaluates the structure and role of bank capital.

Lifeline Accounts

The dramatic rise in service charges has been criticized by consumer groups, who argue that price increases are not justified by increases in costs and that most pricing schemes make even minimal banking services too costly for low-income customers. Several state legislatures responded by passing laws requiring lifeline banking services. In October 1984, Massachusetts implemented a law prohibiting service charges for individuals over 65 and under 18. California has considered a law that requires financial institutions to offer free services to any individuals with an annual income under $11,000, including a checking account with ten checks per month, a maximum 2-day hold on local checks, and a $5-per-day insufficient funds charge for returned checks. Savings accounts with balances below $300 would be exempt from charges.

SUMMARY

This chapter focuses on characteristics of various bank liabilities. Small denomination instruments exhibit fundamentally different risk/return features compared with those of large-denomination liabilities. In both cases, price competition is considerably more important today than in previous years. The chapter introduces the specific features of immediately available funds, Eurodollars, and borrowings from Federal Reserve Banks as sources of funds. Finally, the role of deposit insurance and problems associated with maintaining the viability of the FDIC and FSLIC insurance funds with the recent growth in failures is analyzed.

---

[16]David Cates, president of Cates Consulting Analysts, says that his firm uses no less than 70 ratios when analyzing bank performance (Cates, 1984). The FDIC's proposed risk assessment model is based on three ratios. Such a system will likely produce highly distorted risk classifications.

Questions

Types of Liabilities and Trends

1. Banks compete for liabilities primarily by offering the best possible interest rates. However there are other features of liabilities which banks can change to make them more attractive to various types of depositors. What are some of these other variables?

2. Rank the following types of bank liabilities according to their level of risk for the bank, and identify the types of risks associated with each. Then rank them according to their cost to the bank. Finance theory says that accepting higher risk provides a higher return. Is that true for banks and their solicitation of liability deposits?

    Checking accounts
    NOW accounts
    Savings accounts
    CDs, small
    CDs, large
    Federal funds purchased
    Repos
    Eurodollar liabilities

3. If the liability side of the balance sheet were simplified to these basic accounts, roughly what percent of a bank's funds would come from each category? First examine a large bank, then a small bank. Answer to the nearest whole percent.

    Liabilities
    Core deposits
    Hot deposits
    Fed funds and other borrowings
    Notes, bonds, other, equity
    What is the trend in each of these accounts for each size bank?

4. Bank depositors have always wanted higher rates on their savings. In the good old days, back in the 1960s, banks could ignore the demands, but now they can't. What has changed to cause these demands to be met?

5. Banks are often categorized by size—large or small—but on other occasions banks are categorized by customer type, such as retail or wholesale. Usually retail banks would be of which size? In discussing checking accounts, what would be the difference between a retail and wholesale bank? In savings accounts?

Small Denomination Liabilities

6. What determines whether a transaction account is a demand deposit, a NOW account, or a MMDA?

7. What variables can a bank manipulate to make one checking account look different from another?

8. Summarize the main lesson of Exhibit 11.3 in one sentence. Do the same for Exhibit 11.4.

9. Using the data of Exhibit 11.3, determine the average monthly cost of servicing a typical student's demand deposit account, which generates 25 home debits, 5 transit checks, and 1 deposit a month. Assuming the bank can invest 88 percent of the deposit balance at 9 percent interest and charges the student $3.50 in fees monthly, what is the break-even deposit account balance size? Now compare your average balance with the break-even balance and determine whether your amount is generally profitable to the bank. Discuss the importance of insufficient funds (NSF) charges.

Large Denomination Liabilities

10. Name one advantage and one disadvantage of brokered CDs for a bank. Why would stock brokers want to sell a bank's CDs? What are the disadvantages for the broker? Regulators do not approve of this process of bank fund raising. Why?

11. As a potential jumbo CD depositor, what would your circumstances have to be for you to prefer a variable-rate CD over a fixed-rate CD? How would these circumstances differ for you to prefer a zero-coupon CD over a fixed-rate CD, or over a variable-rate CD?

12. What is the difference between the shorthand definition of Federal funds and the correct definition?

13. What is the main difference between Federal funds purchased and Repos?

14. What would motivate a bank to borrow from the Eurodollar market? What would motivate a person or institution to be a Eurodollar depositor?

15. What was the government's purpose in creating IRAs, and what attribute did the government give them to assure their success? What do IRAs have to do with banks?

Risk

16. Would a bank with a negative or with a positive GAP be more interested in reducing its liquidity risk by borrowing more Eurodollar funds than it can use?

17. Many banks compete aggressively for retail time deposits. What marketing strategies will attract large volumes of deposits from individuals? Why are retail deposits attractive to banks in terms of their liquidity risk?

Fed Borrowing

18. What are the three justifications a bank could use to borrow from the discount window? Which of the three solves technological problems?

19. Does the volume of bank discount window borrowing vary with changes in interest rates? Discuss the impact of variations in the difference between the federal funds rate and the discount rate.

FDIC

20. What is the function of the FDIC fund? Why is its name misleading?

21. As the FDIC fund begins dwindling in size it has been discovered that there are three problems with how the fund was constructed. With perfect hindsight describe these three problems.

22. How large would Sally's uninsured deposits be in these FDIC insured banks if
- she owned a joint account with her sister for $140,000 at 1st Bank?
- she owned an account in her name only for $35,000 at 1st Bank?
- she owned a joint account with her husband for $340,000 at 2nd Bank?
- she owned a joint account with her parents for $600,000 at 2nd Bank?

23. When a bank fails, the regulators have a choice of ways to resolve all claims. In one type of resolution the uninsured depositors get full reimbursement of their deposits but in the other type they only receive their share of residual claims. Explain how the two different systems work. Who are these uninsured depositors? Is the first type of resolution unfair? to whom?

Activity Projects

A. Evaluate the activity you generated in your checking account last month. How many home debits, transit checks, and deposits did you create? What was the average balance in the account? What interest did you earn and what fees did you pay?

B. Did the bank see a profit on your account last month? Use the data from Exhibit 11.3 to determine the bank's break-even deposit balance without insufficient funds (NSF) check charges. Take a survey to determine the range of NSF charges at local banks. How many NSF check charges must a bank collect for the student account to be profitable given the data in Exhibit 11.3?

References

Bennett, Barbara. "Bank Regulation and Deposit Insurance: Controlling the FDIC's Losses." *Economic Review* (Federal Reserve Bank of San Francisco, Spring 1984).

Calem, Paul. "The New Bank Deposit Markets: Goodbye to Regulation Q." *Business Review* (Federal Reserve Bank of Philadelphia, November–December 1985).

Carraro, Kenneth, and Daniel Thornton. "The Cost of Checkable Deposits in the United States." *Review* (Federal Reserve Bank of St. Louis, April 1986).

Cates, David. "Deposit Insurance at the Crossroads: An Issue for Analysts." *American Banker,* March 23, 1984.

Cumming, Christine. "Federal Deposit Insurance and Deposits at Foreign Branches of U.S. Banks." *Quarterly Review* (Federal Reserve Bank of New York, Autumn 1985).

Dotsey, Michael, and Anatoli Kuprianov. "Reforming Deposit Insurance: Lessons from the Savings and Loan Crisis." *Economic Review* (Federal Reserve Bank of Richmond, March/April 1990).

Ely, Bert. "Technology, Regulation and the Financial Services Industry in the Year 2000." *Issues in Bank Regulation* (Fall 1988).

Flannery, Mark, and Aris Protopapadekis. "Risk-Sensitive Deposit Insurance Premia: Some Practical Issues." *Business Review* (Federal Reserve Bank of Philadelphia, September–October, 1984).

Federal Reserve System. *Functional Cost Analysis: 1989 Average Banks.* Washington, D.C.: Government Printing Office, 1989.

Flood, Mark. "On the Use of Option Pricing Models to Analyze Deposit Insurance." *Economic Review* (Federal Reserve Bank of St. Louis, January/February 1990).

Goodfriend, Marvin. "Eurodollars." In *Instruments of the Money Market,* edited by Timothy Cook and Bruce Summers, 5th ed. (Federal Reserve Bank of Richmond, 1981).

Goodfriend, Marvin. "Discount Window Borrowing, Monetary Policy, and the Post—October 6, 1979 Federal Reserve Operating Procedure." *Journal of Monetary Economics*, Volume 12, 1983.

Hilder, David. "Big Banks Are Cooling to Hot Money." *Wall Street Journal*, (April 9, 1991).

Humphrey, Thomas. "Lender of Last Resort: The Concept in History." *Economic Review* (Federal Reserve Bank of Richmond, March/April 1989).

Keeton, William. "Deposit Insurance and the Deregulation of Deposit Rates." *Economic Review* (Federal Reserve Bank of Kansas City, April 1984).

Kuprianov, Anotoli, and David Mengle. "The Future of Deposit Insurance: An Analysis of the Alternatives." *Economic Review* (Federal Reserve Bank of Richmond, May/June 1989).

Lowe, William, and Christopher Svare. "Restructuring Intensifies." *Bank Management* (January 1991).

Lucas, Charles, Marcus Jones, and Thom Thurston. "Federal Funds and Repurchase Agreements." *Quarterly Review* (Federal Reserve Bank of New York, Summer 1977).

Mathews, Gordon. "In Wake of Lombard-Wall Collapse Creditors Ask: What is a Repo?" *American Banker* (August 20, 1982).

Melton, William. "The Market for Large, Negotiable CDs." *Quarterly Review* (Federal Reserve Bank of New York, Winter 1977–1978).

Mengle, David. "The Discount Window." *Economic Review* (Federal Reserve Bank of Richmond, May–June 1986).

Murphy, Neil, and Lewis Mandell. *The NOW Account Decision: Profitability, Pricing and Strategies.* Rolling Meadows, Ill.: Bank Administration Institute, 1980.

"Repurchase Agreements: Taking a Closer Look at Safety." *Economic Review* (Federal Reserve Bank of Atlanta, September 1985).

Summers, Bruce. "Negotiable Certificates of Deposit. *Economic Review* (Federal Reserve Bank of Richmond, July–August 1980).

Stevens, E.J. "Seasonal Borrowing and Open Market Operations." *Economic Review* (Federal Reserve Bank of Cleveland, Quarter 2, 1990).

Taylor, Herb. "The Discount Window and Monetary Control." *Business Review* (Federal Reserve Bank of Philadelphia, May–June 1983).

Thomson, Jason. "Using Market Incentives to Reform Bank Regulation and Federal Deposit Insurance." *Economic Review* (Federal Reserve Bank of Cleveland, Quarter 1, 1990).

FIRST FINANCIAL REVISTED: LIABILITY COMPOSITION

C.W. Hampton noted that the composition of First Financial's liabilities created problems for the bank once it experienced asset quality problems. In particular, First Financial relied heavily on large purchased liabilities rather than consumer deposits. Jumbo CDs and federal funds purchased exceeded industry norms while core deposits were relatively small. The bank was underutilizing its branch banks which could have been used to attract low-cost, stable retail deposits. Instead it bought money through brokers in the money market.

The net effect was that money market investors fled at the first sign of problems because their funds were at risk if the bank failed. Even when the bank offered yield premiums, it could not attract sufficient new funds. Eventually the Federal Reserve had to extend emergency credit to First Financial through the discount window. One lesson is that core deposits are more stable than purchased liabilities because retail customers establish longer-term relationships and are less rate sensitive.

Chapter 12

Managing Capital Risk

Inadequate bank capital is like pornography. You can't accurately define it or measure it. You simply know it when you see it.

—Anonymous Bank Regulator

The large number of bank failures and volume of problem loans has focused increased attention in recent years on the adequacy of bank capital. Regulators want to increase capital requirements to better protect depositors and the viability of the insurance funds and to reduce overall risk-taking. Historically, bankers preferred lower capital requirements which increased financial leverage and thus the multiplier effect on ROE. Low capital requirements also allowed for substantial asset growth. In today's environment of increased competition and consolidation, however, the market rewards banks with substantial capital by valuing their stock highly because they are viewed as the firms most likely to survive as acquirers. Recently, the Federal Reserve, Federal Deposit Insurance Corp. (FDIC) and Office of the Comptroller (OCC) imposed minimum risk-based capital standards that will help control bank risk-taking. These requirements will force consolidation within the banking industry and increase the cost of offering banking services.

Capital plays a significant role in the risk/return trade-off at banks. Increasing capital reduces risk by reducing the volatility of earnings, restricting growth opportunities, and lowering the probability of bank failure. It also reduces expected returns, as equity is more expensive than debt. The fundamental asset and liability management decision regarding capital thus focuses on how much capital is optimal. Firms with greater capital can borrow at lower rates, make larger loans, and expand faster through acquisitions or internal growth. In general, they can pursue riskier investments. A second important decision concerns the form in which new capital is obtained, because regulators allow certain types of debt and preferred stock to qualify as capital to meet the requirements. This chapter examines these decisions in light of capital's regulatory definition, function, and cost.

WHY WORRY ABOUT BANK CAPITAL?

Bank regulators' primary objective is to ensure the safety and soundness of the U.S. financial system. It is generally believed that failures of individual banks, particularly large institutions, might erode public confidence in the financial system. The federal government attempts to limit the magnitude and scope of bank failures and thus ensure confidence in the banking system by imposing minimum capital requirements for individual banks. Requirements are met when banks obtain an acceptable amount of financing in the form of qualifying equity capital and related long-term debt sources. Such capital reduces the risk of failure by acting as a cushion against losses and by providing access to financial markets to meet liquidity needs.

Bank supervision has reached the point where regulators now specify minimum amounts of equity and other qualifying capital that banks must obtain to continue operations.[1] Historically, regulators stipulated minimum capital-to-asset ratios but did not worry about the quality of bank assets. While bank capital-to-asset ratios averaged near 20 percent at the turn of the century, comparable ratios today are closer to 7 percent. Clearly, the solvency risk of the banking system has increased in the aggregate over time because asset quality has not improved sufficiently to compensate for the lower percentages of capital. More importantly, two banks of the same size would have to operate with the same amount of capital independent of their risk profiles. Thus a bank that held only Treasury securities would need the same capital as the same size bank that held speculative real estate loans. Does this seem reasonable? The answer depends on the role that capital is expected to serve and whether regulators want to control bank risk.

Capital-to-asset ratios at commercial banks and thrift institutions are also well below similar ratios at other financial institutions and nonfinancial businesses. This difference reflects the intermediation function of depository institutions and thus is not remarkable. High financial leverage, however, increases the relative riskiness of operations by providing less protection to creditors upon liquidation of the firm. Bankers also recognize that high leverage increases potential profitability, and they therefore attempt to minimize external equity financing. Regulators, in contrast, want to increase bank equity financing and thus focus on balancing solvency risks with an individual bank's profit potential.

This chapter introduces the new risk-based capital requirements that will be fully phased in by the end of 1992. It then examines the function of bank capital and its impact on commercial bank operations. It addresses the following issues: 1) What constitutes bank capital? 2) What functions do capital accounts serve? 3) How much capital is adequate? 4) What is the impact of regulatory capital requirements on bank operating policies? 5) What are the advantages and disadvantages of various sources of internal and external capital? These issues are important because federal regulators appear intent on raising capital standards for banks and other institutions over time.

---

[1]The International Lending Supervision Act of 1983 empowered the Federal Reserve, Federal Deposit Insurance Corp., Office of the Comptroller of the Currency, and Federal Home Loan Bank Board to mandate legally binding minimum capital requirements. Most banks acceded to prior guidelines even though the legal requirement did not exist.

RISK-BASED CAPITAL STANDARDS

Historically, bank regulators specified minimum capital standards for banks that were independent of the riskiness of each institution. Formally, this meant tabulating the dollar value of certain qualifying capital accounts off a bank's balance sheet and comparing the sum to total bank assets. During the last half of the 1980s, for example, all U.S. banks were required to meet a 5.5-percent minimum primary capital requirement and a 6-percent minimum total capital requirement. Primary capital consisted of stockholders equity, perpetual preferred stock, mandatory convertible debt, and loan loss reserves.[2] Each bank was supposed to operate with the dollar value of these primary capital accounts equal to no less than 5.5 percent of total assets. Regulators also recognized secondary capital to include balance sheet items such as long-term subordinated debt and limited-life preferred stock.[3] Primary plus secondary capital equaled total capital with the minimum set at 6 percent of total bank assets.

Note that both ratios were calculated without regard to a bank's asset quality, liquidity risk, and interest rate risk. Thus when banks fell under pressure to increase earnings, as in the case of declining net interest margins and loss of loan demand to the commercial paper and junk bond markets, capital requirements imposed no constraints to risk-taking other than limiting growth. Bank regulators did force banks to have more capital than the minimums when they perceived bank risk to be excessive, but this determination often occurred only after a long lag after management had made risky loans. Exhibit 12.1, for example, demonstrates that bank loan losses rose sharply during the 1980s, exceeding 1 percent of total loans by 1989. Actual bank capital did not keep pace.

The Basle Agreement

In 1986 U.S. bank regulators proposed that U.S. banks be required to maintain capital that reflects the riskiness of bank assets. By 1988 the proposal had grown to include risk-based capital standards for banks in 12 industrialized nations according to the terms of the Basle Agreement. U.S. bank regulators phased in the requirements starting in 1990 with the regulations fully in place by the end of 1992. Importantly, savings and loans must meet the same risk-based capital standards by 1992. The motivation for changing to risk-based standards can be attributed to problems with deposit insurance as noted in Contemporary Issues: Deposit Insurance and Capital Standards.

While the terms varied between nations, primarily in terms of what constitutes capital, the agreement contained several important elements. First, a bank's minimum capital requirement is linked by formula to its credit risk as determined by the composition of assets. The greater is credit risk, the greater is required capital. Second,

---

[2]Perpetual preferred stock has no set maturity date; mandatory convertible debt refers to bonds that must contractually be converted into either common stock or preferred stock; and loan loss reserves refer to the contra-asset account appearing on a bank's balance sheet that represents management's estimate of uncollectible loans.

[3]Subordinated debt refers to bonds for which the claims of bondholders are paid only after insured and uninsured depositors are paid in the case of a bank failure.

Exhibit 12.1 Trends in Problem Loans at U.S. Commercial Banks

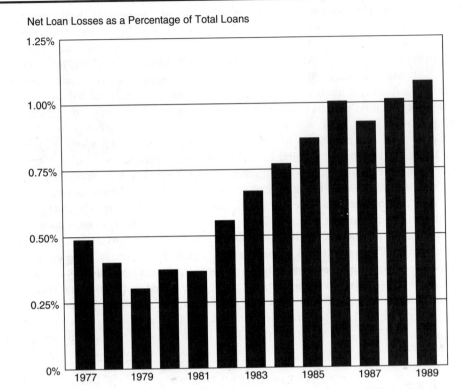

Net Loan Losses as a Percentage of Total Loans

Source: Federal Reserve.

stockholders' equity is deemed to be the most critical type of capital. Each bank is expected to operate with a minimum amount of equity based again on the amount of credit risk. Third, the minimum percentage requirement increased to 8 percent for total capital. Finally, the capital requirements were approximately standardized between countries to "level the playing field," that is, to remove competitive advantages that banks in one country might have over banks in other countries because of regulatory or accounting differences.

Risk-Based Elements of the Plan

To determine minimum capital requirements, bank managers follow a four-step process.

1. Classify assets into one of four risk categories,

2. Classify off-balance-sheet commitments and guarantees into the appropriate risk categories,

CONTEMPORARY ISSUES

Deposit Insurance and Capital Standards

The movement to risk-based capital standards for banks follows from abuses in the use of federal deposit insurance and the increase in bank failures. Throughout the 1980s, the FDIC and FSLIC insured deposits up to $100,000 per account. Depositors were willing to accept lower yields than those available on noninsured investments because their funds were free of default risk. In effect, the federal government subsidized bank borrowing costs.

One peculiar quirk of deposit insurance is that banks were not required to pay insurance premiums that reflected the true riskiness of their operations. In fact, every bank paid the same fixed percentage insurance premium relative to its domestic deposits. This created what is called a *moral hazard* problem in which risky banks used federally insured deposits to make high-risk investments. The system of deposit insurance allowed bank managers to use government guaranteed financing to speculate on risky assets. If the risky investments paid off, they

reported large profits, expanded their operations by buying other businesses, and paid themselves substantial salaries. If the risky investments did not pay off, the bank failed and the FDIC or FSLIC paid insured depositors. From a manager's position as a speculator, it was "heads, I win, and tails, the government (the taxpayer) loses."

Deposit insurance thus created incentives for banks to increase financial leverage by issuing insured deposits, usually jumbo CDs, to the maximum extent allowed by regulators, and to increase the riskiness of their asset holdings. Under the old capital standards, banks were required to have capital equal to some minimum fraction of total assets without any recognition of asset riskiness. Furthermore, if managers moved assets off balance sheet, capital was not required against these activities. Risk-based capital addresses these perverse incentives by linking capital to perceived asset quality. It does not directly address problems with deposit insurance.

---

3. Multiply the dollar amount of assets in each risk category by the appropriate risk weight; this equals risk-weighted assets, and

4. Multiply risk-weighted assets by the minimum capital percentages, either 4 percent or 8 percent.

The process ensures that assets with the highest perceived credit risk have the highest risk weights, and thus require the most capital.

Consider the data in Exhibit 12.2 for Prosperity National Bank (PNB) at the end of 1992. As indicated in the second column, total assets for the bank were just under $5 billion and the bank had almost $656 million in off-balance-sheet items. Under the former capital standards, PNB would have needed 6 percent total capital or approximately $299.6 million in primary and secondary capital. The exhibit demonstrates that the risk-based capital requirements are slightly lower.

The first column indicates the four risk categories and type of assets that fall into each category for PNB. Exhibit 12.3 provides a comprehensive list of the balance sheet items in each category. Beside each category is the applicable risk weight. Note that the lowest risk category carries a zero weight because there is no default risk with cash and U.S. Treasury securities, and U.S. agency securities such as the Government

Exhibit 12.2 Prosperity National Bank: Risk-Based Capital (Dollars in Thousands)

	Assets 12/31/92	Risk Weight	Risk Weighted Assets
Category 1: Zero Percent			
Cash & reserve	$ 104,525	0%	$ 0
Trading account	830	0	0
U.S. Treas. & agencies (GNMA)	45,882	0	0
Federal Reserve stock	5,916	0	0
Category 2: 20 Percent			
Due from/in process	303,610	20	60,722
Interest-bearing deposits/F.F.S.	497,623	20	99,525
U.S. Treasury & agencies (collateralized repos)	329,309	20	65,862
U.S. agencies (govt.-sponsored)	412,100	20	82,420
State & munis secured tax authority	87,515	20	17,503
C.M.O. backed by agency sec.	90,020	20	18,004
Domestic depository institution	38,171	20	7,634
SBAs (govt. guaranteed portion)	29,266	20	5,853
Category 3: 50 Percent			
C.M.O. backed by mortgage loans	10,000	50	5,000
State & munis/all other	68,514	50	34,257
Real estate; 1–4 family	324,422	50	162,211
Category 4: 100 Percent			
Loans: comm/agency/institutional/leases	1,966,276	100	1,966,276
Real estate, all other	388,456	100	388,456
Allowance for credit loss	(70,505)	0	0
Other investments	168,519	100	168,519
Premises, equity, other assets	194,400	100	194,400
Total assets	$4,994,849		$3,276,642
Off-Balance-Sheet Items			
Loan commitments > 1 Year	$ 364,920	50	$ 182,460
Standby letters of credit	165,905	100	165,905
Futures & forwards	50,000	100	50,000
Interest rate swaps	75,000	50	37,500
Contingencies	$ 655,825		$ 435,865
Assets & contingencies	$5,650,674		$3,712,507

Requirement

Tier 1 capital: .04($3,712,507) = $148,500
Total capital: .08($3,712,507) = $297,000

National Mortgage Association (GNMA).[4] Assets in each of the subsequent categories are assumed to exhibit increased default risk. Thus assets in Category 2 are subject to

---

[4]For PNB, trading account securities consist solely of U.S. Treasury securities.

Exhibit 12.3 Risk Categories and Risk Weights for Balance Sheet and Off-Balance-Sheet Items at U.S. Banks

Summary of Risk Weights and Risk Categories

Category 1: Zero %

1. Cash (domestic and foreign).
2. Balances due from, and claims on, Federal Reserve banks.
3. Securities (direct obligations) issued by the U.S. Government or its agencies.
4. Federal Reserve bank stock.

Category 2: 20%

1. All claims (long- and short-term) on domestic depository institutions.
2. Claims on foreign banks with an original maturity of one year or less.
3. Claims guaranteed by, or backed by the full faith and credit of, domestic depository institutions.
4. Local currency claims on foreign central governments to the extent the bank has local currency liabilities in the foreign country.
5. Cash items in the process of collection.
6. Securities and other claims on, or guaranteed by U.S. Government-sponsored agencies (including portions of claims guaranteed).
7. Portions of loans and other assets collateralized by securities issued by, or guaranteed by, U.S. Government-sponsored agencies.
8. General obligation claims on, and claims guaranteed by, U.S., state, and local governments that are secured by the full faith and credit of the state or local taxing authority (including portions of claims guaranteed).
9. Claims on official multilateral lending institutions or regional development institutions in which the U.S. Government is a shareholder or a contributing member.
10. Securities and other claims guaranteed by the U.S. Government or its agencies (including portions of claims guaranteed).
11. Portions of loans and other assets collateralized by securities issued by, or guaranteed by, the U.S. Government or its agencies or by cash on deposit in the lending institution.

Category 3: 50%

1. Revenue bonds or similar obligations, including loans and leases, that are obligations of U.S. state or local governments, but for which the government entity is committed to repay the debt only out of revenues from the facilities financed.
2. Credit equivalent amounts of interest rate and foreign exchange rate related contracts, except for those assigned to a lower risk category.

Category 4: 100%

1. All other claims on private obligors.
2. Claims on foreign banks with an original maturity exceeding one year.
3. Claims on foreign central governments that are not included in item 4 of Category 3.
4. Obligations issued by state or local governments (including industrial development authorities and similar entities) repayable solely by a private party or enterprise.
5. Premises, plant, and equipment, other fixed assets, and other real estate owned.
6. Investments in any unconsolidated subsidiaries, joint ventures, or associated companies—if not deducted from capital.
7. Instruments issued by other banking organizations that qualify as capital.
8. All other assets (including claims on commercial firms owned by the public sector).

(Continued)

a 20-percent risk weight because they are short-term, collateralized, and often carry U.S. government agency guarantees. Included are U.S. agency securities, general obligation municipal bonds, interest-bearing deposits, and federal funds sold, among

Exhibit 12.3 *(Continued)*

Conversion Factors

Credit Conversion Factors for Off-Balance-Sheet Items

100% Conversion Factor

1. Direct credit substitutes (general guarantees of indebtedness and guarantee-type instruments, including standby letters of credit serving as financial guarantees for, or supporting, loans and securities).
2. Acquisitions of risk participations in bankers acceptances and participations in direct credit substitutes (for example, standby letters of credit).
3. Sale and repurchase agreements and asset sales with recourse, if not already included on the balance sheet.
4. Forward agreements (that is, contractual obligations) to purchase assets, including financing facilities with certain drawdown.

50% Conversion Factor

1. Transaction-related contingencies (for example, bid bonds, performance bonds, warranties, and standby letters of credit related to a particular transaction).
2. Unused commitments with an original maturity exceeding one year, including underwriting commitments and commercial credit lines.
3. Revolving underwriting facilities (RUFs). Note issuance facilities (NIFs) and other similar arrangements.

20% Conversion Factor

1. Short-term, self-liquidating trade-related contingencies, including commercial letters of credit.

Zero % Conversion Factor

1. Unused commitments with an original maturity of one year or less or which are unconditionally cancelable at any time.

Credit Conversion for Interest Rate and Foreign Exchange Contracts

The total replacement cost of contracts (obtained by summing the positive mark-to-market values of contracts) would be added to a measure of future potential increases in credit exposure. This future potential exposure measure would be calculated by multiplying the total notional value of contracts by one of the following credit conversion factors, as appropriate.

Remaining Maturity	Interest Rate Contracts	Exchange Rate Contracts
Less than one year	0	1.0%
One year and over	0.5%	5.0%

No potential exposure would be calculated for single currency floating/floating interest rate contracts. The credit exposure on these contracts would be evaluated solely on the basis of their mark-to-market value. Exchange rate contracts with an original maturity of 7 days or less would be excluded. Also, instruments traded on exchanges that require daily payment of variation margin would be excluded.

Source: G. Alexander Cole and Gerald C. Fischer, "Risk-Based Capital: A Loan and Credit Officer's Primer," *The Journal of Commercial Bank Lending*, August 1988, with modifications.

other assets. Each type is low in default risk so that the risk weight is slightly above that for zero default risk assets. First mortgages, collateralized mortgage obligations, and municipal revenue bonds comprise the bulk of 50-percent risk-weight assets under category 3. The final category includes assets with the highest default risk such as commercial loans and real estate loans other than first mortgages, and thus carry a risk weight of 100 percent.

An important element of the risk-based standards is that a bank's off-balance-sheet items must be supported by capital. A bank that exposes its operations to risk by making long-term loan commitments, offering letter-of-credit guarantees, and participating in interest rate swaps and forward or futures transactions must hold capital against the exposure. Management first converts the dollar value of each off-balance-sheet item to a *credit equivalent* amount using the conversion factors in Exhibit 12.3, allocates the converted amount to the appropriate risk category, and then multiplies by the associated risk weight. The bottom of Exhibit 12.2 indicates that PNB's long-term loan commitments and interest rate swaps are classified in category 3, while standby letters of credit, futures and forwards appear in category 4. Figures in the final column represent converted amounts.

The second and third columns indicate the dollar value of each balance sheet figure and the associated risk weight, respectively. Total risk-weighted assets is then calculated by multiplying the values in these two columns, then adding across all assets and off-balance-sheet items. Total risk-weighted assets for PNB thus equaled $3.71 billion at the end of 1992.

Finally, PNB's minimum capital requirements are specified as a fraction of total risk-weighted assets. The next section describes the components of bank capital under the standards. At this point, it is sufficient to know that banks must meet two capital standards; Tier 1 capital must equal no less than 4 percent of risk-weighted assets, while total capital must equal at least 8 percent of risk-weighted assets. Figures at the bottom of Exhibit 12.2 indicate that PNB must have at least $148.5 million in Tier 1 capital and $297.0 million in total capital. Note that this latter figure is $2.8 million below that required under the old standards.

WHAT CONSTITUTES BANK CAPITAL?

According to accounting definition, **capital** or **net worth** equals the cumulative value of assets minus the cumulative value of liabilities and represents ownership interest in a firm. It is traditionally measured on a book-value basis in which assets and liabilities are listed in terms of historical cost. In banking, the regulatory concept of bank capital differs substantially from accounting capital. Specifically, regulators include certain forms of debt when measuring capital adequacy. This policy raises numerous issues regarding bank capital's function and optimal mix.

Accounting capital includes the book value of common equity and preferred stock outstanding. **Common equity** equals the sum of common stock, surplus, undivided profits, and reserves for contingencies and other capital reserves, defined as follows:

- Common stock equals par value of common stock outstanding; thus if there are one million shares outstanding with part value of $10 per share, common stock will show $10 million.

- Surplus equals excess over par value at which common stock was issued plus the value of undivided profits allocated to surplus; suppose in the above case with common stock, the one million shares were originally sold in the market place to net a bank $15 per share. The excess, $5 per share or $5 million, would be allocated to surplus.

- Undivided profits equals the value of cumulative retained earnings minus transfers to surplus; retained earnings increases when a bank reports net income that exceeds dividend payments, and decreases when net income is less than dividends or the bank reports a loss.

- Reserves for contingencies and other capital reserves equals the value of cumulative reserves established for deferred taxes or contingencies; contingencies include expected payments to retire outstanding preferred stock, settle lawsuits, and satisfy other extraordinary obligations. These reserves have been combined with undivided profits for reporting purposes since 1978.

Regulatory capital ratios focus in part on the book value of common equity. This equals the book value of bank assets minus total liabilities. Most analysts today try to estimate the market value of bank equity when assessing financial performance and risk. This can be estimated in several ways. One procedure is to multiply the number of outstanding shares of stock by the most recent stock price per share. Another procedure requires estimating the market value of bank assets and subtracting total bank liabilities. As discussed in Chapter 8, the market value of equity is an important measure of performance in interest rate risk management. Claims of equity stockholders are paid in the case of failure after the claims of all debtholders and preferred stockholders.

Preferred stock includes the book value of aggregate preferred stock outstanding. While it exhibits many of the same characteristics as long-term bonds, preferred stock represents ownership in a firm, with claims superior to common stock but subordinated to all debtholders. Preferred stock is issued either in perpetuity or with a fixed maturity (limited life). Most issues are callable, and some are convertible to common stock. Dividend payments may be fixed, much like coupon payments on bonds, or may vary with some market index over the life of the issue. Unlike coupon payments, dividends are not deductible for corporate income tax purposes.

Regulators also include long-term subordinated debt as bank capital. The term subordinated means that claims of the debtholders are paid only after the claims of depositors. Subordinated debt takes many forms. It includes straight bonds with long maturities that carry fixed rates. It also includes variable-rate bonds, capital notes, or bonds that are convertible into the bank's common or preferred stock. The fact that nonequity accounts constitute capital relates to regulatory perceptions of capital's function. Mandatory convertible debt and subordinated long-term debt are included because they carry relatively long-term maturities and creditors' claims are subor-

Exhibit 12.4 Definition of Qualifying Capital

Components	Minimum Requirements and Limitations after Transition Period
Core Capital (Tier 1).	Must equal or exceed 4% of weighted risk assets
Common stockholders' equity	No limit.
Minority interest in common equity accounts of consolidated subsidiaries.	No limit.
Less Goodwill and other disallowed intangibles.[1]	
Supplementary Capital (Tier 2).	Total of Tier 2 is limited to 100% of Tier 1.[2]
Allowance for loan and lease losses.	Limited to 1.25% of weighted risk assets.[2]
Perpetual and long-term preferred stock (original maturity 20 yrs. or more).	No limit within Tier 2, long-term preferred is amortized for capital purposes as it approaches maturity.
Hybrid capital instruments (including perpetual debt and mandatory convertible securities).	No limit within Tier 2.
Subordinated debt and intermediate-term preferred stock (original weighted average maturity of seven years or more).	Subordinated debt and intermediate-term preferred stock are limited to 50% of Tier 1[2], amortized for capital purposes as they approach maturity.
Revaluation reserves (equity and building).	Not included; regulators would encourage banks to disclose; would evaluate on case-by-case basis for international comparisons; and would take into account in making overall assessment of capital.
Deductions (from sum of Tier 1 and Tier 2):	
Investments in unconsolidated banking and finance subsidiaries.	
Reciprocal holdings of bank-issued capital securities.	
Other deductions (such as other subsidiaries or joint ventures) as determined by supervisor authority.	On case-by-case basis or as matter of policy after formal rulemaking.
Total Capital (Tier 1 + Tier 2—Deductions).	Must equal or exceed 8% of weighted risk assets.

[1]Goodwill on books of bank holding companies before March 12, 1988 would be "grandfathered" for transition period. All goodwill and disallowed intangibles in banks, except previously grandfathered intangibles or goodwill approved in supervisory mergers, would be deducted immediately as under current policies. All deductions are for capital adequacy purposes only; deductions would not affect accounting treatment.

[2]Amounts in excess of limitations are permitted but do not qualify as capital.

Source: G. Alexander Cole and Gerald C. Fischer, "Risk-Based Capital: A Loan and Credit Officer's Primer," *The Journal of Commercial Bank Lending*, August 1988.

dinated to those of depositors. These funding sources therefore provide solvency protection for insured depositors and the insurance funds.

Risk-based capital standards utilize two measures of qualifying bank capital as summarized in Exhibit 12.4. **Tier 1** or **core** capital consists of common equity less intangible assets like goodwill, plus minority interest in consolidated subsidiaries. The book value of Tier 1 capital must equal at least 4 percent of risk-weighted assets. **Tier 2** capital includes loan loss reserves, preferred stock, mandatory convertible debt, and

Exhibit 12.5 Risk-Based Capital Rates for Large U.S. Banks, December 31, 1990

Bank	Tier 1 Capital Ratio	Total Capital Ratio	Leverage Capital Ratio
Citicorp	3.26	6.52	3.62
Security Pacific Corp.	4.10	7.50	3.80
Mellon Bank Corp.	4.30	8.24	4.04
Chase Manhattan Corp.	4.33	8.65	4.30
First Chicago Corp.	4.90	8.30	5.00
Wells Fargo & Co.	5.03	9.27	5.04
NCNB	5.41	9.82	4.14
Manufacturers Hanover Corp.	5.43	9.28	5.36
First Interstate	5.63	9.40	5.00
United Banks of Colorado	5.87	7.72	4.02
Bank America Corp.	6.07	9.46	5.50
C&S/Sovran Corp.	6.27	9.37	5.38
Valley National Corp.	6.51	7.34	4.38
Norwest Corp.	6.51	11.62	4.80
Am South Bancorp.	7.59	10.30	6.04
NBD Bancorp	7.81	9.61	6.00
First Wachovia Corp.	9.08	10.44	7.58
Bank One Corp.	9.27	12.29	8.06
Boatmen's Bancshares Inc.	9.87	12.87	6.86
Fifth Third Bancorp	11.95	13.20	9.80
Regulatory Targets: Year end 1992	4.00%	8.00%	3.00%

Source: *American Banker*, April 18, 1991.

loan loss reserves up to 1.25 percent of risk-weighted assets. As indicated in Exhibit 12.4, there are limits as to how much capital can be obtained from subordinated debt and preferred stock. Total capital includes Tier 1 capital and Tier 2 capital and must equal at least 8 percent of risk-weighted assets.

Exhibit 12.5 documents the capital positions for 20 of the largest U.S. banks at the end of 1990. The first column of data reports Tier 1 capital ratios ranked from the lowest to the highest. Of this group, only Citicorp is below the 1992 regulatory minimum. Contrast its 3.26 percent ratio with Fifth Third Bancorp's at 11.95 percent. The second column reports total capital ratios and again indicates that most banks exceed the 8 percent minimum. Contemporary Issues: Japanese Bank Capital Ratios, in turn, describes capital requirements at Japanese banks.

The final column reports *leverage capital* ratios, which differ from risk-based standards. Regulators are concerned that some banks could acquire so many low-risk assets that risk-based capital requirements would be negligible. Suppose, for example, that PNB from Exhibit 12.2 held all of its assets in the form of cash and due balances and U.S. Treasury securities. Its risk-weighted assets would equal zero. To prevent banks from operating with little or no capital, even though risk-based standards might allow it, they impose a minimum 3-percent leverage ratio, defined as Tier 1 capital,

Exhibit 12.6 Capital Ratios for Different-Sized U.S. Commercial Banks, December 1984 versus December 1990

	Asset Size (Millions of Dollars)				
	≤$25	$25–$300	$300–$1,000	$1,000–$5,000	>$5,000
1984					
Primary capital/total assets	14.5%	8.9%	7.7%	6.9%	6.5%
Number of banks	5,501	8,162	466	209	66
1990				$1,000–$3,000	>$3,000
Primary capital/total assets	10.02%	9.09%	8.08%	7.65%	7.42%
Number of banks	3,104	7,942	620	204	168

Source: Uniform Bank Performance Report.

divided by total assets net of goodwill. Thus all banks must maintain some minimum amount of capital in recognition of risks other than default risk.

Exhibit 12.6 compares the average capital ratios for different-sized banks in 1984 versus 1990. Regardless of how the averages are calculated, three implications stand out. First, capital ratios at banks of all sizes generally exceeded the regulatory minimums. Second, capital ratios at small banks exceeded those at larger banks, on average. This reflects greater regulatory pressure on small banks, which presumably carry less diversified asset portfolios. Finally, except for the smallest banks, capital ratios increased during the 6 years as banks moved to strengthen their financial positions.

WHAT IS THE FUNCTION OF BANK CAPITAL?

Much confusion exists over what purposes bank capital serves. The traditional corporate finance view is that capital reduces the risk of failure by providing protection against operating and extraordinary losses. While this holds for nonfinancial firms that rely on long-term debt with relatively low financial leverage, it is less applicable to commercial banks.

From the regulators' perspective, bank capital serves to protect the deposit insurance funds in the case of bank failures. When a bank fails, regulators can either pay off insured depositors or arrange a purchase of the failed bank by a healthy bank. The greater is a bank's capital, the lower is the cost of arranging a merger or paying depositors. An additional benefit of minimum capital requirements is that the owners of equity and long-term debt impose market discipline on bank managers because they closely monitor bank performance. Excessive risk-taking lowers stock prices and raises borrowing costs, which adversely affect the wealth of these monitoring parties.

The function of bank capital is thus to reduce bank risk. It does so in three basic ways. First, it provides a cushion for firms to absorb losses and remain solvent. Second,

CONTEMPORARY ISSUES

Japanese Bank Capital Ratios

International risk-based capital requirements were agreed upon by regulatory authorities in 12 industrialized nations. While Tier 1 capital components are quite comparable, Tier 2 components vary substantially between banks in different countries. Consider the requirements for Japanese banks, which account for most of the largest banks in the world. Unlike their U.S. counterparts, Japanese banks can own equities. As part of Tier 2 capital, Japan's banks can include 45 percent of unrealized gains on stock investments. Thus when stock prices rise, the banks' capital positions improve. This runs both ways how-

ever, as capital declines when the market falls.

From December 1989 through August 1990 the Nikkei Index, a broad-based index of Japanese stocks, fell almost 40 percent. This produced a $60 billion capital loss for just the five largest Japanese banks. Not surprisingly, growth opportunities were sharply curtailed and Japan's banks were under serious pressure to increase earnings to supplement their capital positions. At its worst, volatility in Japanese stocks translates into volatility in bank capital positions.

---

it provides ready access to financial markets and thus guards against liquidity problems caused by deposit outflows. Third, it constrains growth and limits risk-taking.

Consider the balance sheets for the two firms in Exhibit 12.7. The manufacturing firm has 60 percent current assets and 40 percent fixed assets. Its financing is composed of 60 percent debt and 40 percent equity. Exactly one-half of the debt is short-term, such that its current ratio equals 2. The commercial bank, in contrast, operates with very few fixed assets and finances 92 percent of its assets with debt and just 8 percent with equity. Its current ratio is less than 1. The value of the manufacturing firm's assets would have to decline by more than 40 percent before the firm became technically insolvent. An 8-percent decline in asset values would similarly make the bank insolvent. Equity reduces the risk of failure by increasing the proportion of problem assets that could default before equity is depleted.

The issue, however, is not this simple. Why, for example, do creditors allow banks to operate with far greater financial leverage than manufacturers? Banks exhibit limited operating risk because fixed assets, and in general fixed expenses, are low. Yet several factors suggest that banks should have more equity. First, the market value of bank assets is potentially more volatile than the value of assets at a typical manufacturing firm. Market values of fixed-rate assets change whenever interest rates change and whenever bank borrowers experience difficulties. Manufacturing companies own proportionately fewer financial assets and are not as sensitive to interest rate fluctuations. Second, banks rely proportionately more on volatile sources of short-term debt, many of which can be withdrawn on demand. It seems reasonably probable that banks might be forced to liquidate assets at relatively low values.

This capital discrepancy can be largely explained by federal deposit insurance and bank regulatory policy. Depositors' funds at each member institution are insured up to $100,000. Even if a bank fails, an insured depositor is fully reimbursed. This system prevents massive withdrawals of small-denomination deposits and makes uninsured

Exhibit 12.7 Comparative Balance Sheets: Manufacturing Firm versus Commercial Bank

Manufacturing Firm

Assets	Percent of Total	Liabilities and Equity	Percent of Total
Cash	4%	Accounts payable	20%
Accounts receivable	26	Short-term notes payable	10
Inventory	30	Current	30%
Current	60%	Long-term debt	30
Plant and equipment	40	Stockholders' equity	40
Total	100%	Total	100%

Commercial Bank

Assets	Percent of Total	Liabilities and Equity	Percent of Total
Cash	8%	Short-term deposits	60%
Short-term securities	17	Short-term after borrowings	20
Short-term loans	50	Current	80%
Current	75%	Long-term debt	12
Long-term securities	5	Stockholders' equity	8
Long-term loans	18	Total	100%
Premises and equipment	2		
Total	100%		

creditors the arbiters of bank risk. Just as significantly, through 1987 bank regulators provided de facto insurance for uninsured creditors at the largest financial institutions. Rather than let these banks fail, regulators arranged mergers or acquisitions that allowed such firms to continue operations without liquidation. In the case of Continental Illinois in 1984 and First City Bancorporation in 1987, the U.S. government effectively guaranteed the claims of both debtholders and preferred stockholders, who lost little when the banks collapsed.[5] In these extreme cases, no private capital is technically required for the banks to continue operations. In general, deposit insurance and regulatory policy increase bank liquidity, which reduces the amount of equity financing required.

Interestingly, bank regulators shifted their policy with the failures of First Republic-Bank Corp. in 1988 and MCorp. in 1989. These bank holding companies had $27 billion and $16 billion in assets, respectively, at the time they failed. Still, the regulators created bridge banks that took over the subsidiary banks and stripped the holding companies of their assets. This left common and preferred stockholders to file claims behind bondholders and other uninsured creditors for what little remained. For the first time, investors in the nation's largest banks suffered substantial losses.

---

[5]In 1984 C.T. Conover, the Comptroller of the Currency, suggested indirectly that regulators would not allow the 11 largest banking organizations in the United States to fail.

The role of capital as a buffer against loan losses is clear when put in the context of cash flows rather than accounting capital. Consider a bank whose customers default on their loans. Defaults immediately reduce operating cash inflows because the bank no longer receives interest and principal payments. Cash outflows are largely unaffected except for incremental collection costs. The bank remains operationally solvent as long as its overall operating cash inflows exceed its cash outflows. Capital serves as a buffer because it reduces obligated outflows. Banks can defer dividends on preferred and common stock without being in default. Interest payments on bank debt, in contrast, are mandatory. Banks with sufficient capital can, in turn, issue new debt or stock to replace lost cash inflows and buy time until any asset problems are corrected. Thus the greater a bank's equity capital, the greater the magnitude of assets that can default before the firm is technically insolvent and the lower bank risk.

Recent research on the link between bank capital and the risk of failure suggests mixed conclusions.[6] Some analysts attribute failures to bad management and argue that well-managed banks should be allowed to operate with low capital-to-asset ratios. In these studies, banks with low capital-to-asset ratios do not exhibit any greater tendency toward insolvency compared to banks with higher capital ratios. Other researchers attribute failures to liquidity problems and generally ignore capital. When depositors withdraw their funds, a bank must either liquidate assets from its portfolio or replace the deposit outflows with new borrowings. Forced asset sales can be accomplished only through lowering asset prices. These losses, in turn, would be charged against equity, bringing the bank closer to insolvency. Most banks therefore rely on substitute debt sources. If, however, the volume of required financing is large, the bank must pay an interest premium, which reduces current earnings and depresses potential equity.

Uncertainty regarding the link between capital and liquidity problems and bank failure reflects a misunderstanding of accounting versus economic value. What is important is the market value of bank capital, not its accounting value. As long as the market value is positive, banks can issue debt to offset liquidity problems. This is true regardless of whether accounting capital is positive or negative. If the market value of capital is negative, no private lender would extend credit. Failures, then, are tied directly to market values, not accounting values.

Adequate bank capital minimizes operating problems by providing ready access to financial markets. Hempel and Crosse state that the primary function of bank capital is "to keep the bank open and operating so that time and earnings can absorb losses—in other words, to inspire confidence in the bank on the part of depositors and the (regulatory) supervisor so that it will not be forced into costly liquidation."[7] Capital enables the bank to borrow from traditional sources at reasonable rates. Therefore, depositors will not remove their funds and asset losses will be minimized. Any losses that arise can be charged against current earnings or, ultimately, against equity. Confidence that the bank is an ongoing concern increases with the amount of bank capital and of regulatory assistance via deposit insurance and discount window loans.

---

[6]Wall, 1985, summarizes the conclusions of recent studies suggesting both that capital is and that it is not linked directly to bank failures.

[7]See Hempel and Cross, 1980.

Regulatory interference confuses the true purpose of capital. When regulators guarantee bank debt or create artificial capital, they improve liquidity. The intent is to postpone problems until the firms are self-sufficient. Capital, as such, is meaningless to the firm's continued operation. Capital serves the same purpose as federal guarantees when regulatory assistance is not openly provided.

Finally, capital constrains growth and reduces risk by limiting the amount of new assets a bank can acquire through debt financing. As indicated in Exhibit 12.2, regulators impose equity capital requirements as a fraction of aggregate bank assets. If banks choose to expand loans or acquire other assets, they must support the growth with additional equity financing. Because new equity is expensive, expected asset returns must be high to justify the financing. This restriction is extremely important because many bank failures in the 1980s were linked to speculative asset growth financed by brokered deposits. Rigid capital requirements reduce the likelihood that banks will expand beyond their ability to manage their assets successfully.

HOW MUCH CAPITAL IS ADEQUATE?

The issue of bank capital adequacy has long pitted regulators against bank management. Regulators, concerned primarily with the safety of banks, the viability of the insurance funds, and stability of financial markets, prefer more capital. This reduces the likelihood of failure and increases bank liquidity. Bankers, on the other hand, generally prefer to operate with less capital. As indicated in Chapter 4, the smaller a bank's equity base, the greater its financial leverage and equity multiplier. High leverage converts a normal return on assets into a high return on equity (ROE). Exhibit 12.7 illustrates this point. Suppose that the manufacturing firm and commercial bank each earn 1 percent on assets during the year. The firms' equity multipliers (ratio of total assets to stockholders' equity) equal 2.5 and 12.5, respectively. This difference in leverage produces a 2.5 percent ROE for the manufacturer that equals only one-fifth of the 12.5 percent ROE for the bank. Alternatively, the manufacturer must generate an ROA equal to 5 times that for the bank, 5 percent in this example, to produce the same ROE. Leverage thus improves profitability when earnings are positive.

Whether a specific bank's capital is adequate depends on how much risk the bank assumes. Banks with low-quality assets, limited access to liquid funds, severe mismatches in asset and liability maturities and durations, and high operational risk should have more capital. Low-risk firms should be allowed to increase financial leverage.

The regulatory agencies periodically assess specific bank risks via on-site examinations. A thorough review includes an evaluation of the bank's asset quality—particularly the probability of default on interest and principal payments in the loan portfolio—loan review policies, interest rate risk profile, liquidity profile, cash management and internal audit procedures, and management quality. The FDIC rates banks according to the Uniform Financial Institutions Rating System, which encompasses five general categories of performance, labeled CAMEL: C = capital adequacy, A = asset quality, M = management quality, E = earnings, and L = liquidity. The FDIC numerically rates every bank on each factor, ranging from the highest quality (1) to the lowest quality (5). It also assigns a composite rating for the bank's entire operation. A composite ranking of 1 or 2 indicates a fundamentally sound bank, while a ranking of 3 through 5 signifies a problem bank with some near-term potential for failure.

Weaknesses of the Risk-Based Capital Standards

The risk-based capital requirements have two fundamental weaknesses. First, the formal standards do not account for any risks other than credit risk. Certainly a bank that assumes extraordinary amounts of interest rate risk in volatile rate environments has an abnormal chance of failing. But the bank's formal capital requirement is determined by its asset composition, which does not necessarily address the interest rate risk exposure. Extraordinary liquidity risk exposes banks to similar problems. The regulators can, of course, identify risk-takers and raise required capital above the minimums, except that this recognition rarely occurs prior to problems arising. Second, the book value of capital is not the most meaningful measure of soundness. Among other problems, it ignores changes in the market value of assets, the value of unrealized gains or losses on bank investments, the value of a bank charter, and the value of federal deposit insurance. In practice, book values can be manipulated through accounting ploys and often substantially overstate the firm's true market value.

A related criticism is that many banks have actually seen their capital requirements decrease under the risk-based standards. In fact, a bank with extremely low-risk assets could conceivably get by with very little capital. To see this, suppose a bank owned only cash assets and short-term U.S. Treasury securities. With all assets in risk category one with a zero risk weight, the bank could get by with no capital. To avoid this complication, the regulators imposed an additional leverage ratio requirement on banks and thrifts that must be met along with risk-based minimums. This requirement stipulates that regardless of asset composition and risk-based capital requirements, every bank must operate with a minimum equity-capital-to-total-assets ratio of at least 3 percent. Depending on each bank's CAMEL rating, the minimum leverage ratio requirement increases. Low CAMEL-rated banks, for example, must meet a minimum 4 percent leverage ratio.

THE EFFECT OF CAPITAL REQUIREMENTS ON BANK OPERATING POLICIES

Regulatory efforts to increase capital impose significant restrictions on bank operating policies. Many large banks with access to national markets can issue common stock, preferred stock, or subordinated capital notes to support continued growth and thus are relatively unaffected by minimum capital ratios. Smaller banks, however, do not have the same opportunities. They lack a national reputation, and investors generally shy away from purchasing their securities. These banks often rely instead on internally generated capital and find their activities constrained by a deficiency in retained earnings.

Limiting Asset Growth

Minimum capital requirements restrict a bank's ability to grow. Additions to assets mandate additions to capital for a bank to continue to meet minimum capital-to-asset ratios imposed by regulators. Each bank must limit its asset growth to some percentage of retained earnings plus new external capital.

Consider the $100 million bank in Exhibit 12.8 that just meets the minimum 8-percent total capital requirement. Initially, the bank has $8 million in capital, of which $4 million is undivided profits and $4 million is other capital. Various effects of planned asset growth are shown in the following columns of data, which represent projections of balance sheet and income statement data for the upcoming year. The bank's initial plan, designated as Case 1, calls for 8-percent asset growth with a projected 0.99 percent ROA and 40-percent dividend payout rate. In this scenario, the bank would have $108 million in assets and $640,000 in retained earnings for the year. The 8-percent target capital ratio would be just met.

Suppose that profitable credit opportunities are available to generate 12-percent asset growth within acceptable risk limits. The last three columns of data identify three distinct strategies to grow and still meet minimum capital requirements. One option (Case 2) is for the bank to generate a higher ROA. As indicated at the bottom of the exhibit, the bank would need $960,000 in additional retained earnings to support the $112 million in assets. Because competition prevents banks from raising yield spreads on high-quality loans, they can achieve higher returns only by acquiring riskier assets or generating greater fee income from services. This sample bank would have to increase its ROA by 44 basis points to 1.43 percent if it did not change its dividend policy or obtain additional capital externally. If banks substitute riskier loans for lower-yielding, less risky assets, the benefit from increased capital may be offset by future loan losses.

A second option is for the bank to increase retained earnings by decreasing dividends (Case 3). In this scenario, the bank could lower its 40-percent payment rate to just over 13 percent with the same 0.99 percent ROA, to leave capital ratios unchanged. This option is unattractive because any unanticipated dividend reduction encourages shareholders to sell stock, which lowers share prices immediately. It would thus be extremely difficult and/or costly to issue stock any time in the near future. The final option (Case 4) is to finance part of the asset growth with new capital, such as new common stock or perpetual preferred stock. Here the growth in retained earnings would total $660,000, so $300,000 in new external capital would be needed. Such equity is considerably more expensive than debt, and is available only if the bank actually has access to the stock market.

In practice, a bank would likely pursue some combination of these strategies, or might simply choose not to grow. If the bank in this example decides not to alter its initial policies, asset growth is restricted to 12.5 (100/8) times the addition to retained earnings. In other words, each dollar of retained profits can support $12.50 in new assets.

Exhibit 12.8 Maintaining Capital Ratios with Asset Growth: Applications of Equations (12.2) and (12.3)

Ratio	Initial Position	Case 1 Initial 8% Asset Growth	Case 2 12% Growth: Increase ROA[a]	Case 3 12% Growth: Decrease Dividends	Case 4 12% Growth: Increase External Capital
Asset size (millions of dollars)	100.00	108.00	112.00	112.00	112.00
Asset growth rate (percent)		8.00	12.00	12.00	12.00
ROA (percent)		0.99	1.43	0.99	0.99
Dividend payout rate (percent)		40.00	40.00	13.42	40.00
Undivided profits (millions of dollars)	4.00	4.64	4.96	4.96	4.66
Total capital other than undivided profits (millions of dollars)	4.00	4.00	4.00	4.00	4.30
Total capital/total assets (percent)	8.00	8.00	8.00	8.00	8.00

Case 1: Initial plan parameters.
   108 ROA (1 − DR) = Δ undivided profits
   If DR = 40% and capital ratio = 8% solve for ROA:
   108 ROA(1 − .4) = 0.64
        ROA = 0.99%

Case 2: What ROA is necessary to support 12% asset growth?
   Solve for ROA with DR = 40% and capital ratio = 8%
   112 ROA(1 − .4) = 0.96
        ROA = 1.43%

Case 3: What dividend payment rate will support 12% asset growth?
   Solve for DR with ROA = 0.99% and capital ratio = 8%
   112(.0099)(1 − DR) = 0.96
        DR = .1342

Case 4: What increase in external capital is necessary to support 12% asset growth?
   ΔEC = 0.96 − 112(0.0099)(1 − .4)
       = 0.30

Application of equation (12.3)
Case 2: .12 = ROA(1 −.4)/[.08 − ROA(1 − .4)]; ROA = .0143

Case 3: .12 = .0099(1 − DR)/[.08 − .0099(1 − DR)]; DR = .1342

Case 4: .12 = [.0099(1 − .4) + ΔEC/TA₁]/[.0099(1 − .4)]
        ΔEC/TA₁ = 0.30

[a]ROA = Return on assets

The relationship for internally generated capital can be summarized by the following constraints.[8]
Let

   TA = total assets
   EQ = equity capital
   ROA = return on assets
   DR = dividend payout rate

[8]See the discussion by Bernon, 1978. A simple approximation to Equation (12.2) is DTA/TA1 ¢ ROA(1 − DR)(TA2/EQ2) or the rate of asset growth equals the product of RDA, the earnings retention ratio, and the leverage ratio.

and the subscripts refer to the beginning of the period (1) or the end of the period (2). Capital constraints require that the asset growth rate equal the rate of growth in equity capital:

$$\Delta TA / TA_1 = \Delta EQ / EQ_1 \tag{12.1}$$

If all new capital is retained earnings, then Equation (12.1) can be restated as providing the following sustainable growth rate in assets:

$$\Delta TA / TA_1 = [EQ_2 - EQ_1] / EQ_1$$

$$= \frac{[EQ_1 + ROA(1 - DR)TA_2] - EQ_1}{EQ_1}$$

$$= \frac{ROA(1 - DR)}{[EQ_2 - ROA(1 - DR)TA_2] / TA_2} \tag{12.2}$$

$$= \frac{ROA(1 - DR)}{(EQ_2 / TA_2) - ROA(1 - DR)}$$

The numerator equals the ROA times the earnings retention rate. Equation (12.2) demonstrates the effect of minimum equity capital ratios on asset growth, earnings requirements, and dividend payouts. For example, a bank that targets an 8-percent capital ratio, a 1.2-percent ROA, and a 35-percent dividend payout rate can increase assets by over 10.8 percent. Banks without access to the capital markets can essentially grow only at the rate of growth in equity from retained earnings.

The basic model can be expanded to allow for external capital growth. Letting EC represent additions to external capital, asset growth is constrained by:

$$\Delta TA / TA_1 = \frac{ROA(1 - DR) + \Delta EC / TA_1}{(EQ_2 / TA_2) - ROA(1 - DR)} \tag{12.3}$$

If in the above example the bank also obtains new external capital equal to 0.3 percent of the original assets ($300,000), asset growth can again equal 12 percent, with a 0.99-percent ROA, an 8-percent equity-to-asset ratio, and a 40-percent dividend payout rate. Formulas (12.2) and (12.3) are applied at the bottom of Exhibit 12.8 using the data for each case.

Changing the Capital Mix

Banks that choose to grow faster than the rate allowed with internally generated capital alone must raise additional capital externally. Here, large banks operate with a competitive advantage over smaller banks. In particular, large banks can obtain capital nationally through public offerings of securities. Their name recognition is high and investors willingly purchase the instruments of quality organizations. Small banks, in contrast, can typically issue capital securities to only a few investors, such as existing shareholders, bank customers, and upstream correspondent banks. Limits to growth are far more rigid. One solution, often pursued, is for small bank shareholders to sell their stock to a holding company with greater access to funding sources.

Many large banks responded to the increased capital requirements in 1985 and 1990 by issuing new capital securities. The most popular forms were long-term debt requiring conversion to common stock and adjustable-rate, perpetual preferred stock. Several banks also entered into sale and leaseback arrangements with bank real estate properties to generate one-time infusions of capital. This arrangement typically costs relatively little and can be easily implemented to acquire large amounts of capital. The aggregate effect has been to gradually increase the proportion of total capital represented by common and preferred stock and their hybrids.

Changing Asset Composition

Banks may respond by changing their asset composition. Managers who are risk-averse may shift assets from high-risk categories such as commercial loans with a 100-percent risk weight to lower-risk categories. The natural consequence is that while required risk-based capital declines, potential profitability declines as well. The fear among regulators, however, is that other banks facing higher capital requirements may actually shift assets into higher-risk categories or off-balance-sheet commitments in pursuit of extraordinary returns. This would increase the overall risk profile of the banking industry in contrast to what the regulators desire.

Pricing Policies

One of the advantages of risk-based capital requirements is that they explicitly recognize that some investments are riskier than others. The riskiest investments require the greatest equity capital support. Banks have been forced to reprice assets to reflect these mandatory equity allocations. For example, if a bank has to hold capital in support of a loan commitment, it should raise the fee it charges to compensate for the greater cost of providing that service compared to the time when capital was not required. In fact, all off-balance sheet items should now be priced higher. Remember that equity is expensive. Thus a bank should also raise loan rates on its highest-risk assets that require the greatest capital relative to other asset yields.

Shrinking the Bank

Historically, banks tried to circumvent capital requirements by moving assets off the books. Interest rate and product deregulation encouraged banks to transfer risks off the balance sheet by creating contingent liabilities that produce fee income but do not show up as assets in financial reports. Because off-balance-sheet activity increases risk, bank regulators included off-balance-sheet items in the base when calculating risk-weighted assets. In today's banking environment, the greater a bank's off-balance-sheet commitments, the greater are its capital requirements. In actuality regulators examine a bank's off-balance-sheet exposure and may selectively request additional capital above the risk-based standards when the exposure is deemed to be great.

Alternatively, banks can meet the new standards by shrinking in size. As such, existing capital represents a higher fraction of the smaller asset base. The problem is that a shrinking bank has difficulty generating earnings growth and thus paying shareholders a reasonable risk-adjusted return. Not surprisingly, banks with capital problems often look to merge with stronger banks and may only survive as part of another firm.

CHARACTERISTICS OF EXTERNAL CAPITAL SOURCES

Internally generated capital can support asset growth at a rate implied by Equation (12.2). Banks that choose to expand more rapidly must obtain additional capital from external sources, a capability determined by asset size. Large banks tap the capital markets regularly, but small banks must pay a stiff premium to obtain capital, if it is available at all. While there are many different types of capital sources, they can be grouped into one of four categories: subordinated debt, common stock, preferred stock, and leases. Each carries advantages and disadvantages.

Subordinated Debt

For the past 25 years, banks have been able to use subordinated debt to meet capital requirements. This debt constitutes capital because of its relatively long maturities and funding permanence. It does not qualify as Tier 1 or core capital because it eventually matures and must be replenished, unlike common equity. It also imposes an interest expense burden on the bank when earnings are low. Subordinated debt must possess several specific features before the regulators accept it as capital. First, debtholders' claims must be subordinated to depositors' claims. If the bank fails, insured depositors are paid first, followed by uninsured depositors, then subordinated debtholders. Second, only debt with an original weighted average maturity of at least 7 years qualifies as capital.

Subordinated debt offers several advantages to banks. Most important, interest payments are tax-deductible, so the cost of financing is below that for equity sources. Because they are debt instruments, shareholders do not reduce their proportionate ownership interest, and earnings are not immediately diluted. Furthermore, this type of debt generates additional profits for shareholders as long as earnings before interest and taxes exceed interest payments. Thus shareholders may receive higher dividends, and greater retained earnings may increase the capital base. Fixed-rate debt accentuates this profit potential.

Subordinated debt also has shortcomings. Interest and principal payments are mandatory and, if missed, constitute default. Also, many issues require sinking funds that increase liquidity pressures as banks allocate funds to repay principal. Finally, from the regulators' perspective, debt is worse than equity because it has fixed maturities and banks cannot charge losses against it. Subordinated debt and equity, however, protect depositors and the FDIC equally.

Some subordinated debt pays variable rates that fluctuate with selected interest rate indexes. These securities consequently trade close to par, as the yield changes when market rates change. Banks can pay initial rates below those for comparable fixed-rate debt because they are assuming the interest rate risk. Many bank holding companies also issue mandatory convertible debt in the form of either equity commitment notes or mandatory convertible notes. Both types require that banks issue common stock, perpetual preferred stock, or other primary capital securities to redeem the convertible debt. The average convertible debt issue carries floating rates, matures in 12 years, and contains an option for the debtor to redeem the security any time after 4 years.

Common Stock

Common stock is preferred by regulators as a source of external capital. It has no fixed maturity and thus represents a permanent source of funds. Dividend payments are also discretionary, so that common stock does not require fixed charges against earnings. Losses can be charged against equity, not debt, so common stock better protects the FDIC.

Common stock is not as attractive from the bank's perspective due to its high cost. Because dividends are not tax-deductible, they must be paid out of after-tax earnings. They are also variable in the sense that shareholders expect per-share dividend rates to rise with increases in bank earnings. Transactions costs on new issues exceed comparable costs on debt, and shareholders are sensitive to earnings dilution and possible loss of control in ownership. Most firms wait until share prices are high and earnings performance is strong before selling stock. A positive feature of the Tax Reform Act of 1986 is that it makes common stock more attractive to a firm compared with debt. By lowering corporate marginal income tax rates, the act increased the cost of tax-deductible interest on debt relative to the nondeductible dividend cost of common stock.

Issuing common stock is frequently not a viable alternative for a bank that needs capital. If the current share price is far below book value, new issues dilute the ownership interests of existing shareholders. Stocks of the largest banks are traded in national markets with substantial liquidity. Bank managers attempt to increase share prices through strong earnings, consistent dividend policy, and adequate disclosure of performance to security analysts. Even with these efforts, however, stock prices often fall with adverse economic conditions or disfavor in the industry market. At these times, other capital sources are less expensive.[9] When stock prices are low, many large banks issue debt that is convertible into common stock. Investors accept lower interest payments in view of the option to convert the security into common stock. The conversion price is normally set 20 to 25 percent above the share price at time of issue so that eventual conversions are not as costly.

Small bank stocks are traded over the counter, with far fewer annual transactions. Still, a market for new issues does exist within local communities. Banks can often

---

[9]Many large holding company banks raise new equity by issuing securities via private placements outside the United States. They can lower underwriting fees by as much as 25 percent and shorten the length of time to place an issue.

sell new shares to existing stockholders or current customers. Share prices are less volatile but are sensitive to deviations in current versus historical earnings.

Preferred Stock

Preferred stock is a form of equity in which investors' claims are senior to those of common stockholders. As with common stock, preferred stock pays nondeductible dividends out of after-tax dollars. One significant difference is that corporate investors in preferred stock pay taxes on only 20 percent of dividends. For this reason, institutional investors dominate the market. New issues are effectively restricted to large, well-known banking organizations that are familiar to institutional investors, while smaller banks are excluded.

Since 1982 preferred stock has been an attractive source of primary capital for large banks. Most issues take the form of adjustable-rate perpetual stock. The dividend rate changes quarterly according to a Treasury yield formula. Investors earn a return equal to some spread above or below the highest of the 3-month Treasury bill rate and the 10- or 20-year constant maturity Treasury rates. The size of the spread and whether it is above or below the base yield reflects the perceived quality of the issuing bank. J.P. Morgan & Co., for example, issued adjustable-rate preferred stock at 487.5 basis points below the Treasury formula in February 1983.

Investors are attracted to adjustable-rate preferred stock because they earn a yield that reflects the highest point on the Treasury yield curve under all market conditions. This removes guesswork as to whether short-term yields will move more or less than long-term yields and whether they will all move in the same direction. Unlike fixed-rate issues, these securities trade close to par and thus are more liquid. They effectively represent 3-month securities and have been sold to individuals as well as to corporations.

Preferred stock has the same disadvantages as common stock, but there are instances when it is more attractive. First, if a bank's common stock is priced below book value and has a low price-to-earnings ratio, new equity issues dilute earnings. This earnings dilution is less with perpetual preferred stock than with common stock, so that the cost of common shares is relatively higher. Second, aggregate dividend payments on preferred stock will be less than dividends on common stock over time for any bank that regularly increases common stock dividends. Cash flow requirements on perpetual preferred shares will also be lower because no sinking fund allocations are required to repay principal.

Leasing Arrangements

Many banks enter into sale and leaseback arrangements as a source of immediate capital. Most transactions involve selling bank-owned headquarters and other real estate and simultaneously leasing it back from the buyer. The terms of the lease can be structured to allow the bank to maintain complete control of the property, as if the title never changes hands, yet receive large amounts of cash at low cost. Lease rates run 1 to 2 percent below rates on subordinated debt. A sale and leaseback transaction effectively converts the appreciated value of real estate listed on the bank's books at cost to cash. The price appreciation is taxed at normal income tax rates, with most of the gain flowing to the bottom line as increased earnings. The transaction can be effected quickly when a buyer is located and avoids the high placement costs of stocks and bonds.[10]

CAPITAL PLANNING

Capital planning is part of the overall asset and liability management process. Bank management makes decisions regarding the amount of risk assumed in operations and potential returns. The amount and type of capital required is determined simultaneously with the expected composition of assets and liabilities and forecasts of income and expenses. The greater is assumed risk and asset growth, the greater is required capital.

Capital planning begins with management generating pro forma balance sheets and income statements for the next several years. The bank projects the dollar funding available from alternative deposit and nondeposit sources and the likely asset composition, given the bank's product mix and expertise. Assuming various interest rate scenarios and projections of noninterest income and expense, management forecasts earnings. Asset growth in excess of that financed with new debt or internally generated capital must be financed with external capital. Once a bank recognizes that it needs to obtain additional capital externally, it evaluates the costs and benefits of each source.

The Planning Process

The planning process can be summarized in three steps:

1. Generate pro forma balance sheets and income statements for the bank.
2. Select a dividend payout.
3. Analyze the costs and benefits of alternative sources of external capital.

The first step provides an estimate of how much capital is needed to finance assets. Total equity capital required equals the residual between expected assets and expected debt. The amount of qualifying primary and secondary capital must at least equal the regulatory minimums. If management chooses to shrink the bank by liquidating assets, it may find that total capital required declines. Typically, additional equity capital is needed. The second step identifies how much capital will be generated internally and what amount of external capital is necessary. Dividend payments reduce the amount of retained earnings and add pressure for external capital funding. The third step involves evaluating alternatives. Management should project bank needs over several years so that it can develop a long-term plan. To be flexible, it should not rely extensively on any single source of capital in the short run, so that it can retain that

---

[10]If the sale conforms to FASB statement no. 13, the operating lease does not require capitalization and the transaction further provides off-balance-sheet financing. The capital gains tax advantage was eliminated in 1987.

option in future years. If, for example, a bank is leveraged to the maximum, it may be forced to issue new stock at a time when its share price is low. Chapter 13 introduces quantitative measures of the costs of different capital components.

Applications

Bank capital planning used to be a simple process. Management projected asset growth and retained earnings to show that capital ratios would be strong. Today, capital plans are typically an outgrowth of sophisticated asset and liability management planning models. They are carefully scrutinized by regulators to verify that key assumptions regarding asset quality, loan losses, and net interest margins are realistic. The output itself is the same pro forma balance sheet and income statement data presented in traditional performance reports. (See Chapter 4).

Capital planning can be illustrated using the reporting framework of Exhibit 12.8. Consider a bank that has exhibited a deteriorating profit trend. Classified assets and loan-loss provisions are rising, and earnings prospects are relatively bleak, given the economic environment. Federal regulators who recently examined the bank indicated that the bank should increase its primary capital-to-asset ratio to 8.5 percent from its current 7 percent within 4 years.

The planning process consists of generating pro forma balance sheets and income statements over the next 4 years. Because regulators closely examine historical earnings and are keenly aware of asset problems, the initial pro forma statements should incorporate recent earnings trends slowly, moving the bank toward peer bank averages for key ratios. Often bankers conclude that their bank will meet capital guidelines easily because they overstate earnings. Regulators quickly point out the deficiencies and recommend substantial adjustments.

Suppose that the hypothetical bank reported the summary performance measures listed in Exhibit 12.9 for 1992. Because of asset quality problems, the $80 million bank reported an ROA of just 0.45 percent, less than one-half its average over the past 5 years. The current capital ratio is 7 percent, or 1.5 percent less than the regulatory target. During each of the past 5 years the bank paid $250,000 in common dividends.

The first part of the exhibit simply extrapolates historical asset growth of 10 percent through 1996, assuming that earnings slowly rise to where ROA equals 0.75 percent in the fourth year. Under these conditions and the assumed continued dividend payout, the bank's total capital ratio would decrease to 6.1 percent by 1996. This is clearly unacceptable under the regulatory directive.

The following three parts identify different strategies to meet the required 8.5 percent capital ratio by 1996 and present summary performance measures. The second section examines the impact of shrinking the bank. The quickest way to increase a capital ratio is to reduce the denominator, or shrink the bank's asset base. As discussed earlier, many banks are shrinking to produce this result. Shrinkage can normally be achieved by reducing the bank's loan exposure and letting high-cost purchased liabilities run off. In this example, the bank gradually reduces its assets by $1 million per year until 1996, when the capital ratio reaches 8.55 percent. The capital ratio increases

Exhibit 12.9 Capital Planning: Performance Measures for a Bank with Deficient Capital Ratios (Millions of Dollars)

Historical Growth: $250,000 in Dividends

	1992	1993	1994	1995	1996
Total assets	$80.00	$88.00	$96.80	$106.48	$117.13
Net interest margin	4.40%	4.40%	4.50%	4.60%	4.70%
ROA	0.45%	0.45%	0.60%	0.65%	0.75%
Total capital	$ 5.60	$ 5.75	$ 6.08	$ 6.52	$ 7.15
Capital ratio	7.00%	6.53%	6.28%	6.13%	6.10%

Shrink the Bank: $250,000 in Dividends

	1992	1993	1994	1995	1996
Total assets	$80.00	$79.00	$78.00	$ 77.00	$ 76.00
Net interest margin	4.40%	4.40%	4.50%	4.60%	4.70%
ROA	0.45%	0.45%	0.60%	0.65%	0.75%
Total capital	$ 5.60	$ 5.71	$ 5.93	$ 6.18	$ 6.50
Capital ratio	7.00%	7.22%	7.60%	8.03%	8.55%

Slow Growth: No Dividends

	1992	1993	1994	1995	1996
Total assets	$80.00	$82.00	$84.00	$ 86.00	$ 88.00
Net interest margin	4.40%	4.40%	4.50%	4.60%	4.70%
ROA	0.45%	0.45%	0.60%	0.65%	0.75%
Total capital	$ 5.60	$ 5.97	$ 6.47	$ 7.03	$ 7.69
Capital ratio	7.00%	7.28%	7.71%	8.17%	8.74%

Slow Growth: $250,000 in Dividends, $800,000 External Capital Injection in 1995

	1992	1993	1994	1995	1996
Total assets	$80.00	$82.00	$84.00	$ 86.00	$ 88.00
Net interest margin	4.40%	4.40%	4.50%	4.60%	4.70%
ROA	0.45%	0.45%	0.60%	0.65%	0.75%
Total capital	$ 5.60	$ 5.72	$ 5.97	$ 7.08	$ 7.49
Capital ratio	7.00%	6.97%	7.11%	8.23%	8.51%

continuously because the denominator (total assets) is falling while the numerator (capital) is rising with the growth in retained earnings.

A bank can also increase its capital by cutting its dividend payments. The third section projects the bank's capital position assuming slow asset growth at $2 million annually while eliminating the $250,000 dividend payment. Retained earnings increases more than total assets producing a capital ratio of 8.74 percent in 1996, which exceeds the target.

The final alternative proposes that the bank grow slowly and maintain its dividend, but issue $800,000 in common stock to meet its capital requirement. In this case, the bank would wait until its earnings position had improved sufficiently, 1995 in this pro forma, before issuing external capital. Again, the projected capital ratio just exceeds the regulatory target by 1996.

In practice, a bank's asset and liability management committee will consider numerous other alternatives by varying assumptions until it determines the best plan. What is best depends on a comparison of the costs of each alternative. Eliminating dividends, for example, reduces stock prices and makes it extremely difficult and costly to raise external capital later. If the bank plans to add capital externally, it must carefully measure placement costs and their subsequent impact on share prices. For instance, if a bank issues subordinated debt, it must estimate the direct transactions costs and set aside a portion of future cash flows to service the debt. The same would apply to common stock issues and dividend payments.

Regulatory Policy Toward Capital During the 1990s

Regulators clearly prefer that banks operate with as much capital as possible. The obvious benefit is that capital, particularly stockholders' equity, reduces the risk of failure and thus lowers the need for monitoring by regulators. During the early 1990s, regulators often commented on the need for raising capital requirements even beyond the risk-based minimums. They encouraged banks to obtain additional capital by intimating that only capital-rich banks would be allowed to engage in nontraditional banking activities, such as insurance and corporate securities underwriting. In addition, proposals to modify the deposit insurance system generally favor banks with substantial capital by allowing them to pay lower premiums. In 1991 the U.S. Treasury even proposed, as part of its plan to restructure the banking industry, that banks be allowed to merge with nonfinancial corporations and engage in previously prohibited activities as long as the banks were well-capitalized.

Healthy banks have responded by regularly tapping the capital markets with new issues of common stock, preferred stock, and subordinated debt. Of course, it is a two-tiered market where only healthy banks, the ones that are already well-capitalized and have limited asset quality problems, can issue new stock. These banks will be the acquirers of failed banks through the Resolution Trust Corporation's closing of failed institutions and buyers of assets from problem banks. Customers also have a preference for highly capitalized banks because they know they will be around in times of crisis and will not alter their lending policies or sell cash management services on a whim. Capital is king in the banking industry.

SUMMARY

This chapter addresses six basic issues: What are the features of the new risk-based capital standards? What constitutes bank capital? What function does capital serve? How much capital is adequate? What effect do regulatory capital requirements have on bank operating policies? What considerations are important in capital planning?

Bank capital fulfills three basic functions. It serves as a cushion against loan losses and thus helps protect the interests of depositors and the FDIC. It provides access to financial markets so that management can borrow to offset liquidity problems. It also limits growth by forcing banks to add capital in support of asset expansion. Each purpose serves to reduce bank risk directly and ultimately to protect the viability of the deposit insurance funds.

Because of these functions, federal regulators consider bank capital to be much broader than accounting capital. Regulatory capital therefore includes certain debt and loss reserve components. Effective in 1992 the FDIC, OCC, and Federal Reserve

System changed bank capital standards to conform uniformly to risk-based capital requirements. Each bank must hold common equity equal to a minimum 4 percent of risk-weighted assets, and total capital cannot fall below 8 percent of risk-weighted assets. For the first time, regulators tied capital asset requirements to the perceived default risk of bank assets and off-balance-sheet commitments. Unfortunately, the standards do not take account of interest rate risk or liquidity risk. Banks with special problems, however, need to increase capital more according to specific regulatory directives. These capital requirements have, in turn, forced banks to slow growth, limit their loan exposure, change their asset composition, and find new methods of generating profits and obtaining external capital. A final impact is that banks now actively prepare and analyze capital plans as part of their annual risk/return performance review.

Questions

Capital and Risk

1. Banks, like all businesses, are risky and that risk is a function of the leverage of the business. Operating and financial leverage interact to create total leverage. If a business or industry is structured to use high levels of operating leverage, then it typically tends to use low levels of financial leverage. Define these two types of leverage and explain the amount of each in banking.

2. What are the advantages and disadvantages of using financial leverage? Consider this question from the banker's view and then from a bank regulator's view.

3. What is risk-based capital and why is it suddenly so important?

4. What is the Basle Agreement? What was the motivation for such an agreement? What are the three points of the agreement?

5. For bank regulators there are three types of capital requirements—Tier 1 capital, total capital, and leverage capital. List the balance sheet accounts that are included in Tier 1 capital. What additional accounts are included in total capital? Why are leverage capital requirements important?

Calculating Capital

6. A bank has financed itself in the following manner:

Demand deposits	$ 10,000
Time deposits	500,000
CDs	400,000
Fed funds purchased	30,000
Convertible bonds	300
Subordinated bonds	500
Loan loss reserves	200
Retained earnings	200
Common stock	300
Surplus	600

How much Tier 1 capital does this bank have? How much total capital?

7. How many dollars in risk-weighted assets does the following bank have?

Cash	$ 100
Balances due from Fed	50
Items in the process of collection	60
Treasury bills	5,000
Long-term Treasury securities	3,000
Long-term government agency securities	2,000
Munis (based on taxing authority)	10,000
University dorm bonds (revenue bonds)	4,000
Commercial loans	700,000
Third-world loans	200,000
Premises	400

8. First Student Bank (FSB) has the following balance sheet:

Assets		Liabilities and equity	
Cash	$ 100	Transactions accounts	$ 700
Treasury bills (30 days)	190	CDs	220
Treasury bonds (5 years)	30	Subordinated debt	7
Repos	10	Preferred stock	5
Student tuition loans	500	Retained earnings	48
Student home mortgages	100	Common stock	5
FSB's building and furniture	110	Surplus	15
Loan loss reserves	(40)		
Total	$1,000	Total	$1,000

The bank is only 2 years old and is desperately trying to break into the local market for student loans. As a result it has followed the policy of guaranteeing for 3 additional years tuition loans to every student who promptly paid off his first- year loan. This policy has been a success and the bank has signed agreements guaranteeing $800 in loans. The bank has also tried to encourage the building of one- to four-family homes in the vicinity of campus. The bank is willing to lend money on these properties and to commit to repurchasing the homes when the students graduate. The repurchase price is settled at the time the mortgage is written such that the whole package is expected to be profitable for the bank. Currently the bank has obligated itself to spend $75 to repurchase homes.

a. Since this is a student-owned-and-run bank and since it does not operate in international markets, does it need to comply with the risk-based capital rules?

b. How many dollars of common equity capital does this bank have? How many dollars of Tier 1 capital does it have?

c. How many dollars of total capital does this bank have?

d. Categorize the bank's assets by risk category. How many dollars of category 1, category 2, etc.?

e. How many dollars of contingencies does this bank have? (After applying the appropriate conversion factor.)

f. How many dollars of risk-adjusted assets does FSB own?

g. Does FSB have adequate Tier 1 capital? adequate total capital?

Function and Effect of Capital

9. Explain how capital reduces banking risks. Discuss the importance of cash flows and economic value rather than accounting value.

10. If the FDIC dropped the deposit insurance coverage from $100,000 to $30,000, and if the reduced coverage was redefined to be a dollar limit per depositor, what would be the effect on a bank's liquidity risk? How would the change in liquidity risk affect the bank's optimal level of financial leverage?

11. A bank is forecasting a return on assets of 1.20 percent for next year. From the profits it will pay 30 percent as dividends and retain the rest. If the bank desires to maintain its equity at 8 percent per $100 million in assets, how fast can its assets grow without selling new stock? If all asset growth occurs in the loan portfolio that constitutes 70 percent of total assets, at what rate will the loan portfolio grow? If the bank increases its equity by selling 5,000 new shares for $100 each, how fast could its total assets grow?

12. Many regulators would like to see bank capital requirements raised. A recent proposal suggested that the minimum capital ratio should be set at 10 percent. What impact would this have on bank risk? Would small and large banks share equal opportunity in meeting these requirements?

13. Your bank has been presented with the opportunity to participate with a consortium of banks investing in a local recycling plant. The risk/return profile of the project suggests a better return than any investment the bank has made in the last two years. Advertising the bank's participation in local community development and in the future of an environmentally safe world should allow the bank to attract even more deposits. The loan, however, would be large and the bank is not growing fast enough to accept the loan, maintain its current policies, and meet its capital requirements. Floating new securities is not an option since the bank just sold new shares a few months ago. The only way the bank can participate in this project is to cut its dividend payment by 70 percent. What are the advantages and disadvantages of participating in this loan? If you think the bank should take the loan, what additional actions could the bank take to ameliorate any negative effect of the dividend cut?

14. Two competing commercial banks situated in the same community have comparable asset portfolios, but one operates with a total capital ratio of 8 percent, while the other operates with a ratio of 10 percent. Compare the opportunities and risks of the two banks.

15. Explain why increased regulatory capital requirements lead to a greater consolidation of the banking industry.

16. Risk-based capital requirements may induce bank managers to change their asset composition. Explain why. Determine how a shift in the following would affect a bank's required capital. How would each shift affect the bank's profit potential?
    a. from consumer loans to one- to four-family mortgages
    b. from U.S. agency securities to construction loans
    c. from short-term U.S. Treasury bills to cash

17. Explain why risk-based capital requirements should alter bank pricing of loans and securities.

18. A bank has decided it must raise external capital. Discuss the advantages and disadvantages of each of the following choices:

a. subordinated debt

b. preferred stock

c. common stock

References

Bennett, Barbara. "S&L Accounting." *Weekly Letter* (Federal Reserve Bank of San Francisco, December 21, 1984).

Bernon, David G. "Capacity for Asset Growth Model: A Tool for Internal Bank Management and External Bank Analysis." *The Magazine of Bank Administration* (August 1978).

Charlton, William. "The Pricing Effects of the Risk-Based Capital Regulations." *Journal of Commercial Bank Lending* (April 1991).

Cole, C. Alexander, and Gerald Fischer. "Risk-Based Capital: A Loan and Credit Officer's Primer." *The Journal of Commercial Bank Lending* (August 1988).

Chu, Franklin. "Toward a Flexible Capital Structure." *The Bankers Magazine* (May–June 1986).

Gilbert, Alton, Courtenay Stone, and Michael Trebing. "The New Bank Capital Standards." *Review* (Federal Reserve Bank of St. Louis, May 1985).

Hanley, Thomas, John Leonard, Diane Glossman, and Alan Freudenstein. *Money Center Banks: Capital Adequacy*, Salomon Brothers, (September 1989).

Hempel, George, and Howard Crosse. *Management Policies for Commercial Banks.* New York: Prentice-Hall, 1980.

Keeley, Michael. "Bank Capital Regulation in the 1980's: Effective or Ineffective?" *Economic Review*, (Federal Reserve Bank of San Francisco, Winter 1988).

Keeton, William. "The New Risk-Based Capital Plan for Commercial Banks." *Economic Review*, (Federal Reserve Bank of Kansas City, December 1989).

MacRae, Desmond. "Where's the Capital?" *Bank Administration* (November 1989).

Mahar, Maggie. "Paper Dragons." *Barron's*, (August 27, 1990).

Santomero, Anthony, and Joseph Vinso. "Estimating the Probability of Failure for Commercial Banks and the Banking System." *Journal of Banking and Finance* (1977).

Talley, S.H. "Bank Capital Trends and Financing: Study Summary." *Federal Reserve Bulletin* (February 1983).

Vojta, George. *Bank Capital Adequacy.* New York: First National City Bank, 1973.

Wall, Larry. "Regulation of Banks' Equity Capital." *Economic Review* (Federal Reserve Bank of Atlanta, November 1985).

Wall, Larry, and David Peterson. "The Effect of Capital Adequacy Guidelines on Large Bank Holding Companies." *Journal of Banking and Finance* (December 1987).

Wall, Larry, John Pringle, and James McNulty. "Capital Requirements for Interest-Rate and Foreign-Exchange Hedges." *Economic Review* (Federal Reserve Bank of Atlanta, May/June 1990).

FIRST FINANCIAL REVISITED: CAPITAL PROBLEMS

Bankers occasionally refer to the FDIC as representing the fact that bank regulators are "forever demanding increased capital." At the time C. W. Hampton visits First Financial, the bank is deficient in meeting minimum regulatory capital requirements. In terms of the ratios introduced in this chapter, First Financial meets neither the 5.5-percent and 6-percent primary and secondary capital ratios nor the 4-percent and 8-percent risk-weighted capital ratios. Regulators have encouraged the bank to find a buyer because a sale represents the best potential source of new capital.

Consider the following regarding First Financial's operating performance:

- The bank reported losses for the two most recent years, and management projects losses through two more years. With losses, retained earnings declines, thereby lowering capital.

- Members of the board of directors had recently purchased stock in the bank, which raised capital that was now depleted.

- Depositors were withdrawing funds in large volume, and the bank was forced to borrow emergency funds from the Federal Reserve to remain afloat. If this funding source were removed, the bank would have to liquidate assets at distressed prices. To meet capital requirements, it would have to shrink its assets subsantially.

- The move to risk-based capital requirements will necessitate that the bank have above-average capital because of its heavy exposure to real estate loans, which are in the highest risk class.

Obviously, First Financial is a problem bank that faces serious problems in raising additional capital without a new investor group. Because of the bank's asset quality and funding problems, depositors are generally unwilling to provide uninsured funds. Similarly, the bank has limited access to new external sources of capital unless investors are indemnified against losses on the existing assets. Such investors will often wait until regulators close the bank, then try to underbid other purchasers. First Financial thus has few options, none of which is attractive to current stockholders.

Chapter 13

Measuring the Cost of Funds and Controlling Noninterest Expense

It is extremely important that banks continuously monitor the cost of their funding sources. Changes in the composition of liabilities and equity alter financing costs and may reduce available liquidity. Changes in financing costs require corresponding changes in asset yields to maintain profit margins. With increased competition among financial services companies, both the frequency and magnitude of these changes have increased significantly.

This chapter examines four related issues. First, it discusses the appropriate use of average historical costs and presents a procedure for measuring the weighted marginal cost of funds. Marginal costs for single sources of funds are then compared with average historical costs for a sample commercial bank. Second, it describes internal funds transfer pricing schemes based on marginal funding costs applied to profit centers within a bank. Third, it summarizes the relationship between financing events and a bank's liquidity, credit, and interest rate risk position. In general, the removal of interest rate ceilings on bank liabilities has reduced bank funding stability by increasing the dollar amount of rate-sensitive liabilities, lowering a bank's base of core deposits, and creating an environment in which banks seek higher yields by lowering asset quality. Finally, it describes the importance of controlling noninterest expense and analyzes recent trends toward cost reductions and their impact on bank consolidation and competitiveness.

Managing liabilities used to be relatively routine for most commercial banks. Federal regulators dictated maximum rates banks could pay on deposits, and customers had few alternatives for their savings. Banks competed for depositors primarily through location and personal service. Customers were quite loyal. These factors gave rise to the well-known 3-6-3 method of running a bank: pay 3 percent on deposits, charge 6 percent on loans, and hit the golf course at 3 p.m.

Reading any newspaper or financial publication shows how different the environment is today. Most noticeably, deposit rate ceilings no longer exist. Banks have almost unlimited opportunities to develop new deposit products with any maturity that pay market rates, but they must now compete with a variety of firms offering similar products and services. Any individual wishing to open a simple transaction account can use a commercial bank, credit union, savings and loan, or a money market mutual fund offered by a brokerage house, American Express, or a general retailer such as Sears. While this choice is attractive to consumers, it creates considerable uncertainty for banks regarding the availability and cost of funding sources.

EVALUATING THE COST OF BANK FUNDS

It is important that management understand how to measure the cost of financing bank operations. Accurate cost measurements permit the bank to compare prices between alternative funding sources and to assure that assets are priced high enough to cover costs and pay shareholders a required return. During the 1970s and early 1980s, most banks tied loan rates to prime rates set by large regional or money center banks. They had no control over when the base rate would be changed or by how much. Now, however, many firms use internally generated cost of funds estimates that serve as base rates in pricing loans. These estimates enable them to adjust loan rates, when appropriate, to protect spreads. The following analysis describes two approaches to estimating the cost of total bank funds. Before doing so, it summarizes differences in the concepts of average and marginal cost of funds.

The Average Historical Cost of Funds

The average cost of funds is a measure of average unit borrowing costs for existing funds. Average interest cost for the total portfolio is calculated by dividing total interest expense by the average dollar amount of liabilities outstanding and measures the average percentage cost of a single dollar of debt. Average historical costs for a single source of funds can be calculated as the ratio of interest expense by source to the average outstanding debt for that source during the period. The interest cost rates in Chapter 4 represent such costs.

Many banks incorrectly use average historical costs in their pricing decisions. They simply add historical interest expense with noninterest expense (net of noninterest income) and divide by the investable amount of funds to determine the minimum return required on earning assets. Any profit is represented as a markup.

The primary problem with historical costs is that they provide no information as to whether future interest costs will rise or fall. When interest rates rise, average historical costs understate the actual cost of issuing new debt. Fixed-rate asset yields based on historical costs will not be high enough to cover costs and meet profit targets.[1] When interest rates fall, the opposite occurs. Average historical costs overstate actual interest costs on new debt so that fixed-rate loans might be priced too high to be competitive. The use of average costs assumes that interest rates will be constant at historical levels during the current pricing period.

Pricing decisions should be based on marginal costs compared with marginal revenues. Suppose that a bank can make a new, 1-year loan at 12 percent. The bank's simple average cost of funds equals 8 percent. If the bank compares the new loan rate (marginal revenue rate) with the average cost of funds to determine whether it will make the loan, it estimates a 4 percent spread and accepts the loan. Suppose that it must finance the loan at the margin by issuing a new, 1-year jumbo CD at 13 percent. This represents the marginal interest cost of a single source of new funds. If the bank compares the marginal loan rate with the marginal CD rate, it estimates a negative 1-percent spread and rejects the loan. Because pricing new loans is an incremental decision, it should be based on incremental (marginal) funding costs, not historical average costs. If the bank makes the loan, it loses at least 1 percent on the transaction because its incremental interest expense will exceed its incremental interest income by at least 1 percent of the loan amount.

The best use of average historical costs is in evaluating past performance. It is relatively easy to understand, after the fact, why a bank's expenses and profits differ from peer banks' by comparing average borrowing costs and asset yields. Average costs for noninterest expenses, such as check handling and brokerage fees, can also be evaluated and applied toward measuring expected new debt costs. Typically, these outlays increase by predictable amounts with inflation.

The Marginal Cost of Funds

The marginal cost of debt is a measure of the borrowing cost paid to acquire one additional unit of investable funds. The marginal cost of equity capital is a measure of the minimum acceptable rate of return required by shareholders. Together, the marginal costs of debt and equity constitute the marginal cost of funds, which can be viewed as independent sources or as a pool of funds.[2] Independent sources of funds have distinct marginal costs that vary with market interest rates, handling costs, and reserve requirements. These independent costs can then be combined to yield an overall weighted marginal cost estimate for all new funds. When interest rates are expected to rise,

---

[1]Many analysts attributed the failure of Franklin National Bank in 1974 to its failure to distinguish between average and marginal costs. Franklin's management, using average historical costs to project borrowing costs in a rising interest rate environment, invested in fixed-rate assets yielding less than the incremental cost of new debt. Rose (1974) provides details.

[2]Banking terminology generally refers to the average or marginal cost of funds as the associated cost of liabilities alone. The cost of equity, or required return to shareholders, is incorporated as a required spread over the cost of debt necessary for a bank to meet profit targets and pay shareholders their required return.

Marginal versus Average

Confusion over the terms *average* and *marginal* makes it difficult to evaluate performance measures and understand pricing rules. This is especially true for average costs and weighted marginal costs, which are similar-sounding concepts. With cost and pricing data, readers should view simple averages as referring to historical values. The marginal concept, in contrast, refers to incremental or new values.

Consider, for example, a baseball player's batting average. The press reports a historical average representing the summary performance measure over all games played and a marginal average representing the last game. Suppose that during the first two games in a year, the player gets three hits out of ten batting attempts. His average is 3 divided by 10, or .300. Common usage omits the reference to percentage, so the batter is hitting 300. During the next game, the player gets two hits in five at-bats. His marginal average for the five incremental at-bats is 400, which raises his overall (historical) average to 333 (five hits in 15 at-bats). The player's overall average increases because the marginal performance (400) exceeded the previous historical average (300). If the player gets no hits in his next five at-bats (000 marginal average), his historical average will drop to 250.

---

marginal costs exceed historical costs. When rates are expected to fall, marginal costs are lower.

Marginal costs are especially useful in pricing decisions. If these costs are known, a bank can set asset yields at some markup over marginal costs to lock in a profitable spread. Presumably, the markup reflects default risk as well as the required return to shareholders. Marginal costs also serve as indicators of the relative cost of different funds, which banks can use to target the least expensive sources for financing growth.

Costs of Independent Sources of Funds. Unfortunately, it is difficult to measure marginal costs precisely. Management must include both interest and noninterest costs it expects to pay and identify which portion of the acquired funds can be invested in earning assets. There is also considerable disagreement on whether equity costs are relevant and, ultimately, how to measure equity costs. One researcher introduced a formula similar to that shown below for measuring the explicit marginal cost of a single source of bank liabilities.[3]

$$\text{Marginal cost} = \frac{\text{Interest rate} + \text{Servicing costs} + \text{Acquisition costs} + \text{Insurance}}{1 - \% \text{ of funds in nonearning assets}} \quad \textbf{(13.1)}$$

All elements of the numerator are expected costs annualized as a percentage of each dollar obtained. The denominator measures the fraction of liabilities that can be invested to generate interest income. With transactions accounts, for example, the fraction in nonearning assets will reflect legal reserve requirements plus any allocation

---

[3]Watson (1978) subtracts service charge income from the sum of costs listed in the numerator. This analysis distinguishes between revenues and costs associated with obtaining various sources of funds. This makes it easier to implement the individual account profitability analysis described in Chapter 24.

to such nonearning assets as float or correspondent balances. A bank may also add indirect costs to the numerator, such as the implicit cost of increased risk associated with higher leverage, to obtain an effective marginal cost estimate. Of these costs, only acquisition costs that primarily reflect marketing expenses are truly discretionary. Interest rates are largely determined by market conditions as banks are price takers, servicing costs are determined by the volume of check-processing business handled by a bank, and deposit insurance costs are set by the FDIC.

Consider the following marginal cost estimates associated with obtaining additional NOW account funding:

$$\text{market interest rate} = 6\%$$
$$\text{servicing costs} = 3.4\% \text{ of balances}$$
$$\text{acquisition costs} = 1\% \text{ of balances}$$
$$\text{deposit insurance costs} = 0.2\% \text{ of balances}$$
$$\text{percentage in nonearning assets} = 15\%$$

Equation (13.1) indicates that the estimated marginal cost of obtaining additional NOW balances equals 12.47 percent.

$$\text{marginal cost} = \frac{.06 + .034 + .01 + .002}{.85} = .1247$$

Intuitively, this cost estimate is the all-inclusive incremental cost of obtaining the investable balances from additional NOW funds.

Two problems create potentially large measurement errors. First, the relevant interest rate must be forecast over the entire planning horizon, a task made difficult by volatile interest rates. Thus forecasts need to be modified frequently.[4] Second, a bank must rely on its comptroller or cost accountant to generate meaningful estimates of noninterest costs associated with each debt source. This involves allocating overhead, advertising outlays, and the cost of employee time to handling checks, servicing customer complaints, posting account information, and bidding for public funds. In practice, many banks simply rely on the Functional Cost Analysis averages provided by the Federal Reserve. (See Chapter 11.) Note that some of these costs may be fixed and thus not vary with additional funding. They are still important in pricing issues because asset yields must then be set at a mark-up over the marginal cost of funds to cover the outlays.

The following discussion summarizes general procedures used to estimate the pretax marginal cost of various sources of bank funds. Tax implications are not considered for convenience and because pretax cost estimates are used in asset pricing decisions.

Cost of Debt. The marginal cost of different types of debt varies according to the magnitude of each type of liability. High-volume transactions accounts generate sub-

---

[4]For comparative purposes, all interest rates should be measured identically. Effective rates that recognize differences in discrete and continuous compounding and interest-bearing versus discount instruments should be used.

stantial servicing costs and have the highest reserve requirements and float. The advantage of low interest is offset by other costs and the fact that banks can invest a smaller percentage of investable funds. Purchased funds, in contrast, pay higher rates but carry smaller transactions costs and require lower reserves with greater investable balances.

The cost of long-term nondeposit debt equals the effective cost of borrowing from each source, including interest expense and transactions costs. Traditional analysis suggests that this cost is the discount rate, which equates the present value of expected interest and principal payments with the net proceeds to the bank from the issue. Suppose, for example, that a bank issues $10 million in par-value subordinated notes paying $900,000 in annual interest and carrying a 7-year maturity. It must pay $100,000 in flotation costs to an underwriter. In this case, the effective cost of borrowing (kd), where t equals the time period for each cash flow, is:

$$\$9,900,000 = \sum_{t=1}^{7} \frac{\$900,000}{(1+kd)^t} + \frac{\$10,000,000}{(1+kd)^7}$$

or $kd = 9.20\%$

Cost of Equity. Conceptually, the marginal cost of equity equals the required return to shareholders. It is not directly measurable because dividend payments are not mandatory. Still, several methods are commonly used to approximate this required return, including the dividend valuation model, capital asset pricing model (CAPM), and targeted return on equity model.

Dividend Valuation Model. Returns to common stockholders take the form of periodic dividend receipts and changes in share price during the interval of stock ownership. Dividend valuation models discount the expected cash flows from owning stock in determining a reasonable return to shareholders. The cost of equity equals the discount rate (required return) used to convert future cash flows to their present value equivalent. Specifically, the price of common stock (P) equals the present value of expected dividends over the life of the stock. This holds because the market price at any future point equals the discounted value of expected dividends beyond that point. Recognizing that common stock is issued in perpetuity, the value of a firm's stock is determined by the following formula:

$$P = \sum_{t=1}^{\infty} \frac{D_t}{(1+ke)^t} \qquad\qquad (13.2)$$

where

D_t = the dollar value of the expected dividend in period t
ke = cost of equity, and
t = time period

The dividend valuation model applies for all patterns of expected dividends. A simplified solution to Equation (13.2) exists, however, if dividends are expected to grow at a constant rate in each period.[5] If the periodic growth rate (g) is assumed to be a constant and less than ke, Equation (13.2) reduces to:

$$ke = \frac{Do(1+g)}{P} + g \qquad (13.3)$$

where

Do = the expected percentage dividend yield during the next period
  g = the expected growth in firm earnings, dividend payments, and stock price appreciation[6]

There are many difficulties in applying Equations (13.2) and (13.3) in solving for the required rate of return. No precise estimate of future dividends exists, so different shareholders often have substantially different expectations regarding the firm's prospects. Furthermore, many banks' stock is not actively traded. Dividend streams and quoted share prices may not reflect a true measure of returns to owners who extract benefits from the banks' paying extranormal expenses. The general model does, however, provide an approximation of required shareholder returns.

Consider, for example, a bank's stock that currently trades at $24 per share and pays a $1 annual dividend. It is generally agreed that analysts' forecasts represent the best estimate of future dividends. Suppose that their consensus forecast is that the bank's annual dividends will increase by an average 10 percent annually. With this expectation, the estimated equity cost is:

$$ke = \frac{\$1.10}{\$24} + .10$$

$$= 14.58\%$$

The 14.58 percent represents a payment from after-tax dollars. For pricing purposes, it should be converted to a pretax equivalent. This can be accomplished by dividing by 1 minus the relevant marginal tax rate. Assuming a 34-percent corporate tax rate, the pretax expected return equals 14.58 percent /.66, or 22.09 percent.

Capital Asset Pricing Model. Large institutions with publicly traded stock can obtain an estimate of their cost of equity from the CAPM. This model relates market risk, measured by Beta (β), to shareholders' required returns. Formally, the required return

---

[5]This stock valuation model, developed by Myron Gordon, assumes a constant growth rate in dividend payments. Most corporate finance textbooks analyze the features of this model in detail.

[6]A formal derivation of these equations appears in most corporate finance books. Brigham (1990) analyzes a wide range of modified versions with applications. Analysts frequently distinguish between the cost of retained earnings and the cost of new common stock issues. Equation (13.3) represents the cost of retained earnings. New common stock issues cost more than retained earnings because of flotation costs. The cost of new common stock (ke*) is determined via Equation (13.3) using the share price net of flotation costs (Pn) such that

$$ke^* = \frac{Do(1+g)}{Pn} + g$$

to shareholders (ke') equals the riskless rate of return (rf) plus a risk premium (ρ) on common stock reflecting nondiversifiable market risk:

$$ke' = rf + \rho \tag{13.4}$$

The risk premium equals the product of a security's Beta and the difference between the expected return on the market portfolio (km) and the expected riskless rate of return (rf). Beta measures a stock's historical price volatility relative to the price volatility of the market portfolio as:

$$\beta_i = \frac{\text{Covariance [individual security (i) return, market return]}}{\text{Variance (market return)}} \tag{13.5}$$

where

i = individual security

Covariance represents a statistical measure of how closely two variables move together. If changes in one variable are associated with changes in another variable in the same direction and magnitude, the covariance is high. If β equals 1 over any estimation period, the individual security exhibits the same systematic price volatility as the market portfolio. Here, the covariance of the individual security's return and the market index equals the variance in the market index. If β is greater than 1, the stock's systematic price volatility exceeds the market portfolio's and vice versa. Generally, the greater the absolute value of β, the greater the relative systematic price volatility and market risk.[7]

Banks can use historical β estimates from Equation (13.5) and a projection of the market premium (km − rf) to estimate the required return to shareholders for individual securities:

$$ke'i = rf + \beta(km - rf) \tag{13.6}$$

Most large bank stocks exhibited βs near 1 through the early 1980s. Recently, bank β estimates have taken a wider range of values reflecting greater market risk.

The application of Equation (13.6) is straightforward. Using monthly returns measures for 1985 to 1990, First National Bank of Chicago's estimate equaled 1.42. This means that the bank's stock varied 42 percent more in price relative to the market portfolio over this period. If the differential between the market return and risk-free return—proxied by Standard & Poor's 500-stock composite index minus the 3-month Treasury bill rate—is expected to average 5 percent with the Treasury bill rate expected to equal 8 percent, the CAPM estimate for the bank's cost of equity is:

$$ke = 8.0\% + 1.42(5.0\%) = 15.1\%$$

This cost of equity should again be converted to a pretax equivalent that equals 22.88 percent, using an assumed 34-percent marginal tax rate.

---

[7]Systematic price volatility refers to variation in returns on a security caused by factors that influence the market in general. As such, it is nondiversifiable. Such variation is normally distinguished from nonsystematic price volatility, which is unique to a specific company and is diversifiable.

Targeted Return on Equity Model. Investors require higher pretax returns on common stock than on debt issues because of the greater assumed credit risk. Depending on the business cycle, the differential in returns ranges from 4 to 8 percent. As an approximation, a firm's cost of equity should exceed its cost of debt by some positive differential. Many banks use a targeted return-on-equity guideline based on the cost of debt plus a premium to evaluate the cost of equity. This method simply requires that owners and managers specify a desirable return to shareholders in terms of return on equity. This return is then converted to a pretax equivalent yield. It assumes that the market value of bank equity equals the book value of equity.

Assume that a bank's targeted ROE, derived from a comparison of the bank's cost of debt versus the expected return on equity to shareholders, equals 15 percent and its marginal tax rate equals 34 percent. The pretax required return on bank equity can be determined by:

$$\frac{\text{Targeted net income}}{\text{Equity}} = 15\%$$

$$\frac{\text{Targeted income before taxes}\,(1-.34)}{\text{Equity}} = 15\%$$

$$\frac{\text{Targeted income before taxes}}{\text{Equity}} = \frac{15\%}{(1-.34)} = 22.73\%$$

While this measure has deficiencies, it is easy to calculate for banks without publicly traded stock and serves as a benchmark for other cost-of-equity approximations.

Cost of Preferred Stock. Preferred stock has characteristics of both debt and common equity. It represents ownership, with investors' claims superior to those of common stockholders but subordinated to those of debtholders. Like common stock, preferred stock pays dividends that may be deferred when management determines that earnings are too low. Like long-term bonds, preferred stock stipulates contractual dividend payments over the life of the security and often provides call protection and sinking fund contributions. Recently, preferred issues paying variable-rate dividends have become increasingly common.

The marginal cost of preferred stock (kp) equals the required return to stockholders and can be approximated from Equation (7.3). Consider the case of noncallable, non-sinking-fund preferred stock sold at par with a fixed dividend payment. With dividend payments contractually fixed, expected dividend growth equals 0 and

$$kp = \frac{Dp}{Pp} \tag{13.7}$$

where

Dp = contractual dividend payment
Pp = net price of preferred stock

and Dp is constant over the life of the issue. Management must estimate Dp for variable-rate preferred by forecasting changes in the pricing index, such as the 10-year

Treasury bond yield, and estimate kp using an equation similar to Equation (13.2). As with new common stock issues, Pp is net of placement costs from taking a new issue to market.[8]

Weighted Marginal Cost of Total Funds

Many banks price loans using the marginal cost of a single source of debt funds as the base rate. For example, prime commercial customers are often allowed to choose the interest rate they pay as some mark-up over the marginal cost of either CDs, the London Interbank Offer Rate (LIBOR), or federal funds. Obviously, the customer selects the base rate expected to be the lowest over the credit period. Unfortunately, the cost of any single source of funds may change more or less than the cost of other sources and thus vary substantially from the bank's composite cost of financing.

The best cost measure for asset-pricing purposes is a weighted marginal cost of total funds (WMC). This measure recognizes both explicit and implicit costs associated with any single source of funds. It assumes that all assets are financed from a pool of funds and that specific sources of funds are not tied directly with specific uses of funds.

WMC is computed in three stages. First, management must forecast the desired dollar amount of financing to be obtained from each individual debt source and equity. This requires that the bank specify a planning horizon, such as 1 year, and identify significant changes in composition of liabilities and equity over time. Management should determine a marketing strategy and allocate employees' time to the different account-generating functions. Second, management must estimate the marginal cost of each independent source of funds. It should allocate fundraising and processing costs among the different liability and equity components and project interest and dividend costs for each source, recognizing any perceived changes in risk associated with changes in financial leverage. Each cost estimate should also reflect management's assignment of nonearning assets per Equation (13.1) that indicates the percentage of investable funds. Third, management should combine the individual estimates to project the weighted cost, which equals the sum of the weighted component costs across all sources. Each source's weight (w_j) equals the expected dollar amount of financing from that source divided by the dollar amount of total liabilities and equity. Thus if k_j equals the single-source j component cost of financing, where there are m liabilities plus equity,

$$\text{WMC} = \sum_{j=1}^{m} w_j k_j \qquad (13.8)$$

[8]The effective cost of common and preferred stock should also reflect the portion of these funds that is allocated to nonearning assets. While reserves are not required, banks typically allocate fixed assets and intangibles to equity sources. Computationally, management divides the equity marginal cost estimate by 1 minus the percentage in nonearning assets. To calculate the marginal cost of common and preferred stock when dividends are not constant, the reader should review examples provided in any current corporate finance textbook.

MARGINAL COST ANALYSIS: AN APPLICATION

The following analysis demonstrates the procedures for measuring a bank's cost of funds, using data for Community State Bank introduced in Exhibits 4.1 and 4.2. The analysis consists of projecting the bank's balance sheet composition and marginal costs in order to generate a weighted marginal cost of total funds.

Suppose you are the cashier for Community State Bank and a member of the bank's ALCO. The ALCO has just completed its monthly meeting and asked you to generate an estimate of the bank's weighted marginal cost of funds for the next year. For the first time in several years, there was a consensus among the senior officers that the economy would experience moderate growth throughout the year, which the Federal Reserve would accommodate. Inflation was expected to remain stable at around 5 percent and interest rates would rise only slightly. As part of the meeting, the committee approved a preliminary budget that projected income net of dividends equal to $500,000, representing a lower return on equity and return on assets compared with the prior year. Total average assets were projected to grow by $7 million, of which $6 million was new loans. Liabilities were expected to grow proportionately relative to the past year except that the bank would rely proportionately more on CDs.

Exhibit 13.1 summarizes the ALCO's consensus forecast for the next year. Columns (a) and (b) list the projected composition of funding between debt and equity sources over the next year in dollar amount and percentage. Column (c) lists the interest rates expected to prevail during the year as projected by the senior investment officer. Processing and acquisition costs for each type of liability and the investable percentages are based on the bank controller's estimates, and are reported in columns (d) and (e). Column (f) presents the expected marginal cost for each source, using these projections as defined in Equation (13.1). The weighted marginal cost of funds, obtained by summing the products of figures in columns (b) and (f) for each component, is calculated at the bottom of the exhibit to equal 11.69 percent for the year. This projected marginal cost exceeds historical costs because the bank forecasts an increase in interest rates and expects to obtain a higher percentage of funds from more expensive sources.

The marginal cost of funds estimate should be applied carefully in pricing decisions. The bank in this example should charge at least 11.69 percent on loans (assets) of average risk to cover the marginal costs of debt and pay shareholders a reasonable return. The bank should add a risk premium for loans of greater-than-average default risk to compensate for the increased probability of greater charge-offs. Chapter 24 describes loan pricing models in detail. Whether a bank meets its aggregate profit target depends on the bank's ability to price assets to meet this hurdle rate, its actual default experience, and whether noninterest income covers noninterest expense net of costs allocated to attracting and handling liabilities.

As an ALCO member, however, you have serious reservations that economic stability will persist. Congress and the President have done little to reduce record federal deficits, and with an election year forthcoming, the Federal Reserve is under increased pressure to accelerate money growth. Loan problems at many large regional banks spooked foreign institutions and investors last year to the point where a serious

Exhibit 13.1 Forecast of the Weighted Marginal Cost of Funds: Projected Figures for Community State Bank for the Next Year[a]

Liabilities and Equity	(a) Average Amount	(b) Percent of Total	(c) Interest Cost	(d) Processing and Acquisition Costs	(e) Nonearning Percentage	(f) Component Marginal Costs
Demand deposits	$ 10,900	10.2%		7.0%	18%	8.54%
Interest checking	15,000	14.0	6.0%	5.5	15	13.53
Money market demand accounts	12,300	11.5	8.0	3.0	3	11.34
Other savings accounts	6,400	6.0	8.0	1.2	2	9.39
Time deposits < $100,000	42,400	39.6	9.0	1.4	2	10.61
Time deposits ≥ $100,000	9,500	8.9	11.5	0.3	3	12.16
Total deposits	$ 96,500	90.2%				
Federal funds purchased	$ 200	0.2%	8.0%	0.0%	0%	8.00%
Other liabilities	2,000	1.9		0.0	40	0.00
Total liabilities	$ 98,700	92.3%				
Stockholders' equity	$ 8,300	7.7	21.9%[b]		4%	22.81%
Total liabilities and equity	$107,000	100.0%				

Weighted marginal cost of
capital = .102(8.54%) + .14(13.53%) + .115(11.34%) + .06(9.39%) + .396(10.61%)
     + .089(12.16%) + .002(8.0%) + .077(22.81%)
    = 11.69%

[a]Balance sheet and income statement data for the previous year appear in Exhibits 4.1 and 4.2.

[b]Required pretax return

national liquidity crisis might arise if a single large U.S. bank failed and foreign depositors withdrew their funds. If this occurred, interest rates would rise well above the ALCO's forecast, and the bank would have difficulty issuing new CDs.

Differences in the weighted marginal cost projection generally reflect different interest rate scenarios and variations in the composition of liabilities. Exhibit 13.2 provides a revised cost calculation, assuming higher interest rates and greater shifts of bank financing from lower-cost demand, savings, and small time deposits into interest checking, MMDAs, and CDs. The funds shift and rate increase both have an adverse impact on financing costs. In this scenario, the weighted marginal cost of funds equals 12.66 percent, or almost 1 percent more than the ALCO projection. If the bank acquired fixed-rate assets at 12 percent with the expectation that financing costs would average 11.69 percent, its net interest income would drop with the environment characterized in Exhibit 13.2. Obviously, management should monitor its funding operation and project marginal costs regularly to detect significant deviations from plan.

While this analysis is quite simple once figures on costs and the composition of liabilities are obtained, it glosses over many controversial issues, such as how cost estimates are obtained. In particular, it is extremely difficult to allocate processing and acquisition costs between different liabilities. What is the annual cost of an automatic

Exhibit 13.2 Revised Forecast of the Weighted Cost of Funds

Liabilities	Average Amount	Percent of Total	Interest Cost	Component Marginal Cost
Demand deposits	$ 10,000	9.3%		7.32%
Interest checking	16,000	14.9	7.0%	14.71
Money market demand accounts	12,900	12.1	10.0	13.40
Other savings accounts	6,000	5.6	8.5	9.90
Time deposits < $100,000	40,500	37.9	10.0	11.63
Time deposits ≥ $100,000	11,100	10.4	13.0	13.71
Total deposits	$ 96,500	90.2%		
Federal funds purchased	$ 200	0.2%	11.0%	11.00%
Other liabilities	2,000	1.9		0.00
Total liabilities	$ 98,700	92.3%		
Stockholders' equity	$ 8,300	7.7	21.9%	22.81%
Total liabilities and equity	$107,000	100.00%		

Weighted marginal cost of capital = .093(7.32%) + .149(14.71%) + .121(13.40%) + .056(9.90%)
  + .379(11.63%) + .104(13.71%) + .002(11%) + .077(22.81%)
  = 12.66%

teller machine? How much of a teller's salary should be allocated to the marginal cost of taking deposits? How should utility expenses be allocated among different account categories? It should be recognized that the procedure for estimating marginal costs is not exact. However, useful decisions can be made as long as the data are reported and analyzed in a consistent manner.

MARGINAL COSTS IN TRANSFER PRICING

The previous example views a bank as a single unit and calculates a single, pooled marginal cost of funds measure. Loans are priced at a markup over the estimated cost of funds, with the size of the markup reflecting management's assessment of default risk. This analysis can be easily implemented by banks with a limited volume of daily transactions. Management can reasonably forecast changes in deposit structure and asset growth so that errors in forecasting interest rates determine the accuracy of the total cost estimate.

Many large banks, in contrast, find it difficult to project the types and magnitudes of their assets and liabilities because they are involved in many transactions daily in different product and geographic markets. To facilitate decision-making, they often use internal funds transfer pricing systems, which allocate funds between organizational units of a bank on the basis of marginal costs. Rather than use just the weighted marginal cost of funds, the funding division assigns a transfer price based on a single-source marginal cost of funds or a blended cost of single-source debt and equity. In many cases, funds managers match-fund the assets in question with a funds source of similar maturity or duration.

Profit Centers and Internal Funds Transfer Pricing Systems

Most large banks are divided into organizational units with well-defined sets of responsibilities. Considered separately, each unit typically attracts sources of funds and also uses funds directly. Banks establish internal funds transfer systems to allocate funds between units. Under such systems, a unit that is a user of funds pays an interest charge for the funds while a supplier of funds receives a credit. Marginal cost of funds estimates determine the return to suppliers of funds and the cost to funds users. Because each unit is viewed as a separate profit center, these cost estimates are extremely important.

In a recent examination of profit measurement at banks, Ernst & Whinney (1987) identified the following objectives of transfer pricing systems:

1. Correctly identify the cost of opportunity value of funds.

2. Enhance asset and liability pricing decisions.

3. Separate credit risk from interest rate risk.

4. Facilitate the profitability measurement of various products and components.

The following analysis examines the first three objectives. The fourth indicates that the process can be extended to product lines as well as business units. The real advantage of transfer pricing systems is that they allow senior management to measure the performance of divisional profit centers, individual product managers, and specific customer relationships. They also serve to motivate managers to enhance performance and encourage efficiency.

In the best funds transfer systems, each organizational unit or profit center is assigned specific bank assets and liabilities, which it generates through normal business activity. It then separately sells its liabilities to a funds management unit and buys financing for its assets from the funds management unit at appropriate transfer prices.[9] The funds management unit sets each transfer price, which varies depending on the characteristics of the underlying instruments.

Exhibit 13.3 summarizes a sample funds allocation scheme.[10] Under this system, there are three profit centers, for lending, investments, and deposit gathering. The funds management unit is a fourth profit center, with responsibility for borrowing in the money and capital markets. Each profit center generates revenues and expenses associated with transfer prices as well as normal business activities. The lending and investment centers compare transfer prices plus actual operating costs with revenues obtained directly from assets booked by each unit. The net difference determines the division profit. The deposit-gathering unit receives a credit for supplying funds, which it compares to its actual acquisition and processing costs. The funds management unit makes a profit if the transfer prices it charges on financing loans and investments

---

[9]This discussion analyzes funds flows on a gross basis in which each profit center's total assets are considered separately from total liabilities. Alternatively, pricing systems may apply only to net funds flows. As such, each profit center is assumed to fund its own assets with its own liabilities and transfer the net surplus or fund the net deficiency.

[10]The following analysis is based on Part 3 in Giardini, Pisa, and Schroff (1984).

Exhibit 13.3 A Schematic Diagram of Internal Funds Transfer Systems

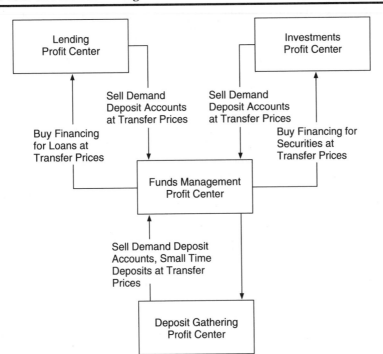

Lending Profit Center: Net Income = Loan Yields + Transfer Prices on Deposits Generated - Transfer Prices on Loan Financing - Actual Costs of Making Loans

Investments Profit Center: Net Income = Security Yields + Transfer Prices on Deposits - Transfer Prices on Security Financing - Actual Cost of Investing

Deposit Gathering Profit Center: Net Income = Transfer Prices on Selling Demand Deposit Accounts and Small Time Deposits - Actual Personnel and Handling Costs

Funds Management Profit Center: Net Income = Transfer Prices on Financing Loans and Securities - Transfer Prices on Deposits - Actual Unit Costs

exceeds the sum of the transfer prices it pays for deposits and its actual borrowing and personnel costs.

Funds transfer pricing schemes may employ a weighted average marginal cost of funds allocation or a single-source marginal cost allocation. If it uses a fully weighted cost system, the funds management unit sets the transfer price equal to the weighted marginal cost of capital. A single-source pricing system is actually a hybrid system: it incorporates both the weighted marginal cost of existing sources of funds and the marginal cost of single-source incremental financing. Funds management sets transfer prices for financing the bank's asset base (at the beginning of each planning cycle) using the WMC. Incremental asset and nonnegotiable deposit growth are then accorded transfer prices based on single funding sources.

The principal advantage of internal funds transfer pricing is that it separates interest rate risk from credit risk in ALCO pricing decisions. Lending divisions can focus on asset quality, while funds management determines how much of a mismatch between asset and liability maturities or durations is appropriate.

An Example. Consider the situations described in Exhibit 13.4. A loan officer is negotiating a $1 million, 1-year, fixed-rate loan with a commercial customer. The officer contacts someone in funds management, who determines a 1-year instrument transfer price based on the prevailing yield curve. This bank uses the marginal cost of jumbo CDs as the single-source cost of funds. It implicitly match-funds the 1-year loan by quoting a transfer price based on 1-year CD rates. If the bank issued a 1-year CD, its effective cost—including interest, required reserves, acquisition costs, and FDIC insurance—would equal 10 percent, which becomes the transfer price. [See Equation (13.1).] The loan officer accepts this 10-percent transfer price and prices the fixed-rate loan at 12 percent, which the borrower accepts. The commercial lending profit center has now locked in a 2-percent spread on the transaction, assuming no default. The 2 percent compensates the bank for default risk and personnel costs and helps pay shareholders a return.[11]

The funds management unit, which is responsible for actually financing the loan at the margin, can issue any type of debt it chooses. If the group can obtain financing cheaper in the Eurodollar market, it may do so and book a profit. If it decides to take on interest rate risk, it may issue CDs at some maturity other than 1 year. Net earnings of the unit indicate its ability both to borrow at the rates quoted to other units (the transfer price) and its ability to mismatch funding profitability. The top part of Exhibit 13.4 assumes that the funds management group actually issues 1-year CDs at 10 percent, thereby earning a zero spread but minimizing interest rate risk.

The bottom part of the exhibit assumes that the group mismatches by issuing a series of $1 million, 3-month CDs rather than a $1 million, 1-year CD. In this example, the 3-month rate was initially 9 percent (annual), which increased by 1 percent each quarter. In this scenario, the funds management group would report a net loss of $5,000 because actual interest expense totals $105,000 rather than the $100,000 originally projected from the yield curve. If instead, the 3-month CD rate were to remain at 9 percent throughout the year, the funds management group would actually pay $90,000 in interest and report a profit of $10,000. The bank's profit would also be $10,000 higher. Regardless of how the loan is financed, the commercial lending unit reports a net profit of $20,000 because it is guaranteed a transfer price of 10 percent. Thus credit risk is separated from interest rate risk.

Funds management units bear the responsibility of estimating funding costs, setting transfer prices between profit centers, actually issuing securities in the money and capital markets, and managing the bank's overall interest rate risk position. In light

---

[11]Depending on bank policy, the quoted transfer price may already include a target return to shareholders by blending the marginal cost of single-source debt and equity. For example, a commercial loan priced at prime plus 1 percent may be match-funded 94 percent out of 1-month CD funds and 6 percent out of equity.

Exhibit 13.4 An Application of Single Source Transfer Pricing to Commercial Lending

A. Loan officer negotiates a $1 million, 1-year loan priced at a 12% fixed rate. The funds management unit match-funds the loan by issuing a 1-year CD at 10%.

Commercial Lending Profit Center			*Funds Management Profit Center*		
Loan interest 0.12($1 million)	= $120,000		Transfer price 0.10($1 million)	= $100,000	
Transfer price 0.10($1 million)	= $100,000		Cost 0.10($1 million)	= $100,000	
Spread	$ 20,000		Spread	$ 0	

B. Loan officer negotiates a $1 million, 1-year loan priced at a 12% fixed rate. The funds management unit mismatches the loan funding by issuing four consecutive 3-month certificates of deposit at 9%, 10%, 11%, and 12%, respectively.

Commercial Lending Profit Center			*Funds Management Profit Center*	
Loan interest 0.12($1 million)	= $120,000		Income 0.10($1 million)	= $100,000
Financing Cost 0.10($1 million)	= $100,000		Cost 0.25(0.09)$1 million	= $ 22,500
Spread	$ 20,000		0.25(0.10)$1 million	= $ 25,000
			0.25(0.11)$1 million	= $ 27,500
			0.25(0.12)$1 million	= $ 30,000
			Spread	−$5,000

of these duties, the chief officer of the funds management group typically heads the ALCO. As indicated above, the unit can use a weighted marginal cost of capital approach, a single-source marginal cost approach, or a combination of the two. For the largest banks, the weighted approach is highly subjective because the composition and cost of incremental funds cannot be easily projected. Many banks therefore attempt to approximately match-fund single-source liabilities with specific assets at the margin.

Single-Pool versus Multiple-Pool Approaches

In the previous example, the funds management group quoted a transfer price based on the assumption that it was matching the maturity of the loan with the maturity of the presumed CD financing. Implicitly, the funds management group has multiple sources of financing, each with a different marginal cost. In the language of transfer funds pricing, this is a multiple-pool system. Financing for specific assets is obtained and matched from a variety of "pools" representing different maturity instruments and thus different interest rate risk. The different pools will reflect the composition of bank liabilities by source and repricing frequency. Alternatively, some banks use a single-pool approach in which all funds are allocated to the same pool and one rate is quoted to all users. While the single-pool system is easy to understand and use, it does not assist in handling interest rate risk, or separating interest rate risk from credit risk. Thus the multiple-pool approach is superior.

FUNDING COSTS AND BANKING RISK

The previous examples demonstrate the difficulty of accurately projecting funding costs. Unanticipated changes in interest rates and the composition of bank liabilities can significantly raise or lower bank profits as interest expense rises or falls more than interest income. The same changes also affect a bank's risk position. This section examines the relationship between the composition of bank funds and banking risk, identifying differences between small and large banks.

Funding Sources and Interest Rate Risk

During the 1980s, most banks experienced a shift in composition of liabilities away from demand deposits into interest-bearing time deposits and other borrowed funds. This reflects three phenomena: the removal of Regulation Q interest rate ceilings, a volatile interest rate environment, and the development of new deposit and money market products. The cumulative effect was to increase the interest sensitivity of funding operations. Today, many depositors and investors prefer short-term instruments that can quickly be rolled over as interest rates change. Banks must offer substantial premiums to induce depositors to lengthen maturities and assume interest rate risk. Many banks choose not to pay the premiums and subsequently reprice liabilities more frequently than in past years.

These changes affect a bank's interest rate risk position to the extent that it does not adjust its asset rate sensitivity. A bank operating with a zero GAP in the late 1970s and 1980s would today have substantial negative GAPs within 1 year if it did not acquire more rate-sensitive assets. For this reason, many institutions attempt to price all loans on a floating-rate basis and no longer purchase bonds for their investment portfolios with maturities beyond 5 years.

One widely recognized strategy to reduce interest rate risk and the long-term cost of bank funds is to aggressively compete for retail core deposits. Individuals are generally not as rate sensitive as corporate depositors. Once a bank attracts deposit business, many individuals will maintain their balances through rate cycles as long as the bank provides good service and pays attention to them. Such deposits are thus more stable than money market liabilities. Core deposits carry an additional advantage to banks because interest rates are lower, but they do cost more to handle.

Funding Sources and Liquidity Risk

The liquidity risk associated with all liabilities has risen dramatically in recent years. Depositors often simply compare rates and move their funds between investment vehicles to earn the highest yields. It is increasingly difficult to establish long-term customer relationships that withstand rate differentials, a problem compounded in virtually every banking market that has at least one firm, typically a savings and loan association, that pays premium deposit rates at all maturities. This firm often operates with lower capital or net worth, which increases its solvency risk, yet it can invest in real estate and other assets not available to commercial banks. Commercial banks feel they are at a competitive disadvantage and, without matching the offered rates, have trouble keeping deposit customers.

The largest banks, which rely on jumbo CDs and Eurodollars, face similar problems. Investors in these instruments are highly rate sensitive. They normally prefer short-term maturities and will move their balances for slightly higher yields elsewhere. Large depositors with uninsured balances, especially foreign investors, frequently react to rumors of financial distress by shifting their funds into less-risky Treasury securities until the crisis passes. For this reason, the largest U.S. banking organizations maintain dealer operations in London, Singapore, and Hong Kong to guarantee access to financial markets 24 hours a day.

The liquidity risk facing any one bank depends on the competitive environment. Many smaller banks operate in communities with only a few competitors that tacitly price deposits comparably. Customers like to invest their funds locally so they can conveniently contact their banker with questions or easily withdraw or move balances. Liquidity risk is relatively low and deposit outflows are predictable. Banks in larger communities normally face more aggressive competition, which increases liquidity risk, and must monitor the composition of funds more closely. Again, it is important to note the liquidity advantage that stable core deposits provide an acquiring bank.

Funding Sources and Credit Risk

Changes in the composition and cost of bank funds can indirectly affect a bank's credit risk by forcing it to reduce asset quality. For example, banks that have substituted purchased funds for lost demand deposits have seen their cost of funds rise. They have not been able to reprice existing high-quality assets to offset this rise because of competitive pressures. Rather than let their interest margins deteriorate, many banks make riskier loans at higher promised yields. While they might maintain their margins in the near term, later loan losses typically rise with the decline in asset quality. This effect is greatest at small banks with limited opportunities to supplement earnings in other ways.

Funding Sources and Bank Safety

Changes in the composition and cost of bank funds have clearly lowered traditional earnings. This decrease slows capital growth and increases leverage ratios. Borrowing costs will ultimately increase unless noninterest income offsets this decline or banks obtain new external capital. Bank safety has thus declined in the aggregate.

CONTROLLING NONINTEREST EXPENSE

Consider the competitive environment in which commercial banks operate. The basic business of banking has always been accepting deposits and making loans. In today's world, banks are high cost producers relative to money market funds run by brokerage houses and relative to the commercial paper and bond markets and worldwide credit

Exhibit 13.5 Noninterest Expenses at U.S. Commercial Banks

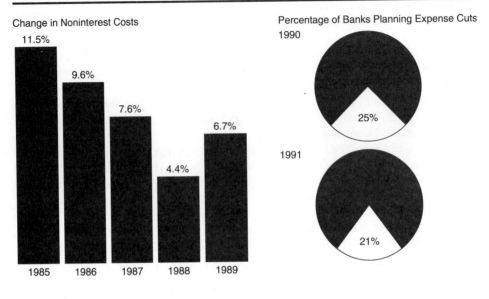

Source: *American Banker* (July 12, 1990).

card enterprises like American Express and AT&T. Noninterest expense, which includes personnel, occupancy, and data processing, is high, and therefore earnings are low. For many bank managers this means that austere budgets directed at controlling expenses are required.

Exhibit 13.5 demonstrates that noninterest expenses at commercial banks grew at a declining rate during most of the last half of the 1980s. In large part this reflects efforts to cut costs and increase profitability driven by a fear of being acquired. Quite simply, senior managers of acquired banks typically find themselves looking for new positions shortly after an acquisition, a fate that most aggressively try to avoid. This begs an obvious question, however. Are there too many banks in the United States? Do we need three competing institutions on every downtown street corner? If banks in the same market combined their operations, they could cut payroll and occupancy expenses, eliminate boards of directors, and use computer technology more efficiently. The cost savings would be recurring and fall right to the bottom line.

When they initially consider noninterest expenses, many managers focus on reducing costs. A more comprehensive strategy, however, is to manage costs in line with strategic objectives. Doesn't it seem sensible, for example, to invest in new technologies if they will reduce long-term operating costs, even if the investment adds to near-term noninterest expense? Gregor and Hedges (1990) demonstrate that there is no systematic link between cost management strategies and the market value of bank equity. Exhibit 13.6 reports two key measures on expense control for 42 of the nation's

Exhibit 13.6 Industry Cost Structure Profile

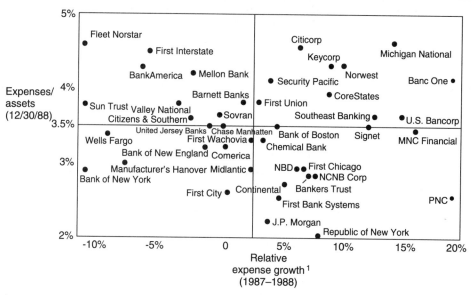

[1]Relative expense growth is defined as 1987–1988 growth in noninterest expense divided by 1987–1988 percentage growth in assets; it is a measure of *relative* expense growth.

Source: The MAC Group.

Source: Gregor & Hedges. "Alternative Strategies for Successful Cost Management." *The Bankers Magazine* (May/June 1990).

largest banks in 1987 and 1988. The measures are year-end ratios of noninterest expense to total assets and relative expense growth, defined as the annualized growth rate in noninterest expense divided by the growth rate in total assets. The exhibit segments the banks into four quadrants. Banks in the lower left quadrant reported the lowest expense ratios for both measures, while banks in the upper right quadrant reported the highest ratios. Banks in the other quadrants reported one high ratio and one low ratio.

Consider the average stock market value to book value ratio of the same banks in each quadrant as reported in Exhibit 13.7. Banks with the highest expenses and relative expense growth actually reported the highest relative stock market values, while banks in the low-expense group reported the lowest. The essential point is that there is no systematic link between reported expenses and the market value of firm equity.

Exhibit 13.7 Impact of Cost Performance on Stock Market Value
Average Market-to-Book Value Ratios (12/30/88)

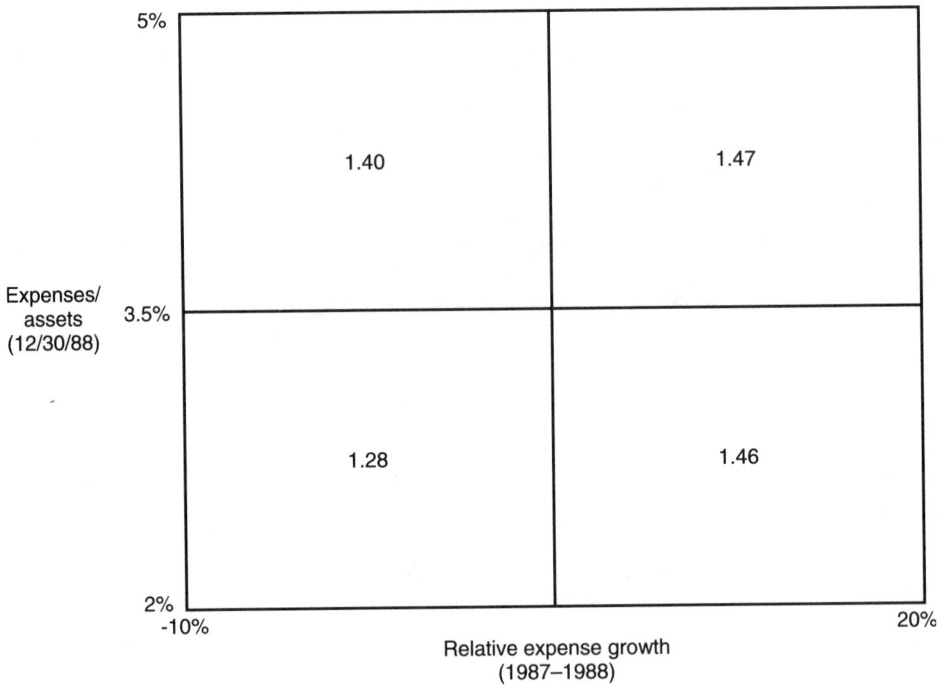

Source: The MAC Group.

Source: Gregor & Hedges. "Alternative Strategies for Successful Cost Management." *The Bankers Magazine* (May/June 1990).

Cost Management Strategies

What then is cost management? In general, it is a philosophy of allocating resources to the most profitable lines of business to achieve improved performance. Ernst & Whinney (1987) in their analysis of bank profitability identify four expense management strategies: expense reduction, operating efficiencies, revenue enhancement, and contribution growth.

Expense Reduction. Many banks begin cost management efforts by identifying excessive expenses and eliminating them. Given that noninterest expenses consist primarily of personnel, occupancy, and data processing costs, these are the areas where cuts are initially made, as summarized in Exhibit 13.8. It is not unusual to hear of banks announcing widespread employee reductions. In 1990, for example, Continental Illinois Corp. announced that it would cut 900 employees, or 13 percent of the holding

Exhibit 13.8 Recent Actions Undertaken to Manage Costs

By Asset Size	All Respondents	Under $100 Million	$100–$500 Million	$500 Million–$1 Billion	$1–$5 Billion	Over $5 Billion
Reduce staff	36%	33%	38%	64%	74%	57%
Improve productivity	49	50	48	29	45	55
Data processing in-house	16	16	16	0	13	10
Improve procedures	51	50	57	50	61	71
Close branches	6	4	8	7	24	38
Consolidate operations	25	25	18	43	50	64
Contract out data processing	6	5	6	21	8	5
Automate manual tasks	18	18	15	0	26	24

By Region	Great Lakes	Midwest	Northeast	Southeast	Southwast	West
Reduce staff	44%	35%	27%	23%	58%	47%
Improve productivity	49	42	40	56	56	54
Data processing in-house	15	21	1	18	15	16
Improve procedures	51	35	62	55	67	54
Close branches	2	1	5	14	7	1
Consolidate operations	27	24	22	16	47	23
Contract out data processing	8	6	3	4	9	8
Automate manual tasks	20	15	40	9	9	26

Source: Miller. "What Banks Say and Do about Operating Costs." *ABA Banking Journal* (October 1989).

company's work force. First Fidelity Bank Corp. similarly announced a staff reduction of 1,400, or 11 percent of its work force. Other common areas for cutting include the number of branch offices and employee medical benefits. Many banks have similarly considered getting rid of their data processing department altogether and contracting to buy data processing services from a nonbank vendor such as IBM or EDS. In industry jargon, this is referred to as *outsourcing*. In the case of Bank South of Atlanta and First Fidelity of Philadelphia, the respective managements estimated immediate cost savings of 8 to 10 percent of total noninterest expense. Contemporary Issues: Expense Reduction Opportunities identifies key areas in which a bank's expense structure can be improved.

Operating Efficiencies. Another strategy is to increase operating efficiency in providing products and services. This can be achieved in one of three ways: by reducing costs but maintaining the existing level of products and services; by increasing the level of output but maintaining the level of current expenses; or by improving workflow. All of these approaches fall under the label of increasing productivity because they involve delivering products at lower unit costs. The first typically involves cutting staff along with increasing work requirements to maintain output. Fewer people do the same amount or more work. The second addresses the issue of economies of scale and economies of scope in banking. Economies of scale are said

CONTEMPORARY ISSUES

Expense Reduction Opportunities

Earnings Performance Group has identified several areas in which expense reduction opportunities typically arise. The following list introduces the broad areas and presents key questions that managers should address when evaluating their existing expense structure.

1. Identify ways to more effectively utilize automated systems.
   - Are you keying data from a computer report into another computer system?

2. Eliminate redundant tasks and functions.

3. Complete a review of all reports to determine if they are actually used.
   - Are multiple copies produced when only one is needed?
   - Would microfiche be just as adequate?
   - Are there on-line screens that provide the same information as reports?
   - Can reports be combined?
   - What happens to paper? Is it recycled?

4. Can the number of statements and/or notices mailed to a customer be decreased?

5. Reevaluate telephone expense, particularly long-distance charges.

6. If you use outside couriers or messengers, when was the last time the routes were rebid? Have the number of stops and/or routes been reviewed in relation to work available?

7. Do you use zip-sorts to reduce postage?

8. Do you have central control of purchases of PCs and related peripherals?

9. What are the opportunities regarding reducing cost of copiers and FAX machines by handling them centrally?

10. Review all contracts with outside vendors to determine the last time they were put out to bid. How are maintenance contracts handled?

---

to exist when a bank's average costs decrease as output increases. Diseconomies exist when average costs increase with greater output. Economies of scope focus on how the joint costs of providing several products change as new products are added or existing product output is enhanced. The argument is that joint costs will grow by much less than the costs associated with producing products or providing services independently. For example, if a bank adds a new product line and it can provide this product and existing products at a lower unit cost than previously, economies of scope exist. Finally, improving workflow involves increasing productivity by accelerating the rate at which a task or function is performed. The intent is to eliminate redundant reviews or tasks and thereby shorten the time to finish a task.

The results of a Booz-Allen study, summarized by Sanford Rose (1989), identified three myths in bank managers' perceptions about noninterest expense. The first is that banks operate with high fixed costs. Fixed costs create problems because they cannot be reduced (that is, controlled) by managers. If banks eliminate some products or services, existing fixed costs must then be allocated to any remaining products. According to the study, however, only 10 percent of costs are shared among products and thus truly fixed. The implication is that banks can eliminate products that are unprofitable or marginally profitable and the average costs of remaining products will be largely unchanged. The second myth is that banks produce many products at the point of minimum unit costs. In the study, just 3 out of 15 large banks were scale producers. The remaining 12 banks would be better off either merging with other banks or outsourcing products. The third myth is that most reductions in expenses are permanent and have a significant impact on overall profitability. In fact, expense reductions are notoriously short-lived until the crisis disappears or the bank fails.

Revenue Enhancement. This strategy involves changing the pricing of specific products and services, while maintaining a sufficiently high volume of business so that total revenues increase. It is closely linked to the concept of price elasticity. Here management wants to identify products or services that exhibit price inelastic demand. For these, an increase in price will lower the quantity demanded of the underlying product, but the proportionate decrease in demand is less than the proportionate increase in price. Revenues thus rise. Alternatively, management can attempt to expand volume while keeping price constant. This can often be achieved by target marketing to enlarge the base of consumers. It also is a by-product of improving product quality. If customers perceive an improvement in quality, they will consume more and/or willingly pay a higher price.

Contribution Growth. With this strategy, management allocates resources to best improve overall long-term profitability. Increases in expenses are acceptable and expected, but must coincide with greater anticipated increases in associated revenues. An example might be investing in new computer systems and technology to provide better customer service at reduced unit costs once volume is sufficiently large. In essence, expenses are cut in the long run but not in the near future.

Clearly, the banks identified in Exhibit 13.6 follow different cost management strategies. This follows from differences in individual bank operating environments as determined by business mix, overall corporate strategic objectives, the geographic markets served, and the history of cost management behavior. Each strategy can be successfully implemented if pursued with long-term objectives. Rather than use traditional measures of expense control to monitor performance, managers should examine noninterest expense relative to operating income, which reflects the volume of business. Remember that cost management does not necessarily mean that expenses decline in absolute terms.

Cost cutting represents normal policy at most banks. In today's banking environment there is too much capacity evidenced by too many banks. With asset quality problems and increased capital requirements, consolidation is slowly shrinking the number of banks and reducing excess capacity. A more direct solution might be for large banks that compete in the same market to merge. Contemporary Issues: The Marriage of Chemical Banking Corp. and Manufacturers Hanover, about a proposed merger, demonstrates why.

Recent Cost Control at Banks

In June 1989 the *ABA Banking Journal* and Price Waterhouse conducted a survey of U.S. commercial banks that addressed cost management philosophies and strategies.

CONTEMPORARY ISSUES

The Marriage of Chemical Banking Corp. and Manufacturers Hanover

In 1991 Gerald Corrigan, president of the Federal Reserve Bank of New York, offered an opinion that large money center banks would merge within the year. At first glance this might seem absurd. A look at the potential financial benefits, however, reveals a different story.

Consider the case of Chemical Banking Corp. and Manufacturers Hanover based in New York City. During 1990, Chemical earned $291 million on $73 billion in assets; Manny Hanny earned $139 million on assets of $62 billion. Tier 1 capital equaled 5 percent and 5.43 percent, respectively. An *American Banker* article reported that analysts estimated that a combined firm could reduce operating costs by 25 percent. Most of the cost savings would come from consolidating branches and back office, or data processing, operations. The combined employee base of 45,866 would have to be cut by 25 percent, but there would be no loss in capacity. The bottom line impact would potentially reach $690 million annually. If this figure is realistic, it represents an annuity. From a financial perspective, the question is Can the cost savings actually be realized, and if so, what might this add to the value of the firm?

There are obvious nonfinancial costs that make such a merger unattractive to many. First, many employees would be laid off. Where do they go? Will outplacement services and job training be offered? The human resources costs are enormous. Second, who would manage the combined bank? Both firms already have entrenched management teams that will likely fight for turf. Can the senior managers work together? Who will be CEO of the combined firm? Finally, which bank's systems and policies will be used? Earlier mergers have struggled with consolidating computer operations far longer than originally anticipated.

Such mergers have not taken place because the presumed costs outweigh the benefits. Increased capital pressures, however, might change this dramatically if real cost savings in the magnitude suggested can be realized.

The results indicate that most banks start by improving productivity and streamlining procedures. They then focus on reducing staff size and closing branches. Exhibit 13.8 documents the range of actions taken to manage costs by size of bank and geographic region. Banks over $1 billion exhibited the greatest tendency to address cost control issues, in part because they have more branches and a larger employee base to trim.

Exhibit 13.9 indicates the type of actions by which management planned to control future costs. Again, the most frequently mentioned strategies were to improve productivity and streamline operating procedures as roughly four out of five respondents planned these actions. Only 19 percent intended to reduce staff and just 3 percent planned to close branches. This is not surprising as most banks that have implemented cost management actions have already taken these steps.

The net result of cost management is that banks will operate as leaner competitors. This should enhance long-term profitability and survival prospects in the consolidating banking industry. The negative aspects include the painful effects of replacing people with machines, requiring greater work effort that potentially increases employee stress, and in many cases reduced support of community activities.

Exhibit 13.9 Actions Planned by Banks for Future Control of Costs

Percent of those planning some actions to improve cost ratios

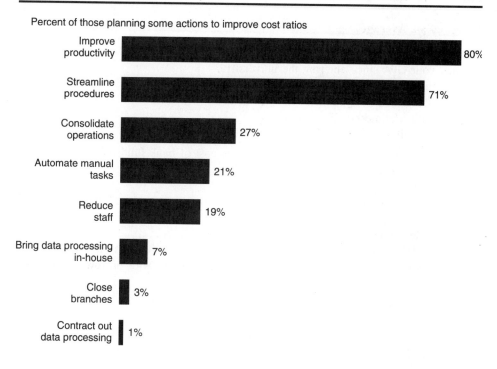

Improve productivity	80%
Streamline procedures	71%
Consolidate operations	27%
Automate manual tasks	21%
Reduce staff	19%
Bring data processing in-house	7%
Close branches	3%
Contract out data processing	1%

Source: Miller. "What Banks Say and Do about Operating Costs." *ABA Banking Journal* (October 1989).

SUMMARY

Banks constantly measure their operating costs. This chapter analyzes the measurement of costs associated with bank liabilities and equity capital. It discusses average costs and their application to understanding historical bank performance, then focuses on estimating marginal costs which are used in pricing decisions. Marginal costs represent the incremental cost of obtaining financing. Each individual source of debt funds has a distinct cost that reflects interest expense, acquisition and processing costs, and restrictions regarding the amount of funds a bank can invest. Equity capital has a marginal cost that reflects shareholders' required returns. Individual cost estimates are combined into a weighted marginal cost of capital, which is used in pricing. The chapter provides applications of the estimation process. It also discusses internal funds transfer pricing systems used by large banks that rely on single-source marginal cost analysis. Finally, the chapter examines bank efforts to manage or control noninterest expense.

Questions

Marginal vs. Average

1. Identify the following as either average (A) or marginal (M) measures.
   a. your GPA since entering the university
   b. the current interest rate on your MMDA
   c. your taxes last year divided by your taxable income
   d. your lifetime bowling average
   e. the miles-per-gallon your car is currently getting

2. Identify whether you should use an average cost of bank funds (A) or a marginal cost of funds (M) in the following situations.
   a. Setting the rate on a new loan.
   b. Evaluating the profitability of a long-standing customer's relationship with the bank.
   c. Calculating the bank's income tax liability.
   d. Deciding whether to build a new bank building or refurbish the old.
   e. Deciding whether to advertise the bank's jumbo CDs or borrow funds in the Eurodollar market instead.
   f. Deciding whether your bank has been performing as well as the competition down the street.

3. What are the consequences of a bank mistakenly pricing loans based on the historical cost of funds?

Calculating the Marginal Cost of Types of Bank Funding

4. Besides the explicit interest rate, what other costs must be considered when calculating the marginal cost of bank funds? How might a bank derive the value of these other costs?

5. Which source of bank funds generates the largest servicing costs? the largest acquisitions costs?

6. Calculate the pretax marginal cost of each of the following types of bank debt for a 1-year planning period.

	Interest Rate	Dollars Raised	Dollars Spent in Acquiring	Required Reserves	FDIC	Servicing Cost
NOW account	8%	$5 million	$10,000	12%	0.1%	$134,000
CD	9	10 million	1,000	0	0.1	2,000
Subordinated debentures	12	25 million	80,000	0	0.0	15,000

7. A bank plans to issue $20 million in 10-year perpetual subordinated bonds. The issue is priced at a discount to provide $19.2 million to the bank. The bonds pay $1.5 million in coupon interest at the end of each year and $200,000 each year to a computer service to send the coupon payments. Flotation costs will total $150,000. What is the pretax marginal cost of these funds if the bank is in the 40 percent marginal tax bracket?

8. A bank plans to issue perpetual preferred stock carrying a $40.00 per share price and paying $3.60 in annual dividends. Flotation costs are expected to be $1.85 per share. What is the bank's pretax marginal cost of these funds if the bank is in the 40 percent marginal tax bracket?

9. The common stock of a major bank currently sells for $38.50 per share and paid a $1.40 dividend at the end of last year. Most analysts expect the bank to increase its dividends by 5 percent each year. Flotation costs of new issues will average $1.50 per share. What is the bank's pretax marginal cost of these funds if the bank is in the 40 percent marginal tax bracket?

10. You have collected the following information, at least some of which you think will be useful in estimating the pretax cost of issuing new equity for your bank. What is that cost?

T-bill rate	8%
Bank's CD rate	9%
Banks' bond rate	9.4%
S&P 500 rate	12%
Bank's tax rate	40%
Bank's stock price	$25
Bank's Beta	1.2

11. A bank has calculated the pretax marginal cost of all its sources of funds and generated the following results:

Source	Amount to Be Raised	Amount Current on Balance Sheet	Pretax Cost
Deposits	$10 million	$400 million	9%
Debentures	2 million	1 million	12
Equity	5 million	33 million	16

What is this bank's weighted marginal cost of funds?

12. How should the weighted marginal cost of funds be used to price a loan of average risk? a loan of above-average risk?

Transfer Pricing

13. What type of bank benefits from an internal funds transfer system? What are the objectives of such a system?

14. Your bank has three organizational units—lending, deposit gathering, and funds management—that determine internal funds transfer prices. Assume that the lending area books a 2-year $5 million loan at 13.5 percent, the deposit-gathering area obtains $5 million in 1-year deposits at 9 percent, and the funding area (1) allocates $5 million to lending for 2 years at 11 percent (the 2-year CD rate), (2) accepts $5 million from deposits at 10.4 percent (the 1-year CD rate), and (3) plans to receive $5 million in additional 1-year deposits when these funds expire.
  a. Calculate the profit of each of these organizational units over the next year.
  b. Is this bank committed to a positive or negative duration over the 2-year planning period? What can the funds lending unit do if it wants a duration of zero?

c. If the CD rate declines during the second year and the deposit unit issues $5 million in 1-year deposits at 8.4 percent that it transfers to the funding area at 9.8 percent, which of these three units benefits from the declining rate? Is this the unit that should benefit? Why?

15. The funds transfer unit wields a great deal of power by setting the rates and thus the profits for other divisions. How should the funds management unit determine what portion of profits should go to lending, what portion to deposits, and what portion it should keep for itself?

Funding and Risk

16. As banks change their funding sources they affect the risks of the bank. Name the three risks that are directly affected and explain how using more short-term, "hot" funding affects each type.

17. As banks rely more on "hot" funds their ability to grow is curtailed. Explain this relationship.

Noninterest Expense

18. When confronted with runaway noninterest expense, a bank's first impulse is to cut costs. What are the advantages and disadvantages of this approach? What other approach is possible?

19. The operating efficiencies method of cost management can succeed through one of two approaches. What are the two?

20. What is the relationship between revenue enhancement and price elasticity of bank products?

Activity Projects

1. Calculate the total cost of one of your loans including both explicit and implicit costs. What is the explicit interest rate? What implicit costs should you consider? Try to estimate these costs. What problems do you have in the estimation? Are the implicit costs a substantial portion of the total cost?

2. Analyze financial data for a local commercial bank from its most recent annual report by calculating the average annual cost of alternative bank liabilities. Given current economic conditions and the risk-return profile of the bank, estimate whether the marginal cost of bank funds is above or below the average cost.

References

Berger, Allen, Gerald Hanweck, and David Humphrey. "Competitive Viability in Banking." *Journal of Monetary Economics* (June 1987).

Brigham, Eugene F. *Financial Management Theory and Practice*. Hinsdale, Ill.: The Dryden Press, 1990.

Clark, Jeffrey. "Economies of Scale and Scope at Depository Financial Institutions: A Review of the Literature." *Economic Review* (Federal Reserve Bank of Kansas City, September/October 1988).

Cole, Leonard. *Management Accounting in Banks*. Rolling Meadows, Ill.: Bank Administration Institute: Bankers Publishing Company, 1988.

Dyl, Edward. "The Marginal Cost of Funds Controversy." *Journal of Bank Research* (Autumn 1978).

Giardini, Valerie, John Pisa, and Casey Schroff. "A Critical Factor of Bank Profitability Measurement: Parts 1, 2 and 3." *Magazine of Bank Administration* (September–October–November 1984).

Goldstein, Stephen, James McNulty, and James Verbrugge. "Scale Economies in the Savings and Loan Industry Before Diversification." *Journal of Economics and Business* (February 1987).

Gregor, William, and Robert Hedges. "Alternative Strategies for Successful Cost Management." *The Bankers Magazine* (May/June 1990).

Horowitz, Jed. "Manny Hanny, Chemical: Does Marriage Make Sense?" *American Banker* (March 5, 1991).

Humphrey, David. "Intermediation and Cost Determinants of Large Bank Liability Composition." *Journal of Banking and Finance* (June 1981).

Humphrey, David. "Cost Dispersion and the Measurement of Economies in Banking." *Economic Review* (Federal Reserve Bank of Richmond, May/June 1987).

Humphrey, David. "Costs and Scale Economies in Bank Intermediation." In *Handbook for Banking Strategy*, edited by Richard Aspinwall and Robert Eisenbeis. New York: John Wiley & Sons, 1985.

Johnson, Bradford. "An Analysis of Modern Concepts of Loan Yields." *Magazine of Bank Administration* (August 1977).

Kim, Youn. "Economies of Scale and Scope in Multiproduct Financial Institutions: Further Evidence from Credit Unions." *Journal of Money, Credit, and Banking* (February 1986).

Kolari, James, and Asghar Zardhooki. *Bank Cost, Structure, and Performance*. Lexington, Mass.: D.C. Heath, 1987.

Mester, Loretta. "Efficient Production of Financial Services: Scale and Scope Economies." *Business Review* (Federal Reserve Bank of Philadelphia, January/February 1987).

Miller, William. "What Banks Say and Do about Operating Costs." *ABA Banking Journal* (October 1989).

Profitability Measurement for Financial Institutions: A Management Information Approach. Rolling Meadows, Ill.: Ernst & Whinney, Bank Administration Institute, 1987.

Roosevelt, Joseph. "Product Cost and Profitability: Developing Accurate Information in a Changing Environment." *The Bankers Magazine* (January–February 1985).

Roosevelt, Phil. "Cost Cutting Gains Momentum as Sources of Revenue Dry Up." *American Banker* (July 12, 1990).

Rose, Sanford. "What Really Went Wrong at Franklin National." *Fortune* (October 1974).

Rose, Sanford. "Rethinking Cost Control." *American Banker* (November 21, 1989).

"65 Ways to Cut Costs." *American Banker* (February 28, 1991).

Watson, Ronald. "Estimating the Cost of Your Bank's Funds." *Business Review* (Federal Reserve Bank of Philadelphia, May–June 1978).

Chapter 14

Why Hold Cash Assets?

Have you ever written a check against an account balance that you didn't have, then scrambled to deposit funds before the check cleared? Or have you ever charged certain expenses on your credit card, then been shocked at how much you owed when the bill came due? Consider the shock at Bank of New York when its deposit balance at the Federal Reserve went negative.

On November 20, 1985, officers at the Bank of New York, a $16 billion firm, determined that the bank was deficient in its required reserve holdings by $23.6 billion. The deficiency resulted from a computer malfunction that did not permit the bank to collect payments from other banks for transferring government securities. While checks drawn on it cleared, it received few of the deposits it expected. The Federal Reserve Bank of New York stepped in and loaned the bank $23.6 billion overnight (with interest) to cover the deficiency. This sum represented the largest single discount window loan in history.

Banks own four types of cash assets: vault cash, demand deposit balances at Federal Reserve Banks, demand deposit balances at private financial institutions, and cash items in the process of collection (CIPC). None of these assets earns any interest, so the entire allocation of funds represents a substantial opportunity cost for banks. Why then do banks hold cash assets? If cash assets involve a large opportunity cost, how can a bank determine its required holdings and minimize any excess? This chapter examines the nature of cash assets and the rationale underlying holding each type. It looks at legal reserve requirements, the source and impact of float, and the pricing of correspondent balances. The discussion provides a background for Chapter 15 because cash assets are linked closely with a bank's liquidity requirements.

Why does a bank hold cash assets? This chapter examines the role of cash assets and various strategies to minimize holdings and implicit costs.

OBJECTIVES OF CASH MANAGEMENT

Banks hold cash assets to satisfy four objectives. First, banks supply coin and currency to meet customers' regular transactions needs. The amount of cash in a bank's vault corresponds to customer cash deposits and the demand for cash withdrawals. Both exhibit considerable seasonal fluctuations, rising prior to holidays such as Christmas and falling immediately thereafter. Second, regulatory agencies mandate legal reserve requirements that can only be met by holding qualifying cash assets. Third, banks serve as a clearinghouse for the nation's check payment system. Each bank must hold sufficient balances at Federal Reserve Banks or other financial institutions so that checks written by its depositors will clear when presented for payment. Finally, banks use cash balances to purchase services from correspondent banks.

Banks prefer to hold as little cash as possible without creating transactions problems. Because cash does not generate interest income, excess holdings have a high opportunity cost represented by the interest that could be earned on an alternative investment. As interest rates rise, so do the opportunity cost and the incentive to economize on cash assets. There are, however, significant risks in holding too little cash. Imagine depositors' concerns if they were told that their bank did not have enough currency on hand for withdrawals. A bank must similarly keep enough deposit balances at other banks and the Federal Reserve to cover deposit outflows or it will be forced to replenish its balances under duress. Owning too few cash assets potentially creates liquidity problems and increases borrowing costs. Continued deficiencies are attributed to poor management, which ultimately leads to close regulatory scrutiny and deteriorating business relationships.

Fortunately, vault cash needs are fairly predictable. Local businesses make regular cash deposits and bank customers generally withdraw cash at predictable intervals near weekends, holidays, and when they receive their paychecks. Vault cash shortages can be avoided by requesting a currency shipment from the closest Federal Reserve Bank or correspondent bank. The Lone Star Bank (see Contemporary Issues: A Cashless Bank) has gone to the extreme in reducing vault cash holdings by handling no cash within the bank.

It is much more difficult to predict accurately the timing and magnitude of deposit inflows and outflows that influence deposits held at Federal Reserve Banks and other financial institutions. Deposit inflows raise legal reserve requirements but also increase actual reserve assets and correspondent deposits. Deposit outflows lower reserve requirements and reduce actual deposit holdings. Because deposit flows are determined by customer credit and payment transactions, banks cannot directly control the timing of clearings and float. Management is thus continually aiming at a moving target in projecting cash needs.

When banks realize unexpected deposit shortages, they must have access to balances at Federal Reserve or correspondent banks via either new borrowings or the sale of noncash assets. Unfortunately, borrowing costs typically increase and funding sources disappear when a bank experiences credit problems or operating difficulties. Similarly, assets that can easily be sold near par value typically earn lower yields. A bank's cash needs are thus closely related to its liquidity requirements and sources, as

A Cashless Bank

Lone Star National Bank in Dallas, Texas, has added a new twist to cash management. It handles no cash. Customers cannot make cash deposits, withdraw cash from deposit accounts, or even cash checks. All transactions are handled via checks. The only concession is that customers can withdraw cash from automatic teller machines.

Management initially decided to go cashless when it opened for business in a small, temporary mobile home facility. The bank's customer base is comprised of small businesses and professionals who handle the bulk of their business by mail. Going cashless cuts overhead by reducing the number of employees and lowering expenses for security guards, armored cars, and insurance.

discussed in Chapter 15. The fundamental management goal underlying cash and liquidity management is to accurately forecast cash needs and to arrange for readily available sources of cash at minimal cost.

THE RELATIONSHIP BETWEEN CASH AND LIQUIDITY REQUIREMENTS

The amount of cash management chooses to hold is heavily influenced by the bank's liquidity requirements. The liquidity position is, in turn, affected by the potential size and volatility of its cash requirements. Transactions that reduce cash holdings normally force a bank to replenish cash assets by issuing new debt or selling assets. Transactions that increase cash holdings provide new investable funds. From the opposite perspective, banks with ready access to borrowed funds can enter into more transactions because they can borrow at the margin quickly and at low cost to meet cash requirements.

Consider the simplified balance sheet in Exhibit 14.1. The bank holds $55 million in non-interest-bearing cash assets, most of which are correspondent balances at other institutions and deposits at the Federal Reserve. Vault cash is held for transactions requirements. If a bank needs currency, it requests a shipment from the Federal Reserve or a correspondent bank that has the impact outlined at the bottom of the exhibit. The transaction is reversed when the bank delivers excess currency. Neither transaction alters total cash holdings or the bank's liquidity requirements.

The bank holds demand deposits at the Federal Reserve in part because the Federal Reserve imposes legal reserve requirements and deposit balances qualify as legal reserves. The purpose of required reserves is to enable the Federal Reserve to control the nation's money supply. By forcing banks and other depository institutions to hold deposit balances in support of transactions accounts and time deposits, the Federal Reserve hopes to control credit availability and thereby influence general economic conditions.

The Federal Reserve sets required reserves as a fraction of the dollar amount of selected bank liabilities. The nature of the impact can be shown using the data from

**Exhibit 14.1 Transactions Affecting a Bank's Cash
Holdings (Millions of Dollars)**

ASSETS		LIABILITIES AND EQUITY	
Vault cash	$ 2	Demand deposits	$100
Demand deposits held at Federal Reserve	17	Time deposits	500
Demand deposits held at other financial institutions	28	Federal funds purchased	60
Cash in process of collection	8	Other liabilities	30
Total	$ 55	Total	$690
Securities and interest-bearing time deposits	$270	Equity	$ 60
Net loans	375		
Other assets	50		
Total	$750	Total	$750

Impact of $0.5 Million Currency Shipment		*Impact of $10 Million Demand Deposit Outflow*	
ΔASSETS	ΔLIABILITIES	ΔASSETS	ΔLIABILITIES
Vault cash $0.5		Demand deposits held at Federal Reserve −$10	Demand deposits −$10
Demand deposits held at Federal Reserve −$0.5			

Exhibit 14.1 and several simplified assumptions. Assume that the legal reserve requirement equals 10 percent for demand deposits and 1 percent for all time deposits. (Actual percentage requirements are introduced in Exhibit 14.3.) Ignore also the role of vault cash. Total required reserves thus equal $15 million, the minimum amount the bank must keep on deposit at the Federal Reserve. In this example, the bank actually holds $17 million, or $2 million more than the requirement. If the volume of outstanding deposits at the bank rises or falls, the bank's required reserves rise and fall, respectively. Thus deposit balances at the Federal Reserve will vary directly with the magnitude of reservable bank liabilities.

A bank also holds deposit balances to help process deposit inflows and outflows caused by check clearings, maturing time deposits and securities, wire transfers, and other transactions. Deposit flows are the link between a bank's cash position and its liquidity requirements. Consider the T-account at the bottom of Exhibit 14.1, which documents the impact of a $10 million demand deposit outflow that clears through the bank's reserve account at the Federal Reserve. The outflow may represent a daily net clearing drain, in which the value of checks written on deposits at the sample bank exceeds the value of checks drawn on other banks which are deposited at the sample bank and presented to the Federal Reserve for payment. The offsetting adjustment to the deposit loss is a $10 million decrease in reserve balances. In this simplified example, required reserves now decline by $1 million. A liquidity problem arises, however, because actual deposit balances held at the Federal Reserve decrease by $10 million. The bank is now $7 million deficient ($14 − $7) in required reserves, which represents its immediate liquidity need.

All such deposit outflows directly reduce a bank's deposit balances at either the Federal Reserve or correspondent banks and raise its liquidity needs. A deposit inflow has the opposite impact. Chapter 15 examines how banks can replenish cash assets by issuing new debt and selling assets.

MEETING LEGAL RESERVE REQUIREMENTS

The actual computation of legal reserve requirements is more complex than suggested above. Reserve percentages are multiplied by outstanding deposit balances, but not all deposits are subject to reserves. Banks reduce the volume of liabilities subject to required reserves by subtracting correspondent balances, and vault cash qualifies as a reserve asset. Most importantly, required reserves can be met over a 2-week period, so a bank does not have to hold a specific amount of cash assets on each day. This section analyzes current reserve requirements in detail and provides a comprehensive example. Important terminology is introduced in Exhibit 14.2.

Federal Reserve Regulations D and M specify minimum reserve requirements for commercial banks. The regulations stipulate that each bank must hold cash reserves equal to a fraction of its base liabilities. There are three elements of required reserves: the dollar magnitude of base liabilities, the dollar magnitude of qualifying cash assets, and the required reserve fraction. Base liabilities are comprised of net transactions accounts, nonpersonal time deposits, and Eurocurrency liabilities (borrowings from foreign branches or foreign banks). Net transactions accounts equal the sum of the balances that are listed on the bank's books, referred to as ledger balances, in the form of demand deposits, NOW accounts, automatic transfers, and other accounts subject to preauthorized transfers minus the sum of a bank's CIPC and collected balances due from private depository institutions. Nonpersonal time deposits are nontransactions accounts owned by a depositor that is not a natural person. Only accounts with less than $1\frac{1}{2}$ years original maturity require reserves. No reserves are required against personal time deposits, money market deposit accounts (MMDAs), federal funds purchased, security RPs, and all other liabilities.

A bank's qualifying reserve assets include vault cash and demand deposits due from Federal Reserve Banks. The relevant percentages (required reserve ratios) appear in Exhibit 14.3. In 1990, for example, each bank was required to hold 3 percent reserves against its first $40.4 million of daily average net transactions accounts and 12 percent on any excess. It had to hold only 3 percent reserves against nonpersonal time deposits with original maturity under $1\frac{1}{2}$ years and all Eurocurren-

Exhibit 14.2 Important Terminology

Base computation period: the 14-day period during which a bank's outstanding liabilities determine the amount of required reserves to be held during the reserve maintenance period.

Collected balances: the dollar value of ledger balances minus float.

Correspondent bank: a bank that provides services to other financial institutions and receives payment in the form of either deposit balances or direct user fees.

Daylight overdrafts: the process of authorizing payments within a business day from deposit accounts held at the Federal Reserve or correspondent banks in excess of actual balances held.

Deferred availability credit items: the dollar amount of checks deposited at the Federal Reserve Bank for which the Federal Reserve has not yet granted credit.

Earnings credit: the assumed interest rate at which a bank can invest customer deposit balances to earn interest income.

Investable balances: the dollar value of collected balances minus required reserves.

Reserve maintenance period: the 14-day period during which a bank must hold sufficient deposit balances at the Federal Reserve to meet its legal reserve requirement.

Respondent bank: a bank that buys services from other financial institutions and pays by holding nonearning deposit balances at the correspondent or via direct user fees.

Transactions accounts: all deposits on which the account holder is allowed to make withdrawals by negotiable instruments and more than three monthly telephone and preauthorized funds transfers.

cy liabilities.[1] The Board of Governors can vary these reserve ratios within established regulatory limits.

Recent Problems with Reserve Requirements

Historically, commercial bank reserve requirements varied with the type of bank charter and the bank's geographic location. The states stipulated reserve requirements for banks that were not members of the Federal Reserve System (state-chartered nonmembers), which were generally less restrictive than those for members. Nonmember reserve ratios were lower, and more assets, even interest-bearing government securities, often qualified as legal reserves for nonmember banks. Only vault cash and demand balances held at the Federal Reserve constituted reserves for member banks. Thus nonmembers could invest more funds in earning assets than could similar member banks. This discrepancy represented a substantive opportunity cost of Federal Reserve membership, which was compounded further because nonmembers had access to Federal Reserve services through correspondent bank relationships.

Not surprisingly, many member banks switched charters and withdrew their Federal Reserve memberships. This withdrawal peaked during 1977 to 1979, when the level of interest rates reached historical highs and the opportunity cost became prohibi-

---

[1]Financial institutions that are not members of the Federal Reserve System can use pass-through balances to meet reserve requirements. Pass-through balances are deposits held at either the Federal Home Loan Bank, the National Credit Union Administration Central Liquidity Facility, or any bank that keeps balances at the Federal Reserve Bank. The first $3.4 million in reservable liabilities in 1990 was exempt from required reserves for all firms.

**Exhibit 14.3 Reserve Requirement Percentages for
Depository Institutions after DIDMCA[a]**

Type of Deposit	Percentage	Effective Date of Applicable Percentages
Net transactions accounts[a]		
$0–$40.4 million	3%	12/31/89
> $40.4 million	12	12/31/89
Nonpersonal time deposits by original maturity[b]		
< 1.5 years	3	10/6/83
≥ 1.5 years	0	10/6/83
Eurocurrency liabilities (all types)	3	11/13/80
All other liabilities	0	10/6/83

[a]DIDMCA specified that the 3 percent requirement would be applied against a base amount of transactions accounts that increases annually by 80 percent of the change in total transactions accounts of all depository institutions.

[b]The Garn–St Germain Act specified that no reserves would be required against the first $2 million of reservable liabilities. This base amount would increase annually by 80 percent of the increase in total reservable liabilities at all depository institutions. The exempt amount equaled $3.4 million in 1990.

Source: *Federal Reserve Bulletin*, Table 1.15, with modifications.

tive. Congress eliminated this problem by passing the Depository Institutions Deregulation and Monetary Control Act (DIDMCA) in 1980. DIDMCA mandated that all depository institutions offering transactions accounts be subject to uniform reserve requirements, regardless of charter. The figures in Exhibit 14.3 now apply to both member and nonmember banks as well as savings and loan associations, and credit unions.[2]

During the late 1970s, the Federal Reserve experienced related problems in controlling the banking system's aggregate reserves. This trouble resulted from its reserve accounting system and monetary policy operating strategy. From 1968 through February 1984, the Federal Reserve employed lagged reserve accounting (LRA), under which an individual bank held reserves against its deposit liabilities outstanding 2 weeks earlier. It could average its actual reserve holdings over a 7-day period (the reserve maintenance week) based on its actual liabilities outstanding during the 7-day base period 2 weeks prior. The timing is represented in Exhibit 14.4. Each bank knew its total reserve requirement with certainty during the maintenance week because changes in deposit liabilities during the week did not alter reserve needs until 2 weeks later. A bank simply had to manage its clearing balances to avoid problems.

LRA made it difficult for the Federal Reserve to control the money supply after the change in operating strategies in October 1979, when it began targeting monetary aggregates rather than short-term interest rates. With LRA, Federal Reserve purchases or sales of securities immediately altered the amount of total reserves in the system but did not affect required reserves. Banks found that the cost of reserves varied depending on the amount of excess reserves available, but they did not have to alter

---

[2]The requirements were phased in gradually through 1987 to where firms of similar size are now treated equally.

Exhibit 14.4 The Relationship Between the Reserve Maintenance Period and Base Computation Periods under Lagged Reserve Accounting

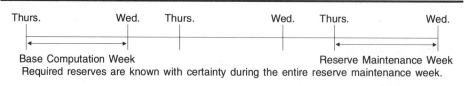

their required holdings until 2 weeks later, when deposit fluctuations affected reserve requirements. To help offset this imbalance, the Federal Reserve moved to a contemporaneous reserve accounting (CRA) system in February 1984. Now open market operations affect both current deposit levels and required reserves coincidentally.

Contemporaneous Reserve Accounting

The current CRA procedure mixes elements of LRA and fully contemporaneous accounting systems. Under CRA, banks must maintain reserves on a daily average basis for a 14-day period beginning on a Thursday and ending on the second Wednesday following.[3] This 2-week interval is called the *reserve maintenance* or *settlement period*. The amount of required reserves is determined by the magnitude of daily average reservable liabilities over two separate base computation periods. The computation period for nontransactions accounts lasts 2 weeks but leads the maintenance period by 30 days, beginning on a Tuesday and ending on a Monday 17 days before the start of the maintenance period. Thus a bank knows its required reserves against nontransactions accounts with certainty over the entire settlement period. The base computation period for net transactions accounts virtually coincides with the maintenance period. It begins 2 days before the beginning of the maintenance period and ends 2 days before the end of the maintenance period. A bank can compute its required reserves against these accounts with certainty only during the last 2 days of the settlement period. Exhibit 14.5 demonstrates the timing of these intervals. Note that Friday balances carry over to Saturday and Sunday such that Friday's balances have a 3-day impact on the daily average.

The procedure to determine required reserves involves multiplying the percentages from Exhibit 14.3 by the daily average amount outstanding for each reservable liability during the base computation period. Banks can vary from the daily average requirement on any day of the maintenance period as long as their average reserve holdings meet the minimum daily requirement over the entire period. Both vault cash and demand balances at the Federal Reserve qualify as reserve assets. However, vault cash actually held during the lagged computation period for nontransactions accounts is used to offset total required reserves during the maintenance period. For example, if a bank's daily average required reserves based on reservable liabilities total $20 million during the reserve maintenance

---

[3]Banks with reservable liabilities of $15 million or less compute and meet reserve requirements only quarterly.

Exhibit 14.5 The Relationship Between the Reserve Maintenance and Base Computation Periods under Contemporaneous Reserve Accounting

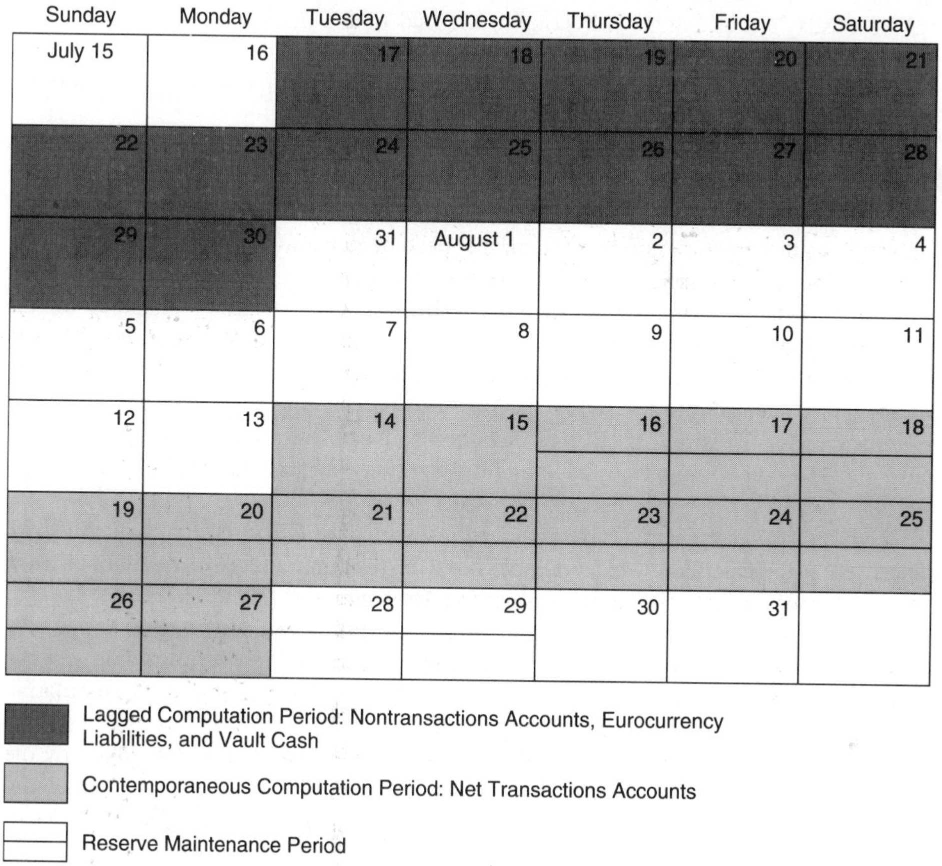

Sunday	Monday	Tuesday	Wednesday	Thursday	Friday	Saturday
July 15	16	17	18	19	20	21
22	23	24	25	26	27	28
29	30	31	August 1	2	3	4
5	6	7	8	9	10	11
12	13	14	15	16	17	18
19	20	21	22	23	24	25
26	27	28	29	30	31	

Lagged Computation Period: Nontransactions Accounts, Eurocurrency Liabilities, and Vault Cash

Contemporaneous Computation Period: Net Transactions Accounts

Reserve Maintenance Period

period, required demand balances at the Federal Reserve would equal $18 million if the bank held an average $2 million in vault cash during the lagged computation period.

Finally, actual reserve holdings during the maintenance week can deviate slightly from the exact percentage requirement, with any excess or deficiency carried forward to the next period. The present allowance is 2 percent of daily average required reserves before past excesses or deficiencies and the vault cash offset, or $25,000, whichever is greater. If a bank is deficient by more than this amount, it must pay a nondeductible interest penalty equal to the discount rate plus 2 percent times the extraordinary deficiency. More importantly, if a bank consistently holds too little reserves, the Federal Reserve will penalize it further by restricting its operating procedures and allowable business activities. If a bank holds more reserves than the allowable excess, it cannot carry this difference forward and thus loses any interest income it could have earned by investing the balances. The timing of these requirements places a premium on Wednesday's transactions just prior to the end of the maintenance week. Because federal funds are an important source of reserves, federal funds trading is very active on Wednesdays and the federal funds rate is typically more volatile compared to other days.

An Application: Reserve Calculation under CRA

Reserve maintenance requirements can be best demonstrated through an example. Consider the time frame outlined in Exhibit 14.5, with August 16 to 29 representing the 14-day reserve maintenance period. Exhibit 14.6 presents daily balances for all reservable liabilities during the relevant lagged and contemporaneous reserve computation periods for a sample bank. The final column lists the cumulative totals for each balance sheet item over the 2-week period.[4] The base period for reservable nontransactions accounts ends on July 30, 17 days before the maintenance period begins. The base period for net transactions accounts begins 2 days before the maintenance period starts.

Exhibit 14.7 demonstrates the required reserves calculation. Actual balance sheet data used in the calculation are available only for the final 2 days of the maintenance period, August 28 and 29. The procedure has four steps: 1) calculating daily average balances outstanding during the computation period, 2) applying the reserve percentages, 3) subtracting vault cash, and 4) adding or subtracting the allowable reserve carried forward from the prior period. Daily average balances equal each cumulative total divided by 14, the number of days in the base period. Weekends count even if a bank is not open for business. These daily average balances are then multiplied by the percentages from Exhibit 14.3. In 1990 the first $3.4 million of nonpersonal time and savings deposits was exempt from required reserves, while the first $40.4 million of net transactions accounts was subject to the lower 3-percent requirement. Both base amounts increase annually with economic growth, as indicated in Exhibit 14.3.

In this example, total daily average required reserves equal $188.438 million. Average vault cash of $32.214 million during the lagged computation period is then subtracted to yield a net requirement of $156.224 million. Banks can deviate from the exact requirement as long as they make up deficiencies in the following maintenance period. Excess reserve holdings or surpluses of up to 2 percent of gross required reserves can be carried forward to reduce the next period's minimum requirement. The computation in Exhibit 14.7 assumes that the prior period deficiency totaled $2.276 million. The sample bank must hold minimum reserves equal to the net requirement plus the daily deficiency—a total of $158.500 million. The last item in the exhibit, maximum reserves at the Federal Reserve, equals the minimum requirement plus 2 percent of $188.438 million. Of course, there is no limit on how much in balances a

---

[4]Banks can report balance sheet figures to the nearest thousand dollars. Exhibit 14.6 rounds figures to the nearest million.

Exhibit 14.6 Report of Reservable Liabilities and Offsetting Asset Balances (Millions of Dollars)

Balances at Close of Business Each Day

Lagged Computation Period[a]	July 17	18	19	20	21	22	23	24	25	26	27	28	29	30	Two-Week Total	Daily Average
Nonpersonal money market deposit accounts	$ 305	$ 314	$ 316	$ 316	$ 316	$ 316	$ 312	$ 309	$ 312	$ 318	$ 319	$ 319	$ 319	$ 311	$ 4,402	$ 314.43
Nonpersonal other savings	28	27	27	27	27	27	28	28	28	28	28	28	28	28	387	27.64
Nonpersonal time deposits of < 1.5 years' original maturity	1,844	1,839	1,840	1,841	1,841	1,841	1,847	1,847	1,851	1,851	1,851	1,851	1,851	1,856	25,851	1,846.50
Eurocurrency liabilities	572	572	570	565	565	565	549	552	552	552	552	552	552	568	7,838	559.86
Vault cash	28	30	31	33	33	33	38	30	31	32	32	32	32	36	451	32.21

Contemporaneous Computation Period	August 14	15	16	17	18	19	20	21	22	23	24	25	26	27	Two-Week Total
Demand deposits	$992	$955	$956	$954	$954	$954	$989	$996	$960	$959	$958	$958	$958	$990	$13,533
Automatic transfers from savings accounts	0	0	0	0	0	0	0	0	0	0	0	0	0	0	0
Telephone and preauthorized transfers	0	0	0	0	0	0	0	0	0	0	0	0	0	0	0
NOW and Super NOW accounts	221	221	222	223	223	223	223	224	225	225	225	225	225	225	3,130
Deductions															
Demand balances due from U.S. depository institutions	163	281	190	186	186	186	159	159	274	178	182	182	182	164	2,664
Cash items in process of collection	96	96	78	78	78	78	95	98	92	79	81	81	81	88	1,198
Net transactions accounts	954	805	910	913	913	913	966	963	819	927	920	920	920	958	12,801

[a] The bank has no ineligible acceptances or reservable obligations of affiliates.

Exhibit 14.7 Required Reserves Report: August 16–29 (Millions of Dollars)

Reservable Liabilities For	Daily Average Deposits	Reserve Percentage	Daily Average Requirement
July 17-30			
Nonpersonal money market deposit accounts			
Exempt	$ 3.40	0.0%	$ 0.000
Remaining balance	311.03	3.0	9.331
Total	$ 314.43		
Nonpersonal other savings	$ 27.64	3.0	0.829
Nonpersonal time deposits up to 1.5 years' maturity	1,846.50	3.0	55.395
Eurocurrency liabilities	559.86	3.0	16.796
August 14-17			
Net transactions accounts			
Up to $40.4 million	40.40	3.0	1.212
Over $40.4 million	873.96	12.0	$104.875
Total	$ 914.36		
Gross reserve requirement			$188.438
Daily average vault cash for July 17–30			32.214
Net reserve requirement			$156.224
Reserve carry-forward from prior period: Daily average amount = –2,276 (deficit)			2.276
Minimum reserve to be maintained with the Federal Reserve			$158.500
Maximum reserves to be maintained [0.02(188.438) = 3.769]			$162.269

bank may hold at the Federal Reserve. The term *maximum* refers to the fact that no more than a 2-percent surplus can be used to reduce future balance requirements.

The calculations would be slightly different if the bank carried forward a surplus from the previous maintenance period. In this case, a bank is allowed to be deficient by 2 percent of gross reserves during the current maintenance period. If, for example, the bank in Exhibit 14.7 reported a carry-forward surplus of $1 million, it could have used the $1 million to reduce its total requirement and still be deficient 2 percent more. Thus the minimum point in the target range would equal $151.455 million and the maximum would equal $158.993 million.

Reserves Planning

The greatest difficulty in meeting reserve requirements derives from not knowing what the average periodic requirement will be during the first 12 days of the maintenance period. Unlike LRA, changes in the volume of net transactions accounts simultaneously change actual requirements. This is the essential point regarding the impact of deposit outflows in Exhibit 14.1. A bank must therefore continuously monitor its deposit inflows and outflows and make corresponding adjustments to its cash position. Typically, weekly patterns reflect large commercial deposit inflows from weekend transactions or regular payroll payments. Changes in float naturally follow. Management can incorporate these systematic funds flows into a planning model to time federal funds sales and purchases.

For example, if a bank experiences net clearing surpluses early in the week and deficiencies later, it can either use the surpluses to offset later period reserve deficiencies or temporarily invest balances in earning assets and rely on future borrowings to cover deficiencies. A planning model might simply extrapolate actual net transactions balances from 2 weeks prior for the unknown daily outstandings to project requirements during the maintenance period. Significant deviations can easily be noted and adjustments made.

Every bank should manage reserves to keep actual Federal Reserve balances within the range represented by the theoretical minimum and maximum of Exhibit 14.7. In this case, every dollar of reserves counts. Deficiencies and interest penalties are avoided, while all excesses reduce future requirements. This means that banks should alternate between deficiencies and excesses over successive maintenance periods. An actual reserve average of $161 million during August 16 to 29 in Exhibit 14.7 would allow the sample bank to reduce its daily requirement the following period by $2.5 million plus 2 percent of gross reserves required. In this case, every dollar of reserves is fully used.

MANAGING FLOAT

During any single day approximately $90 million of checks drawn on U.S. commercial banks are waiting to be processed. Individuals, businesses, and governments deposit the checks but cannot use the proceeds until banks give their approval, typically in several days. Checks in process of collection, called *float,* are a source of both income and expense to banks.

The Payment System

To understand float management and recent criticism of bank policies, it is necessary to explain banking's payment system. Payments between banks can be made either by check or electronically. Checks drawn against transactions accounts are presented to the customer's bank for payment and ultimately "cleared" by reducing the bank's deposit balance at the Federal Reserve or a correspondent bank. Payments made electronically directly and immediately alter balances held at Federal Reserve Banks. This network for transferring funds electronically is called the Fedwire.

The standard check-clearing process is outlined in Exhibit 14.8. An individual visiting San Jose, California, purchases goods from a local business for $500 by writing a check on his demand deposit held at Community National Bank (CNB) in Portland, Oregon. The check-clearing process begins when the business deposits this check at the Bay Area National Bank (BANB). Because BANB assumes the risk that the check is not good, it does not allow the depositor to use the funds immediately. Normally, a bank places a hold on the check until it verifies that the check writer has enough funds

Exhibit 14.8 An Example of the Check-Clearing Process[a]

Bay Area National Bank, San Jose		
ΔASSETS	ΔLIABILITIES	
1. CIPC +$500	Demand deposit owed the business	+$500
4. CIPC −$500		
Demand deposit at BOC +$500		

Bank of California, San Francisco		
ΔASSETS	ΔLIABILITIES	
2. CIPC +$500	Demand deposit (BANB)	+$500
5. CIPC −$500		
Demand deposit at FRB of San Francisco +$500		

Federal Reserve Bank of San Francisco		
ΔASSETS	ΔLIABILITIES	
3. CIPC +$500	DACI	+$500
5.	DACI	−$500
	Demand depoist (BOC)	+$500
6. CPIC −$500	Demand deposit (CNB)	−$500

Community National Bank, Portland		
ΔASSETS	ΔLIABILITIES	
6. Demand deposit at FRB of San Francisco −$500	Demand deposits owed the individual	−$500

[a] CIPC indicates checks in the process of collection; BOC, Bank of California; FRB, Federal Reserve Bank; BANB, Bay Area National Bank; DACI, deferred credit availability items; and CNB, Community National Bank.

on deposit to cover the draft. BANB thus increases the ledger balances of the business's demand deposit account and its own CIPC. The business's usable collected balances, ledger balances minus float, are unchanged.

During stage 2, BANB forwards the check to its upstream correspondent, the Bank of California (BOC) in San Francisco. This bank replicates BANB's procedures, deferring credit to BANB for several days until the check clears. In stage 3, BOC presents the check to the Federal Reserve Bank of San Francisco. The Federal Reserve follows a timetable indicating how long a bank must wait before it can receive credit on deposited items. The dollar amount of deferred credit is labeled *deferred credit availability items (DACI)*. Until the Federal Reserve provides credit, it increases its CIPC and DACI equally so that Federal Reserve float (CIPC minus DACI) equals zero.

Up to this point, no depositor can spend its funds, and the check has not been presented to CNB for payment. Frequently, correspondent banks and the Federal Reserve give credit on checks deposited by other banks prior to actually verifying that the checks are good. This is indicated as stages 4 and 5 in Exhibit 14.8. BANB, however, does not provide the same credit to the business depositor until the check clears. After stage 4, BANB can invest its deposit at BOC while it defers crediting the business account. BOC, in turn, receives reserve credit before the check actually clears.

During stage 6, the Federal Reserve Bank presents the original check to CNB, which verifies that the individual has enough funds on deposit to cover the payment.

Most checks complete this trip in 2 to 6 days. The actual length of time varies with the number of financial institutions that handle an item and the geographic distance between banks. The greater the number of handlers and distance, the longer it takes to transfer and verify a check. To accelerate the process, banks encode checks with magnetic numbers that can be read by high-speed machines and often move checks via overnight couriers between destinations. Unfortunately, the process does not work as quickly in reverse. If the bank on which the original check is drawn (CNB in the above example) discovers that the check writer has insufficient funds to cover the draft, it sends the check back to the bank accepting the initial deposit (BANB in the example). In most instances, the check must again go through each intermediate institution that handled it earlier.[5] This may take another 7 to 14 days because returned checks are physically analyzed for endorsements.

Many payments are effected electronically without any checks. Customers simply advise their banks to transfer funds via telephone or computer hook-ups between institutions. The exchange is completed on the same day as payment authorization using immediately available funds. Customers who use the Federal Reserve's wire transfer system pay a fee to their bank. Most large-denomination transactions are handled via the Fedwire. Consider the payment outlined in Exhibit 14.8. In this case, the individual could have authorized CNB to have the Federal Reserve immediately transfer $500 from CNB's reserve account to BANB's reserve account. The Federal Reserve's computer records the funds transfer and notifies BANB of payment.[6] Reserve credit is immediate because the payment comes from immediately available funds.

Holds on Deposited Checks

A bank that accepts a deposit accepts the risk that supporting funds will eventually appear. If the individual in Exhibit 14.8 does not have sufficient funds to cover the $500 draft, BANB must collect from its business depositor and may suffer losses. To reduce this risk, banks typically place a hold on deposited funds. Essentially, they do not let depositors spend the proceeds until there is reasonable certainty the deposit is good.

Consumer groups and legislators have long criticized banks for lengthy delays in making deposits available. Prior to 1989, banks often forced customers to wait 20 business days for availability. Averages for checks drawn on out-of-state banks typically ranged from 8 to 10 days.[7] Because banks can normally invest deposited items

[5]The Federal Reserve Bank of Dallas implemented a test program in 1984 for the final payer bank to return items directly to the bank of first deposit without following the chain of endorsements. The payer bank is required to notify the first bank within 3 business days of a check's receipt if a check is not honored. Notification is required for all checks over $2,500. Failure to notify makes the payer bank liable.

[6]Large payments involving international participants are handled through the New York Clearing House Interbank Payment System (CHIPS).

[7]Averages come from a 1985 Bank Administration Institute study summarized in the *American Banker*, April 1, 1985. At that time it took an average 6.8 days for a returned item to make the round trip from the initial deposit payer bank and back.

in 2 to 3 days, they earned substantial amounts of interest while delaying availability and interest payments on deposits. In the previous example, BANB may be able to invest the initial deposit after 2 days via its correspondent bank. It may coincidentally delay availability to the depositor for 6 or more days, during which time it pays no interest and prohibits transactions.[8]

Several states subsequently passed laws forcing banks to publish their check-clearing schedules and, in turn, set maximum delays on deposited items. New York, for example, requires banks to credit accounts within 1 business day for checks under $100 and all government checks. Checks for greater amounts are subject to a maximum hold at commercial banks of 3 days on local items and 6 days on out-of-state items. Effective in September 1990, Congress passed the Expedited Funds Availability Act, which stipulated maximum time limits under Regulation CC for banks to make funds available on deposited checks. There are several basic limits that all banks must meet.

1. Local checks must be cleared in no more than 2 business days. A local check is one written on a firm in the same metropolitan area or within the same Federal Reserve check-processing region.

2. Non-local checks must be cleared in no more than 5 business days.

3. Funds deposited in the form of government checks, certified checks, and cashiers checks must be available by 9 a.m. the next day.

There are exceptions to these schedules, such as with habitual check bouncers, but the law generally lets account holders know the longest they will have to wait to access their funds. The Act also required banks to disclose their hold policy to all transactions account owners, required banks to start accruing interest when the firm receives credit for its deposited checks, and established penalties for failure to comply with its provisions.

Daylight Overdrafts

Most individuals at one time or another have played the float game, writing checks against insufficient balances, then rushing to deposit funds that permit the checks to clear. Banks play the same game with electronic funds transfers—for far greater dollar amounts—by authorizing payments from deposits held at the Federal Reserve or correspondent banks in excess of their balances. In doing so, they drive their collected balances below zero. These negative balances are called daylight overdrafts. Normally, enough funds are transferred into the account by the end of each day to cover the overdraft. In early 1985 daylight overdrafts averaged around $120 billion daily, of which $85 billion originated over the Fedwire.[9] In November 1985 the Federal Reserve

---

[8]Interest is applicable only on NOW, Super NOW, and MMDA accounts. If the business had immediate availability and liquidated the deposit, BANB's actual reserves would decline, forcing the bank to replenish nonearning assets.

[9]Richard Smoot, 1985, discusses overdrafts arising over the major wire transfer systems and analyzes the risks assumed in each case.

was forced to lend the Bank of New York $23.6 billion to cover overdrafts caused by a computer malfunction. (See Contemporary Issues: A $24 Billion Overdraft.)

These overdrafts could potentially close down the electronic payments system. The primary risk is that some financial institution might fail because it cannot meet a payments obligation. A failure might produce liquidity problems at other banks and have a ripple effect, generating other losses and failures. Suppose, for example, that CNB from Exhibit 14.8 transfers funds over the Fedwire to BANB before the individual makes sufficient balances available to cover the original $500 check to the San Jose business. Once the wire transfer is received, BANB can release funds to the business without risk. Settlement is immediate and final. If the individual does not provide the underlying balances, CNB could lose the amount of the transfer. When extended to all transactions, any single bank may have daylight overdrafts two or three times larger than its capital base.

There are two main electronic funds transfer networks, the Fedwire and CHIPS (Clearing House Interbank Payment System). Most of the transactions on Fedwire involve transfers of immediately available funds between financial institutions and balance adjustments from the purchase or sale of government securities. Most of the wire transfers on CHIPS involve either transfers of Eurodollar balances or foreign exchange trading. While participants are required to maintain positive balances at the Federal Reserve and correspondent banks at the end of each business day, they may create negative balances during a day by transferring funds in excess of their initial balance before any deposits are received. This negative balance is a daylight overdraft. Conceptually, the overdraft is a loan, but under current regulation it is costless to the deficient bank because no interest or fees are paid. Daylight overdrafts may be intentional or unintentional, but they clearly pose risk to the Federal Reserve or CHIPS system. The Fed assumes risk because recipients of wire transfers retain legal title to the funds. The Fed thus essentially guarantees wire transfers.

The Federal Reserve endorsed guidelines on overdrafts in 1986 which limited the size of daylight overdrafts while transferring funds over the Fedwire. VanHoose and Sellon (1989) describe the types of policies the Fed uses to control payment system risk over the Fedwire and CHIPS. The policies consist primarily of caps on the size of any single firm's overdrafts. Interestingly, the Fed chooses not to use the price mechanism by charging interest on overdrafts to influence their usage. Still, the Fed identifies large overdrafts on the Fedwire and discusses the potential risks with the guilty bank's senior management. If the overdrafts arise because of computer problems, it will extend discount window credit at the current discount rate plus 2 percent. Its ultimate weapon, however, is to restrict bank operations.

Pricing Federal Reserve Check-Clearing Services

One important facet of DIDMCA was to promote competition in check-clearing services. Prior to the Act, the Federal Reserve provided free check collection to member banks. Banks did pay indirectly through owning nonearning reserve deposits. Still, many banks also chose to clear checks through correspondent banks. Correspon-

A $24 Billion Overdraft

The Bank of New York serves as a clearing agent for numerous brokers that buy and sell U.S. government securities, transferring ownership of securities between buyers and sellers. Normally, sellers of securities route the instruments through the bank's securities account at the Federal Reserve Bank of New York and simultaneously receive payment through debits against the Bank of New York's reserve account. The Bank of New York promptly routes the securities to the buyers, from whom it collects payment.

On November 20, 1985, the bank experienced a computer malfunction that short-circuited the normal sequence of transactions. While the computer allowed sellers to route securities to the bank's account and debit the bank's reserves in payment, it did not allow the bank to route the same securities to the ultimate buyers. Thus the bank saw its reserves decline, but it could not generate sufficient cash receipts to replenish the deductions. By the end of the day, the bank reported a $22.6 billion overdraft in its reserve account. The Federal Reserve Bank of New York stepped in and made a $22.6 billion overnight discount window loan at 7.5 percent. Later it was determined that the actual deficiency was $23.6 billion, and the bank was charged interest on an additional $1 billion loan.

The $23.6 billion loan was 2,300 percent of the bank's capital, and it cost the bank almost $5 million in unanticipated interest expense. If a bank were unable to cover its exposure, it could lose an amount far in excess of its capital and thus quickly become insolvent. Because Bank of New York's loan was fully collateralized with U.S. government securities, the Federal Reserve was never at risk of loss. In response to the bank's problems, the Federal Reserve imposed operational standards on the allowable size of daylight overdrafts that clearing banks could run. The applicable interest charge was also increased to 2 percent over the prevailing discount rate.

---

dents generally provided deposit credit sooner than the Federal Reserve, and banks could invest funds earlier.

DIDMCA authorized the Federal Reserve to price float by charging interest at the federal funds rate for reserves that banks received in the form of float. The catalyst was the rise in Federal Reserve float during the late 1970s, when interest rates rose to historical highs. At the time, corporate cash managers set up remote disbursement facilities, which allowed them to write checks on remotely located banks. This method increased the time it took for checks to clear (increased CIPC) and simultaneously increased Federal Reserve float. Unpredictable changes in float, in turn, made it more difficult for the Federal Reserve to control the nation's money supply. Banks now pay for float on a per-item basis, which has substantially lowered Federal Reserve float.

After this pricing began in 1981, correspondent banks argued that the Federal Reserve was undercutting private sector prices to maintain its market share. By 1984 the debate subsided, after the Federal Reserve reported a $25-million surplus on check-collection services. This surplus came after direct operating expenses, the cost of float, and a private sector adjustment factor were netted out. The adjustment factor is a cost surcharge the Federal Reserve recoups in pricing to cover capital requirements, that is, to pay a targeted return on equity and substitute for taxes it would pay if it operated privately.

In 1988 the Federal Reserve received $801.7 million in fees for services provided and estimated its costs at $796.6 million. Preliminary data for 1989 indicate that this profit increased slightly over 1988. The Federal Reserve's market share in 1989 differed little from that in 1981, suggesting that it and large correspondent banks are making money on checking services. Correspondents, however, appear to be making less than they did prior to the new pricing environment.

MANAGING CORRESPONDENT BALANCES

In addition to holding deposit balances at the Federal Reserve, most banks maintain demand deposit accounts at other financial institutions. The balances are held as payment for services purchased from the issuing bank. This interbank deposit network links the activities of small and large banks and banks located in different geographic areas. A bank that owns deposit balances is a *respondent bank*. A bank that accepts deposits is a *correspondent bank*. Larger banks typically fill both roles, providing basic services to smaller banks and buying services from large firms that are either located in other geographic markets or able to offer a broader range of services.

Correspondent Banking Services

Correspondent banking is the system of interbank relationships in which a bank sells services to other financial institutions. The institution providing the services is the correspondent bank or upstream correspondent, while the institution buying the services is the respondent bank or downstream correspondent.

Respondent banks purchase services from correspondents for a variety of reasons. Some services, such as check collection, carry advantages over those provided directly by the Federal Reserve System, which generally takes longer to grant credit. Other services are either too expensive to provide independently or cannot be provided because of regulatory constraints. Small banks, for example, want to offer a full range of services to their customers, but the demand for specialty transactions is sporadic. It would be too costly to invest in the technology and manpower for international transactions or investment banking advice on mergers and acquisitions if those services are used infrequently. These services are only provided in large volume to take advantage of economies of scale, which lower unit costs. Even when priced at a markup over correspondents' costs, these services are cheaper than if provided independently. Respondent banks similarly sell loan participations to correspondent banks when individual loans exceed a bank's legal lending limit.

The correspondent banking system evolved before the establishment of the Federal Reserve, largely to help process checks. Respondent banks paid for the service by maintaining balances above those needed to clear items. Correspondent banks could invest the excess, with interest income covering their costs. The fundamental relationships are the same today. Respondent banks choose services they need from menus provided by correspondents. They shop around for quality service at the lowest available price and hold balances that pay for the supplier's costs plus profit.

The most common correspondent banking services are:

1. Check collection, wire transfer, and coin and currency supply
2. Loan participation assistance
3. Data processing services
4. Portfolio analysis and investment advice
5. Federal funds trading
6. Securities safekeeping
7. Arrangement of purchase or sale of securities
8. Investment banking services: swaps, futures, and mergers and acquisitions
9. Loans to directors and officers
10. International financial transactions

The predominant services purchased can be grouped into three broad categories: check clearing and related cash transactions, investment services, and credit-related transactions. Check-clearing services are attractive because respondent banks can reduce float. Correspondent banks often make funds available for respondent investment before the Federal Reserve's scheduled availability. Additional interest earned more than compensates for the required compensating balances.

Respondents purchase other services when the price is below the unit cost of supplying the service directly. Small banks with a limited customer base cannot justify large investments in equipment or manpower to provide infrequently used services. They must, however, be able to provide these services to remain full-service banks, and it is cheaper to buy them on demand. Many large banks, in contrast, view correspondent banking as a profit center. The demand for basic correspondent services and related leasing, international banking, stock brokerage, and real estate services by other banks and their customers is sufficiently large to justify offering these services worldwide.

Payment for Services

Many banks act as both a correspondent and respondent bank as determined by size and geographic market. Small banks typically purchase services from larger correspondents, which take advantage of scale economies, and from banks located in distant geographic markets where bank customers do significant business. Respondents pay for services either with explicit fees or by maintaining deposit balances at the correspondent. In most cases, compensation takes the form of demand deposit balances, which provide an investment return to the correspondent. These due-to and due-from relationships represent the lifeblood of correspondent banking.

Exhibit 14.9 documents the deposit relationships for three hypothetical banks in Illinois. Community Bank in Moline purchases services from First National Bank in Champaign, which in turn purchases services from City Bank in Chicago. Community Bank maintains a demand deposit balance of $200,000 at First National to pay for

Exhibit 14.9 Interbank Deposit Relationships

First National Bank—Champaign

Assets	*Liabilities + Equity*
Demand deposits due from City Bank	Demand deposits due to Community Bank
$800,000	$200,000

Community Bank—Moline

Assets	*Liabilities + Equity*
Demand deposits due from First National Bank	
$200,000	

City Bank—Chicago

Assets	*Liabilities + Equity*
	Demand deposits due to First National Bank
	$800,000

services rendered. This represents an implicit payment because First National earns interest on the investable portion of the balance ($200,000 minus float and required reserves). First National similarly maintains a deposit balance at City Bank as payment for services it uses. Its $800,000 balance is larger than Community Bank's because First National acquires a greater volume and range of services. City Bank would, in turn, normally maintain correspondent relationships with banks in other money market centers as well as overseas. Some banks view correspondent services as one of their basic profit centers.

Correspondent banking has traditionally relied on personal friendships among bankers. Increased competition resulting from deregulation and interstate mergers and acquisitions, however, has shrunk the pool of commercial bank respondents and put pressure on profit margins. Banks that acquire a firm in another state no longer need the services previously obtained through a correspondent. In response, many correspondent banks no longer provide a full range of services and have scaled back the size of their correspondent departments, focusing only on profitable product lines. Other correspondents have aggressively gone after business from savings banks and credit unions.

Small banks have also become increasingly sensitive to competition from correspondent banks for their customers' business. A community banker who acquaints an upstream correspondent with his or her customer base will frequently discover that the correspondent has tried to market services directly to the customer and completely circumvent the respondent bank. This situation has produced two results. First, respondents now unbundle the services of upstream correspondents, purchasing different services from different correspondents rather than dealing with only one firm. Second, community banks are forming and buying services from cooperative institutions known as *bankers' banks,* which are owned by independent commercial banks in a state and are authorized to provide services only to financial institutions. They do not market services directly to bank customers and compete only with other correspondent banks.

Bankers' banks maintain a staff that handles check collection, analyzes the credit quality of loan participations, trades in government securities, and offers other services, such as discount brokerage, at competitive prices. Independent bankers serve as directors and offer guidance regarding product selection, pricing, and portfolio policies.

Computing Balance Requirements

It is relatively easy to calculate the dollar amount of balances required to pay for correspondent services. Important variables include the volume and type of services used, unit prices charged by the correspondent, direct fees paid for specific services, and the applicable (assumed) earnings rate applied to investable balances. Consider the pricing analysis presented in Exhibit 14.10. The respondent bank uses services valued at $637.30 for the month of June. Of this total, $100 is covered by fees, so that the correspondent needs to earn $537.30 in interest on balances to meet costs. Panel C calculates the respondent's required ledger balances, assuming an 8-percent earnings credit applied to ledger balances less $7,200 float and 12 percent required reserves. During the month, the respondent should have maintained approximately $100,000 in balances to pay for its services.

Of course, several elements are subject to negotiation, particularly unit costs for each service applied by the correspondent and the applicable earnings credit. Respondent banks prefer lower costs and higher assumed investment yields. Normally, the earnings credit floats with money market yields and is often specified as the monthly average federal funds or Treasury bill rate. High-volume purchasers can obtain unit cost discounts to lower balance requirements.

In recent years correspondent banks have tried to move to fee-based pricing of correspondent services. Respondent banks, however, have generally resisted, so that less than 10 percent of all correspondent relationships currently use direct fee pricing. Competition continues to dictate payment in the form of demand deposit balances.

Credit Services

With recent changes in the competitive environment, the nature of interbank credit relationships has changed. Small banks historically looked to larger correspondents to purchase a portion of their large loans that exceeded lending limits (overlines). Small banks, in turn, would take participations from the same correspondents. In addition, correspondents sometimes made low-interest loans to directors and officers of respondent banks in return for compensating balances. Often these correspondent relationships depended on informal agreements secured by long-standing personal and institutional friendships.

Two developments permanently altered this environment. First, Bert Lance, President Carter's budget director, was accused in 1977 of using his political and business connections to obtain loans at below-market rates from correspondent banks he had done business with as a private banker. Even though Lance was not convicted of any illegalities, Congress passed laws restricting preferential treatment for credit activities between banks. The Financial Institutions Regulatory and Interest Rate Control Act of

Exhibit 14.10 Pricing Correspondent Services: Monthly Analysis

	Cost (Dollars)
A. Services Provided: June	
Check clearing 10,540 items at $0.0045 per item	$474.30
Wire transfers 28 items at $1.50 per item	42.00
Security safekeeping 7 items at $3.00 per item	21.00
Data processing services/microcomputer software	100.00
Total monthly cost	$637.30
B. Correspondent Bank Revenues	
Fees for computer services	$100.00
Required investment income from compensating balances	537.30
Total	$637.30

C. Required Ledger Balances (B)

Investment income = (Earnings credit)(30/365)(Ledger balances – Float – Required reserves)

If earnings credit = 8%, average float = $7,200 and required reserves = (.12)(B – 7,200)

$$537.30 = (.08)(30/365)(.88)(B - 7,200)$$
$$B = \$100,059$$

1978 specifically forced banks to charge market interest rates on loans to any officers, directors, or shareholders with at least 10 percent ownership of a correspondent bank; required banks to advise regulators of any such insider loans; and prohibited correspondent relationships if insider loan terms were not equivalent to terms for outsiders.

A second development was the increase in bank failures in the early 1980s and treatment of failed banks' loan participations, which forced banks to reassess the risk of correspondent activities. The failure of Penn Square Bank of Oklahoma City in 1982 served as the catalyst. Penn Square was notable for selling loan participations to other banks that did not perform careful credit analyses. Prior to Penn Square, tradition held that a participation sold downstream belonged to the seller's bank. Even though formal contracts noted that a credit was the respondent's when purchased, the informal gentleman's agreement was that the correspondent would buy it back if the credit went sour. Correspondents cut 10 to 15 basis points off the yield and required balances for the service. After Penn Square and other large banks failed, regulators would not let the problem banks buy the participations back, and forced respondent banks to absorb any losses. Banking circular 181 from the U.S. Comptroller's Office was introduced, stating, "the purchase of loans and participations in loans may constitute an unsafe and unsound banking practice in the absence of satisfactory documentation, credit analysis, and other controls over risk."

This second development sharply curtailed downstream participations to small independent banks. Traditionally, these banks did not do any credit analysis of the correspondent's participation because the loans were short term.[10] The sale was a service. Small-bank overlines, in contrast, went through the correspondent's loan committee before being approved. Tradition held that these sales constituted formal credits and belonged to the buyer.

Multibank holding company growth accentuated this change. Major holding companies now operate subsidiaries in major markets throughout a state. The groups take care of their own operations first, and smaller independent banks often do not feel that they are given the same high-quality treatment and opportunities. This has led to the establishment of bankers' banks.

SUMMARY

Banks manage their cash position to minimize required holdings because cash assets do not generate interest income. Vault cash is held to meet customer transaction needs. Banks hold demand deposit balances at the Federal Reserve and other financial institutions to meet the Federal Reserve's legal reserve requirements and to purchase services such as check clearing. Float, or checks in the process of collection, is a natural product of the check-clearing process.

This chapter examines the characteristics of cash assets and explains why banks hold each type and how the magnitudes can be minimized. It focuses on the link between cash holdings and a bank's liquidity needs as well as the mechanics of meeting reserve requirements and determining correspondent balance requirements. Problem areas for bank management include estimating the bank's required reserve position during the first 12 days of the 2-week reserve maintenance period, when requirements are not known with certainty. Large banks have also had problems with daylight overdrafts, attributable to authorizing payments from deposit accounts in excess of actual balances on hand. These difficulties can be reduced with acceptable liquidity planning.

Questions

1. What are the four bank needs that require holding cash or near-cash?

2. What are the advantages and disadvantages for a bank contemplating holding more cash?

3. If a bank develops a highly predictable depositor base and predictable borrowers, does the bank need higher or lower levels of cash than before?

Required Reserves

4. A bank is currently operating with precisely the amount of reserves it feels it needs to meet requirements. Unexpectedly a depositor enters the bank and wishes to open

---

[10]In the case of Penn Square, large multinational banks such as Continental Illinois in Chicago and Chase Manhattan in New York also performed very little credit analysis of Penn Square's energy loan participations. They were ultimately forced to charge off millions of dollars of loans.

an account with a $6 million check she received for winning the state lottery. The account she has in mind requires 10 percent in reserves. As the money desk manager is sending the check to the Fed for collection he realizes that his reserve balance will now be at an inappropriate amount. Should he plan on borrowing or lending in the federal funds market and how much?

5. Which of the following activities will affect a bank's required reserves?

   a. The local Boy Scout troop has collected pennies to fund the purchase of a new tent. Today they bring in $400 worth of pennies and take out a 6-month CD.

   b. You have just started a business that has taken off. You find yourself with a great deal of cash but are reluctant to purchase any fixed assets until you are sure the business will continue to succeed. You decide the business should take the money out of the cash register and put it in a 2-year CD to assure that you do not rashly purchase any assets.

   c. Tom decides he needs more readily available cash and switches $100 from his MMDA to his NOW account.

   d. Joan sells her car to a teller at her bank. The teller pays with a check which Joan immediately deposits into her checking account.

   e. GM is opening an assembly plant in town and your bank has just gotten notice to open a checking account for them with a $400,000 check drawn on their Flint bank.

   f. The university takes 60 percent of the fall tuition money and invests in a 45-day CD.

6. Today, October 21, begins a reserve maintenance period. What day of the week is it? What was the date at the beginning of the lagged computation period? What was the date at the beginning of the contemporaneous computation period?

7. Today, November 10, begins a lagged computation period for a later reserve maintenance period. What day of the week is it? On what date will the maintenance period begin?

8. You are new at the money desk and have just learned how to use the bank's computer system. You call up the file entitled "Calculations for Required Reserves." The file contains the following information:

Accounts recorded in millions of dollars

(L1) Date: January	1st	2nd	3rd	4th	5th
(L2)Transactions accounts	$40	$50	$60	$90	$40
Nonpersonal time deposits					
(L3) Less than 1.5 years	20	10	7	7	7
(L4) More than 1.5 years	30	50	60	10	20
(L5) Eurocurrency liabilities	4	7	2	1	8
(L6) All other liabilities	15	12	11	16	10
(L7) Cash	1	1	2	1	1

(L1)	8th	9th	10th	11th	12th	15th	16th	17th
(L2)	30	45	50	20	25	30	40	50
(L3)	5	5	5	5	6	6	7	7
(L4)	20	20	40	40	40	40	30	30
(L5)	3	6	4	2	1	8	6	3
(L6)	20	40	52	68	73	47	53	46
(L7)	1	1	1	0	0	0	1	1

(L1)	18th	19th	22nd	23rd	24th	25th	26th	29th
(L2)	10	10	10	20	30	35	65	85
(L3)	3	4	3	4	5	5	5	6
(L4)	25	26	28	30	30	35	40	20
(L5)	8	6	7	4	7	3	6	2
(L6)	34	52	75	48	93	25	45	32
(L7)	1	0	1	1	1	2	2	2

(L1)	30th	31st	1st	2nd	5th	6th	7th	8th
(L2)	95	10	10	20	25	45	45	45
(L3)	4	6	4	6	5	5	5	5
(L4)	10	10	20	20	30	30	40	40
(L5)	5	6	4	2	8	5	7	8
(L6)	24	42	35	54	47	54	34	67
(L7)	2	3	3	2	1	1	1	1

(L1)	9th	12th	13th	14th	15th	16th	19th	20th
(L2)	35	45	55	65	75	80	60	?
(L3)	10	10	10	10	10	10	10	
(L4)	20	25	25	35	35	35	35	
(L5)	3	2	5	4	7	5	8	
(L6)	22	33	43	25	54	56	67	
(L7)	1	2	2	2	2	2	2	2

Today is February 20th and you note that it is a Tuesday. Just as you are considering this, your new boss walks by and sees the file you have loaded.

"Good," he says. "Tomorrow is the last day of the reserve maintenance period and we need to decide what actions we will take. We have kept a 12-day average of $0.515 million in reserves with the Fed for this maintenance period. Calculate what we need to average over the 14 days and figure out if we need to keep more or less during these last 2 days. Let me know by 2 p.m. so we can enter the federal funds market this afternoon if necessary."

a. Figure out which days to include in the lagged computation period and which in the contemporaneous period.
b. Calculate the average daily reserve balances needed for these two periods.
c. What range of average daily reserves would be acceptable for this maintenance period?
d. Compare this requirement with the average reserves the bank has kept so far during this maintenance period. If it keeps the same level of reserves today and tomorrow will it be in the acceptable range of reserves? If not, what should you do in the federal funds market today and tomorrow?

    e. Just as you are finishing the report your boss stops by again and says, "By the way did I tell you that we had a daily deficit of reserves of $0.040 million last maintenance period, all of which will be carried forward to this period?" Now what would you do in the federal funds market?

9. What would the required reserve ratio be on the following accounts if they belonged to an individual?
    a. demand deposit
    b. NOW account
    c. MMDA
    d. 6-month CD
    e. 2-year CD
    f. jumbo CD
    g. bank bond
    h. preferred stock
    i. common stock

10. Which of the following accounts would be added as cash for calculating required reserves?
    a. currency
    b. checks in the process of being collected
    c. deposits with the Fed
    d. deposits with a correspondent
    e. deposits with a banker's bank
    f. loan from the discount window
    g. federal funds purchased
    h. repos
    i. Treasury bills

Float

11. What is float? Have you ever benefited from its creation? What did you do to get this benefit?

12. Have you ever taken a check into the bank and not been given an immediately available credit? What is the longest the bank can procrastinate in giving you a spendable credit?

13. Describe a daylight overdraft. How does it differ from check float? Who might be the cause of a daylight overdraft? Why has the Fed taken steps to limit these overdrafts?

Correspondent Services

14. What is the difference between a correspondent, respondent, and banker's bank?

15. What are the advantages and disadvantages of using a correspondent bank?

16. Identify three services it is likely that your bank buys from a correspondent.

17. Bill Holmstrom is responsible for monitoring Hawkeye National Bank's respondent bank account relationships. Hawkeye priced correspondent services monthly using cost allocations derived by its accounting department. Respondents paid for services by maintaining demand deposit balances with Hawkeye for which they were credited with earnings at the average 3-month Treasury bill rate on investable balances (demand deposits require 12 percent reserves).

Bill was concerned that Valley State Bank was not keeping adequate balances and decided to review their account in April. Did Hawkeye's revenue from this account cover its cost of services? How much could Valley change its balance to produce a break-even relationship?

Services Provided	Cost per Item
Check clearing—14,785 items	$ 0.0056
Wire transfers—43 items	2.0000
Currency shipment—1 item	75.0000
Security safekeeping—11 items	4.5000
Data processing—1 item	150.0000
Letters of credit—2 items	100.0000

Memoranda

Valley State's average ledger balance was $107,500.
Average float associated with the account was $35,808.
Fee income generated by Hawkeye was $150.
Applicable earnings credit was 7.1 percent.

Activity

Determine how long it takes your bank to process your checks. Find some old checks you wrote to local people, to distant people still in your Federal Reserve District, and to some even more distant people outside of your Federal Reserve District. Note the date on which you wrote the check and then find the date on your monthly check statement when the bank deducted the amount from your account. How might you use this information to manage your personal float? Compare this with the funds availability schedule provided at your bank.

References

Bennett, Veronica. "Check Safekeeping: Transition to the Electronic Future." *Economic Review* (Federal Reserve Bank of Atlanta, October 1982).

Evanoff, Douglas. "Priced Services: The Fed's Impact on Correspondent Banking." *Economic Perspectives* (Federal Reserve Bank of Chicago, September/October 1985).

Evanoff, Douglas. "Daylight Overdrafts: Rationale and Risks." *Economic Perspectives* (Federal Reserve Bank of Chicago, May/June 1988).

Fasbee, Pamela. "Bankers' Banks: An Institution Whose Time Has Come." *Economic Review* (Federal Reserve Bank of Atlanta, April 1984).

Feddis, Nessa. "Analyzing the Revised Reg CC." *ABA Banking Journal* (July 1988).

Frodin, Joanna. "Fed Pricing and the Check Collection Business: The Private Sector Response." *Business Review* (Federal Reserve Bank of Philadelphia, January–February 1984).

Gilbert, Alton. "Payments System Risk: What Is It and What Will Happen If We Try to Reduce It?" *Review* (Federal Reserve Bank of St. Louis, January/February 1989).

Goodfriend, Marvin. "The Promises and Pitfalls of Contemporaneous Reserve Requirements for the Implementation of Monetary Policy." *Economic Review* (Federal Reserve Bank of Richmond, May–June 1984).

Jones, David S. "Contemporaneous vs. Lagged Reserve Accounting: Implications for Monetary Control." *Economic Review* (Federal Reserve Bank of Kansas City, November 1981).

Laurent, Robert D. "Lagged Reserve Accounting and the Fed's New Operating Procedure." *Economic Perspectives* (Federal Reserve Bank of Chicago, midyear 1982).

Ledford, Stephen. "Getting Ready for Expedited Funds Availability." *Bank Administration* (March 1988).

Mengle, David. "Daylight Overdrafts and Payment System Risks." *Economic Review* (Federal Reserve Bank of Richmond, May–June 1985).

"Pricing Services, 1988 and 1989." *Federal Reserve Bulletin* (August 1989).

Smoot, Richard L. "Billion-Dollar Overdrafts: A Payments Risk Challenge." *Business Review* (Federal Reserve Bank of Philadelphia, January–February 1985).

Tarhan, Vefa. "Individual Bank Reserve Management." *Economic Perspectives* (Federal Reserve Bank of Chicago, July–August 1984).

VanHoose, David, and Gordon Sellon, Jr. "Daylight Overdrafts, Payments System Risk, and Public Policy." *Economic Review* (Federal Reserve Bank of Kansas City, September/October 1989).

Young, John E. "The Rise and Fall of Federal Reserve Float." *Economic Review* (Federal Reserve Bank of Kansas City, February 1986).

Chapter 15

Liquidity Planning

During the early 1980s, Home State Savings Bank in Cincinnati, Ohio, dealt closely with E.S.M. Government Securities Inc. in the market for repurchase agreements. Home State, a $1.4 billion thrift institution, bought and sold securities through E.S.M., speculating on short-run interest rate movements. On March 4, 1985, the Securities and Exchange Commission (SEC) closed E.S.M., citing huge losses on speculative securities trades. That same week Home State's depositors withdrew approximately $90 million out of concern that E.S.M.'s problems would harm the thrift. On March 10, the regulators closed Home State.

Home State was one of 72 thrifts that were privately insured by the Ohio Deposit Guarantee Fund and not the Federal Savings and Loan Insurance Corp. or the Federal Deposit Insurance Corp. At that time, the insurance fund had only $136 million in reserves. The fund allocated $45 million to Home State before the thrift closed, which helped create the impression that private deposit insurance and the fund itself were insufficient to cover customer deposits. Before long, depositors were lining up at the 71 other privately insured thrifts in Ohio to withdraw their deposits. Two weeks after E.S.M. failed, Ohio's governor invoked emergency powers to close the remaining 71 thrifts temporarily until the viability of the private insurance fund and consumer confidence could be restored.

Liquidity planning is an important facet of asset and liability management. While public confidence is essential for preventing deposit runs, there are steps managers can take to reduce the likelihood of unanticipated deposit outflows and to gain access to additional sources of cash assets. They must be able to estimate liquidity needs accurately and to structure their bank's portfolio to meet the anticipated needs.

This chapter examines liquidity planning, both over the 2-week reserve maintenance period and throughout the course of a year.

Bank liquidity is a bank's capacity to acquire immediately available funds from the Federal Reserve or correspondent banks at a reasonable price. It encompasses the potential sale of liquid assets, federal funds purchases, and new issues of CDs, Eurodollars, subordinated debt, and stock offerings. Assets are liquid if they can be quickly converted into immediately available funds with limited price depreciation. Liabilities similarly represent liquid sources of funds if a bank can easily borrow at rates comparable to those paid by peers.

The large number of bank failures and occasional deposit runs during the 1980s made bankers and regulators especially sensitive to liquidity planning. When the FDIC closed Penn Square Bank in 1982, it paid only a fraction of the claims of uninsured depositors. This move was generally interpreted as a signal that the FDIC was imposing market discipline by placing uninsured depositors at risk. The regulators reinforced this view with the closings of First RepublicBank Corp. and MCorp in 1988 and 1989, respectively. Depositors, bondholders, and stockholders are now much more sensitive to perceived problems and willing to move balances or liquidate their investments at the slightest hint of problems.

Exhibit 15.1 lists the emergency borrowings of problem banks resulting from net deposit losses in recent years. Continental Illinois, for example, borrowed $15 billion against emergency credit lines at the peak of its liquidity troubles in 1984. First National Bank in Midland, Texas, similarly lost $800 million in net deposits, largely in the form of CDs withdrawn by money brokers, which equaled almost 50 percent of the bank's total assets prior to the run. In 1988 First RepublicBank needed to borrow $3.5 billion from the Federal Reserve. Deposit runs demonstrate the effects of limits on FDIC insurance. When banks exhibit financial problems, customers restrict their balances to fully insured deposits at any single bank and move any excess to presumably safer institutions.

This chapter examines liquidity planning. The first section outlines the link between liquidity and banking risks and returns. The second describes the strengths and weaknesses of traditional measures of liquidity. The next section applies bank liquidity planning to reserves management and estimates of longer-term funds requirements. The chapter ends with a case study of Continental Illinois National Bank & Trust's liquidity crisis and the regulatory response.

THE LINK BETWEEN LIQUIDITY AND BANKING RISKS AND RETURNS

Liquidity needs arise from net deposit outflows. Most withdrawals are predictable because they are either contractually based or follow well-defined patterns. For example, banks that purchase securities typically pay for them with immediately available funds. Maturing investments similarly are credited to deposit balances held at the Federal Reserve. Transactions accounts normally exhibit weekly or monthly patterns that follow the payroll and billing activities of large commercial customers.

Exhibit 15.1 Maximum Borrowings from Emergency Credit Lines Provided by Federal Agencies and Banks (Millions of Dollars)

Date	Bank	Size of Borrowing	Total Assets: December 31, Year Prior to Deposit Loss
1974	Franklin National Bank, New York, N.Y.	$ 1,700	$ 5,007
1980	First Pennsylvania Bank, Philadelphia, Pa.	925	8,406
1983	First National Bank, Seattle, Wash.	900	9,841
1983	First National Bank, Midland, Tex.	800	1,800
1984	Continental Illinois, Chicago, Ill.	15,000	40,643
1986	First National Bank & Trust Co., Oklahoma City, Okla.	300	1,400
1987	First City Bancorporation, Houston, Tex.	950	12,200
1988	First RepublicBank Corp., Dallas, Tex.	3,500	26,900
1989	MCorp., Dallas, Tex.	1,200	15,400

Source: G. Christian Hill and Edwun A. Finn, "Big Depositors Runs on Beleaguered Banks Speed the Failure Rate." *The Wall Street Journal*, August 23, 1989.

Still, some outflows are totally unexpected. Often management does not know whether customers will reinvest maturing CDs and keep the funds with the bank or withdraw them. Management also cannot predict when loan customers will borrow against open credit lines. This uncertainty increases the risk that a bank may not have adequate sources of funds available to meet payments requirements. This risk, in turn, forces management to structure its portfolio to access liquid funds easily, which lowers potential profits.

Exhibit 15.2 portrays the effects of customer deposit withdrawals and loan usage on a bank's deposit balances at the Federal Reserve. The first part indicates that a maturing CD is not rolled over directly and immediately reduces a bank's reserves. Here the CD holder directs the Federal Reserve to transfer the funds by wire to another institution, which directly lowers CDs outstanding as well as deposit balances held at the Federal Reserve. Loan usage produces the same result. In the second part a loan customer borrows $250,000 against an outstanding credit line by requesting a wire transfer to cover the purchase of some good or service. The bank authorizes the payment, lowering its deposit balance at the Federal Reserve by $250,000 while simultaneously booking the loan. In the last part the bank first allocates $500,000 in loan proceeds to the borrower's account. The bank's deposit at the Federal Reserve falls when the customer writes a check against the proceeds and the check clears after being deposited in another bank. Each transaction reduces immediately available funds, creating the possibility that the bank is reserves deficient and, perhaps, short of balances needed to cover future deposit outflows.

The Development of Liquidity Strategies

Historically, liquidity management focused on assets and was closely tied to lending policies. Under the *commercial loan theory* prior to 1930, banks were encouraged to

Exhibit 15.2 The Effect of Maturing Certificates of Deposit and Loan Usage on a Bank's Deposit Balances at the Federal Reserve

*Maturing Certificates of Deposit
Not Rolled Over*

Commercial Bank

Δ ASSETS	Δ LIABILITIES
Demand deposit at Federal Reserve −$100,000	Certificates of deposit −$100,000

*Loan Customer Borrows
against a Credit Line*

Commercial Bank

Δ ASSETS	Δ LIABILITIES
Demand deposit at Federal Reserve −$250,000 Commercial loans +$250,000	

Borrowing against a New Term Loan

Commercial Bank

Δ ASSETS	Δ LIABILITIES	
Commercial loan +$500,000	Demand deposit +$500,000	Bank grants loan and deposits proceeds in customer's account.
Demand deposits at Federal Reserve −$500,000	Demand deposit −$500,000	Customer spends full amount of loan proceeds by writing check.

make only short-term, self-liquidating loans. Such loans closely matched the maturity of bank deposits and enabled banks to meet deposit withdrawals with funds from maturing loans. An inventory loan, for example, would be repaid when the borrower sold the items that coincided with the need for financing to accumulate additional inventory. A bank was liquid if its loan portfolio consisted of short-term loans.

The *shiftability theory* represented the next extension by recognizing that any liquid asset could be used to meet deposit withdrawals. In particular, a bank could satisfy its liquidity requirements if it held loans and securities that could be sold in the secondary market prior to maturity. The ability to sell government securities and eligible paper effectively substituted for illiquid, longer-term loans with infrequent principal payments. Not surprisingly, the application of this theory coincided with the growth of the U.S. government securities market after 1930. The effect was to lengthen loan maturities and expand bank portfolios to include marketable securities.

Around 1950 the focus shifted to the *anticipated income theory,* which suggested that liquidity requirements and thus loan payments should be tied to a borrower's expected income. Banks were still encouraged to invest in marketable instruments but now structured loans so that the timing of principal and interest payments matched the borrower's ability to repay from income. The primary contribution was the emphasis on cash flow characteristics of different instruments because a borrower's cash flow generally varied closely with his or her income. This encouraged the growth in amortized loans with periodic interest and principal payments and staggered maturities in a bank's bond portfolio.

More recently, banks have focused on liabilities. According to the *liability management theory,* banks can satisfy liquidity needs by borrowing in the money and capital markets. When they need immediately available funds, they can simply borrow via federal funds purchased, RPs, jumbo CDs, commercial paper, and Eurodollars. This theory became increasingly popular as banks gained the ability to pay market interest rates on large liabilities. The fundamental contribution was to consider both sides of a bank's balance sheet as sources of liquidity.

Today, banks use both assets and liabilities to meet liquidity needs. Available liquidity sources are identified and compared to expected needs by a bank's asset and liability management committee (ALCO). Management considers all potential deposit outflows and inflows when deciding how to allocate assets and finance operations. Key considerations include maintaining high asset quality and a strong capital base that both reduces liquidity needs and improves a bank's access to funds at low cost.

Liquidity versus Profitability

There is a short-run trade-off between liquidity and profitability. The more liquid a bank is, the lower are its return on equity and return on assets, all other things being equal. Both asset and liability liquidity contribute to this relationship. Asset liquidity is influenced by the composition and maturity of funds. Large holdings of cash assets clearly decrease profits because of the opportunity loss of interest income. In terms of the investment portfolio, short-term securities normally carry lower yields than comparable longer-term securities. Investors value price stability, so long-term securities pay a yield premium to induce investors to extend maturities. Banks that purchase short-term securities thus increase liquidity, but at the expense of higher potential returns. Consider an environment where market expectations are for short-term Treasury yields to remain constant at present levels. The Treasury yield curve will slope upwards, reflecting liquidity premiums that increase with maturity.[1] A bank that buys 6-month bills at 8 percent rather than a 1-year bill at 8.2 percent gives up 20 basis points for the greater price stability (lower risk).

A bank's loan portfolio displays the same trade-off. Loans carrying the highest yields are the least liquid. Yields are high because default risk or interest rate risk is substantial and the loan administration expense is high. Loans that can readily be sold usually are short-term credits to well-known corporations or government-guaranteed instruments and thus carry minimal spreads. Amortized loans, in contrast, may improve

---

[1]Recent research by Cook, et al. (1987) and Toevs (1986) demonstrates that Treasury bill rates include a liquidity or term premium through at least 1 year.

liquidity even though they are frequently long term because the periodic payments increase near-term cash flow.

In terms of liability liquidity, banks with the best asset quality and highest equity capital have greater access to purchased funds. They also pay lower interest rates and generally report lower returns in the short run. Promised yields on loans and securities increase with the perceived default risk of the underlying issuer. Banks that acquire low-default risk assets, such as U.S. government securities, forego the risk premium that could be earned. Interestingly, many banks buy U.S. agency securities because the incremental yield more than compensates for perceived differences in default risk relative to U.S. Treasuries. Similarly, banks with greater equity financing exhibit lower equity multipliers (see Equation 4.3) and thus generate lower returns on equity, even with identical returns on assets. These banks can borrow funds more cheaply because a greater portion of their assets have to be in default before they might fail.

Liquidity planning focuses on guaranteeing that immediately available funds are available at the lowest cost. Management must determine whether liquidity and default risk premiums more than compensate for the additional risk on longer-term and lower-quality bank investments. If management is successful, long-term earnings will exceed peer banks' earnings, as will bank capital and overall liquidity. The market value of bank equity will increase relative to peers as investors bid up stock prices.

Liquidity Risk, Credit Risk, and Interest Rate Risk

Liquidity management is a day-to-day responsibility. Banks routinely experience fluctuations in their cash assets, depending on the timing and magnitude of unexpected deposit outflows. Deviations from expectations can normally be attributed to large payments or deposits that clear through the Federal Reserve or local clearinghouse. Most shortages can be met by accelerating planned borrowings or deferring asset purchases. Excess cash can easily be invested in earning assets. A well-managed bank monitors its cash position carefully and maintains low liquidity risk.

Liquidity risk for a poorly managed bank closely follows credit and interest rate risk. In fact, banks that experience large deposit outflows can often trace the source to either credit problems or earnings declines from interest rate gambles that backfired. The normal sequence of events underlying liquidity problems is 1) bank management assumes substantial risk by mismatching asset and liability maturities and durations or by extending credit to high-risk borrowers, 2) the bank reports reduced earnings, 3) the media publicizes the credit and interest rate difficulties, 4) the bank must pay higher rates to attract and keep deposits and other purchased funds, 5) bank earnings decline further with reduced interest margins and nonaccruing loans, and 6) uninsured depositors move their funds, forcing the bank to sell assets at fire-sale prices and obtain temporary financing from government sources until a merger can be arranged or the bank fails.

Few banks can replace lost deposits independently if an outright run on the bank arises. Liquidity planning forces management to monitor the overall risk position of the bank such that credit risk partially offsets interest rate risk assumed in the bank's overall asset and liability management strategy. If credit risk is high, interest rate risk should be low and vice versa. Potential liquidity needs must reflect estimates of new loan demand and potential deposit losses. The following list identifies factors affecting certain liquidity needs:

New Loan Demand

- Unused commercial credit lines outstanding
- Consumer credit available on bank-issued cards
- Business activity and growth in the bank's trade area
- The aggressiveness of the bank's loan officer call programs

Potential Deposit Losses

- The composition of liabilities
- Insured versus uninsured deposits
- Deposit ownership between money fund traders, trust fund traders, public institutions, commercial banks by size, corporations by size, individuals, foreign investors, and Treasury tax and loan accounts
- Large deposits held by any single entity
- Seasonal or cyclical patterns in deposits
- The sensitivity of deposits to changes in the level of interest rates

Each of the factors under new loan demand signify a potential increase in borrowing that might deplete a bank's cash reserves. Suppose, for example, that the Federal Reserve tightens credit policy and pushes short-term interest rates higher. Businesses often choose to borrow under outstanding loan commitments rather than use commercial paper, so that bank loans increase. During recessions, individuals might similarly increase outstanding borrowings under credit card agreements. Loan demand closely follows the economic development and growth in a community such that good economic times accelerate borrowing requests. Finally, some banks require loan officers to systematically call on customers to solicit new business. If such call programs are successful, loan demand will increase accordingly.

The factors under potential deposit losses similarly convey information regarding potential cash deficiencies. Banks with substantial core deposits and few purchased liabilities will experience smaller proportionate deposit losses. If the majority of the deposits are federally insured, unanticipated outflows will decline further. Large purchased liabilities are more sensitive to changes in market interest rates. When rates rise, for example, a bank must increase the rates it pays on these rate-sensitive balances or customers will quickly move their balances in search of higher yields. Finally, many banks are located in markets that experience seasonal or cyclical deposit outflows that track changes in regional economic conditions. Consider a bank in a resort community. Deposits flow into the bank during the resort season, but flow out afterwards. Managers must thus monitor these influences in order to plan for cash needs.

TRADITIONAL MEASURES OF LIQUIDITY

As described earlier, banks rely on both assets and liabilities as sources of liquidity. Small banks generally have limited access to purchased funds and thus rely primarily on short-term assets. Larger banks, in contrast, obtain liquid funds mainly via liabilities rather than selling assets. Traditional liquidity measures focus on balance sheet accounts and measure liquidity in terms of financial ratios.

Asset Liquidity Measures

Asset liquidity refers to the ease of converting an asset to cash with a minimum of loss. The most liquid assets mature in the near term and are highly marketable. Liquidity measures are normally expressed in percentage terms as a fraction of total assets. Most small banks maintain substantial investments in highly liquid assets because they provide liquidity in times of duress. Highly liquid assets include

1. Cash and due from banks in excess of required holdings

2. Due from banks—interest bearing; these typically have short maturities

3. Federal funds sold and reverse repurchase agreements

4. U.S. Treasury securities maturing within 1 year

5. U.S. agency obligations maturing within 1 year

6. Corporate obligations maturing within 1 year, rated Baa and above

7. Municipal securities maturing within 1 year, rated Baa and above

8. Loans that can be securitized

In general, the most marketable assets exhibit low default risk, short maturities, and large trading volume in the secondary market. Cash and due from banks is liquid in the sense that a bank needs clearing balances to process transactions on a daily basis. Without deposits at the Federal Reserve or other financial institutions, a bank could not conduct business. Banks normally minimize cash holdings because they do not earn interest. Only excess cash is truly liquid. This excess includes balances held above legal reserve requirements and the amounts required by correspondent banks for services. Cash balances can decline during any single day without presenting serious problems but must quickly be replenished to sustain operations. Thus cash and due meets daily liquidity requirements, but banks rely on other assets for longer-term or permanent liquidity needs.

Federal funds and reverse RPs typically mature overnight and increase cash and due at maturity if they are not rolled over. The other securities exhibit low default risk and short maturities. Thus they typically trade at prices close to par and if sold, have a negligible impact on noninterest income. Treasury obligations are supported by federal taxing authority and borrowing capability. U.S. agency securities are issued by quasi-public entities, such as the Federal Home Loan Mortgage Corporation and Federal Land Bank, and have a long history of low defaults. Liquid corporate and municipal securities are high-rated, investment-grade obligations (rated Baa and above) that are well-known nationally. Other securities are similarly liquid if their current market value exceeds their book value. This results from management's willingness to sell securities at a gain, which adds to reported net income, but unwillingness to take losses. Finally, standardized loans such as credit card receivables may be liquid if a bank regularly packages these assets and securitizes them.

Historically, banks and regulators focused on loan-to-deposit ratios. Because loans are relatively illiquid in general, the greater a bank's loan-to-deposit ratio, the lower the assumed liquidity. As discussed below, the key issue is whether loans generate cash inflows and exhibit high or low default risk.

Pledging Requirements. Not all of a bank's securities can easily be sold. Like their credit customers, banks are required to pledge collateral against certain types of borrowing. U.S. Treasuries or municipals normally constitute the least cost collateral and, if pledged against a debt, cannot be sold until the bank removes the claim or substitutes other collateral. Collateral is required against three different liabilities: securities sold under agreement to repurchase, borrowing from Federal Reserve Banks at the discount window, and public deposits owned by the U.S. Treasury or any state or municipal government unit.

In most cases, each depositor stipulates which assets qualify as collateral and what the pledging ratio is. For example, cities often stipulate that a local bank can pledge either U.S. Treasury securities or municipals against 100 percent of the city's uninsured deposits at the bank. Treasuries are valued at par, while A-rated or better in-state municipal securities are valued at 110 percent of par. This collateral must, in turn, be held by a third-party trustee. While these terms favor municipal securities, the bank can choose among its securities to pledge any short-term or long-term bonds. Pledging requirements against RPs and discount window borrowing establish Treasury securities as preferred collateral against 100 percent of qualifying liabilities. All pledged securities should be subtracted from the above list of liquid assets to obtain the dollar value of net liquid assets.

Loans. Many banks and bank analysts monitor loan-to-deposit ratios as a general measure of liquidity. Loans are presumably the least liquid of assets, while deposits are the primary source of funds. A high ratio indicates illiquidity because a bank is fully loaned up relative to its stable funding. Implicitly, new loans or other asset purchases must be financed with large, purchased liabilities. A low ratio suggests that a bank has additional liquidity because it can grant new loans financed with stable deposits.

The loan-to-deposit ratio is not as meaningful as it first appears. It ignores the composition of loans and deposits. Some loans, such as dealer call loans and government-guaranteed credits, either mature soon or can easily be sold if needed. Others are longer term, with deferred payments, and can be sold only at a substantial discount. Two banks with identical deposits and loan-to-deposit ratios may have substantially different loan liquidity if one bank has highly marketable loans while the other has risky, long-term loans. An aggregate loan figure similarly ignores the timing of cash flows from interest and principal payments. Installment contracts generate cash faster than balloon notes, which defer the principal payment until maturity. The same is true for a bank's deposit base. Some deposits, such as long-term nonnegotiable time deposits, are more stable than others, so that there is less risk of withdrawal. Aggregate ratios thus ignore the difference in composition of both assets and liabilities.

Finally, loan-to-deposit ratios have generally increased recently with interest rate deregulation. While ratios averaged 60 to 70 percent in the 1970s, many banks run ratios near 100 percent today. This increase resulted from the loss of demand and savings deposits and the increased reliance on purchased funds. The corresponding pressure on net interest margins induced many banks to seek more loans, which were the only assets offering high enough yields to maintain interest spreads. It is thus difficult to compare loan-to-deposit ratios over time.

In summary, the best measures of asset liquidity identify the dollar amounts of unpledged liquid assets as a fraction of total assets. The greater the fraction, the greater the ability to sell assets to meet cash needs. Alternatively, liquid assets as a fraction of purchased liabilities conveys whether net liquidity sources are available from assets. In particular, this ratio should exceed 1, indicating that if the bank experiences a run-off of all purchased funds, liquid assets will be sufficient to cover the cash loss.

Liability Liquidity Measures

Liability liquidity refers to the ease with which a bank can issue new debt to acquire clearing balances at reasonable cost. Measures typically reflect a bank's asset quality, capital base, and composition of outstanding deposits and other liabilities. The following ratios are commonly cited:

1. Total equity to total assets
2. Risk assets to total assets
3. Loan losses to net loans
4. Reserve for loan losses to nonperforming loans
5. The percentage composition of deposits
6. Total deposits to total liabilities
7. Core deposits to total assets
8. Federal funds purchased and RPs to total liabilities
9. Commercial paper and other short-term borrowings to total liabilities

A bank's ability to borrow at reasonable rates of interest is closely linked to the market's perception of asset quality. Banks with high-quality assets and a large capital base can issue more debt at relatively low rates, compared with peers. The reason is that investors believe there is little chance that such banks will fail. Thus analysts focus on measures of loan quality and risk assets along with a bank's equity base when assessing future borrowing capabilities.

Banks with stable deposits such as transactions accounts, savings certificates, and nonnegotiable time deposits generally have the same widespread access to borrowed funds at relatively low rates. Those that rely heavily on purchased funds, in contrast, must pay higher rates and experience greater volatility in the composition and average cost of liabilities. For this reason, most banks today compete aggressively for retail core deposits. *Core deposits* are funds that management feels are not rate sensitive and will remain on deposit regardless of economic conditions or seasonal trends. They are typically associated with retail customers who exhibit greater loyalty and prefer to deal with one institution. It is well known that individuals exhibit considerable inertia in their choice of banks as long as they perceive that the bank offers quality, friendly service. The last five ratios listed above provide information regarding the breakdown of liabilities between core deposits and purchased liabilities.

One procedure to estimate the magnitude of stable, core deposits is diagrammed in Exhibit 15.3. The procedure involves plotting total deposits against time and drawing a line through the low points in the graph. This base line represents core deposits, equal to the minimum trend deposit level under which actual deposits never fall. Future stable deposits can be forecast by extending the base line on trend. *Volatile* and *rate-sensitive deposits* equal the difference between actual current deposits and the base estimate of core deposits. A curved base line is used in Exhibit 15.3 to emphasize the lack of growth in stable deposits. Many banks calculate liquidity ratios that use an estimate of volatile deposits as the base.

It is also important to recognize that different institutions have different access to specific funding sources. Allen, Peristiani, and Saunders (1989) demonstrate, for example, that banks with over $1 billion in assets are the largest proportionate purchasers of federal funds. Regardless of size, banks located in primary banking centers are heavier federal funds borrowers. In the RP market, however, the smallest banks are the largest net borrowers.

The real difficulty in managing liabilities is estimating the interest elasticity of different sources of funds. Management would like to know the quantity response to a change in the level of rates. For example, if interest rates increase by an average of 1 percent during the next 6 months, how much will demand deposits and NOW accounts change? Similarly, if a bank pays one-half of 1 percent more on CDs relative to competitors, how many new funds will it attract? Some information is available from historical relationships. Management can document the magnitude of disinter-mediation when interest rates rose in past years as an approximation of potential deposit losses, given expected rate changes. Management can also periodically conduct market tests of rate sensitivity by offering yield premiums on selected liabilities independently and observing the quantity response. These estimates are imprecise, however, and actual rate sensitivity can change quickly with economic conditions or changes in the public's evaluation of the bank's financial health. If the market perceives that a bank is not sound, most borrowing sources immediately dry up regardless of the rate premiums paid. In response, many banks aggressively solicit retail deposits using innovative marketing strategies (see Contemporary Issues: Competing for Retail Deposits) because individuals are less rate sensitive and their deposits are more stable.

Large banks attempt to maintain a base of unused borrowing capacity. Many simply expand their funding sources beyond routine loan needs and invest any excess at other banks. When their own loan demand increases, the financing is there. A bank's

Exhibit 15.3 Measuring Core Deposits

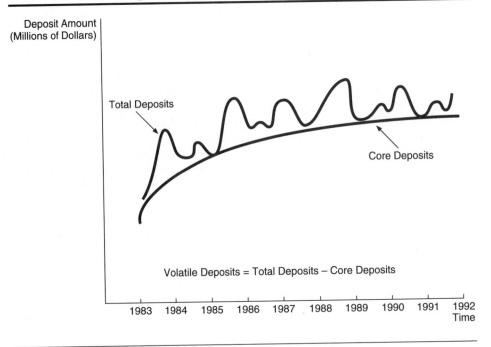

Volatile Deposits = Total Deposits − Core Deposits

unused borrowing capacity by source can be approximated as the maximum amount ever borrowed minus current borrowings. Banks occasionally use all sources, even though they do not have extraordinary funding needs, just to keep channels open.

Liquidity Analysis of Valley National Corporation and Community State Bank

Small banks rely on different sources of liquidity than do larger money center banks. This section analyzes liquidity measures for Valley National Corporation with $11 billion in assets and Community State Bank with $100 million in assets using the balance sheet and risk figures from Exhibits 4.1 and 4.5 of Chapter 4. The relevant ratios appear in Exhibit 15.4.

Consider first the asset liquidity measures. As indicated in Exhibit 15.4, each banking organization holds over 20 percent of its assets as cash and due plus non-municipal securities. Small banks rely proportionately more on short-term, interest-bearing assets to meet normal liquidity needs, so this total of gross liquid assets for Community State Bank exceeds that for Valley National Corp. by almost 6 percent. The higher cash and due percentage for the Valley National Corp. reflects two phenomena. First, large banks hold relatively more legal reserves because the first 40 million of net transactions accounts is reservable at only 3 percent. The higher 12

CONTEMPORARY ISSUES

Competing for Retail Deposits: Gifts for Cash Using Federal Deposit Insurance

With the collapse in energy prices during the early 1980s, First City Bancorporation of Texas saw its asset quality deteriorate and its ability to attract funds on Wall Street virtually disappear. Recognizing that it needed a more stable deposit base, the group's management introduced several innovative deposit programs that offered luxury gift items to customers who made large cash deposits. All gifts were in addition to interest earned.

For opening a 5-year CD of $6 million in 1986, a customer could select either a 1986 Rolls-Royce Corniche convertible, valued at $164,000, or a 40-foot Hatteras motor yacht, valued near $200,000. First City is a bank holding company with 63 subsidiary banks in Texas and one in South Dakota. To improve the CDs' marketability, it allocated the deposits among its subsidiary banks in $100,000 increments so that a single customer's entire $6 million was fully insured by the FDIC. Customers wishing to make smaller deposits could receive a Procraft bass boat with trailer ($500,000 for 5 years), a Honda three-wheeler ($75,000 for 5 years), an RCA video camcorder ($20,000 for 5 years), and many other gifts for simply opening a savings account.

The incentive for First City was obvious: Gift items would attract long-term deposits, which should remain with the group of banks until its problems disappeared. Depositors, in turn, viewed the gifts as implicit interest and compared the total return to that available on competing instruments. First City's gift program for the first year attracted over $300 million. Clearly, however, the attractiveness of these programs depends on FDIC insurance and the holding company system of ownership. The funding from these programs was insufficient, as First City failed in 1987.

percent requirement thus applies to proportionately fewer of a small bank's outstanding accounts. Second, large banks hold more interbank deposits to support national and international correspondent relationships. Cash balances do not provide much liquidity to meet permanent needs, and the smaller independent bank owns less cash and more securities. The largest difference in gross liquid assets is in the proportion of Treasury and agency securities. Here Community State Bank holds more than twice as much as Valley National Corp. because these assets provide the bank's primary liquidity buffer.

The data in rows 1e through 1g adjust the gross liquid asset ratios by identifying unpledged securities with maturities of 1 year or less. The contribution of federal funds sold is also offset by subtracting any overnight borrowing via federal funds purchased. With these adjustments the independent bank owns 13.4 percent of its assets in liquid form, or 2.4 percent more than Valley National. When cash and due balances are subtracted, the small bank has 9.4 percent liquid assets, while Valley National has just 4.2 percent.

Both banks exhibit high net loan-to-deposit ratios. Valley National Corp. holds relatively more consumer, real estate, and international loans, while the independent bank has more business loans. This is atypical because most large institutions focus on commercial customers and not on individual borrowers. It is difficult to assess actual loan liquidity without knowing all contract terms including the cash flow

Exhibit 15.4 Liquidity Measures for Valley National Corporation and Community State Bank[a]

Asset Liquidity Measures	Bank Holding Company and Subsidiaries (%)	Independent Community Bank
1. Percentage of total assets		
a. Cash and due from banks	6.8%	4.0%
b. Due from banks (interest bearing)	2.0	1.5
c. Federal funds sold and reverse repurchase agreements	3.7	4.1
d. Treasuries and U.S. agencies[b]	8.3	17.0
Total gross liquid assets (a + b + c + d)	20.8%	26.6%
e. Unpledged treasuries and U.S. agencies (maturity ≤ 1 year)[b]	1.4%	2.8%
f. Unpledged state and municipals (maturity ≤ 1 year)	0.2	1.0
g. Federal funds sold and reverse RPs minus federal funds purchased and RPs	0.6	4.1
Total (a + b + e + f + g)	11.0%	13.4%
Total (b + e + f + g)	4.2%	9.4%
2. Percentage of total deposits		
a. Net loans	80.0%	65.9%
b. Business loans	25.8	34.1
c. Real estate loans	23.3	12.8
d. Consumer loans	29.8	20.0
e. International loans	1.4	—
f. Leases	1.9	0.6
Liability Liquidity Measures		
1. Percentage of total liabilities		
a. Total deposits	85.4	90.4
b. Federal funds purchased and RPs	3.1	
c. Commercial paper and other borrowings	1.1	0.3
2. Percentage of total deposits		
a. Demand deposits	18.7	11.8
b. Interest/checking deposits	8.6	15.8
c. Insured money market deposit accounts	24.2	13.2
d. Other savings deposits	5.6	6.8
e. Time deposits < $100,000	28.7	44.5
f. Time deposits ≥ $100,000	14.2	7.9
3. Total equity to total assets	5.4	7.8
4. Past due & nonaccrual loans to total loans	5.5	1.6
5. Net loan charge-offs to total loans	1.3	0.9
6. Reserve for loan losses to total loans	2.5	2.3
7. Core deposits to total assets	73.3	83.3
8. Purchased liabilities to total assets	17.2	7.4

[a]The banking organizations were introduced in Exhibit 4.1

[b]Ignores trading account securities.

[c]Figures obtained from detailed financial statements.

characteristics of specific loans, whether any loans can be securitized, and whether any loans are government guaranteed.

Liability liquidity measures focus on the composition of funding sources. Not surprisingly, Community State Bank relies proportionately more on deposits, while Valley National obtains more of its funding from nondeposit liabilities such as federal funds and commercial paper. More of the large bank's deposit base consists of demand deposits owned primarily by commercial customers, money market deposit accounts, and large time deposits, while less comes in the form of interest checking, other savings, and small time deposits. The core deposit base contributes 10 percent more with purchased liabilities almost 10 percent less at Community State Bank, which is consistent with aggregate figures nationally. Community State Bank similarly operates with proportionately more equity, fewer past-due and nonaccrual loans, and lower loan losses. Still, Valley National Corp. probably has greater borrowing capacity because of its worldwide market presence and market reputation.

LIQUIDITY PLANNING

Banks actively engage in liquidity planning at two levels. The first relates to managing the required reserve position. Chapter 14 describes contemporaneous reserve accounting and the procedure for calculating legal requirements. The planning horizon is 2 weeks, during which a bank must hold a minimum amount of deposit balances at the Federal Reserve. Actual balances vary daily, with many transactions affecting outstanding liabilities and the investment portfolio. Short-term liquidity planning focuses on forecasting daily closing balances at the Federal Reserve relative to potential legal reserves. The second stage involves forecasting net funds needs derived from seasonal or cyclical phenomena and overall bank growth. The planning horizon is considerably longer, encompassing monthly intervals throughout an entire year.

Liquidity Planning over the Reserve Maintenance Period

The fundamental objective in managing a legal reserve position is to meet the minimum requirement at lowest cost. Because vault cash needs are determined by customer preferences, they vary largely with the payments patterns of the bank's customers and local businesses. They also exhibit well-defined seasonal patterns that are easily forecast. When a bank needs additional vault cash, it simply requests a cash delivery from its local Federal Reserve Bank or a correspondent bank. It similarly ships any excess cash when appropriate. The primary difficulty in meeting required reserves derives from forecasting required deposit balances at the Federal Reserve resulting from volatile shifts in bank liabilities. The process involves forecasting daily clearing balances and either investing any excess at the highest yield or obtaining additional balances at the lowest cost to cover any deficits. Contemporaneous reserve accounting further complicates the process because the magnitude of any cumulative excess or deficiency is not known with certainty until the last 2 days of the reserve maintenance period.

Exhibit 15.5 identifies several factors that alter a bank's actual and required reserve assets. These factors are separated into nondiscretionary items, over which a

Exhibit 15.5 Factors Affecting Daily Reserves Held at the Federal Reserve

Factors Increasing Reserves	Factors Decreasing Reserves
Nondiscretionary	**Nondiscretionary**
Yesterday's immediate cash letter	Remittances charged
Deferred availability items	Deficit in local clearinghouse
Excess from local clearinghouse	Treasury tax and loan account calls
Deposits from U.S. Treasury	Maturing certificates of deposit, Eurodollars not rolled over
Discretionary	**Discretionary**
Currency/coin shipped to Federal Reserve	Currency and coin received from Federal Reserve
Security Sales	Security purchases
Borrowing from Federal Reserve	Payment on loans from Federal Reserve
Federal funds purchased	Federal funds sold
Securities sold under agreement to repurchase	Securities purchased under agreement to resell
Interest payments on securities	
New certificates of deposit, Eurodollar issues	

bank has virtually no control, and discretionary items, over which it has at least partial control. The most important nondiscretionary items are checks presented for payment. Exhibit 15.5 differentiates between the Federal Reserve's cash letter and local clearings.[2] Because the Federal Reserve provides a schedule for the timing of clearings, a bank knows when previously deferred items will be available. Check clearings are uncontrollable in that bank customers determine the timing and magnitude of check payments. Customers do not normally notify a bank at the time of payment or prior to making deposits.

This uncontrolled activity presents serious problems when large withdrawals or new deposits catch a bank unaware and force it to scramble for additional reserves or invest new-found funds. It is thus important that banks have good data bases and communications systems from tellers and automatic teller machines (ATMs) to management. Managers should monitor activity in large deposit accounts routinely. They should know when large CDs mature, when the Treasury transfers deposits to the Federal Reserve, and when loan customers make large loan payments. They should also identify any weekly patterns in deposit flows that arise from normal business activity. This may allow them to use balances from inflows during one part of the maintenance period to offset outflows during another part, rather than jump into and out of federal funds trading.

When managers need to adjust a bank's reserve assets, they use the discretionary items listed in Exhibit 15.5. Managers have some control over these transactions and use them to complement uncontrollable deposit flows. In most cases, a bank receives information on clearing surpluses or deficiencies twice daily. Summary figures from yesterday's check clearings are available each morning, along with balances from

---

[2]A cash letter is a letter or data tape on which a bank lists and describes transit checks.

federal funds trades and securities transactions. In most urban areas, local clearing-houses report net clearings each afternoon from checks submitted that day. Once this information is available, managers may actively increase or decrease daily reserves by choosing among the items in Exhibit 15.5. While federal funds and RP transactions are the most popular, the choice depends on a comparison of costs and returns.

Consider, for example, the planning sheet for a sample bank in Exhibit 15.6. This format compares debits and credits posted to the reserve account at the Federal Reserve with a bank's forecasted reserve position during the first 4 days of the 2-week maintenance period. It is thus comparable in form to a corporate cash budget. The first four columns of data document the impact of transactions affecting reserves on the bank's daily closing reserve balance. The final three columns represent forecasts of the bank's net reserve position for the maintenance period. The bank's beginning reserve balance is $160.458 million. On Thursday the bank realized a net decrease in reserves of $134,000 because it purchased securities and received a currency shipment in excess of its net clearing surplus for the day. At the end of the same day, the reserve manager forecast that the daily minimum required reserves would total $160.22 million (ignore the figure in parentheses for now). Through Thursday, the funds manager knows the bank's actual net transaction balances for only the first 3 days and must forecast balances for the next 11 days.[3] The preliminary estimate is consistent with a daily reserve excess of $104,000.

On Friday the bank's reserve assets fell by $1.649 million because of a large clearing drain and maturing CDs that were withdrawn. With no adjustments, the daily deficit would reach almost $10 million. The bank partially offset the deficit by purchasing $8 million in federal funds. Because the bank is not open on weekends, Friday's closing balance carries over for Saturday and Sunday. The bank pays 3 days' interest on the federal funds transaction, which reverses on Monday. The money manager lowers the required reserves forecast to $160.1 million due to the deposit outflow. This has a cumulative effect for all prior days in the maintenance period, indicated by the forecast data in parentheses for Thursday where the daily excess is now estimated at $224,000. At the end of the weekend, the bank is over $4 million dollars short in its cumulative expected reserves.

This format can be used to project the bank's cumulative reserve position for the entire maintenance period. A manager can incorporate all known transactions affecting reserves in future days to obtain a projected cumulative deficit or surplus prior to any adjusting transactions. Again, the biggest difficulty centers around forecasting daily clearing balances, which requires careful analysis of daily payments patterns. In Exhibit 15.6, the bank will need to offset Friday's deposit loss with a clearing surplus sometime during the next 10 days. Otherwise, it will be forced to borrow additional reserves or sell assets.

---

[3]The simplest forecast is to assume that daily balances for the current maintenance period will equal the same amounts that appeared on similar days during the prior maintenance period. The analyst can then substitute the figures for current closing balances as they arise to revise the forecast daily.

Exhibit 15.6 Liquidity Planning over the Reserve Maintenance Period (Millions of Dollars)

					Forecasts	
Date	Transactions Affecting Reserves	Amount	Actual Reserves at Federal Reserve	Minimum Daily Required Reserves at Federal Reserve	Daily Excess (+) or Deficiency (−)	Cumulative Excess or Deficiency
Thursday, 8/30			Beginning Balance $160.458			
	Yesterday's cash letter	+$10.250				
	Deferred availability items	+ 2.114				
	Remittances charged	− 9.729				
	Securities purchased	− 3.000				
	Currency/coin received	− 0.500				
	Local clearinghouse credit	+ 0.731				
	Total	−$ 0.134	$160.324	$160.220 (160.100)	+$0.104 (0.224)	+$0.104 (0.224)
Friday, 8/31						
	Yesterday's cash letter	+$ 7.056				
	Deferred availability items	+ 0.337				
	Remittances charged	− 10.625				
	Local clearinghouse deficit	− 1.437				
	Maturing certificates of deposit	− 5.000				
	Federal funds purchased	+ 8.000				
	Total	−$ 1.649	$158.675	$160.100	−$1.425	−$1.201[a]
Saturday, 9/1			158.675	160.100	− 1.425	− 2.626
Sunday, 9/2			158.675	160.100	− 1.425	− 4.051
Monday, 9/3						

[a]Recognizes adjustment in forecast daily required reserves: −1.425 + 0.224 = −1.201.

Liquidity Planning: Monthly Intervals

The second stage of liquidity planning involves projecting funds needs over the coming year and beyond if necessary. ALCO members are responsible for forecasting deposit growth and loan demand and arranging for adequate liquidity sources to meet potential needs. Projections are separated into three categories: base trend, short-term seasonal, and cyclical values. The analysis assesses a bank's liquidity gap, measured as the difference between potential uses of funds and anticipated sources of funds, over monthly intervals. In practice, many large banks perform their analysis weekly. Deposit and loan data are aggregated to simplify the calculations.

Exhibit 15.7 summarizes the basic procedure for projecting liquidity needs over a 12-month planning horizon. The sample bank's year-end balance sheet, which serves as the reference point in the planning model, is provided at the top. Total deposits and loans are forecast monthly during 1992 at the bottom, with the deposit forecast excluding CDs. The base trend forecast examines the regular annual growth component of deposits or loans. Deposits are expected to grow at a 6 percent annual rate, and loans at 12 percent. These growth rates are calculated from historical data consistent with drawing a trend growth line through annual December figures, as in Exhibit 15.3. The estimates indicate what the monthly balances would equal if no seasonal or cyclical fluctuations existed and trend growth continued.

Seasonal influences net of trend are identified in the third column of data. Column 2 provides a seasonal index for each month relative to December totals. This index represents the average of the monthly figure relative to the average of the December figure over the past 5 years. Independent of trend, January deposits average 99 percent of December deposits while January loans equal 101 percent of December loans. Column 3 lists the difference between the monthly seasonal estimate and the respective December 1991 deposit or loan figure. Finally, in column 4 cyclical deposits are measured as monthly deviations of the prior year's actual deposit or loan balance and the implied trend plus seasonal component. In this example, the January 1991 trend plus seasonal estimate for loans equaled $6 million less than the actual 1991 balance. This $6 million represents the 1992 forecast of unanticipated cyclical loan needs. Column 5 lists the forecast of total deposits and total loans, respectively, equal to the sum of figures in columns 1, 3, and 4.

Exhibit 15.8 presents summary estimates of monthly liquidity needs. The cumulative need equals the forecast change in loans plus required reserves minus the forecast change in deposits.

$$\text{Liquidity needs} = \text{Forecast } \Delta\text{loans} + \Delta\text{Required reserves} - \text{Forecast } \Delta\text{deposits}$$

All changes are calculated relative to December 1991 figures. A positive figure means the bank needs additional liquid funds. Thus the July estimate of $279.4 million indicates that the bank will need to sell assets, issue CDs, or borrow via other sources in this amount, if it attempts to meet historical loan growth. A negative figure suggests that the bank will have surplus funds to invest. The pattern of liquidity estimates for this sample bank indicates large surpluses early in the year followed by large liquidity requirements from June through September.

Exhibit 15.7 Forecasts of Trend, Seasonal, and Cyclical Components of Deposits and Loans for 1992

Reference Balance Sheet: December 31, 1991 (Millions of Dollars)

Assets		Liabilities	
Cash and due from banks	$ 160	Transaction accounts and nonnegotiable deposits	$1,600
Loans	1,400	Certificates of deposit and other borrowing	280
Investment securities	400	Stockholders' equity	120
Other assets	40	Total	$2,000
Total	$2,000		

Deposit Forecast

End of Month	(1) Trend Deposits[a]	(2) Seasonal Deposit Index[b]	(3) Seasonal Deposits – Dec. 1991 Deposits	(4) Cyclical Deposits	(5) Total
January	$1,608	99%	–$16	–$3	$1,589
February	1,616	102	+32	8	1,656
March	1,623	105	+80	7	1,710
April	1,631	107	+112	10	1,753
May	1,639	101	16	1	1,656
June	1,647	96	–64	–8	1,575
July	1,655	93	–112	–15	1,528
August	1,663	95	–80	–9	1,574
September	1,671	97	–48	–4	1,619
October	1,680	101	+16	0	1,696
November	1,688	104	+64	+3	1,755
December	1,696	100	0	0	1,696

Loan Forecast

End of Month	Trend Loans[a]	Seasonal Loan Index[b]	Seasonal Loans – Dec. 1991 Loans	Cyclical Loans	Total
January	$1,413	101%	$14	$6	$1,433
February	1,427	97	–42	–9	1,376
March	1,440	95	–70	–18	1,352
April	1,454	94	–84	–21	1,349
May	1,467	97	–42	–15	1,410
June	1,481	102	28	–3	1,506
July	1,495	108	112	9	1,616
August	1,510	106	84	17	1,611
September	1,524	103	42	11	1,577
October	1,538	99	–14	5	1,529
November	1,553	98	–28	0	1,525
December	1,568	100	0	0	1,568

[a]Growth trend for December to December averaged 6 percent for deposits and 12 percent for loans from 1987 to 1991.

[b]Multiply by the preceding December figure.

While this analysis is somewhat general, it identifies longer-term trends in fund flows. In practice, forecasts are prepared for each distinct deposit account and loan

Exhibit 15.8 Estimates of Liquidity Needs (Millions of Dollars)

End of Month	Δ Deposits	Δ Required Reserves	Δ Loans	Liquidity Needs[a]
January	-$ 11.0	-$ 1.3	$ 33.0	$ 42.7
February	56.0	6.7	-24.0	-73.3
March	110.0	13.2	-48.0	-144.8
April	153.0	18.4	-51.0	-185.6
May	56.0	6.7	10.0	-39.3
June	-25.0	-3.0	106.0	128.0
July	-72.0	-8.6	216.0	279.4
August	-26.0	-3.1	211.0	233.9
September	19.0	2.3	177.0	160.3
October	96.0	11.5	129.0	44.5
November	155.0	18.6	125.0	-11.4
December	96.0	11.5	168.0	83.5

[a]Estimates of liquidity needs equal the change in loans plus change in required reserves minus the change in deposits. The reserve ratio equals 12 percent. A positive figure represents a shortage, while a negative figure means the bank has surplus funds to invest.

category, then summed to yield a total estimate. This allows management to incorporate different trend and seasonal patterns for demand deposits, NOWs, and MMDAs, and thus reduce the aggregate forecast error. For example, demand deposit growth has slowed in recent years while the growth in MMDAs, IRAs and other deposits has accelerated. Separate estimates capture this diverse behavior.

Management can supplement this analysis by including projected changes in purchased funds and investments with specific loan and deposit flows. One procedure is to calculate a liquidity gap measure over different time intervals. This format is comparable to the funding GAP analysis introduced in Chapter 8. It begins by classifying potential uses and sources of funds into separate time frames according to their cash flow characteristics. The liquidity gap for each interval equals the dollar value of uses of funds minus the dollar value of sources of funds.

Exhibit 15.9 demonstrates this format and extends the analysis of Exhibit 15.8 by segmenting account categories and adding information on maturing CDs, Eurodollar deposits, and bank investments. By using specific account information, managers can trace the source of any significant outflow or inflow and take remedial action. Consider the data representing the next 30 days for the hypothetical bank. The bank has $50 million in maturing CDs and Eurodollars and $5.5 million in small time deposits that mature. It expects to fund $113 million in new loans and see transactions accounts fall by $4.5 million for a total $173 million in uses. Expected sources of funds include $18 million in maturing securities and $80 million in loan principal payments. The liquidity gap for the next 30 days thus equals $75 million.[4] The bank needs to replace the maturing CDs and Eurodollars plus find an additional $25 million in liquid funds to finance this loan growth.

---

[4]This figure is comparable to the $42.7 million liquidity need estimate in Exhibit 15.8, which can be approximated by subtracting maturing certificates of deposit and Eurodollars and adding maturing investments.

Exhibit 15.9 Liquidity Gap Estimates (Millions of Dollars)

	0–30 Days	31–90 Days	91–365 Days
Potential Uses of Funds			
Add: Maturing time deposits			
Small time deposits	$ 5.5	$ 8.0	$ 34.0
Certificates of deposit over $100,000	40.0	70.0	100.0
Eurodollar deposits	10.0	10.0	30.0
Plus: Forecast new loans			
Commercial loans	60.0	112.0	686.0
Consumer loans	22.0	46.0	210.0
Real estate and other loans	31.0	23.0	223.0
Minus: Forecast net change in transactional accounts[a]			
Demand deposits	–6.5	105.5	10.0
NOW accounts	0.3	4.5	5.0
Super NOW accounts	0.1	1.0	2.0
Money market deposit accounts	1.6	3.0	6.0
Total uses	$173.0	$155.0	$1,260.0
Potential Sources of Funds			
Add: Maturing investments			
Money market instruments	$ 8.0	$ 16.5	$ 36.5
U.S. Treasury and agency securities	7.5	10.5	40.0
Municipal securities	2.5	1.0	12.5
Plus: Principal payments on loans	80.0	262.0	903.0
Total sources	$ 98.0	$290.0	$ 992.0
Periodic Liquidity Gap[b]	$ 75.0	–$135.0	$ 268.0
Cumulative Liquidity Gap	75.0	–60.0	208.0

[a]Net of required reserves.

[b]Potential uses of funds minus potential sources of funds.

Comparable figures for 31 to 90 days out and 91 to 365 days out are also shown in the exhibit. The cumulative gap summarizes the total liquidity position from the present to the farthest day within each time interval. The bank expects to experience a liquidity surplus 2 to 3 months out and a $208 million liquidity shortage for the entire year.[5]

Once normal liquidity needs are forecast, a bank should compare the estimates with potential funding sources and extraordinary funds needs. One researcher introduced a simple format, modified as Exhibit 15.10, that requires each bank to project its borrowing capacity via federal funds purchased, RPs, and unused CDs and combine it with funds available from reducing federal funds sold and selling loan participations, money market securities, and unpledged securities.[6] This total is then compared with potential draws against unused loan commitments and letters of credit. Of course, no

---

[5]The cumulative liquidity gap numbers are comparable to the liquidity estimates in Exhibit 15.8.

[6]See Temple (1983).

Exhibit 15.10 Potential Funding Sources (Millions of Dollars)

	Time Frame		
	0–30 Days	31–90 Days	91–365 Days
Purchased Funds Capacity			
Federal funds purchased (overnight and term)	$ 20	$ 20	$ 30
Repurchase agreements	10	10	10
Negotiable certificates of deposit			
Local	50	50	60
National	20	20	25
Eurodollar certificates of deposit	20	20	20
Total	$120	$120	$145
Additional Funding Sources			
Reductions in federal funds sold	$ 5	$ 5	$ 5
Loan participations	20	20	20
Sale of money market securities	5	5	5
Sale of unpledged securities	10	10	10
Total	$ 50	$ 50	$ 50
Potential Funding Sources[a]	$170	$170	$195
Potential Extraordinary Funding Needs			
50% of outstanding letters of credit	5	10	15
20% of unfunded loan commitments	25	30	35
Total	$ 30	$ 40	$ 50
Excess Potential Funding Sources	$140	$130	$145

[a]Purchased funds capacity plus additional funding sources.

bank wants to utilize its borrowing capacity fully or sell all of its available assets. It should always leave some potential funding available for extraordinary events.

Applying the data from Exhibit 15.10 to the 30-day gap in Exhibit 15.9, the sample bank has considerable flexibility in meeting its liquidity need. First, it could simply replace the maturing CDs and Eurodollars with similar borrowings, for which it has an estimated $90 million capacity. Second, the bank could borrow via federal funds or RPs, eliminate federal funds sold, and make up the difference with new CDs. The best alternative is the one with the lowest cost. In general, large banks prefer to borrow rather than liquidate assets, while small banks sell assets or restrict growth. The best use of this information is to conduct "what if" analysis to determine the cost implications of various alternatives and assess how much flexibility management has in adjusting its cash position.

Considerations in Selecting Liquidity Sources

The previous analysis focuses on estimating the dollar magnitude of liquidity needs. Implicit in the discussion is the assumption that the bank has adequate liquidity sources. For most banks, loan growth exceeds deposit growth net of CDs and Eurodollars. In the short run, banks have the option of financing this net growth either by selling securities or by obtaining new deposits. In the long run, this net growth must be financed out of purchased liabilities because banks own a limited amount of securities. Yet most banks have limited access to new purchased funds because they are small with no market reputation, or they have exhausted their borrowing capacity in terms of their capital base and earnings potential. There are two possible solutions to this dilemma. Management can either restrict asset growth or seek additional core deposits or equity. Regulatory actions to raise bank capital requirements, discussed in Chapter 12, have the beneficial side effect of improving access to the money and capital markets.

Banks with options in meeting liquidity needs evaluate the characteristics of various sources to minimize costs. The following factors should be considered in asset sales or new borrowings:

Asset Sales

1. Brokerage fees

2. Securities gains or losses

3. Foregone interest income

4. Any increase or decrease in taxes

5. Any increase or decrease in interest receipts

New Borrowings

1. Brokerage fees

2. Required reserves

3. FDIC insurance premiums

4. Servicing or promotion costs

5. Interest expense

The costs should be evaluated in present-value terms because interest income and expense may arise over substantially different time periods. The choice of one source over another often involves an implicit interest rate forecast.

Suppose, for example, that a bank temporarily needs funds for 6 months. Management has decided to sell $1 million of Treasuries from the bank's portfolio. The choice is between securities with either 1 year or 5 years remaining to maturity. Both securities sell at par and earn 10 percent annually. If the bank sells the 1-year security, it implicitly assumes that the level of short-term Treasury rates is going to fall far enough below 10 percent so that any eventual reinvestment of funds would yield less than that on a 5-year security. If the bank sells the 5-year bond, it assumes that the level of short-term rates will rise above 10 percent, on average.

Suppose instead that the bank decides to issue either a 6-month CD or a 1-month CD. Clearly, the 6-month CD locks in interest expense and requires only one transaction. A 1-month CD will need to be rolled over, with uncertain future interest expense.

Transactions costs will also be higher. The rationale for issuing any shorter-term CD can only be that the present value of expected interest expense plus transactions costs will be lower with this alternative.[7]

CONTINENTAL ILLINOIS: THE MAKING OF A LIQUIDITY CRISIS

On Friday, May 11, 1984, Continental Illinois National Bank & Trust Co. of Chicago borrowed $3.6 billion from the Federal Reserve system to replace overnight deposits at the bank that could not be rolled over. The largest run ever on a single bank had begun. By the end of 1984, Continental's deposit base had shrunk by almost $12 billion and the bank had effectively been nationalized. The story behind Continental's problems is a simple one: bad loans produce earnings problems, which decrease the market value of bank equity, undermine customer confidence, and subsequently bring about net deposit outflows. The story behind Continental's rescue demonstrates the inconsistencies of current regulatory policy.

The Loan Problems

Continental's problems largely reflect management's pursuit of growth through aggressive lending initiated in the early 1970s. Roger Anderson, named chairman in 1973, targeted the bank to become one of the top three domestic lenders in the United States. Loan officers were given considerable leeway in booking new credits. Individual officers had authority to approve larger loans than their counterparts at other banks and often offered lower rates to win new business. If the bank was part of a loan syndicate, it often insisted on a disproportionately large share of the credit.[8] Not surprisingly, Continental's loan growth far outpaced that at other multinational banks. From 1977 to 1981, Continental's loans grew at a 19.8 percent average annual rate, while the comparable rate for peer banks was 14.7 percent. Exhibit 15.11 compares Continental's performance ratios with those of peer banks.[9] It indicates that through 1981 Continental was a high-performance bank, operating with greater leverage and earning more with comparable loan quality.

Still, the reported profit figures disguised potentially serious earnings and liquidity problems in funding the loan growth. Unlike other large banks, Continental had few core deposits. The state of Illinois imposed strict limits on branch banking, which gave Continental a relatively small stable consumer deposit base. The bank subsequently

---

[7]The yield curve incorporates both liquidity premiums and interest rate expectations. Thus 1-month yields at 9 percent and 6-month yields at 9.2 percent signify that traders expect 1-month rates to increase. By issuing a 1-month security, the borrower implicitly assumes that rates will not increase as much as that implied by the yield curve.

[8]In most cases, syndicate partners split the credit into shares in proportion to each bank's relative asset size.

[9]The comparisons are between Continental Illinois Corp. (Continental Bank's holding company) and other large bank holding companies. The data are from *Inquiry into Continental Illinois* (1984). Peer banks are the 16 largest U.S. multinational banking organizations not including Continental Illinois.

**Exhibit 15.11 A Comparison of Performance Measures:
Continental Illinois versus Peer Banks**[a]

Ratios	1977–1981	1982	1983
Growth[a]			
Loan growth			
Continental	19.82%	2.70%	−7.15%
Peers	14.67	9.26	5.99
Asset growth			
Continental	16.41	−8.67	−1.87
Peers	13.04	7.56	4.59
Earnings growth			
Continental	14.74	−69.41	39.07
Peers	18.26	4.19	10.79
Profitability			
Return on equity			
Continental	14.38	4.56	5.95
Peers	12.65	11.53	11.15
Return on assets			
Continental	0.54	0.18	0.26
Peers	0.50	0.49	0.52
Capital Adequacy			
Equity/Total assets			
Continental	4.36	4.81	5.17
Peers	4.55	4.86	5.39
Equity/Total loans			
Continental	6.16	5.26	6.03
Peers	7.00	6.98	7.62
Asset Quality			
Net charge-offs/Total loans			
Continental	0.33	1.28	1.37
Peers	0.45	0.55	0.64
Allowance for possible loan losses/Total loans			
Continental	0.97	1.15	1.24
Peers	1.01	1.08	1.21
Nonperforming assets/Total assets			
Continental	1.4	4.6	4.5
Peers	1.4	2.1	2.3
(Liquid assets − Volatile liabilities)/Total assets			
Continental	−43.83	−58.16	−52.61
Peers	−23.63	−31.51	−30.88

[a]Peer banks' data are averages for 16 largest U.S. banking organizations at year-end 1983, excluding Continental Illinois.

[b]Average annual growth rates.

financed its loan growth with short-term CDs, Eurodollars, and overnight borrowings from commercial customers and financial institutions. Through 1981 its net reliance on this "hot money" was almost double that of comparable banks, indicated by the liquidity measure net of these volatile liabilities at the bottom of Exhibit 15.11.

The bank's reported earnings also masked problems with loan quality. Aggressive lending in a volatile economic environment like the late 1970s virtually mandates that a bank take on marginal credits. Ultimately, Continental had heavy loan exposure to problem companies like Braniff, International Harvester, Nucorp Energy, and Wickes. Still, much of the loan growth was fueled by energy lending, an area in which Continental had a long-standing interest and recognized expertise. Lending in this area coincided nicely with the oil boom's rising prices and profitable-looking borrowers, which included major oil companies, wildcat drillers, and oil field servicing operators.

With the downturn in oil prices, many energy customers began having serious problems. Continental subsequently had problems with its own customers, as well as with Penn Square Bank, a downstream correspondent in Oklahoma City. By 1981 Continental had purchased over $600 million in loan participations from Penn Square Bank. In many cases, loan officers failed to obtain or review loan documentation. This documentation provides collateral information, cash flow projections, and the reason for granting the loan. Bank auditors often did not verify that collateral existed, and bank lawyers did not complete the paperwork to ensure the bank's security interest. When Penn Square Bank failed in July 1982, Continental held more than $1 billion in loans originated by Penn Square. By December 1982, Continental had written off or listed as nonperforming over $500 million of this total. Losses on other marginal credits followed.

Exhibit 15.11 documents the deterioration in Continental's performance during 1982 and 1983. Earnings fell by over 60 percent as the bank charged-off more loans and restricted its growth. Nonperforming assets (those with interest payments more than 90 days past due) increased to 4.6 percent of total assets, more than double that of peer banks. Even with the decrease in loans and other assets in 1983, the bank's liquidity position worsened to where volatile liabilities exceeded liquid assets by almost 53 percent of total assets.

Two events foretold Continental's eventual liquidity trouble. First, in July 1982 Continental's CDs were removed from the list of CDs traded "on the run." This list represents CDs of the largest, well-known U.S. banking organizations that are traded interchangeably by dealers without reference to the specific underlying banks. Removal reduced the effective demand for Continental's CDs and increased the bank's borrowing costs. It also signified that investors were not eager to acquire Continental's CDs. Second, the bank announced in response that it would rely more heavily on Eurodollars. Continental was then paying a premium on its deposits, and investors demanded much shorter maturities.

The Liquidity Crunch

The Penn Square failure forced Continental to examine its loan policies and asset quality closely. Regulators pressured the bank to clean up its operations while management played down its problems. Nonperforming loans increased to $1.9 billion at the end of 1983, leading to the early retirement of chairman Anderson in February 1984.

During the first 3 months of 1984, problem loans rose to $2.3 billion, net interest income fell $80 million below that for the first quarter of 1983, and the bank reported an operating loss. Many of the newer problem loans were to Third World borrowers. Although the bank's loan loss reserve increased, it equaled only the industry norm. To report a quarterly profit and pay dividends, Continental sold its credit card operation to Chemical Bank of New York. The economic value of shareholder equity was deteriorating rapidly.

Continental's deposit-gathering problems surfaced during this period. As of December 31, 1983, the bank obtained only 25 percent of its borrowings from relatively stable, domestic sources. An incredible 64 percent came from CDs, Eurodollars, commercial paper, and overnight borrowings, as indicated below.

Funding Source	Percentage of Liabilities
Non-Interest-bearing accounts	9.8%
Domestic time and savings deposits, nonnegotiable	15.5
Commercial CDs	8.8
Time deposits in foreign branches	38.1
Federal funds purchased and RPs	15.5
Commercial paper	1.3
Other interest-bearing debt	11.0
	100.0%

The market was constantly bombarded with Continental's problems. When rumors circulated on May 8, 1984, that the bank was about to fail, foreign banks called in credit lines extended to Continental and refused to buy the bank's new CDs. Over the next few days, depositors refused to roll over maturing CDs and Eurodollars, and Continental had to borrow $3.6 billion from the Federal Reserve to replace the deposit outflow. In short, the market had lost confidence in Continental's future.

The Rescue

The first step in Continental's rescue was to calm the money markets. Without public confidence, Continental could not sell its CDs or borrow unsecured federal funds overnight. A group of banks led by Morgan Guaranty Trust Co. quickly put together a $4.5 billion line of credit to Continental. The Federal Reserve allocated $17 billion of Continental's assets deposited with it as collateral against potential borrowing. Still, this was not enough to stem the panic. On May 17, regulators stepped in with a four-part, government-arranged rescue. First, the FDIC guaranteed all of Continental's depositors and general creditors against any loss, regardless of size. This effectively removed the $100,000 per account limit on FDIC insurance. Second, the FDIC and seven large banks injected $2 billion into the bank's capital base.[10] Third, the initial private bank credit line was extended to $5.5 billion with 28 banks participating. Finally, the Federal Reserve pledged to continue funding Continental's discount window borrowing.

---

[10]The Federal Deposit Insurance Corp. stated that its capital contribution would be available only until Continental obtained permanent capital "by merger or otherwise."

This package represented only a temporary solution, as the deposit outflow continued even with this support. In early July, after liquidating $5 billion in assets, Continental still owed $4 billion to the Federal Reserve, $4 billion to the 28 banks, and $2 billion to the FDIC. In just 2 months, the bank had lost around $15 billion in deposits.[11]

Permanent Financial Restructuring

In July 1984 the regulators proposed a permanent restructuring of Continental that was later approved by shareholders. This agreement made the FDIC an owner in Continental through a complex series of transactions, yet it forced the bank's existing shareholders to bear most of the risk of loss. The plan contained the following elements:

1. The FDIC immediately purchased $3 billion (book value) of Continental's problem loans. The FDIC paid for the loans by assuming $2 billion of Continental's existing debt from the Federal Reserve. It immediately charged off $1 billion as a loss, which reduced the book value of its capital to $800 million.

2. Continental retained the option to sell an additional $1.5 billion in problem loans during the next 3 years.

3. The FDIC purchased $1 billion of newly issued preferred stock in Continental, convertible into 160 million common shares. Holders of Continental's existing 40 million shares exchanged their shares for stock in a newly created holding company, which owned the remaining 40 million shares. The FDIC thus immediately owned 80 percent of the bank.[12]

4. The FDIC kept the right to purchase the 40 million shares in the new holding company, depending on its losses on the problem loans it purchased. The FDIC's total loss, including interest expense paid to the Federal Reserve and collection costs, will be calculated after 5 years. The FDIC may repurchase one share, for 1/1000 of a cent, for each $20 in loss.[13]

5. Existing shareholders received one right for each share owned to purchase a share in Continental for $4.50 within 60 days and for $6 afterwards.

In addition to these changes, Continental continued to borrow from private banks and the Federal Reserve. It was essentially nationalized even though it changed management and the FDIC did not play a role in supervising day-to-day operations.

---

[11]Investor uncertainty explains why depositors pulled their funds even with a government guarantee. The initial guarantee was extremely vague, providing no detail for a formal legal challenge if necessary. If Continental failed, depositors did not know whether they would lose interest until restitution or how long their funds would be tied up. If Continental were sold, there was no assurance the government guarantee would still apply. The premium for rolling over deposits was not worth the risk or worry.

[12]Interestingly, in 1932 the Reconstruction Finance Corp., a federal government agency, purchased $50 million of preferred stock in Continental under similar circumstances to help prevent the bank's failure.

[13]If the total loss reaches $800 million, the Federal Deposit Insurance Corp. can repurchase all 40 million shares and effectively own 100 percent of the bank. This ignores the rights offer to existing shareholders that was part of the agreement. Even if all rights are exercised, the FDIC would still own over 83 percent of Continental.

From 1985 through 1990 Continental Illinois reported profits. It shrunk its asset base to $29 billion in 1990, one-third less than the asset base in 1981. In 1986 Continental's management announced, with the FDIC's approval, its intent to purchase several Chicago area suburban banks with cumulative assets of over $150 million. The strategy was to start building a stable retail deposit base. From 1987 to 1989 Continental redirected its business strategy by focusing on commercial lending, particularly highly leveraged transactions, and offering investment advisory services in the area of futures and options through its First Options Corp. subsidiary. During 1990 Continental's management announced that it was selling First Options, cutting 900 employees (13 percent of its total), and it reported a doubling of its nonperforming loans to over $450 million. Clearly, the bank's performance continued to be highly volatile as management searched for a viable long-term strategy.

After the 1984 rescue, the FDIC owned Continental at a cost of approximately $4.5 billion. As the bank became profitable through 1990, the FDIC sold common and preferred stock to the public so that it owned only 26 percent of Continental by 1991. Continental's management offered $22 per share for the FDIC's stake in 1988 but was turned down. The bank's officers believe that FDIC ownership prevents the bank from expanding its operations via acquisitions. Eventually the FDIC will sell its shares to the public and Continental will again be privately owned and managed.

Public Policy Issues

The FDIC's bail-out of Continental raises numerous policy issues. Should the bank have been allowed to fail? Throughout the crisis, the regulators guaranteed that none of Continental's depositors or other creditors would lose anything. This promise conflicts directly with the modified-payout solution imposed in other bank failures, in which uninsured depositors lost their investments. Because most failures involve small banks, Continental's special treatment constitutes discrimination against small banks. The rescue also leaves unanswered what the consequences would have been had Continental failed. The regulators argued that failure would have led to a chain reaction of small bank failures because so many banks held correspondent balances with Continental. Finally, what is the ultimate cost of this type of bail-out to the U.S. Treasury? What is the impact on the federal deficit?

Another lesson for bank managers is the value of a stable deposit base. Banks that rely heavily on large, purchased liabilities subject the firm to the whims of creditors with little allegiance. These investors are quite willing to move their funds when a bank reports problems or another institution offers higher rates. Extreme reliance on "hot" money increases a bank's liquidity risk and risk for the entire banking system. Many banks have had to seek stable retail deposits, limit their asset growth, and generally increase their capital base to reduce potential funding problems. Today, all banks recognize the value of core deposits, so competition has increased, benefiting consumers.

SUMMARY

Liquidity planning is an ongoing part of a bank's asset and liability management strategy. It involves monitoring net deposit outflows and inflows and deciding how to finance deficiencies or invest excess funds. This chapter examines two different stages of liquidity planning. The first focuses on managing a bank's required reserve position over the 2-week maintenance period. The second analyzes monthly liquidity gaps throughout the coming year. A liquidity gap measures the difference between the dollar value of expected cash outflows and expected cash inflows within a given time interval. Positive liquidity gaps indicate a net liquidity need, while negative liquidity gaps indicate surplus investable funds. Planning models for each stage of analysis are applied to a hypothetical bank's data. The problems faced by Continental Illinois in 1983 and 1984 provide a dramatic example of a liquidity crisis and outline important public policy issues regarding regulatory policy toward bank failures.

Questions

1. Liquidity planning requires monitoring deposit outflows. Of the following causes for outflows, which are discretionary and which are not? If the outflow is not discretionary, is it predictable or unexpected?

    a. In April a farmer draws down his line of credit in order to purchase seeds.

    b. Students borrow money for fall tuition.

    c. The bank makes a preferred stock dividend payment.

    d. The rent on the bank's offices must be paid.

    e. A major fire destroys a portion of the local manufacturing district and several firms apply for reconstruction loans.

    f. It is the Friday before the annual city-wide festival and all of the ATMs in town have been drained of cash.

    g. A New York bank has just opened a local office and is offering a VCR to anyone who transfers funds from a CD at another bank.

    h. The largest corporate customer of the bank has just lost a legal suit to a French firm and will have to pay charges of $1 million by the end of the week.

    i. The bank buys most of the newly issued local municipal securities.

    j. The bank initiates a massive loan officer call program.

2. What are the fundamental differences and similarities among the commercial loan theory, shiftability theory, anticipated income theory, and liability management theory?

3. Which of the four theories of liquidity management—the commercial loan theory, shiftability theory, anticipated income theory, or liability management theory—is exemplified by each of the following actions?

    a. A borrower applies for a balloon-payment loan and the bank officer convinces him that a monthly payment loan would be easier to repay.

    b. A bank only writes loans against short-term productive assets; it does not write loans to purchase consumption goods.

   c.   Bank policy states that every loan officer is allotted a quota of equity capital and liquid securities. For every 2-year or longer loan the officer accepts, she must allocate equity to equal 10 percent of the loan balance and liquid securities to equal 25 percent.

   d.   Before a loan officer can approve a line of credit, she must ascertain if the ALCO can acquire deposits of an equivalent amount in the Eurodollar market.

   e.   The bank only writes corporate loans and only those that mature in 90 days or less.

   f.   The bank only writes installment loans.

   g.   The bank maintains a strict ratio between loans and Treasury securities.

4. Discuss the trade-off between a bank's profitability and its asset liquidity, liability liquidity, and equity capital position.

5. Explain how credit risk and interest rate risk can spread into liquidity risk.

6. Discuss the relative importance of liquidity versus capital problems in causing bank failures. Explain the normal sequence of events leading to failure and the importance of market value measures.

7. Identify three changes in the loan portfolio and three changes in the deposit portfolio which would produce liquidity needs.

8. Rank the following types of depositors by the liquidity risk they typically pose for a bank. Start with the depositor creating the highest liquidity risk.

   a.   A CD depositor attracted through a stock broker.

   b.   Local school children.

   c.   Foreign investors trading with a local corporation.

   d.   A two-person yuppie family.

9. Explain how each of the following will affect a bank's deposit balances at the Federal Reserve.

   a.   The bank ships excess vault cash to the Federal Reserve.

   b.   The bank buys U.S. government securities in the open market.

   c.   The bank realizes a surplus in its local clearinghouse processing.

   d.   The bank sells federal funds.

   e.   A $100,000 CD at the bank matures and is not rolled over.

   f.   Local businesses deposit tax payments in the Treasury's account at the local bank.

Measuring Liquidity

10. If you were forced to measure the liquidity of a bank using one ratio, what would it be and why? Create your own ideal ratio.

11. A traditional measure of liquidity risk is the loan/deposit ratio. Give two reasons why this is a poor measure of risk. Give one reason why it is a good measure.

12. What do the terms *core deposits* and *volatile deposits* mean? Explain how a bank might estimate the magnitude of each. Liquidity measures and potential sources of liquidity differ for large multinational banks and small community banks. List the key differences and explain why they appear.

13. What can bank management do to increase core deposits? Generally, how might management estimate the relative interest elasticity of various deposit liabilities of a bank?

14. Liquidity measures and potential sources of liquidity differ between large multi-national banks and small community banks. List the key differences and explain why they appear.

15. In Exhibit 15.11 Continental Illinois' liquidity is measured with the ratio (liquid assets - volatile liabilities)/total assets. Give one reason this is a good measure of liquidity and one reason why it is not. Would you expect small banks to have a larger or smaller ratio than that shown in the exhibit?

16. Cash is certainly the most liquid of assets, yet for many banks their cash account offers little or no liquidity. Why?

17. The secondary market in Treasury securities is exceedingly active, yet a bank's holdings of Treasury securities may offer limited or no liquidity. Why?

18. You are analyzing the following bank. Is this bank more or less liquid than the bank holding company reported in Exhibit 15.4? Explain your reasoning.

Assets

Cash and due from banks	$100
Federal funds sold and reverse RPs	45
U.S. government securities	95
Balloon loans	100
Installment loans	600
Fixed assets	60
Total	$1,000

This bank has required reserves of $90 and has pledged $90 in government securities.

Liquidity Planning

19. Exhibit 15.6 summarizes a hypothetical bank's reserve planning information for August 30 through September 2, the first 4 days of a 2-week reserve maintenance period. At the end of the fourth day, management projects that the minimum daily required reserves will average $160.1 million. Monday's opening reserve balance is $1.425 million short of this estimate, and the cumulative deficiency exceeds $4 million.

Use the information in Table 1 to complete the reserves planning analysis for the entire maintenance period. The dollar amounts of each transaction are indicated, but you must determine whether actual reserves are increased or decreased. All federal funds and security RP transactions have a 1-day maturity and thus are reversed the following business day.

Table 1 Transactions Affecting the Bank's Reserve Balances at the Federal Reserve

Date	Transactions	Amount (Millions)	Estimated Minimum Daily Required Reserve
Monday, 9/3	Bank holiday		
Tuesday, 9/4	Yesterday's (Friday's) cash letter	$ 5.250	
	Deferred availability items	0.496	
	Remittances charged	6.771	
	Local clearinghouse deficit	1.088	
	Deposit from the U.S. Treasury	4.526	$160.0
Wednesday, 9/5	Yesterday's cash letter	8.623	
	Deferred availability items	0.757	
	Remittances charged	6.209	
	Local clearinghouse credit	2.540	160.3
Thursday, 9/6	Yesterday's cash letter	8.915	
	Deferred availability items	0.096	
	Remittances charged	11.166	
	Local clearinghouse credit	0.742	
	Securities sold under agreement to repurchase	2.000	160.3
Friday, 9/7	Yesterday's cash letter	10.933	
	Deferred availability items	2.005	
	Remittances charged	9.891	
	Local clearinghouse deficit	1.218	
	Maturing CDs	6.500	160.2
Saturday, 9/8			
Sunday, 9/9			
Monday, 9/10	Yesterday's cash letter	7.696	
	Deferred availability items	0.400	
	Remittances charged	8.237	
	Local clearinghouse credit	0.335	
	Federal funds sold	6.000	160.1
Tuesday, 9/11	Yesterday's cash letter	10.105	
	Deferred availability items	1.134	
	Remittances charged	9.642	
	Local clearinghouse credit	0.808	
	Treasury tax and loan call	4.000	
	Federal funds sold	7.000	160.1
Wednesday, 9/12	Yesterday's cash letter	8.353	
	Deferred availability items	0.311	
	Remittances charged	11.909	
	Local clearinghouse credit	0.568	
	Federal funds	?	160.1

a. Forecast the daily and cumulative reserve excess or deficiency for each day in the maintenance period.

b. Based on the estimated cumulative position on Wednesday, September 12, indicate whether the bank should sell or borrow federal funds and the appropriate amount needed to meet the legal reserve requirement.

20. What are the conceptual differences between the trend, seasonal, and cyclical components of a bank's loans and deposits? Discuss why a bank should examine each component rather than simply look at total loans and deposits.

21. Which of the following would represent trend, seasonal, and cyclical components of liquidity and which would not be relevant to liquidity planning?
   a. It is the Friday before Easter.
   b. Inflation and interest rates have just hit an all-time high.
   c. The stock market always rebounds in the first week of January.
   d. The local economy is feeling the results of the shift of population toward the southwest.
   e. It is the 15th of the month.
   f. The school year is drawing to a close.
   g. This is the triple-witching Friday on the options and futures exchanges when large volumes of futures and options contracts expire simultaneously.
   h. The baby boom generation is beginning to retire.
   i. Local unemployment has just hit a 4-year high.

22. Your bank's estimated liquidity gap over the next 90 days equals $180 million. You estimate that funding sources over the same 90 days will equal only $150 million. What planning and policy requirements does this impose on your $3 billion bank?

23. The cost associated with liquidity management could be subdivided into those associated with maintaining liquidity and those associated with acquiring it. Name one of each type for liquidity acquired through asset management and liquidity acquired through liability management.

24. The failure of Continental Illinois is a classic. What management policy led to this failure? Suggest a better policy the bank could have pursued. What did regulators do that set a precedent that still haunts them today? Do you think the regulators did the right thing? If so, why? If not, then what would you suggest? In what way is a bank failure different from the failure of other large U.S. corporations?

Activity

1. Liquidity planning is not a unique banking problem—all financial entities must plan for liquidity. Individuals are no exception, whether the planning is formal or informal. How much cash do you have in your pocket now? Why? Do you have other sources of liquidity in your pocket at this time? If so, what are they?

2. Plan your daily liquidity needs for the next week. Be sure to identify all incoming and outgoing cash flows. How will you meet any shortages? What will you do with any excess cash? Approximately what does it cost you to maintain your personal liquidity for a year?

3. In 1990 several credit unions located in Rhode Island experienced severe liquidity problems. Much like Home State Savings' experience in Ohio, private deposit insurance was again involved. Research the causes and problems experienced by these credit unions and the eventual solution to the problems.

References

Allen, Linda, Stavros Peristiani, and Anthony Saunders. "Bank Size, Collateral, and Net Purchase Behavior in the Federal Funds Market: Empirical Evidence." *Journal of Business* (October 1989).

Bender, Roxanne. "Bank Liquidity: Learning to Love It." *Bankers Monthly* (December 1985).

"Closing of Ohio S&Ls after Run on Deposits Is One for the Books." *Wall Street Journal* (March 18, 1985).

"Continental Illinois: How Bad Judgments and Big Egos Did It In." *Wall Street Journal* (July 30, 1984).

Cotes, David. "Liquidity Lessons for the '90s." *Bank Management* (April 1990).

Federal Deposit Insurance Corp. *Regulators Statement on the Permanent Assistance Program for Continental Illinois National Bank and Trust Co.* Washington, D.C.: July 26, 1984.

Gendreau, Brian, and Scott Prince, "The Private Costs of Bank Failure." *Business Review* (Federal Reserve Bank of Philadelphia, March–April 1986).

Hill, G. Christian, and Edwin Finn. "Big Depositors Runs on Beleagured Banks Speed the Failure Rate." *The Wall Street Journal* (August 23, 1989).

Horvitz, Paul. "FDIC's Solution for Continental Illinois was a Masterful Deal." *American Banker* (August 28, 1984).

Humphrey, David, "Lender of Last Resort: The Concept in History." *Economic Review* (Federal Reserve Bank of Richmond, March/April 1989).

Inquiry into Continental Illinois Corp. and Continental Illinois National Bank. Hearings Before the Subcommittee on Financial Institutions Supervision, Regulation, and Insurance of the Committee on Banking, Finance, and Urban Affairs, House of Representatives, 98th Congress, second session. Washington, D.C., September 18 and 19 and October 4, 1984.

Kantron, Yvette. "As U.S. Consumers Change, So, Too, Must Banks' Tactics." *American Banker* (April 23, 1991).

Luckett, Dudley. "Approaches to Bank Liquidity Management." *Economic Review* (Federal Reserve Bank of Kansas City, March 1980).

McKinney, George. "A Perspective on the Use of Models in the Management of Bank Funds." *Journal of Bank Research* (Summer 1977).

Ratti, Ronald. "Pledging Requirements and Bank Asset Portfolios." *Economic Review* (Federal Reserve Bank of Kansas City, September–October 1979).

Roe, Timothy, Thomas Lawler, and Timothy Cook. "Treasury Bill versus Private Money Market Yield Curves." *Economic Review* (Federal Reserve Bank of Richmond, July/August 1986).

Rose, Sanford. "To Mismatch or Not to Mismatch." *American Banker* (February 2, 1988).

Rose, Sanford. "Mismatching Revisited." *American Banker* (June 7, 1988).

Temple, W. Robert. "Bank Liquidity: Where Are We?" *American Banker* (March 8, 1983).

Part IV

Managing the
Investment Portfolio

Chapter 16

The Investment Portfolio and Policy Guidelines

The world of bank investments has changed dramatically since 1986. At that time, Congress changed the tax laws so that banks no longer found most municipal bonds to be attractive. Because banks had historically invested substantial sums in municipals, the tax change forced a fundamental restructuring of the composition of bank investments. Today there are few tax-sheltered investments remaining. Banks must rely on taxable investments to meet their portfolio objectives.

This has presented both problems and opportunities. Problems generally center around the fact that many banks purchase securities without fully understanding their risk and yield features. For example, banks in the aggregate have purchased enormous amounts of mortgage-backed securities in a variety of forms. Unfortunately, these securities include a prepayment option for the mortgage borrower that makes it extremely difficult to accurately forecast both the magnitude of interest and principal payments and when they will be received. Opportunities arise with other innovative investment alternatives that have appeared, such as securities backed by car loans, leases, and credit card receivables, to further complicate the investment decision.

Furthermore, during the 1980s asset quality at commercial banks, particularly the loan portfolio, generally deteriorated, forcing banks to raise loan charge-offs. This reduced the need for tax-exempt interest, forcing many banks to cut back their demand for municipals. The net effect was twofold: the size of the investment portfolio often increased relative to loans, and portfolio managers sought out higher yields among taxable alternatives including old standbys like U.S. Treasury and agency securities as well as newer instruments such as mortgage-backed securities, corporate and foreign bonds, securities collateralized by loan receivables, and mutual funds.

This chapter examines why banks own marketable securities. It discusses trading account securities and provides an overview of the risk and return factors that influence the choice of securities in the investment portfolio. As such, it follows the discussion of interest rates and security pricing in Chapters 6 and 7. It further introduces policy guidelines that should help identify the appropriate investment decisions. Subsequent chapters describe the specific features of each type of taxable and tax-exempt security and examine the effects of recent tax laws on relative tax-exempt and taxable security yields.

Most commercial banks concentrate their asset management efforts on meeting loan customers' credit needs. Because this involves detailed credit analysis and direct negotiation of terms with borrowers, they maintain a large staff of loan officers. Managing investment securities typically plays a secondary role, especially at small banks. Banks operate as price-takers because security yields are normally determined nationally in the money and capital markets. Basic investment decisions, including what amount and type of securities to purchase, can be determined by senior management or the board of directors and implemented by a smaller staff.

The securities activities of large banks and small banks are fundamentally different. Small banks generally purchase securities and hold them until maturity. In many cases, they work with large correspondent banks in deciding which securities to buy and how many. Large banks, in contrast, not only buy securities for their own portfolios, they frequently manage a securities trading account and an underwriting subsidiary that helps municipalities issue debt in the money and capital markets. All of these activities are grouped under a single division, which is also responsible for the bank's funding and interest rate risk management. (See the discussion of transfer pricing in Chapter 13.)

Historically, bank regulators have emphasized the risks associated with owning securities. Investment policy guidelines thus focus on controlling risk within the securities portfolio. Regulators prohibit banks from purchasing common stock for income purposes and effectively limit investments in debt instruments to investment grade securities (designated as bonds rated Baa or above).[1] Maturities are often kept short to reduce price volatility and provide greater liquidity. As a result, many banks pursue passive investment portfolio management strategies, under which managers react to events, rather than active strategies in which they manage the risk and return trade-off in anticipation of economic conditions.

Interest rate deregulation and problem loans, however, have encouraged an increasing number of banks to pursue active strategies in managing investments. Bank managers now look to marketable securities to generate more interest income. Consequently, they manage their portfolio maturity and composition more aggressively

---

[1]In certain situations, such as when common stock is taken as collateral against a loan, commercial banks can own equities. They must, however, liquidate equities within a reasonable period of time. Banks can also own noninvestment-grade securities, but must show they are comparable in quality to similar investment-grade instruments.

relative to their preferred interest rate risk position. The following analysis describes the function of bank trading accounts and then outlines the objectives and structure of the investment portfolio. The final section identifies the key facets and importance of a bank's formal investment policy statement.

DEALER OPERATIONS AND THE SECURITIES TRADING ACCOUNT

Many large banks hold securities as part of a trading account. A *trading account* represents an inventory of securities that a bank holds for resale to other investors. The securities can be of any type including Treasury, agency, and municipal securities, but the bank expects to own them only briefly until a long-term buyer is found. Such securities are listed separately on a bank's balance sheet as trading account securities. The bank profits from this activity by buying the securities at prices below the sales price, which is referred to as a trading profit. For accounting purposes, trading account securities are valued at the lower of cost or market value on the balance sheet and any appreciation or depreciation in value is reported on the income statement whether realized or not. During 1990, regulators proposed that any security not held to maturity be marked to market in financial reports.

In this capacity, banks operate both as primary dealers with the Federal Reserve and as market makers with other participants. As a primary dealer, a bank (or bank subsidiary) normally buys U.S. Treasury securities at auction and in the secondary market and sells the securities to its customers. The Federal Reserve System trades only with primary dealers through its New York Bank when implementing open market purchases and sales. As market makers, banks perform the same service with U.S. Treasury, agency, and selected municipal securities, trading with all interested parties.

Banks perform three basic functions within their trading activities. First, they offer investment advice and assistance to customers managing their own portfolios. With their market expertise they can help a smaller bank determine the appropriate type of investment and select specific instruments. If a customer needs to sell a security, the banks stand willing to buy. Second, they maintain an inventory of securities for possible sale to investors. The willingness to buy and sell securities is called *making a market*. Third, traders speculate on short-term interest rate movements by taking positions in various securities.

Banks earn profits from their trading activities in several ways. When making a market, they price securities at an expected positive spread, charging a higher price (lower interest rate) on securities sold than the price paid on securities purchased. Thus a customer who contacts a bank's trading department will get two price quotes for the same instrument: a bid price reflecting what the dealer is willing to pay and an ask or offer price representing the price at which a dealer will sell. Profits arise from a positive spread between the ask minus the bid prices.

Traders can also earn profits if they correctly anticipate interest rate movements. This is accomplished by taking long (ownership) and short (borrowed) positions consistent with their expectations or by adjusting maturities on RPs. Both long and short positions are normally financed via RPs. When traders expect interest rates to decline (prices to rise), they want to own securities so they take a long position in selected instruments. In most cases, overnight financing is used so that the bank earns net interest from the spread between the yield on the asset owned and the cost of financing, as well as being able to sell the asset for a price above that initially paid. When traders expect interest rates to rise, they want to sell securities or go short (sell securities not owned) to avoid holding assets that depreciate in value. Traders typically negotiate reverse RPs to obtain securities to short and earn interest that varies daily with financing costs on the short position. The bank profits if rates rise and traders buy back the securities shorted at a lower price than that initially paid.

OBJECTIVES OF THE INVESTMENT PORTFOLIO

A bank's investment portfolio differs markedly from a trading account as investment securities are held to meet one of six general objectives:

1. safety or preservation of capital
2. liquidity
3. yield
4. diversification of credit risk
5. managing interest rate risk exposure
6. meeting pledging requirements.

Not surprisingly, securities with different return and risk features meet each objective differently so that the average portfolio is quite varied in terms of composition and price sensitivity. Banks generally hold the securities for longer periods of time so that they are valued at cost for accounting purposes on the balance sheet.[2] Periodic interest payments appear on the income statement as interest income, while any gains or losses from sale prior to maturity appear as noninterest income.

Safety or Preservation of Capital

Banks assume considerable default risk in their commercial and consumer loan portfolios. They balance this by accepting much lower default risk in their investment portfolios. Thus a primary objective is to preserve capital by purchasing securities having only a small risk of principal loss. Regulators encourage this policy by requiring that banks concentrate their holdings in investment-grade securities, or those rated Baa or higher (see Exhibit 7.8). When they buy nonrated securities, banks must maintain

---

[2]During 1990 the Securities and Exchange Commission (SEC) and Financial Accounting Standards Board (FASB) proposed that banks be required to report most of their assets and liabilities at market values in periodic financial statements. This would improve investors' and regulators' ability to evaluate the economic worth of a bank, but would add considerable volatility to reported stockholders' equity and periodic net income. While the issue has not yet been resolved, banks will likely be forced to provide much more market value data in their periodic statements.

a credit file which indicates that management periodically evaluates the borrowers' ability to meet debt service requirements, and that this ability is equivalent to an investment-grade credit.

Liquidity

Commercial banks purchase debt securities to help meet liquidity requirements. Liquidity needs are determined by unanticipated deposit outflows and unanticipated loan demand. Most banks, particularly small institutions that do not have ready access to the money and capital markets to borrow funds, must rely on securities to sell if a liquidity shortage appears. Because securities are more marketable than most commercial and consumer loans, banks often designate a portion of their investment portfolio as a liquidity reserve.

As indicated in Chapter 15, securities with maturities under 1 year can readily be sold for cash near par value and are classified as liquid investments. In reality, most securities with a market value above book value can also quickly be converted to cash, regardless of maturity. While at first glance a security's market value may not appear to affect its liquidity, in practice most banks choose not to sell securities if their market values are below book values. Their rationale is that they would have to report securities losses on the income statement, which would reduce net income and the bank's aggregate profit measures. In contrast, they are much more willing to sell securities at a gain when market values exceed book values, and thus artificially inflate periodic net income.[3]

When evaluating the potential liquidity in a bank's investment portfolio, most managers simply compare a security's current market value with its book value. If it trades at a premium, it is liquid. Consider the four securities summarized in Exhibit 16.1. As indicated, the bonds were purchased 2 to 7 years before the statement data. Because market interest rates changed significantly during the interim, the Treasury note and the State of Illinois municipal sell at a premium, while the other two sell at a discount. If the bank sold the premium bonds on September 30, 1991, it would report a gain from securities sales under noninterest income in its income statements. If the bank held the premium bonds but sold either of the discount bonds, it would report a loss from securities sales. Because securities losses lower reported net income in the short run, most banks are unwilling to sell securities at a discount. Thus liquid securities are often viewed as only those which can be sold at a gain, regardless of the remaining term to maturity, credit quality, and issue size. This again ignores the fact that low-rate, discount securities often carry an opportunity loss in the form of reduced interest income.

---

[3]The costs and benefits of selling securities for a gain versus a loss and reinvesting the proceeds are discussed in Chapter 19 in the section on security swaps. In general, selling to realize short-term gains is short-sighted because a bank sacrifices longer-term cash flow.

Exhibit 16.1 Investment Portfolio for a Hypothetical Commercial Bank

Current Date: September 30, 1991

Purchase Date	Book Value	Description	Annual Coupon Income	Market Value
12/15/89	$4,000,000	$4,000,000 par value U.S. Treasury note at 11%, due 11/15/92	$440,000	$4,099,000
10/15/89	2,000,000	$2,000,000 par value Federal National Mortgage Association bonds at 8.75%, due 10/15/04	175,000	1,824,000
3/1/89	500,000	$500,000 par value Allegheny County, PA, A-rated general obligations at 5.15%, due 3/1/00	25,750	482,500
7/1/84	1,000,000	$1,000,000 par value State of Illinois Aaa rated general obligations at 11%, due 7/1/12	110,000	1,190,000

Yield

To be attractive, investment securities must pay a reasonable return for the risks assumed. The return may come in the form of price appreciation or periodic coupon interest. It may be fully taxable or exempt from federal income taxes and/or state and local income taxes. Chapter 6 documents how yields are quoted on different types of securities, and Chapter 7 explains why yields differ across securities depending on default risk, marketability, tax treatment, maturity, and whether the securities carry call or put features. Clearly, bank managers must evaluate each security to determine whether its yield is attractive given the other features of the security and the overall profile of the bank's portfolio.

Diversify Credit Risk

The diversification objective is closely linked to the safety objective and difficulties that banks have with diversifying their loan portfolios. Too often, particularly at small banks, loans are concentrated in one industry such as agriculture, energy, or real estate, that reflects the specific economic conditions of the region. In these situations, the loan portfolio is not adequately diversified even when loans are not concentrated among single borrowers because its value will deteriorate if conditions adversely affect the industry in question. Banks view the securities portfolio as an opportunity to spread credit risk outside their geographic region and into other industries.

Help Manage Interest Rate Risk Exposure

Investment securities are very flexible instruments in managing a bank's overall interest rate risk exposure. While some are private placements by the borrower directly with a lender, as may be the case with a local municipal bond, most are standardized contracts purchased through brokers. Thus banks can select terms that meet their specific needs without fear of antagonizing the borrower. They can readily sell the security if their needs change. If management chooses to narrow the GAP in anticipation of falling rates, for example, the bank can easily and quickly lengthen the maturity or duration of its securities portfolio. Contrast this with the difficulty in adjusting commercial or consumer loan terms, or calling a loan with undesirable pricing features. As a consequence, managers change the composition and price sensitivity of the investment portfolio at the margin to achieve the desired rate sensitivity profile.

Pledging Requirements

By law, commercial banks must pledge collateral against certain types of liabilities. Banks that sell RPs essentially pledge part of its government securities portfolio against this debt. Similarly, banks that borrow at the discount window must collateralize the loan with qualifying assets. While some loans meet the collateral requirements, most banks pledge Treasury securities, which are already registered at the Federal Reserve in bookkeeping form. Finally, banks that accept public deposits must also pledge government securities against the uninsured portion of deposits. Under federal regulations, 100 percent of uninsured federal deposits must be secured with Treasury and agency obligations valued at par or with municipals valued at 80 to 90 percent of par for collateral purposes. Pledging requirements for state and local government deposits vary according to specific regulations established by each deposit holder. In many instances, the public depositor values local municipal securities above par while valuing Treasury and agency securities at less than par for collateral purposes. The intent is to increase the attractiveness of local issues to potential bank investors.

COMPOSITION OF THE INVESTMENT PORTFOLIO

A commercial bank's investment portfolio consists of many different types of instruments. Money market instruments with short maturities and durations include Treasury bills, large negotiable CDs, bankers acceptances, commercial paper, security repurchase agreements, and tax anticipation notes. Capital market instruments with longer maturities and duration include long-term U.S. Treasury securities, obligations of U.S. government agencies, obligations of state and local governments and their political subdivisions labeled municipals, mortgage-backed securities backed both by government and private guarantees, corporate bonds, and foreign bonds. At the end of 1990, banks in the aggregate owned almost $670 billion of investment securities. They also held almost $30 billion of securities in inventory for trading account purposes.

The top part of Exhibit 16.2 documents the changing composition of bank investments from 1965 through 1990 in four broad categories by issuer. There are several obvious trends. First, the investment portfolio has consistently shrunk as a fraction of total bank assets from a high of 31.1 percent in 1965 to just 20 percent in 1990. This coincides with an increase in the proportionate contribution of loans. Second, municipal securities were the dominant bank investment through 1985, after which bank

Exhibit 16.2 Composition of U.S. Commercial Bank Investments: 1965–1990

A. All Banks Over Time[a]	Percentage of Total Assets					
	1965	**1970**	**1975**	**1980**	**1985**	**1990**
U.S. Treasury securities	17.6%	12.1%	9.8%	7.8%	8.3%	5.4%
Agency securities	1.7	2.7	3.9	4.1	3.2	8.4
Municipal securities	11.4	13.6	11.6	10.0	9.7	3.5
Corporate & foreign securities	0.4	0.6	0.9	0.5	1.0	2.7
	31.1%	29.0%	26.4%	22.4%	22.2%	20.0%
Total financial assets (billions of dollars)	$341.8	$517.4	$885.5	$1,484.6	$2,379.1	$3,356.2

B. Percentage of Total Assets, December 31, 1990[b]

	Asset Size (Millions of Dollars)						
	≤ 99	100–299	300–499	500–999	1,000–2,999	3,000–9,999	≥ 10,000
Trading account securities					0.1%	0.2%	1.0%
Investment securities							
U.S. Treasury & agency securities	22.8%	17.7%	15.3%	12.4%	13.2	10.8	8.8
Municipal securities	5.0	4.3	3.4	2.6	2.2	2.0	1.4
Other securities	2.3	2.7	2.2	2.8	2.3	2.5	2.5
	30.1%	24.7%	20.9%	17.8%	17.8%	15.5%	13.7%

[a] Source: Flow of Funds Accounts, Board of Governors of the Federal Reserve System.

[b] Source: Uniform Bank Performance Report.

holdings fell sharply. As discussed later, this reflects the impact of the Tax Reform Act of 1986, which induced banks to withdraw as investors in most municipal securities. Third, banks have slowly reduced their proportionate investment in Treasury securities over time. Finally, both agency and corporate/foreign securities increased sharply after 1985 as a fraction of total assets as banks sought out alternatives to municipals. The growth in agency securities consists primarily of mortgage-backed securities, which have far different characteristics than traditional bank investments.

The bottom part of the exhibit indicates the proportionate security holdings of different-sized banks at the end of 1990. The figures document significant differences, including the fact that the proportionate size of the investment portfolio decreases with bank size, ranging from over 30 percent of total assets at banks under $100 million to just 13.7 percent at banks over $10 billion. This is not surprising because smaller banks rely much more heavily on securities to meet liquidity needs. Money center and large regional banks routinely borrow in the money market to help meet deposit outflows and finance incremental loan demand. In addition, while U.S. Treasury and agency securities are the dominant investment for all banks, they comprise over two-thirds of the investment portfolio at small banks but just over one-half the portfolio at the largest banks. Much of this represents mortgage-backed instruments. Municipals rank second at all but the largest banks. The heavy concentration in municipals reflects the high demand for tax-exempt interest income at all banks. The ratio of municipals to total assets is greater at small banks because they do not use other means to shelter income. Large banks shelter proportionately more income via investment tax credits and accelerated depreciation generated from foreign operations and leasing activities. Other securities, including corporate and foreign bonds, comprise a similar portion of the investment portfolio at all banks. Finally, note that only banks over $1 billion operate trading accounts.

THE RISK/RETURN CHARACTERISTICS OF INVESTMENT SECURITIES

The fundamental objective of the investment portfolio is to maximize earnings while limiting risk within guidelines set by management. Earnings come in the form of both periodic interest income and capital gains or losses. Managing returns thus involves selecting the appropriate mix of taxable and tax-exempt securities, optimal maturities/durations, and the timing of purchases and sales. Portfolio risk is evidenced by deviations in actual returns from that expected. Such deviations may result from unanticipated changes in interest rates, defaults on promised interest and principal payments, and unanticipated inflation. Managing risk focuses on ensuring the safety of principal, guaranteeing access to cash to meet liquidity needs, and timing security purchases relative to the business cycle. It also involves diversifying the portfolio with different types of securities, types of issuers, and issue maturities/durations.

General Return Characteristics

Bank investments contribute to earnings in the form of periodic interest income and principal appreciation or depreciation. Most debt instruments either accrue interest at fixed rates against the principal invested with a lump sum distribution at maturity, or carry fixed coupon payments with the return of principal at final maturity. Some securities, such as Treasury bills, are purchased at a discount and pay interest in the form of principal appreciation. In recent years banks have acquired larger amounts of variable-rate securities, whose returns fluctuate with market conditions.

Chapter 6 describes how different securities generate periodic income and the nature of their associated yield calculations. It is important to note that returns vary substantially across securities. In order to accurately compare returns an analyst must know how interest accrues, the frequency of compounding, whether yields are quoted on a 360- or 365-day basis, and whether the interest is subject to taxes or is tax-exempt.

Aggregate returns are also affected by capital gains and losses on securities sold prior to final maturity. Realized principal appreciation or depreciation is reported separately under noninterest income on the income statement as a securities gain or loss. Whether securities increase or decrease in value after purchase depends on the general movement in the level of interest rates and specific features of individual securities. If market interest rates on comparable debt securities increase after purchase, the market value of fixed-rate option-free debt decreases. If comparable interest rates decrease, market value increases. Variable-rate debt instruments normally trade at prices close to maturity value because periodic interest payments change directly with the level of interest rates. The magnitude of reported gains or losses thus depends on whether portfolio managers purchase securities at interest rate peaks or troughs and whether they sell securities prior to maturity to realize principal appreciation or depreciation. Only if a bank sells securities from its portfolio will it report a securities gain or loss.

In general, bank managers are reluctant to report securities losses, even in the face of superior reinvestment opportunities. Securities losses directly lower reported profits and, in the near term, earnings may appear depressed. In reality, market values are low because interest rates on comparable securities are higher than when the securities owned were originally purchased. By not selling low-rate instruments, banks accept the opportunity loss of higher interest income over future reporting periods. Management substitutes reduced net interest income for not reporting securities losses, even though the bank may gain by improving its current cash flow and later profits. Chapter 19 demonstrates that there are often substantial long-term benefits from selling securities at a loss and reinvesting the proceeds, while long-term losses are typically associated with selling for a near-term gain.

General Risk Characteristics

Portfolio managers attempt to maximize returns while controlling risk, which is evidenced by variations in cash inflows. The real concern, however, is that actual returns will fall short of expected returns. Expected returns reflect promised interest and principal payments, a real rate of return after inflation, and potential returns available when interest rates fluctuate. Specific risk factors are discussed briefly in the following sections.

Credit Risk. Credit risk is the potential variability in returns resulting from debt issuers not making promised principal and interest payments. Such nonpayment is normally caused by a deterioration in general economic conditions. Because most banks concentrate their investments in federal or state and local government securities, actual defaults occur infrequently. Still, banks purchase some corporate and foreign bonds for which nonpayment is a real possibility, and municipal borrowers occasionally default because of deficient revenues supporting the bonds.

Most banks do not directly analyze the probability of timely repayment attributable to potential default for different corporate and municipal securities. Instead they rely on quality assessments provided by private agencies, such as Standard & Poor's Corp. and Moody's Investors Service. Ratings are based on a corporation's financial condition, demographic trends, the local economic base, and the tax and borrowing powers of issuers. Exhibit 7.8 in Chapter 7 summarizes the various ratings provided by Standard & Poor's and Moody's for municipal bonds. The lowest risk Aaa-rated securities offer the lowest promised yields, while noninvestment grade securities offer the highest promised yields.

Regulators strongly encourage banks to restrict their investments to the four top categories, which are labeled investment grade securities. Many securities are not rated, usually because the issuer is small and unwilling to pay the required fees. In some cases the issuer can place its debt privately with a local institution. Regulators permit banks to purchase these nonrated securities, but the banks must maintain a credit file on the issuer and be able to demonstrate the economic soundness of the investment. Sound investments require the same detailed credit analysis normally associated with commercial loans.

Purchasing Power Risk. Purchasing power risk refers to the potential variability in returns caused by unanticipated changes in inflation. It arises when actual inflation does not equal expected inflation. Investors who buy fixed-rate securities lose purchasing power when the actual inflation rate exceeds the after-tax expected rate of return from interest and principal payments. They have deferred consumption expenditures by purchasing securities, yet their realized return buys less when it is actually received. Accordingly, banks as investors should require a nominal after-tax return on investments that exceeds the expected inflation rate. Purchasing power risk at banks is mitigated by the intermediation function. As long as depositors' inflation expectations are identical to bank management's, both asset yields and interest costs of liabilities incorporate the same inflation premiums. Inflation poses serious problems to a bank when its inflation expectations are below those of its depositors and actual inflation is high. In this instance, a bank is willing to accept lower yields on its investments (a smaller spread) relative to its deposit rates. Higher than expected inflation reduces the spread even more, and the bank's profitability worsens.

Interest Rate Risk. Interest rate risk in the investment portfolio is the potential variability in returns caused by changes in the level of interest rates. Interest rate changes affect returns in two ways. First, the market value of outstanding debt changes in the opposite direction from interest rate changes on comparable securities. As demonstrated in Chapter 6, the market value of fixed-rate debt securities decreases when interest rates increase, and vice versa. Second, investors are subject to reinvestment risk on securities that make periodic coupon payments. If the level of interest rates decreases, for example, an investor must reinvest the coupon payments at lower rates over the life of the security to maintain the same quality of investment.

These two facets of interest rate risk are embodied in the concepts of duration and convexity, which signify the overall price sensitivity of a security to changing interest rates. In general, the longer is duration, the greater is the percentage fluctuation in a security's market value for a given change in interest rates. A security's duration is in turn closely linked to its coupon rate. Zero coupon securities that pay no periodic interest have a duration equal to final maturity, while coupon-bearing securities have a duration less than maturity. Thus a 5-year maturity bond that pays semiannual interest at 4 percent (8 percent annually) will have a shorter duration than a 5-year zero coupon security paying 4 percent semiannually. There is no reinvestment risk with the zero coupon security because there are no interim cash flows that must be reinvested. In general, high-coupon securities have relatively short durations while low-coupon securities have longer durations. Thus high-coupon securities exhibit relatively stable prices compared with otherwise similar low-coupon securities.

Exhibit 16.3 demonstrates the general price sensitivity of bonds with the same final maturity but different-sized periodic payments. The vertical axis measures the percentage price change on various securities when interest rates rise by 2 percent and fall by 2 percent, respectively. The securities are positioned from highest coupon (high-coupon corporate bond) to lowest coupon (zero coupon Treasury bond). Regardless of the direction of rate changes, low-coupon instruments change proportionately more in price than high-coupon instruments for a given change in interest rates.

In most cases, the variation in return caused by securities gains or losses is at least partially offset by the variation in reinvestment returns. If, for example, interest rates increase and the portfolio manager sells bonds at less than cost, part of the loss can be recovered by reinvesting the proceeds and future coupon payments at the higher rates. The opposite occurs when rates decrease and investors sell securities at a gain. Part of the gain is lost because reinvestment income drops with the lower rates. Thus price risk and reinvestment risk must be viewed jointly. If desired, portfolio managers can "immunize" their portfolios through the use of duration analysis.[4] This is accomplished by acquiring securities with a combined duration equal to the bank's planned holding period. If the bank holds the securities as planned, changes in interest rates will not affect the portfolio's planned return because price changes will be exactly offset by changes in reinvestment income. Of course, a bank with an immunized portfolio will not realize speculative gains.

Securities with imbedded options, such as call and put features, may exhibit substantially different price sensitivity than option-free securities. Mortgage-backed securities, for example, may vary widely in price due to sharp swings in mortgage prepayments as a result of rising or falling interest rates. In essence the securities' durations may change substantially when interest rates change so that the relative price sensitivity varies widely with rate movements. The concept of convexity is used to characterize these variations in duration. It is applied to mortgage-backed securities in Chapter 17.

Liquidity Risk. Some securities cannot easily be traded prior to maturity. This may occur because the security is small in size and nonrated. To induce another investor to buy it, the owner may have to reduce the price substantially. The risk of potential variability in returns caused by this lack of marketability represents a component of liquidity risk.

Liquidity risk is also affected by pledging requirements that limit the pool of securities banks can sell to obtain cash. In most cases, pledged securities are held by a third-party trustee. Banks must substitute other collateral before selling a pledged security. For this reason, banks normally pledge securities they intend to hold for long

---

[4]Chapter 6 introduces Macaulay's duration and Chapter 8 applies it to managing a bank's total balance sheet. The duration concept can be applied to the investment portfolio alone. See Bierwag, Kaufman, and Toevs (1983) for a discussion and applications.

Exhibit 16.3 The Impact of Interest Rate Changes on Fixed-Rate Option-free Bond Prices

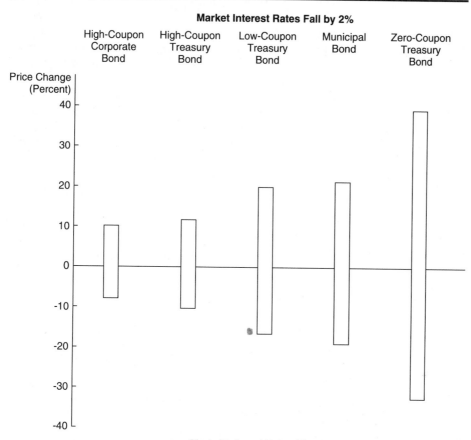

All bonds have the same final maturity. For a given change in interest rates, low-coupon securities change proportionately more in price than high-coupon securities with the same final maturity.

periods. The key point, however, is that any pledged security is illiquid over the near term.

Regulatory Guidelines

Bank investments differ markedly in their risk/return features. Regulators attempt to limit the range of options by specifying what securities qualify as investments and conducting periodic examinations. They examine three classes of securities for banks that are members of the Federal Reserve System.

Type I securities include U.S. Treasury, federal agency, and general obligation municipal obligations, which presumably carry the lowest default risk. Banks can own unlimited quantities of these securities and underwrite new issues or make a market in outstanding obligations. Type II securities consist of obligations issued by quasi-public federal and municipal agencies such as the International Bank for Reconstruction and Development, the Tennessee Valley Authority, and selected state agencies associated with housing and general university projects. The amount owned from any single issuer is limited to 15 percent of a bank's capital plus surplus. In addition, banks can underwrite and deal in these obligations. Type III securities include all other investment-grade equivalent obligations. While there is no specific restriction to a BBB/Baa or better rating, this grouping is normally followed. Banks can invest only 10 percent of capital and surplus in any single issue and are not allowed to underwrite or deal in these securities. As indicated in Exhibit 16.2, banks concentrate their Type III investments in municipal bonds.

Regulators do not restrict banks in their maturity choices. Banks are required, however, to understand their overall interest rate risk position as part of the regular examination process. Different securities are affected by different credit and liquidity factors.

ESTABLISHING INVESTMENT POLICY GUIDELINES

Each bank's asset and liability management committee (ALCO) is responsible for establishing investment policy guidelines. These guidelines define the parameters within which investment decisions help meet overall return and risk objectives. Because securities are impersonal loans that are easily bought and sold, they can be used at the margin to achieve a bank's liquidity, credit risk, and funding GAP or duration gap targets. Investment guidelines identify specific goals and constraints regarding the composition of investments, preferred maturities, quality ratings, pledging requirements, and strategies underlying any portfolio adjustments.

Return Objectives

A bank's ALCO policy statement specifies overall return objectives in terms of return on equity, return on assets, and net interest margin. Investment policy guidelines complement this by identifying what portion of interest income should be generated by securities. In particular, they establish targets for the contribution of both taxable interest and tax-exempt interest to net income. Guidelines also outline the potential costs and benefits of taking tax losses or gains on security sales. Guidelines assume that the bank has an interest rate forecast and structures its portfolio to take advantage of rate changes.

Portfolio Composition

Investment guidelines concerning portfolio composition directly address the bank's targeted liquidity, credit risk, and interest rate risk position. The guidelines generally specify 1) what types of securities can be purchased, 2) what credit ratings are acceptable, 3) what maturity range is acceptable at different stages of the interest rate cycle, and 4) which securities should be pledged as collateral against public deposits. Examples of areas for specific guidelines follow.

Liquidity Considerations

1. What volume of federal funds transactions is desirable?
2. To what financial institutions should the bank sell federal funds and purchase security RPs?
3. Which Treasury, agency, or municipal securities should the bank pledge as collateral?
4. What amount of short-term securities (under 1 year) should be held as a potential liquidity reserve?
5. With which banks or securities dealers should the bank establish a trading relationship?

Credit Risk Considerations

1. What amount of municipal, corporate, and foreign securities is optimal?
2. How much (what percentage) should the bank hold in each of the top four rating categories?
3. What is the maximum amount that can be invested in any one issuer's securities?
4. What information should credit files for nonrated municipals and all corporate bonds contain?
5. Which issuer's securities should be avoided?
6. Should the bank purchase insured municipals?

Interest Rate Risk Considerations

1. What maturity distribution of Treasuries, agencies, and municipals (separately) is desired?
2. What duration characteristics are desirable?
3. What planned holding period is desirable?
4. To what extent should the bank purchase discount (or zero coupon) securities?
5. What prepayment probabilities are associated with specific mortgage-backed securities?
6. What is the convexity of specific mortgage-backed securities and how does it vary according to the underlying coupon rate on the mortgages?

GENERAL PORTFOLIO CONSIDERATIONS

Investment policies must be flexible because no bank can exactly forecast its operating environment. Interest rates rise and fall, the yield curve changes shape, loan demand fluctuates, and the risk features of securities change when issuers' economic circumstances improve or deteriorate. A bank should establish guidelines that specify what and when portfolio adjustments are appropriate. Adjustments normally take the form of lengthening or shortening acceptable maturities, swapping securities, and security sales. Chapter 19 examines these adjustment strategies in detail. The following items influence each portfolio decision.

Optimum Size of the Loan Portfolio

Most bankers consider meeting the credit needs of businesses and individuals within risk guidelines the most important part of asset management. Thus considerable effort is directed at determining the optimal size of the loan portfolio. Obvious factors that influence the decision include international, national, and regional economic conditions, seasonality of loan demand, local demographic trends characterizing population growth and new business formation, and specific risks and returns associated with individual credits. Decisions regarding how much to invest in securities and what specific instruments to buy typically follow credit decisions.

The issue is often couched in terms of the optimum loan-to-deposit ratio. Deposits presumably measure the stable source of bank funds which can support loans. The greater are loans as a fraction of deposits, the greater is the presumed default risk of assets and the greater is liquidity risk. Aggressive banks in high-growth areas frequently report loan-to-deposit ratios above 100 percent. Obviously, a high ratio indicates that a bank will own proportionately fewer securities. In addition, however, the composition of securities will reflect the presumed riskiness of loans as banks with high loan-to-deposit ratios will generally hold more shorter-term and higher-rated securities to balance overall risk.

Stability of Deposits

The stability of a bank's deposits affects the investment portfolio by raising or lowering liquidity risk. A bank with a large amount of stable core deposits does not experience the same unanticipated deposit outflows as a bank with fewer core deposits. The more stable is the deposit base, the less management has to rely on securities to meet liquidity needs. Such a bank can make more loans, hold longer-duration securities, and potentially hold lower rated (Aa to Baa) investment-grade securities in search of higher promised yields.

Optimal Federal Funds Position

As indicated in Chapter 11, federal funds refer to immediately available funds (certain collected deposits) at Federal Reserve Banks and financial institutions. Banks buy and sell federal funds as part of managing their reserve positions. The transactions usually involve overnight loans in some multiple of $1 million. Large banks typically borrow federal funds from smaller banks as a permanent source of financing. Small banks in turn lend federal funds to earn interest on otherwise idle balances.

Two aspects of a bank's federal funds position affect the investment portfolio: whether the bank borrows or lends federal funds, and the size of the position. Lenders (federal funds sold) actually treat the loans as short-term investments. It is the ultimate rate-sensitive asset that reprices daily. When the federal funds rate rises, interest income rises, and when the rate falls, interest income falls. Thus during tight money periods, sellers of federal funds do quite well. This was evidenced from 1979–1981 as many small banks earned considerable interest by selling federal funds to large banks when the federal funds rate varied from 17 percent to 22 percent. Not surprisingly, when rates were high many small banks held large fed funds sold positions. Borrowers in turn view federal funds purchased as volatile funds that can disappear quickly. Banks with a large exposure often reduce the risk of their securities portfolio by holding highly liquid, high-rated instruments that can readily be sold to obtain cash. The essential point is that banks should use the investment portfolio to balance the bank's overall risk and return profile.

Capital Requirements

Risk-based capital standards require different amounts of equity and total capital in support of different bank assets.[5] Because loans generally require more capital backing than do securities, the standards impart a bias for banks to increase their securities portfolios at the expense of loans. The preferential treatment of certain "low risk class" securities in turn induces banks to direct a greater share of their investments to these instruments. Thus banks have purchased large amounts of government-guaranteed mortgage-backed securities that require only 20 percent capital backing. In general, capital requirements influence the allocation of bank investments because banks operate as price takers and cannot independently raise security yields to offset the higher capital requirements.

SUMMARY

Bank investment activities consist of two distinct functions. Large banking organizations manage trading accounts in which they offer investment advice to other market participants, make a market in government securities, and speculatively trade instruments in the short run to take advantage of perceived changes in interest rates. All banks, regardless of size, also own marketable securities for their own portfolios and generate substantial interest income that supplements earnings from their loan portfolios.

---

[5]Chapter 12 documents the specific risk classifications for different bank assets. It is sufficient to note here that Treasury securities are in the zero risk class, while other government-guaranteed securities are in the 20 percent risk class. Municipal revenue bonds are in the 50 percent risk class.

Historically, commercial banks were the dominant investors in municipal securities. They also owned large amounts of U.S. Treasury and agency securities. With the Tax Reform Act of 1986 banks shifted the composition of investments more toward mortgage-backed and straight corporate securities. This chapter examines the general risk and return features of different instruments and general policy guidelines for assessing their liquidity, credit, and interest rate risk characteristics.

Questions

Introduction

1. Why do banks own marketable securities? Why do they differentiate between securities held in trading accounts and those held in an investment portfolio?

2. How do the marketable securities policies of small banks differ from those of large banks? Why do they differ? What is the effect of each policy on the banks' profits and risks?

3. What two types of securities are banks prohibited by bank regulators from holding?

Trading Account

4. What two changes in the banking environment led to the development of trading accounts? How do these accounts differ from traditional investment portfolios?

5. Describe three ways a bank makes a profit with its trading account. What are the risks? How do banks account for trading account securities?

Objectives

6. What are the six objectives of a bank's investment portfolio? How do investments satisfy each of these objectives?

7. Only two of the six objectives of the investment portfolio are not risk avoidance considerations—which two? Are these more or less important than the other four?

8. Explain why bank managers are reluctant to sell securities that involve a capital loss. What is one advantage and one disadvantage of only selling securities with capital gains? What is the cost of holding securities that are trading at a discount?

Composition of the Portfolio

9. Identify three trends in the investment portfolio and explain the driving force behind each.

Risk and Return

10. For the investment portfolio, what is one advantage and one disadvantage of variable-rate securities over fixed-rate securities?

11. How do banks judge the credit risks of their investments? What agencies help them?

12. What is purchasing power risk? Is it higher when inflation is steadily high or when inflation fluctuates between high and low?

13. You overhear an investor say, "Fortunately reinvestment risk offset the devastating effect of interest rate risk in my portfolio." Define the two types of risk. Explain how each would affect the value of a 5-year 8 percent coupon bond.

14. Give an example of a security for which interest rate risk and reinvestment risk might both work to the detriment of the investor.

15. Explain the three types of securities defined by the Federal Reserve. What limitations and opportunities does the Fed offer for each type?

Investment Policy

16. What group within the bank sets investment policy? What issues does the policy address?

17. Explain how a bank's loan-to-deposit ratio is likely to affect both the size and composition of its investment portfolio.

18. Large banks often borrow heavily in the federal funds market and maintain small investment portfolios. Are these offsetting risk positions? Why do large banks organize themselves this way?

19. Under currently instituted rules, how do regulators influence the level and risk of banks' investment portfolios?

Activities

20. Check the annual report of a local bank and determine if the bank
   a. operates a trading account,
   b. has recently recognized security gains or losses,
   c. invests in municipal securities,
   d. has a safe or risky investment portfolio, compared to the ratios in Exhibit 16.2.

21. Check the tombstone advertisements in *The Wall Street Journal* and analyze the price/yield characteristics of recent agency, corporate, and municipal securities.

References

Aberth, John. "Searching for an Investment Strategy." *ABA Banking Journal* (July 1988).

Berquist, Lizbeth. "Trends in Investment Portfolio Management." *Bank Management* (January 1991).

Bierwag, George, George Kaufman, and Alden Toevs. "Duration: Its Development and Use in Bond Portfolio Management." *Financial Analysts Journal* (July–August 1983).

Clark, Daniel. "A Farewell to Municipals and Other Tax Effects." *ABA Banking Journal* (February 1987).

Cook, Timothy, and Timothy Rowe, eds. *Instruments of the Money Market*, Chapters 7, 8, 11. Richmond, Va.: Federal Reserve Bank of Richmond, 1986.

Fortune, Peter. "An Assessment of Financial Market Volatility: Bills, Bonds, and Stocks." *New England Economic Review* (Federal Reserve Bank of Boston, November/December 1989).

Hempel, George, ed. *The Impact of Increased Insurance on Public Deposits.* Washington, D.C.: Advisory Commission on Intergovernmental Relations, 1977.

Hoffland, David. "A Model Bank Investment Policy." *Financial Analysts Journal* (May–June 1978).

Hueglin, Steven, and Karyn Ward. *Guide to State and Local Taxation of Municipal Bonds.* New York: Gabriele, Hueglin, and Cashman, 1981.

Kidwell, David, and Timothy Koch. "State and Local Government Financing." In *Handbook of Modern Finance*, edited by Dennis Logue. New York: Warren, Gorham & Lamont, 1984.

Lumpkin, Stephen. "Repurchase and Reverse Repurchase Agreements." *Economic Review* (Federal Reserve Bank of Richmond, January/February 1987).

McEnally, Richard. "Duration as a Practical Tool for Bond Management." *Journal of Portfolio Management* (Summer 1977).

Moran, Michael, "The Federally Sponsored Credit Agencies." In *Instruments of the Money Market*, edited by Timothy Cook and Timothy Rowe. Richmond, Va.: Federal Reserve Bank of Richmond, 1986.

Naylor, Bartlett. "Minimum Tax Will Put Banks on the Horns of a Dilemma." *American Banker* (August 27, 1986).

Syron, Richard, and Sheila Tschinkel. "The Government Securities Market: Playing Field for Repos." *Economic Review* (Federal Reserve Bank of Atlanta, September 1985).

Van Horne, James. *Financial Market Rates and Flows.* Englewood Cliffs, N.J.: Prentice-Hall, 1990.

Walter, John. "Short-Term Municipal Securities." *Economic Review* (Federal Reserve Bank of Richmond, November–December 1986).

Chapter 17

Taxable Securities

The Tax Reform Act of 1986 turned the world of bank investments upside down. Previously, municipals comprised from 40 percent to 60 percent of security holdings. Because banks could no longer deduct interest expense used to finance most municipals, they were forced to find substitute investments. In addition, banks were allowed to buy mutual funds for the first time. Many banks simply added to their Treasury and U.S. agency security holdings. Others aggressively sought out the higher yields promised on mortgage-backed securities, corporate bonds, and other asset-backed securities. With no history of investing in these instruments, banks often purchased securities without a clear understanding of their risk and return features.

Many banks, for example, acquired mortgage backed securities without any understanding of prepayment risk associated with the underlying mortgages. While banks believed the securities had effective maturities of 10 to 12 years, they often had much shorter lives. This dramatically altered the cash flow characteristics of the securities so that their market prices fluctuated widely from that expected.

The objective of this chapter is to introduce the specific characteristics of taxable investment instruments that banks hold in portfolio. The term taxable refers to the fact that interest income is subject to federal income tax. Importantly, some securities pay interest that is exempt from state and local income taxes, which is addressed in Chapter 18. The analysis begins with a description of the risk and return features of popular money market instruments. The latter parts examine the characteristics of capital market instruments. The reader should be able to differentiate between the specific risks associated with each security and the comparative promised returns. Because market participants commonly use a wide range of acronyms and abbreviations to label securities and transactions, important terminology is presented in Exhibit 17.1.

Exhibit 17.1 Important Terminology

ARM: Adjustable rate mortgage—a mortgage in which the contractual interest rate is tied to some index of interest rates and changes when supply and demand conditions change the underlying index.

CD: Certificate of deposit—a large negotiable time deposit issued by a financial institution.

CMO: Collateralized mortgage obligation—a security backed by a pool of mortgages, which is structured to fall within an estimated maturity range (tranche) based on the timing of allocated interest and principal payments on the underlying mortgages.

Conventional mortgage: A mortgage or deed of trust that is not obtained under a government-insured program.

FHA: Federal Housing Administration—a federal agency that insures mortgages.

FHLMC: Federal Home Loan Mortgage Corporation (Freddie Mac)—a private corporation operating with an implicit federal guarantee that buys mortgages, financed largely by mortgage-backed securities.

FNMA: Federal National Mortgage Association (Fannie Mae)—A private corporation operating with an implicit federal guarantee that buys mortgages, financed by mortgage-backed securities.

GNMA: Government National Mortgage Association (Ginnie Mae)—a government entity that buys mortgages for low-income housing and guarantees mortgage-backed securities issued by private lenders.

IO: Interest-only security representing the interest portion of a stripped Treasury or stripped mortgage-backed security.

MBS: Mortgage-backed security—a security that evidences an undivided interest in the ownership of a pool of mortgages.

PAC: Planned amortization class CMO—a security that is retired according to a planned amortization schedule, while payments to other classes of securities are slowed or accelerated. The objective is to ensure that PACs exhibit highly predictable maturities and cash flows.

PO: Principal-only security representing the principal portion of a stripped Treasury or stripped mortgage-backed security.

RP: Repurchase agreement (Repo)—an agreement by one party to buy back, under certain terms, the item that is originally sold to a second party. The underlying item is generally a U.S. Treasury, agency, or mortgage-backed security.

Tranche: The principal amount related to a specific class of stated maturities on a collateralized mortgage obligation.

VA: Veterans Administration—a federal agency that insures mortgages.

Z-Tranche: The final class of securities in a CMO exhibiting the longest maturity and greatest price volatility. These securities often accrue interest until all other classes are retired.

TAXABLE MONEY MARKET INVESTMENTS

In order to meet liquidity and pledging requirements and earn a reasonable return, banks hold significant amounts of government and corporate securities that mature within 1 year and thus are labeled money market instruments. Most are highly liquid because they are issued by well-known borrowers and a deep secondary market exists. An investor must be careful, however, because the quoted yields are calculated in a variety of ways that make yield comparisons confusing. Chapter 6 describes the specific yield calculations for different securities.

Repurchase Agreements

Repurchase agreements (RPs or Repos) involve a loan between two parties, with one typically either a securities dealer or a commercial bank. The lender or investor buys securities from the borrower, and simultaneously agrees to sell the securities back at a later date at an agreed-upon price plus interest. The transaction essentially represents a short-term loan collateralized by the securities because the borrower receives the principal in the form of immediately available funds, while the lender earns interest on the investment. If the borrower defaults, the lender gets title to the securities.

Consider an overnight RP transaction for $1 million at 7.6 percent between a bank as lender and a foreign government as borrower. RP rates are quoted on an add-on basis assuming a 360-day year. The bank would book an asset, securities purchased under agreement to resell, and would lose deposit balances held at the Fed equal to $1 million. After one day the transaction would reverse so that deposit balances would rise by $1 million and the RP loan would disappear, plus the foreign government would pay the bank $211.11 in interest.

$$\text{Interest} = \$1,000,000 \times (.076 / 360) = \$211.11 \qquad \textbf{(17.1)}$$

If the foreign government defaults, the bank retains the securities as collateral on the loan. This transaction is technically labeled a reverse RP to a bank because it is the lender while another party is the borrower. In a regular repurchase agreement a bank or securities dealer sells securities under an agreement to repurchase at a later date, and thus represents the borrower. Every RP transaction involves both a regular RP and reverse RP depending on whether it is viewed from the lender's or borrower's perspective.[1]

Banks operate on both sides of the RP market as borrowers and lenders. While any securities can serve as collateral, most RPs involve Treasury or U.S. agency securities. Typically, small banks lend funds aggressively in the RP market because they operate their reserves position more conservatively with positive excess reserves, and own proportionately more of the securities used as collateral. Every RP transaction is negotiated separately between parties. The minimum denomination is generally $1 million, with maturities ranging from 1 day to 1 year. The rate on 1-day RPs is referred to as the *overnight RP rate,* which plays an important role in arbitrage transactions associated with financial futures and options. Longer-term transactions are referred to as *term RPs* and the associated rate the *term RP rate.* The RP rate varies from 15 to 50 basis points below the comparable federal funds rate because RP transactions are secured.

Treasury Bills

At the end of 1990, commercial banks owned approximately $200 billion in securities issued directly by the U.S. Treasury—8.5 percent of total Treasury securities outstanding. While no precise breakdown is available, commercial banks are significant investors both in short-term Treasury bills and longer-term Treasury notes and bonds. Banks find Treasuries attractive because they pay market rates of interest, are free of default risk, and can easily be sold in the secondary market. Because they are

---

[1]Market terminology for RP transactions is viewed from the perspective of the Federal Reserve's relationship with securities dealers or banks. Reverse RPs are formally labeled matched sales-purchase agreements because they involve the Fed initially selling securities to banks or securities dealers to contract the reserve base, then buying them back.

default-risk-free, Treasury securities pay a lower pretax yield than otherwise comparable taxable securities. They do, however, carry a tax advantage: all interest is subject to federal income taxes but exempt from state and local income taxes. This raises the effective return relative to fully taxable securities. In addition, the primary and secondary market for Treasury instruments is very competitive. Dealers keep bid-ask spreads low and maintain substantial inventories. This ease of purchase and sale lowers transactions costs and makes Treasuries highly liquid.

Treasury bills are marketable obligations of the U.S. Treasury that carry original maturities of 1 year or less. They exist only in book-entry form, with the investor simply holding a dated receipt. Treasury bills are discount instruments, and the entire return is represented by price appreciation as maturity approaches. Investors can purchase bills in denominations as small as $10,000, but most transactions involve much larger amounts.

Each week the Treasury auctions bills with 13-week and 26-week maturities. Investors submit either competitive or noncompetitive bids. With a competitive bid, the purchaser indicates the maturity amount of bills desired and the discount price offered. Noncompetitive bidders indicate only how much they want to acquire. They agree to pay the average price posted for all competitive offers that the Treasury accepts but are limited to no more than $500,000 in maturity value. The auctions are closed in that sealed bids must be submitted by 1:30 p.m. each Monday, the normal sale date. The Treasury accepts all noncompetitive bids. It then ranks the competitive bids from the highest discounted price offered to the lowest price and accepts bids until the desired financing objective is met. Noncompetitive bidders then pay the average price of the accepted competitive bids. Exhibit 17.2 documents the auction results for the April 2, 1991 Treasury auction. On this date, the Treasury sold over $18 billion in T-bills at an average rate of 5.80 percent for 13-week bills and 5.79 percent for 26-week bills. Just 16 percent of the accepted bids were noncompetitive. Similar auctions occur monthly for 52-week bills. Occasionally, the Treasury offers cash management bills with maturities under 18 weeks that supplement the regular bill offerings.

Banks participate in the auction process in two ways: by buying bills directly for their own portfolios or by buying bills for inventory in their securities trading activity. Treasury bills are purchased on a discount basis so that the investor's income equals price appreciation. As with most money market yields, the Treasury bill discount rate is quoted in terms of a 360-day year, as indicated below:

$$dr = \frac{FV - P}{FV}(360/n) \qquad (17.2)$$

where

dr = discount rate
FV = dollar amount of face value
P = dollar purchase price, and
n = number of days to maturity.

**Exhibit 17.2 Results of the April 2, 1991 Auction for
13-Week and 26-Week Treasury Bills**

Rates are determined by the difference between the purchase price and face value. Thus, higher bidding narrows the investor's return while lower bidding widens it. The percentage rates are calculated on a 360-day year, while the coupon equivalent yield is based on a 366-day year.

	13-Week	26-Week
Applications	$25,311,500,000	$23,525,765,000
Accepted bids	$7,637,655,000	$7,612,095,000
Accepted at low price	53%	70%
Accepted noncompet'ly	$1,679,215,000	$1,280,365,000
Average price (Rate)	98.518 (5.80%)	97.073 (5.79%)
High price (Rate)	98.523 (5.78%)	97.083 (5.77%)
Low price (Rate)	98.518 (5.80%)	97.073 (5.79%)
Coupon equivalent	5.98%	6.06%
CUSIP number	912794WR1	912794XH2

Both issues are dated April 4, 1991. The 13-week bills mature July 5, 1991, and the 26-week bills mature Oct. 3, 1991.

Source: *The Wall Street Journal.*

For example, a bank that purchases $1 million in face value of a 26-week (182-day) bill at $970,730, the low auction price in Exhibit 17.2, earns a discount yield of 5.79 percent.[2]

$$dr = \frac{\$1,000,000 - \$970,730}{\$1,000,000}(360/182)$$
$$= 0.0579$$

The bank reports interest of $29,270 over the 182 days if the bill is redeemed at maturity. The bank includes this interest as taxable income for federal income tax purposes but omits it where state and local income taxes apply.

Treasury bills are attractive investments to banks because they are low risk, earn interest that fluctuates with market conditions, and can be used to meet pledging requirements. Panel A of Exhibit 17.3 plots movements in selected money market rates for 1989 and 1990. Note that T-bill rates are below rates on other money market instruments of the same maturity because of the lower risk. All of these rates respond quickly to changes in economic conditions, generally falling during recessions and

---

[2]Alternatively, a known discount rate produces a purchase price (P):

$$P = FV\left[1 - dr\left(\frac{n}{360}\right)\right]$$

The discount rate (dr) understates the true percentage yield to an investor. The *Wall Street Journal* publishes a bond-equivalent yield for Treasury bills at each auction, calculated in terms of Equation (17.2), but instead compares the dollar return to the actual purchase price and uses a 365-day year. (366 days for leap years.) The coupon-equivalent rate (cer) for the 182-day bills in this example (366-day leap year) equals 6.06 percent.

$$cer = \frac{\$1,000,000 - \$970,730}{\$970,730}\left[\frac{366}{182}\right] = 0.0606$$

The true (effective) yield is even greater, calculated generally as

$$\text{Effective yield} = \left[1 + \frac{(FV - P)}{P}\right]^{366/k} - 1$$

where k = the number of days until maturity. In this example, the effective yield equals 6.15 percent.

Exhibit 17.3 Selected Money and Capital Market Interest Rates: 1989–1990

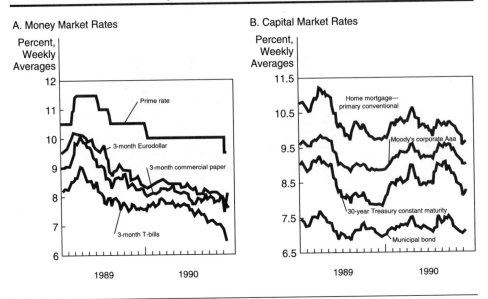

Source: Board of Governors of the Federal Reserve System, Federal Reserve Statistical Release H. 15. December 31, 1990.

rising during the high-growth stage of the business cycle. Banks also use T-bills to pledge as collateral against RPs, borrowing from the Fed, and public deposits.

CDs and Eurodollars

Many commercial banks, particularly smaller institutions, buy negotiable certificates of deposit (CDs) and Eurodollars issued by other commercial banks. Domestic CDs are dollar-denominated deposits issued by U.S. banks in the United States with fixed maturities ranging from 14 days to several years. They are attractive because they pay yields above Treasury bills and, if issued by a well-known bank, can easily be sold in the secondary market prior to maturity. As with federal funds, interest is quoted on an add-on basis assuming a 360-day year. Eurodollars are dollar-denominated deposits issued by foreign branches of banks outside the United States. Because only the largest banks can tap this market, the secondary market is quite deep. The Eurodollar market is less regulated than the domestic market so that the perceived riskiness is greater. Eurodollar rates thus exceed domestic CD rates for comparable banks.

Investing banks can choose from a variety of CDs in terms of yield characteristics and issuer. While most CDs pay fixed rates to term, some carry floating rates that are pegged to an index such as LIBOR or a commercial paper rate. An investor commits the funds for up to 5 years but the rate is reset periodically according to a preestablished formula. For example, a floating-rate CD may carry a rate equal to the prevailing 3-month commercial paper rate plus 50 basis points with interest paid quarterly, at which time the rate is reset. Two other CDs that pay above-average rates are *Yankee CDs* and *Asian Dollar CDs*. Yankee CDs are dollar-denominated deposits issued by branches of foreign banks in the United States, while Asian Dollar CDs are issued by banks located in Singapore that pay interest in dollars that varies with the Singapore interbank offer rate (SIBOR) as an index. Even though the issuers are well-known institutions, investors demand a risk premium over rates paid by the safest domestic institutions.

Commercial Paper

Commercial paper refers to unsecured promissory notes issued by corporations. Most firms use the proceeds to finance short-term working capital needs. Because these instruments are neither insured nor backed by collateral, the issuers are presumably the highest-quality firms. During recent years, however, several commercial issues have defaulted. In fact, the market is extremely sensitive to deterioration in any well-known borrower's financial condition. When a large firm is known to be in distress, such as Citicorp in 1990, virtually all issuers of new commercial paper must pay a substantial premium over T-bills to place their debt regardless of their financial condition.[3] Today, most commercial paper is rated by several rating agencies to help investors gauge default risk. Issuers also typically obtain an irrevocable letter of credit from a bank that guarantees payment in case the issuer defaults. This guarantee mitigates default risk and improves marketability. Still, most investors hold commercial paper to maturity because the secondary market is thin.

Small banks purchase large amounts of commercial paper as investments. The minimum denomination is $10,000 and maturities range from 3 to 270 days. Interest rates are fixed to term and quoted on a discount basis as with T-bills. Thus the market price is always less than face value and the entire principal plus interest is paid at maturity. The primary attraction is the yield premium over T-bills and the ability to match specific commercial paper maturities with the bank's planned holding period.

Bankers' Acceptances

According to Federal Reserve Board Regulation A, a *bankers' acceptance* is a "draft or bill of exchange . . . accepted by a bank or trust company, or a firm, company, or corporation engaged generally in the business of granting bankers' acceptance credits." In essence it is a draft drawn on a bank by a firm that either exports or imports goods and services. Chapter 26 describes in detail how a bankers' acceptance arises to assist in financing international trade.

From an investor's perspective, a bankers' acceptance is a short-term interest bearing time draft created by a high-quality bank. The acceptance has a fixed maturity ranging up to 9 months and is priced as a discount instrument like T-bills. Because

---

[3]There are two basic types of commercial paper—direct paper and dealer paper. Direct paper comprises the bulk of new commercial paper and is issued primarily by finance companies and large bank holding companies. Thus firms such as General Motors Acceptance Corp., Ford Motor Credit Corp., and the Associates Corp. along with the nation's largest bank holding companies borrow heavily in this market. Dealer paper (or industrial paper) refers to commercial paper issued primarily by nonfinancial firms through securities dealers.

default risk is relatively low, the promised rate is only slightly above the rate on a comparable-maturity T-bill. Banks find bankers' acceptances attractive investments because they exhibit low default risk, pay a premium over T-bills, and can be used as collateral against discount window borrowings.

TAXABLE CAPITAL MARKET INVESTMENTS

The largest portion of bank securities consists of instruments with original maturities greater than 1 year that are labeled capital market instruments. By regulation, banks are restricted to investment-grade securities—those rated Baa or above—and thus do not own junk bonds. The long-term taxable portfolio is consequently dominated by Treasury and U.S. agency securities, corporate and foreign bonds, and mortgage-backed securities. Each of these exhibits broadly different risk and return features.

Treasury Notes and Bonds

Treasury notes and bonds differ from Treasury bills in terms of original maturity and the form of interest payment. Notes have original maturities of 1 to 10 years. Bonds can carry any original maturity but typically are issued to mature well beyond 10 years. Most notes and bonds pay coupon interest semiannually. Since 1985 the Treasury has also issued zero coupon discount bonds that are comparable in form to bills. These zeros, labeled STRIPs (separate trading of registered interest and principal of securities), typically mature 20 to 30 years from origination and carry reported yields that assume semiannual compounding.

Like bills, Treasury notes and bonds are sold via closed auctions. In most cases, securities with a variety of maturities and coupon payments are sold, with buyers submitting either competitive or noncompetitive bids. The auctions normally take place every 3 months when large amounts of outstanding notes and bonds mature. The secondary market is extremely deep due to the large volume of securities outstanding, low default risk, and wide range of investors who trade these securities. Banks buy these notes and bonds in both the auction and secondary markets. They are attractive because they exhibit low default risk, are highly liquid, and pay a market return.

Unlike Treasury bill rates, yields are quoted on a coupon-bearing basis with prices expressed in thirty-seconds of a point. Each thirty-second is worth $31.25 per $1,000 face value ($1,000/32). Coupon interest is paid semiannually. For example, an investor might obtain a price quote of 96.24 on a 10 percent coupon, $10,000 par value Treasury note with exactly 2 years remaining to maturity. Interest equals 5 percent semiannually so that the investor receives four coupon payments of $500 at 6-month intervals and $10,000 principal after 2 years. The quoted price equals 96.75 percent (96 plus 24/32) of par value or $9,675. The effective pretax yield to maturity can be calculated from the present value formula presented in Chapter 6 and equals

11.87 percent.[4] Panel B in Exhibit 17.2 plots selected capital market rates in recent years. Treasury rates exceed only municipal bond rates, which are lower because interest on municipals is exempt from federal income taxes.

During recent years, many banks have purchased zero coupon Treasury securities as part of their interest rate risk management strategies. Since 1985 the U.S. Treasury has allowed any Treasury with an original maturity of at least 10 years to be "stripped" into its component interest and principal pieces and traded via the Federal Reserve wire transfer system. Each component interest or principal payment thus constitutes a separate zero coupon security and can be traded separately from the other payments.

Consider a 10-year, $1 million par value Treasury bond that pays 9 percent coupon interest or 4.5 percent semiannually ($45,000 every 6 months). This security can be stripped into 20 separate interest payments of $45,000 each and a single $1 million principal payment, or 21 separate zero coupon securities.

Time Line

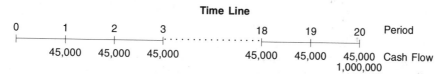

Each zero coupon security is priced by discounting the promised cash flow at the appropriate interest rate. If the market rate on the 2-year zero—fourth periodic cash flow—equals 8 percent (4 percent semiannually), the associated price of the $45,000 promised payment would equal $38,466.[5]

The primary advantage of zero coupon Treasury securities is that a bank can lock in a fixed interest payment and rate for whatever maturity is selected. The above 2-year zero, for example, would pay $45,000 at maturity, thus providing $6,534 in interest. Because there are no interim cash flows, there is no reinvestment risk and the bank can be assured of receiving its promised yield of 8 percent. In terms of interest rate risk management advantages, the Macaulay duration of zero coupon securities equals maturity so a bank can more precisely balance its GAP profile with such STRIPs.

---

[4]The yield to maturity formula follows from Equation (6.8) from Chapter 6 and can be expressed as:

$$PO = \sum_{t=1}^{n} \frac{C_t}{(1+y)^t} + \frac{P_n}{(1+y)^n}$$

where

PO = current price,
P_n = cash flow at maturity,
C_t = dollar value of the cash flow (interest payment) received in period t,
n = number of periods until the final cash flow, and
y = periodic yield to maturity.

Applied to the Treasury note, the annualized yield to maturity (y*) is determined:

$$\$9,675 = \sum_{t=1}^{4} \frac{\$500}{(1+y*/2)^t} + \frac{\$10,000}{(1+y*/2)^4} \quad \text{or}$$

$$y* = 11.87\%$$

[5]The calculator is $\dfrac{\$45,000}{(1.04)^4} = \$38,466.$

U.S. Government Agency Securities

At the end of 1990 commercial banks owned just under $300 billion in U.S. government agency securities. The bulk of these securities exhibit characteristics similar to those of U.S. Treasury securities, which is why they are attractive investments. Others, such as mortgage-backed securities, exhibit characteristics that are more comparable to corporate bonds. The wide range of mortgage-backed securities is described in the next section.

Federal agencies can be separated into two groups. Members in the first group are formally part of the federal government. As such, they obtain operating funds from the Treasury and borrow from the Federal Financing Bank, a political subdivision of the Treasury that borrows from the Treasury and lends to selected agencies. This intermediation function enables agencies to borrow at the Treasury rate but also raises total Treasury financing requirements. These agencies, including the Federal Housing Administration, Export-Import Bank, and Government National Mortgage Association (Ginnie Mae), are effectively owned by the U.S. government.

Members in the second group are *government-sponsored agencies* that are quasi-public entities. The quasi-public label represents the fact that even though the agencies are federally authorized and chartered, they are privately owned, often with publicly traded stock. They operate like any private corporation, issuing debt and acquiring assets that presumably provide revenues to cover operating expenses, pay interest and dividends, and add to capital. The U.S. government sponsors the agencies by encouraging and often subsidizing activities in favored markets such as housing and agriculture. Sponsorship also involves an implied guarantee to bail out any agency with financial problems. Government-sponsored agency issues are not direct obligations of the Treasury and thus are not backed by the Treasury's tax and credit authority. Default risk is considered low, however, because investors believe that the U.S. Congress has a moral obligation to provide financial aid in the event of problems at specific agencies. These agency issues normally carry a risk premium of 10 to 100 basis points over comparable-maturity direct Treasury obligations due to this lack of a direct guarantee. In recent years, however, certain federal agencies have experienced large operating losses and investors have dumped their securities, driving default risk premiums much higher. As an example, the farm crisis throughout the Midwest and Mideast severely strained the financial condition of the Farm Credit Banks in Omaha, Nebraska and Jackson, Mississippi to the point that they became insolvent and had to be subsidized by other government entities.

Exhibit 17.4 lists the major U.S. agencies and their status. Those specially marked are true agencies of the federal government and not sponsored. The agencies listed are generally active in the areas of housing, agriculture, education, and small business. Recently, a variety of agency securities have been offered by the Financing Corporation (FICO) and the Resolution Funding Corporation (RefCorp) to assist in the bail-out of troubled savings and loans. These agencies generally borrow in both the money and capital markets. Most money market instruments are discount securities comparable to Treasury bills. Capital market instruments are similar to Treasury notes and bonds, except that original maturities are typically shorter. They represent attractive invest-

Exhibit 17.4 Federal Status of U.S. Government Agency Securities

Agency	Full Faith and Credit of the U.S. Govt.	Authority to Borrow from the Federal Treasury	Interest on Bonds Generally Exempt from State and Local Taxes
Farm Credit System	No	Yes—$260 million revolving line of credit.	Yes
Farm Credit System Financial Assistance Corporation (FCSFAC)	Yes	Yes—FCSFAC began issuing bonds in late 1988.	Yes
Federal Home Loan Banks (FHLB)	No	Yes—the Treasury is authorized to purchase up to $4 billion of FHLB securities.	Yes
Federal Home Loan Mortgage Corporation (Freddie Mac)[a]	No	Yes—indirect line of credit through the FHLBs.	No
Federal National Mortgage Association (FNMA) (Fannie Mae)[a]	No	Yes—at FNMA request the Treasury may purchase $2.25 billion of FNMA securities	No
Financing Corporation (FICO)	No	No	Yes
Student Loan Marketing Association (Sallie Mae)	Not since 1/9/82	Yes—at its discretion the Treasury may purchase $1 billion of Sallie Mae obligations.	Yes
United States Postal Service[b]	Guarantee may be extended if Postal Service requests and Treasury determines this to be in the public interest.	Yes—the Postal Service may require the Treasury to purchase up to $2 billion of its obligations.	Yes
Resolution Funding Corporation (RefCorp)	No	No	Yes
Farmers Home Administration[b] (FmHA) CBOs	Yes	No	No
Federal Financing Bank (FFB)	Yes	Yes—FFB can require the Treasury to purchase up to $5 billion of its obligations. The Treasury Secretary is authorized to purchase any amount of FFB obligations at his discretion.	Yes
General Services Administration[b] (GSA)	Yes	No	Yes
Government National Mortgage Association[b] (GNMA)	Yes	No	No
Maritime Administration Guaranteed Ship Financing Bonds issued after 1972	Yes	No	No
Small Business Administration (SBA)	Yes	No	No, with exceptions
Tennessee Valley Authority (TVA)	No	Yes—up to $150 million.	Yes
Washington Metropolitan Area Transit Authority (WMATA) Bonds	Yes	No	No, except for states involved in the interstate compact

[a] Fully modified pass-through mortgage-backed securities and certain mortgage-backed bonds of Freddie Mac and Fannie Mae are guaranteed as to timely payment of principal and interest by Ginnie Mae.
[b] True federal agencies.

Source: *Handbook of Securities of the United Sates Government and Federal Agencies,* First Boston, 1988.

ments because of the low default risk, high marketability, and attractive yields relative to Treasury securities.

Conventional Mortgage-Backed Securities

Since passage of the Tax Reform Act of 1986 and implementation of risk-based capital standards, banks have been aggressive buyers of mortgage-backed securities (MBSs). Data for 1990 in fact indicate that these instruments comprise almost 40 percent of bank investment holdings. This is not surprising given their preferential treatment under capital regulation, where certain MBSs require no capital backing and others are in the 20-percent risk class which is below that for many other investments. Still, even though default risk might be low, mortgage-backed securities exhibit fundamentally different interest rate risk features than other investments due to mortgage prepayments. The following discussion thus focuses on the characteristics of different MBSs and the nature of prepayment risk.

In order to understand prepayment risk, it is necessary to understand the characteristics of mortgages. Formally, a mortgage is the pledge of property, typically real estate, to secure a debt. Thus a mortgage on a house represents the pledge of the house as payment for the loan in case of default by the borrower. Mortgage loans generally take the form either of fixed-rate loans where the associated interest rate is constant over the life of the loan, or adjustable-rate loans where the interest rate varies over time based on movements in market interest rates. Mortgages are typically amortized with monthly payments that include both interest and principal. A 30-year fixed-rate mortgage, for example, will have a constant monthly payment in which the portion that is interest is quite high during the early years of the loan because the outstanding loan balance is large. The interest portion declines with each successive payment as the principal remaining declines, while the principal portion rises over the life of the loan.

A mortgage-backed security is any security that evidences an undivided interest in the ownership of mortgage loans. The most common form of MBS is the *pass-through security* in which mortgages are pooled and investors buy an interest in the pool in the form of certificates or securities. The originator of the mortgages or another firm collects the underlying mortgage payments and passes through the actual interest and principal received, less a servicing fee and other charges such as insurance. This structure creates substantial differences in the features of specific mortgage-backed securities as well as differences with conventional bonds. Two fundamental differences with conventional bonds are monthly rather than semiannual payments and price volatility differences due to prepayment risk. Characteristics of the most popular forms of MBSs are discussed below.

Most mortgages are originated by savings and loans, commercial banks, and mortgage bankers. These private institutions can issue pass-through securities directly or work through government-sponsored agencies. Specific features of the securities issued will differ sharply depending on which alternative is selected.

GNMA Pass-Through Securities. The Government National Mortgage Association (GNMA or Ginnie Mae) was established as part of the Department of Housing and Urban Development to provide support for the residential mortgage market. It does so primarily by guaranteeing the timely payment of interest and principal to the holders of pass-through securities regardless of whether the promised mortgage payments are made.[6] As such, even though GNMA pass-through securities are issued by private institutions, they are backed by the federal government and thus exhibit low default risk and high liquidity. Investors willingly pay for this guarantee so yields on GNMA pass-throughs are lower than yields on otherwise comparable MBSs.

The underlying mortgages in GNMA pools consist of mortgages insured by either the Federal Housing Association (FHA), Veterans Administration (VA), or Farmers Home Administration (FmHA). They can be of virtually any form including both fixed-payment and adjustable-rate mortgages (ARMs). Generally, mortgages in the pool are quite homogeneous in that they are issued at roughly the same time, have approximately the same maturity, and carry coupon rates that are similar.

FHLMC Securities. The Federal Home Loan Mortgage Corporation (FHLMC or Freddie Mac) was established to support the market for conventional mortgages. Unlike GNMA, FHLMC is formally a private corporation, albeit one that operates with an implicit federal guarantee. Although its stock is publicly traded today, it was originally owned by the Federal Home Loan Banks and member savings and loans, and Congress still selects a portion of its Board of Directors that helps set policy. FHLMC provides support by buying mortgages in the secondary market. It finances its purchases by issuing a variety of securities. It is these securities that banks and others purchase as investments.

FHLMC participation certificates are pass-through securities issued by FHLMC that are secured by conventional residential mortgages. Each participation certificate (PC) represents an undivided interest in the mortgages that comprise the mortgage pool used as collateral. FHLMC guarantees monthly interest and principal payments to security holders whether or not the payments are actually received on the underlying mortgages. This is, however, not the same as a federal guarantee so investors demand a risk premium. This risk premium can be volatile due to uncertainty regarding the credit quality of FHLMC's mortgage portfolio and the viability of the implied federal guarantee.

FHLMC guaranteed mortgage certificates are mortgage-backed securities issued by FHLMC that are similar to bonds. Interest and principal payments on the certificates are again backed by a pool of mortgages, but interest is paid just semiannually and principal is repaid annually. FHLMC also backs these payments with its guarantee.

FHLMC collateralized mortgage obligations are debt issues originated by FHLMC that are secured by a pool of mortgages, but the securities are grouped into classes according to estimated stated maturities. The purpose of these classes is described after the discussion of prepayment risk. Investors in all classes of collateralized mortgage

---

[6]The term *modified pass-through securities* is used to describe this guarantee feature. GNMA also purchases mortgages directly at below-market interest rates where the mortgages are used to finance low-income housing.

obligations (CMOs) receive semiannual interest payments until maturity.[7] Principal payments are also semiannual but are allocated initially to the class of CMOs with the shortest stated maturity, then sequentially to the remaining outstanding classes by maturity. Investors find CMOs attractive because they can better estimate the effective maturity of the securities compared with other types of pass-throughs.

FNMA Securities. The Federal National Mortgage Association (FNMA or Fannie Mae) was created by the federal government in 1938 to support housing, but today is another private corporation that operates with an implicit federal guarantee. It operates much like FHLMC, buying mortgages and financing the mortgages with securities backed by pools of mortgages with features similar to FHLMC's participation certificates. FNMA similarly guarantees timely interest and principal payments so that default risk is generally perceived to be low.

Privately Issued Pass-Throughs. Commercial banks, savings and loans, and mortgage banks also issue mortgage-backed pass-through securities secured by pools of mortgages. The primary difference with federal agency MBSs is that there is no actual or implied guarantee by the federal government or agency. Instead, private issuers purchase mortgage insurance either in the form of pool insurance by such groups as the Mortgage Guarantee Insurance Corporation or via letters of credit. In most cases, it is more profitable for mortgage lenders to use the agency programs. With certain mortgages, such as large mortgages for which the outstanding principal balance exceeds the acceptable maximum set by the agencies, a private pass-through program is the only one available.

Prepayment Risk on Mortgage-Backed Securities

As indicated earlier, most mortgage-backed securities (MBSs) carry a guarantee that principal and interest payments will be made to investors regardless of whether the payment on the underlying mortgages is made. Despite these guarantees, MBSs exhibit considerable risk because they may fluctuate widely in price when interest rates change. This results from uncertainty over the timing of prepayments and thus what cash flows will actually be passed through to investors at various points in time.

Remember that investors receive the actual principal and interest payments made by borrowers on the underlying mortgages minus a servicing fee. Borrowers may, in fact, prepay the outstanding mortgage principal at any time, for any reason, and generally without penalty. Prepayments generally occur because of fundamental demographic trends as well as from movements in interest rates. Demographic phenomena include factors affecting general labor mobility as individuals change jobs with fluctuations in regional economic activity, as well as changes in family structure attributable to events such as children leaving home or divorce. The important point is

---

[7]Holders of certain classes of interest accrual securities do not receive any interest payments until all interest and principal payments are made on the other classes of bonds. Interest continues to accrue, however, until received.

that the prepayment feature represents an option that is quite valuable to the borrower. It is risky to an investor, however, because it causes cash flows to be unpredictable.

Consider the case in which an investor buys a Ginnie Mae MBS based on a pool of mortgages paying 12.5 percent. Current mortgage rates are lower so that the security trades at 110 for a promised yield of 11.1 percent. If rates remain constant, an investor might receive interest on the outstanding principal at the higher rate for 7 or 8 years. Suppose instead that mortgage rates fall sharply. Some mortgage borrowers will exercise their option and refinance their properties with new mortgages at lower rates so they can save on monthly interest payments. They prepay principal on the 12.5 percent mortgages so that investors receive smaller interest payments. If prepayments are substantial, all outstanding principal may quickly be repaid so that the MBS effectively matures. Investors lose because they paid a premium expecting to receive high interest payments for several years. With the decline in rates, they not only receive considerably less interest over a shorter period of time, but they have to reinvest their cash receipts at lower rates. If prepayments are high enough, they may not even recover the premium paid.

Suppose alternatively that mortgage rates rise substantially. Prepayments will either slow or remain constant because fewer individuals will move and interest rates will induce fewer refinancings. The effect on investors in MBSs is threefold. First, the outstanding principal will be higher than originally anticipated. Thus interest received will be higher as repayment slows. Second, the security will remain outstanding longer so that interest payments will be received for more periods. Third, all cash receipts can be reinvested at higher rates. Of course, the increase in rates lowers the market value of the MBS.

Panel A of Exhibit 17.5 demonstrates the general interest sensitivity of a MBS. The vertical axis represents the market value of a $100,000 interest in a pool of 30-year mortgages carrying 9-percent rates. Assume that the expected rate of prepayments over the life of the mortgages is 6 percent per year. This type of constant prepayment rate (CPR) is typically measured as the annualized fraction of principal prepaid during a specific period, such as a year.[8] The dashed line represents the value of the MBS if the prepayment rate remains at 6 percent regardless of the level of mortgage rates. The solid line indicates the value of the MBS if the prepayment rate varies from 6 percent at different interest rate levels. At a current market rate of 9 percent, the MBS is valued at $100,000. As interest rates rise or fall, the value of the MBS declines or rises, respectively. Note, however, the differences in the two values at different rate levels. An increase in rates lowers the actual price of the MBS below the price at a constant prepayment rate because prepayments will slow and an investor will receive below-market interest payments for a longer period of time than originally anticipated. A decrease in rates raises value, but the sharp increase in prepayments at low rates limits the price appreciation. Thus prepayments increase potential capital losses to investors while they decrease potential capital gains.

---

[8]Suppose that a pool of mortgages contained $100 million in principal. A 6 percent annual CPR means that prepayments equal $6 million during the first year, $5.64 million (.06 x $94) during the second year, etc. If $6 million in principal were prepaid during the first 3 months, the annualized CPR would equal 24 percent. CPR does not include normal amortization.

Exhibit 17.5 Prepayment Risk on Mortgage-Backed Securities

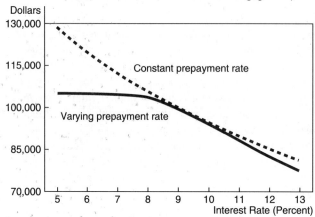

Panel A. The Interest Sensitivity of Mortgage Pass-Throughs
(Dollar Value of $100,000 Share in a Mortgage Pool)

Constant prepayment rate

Varying prepayment rate

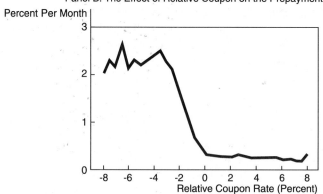

Panel B. The Effect of Relative Coupon on the Prepayment Rate

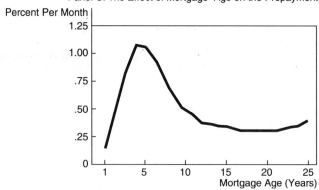

Panel C. The Effect of Mortgage Age on the Prepayment Rate

Source: Becketti, "The Prepayment Risk of Mortgage-Backed Securities." *Economic Review* (Federal Reserve Bank of Kansas City, February 1989).

This would not be a problem if investors could accurately forecast prepayments. Unfortunately, this is difficult to do. Pools of mortgages differ by geographic region, by the type of home or commercial property financed, by the age of the mortgages or how long they have been in existence, and by the interest rates on the underlying mortgages. Thus prepayment experience will vary widely between pools of mortgages even at the same point in time. This problem is mitigated somewhat by the fact that the U.S. Department of Housing and Urban Development (HUD) collects and reports data on the prepayment experience of selected mortgage pools. Securities dealers similarly track prepayment experience to assist investors when buying MBSs. While such information helps distinguish between pools, past prepayment experience is not always useful in predicting prepayments.

The bottom two panels of Exhibit 17.5 document the relationship between the prepayment rate on the vertical axis and different coupon rates on the underlying mortgages and mortgage age. The horizontal axis in panel B indicates the difference between the current rate on new mortgages and the rate on the underlying mortgages, while mortgage age in panel C refers to the length of time the mortgages have been outstanding since origination. Not surprisingly, prepayment rates rise sharply when mortgage rates fall. Prepayments are relatively low until mortgage rates fall by at least 2 percent, then jump to almost 3 percent per month. Prepayments are virtually unchanged when rates rise because there are no rate-induced prepayments, only prepayments resulting from demographic events. According to panel C, prepayment experience is low on new mortgages, but rises consistently through 5 years, after which it declines. This reflects the fact that rate changes are typically small near term and that most individuals must remain in their homes for a while before they can cover the costs of refinancing.

Impact of Prepayments on Duration and Yield

Even though prepayments cannot be forecast precisely, it is important to know how they affect the duration and thus the price and yield of MBSs.[9] In general, MBSs are priced near par when prepayments are relatively low. They are priced at a spread over Treasury securities with similar estimated durations when prepayments are expected to be high. The greater are prepayments the shorter is a security's duration because an investor receives the underlying principal and interest payments earlier. If prepayments slow, duration lengthens because larger cash flows are received later.

Different MBSs will exhibit different durations and thus different prices depending on their specific characteristics. Exhibit 17.6 documents differences in pricing associated with GNMA mortgage-backed securities carrying coupon rates between 8 and 12 percent. All mortgages are assumed to have a CPR of 6 percent due to demographic effects. Falling interest rates, in turn, are assumed to raise the CPR to as high as 55 percent. The data in panel A represent the price and yield relationships when the

---

[9]See Chapter 6 and particularly Exhibit 6.6 for a review of duration and sample duration calculations. Mathematically, duration equals the weighted average of the time until cash flows are received where the weights equal the present value of each cash flow divided by the security's price. Conceptually, duration is an elasticity measure that indicates the approximate price sensitivity of a security to a change in interest rates.

Exhibit 17.6 Pricing of GNMA Mortgage-Backed Securities

Table 1

GNMA 9's at Par

GNMA Coupon	8	9	10	11	12
CPR (%)	6%	6%	6%	20%	40%
Duration (Years)	5.4	5.9	6.0	3.2	1.8
Purchase Yield	8.99	9.28	9.42	8.75	7.54
Purchase Price	95–08	99–00	104–04	107–08	107–18

Table 2

GNMA 11's go to Par

GNMA Coupon	8	9	10	11	12
CPR (%)	6%	6%	6%	6%	6%
Duration (Years)	5.4	5.9	6.0	5.8	5.6
Yield at Purchase Price	8.99	9.28	9.42	9.87	10.80
Market Yield	10.25	10.50	10.75	11.17	11.25
Market Price	88–12	91–14	95–15	100	103–18

Table 3

GNMA 7's go to Par

GNMA Coupon	8	9	10	11	12
CPR(%)	6%	2%	40%	50%	55%
Duration (Years)	5.4	3.1	1.8	1.4	1.2
Yield at Purchase Price	8.99	9.38	7.53	5.56	5.57
Market Yield	7.25	7.00	6.00	6.00	6.00
Market Price	104–00	106–09	106–25	106–16	106–29

Source: James Vining and C. J. Pickering, "Maximizing Investment Income with Mortgage-Backed Securities," *Texas Banking*, (December 1986).

prevailing mortgage rate equals 9 percent. Note initially that the estimated CPRs equal 6 percent for the three lowest coupons, while they increase to 20 and 40 percent for the two highest coupon pools. This reflects the fact that homeowners typically refinance in greater numbers only when rates fall by at least 2 percent. As CPR increases duration decreases, ranging from 6 years down to under 2 years. If MBSs with high CPRs are priced off of Treasury securities with the same duration, the yield at the purchase price will reflect the Treasury yield curve. Thus the 12-percent GNMA carries a 7.54 percent yield because it is effectively a short-term security. The lowest coupon GNMAs, in turn, carry yields near 9 percent and lower prices.[10]

---

[10]The pattern of prices shown reflects actual prices in September 1986. The GNMA 9s were priced slightly below par of 100. The differences in duration between the 8s, 9s, and 10s reflect characteristics specific to each pool. The market prices in panels B and C when the market rate rises to 11 percent and falls to 7 percent are estimates that incorporate *premium resistance*. When MBSs are purchased at a premium, an investor has to write off the premium over time. If prepayments are high, the write-off must occur quickly. Investors in high-coupon MBSs price this risk accordingly.

Panel B outlines the change in prices and yields when the market rate increases to 11 percent. Here each MBS exhibits a CPR of 6 percent because its underlying mortgage rate is less than 2 percent over the market rate. The estimated durations are thus close to 6 years. Note that any original investors in the three lowest coupons would still receive the same yield if held to maturity because there is no change in expected cash flows. Investors in the GNMA 11s and 12s, however, would see their effective yields rise. This occurs because while they originally purchased high-coupon securities with short expected durations, the increase in rates lengthens the time over which they will receive the high interest payments. Thus while market prices for all the MBSs fall, they fall most for the low coupon GNMAs and least for the high-coupon GNMAs.

If instead the market rate declines to 7 percent from its original level, the pricing is substantially different. Panel C demonstrates that only the GNMA 8s have a CPR of 6 percent while the others range from 20 to 55 percent. The estimated durations decline systematically from 5.4 years to 1.2 years with the increase in coupons. Consistent with the change in durations, the yields at the original purchase price drop sharply for the highest-coupon GNMAs because they are very-short-term securities and thus are priced off of very-short-term Treasuries which carry low yields.

The general implication is that different coupon MBSs exhibit fundamentally different price/yield characteristics. In particular, yields on low-coupon MBSs do not differ substantially from the original purchase yield because prepayments and hence duration do not vary much. Yields on high-coupon MBSs, in contrast, may vary widely as market rates change because estimated duration changes considerably. When rates increase, duration lengthens and yields increase. When rates decrease, duration shortens and yields decrease. High-coupon MBSs are thus priced much like floating-rate securities while low-coupon MBSs are priced more like traditional fixed-rate securities.

Option-Adjusted Spreads. The previous discussion demonstrates that the standard calculation of yield to maturity is inappropriate with prepayment risk. Analysts instead use an option-adjusted spread approach when pricing mortgage-backed securities that accounts for factors that potentially affect prepayments. Briefly, the approach assigns probabilities to various cash flows based on different interest rate scenarios. A discount rate is determined that equates the average present value of these option-adjusted cash flows with the prevailing price of the underlying security. This discount rate represents an option-adjusted yield in the mortgage. The option-adjusted spread represents the difference between the option-adjusted yield and the yield on a Treasury bond of similar duration. The advantage is that an option-adjusted yield reflects consensus expectations regarding the interest-rate environment. The option-adjusted spread allows a comparison of the attractiveness of mortgage-backed securities relative to Treasuries over different time periods. Stephen Smith (1991) describes the basic models for calculating these spreads and presents the sequence of steps for evaluating expected returns in Exhibit 17.7.

Exhibit 17.7 Steps in Option-Adjusted Spread Calculation

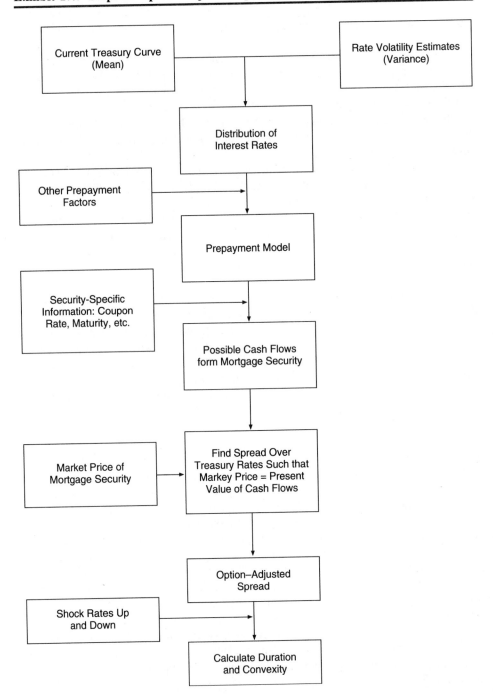

Source: Stephen Smith, "Mortgage-Backed Securities: Analyzing Risk and Return." *Economic Review* (Federal Reserve Bank of Atlanta, January/February 1991).

Collateralized Mortgage Obligations

The Federal Home Loan Mortgage Corporation first introduced CMOs in 1983 to try to circumvent some of the prepayment risk associated with the traditional pass-through security. This was accomplished by converting pass-throughs to securities with more predictable maturity and yield features comparable to those of well-known fixed-income securities. CMOs are essentially bonds. An originator combines various mortgage pools together that serve as collateral and creates classes of bonds with different maturities secured by the collateral. The first class of bonds or *tranche,* has the shortest maturity because all principal payments on the underlying mortgages are allocated to these securities so that repayment occurs on schedule. Interest is paid on these and other bonds at all times that the securities are outstanding. Once these bonds have been fully repaid, principal payments are allocated to a second class of bonds until they are paid off, and so forth. The primary advantage is that bonds in separate CMO tranches exhibit less prepayment uncertainty. An investor can therefore better forecast the effective maturity and overall yield.

As an example, consider the CMO prospectus in Exhibit 17.8. These CMO bonds were issued by Freddie Mac in January 1990, have $896 million in principal, and are divided into four tranches. Bonds in the first tranche (Series 123) carry a coupon rate of 8.25 percent but are priced to yield slightly more. Note that the final payment date is listed at February 1995, roughly 5 years after issue. This is an approximate maturity date assuming there are no prepayments. According to the structure of this issue, investors in first tranche bonds receive all principal payments until the $330 million in principal is paid off. If there are prepayments, all principal is allocated to repaying these bonds. Because there will be some prepayments, 5 years represents the longest an investor would have to wait for a return of all principal. After these bonds are retired, all principal payments are allocated to the Series 124 bonds representing the second tranche until they are retired. The estimated (longest) final maturity here is 7 years assuming no prepayments. The process continues until bonds in the third and fourth tranches are paid off. The longest possible maturity for the Series 126 bonds is 25 years.

The structure essentially creates 4 classes of bonds with different maturities and cash flow features. The coupon rates and promised yields increase with estimated maturity to compensate investors for additional risk. The bonds are guaranteed by Freddie Mac such that investors assume little default risk. There is still interest rate risk, however, with the uncertain prepayments, it is relatively low for the first tranche bonds. Interest rate risk clearly increases with bonds in each successive tranche.

There are many different types of CMOs. The least risky are *planned amortization classes* (PACs) in which principal payments are allocated according to a fixed amortization schedule. If actual prepayment rates differ from that expected, principal allocated to other tranches is reduced or accelerated to ensure that PAC CMOs are paid as scheduled. The last class of CMO bonds is often a Z-tranche, which represents accrual bonds that pay no interest or principal until all other bonds are retired. Such Z-bonds accrue interest while the other CMO bonds remain outstanding so that the principal owed increases over time. An investor in Z-bonds subsequently assumes

Exhibit 17.8 CMO Prospectus

New Issue

$896,000,000

Freddie
Mac

Federal Home Loan Mortgage Corporation

Multifamily Plan C REMIC
Mortgage Participation Certificates
(Guaranteed), Series 123 through 126

Series 123
$330,000,000 8.25% Class 123-A Final Payment Date February 15, 1995 — Price 99.781250%

Series 124
$307,000,000 8.50% Class 124-A Final Payment Date March 15, 1997   — Price 99.093750%

Series 125
$220,000,000 8.75% Class 125-A Final Payment Date March 15, 2000   — Price 99.031250%

Series 126
$ 39,000,000 9.00% Class 126-A Final Payment Date March 15, 2005   — Price 99.390625%

(plus accrued interest at the applicable rate from January 15, 1990)

Freddie Mac, in its corporate capacity, will be contractually obligated to pay PC Yield Maintenance Premiums, if any, to each Holder of the Class 123-A, Class 124-A, Class 125-A and Class 126-A Plan C REMIC PCs.

The obligations of Freddie Mac under its guarantee of the Plan C REMIC PCs, and its obligations to pay PC Yield Maintenance Premiums, are obligations of Freddie Mac only and are not backed by the full faith and credit of the United States.

The residual interest for each Plan C REMIC PC Pool is not offered by the Offering Circular Supplement and the related Offering Circular and will initially be retained by Freddie Mac.

The Class 123-A, Class 124-A, Class 125-A and Class 126-A Plan C REMIC PCs will each be a regular interest in one of the Plan C REMIC PC Pools.

Elections will be made to treat the Plan C REMIC PC Pools as REMICs.

Copies of the Offering Circular Supplement and the related Offering Circular describing these securities and the business of the Corporation may be obtained from any of the undersigned in States in which such underwriters may legally offer these securities. This announcement is neither an offer to sell nor a solicitation of an offer to buy these securities. The offer is made only by the Offering Circular Supplement and the related Offering Circular.

Prudential-Bache Capital Funding

The First Boston Corporation

Goldman, Sachs & Co.

Merrill Lynch Capital Markets

Salomon Brothers Inc

Shearson Lehman Hutton Inc.

BT Securities Corporation	Bear, Stearns & Co. Inc.	Citicorp Securities Markets, Inc.
Donaldson, Lufkin & Jenrette		Drexel Burnham Lambert
Freddie Mac Security Sales and Trading Group		Greenwich Capital Markets, Inc.
Kidder, Peabody & Co.	J.P. Morgan Securities Inc.	Morgan Stanley & Co.
Nomura Securities International, Inc.	PaineWebber Incorporated	UBS Securities Inc.

January 9, 1990

considerable interest rate risk. Because maturity or duration is difficult to forecast, these bonds are priced off of 20-year Treasury securities. In addition, floating rate CMOs have been developed to appeal to investors outside the United States. These securities generally constitute a class of a typical CMO issue in which the interest payment is set at a markup over LIBOR.

CMOs provide advantages over traditional MBSs in a variety of ways. First, they exhibit less prepayment risk. Second, by segmenting the securities into maturity classes CMOs appeal to different investors who have different maturity preferences. Banks, for example, often prefer first-tranche securities because the short maturities and durations better match their cash-flow obligations with deposit liabilities. Insurance companies, in contrast, often prefer later tranches where the bonds have much longer effective maturities. Third, CMOs exhibit little default risk because the collateral backing the bonds is generally agency securities that carry explicit guarantees or the issuer purchases private insurance. Thus most CMOs are Aaa-rated. In addition, many early classes of bonds are overcollateralized because the actual cash flows from the collateral exceed cash flow required to pay bondholders. Fourth, like MBSs, CMOs are priced at a spread over Treasury securities so that changes in yields are fairly predictable.

CMOs have several disadvantages. They are less liquid because the secondary market is less developed. Transactions costs are consequently higher. In addition, an investor may find it difficult to obtain an accurate price quote when trying to sell a CMO. This is particularly true for the latter tranches, which exhibit far greater price volatility. Finally, all CMO interest is taxable at both the federal and state and local government levels, unlike Treasury securities which are subject only to federal income taxes.

Corporate, Foreign, and Taxable Municipal Bonds

Banks also purchase small amounts of taxable fixed-income securities in the form of corporate bonds and foreign government bonds. Banks do not purchase junk bonds because they are restricted to investment-grade securities. Banks are also constrained by regulation concerning legal lending limits to investing no more than 10 percent of capital in the securities of any single firm. These bonds typically pay interest semiannually and return the entire principal at maturity. In most cases, banks purchase securities that mature within 10 years.

Occasionally, banks also purchase municipal bonds that pay taxable interest. The Tax Reform Act of 1986 eliminated the tax-exempt status of certain types of municipal revenue bonds. These entities have subsequently issued debt that pays taxable interest to meet their financing needs. The pretax yields are comparable to those on corporate securities even though the borrower is affiliated with a municipal government. Exhibit 17.9 compares the features of corporate securities with those of Treasury securities and pass-throughs.

Asset-Backed Securities

One of the dominant trends in financial markets is the securitization of bank loans. Chapter 3 describes the process and rationale given the recent increase in regulatory

Exhibit 17.9 Features of Pass-Through, Government, and Corporate Securities

	Pass-Throughs	Treasuries	Corporates	Stripped Treasuries
Credit risk	Generally high grade; range from government guaranteed to A (private pass throughs).	Government guaranteed.	High grade to speculative.	Backed by government guarantees.
Liquidity	Good for agency issued/guaranteed pass-through.	Excellent.	Generally limited.	Fair.
Range of coupons (discount to premium)	Full range.	Full range.	Full range for a few issuers.	Zero coupons (discount securities).
Range of maturities	Medium and long term (fast-paying and seasoned pools can provide shorter maturities than stated).	Full range.	Full range.	Full range.
Call protection	Complex prepayment pattern; investor can limit through selection variables such as coupon, seasoning, and program.	Noncallable (except certain 30-year bonds).	Generally callable after initial limited period of 5 to 10 years.	Noncallable.
Frequency of payment	Monthly payments of principal and interest.	Semiannual interest payment.	Semiannual interest (except Eurobonds, which pay interest annually).	No payments until maturity.
Average life	Lower than for bullets of comparable maturity; can only be estimated due to prepayment risk.	Estimate only for small number of callable issues; otherwise, known with certainty.	Minimum average life known, otherwise a function of call risk.	Known with certainty.
Duration/interest rate risk	Function of prepayment risk; can only be estimated; can be negative when prepayment risk is high.	Unless callable, a simple function of yield, coupon and maturity; is known with certainty.	Function of call risk; can be negative when call risk is high.	Known with certainty; no interest rate risk if held to maturity.
Basis for yield quotes	Cash flow yield based on monthly prepayments and constant CPR assumption (usually most recent 3-month historical prepayment experience).	Based on seminannual coupon payments and 365-day year.	Based on semiannual coupon payments and 360-day year of twelve 30-day months.	Bond equivalent yield based on either 360- or 365-day year depending on sponsor.
Settlement	Once a month.	Any business day.	Any business day.	Any business day.

Source: *Handbook of Securities of the United States Government and Federal Agencies.* First Boston Corporation (1988).

capital requirements. While some banks have been active in securitizing nontraditional types of loans, others view these securities as potential investments. Conceptually, an asset-backed security is comparable to a mortgage-backed security in structure. The securities are effectively pass-throughs because promised interest and principal payments are secured by the payments on the specific loans pledged as collateral.

Two of the more popular forms of asset-backed securities are collateralized automobile receivables (CARS) and certificates for amortizing revolving debt (CARDS).[11] As the names suggest, CARS are securities backed by automobile loans to individuals. CARDS are, in turn, securities backed by credit card loans to individuals.

CARS may be structured either as conventional pass-throughs or CMOs. Automobile loans representing installment contracts with maturities up to 60 months are placed in a trust. CARS represent an undivided interest in the trust. An investor receives the underlying monthly principal and interest payments less a servicing fee. As with CMOs, CARS may be multiple-class instruments in which cash flows pay interest to all security holders, but repay principal sequentially from the first class of bonds to the last. Default risk is reduced because the issuer may either set up a reserve fund out of the payments to cover losses, purchase insurance, or obtain a letter of credit. Such credit enhancements typically provide the securities an Aaa credit rating. CARS are attractive to investors because they have maturities of 5 years or less, exhibit little prepayment risk, and carry rates that are approximately 1 percent over rates on comparable duration Treasury securities. Prepayment risk is low because automobile loan rates are somewhat sticky and there are limited incentives to prepay. The primary negative is that liquidity is reduced compared with many other securities.

CARDS are structured much like CARS except that the collateral is credit card receivables. An issuer places credit card accounts in a trust and sells participations. The securities generally have stated maturities around 5 years with only interest being paid monthly during the first 1 1/2 to 2 years. Principal payments begin thereafter. Because many cardholders repay their debts quickly, the principal may be repaid well before the stated maturity. Thus prepayment risk is higher for CARDS than for CARS. Still, issuers establish a reserve fund or obtain explicit guarantees via letters of credit so that the securities are similarly rated Aaa.

NEWER INVESTMENT VEHICLES

The search for higher yields has led banks to many different types of investments. Brokerage houses have successfully marketed many securities to banks as having attractive risk and return features that are in fact difficult to comprehend and measure. Two such types include stripped mortgage-backed securities and mutual funds.

---

[11]CARS and CARDS are formally the labels copyrighted by Salomon Brothers for their specific issues of asset-backed securities, but will be used generically in the discussion to refer to all such securities.

Stripped Mortgage-Backed Securities

Stripped Treasury securities, introduced earlier, are nothing more than zero coupon instruments that represent either a principal payment or coupon interest payment on a Treasury obligation. The general label is principal-only (PO) and interest-only (IO) security. The time line for the 10-year Treasury on page 547 revealed 20 distinct IOs paying $45,000 each at maturity and one PO of $1 million. These stripped Treasury securities exhibit no default risk and no interest rate risk if held to final maturity. An investor can therefore lock in a guaranteed return if he matches his holding period with a stripped Treasury of the same maturity.

Stripped mortgage-backed securities are much more complicated in terms of their pricing characteristics. This reflects the structure of mortgage contracts and the impact of mortgage prepayments. Consider a 30-year, 12 percent fixed-rate mortgage that is fully amortized. There will be 360 scheduled principal and interest payments equal to a fixed dollar amount per month (PY). The following time line demonstrates the cash flow pattern of interest (I) and principal (P) payments where the subscripts refer to the month in which the payment is made.

Time Line

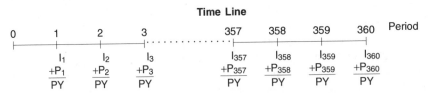

Loan amortization requires that the early period principal payments are small relative to the total payment so that $P_1 < P_2 < \ldots < P_{360}$. Interest payments are large during the early periods when the outstanding principal is high, and decline over time as the principal is reduced. Thus $I_1 > I_2 > I_3 > \ldots > I_{360}$.

Unlike Treasury securities, there is more than one principal component as each payment is part principal. Furthermore, MBSs are typically stripped into just two securities with the PO representing the entire stream of principal payments, and the IO representing the entire stream of interest payments. Thus each payment is not a separate security and the strips are no longer simple zero coupon instruments. More importantly, MBSs are subject to prepayment risk, which affects the underlying principal and interest payments and thus makes mortgage-backed POs and IOs highly interest sensitive.

Suppose that an investor purchased the PO security represented by the stream of principal payments in the above time line when the market rate equaled 12 percent. Given normal demographic trends, prepayments are expected to equal 6 percent annually. Now suppose that the prevailing mortgage rate drops to 9 percent so that prepayments accelerate and the CPR jumps to 20 percent. The investor will receive principal payments earlier than originally anticipated. In addition, the payments will be discounted at a lower rate so that the price of the PO will rise substantially. Similarly a rise in mortgage rates will not slow prepayments because they are already at the minimum 6 percent, but the cash flows will be discounted at a higher rate so the price of the PO will fall. If the PO originally carried a higher rate, prepayments would have slowed and the price decline would be even greater. In short, a mortgage-backed PO behaves much like a typical MBS except it is more price sensitive.

Suppose that another investor bought the IO security represented by the stream of interest payments at 12 percent. The decline in rate to 9 percent would accelerate principal payments such that the IO investor would receive much lower interest payments than originally anticipated because the outstanding principal balance would be reduced. In the extreme case when the entire outstanding principal balance is repaid, the IO investor would receive no interest payments. Not surprisingly, the price of an IO is quite volatile. If prepayments are high enough, the drop in the dollar value of interest received can swamp any effect from discounting at a lower rate so that the price of an IO will fall. In a similar vein, suppose that the investor purchased the IO when the prevailing mortgage rate was 8 percent, or 4 percent below the rates on the underlying mortgages. If the market rate rose to 11 percent, prepayments would slow substantially, outstanding principal would be greater than that initially anticipated, and interest payments would rise sharply. If the prepayment effect were large enough, it could swamp discounting at a higher rate such that the value of the IO might rise.

The essential point is that mortgage-backed IOs are extremely price sensitive to changes in interest rates. When prepayments rise sharply with a drop in rates compared to that anticipated, the value of the IO will similarly fall. When prepayments fall sharply with an increase in rates relative to expectations, the value of the IO will similarly rise. Thus IOs may vary in price in the opposite direction of that normally observed for traditional fixed-income securities. In securities parlance, these IOs exhibit *negative convexity*. The concept of convexity is described below and is applied to mortgage-backed securities.

Unfortunately, many banks and savings and loan managers purchased IOs for interest rate hedges without understanding their features. IOs could presumably be used to hedge a negative GAP or positive duration gap because a bank with this risk profile would lose when interest rates increased. An IO would presumably rise in value as rates increased as an offset. Of course, if rates fell a bank would win with its GAP profile, but this would be offset by losses on the IO. The success of IOs as hedges, however, depended on wide swings in rates. Small rate changes typically moved IO prices in the same direction as a bank's cash flows from normal operations so that no hedge was in place.

It is extremely difficult to predict prepayments and thus the value of IOs and POs when rates change. They are extremely risky because they are extremely interest sensitive. There are many better hedging tools, such as interest rate swaps and options on futures, with more predictable cash flows and changes in value. Bank regulators have consequently encouraged banks to stay away from IOs.

Mutual Funds

In recent years, regulators have allowed banks to purchase certain types of mutual fund shares as an investment. The shares must be in funds that purchase only securities that banks would be allowed to own directly for their own account, such as Treasury and agency obligations, mortgage-backed securities, and investment-grade corporates. The presumed benefit is that small banks might be able to better diversify credit risk because they would own shares in a pool of securities rather than individual securities. Regulators further limited mutual fund purchases to no more than 10 percent of a bank's capital plus surplus.

After initial interest during the latter 1980s, banks have generally ignored mutual funds as investments. The primary reason is that regulations require that mutual fund shares be marked to market rather than reported at book values. Funds that do not have fixed share prices fluctuate in value with changes in interest rates, which translates into fluctuating values reported on a bank's balance sheet. Such volatility looks bad in periodic financial statements because it presents an appearance of high risk. Banks thus avoid most mutual funds as investments.

THE ROLES OF DURATION AND CONVEXITY IN ANALYZING BOND PRICE VOLATILITY

Most option-free bonds exhibit predictable price/yield relationships because valuation involves straightforward present value analysis of promised cash flows. The analysis is complicated, however, when bonds with call and put options are valued. Prepayments with mortgage-backed securities, for example, distort simple present value analysis because prepayment effects can swamp discounting effects resulting from the same change in interest rates. The case in which an IO decreases in value when mortgage rates decrease serves as an example. Many bond analysts use the concepts of duration and convexity to measure price sensitivity. This section reviews duration and demonstrates how convexity provides additional information.[12]

Duration and Convexity Measures

Duration measures the weighted average of the time until cash flows are made on a security. The weights equal the present value of each cash flow divided by the original price of the security. Alternatively, duration is an approximate elasticity measure. As such, it measures the relative price sensitivity of a security to a change in the underlying interest rate. Consider a 3-year, $10,000 par bond with a 10 percent coupon, that pays $500 interest at 6-month intervals and $10,000 at maturity. The bond carries no call or put options. The curved line in Exhibit 17.10 shows the relationship between the bond's price and market yield according to the present value formula. Notice that the shape of the curve is nonlinear. The Macaulay duration of the bond appears at the bottom of the exhibit measured in semiannual periods. Duration can be represented by the slope of the price-yield relationship at various yields, and approximated by the following formula:

---

[12]The following examples are taken from Koch (1989).

Exhibit 17.10 Price-Yield Relationships and Duration

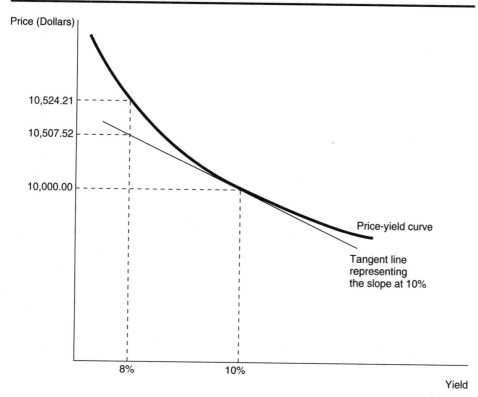

Yield	Price	Price - $10,000	Duration*
8%	$10,524.21	$524.21	5.349
9	10,257.89	257.89	5.339
10	10,000.00	0.00	5.329
11	9,750.00	(249.78)	5.320
12	9,508.27	(491.73)	5.310

* Macaulay's duration in semiannual periods.

Source: Koch, Timothy. "The Roles of Duration and Convexity in Analyzing Bond Price Volatility." *Bank Asset/Liability Management* (Warren, Gorham & Lamont, Inc., June 1989).

$$\text{Duration} = -\left[\frac{\Delta P/P}{\Delta i/(1 + i)} \right] \qquad (17.3)$$

where P equals the price of the bond and i equals the market yield. Rearranging terms,

$$\Delta P = -\text{Duration} \left[\Delta i/(1 + i)\right]P \qquad (17.4)$$

Formula (17.4) can be applied in the following manner. Suppose that the prevailing yield on the bond is 10 percent so that duration equals 5.329 six-month periods (2.665 years). If the underlying market rate falls to 8 percent, the bond's price increases to $10,524.21 according to the present value formula. Formula (17.4) approximates the price change as:

$$\Delta P = -5.329(-0.01/1.05)\$10,000 = \$507.52$$

The estimated price of $10,507.52 can be read off the straight line in Exhibit 17.10 representing the slope of the price-yield curve at a 10-percent yield. The pricing error is thus $16.69. Interestingly, a 2 percent increase in market rate will lower the bond price by only $491.73, which is less in absolute value than the price increase when the market rate fell by 2 percent. The pricing error ($15.79 in this instance) is thus also lower when rates increase.

A careful inspection of Exhibit 17.9 reveals several important conclusions.

- The difference between the price-yield curve and the straight line representing duration at the point of tangency equals the error in applying (17.4) to estimate the change in bond price at each new yield;

- For both rate increases and rate decreases, the estimated price based on duration will be below the actual price;

- For small changes in yield, such as yields near 10 percent, the error is small; and

- For large changes in yield, such as yields well above or well below 10 percent, the error is large.

The fundamental implication is that duration reasonably approximates price volatility on an option-free bond only when yield changes are small.

Convexity, in contrast, characterizes the rate of change in duration when yields change. It thus attempts to improve upon duration by itself as an approximation of price volatility. Notice from Exhibit 17.10 that the slope of a line tangent to the price-yield curve will increase as yields fall below 10 percent, and will decrease as yields rise above 10 percent. In essence, the duration of the bond lengthens as yields fall and shortens as yields rise. This characteristic is called *positive convexity,* signifying that the underlying bond becomes more price sensitive when yields decline and less price sensitive when yields rise.

Formally, convexity can be defined as one-half times the second derivative of a bank's price with respect to the interest rate, divided by the bond's price.[13] A bond's convexity can be combined with duration to better estimate true price volatility from yield changes. The additional convexity measure captures a portion of the error associated with using duration alone. The previous example demonstrates the value of convexity. From 10 percent to 8 percent, the estimated price change due to duration equals $507.52 as described earlier. At 10 percent, the estimated convexity of the bond in Exhibit 17.10 is 16.23 semiannual periods. The estimated price change due to

---

[13]Fabozzi and Fabozzi (1989) provides details.

convexity thus equals $16.23 with the assumed 1 percent decline in the semiannual rate.

$$\Delta P \text{ due to convexity} = \text{convexity} (\Delta i)^2 P \qquad (17.5)$$

or

$$= 16.23(.01)^2 \$10,000$$
$$= \$16.23$$

in this example. The estimated price change due to duration and convexity together equals $523.75, or just $0.46 less than the actual price change. Knowing a bond's duration and convexity allows for improved forecasts of price sensitivity even when yields change substantially.

The above discussion used option-free bonds. Securities with options, such as mortgage-backed securities with a prepayment option, often exhibit *negative convexity*. A bond that exhibits negative convexity is difficult to price and potentially dangerous to investors. With negative convexity duration lengthens when yields increase and shortens when yields decrease. The price-yield relationship of a bond with negative convexity does not take the simple convex shape from Exhibit 17.10, but rather curves back toward the origin at certain lower interest rate levels. In order to price these mortgage-backed bonds, analysts must accurately forecast the degree of negative convexity by precisely estimating the dollar magnitude and timing of prepayments. Duration and convexity are thus important because market participants price this relative price sensitivity and establish trading positions based on expected rate movements and interest rate volatility.

SUMMARY

With the Tax Reform Act of 1986 banks were forced to concentrate their investment portfolio on taxable securities rather than tax-exempt municipals. Traditionally, banks have invested heavily in taxable money market securities, such as Repos, Treasury bills, bankers' acceptances, CDs, and Eurodollars, and capital market instruments such as Treasury notes and bonds and federal agency securities. More recently they have shifted the composition of investments toward mortgage-backed securities.

This chapter examines the risk and return features of various taxable securities. In general, banks purchase securities with low default risk because they are restricted to buying investment-grade securities or their equivalents. Many instruments carry explicit federal guarantees of interest and principal payments, while most agency and mortgage-backed securities offer at least implicit guarantees. Non-Treasury securities are attractive because they pay rates above Treasury rates, yet exhibit little default risk. They are, however, less liquid. Interest rate risk associated with individual securities may also be substantial as most securities carry fixed rates, and some have maturities and durations that are relatively long term. Mortgage-backed securities exhibit the greatest interest rate risk because mortgage borrowers can prepay principal at any time.

Uncertainty over prepayments makes it difficult to forecast a security's effective maturity and actual cash flows. This has been somewhat mitigated by the development of collateralized mortgage obligations that allocated principal payments to classes of securities sequentially. Banks buy CMO bonds in the first classes that have the most predictable cash flows and thus the shortest maturities. Still, banks must be extremely cautious when buying mortgage-backed securities because prepayment rates and thus yields and prices vary widely between different instruments.

Questions

Money Market Investments

1. Would you expect to find repurchase agreements or reverse repurchase agreements in a bank's investment portfolio? Would you expect to find a larger portion of these in small banks or large banks? How do RP rates compare to fed fund rates?

2. What are the advantages of holding Treasury bills in the investment portfolio? Why doesn't a bank invest exclusively in Treasury bills?

3. T-bills can serve as collateral for three other banking needs. What are they?

4. Suppose the Treasury is auctioning $15 billion in 13-week Treasury bills. They receive non-competitive bids for $2 billion and the following competitive bids:

Amount in Billions	Price
$5	98.45
$6	98.43
$8	98.41
$3	98.40

What annual discount rate did the non-competitive bidders receive?

What is the bond-equivalent yield?

5. How are the following securities alike and how do they differ: CDs, Eurodollars, Yankee CDs, and Asian Dollar CDs?

6. Why do banks buy corporate commercial paper rather than loaning money to the corporation? Which types of banks, small or large, are heavy investors in the commercial paper market?

7. What is a bankers' acceptance? Do you suspect they are becoming more or less important in today's global society?

Capital Market Investments

8. What is a "stripped" Treasury bond? What are the advantages of buying the components rather than the whole bond?

9. What is the difference in risk and return among the securities issued by the Treasury, a government agency, and a quasi-agency? What default-guarantees does each carry?

10. What is one advantage and one disadvantage to a bank of owning a mortgage-backed security rather than a mortgage?

11. What differences exist among GNMA, FHLMC, and FNMA?

12. If timely payment of interest and principal are guaranteed in pass-through securities, what risk remains?

13. Investors were having problems with pass-throughs, and CMOs were invented to eliminate them. What were these problems? How do CMOs work?

14. What are the disadvantages of CMOs?

15. What are CARS and CARDS? What are their advantages and disadvantages compared with CMOs?

16. How do stripped mortgage-backed securities differ from stripped Treasuries?

17. Bankers indicate that they are not interested in purchasing shares in mutual funds because they are required to mark them to market value on their books. Why do bankers care how securities are accounted for?

Duration and Convexity

18. For each of the following pairs of securities, identify the one that most likely exhibits the largest positive convexity:
    a. You own a bond when interest rates fall 2 percent; you own a bond when interest rates rise 2 percent.
    b. You own a 2-year bond; you own a 20-year bond.
    c. You own a traditional bond; you own a putable bond.
    d. You own a 5-year CARS security; you own a 5-year IO security.

19. You are considering purchasing pass-throughs on a pool of 8 percent mortgages with all principal paid at maturity that mature 3 years from today. These mortgages are unique in that all principal and interest will be repaid in one terminal payment. They are also unique in that the homeowners can only prepay their mortgages on the annual anniversary dates. Currently market interest rates are 8 percent and you expect 10 percent of the mortgages to prepay a year from today and 20 percent 2 years from today. However, if interest rates rise substantially, you expect to see no prepayments. If interest rates fall substantially, you expect next year's prepayments to be 30 percent and the following year's to be 50 percent of the total with only 20 percent being left in the pool at its maturity. What would the duration of this investment be under the three interest rate forecasts? For simplicity assume you will invest $10,000 and assume that the highest interest rates would go would be up to 10 percent, and the lowest would be down to 6 percent. Does this investment exhibit positive or negative convexity?

20. You have been put in charge of a bank's investment portfolio and have been given total control. In your review of the current portfolio you discover that your predecessor has invested exclusively in 90-day T-bills. Name five different suitable investments for your portfolio and explain why you might consider adding each of them to the portfolio.

Activity

Check a recent *Wall Street Journal* for the secondary market yields on the following securities:

    90-day T-bills

    5-year T-notes

    5-year Treasury STRIPs of interest

    5-year Treasury STRIPs of principal

    5-year FNMA pass-throughs

    5-year Student Loan Marketing securities

    Municipal bonds

    Conventional fixed-rate mortgages

References

Becketti, Sean. "The Role of Stripped Securities in Portfolio Management." *Economic Review* (Federal Reserve Bank of Kansas City, May 1988).

Becketti, Sean. "The Prepayment Risk of Mortgage-Backed Securities." *Economic Review* (Federal Reserve Bank of Kansas City, February 1989).

Cook, Timothy, and Timothy Rowe, eds. *Instruments of the Money Market.* Richmond, Va.: Federal Reserve Bank of Richmond, 1986.

Domingo, Gregory, and Lisa Wolfson. "Stripped Mortgage Securities and Their Use in Thrift Portfolio Management." In *Review* (Federal Home Loan Bank of Atlanta, October 1987).

Fabozzi, Frank, and T. Dessa Fabozzi. *Bond Markets, Analysis and Strategies*, Englewood Cliffs, N.J.: Prentiss-Hall, Inc., 1989.

Fabozzi, Frank, editor. *The Handbook of Mortgage-Backed Securities.* Chicago, Ill.: Probus Publishing Company, 1988.

Handbook of Securities of the United States Government and Federal Agencies. The First Boston Corporation, 1988.

Koch, Timothy. "The Roles of Duration and Convexity in Analyzing Bond Price Volatility." *Bank Asset/Liability Management* (Warren, Gorham & Lamont, Inc., June 1989).

Lumpkin, Stephen. "Repurchase and Reverse Repurchase Agreements." *Economic Review.* (Federal Reserve Bank of Richmond, January/February 1987).

Mortgage Product Spotlight. *CMO Residuals.* Atlanta, Ga.: Federal Home Loan Bank of Atlanta, November 1989.

Roosevelt, Phil. "Filings Reveal Banks Hold 30% of Collateralized Mortgage Bonds." *American Banker* (August 24, 1990).

Smith, Stephen. "Analyzing Risk and Return for Mortgage-Backed Securities." *Economic Review* (Federal Reserve Bank of Atlanta, January/February 1991).

Syron, Richard, and Sheila Tschinkel. "The Government Securities Market: Playing Field for Repos." *Economic Review* (Federal Reserve Bank of Atlanta, September 1985).

Vining, James, and C.J. Pickering. "Maximizing Investment Income with Mortgage-Backed Securities." *Texas Banking*, December 1986.

Chapter 18

Tax-Sheltered Investments

Suppose that you could borrow funds at 8 percent, deduct your interest expense at a 40-percent tax rate, and buy securities that paid tax-exempt interest at 7 percent. Ignoring credit and interest rate risk issues, you would effectively pay 4.8 percent on your borrowing and thus earn a 2.2 percent spread. For each $1 million this would amount to $22,000 that would filter right to the bottom line. If you were a bank, you could conceivably do this in sufficiently large volume to add many basis points to your ROE and ROA.

For many years, banks were allowed to borrow funds, buy municipals, and deduct their interest expense, just as in the above case. Because they paid taxes at the highest corporate rate and this tax rate exceeded those paid by most individuals, they were often first in line when state and local governments issued debt. Not surprisingly, banks used to dominate the municipal market among investor groups and were able to shelter a very large fraction of their income.

During the 1980s Congress grew frustrated with banks that seemed to pay little in federal income tax, so it slowly modified banks' ability to arbitrage the rate difference. Effective in 1983, Congress changed the tax laws so that banks could deduct just 85 percent of their interest expense associated with municipal purchases. The deductible portion was further lowered to 80 percent in 1985. Both changes served to reduce the net spread, but still left municipals attractive investments. The Tax Reform Act of 1986, however, eliminated the deductibility of interest on borrowing to finance municipal purchases, except for certain small-issue, public purpose securities issued by qualifying municipalities. Only these securities retained the 80 percent deductibility. The net effect was to lower after-tax yields on most municipals, but more importantly to eliminate one of the few tax shelters left for commercial banks so that banks are now relatively small players in the municipal market.

The purpose of this chapter is to introduce the specific characteristics of municipal securities, describe the nature of the their tax treatment at banks, demonstrate how municipal yields compare with yields on alternative taxable securities, and finally to describe other tax-sheltered investments such as employee stock ownership plan (ESOP) loans and lease contracts. Both of these alternative investments recently lost part of their tax shelter due to changes in tax laws. After reading the chapter, it should be clear why aggregate bank holdings of municipals have declined. It should also be easy to identify what types of municipals are attractive and what their incremental yield advantage is.

CHARACTERISTICS OF MUNICIPAL SECURITIES

At year-end 1985 commercial banks owned $232 billion in municipal securities or 35 percent of total municipals outstanding, more than any other investor group. By year-end 1990, bank municipal holdings had fallen below $120 billion to around 14 percent of outstandings. This reflects changes in the tax laws to where many municipals offer low after-tax yields to banks, and a general deterioration in bank earnings to where banks need fewer tax-sheltered investments.

Municipals are generally attractive investments because their interest is exempt from federal income taxes. Interest on in-state issues is also normally exempt from state and local income taxes. This tax treatment lowers quoted yields below pretax yields on taxable securities of comparable maturity and risk because municipal yields effectively represent after-tax returns. Such investments also support local business development and growth, in addition to essential public services.

Municipal securities are formally issued by state and local governments and their political subdivisions, such as school corporations, water treatment authorities, and river authorities. Nonprofit organizations and nonfinancial corporations also effectively issue municipals because they get the use of the proceeds at reduced rates, even though a municipal unit's name actually goes on the debt. Government units distinguish between short-term and long-term municipals because they are used for different purposes and are subject to different restrictions. Short-term securities are used to finance temporary imbalances between the timing of operating receipts and expenditures or to provide interim financing of construction outlays. By law, most government units are forced to run balanced operating budgets, meaning that current operating revenues must be sufficient to cover operating expenses. State and local governments are not allowed to issue long-term bonds to finance short-term operating budget deficits.

Today, long-term municipals are used primarily to finance capital expenditures for such purposes as education facilities, hospitals, housing, and public utilities. The benefits to these facilities presumably arise over long periods so that future taxes that should cover the interest and principal payments will be paid by those who benefit. Through 1985 an increasing share of long-term municipal debt effectively financed the expenditures of private corporations in the form of industrial development bonds. It was not unusual, for example, for Kmart to negotiate a deal with a municipality to locate a store within the city limits if the municipality would form a local economic development unit, have the unit issue debt, and then let Kmart pay the debt service with lease payments to the economic development unit. The advantage to Kmart was that it could effectively borrow at lower tax-exempt interest rates. The advantage to the community was that it had attracted a new business which presumably brought jobs and services. The Tax Reform Act of 1986 sharply reduced the issuance of tax-exempt industrial development bonds so that they now comprise a much smaller share of the municipal market.[1]

Most long-term municipals are serial bonds, with a fraction of the total principal maturing in consecutive years. This is shown in Exhibit 18.1 for the $120 million issue by the state of Washington. This new issue tombstone ad indicates that the offering has 20 serial components of different amounts that mature annually from 1991 through the year 2010. Serialization enables a municipality to spread out principal and interest payments to stay within annual debt service capability. Issues may also have term components for which the entire principal comes due at a set maturity. The state of Washington issue has a separate term component of bonds with just under $41 million in principal that mature 35 years after the issue date. The firms listed at the bottom are the investment banks that served as underwriters.

From a bank's perspective, serial issues allow portfolio managers to select instruments with the precise maturities that best meet the bank's risk and return preferences. For example, a bank with many short-term liabilities may choose to concentrate investments near term. Similarly, banks that choose to use municipals to lengthen their asset rate sensitivity profile may select longer-term issues. With a serial issue, the manager can simply select the appropriate maturity instrument because credit and liquidity risk are comparable across maturities.

Short-Term Municipals

Municipal notes are issued to provide operating funds for government units. Tax and revenue anticipation notes are issued in anticipation of tax receipts or other revenue generation, typically from the federal government. These securities enable governments to continue to spend funds even when operating revenues decline, then repay the debt as revenues are received. Bond anticipation notes provide interim financing for capital projects that will ultimately be financed with long-term bonds. For example, a school district may begin construction of new schools with note proceeds because it believes that current long-term municipal rates are temporarily high. Long-term bonds will be issued after rates decline, with the proceeds used to retire the notes. Most notes carry a minimum denomination of $25,000, with maturities ranging from 30 days to 1 year. Maturities on bond anticipation notes may extend to 3 years.

Project notes and tax-exempt commercial paper also play important roles in the municipal market. Local housing authorities issue project notes to finance federal expenditures for urban renewal, local neighborhood development, and low-income housing. The notes are repaid out of revenues from the projects financed. In the event

---

[1]Most analysts agree that industrial development bonds misallocate resources, reduce federal tax revenues, and increase borrowing costs of traditional general obligation debt. Kidwell and Koch (1984) describe the structure, costs, and benefits of IDB issues.

Exhibit 18.1 State of Washington Bond Issue

C18   THE WALL STREET JOURNAL THURSDAY, JANUARY 11, 1990

In the opinion of Bond Counsel, interest on the Bonds, including original issue discount properly allocable to a holder thereof, is excluded from gross income subject to federal income taxation pursuant to the Internal Revenue Code of 1986, as amended, subject to certain conditions and assumptions as described in the Official Statement. The Bonds are not private activity bonds. Interest on the Bonds is included in the computation of certain federal taxes on corporations.

NEW ISSUE

$120,000,000

State of Washington

Various Purpose General Obligation Bonds, Series 1990A

Dated: February 1, 1990

Due: February 1, as shown below

The Bonds are general obligations of the State to which the full faith, credit and taxing power of the State is unconditionally pledged. Interest on the Bonds is payable on August 1, 1990 and semiannually thereafter on the first day of each succeeding February and August. The Bonds are not subject to redemption prior to their stated date of maturity.

The Bonds are issuable only as fully registered bonds, and when issued, will be registered in the name of Cede & Co., as Bond-owner and nominee for The Depository Trust Company, New York, New York, which will act as securities depository for the Bonds. The Bonds will be issued in book-entry form, in the denomination of $5,000 or any integral multiple thereof. Purchasers will not receive certificates representing their interest in the Bonds purchased. The principal of and interest on the Bonds are payable by Seattle-First National Bank, Seattle, Washington, or The Bank of New York, New York, New York, as Paying Agent, to DTC, which will in turn remit such principal and interest to the DTC participants for subsequent disbursement to owners of the Bonds as described in the Official Statement.

Amount	Maturity	Interest Rate	Price or Yield	Amount	Maturity	Interest Rate	Price or Yield	Amount	Maturity	Interest Rate	Price or Yield
$1,575,000	1991	5¾ %	100%	$1,895,000	1998	6.30%	6.35%	$3,710,000	2004	6.60%	6.70%
1,730,000	1992	5.80	5.85	2,425,000	1999	6.40	100	4,045,000	2005	6.70	6.75
1,900,000	1993	5.90	5.95	945,000	2000	6.40	6.45	4,400,000	2006	6.70	6.75
1,890,000	1994	6	6.05	2,850,000	2001	6½	6.55	4,780,000	2007	6¾	6.80
9,455,000	1995	6.10	6.15	3,120,000	2002	6.60	100	5,875,000	2008	6¾	6.80
9,535,000	1996	6¼	100	3,400,000	2003	6.60	6.65	6,605,000	2009	6¾	6.80
2,060,000	1997	6.30	100					6,890,000	2010	6¾	6.80

$40,915,000 6¾% Term Bonds due February 1, 2015 to yield 6.93%

Bonds may or may not be available from the undersigned or others at the above prices on and after the date of this announcement.

The Bonds are offered when, as and if issued, subject to approval of legality by Lane Powell Moss & Miller, Olympia, Washington, Bond Counsel, and certain other conditions. The offering of the Bonds is made only by the Official Statement, copies of which may be obtained in any state from such of the undersigned as may lawfully offer these securities in such state.

Goldman, Sachs & Co.

Smith Barney, Harris Upham & Co.
Incorporated

The First Boston Corporation

Shearson Lehman Hutton Inc.

PaineWebber Incorporated

Kidder, Peabody & Co.
Incorporated

Chemical Securities Inc.

Manufacturers Hanover Securities Corporation

Marine Midland Capital Markets Corporation

The Bank of New York

Alex. Brown & Sons
Incorporated

Grigsby Brandford Powell Inc.

Mabon, Nugent & Co.

Rauscher Pierce Refsnes, Inc.

The GMS Group Inc.
Affiliate of Gruntal & Co., Inc.

Masterson Moreland Sauer Whisman, Inc.

Mesirow Capital Markets

Morgan Keegan & Company, Inc.

Williams Capital Markets, Inc.

January 9, 1990

that revenues are not forthcoming, the Department of Housing and Urban Development agrees to make the obligated interest and principal payments, so the notes carry an implied federal guarantee. Tax-exempt commercial paper is issued by the largest municipalities, which regularly need blocks of funds in $1 million multiples for operating purposes. Because only large, well-known borrowers issue this paper, yields are below those quoted on comparably rated municipal notes.

Banks buy large amounts of short-term municipals. They often work closely with municipalities in placing these securities and have a built-in need for short-term liquidity given that most bank liabilities are highly rate sensitive near term. Thus short-term municipals are in high demand, and short-term municipal rates are relatively low compared with rates on longer-term municipals. The state of Washington issue in Exhibit 18.1 demonstrates this rate relationship. Consider the serial bond issues that mature from 1991 through 2010. The interest rate column refers to the coupon rate while the price/yield column indicates the market rate. A price of 100 means that the security sells at par, or that the market rate equals the coupon rate. Note that the 1-year serial bond pays 5.75 percent, which is lower than all other market rates.

Long-Term Municipals

Long-term municipal securities include general obligation bonds and revenue bonds. Until the mid-1970s general obligations dominated the municipal market. Since 1976, however, revenue bonds have comprised more than one-half of all new issues. By 1985 new revenue bond issues equaled 75 percent of all new municipal issues. Much of this growth represented bonds issued to finance private-sector expenditures. As discussed earlier, these industrial development bonds (IDBs) were heavily criticized as an abuse of the tax exemption privilege so that new issues were restricted by the Tax Reform Act of 1986. Revenue bonds still constitute almost 70 percent of new municipal issues, but the proceeds are directed more to public facilities than are industrial revenue bonds.

General Obligation Bonds. Interest and principal payments on general obligation bonds are backed by the full faith, credit, and taxing power of the issuer. This backing represents the strongest commitment a government can make in support of its debt. At the extreme, governments promise to raise taxes, attach real property, and issue new debt to meet promised debt service payments. The state of Washington issue in Exhibit 18.1 is such a bond. Because this guarantee is so broad, issuers must generally obtain voter approval via referendum to issue new general obligation debt. Actual default risk depends on the viability of the issuer's tax base and its willingness to live up to the terms of the debt.

Occasionally, a municipality's taxing authority is limited, typically by a maximum allowable tax rate. In these cases, the bonds are still classified as general obligations but are referred to as *limited tax bonds*. In addition, municipalities often issue general obligations that are also secured by revenues independent of issuer general funds. Such bonds are referred to as *double barrel bonds* because of the dual backing.

Revenue Bonds. Revenue bonds are issued to finance projects whose revenues are the primary source of repayment. An example is bonds issued to finance airport expansion that are supported by fees obtained from the sale of landing rights and the city's share of parking and concessions. Other common public purpose revenue bond projects include toll roads and bridges, port facilities, hospital facilities, university dormitories, and water treatment plants. The revenue sources of these bonds can be identified by the label: tolls, port entry and exit charges, hospital charges, student fees, and water/sewer user charges, respectively. In general, revenue bonds exhibit greater default risk than do general obligations. The risk associated with specific bonds, however, depends on the strength of the revenue source supporting each project. Thus some revenue bonds supported by substantial cash flows trade at rates below those on general obligations. Many revenue bonds are sufficiently complex that an investor must read the bond prospectus carefully to determine what the primary revenue source is and what group is ultimately responsible for ensuring that investors are paid. Unlike general obligations bonds, revenue bonds do not need voter approval prior to issue.

Banks buy both general obligation and revenue bonds. The only restriction is that the bonds be investment grade or equivalent. Banks generally have a preference, however, for general obligations because they are more marketable and more closely associated with essential public purposes.

Historically, IDB investments at commercial banks represented direct loans rather than investment securities. Corporations generally approached a local government with a financing proposal. The firm's legal and financial staff prepared materials that demonstrated the project's economic benefits and met legal requirements. The firm then negotiated the terms of the bond issue, including maturities, pricing, and collateral, for direct placement with a local commercial bank. Loan officers analyzed the firm's financials and made a credit decision on whether the bank should make the loan. Most of these IDBs in bank portfolios are priced at floating rates equal to 65 to 75 percent of the bank's prime rate. Due to direct placement, these securities are typically nonrated and thus relatively illiquid. Existing IDB loans are regularly reviewed by the credit department, not the investment department.[2]

Credit Risk in the Municipal Portfolio

Until the 1970s, few municipal securities went into default. This was followed by deteriorating conditions in many large cities that ultimately resulted in defaults by New York City (1975) and Cleveland (1978). The Washington Public Power and Supply System (WHOOPS) similarly defaulted in 1983 on $2.25 billion of bonds issued to finance two nuclear power plants. During the decade of the 1980s, over 600 distinct municipals went into default. Past defaults and deteriorating economic conditions during the early 1990s raised investor concerns regarding the quality of municipal

---

[2]The practical treatment of industrial development bonds as loans while banks report them as investment securities raises the issue as to whether banks hold adequate loan-loss reserves against IDBs. Banks no longer acquire IDBs due to the Tax Reform Act of 1986. IDBs purchased before August 7, 1986, continue to generate tax-exempt interest.

issues and the accuracy of bond ratings.[3] Since WHOOPS' difficulties, the rating agencies have intensified their periodic reviews of issuer characteristics and conditions and revised their ratings with greater frequency after initial issue. During 1990 Standard & Poor's Corporation downgraded almost three times as many municipal issues as it upgraded.

Unfortunately, the diversity of municipal borrowers and disparate types of issues make it difficult to categorize municipal securities. Many issuers do not purchase bond ratings, so their securities are nonrated. While these securities may be low risk, an investing bank is responsible for documenting that they are equivalent to investment-grade securities. Much like the rating agencies, banks must examine the issuer's existing debt burden, the soundness of the operating budget, the strength of the tax base, cash flow support for revenue issues, and local demographic trends, all of which is recorded in a credit file. With many securities, it is extremely difficult for an investor to trace the web of revenue sources and guarantees to determine which group is ultimately responsible for meeting debt service requirements. Thus it is often difficult to assess the credit risk associated with nonrated issues.

Many municipal issuers purchase bond insurance to reduce perceived default risk and increase the marketability of their debt. The insurance is an unconditional guarantee by a property and casualty insurance company to pay promised coupon interest and principal if the issuer defaults. The municipality pays for the insurance when the securities are issued, and the policy is nonrefundable and noncancelable over the life of the securities. During 1990 approximately 30 percent of new issues carried some form of insurance or third-party guarantee. Municipalities that purchase insurance benefit from reduced interest costs because ratings on most insured bonds improve to the AAA or AA level. Such issues paid rates 10 to 25 basis points below rates on otherwise comparable noninsured bonds, which can alternatively be viewed as the price investors pay for the reduced credit risk. Of course, the value of the guarantee is only as good as the insurance company. Three well-known insurers, the American Municipal Bond Assurance Corp. (AMBAC), the Municipal Bond Insurance Association (MBIA), and Financial Guarantee Insurance Corporation (FGIC) provide most insurance coverage in the municipal market.

Liquidity Risk

Municipals exhibit substantially lower liquidity than Treasury or agency securities. The secondary market for municipals is fundamentally an over-the-counter market. Small, nonrated issues trade infrequently and at relatively large bid-ask dealer spreads. Large issues of nationally known municipalities, state agencies, and states trade more actively at smaller spreads. Name recognition is critical, as investors are more comfortable when they can identify the issuer with a specific location. Insurance also helps by improving the rating and by association with a known property and casualty insurer. Most dealers advertise their municipals inventory in the *Blue List,* a weekly booklet published by Standard & Poor's.

---

[3]The WHOOPS bonds were rated A+ and A1 by Standard & Poor's and Moody's at the time of default.

Still, municipals are less volatile in price than Treasury securities. This is generally attributed to the peculiar tax features of municipals.[4] The municipal market is segmented. On the supply side, municipalities cannot shift between short- and long-term securities to take advantage of yield differences because of constitutional restrictions on balanced operating budgets. Thus long-term bonds cannot be substituted for short-term municipals to finance operating expenses. On the demand side, banks once dominated the market for short-term municipals so that their rates were a set fraction of Treasury rates. Today, individuals via tax-exempt money market mutual funds dominate the short maturity spectrum. The investment activity of banks and money market mutual funds at the short end stabilizes municipal bond prices because these groups purchase most of the short-term municipals offered. This does not hold at longer maturities, where individuals represent the marginal investor. Therefore, short-term municipals do not vary sharply in price over time relative to short-term Treasuries.

COMPARATIVE YIELDS ON TAXABLE VERSUS TAX-EXEMPT SECURITIES

A bank's effective return from investing in securities depends on the amount of interest income, potential capital gains or losses, whether the income is tax-exempt or taxable, and whether the issuer defaults on interest and principal payments. When making investment decisions, a bank compares expected risk-adjusted, after-tax returns from alternative investments. It purchases securities that provide the highest expected risk-adjusted returns.

Municipal interest is exempt from federal income taxes and, depending on state law, state income taxes. Some states exempt all municipal interest. Most states selectively exempt interest from municipals issued in-state but tax interest on out-of-state issues. Other states either tax all municipal interest or do not impose an income tax. Capital gains on municipals are taxed as ordinary income under the federal income tax code. This makes discount municipals less attractive than par municipals because a portion of the return, the price appreciation, is fully taxable.

The net effect of the tax treatment is that municipal securities trade at yields well below yields on comparable-risk taxable securities. Thus when a 10-year taxable yields 10 percent, a 10-year municipal might yield just 7.5 percent. The difference in pretax yields reflects the tax benefit to an investor in municipals.

After-Tax and Tax-Equivalent Yields

The importance of income taxes on yields can easily be shown. Suppose that we are comparing yields on two securities of comparable maturity and risk. For the moment ignore state and local income taxes as well. Let

---

[4]Stock and Schrems (1987) compare the relative price volatility of municipals and Treasuries. They conclude that the volatility of short-term municipals is much lower, which is attributed to substantial short-term municipal investments by commercial banks. Relative volatility with longer-term securities is more similar.

R_m = pretax yield on a municipal security
R_t = pretax yield on a taxable security
  t = investor's marginal federal income tax rate

Once an investor has determined the appropriate maturity and risk security, the investment decision involves selecting the security with the highest after-tax yield. The relevant yield comparison is

$$R_m \gtreqless R_t(1-t) \tag{18.1}$$

Using the above data for R_m and R_t, an investor who pays taxes at the 31 percent rate would buy the municipal because it pays 0.6 percent more after taxes.

$$7.5\% > 10\%(1-.31) = 6.9\%$$

An investor who pays taxes at the 15 percent rate would prefer the taxable security because it offers 1 percent more in yield.

Municipals are often marketed to investors using a modified form of relationship (18.1). Suppose that the following question were posed. What tax rate would make an investor indifferent between buying a taxable or a municipal security? Indifference here means that the after-tax yields would be equal. The answer is obtained by solving (18.1) as an equality. Using the above data, an investor would be indifferent at the margin if his tax rate were 25 percent. In general, this indifference tax rate (t*) is solved by (18.2)

$$t* = 1 - \frac{R_m}{R_t} \tag{18.2}$$

The investment decision is then made by comparing an investor's marginal tax rate with this indifference rate. The following rules determine the appropriate choice.

- If t > t* then buy the municipal

- If t < t* then buy the taxable

- If t = t* then indifferent

With R_m equal to 7.5 percent and R_t equal to 10 percent, any investor with a marginal tax rate over 25 percent prefers municipals while any investor with a tax rate below 25 percent prefers taxables.

The analysis is complicated only slightly when state and local income taxes are taken into account. Let t_m equal the marginal state and local tax rate on municipal interest. Then the relevant yield comparison, assuming no state and local tax against taxable interest as with Treasury securities, is

$$R_m(1-t_m) \gtreqless R_t(1-t) \tag{18.3}$$

Suppose that t_m equals 5 percent in the above case in which the marginal federal income tax rate equals 31 percent. The after-tax yield comparison now becomes

$$7.5\%(1 - .05) > 10\%(1 - .31)$$
$$7.125\% \quad > \quad 6.9\%$$

The municipal still yields more, but the incremental advantage is reduced to just 22.5 basis points.

Many analysts compare returns on municipals with taxables in terms of tax-equivalent yields. This involves nothing more than restating relationships (18.1) and (18.3) when the equality of after-tax yields is enforced. Specifically, municipal yields are converted to their tax-equivalent values by solving (18.4).

$$\text{tax-equivalent yield} = \frac{R_m(1 - t_m)}{(1 - t)} \qquad \textbf{(18.4)}$$

In the above example, the tax-equivalent municipal yield equals 10.33 percent $[.075(1 - .05)/(1 - .31)]$. This figure means that the investor would have to earn 10.33 percent on a comparable taxable security to produce the same 7.125 percent after-tax yield.[5]

The Yield Comparison for Commercial Banks

Suppose that a bank portfolio manager wants to compare potential returns between a taxable security and a municipal security that currently yield 10 percent and 8 percent, respectively. Both securities are new issues trading at $10,000 par with identical maturities, call treatment, and default risk. The primary difference is that the bank pays federal income taxes at a 34 percent marginal rate on the taxable security while municipal interest is entirely tax-exempt. Part A of Exhibit 18.2 shows that the portfolio manager would earn $140 more in after-tax interest from buying the municipal.

Applying (18.3) using this data, the yield comparison is

$$8\%(1 - 0) = 8\% > 10\%(1 - 0.34) = 6.6\%$$

The after-tax yield differential times the principal invested produces the $140 difference in after-tax income.

The tax-equivalent yield, which essentially converts the municipal yield to a pretax yield that would produce an after-tax return equal to that on an otherwise identical taxable security, equals 12.12 percent from (18.4).

The Effective Tax on Incremental Municipal Interest Earned by Commercial Banks.
Prior to 1983, commercial banks could invest in tax-exempt securities and deduct the full amount of interest paid on liabilities used to finance their purchases. Virtually all other investors, including individuals, were (and are still) denied a deduction for any indebtedness to carry or purchase tax-exempts. The deduction enabled many banks to arbitrage between the after-tax cost of borrowing and municipal

---

[5]In most published reports, taxes on municipal interest are ignored (t_m is set equal to 0) so that the reported tax-equivalent yield equals the municipal rate divided by 1 minus the federal income tax rate. In this example, such a tax-equivalent yield would equal 10.87 percent $[7.5\%/(1 - .31)]$. This clearly overstates the true tax-equivalent yield with nonzero state and local taxes.

Exhibit 18.2 A Comparison of After-Tax Returns on Taxable and Tax-Exempt Securities for a Bank as Investor

A. After-Tax Interest Earned on Taxable versus Exempt Municipal Securities

	Taxable Security	Municipal Security
Par value	$10,000	$10,000
Coupon rate	10%	8%
Annual coupon interest	$ 1,000	$ 800
Federal income taxes at 34%	$ 340	Exempt
After-tax interest income	$ 660	$ 800

B. Disallowing Deduction of Interest on Indebtedness to Finance Municipal Purchases for a Bank: Total Portfolio and Income Statement Effect

Factors affecting allowable deduction for 1991.

- Total interest expense paid in 1991: $1,500,000
- Average amount of assets owned during 1991: $20,000,000
- Average amount of tax exempt securities owned that were acquired after the change in tax laws affecting interest deductibility: $800,000
- Weighted-average cost of financing assets: $\dfrac{\$1,500,00}{\$20,000,000} = 7.5\%$

Nondeductible interest expense:

- Pro rata share of interest expense to carry municipals purchased after 1982: $\dfrac{\$800,000}{\$20,000,000} = 4\%$
- Nondeductible interest expense at 20 percent: $1,500,000(.04)(0.2) = $12,000

Deductible interest expense: $1,500,000 − $12,000 = $1,488,000

C. After-Tax Interest Earned Recognizing Partial Deductibility of Interest Expense: Individual Asset

	Taxable Security	Municipal Security
Par value	$10,000	$10,000
Coupon rate	10%	8%
Annual coupon interest	$ 1,000	$ 800
Federal income taxes at 34%	$ 340	Exempt
Pooled interest expense (rate = 7.5%)	$ 750	$ 750
Lost interest deduction (20%)	$ 0	$ 150
Increased tax liability at 34%	$ 0	$ 51
Effective after-tax interest income	$ 660	$ 749

yields at the margin to supplement earnings and reduce their effective income tax liability.

In 1983 Congress rewrote the tax law to deny banks a deduction for 15 percent of their interest expense allocated to indebtedness for the purpose of acquiring and holding new municipal issues. This nondeductible portion was increased to 20 percent in 1985. The Tax Reform Act of 1986 went one step farther and eliminated the deduction for most municipal bonds.

The following calculations demonstrate the impact of the lost deduction on a bank's total after-tax income and on the effective yield on municipal securities. For income tax purposes, interest expense allocated to municipal investments is prorated against total interest expense according to the ratio of average tax-exempt securities purchased after the change in tax laws that are owned by a bank to its average total assets. Part B of Exhibit 18.2 provides an example that uses data on a bank's total portfolio and calculates the total amount of lost deductions for the year assuming 20 percent lost interest deductibility. The bank is relatively small with only $20 million in assets. During 1991 the bank paid $1.5 million in total interest expense so that its weighted average cost of financing assets equaled 7.5 percent. The amount of interest expense that is nondeductible depends on how many bonds were purchased after the tax change, which is $800,000 in this example. A 4 percent pro rata share of total interest expense is allocated to municipal financing costs, which produces a disallowed deduction of $12,000. The remaining $1.488 million in interest was tax deductible. The $12,000 lost deduction has a tax value of $4,080 (.34 × $12,000) which represents the increase in taxes owed by the bank.[6]

Part C of Exhibit 18.2 indicates the effect of this lost interest deductibility on the expected return from municipal investments. It replicates Part A except that the bank as an investor can deduct only 80 percent of its interest expense applicable to financing the municipal security. The analysis is identical through the federal income tax calculation. Beyond that, the bank pays a pooled interest cost of 7.5 percent (the same as in part B; $1.5 million/$20 million). Thus interest paid to finance the $10,000 in municipals equals $750, of which $150 is nondeductible. This lost deduction raises the bank's effective tax liability by $51 (34 percent of $150) and reduces the realized return on the municipal to $749, or 7.49 percent.

This lost interest deduction essentially represents a tax on incremental municipal interest. A good analogy is a home buyer who obtains a mortgage to finance the purchase. Each month the homeowner makes a mortgage payment that includes interest and principal on the debt. Suppose that Congress suddenly changed the tax laws and no longer allowed individuals to deduct home mortgage interest. The homeowner would still make the obligated mortgage payments, but could no longer itemize the interest deduction on her income statement. The lost deduction essentially represents an increase in taxes owed because reported taxable income increases without any additional cash receipts. The cost of owning a home would increase, or alternatively, the after-tax return from owning a home would decrease.

In order to compare yields on municipal and taxable securities, the lost interest deduction is converted to a marginal tax on municipal interest. Setting

c = bank's pooled interest cost rate
n = the nondeductible portion of interest expense
t_c = the marginal corporation income tax rate
t_s = state/local government income tax rate

---

[6]Note that the bank must pay the entire $1.5 million in interest, which represents its actual cash outflow. It is just allowed a deduction for $1.488 million, however, so that its reported income is $12,000 higher. This produces the $4,080 additional tax payment.

the federal tax value of the lost interest deduction equals the product of c, n, and t_c, divided by the pretax municipal rate (R_m). When state and local income taxes are added, the effective bank tax rate on municipal interest (t_b) can be expressed as

$$t_b = \frac{c(n)t_c}{R_m} + t_s \qquad\qquad (18.5)$$

Applying the data from part C with no state/local income taxes:

$$t_b = \frac{[0.34(0.2)(0.075)]}{.08} = 0.06375$$

and

$$8\%(1 - 0.06375) = 7.49\% > 10\%(1 - 0.34) = 6.6\%$$

The true tax-equivalent municipal yield for this bank paying no state and local income taxes is 11.35 percent.[7]

THE IMPACT OF THE TAX REFORM ACT OF 1986

The Tax Reform Act of 1986 dramatically altered commercial banks' investment strategies and the attractiveness of different types of securities. This section describes factors that lowered returns on most municipal securities. In general, the Act reduced the pool of municipal securities that kept their tax exemption and eliminated banks' ability to deduct carrying costs on new municipal purchases except for qualifying small issues that meet essential public purpose requirements. The discussion focuses only on commercial banks as the distinction between qualified and nonqualified issues does not apply to other investors.

Qualified versus Nonqualified Municipals

All municipal interest is still tax-exempt for federal income tax purposes. There are, however, a variety of ways in which banks may be subject to tax when they buy municipals. The Tax Reform Act created different categories of municipal bonds. The more essential a given type of bond is for states and localities, the broader is its tax exemption. The first distinction is between municipals issued before and after August 7, 1986. Municipals issued before this date retain their tax exemption. They are essentially grandfathered because banks can still deduct 80 percent of their associated financing costs regardless of the Act. Securities issued after this date are categorized as qualified or nonqualified depending on whether they meet certain criteria.

Qualified Municipals. Banks can still deduct 80 percent of their carrying costs associated with the purchase of certain essential, public-purpose bonds. There are two important criteria for bonds to qualify. First, the proceeds must be used to finance

---

[7][8% (1 − .06375)/10% (1 − .34)] = 11.35%.

essential government services including schools, highways, sewer systems, and so forth. In most cases, traditional general obligation bonds meet this standard. Second, the municipality cannot issue more than $10 million in municipal securities per year. Thus only small-issue municipals qualify. They are labelled *bank qualified* municipals. State government issues do not qualify regardless of total debt issuance. The purpose of this distinct treatment was to help small government units obtain financing. In many communities banks are the only investors in local government securities because they are the only ones with the resources and some knowledge of the financial condition of the borrower. If this exception to the lost deduction had not been granted, it was feared that many such units would have had to cut back services drastically.

The effective bank tax rate against qualified municipals uses a nondeductible portion of interest equal to 20 percent ($n = 0.20$). Thus the after-tax yield calculation in Exhibit 18.2 and the above examples is relevant for qualified municipals. The net impact is that even though banks lose a portion of their interest deductibility, with $n = .20$ the bank tax rate on municipal interest is so low that qualified municipals still yield more than fully taxed alternative investments. Thus qualified municipals are attractive investments for profitable banks. The problem is that transactions costs are high when banks search out qualified municipals. This occurs because only smaller, lesser-known municipalities can issue qualifying debt.

Nonqualified Municipals. All municipals that do not meet the criteria as bank-qualified bonds are labeled nonqualified municipals. If banks buy these securities, they can deduct none of their associated carrying costs. In terms of Exhibit 18.2 and the after-tax yield comparison, nondeductible interest on nonqualified municipals equals 100 percent. This sharply raises the effective tax rate on nonqualified municipals purchased by banks to such an extent that they are no longer viable investments. If the 8 percent municipal bond in Exhibit 18.2 (part C) were nonqualified, the lost interest deduction would have totaled $750 and the tax liability would have increased to $255 ($t_b$ equals 0.3188). The effective after-tax income would have equaled only $545, or $115 less than that from the taxable security.

$$R_m(1 - t_b) = 8\%\left(1 - \frac{.075(1.0).34}{.08}\right) = 5.45\%$$

As demonstrated, the effective bank tax rate on nonqualified municipal interest is quite high. Because these securities are still attractive to nonbank investors looking for tax-sheltered income, they continue to carry yields below those on comparable taxable securities. The combination of tax-exempt yields and a high effective tax rate make nonqualified municipals unattractive to banks. Banks thus no longer buy nonqualified municipals because they can get higher yields elsewhere.

A second important change under the Act is the expanded alternative minimum tax. Banks must now compute their tax liability in two ways, according to regular income tax guidelines and according to minimum tax rules, which add preference items back to normal taxable income and apply a 20 percent minimum tax rate. Banks pay the higher of the two taxes. The importance for the investment portfolio is that tax-exempt interest is a preference item and banks must include one-half of tax-exempt interest earned in the taxable base. Thus the effective tax on qualified, essential public-purpose bond interest potentially rose by 10 percent.

The Tax Reform Act of 1986 will have several long-term effects on bank investments and relative security yields. Pretax municipal yields have risen relative to taxable yields to reflect reduced demand by commercial banks. Banks have also shifted their investment portfolios to taxable securities, such as mortgage-backed pass-through securities and CMOs, to earn higher risk-adjusted yields.

A COMPARISON OF TREASURY AND MUNICIPAL YIELD CURVES

When selecting specific investment securities, portfolio managers must decide what maturities best meet the bank's return and risk objectives. Yield considerations involve forecasting the direction of interest rates, then comparing the forecasts to existing opportunities at various maturities. Knowledge of the term structure of interest rates on Treasury and municipal securities provides a framework for analyzing various strategies.

The term structure of interest rates, or yield curve, is represented by a two-dimensional graph, with the percentage yield on the vertical axis and the term to maturity on the horizontal axis for securities that differ only in terms of maturity. The Treasury yield curve compares market interest rates on Treasury securities of varying maturities at a fixed point in time. Yield curves on Treasury securities were introduced in Chapter 7, and Exhibit 7.9 compares alternative shapes in recent years. Any yield/maturity relationship can change over time as economic conditions and market expectations vary. Because municipal securities differ in terms of default risk, no pure yield curve for all municipals exists. An approximate yield curve using averages of market interest rates characterizes average yield/maturity relationships. Yield curves for individual securities can be extrapolated from serial bond issues.

The Treasury Yield Curve

Treasury securities provide the purest yield curve because all Treasuries are free of default risk. Treasury yields do not include default risk premiums and are directly comparable across maturities. Diagrams A, B, and C in Exhibit 18.3 indicate the three most common shapes of the Treasury yield curve.[8]

A normal yield curve is continuously upsloping, indicating that market yields on short-term securities are below market yields on longer-term securities. The yield curve generally takes this ascending shape when interest rates are low and market participants expect short-term rates to rise. Rates are low because economic growth is low, loan demand is weak, inflation is low, and the Federal Reserve is accelerating money

---

[8]Van Horne, 1990, summarizes recent empirical research on specific determinants of the various shapes yield curves take.

Exhibit 18.3 Shapes of Treasury and Municipal Yield Curves

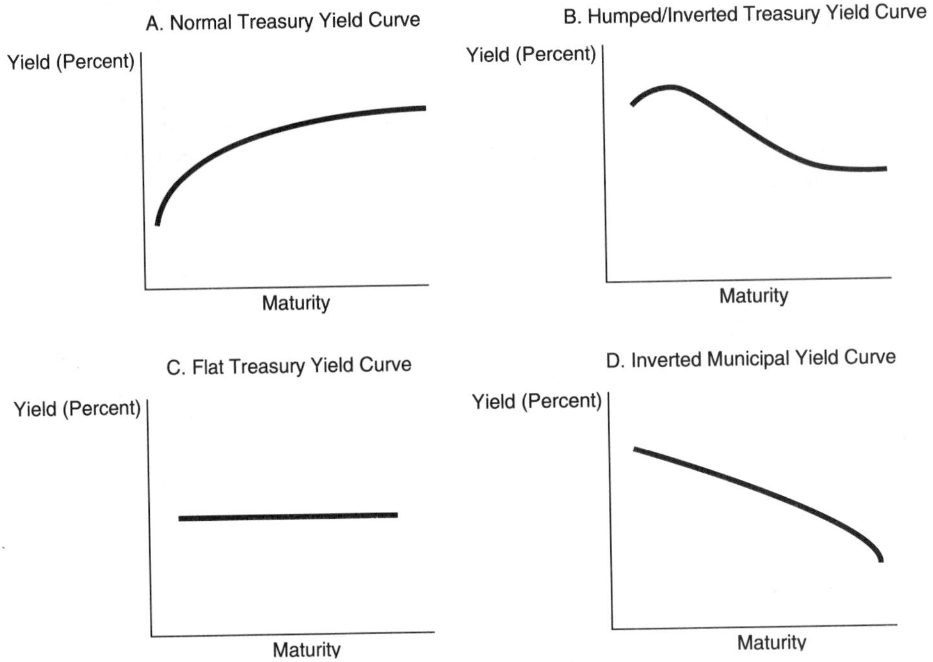

A. Normal Treasury Yield Curve

Yield (Percent)

Maturity

B. Humped/Inverted Treasury Yield Curve

Yield (Percent)

Maturity

C. Flat Treasury Yield Curve

Yield (Percent)

Maturity

D. Inverted Municipal Yield Curve

Yield (Percent)

Maturity

growth. Banks typically have considerable liquidity and limited opportunities to extend credit to creditworthy borrowers. Rates typically increase over time as consumer spending, real investment, and loan demand pick up.

An inverted yield curve is frequently humped as rates rise over very short maturities, then downsloping throughout the longest maturity. Diagram D indicates a completely inverted yield curve. Inverted yield curves typically appear when interest rates are relatively high and market participants expect rates to decline. This coincides with periods of high economic growth, strong loan demand, high inflation, and tight Federal Reserve monetary policy. Banks need liquidity and bid short-term rates higher as they compete for funds in the short-term deposit markets. Rates are expected to decline over time as economic growth slows.

A flat yield curve indicates that yields are approximately equal across all maturities. Treasury yields are often constant during transition periods when the yield curve is switching from a normal to inverted shape or vice versa.

A bank portfolio manager must be especially mindful of the yield curve's shape and potential economic conditions when making maturity decisions. The temptation is to lengthen maturities during periods of slack loan demand and high liquidity when the yield curve is upsloping. Long-term securities offer the highest rates and appear to best supplement earnings the bank loses from declining loan demand. In general, however, when available liquidity is highest, interest rates at all maturities are lower than during other periods. If economic growth accelerates and loan demand picks up, all interest rates will rise and the bank may be stuck with bonds paying below-market rates. Selling a bond after a rate increase entails taking a capital loss. The opposite temptation exists when the yield curve is inverted. Portfolio managers typically limit purchases to short-term instruments because their yields are the highest and the bank needs additional liquidity. These periods, however, represent the best opportunities to lock in high yields and realize potential capital gains. Interest rates at all maturities are generally higher compared with other periods. When economic growth and loan demand weaken, rates will fall, providing relatively greater excess returns to long-term bond holders.

The Municipal Yield Curve

Unlike the Treasury yield curve, municipal yields almost always increase monotonically with maturity. This is true for averages of market rates on similarly rated municipals and for reoffering yields on individual serial bond issues. Diagram A in Exhibit 18.3 displays the shape of the term-structure of reoffering yields on the state of Washington general obligation bonds presented in Exhibit 18.1. Note, for example, that the 1-year yield is just 5.75 percent, but subsequent market yields rise throughout the 20-year term to 6.80 percent. The shape of the yield curve does not vary dramatically over the business cycle. When the Treasury yield curve inverts, however, short-term municipal yields rise relative to long-term yields so that the municipal yield curve is flatter, but still upsloping.

Prior to the Tax Reform Act of 1986, most analysts attributed the positive slope of the municipal yield curve to the investment behavior of commercial banks in the municipal market. Regardless of maturity, banks that paid the full corporate income tax rate found that municipals provided higher after-tax returns than comparable taxable securities. In terms of the yield comparison implied by Equation 18.2, the maximum corporate tax rate always exceeded the indifference tax rate (t^*) so that municipals always yielded more for banks after taxes than did taxable securities. Bank municipal investments were thus largely insensitive to the relationship between municipal yields and taxable security yields. The fundamental decision was how many municipals to acquire and which maturities were optimal. Since 1986 the role formerly played by banks has been filled by money market mutual funds. Their impact on the municipal yield curve derives from their concentrated investment in municipals at the shortest maturities.

Market segmentation arguments provide the fundamental explanation of the continuously upsloping yield curve. Market segmentation theory suggests that investors and borrowers restrict their activity to specific maturities and do not substitute between maturities based on small yield changes. Before tax reform banks were the dominant investor at the shortest maturities and purchased proportionately smaller shares at successively longer maturities. In terms of Equation 18.2, bank investments drove t^* close to the full corporate tax rate for short-term securities. As maturity lengthened, banks purchased proportionately fewer municipals, and t^* decreased to induce additional purchases from individual investors in lower marginal tax brackets. After 1986 money market mutual fund purchases of short-term municipals accelerated to replace the lost purchases of commercial banks. The segmentation relationships appear to have remained. State and local government borrowers, in turn, are required by constitutional provisions to use short-term debt for operating expenses and long-term debt for capital expenditures. They consequently do not freely substitute between maturities to take advantage of the lower short-term rates.[9]

The fact that t* decreases with maturity is well documented. Exhibit 18.4 plots the ratio of municipal to Treasury yields (R_m/R_t) from 1971 through 1990 for 1-, 10-, and 20-year maturity securities. Each rate ratio equals $(1 - t^*)$ according to Equation 18.2. Note that the 1-year ratio is always less than the other ratios, and the 10-year ratio is always less that the 20-year ratio except for one brief period. The fact that municipal yields increase relative to Treasury yields the longer the term to maturity indicates that t* declines with maturity. At 1 year, the rate ratio averages around .6, suggesting that t* averages 40 percent. At 10 and 20 years, t* is closer to 30 percent and 20 percent, respectively.

This systematic relationship imparts an upward bias to the slope of the municipal yield curve. Suppose, for example, that the Treasury yield curve is flat at 10 percent. Assume also that t* equals .4, .3, and .2 at 1-, 10-, and 20-year maturities, respectively. The simple application of Equation 18.2 requires that R_m equal 6 percent, 7 percent, and 8 percent at the respective maturities. Thus the municipal yield curve is upsloping even when the Treasury yield curve is flat. Given historical values for t* at different maturities, the taxable yield curve would have to invert dramatically to induce even a flat municipal yield curve.

The large reduction in corporate and individual tax rates after 1986 and the lost interest deduction for banks changed the normal level of municipal yields relative to taxable yields. As revealed in Exhibit 18.4, it generally made the slope of the municipal yield curve flatter. This is due to a decline in the difference between the maximum corporate tax rate and the effective individual tax rate, and banks' general withdrawal from the municipal market.

LOANS TO EMPLOYEE STOCK OWNERSHIP PLANS

An employee stock ownership plan (ESOP) is a defined-contribution employee benefit plan set up as a trust that invests the bulk of its assets in the employer's stock. A leverage ESOP is one in which an employer borrows the funds to buy its stock and guarantees the loan. The stock is typically pledged as collateral on the loan. In either case, employees become owners of the firm. Over time the employer makes contribu-

---

[9]In recent years municipal put bonds have evolved which indirectly accomplish this substitution. A put bond gives the investor the option to put the bond back to the issuer at predetermined intervals and thus to receive invested principal prior to final maturity. Put bonds are priced off of the time until the bond can be tendered as if that term were its maturity. Thus a 20-year bond that is puttable annually is effectively priced as a 1-year municipal when the rate floats at each put interval.

Exhibit 18.4 Ratio of Municipal Yields (R_m) to Treasury Yields (R_t) on Securities of Comparable Maturity (Maturity in Years Appears in Parentheses)

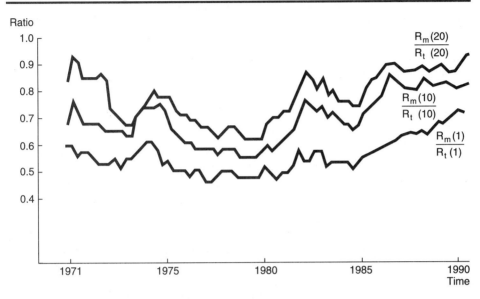

Source: An Analytical Record of Yields and Yield Spreads, Salomon Brothers

tions to the ESOP which are used to repay the loan. As the loan payments are made the ESOP directly allocates shares of stock to each employee on the payroll.

In recent years ESOPs have grown in popularity for a variety of reasons. They have been used primarily as an antitakeover device. By putting additional stock in the hands of a friendly trustee who will presumably vote with current management, it is more difficult for an outsider to gain control of the firm. ESOPs have the added advantage, however, of reducing costs. Employers can deduct any interest on their borrowings to fund the ESOP and can even deduct dividends paid on shares of stock held by an ESOP when the dividends are used to repay the loan or paid directly to employees.

While some banks have established ESOPs for their own employees, their importance as an investment derives from a bank lending another company the proceeds to purchase stock for an ESOP. Once again, there are two sets of rules depending on when an ESOP was established. Loans to ESOPs established by an employer that had a binding commitment for the ESOP by June 6, 1989 are treated differently than those established later. Specifically, any company that made a loan to a grandfathered ESOP for the purchase of employer securities could exclude 50 percent of the interest earned from taxable income. For loans made after this date, the 50 percent interest exclusion only applies if the ESOP owns more than 50 percent of each class of the employer's stock.

The many banks that made ESOP loans throughout the 1980s can thus still exempt one-half of the interest earned so that these loans are effectively revenue bonds with a partial exemption. Typically, banks pass on part of the tax exemption by charging a lower rate on an ESOP loan. Thus an ESOP loan rate might be set at 85 percent of the bank's prime rate. By mid-year 1989 ESOP loans exceeded $20 billion, of which banks were major creditors. Qualifying loans after the June 1989 cut-off date have the same impact, but there are fewer of these loans outstanding because few ESOPs own 50 percent of an employer's stock.

LEASING ACTIVITIES

Many banks are actively involved in originating leases for customers, typically through a bank subsidiary. While there are many types of leases, the basic concept is that a customer gets to use some asset for a stated period of time without ever owning it. A lease contract stipulates that a lessor, or owner of the asset, authorizes a lessee to use the asset in return for regular lease payments. A simple parallel is an apartment rental agreement.

Banks generally operate as lessors by acquiring capital assets that they lease to corporate customers. Such leases serve as alternatives to loans. Leases do not directly provide tax-sheltered income to a bank. The tax shelter arises because a lessor can depreciate the capital assets on an accelerated basis. Depreciation is a noncash expense and thus serves to defer any tax liability. The extent to which a bank realizes the benefit of the deductions depends on how the lease contract is priced. In many cases, a lessor must pass through much of the value of accelerated depreciation in the form of lower periodic lease payments. In this environment, the lessor ends up speculating on the salvage value of the capital asset after it is fully depreciated.

The Alternative Minimum Tax

The Tax Reform Act of 1986 expanded the attack on taxpayers that receive tax-sheltered income by creating an alternative minimum tax (AMT). Under this system, a bank must calculate its tax liability under the normal federal corporate income tax code, then calculate its tax liability under AMT provisions. Alternative minimum taxable income essentially equals reported taxable income plus certain preference items representing tax-sheltered income. Examples of preference income are tax-exempt interest on certain types of private-purpose municipals, the excess of a bank's addition to its bad debt reserve over its actual loss experience, and the excess of accelerated depreciation over straight-line depreciation. There are some adjustments for foreign tax credits. The AMT liability then equals 20 percent of this version of taxable income.

The purpose of the AMT is to ensure that all corporations pay some minimum amount of taxes. Banks that once were able to shelter virtually all of their income from taxes now must pay at least the AMT. The practical impact has been to force banks to closely monitor their taxable income under both tax systems. When the AMT comes close to applying, banks often adjust their portfolios away from generating tax-sheltered income.

SUMMARY

Banks, like other investors, constantly try to identify tax-sheltered investments that offer attractive after-tax returns with limited risk. Historically, they relied on tax-exempt interest income from municipal securities, partially tax-exempt interest on loans to ESOPs, investment tax credits and accelerated depreciation allowances associated with capital expenditures. During the latter part of the 1980s, the value of these tax-sheltered investments was sharply reduced and even eliminated in some instances.

Today, banks earn tax-exempt interest on qualified municipal securities that meet a small-issue, public-purpose exception to the Tax Reform Act of 1986. This chapter analyzes procedures to compare after-tax returns on qualified municipals versus taxable securities. The nondeductibility of 20 percent of municipal carrying costs is seen to represent a tax on municipal interest. Interest earned on other, nonqualified municipals is effectively subject to a high marginal tax rate so that they yield less than alternative investments. Banks have consequently shifted much of their securities portfolio to taxable instruments, such as mortgage-backed securities. Banks can still exempt 50 percent of the interest they receive on loans to ESOPs if the loans were authorized before June 1989. Loans to newly formed ESOPs are partially exempt only when the ESOP owns at least 50 percent of the employer's stock. Leasing activities that generate substantial accelerated depreciation benefits are attractive because depreciation is a non-cash expense and thus serves to defer tax payments. Finally, even when a bank generates sufficient tax-sheltered income, it may have to pay the alternative minimum tax that penalizes preference income like tax-exempt interest on certain municipals.

Banks must thus evaluate their tax profile carefully before making tax-sheltered investments. They must also focus more closely on alternative taxable investments that will eventually provide comparable after-tax returns.

FIRST FINANCIAL REVISTED: MUNICIPAL BONDS

Joan Nystrom was in charge of First Financial's investment portfolio. At the time C.W. Hampton examined the bank's risk and return profile, First Financial was reporting losses due largely to large provisions for loan losses. Yet the bank owned significant amounts of municipal bonds.

If a bank reports negative net income, its marginal tax rate is zero. If it pays no taxes, it has no need for tax-sheltered interest income from municipals. The fact that First Financial owned municipals means that it realizes an opportunity loss from not using the same investible funds to buy taxable securities. In essence, the taxable income that could be generated would be offset or sheltered by the provisions for loan losses. Thus if First Financial could sell its municipal portfolio and reinvest the proceeds in Treasury or mortgage-backed securities, it would generate more in periodic interest income.

First Financial would pursue such a strategy except that its municipal portfolio is currently under water. That is, the municipal bonds sell at a discount from the bank's historical cost of buying the securities. If they are sold, First Financial must report a loss on sale of securities (a reduction in noninterest income) and the bank's profit position and capital position would deteriorate even further. The bank is caught in a bind where it should sell its municipal bonds to improve cash flow, but it feels prevented from doing so because it cannot absorb the additional losses.

Questions

Characteristics of Municipals

1. Which investor would offer a higher price to buy a tax-exempt municipal revenue bond?
   a. a state university
   b. a pension fund
   c. a corporation in the 34% tax bracket
   d. an individual in the 28% tax bracket
   e. a bank in the 34% tax bracket

2. Why are municipalities allowed to issue tax-exempt securities? Why were banks originally encouraged to purchase them? Why are they no longer encouraged to do so? How is this change in regulation related to the current banking crisis?

Taxable vs. Tax-exempt Yields

3. A bank is considering investing in two securities of comparable maturity and risk. The first, paying 10% interest, is taxable at the federal and state levels; the second, a municipal, is exempt from both taxes.
   a. The bank is in the 40% marginal tax bracket and the 30% average tax bracket, including both federal and state taxes. What is the minimal acceptable yield on the municipal?
   b. If the municipal is only exempt from federal taxes, not state taxes, will its minimal acceptable yield increase or decrease?

4. Suppose the tax laws applying to banks were changed to designate three types of municipal securities:

   Type A: all interest is tax-exempt

   Type B: 20% of interest is not tax-exempt

   Type C: 100% of interest is not tax-exempt

   A municipality is issuing all three types and each type is equally risky to the investor. If the Type A security is yielding a going market rate of 8%, what rates would the other two types have to offer to make them equally attractive to a bank in the 40% marginal tax bracket?

5. A bank is anticipating its annual taxes while formulating its investment policies. It has collected the corporate tax rates as follows:

If taxable income is:	Taxes are:	
	Base	**Plus this percentage over base**
0–$50,000	$ 0	15%
50,000–75,000	7,500	25
75,000–100,000	13,750	34
100,000–335,000	22,250	39
Over $335,000	113,900	34

It also is very much aware that it has to pay the higher of the above tax or 20% of taxable income plus preferred income. Half of municipal interest income is considered preferred income. Currently this bank's taxable income is $55,000, but the bank is planning to receive $400,000 of new deposits and these funds will be placed in the bank's investment portfolio. The new investments can be placed in Aaa bonds yielding 10% return or in eligible municipals yielding 8%.

a. Without the additional funds what is the bank's tax liability? What are its after-tax profits?

b. If all of the funds are invested in the Aaa bonds, what will be the bank's tax liability? What will be its after-tax profits?

c. If all of the funds are invested in the municipals, what will be the bank's tax liability? What will be its after-tax profits?

d. If the bank must put all of these funds in one or the other, do you prefer the bonds or the munis? If the bank can split the funds between the two investments, is that a better alternative?

6. Carol Frantz manages Community Bank's investment portfolio and reports monthly to the bank's asset and liability committee on recent acquisitions, sales, and maturing instruments. Community Bank is a $90 million organization that has traditionally used investments to shelter as much income as possible. At the end of the current month, $1 million in municipals purchased in 1980 will mature.

Carol's immediate concern is whether or not she should reinvest the proceeds in new municipals that qualify for the small issue exception to the Tax Reform Act of 1986. She has identified two comparable risk and maturity instruments. One is a 5-year Federal Land Bank bond paying 11.45 percent in taxable interest. The other is a 5-year municipal bond paying 9.5 percent issued by the State Park Independent School District in Pennsylvania. Because the school district will issue less than $10 million in bonds during the year and the proceeds will be used to build a new school, the issue qualifies under the small issue, public-purchase bond exception. Community Bank can deduct 80 percent of the interest income from this investment.

Carol decides to compare the after-tax income contribution of the two securities. Community Bank pays federal taxes at the 34 percent rate and no state or local income taxes.

a. What is Community Bank's effective tax rate on the school district's municipal bond? Does the municipal or the federal security offer the higher after-tax yield?

b. What would be the tax equivalent yield on the municipal if it did not qualify for any deduction? If it qualified for 100% deduction?

Tax Reform

7. Why are banks required to pay the higher of the taxes calculated as:
   a. regular corporate rates
   b. 20% of taxable income plus preference items
   Name one of the preference items used in the alternative minimum tax. Is this distinction meaningful since 20% is far below the marginal corporate tax rate of 34%?

Treasury and Municipal Yield Curves

8. When loan demand is weak, banks tend to supplement their portfolios by purchasing long-term securities. What is the justification for doing this? What caution should be given to such a bank?

9. How does the municipal yield curve compare to the Treasury yield curve during periods of low inflation? During periods of high inflation? What would explain this anomaly?

10. The maximum advantage can be obtained from the tax-exempt status of municipals by investing in the short-term municipals or long-term ones? Has this differential narrowed or widened as a result of the 1986 tax changes?

Loans to ESOPs

11. Why does the chapter discuss ESOPs? Is the bank role in this market increasing or decreasing and why?

12. What is the benefit to a bank of leasing an asset to a customer rather than making the customer to borrow the money? Consider the benefit in terms of both profits and risk. In light of the Alternative Minimum Tax does this benefit still exist?

References

Clark, Danial. "A Farewell to Municipals." *ABA Banking Journal* (February 1987).

Hueglin, Steven, and Karyn Ward. *Guide to State and Local Taxation of Municipal Bonds.* New York: Gabriele, Hueglin, and Cashman, 1981.

Hsueh, Paul, and David Kidwell. "The Impact of State Bond Guarantees on State Credit Markets and Individual Municipalities." *National Tax Journal* (June 1988).

Jordan, Brad, and Richard Pettway. "The Pricing of Short-Term Debt and the Miller Hypothesis: A Note." *Journal of Finance* (June 1985).

Kidwell, David, and Timothy Koch. "Market Segmentation and the Term-Structure of Municipal Yields." *Journal of Money, Credit and Banking* (February 1983).

Kidwell, David, and Timothy Koch. "State and Local Government Financing." Chapter 8 in *Handbook of Modern Finance*, Warren, Gorham & Lamont. Boston, MA, 1984.

Kidwell, David, Timothy Koch, and Duane Stock. "The Impact of State Income Taxes on Municipal Borrowing Costs." *National Tax Journal* (December 1984).

Kidwell, David, Eric Sorensen, and John Wachowitz. "Estimating the Signalling Benefits of Debt Insurance: The Case of Municipal Bonds." *Journal of Financial and Quantitative Analysis* (September 1987).

Koch, Timothy. "The Tax Subsidy Associated with Bank Qualified Municipal Bonds." University of South Carolina working paper, January 1991.

Livingston, Miles. "The Pricing of Municipal Bonds." *Journal of Financial and Quantitative Analysis* (June 1982).

Neubig, Thomas, and Martin Sullivan. "The Implications of Tax Reform for Bank Holdings of Tax-Exempt Securities." *National Tax Journal* (September 1987).

Stock, Duane, and Edward Schrems. "Municipal Bond Demand Premiums and Bond Price Volatility: A Note." *Journal of Finance* (June 1984).

Van Horne, James. *Financial Market Rates and Flows.* Englewood Cliffs, N.J.: Prentice-Hall, Inc., 1990.

Yawitz, Jess, Kevin Maloney, and Louis Ederington. "Taxes, Default Risk, and Yield Spreads." *Journal of Finance* (September 1985).

Chapter 19

Investment Strategies

Suppose that you make the investment decisions for your bank and currently have $15 million to invest in Treasury securities for 5 years. The current yield curve is upsloping with 1-year Treasuries yielding 7.0 percent, 5-year Treasuries yielding 7.6 percent, and 10-year Treasuries yielding 8.0 percent. Based on your reading of economic conditions, you believe that interest rates will rise in the foreseeable future. Should you buy short-term or long-term Treasuries? When do you win and when do you lose? The natural tendency is to invest long-term to capture the higher promised yields. If, however, the yield curve is correct in the sense that forward rates accurately forecast future cash market rates, then your choice of investments doesn't matter. Your return over 5 years from buying the 7.6 percent 5-year bond will exactly match the return from buying a 1-year Treasury at 7.0 percent and reinvesting the proceeds each year in another 1-year Treasury. Both returns will match that from buying a 10-year Treasury at 8.0 percent and selling it after 5 years. The only case in which you can earn an above-average return is when forward rates are incorrect, and you out-predict the market. This involves speculating that rates will rise more than that expected and staying short, or speculating that rates will be lower than that expected and going long-term.

Commercial banks, like individual investors, constantly search for good investments to supplement earnings. As in the above situation, portfolio managers often speculate on short-term interest rate changes in the hope of guessing correctly. They also alter the composition of the portfolio as circumstances dictate. A bank that experiences large unanticipated loan losses, for example, may no longer need to shelter as much income with municipal securities. Another bank may want to shift its portfolio into higher-rated instruments when quality spreads are low or shorten maturities when interest rates are expected to rise. Successful securities transactions depend on using the flexibility inherent in the investment portfolio to alter strategies.

This chapter addresses several basic questions facing investment portfolio managers. What maturity securities should be acquired? What is the optimal portfolio composition between tax-exempt and taxable securities? How can the bank change its portfolio risk and return profile at least cost when economic conditions change? Specific strategies with applications cover each of these topics. The discussion focuses on distinctions between active and passive investment strategies and the costs or benefits of each.

Unlike loans and deposits that have negotiated terms, bank investments generally represent impersonal financial instruments. As such, portfolio managers can buy or sell securities at the margin to achieve aggregate risk and return objectives without the worry of adversely affecting long-term depositor or borrower relationships. Investment strategies can consequently play an integral role in meeting overall asset and liability management goals regarding interest rate risk, liquidity risk, credit risk, the bank's tax position, expected net income, and capital adequacy.

Unfortunately, not all banks view their securities portfolios in light of these opportunities. Many small community banks passively manage their portfolios using simple buy-and-hold strategies. The purported advantages are that such a policy requires limited investment expertise and virtually no management time, lowers transaction costs, and provides for predictable liquidity. Regulators reinforce this approach by emphasizing the risk features of investments and not the available returns. The *Comptroller's Handbook,* for example, states that "the investment account is primarily a secondary reserve for liquidity rather than a vehicle to generate speculative profits. Speculation in marginal securities to generate more favorable yields is an unsound banking practice."[1] Large regional banks and multinational banks, in contrast, actively manage their portfolios by adjusting maturities, changing the composition of taxable versus tax-exempt securities, and swapping securities to meet asset and liability management objectives that change with the external environment. The presumed advantage is that active portfolio managers can earn above-average returns by capturing pricing discrepancies in the marketplace. The disadvantages are that in many cases managers must consistently out-predict the market for many strategies to be successful, and transactions costs are high.

This chapter examines general factors that affect most investment decisions and active portfolio strategies that help achieve specific risk and return objectives. The analysis begins with a discussion of the traditional interest rate cycle and difficulties in forecasting the level of interest rates. The following sections address the maturity choice and how to determine the optimal amounts of taxable and tax-exempt security holdings. The final sections discuss the sale of securities with put options and security swaps as strategies to meet risk and return targets.

---

[1] See the *Comptroller's Handbook for National Bank Examiners,* section 203.1, U.S. Department of Treasury, Washington, D.C.

THE MATURITY OR DURATION CHOICE FOR LONG-TERM SECURITIES

Portfolio managers consider many factors when determining which securities to buy or sell. Perhaps the most difficult to quantify is the optimal maturity or duration instrument. Difficulties arise because it is virtually impossible to outperform the market when forecasting interest rates. Management must also be aware of the bank's overall interest rate risk position to make investments that offset the prevailing risk or enhance returns as targeted. Many managers justify passive buy-and-hold strategies because they lack the time and expertise to evaluate investment alternatives and monitor performance in an attempt to outperform the market. As a result, they select maturities that generate average returns over the entire business cycle. Other managers actively trade securities in an effort to earn above-average returns.

Passive Maturity Strategies

Specific policies frequently follow one of two models. The first model, the *laddered (or staggered) maturity strategy,* stipulates that management should initially specify a maximum acceptable maturity. Securities are held to maturity, and managers acquire bonds expecting to earn fixed yields over the life of the instruments. Under this strategy, securities are spaced approximately evenly throughout the maturity range so that an equal proportion of the entire portfolio matures each year. Bonds near maturity represent a liquidity buffer, with the proceeds simply reinvested at maturity in securities with the longest acceptable maturity, regardless of prevailing yields. If, for example, management wants all securities to mature within 10 years, it will have 10 percent of the portfolio maturing each year. As securities mature, the proceeds will be reinvested in new 10-year maturity instruments. The only remaining decision involves selecting securities of acceptable credit quality. Managers do not attempt to forecast interest rates but rather recognize that the bank earns average yields over the interest rate cycle.[2]

The second model, the *barbell maturity strategy,* differentiates between bonds purchased for liquidity versus pure income purposes. Management invests a fraction of the portfolio, typically 25 to 40 percent, in shorter term securities ≤ four years that pay market rates and normally trade at prices close to par. These instruments are held primarily to meet liquidity requirements. All remaining funds are invested at long-term maturities, with the majority out 10 to 15 years, to maximize coupon interest income. The long-term bonds are sold prior to maturity and the proceeds reinvested long term once the remaining maturity falls into the intermediate (5 to 9 years) range. With an upsloping yield curve, long-term securities pay higher initial yields. If the level of interest rates does not increase, banks sell the securities at a capital gain when less than 10 years remain to maturity, thereby increasing the gross return. During relatively stable interest rate environments, this barbell, or short-and-long strategy, yields returns

---

[2]This strategy earns average yields as long as the yield curve does not change. This, of course, is highly unlikely. Few banks use duration analysis.

above those for the laddered maturity strategy.[3] Risk is also greater. If a liquidity crisis arises and the bank has to sell long-term securities, it may have to take unexpected gains or losses.

Exhibit 19.1 graphically demonstrates the differences between the two strategies. With the laddered maturity strategy, a constant portion of the portfolio matures each year. With the barbell strategy, short and long maturities dominate as most of the portfolio matures at these extreme periods. The laddered strategy simply picks yields off the long maturities whenever a bond matures. The barbell strategy picks yields off the short and long end of the maturity spectrum so that managers are reinvesting proceeds more frequently. Both strategies are mechanical and thus have the advantage of reducing transactions costs over active portfolio management. In addition, there is little likelihood that losses will arise from selling securities prior to maturity. The disadvantage is that banks that follow these strategies sacrifice short-term returns for risk reduction and extraordinary profit opportunities may be missed. Small banks typically follow the laddered maturity strategy.

Active Maturity Strategies

Today, many banks actively manage their portfolios in response to the general economic climate and their interest rate risk position. Active portfolio management involves taking risks to improve total returns by adjusting maturities, swapping securities, and periodically liquidating discount instruments. To do this successfully, a bank should exhibit a strong capital base and broad-based earnings power. It must also avoid the trap of aggressively buying fixed-income securities at relatively low rates when loan demand is low and deposits are high.

Much like the previous examples, active portfolio strategies recognize both liquidity needs and income requirements. A primary focus is liquidity in which a bank maintains a portion of its portfolio with market values at or above book values. Such instruments can always be sold at a gain, regardless of maturity. While this is not always easily accomplished, banks can keep their portfolios trading near par if they purchase instruments of short maturity or duration, variable rate instruments, or if they willingly sell securities at a loss and reinvest the proceeds in other marketable securities when rates increase. The primary advantage of this liquidity focus is that a bank can substitute between long- and short-duration instruments as long as a portion of the portfolio exhibits price appreciation. If an acceptable amount of long-term securities is currently priced above book value, management can invest any remaining funds at maturities or durations consistent with its interest rate forecasts and desired risk position. The primary disadvantage is that losses may arise from inaccurate forecasts.

One active strategy has banks actively adjust their GAP profile in line with interest rate forecasts. Regular asset and liability management committee (ALCO) meetings identify the portfolio interest sensitivity and thus interest rate exposure of bank net

---

[3]Bradley and Crane (1975) compared the performance of these two strategies and concluded that the barbell strategy generally dominated.

Exhibit 19.1 A Comparison of Laddered and Barbell Maturity Strategies

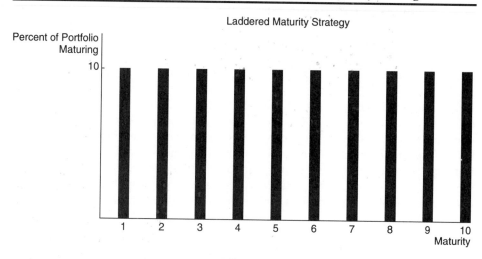

Laddered Maturity Strategy

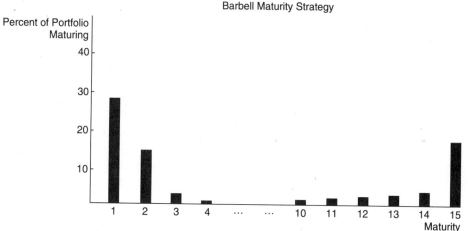

Barbell Maturity Strategy

interest margin to potential rate changes. Banks operating with a negative GAP and/or positive duration gap may choose to shorten maturities and reduce the aggregate duration of assets by purchasing short-duration securities to reduce their risk exposure. This would be consistent with an environment in which rates are expected to rise above those suggested in market. Alternatively, banks may choose to increase their exposure by buying long-term and long-duration securities, thereby increasing the funding and duration gaps. This might occur when the bank has sufficient liquidity and management forecasts a long-term decrease in interest rates. Banks operating with a positive GAP and/or negative duration gap might similarly lengthen maturities and acquire long-duration securities to reduce their risk exposure when rates are expected to decline, or do the opposite when rates are expected to rise. The key point is that a bank's maturity or duration choice depends on its goals for interest rate risk and return. By adjusting security maturities and durations it is generally speculating on future rate movements. If management consciously assumes greater risk in the security portfolio, it assumes that it can outperform the market; that is, its interest rate forecast is better than that implied by current yields.

Riding the Yield Curve. Another example might be a portfolio manager who attempts to *ride the yield curve*. This works best when the yield curve is upsloping and rates are relatively stable. The strategy involves buying securities with a maturity longer than the planned holding period and selling the security at a gain prior to maturity. There are three basic steps. First, identify the preferred investment horizon, such as 5 years. Second, buy a par security with a maturity longer than the investment horizon for which the coupon yield is high in relation to the overall yield curve. Third, sell the security after time elapses with time still remaining until maturity. If yields remain relatively constant, the overall return will exceed that from simply buying the security that matches the planned investment horizon.

Consider the example summarized in Exhibit 19.2. A portfolio manager has a 5-year investment horizon or holding period. A risk reduction strategy might involve buying a 5-year security yielding 7.6 percent and holding it to maturity. Alternatively, if the manager felt that rates would remain roughly constant over the next 5 years, another alternative would be to buy a 10-year security paying 8 percent and sell the security after 5 years. If rates are stable, a 5-year security will yield the same 7.6 percent in 5 years and the bond can be sold at a gain. In addition, the 10-year security carries a higher coupon so that periodic interest payments are higher and reinvestment income will be greater. As indicated, the 5-year security pays $7,600 in interest each year, which is assumed to be reinvested the following year at 7 percent. The 10-year security, in contrast, pays $8,000 in annual interest so that actual coupon and reinvestment income will be greater. After 5 years, the 5-year bond returns principal of $100,000. If rates are constant, the 10-year bond sells for $101,615 with 5 years remaining to maturity. The bottom part of the Exhibit demonstrates that the effective return to riding the yield curve is 58 basis points greater than that for the matched holding period strategy. Of course, this active strategy involves greater risk. If rates rise substantially, the bond would have to be sold for a loss that could potentially wipe out the incremental coupon and reinvestment income earned.

To implement active investment strategies, portfolio managers must understand the interest rate environment in which they operate. They continuously monitor recent movements in the level of rates and the magnitude of specific rate differentials to formulate an interest rate forecast. Most importantly, portfolio managers must understand their bank's specific risk and return objectives and current financial position. No one can accurately forecast specific interest rates continuously over time. Managers can, however, position their portfolios to take advantage of long-term trends in rates.

Exhibit 19.2 Effect of Riding the Yield Curve when Interest Rates Are Stable

Initial conditions and assumptions: Bank has a planned 5-year investment horizon. The yield curve is upsloping with 5-year securities yielding 7.6 percent and 10-year securities yielding 8 percent. Coupon interest is payable annually and can be reinvested at 7 percent annually. The investment choice is to invest $100,000 in a 5-year security and hold it to maturity or to invest $100,000 in a 10-year security and sell it after 5 years.
Objective: Compare overall return.

Cash Flows

	Buy a 5-Year Security		Buy a 10-Year Security and Sell It after 5 Years	
Period: Year-End	**Coupon Interest**	**Reinvestment Income at 7%**	**Coupon Interest**	**Reinvestment Income at 7%**
1	$ 7,600	—	$ 8,000	—
2	7,600	$ 532	8,000	$ 564
3	7,600	1,101	8,000	1,159
4	7,600	1,710	8,000	1,800
5	7,600	2,362	8,000	2,486
	$38,000	$5,705	$40,000	$6,005
5	Principal at Maturity = $100,000		Price at Sale after 5 years = $101,615 when rate = 7.6%	

Realized Compound Yield[a]

Solve for yield:

5-Year Security:

$$i = \left[\frac{(100,000 + 38,000 + 5,705)}{100,000}\right]^{1/5} - 1$$

$$i = .0752$$

10-Year Sold after 5 years:

$$y = \left[\frac{(101,615 + 40,000 + 6,005)}{100,000}\right]^{1/5} - 1$$

$$y = .0810$$
$$y - i = .0058$$

[a]Realized yield with an assumed reinvestment rate different from the yield to maturity.

Interest Rates and the Business Cycle

Most portfolio managers structure security maturities relative to the business cycle. Exhibit 7.5 from Chapter 7, reproduced here as Exhibit 19.3, characterizes the general relationship between movements in interest rates at different stages of the cycle. The Exhibit suggests that the term-structure of Treasury yields follows predictable patterns within the business cycle. Upsloping yield curves appear during periods that coincide with monetary ease, when rates are low. Inverted yield curves appear as interest rates rise to their cyclical peak and thereafter as the Federal Reserve restricts money growth. The shape of each yield curve contains information regarding the market's consensus forecast of interest rates.[4] When the yield curve is upsloping, the market forecast is

---

[4]Three theories of yield curves, the unbiased expectations theory, the liquidity premium theory, and the market segmentation theory, are described in Chapter 7. This analysis focuses only on the role of expected interest rates. Chapter 7 and Van Horne (1990) demonstrate how to derive forward rates from prevailing yields.

Exhibit 19.3 Interest Rates over the Business Cycle with Constant Inflation Expectations

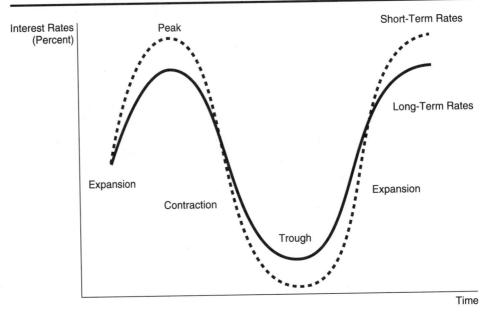

that short-term rates are going to rise from their relatively low levels. Because long-term rates represent an average of current and expected short-term rates, they too will increase with expected increases in short-term rates. When the yield curve is downsloping, the market forecast is that short-term rates will decline, thus lowering long-term rates.

Consensus forecasts obviously represent averages. Individual traders may have substantially different views of economic conditions and the likely movement in interest rates. As they take different positions, the yield curve shifts to reflect the new, market-driven consensus. Thus, any implied interest rate forecast simply reflects the market's current guess about future rates based on prevailing information.

Passive Strategies over the Business Cycle. One popular passive investment strategy follows from the traditional belief that a bank's securities portfolio should consist of primary reserves and secondary reserves. This view suggests that banks hold short-term, highly marketable securities primarily to meet unanticipated loan demand and deposit withdrawals. Once these primary liquidity reserves are established, banks invest any residual funds in long-term securities that are less liquid but offer higher yields. These residual investments, or secondary reserves, thus focus on generating income.

A problem arises because banks normally have excess liquidity during contraction-ary periods when the level of rates is low, loan demand is declining, and deposit growth is stable. Banks employing this strategy add to their secondary reserves by buying long-term securities near the low point in the interest rate cycle. In the normal cycle, long-term rates are typically above short-term rates, but all rates are relatively low. With a buy-and-hold orientation, these banks lock themselves into securities that depreciate in value as interest rates move higher. Bankers who follow these passive strategies are furthermore unwilling to sell securities at a loss. They wrongfully end up holding the low-coupon securities until maturity instead, thereby foregoing oppor-tunities to enhance investment returns.

Passive investment strategies can avoid these difficulties only if the bank buys securities when yields are at cyclical peaks or if the bank restricts its purchases to securities with short maturities. In both cases the bank will find that the market value of its portfolio consistently exceeds or at least equals its book value. Of course, it is extremely difficult to accurately forecast interest rate turns, so banks cannot systemati-cally time investments at interest rate peaks. The fundamental problem with short-term investments is that interest income is relatively unpredictable beyond 1 year. The bank also foregoes any opportunity to earn above-average returns by locking in high-coupon yields or selling securities with substantial price appreciation.

Active Strategies and the Business Cycle. Many portfolio managers attempt to time major movements in interest rates relative to the business cycle and adjust security maturities accordingly. Some try to time interest rate peaks by following a contracycli-cal investment strategy defined by changes in loan demand. The strategy entails both expanding the investment portfolio and lengthening maturities when loan demand is high, and alternatively contracting the portfolio and shortening maturities when loan demand is weak. The advantage is that a bank is much more likely to purchase securities when the level of interest rates is high. These yields can in turn be locked in for long periods of time. The disadvantage is that a bank either has to restrict credit to loan customers or rely on relatively expensive, short-term debt instruments such as federal funds to finance the loans. It is at these times, however, that the yield curve is inverted and investment officers feel pressure to stay short term because of the high yields. If rates follow the cycle, though, these high short-term rates will only be temporary.

When loan demand is weak, banks should keep investments short term. The obvious problem is that without loans banks need to find higher-yielding investments to maintain net interest income. Thus the tendency is to lengthen maturities because the yield curve is upsloping. This is a time of relatively low yields so that if rates do increase, the bank will ultimately have to sell the securities at a loss or keep them in portfolio and not realize the loss but earn a below-market yield.

It is important to remember that efforts to time interest rate changes are risky. If management guesses incorrectly and positions the bank accordingly, it may have to take capital losses when it sells securities or it will forego income that it could have earned alternatively. Because it is a riskier strategy, the volatility of returns will be greater than passive strategies. Contemporary Issues: An Interest Rate Gamble That

CONTEMPORARY ISSUES

An Interest Rate Gamble That Lost

There are many ways to bet the bank. During the 1980s, senior management of First Bank System, Inc. of Minneapolis chose to speculate on interest movements in its bond portfolio. In 1986 the bank sold enough government securities to report a gain of almost $400 million, which just exceeded its loan losses of $385 million. For the year it reported a record profit over $200 million—not bad for a $25 billion bank that had loan quality problems. The gamble consisted of buying long-term securities and hoping that interest rates remained stable or fell. In this case it worked. So willing was the bank to take risk that it did not hedge its position.

In April 1987, interest rates climbed higher, pushing the value of fixed-rate bonds lower. By September 1987 First Bank Sys-

tem reported $640 million in unrealized paper losses on its $8 billion bond portfolio. Again, it chose not to hedge in the belief that interest rates would soon fall. They instead rose.

After the dust settled in 1988, First Bank System reported a $500 million pretax loss. This arose from a combination of loan losses and the sale of over 50 percent of its investment portfolio. To shore up capital, the bank sold a 50 percent interest in its headquarters building in Minneapolis, laid off employees, and shrunk the bank's asset base. By 1989 both the president and chief executive officer had resigned. The basic lesson is that high risk involves greater volatility in earnings, potentially to the detriment of the investor.

Lost demonstrates how one bank, First Bank System, Inc. of Minneapolis, gambled heavily on interest rates and lost.

DETERMINING THE OPTIMAL AMOUNT OF TAX-EXEMPT AND TAXABLE SECURITY HOLDINGS

One of the most important decisions in managing the investment portfolio involves determining the mix between tax-exempt and taxable securities. Prior to 1986, the decision was relatively simple. Banks that paid taxes at the full corporate income tax rate always found that tax-exempts provided higher after-tax yields than comparable maturity and risk taxable securities. This was true because the maximum corporate tax rate always exceeded the indifference tax rate (t^*) at all maturities, where:

$$\text{Maximum corporate tax rate} > t^* = 1 - R_m / R_t$$

[from Equation (18.2)]. Banks consequently purchased taxable securities only to the extent that taxable income did not produce a tax liability. They would buy Treasury, Agency, and other taxables to generate income to cover deductible expenses plus income sheltered by investments other than municipals and to put the bank in the highest corporate tax bracket. At the margin, the remaining funds were invested in tax-exempts, and additional income was tax-sheltered.

The Tax Reform Act of 1986 complicated the analysis by changing the tax status of many municipal bonds. As indicated in Chapter 18, banks can no longer deduct any borrowing costs associated with financing new municipal purchases after August 7, 1986, unless the municipals meet the small-issue, public-purpose exception. The maximum corporate tax rate still exceeds the indifference rate for municipals that meet the small-issue exception, and thus banks still have a clear preference for these securities.[5] The corporate tax rate is below the indifference rate that applies to all other municipals, so that banks prefer taxable securities to these instruments.

The optimal amount of taxable versus tax-exempt securities depends on a bank's need for taxable income, pledging and liquidity requirements, and preferences for diversification. The underlying strategy for determining the optimal portfolio mix can be demonstrated by the following example. The example assumes that municipals that generate higher after-tax yields than taxable securities exist in sufficient volume to meet bank demand and that transactions costs are negligible. Taxable securities also satisfy pledging and liquidity requirements.

A bank's portfolio manager knows with certainty that the bank will earn sufficient taxable income to increase its marginal income tax rate to 34 percent. The bank plans to issue $10 million in 1-year CDs and invest the proceeds, net of required reserves, in either 1-year qualified, small-issue municipals or taxable securities. The bank must pay 8.2 percent on the CDs and can earn 10 percent on the taxables and 8 percent on the municipals. The bank must hold reserves equal to 3 percent of the CDs. How should the bank invest the proceeds to maximize after-tax income on this transaction?

Exhibit 19.4 presents the bank's incremental income statement impact for three separate portfolios. Ignore for the moment the limitation on interest deductibility for municipal purchases. In the first case, the entire $9.7 million of investable funds, $10 million net of $300,000 in reserves, is allocated to taxables. Interest income exceeds the deductible CD interest expense by $150,000 so that net income equals $99,000 after taxes. In the second case, the bank invests the full $9.7 million in tax-exempts and loses $44,000 because tax-exempt interest does not even cover the CD interest. The final column presents the optimal portfolio composition and resulting income. Given the assumptions in this example, the bank maximizes net income when it purchases sufficient taxables so that taxable interest income just equals the deductible CD interest. Algebraically, the yield on taxables multiplied by the taxable investment should equal the deductible expense. In this example,

$$0.10 \text{ (Taxable securities)} = \$820,000, \text{ or}$$
$$\text{Taxable securities} = \$8.2 \text{ million}$$

so that the dollar investment in taxable securities should equal $8.2 million, at which point the bank earns $820,000 in taxable interest.

Until this investment level is reached, the bank effectively pays no additional taxes. However, once its taxable interest exceeds $820,000, the bank's tax rate increases to 34 percent. Thus the bank's tax rate is less than t* (t* = 1 − 8%/10%) for the first $820,000 in taxable interest and greater than t* for additional taxable interest. After investing the remaining $1.5 million in tax-exempts, the bank reports net income

[5]Banks can deduct 80 percent of their carrying costs related to purchases of qualified municipals issued by state and local subdivisions which limit borrowing to $10 million or less per year. Exhibit 18.2 analyzes the effect of the limited deductibility of interest expense.

Exhibit 19.4 Investment Portfolio Mix between Tax-Exempt and Taxable Securities: Incremental Income Statements from Alternative Portfolios

	All Taxable Securities	All Tax-Exempt Securities	Optimal Portfolio Mix
Portfolio Mix			
Taxable securities	$9,700,000	0	$8,200,000
Tax-exempt securities	0	$9,700,000	1,500,000
Projected Incremental Income Statement Items			
Interest income			
Taxable interest at 10%	$ 970,000	$ 0	$ 820,000
Tax exempt interest at 8%	0	776,000	120,000
Total	$ 970,000	$ 776,000	$ 940,000
Interest expense			
Certificate of deposit interest at 8.2%	$ 820,000	$ 820,000	$ 820,000
Net interest income	150,000	−44,000	120,000
Income tax at 34%	$ 51,000	0	0
Net income	$ 99,000	$ −44,000	$ 120,000

Application of the Limit on Interest Expense Deductibility

All Tax-Exempt Securities

Applicable interest expense for municipals (0.082)($9,700,000) = $795,400
Lost deduction at 20%   (0.20)($795,400) = $159,080
Increased tax liability   (0.34)($159,080) = $ 54,087
Actual net income   = $−98,087

Optimal Portfolio Mix

Applicable interest expense for municipals (0.082)($1,500,000) = $123,000
Lost deduction at 20%   (0.20)($123,000) = $ 24,600
Increased tax liability   (0.34)($24,600) = $ 8,364
Actual net income   = $111,636

of $120,000. The bank pays no taxes on this series of transactions because the entire amount of income before taxes is tax-exempt interest.

This type of arbitrage is possible only because banks can borrow, invest in tax-exempts, and still deduct some of their interest expense. The actual comparison of returns in Exhibit 19.4 differs from that reported because, as Chapter 18 indicates, banks can deduct only 80 percent of their carrying costs when they purchase new qualified municipals. The bottom part of Exhibit 19.4 indicates what the actual net income, or true net cash flow, from investing in municipals would be when the 80 percent deduction limit applies.[6] Net income is unchanged in the first case, in which only taxable securities were purchased. Net income declines to a loss of $98,087 when only municipals are purchased because the bank loses a deduction of $159,080. The

---

[6]Exhibit 18.2 in Chapter 18 summarizes these effects.

relevant case is the optimal portfolio allocation. If the bank buys $1.5 million in new municipals, it will not be able to deduct $24,600 in interest expense associated with financing the tax-exempts. The bank's incremental tax liability would actually be $8,364, which produces an actual net return of $111,636. This still exceeds the $99,000 earned from the fully taxable portfolio and any other alternative. If the municipal securities did not qualify for the small issue exception, 100 percent of the applicable interest expense would be nondeductible and the actual net return on the mixed portfolio would be only $78,180.

The key concept is that until income from taxable investments equals deductible expenses a bank's marginal tax rate is zero. Taxable yields thus exceed tax-exempt yields after-tax. Any additional taxable income is taxed at the 34 percent rate, however, so that qualified tax-exempt yields exceed taxable yields. Banks should make taxable investments until they cover deductible expenses, then make tax-sheltered investments. This is not the same as simply minimizing taxes owed, which could be achieved by buying only tax-exempts.

Application to the Total Investment Portfolio

The strategy suggested by the previous example can be extended to a bank's entire portfolio. Tax-exempt and taxable securities are simply two of the elements involved in the overall asset allocation decision. The general rule for a bank is to structure its asset holdings so that aggregate taxable income exactly equals the sum of 1) tax-de-ductible expenses, 2) taxable income sheltered by tax credits, and 3) the first $75,000 of taxable income, at which point a bank pays the full corporate income tax rate.[7] Only after banks pay the full corporate tax rate do tax-exempts yield more after taxes than do taxables. Any remaining investable funds are allocated to tax-exempt securities. Essentially, after-tax yields from tax-sheltered investments exceed comparable after-tax yields net of expenses from loans and taxable securities. Qualified tax-exempts are viewed as substitutes for alternative tax-sheltered investments such as leasing operations. In practice, problems may arise with the alternative minimum tax, which is ignored in this discussion.

Determining the optimal composition of securities is part of a bank's overall profit plan and strategic planning function. The ALCO initially determines the expected composition of the bank's funding base and projects interest expense. It then projects net noninterest expense, incorporating expectations regarding noninterest income and provisions for loan losses in addition to wages, salaries, and occupancy expense. Interest expense plus provisions for loan losses and net noninterest expense equals anticipated net deductible expense. The third step involves forecasting the value of tax credits the bank will claim during the tax year. The purpose here is to use taxable income to cover income already sheltered by tax credits. Historically, tax credits arose from taxes paid on foreign operations and investment tax credits from acquiring capital assets. Since the Tax Reform Act, only foreign tax credits apply. At this stage the

---

[7]The Tax Reform Act of 1986 lowered marginal corporate income tax rates to 15 percent of the first $50,000 of taxable income, 25 percent of the next $25,000, and 34 percent of all taxable income over $75,000.

ALCO projects loan demand given general economic conditions and the overall interest rate environment. With this information the bank can compare taxable loan fees and interest with deductible expenses and income sheltered by tax credits. The bank acquires sufficient taxable securities so that taxable investment income equals the difference. Any remaining funds are then invested in tax-exempt securities.

A Simplified Example

Determining the optimal portfolio mix involves forecasting a bank's financial position over the relevant tax year. In practice, there is considerable uncertainty because banks cannot accurately predict interest rates or loan losses. Banks can minimize these difficulties through the use of sensitivity analysis and by continuously updating their forecasts. The following example incorporates only one interest rate environment and thus one possible portfolio composition.

A bank has generated strong earnings for the past several years. Its ALCO projects an average of $500 million in financing for the upcoming year, as summarized in part A of Exhibit 19.5. Of the total, $70 million is obtained from demand deposits paying no interest, $250 million from interest-bearing deposits paying a projected 8 percent, and $150 million in CDs paying an estimated 10 percent. With this funding base the bank expects to hold $75 million in nonearning assets, $300 million in loans, and $125 million in securities. The fundamental issue is, how should the bank allocate the $125 million between taxable and tax-exempt securities to maximize its after-tax income?

Part B of Exhibit 19.5 summarizes the steps in arriving at an optimal portfolio mix.

- Step 1. Interest expense is calculated as the average rate paid on each liability times the dollar amount of financing from that source and is projected at $35 million.

- Step 2. Net noninterest expense equals the difference between noninterest expense and noninterest income, or the bank's burden. This bank projects noninterest income equal to 1 percent of average assets and noninterest expense at 3 percent. The net expense thus equals $10 million.

- Step 3. The bank expects to claim $1.46 million in tax credits. The value of each tax credit is the amount of pretax income a bank would have to earn to generate that amount of tax liability. If the bank's marginal tax rate equals 34 percent, .34 times the pretax value of the tax credit should equal $1.46 million. In this case, the tax credit shelters $4.3 million in taxable income.

- Step 4. The bank next projects earning $39 million from loans at a pretax yield of 13 percent.

- Step 5. Given these forecasts, the ALCO can determine the bank's optimal taxable security holdings. Specifically, the bank should own enough taxables to earn $10.375 million in interest income. This figure equals the sum of deductible expense, the pretax value of tax credits claimed, and the first $75,000 of taxable income that puts the bank in the highest marginal tax bracket. If the yield on the

Exhibit 19.5 A Procedure for Determining the Optimal Tax-Exempt and Taxable Security Portfolio for a Bank (Millions of Dollars)

A. Projected Balance Sheet

Assets		Liabilities and Equity	
Nonearning	$ 75	Demand deposits	$ 70
Loans	300	Nonnegotiable interest-bearing deposits	250
Investments	125	Large certificates of deposit	150
Taxable	X	Equity	30
Tax-exempt	Y	Total	$500
Total	$500		

B. Projected Income Statement Elements

1. Projected interest expense
   Interest on nonnegotiable deposits at 8%: $0.08(\$250) = \$20$
   Interest on large certificates of deposit at 10%: $0.10(\$150) = \underline{15}$
      Total $\$35$

2. Projected net noninterest expense
   Noninterest income (1% of assets): $0.01(\$500) = (\$5)$
   Noninterest expense (3% of assets): $0.03(\$500) = \underline{15}$
      Total $\$10$

3. Estimated pretax value of tax credits claimed
   Tax credits to be claimed: $1.462
   Pretax value: $1.462/Marginal income tax rate = $1.462/0.34 = $4.3

4. Projected loan demand and loan interest
   Interest and fees on loans at 13%: $0.13(\$300) = \$39$

5. Projected investment in taxable securities[a]
   Targeted investment income from taxables: $35 + $10 + $4.3 + $0.075 − $39 = $10.375
   Targeted holdings of taxable securities if average yield equals 11%: X = 10.375/0.11 = $94.3

6. Projected investment in tax-exempt securities
   Targeted investment portfolio − Targeted taxable security holdings: Y = $125 − $94.3 = $30.7
   Targeted investment income from tax-exempts at 8.8%: $30.7(0.088) = $2.7

C. Projected Income Statement

Interest income	
Interest and fees on loans	$39.000
Interest on taxable securities	10.375
Interest on tax-exempt securities	2.700
Total	$52.075
Interest expense	
Interest on deposits	$20.000
Interest on certificates of deposit	15.000
Total interest expense	$35.000
Net interest income	$17.075
Noninterest income	$ 5.000
Noninterest expense	$15.000
Income before income taxes	$ 7.075
Income taxes[a]	0.160
Net income	$ 6.915

---

[a]Taxable income should also cover the first $75,000 (0.075) to put the bank in the highest marginal income tax bracket.

[b]Actual taxes equal $13,750 on the first $75,000 of taxable income and $146,132 on the nondeductible portion of interest expense. The nondeductible interest expense equals $429,800, assuming that the entire $30.7 million municipal portfolio was acquired after 1982 and is subject to a lost 20% deduction of associated carrying costs. The tax liability on the remaining $4.3 million of taxable income is exactly offset by the tax credit of $1.46 million.

bank's taxable security holdings is projected to average 11 percent during the year, the bank needs to own an average $94.3 million in taxables.

- Step 6. The final step is to determine how many tax-exempt securities to buy. The bank estimates the total size of its investment portfolio at $125 million. The allocation of $94.3 million to taxables leaves a tax-exempt portfolio of $30.7 million, which generates an expected $2.7 million in interest at 8.8 percent.

Note that a bank will still pay some taxes even in this world of perfect foresight. With this portfolio allocation, it will simply have lowered its tax liability as much as possible. Part C presents the bank's projected income statement. Given the above forecasts, the bank expects to earn $7.075 million before taxes. Of this amount, $2.7 million is tax-exempt interest while $4.3 million is sheltered by the $1.46 million in tax credits claimed. The remaining $75,000 reflects taxable income, which is taxed at marginal tax rates below 34 percent.[8] Net income is maximized because all possible taxable income is tax sheltered. The bank makes sufficient taxable investments so that its taxable income from loans and securities of $49.375 million just equals the sum of its deductible expenses, the pretax value of tax credits, and the first $75,000 of taxable income. After this earnings level is reached, the bank's marginal income tax rate equals 34 percent. Net income is expected to be slightly below $7 million because the bank will pay $160,000 in taxes, primarily due to the 20 percent lost interest deductibility on municipals.

It is virtually impossible for any bank to consistently meet its theoretically optimal portfolio mix. Rapidly changing interest rates alter the projected composition and cost of funds as well as available loan and security yields. Noninterest expense is also difficult to forecast, especially in a declining economy when loan losses rise. A bank's ALCO should therefore modify its forecasts regularly. Furthermore, banks do not always want to substitute between taxable and tax-exempt securities. If, for example, a bank buys 5- to 10-year securities to achieve its yield and composition targets, it may be reluctant to sell the securities at a capital loss when rates increase. In many cases, management circumvents this problem by investing heavily in short-term securities. Unfortunately, a bank then gives up interest income because the yield curve normally is upsloping. Alternatively, many banks wait until the second 6 months of each year to aggressively purchase tax-exempt securities. After 6 months of operations, management can better forecast net earnings and reduce the risk of owning too many municipals if yield spreads narrow or loan losses exceed expectations.

The relationships summarized in Exhibit 19.5 still provide a useful framework for assessing a bank's optimal portfolio composition. An overall planning model that incorporates alternative scenarios regarding the balance sheet composition, effective asset yields, and borrowing costs emphasizes the trade-offs that must be considered. If, for example, the spread between loan yields and the bank's cost of funds is expected to narrow, management can approximate the necessary increase in taxable securities

---

[8]The bank actually pays taxes on the first $75,000 of taxable income. Any taxable income above this is taxed at the 34 percent corporate rate. Taxes on the $75,000 in 1991 would equal $13,750. In the model just developed, tax credits should first be offset against any actual tax liability including this $13,750. For ease of analysis, this adjustment is ignored.

relative to tax-exempts. A reduction in loan interest in Exhibit 19.5 to $37 million, other factors being equal, increases the targeted taxable securities by over $12 million. Similar comparisons can be made in other scenarios.

Municipals versus Other Tax-Sheltered Investments

The example provided in Exhibit 19.5 demonstrates that banks effectively choose among alternative tax-sheltered investments when determining the size of their municipal portfolios. Management structures the portfolio so that taxable income from loans, taxable securities, and noninterest revenues equals deductible expenses. A bank's expected net income is generated by tax-exempt interest or sheltered by tax credits. Of course, banks do not have perfect foresight.

The fundamental decisions facing the ALCO regarding the value of a bank's municipal holdings can be characterized in terms of Equation (19.1). The term in brackets on the right hand side of the equality represents pretax income less the pretax value of tax credits.

$$EXINT = \Phi[OI - OE - TC / t] \qquad (19.1)$$

where

$EXINT$ = expected tax–exempt interest from municipal holdings
TC = expected tax credits claimed
t = marginal income tax rate
Φ = desired proportion of net income that is tax–sheltered
OI = expected operating income
OE = expected operating expenses plus provisions for loan losses

The ALCO evaluates different interest rate scenarios to establish an optimal portfolio. If it chooses to shelter all its income from taxes (Φ will be close to 1), then net income approximately equals municipal interest plus taxable income sheltered via tax credits. This can be demonstrated using the data from the income statement in Exhibit 19.5. In terms of the factors listed above:

$$2.7 = \Phi[57.075 - 50 - 4.3]$$

such that Φ is slightly less than 1. It differs only by the $75,000 in targeted taxable income that puts the bank in the highest marginal income tax bracket. In general, the demand for tax-exempt interest will increase as expected taxable income increases, as operating expenses decline, and as the value of tax credits declines.

Historically, along with municipal securities, banks looked to loan loss reserves, capital expenditures, leasing operations, and foreign activities to shelter income. Chapter 23 indicates that most banks claimed tax deductions for transfers to loss reserves that exceeded the amount of actual net charge-offs. Normal capital expenditures and leasing operations generated investment tax credits and accelerated depreciation deductions. Banks with foreign operations could claim tax credits for tax payments made to foreign governments. These tax-sheltering vehicles were largely eliminated by the Tax Reform Act of 1986.

Income that is sheltered via any activity reduces the need for alternative tax-sheltered investments. A bank or bank holding company with significant leasing activity, for example, will report greater depreciation expense, thereby increasing OE in Equation (19.1). This directly reduces the need for tax-exempt interest and thus the demand for municipal securities while increasing the demand for taxable investments. Conversely, the demand for municipal interest increases when banks move completely to the experience method in accounting for loan loss reserves, as OE decreases with lower provisions for loan losses. Banks' demand for municipals should decrease near term because they are required to recapture excess deductions in prior years as taxable income.

Income sheltering alternatives explain, in part, why small banks invest more heavily in municipals than do the largest banks. Many large banks, especially multibank holding companies, conduct leasing operations, own data-processing facilities, and pay taxes on foreign operations that generate substantial deductions and foreign tax credits. They consequently own fewer municipals. Exhibit 16.2 in Chapter 16 indicates that banks with assets below $100 million held 5 percent of their assets in municipals in 1990. The comparable percentage declined for larger banks. Banks with more than $10 billion in assets held just 1.4 percent of their assets in municipals.

The data in Exhibit 16.2 also demonstrate that commercial banks have reduced their investment in municipals relative to other securities. The fundamental causes are implied by Equation (19.1). First, banks in the aggregate now rely proportionately more on other investments to shelter income. Large multibank holding companies, which dominate the data for aggregate municipal holdings, rely less on municipals because they generate accelerated depreciation deductions and foreign tax credits. Both operating expenses (OE) and tax credits claimed (TC) reflect these activities. Second, since 1981 interest rate deregulation generally raised bank funding costs and increased the pressure to earn higher yields. Many banks responded by raising loan-to-asset ratios, thereby increasing expected net interest margins. This increase in loans effectively substituted for security purchases. It also increased loan losses, which directly reduced earnings and the demand for tax-exempt interest. Banks in many areas also experienced dramatic losses on agriculture, energy, and real estate loans. This was particularly true for banks in the Southwest that saw their loan portfolios deteriorate with declining oil prices and subsequent drops in real estate values and associated business activity, and the Eastern Seaboard and West Coast with declining real estate values. Finally, the Internal Revenue Service (IRS) limited the deductibility of interest paid by banks to purchase new municipals. This policy, described in Chapter 18, reduced the differential return between tax-exempt and comparable taxable securities making municipals less attractive.

SELLING TAX-EXEMPT SECURITIES WITH PUT OPTIONS

On many occasions banks have discovered that they own too many municipal bonds. This situation typically arises when a bank experiences a dramatic decrease in profits or periodic losses caused by unanticipated loan charge-offs. Frequently, interest rates have increased since the bank acquired the bonds, and most portfolio holdings can only be sold at a capital loss. If the bank sells its depreciated municipals, it must report securities losses, which will lower reported earnings further. If it continues to hold the securities, it foregoes the higher yields it could potentially earn on taxable instruments. One solution that meets the needs of banks in this situation is the sale of municipal bonds from the bank's portfolio with a put option attached.[9] The put allows the bank to convert the bond to cash immediately without having to report any losses.

Municipal put bonds are popular because both buyers and sellers benefit from the exchange. (The IRS, or other taxpayers, is the loser.) Banks selling the bonds get rid of unwanted tax-exempt interest, receive higher prices than they would without the put option, and do not report securities losses. Investors earn higher-than-normal yields and retain the right to put the bonds back to the issuer without risk of capital loss.

This apparent free lunch exists because the IRS views the transaction differently from generally accepted accounting principles. According to the IRS, a sale of bonds, with or without a put option, is a legitimate sale for tax purposes. Thus any capital loss can be used to reduce current tax liabilities or can be carried forward. Generally accepted accounting principles, in contrast, view a sale with option as a collateralized financing arrangement with no recognized gain or loss. Thus a bank can sell put bonds and improve earnings without adverse reporting requirements.

Several conditions must be met to guarantee this treatment. First, the term of a put option should be considerably shorter than the remaining maturity of the underlying bonds. For example, investors should be permitted to exercise puts only at intervals during the first 5 years for bonds with 10-year maturities. Second, it should appear that there is a reasonable probability that a put will be exercised. This can be met if the price of a put bond is set substantially above the price of a comparable nonput bond. Finally, the seller must disclose in financial statements which bonds have been pledged as collateral under these put arrangements.

Benefits to Investors

An investor who buys the bonds with a put has the option, at specified times before maturity, to put the bonds back to the seller at the same price for which they were purchased. Option exercise dates are typically set for near-term anniversaries of the transaction closing date. If interest rates rise, investors can sell the bonds back and suffer no capital loss. If interest rates fall, investors can continue to hold the bonds or sell them in the open market to realize a capital gain.

In addition to eliminating capital losses, investors can earn above-market yields. This occurs because the municipal yield curve is upsloping. Securities sold in the option package typically carry maturities from 5 to 10 years and are priced at yields slightly below 5- or 10-year investments. With the option, however, the securities effectively mature at the first exercise date, 1 or 2 years out. Thus investors receive long-term yields with a much shorter holding period.

---

[9]This discussion is based on Koch, 1985.

Benefits to Sellers

A sale with put option enables banks to sell municipal discount bonds, reinvest the proceeds at higher (possibly taxable) yields, and generate a tax loss but defer any reporting losses on the income statement. The asset liability management advantages are obvious. A bank that sells put bonds can:

- reinvest the proceeds at higher yields
- substitute taxable for tax-exempt income
- increase the rate sensitivity of assets by shortening the maturity/duration of bond investments
- reduce taxes

The bank must, of course, stand ready to redeem the bonds at each exercise date. Most banks obtain a standby commitment or letter of credit from another institution to make funds available when bonds are put. This imposes additional liquidity requirements but appears to be worth the asset liability management benefits.

An Example: Selling Tax-Exempt Securities with Put Options

Exhibit 19.6 illustrates the effect of a hypothetical sale of tax-exempt securities from a bank's portfolio. This bank currently owns $1 million of 6 percent Tarrant County School District Bonds with 10 years remaining to maturity but does not need the tax-exempt income. If it sold the bonds outright, it would realize a tax loss of approximately $164,000 at a current yield of 8.5 percent.

Instead, the bank chooses to sell the securities with a put option. An investor group agrees to buy the bonds with an annual put option for 5 years for $929,764, yielding 7 percent to maturity. This yield is lower because investors view the securities as being repriceable annually and thus the market rate is closer to the yield on a newly issued 1-year municipal. At each of the next five anniversaries of the sale, the investors can sell the bonds back to the bank for $929,764. This should qualify as a sale for the IRS because the purchase price exceeds the current $835,966 market value of the bonds without a put. The bonds are attractive to investors for two reasons. First, the put option effectively converts the original 10-year maturity to just 1 year with no price risk. Second, investors earn a 7 percent yield, which is well above the current 5.75 percent yield on 1-year maturity, new issue municipals.

The transaction is attractive to the bank for similar reasons. First, it generates a tax loss of $70,236, the difference between the bonds' book value and sale price of $929,764, and thus reduces income taxes without the bank having to report the loss in its financial statements. Second, the bank can reinvest the sale proceeds in taxable securities to increase its after-tax return. Third, the bank can increase or decrease the rate sensitivity of its assets as desired by purchasing securities with a different duration.

Exhibit 19.6 Sale of Tax-Exempt Securities with a Put Option: Bank Currently Owns Tarrant County Bonds

A. Bank Sells Tarrant County School District Bonds Outright

	Book Value	Annual Coupon[a]	Current Market Value[b]	Yield to Final Maturity
10-year Tarrant County School District bonds	$1,000,000	$60,000	$835,966	8.5%

B. Bank Sells Tarrant County School District Bonds with a Put Option

	Annual Coupon Income[a]	Purchase Price	Yield to Final Maturity
Investors purchase bonds with annual put options for 5 yrs.	$60,000	$929,764	7.0%

	Purchase Price	Annual Income	Yield to Final Maturity	Tax Loss on Sale
Bank reinvestment of sale proceeds with puts				
1-year Treasury	$929,764	$ 83,679	9.0%	$70,236
5-year Treasury	929,764	102,274	11.0	70,236

[a] End-of-year payment.

[b] If the bank sells the bonds outright, the relevant discount rate is 8.5%. If the bonds are sold with a put option, the discount rate (market yield) is 7%. Thus the market price is greater for the sale under a put as the bank is moving the security down the yield curve in terms of effective maturity.

Exhibit 19.6 lists two reinvestment alternatives with different consequences. The bank is assumed to need taxable income rather than tax-exempt interest. In one, the bank buys a 1-year Treasury yielding 9 percent. The annual income from this investment equals $83,679, or $23,679 more than interest on the original municipal bonds. This has the further advantage of offsetting the risk that the put bonds will be redeemed at the first anniversary of the sale. In the other, the bank purchases a 5-year Treasury yielding 11 percent. The incremental income is $42,274, but the bank assumes additional interest rate risk relative to the put bonds. In any case, the asset and liability opportunities are unlimited, as the bank can choose whatever investment produces the best maturity mix relative to its payment obligations.

STRATEGIES UNDERLYING SECURITY SWAPS

Active portfolio strategies also enable banks to sell securities prior to maturity whenever economic conditions dictate that additional returns can be earned without a significant increase in risk, or risk can be lowered without reducing expected returns. In most cases, banks reinvest the sale proceeds in securities that differ in terms of maturity, credit quality, or even tax treatment.[10] Such portfolio restructuring improves long-term profitability beyond that available from buy-and-hold strategies.

Banks are generally willing to sell securities that have appreciated in price yet are unwilling to sell depreciated securities. Since 1983, banks have reported securities gains and losses under noninterest income prior to earnings before taxes. While gains are quite popular and enhance earnings, senior bank officers usually believe that stockholders will attribute security losses to poor management. They are thus extremely reluctant to take any losses. It does not, however, prevent the same banks from taking securities gains to supplement normal operating income and capital in low-profit periods.

This is perverse behavior in terms of financial economics. The reason that a security is priced at a discount is that the prevailing market rate exceeds the coupon rate on the security. The bank is earning below-market interest. A security is priced at a premium when its coupon rate exceeds the market rate so that the holder earns an above-average return. An investor who holds a security to maturity may suffer an opportunity loss by not selling the security at a loss, or may give up substantial value by selling at a premium to capture the gain. The appropriate financial decision can be viewed as a straightforward capital budgeting problem.

ANALYSIS OF A CLASSIC SECURITY SWAP

In its classic form, a security swap involves the sale of a depreciated bond and the simultaneous purchase of a similar par bond to improve long-term earnings. The basic principle is to take advantage of the tax laws and the time value of money. Consider the two bonds identified in panel A of Exhibit 19.7. A bank currently owns the 10.5 percent Treasury with 3 years remaining until maturity and is considering buying a 3-year FHLMC bond yielding 12.2 percent. If the bank sells the Treasury, it gives up $105,000 in semiannual interest and realizes a capital loss of $73,760. This loss directly lowers taxable income as banks do not distinguish between the tax treatment of short- and long-term capital gains or losses. A loss results because comparable instruments yield 12 percent annually, or 1.5 percent more than the Treasury coupon rate. The paper loss, in turn, produces a tax savings of $25,078, which can be reinvested with the direct proceeds from the sale in a FHLMC security at par that pays $119,030 in semiannual interest. The cost to the bank includes transactions costs plus potential negative ramifications from the reported capital loss. The benefits include the $14,030 increase in semiannual interest.

The simple net present value analysis in panel C of Exhibit 19.7 demonstrates how much added value the swap provides for the slightly greater default risk and adverse reporting consequences. The calculation essentially compares the cash flow from the Treasury if the bank held it to maturity with the cash from selling the Treasury and

---

[10]The following discussion focuses on securities that banks hold as part of their investment portfolio, as opposed to trading account securities. Investment securities generate a return via coupon interest or price appreciation on discount instruments. Current accounting procedures value investment securities at cost when they are purchased at par, and at their amortized value taking discounts or premiums into account when not purchased at par.

Exhibit 19.7 Evaluation of Security Swaps

	Par Value	Market Value	Remaining Maturity	Semiannual Coupon Income	Yield to Maturity
A. Classic Swap Description					
Sell U.S. Treasury bonds at 10.5%	$2,000,000	$1,926,240	3 yrs.	$105,000	12.0%
Buy FHLMC bonds at 12.2%[a]	1,951,318[b]	1,951,318	3 yrs.	119,030	12.2
				$ 14,030[c]	
B. Swap with Minimal Tax Effects					
Sell U.S. Treasury bonds at 10.5%	$2,000,000	$1,926,240	3 yrs.	$105,000	12
Sell FNMA at 13.8%	3,000,000	3,073,060	4 yrs.	207,000	13
Total	$5,000,000	$4,999,300		$312,000	
Buy FNMA at 13%	$5,000,000	$5,000,000	1 yr.	$325,000	12
				$ 13,000[c]	

C. Present Value Analysis

Time Line: Semiannual Periods

Period	0	1	2	3	4	5	6
Incremental Cash Flows Treasury:	1,926,240	−105,000	−105,000	−105,000	−105,000	−105,000	−2,105,000
Tax saving:	27,078						
FHLMC:	−1,951,318	119,030	119,030	119,030	119,030	119,030	2,070,348
Difference:	0	14,030	14,030	14,030	14,030	14,030	−34,652

Present value calculation: discounted at 4.025 percent[d]

$$\sum_{t=1}^{5} \frac{14,030}{(1.04025)^t} - \frac{34,652}{(1.04025)^6} = \$35,028$$

[a] FHLMC indicates Federal Home Loan Mortgage Corporation: FNMA indicates Federal National Mortgage Association.

[b] Reported security loss equals $73,760, which generates a tax savings of $25,078 at 34 percent. The loss recovery period equals $48,682/14,030 or 3.5 periods.

[c] Incremental coupon income.

[d] [12.2%/2](1 −.34) = 4.025%.

buying the FHLMC bond. Note that the cash flows reduce to a comparison of the present value of the incremental coupon payments versus the lower principal received at the end of the 3 years. In this case, the net present value equals $35,028 using a discount rate equal to the after-tax yield on the FHLMC bond.

The attractiveness of such a swap is often viewed in terms of a calculated loss-recovery period for the combined transaction. This is comparable to payback analysis in capital budgeting and thus ignores the time value of money. Still, in this example, the after-tax security loss equals $48,682 which the bank can recover entirely in four semiannual periods. Obviously, the net benefits might increase if the bank chose to reinvest the proceeds in a riskier asset, such as a loan that offered an even higher yield. A bank could also search out higher yields by lengthening maturities with an upsloping yield curve. Alternatively, a bank in need of tax-sheltered income could reinvest the proceeds in a municipal bond of similar maturity that offers a higher after-tax yield.

These alternatives point out the attractiveness of security swaps. In general, banks can effectively improve their portfolios by

1. upgrading bond credit quality by shifting into high-grade instruments when quality yield spreads are low,
2. lengthening maturities when yields are expected to level off or decline,
3. obtaining greater call protection when management expects rates to fall,
4. improving diversification when management expects economic conditions to deteriorate, and
5. generally increasing current yields by taking advantage of the tax savings.

Any swap thus involves a comprehensive assessment of a bank's overall risk position and explicit interest rate forecast. As a rule, banks normally lengthen maturities and shift to higher-quality securities when they expect market rates to decline. They alternatively shorten maturities and move into lower-grade securities when they expect market rates to rise.

Consider, alternatively, a swap that involves the sale of a security at a gain and the simultaneous purchase of another security at par. A gain produces an increased tax liability so that the seller receives more than cost, but less than the market price of the security after taxes. Because the government gets its cut up front, there are fewer funds to invest. The reason there was a gain is that prevailing interest rates are below the liquidated bond's coupon rate. Thus periodic interest income from the reinvested proceeds will decline from that generated by the bond alone. The net present value comparison is again straightforward. Is the present value of the incremental principal cash flow at maturity greater than the present value of the negative interim cash flows? In most cases, the answer is no. It does not add value to sell securities at a gain.

Swap with Minimal Tax Effects

Because most banks are reluctant to take capital losses regardless of the financial opportunities, swaps can occasionally be constructed that have no tax or reporting impacts. Panel B of Exhibit 19.7 outlines a swap for which the net tax impact is negligible. This possibility arises because the bank acquired securities at different times in the past. Over time, rates have changed, so that some securities have appreciated in value relative to cost while others have depreciated. The simultaneous sale of two such instruments minimizes any tax effects and frees up funds for reinvestment. In the example, the bank sells a Treasury bond at a pretax loss of $73,760 and a Federal National Mortgage Association (FNMA) bond at a pretax gain of $73,060. The net loss equals only $694, and the bank has almost $5 million to reinvest. Because management

Marking to Market

During 1990 Richard Breeden, Chairman of the Securities and Exchange Commission (SEC), and the Financial Accounting Standards Board lobbied aggressively to have banks report market value data for certain balance sheet items. In its more extreme form, market value accounting would be required for all assets, liabilities, and off-balance sheet items. In a modified form, market value accounting would be imposed only on the investment portfolio. The fundamental complaint was that historical cost accounting data do not provide adequate information to accurately assess a bank's financial condition. Under market value accounting, balance sheet data would provide a snapshot of the value of the bank if it was liquidated on that day.

Accounting conventions through 1991 allowed bank portfolio managers to decide whether a security is held for investment purposes or as part of a trading account. Anything held as part of the trading account was valued at market prices for financial statements. If an asset was being held for sale, such as mortgages, it was recorded at the lower of cost or market. Any investment, loan, or other asset was recorded at historical cost. The difference is that when interest rates change, market values change, but these changes do not show up as affecting the value of the majority of bank assets and liabilities.

Bankers were obviously frantic about the proposal. Market value accounting would increase the volatility of earnings as unrealized gains and losses are added to or subtracted from normal operating income. It would also add volatility to the balance sheet as market values drop when rates rise and rise when rates fall, such that the market value of equity might fluctuate wildly. Many bankers argued that it would force banks to shorten maturities and durations of both assets and liabilities in order to reduce price sensitivity and thus stem market value fluctuations. The regulators argued alternatively that market value accounting would force banks to monitor interest rate and credit risk more carefully and improve their hedging capabilities—all desirable outcomes.

In actuality, there are both costs and benefits to forcing banks to provide market value data. The primary benefit is that such data provide a better picture of the bank's financial health. Investors should thus gain. Regulators would know sooner which firms are in trouble and whether they should be closed. Reporting market value results would also force managers to improve risk management practices. The primary cost is that accurate market value data are difficult to obtain and even if determined do not reflect the *going concern* value of a bank. Market value data are simply not readily available for most loans and assets without a liquid secondary market. Hence the focus initially on securities where these criticisms do not apply.

Clearly, banks need to provide better market value data for both regulators and investors. A compromise might be not to require market value information in reported balance sheet and income statement data, but to require detailed footnotes to financial statements that provide best estimates of market values, thereby enabling a better approximation of a bank's aggregate market value of equity.

anticipates rising rates, it reinvests the proceeds in a 1-year FNMA security, thereby shortening the maturity and duration of its assets. It is difficult to conduct a net present value analysis until management specifies what it will do with the proceeds after the first year. Of course, sensitivity analysis involving a variety of rate forecasts is extremely relevant here.

The essential point is that with swaps, active portfolio management allows a bank to adjust its interest rate risk, liquidity risk, and credit risk profile via buying and selling securities. Portfolio managers must also recognize that securities not sold simply because they are priced at a discount entail losses in the form of reduced periodic interest income. Similarly, securities sold for a gain typically involve substitution of a larger current-period cash inflow for reduced interest income in later periods. Contemporary Issues: Marking to Market suggests, however, that this fear of accounting for realized gains and losses may soon disappear because banks may have to formally account for unrealized gains and losses on a regular basis.

SUMMARY

With the changing competitive environment, commercial banks are looking to manage their investment portfolios more aggressively. Passive strategies, which view the portfolio as a simple supplement to loans, earn average returns over time relative to the interest rate cycle. Active strategies, if implemented carefully, can enhance returns by taking advantage of perceived changes in interest rates and required adjustments in portfolio composition. Still, taking large speculative positions based on interest rate forecasts is inappropriate. The higher risk will inevitably come back to haunt managers in the form of losses.

Banks can generally improve the timing of their investments if they buy securities contracyclically, when loan demand is high. They should use municipal securities to shelter as much income as possible, given expectations of deductible expenses and tax benefits from alternative investments. A bank holding too many municipals can sell the securities with put options to improve total returns. Finally, portfolio managers should recognize that holding low-rate discount instruments produces opportunity losses in the form of reduced interest income in future years. If possible, they should take advantage of security swaps, which allow a bank to realign its overall risk and return position.

Questions

Active vs. Passive Strategies

1. Explain the differences between active and passive investment strategies. Give an example of each.

2. Why is it advantageous to actively manage the investment portfolio rather than the loan or deposit portfolio of a bank?

3. Discuss one reason for and one reason against using the investment portfolio to speculate. Which do you believe? What do you think about the existence of efficient markets and how does this opinion relate to your view of speculation?

4. The local community issues 10-year tax-exempt municipals every two years. It is the bank's policy to invest all of its available investment portfolio funds into these

securities. Is the bank following an active or passive investment strategy? What is the name of this strategy?

5. The ALCO reports that the bank duration gap is too positive. What might the investment manager do to bring the gap closer to zero? Would this be active or passive investment management? Would this be speculating?

6. The term-structure of U.S. Treasury interest rates generally exhibits certain shapes during different stages of the business cycle. Discuss this relationship and explain why it holds, on average.

7. What rationale suggests that a contracyclical investment strategy should outperform the market, on average? Is it possible to consistently earn above average returns by timing securities purchases?

8. Suppose the U.S. Treasury yield curve is continuously downsloping. Should a bank portfolio manager buy securities with maturities under one year or securities with maturities of 10 years to maximize interest income over the next 10 years? Explain what factors should be used to make a decision.

Laddered, Barbell and Riding the Yield Curve

9. What are the fundamental differences between the laddered maturity strategy and the barbell strategy? Why will a barbell strategy typically outperform the laddered strategy in a stable interest rate environment?

10. Both the laddered and barbell investment strategies require the bank to determine the maximum length of securities it will purchase. What factors might influence this decision? What additional decisions must the bank using the barbell strategy make?

11. Explain the technique of riding the yield curve. The chapter says, "It works best when the yield curve is upsloping and rates are relatively stable." Could you ride the yield curve if the yield curve was downsloping? What happens if interest rates are not stable?

12. Your bank prefers securities that mature in 8 years. You, as investment manager, feel that now is a particularly good time to ride the yield curve.
    a. What conditions might make you feel like riding the curve?
    b. Currently the yield curve looks like:

Maturity	Rate
1 year	8.0%
3 years	8.4%
6 years	8.8%
8 years	9.0%
10 years	9.2%
12 years	9.2%
14 years	9.3%
16 years	9.3%

    i.   What maturity would you suggest buying?

ii. The ALCO has given you permission to buy $1 million in 14-year bonds at par value. How many additional dollars can you earn with 14-year versus 8-year securities if interest rates do not change in the next two years? (Assume that two years from now you will sell what you buy today. Also assume that these bonds only pay interest once a year.) How long do interest rates have to stay steady for this strategy to work?

iii. If the interim cash flows from these bonds are reinvested at 8 percent interest, what interest rate return would you earn from riding the yield curve?

iv. What would the results have been if you originally invested for 10 years rather than 14 years?

13. Suppose you institute the above strategy but interest rates change. Rates were particularly unfavorable for quite a while and now you are forced to sell. The 14-year securities now have 6 years until they mature and the yield curve is:

Maturity	Rate
1 year	10.0%
3 years	10.1%
6 years	10.1%
8 years	10.2%
10 years	10.2%
12 years	10.2%
14 years	10.3%
16 years	10.3%

With the same reinvestment how did the 14-year strategy compare to the 8-year strategy?

Municipals

14. What impact should each of the following have on a bank's demand for tax-exempt securities? Explain why in each case.
   - The bank increases its loan charge-offs by 20 percent.
   - The bank claims twice as many foreign tax credits as previously expected.
   - A leasing subsidiary acquires equipment that substantially raises the bank's depreciation expense.
   - Municipal interest rates increase relative to all taxable rates.

15. Charter Bank issued $4.5 million in 2-year certificates of deposit paying 7.7 percent annually. It will use the proceeds to buy FNMA securities at par yielding 8.4 percent or 2-year qualifying tax-exempt bonds yielding 7.6 percent. (They generate an 80 percent tax exemption.) Charter must hold 3 percent reserves in support of CDs. What is the optimal mix of investments for the profit maximizing bank? What will the expected profits equal? Assume a 34 percent tax rate.

16. During the past year the ALCO of Bridgeport Bank & Trust determined that the bank held too many municipal bonds given its expected expenses. Although they expect earnings to improve, they plan to liquidate part of their municipal portfolio. Currently they are trying to determine how many municipals the bank should own.

Table 1 Bridgeport Bank & Trust: Balance Sheet and Interest Rate Forecasts for the Next Year (Millions of Dollars)

Assets	Amount	Average Interest Yield	Liabilities and Equity	Amount	Average Interest Cost
Cash and due	$ 105	0%	Demand deposits	$ 155	0%
			NOWs	160	5.6
Other nonearning	20	0	Small time deposits	475	7.7
Investments	350		Large CDs	225	9.5
Taxable		8.8	Federal funds purchased	85	9.2
Tax exempt[a]		7.0	Liabilities	$1,100	
Loans	725	12.0	Equity	90	0
Total	$1,200		Total	$1,200	

Noninterest Income and Expanse Component Forecasts (Millions of Dollars)

1. Noninterest income: $13.5
2. Noninterest expense (excluding loan loss provisions): $42.6
3. Provisions for loan losses: $3.2
4. Tax credits expected to be claimed: $1.0
5. Income taxes: $13,750 on the first $75,000 of taxable income; a 34 percent marginal tax rate applies to all other taxable income.

[a]All municipals owned were purchased after 1982 such that the bank can deduct only 80% of the associated carrying costs.

To forecast next year's expected earnings the ALCO has agreed to the balance sheet composition and associated interest rates summarized in Table 1. Management expects to allocate $350 million to investment securities but does not know the optimal composition to maximize after-tax income. Expected noninterest income and expense components are listed in the middle of the table along with information regarding the bank's tax position. At present, Bridgeport Bank & Trust owns $115 million in municipals. Of this total, $10 million will mature during the upcoming year. All of the municipals were purchased after 1982 so the bank can only deduct 80 percent of the interest. If it buys additional municipals, it will purchase only qualifying, small-issue public-purpose bonds.

a. Follow the format in Exhibit 19.5 of the text to determine the target holdings of municipal securities which will maximize expected after-tax income.

b. Calculate the bank's projected net income for the upcoming year.

c. Should the bank buy or sell munis during the year?

Puts on Municipals

17. What rationale justifies selling municipal bonds with put options? How can a portfolio manager use the transaction to alter a bank's overall risk and return profile?

18. What are the benefits to investors in put municipal bonds? Would investors prefer some types of municipalities over others?

19. If banks must "mark to market" their investment portfolio, what effect will this have on the use of selling munis with puts? What impact will it have on any security swap?

Security Swaps

20. Suppose that a bank currently owns a $1 million par value Treasury note, purchased at par, with 3 years remaining to maturity that pays $50,000 in interest every 6 months. Currently the bank could sell this bond for $1.09 million and reinvest the proceeds in a 3-year taxable bond paying 8.2 percent annually, with semi-annual payments. Determine the incremental cash flows which would result from this swap if the bank is in the 34 percent tax bracket.

21. Suppose the above bank owns a $1 million par value Treasury note, purchased at par, with 3 years to maturity, paying $39,000 in semiannual interest, and a market value of $960,000. Determine the incremental cash flow effects if the bank sold this note and bought the 8.2 percent security described above.

22. The ALCO members of Bridgeport Bank & Trust, presented in question 16, agree that market interest rates are going to rise by 100 to 150 basis points during the upcoming year. Committee members decided to swap securities in the bank's investment portfolio to increase its rate sensitivity. Below are listed selected security holdings and market interest rates currently available on Treasury and agency instruments.

Security	Par Value	Market Value	Semiannual Coupon
2-year U.S. Treasury note	$2,000,000	$1,982,625	$ 81,500
8-year U.S. Treasury bond	$3,000,000	$3,067,250	$148,200
3-year Federal National Mortgage Assoc. bond	$1,000,000	$ 972,450	$ 42,000
3-year Federal Land Bank (FLB) bond	$2,000,000	$1,938,875	$ 80,000

Current Market Rates[a]
3-month Treasury bills: 8.25%
6-month Treasury bills: 8.40%
52-week Treasury bills: 8.55%
2-year Treasury note: 8.70%
3-year FLB bond: 9.25%

---

[a]The bank's marginal income tax rate equals 34%.

a. What will the incremental cash flow effects be over the next year if the bank sells both 3-year bonds from its portfolio and invests the entire after-tax proceeds in a new 3-year FHLB bond? What are the advantages and disadvantages of the bank doing this?

b. Suppose the bank sells the 2-year Treasury note, the 8-year Treasury bond, and the 3-year FNMA bond. Determine what dollar amount the bank will report under securities gains or losses. Analyze the incremental cash flow effects if the bank uses the proceeds after tax to 1) buy 3-month T-bills, 2) buy 6-month T-bills, 3) buy 52-week T-bills, and 4) buy 2-year Treasury notes. In each case explain how the bank's risk profile will have changed.

FIRST FINANCIAL REVISTED: INVESTMENT POLICIES

At the time C.W. Hampton visited First Financial, the bank's investment portfolio was providing the bulk or revenues because of the extensive loan problems. The majority of bond holdings were Treasury, agency, and CMO securities with some municipals. Joan Nystrom, the investment manager, was particularly bothered by four problems that prevented her from actively managing the portfolio.

1. Most of the Treasury securities were pledged as collateral against RP transactions and the bank's substantial borrowing from the Federal Reserve Bank. Thus she could not sell these Treasuries without substituting other collateral. They were illiquid.

2. The bank owned municipals that generated tax-exempt interest when the bank was operating at a loss. First Financial would have no need for tax-sheltered income for the next few years. Ideally, she would like to sell the municipals and reinvest the proceeds. Unfortunately, they were currently priced at a discount and the bank would have to report a securities loss at sale. First Financial did not have the capital to absorb additional losses even though a security swap would improve its cash flow.

3. Various members of the Board of Directors were strongly pushing her to buy CMOs because they offered higher yields than Treasuries. She felt uncomfortable with the risk and return features of CMOs because she could not accurately forecast prepayments and she did not believe that the secondary market for CMOs was very liquid.

4. Members of the Board of Directors were recommending that she extend maturities in the bond portfolio to capture the higher yields from an upsloping yield curve. The economy was in the early stages of recession so the general level of interest rates was low. Nystrom believed that buying long-term securities in this environment was extremely risky.

What should she do? Clearly, First Financial needs a formal investment policy to establish acceptable risk and return guidelines. Without this, management has no reference base to evaluate acceptable performance. She must clearly articulate the risks of investment choices that vary: security maturity, portfolio composition, and average credit rating. She must also evaluate the risks of CMOs and communicate this to senior management. Finally, she should look into selling municipals with a put option and reinvest the proceeds.

Project

Obtain a copy of a large bank's recent annual report. Analyze data for the securities portfolio and footnotes to determine whether marked values of assets either exceed or fall below reported book values on the balance sheet. What impact would full market value accounting have on the bank's reported earnings for the most recent year?

References

Bergquist, Lizbeth. "Trends in Investment Portfolio Management." *Bank Management* (January 1991).

Bradley, Stephen, and Dwight Crane. "Simulation of Bond Portfolio Strategies: Laddered versus Barbell Maturity Structure." *Journal of Bank Research* (Summer 1975).

Darling, George, John Lastivica, and Alan Udall. "Marking to Market Will Erode Public Confidence." *American Banker* (December 12, 1989).

Hendershott, Patric, and Timothy Koch. "The Demand for Tax-Exempt Securities by Financial Institutions." *Journal of Finance* (June 1980).

Holland, Kelley. "Accounting Proposal Still Alive Despite Panel's Move." *American Banker* (September 17, 1990)

Hoffland, David. "A Model Bank Investment Policy." *Financial Analysts Journal* (May–June 1978).

Koch, Timothy. "Commercial Bank Size, Relative Profitability and the Demand for Tax-Exempt Securities." *Journal of Bank Research* (Spring 1982).

Koch, Timothy. "Selling Tax-Exempt Securities with Put Options." In *Bank Asset/Liability Management*. Boston, Mass.: Warren, Gorham & Lamont, 1985.

Loughran, Tim. "Marking to Market: Will Banks Get Mauled?" *Bankers Monthly* (April 1989).

McEnally, Richard. "Duration as a Practical Tool for Bond Management." *The Journal of Portfolio Management* (Summer 1977).

Meyer, K.R. "Forecasting Rates: Key to Active Bond Management." *Financial Analysts Journal* (November 1978).

Salwen, Kevin, and Robin Blumenthal. "Tackling Accounting, SEC Pushes Changes With Broad Impact." *Wall Street Journal* (September 27, 1990).

Sorenson, Eric. "Who Puts the Slope in the Municipal Yield Curve?" *The Journal of Portfolio Management* (Summer 1983).

Van Horne, James. *Financial Market Rates and Flows*. Englewood Cliffs, N.J.: Prentice-Hall, Inc., 1990.

White, Lawrence. "Marking to Market Recognizes Realities." *American Banker* (December 12, 1990).

Part V

Extending Credit to Business and Individuals

Chapter 20

Overview of Credit Policy and Loan Characteristics

For most people in commercial banking, lending represents the heart of the industry. Loans dominate asset holdings and generate the largest share of operating income. Loan officers are among the most visible bank employees, while loan policies typically determine how fast a community grows and what type of business develops. Historically, senior management has selected future replacements from the lending staff.

With increased competition among commercial banks, savings and loan associations, credit unions, and investment banks, lending policies and loan portfolios have changed. Following World War II through the 1970s, commercial banks controlled commercial lending in the United States. When confronted with earnings pressure, they often raised loan-to-asset ratios by extending credit to marginal borrowers in the search for higher returns. Rising loan losses necessarily followed, in many cases causing banks to fail. The credit environment during the early 1990s can be summarized as having too many high-risk loans, few creditworthy customers, historically high loan losses, and aggressive pricing producing low risk-adjusted returns. The biggest challenge today is making profitable loans at reasonable risk in the face of intense price competition. The fundamental trade-off is loan quality versus loan volume and profitability.

Different management teams pursue different strategies. Many banks have pulled in their reins by restricting new loans to well-defined markets where they have specialized experience. They consciously limit growth in hopes of building capital to support future expansion. At the extreme, some banks have gravitated toward investment banking, underwriting securities and making loans but moving them off the balance sheet by selling them to other investors and earning a profit from servicing fees. Other banks see loan growth as their primary path to long-term survival and

633

aggressively court new consumer and commercial business. Many hope eventually to be allowed to make an equity investment in some of the companies to whom they currently lend.

This chapter provides an overview of the credit process and the types of credit extended by commercial banks. It describes recent problems banks have faced in certain credit areas and issues related to default risk and interest rate risk. The trend toward increased involvement in off-balance sheet activities including loans is analyzed in Chapter 25.

RECENT TRENDS IN LOAN GROWTH AND QUALITY

Commercial banks extend credit to different types of borrowers for many different purposes. For most customers, bank credit is the primary source of available debt financing. For banks, good loans are the most profitable assets. Still, banks' share of total loans extended has declined sharply during the 1980s. High-quality commercial borrowers issue commercial paper directly. The availability of junk bond financing has similarly reduced the demand for bank loans.

As with any investment, extending loans to businesses and individuals involves taking risks to earn high returns. Returns come in the form of loan interest, fee income, and investment income from deposits. The most prominent assumed risk is credit risk. Many factors can lead to loan defaults. An entire industry, such as energy or agriculture, can decline because of general economic events. Firm-specific problems may arise from changing technology, labor strikes, or fraudulent management. Individual borrowers find that their ability to repay closely follows the business cycle as personal income rises and falls. Loans as a group thus exhibit the highest charge-offs among bank assets, so banks regularly set aside substantial reserves against anticipated losses.

Interest rate risk also arises from credit decisions. Loan maturities, pricing, and the form of principal repayment affect the timing and magnitude of a bank's cash inflows. Floating-rate and variable-rate loans, for example, generate cash flows that vary closely with borrowing costs. Fixed-rate balloon payment loans, in contrast, involve far fewer cash flows. Longer-term consumer loans need to be funded with stable deposits to reduce exposure to rate changes.

Loans are the dominant asset in most banks' portfolios, comprising from 50 to 70 percent of total assets. Loan composition varies between banks depending on size, location, trade area, and lending expertise. Exhibit 20.1 summarizes proportionate differences among general loan categories for different-sized banks at the end of 1990. Several aggregate trends stand out. First, the ratio of loans to assets generally increases with bank size. The range is from 51 percent for banks with assets under $50 million to 66 percent for banks from $500 million to $1 billion, with larger banks exhibiting ratios just under 66 percent. Second, real estate loans represent the largest single loan category for banks under $10 billion in assets. Commercial and industrial loans exceed real estate loans at banks with more than $10 billion in assets. Third, agriculture loans make up a significant portion of the smallest banks' loans but are negligible at larger banks. Fourth, banks under $10 billion invest 10 to 14 percent of their loans to finance

**Exhibit 20.1 Commercial Bank Loans as a Percentage
of Total Assets: December 31, 1990**

Loan Category	**Bank Asset Size (Millions of Dollars)**						
	≤$50	$50–$100	$100–$500	$500–$1,000	$1,000–$3,000	$3,000–$10,000	>$10,000
Commercial & industrial	8.8%	8.7%	10.4%	15.2%	15.9%	17.8%	18.7%
Real estate	22.1	28.1	29.3	30.5	26.2	23.9	18.1
Individuals	10.8	10.6	11.5	12.4	13.3	12.2	7.9
Agriculture	8.8	2.8	1.8	0.1	0.1	0.1	0.1
Foreign office	—	—	—	—	—	0.1	3.1
Other	1.3	4.6	5.0	7.7	8.5	9.7	15.0
	51.8%	54.8%	58.0%	65.9%	64.0%	63.8%	62.9%

Source: Uniform Bank Performance Report.

consumer expenditures. The comparable percentage is lower but rising over time at the largest banks. Finally, international and other loans are significant only at the largest banks. Other loans include primarily loans to other financial institutions and lease receivables.

These comparisons at a point in time mask several important trends in bank lending over time. Exhibit 20.2 demonstrates how bank risk assets and real estate loans have increased as a fraction of bank assets during the past 30 years, particularly after 1985 for real estate. Not surprisingly, the decline in real estate values during the early 1990s produced significant problem loans and losses for commercial banks throughout the United States. The bottom part of the exhibit shows that the buffer against loan losses has declined sharply over the same interval. This figure plots the ratio of bank equity capital plus loan loss and FDIC reserves against deposit losses to net loan charge-offs. Note that the ratio is just 20 percent of its value in 1970. Exhibit 20.3, in turn, compares noncurrent loan rates and net loan charge-off rates across types of loans for most of the 1980s. A noncurrent loan is one in which some principal and interest payments are past due. Net charge-offs represent the dollar amount of loans that are formally charged off as uncollectable minus the dollar value of recoveries on loans previously charged off. Since 1987 foreign loans and real estate loans have exhibited the greatest problems and highest loss rates. Note, however, the volatility in these measures.

Recent deregulation and regulation have increased the importance of lending to overall performance. In response to interest rate deregulation during the early 1980s, most banks raised their loan-to-asset ratios. Because banks now pay market rates on their liabilities, their cost of funds has increased and they must earn higher yields on investments to maintain a positive spread and stable net interest income. Loans offer the highest promised yields. If banks can find enough good loans and price them appropriately, they can continue historical earnings growth. The problem is that banks face increased competition from other lenders, many of whom cut prices to establish

Exhibit 20.2 The Growth in Loans and the Buffer against Loan Losses

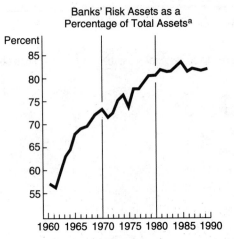

Banks' Risk Assets as a
Percentage of Total Assets[a]

[a] Risk Assets are defined as total assets less government securities and cash items

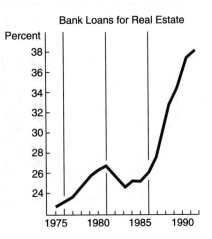

Bank Loans for Real Estate

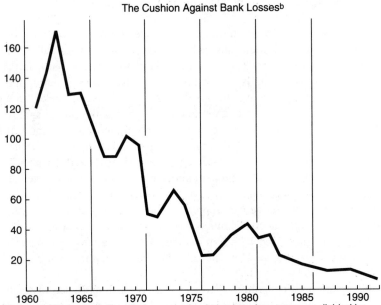

The Cushion Against Bank Losses[b]

[b] Banks' equity capital plus FDIC reserve fund plus loan loss reserves divided by net loan charge-offs.

Source: Federal Deposit Insurance Corporation.

**Exhibit 20.3 Noncurrent Loan Rates and Net Charge-off
Rates at Commercial Banks: 1982–1990**

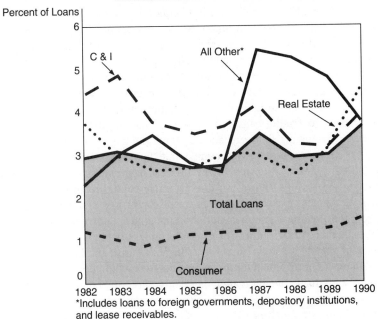

Noncurrent Loan Rates at Year-end 1982–1990

*Includes loans to foreign governments, depository institutions,
and lease receivables.

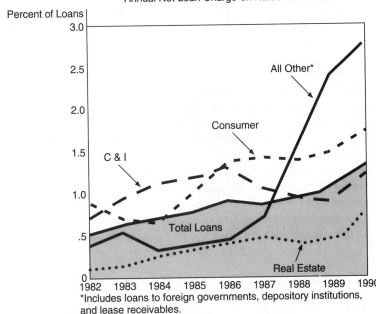

Annual Net Loan Charge-off Rates 1982–1990

*Includes loans to foreign governments, depository institutions,
and lease receivables.

Source: The FDIC Quarterly Banking Profile.

a market presence. Many quality borrowers also have access to alternative sources of funds by directly borrowing in the commercial paper or long-term bond markets. Alternatively, banks must increase services to generate additional fee income.

Regulators have also raised mandatory capital-to-asset ratios and implemented risk-based capital requirements. As indicated in Chapter 12, risk-based capital standards require that banks hold a minimum amount of equity capital for each loan kept on the books. More generally, strict capital ratios restrict loan growth and force banks to change the pricing based on increased capital required to support loans. The bottom line is that banks choosing to make loans must obtain additional capital to continue growing. Many banks have responded by acting as loan brokers rather than keeping all loans on their books. This process involves originating large loans or large volumes of loans and selling parts to smaller banks, thrift institutions, or other investors. Banks typically earn fees for originating the loans and servicing the payments. In many cases, they can sell part of the loan at a lower interest rate than that negotiated with the borrower. If so, the bank keeps a portion of the interest payment as well as the loan fee. Loan sales increase earnings but do not directly raise capital requirements.

Banks further supplement earnings but circumvent capital requirements by engaging in off-balance sheet lending arrangements and financial guarantees. Here a bank does not directly extend credit but either serves as an underwriter arranging financing or attaches a letter of credit to a loan agreement. In both cases, the bank earns a fee for its role but retains a contingent liability. If the borrower defaults, the bank must take over the asset and make the obligated payments. Contingent liabilities do not appear on the balance sheet and thus do not affect the capital-to-asset ratio calculated from balance sheet items. Regulators do selectively increase capital requirements if these contingent liabilities are large.[1] Chapter 25 offers examples of off-balance sheet activities and their impact on performance.

THE CREDIT PROCESS

The fundamental objective of commercial and consumer lending is to make profitable loans with minimal risk. Management should target specific industries or markets in which lending officers have expertise. The twin goals of loan volume and loan quality should be balanced with the bank's liquidity requirements, capital constraints, and rate-of-return objectives. The credit process relies on each bank's systems and controls that allow management and credit officers to evaluate risk and return trade-offs.

The credit process includes three functions: business development and credit analysis, credit execution and administration, and credit review (Exhibit 20.4). Each reflects the bank's written loan policy as determined by the Board of Directors. A loan policy formalizes lending guidelines that employees follow to conduct bank business and reduce risk. It identifies preferred loan qualities and establishes procedures for

---

[1]Banks do report off-balance sheet terms related to standby letters of credit, bankers acceptances, and loan commitments on the Federal Reserve's Schedule L.

Exhibit 20.4 The Credit Process

Business Development and Credit Analysis	Credit Execution and Administration	Credit Review
Market research	Loan committee reviews proposal/recommendation	Review loan documentation
Advertising, public relations	Accept/reject decision made, terms negotiated	Monitor compliance with loan agreement:
Officer call programs		Positive and negative loan covenants
Obtain formal loan request	Loan agreement prepared with collateral documentation	Delinquencies in loan payments
Obtain financial statements, borrowing resolution, credit reports	Borrower signs agreement, turns over collateral, receives loan proceeds	Discuss nature of delinquency or other problems with borrower
Financial statement and cash flow analysis	Perfect security interest	Institute corrective action:
Evaluate collateral	File materials in credit file	Modify credit terms
Line officer makes recommendation on accepting/rejecting loan	Process loan payments, obtain periodic financial statements, call on borrower	Obtain additional capital, collateral, guarantees
		Call loan

granting, documenting, and reviewing loans.[2] Specific elements within each function are listed in the exhibit.

Business Development and Credit Analysis

Where would a bank be without customers? Business development is the process of marketing bank services to existing and potential customers. With lending, it involves identifying new credit customers and soliciting their banking business, as well as maintaining relationships with current customers and cross-selling noncredit services. Every bank employee, from tellers handling drive-up facilities to members of the Board of Directors, is responsible for business development. Each employee regularly comes into contact with potential customers and can sell bank services. To encourage marketing efforts, many banks use cash bonuses or other incentive plans to reward employees who successfully cross-sell services or bring new business into a bank.

The normal starting point for any business development effort is market research. Management should establish targets for loan composition and identify areas of potential business. The research may formally analyze economic conditions, local demographic trends, and customer surveys. Alternatively, it may simply evolve from normal customer contacts and any communications link with local businesses about forthcoming opportunities. The purpose is to forecast the demand for bank services. The second step is to train employees regarding what products are available, what customers are likely to need or want and how they should communicate with customers. Finally, the bank should make customers aware of its services. The most obvious means is through effective advertising and public relations. Many banks also

[2]In their periodic examinations, regulators evaluate each bank's written loan policy to see if existing loans conform to management's objectives and acceptable guidelines. Typical guidelines and sample loan policies are provided in *A Guide to Developing a Written Lending Policy* (1977).

incorporate formal officer call programs, in which lending officers are required to make regular face-to-face contact with current and potential borrowers. Borrowers are often hesitant in revealing personal or business financial backgrounds. Before doing so, they like to know and trust the bank official with whom they are dealing.

Call programs require constant personal contact with potential borrowers, either through civic groups and trade associations or through direct appointments. Formal programs involve bank-determined numerical objectives and officer implementation of customer contact procedures. The numerical objectives often stipulate a minimum number of calls each month. Some are directed at current customers, while others target potential customers identified through research. The calling officer establishes the personal contact, makes the call, and files a report. After each call, the officer logs the date and time of the meeting, the issues discussed, and notes the opportunities for obtaining new business. Typically, officers must call on new customers several times before an opportunity develops. The bank is essentially positioning itself for the times when customers become dissatisfied with their prior bank relationships or qualify as good credits.

Credit Analysis. Once a customer requests a loan, bank officers analyze all available information to determine whether the loan meets the bank's risk/return objectives. Credit analysis is essentially default risk analysis in which a loan officer attempts to evaluate a borrower's ability and willingness to repay. One author has identified three distinct areas of commercial risk analysis related to the following questions:[3]

1. What risks are inherent in the operations of the business?

2. What have managers done or failed to do in mitigating those risks?

3. How can a lender structure and control its own risks in supplying funds?

The first question forces the credit analyst to generate a list of factors that indicate what could harm a borrower's ability to repay. The second recognizes that repayment is largely a function of decisions made by a borrower. Is management aware of the important risks and has it responded? The last question forces the analyst to specify how risks can be controlled so the bank can structure an acceptable loan agreement.

Traditionally, key risk factors have been classified according to the five "Cs" of credit: character, capital, capacity, conditions, and collateral. Character refers to the borrower's honesty. An analyst must assess the borrower's integrity and intent to repay. If there are any serious doubts, the loan should be rejected. Capital refers to the borrower's wealth position measured by financial soundness and market standing. Can the firm or individual withstand any deterioration in its financial position? Capacity involves both the borrower's legal standing and management's expertise in maintaining operations so the firm or individual can repay its debt obligations. A business must have identifiable cash flow or alternative sources of cash to repay debt. An individual must be able to generate income. Conditions refers to the economic environment or industry-specific supply, production, and distribution factors influencing a firm's opera-

---

[3]The discussion is based on Compton, 1985.

tions. Repayment sources of cash often vary with the business cycle or consumer demand. Finally, collateral is the lender's secondary source of repayment or security in the case of default.

The formal credit analysis procedure includes a subjective evaluation of the borrower's request and a detailed review of all financial statements. The initial quantitative analysis may be performed by credit analysts for the loan officer. The process consists of

1.   Collecting information for the credit file

2.   Spreading financial statements (analyzing financial ratios)

3.   Projecting the borrower's cash flow

4.   Evaluating collateral

5.   Writing a summary analysis and making a recommendation

The credit file contains background information on the borrower, including summaries of information obtained from officer calls, past and present financial statements, pertinent credit reports, and supporting schedules such as an aging of receivables, a breakdown of current inventory and equipment, and a summary of insurance coverage. If the customer is a previous borrower, the file should also contain copies of the past loan agreement, cash flow projections, collateral agreements and security documents, any narrative comments provided by prior loan officers, and copies of all correspondence with the customer. The credit analyst uses the credit file data to spread the financial statements, project cash flow, and evaluate collateral.[4] The last step is to submit a written report summarizing the loan request, loan purpose, and the borrower's comparative financial performance with industry standards, and to make a recommendation.

The loan officer evaluates the report and discusses any errors, omissions, and extensions with the analyst. If the loan does not satisfy the bank's risk criteria, the officer notifies the borrower that the original request has been denied. The officer may suggest procedures that would improve the borrower's condition and repayment prospects and solicit another proposal if circumstances improve. If the credit satisfies acceptable risk limits, the officer negotiates specific preliminary credit terms including the loan amount, maturity, pricing, collateral requirements, and repayment schedule.

Many small banks do not have formal credit departments and full-time analysts to prepare financial histories. Loan officers personally complete the steps outlined above before accepting or rejecting a loan. Often loan requests are received without detailed information on the borrower's condition. Financial statements may be hand-written or unaudited and may not meet generally accepted accounting principles. Yet the borrower may possess good character and substantial net worth. In such instances, the loan officer works with the borrower to prepare a formal loan request and obtain the best financial information possible. This may mean personally auditing the borrower's receipts, expenditures, receivables, and inventory.

---

[4]This detailed data analysis is discussed in Chapter 21 for commercial loans and Chapter 22 for consumer loans, with several examples.

Credit Execution and Administration

The formal credit decision can be made by individual loan officers or by committee, depending on a bank's organizational structure. This structure varies with a bank's size, number of employees, and the type of loans handled. A bank's Board of Directors normally has the final say over which loans are approved, but most boards do not effectively exercise such control. Typically, each lending officer has independent authority to approve loans up to some fixed dollar amount. Junior officers at a large bank might have authority to approve loans up to $100,000, while senior lending officers might independently approve loans up to $500,000. Larger loans are often formally reviewed by a committee made up of the bank's senior loan officers. This committee reviews each step of the credit analysis as presented by the loan officer and supporting analysts and makes a collective decision. Loan committees meet regularly to monitor the credit approval process and asset quality problems when they arise. When required, the Board of Directors or a directors' loan committee reviews this decision and grants final approval.

Once a loan has been approved, the officer notifies the borrower and prepares a loan agreement. This agreement formalizes the purpose of the loan, the terms, repayment schedule, collateral required, and any loan covenants. It also states what conditions bring about a default by the borrower. These conditions may include late principal and interest payments, the sale of substantial assets, a declaration of bankruptcy, and breaking any restrictive loan covenant. The officer then checks that all loan documentation is present and in order. The borrower signs the agreement along with other guarantors, turns over the collateral if necessary, and receives the loan proceeds.

Documentation. A critical feature of executing any loan involves perfecting the bank's security interest in collateral. A security interest is the legal claim on property that secures payment on a debt or performance of an obligation, that is, collateral. When the bank's claim is superior to that of other creditors and the borrower, its security interest is perfected.[5]

Because there are many different types of borrowers and collateral, there are different methods of perfecting a security interest. In most cases, the bank requires borrowers to sign a security agreement that assigns qualifying collateral to the bank. This agreement describes the collateral and relevant covenants or warranties. Formal closure may involve getting the signature of a third-party guarantor on a loan agreement or having a key individual assign the cash value of a life insurance policy to the bank. In other cases, a bank may need to obtain title to equipment or vehicles. Whenever a security agreement is signed by all parties and the bank holds the collateral, the security interest is perfected. When the borrower holds the collateral, the bank must file a financing statement with the state that describes the collateral and the rights of the bank and borrower. It must be signed to establish the bank's superior interest.

---

[5]The Uniform Commercial Code (UCC) establishes what documentation is required to obtain a security interest in commercial lending. The UCC applies in every state, although various states have revised certain conditions. Each lending officer must understand what conditions apply wherever the bank conducts business.

Loan Covenants. Once a bank lends funds to a customer, the bank and borrower effectively become partners. The bank wants the customer to repay the debt service and purchase other bank services. The customer looks to the bank to provide useful accounting, financial, and tax advice.

Both the bank and borrower should recognize this partnership when negotiating credit terms. Still, it is important that each party protect its interests. For this reason, the bank often includes covenants in the loan agreement. Covenants may either be negative, indicating financial limitations and prohibited events, or positive, indicating specific provisions to which the borrower must adhere. The intent is to protect against substantive changes in the borrower's operating environment that damage the bank's interests. Most covenants address target financial ratios, limitations on asset sales, and maintenance of management quality. Exhibit 20.5 provides a partial list of covenants. The first three negative covenants, for example, attempt to limit discretionary cash payments by a firm. If effective, more cash is available for debt service. The first affirmative covenant example prevents management from altering a firm's balance sheet adversely.

Credit Review

The loan review effort is used after loan approval and is directed at reducing credit risk as well as handling problem loans and liquidating assets of failed borrowers. Effective credit management separates loan review from credit analysis, execution, and administration. The review process can be divided into two functions: monitoring the performance of existing loans and handling problem loans. Many banks have a formal loan review committee, independent of calling officers, that reports directly to the chief executive officer and directors' loan committee. Loan review personnel audit current loans to verify that the borrower's financial condition is acceptable, loan documentation is in place, and pricing meets return objectives. If the audit uncovers problems, the committee initiates corrective action. Removing the problem may simply involve getting signatures on omitted forms or filing required documents with the state. If the borrower has violated any loan covenants, the loan is in default. The bank can then force the borrower to correct the violation or it can call the loan. Calling a loan is normally a last resort and done only when the borrower does not voluntarily correct the problem. It allows the bank to request full payment before repayment prospects worsen.

The problem is much more serious when the borrower's financial condition deteriorates. These loans are classified as problem loans and require special treatment. In many cases, the bank has to modify the terms of the loan agreement to increase the probability of full repayment. Modifications include deferring interest and principal payments, lengthening maturities, and liquidating unnecessary assets. Often the bank requests additional collateral or guarantees and asks the borrower to contribute additional capital. The purpose is to buy time until the borrower's condition improves. Chapter 23 examines problem loans in detail. Banks separate loan work-out specialists from traditional loan officers because they are liquidation oriented and often involved in intense negotiations.

Exhibit 20.5 Sample Loan Covenants

Negative	Affirmative
Capital outlays cannot exceed $3 million annually	Borrower must maintain following financial ratios:
Cash dividends cannot exceed 60% of periodic earnings	Current ratio ≥ 1.0
Total officers' salaries cannot exceed $300,000 annually	Days receivables outstanding ≤ 50 days
No liens on assets beyond existing liens	Inventory turnover ≥ 4.5 times
No mergers, consolidation, or acquisition without bank approval	Debt to total assets ≤ 70%
No sale, lease, or transfer of more than 10% of existing assets	Net worth ≥ $1 million
No change in senior management	Fixed charge coverage ≥ 1.3 times
	Cash flow from operations ≥ dividends + current maturities of long-term debt
	Certified financial statements must be provided within 60 days of end of each fiscal year
	Borrower will maintain $500,000 "key man" life insurance policy on company president, with bank named as beneficiary
	Bank will be allowed to inspect inventory, receivables, and property periodically
	Borrower must pay all taxes and government fees unless contested in good faith and comply with all laws
	Borrower must inform bank of any litigation or claim that might materially affect its performance
	Borrower must maintain all property in good condition and repair

CHARACTERISTICS OF DIFFERENT TYPES OF LOANS

This section describes the basic characteristics of commercial bank loans. While there are many ways to classify loans, the analysis focuses on the borrower's use of loan proceeds and loan maturity. Each type of loan has different features that necessitate different repayment schemes, collateral, and loan covenants.

Commercial Loans

There are as many types of commercial loans as there are business borrowers. Banks lend large amounts to manufacturing companies, service companies, farmers, securities dealers, and other financial institutions. The loans may finance short-term uses such as temporary working capital needs and construction expenses in which the borrower has obtained a commitment for long-term financing from another lender, or long-term uses such as new equipment purchases and plant expansion. Short-term business loans often take the form of loan commitments or line-of-credit agreements. These loans may be formal or informal and operate much like a credit card arrangement. A bank and borrower agree in advance that the customer can draw against the line as needed up to some maximum credit limit. The borrower determines the timing of borrowings and the actual amount. The obvious advantage to the borrower is flexibility. For example, the firm may only need temporary financing as it accumulates inventory prior to its major sales period. Once sales occur, it can repay the loan. These loans also take up less of the loan officer's time. Bankers must still complete a detailed analysis before extending credit. Prior to formal approval, the loan officer evaluates the purpose and repayment prospects and negotiates the size of the commitment, the term the commitment is outstanding, any fees or compensating balance requirements, and the interest rate charged.

Because many commercial loans finance current assets, the following discussion analyzes normal working capital requirements and several types of loans associated with this financing. Additional sections analyze the general features of term commercial loans, real estate loans, and agriculture loans.

Working Capital Requirements. A company's net working capital equals its current assets minus its current liabilities.[6] For most firms, working capital is positive, suggesting that current assets are financed partially by current debt and partially by long-term debt and equity. If current assets are liquidated, the proceeds exceed current liabilities. Working capital is thus a net liquidity measure. Consider the daily average balance sheet information in Exhibit 20.6 for Biotech Inc., which has $200 in working capital. Implicitly, $200 of long-term debt and equity is financing $200 of cash, receivables, and inventory, and the firm's current assets exceed its current liabilities. Note that $250 of the current liabilities are notes payable to a bank indicating short-term financing currently provided for operating purposes. Virtually all businesses must invest in current assets to operate. Manufacturers purchase materials to produce goods that are typically sold on credit. Retail firms purchase display merchandise and often rely on credit sales to stimulate business. Service companies need operating cash and small inventories of supplies. Each type of business relies on different financing methods depending on its operating policies and growth. If the financing needs are truly short term, a working capital loan is often appropriate.

Exhibit 20.7 summarizes the normal working capital cycle for a manufacturing firm. This cycle compares the timing difference between converting current assets to cash and making cash payments on normal operating expenses. All sales are assumed to be credit sales. Initially, a firm accumulates operating cash. It then invests in inventory by purchasing materials that are converted into finished goods. Accounts receivable appear when the firm sells the inventory on credit. Finally, the receivables revert to cash as customers pay off their credit purchases. Many factors influence how long it takes to complete the cycle, including the complexity of the production process, the terms of credit sales, and the firm's collection efforts on outstanding receivables. The longer it takes to produce a finished good, sell it, and collect on the sale, the longer the firm has to wait to get its cash investment back. If a timing difference exists, a loan may be necessary to help a firm manage the mismatch in cash flows.

In most industries, the cash-to-cash asset cycle takes longer than the comparable cycle for nonbank current liabilities. The cash-to-cash liability cycle essentially mea-

---

[6]Throughout the chapter the term *working capital* is used for *net working capital*, which actually equals current assets minus current liabilities.

Exhibit 20.6 Balance Sheet and Income Statement Data for Biotech Inc.

Assets		Liabilities + Equity		Selected Income Statement Data[a]
Cash	$ 50	Accounts payable	$ 290	Net sales = $5,475
Accounts receivable	350	Accrued expenses	40	Cost of goods sold = $3,650
Inventory	400	Notes payable—bank	250	Operating expenses = $1,460
		Current maturities—Long-term debt	20	Purchases = $3,688
Current assets	$ 800			Average daily sales = $15
Fixed assets	700	Current liabilities	$ 600	Average daily cost of goods sold = $10
		Long-term debt	300	Average daily operating expenses = $4
Total	$1,500	Equity	600	Average daily purchases = $10.1
		Total	$1,500	

Working Capital Cycle[b]

Current Assets

Cash= $ 50
Inventory= $400
Receivables= $350

Current assets = $800

Days cash=   3.3
Days inventory= 40.0
Days receivables= 23.4

Days cash-to-cash= 66.7

Current Liabilities

Accounts payable= $290
Accruals= $ 40

Days payables= 28.7
Days accruals= 10.0

Days cash-to-cash= 38.7

Difference in cash-to-cash cycles = 28 days

---

[a] Assumes a 365-day year.
[b] Ratio Definitions:

Days cash = Cash /Average daily sales
Days inventory = Inventory/Average daily cost of goods sold
Days receivables = Accounts receivable /Average daily sales
Days payables = Accounts payable /Average daily purchases
Days accruals = Accruals /Average daily operating expenses

Exhibit 20.7 Cash-to-Cash Working Capital Cycle

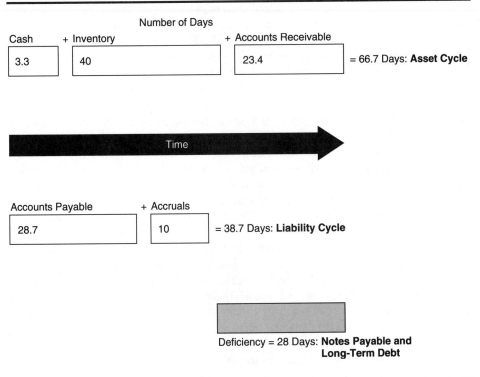

sures how long a firm can obtain interest-free financing from suppliers in the form of accounts payable and accrued expenses. Firms use trade credit to finance materials purchases temporarily, but must normally pay their suppliers within 30 days to receive any discounts. Even when they can ride suppliers longer, they still pay down accounts payable well before their current asset cycle is completed. Firms may also be able to accrue expenses rather than make immediate cash payments, but the deferment period is quite short. The net effect is that most businesses receive cash from an asset sale long after they have paid suppliers, associated labor costs, and other operating expenses. With the timing discrepancy, firms must rely on bank credit or long-term debt to finance current assets during this period of mismatched cash flows.

This cash-to-cash comparison is demonstrated at the bottoms of Exhibit 20.6 and Exhibit 20.7 using data for Biotech Inc. Exhibit 20.6 shows that it takes almost 67 days for Biotech's current assets to turn over. In comparison, the company rides its suppliers for an average of 29 days and defers operating expenses for 10 days. Notes payable to the bank and long-term debt finance this 28-day deficiency in underlying cash flows.

One procedure for estimating working capital loan needs is to multiply the number of days deficiency between the asset and liability cash-to-cash cycle by the firm's average daily cost of goods sold. In this example the product equals $280, which is close to the sum of the notes payable and current maturities of long-term debt currently outstanding. Of course, this calculation ignores the firm's capital structure. If a company has above-average equity or more long-term debt financing than the norm, working capital financing needs can be met by these more permanent sources of funds. In this case, the estimate based on the above calculation will overstate true short-term funding needs.

Seasonal versus Permanent Working Capital Needs. Many businesses find that their working capital fluctuates over time. This may be caused by events such as an unexpected increase in credit sales relative to cash sales, an increase in inventory resulting from defective materials, or changes in payment patterns to suppliers. Working capital may also vary during the year because of seasonal sales. Businesses temporarily build up inventories and pay higher operating expenses prior to the peak sales season. Working capital needs rise because accounts payable increase at a slower pace. The deficiency rises further with an increase in receivables, then declines to normal as the firm collects on receivables and inventory contracts. An important facet of working capital financing is thus to assess any seasonal pattern in inventory accumulation, production, sales, and collection of receivables. If seasonal patterns exist, a lender must obtain interim financial statements that reveal peak holdings of current assets. Consider, for example, a company that manufactures fireworks or a restaurant in a ski resort area. The maximum working capital loan will normally apply during or just preceding their peak business activity.

Most businesses have a stable amount of working capital that persists regardless of unexpected events and seasonal fluctuations. This base or permanent working capital need equals the minimum level of current assets minus the minimum adjusted level of current liabilities, defined as current liabilities minus short-term bank credit and current maturities of long-term debt. It is important that businesses and their lenders recognize this permanent need because it represents the amount of long-term debt financing required for current assets. Firms should try to raise funds for these permanent needs in the bond or stock market as banks are reluctant to make term loans for this purpose. Any working capital requirement in excess of this base amount should be financed with short-term credit.

A time series plot of a firm's working capital position helps quantify permanent and temporary needs. It also identifies any seasonal patterns that appear. Exhibit 20.8 shows this concept graphically. The base trend lines through the minimum amounts of current assets and adjusted current liabilities designate the permanent components of these balance sheet items. These amounts jump at period q when the firm is assumed to expand its physical plant. The curved lines represent total current assets and total current liabilities. The peak value of current liabilities comes before the peak in current assets, reflecting the fact that receivables growth typically lags behind increases in inventory and trade credit.

Permanent working capital needs equal the difference between minimum current assets and minimum adjusted current liabilities. Seasonal needs equal the difference in

Exhibit 20.8 Trends in Working Capital Needs

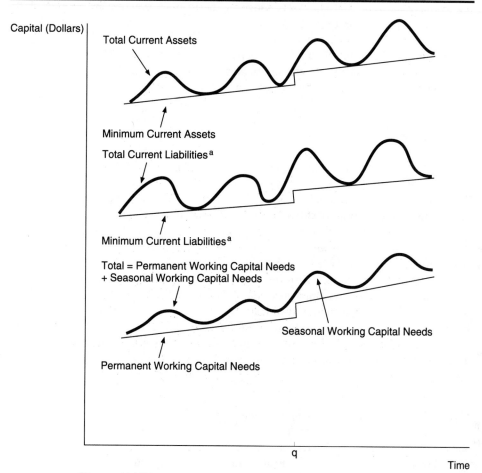

Capital (Dollars)

Total Current Assets

Minimum Current Assets

Total Current Liabilities[a]

Minimum Current Liabilities[a]

Total = Permanent Working Capital Needs + Seasonal Working Capital Needs

Seasonal Working Capital Needs

Permanent Working Capital Needs

q

Time

[a]Current Liabilities are net of notes payable and current maturities of long-term debt (adjusted current liabilities).

total current assets and total adjusted current liabilities. Peak needs coincide with the peak level of current assets.

Short-Term Commercial Loans. Banks try to match credit terms with a borrower's specific needs. The loan officer estimates the purpose and amount of the proposed loan, the expected source of repayment, and the value of collateral. The loan amount, maturity, and repayment schedule are negotiated to coincide with the projections. Short-term funding needs are financed by short-term loans, while long-term needs are financed by term loans with longer maturities.

Seasonal Working Capital Loans. Seasonal working capital loans finance a temporary increase in net current assets above the permanent requirement (Exhibit 20.8). A borrower uses the proceeds to purchase raw materials and build up inventories of finished goods in anticipation of later sales. Trade credit also increases, but by a smaller amount. Funding requirements persist as the borrower sells the inventory on credit and accounts receivable remain outstanding. The loan declines as the borrower collects on the receivables and stops accumulating inventory.

This type of loan is seasonal if the need arises on a regular basis and if the cycle completes itself within 1 year. It is self-liquidating in the sense that repayment derives from sales of the finished goods that are financed. Because the loan proceeds finance an increase in inventories and receivables, banks try to secure the loan with these assets. However, seasonal working capital loans are often unsecured because the risk to the lender is relatively low.

When evaluating seasonal loans it is necessary to compare the borrower's working capital position over time (Exhibit 20.8). If the bank only obtained year-end historical financial statements when current assets were at seasonal lows, an analysis would demonstrate that the borrower did not need seasonal financing. To estimate maximum seasonal needs, the bank needs comparative statements for periods when current assets are at their highs and lows. The difference in total working capital needs between the two periods equals the maximum seasonal loan requirement. This means that the bank must normally request interim financial statements. Suppose, for example, that the balance sheet data for Biotech Inc. in Exhibit 20.6 represent the company's minimal seasonal working capital needs. If the peak needs arise 4 months later when current assets equal $1,500 and current liabilities equal $900, the maximum seasonal requirement totals $600.

Open Credit Lines. Seasonal loans often take the form of open credit lines.[7] Under these arrangements, the bank makes a certain amount of funds available to a borrower for a set period of time. The customer determines the timing of actual borrowings, or "takedowns," by writing checks against the account. Typically, borrowing gradually increases with the inventory buildup, then declines with the collection of receivables. The bank likes to see the loan fully repaid at least once during each year. This confirms that the needs are truly seasonal.

The terms of credit lines vary between borrowers and arrangements may be informal or contractual. Informal lines are not legally binding but represent a promise that the bank will advance credit. The customer pays for the service only by paying interest on the funds actually borrowed. A contractual or formal credit line is legally binding even though no written agreement is signed. The bank charges a fee for making credit available, regardless of whether the customer actually uses the line. The customer also pays interest on actual borrowings. In both cases, credit lines are typically renegotiated each year when the bank reassesses the firm's credit needs. Borrowers

---

[7]Credit lines are used to meet many types of temporary needs in addition to seasonal needs. One popular type is the back-up credit line used by large corporations that regularly issue commercial paper. This credit is available to pay investors when commercial paper matures if the corporation does not or cannot roll over its outstanding paper.

pay interest at variable rates and often must hold compensating deposit balances with the bank as part of the arrangement. These pricing characteristics are discussed in Chapter 24.

Asset-Based Loans. An asset-based loan is any loan secured by the customer's assets. In practice, the term has come to mean short-term loans secured by inventories and/or accounts receivable. The key is that such loans rely on asset conversion for repayment. Banks require collateral when borrowers cannot qualify for unsecured loans. Loans to finance leveraged buyouts are also classified in this category. In the case of inventory loans, the security consists of raw materials, goods in process, and finished products. The value of the inventory depends on the marketability of each component if the borrower goes out of business. Banks will lend from 40 to 60 percent against common raw materials and against finished goods that are marketable, and nothing against unfinished inventory. With receivables, the security consists of paper assets that presumably represent sales. The quality of the collateral depends on the borrower's integrity in reporting actual sales and the credibility of billings.

Making asset-based loans requires a loan officer to examine inventory on site and personally confirm that the customer's figures for receivables are purged of uncollectable or nonexistent accounts. A bank normally lends against 50 to 80 percent of a borrower's receivables depending on the aging schedule and collection experience. An aging schedule is a list of accounts receivable segregated according to the month in which the invoice is dated (invoice aging) or in which the invoice is payable (due-date aging). An analyst can quickly determine the volume of past-due accounts and trends in collection experience by comparing the fraction of total receivables in each month over time.

Banks frequently require lock-box arrangements to assure that borrowers repay receivables loans when payments are received. With a lock box the borrower requests that its customers mail payments directly to a post office box controlled by the bank. The bank processes the payments and reduces the borrower's loan balance but charges the borrower for handling the items. Furthermore, because banks spend more time monitoring asset-based loans, they charge rates above those available on open credit lines. The standard interest pricing is a rate that floats from 2 to 6 percent above a bank's base rate.[8]

Highly Leveraged Transactions. During the early 1980s, one growth area in asset-based lending was leveraged buyouts (LBOs). A leveraged buyout involves a group of investors, often part of the existing management team, buying a target company and taking it private with a minimum amount of equity and a large amount of debt. Target companies are generally those with undervalued real assets. The investors typically sell off specific assets or subsidiaries to pay down much of the debt quickly. If key assets have been undervalued, the investors may then own a down-sized company whose

---

[8]The term *base rate* refers to an index rate used to price loans. The index can be any rate that approximates a bank's cost of debt financing, including the federal funds rate, CD rate, weighted marginal cost of debt, and a bank's own prime rate. Historically, loans were priced as a markup over prime. For reasons discussed in Chapter 24, the term *base rate* has generally replaced *prime rate* in loan agreements.

earnings prospects have improved and whose stock has increased in value. The investors sell the company or take it public once the market perceives its greater value. If investors misforecast and pay too much, the target company goes bankrupt.

Many of the earliest LBOs produced returns as high as 50 percent for the equity investors. The development of the junk bond market during the early 1980s gave corporate raiders the capacity to finance highly leveraged takeovers so that both friendly and hostile takeovers were common. As more players entered the game, prices increased and the returns declined. By the late 1980s the junk bond market collapsed and takeover financing was restricted to the soundest deals. Many large, highly leveraged corporations, such as the Campeau group and Revco, declared bankruptcy. The descriptions of the Allied-Signal and RJR LBOs in Contemporary Issues: Not All Leveraged Buyouts Are Immediate Successes and Contemporary Issues: RJR—Deleveraging an LBO demonstrate the risks and returns of two well-known transactions.

With the bidding wars and onslaught of bankruptcies, lenders and bank regulators grew concerned with the credit risks that banks were assuming in these transactions. Bank regulators eventually grouped LBOs with other transactions involving extensive borrowings under the label highly leveraged transactions (HLTs). HLTs arise from three types of transactions; LBOs in which debt is substituted for privately held equity, leveraged recapitalizations in which borrowers use loan proceeds to pay large dividends to shareholders, and leveraged acquisitions in which a cash purchase of another related company produces an increase in the buyer's debt structure. According to regulatory definition, an HLT involves the buyout, recapitalization or acquisition of a firm in which either 1) the firm's subsequent leverage ratio exceeds 75 percent, 2) the transaction more than doubles the borrower's liabilities and produces a leverage ratio over 50 percent, or 3) the regulators or firm that syndicates the loans declares the transaction an HLT. Because of highly visible HLT failures, regulators closely monitor these loans.

Commercial banks play a variety of roles in leveraged buyouts. They may act as investment bankers in putting deals together by obtaining commitments from wealthy individuals, pension funds, and insurance companies for financing. More typically, they extend credit directly in support of the buyer's equity investment. These loans are asset-based because they are secured by the firm's underlying assets and thus represent senior debt in HLTs. It is these loans that have become problem loans and adversely affected bank profits in recent years. Most HLTs also involve *mezzanine financing*, a type of credit that is subordinated to the claims of bank debt but senior to the investor's common stock. It is appealing because it usually carries an equity participation option. However, as the number of leveraged buyouts rises, the riskiness of the deals also rises. There are more potential buyers, prices are bid higher, financing costs increase, and fewer deals generate the necessary cash flow to service the debt.

Two of the biggest players in leveraged buyouts are the corporate finance divisions of Bankers Trust Co. and Citicorp. Each routinely commits up to $500 million per deal in financing to attract additional buyout customers. If they cannot sell portions of the financing to other groups, they keep the loans in their own portfolio. Fee income makes the deals attractive. Typically a borrower selects a lead bank that puts an underwriting syndicate together which arranges the total financing. The lead bank earns a substantial

CONTEMPORARY ISSUES

Not All Leveraged Buyouts Are Immediate Successes

In 1985 Allied-Signal Corp. sold a 50 percent interest in Union Texas Petroleum to a group of investors headed by Kohlberg Kravis Roberts & Co. for $1.7 billion. The investors invested $250 million in common equity, issued $300 million in preferred stock to Allied, and borrowed just under $1.2 billion from banks. The leverage buyout ratio was roughly five parts debt to one part common equity.

At the time, Union Texas Petroleum owned almost 600 million barrels of oil, which was selling for around $30 per barrel. During 1984 its profits exceeded $150 million. By 1986 oil prices had dropped to $14 a barrel. Union Texas was forced to write down the value of oil and gas reserves because sales contracts with gas purchasers had to be renegotiated. As Union Texas reported losses, it came under pressure to sell other parts of its business to help service its heavy debt load. The viability of the buyout was clearly based on the level of oil prices. Cash flow dropped with declining oil prices, and both investors' and bank lenders' risk exposure increased. The lesson is the same with all conservative lending: know your risk exposure.

---

up-front agent fee while all underwriters receive fees for placing the debt. Bankers Trust generated as much as 20 percent of its pretax income as fees from HLTs in 1989.

Term Commercial Loans. Many businesses have credit needs that persist beyond 1 year. Term commercial loans, which have an original maturity of more than 1 year, are normally used in these cases. Most term loans have maturities from 1 to 7 years and are granted to finance either the purchase of depreciable assets, start-up costs for a new venture, or a permanent increase in the level of working capital. Because repayment comes over several years, lenders focus more on the borrower's periodic income and cash flow than on the balance sheet. Chapter 21 examines the traditional credit analysis underlying a term loan from basic ratio analysis to cash flow projections. Term loans often require collateral, but this represents a secondary source of repayment in case the borrower defaults.

The characteristics of term loans vary with the use of the proceeds. For asset purchases, the loan principal is advanced in its entirety after an agreement is signed. The amount equals the net purchase price on the asset acquired. The maturity is determined by the asset's useful life and the borrower's ability to generate cash to repay principal and interest. The interest charged reflects the bank's cost of funds plus a risk premium to compensate for default risk and interest rate risk. Virtually all term loans use formal loan agreements that stipulate what is expected of each party and provide remedies when the agreement is breached. These are necessary because most term loans are complex.

Loan payments are structured in several forms. Many are scheduled over several years so that the borrower's cash flow is sufficient to cover the interest and principal in each year. Many term loans are repaid on an installment basis and fully amortized. Each periodic payment includes interest plus principal in varying amounts. Other term loans may use equal annual principal payments with interest computed on the declining

CONTEMPORARY ISSUES

RJR—Deleveraging an LBO

At the end of 1988, Kohlberg Kravis Roberts & Co. (KKR) acquired RJR Nabisco for $24.7 billion, the largest LBO in history. In October 1988, RJR's chairman and other insiders offered to buy the firm for $75 a share. After an aggressive bidding war that ended 2 months later, the eventual sales price was the equivalent of $114 in securities per share. RJR obtained $24.7 billion in financing and immediately announced a plan to sell corporate assets to pay down the debt. The following chart demonstrates how RJR's stock price reacted initially versus prices on its outstanding bonds with a 13-year maturity. The stock price rose over the offer price because arbitragers bought shares in anticipation of a bidding war for the company. The bond prices plummeted because any firm that acquired RJR would load up on debt to finance the purchase. Existing bondholders' claims would be adversely affected and RJR's ability to service interest and principal payments on debt would be hampered. In fact, when KKR announced a 1.25 billion senior note offering in January 1989, Moody's rated the bonds as speculative thereby raising KKR's borrowing costs based on the firm's reduced ability to cover debt payments.

By 1991 KKR was in the middle of deleveraging, or substituting equity for debt. Asset sales had gone slower than expected

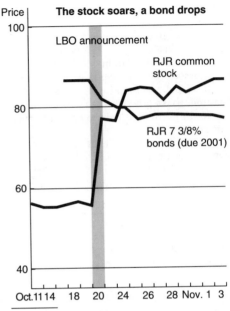

Source: Diana Fortier (1989).

and prices were generally lower than expected. To reduce interest payments KKR decided to inject $1.18 billion in equity with the proceeds used to pay down its debt. KKR had come full circle from increasing leverage back to decreasing leverage.

---

principal balance. Occasionally, term loans will call for balloon payments of principal. In these cases, the borrower pays only the periodic interest until maturity when the full principal comes due (bullet loan). Frequently, the borrower makes amortized principal and interest payments based on a very long maturity (30 years), then pays the principal still remaining in a lump sum at a shorter maturity (5 years). Such loans work for assets that are stable or increase in value over time. The normal source of repayment is cash flow generated from a company's operations.

For new ventures and permanent increases in working capital, banks advance the loan principal as needed. If the borrower needs different amounts over time, a bank usually structures the agreement as a loan commitment during the early stages, then converts the outstanding principal to a term loan. With this type of term loan—often called a revolving credit—repayment still derives from future cash flows and the agreement is priced at higher yields because of the greater risk.

Revolving Credits. Revolving credits are a hybrid of short-term working capital loans and term loans. Typically, they involve a commitment of funds (the borrowing base) for 1 to 5 years. At the end of some interim period, the outstanding principal converts to a term loan. During the interim period, the borrower determines usage much like a credit line. Mandatory principal payments begin once the commitment converts to a term loan. The revolver has a fixed maturity and often requires the borrower to pay a fee at the time of conversion to a term loan. This agreement reduces paperwork and simplifies loan servicing for creditworthy customers, who like its flexibility during the interim period. Revolvers have often substituted for commercial paper or corporate bond issues.

Real Estate Loans

Exhibits 20.1 and 20.2 indicate that real estate loans represent a high percentage of total loans at most commercial banks. They are classified separately from commercial and consumer loans because the collateral is some form of real property and the loans are subject to different risks and regulation. During prosperous times, short-term real estate loans are among the most profitable investments and thus are extremely attractive to growth-oriented banks. Many banks also extend long-term mortgage credit to residential homeowners or to holders of commercial property.

Real estate loans can be highly speculative, however, if banks lend against properties that do not generate predictable cash flows. Many banks, savings and loans, insurance companies, and pension funds, in fact, now own significant amounts of real estate, with other credits still on the books that are not producing sufficient cash to service debt. Often the underlying real estate is commercial property built under the assumption that lease rates and occupancy would quickly rise. Banks can only sell the properties at depressed prices, so they keep them on their books to avoid taking losses. The failures of numerous banks, such as the Bank of New England in 1991, have been attributed largely to problem real-estate loans.

Short-Term Real Estate Loans. Many banks lend heavily to businesses for new building construction and land development. Construction loans represent interim financing on commercial, industrial, and residential property. A bank extends credit to a builder to pay for the materials and labor necessary to complete a project. The builder repays the loan when the project is completed, and permanent (long-term) financing is arranged. Land development loans finance the construction of roads and public utilities in areas where developers plan to build houses. The developer repays the loan as homeowners or investors buy lots. Maturities on these loans normally range from 12 months to 2 years but are often extended if developers cannot find permanent financing.

The credit analysis of construction and land development loans follows that described in Chapter 21.[9] There are, however, peculiar features of these projects that deserve mention. Most importantly, these loans may be extremely risky. Individual projects, such as the construction of an office building in a metropolitan area's downtown business district, are often quite costly. Few banks choose to assume that risk alone, so most enter into joint financing agreements. The primary source of repayment is permanent financing provided by a third party. If this is not forthcoming, the bank must look either to the developer's cash flow from other projects or, ultimately, the outright sale of the building. If the developer defaults on the loan before construction is completed, the bank must pay for someone to finish the project. Banks prefer a project in which customers have already committed to lease space and the developer has arranged for a takeout commitment. A takeout commitment is an agreement whereby a different lender, such as a life insurance company or pension fund, agrees to provide long-term financing after construction is finished. The construction loan is speculative when the builder does not have a commitment or the ultimate owner of the structure is not known.

Most banks attempt to limit their risk by working closely with a select group of developers and by requiring third-party appraisals of projects. A bank that makes a construction loan essentially underwrites the developer. Maintaining a close working relationship allows the bank to assess whether the developer can complete a specific project and has cash flow from other projects to cover losses if this one fails. Third-party appraisals provide an estimate of the project's value at completion and offer assurance that the structure's value can cover loan payments in the event of default.[10]

Banks try to compensate for high default risk by requiring up-front fees and pricing construction loans at substantial mark-ups over their funding costs. It is not uncommon, for example, for a bank to charge an origination fee of 1 percent of the loan and float the interest rate at 4 percent over the bank's base rate. Interest rate risk is lessened because interest income varies with changes in the level of interest rates. Still, if the structure is not sold or adequately leased, cash flows will not cover debt service requirements.

The quality of these loans closely follows the business cycle. During the first half of the 1980s, many developers overbuilt office space in major metropolitan areas. Normal business growth did not absorb the new construction, and many borrowers defaulted because of high vacancy rates. These problems resulted, in part, from liberal lending policies pursued by S&Ls, insurance companies, and some commercial banks. Lenders and their developers speculatively built apartments and office buildings with

---

[9]The financial statements of developers differ markedly from those of most nonfinancial businesses. Analysts must be familiar with how specific firms allocate costs for projects under construction and how they report gross profit. Generally accepted accounting principles allow builders to estimate profit on unfinished projects. An analyst must know what portion of gross profit can be attributed to completed contracts and should compare this with past estimates to assess the efficiency of the builder's historical profit estimates.

[10]Unfortunately, there is no guarantee that appraisals are meaningful. Appraisers are not regulated, and many instances of abuse are known. Bank of America, for example, charged off $95 million in the last 3 months of 1984 based on faulty mortgages involving inflated property appraisals.

little or no preleased space. In many cases, banks even lent funds for origination fees and loan interest in addition to normal materials and labor costs. Developers were often not required to invest any of their own equity in the projects. Banks expected to be repaid when the developer sold the project at completion of construction or when the project generated sufficient cash flow from rentals. High vacancy rates lowered real estate values and the quality of these loans.

Long-Term Real Estate Loans. Most bank real estate loans are long-term mortgages, primarily on single-family houses. A mortgage is a legal document through which a borrower gives a lender a lien on real property as collateral against a debt. The borrower gets to use the property as long as the scheduled interest and principal payments are met. If the borrower defaults, the lender can exercise the lien and claim the property.[11] Banks can make conventional mortgages or mortgages insured by the Federal Housing Authority or Veterans Administration. These last two carry long maturities and require small down payments by borrowers. They are costly in terms of officer time because management must complete considerable paperwork before the loans are officially approved.

Many banks lend on commercial real estate, such as motels warehouses, and apartment complexes. Such loans are amortized over 20 to 30 years, but are callable after 3 to 7 years for a much shorter effective maturity. They carry adjustable rates priced at 1 to 3 percent over the comparable maturity Treasury security.

Residential mortgage loans are attractive investments when priced correctly. When their deposit base was relatively stable, banks made fixed-rate loans with 30-year maturities. They paid below market rates on their deposits but effectively passed on some of the savings by charging artificially low fixed rates on mortgages. Mortgage rates did not include long-term premiums because deposit rates could not rise above regulatory ceilings. Such banks operated with negative funding GAPs but were not penalized as long as interest rates remained low. With the gradual removal of deposit rate ceilings and the increased volatility of interest rates in the 1970s, banks at times found that they were paying 15 to 18 percent on CDs and money market certificates, while their mortgages earned 6 to 9 percent.

Not surprisingly, lenders have developed contracts that increase the rate sensitivity of their mortgage portfolio. Mortgages now may provide for 1) periodic adjustments in the interest rate charged, 2) adjustments in periodic principal payments, or 3) lender sharing in any price appreciation of the underlying structure at sale. The purpose is to increase cash flow when the level of interest rates rises or inflation accelerates.[12] Most banks now offer borrowers a choice between fixed-rate and adjustable-rate mortgages. Because borrowers assume interest rate risk with adjustable-rate mortgages, banks offer inducements, such as lower initial rates and caps on how high the rate might go, to

---

[11]A borrower has the right of redemption, whereby foreclosure is prevented if the debt is repaid within a reasonable time after default.

[12]Many types of adjustable-rate mortgages have evolved. Some tie the interest rate to an index that changes when the general level of rates changes. Others establish rates that change according to a fixed schedule. Principal payments may likewise be indexed to inflation. Barnett and McKenzie (1985) discuss various features in detail.

**Exhibit 20.9 Fixed-Rate versus Adjustable-Rate Mortgages
and the Level of Interest Rates**

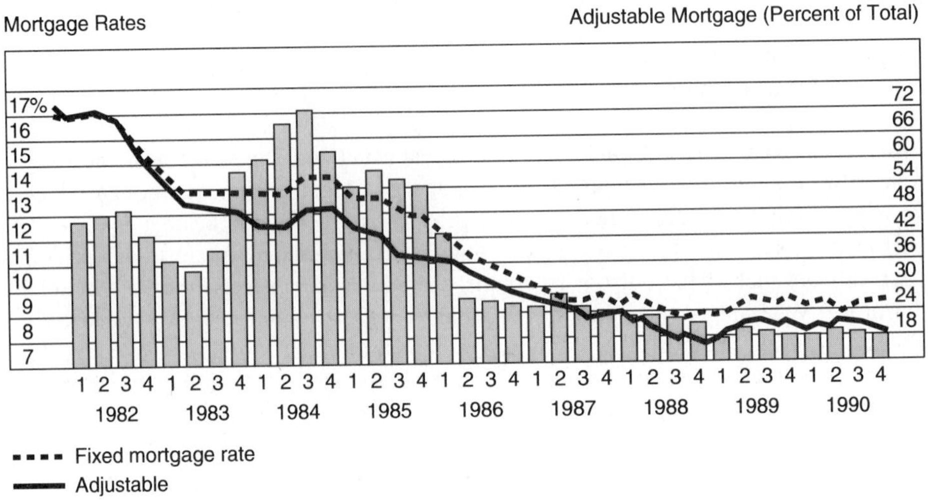

Source: Federal Home Loan Bank Board; with updates.

increase their attractiveness. As Exhibit 20.9 indicates, however, mortgage lenders often fall into the trap of speculating on rate movements. Adjustable-rate mortgage closings as a percentage of all closings have decreased since 1984, along with the level of mortgage rates. Lenders are making fewer adjustable-rate loans and more fixed-rate loans as the rates drop, which exposes them to substantial risks if rates rise sharply.

The credit analysis of residential mortgages resembles that of any consumer loan. Most mortgages are amortized with monthly payments including both principal and interest. Because of the long maturity, banks look carefully at the borrower's cash flow, character, and willingness to repay. The evaluation concentrates on three significant features of the loan: the appraised property value, the borrower's down payment, and the borrower's cash flow relative to required interest and principal payments. Banks assume less credit risk when the down payment is high and debt service payments are small relative to the buyer's income.

Unfortunately, the economic environment and competition have recently reduced downpayments, thereby raising monthly payments and the level of risk. From 1970 to 1980 the price of the average U.S. home more than doubled with inflation. Home buyers viewed their houses as assets that would regularly appreciate from 10 to 15 percent annually. Lenders who normally required 20 percent down payments, in turn, lowered the requirement to 5 percent so more borrowers qualified. In their rush to buy a house, borrowers often took out mortgages with payments that increased over the life of the loan. When they could not make the payments, they simply sold the house at a higher price and repaid the outstanding debt. Everyone was happy.

After 1980 the rate of appreciation in house prices slowed dramatically. Many home-buyers who had relied on inflation found that their income did not rise enough to make the obligated mortgage payments affordable. Even if they sold their houses, they could not entirely repay their debt. In this environment mortgage delinquencies rose; by 1990, nine percent of all outstanding mortgages had payments more than 30 days past due. The comparable figure for 1980 was 4.7 percent.

The Secondary Mortgage Market. Real estate problems were compounded by the growth of the secondary mortgage market and the increased number of players in the mortgage banking business. The secondary mortgage market involves the trading of previously originated residential mortgages. Lenders who originate mortgages can either sell them directly to interested investors or package them into mortgage pools. With a mortgage pool, the original lender issues long-term securities that evidence a claim on the mortgages in the pool. Investors in the securities receive the interest and principal payments on the underlying mortgages net of servicing fees. In most cases, the pool originator collects the mortgage payments from home buyers, keeping a portion as a servicing fee, pays the relevant property taxes, and apportions the remainder to insurers and holders of the securities.

With risk-based capital requirements, many banks follow a strategy of originating mortgages for the purpose of securitizing them. Their earnings come from origination and servicing fees. Chapter 17 documents recent growth in the secondary mortgage market including the nature of securities created by the securitization process.

Equity Investments in Real Estate. For many years government regulations prevented commercial banks from owning real estate except for their corporate offices or property involved in foreclosure. State-chartered S&Ls and insurance companies, in contrast, have long been able to take equity positions in real estate projects. This enabled them to charge lower loan rates in exchange for unlimited profit potential from price appreciation. Federal regulators want banks to engage in these more speculative real-estate activities only through separate subsidiaries, if at all. By the end of 1989, laws had been passed by 20 states permitting state-chartered banks to invest in real estate, in many cases restricting the dollar investment to a fixed percentage of assets.

Agriculture Loans

Agriculture loans are similar to commercial and industrial loans in that short-term credit finances seasonal operating expenses, in this case those associated with planting and harvesting crops. Much like working capital loans, the proceeds are used to purchase inventory in the form of seed, fertilizer, and pesticides and to pay other production costs. Farm operators expect to repay the debt when the crops are harvested and sold. Long-term credit finances livestock, equipment, and land purchases. The fundamental source of repayment is cash flow from the sale of livestock and harvested crops in excess of operating expenses. These loans differ, however, because agriculture is perceived to be a vital national industry. The federal government lends considerable sums to farmers through its farm credit system. Federal agencies involved with agriculture lending include the Farmers Home Administration, the Farm Credit Banks, and Federal Land Banks. Commercial banks often work with these agencies to keep farmers operating, even when it appears that they will sustain large near-term losses.

The profitability of agriculture loans follows cyclical trends in the farm economy. During the 1970s when inflation was high, farm land values more than doubled in many regions of the United States. Using land as collateral, banks encouraged farmers to expand their operations, financed with term loans. Both farmers and banks expected land values to continue rising and virtually ignored whether cash flow from production was sufficient to cover the debt service. A series of events—beginning with the Soviet grain embargo in 1980, the worldwide recession in 1982, and the strong U.S. dollar lowering net exports—reversed the trend. Farm commodity prices fell so far that farm revenues were frequently less than the cost of seed, fertilizer, and loan interest. Land values fell with this negative operating cash flow, reducing the farmer's borrowing base just when he needed more credit for operating expenses.

The problem was that banks lent against the perceived value of land, but farmers never expected to sell the land to repay the debt. As cash flow deteriorated from 1984 to 1987, land values fell and the loans were undercollateralized. The obvious lesson is that farm loans, like term commercial loans, are repaid out of cash flow. Before lending, a bank should verify that cash flows will be sufficient to service debt under both good and bad circumstances.

From 1984 to 1987 many small agriculture banks throughout the United States experienced severe credit problems with their farm loans. During this time over 40 percent of the nation's bank failures were agriculture banks, and many that did not fail had more problem loans than capital.[13] In 1985 the Farm Credit System, which consists of 12 Federal Land Banks, 12 Federal Intermediate Credit Banks, and 13 Banks for Co-ops and affiliated associations, lost $2.7 billion in loan and mortgage defaults on a portfolio of approximately $70 billion. The U.S. Congress had to reorganize the system and give it access to Treasury credit. Even with these losses, many commercial banks and the government's farm lending agencies deferred charging off more loans by extending credit to borrowers, with little chance of repayment. Agriculture lenders and farmers hoped to wait out the cycle until commodity prices increased either from expanding foreign markets or reduced production.

Consumer Loans

Nonmortgage consumer loans differ substantially from commercial loans. Their usual purpose is to finance the purchase of durable goods, although many individuals borrow to finance education, medical care, and other expenses. The average loan to each borrower is relatively small. Most loans have maturities from 1 to 4 years, are repaid in installments, and carry fixed interest rates. In recent years, states have removed usury ceilings that set maximum rates banks can charge so that consumer loan rates are now high relative to historical norms. This leads to different risk and return features than with other loans. In

---

[13]McCoy and Charlier (1985) describe farm loan delinquencies and farm bank problems.

general, an individual borrower's default risk is greater than a commercial customer's. Consumer loan rates are thus higher to compensate for the greater losses.

While most consumer loans carry fixed rates, installment payments increase their rate sensitivity so their average duration is relatively short. Long-term loans, however, may subject banks to considerable interest rate risk. Finally, consumer loans are relatively illiquid. Banks generally cannot sell them near face value because no secondary market exists. This is slowly changing, however, as more banks attempt to securitize automobile loans and credit card receivables. (See Chapter 3).

Consumer loans are normally classified as either installment, credit card, or noninstallment credit. Installment loans require a partial payment of principal plus interest periodically until maturity. Other consumer loans require either a single payment of all interest plus principal or a gradual repayment at the borrower's discretion, as with a credit line. Exhibit 20.10 presents a breakdown of installment credit by type and holder in March 1990. Even with many competitors, commercial banks held 47 percent of the total credit outstanding and were the largest single holders of each type of credit. Automobile loans are either direct loans extended by bank officers to walk-in customers or indirect loans purchased from automobile dealers. Revolving credit consists of credit card loans or overdraft loans to deposit customers. Mobile home loans are dealer-generated paper. The other loan category includes such items as home equity, home improvement, and personal loans to consolidate debts. Noninstallment loans are for special purposes in which the individual normally expects a large cash receipt to repay the debt, such as a temporary bridge loan for the down payment on a new house that will be repaid from the sale of the previous house. Chapter 22 discusses additional features of consumer loans and selected credit analysis procedures.

Home Equity Loans. The Tax Reform Act of 1986 gradually phased out the deductibility of interest on consumer debt when computing federal income taxes, except for mortgages. As might be expected, individual lenders quickly packaged home equity loans that substituted for many traditional forms of consumer borrowing. Home equity loans are secured by real estate so that any interest payments meet the requirement for deductibility. They have been structured to resemble direct installment loans, but even more to function as credit lines in which an individual has a credit limit and can borrow up to the limit for any purpose.

From the lender's perspective, home equity loans are fully secured and thus low risk. In reality, the loans encourage many consumers to spend beyond their normal ability to generate income so that borrowers may default on loans. With declining property values in the late 1980s and early 1990s, lenders tightened standards because of concern over their risk exposure and the economic downturn. Exhibit 20.11 documents the growth in home equity loans after tax reform and the trend of delinquencies.

SUMMARY

Lending involves more risk than virtually any other banking activity. Management therefore analyzes the nature of risks carefully before extending credit. The credit

Exhibit 20.10 Consumer Installment Credit Outstanding (Millions of Dollars), March 31, 1990

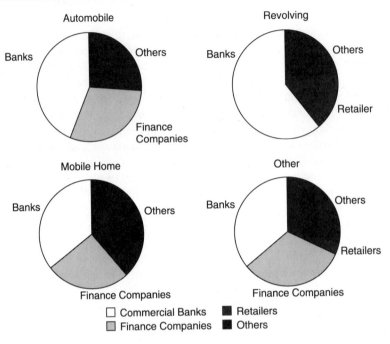

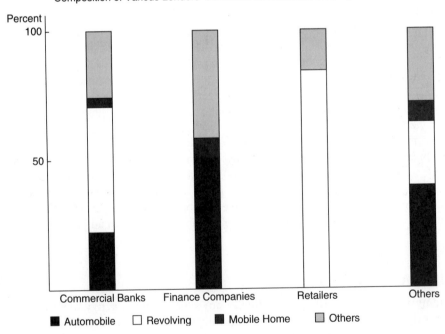

Composition of Various Lenders' Consumer Investment Portfolio; December 1990

Source: *Federal Reserve Bulletin*, Table 1 55.

Exhibit 20.11 The Growth in Home Equity Loans and Delinquencies

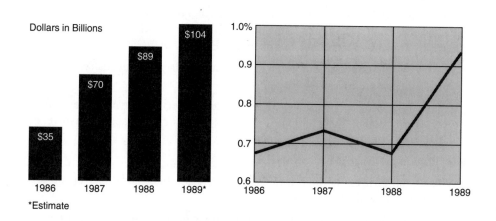

Source: Kantrow, Yvette, "Home Equity Lending Tightens as Property Values Head Down." *American Banker* (January 5, 1990).

process includes three functions: business development and credit analysis, credit execution and administration, and credit review. Business development activities concentrate on identifying profitable customers and encouraging credit relationships. Credit analysis is the process of assessing risk and includes a review of financial data and subjective evaluation of the borrower's character. The credit staff formally accepts or rejects a loan request and executes the necessary documents with approvals. Finally, loan officers periodically review each outstanding loan, especially when it comes up for renewal or reaches problem status, demanding action. At times, loan terms may need to be modified to recognize a change in the borrower's status.

Banks make many different types of loans, which are the dominant asset in most bank portfolios. This chapter describes the basic features of short-term working capital loans, asset-based loans, real estate loans, term commercial loans, consumer loans, and agriculture loans. Subsequent chapters address specific credit analysis and pricing issues with various types of loans.

Questions

Trends

1. Loans make up what percent of a typical bank's assets? What is the relationship between this percent and the size of the bank?

2. What type of loan is most common in the smallest banks? in the largest?

3. List the types of real estate loans made by banks. What are the special risks?

4. Two types of loans have dominated the "problem loan" lists of banks in the past two or three years. Which type has hurt the smallest banks? Which type has hurt the largest?

5. During the 1980s banks increased the loan portion of their portfolios. Why? What are the disadvantages of increasing loans? Over time banks' share of total loans made by financial institutions has declined. Explain why.

6. Banks have found non-traditional ways to make money from loans. What are two general methods they use?

7. Explain how banks move loans off the balance sheet. What motivates different types of off-balance sheet activities? Discuss the risks these actions involve.

Credit Process

8. What is the goal of the loan officer? What are the three functions of the credit process and how do they relate to the goal?

9. Describe the basic features of the three functions of the credit process at commercial banks.

10. What are the five Cs of credit? Discuss their importance in credit analysis.

11. Why might a bank choose to include the following covenants in a loan agreement?
    a. Cash dividends cannot exceed 60 percent of pretax income.
    b. Interim financial statements must be provided quarterly.
    c. Inventory turnover must be greater than five times annually.
    d. Capital expenditures may not exceed $5 million annually.

Types of Loans

Commercial Loans

12. Explain how a company's permanent working capital needs differ from its seasonal working capital needs.

13. A firm with the following balance sheet approaches a bank for a loan.

Assets:		Liabilities:	
Cash	$100	Accounts payable	$180
Accounts receivable	700	Notes payable	300
Inventory	600	Long-term debt	10,700
Fixed assets	12,000	Equity	2,220

Assuming a 360-day year, what is the cash-to-cash cycle for the assets and what is it for the liabilities if:
a. sales are $6,000;
b. cost of goods sold are $2,000;
c. operating expenses are $1,800; and
d. purchases are $1,900?

What percentage of this firm's current assets are being funded with long-term debt and equity? Estimate the working capital loans needs for this firm using the method suggested in the chapter. Would you consider loaning bank funds to this firm?

14. You are considering making a working capital loan to a company that manufactures and distributes chemical fertilizers. The loan will be secured by the firm's inventory and receivables. What risks are associated with this type of collateral? How would you minimize the risk and periodically determine that the firm's performance was not deteriorating?

15. Describe the basic features of:
  a. Open credit lines
  b. Asset-based loans
  c. Highly leveraged transactions
  d. Term commercial loans
  e. Revolving credits

Real Estate Loans

16. Banks create both short-term and long-term real estate loans. Who gets each type? Which is more risky for the bank and why?

17. What motivates commercial banks to make adjustable-rate mortgages? Examine Exhibit 20.9. Why are adjustable mortgage rates normally below fixed rates? As the level of rates declines, would you expect banks to increase or decrease the adjustable rate proportion of their mortgage portfolios?

18. Some bankers claim the secondary mortgage market has been a blessing and some claim it has been a curse. Explain the two views.

Agriculture Loans

19. Explain why such a high percentage of bank failures from 1982 to 1986 were agriculture banks.

20. What type of inventory does a farmer need? Does this type of inventory qualify the farmer for working capital loans? Beside the economy, what should a banker be watchful of before extending credit to a farmer?

Consumer Loans

21. Explain the difference between installment, credit card and noninstallment consumer credit. What is the major purpose of each loan type and how and why do the repayment streams differ?

22. Explain the structure of a home equity loan and discuss its economic justification.

Project

Obtain copies of the annual reports for a small community bank and a large regional or money center bank. Compare the composition of their loan portfolios. What differences do you detect? What is the loan loss experience for each type of loan at each bank? Determine why differences appear.

FIRST FINANCIAL REVISITED: THE CREDIT PROCESS

According to Ralph Treadway, president of First Financial, the bank's problems were due largely to bad real estate loans. While economic conditions likely worsened the bank's credit problems, First Financial had virtually no credit controls in place to monitor risk. Consider the following:

1. The bank had only a brief, incomplete credit policy statement.

2. Real estate loans were concentrated among two developers in the same geographic market. Diversification was thus inadequate.

3. Credit approval was controlled by one senior officer because the Board of Directors simply rubber-stamped his decisions.

4. Credit terms seemed to be negotiated in a haphazard fashion with little emphasis on documentation or the use of loan covenants. Incomplete financial information was required and loans were routinely renewed when problems arose.

5. The bank had violated regulatory guidelines regarding the maximum size loan to any single borrower.

6. The bank had CRA problems because it was making a disproportionate share of loans outside its trade area where it collected its deposits.

7. The bank was the defendant in two lender liability suits. One accused the bank of seizing collateral inappropriately. In another case the bank was accused of seizing control of the borrower's Board of Directors and dictating operating policy to the detriment of the borrower.

Each of the above credit issues represents a serious problem by itself for any bank. When viewed in concert, it is not surprising that First Financial experienced large loan losses regardless of economic conditions. Common sense suggests that senior management should institute policies that control risk and provide for routine monitoring. See if you can make a list of recommended policy changes.

References

Alcott, Kathleen. "An Agricultural Loan Rating System." *Journal of Commercial Bank Lending* (February 1985).

Barnett, Peter, and Joseph McKenzie. *Alternative Mortgage Instruments.* Boston: Warren, Gorham & Lamont, 1985.

Conner, Glenn, and Charles Luckett. "Mortgage Refinancing." *Federal Reserve Bulletin.* Board of Governors of the Federal Reserve System (August 1990).

Compton, Eric N. "Credit Analysis is Risk Analysis." *The Bankers Magazine* (March–April 1985).

Economic Perspectives. A series of articles on the farm credit crunch. (Federal Reserve Bank of Chicago, November–December 1985).

FDIC Quarterly Banking Profile. FDIC Division of Research & Statistics, quarterly publication.

Fortier, Diana. "Buyouts and Bondholders." *Chicago Fed Letter* (January 1989).

Foust, Dean. "Leveraged Buyouts Fall to Earth." *Business Week* (February 12, 1990).

Gill, Edward. *Commercial Lending Basics.* Reston, Va.: Reston Publishing Co., 1983.

A Guide to Developing a Written Lending Policy. Washington, D.C.: American Bankers Association, 1977.

Kantrow, Yvette. "Home-Equity Lending Tightens As Property Values Head Down." *American Banker* (January 5, 1990).

Kester, George, and Thomas Bixler. "Why 90-Day Working Capital Loans Are not Repaid on Time." *Journal of Commercial Bank Lending* (August 1990).

Logan, John, and Richard Dongan. "Asset-Based Lending: You're Doing It, But Are You Doing It Right?" *Journal of Commercial Bank Lending* (June 1984).

McCoy, Charles, and Marj Charlier. "Banks Give Farmers Loans and Pray for a Bailout." *Wall Street Journal* (June 6, 1985).

Merris, Randall. "Loan Commitments and Facility Fees." *Economic Perspectives* (Federal Reserve Bank of Chicago, March–April 1978).

Newburgh, Conrad. "Character Assessment in the Lending Process." *Journal of Commercial Bank Lending* (April 1991).

Sorenson, Richard. "Why Real Estate Projects Fail." *Journal of Commercial Bank Lending* (April 1990).

Springer, Claudia. "Court Rulings Erode Collateral Protection." *ABA Banking Journal* (February 1991).

Tannenbaum, Carl. "The Changing Face of Corporate Debt." *Bank Management* (November 1990).

Todd, Richard M. "Taking Stock of the Farm Credit System: Riskier for Farm Borrowers." *Quarterly Review* (Federal Reserve Bank of Minneapolis, Fall 1985).

Chapter 21

Evaluating Commercial Loan Requests

Though my bottom line is black, I am flat upon my back,
My cash flows out and customers pay slow.
The growth of my receivables is almost unbelievable;
The result is certain—unremitting woe!
And I hear the banker utter an ominous low mutter,
"Watch cash flow."

—Herbert S. Bailey Jr. with apologies to "The Raven" by Edgar Allan Poe[1]

The financial press pays great attention to corporate earnings announcements as indicators of past performance and future growth opportunities. Most analysts, however, recognize that cash flow information is equally important when evaluating a firm's prospects. Reported earnings and earnings per share can be manipulated by management and may not depict the firm's true ability to meet payments obligations. Debts are repaid out of cash flow, not earnings.

Many firms, for example, book credit sales as revenues, even though no cash is immediately generated. A firm with large increases in receivables might report rising profits but have no cash to cover operating expenses. Similarly, some companies report as income their share of undistributed profits in companies in which they have a limited equity interest, even though no cash is received. Cash flow analysis used in conjunction with trends in net income is helpful in determining the quality, and thus permanence, of earnings.

This chapter provides guidelines for evaluating commercial credit requests. It ignores the qualitative aspects of loans. As Bailey's banker advised, "Watch cash flow" is an important motto.

---

[1]Cited in R. Green, "Are More Chryslers in the Offing?" *Forbes* (February 2, 1981).

The basic objective of credit analysis is to assess the risks involved in extending credit to bank customers. In finance, risk typically refers to the volatility in earnings. Lenders are particularly concerned with adverse fluctuations in net income or cash flow which hinder a borrower's ability to service a loan. Such risk manifests itself by a borrower defaulting, or not making timely interest and/or principal payments. Credit analysis assigns some probability to the likelihood of default based on quantitative and qualitative factors. Some risks can be measured with historical and projected financial data. Other risks, such as those associated with the borrower's character and willingness to repay a loan, are not directly measurable. The bank ultimately compares these risks with the potential benefits when deciding whether or not to approve a loan. A formal comparison of loan revenues with loan expenses and estimated risk, called loan profitability analysis, appears in Chapter 24.

This chapter introduces a procedure that can be used to analyze the quantifiable aspects of commercial credit requests. The procedure incorporates a systematic interpretation of basic financial data and focuses on issues that typically arise when determining credit worthiness. The results supplement qualitative information regarding the borrower's character and history of financial responsibility. The key issues include:

1. What are the loan proceeds going to be used for?
2. How much does the customer need to borrow?
3. What is the primary source of repayment, and when will the loan be repaid?
4. What collateral is available?

The first section discusses these questions in detail. The second section introduces an evaluation procedure. The final section provides an application and interpretation of the analysis for a hypothetical loan request. The appendix reviews basic terminology and discusses sources of financial data.

FUNDAMENTAL CREDIT ISSUES

Virtually every business in the United States has a credit relationship with a financial institution. Some firms use only back-up credit lines in support of commercial paper issues. Some rely on periodic short-term loans to finance temporary working capital needs. Others primarily use term loans with a maturity beyond 1 year to finance capital expenditures, new acquisitions, or permanent increases in working capital. Regardless of the type of loan, all credit requests mandate a systematic analysis of the borrower's ability to repay.

When evaluating loan requests, bankers can make two types of errors in judgment. The first is extending credit to a customer who ultimately defaults. The second is denying a loan request to a customer who ultimately would repay the debt. In both cases, the bank loses a customer and its profits are less. Many bankers focus on eliminating the first type of error, applying rigid credit evaluation criteria and rejecting applicants who do not fit the mold of the ideal borrower. A well-known axiom in banking is that the only time borrowers can get financing is when they really do not need the funds. The purpose of credit analysis is to identify the meaningful, probable circumstances under which the bank might lose. Lenders also use credit analysis to restructure a weak loan application into a good loan when the borrower is strong, but does not fully understand the true borrowing needs.

Character

The foremost issue in assessing credit risk is determining a borrower's commitment and ability to repay debts in accordance with the terms of a loan agreement. Commitment is typically evidenced by an individual's honesty, integrity, and work ethic. Still, while a borrower may sincerely make every effort to repay a loan, the promise is weak if he or she has misjudged the ability to generate cash for payment. An important facet of character is thus credibility. For a business, commitment is evidenced by the owners and senior management. Bankers who say that they make many credit decisions quickly implicitly state that many potential borrowers are of dubious character. Even if the numbers look acceptable, a bank should lend nothing if the borrower appears dishonest. Such assessments reflect both deception and ineptitude or the lack of credibility.

It is often difficult to identify dishonest borrowers. The best indicators are the borrower's financial history and personal references. When a borrower has missed past debt service payments and been involved in default or bankruptcy, a lender should carefully document why, to see if the causes were reasonable. Borrowers with a history of credit problems are more likely to see the same problems arise later. Similarly, borrowers with a good credit history will have established personal and banking relationships that indicate whether they fully disclose meaningful information and deal with subordinates and suppliers honestly. A loan officer should begin the credit analysis by analyzing the firm's prior banking relationship, dealings with suppliers and customers, and current record from appropriate credit bureaus.

Lenders often look for signals of a borrower's condition beyond basic balance sheet and income statement data. For example, negative signals may appear in the following forms.[2]

- A borrower's name consistently appears on the list of bank customers who have overdrawn their accounts

- A borrower makes a significant change in the structure of the business, such as a change in accountant or change in key manager or advisor

---

[2]See Thomas Bennett (1987) for a lender's view of these issues. Conrad Newburgh (1991) further presents procedures for evaluating character and maintaining control.

- A borrower appears to be consistently short of cash which might be indicated by frequent requests for small loans or keeping small balances in checking accounts when net worth is high

- A borrower's personal habits have changed for the worse; red flags include behavior suggesting drug use, heavy gambling, alcoholism, or break-up in a marriage

- A firm's goals are incompatible with those of stockholders, employees, and customers

In addition to character, four basic issues must be resolved prior to extending credit: the use of loan proceeds, loan amount, source and timing of repayment, and collateral. These issues draw attention to specific features of each loan that can be addressed when structuring the loan agreement terms.

Use of Loan Proceeds

The range of business loan needs is unlimited. Firms may need cash for operating purposes to pay overdue suppliers, make a tax payment, or pay employee salaries. Similarly, they may need funds to pay off maturing debt obligations or to acquire new fixed assets. Frequently, a firm recognizes that it is short of cash but cannot identify why.

The first issue facing the credit analyst is, what are the loan proceeds going to be used for? Loan proceeds should be used for legitimate business operating purposes, including seasonal and permanent working capital needs, the purchase of depreciable assets, physical plant expansion, acquisition of other firms, and extraordinary operating expenses. Speculative asset purchases and belated debt substitutions should be avoided. The true need and use determines the loan maturity, the anticipated source and timing of repayment, and the appropriate collateral.

Most commercial loans are made for working capital purposes. The analyst must determine whether the bank is financing an increase in inventory or receivables or replacing outstanding payables and debt. Banks all too often originate working capital loans as seasonal credits, only to find that they are never fully repaid as anticipated. Term loans should be made for asset acquisitions, which require a longer repayment schedule. One common pitfall is for banks to focus too much on collateral and end up financing a firm's long-term needs with short-term notes. A careful review of a firm's financial data typically reveals why a company needs financing.

Loan Amount

In many cases, borrowers request a loan before they clearly understand how much external financing is actually needed and how much is available internally. The amount of credit required depends on the use of the proceeds and the availability of internal sources of funds. For example, if a firm wants to finance new equipment, the loan request is typically for the purchase price less the resale value of any replaced assets. For a shorter-term loan, the amount might equal the temporary seasonal increase in receivables and inventory net of that supported by increased accounts payable. With term loans, the required amount can be determined via pro forma analysis. Borrowers often ask for too little in requesting a loan. The lender's job is to help determine the correct amount, such that a borrower has enough cash to operate effectively but not too much to spend wastefully.

Once a loan is approved, the amount of credit actually extended depends on the borrower's future performance. If the borrower's cash flows are insufficient to meet operating expenses and debt service on the loan, the bank will be called upon to lend more and possibly lengthen the loan maturity. If cash flows are substantial, the initial loan outstanding might decline rapidly and even be repaid early. The required loan amount is thus a function of the initial cash deficiency and the pattern of future cash flows.

The Primary Source and Timing of Repayment

Loans are repaid from cash flows. The four basic sources of cash flow are the liquidation of assets, cash flow from operations, new debt issues, and new equity issues. Credit analysis evaluates the risk that a borrower's future cash flows will not be sufficient to meet mandatory expenditures for continued operations and interest and principal payments on the loan.

Specific sources of cash are typically associated with certain types of loans. Short-term, seasonal working capital loans are normally repaid from the liquidation of receivables or reductions in inventory. Term loans are typically repaid out of cash flows from operations, specifically earnings and noncash charges in excess of net working capital needs and capital expenditures to maintain the existing fixed asset base. A comparison of projected cash flows with interest and principal payments on prospective loans indicates how much debt can be serviced and the appropriate maturity. Unless specifically identified in the loan agreement, it is inappropriate to rely on new equity from investors or new debt from other creditors for repayment. Too often these external sources of cash disappear if the firm's profitability declines or economic conditions deteriorate.

Collateral

Banks can lower the risk of loss on a loan by requiring back-up support for a loan beyond normal cash flow. This can take the form of assets held by the borrower or an explicit guarantee by a related firm or key individual. Collateral is the security a bank has in assets owned and pledged by the borrower against a debt in the event of default. Banks look to collateral as a secondary source of repayment when primary cash flows are insufficient to meet debt service requirements. Banks select collateral that retains its value over the business cycle. Receivables and inventory are preferred because of their liquidity. Plant, equipment, and real estate are also valuable.

Virtually any asset or the general capacity to generate cash flow can be used as collateral. From a lender's perspective, however, collateral must exhibit three features. First, its value should always exceed the outstanding principal on a loan. Any bank that must take possession of the collateral can sell it for more than the balance due and losses are reduced. Recent car loans with 5-year maturities stretch this limit, as the value of the car used as collateral often declines faster than the loan principal. Second, a lender should be able to easily take possession of collateral and have a ready market for sale. Highly illiquid assets are worth far less because they are not portable and often are of real value only to the original borrower. Chapter 23 provides examples of unusual collateral obtained in loan defaults. Third, a lender must be able to clearly mark collateral as its own. This means that the claim must be legal and clear. Careful loan documentation is the requirement here.

When physical collateral is not readily available, banks often look for personal guarantees. They generally rely on the borrower's cash flow to cover debt service with the borrower's net worth in reserve. Banks attempt to protect themselves against potential adverse changes in a borrower's financial condition by imposing loan covenants in the loan agreement that restrict a borrower's ability to make extreme decisions and thereby alter its fundamental operating profile.

Liquidating collateral is clearly a second-best source of repayment for three reasons. First, there are significant transactions costs associated with foreclosure. Banks must often allocate considerable employee time and pay large legal expenses that reduce the collateral's net value. Thus when negotiating loan agreements, the bank should select collateral with a value above the anticipated loan amount. Second, bankruptcy laws allow borrowers to retain possession of the collateral long after they have defaulted. During that time, the collateral often disappears or deteriorates in value. Third, when the bank takes possession of the collateral, it deprives the borrower of the opportunity to salvage the company. The bank must hire new managers or manage the firm temporarily with its own personnel until sale, a poor alternative.

In general, a loan should not be approved on the basis of collateral alone. Unless the loan is secured by collateral held by the bank, such as bank CDs, there is risk involved in collection. In most cases, it is essential that lenders periodically examine the quality of collateral to determine whether it truly exists or has deteriorated over time. This involves on-site inspections of a borrower's inventory, receivables, and operating facilities. In addition to assessing collateral, the lender can reevaluate the borrower's character by the nature of the business and collateral. Collateral improves the bank's position by lowering its net exposure. It does not improve the borrower's ability to generate cash to repay the loan.

In addition to these issues, credit analysis should examine risks that are unique to each loan. Each analysis should identify questions regarding the quality of management and of the business, sensitivity to economic conditions, the firm's relationship with other creditors, and any other information that is not available in the financial statements.

PROCEDURE FOR FINANCIAL ANALYSIS

The purpose of credit analysis is to identify and define the lender's risk in making a loan. There is a four-stage process for evaluating the financial aspects of commercial loans:

1. Overview of management and operations
2. Financial ratio analysis
3. Analysis of the statement of changes reconciled to cash
4. Financial projections

During all phases the analysis should examine facts that are relevant to the credit decision and recognize information that is important but unavailable. The analyst should prepare a list of questions to be presented to the borrower for clarification. Financial calculations using historical data should examine the absolute magnitudes of ratios and funds flows and pertinent changes in the magnitudes over time (trend analysis), and compare these measures to industry averages for the firm's competitors. Much of the information is available from the bank's credit files and conversations with the firm's management and chief financial officer. Sources of financial data on comparable firms are described in the appendix.

Financial projections involve making reasonable assumptions about a firm's future sales, working capital needs, capital expenditures, operating expenses, taxes, and dividends. The projections are used to forecast cash flows when addressing the issues described earlier. These cash flows are formally compared with interest and principal payments on all debt obligations. The same ratio analysis can then be performed using the projections. This procedure provides a check on the reasonableness of the forecasts.

Overview of Management and Operations

Before analyzing financial data, an analyst should gather background information on the firm's operations, including specific characteristics of the business and the intensity of industry competition, management quality, the nature of the loan request, and the data quality. Relevant historical developments and recent trends should also be examined.

This evaluation usually begins with an analysis of the organizational and business structure of the borrower. Is it a holding company with subsidiaries or a single entity? Does it operate as a corporation or a partnership? Is the firm privately or publicly held? When did the firm begin operations, and in what geographic markets does it now compete? The evaluation should also identify the products or services provided and the firm's competitive position in the marketplace as measured by market share, degree of product differentiation, presence of economies of scale in cost structure, and the bargaining power of buyers and sellers that the firm deals with.[3]

This inquiry leads to a brief analysis of industry trends. How many firms offer competitive products? Are there differences in product quality or life? The analysis should examine historical sales growth, the relationship between industry sales and the business cycle, and an implied forecast for the industry. A logical extension is to evaluate suppliers and the production process. Has the firm contracted for the appropriate raw materials at good prices? How many suppliers can provide the necessary

---

[3]Arnold (1988) describes how the intensity of competition affects a firm's business risk. Lenders should incorporate the results of this analysis in their forecasts of sales, costs, and product pricing.

materials? What is the quality of the firm's labor force and employee relations? Are the firm's fixed assets obsolete?

Particular attention should be focused on management quality. The backgrounds of the chief executive, financial, and operating officers should be examined in terms of key individuals' ages, experience in the business, service with the company, and apparent line of succession. Businesses frequently are dominated by one individual even though others hold officer titles. When possible, it is useful to identify the top officers' equity interest in the firm and the type of compensation received. This helps to identify motivating factors underlying firm decisions.

Finally, the overview should recognize the nature of the borrower's loan request and the quality of the financial data provided. It should indicate the proposed use and amount of credit requested and the borrower's anticipated source of repayment. It should specify whether the financial statements are audited and, if so, the type of opinion issued. A brief discussion of generally accepted accounting principles and audited statements appears in the appendix.

Financial Ratio Analysis

Most banks initiate the data analysis with statement spread forms, which array the firm's balance sheet and income statement items in a consistent format for comparison over time and against industry standards. Data for each reporting period are provided in two columns. The first column lists the actual dollar value of the accounting entry. The second column converts the figure to a common size ratio by dividing by total assets (balance sheet) or net sales (income statement). Comparable figures from the most recent period for specific competitors or industry standards are usually listed in the final two columns. A reconciliation of shareholders' equity is provided at the bottom of the income statement spread form.

The next step is to calculate a series of ratios that indicate performance variances. This analysis should differentiate between at least four categories of ratios that focus on liquidity, activity, leverage, and profitability.[4] Liquidity indicates the firm's ability to meet its short-term obligations and continue operations. The proceeds of short-term loans are typically used to finance current assets or to reduce other current liabilities. Notes are repaid by systematically reducing inventories following increases in sales and reducing receivables following the collection of credit sales. Measures of net working capital, current and quick ratios, inventory turnover, the average receivables collection period, the days payables outstanding, and the days cash-to-cash cycle help indicate whether current assets will support current liabilities.

Activity ratios signal how efficiently a firm is using assets to generate sales. A highly efficient firm, for example, will report sales-to-asset ratios that exceed industry norms, indicating that its asset base produces proportionately more revenue. Low turnover ratios indicate that the asset mix is not efficient in the sense that too much is allocated to that asset. Key ratios include accounts receivable turnover, inventory turnover, and fixed asset turnover.

---

[4]Key ratios are defined in the appendix.

Leverage ratios indicate the mix of the firm's financing between debt and equity and potential earnings volatility. The greater a firm's leverage, the more volatile its net profit (or loss). Ratios that should be examined include debt to total assets, times interest earned, fixed charge coverage, net fixed assets to tangible net worth, and the dividend payout percentage.

Profitability ratios provide evidence of the firm's sales and earnings performance. Basic ratios include the firm's return on equity, return on assets, profit margin, asset utilization, and sales growth rate. Profit ratios indicate the return to stockholders and the average return per dollar of assets invested. Profit margin is a measure of expense control, while asset utilization reveals the gross yield on assets. Finally, sales growth figures demonstrate whether the firm is expanding or contracting and provide evidence of industry competitiveness.

An analyst should evaluate these ratios with a critical eye, trying to identify firm strengths and weaknesses. All ratios should be evaluated on trend to detect shifts in competitiveness and/or firm strategy, and relative to industry standards. The latter comparison indicates where significant deviations occur, both positively and negatively. When reviewing the ratios, an analyst should prepare a list of questions to ask the firm's managers, suppliers, and creditors that fill in information not revealed by the data.

Cash-Based Income Statement

Most analysts focus on cash flow when evaluating a nonfinancial firm's performance. Bank regulators now insist that banks support credit decisions with cash flow information for each borrower. This section presents a framework for calculating a firm's cash flow from operations that essentially converts a company's income statement to a cash basis. Cash flow estimates are subsequently compared to principal and interest payments and discretionary expenditures to assess a firm's borrowing capacity and financial strength.

The importance of cash flow has recently been emphasized by the introduction of the statement of financial accounting standards (SFAS) 95. Since 1988, firms have been required to report a statement of cash flows alongside balance sheet and income statement data. Accounting standards mandate that the statement distinguish between a firm's operating, investing, and financing activities. The intent is to allow the reader to distinguish between profits and cash flow. Reported net income is reconciled to cash flow from operations and the entire statement is reconciled to cash and cash equivalents.

The cash-based income statement introduced in this chapter is a modified form of a statement of cash flows. It is essentially a statement of changes reconciled to cash that combines elements of the income statement and balance sheet items. In general, a statement of changes records changes in balance sheet accounts over a specific time period. Its purpose is to indicate how new assets are financed or liabilities repaid. Actual funds flows are measured by the absolute differences between balance sheet entries in two different time periods, such as year-end 1990 versus year-end 1991. Income statement data can be combined by substituting the revenues and expenses that

Illusory Profits at Charter Co.

In 1984 the Securities and Exchange Commission requested that Charter Co. restate its earnings for 1981 to 1983 and adopt a more conservative method of reporting income. The problems arose from Charter's single-premium annuity contracts. These contracts are insurance policies for which individuals pay a single up-front premium averaging almost $20,000, which generates tax-deferred interest until the policy is paid out. Charter made a profit by investing the funds at yields above those paid annuity holders over the life of the contract. Whenever it sold a policy, Charter immediately booked 35 percent of the total estimated profit over the entire annuity term. Obviously, this profit did not yet exist and would only appear if Charter successfully invested the funds at a positive spread.

In 1983 many policy holders redeemed their contracts. Because the contracts were not held to term, redemptions forced Charter to book a loss immediately by writing down the profits it had recorded earlier. The fundamental point is that the sales and profits reported on financial statements may differ substantially from realized cash flow. Paper profits cannot be used to support expenditures that must be backed by cash.

---

determine net income and subtracting dividends for the change in retained earnings on the balance sheet.

The key element in the analysis is to determine how much cash flow a firm generates from its normal business activity, that is, cash flow from operations. This cash flow must be sufficient to make interest and principal payments on debt. It may differ substantially from reported profits, as Charter Co. revealed (see Contemporary Issues: Illusory Profits at Charter Co.). A cash-based income statement also provides insights into whether a firm has adequately structured its financing. In a normal operating environment, any firm should repay short-term debt by liquidating its receivables and inventory. Long-term debt, in contrast, should be repaid from operating cash flow in excess of financing costs and that needed to maintain capital assets.

Statement Format. Consider the balance sheet and income statements for Donzi Inc. in Exhibit 21.1. These data are used to generate a statement of changes reconciled to cash in Exhibit 21.2. This statement incorporates specific income statement items through substitution for the change in net worth on the balance sheet. Because most firms prepare financial statements on an accrual rather than cash basis, revenues and expenses are recognized when earned or incurred rather than when a cash payment is made. Thus reported net income may differ substantially from operational cash flow. This format combines traditional balance sheet and income statement figures into a cash-based income statement. It emphasizes cash flow from operations, not reported net income.

With a statement of changes reconciled to cash, a source of funds is any transaction that increases cash (or cash-equivalent) assets. A use of funds is any transaction that decreases cash assets. As noted below, sources of funds include any decrease in an asset, increase in liability, noncash expense, or any revenue item. Selling receivables

Exhibit 21.1 Balance Sheet and Income Statement Data
for Donzi Inc. (Thousands of Dollars)

Balance Sheet	1990	1991	Income Statement	1991
Cash and market securities	$ 85	$ 90	Sales	$2,800
Accounts receivable	141	167	Cost of goods sold	2,380
Inventory	306	295	Gross profit	420
Prepaid expenses	22	18	Selling and administrative expenses	210
Current assets	$ 554	$ 570	Depreciation and amortization	45
Gross fixed assets	$ 575	$ 645	Other operating expenses	40
Less accumulated depreciation	−115	−160	Operating profit	125
Net fixed assets	460	485	Other income	5
Long-term investments	11	20	Interest expense	34
Total assets	$1,025	$1,075	Other expense	12
Notes payable (bank)	$ 50	$ 80	Profit before taxes	84
Accounts payable	99	96	Income taxes	29
Accruals	15	32	Net profit[a]	55
Income tax payable	6	12		
Current maturity (long-term debt)	35	40		
Current liabilities	$ 205	$ 260		
Long-term debt	$ 280	$ 240		
Total liabilities	$ 485	$ 500		
Common stock	$ 325	$ 325		
Retained earnings	215	250		
Net worth	$ 540	$ 575		
Liabilities and net worth	$1,025	$1,075		

[a]Dividends paid = $20.

or issuing new debt represent sources of cash. Uses of funds include any increase in an asset, decrease in a liability, or cash expense item. Thus the purchase of a building and principal payment on debt use cash. Sources of funds must equal uses of funds. Equivalently, the balance sheet identity requires that the sum of the changes in each asset equal the sum of the changes in each liability and the change in net worth (stockholders' equity). Let:

A_i = the dollar value of the ith type of asset A
L_j = the dollar value of the jth type of liability L
NW = the dollar value of net worth

There are n different assets and m different liabilities. Then:

$$\sum_{i=1}^{n} \Delta A_i = \sum_{J=1}^{m} \Delta L_j + \Delta NW \qquad (21.1)$$

ΔNW equals net income minus dividends paid plus the change in common and preferred stock outstanding plus the change in paid-in surplus. Thus Equation (21.1) can be written as:

Exhibit 21.2 Statement of Changes Reconciled to Cash: Data for Donzi Inc. (Thousands of Dollars)

	1991	Cash Flow Impact
Net sales	$2,800	Revenue
Change in accounts receivable	−26	Asset increased
Cash receipts from sales	$2,774	
Cost of goods sold	−$2,380	Expense
Change in inventory	11	Asset decreased
Change in accounts payable	−3	Liability decreased
Cash purchases	−$2,372	
Cash margin	$ 402	
Total operating expenses[a]	−295	Expense
Depreciation and amortization[a]	45	Noncash expense
Change in prepaid expenses	4	Asset decreased
Change in accruals	17	Liability increased
Cash operating expenses	−$ 229	
Cash operating profit	$ 173	
Other income	5	Revenue
Other noninterest expense	−12	Expense
Cash before interest and taxes	166	
Interest expense	−34	Expense
Income taxes reported	−29	Tax expense
Change in income tax payable	6	Liability increased
Change in deferred income taxes		
Cash flow from operations	**$ 109**	
Payment for last period's current maturity of long-term debt	−35	Liability decreased
Dividends paid	−20	Dividend
Capital expenditures	−70	Asset increased
Change in long-term investments	−9	Asset increased
Change in other noncurrent assets		
Discretionary cash expenditures	−$ 134	
Cash before external financing	−$ 25	
Change in short-term debt	30	Liability increased
Change in long-term debt plus end-of-period current maturity of long-term debt		
Change in stock		
Change in surplus		
External financing	$ 30	
Change in cash	5	Asset increased

[a]Total operating expenses include all noncash expenses as well as cash expenses. Cash expenses equals $295 − $45, or $250.

$$\sum_{i=1}^{n} \Delta A_i = \sum_{j=1}^{m} \Delta L_j + \Delta Stock + \Delta Surplus + NI - DIV \qquad (21.2)$$

where

NI = reported net income

DIV = actual cash dividends paid

$\Delta Stock$ = change in common and preferred stock outstanding between reporting periods

$\Delta Surplus$ = change in paid-in surplus between reporting periods

Cash flow from operations is derived using Equation (21.2) and the components of net income from the income statement. Each source of cash has a positive sign and each use of cash has a negative sign. The statement of changes format simply rearranges the elements of Equation (21.2) in terms of a cash-based income statement. Conceptually, Equation (21.2) is solved for the change in cash. Designating the first asset type as cash and decomposing net income:

$$\Delta Cash = \sum_{j=1}^{m} \Delta L_i - \sum_{i=2}^{n} \Delta A_j + \Delta Stock + \Delta Surplus \qquad (21.3)$$
$$+ \, Revenues - Expenses - Taxes - DIV$$

where

NI = Revenues − Expenses − Taxes.

As the signs before each element indicate, any increase in a liability or decrease in a noncash asset is a source of cash. A decrease in a liability or increase in a noncash asset is a use of cash. Issues of stock or positive additions to surplus represent a source of cash. Finally, revenues are a source of cash, while cash expenses, taxes paid, and dividends are a use of cash. These general relationships are summarized below:

Sources of Cash	Uses of Cash
Increase in any liability	Decrease in any liability
Decrease in any noncash asset	Increase in any noncash asset
New issue of stock	Repayments/refunding of stock
Additions to surplus	Deductions from surplus
Revenues	Cash expenses
	Taxes
	Cash dividends

Application to Donzi Inc. The cash flow format is presented in Exhibit 21.2 using balance sheet and income statement data for Donzi Inc. from Exhibit 21.1. The focal point of the statement is cash flow from operations. The far right column identifies the type of cash flow impact in terms of Equation (21.3) for each entry in the exhibit.

The top part of the statement shows why reported net income for Donzi differs from cash flow from operations. The first item listed is net sales. Donzi collected less on credit sales than it billed its customers because outstanding accounts receivable increased from 1990 to 1991. Thus net sales are offset by the $26 million increase in receivables to obtain actual cash receipts. Had receivables declined, actual cash receipts from sales would have exceeded the reported sales figure. The next series of figures recognizes that actual cash purchases differ from reported cost of goods sold. The comparison is shown as follows:

Production Budget Summary, 1991 (Thousands of Dollars)

Beginning inventory	$ 306	
+ Purchases	2,369	
= Goods available for sale	2,675	= − $11
− Cost of goods sold	2,380	
= Ending inventory	295	

Donzi started the year with $306,000 in inventory. During 1991 the firm purchased $2,369,000 from suppliers such that after the cost of goods sold was subtracted it held $295,000 in inventory. The statement of changes adds the change in inventory to the cost of goods sold to get total purchases.[5] If inventory decreases, as it does for Donzi, actual purchases are less than cost of goods sold, and vice versa. In this example, purchases equal $2,380,000 − $11,000. The statement then subtracts the change in outstanding accounts payable from total purchases to get actual cash purchases. An increase in payables indicates that a portion of purchases is financed by additional trade credit from suppliers. Donzi's cash purchases thus equaled $2,372,000 [$2,369,000 − (−$3,000)]. The reduction in accounts payable indicates that Donzi spent $3,000 more than the cost of supplies in 1991. Net cash purchases thus equal the cost of goods sold adjusted for inventory accumulation not financed by additional trade credit.

The statement format mimics an income statement. The next step is to subtract cash operating expenses. In this case, reported operating expenses overstate actual cash expenses by the amount of noncash charges, including depreciation and amortization. The format subtracts total operating expenses, which includes all noncash charges, then adds noncash charges back to yield a net figure for cash expenses. Prepaid expenses fell as Donzi paid more expenses than were reported on the income statement. The increase in accruals indicates that Donzi paid $17,000 less than costs incurred. The resulting cash operating profit is then adjusted by other income and noninterest expense that arises from normal business activity. Finally, actual interest expense and an estimate of income taxes paid are subtracted to obtain cash flow from operations. The data indicate that income taxes reported on the income statement exceeded actual taxes paid. This typically occurs because firms take greater deductions for tax purposes than they report in published statements. Tax payments are thus effectively deferred, and the net tax expense is $23,000, or $6,000 less than reported.

The resulting net figure, cash flow from operations, indicates whether the firm was able to service its debt and is useful in forecasting whether the firm can assume additional debt. As Contemporary Issues: The Many Faces of Cash Flow suggests, cash flow from operations is one of many cash flow measures. As a rule, any transaction representing a normal business activity should be recognized prior to calculating cash flow from operations. The items listed in Exhibit 21.2 are not all-inclusive, as financial statements for different firms contain different line items. Every balance sheet and income statement account must appear somewhere in the cash-based income statement. The key criteria is that normal activities are listed above cash flow from operations, while extraordinary items should be listed after cash flow. Thus if other income comes from the one-time sale of real estate, it should appear below cash flow.

At a minimum, cash flow from operations must be sufficient to cover dividends and current maturities of long-term debt. Other cash flows are unpredictable and cannot be relied on. In the case of Donzi, cash flow from operations of $109,000 exceeded dividends paid and the principal payment on long-term debt by $54,000. The excess

---

[5]Beginning and ending inventory and cost of goods sold are reported in the financial statements. Purchases and goods available for sale can be obtained from these three figures.

CONTEMPORARY ISSUES

The Many Faces of Cash Flow

What is cash flow? The classic definition is net income plus depreciation, amortization, and deferred taxes. According to a statement of changes reconciled to cash, cash flow from operations approximately equals classical cash flow adjusted for changes in working capital. In practice, the meaning of cash flow varies according to which analyst reviews the data.

Four commonly accepted definitions of cash flow are listed below, along with the associated value, using the data for Donzi Inc. in 1991 (in thousands of dollars).

1. Net income + (Depreciation + Amortization + Deferred taxes): $55 + $45 = $100

2. No. 1 total − All capital expenditures: $100 − $70 = $30

3. No. 2 total − ΔAccounts receivable − ΔInventory − ΔPrepaid expenses + ΔAccounts payable + ΔAccruals: $30 − $26 + $11 + $4 − $3 + $17 = $33

4. Pretax income + Depreciation + Amortization − Maintenance capital expenditures: $84 + $45 − $70 = $59

Maintenance capital expenditures equals that portion of capital outlays that maintains production operations at the current level (assumed equal to $70,000 for Donzi). This last measure is often referred to as *free cash flow*. Donzi's cash flow from operations is calculated before subtracting capital expenditures, and thus at $109,000 exceeds values obtained for cash flow according to definitions 2, 3, and 4.

Which is the best measure? Like most data analysis, there is no obvious answer. Definitions 3 and 4 provide the best estimates of how much new debt a firm can support with existing cash flow. However, firms can generally manipulate both balance sheet and income statement data and thus bias cash flow estimates. The statement of changes format incorporates all balance sheet and income statement data. When viewed comprehensively, an analyst can examine transactions relationships across the entire portfolio. Cash flow from operations is the appropriate estimate but must be compared with dividends, mandatory principal payments, and capital expenditures to determine debt service capabilities.

---

cash flow along with an increase in short-term debt was used to purchase new capital assets and fund an increase in long-term investments. In this example, the $70,000 capital expenditure equals the change in gross fixed assets. If a firm sells fixed assets, depreciation reported in the income statement will typically exceed the change in accumulated depreciation, and capital expenditures will exceed the change in gross fixed assets.[6]

The bottom part of Exhibit 21.2 completes the statement of changes. Discretionary expenditures totaling $134,000 include the payment for current maturities of long-term debt, capital outlays, and increases in long-term investments. This leaves a cash deficiency of $25,000, which is offset by a $30,000 increase in short-term debt. The statement balances by reconciliation to cash because the change in cash of $5,000 from the cash-based income statement equals the change in cash calculated from 1990 and 1991 balance sheet figures.

---

[6]A general formula to determine capital expenditures is:

$$\text{capital expenditures} = \Delta \text{ net fixed assets} + \text{depreciation.}$$

While short-term debt is typically rolled over, cash flow from operations might ultimately be needed to cover these maturing obligations. In 1991 Donzi Inc.'s cash flow was sufficient to pay $20,000 in dividends, $35,000 in maturing principal on long-term debt, and the entire $50,000 in notes payable outstanding at the beginning of the year. Thus Donzi Inc. was in excellent operating condition and could have supported new borrowing.

This analysis suggests two additional ratios: 1) cash flow from operations divided by the sum of dividends paid and last period's current maturities of long-term debt, and 2) cash flow from operations divided by the same two terms plus short-term debt outstanding at the beginning of the year. If these ratios exceed 1, as is the case with Donzi, the firm's operational cash flows can pay off existing debt and support new borrowing.

Financial Projections

The three-stage process described previously enables a credit analyst to evaluate the historical performance of a potential borrower. The final step, which addresses the basic issues introduced at the beginning of the chapter, is generating pro forma statements. Projections of the borrower's financial condition reveal how much financing is required and how much cash flow can be generated from operations to service new debt, and determine when, if at all, a loan can be repaid. In order to understand the range of potential outcomes, an analyst should make forecasts that incorporate different assumptions about sales, inventory growth, the level of interest rates, and the growth in operating expenses.

Consider the prospective use of loan proceeds. Firms with a legitimate need for working capital financing should demonstrate a decline in cash flow from operations caused by some combination of increased receivables and inventory or decreased accounts payable and accruals. Seasonal needs should appear from interim financial statements. Firms with positive and stable cash flow from operations do not generally need working capital financing but do have the capacity to service new debt. Specific cash outflows associated with term loans are easily identified in the bottom part of the statement of changes as discretionary expenditures increase or external financing declines.

The amount of financing required and the source and timing of repayment can similarly be determined with financial projections. In essence, each element of the cash flow statement is projected over the future. Projections are normally obtained by associating balance sheet items with sales or with external sources such as capital budgets. For example, current assets frequently equal a relatively constant percentage of sales or exhibit a stable turnover rate. In a stable environment, net income varies directly with sales. An analyst can determine an approximate percentage or turnover rate from historical data or comparable firm standards. Sales forecasts will then determine the projected growth in receivables, inventories, and profits. Similarly, the amount of trade credit provided may be tied to inventory growth, and thus accounts payable will also vary with sales forecasts. Principal payments on debt are known and planned fixed asset purchases can be obtained from the capital budget.

The differences in the projected asset base and total funding without new debt indicate how much additional credit is required at each future interval. This is an iterative procedure as new debt, in turn, increases projected interest expense and lowers net income. For working capital financing, projections should be made using peak and trough estimates of current asset needs over the next year. For term loans, projections should be made over several years. The projected credit requirement must approach zero in a reasonable period or the firm will have to restructure its existing financing and operations to service new debt.

Pro forma analysis is a form of sensitivity analysis. The analyst formulates a set of assumptions that establishes the relationships between different balance sheet and income statement items. At a minimum, three alternative scenarios or sets of assumptions should be considered: a best-case scenario in which optimistic improvements in planned performance and the economy are realized; a worst-case scenario that represents the environment with the greatest potential negative impact on sales, earnings, and the balance sheet; and a most-likely scenario representing the most reasonable sequence of economic events and performance trends. The three alternative forecasts of loan needs and cash flow establish a range of likely results that indicates the riskiness of the credit.

Risk-Classification Scheme

Most banks use a risk-classification scheme as part of the analysis process for commercial loans. After evaluating the borrower's risk profile along all dimensions, a loan is placed in a rating category ranked according to the degree of risk. Such a system is presented below and used for credit granting and pricing decisions.

Rating Category	Rating Scale	Collateral Support	Descriptive Indicators of Loan Quality
Highest Quality	1	Gov't. securities; cash	Highest quality borrowers. 5 years of historic cash flow data. Strong balance sheet & liquidity.
	2	Agency & high quality municipal securities; insured CDs	Highest quality; differs from class 1 only by degree of financial strength.
	3	Uninsured CDs; high quality stocks & bonds	Highest quality; cash flow average is slightly below classes 1 and 2.
Acceptable Quality	4	Gov't. guaranteed loans; may be unsecured	High degree of liquidity; assets readily convertible to cash; unused credit facilities. Strong equity capital and management.
	5	Secured by trading assets (A/R & Inv.) and/or real estate	Adequate liquidity; adequate equity capital with comfortable cash flow coverage; proactive management; cyclical industry with smaller margins.
	6	Heavily dependent on collateral and/or guarantees	Partially strained liquidity; limited equity so leverage exceeds industry norms; limited management strength; loss of business is cyclically vulnerable.
Poor Quality	7	Inadequate collateral	Strained liquidity, inadequate capital, and weak management. Adverse trends in industry and borrower financials.
	8	Inadequate collateral	Same as class 7, except financials are weaker.
	9	Inadequate collateral	Totally inadequate profile; well-defined weaknesses.

CREDIT ANALYSIS: AN APPLICATION

The following analysis presents a systematic application of the credit evaluation procedure just described. Each of the four key issues is addressed. Nonquantitative aspects of the evaluation are ignored.

Suppose that you are the bank loan officer who handles the account for Wade's Office Furniture, a small manufacturer of metal office furniture. On March 1, 1991, Marcus Wade, president and majority owner of the firm, met with you and requested an increase in the company's credit line from $900,000 to $1.2 million and a term loan of $400,000 for the purchase of new equipment. Mr. Wade reported that sales rose 50 percent in 1990 after 2 consecutive years of slow growth. He also showed you the balance sheet and income statement data provided in Exhibits 21.3 and 21.4, along with a list of backlogged orders totaling $250,000. He projected sales to increase another 50 percent in 1991 and felt that this would quickly reduce the outstanding note payable to the bank and help repay the term loan.

Financial Ratios Analysis: Wade's Office Furniture

The analysis begins with common size ratios from the balance sheet and income statement (Exhibits 21.3 and 21.4). Comparable figures from the *Annual Statement Studies* by Robert Morris Associates (RMA) for 1990 are listed in the final columns. The balance sheet data indicate that Wade's net receivables and inventory exceeded the industry norms in 1990 and increased each year from 1988 to 1990. Net fixed assets were well below industry standards in each year. In terms of financing, Wade's relied proportionately more on trade credit and short-term bank loans and less on long-term debt than did comparable firms. The firm's net worth-to-asset ratio was 8 percent less than the norm in 1990.

The income statement reveals two important factors. First, the cost of goods was a substantially lower percentage of sales compared with the industry average, reflecting higher mark-ups on finished products. Second, Wade's operating expenses far exceeded the industry percentage. This may reflect a large salary for Marcus Wade in that the firm pays no dividends and the company provides his only source of income. The net effect is that the firm earns proportionately less before taxes than do comparable firms.

One weakness of common size ratios is that they may be distorted by any one account that takes an extreme value. Wade's, for example, leases a disproportionately large amount of equipment, so net fixed assets are relatively low. This necessarily increases the relative contribution of current assets. For this reason, the analyst must examine all financial ratios in concept before drawing conclusions.

Exhibit 21.5 shows selected ratios for Wade's and comparable RMA figures. The first set of measures indicates that Wade's liquidity position has been relatively stable over time. Relative to its peers, the firm's current and quick ratios are low. This apparently contradicts the common size data. In fact, the ratios jointly reflect the dominant impact of the proportionately high accounts payable. The slower collection of receivables by 11 days and the greater number of days that inventory is outstanding in 1990 evidence current assets that exceed industry norms. High payables outstanding

Exhibit 21.3 Comparative Balance Sheet

Name: Wade's Office Furniture, SIC #2522   Auditor: Expressed in: 000

ASSETS	Audit Opinion	Unaudited	%	Unaudited	%	Unaudited	%	RMA	%
	Date	12/31/88		12/31/89		12/31/90		6/30/90-9/30/91	
Cash		141	4.3	133	3.9	72	1.6		5.5
Marketable Securities									
Net A/R—Trade		1254	38.4	1399	40.8	1896	42.3		28.8
Inventory		1160	35.6	1205	35.2	1764	39.4		29.7
Prepaid Expenses		47	1.5	50	1.5	15	0.3		
								Other	2.4
TOTAL CURRENT ASSETS		2602	79.8	2787	81.4	3747	83.6		66.4
Gross Fixed Assets		629		674		795			
Leasehold Improvements		198		202		238			
Less Accum. Deprec.		206		277		350			
NET FIXED ASSETS		621	19.0	599	17.5	683	15.2		28.2
Investments									
Prepaid Expenses									
Intangible Assets		40	1.2	39	1.1	50	1.2		0.4
Other Noncurrent								5.0	
TOTAL NON-CURRENT ASSETS		661	20.2	638	18.6	733	16.4		33.6
TOTAL ASSETS		3263	100	3425	100	4480	100		100
LIABILITIES									
Notes Payable—Banks		643	19.7	582	17.0	892	19.9		6.0
Notes Payable—Other									
Current Maturities—L.T.D.		75	2.3	75	2.2	75	1.6		3.6
Accounts Payable—Trade		836	25.6	908	26.5	1282	28.6		14.0
Accruals		205	6.3	258	7.5	348	7.8		
Federal Income Tax—Payable		41	1.3	62	1.8	79	1.8		1.7
Other									11.8
TOTAL CURRENT LIABILITIES		1800	55.2	1885	55.0	2676	59.7		37.1
Long Term Debt—Unsecured									
Long Term Debt—Secured									
Long Term Debt—Mortgage		450		375		300			
Long Term Debt—Subordinated									
TOTAL LONG TERM BORROWINGS		450	13.8	375	11.0	300	6.7		20.1
Reserves—Deferred Taxes									
Reserves—Other									
Reserves—									
Total Other Long Term Liabilities									0.9
TOTAL LIABILITIES		2250	69.0	2260	66.0	2976	66.4		58.1
MINORITY INTEREST									
Capital Stock—Preferred									
Capital Stock—Common		700		700		700			
Paid—In Surplus									
Retained Earnings		313		465		804			
Less Treasury Stock									
NET WORTH		1013	31.0	1165	34.0	1504	33.6		41.9
TOTAL LIABILITIES, MI, & N.W.		3263	100	3425	100	4480	100		100
DATE PREPARED & BY									

Exhibit 21.4 Comparative Income Statement

Name: Wade's Office Furniture, SIC #2522   Expressed in: 000

OPERATIONS	Length of Period	12 mths	%	12 mths	%	12 mths	%	RMA	%
	Period Ending	1988		1989		1990		6/30/90-9/30/91	
NET SALES/REVENUES		7571	100	8184	100	12,430	100		100
COST OF GOODS SOLD		5089	67.2	5424	66.3	8255	66.4		67.3
GROSS PROFIT		2482	32.8	2760	33.7	4175	33.6		32.7
Selling Expenses		906	12.0	1026	12.5	1628	13.1		
General & Admin. Expenses		1019	13.5	1211	14.8	1689	13.6		
Depreciation		70	0.9	71	0.9	73	0.6		
Total Operating Expense		1995	26.4	2308	28.2	3390	27.3		25.7
OPERATING PROFIT		487	6.4	452	5.5	785	6.3		7.0
Other Income									
Interest Expense		141	1.9	119	1.5	157	1.3		
Other Expense		63	0.8	86	1.0	101	0.8		
PROFIT BEFORE TAX		283	3.7	247	3.0	527	4.2		6.2
Income Taxes		100	1.3	95	1.1	188	1.5		
NET PROFIT BEFORE EX. ITEMS		183	2.4	152	1.9	339	2.7		
NET PROFIT		183	2.4	152	1.9	339	2.7		
N/W RECONCILIATION									
Beginning Net Worth		830		1013		1165			
Add—Net Profit		183		152		339			
Less—Net Loss									
—Cash Dividend									
Ending Net Worth		1013		1165		1504			
SOURCE/USE STATEMENT									
SOURCES									
Net Profit (Loss)									
Depreciation									
Deferred Taxes									
TOTAL FROM OPERATIONS									
Issue L.T.D.									
Sale of Stock									
Disposals									
TOTAL SOURCES									
Dividends									
Retirement L.T.D.									
Capital Expenditures									
TOTAL USES									
NET CHANGE W/C									
DATE RECEIVED & BY:									

Exhibit 21.5 Ratio Analysis: Wade's Office Furniture

	1988	1989	1990	RMA*
Liquidity and Activity				
Net working capital (thousands of dollars)	$802	$902	$1,071	
Current ratio	1.45	1.48	1.40	1.7
Quick ratio	0.78	0.81	0.74	0.9
Inventory turnover (days)	4.4×(83)	4.5×(81)	4.7×(78)	5.6×(65)
Accounts receivable collection (days)	60	62	56	45
Cost of goods sold to accounts payable	6.1×	5.9×	6.9×	11.3×
Days accounts payable outstanding	60	61	53	32
Days cash-to-cash cycle	150	149	136	
Sales/net fixed assets	12.2×	13.7×	18.2×	9.1×
Sales/total assets	2.3×	2.4×	2.8×	2.1×
Leverage				
Debt to tangible net worth	2.3×	2.0×	1.9×	1.7×
Times interest earned (coverage)	3.0×	3.1×	4.4×	5.3×
Fixed charge coverage[b]	1.4×	1.2×	1.8×	1.7×
Net fixed assets/net worth (%)	0.6	0.5	0.5	0.5
Dividend Payout				
Profitability				
Sales growth (%)	1.4	8.1	51.9	
Earnings before taxes/net worth (%)	29.1	21.9	36.2	27.7
Earnings before taxes/total assets (%)	8.7	7.2	11.8	12.1
Income taxes/Earnings before taxes (%)	35.3	38.5	35.7	
Return on average net worth (%)	18.8	14.0	25.4	

[a]RMA indicates figures for comparable firms from Robert Morris Associates. Comparable firms are those with total assets between $1 million and $10 million, reporting June 4, 1990, through September 30, 1991; median figure reported.

[b]Fixed charges include lease payments of $154,000, $192,000, and $325,000 from 1988 to 1990, respectively.

indicate that Wade's rides suppliers longer than comparable firms do and account for the low current and quick ratios.

The set of leverage ratios confirms the minimal net worth supporting the firm's operations. Debt exceeds tangible net worth by almost 100 percent in each year, well above the RMA average. Both the interest earned and fixed charge coverage are low compared with competitors, indicating greater interest expense and lease payments on equipment relative to earnings.

The profitability ratios indicate that Wade's profits before taxes exceeded the standard relative to net worth but fell below the standard relative to total assets. This again evidences the firm's relatively high degree of financial leverage. Reported profits did increase substantially in 1990, due in large part to the dramatic increase in net sales.

In summary, Wade's has invested more in receivables and inventory and less in fixed assets than have comparable firms. It likewise relies proportionately more on trade credit and short-term bank loans and less on long-term debt for financing. Its net worth is also substantially lower. Possible explanations are that the firm's terms of credit sales are too lenient or that the firm has poor collection policies. Similarly, Wade's may hold obsolete inventory or simply acquire it too far in advance of sales. Profitability has been relatively low, adversely affecting the equity base. On the positive side, the firm's sales growth and mark-up on sales are excellent. If the receivables and inventory are good quality, Wade's exhibits excellent potential. However, it is important for the banker to obtain a receivables aging schedule and personally audit the composition and quality of inventory.

The data suggest two specific risks. First, if suppliers refuse to grant Wade's the same volume of trade credit in the future, the firm will need additional bank loans to support operations. Second, the firm's low net worth and high debt provide limited support for the planned growth and expose the firm to declining profits if interest rates rise.

Cash-Based Income Statement: Wade's Office Furniture

Exhibit 21.6 presents a cash-based income statement for Wade's and documents changes in cash flow from operations. Consider the first two columns of historical data. In 1989 cash flow from operations equaled $176,000, which was $24,000 more than reported net income. However, cash flow fell to -$128,000 in 1990, even though sales rose by over $4 million and profits increased by almost 125 percent. A close examination of the statement reveals that the decline in 1990 was caused by a combined increase in receivables and inventory of almost $1.1 million. The $374,000 increase in accounts payable, while substantial, left $682,000 in new trading assets to be financed either externally or out of cash flow. The cash margin did rise by $850,000 but cash operating expenses increased by over $1 million, leading to a decline in cash operating profit. Increases in noninterest and interest expense and income taxes paid then produced the negative cash flow from operations. The additional $310,000 in notes payable to the bank financed a portion of this cash deficiency, payments for maturing principal on term debt, and $157,000 in capital expenditures. The residual financing came from reduced cash holdings.

The ratios at the bottom of the exhibit demonstrate that Wade's generated enough cash from operations to pay off current maturities of long-term debt in 1989 but fell far short in 1990. The negative cash flow from operations in 1990 indicates that the firm should not take on additional debt unless it can successfully restructure its operating policies.

Negative cash flow does not necessarily eliminate the possibility that the bank may want to make a loan. Under proper operating policies, Wade's may be able to expand and pay off new debt on a timely basis. Exhibit 21.7 outlines a set of financial projections that describes a most likely set of circumstances regarding the economic environment and revisions in Wade's operating policies. In this case, the loan should be repaid. The projections are based on the following assumptions drawn from the conclusions of the previous analysis:

1. Sales increase by 20 percent annually. All sales are credit sales. Wade's forecasts a 50 percent rise.

**Exhibit 21.6 Wade's Office Furniture: Cash-Based
Income Statement (Thousands of Dollars)**

	Historical Data		Forecasts	
	1989	**1990**	**1991**	**1992**
Net sales	$8,184	$12,430	$14,916	$17,899
Change in accounts receivable	−145	−497	−147	−213
Cash receipts from sales	$8,039	$11,933	$14,769	$17,686
Cost of goods sold	−$5,424	−$ 8,255	−$10,143	−$12,171
Change in inventory	−45	−559	−306	−317
Change in accounts payable	72	374	235	296
Cash purchases	−$5,397	−$ 8,440	−$10,214	−$12,192
Cash margin	$2,642	$ 3,493	$ 4,555	$ 5,494
Total operating expenses	−$2,308	−$ 3,390	−$ 3,869	−$ 4,621
Depreciation	71	73	110	110
Change in prepaid expenses	−3	35	−5	−5
Change in accruals	53	90	20	20
Cash operating expenses	−$2,187	−$ 3,192	−$ 3,744	−$ 4,496
Cash operating profit	$ 455	$ 301	$ 811	$ 998
Other noninterest expense	−86	−101	−110	−135
Cash before interest and taxes	$ 369	$ 200	$ 701	$ 863
Interest expense	−$ 119	−$ 157	−$ 186	−$ 123
Income tax reported	−95	−188	−219	−306
Change in income tax payable	21	17	22	27
Cash flow from operations	**$ 176**	**−$ 128**	**$ 318**	**$ 461**
Payment for last period's current maturity long-term debt	−$ 75	−$ 75	−$ 75	−$ 125
Dividends paid				
Capital expenditures	−49	−157	−400	
Change in other noncurrent assets	1	−11		
Discretionary expenditures	−48	−168	−400	
Cash flow before external financing	$ 53	−$ 371	−$ 157	$ 336
Change in notes payable	−$ 61	$ 310	−$ 195	−$ 336
Change in long-term debt plus end-of-period current maturity long-term debt			400	
External financing	−61	310	205	−336
Change in cash	−8	−61	48	0
Cash flow from operations/Dividends plus current maturity long-term debt (last period)	2.35	−1.71	4.24	3.69
Cash flow from operations/Dividends plus current maturity long-term debt (last period) plus notes payable	0.27	−0.13	0.41	0.95

2. Cost of goods sold equals 68 percent of sales.

3. Selling expenses average 13 percent of sales, general and administrative expenses average 12.2 percent of sales, and depreciation equals $110,000 annually.

4. Noninterest expense equals $110,000 in 1991 and $135,000 in 1992.

**Exhibit 21.7   Financial Projections: Wade's Office
Furniture (Thousands of Dollars)**

Balance sheet	1991	1992	Income Statement	1991	1992
			Sales	$14,916	$17,899
Assets			Cost of goods sold	10,143	12,171
Cash	$ 120	$ 120	Gross margin	4,773	5,728
Accounts receivable	2,043	2,256	Operating expense	3,869	4,621
Inventory	2,070	2,387	Interest	186	123
Prepaid expenses	20	25	Other expenses	110	135
Current assets	$4,253	$4,788	Profit before taxes	608	849
Fixed assets (net)	$ 973	$ 863	Income tax	219	306
Other assets	50	50	Net profit	389	543
Total assets	$5,276	$5,701	**Cash Flow Comparison**	**1991**	**1992**
Liabilities and Net Worth			Principal payment	$125	$125
Current maturity long-term debt	$ 125	$ 125	Interest payment	186	123
			Cash flow from operations		
Accounts payable	1,517	1,813	Before interest	504	584
Accruals	368	388	Surplus/deficit	193	330
Income tax payable	101	128	Dividends		
Current liabilities	$2,111	$2,454	Capital expenditures	400	
Long-term debt	225	150			
Net worth	1,893	2,436			
Total	$4,229	$5,040			
Short-term bank loan required	$ 697	$ 361			
Assumed term loan at bank[a]	350	300			
Total liabilities and net worth	$5,276	$5,701			
Total bank loan	$1,097	$ 711			

[a]Excludes $50 in current maturity long-term debt.

5. Interest expense equals 14.5 percent of outstanding bank debt and 9 percent of other long-term debt.

6. Income taxes equal 36 percent of earnings before taxes; income tax payable increases annually by the rate of change in 1990.

7. Receivables collection improves so that days receivables outstanding equals 50 in 1985 and 46 in 1986.

8. Inventory turnover increases to 4.9 times in 1991 and 5.1 times in 1992.

9. Days accounts payable outstanding remains constant at 53.

10. Prepaid expenses and accruals increase by $5,000 and $20,000 annually, respectively.

11. No dividends are paid.

12. $400,000 is lent to purchase new equipment, with the principal repaid over 8 years in equal annual installments. The first payment is due March 1, 1992.

13. Reported depreciation on the new equipment equals $40,000 a year for 10 years. Depreciation on old assets equals $70,000 per year.

14. The minimum cash required is $120,000.

15. Other assets remain constant at $50,000.

Each of these assumptions reflects a conservative estimate of future performance, in which Wade's operating ratios more closely approximate industry norms. Implicitly, the bank will lend money only if Wade's restricts its growth in current assets by tightening credit policies and slowing inventory growth. Restrictions on credit sales, in turn, are assumed to lower sales below Marcus Wade's forecast and to decrease the effective mark-up over cost of goods sold. Both receivables and inventory turnover will increase to the industry norm by 1992. Net profit will increase proportionately because of decreases in expenses as Wade's salary is unchanged and nonoperating expenses decline proportionately.

Balance sheet and income statement projections appear in Exhibit 21.7. Calculations that generate the projected values for selected balance sheet accounts in 1991 follow.

$$\text{Accounts receivable} = \text{Days outstanding (Daily average credit sales)}$$
$$= 50(14{,}916/365)$$
$$= 2{,}043$$

$$\text{Inventory} = \text{Cost of goods sold} / \text{Inventory turnover}$$
$$= 10{,}143/4.9$$
$$= 2{,}070$$

$$\text{Net fixed assets} = \text{Prior year's value} + \text{Capital expenditures}$$
$$- \text{Accumulated depreciation}$$
$$= 683 + 400 - 110$$
$$= 973$$

$$\frac{\text{Current maturity}}{\text{long--term debt}} = \text{Payment on old term debt} + \text{Payment on new term debt}$$
$$= 75 + 50$$
$$= 125$$

$$\text{Accounts payable} = \text{Days outstanding (Daily average purchases)}$$
$$= 53(10{,}449/365)$$
$$= 1{,}517$$

$$\text{Net worth} = \text{Old net worth} + \text{Retained earnings}$$
$$= 1{,}504 + 389$$
$$= 1{,}893$$

If the projected cash flow from operations (listed on the right side of Exhibit 21.6) is realized, it will total $318,000 in 1991 and $461,000 in 1992, considerably more than current maturities of long-term debt. Cash flow increases with sales because new trading assets are presumably financed almost entirely by additional trade credit. Thus the cash margin rises more than cash operating expense, interest expense, and taxes paid. The bank's short-term loan exposure will decrease in 1991 and 1992 to $697,000 and $361,000, respectively. Of course, the total bank loan outstanding will equal almost $1.1 million at the end of 1985 and $0.711 million at the end of 1992. This is substantially less than the requested $1.6 million.

The cash flow comparison at the bottom of Exhibit 21.7 indicates the relative size of cash flow from operations versus principal and interest payments. In 1991 cash flow from operations of $504,000 is forecast to exceed principal and interest payments by $193,000. The excess is forecast to reach $330,000 in 1992. Both estimates reveal Wade's ability to take on additional debt.

In this scenario, the loan proceeds would be used to finance the new equipment and current assets. The projected decrease in notes payable represents reduced working capital financing needs. Alternatively, the bank could shorten the maturity of the term loan and increase the annual principal payment. The projected cash flows would be sufficient to repay the term loan by 1992 and not increase short-term note exposure. The projections simply provide an estimate of total loan needs; the composition is determined through negotiations. If the assumed conditions hold for several years, the entire loan could be repaid from internal cash flow by 1994, shown by projecting the statement items through that year.

It is further likely that the bank would secure both the short-term and term loans with all available collateral, including receivables, inventory, and new equipment. The bank must consequently determine the quality of Wade's trading assets. Again, receivables agings and an assessment of inventory are required.[7]

These projections represent only one possible outcome. In all likelihood, Wade's performance in 1991 and 1992 will differ materially from that described above. The bank should always perform sensitivity analyses by adjusting assumptions regarding key factors, such as sales growth and receivables collection, and recalculating the projected financial statements. If the above projections are a most-likely scenario, management should compare the results with worst- and best-case scenarios. This generates a range of projected outcomes for the loan magnitude and repayment schedule. For example, if Wade's accounts receivable collection remained stable at its 1990 pace, its projected short-term loan requirement would exceed $800,000 in both 1991 and 1992. Not surprisingly, repayment would take much longer. The bank ultimately assigns probabilities (at least implicitly) to each potential outcome to arrive at an expected result.

SUMMARY

Credit analysis is the evaluation of risk associated with a borrower's willingness and ability to repay debts. Before analyzing financial data, the analyst should assess the borrower's character and the quality of corporate management. The subsequent financial analysis consists of spreading financial statements and determining cash flow from

---

[7]An aging schedule is a listing of accounts receivable grouped according to the month in which the invoice is either dated or payable. A comparison of aging schedules indicates whether the volume of past-due accounts is rising or falling and whether the general quality of receivables is deteriorating.

operations using historical data, followed by a review of pro forma balance sheet and income statement data. The entire procedure provides a framework for determining how large a loan is needed, what the proceeds will finance, how and when the loan should be repaid, and what collateral is available. This information and answers to specific questions about the firm's production process, supply relationships, and related concerns generally enable the lending officer to determine whether the credit request falls within acceptable risk limits.

One important facet of the analysis is evaluating cash flow. Principal and interest payments on debt plus dividends and a portion of other discretionary expenditures should be paid out of cash flow from operations. Term loans should generally not be approved unless the analysis indicates that projected cash flow will be sufficient to cover debt service requirements. Term loan analysis requires pro forma analysis. A statement of changes reconciled to cash generates cash flow estimates by constructing a cash-based income statement. The ratio of cash flow from operations to dividends and principal payments on loans reveals whether the firm's underlying operating position is healthy.

Questions

Fundamental Credit Issues

1. A former borrower of the bank applied for a new loan and presented financial statements that forecast outstanding cash flows. The applicant paid off his previous loan in a timely fashion. However, after granting the last loan for inventory purchases in his small business, you saw him driving an expensive new sports car. At the time you couldn't help wondering if the bank loan went to buy the car rather than inventory. Should you grant this loan? What additional information might you desire?

2. Rank the importance of the four basic credit issues described in the text.

3. Which of the following loan requests by an off-campus pizza parlour would be unacceptable to a banker?
   a. to buy cheese for inventory
   b. to buy a pizza warming oven
   c. to buy a car for the owner
   d. to buy the next-door building for expansion
   e. to buy stock in Leprino Cheese—the cheese supplier
   f. to repay the original loan used to purchase pizza ovens
   g. to pay employees—because of a temporary cash flow problem

4. Do borrowers tend to make loan requests that are too large or too small? Why do you think this is so?

5. What role should collateral play in a loan approval? How does the agriculture loan crisis from the mid-1980s illustrate this point?

6. What difficulties does a bank face in seizing collateral from a borrower in default?

Procedure for Financial Analysis

7. What should a bank be trying to learn in its overview of management and operations?

8. Ratio analysis usually groups ratios into the four categories of liquidity, activity, leverage, and profitability. How does each of these categories relate to the basic finance concerns of risk and return?

9. Suppose a borrower approaches a bank with two potential investment projects and asks for bank funding. The borrower has calculated the following expected net present values for the projects:

NPV of project A = $10,000 using a risk-adjusted discount rate of 10 percent

NPV of project B = $30,000 using a risk-adjusted discount rate of 14 percent

The bank has agreed to fund one of these projects: Which one do you think the bank will prefer if they both require the same initial investment?

10. When generating a statement of changes reconciled to cash, what items represent sources of cash? What items represent uses of cash?

11. Complete a Statement of Changes Reconciled to Cash for Grand Marina, whose financial statements are as follows:

	19X1	19X2			19X2
Cash	$ 100	$ 75	Sales		$5,000
Accounts receivable	75	85	Cost of goods sold		4,500
Inventory	700	800	Selling expense		100
Current assets	875	960	Depreciation		45
Net fixed assets	755	710	Interest expense		75
			Taxes		95
Total assets	$1,630	$1,670	Net income		$ 185
Notes payable (bank)	$300	$155			
Accounts payable	130	230	To dividends		$100
Current liabilities	430	385	To retained earnings		85
Long-term debt	700	700			
Equity	500	585			

12. What is the minimum acceptable amount of cash flow from operations for a firm requesting a loan?

13. Why are pro forma balance sheets and income statements useful in evaluating term loan requests? Do pro forma statements give you the same information as cash budgets?

14. Why are spreading financial statements useful in evaluating performance?

15. Is it possible for a firm to report rising net income each year yet continue to need more working capital financing from a bank?

16. Suppose that you have generated the estimates listed below from a pro forma analysis for a manufacturing company that had requested a 3-year term loan. What repayment plan would this borrower be able to handle?

	Year 1	Year 2	Year 3
Principal payment	$500,000	$500,000	$500,000
Interest payment	180,000	130,000	70,000
Capital expenditures	250,000	20,000	200,000
Dividends	120,000	120,000	120,000
Cash flow from operations (before interest expense)	705,000	740,000	800,000

Credit Analysis: An Application

17. Develop a list of questions that a loan officer should ask Marcus Wade, from the example in the text, to gain a better understanding of the risk in lending to Wade's Office Furniture.

18. Using the following data for Cramden's Booknook, calculate a statement of changes reconciled to cash for the second and fourth quarter of operations. Interpret the figures.

Problems

Cramden's Booknook Inc.

I. In late 1990, Howard Cramden was finalizing plans for opening his own bookstore in Wellesley, Massachusetts, just outside Boston. Even though it was his first effort at entrepreneurship, Cramden was well aware of the pitfalls in starting a small business. He had spent much of the last 2 years researching the market and identifying a niche where his firm could succeed. Cramden's Booknook would specialize in retailing hardbound and paperback books written for general audiences as well as reprints of classic fiction and nonfiction. It would also carry a wide range of stationery and greeting cards. As part of his marketing effort, Cramden planned to display rare books from his personal collection and provide a computer search service to help customers locate out-of-print titles.

Cramden intended to plan the first years of operation very carefully. He knew that most small businesses failed for lack of initial capital and managerial skill. He felt comfortable with his business background and wanted to impress his banker by preparing a comprehensive business plan. After graduating from college with a degree in economics, Cramden had gone to work as a sales representative in Boston for a major college textbook publisher. He was eventually promoted to publisher of the firm's economic and finance group. Having served in that capacity for 10 years, he was now ready, at age 48, to start his own business.

Cramden recently learned of an opportunity to buy a small building next to a large shopping mall in Wellesley. The building, which had previously been occupied by a franchise of a national computer chain, was located in a growth area with many young families and college students nearby. At present, the mall was fully leased and did not have a bookstore. The asking price for the building and land on which it was located was $280,000. Cramden, however, had reached a tentative agreement with the current owner to acquire the building for $230,000, contingent upon negotiations being completed by December 31, 1990.

Cramden arranged a meeting with the chief loan officer of Wellesley National Bank to discuss financing needs for the building and residual cash flow requirements for the first year of operations. He estimated that he would need $50,000 to modify the layout of the building's interior, $200,000 in inventory to begin operations, and a $25,000 cash balance to meet daily transactions requirements. Cramden also prepared the following estimates for projecting the firm's balance sheet and income statement:

1. Cost of goods sold will equal the industry standard of 62 percent of sales.
2. Cramden's inventory will equal 170 percent of next quarter's estimated cost of goods sold.
3. Forty percent of all merchandise purchases other than the initial stock will be paid for in cash in the quarter they are acquired, with the remaining 60 percent paid in the following quarter.
4. Sixty percent of sales will be for cash. The remaining 40 percent of credit sales will be collected during the following quarter.
5. Selling and administrative expenses will average $15,000 per month with all other operating expenses, including advertising, equal to 10 percent of sales. Financing costs are included in other operating expenses.
6. Depreciation charges for the first year of operation will equal $36,000, or $9,000 per quarter. This amount is not included in the expenses listed above.
7. Special promotion and grand opening expenses of $15,000 will be paid in January and expensed for accounting purposes. All expenses other than merchandise purchases will be paid for in cash. The applicable income tax rate is 34 percent.

Cramden projected that sales for the first 3 months of operation would be only $120,000. He expected sales to increase slowly during the second, third, and fourth quarters at $140,000, $180,000, and $220,000, respectively. Cramden planned to invest $300,000 of his life savings in the new business and had raised $100,000 from his brother in return for unsecured notes of the proposed firm. All remaining funds needed to run the bookstore would be provided by the bank and company profits. Principal payments on the $100,000 note were set at $20,000 per year beginning in 1993. Estimated interest expense on the $100,000 and bank financing were included in Cramden's estimate of operating expenses. Cramden intended to open the bookstore's doors on January 1, 1991, with the building remodeling completed and the initial inventory in place. Both the remodeling contractor and the inventory vendors would have to be paid in full during December.

1. Estimate how much bank financing is required for Cramden Booknook to open its doors for business on January 1, 1991.
2. Calculate quarterly pro forma income statements and balance sheets for the four quarters of 1991. The bank financing requirement is a plug figure to ensure that total assets equal total liabilities plus equity. Make assumptions and run projections beyond 1991. Use this information to answer the following questions:
   a. What size loan is required?

    b. What will the loan proceeds be used to finance?

    c. When will the loan be repaid?

    d. How will the loan be repaid? What is the source of repayment?

    e. What collateral should the bank require?

3. Generate a cash budget for the four quarters of 1991. Compare the results to those from the pro forma statements.

4. Develop a list of questions you would ask Howard Cramden or other relevant parties.

II. Table 1 presents balance sheet and income statement data for Growth Resources, Inc., a manufacturer of herbal dietary supplements that recently bought out an existing chain of health stores. During 1992 the firm instituted a national marketing campaign to enroll individuals to sell the firm's products from their homes. Chief Executive Officer Patrice King was pleased with sales in 1992, noting the 20 percent increase over 1991 sales. Individuals enroll in the new program for 1 year, and Growth Resources recognizes the entire membership fee immediately, even though the sales people have the right to cancel without obligation during the first 3 months. King feels that this policy has helped the firm's marketing efforts and sales.

  1. Using the data in Table 1, calculate a statement of changes reconciled to cash for Growth Resources, Inc. for 1992.

  2. Interpret the figures by evaluating the firm's cash flow for operations and key financial ratios.

  3. Identify potential problems that the firm faces.

Activity

Collect balance sheets and an income statement from a local business and convert them into a Statement of Changes Reconciled to Cash. If this business approached your bank for a loan that would increase the firm's total short-term liabilities by 10 percent, would you grant the loan? Support your decision.

References

Arnold, Jasper. "Assessing Credit Risk in a Complex World." *Commercial Lending Review* (June 1988).

Bennett, Thomas. "Mixed Signals." *Inc.* (October 1987).

Coleman, A. "Restructuring the Statement of Changes in Financial Position." *Financial Executive* (January 1979).

Compton, Eric. "Credit Analysis is Risk Analysis." *The Bankers Magazine* (March–April 1985).

Emmanuel, Christine. "Cash Flow Reporting, Part 2: Importance of Cash Flow Data in Credit Analysis." *Journal of Commercial Bank Lending* (June 1988).

Gill, Edward. *Commercial Lending Basics*. Reston, Va.: Reston Publishing Co., 1983.

Greene, R. "Are More Chryslers in the Offing?" *Forbes,* (February 2, 1981).

"How Banks Lend." *The Economist* (February 4, 1989).

Table 1 Balance Sheet and Income Statement Data for Growth Resources, Inc. (Millions of Dollars)

Balance Sheet	1991	1992	Income Statement	1992
Assets				
Cash and marketable securities	$ 27	$ 6	Net sales	$784
Accounts receivable	118	203	Cost of goods sold	604
Merchandise Inventory	97	99	Gross margin	180
Prepaid expenses	8	5	Selling expenses	47
Gross fixed assets	130	139	General & adm. expenses	59
Less accumulated depreciation	42	57	Depreciation	23
Net fixed assets	88	82	Operating profit	51
Intangible assets	4	3	Interest income	3
Total	$342	$398	Interest expense	21
Liabilities and Net Worth				
Notes payable—bank	121	154	Profit before taxes	33
Current maturities of long-term debt	9	11	Income taxes	8
Accounts payable	42	48	Net profit[a]	25
Accruals	2	8		
Federal income tax payable	3	6		
Long-term mortgage	19	17		
Long-term debt	48	39		
Liabilities	$244	$283		
Common stock	50	50		
Retained earnings	48	65		
Net worth	98	115		
Total	$342	$398		

[a]Net worth reconciliation

Beginning net worth	48
+ Net profit	25
– Dividends paid (cash)	8
Ending net worth	65

Iannuccilli, Joseph. "Asset-Based Lending: An Overview." *Journal of Commercial Bank Lending* (March 1988).

Kohl, David. "Lending to Agribusiness." *Journal of Commercial Bank Lending* (April 1990).

Laderman, Jeffrey. "Earnings, Schmernings—Look at the Cash." *Business Week* (July 24, 1989).

Lunzer, Francesca. "Confusing Flows the Cash Flow." *Forbes* (April 7, 1986).

Newburgh, Conrad. "Character Assessment in the Lending Process." *Journal of Commercial Bank Lending* (April 1991).

O'Connell, J. Brian. "How Inventory Appraisals Are Done." *Journal of Commercial Bank Lending* (April 1990).

O'Leary, Carolyn. "Cash Flow Reporting, Part 1: An Overview of SFAS 95." *Journal of Commercial Bank Lending* (May 1988).

Strischek, Dev. "Assessing Creditworthiness: Importance of Evaluating Management." *Journal of Commercial Bank Lending* (March 1990).

Viscione, Jerry A. "Assessing Financial Distress." *The Journal of Commercial Bank Lending* (July 1985).

White, Larry. "Credit Analysis: Two More 'Cs' of Credit." *Journal of Commercial Bank Lending* (October 1990).

APPENDIX TO CHAPTER 21

Background Information for Financial Analysis

A quantitative analysis of financial data serves as the basis for most credit decisions. Its effectiveness depends largely on the quality of the data. Before proceeding with the ratio and cash flow evaluation, an analyst should examine the nature of available information and its completeness. This appendix summarizes background information regarding financial analysis.

Financial Statements

Accountants prepare formal financial statements with an eye toward "generally accepted accounting principles" (GAAP). The intent of GAAP is to establish a set of policies and procedures that require the consistent, systematic presentation of accounting information. Even with GAAP, however, two problems frequently arise. First, many financial statements are prepared by individuals who are not familiar with GAAP, let alone fundamental accounting identities such as assets equal liabilities plus net worth. Thus asset classifications and expenses claimed in many reports vary from allowable provisions. Second, even GAAP allow different procedures for presenting information. For example, if a company sells a product under an installment contract, it can book sales when the order is signed or when delivery is actually made. Similarly, a company has a choice in how it accounts for inventory. Last-in-first-out systems have far different reporting and cash flow impacts than first-in-first-out systems.

The implication is that an analyst must examine the nature of financial data before spreading statements. Following are some recommended guidelines:

1. Determine who prepared the statements.

2. Determine if the statements are audited.

3. If audited, assess what type of opinion was issued and the nature of any qualification or disclaimer. In general, an unqualified opinion means that the auditor determined that the reported statements conformed with GAAP. A qualified opinion means that either some item in the report does not conform to GAAP or selected figures cannot be determined with a reasonable degree of certainty. The second case occurs, for example, when the value of inventory cannot be adequately

determined. Adverse opinion means that the financial statements are not presented in accordance with GAAP, and a disclaimer appears when the auditor expresses no opinion.

4. Determine areas where a firm has used its discretion to select a particular accounting policy within GAAP that might significantly affect reported figures. This requires the careful examination of footnotes to financial statements. Discretionary policies frequently arise in the areas of revenue recognition, income tax reconciliation, inventory valuation, accounts receivable classification, depreciation of plant and equipment, goodwill, consolidation of entities, and pension, profit sharing, and stock option plans.

5. Determine all outstanding commitments and contingent claims.

6. Identify any unusual balance sheet entries or transactions.

Calculation of Financial Ratios[1]

Liquidity

1. Current ratio = Current assets/Current liabilities

2. Quick ratio $= \dfrac{\text{Cash} + \text{Accounts receivable}}{\text{Current liabilities}}$

3. Accounts receivable aging schedule: a comparison of the dollar amount and percentage of total receivables outstanding across the number of days they have been outstanding (less than 30, 31–60, etc.)

Activity

1. Inventory turnover = Cost of goods sold/Inventory

2. Days inventory outstanding = 365/Inventory turnover

3. Accounts receivable turnover $= \dfrac{\text{Credit sales}}{\text{Accounts receivable}}$

4. Accounts receivable collection period = 365/Accounts receivable turnover

5. Days accounts payable outstanding $= \dfrac{365}{(\text{Purchases/Accounts payable})}$

6. Days cash-to-cash cycle (assets) = (Cash/Daily sales) + Days inventory outstanding + Accounts receivable collection period

7. Sales to net fixed assets = Sales/Net fixed assets

Leverage

1. Debt to tangible net worth = Total liabilities/Net worth

---

[1]An interpretation of each ratio along with its corresponding deficiencies is provided in Robert Morris Associates' *Annual Statement Studies.*

2. Times interest earned $= \dfrac{\text{Profit before taxes} + \text{Interest}}{\text{Interest expense}}$

3. Fixed charge coverage $= \dfrac{\text{Profit before taxes} + \text{Interest} + \text{Lease payments}}{\text{Interest expense} + \text{Lease payments}}$

4. Net fixed assets to tangible net worth $= \dfrac{\text{Net fixed assets}}{\text{Tangible net worth}}$

5. Dividend payout = Dividends paid/Net profit

Profitability

1. Sales growth = Change in sales/Last period's sales

2. Profit before taxes to net worth $= \dfrac{\text{Profit before taxes}}{\text{Tangible net worth}}$

3. Profit before taxes to total assets $= \dfrac{\text{Profit before taxes}}{\text{Total assets}}$

4. Income taxes to profit before taxes $= \dfrac{\text{Reported income tax}}{\text{Profit before taxes}}$

5. Return on average net worth $= \dfrac{\text{Net profit}}{\text{Tangible net worth}}$

References

Annual Statement Studies, Robert Morris Associates, annual.

Key Business Ratios, Dun & Bradstreet, annual.

Analyst's Handbook, Standard & Poors, annual.

Almanac of Business and Industrial Ratios, Troy, annual.

Chapter 22

Evaluating Consumer Loans

Between 1980 and 1990 commercial banks' share of car loans to individuals dropped from 53 percent to 35 percent, largely due to competition from the big three domestic car manufacturers' captive finance subsidiaries. In order to move inventory, General Motors, Ford, and Chrysler routinely offer low-interest financing and/or substantial price rebates that entice buyers and effectively takes business from banks.

At the same time, the consumer credit card business is consolidating with fewer card issuers controlling an increasing share of credit card receivables. Citicorp had an estimated $43 billion in outstanding credit card loans at year-end 1990 with over 32 million cardholders. During 1989, Chase Manhattan spent $2.3 billion to acquire the credit card portfolios of five banks and thrifts. The ten largest bank card issuers subsequently held 51 percent of credit card loans—up 4 percent from the previous year.

Lenders, ranging from credit unions to investment banks and finance companies, aggressively compete with commercial banks and savings and loans for consumer credit. In part, this reflects the extraordinary profitability of most consumer loans during the 1980s. It also reflects the attraction of relatively low-cost, stable consumer deposits. This chapter analyzes the characteristics and profitability of different types of consumer loans and introduces general credit evaluation techniques to assess risk. In doing so, it demonstrates why consumer banking relationships are attractive to banks.

For many years banks viewed consumer loans with skepticism. Commercial loans were available in large volume, net yields were high, and the loans were highly visible investments. Consumer loans, in contrast, involved small dollar amounts and a large staff to handle accounts, and less prestige was associated with lending to individuals. This perception changed with the decline in profitability of commercial loans. In recent years, competition among lenders has lowered spreads on commercial loans to where potential profits are small relative to credit risk. Most states no longer have effective usury ceilings on consumer loans so that lenders have increased interest rates and risk-adjusted returns have exceeded those on commercial loans. Even with high relative default rates, consumer loans in the aggregate currently produce greater profits than do commercial loans.

Today, many banks target individuals as the primary source of growth in attracting new business. This reflects the attraction of consumer deposits as well as consumer loans. Interest rate deregulation forced banks to pay market rates on virtually all their liabilities. Corporate cash managers, who are especially price sensitive, routinely move their balances in search of higher yields. Individuals' balances are much more stable. While individuals are price sensitive, a bank can generally retain deposits by varying rates offered on different-maturity time deposits to meet the customer's needs. Consumers thus hold substantial demand deposits and NOW accounts that are relatively inexpensive to the bank. A consumer who maintains a deposit relationship and borrows from the same institution is typically quite loyal.

From a lender's perspective, the analysis of consumer loans differs from that of commercial loans. First, the quality of financial data is lower. Personal financial statements are typically unaudited so that it is easy for borrowers to hide other loans. It is similarly easy to inflate asset values undetectably. Second, the primary source of repayment is current income. There is rarely cash flow from projects. The net effect is that capacity and character are more difficult to assess, but extremely important.

TYPES OF CONSUMER LOANS

When evaluating the measurable aspects of consumer loan requests, an analyst addresses the same issues discussed with commercial loans: the use of loan proceeds, the amount needed, and the primary and secondary sources of repayment. Consumer loans, however, differ so much in design that no comprehensive analytical format applies to all loans. With credit cards, for example, a bank does not know what the loan proceeds will be used for or how much the customer will borrow at any point in time. A boat loan with fixed installment payments, in contrast, has a maximum borrowing amount and a regular repayment schedule. Credit analysis thus differs across loan types. Many banks mass market their credit cards knowing that losses will rise but hoping to attract enough affluent customers to offset charge-offs. Other than purchasing names from a mailing list, no formal analysis of individual borrower characteristics occurs. In contrast, lenders treat direct installment loans much like commercial loans by evaluating each facet of the credit request, such as estimating discretionary income (cash flow) relative to debt service requirements.

As discussed in Chapter 20, consumer loans can be classified into one of three types: installment loans, credit cards/revolving credit lines, and noninstallment loans. Each type requires a different approach for credit analysis and provides different answers to the fundamental credit issues.

Installment Loans

Installment loans require the periodic payment of principal and interest. In most cases, a customer borrows to purchase durable goods or cover extraordinary expenses and agrees to repay the loan in monthly installments.[1] While the average loan is quite small, some may be much larger, depending on the use of the proceeds. It is not unusual, for example, to see loans for aircraft, boats, and personal investments exceed $250,000. The typical maturity ranges from 2 to 5 years. Except for revolving credit, most consumer loans are secured.

Installment loans may be either direct or indirect loans. A *direct loan* is negotiated between the bank and the ultimate user of the funds. An individual who borrows from a bank to finance an automobile must formally request credit and provide supporting personal financial information. The loan officer analyzes the information and approves or rejects the request. An *indirect loan* is funded by a bank through a separate retailer that sells merchandise to a customer. The retailer, such as an automobile dealer, takes the credit application, negotiates terms with the individual, and presents the agreement to the bank. If the bank approves the loan, it buys the loan from the retailer under prearranged terms.

Exhibit 20.10 provides a breakdown of installment credit by use of proceeds. As indicated, automobile loans exceed any other type of installment loan, followed by revolving credit and mobile home loans. Approximately 60 percent of automobile loans are indirect loans purchased from dealers. The figure for indirect mobile home loans is considerably higher.

Revenues and Costs from Installment Credit. Installment loans can be extremely profitable. Exhibit 22.1 summarizes revenue and cost data for different-sized banks from the Federal Reserve's 1989 *Functional Cost Analysis.* In 1989 the average size loan was approximately $5,000. Depending on the size of bank, it cost from $118 to $155 to originate each installment loan. Acquisition costs include salaries, occupancy, computer, and marketing expenses associated with soliciting, approving, and processing loan applications. It also cost from $6 to $10 to collect payments, and the bank charged-off an average of $13 to $31 per loan.

Even though these costs are high, banks were able to earn excellent spreads on the average loan. Interest and discounts, for example, averaged around 12 percent. After subtracting acquisition costs, collection costs, and net charge-offs, the net yield was 8 to 9 percent. Because the average cost of financing the loans averaged around 7 percent, the net spread ranged from 0.52 percent to 2.15 percent, depending on the size of the bank. Anything over 1 percent exceeds historical norms, and thus the average consumer installment loan was highly profitable in 1989 for banks over $50 million in deposits.

---

[1] Credit card loans and overdraft lines are formally installment loans because they require periodic monthly payments. They are discussed separately because their other features differ widely from other installment loans.

Exhibit 22.1 Costs and Returns on Consumer Installment Loans: Functional Cost Analysis Data for 1989

	Deposit Size (Millions of Dollars)		
	<$50	$50–$200	>$200
Data			
Average size of loan	$4,724	$4,638	$5,764
Percent of applications accepted	76.2%	72.0%	60.4%
Number of banks surveyed	48	119	37
Costs Per Loan			
Cost to make a loan	$124.50	$117.99	$155.04
Cost to collect a payment	9.95	6.70	6.41
Loan loss (average size loan)	31.18	19.46	12.72
Total	$165.63	$144.15	$174.17
As a % of Total Loans Outstanding			
Loan income[a]	12.38%	12.29%	11.74%
Expenses			
Cost of making loans	1.75	1.52	1.15
Cost of maintenance/collecting	2.09	1.64	1.15
Loan loss rate (3 year average)	0.66	0.53	0.32
Total	4.50%	3.69%	2.62%
Net yield	7.88%	8.60%	9.12%
Cost of funds	7.36	6.95	6.97
Net spread	0.52%	1.65%	2.15%

[a]Loan income includes installment plus other income.

Credit Cards and Other Revolving Credit

Credit cards and overlines tied to checking accounts are the two most popular forms of revolving credit agreements. In 1989 consumers charged over $360 billion on credit cards. Many pay only a fraction of their monthly bill and thus incur finance charges on the remainder. Credit lines against demand deposit accounts at banks are less common but function identically to credit cards. Customers can write checks in excess of actual balances held but must pay interest on the overdraft, usually against lump sums at $50 or $100 increments.

Banks offer a variety of credit cards. While some banks issue cards with their own logo and supported by their own marketing effort, most operate as franchises of MasterCard and/or Visa. To become part of either group's system, a bank must pay a one-time membership fee plus an annual charge determined by the number of its customers actively using the cards. MasterCard and Visa, in turn, handle the national marketing effort. All cards prominently display the MasterCard and Visa logos with the issuing bank's name imprinted on the front. The primary advantage of membership is that an individual bank's card is accepted nationally and internationally at most retail stores without each bank negotiating a separate agreement with every retailer. U.S.

CONTEMPORARY ISSUES

Smart Cards and the Computer Generation

Banks throughout the world are investing in technologies that promote *debit cards* and *smart cards*. Debit cards are widely available, but not very attractive to consumers. As the name suggests, when an individual uses the card his or her balance at a bank is immediately debited, that is, funds are instantaneously transferred from the card user's account to the account of the retailer. The obvious disadvantage to a consumer is the loss of float, which explains why debit cards are not yet popular.

A smart card is an extension of the debit card that contains a computer memory chip which stores and manipulates informa-tion. When inserted in a terminal, the cardholder can pay for goods and services, dial the telephone, make airline arrangements, and authorize currency exchanges. It is programmable so that users can store information regarding their complete financial history and recall this information when effecting transactions. Over 60 million smart cards were in use in Europe and Japan in 1990, but they have yet to arrive in the United States. This largely reflects the U.S. consumer's satisfaction with existing technology and banks' unwillingness to invest in the computer terminals necessary to process transactions.

banks have not been aggressive in developing alternatives to credit cards, such as the smart card, which is currently dominated by foreign competitors (see Contemporary Issues: Smart Cards and the Computer Generation).

Exhibit 22.2 lists the major issuers of bank-related credit cards, their outstanding loans relative to the net charge-off percentage, and the number of accounts at the end of 1990. By 1990 MasterCard and Visa together had issued 220 million cards through thousands of financial institutions across the United States, American Express had 37 million cards outstanding, and Sears had 23 million Discover cardholders. AT&T, which introduced its Universal Master Card earlier in 1990, had signed 4.7 million cardholders by year-end 1991. Citicorp, the largest card-issuing commercial bank, offered five different VISA and MasterCards plus Diners Club and Carte Blanche. Diners Club and Carte Blanche have their strongest markets overseas in the travel and entertainment areas.

Credit cards are attractive because they provide higher risk-adjusted returns than other types of loans. Card issuers earn income from three sources: charging cardholders annual fees, charging interest on outstanding loan balances, and discounting the charges merchants accept on purchases. In 1990 annual fees averaged $20 per account, annual interest rates averaged around 19 percent, and the discount to merchants ranged from 2 to 5 percent. Even though other interest rates may fall, credit card rates are notoriously sticky. Thus the spread between the rate charged and bank's cost of funds widens. The *Nilson Report* estimated that credit card business generated around 70 percent of the net profits at Citicorp and Chase Manhattan Corp. in 1989, obviously swamping profits in any other line of business.

The three largest nonbank competitors are American Express, Sears, and AT&T. In 1985 Sears developed its Discover card, which provides the same transactions privileges as bank cards. During 1986 Sears announced that over 380,000 merchants

Exhibit 22.2 Widely Held Bank-Related Credit Cards[a]

Company Card	1990 Billings[a]	Outstanding Loans December 31, 1990	Net Charge-offs as Percentage of Loans	Number of Accounts[b]
American Express	$111.5	$6.0	4.8%	37.1
Citicorp: VISA/MasterCard	43.0	31.7	4.0	22.5
Sears: Discover	19.4	11.5	2.2	22.9
First Chicago	13.0	7.1	3.0	7.2
Bank America	10.4	6.7	2.9	6.1
Chase Manhattan	11.4	9.4	2.7	10.0
MBNA	11.5	6.8	2.1	5.3
AT&T Universal: MasterCard	—	7.7	0.9	4.7

[a] Billions of dollars

[b] Millions

Source: Saparito, Bill. "Melting Point in the Plastic War." *Fortune* (May 20, 1991).

accepted the card, but the entire program was expected to lose more than $100 million for the year. To increase usage, Sears offered rebates up to 1 percent on purchases made with the Discover card and did not charge an annual user fee. By 1990 the Discover card had captured 6 percent of the market and added $80 million in profits to Sears' bottom line. The American Express card is the dominant travel and entertainment card and comes in three versions—green, gold, and platinum—each with different basic services and different fee. The gold and platinum cards offer such services as extended warranties on purchases, car rental collision insurance, buyers' assurance (guarantees), and medical monitoring and evacuation. Many banks have tried to attract similar affluent cardholders by offering "premium" or "prestige" MasterCards and Visa cards with different features than the basic charge card (see Contemporary Issues: Prestige Cards).

Credit card lending involves issuing plastic cards to qualifying customers. The cards have preauthorized credit limits that restrict the maximum debt outstanding at any time. An individual can use the card to purchase goods and services from any merchant that accepts the card. Thus the individual determines the timing and amount of actual borrowing. Many cards can be used in electronic banking devices, such as automatic teller machines, to make deposits or withdrawals from existing transactions accounts at a bank.

The recent regulatory and competitive environment has made credit cards extremely attractive. Many banks view credit cards as a vehicle to generate a nationwide customer base. They offer extraordinary incentives to induce consumers to accept cards in the hope that they can cross-sell mortgages, insurance products, and eventually securities. Some banks also use the card relationship to solicit money market deposits or small CDs. Credit cards are profitable because many customers are price insensitive. Most banks charge annual user fees, and credit card interest rates are among the highest rates quoted. People simply are willing to pay for the convenience of buying goods whenever they wish, and many believe that the periodic interest is too small to cause

CONTEMPORARY ISSUES

Prestige Cards

The credit card business has undergone a dramatic transition in recent years as commercial banks and travel service companies, such as American Express, compete for affluent customers. The standard is a firm's "prestige" or "premium" credit card targeted to individuals who travel frequently or regularly purchase big-ticket items. The cards carry high membership fees ranging up to $300 a year, which individuals who demand status symbols pay without a second thought.

Visa International offers a Premier Visa card; MasterCard International, a gold Preferred Customer card; and American Express, a Gold Card and Platinum Card. The cards carry substantial credit lines that start at $5,000 and enable holders to purchase travel insurance, hotel services, travelers' checks, car rentals, and other services at substantial discounts. In most cases, these services do not differ significantly from services available through less-expensive cards. The appeal is primarily status and prestige from being able to afford the card.

---

them to give up the spending convenience. Credit card losses, however, are among the highest of all loan types. Fraud is prevalent, and many individuals eventually default on their debts because their incomes do not cover their spending habits.

Credit Card Systems and Profitability. The returns to credit card lending depend on the specific roles a bank plays. According to Federal Reserve classifications, a bank is called a card bank if it administers its own credit card plan or serves as the primary regional agent of a major credit card operation, such as Visa or MasterCard. A noncard bank, in contrast, operates under the auspices of a regional card bank and does not issue its own card. Noncard banks do not generate significant revenues from credit cards. Because default risk is borne by the card-issuing bank, noncard banks do not assume much risk in this product line.

The types of revenues available are described in Exhibit 22.3, which summarizes the clearing process for a credit card transaction. Once a customer uses a card, the retail outlet submits the sales receipt to its local merchant bank for credit. A retailer may physically deposit the slip or electronically transfer the information via a card-reading terminal at the time of sale. The merchant bank discounts the sales receipt by 2 to 5 percent as its fee. Thus a retailer will receive only $97 credit for each $100 sales receipt if the discount is 3 percent. If the card was not issued by the merchant bank, the retailer sends the receipt to the card-issuing bank through a clearing network, paying an interchange fee. The card-issuing bank then bills the customer for the purchase. Card revenues thus arise from these sources; merchant discounts, annual fees, and interest on outstanding balances. The bank earns interest at rates ranging from 11 to 22 percent and normally charges each individual an annual fee for use of the card. As mentioned earlier, interest rates are sticky. Thus when money market rates decline and lower a bank's cost of funds, the net return on credit card loans rises because credit card rates do not fall coincidentally. Interest income and annual fees comprise approximately 80 percent of credit card revenues. The remaining 20 percent is merchant discounts.

Exhibit 22.3 The Credit Card Transaction Process

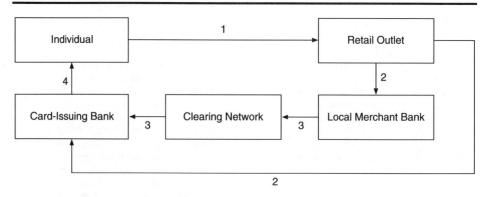

Steps	Fees
1. Individual uses a credit card to purchase merchandise from a rental outlet.	1. None
2. Retail outlet deposits the sales slip or electronically transmits the purchase data at its local bank.	2. The merchant bank discounts the sales receipt. A 3 percent discount indicates the bank gives the retailer $97 in credit for each $100 receipt.
3. Local merchant bank forwards the transaction information to a clearing network, which routes the data to the bank that issued the credit card to the individual.	3. The card-issuing bank charges the merchant bank an interchange fee equal to 1 to 1.5 percent of the transaction amount for each item handled.
4. The card-issuing bank sends the individual an itemized bill for all purchases.	4. The card-issuing bank charges the customer interest and an annual fee for the privilege of using the card. A card-issuing bank also serves as a merchant bank.

Source: Weinstein, Michael, "Credit Card Business Mushrooms at Large Banks." *American Banker* (August 14, 1986).

Exhibit 22.4 presents *Functional Cost Analysis* data for a sample of card-issuing banks in 1984 and 1989. In 1989 just under two-thirds of card users paid interest on outstanding balances such that banks earned an average 13.32 percent in interest on loans outstanding. Gross revenues, including merchant discounts and all fees, totaled 25.51 percent of outstanding loans. After subtracting operating expenses and loan charge-offs, the net yield still exceeded the banks' average cost of funds by 0.43 percent. Even with fraud and credit losses equal to 1.5 percent of outstanding loans, credit card loans were profitable. The data substantially understate the profit potential for banks with a large cardholder base. Fixed expenses decline as a fraction of outstanding loans the greater is the volume of business, while income is unchanged.

Exhibit 22.4 Costs and Returns on Credit Card Operations at Card-Issuing Banks with \$50–\$200 Million in Deposits: 1984 versus 1989

	1984	1989
Average size of active account	\$493	\$605
Average size of cash advance	352	308
Percent of active accounts paying interest	67.9%	63.9%
As a Percentage of Total Credit Card Loans Outstanding		
Outstandings	93.60%	97.36%
Cash advances	6.40	2.64
Total	100.00%	100.00%
Income		
Merchant discount	6.01%	9.01%
Finance charge interest	15.56	13.32
Net interchange fees	0.65	0.71
Other income	2.99	2.47
Total	25.21%	25.51%
Expenses		
Total operating expense	13.57%	16.64%
Net credit losses	1.06	1.46
Net fraud losses	0.14	0.03
Total	14.77%	18.13%
Net yield	10.44%	7.38%
Cost of funds	8.34	6.95
Net spread	2.10%	0.43%

Thus the net profit for many of the largest card issuers is closer to 2 percent of the loan balance.

Contrast the results with those of 1984. While the average size of account increased, 3 percent fewer accounts paid interest. Income was almost the same, but operating expense rose by over 3 percent such that the net yield on outstanding loans and overall net spread fell sharply. This increase in operating costs largely explains the drop in net spread to 2.1 percent.

Overdraft Protection and Open Credit Lines. Revolving credit also takes the form of overdraft protection for checking accounts. A bank authorizes qualifying individuals to write checks in excess of actual balances held in a checking account up to a prespecified limit. The customer must pay interest on the loan from the date of the draft's receipt and can repay the loan either by making direct deposits or by periodic payments. One relatively recent innovation is to offer open credit lines to affluent individuals whether or not they have an existing account relationship. These loans are the functional equivalent of loan commitments to commercial customers. In most instances, the bank provides customers with special checks that activate a loan when presented for payment. The maximum credit available typically exceeds that for overdraft lines, and the interest rate floats with the bank's base rate.

Home Equity Loans and Credit Cards. Home equity loans grew from virtually nothing in the mid-1980s to over $100 billion in 1990 spurred by the Tax Reform Act of 1986, which limited deductions for consumer loan interest paid by individuals unless the loan was real-estate related. Home equity loans meet the tax deductibility requirements because they are secured by equity in an individual's home. Many of these loans are structured as open credit lines where a consumer can borrow up to 75 percent of the market value of the property less the principal outstanding on the first mortgage. Individuals borrow simply by writing checks, pay interest only on the amount borrowed, and can repay the principal at their discretion. The loans generally carry adjustable rates tied to the bank's base rate. In some cases, home equity credit lines can be accessed by using a credit card. Because consumers can take out only one such loan, the lender that initiates the credit relationship has locked in a long-term customer.

These credit arrangements combine the risks of a second mortgage with the temptation of a credit card, a potentially dangerous combination. Home equity loans place a second lien on a borrower's home. If the individual defaults, the creditor can foreclose so that the borrower loses his or her home. Yet ready access to the financing through credit cards encourages consumers to spend and ultimately take on too much debt. Federal Reserve studies have generally shown that consumers borrow primarily to improve their existing homes, consolidate debts, or finance a child's college education. In either case, the typical home equity loan represents a large initial borrowing that is paid down over several years.

In order to attract customers immediately after the Tax Reform Act of 1986 passed, many banks priced loans at just 1 or 2 percent over the prime rate, which was well below other consumer loan rates. Some additionally required only interest payments during the first few years. Low rates have been justified by historically low losses and good collateral, a home. Of course, delinquency rates increase during economic downturns when real estate values often decline. In addition, there is always the risk that customers will borrow the maximum, especially under credit card arrangements, for short-run lifestyle expenses. If they take on too much debt and interest rates rise or housing values fall, many borrowers may default and lenders will see losses rise.

Noninstallment Loans

A limited number of consumer loans require a single principal and interest payment. Typically, the individual's borrowing needs are temporary. Credit is extended in anticipation of repayment from a well-defined future cash inflow. Bridge loans are representative of single-payment consumer loans. Bridge loans often arise when an individual borrows funds for the down payment on a new house. The loan is repaid when the borrower sells an existing home, hence the term *bridge*. The quality of the loan depends on the certainty of the timing and amount of the anticipated net cash inflow from the sale.

CONSUMER CREDIT REGULATIONS

The federal government has approved a wide range of regulations to protect individuals when obtaining credit. Most of the regulations address discrimination, billing practices, customer liability, and the proper disclosure of finance charges and reasons for denying credit. The need for such regulation arose from abuses of the credit system. At one time, many lenders refused to extend credit to women who did not have a personal credit record because loans were credited to a husband. Loans were sometimes denied because of the borrower's race or age. Lenders would refuse to extend credit in deteriorating neighborhoods and made it difficult for borrowers to determine the effective cost of credit. This section discusses several important regulations that address these abuses.

Equal Credit Opportunity

Ideally, credit will be available to any borrower who satisfies acceptable risk criteria. To ensure this, Congress passed the Equal Credit Opportunity Act (ECOA), which makes it illegal for lenders to discriminate against potential borrowers because of race, religion, sex, marital status, age, or national origin. The Federal Reserve's Regulation B specifies conditions that must be met in structuring credit applications and establishing creditworthiness. In doing so, it focuses on three different aspects of credit transactions. First, it indicates what information a creditor may not request. Implicitly, this information is not relevant to the credit evaluation and would, if available, be used primarily to discriminate. Second, it specifies how certain information can be used in credit scoring systems. Finally, it provides for proper credit reporting. For example, lenders must include spouses in the credit records whenever a spouse is jointly liable for any debts. Lenders must also notify applicants of adverse action on a loan within 30 days of the request. The following list identifies specific items that are prohibited or required.

Prohibited Information Requests

1. Lenders may not request information about the applicant's marital status unless credit is being requested jointly, the spouse's assets will be used to repay the loan, or the applicant lives in a community property state.[2] This popularized the term "cohabitant" on many application forms.

2. Lenders may not request information about whether alimony, child support, and public assistance payments are included in an applicant's reported income. Applicants can voluntarily provide this information if they believe it will improve perceived creditworthiness.

3. Lenders may not request information about a woman's childbearing capability and plans or birth control practices.

4. Lenders may not request information about whether an applicant has a telephone.

---

[2]In community property states, couples own assets jointly. Assets listed on an application are often only partly owned by a married applicant, which would restrict a lender's access to collateral.

Credit Scoring Systems

1. Credit scoring systems are acceptable if they do not require prohibited information and are statistically justified. The statistical soundness should be systematically reviewed and updated.

2. Credit scoring systems can use information about age, sex, and marital status as long as these factors contribute positively to the applicant's creditworthiness.

Credit Reporting

1. Lenders must report credit extended jointly to married couples in both spouses' names. This enables both individuals to build a credit history.

2. Whenever lenders reject a loan, they must notify applicants of the credit denial within 30 days and indicate why the request was turned down. An applicant may request written notification, and the lender must comply.

In practice, the ECOA includes many complex provisions that are difficult to comprehend. To make compliance easier, the Federal Reserve provides model loan application forms that conform to Regulation B.

Truth in Lending

The intent underlying truth-in-lending legislation is for lenders to disclose consumer loan finance charges in a standardized format. This enables borrowers to compare credit terms and the cost of credit between loans and between lenders. Truth-in-lending regulations apply to all loans up to $25,000 extended to individuals, where the borrower's primary residence does not serve as collateral.[3]

Legislation arose because lenders quoted interest rates in many different ways and often included supplemental charges in a loan that substantially increased the actual cost. Consumers could not easily determine how much they were paying and what the effective interest rate was on a loan. This confused borrowers and potentially led to inferior credit decisions.

Historically, consumer loan rates were quoted as add-on rates, discount rates, or simple interest rates. Add-on rates are applied against the entire principal of installment loans. The gross interest is added to the principal with the total divided by the number of periodic payments to determine the size of each payment. For example, suppose that a customer borrows $3,000 for 1 year at a 12 percent add-on rate with the loan to be repaid in 12 equal monthly installments. Total interest equals $360, the monthly payment equals $280, and the effective annual interest cost is approximately 21.5 percent. Exhibit 22.5 presents these calculations and similar ones for discount rate and simple interest examples.

With the discount rate method, the quoted rate is applied against the sum of principal and interest, yet the borrower gets to use only the principal, as interest is

---

[3]The Truth in Lending Act, passed in 1968, is implemented through the Federal Reserve's Regulation Z. Originally, it applied to agriculture loans as well as personal credit, but in 1980 Congress exempted agriculture from the reporting requirements.

Exhibit 22.5 A Comparison of Interest Rate Quotes

Add-On Rate

$3,000 loan for 1 year, 12% add-on rate, repaid in 12 equal monthly installments

Interest charge: $360

$$\text{Monthly payment:} \frac{[0.12(\$3,000) + \$3,000]}{12} = \frac{\$3,360}{12} = \$280$$

$$\text{Effective interest rate (i):} \sum_{t=1}^{12} \frac{\$280}{(\$1 + i)^t} = \$3,000$$

$$i = 1.796\%$$

$$\text{Annual rate} = 21.55\%$$

Discount Rate

$3,000 to be repaid at the end of 1 year, 12% discount rate.

$$\text{Interest charge:} 0.12(\$3,000) = \$360$$

Year-end payment: $3,000

$$\text{Effective annual interest rate (i}_n\text{):} \$2,640 = \frac{\$3,000}{(1 + i_n)}$$

$$i_n = 13.64\%$$

Simple Interest Rate

$3,000 loan for 1 year, 12% simple interest, repaid at end of year in one payment.

$$\text{Interest (i}_s\text{):} = \$3,000(0.12)(1) = \$360$$

$$\$3,000 = \frac{\$3,360}{(1 + i_s)}$$

$$i_s = 12\%$$

$3,000 loan for 1 year, 1% monthly simple interest rate, repaid in 12 equal monthly installments.

Repayment Schedule

End of Month	Monthly Payment	Interest Portion	Principal	Outstanding Principal Balance
January	$ 266.55	$ 30.00	$ 236.55	$2,763.45
February	266.55	27.63	238.92	2,524.53
March	266.55	25.25	241.30	2,283.23
April	266.55	22.83	243.72	2,039.51
May	266.55	20.40	246.15	1,793.36
June	266.55	17.93	248.62	1,544.74
July	266.55	15.45	251.10	1,293.64
August	266.55	12.94	253.61	1,040.03
September	266.55	10.40	256.15	783.88
October	266.55	7.84	258.71	525.17
November	266.55	5.25	261.30	263.87
December	266.51	2.64	263.87	0.00
Total	$3,198.56	$198.56	$3,000.00	

Effective interest rate: Monthly rate = 1%

Annual rate = 12%

$$\text{Monthly payment} = \$3,000 / \sum_{i=1}^{12} \frac{1}{(1.01)^t}$$

immediately deducted from the total loan. Exhibit 22.5 considers a 1-year loan with a single $3,000 payment at maturity. The borrower receives only $2,640, or the total loan minus 12 percent discount rate interest. The effective annual rate equals 13.64 percent. The bottom part of Exhibit 22.5 demonstrates simple interest calculations. Simple interest is interest paid on only the principal sum. A $3,000 loan at 12 percent simple interest per year produces $360 in interest, or a 12 percent effective rate. At the bottom of the exhibit, the quoted rate is adjusted to its monthly equivalent, which is applied against the unpaid principal balance on a loan. A $3,000 loan, repaid in 12 monthly installments at 1 percent monthly simple interest, produces interest under $200. The monthly interest rate equals 1 percent of the outstanding principal balance at each interval. Depending on how it is quoted, a 12 percent rate exhibits a noticeably different effective rate, ranging from 12 percent to 21.5 percent in the examples.

Truth-in-lending legislation requires that lenders disclose to potential borrowers both the total finance charge and an annual percentage rate. The total finance charge equals the dollar amount of interest costs plus all supplemental charges that are imposed as part of a loan, including loan origination fees, service charges, and insurance premiums if the lender demands the customer take out a policy as part of the agreement. The *annual percentage rate (APR)* equals the total finance charge computed against the loan balance as a simple annual interest rate equivalent.

The regulations also stipulate that advertisements must include all relevant terms of a loan if any single payment or pricing feature is mentioned. These terms include the finance charge, APR, dollar magnitude of any down payment requirement, number of payments, and final maturity. This prevents a lender from using one very attractive feature, such as no required down payment, to lure customers without disclosing all terms. Assuming the borrower does not pay additional fees, the effective interest rates in Exhibit 22.5 are APRs.

Fair Credit Reporting

Lenders can obtain information on an individual's prior credit relationships from local credit bureaus when evaluating consumer loan requests. The Fair Credit Reporting Act enables individuals to examine their credit reports provided by credit bureaus. If any information is incorrect, the individual can have the bureau make changes and notify all lenders who obtained the inaccurate data. If the accuracy of the information is disputed, an individual can permanently enter into the credit file his or her interpretation of the error. The credit bureau, when requested, must also notify an individual which lenders have received credit reports.

Community Reinvestment

The Community Reinvestment Act (CRA) was passed in 1977 to prohibit redlining and to encourage lenders to extend credit within their immediate trade area and the markets where they collect deposits. Redlining is the practice of not extending credit within geographic areas that are felt to be deteriorating. Its name comes from the reputed practice of outlining in red those areas of a city where a lender would automatically refuse credit because of location. It discriminates against borrowers from economically declining neighborhoods that represent the redlined areas. Community reinvestment has played an important role in the interstate banking movement. Out-of-state banks that acquire local banks must commit to continued lending in the area and not use acquired banks simply as deposit gatherers.

The Financial Institutions Reform, Recovery, and Enforcement Act (FIRREA) of 1989 raised the profile of the CRA by mandating public disclosure of bank lending policies and regulatory ratings of bank compliance. Specifically, regulators now rate banks as outstanding, satisfactory, needs improvement, or substantial noncompliance in terms of their compliance with nondiscriminatory lending practices. These ratings are publicized to put pressure on banks that are not in compliance through fear that negative publicity will harm their image and subsequent performance. Consumer groups now routinely use claims of noncompliance under CRA to delay bank mergers and acquisitions, forcing an acquirer to demonstrate how performance will be improved. It is both good business and necessary for the bank's future to comply with nondiscrimination legislation.

Bankruptcy Reform

Individuals who cannot repay their debts on time can file for bankruptcy and receive court protection against creditors. Court protection takes the form of exempting selected personal assets from creditors' claims and providing for an orderly repayment of debts. In 1978 and 1985 Congress modified the Federal Bankruptcy Code. The 1978 legislation liberalized the volume and type of assets that individuals could exempt and made unsecured loans extremely risky.

Individuals can file for bankruptcy under Chapter 7 or Chapter 13. Chapter 7 authorizes individuals to liquidate qualified assets and distribute the proceeds to creditors. The 1978 Bankruptcy Reform Act specifically exempted such assets as an automobile, household furnishings, some jewelry, and a fraction of the individuals' equity in a primary residence from liquidation. In some states, state exemptions are even more liberal, and individuals can take advantage of the broadest exemptions.[4] An individual must pay all taxes, alimony, and child support owed in full. Cash received from the sale of nonexempt assets is allocated to other creditors on a pro rata basis with secured creditors paid first. Because the list of exemptions was so broad after 1978, unsecured creditors rarely received any payment. Once the cash is distributed, the remaining debts are discharged.

Under Chapter 13 an individual works out a repayment plan with court supervision. The individual gets to keep his or her assets but commits to repay selected debts out of future earnings according to a schedule approved by all secured creditors. Once the scheduled debts are repaid, the remaining debt is discharged. Under the 1978

---

[4]The 1978 regulations actually allowed one spouse to file for bankruptcy in state court while the other filed in federal court, thereby doubling their exemptions. The 1985 provisions force a couple to file in only one jurisdiction.

regulations, unsecured creditors again had no recourse and often received nothing under Chapter 13.

Reforms to the bankruptcy code in 1985 made it more costly for an individual to walk away from outstanding debt. Under Chapter 13 plans, lenders can obtain a court order that assigns a large fraction of a debtor's income to repay debt for 3 years after the date of filing. The reforms shortened the list of exempt assets and permitted the court to switch a Chapter 7 filing to Chapter 13 when it determined that an individual, who was financially able was using bankruptcy simply to avoid paying all debts. Unsecured lenders were also protected by provisions that forced borrowers to repay all credit card purchases made during the 3 weeks prior to filing for bankruptcy.

CREDIT ANALYSIS

The objective of consumer credit analysis is to assess the risks associated with lending to individuals. Not surprisingly, these risks differ substantially from those of commercial loans. Most consumer loans are quite small, averaging around $5,000 in 1990. Because the fixed costs of servicing consumer loans is high, banks must generate substantial loan volume to reduce unit costs. This means dealing with a large number of distinct borrowers with different personalities and financial characteristics.

When evaluating loans, bankers cite the Cs of credit: character, capital, capacity, conditions, and collateral. The most important, yet difficult to assess, is character. A loan officer essentially must determine the customer's desire to repay a loan. The only quantitative information available is the borrower's application and credit record. If the borrower is a bank customer, the officer can examine internal information regarding the customer's historical account relationship. If the borrower is not a current customer, the officer must solicit information from local credit bureaus or other businesses that have extended credit to the individual. The ECOA stipulates what information can be required and prohibits discrimination. It also mandates how lenders must report information to the credit reporting agencies. Banks also rely heavily on subjective appraisals of the borrower's character. They normally obtain personal references, verify employment, and check the accuracy of the application. This is necessary because fraud is prevalent, and it is relatively easy for an individual to disguise past behavior. If the officer determines that a potential customer is dishonest, the loan is rejected automatically.

Capital refers to the individual's wealth position and is closely related to capacity, an individual's financial ability to meet loan payments in addition to normal living expenses and other debt obligations. For almost all consumer loans, the individual's income serves as the primary source of repayment. A loan officer projects what income will be available after other expenses and compares this with periodic principal and interest payments on the new loan. To assure adequate coverage, the lender often imposes minimum down payment requirements and maximum allowable debt-service-to-income ratios. The loan officer verifies that the borrower's income equals that stated on the application and assesses the stability of the income source. Conditions refers to the impact of economic events on the borrower's capacity to pay when some income sources disappear as business activity declines.

The importance of collateral is in providing a secondary source of repayment. Collateral may be in the form of the asset financed by the loan, other assets owned by the individual, or the personal guarantee of a cosigner on the loan. Collateral gives banks another source of repayment if the borrower's income is insufficient. Normally, a loan is not approved simply because the collateral appears solid. Often the collateral disappears or deteriorates in value prior to the bank taking possession, as with a damaged or older automobile. Finally, the bankruptcy code enables individuals to protect a wide range of assets from creditors, and it may be difficult to obtain a judgment.

Two additional *C*s have been added, customer relationships and competition.[5] A bank's prior relationship with a customer reveals information about past credit and deposit experience which is useful in assessing willingness and ability to repay. Competition has an impact by affecting the pricing of a loan. All loans should generate positive risk-adjusted returns. Lenders periodically react to competitive pressures, however, by undercutting competitors' rates to attract new business. Still, such competition should not affect the accept/reject decision.

Policy Guidelines

Consumer loans are extended for a variety of purposes. The most common purposes are for the purchase of automobiles, mobile homes, home improvements, furniture and appliances, and home equity loans. Before approving any loan, a lending officer requests information regarding the borrower's employment status, periodic income, the value of assets owned and outstanding debts, personal references, and specific terms of the expenditure that generates the loan request. The officer verifies the information and assesses the borrower's character and financial capacity to repay the loan. Because borrowers' personal and financial characteristics differ widely, most banks have formalized consumer lending guidelines. As an example, guidelines for acceptable and unacceptable loans might appear as listed below.

Acceptable Loans

Automobile

1. Limited to current-year models or models less than 5 years old.

2. Made on an amortizing basis with a minimum 10 percent down payment.

3. Advances against used models should not exceed National Automobile Dealer Association loan value.

4. New automobiles for business purposes are limited to 30-month amortization.

5. Insurance must be obtained and verified with a $250 maximum deductible.

---

[5]See Larry White (1990) for a general discussion of the 7 *C*s of credit.

Boat

1. Limited to current-year models or models less than 3 years old.

2. Made on an amortizing basis with a minimum 20 percent down payment.

3. Marine survey must be obtained with large craft.

4. Insurance must be obtained and verified.

Home Improvement

1. Loans in excess of $2,500 should be secured by a lien.

2. Loans in excess of $10,000 require a property appraisal and title search.

3. A third lien position is not acceptable.

4. Bank retains the right to cancel in all cases.

Personal—Unsecured

1. Minimum loan is $2,500.

2. Made only to deposit customers.

3. Limited to 1/12 of the applicant's annual income.

Single Payment

1. Limited to extraordinary purposes.

2. Require a verified, near-term source of repayment.

3. Insurance claims, pending estate settlements, and lawsuit settlements are not acceptable sources of repayment.

Cosigned

1. Applicant exhibits the potential to be a qualified, long-term bank customer.

2. Both the applicant and cosigner are depositors of the bank.

3. Applicant does not have an established credit history but does have the capacity to pay.

4. Cosigner has qualified credit history and the capacity to pay.

5. Cosigner is informed that the bank is relying totally on the cosigner for repayment in case of default.

Unacceptable Loans

1. Loans for speculative purposes.

2. Loans secured by a second lien, other than home improvement or home equity loans.

3. Any participation with a correspondent bank in a loan that the bank would not normally approve.

4. Accommodation loans to a poor credit risk based on the strength of the cosigner.

5. Single-payment automobile or boat loans.

6. Loans secured by existing home furnishings.

7. Loans for skydiving equipment and hang gliders.

Evaluation Procedures

Banks employ judgmental procedures and quantitative credit scoring procedures when evaluating consumer loans. In both cases, a lending officer collects information regarding the borrower's character, capacity, and collateral. With a pure judgmental analysis, the loan officer subjectively interprets the information in light of the bank's lending guidelines and accepts or rejects the loan. This assessment can often be completed shortly after receiving the loan application and visiting with the applicant. With a pure quantitative analysis, the loan officer grades the loan request according to a statistically sound credit scoring model that assigns points to selected characteristics of the prospective borrower. The officer simply adds the points and compares the total with statistically determined accept/reject scores.[6] If the total exceeds the accept score, the officer approves the loan. If the total is below the reject score, the officer denies the loan. Typically, there is a gap between the accept/reject scores representing an inconclusive evaluation of characteristics. If the total falls within this gap, the officer makes a decision based on judgmental factors.

When developing the accept/reject scores, banks must obtain data on applicant characteristics when loans were originally requested for both accepted and rejected loans. Actual performance on the loans is then evaluated to determine the extent to which different factors influenced the individual's ability to repay. These weights determine the credit scoring formula.

Clearly, credit scoring procedures are more objective than judgmental evaluations. Credit decisions can be made quickly once the information is verified, often in less than 10 minutes when computers are used. Discrimination is largely eliminated because the ECOA does not allow credit scoring models to grade race, religion, sex, or national origin. The primary difficulty is that credit scoring models must be statistically verified and continually updated, which can be expensive. Many small banks are, in fact, precluded from developing their own models because of the high cost and a limited data base.

An Application: Credit Scoring. Credit scoring models are based on historical data obtained from applicants who actually received loans.[7] Statistical techniques assign weights to various borrower characteristics that represent each factor's contribution toward distinguishing between good loans that were repaid on time and problem loans that produced losses. These weights are then used as predictors of high-risk and low-risk loans, using data from new loan applications.

The use of credit scoring models can be demonstrated with an example. Suppose that a bank officer receives a loan application for the purchase of an automobile, as

---

[6]Credit scoring systems and accept/reject scores are empirically derived from either multiple regression analysis or multiple discriminant analysis. These statistical techniques use historical data regarding a bank's good and bad consumer loans to assess what characteristics identify a high percentage of good or bad borrowers. The accept/reject scores represent the weighted value of borrowers' characteristics. See Grablowski (1979).

[7]The fact that the sample excludes applications that were rejected biases the model parameters because the characteristics of these applicants are ignored. The extent of the bias depends on whether good borrowers who would have repaid the loan on a timely basis were eliminated or whether all rejects were bad credits.

Exhibit 22.6 Credit Application—University National Bank

IMPORTANT: Please read these directions before completing this Application, and check (✔) the appropriate box below.

☒ If you are applying for individual credit in your own name, are not married, and are not relying on alimony, child support, or separate maintenance payments or on the income or assets of another person as the basis for repayment of the credit requested, complete only Sections A and D. If the requested credit is to be secured, also complete Section E.

☐ In all other situations, complete all Sections except E, providing information in B about your spouse, a joint applicant or user, or the person on whose alimony, support, or maintenance payments or income or assets you are relying. If the requested credit is to be secured, also complete Section E.

AMOUNT REQUESTED	PAYMENT DATE DESIRED	PROCEEDS OF CREDIT TO BE USED FOR
$ 8500	Nov. 15, 1990	Purchase of a 1988 Buick Skylark

SECTION A — INFORMATION REGARDING APPLICANT

FULL NAME	AGE	BIRTH DATE	SOCIAL SECURITY NO.
Sarah Ann Johnson	28	July 12, 1958	496-62-0448

PRESENT ADDRESS (Street, City, State, & Zip)	How Long At Present Address?	HOME PHONE
#115 Woodhaven Lane Apts., Tempe, Arizona	10 mths	765-1191

PREVIOUS ADDRESS (Street, City, State, & Zip)	How Long At Previous Address?
Circle Townhouses, #820A, Broken Arrow, Oklahoma	2 years

PRESENT EMPLOYER (Company Name & Address)
James O'Malley, DDS 650 University Avenue, Tempe, Arizona

How Long With Present Employer?	YOUR POSITION OR TITLE	NAME OF SUPERVISOR	BUSINESS PHONE
8 mths	Dental assistant	James O'Malley	765-8014

PREVIOUS EMPLOYER (Company Name & Address)
Homemaker

Your Present Gross Salary or Commission	Your Present Net Salary or Commission	No. Dependents	Ages of Dependents
$ 18,500 PER year	$ 983 PER month	1	6 years

Alimony, child support, or separate maintenance income need not be revealed if you do not wish to have it considered as a basis for repaying this obligation. Alimony, child support, separate maintenance received under: ☐ Court Order ☐ Written Agreement ☐ Oral Understanding

OTHER INCOME	SOURCES OF OTHER INCOME
$ 150 PER year	savings interest

Is any income listed in this Section likely to be reduced before the credit requested is paid off? ☒ No ☐ Yes (Explain)

Have you ever received credit from us? ☒ No ☐ Yes — When?

Checking Account No. 355 0114 8 Where? UNB
Savings Account No. 457 1988 Where? UNB

NAME & ADDRESS OF NEAREST RELATIVE NOT LIVING WITH YOU
Albert F. Johnson, RR#10, Adair, Oklahoma

RELATIONSHIP
Uncle

OUTSTANDING DEBTS (Include charge accounts, installment contracts, credit cards, rent, mortgages, etc. Use separate sheet if necessary.)

CREDITOR	BALANCE	PAYMENT	PAID OFF ACCOUNTS
Sears	$450	$50/mth	

SECTION B — INFORMATION REGARDING JOINT APPLICANT OR OTHER PARTY

FULL NAME	BIRTH DATE	RELATIONSHIP

ADDRESS	PHONE NUMBER

PRESENT EMPLOYER — ADDRESS	PHONE NUMBER

HOW LONG	PREVIOUS EMPLOYER	HOW LONG	SOCIAL SECURITY NUMBER

GROSS SALARY	SOURCE AND AMOUNT OF OTHER INCOME
$_____ PER _____	$_____ PER _____

NAME & ADDRESS OF NEAREST RELATIVE NOT LIVING WITH YOU

Alimony, child support, or separate maintenance income need not be revealed if you do not wish to have it considered as a basis for repaying this obligation. Alimony, child support, separate maintenance received under: ☐ Court Order ☐ Written Agreement ☐ Oral Understanding

SECTION C — MARITAL STATUS

| APPLICANT | ☐ Married | ☐ Separated | ☐ Unmarried, including single, divorced, and widowed. |
| OTHER PARTY | ☐ Married | ☐ Separated | ☐ Unmarried, including single, divorced, and widowed. |

Are you a co-maker, endorser, or guarantor on any loan or contract? ☐ No ☐ Yes — For Whom?   To Whom?

Are there any unsatisfied judgements against you? ☐ No ☐ Yes — Amount $ If "Yes", To Whom Owed?

SECTION D — ASSET & DEBT INFORMATION

If Section B has been completed, this Section should be completed, giving information about both the Applicant and Joint Applicant or Other Person. Please mark Applicant-related information with an "A". If Section B was not completed, only give information about the Applicant in this section.

ASSETS OWNED (Use separate sheet if necessary)

DESCRIPTION OF ASSETS	VALUE	SUBJECT TO DEBTS	NAMES OF OWNERS
Cash	$		
Automobiles 1. 1971 Chevrolet Impala	200	No	SAJ
2.			
3.			

Landlord or Mortgage Holder		Name Account Carried	Balance	Monthly Payment	Past Due
Woodhaven Lane Apts	☐ Rent Payment ☒ Mortgage	Sarah A. Johnson	$	$	$ 450	$ 0

SECTION E — SECURED CREDIT (Complete only if credit is to be secured.) Briefly describe the property to be given as security:

Property Description
1988 Buick Skylark

NAMES AND ADDRESSES OF ALL CO-OWNERS OF THE PROPERTY

IF THE SECURITY IS REAL ESTSTE GIVE THE FULL NAME OF YOUR SPOUSE (If any):

SIGNATURES

outlined in Exhibit 22.6. The application identifies the purpose, amount, and maturity of the loan as well as information regarding the applicant's personal and financial circumstances and recognizes ECOA guidelines. Before providing any information, Sarah Johnson indicates that she is applying for individual credit and not relying on alimony, child support, or government income maintenance payments to repay the debt. The bank, therefore, cannot demand information regarding her marital status or information about joint applicants or cosigners.

The Credit Score. Exhibit 22.7 lists the factors and corresponding weights for the bank's credit scoring model. A loan is automatically approved if the applicant's total score equals at least 200. The applicant is denied credit if the total score falls below 150. Scores in between these accept/reject values are indeterminate. The weights indicate the relative importance of each characteristic. At University National Bank five factors, including employment status, principal residence, monthly debt relative to monthly income, total income, and banking references, are weighted most heavily. Not surprisingly, these characteristics represent financial capacity and personal stability, which are important in determining repayment prospects. The bank also uses a local retail merchants association and a similar national association to check credit histories. Subsequent reports reveal the applicant's current list of outstanding debts, the highest balance outstanding at any one point, and whether the individual was ever late in making payments.

Sarah Johnson's credit score totals 155, as the scores from her application within each category in Exhibit 22.7 denote. Given the accept/reject scores, the model provides an inconclusive evaluation of the credit risk, and the loan officer must rely on judgmental factors. When discussing the application, Sarah Johnson revealed that she moved to Tempe after her husband, who worked for an oil field services company, died in a automobile accident. After searching for 2 months, she found work as a dental assistant with a dentist who had recently started his own business. She had experience in this field before she met her husband but quit her job to stay at home with their son. She is currently attending evening classes at the local university to complete a degree in accounting. She further indicated that the total cost of the car she wanted to purchase was $14,500 but she intended to make a $4,000 down payment. This would lower her savings balance at the bank to $1,200. The loan officer had his secretary verify this and determined that Sarah's monthly checking account balance averaged around $150. Her monthly rent payment was $450.

The Credit Decision. The credit decision rests on the loan officer's evaluation of the applicant's character and capacity to repay the debt. The officer estimates that the monthly installment payment on the loan at current rates would equal $185 for the next 4 years. The officer ponders the following questions. Will the applicant remain in Tempe long enough to repay the loan? How stable is her job and income? Is her income high enough to cover normal monthly living expenses, debt payments, and extraordinary expenses? Should the officer reject the loan and encourage the applicant to reapply with a cosigner?

Exhibit 22.7 University National Bank Credit Scoring System[a]

Category	Characteristics/Weights					
Annual Gross Income	< $10,000 / 5	$10,000–20,000 / 15	$20,000–40,000 / 30	$40,000–60,000 / 45	> $60,000 / 60	
Monthly Debt Payment Monthly Net Income	> 40% / 0	30–40% / 5	20–30% / 20	10–20% / 35	< 10% / 50	
Bank Relationship Checking/Saving	None / 0	Checking only / 30	Saving only / 30	Checking & Saving / 50	No answer / 0	
Major Credit Cards	None / 0	1 or more / 30	No answer / 0			
Credit History	Any derogatory within 7 yrs. / −10	No record / 0			Met obligated payments / 30	
Applicant's Age	< 50 yrs. / 5	> 50 yrs. / 25	No answer / 0			
Residence	Rent / 15	Own/Buying / 40	Own outright / 50	No answer / 15		
Residence Stability	< 1 yr. / 0	1–2 yrs. / 15	2–4 yrs. / 35	> 4 yrs. / 50	No answer / 0	
Job Stability	< 1 Yr. / 5	1–2 yrs. / 20	2–4 yrs. / 50	> 4 yrs. / 70	Unemployed / 5	Retired / 70

[a]Minimum score for automatic credit approval is 200; score for judgmental evaluation, 150 to 195; and score for automatic credit denial, less than 150. Sara Johnson's credit score is 155.

The loan officer has numerous grounds to deny credit. The applicant's credit history is inadequate, her local residence was established too recently, and she was employed too recently to establish job stability. Even if she were to get a cosigner, such as her employer, experience shows that many cosigners renege on their commitments. On the positive side, Sarah Johnson appears to be a hard worker who is the victim of circumstances resulting from her husband's death. It is also unlikely that anyone who puts almost 30 percent down on a new-model car is going to walk away from a debt. The bank will likely lose Sarah as a depositor if it denies the application. The resolution depends on the careful weighting of the costs and benefits. What would you recommend?

An Application: Indirect Lending. Indirect lending is an attractive form of consumer lending when a bank deals with reputable retailers. A retailer sells merchandise and takes the credit application when the consumer decides to finance the purchase. Because many firms do not have the resources to carry their receivables, they sell the loans to banks or other financial institutions. In most instances a bank analyzes the credit application and makes the credit decision. These loans are collectively referred to as dealer paper. Banks aggressively compete for paper originated by well-established automobile, mobile home, and furniture dealers.

Most banks involved in indirect lending provide a wide range of services to dealers in addition to buying their paper. Automobile dealers, for example, often finance their display inventory under floor plan arrangements. When the dealer sells a vehicle, the bank buys the paper and reduces the dealer's inventory loan by the loan value of the vehicle.

Dealers negotiate finance charges directly with their customers. A bank, in turn, agrees to purchase the paper at predetermined rates that vary with the default risk assumed by the bank, the quality of the assets sold, and the maturity of the consumer loan. A dealer normally negotiates a higher rate with the car buyer than the determined rate charged by the bank. This differential varies with competitive conditions but potentially represents a significant source of dealer profit.

Most indirect loan arrangements provide for dealer reserves that reduce the risk in indirect lending. The reserves are derived from the differential between the normal, or contract, loan rate and the bank rate and help protect the bank against customer defaults and refunds. Consumers make their loan payments directly to the bank. Instead of immediately giving up the dealer's share of interest, a bank retains the interest in reserve. The reserve is used to cover defaults and the unearned portion of the dealer's share of interest. If the dealer chooses to approve a loan at a rate below the predetermined rate set by the bank for a preferred customer, this negative interest earned also reduces the reserve. A bank refunds a dealer's share of the differential only after the reserve equals some minimum amount, normally a negotiated fraction of total loans purchased.

Consider the following example in Exhibit 22.8 using automobile dealer paper. The dealer charges a customer a 15 percent annual rate (1.25 percent monthly) to finance the purchase of an automobile for $8,000. The bank has evaluated the credit application, and the transaction qualifies for a discounted 12 percent rate. By agree-

Exhibit 22.8 The Role of Dealer Reserves in Indirect Lending: Automobile Paper

Terms of the Dealer Agreement:
  Bank buys dealer paper at a 12% rate. Dealer charges customers a higher rate, with 25% of difference allocated to a reserve.

Sample Automobile Loan:
Principal   = $8,000
Maturity   = 3 years, 36 monthly installments
Loan rate   = 15% annual rate
Monthly payment = $8,000/[(1/.0125) − (1/.0125(1.0125)^{36})] = $277.32

Allocation to the Dealer Reserve
Total interest expense to customer = $1,983.52
Total interest income for bank   =   1,565.72
Differential interest   = $ 417.80

75% allocated to dealer: 0.75(417.80) = $313.35
25% allocated to reserve: 0.25(417.80) = $104.45

Interest Refunds on Prepayments with Add-on Rates
  Loan is written on a precomputed basis, and bank accrues interest using "rule of 78s."[a]
Interest expense to customer = 0.09($8,000)(3) = $2,160
Interest income for the bank = 0.07($8,000)(3) =   1,680
Differential interest   = $ 480
75% allocated to dealer: 0.75($480) = $360
25% allocated to reserve: 0.25($480) =   120

End of Year	Interest Earned[a]	Total	Bank	Difference
1	54.96%	$1,187.14	$ 923.33	$263.81
2	33.33	719.33	559.94	159.99
3	11.71	252.93	196.73	56.20
	100.00%	$2,160.00	$1,680.00	$480.00

[a]Rule of 78s factors are 366/666, 222/666, and 78/666, respectively.

ment, the bank retains 25 percent of the interest differential and transfers 75 percent to the dealer's account. The loan is written for 3 years with 36 monthly payments of $277.32. The borrower pays $1,983.52 in total interest expense, of which $1,565.72 is credited to the bank, to yield 12 percent. Of the $417.80 interest differential, 75 percent is immediately allocated to the dealer, while 25 percent is retained in the reserve.

   The reserve serves primarily to cover charge-offs. If the borrower defaults on the loan, the bank reduces the reserve by the unpaid principal outstanding. This ultimately lowers the dealer's profits because the reserve must be replenished. The reserve also covers rebates of unearned interest. Suppose, for example, that the dealer charges the borrower a 9 percent add-on rate for 3 years and the bank discounts it at a 7 percent add-on rate. With add-on interest, a lender receives some unearned interest if the borrower prepays. Interest rebates are commonly calculated according to the rule of 78s, which determines the fraction of total interest to be refunded at a point in time prior to maturity.[8] Applicable rebate percentages at the end of each year are determined at the bottom of Exhibit 22.8 in the second column, assuming 36 monthly payments. If a 3-year loan is prepaid after 2 years, 11.71 percent of the interest is unearned (88.29 percent is earned). If, in this example, a borrower prepays the entire loan after 2 years and the bank takes interest into income by the sum of the digits method, the bank must rebate $252.93 to the customer at the 9 percent add-on rate. Because the bank earns interest at the 7 percent add-on rate, its unearned interest income equals only $196.73 after 2 years. The $56.20 difference between the rebate amount and unearned bank interest would be charged against the reserve. The rule of 78s incorporates a charge for the borrower having a prepayment option. It penalizes borrowers by assuming that earned interest is greater than that actually generated on a loan's outstanding principal. For short-term loans, however, the error is small.

There are many different reserve agreements, the most common being full-recourse and no recourse arrangements. As the name suggests, full-recourse agreements place the dealer at risk. If a borrower defaults, the dealer absorbs the loss by either reducing the reserve at the bank or paying off the note on the bank's terms. No-recourse agreements, in contrast, stipulate that banks assume the credit risk. All losses are charged directly against bank earnings. Finally, some reserve arrangements involve limited recourse. A bank may negotiate a plan whereby dealers are liable for any losses only during the first 3 months of the loan. While these losses are immediately charged to the reserve, later losses are absorbed by the bank. The above example represents a full-recourse arrangement.

Banks prefer to deal with well-established retailers that generate paper of predictable quality. Banks vary the predetermined discount rate according to the dealer's reputation and the nature of the recourse agreement. They charge lower rates under full-recourse plans because they assume less credit risk. Dealers that have the capability to assess credit quality prefer these arrangements because their profits are potentially greater. Under no-recourse arrangements, banks charge higher rates and review each application carefully, as if the loan were a direct one.

RECENT RISK AND RETURN CHARACTERISTICS OF CONSUMER LOANS

Historically, banks differentiated among themselves as being either wholesale or retail institutions, focusing on commercial and individual customers, respectively. Recent developments, however, have blurred the distinction, as traditional wholesale banks have aggressively entered the consumer market. The attraction is twofold. First,

---

[8]According to the rule of 78s, the applicable rebate percentage equals the sum of the integers from one to the number of payments remaining after prepayment, divided by the sum of integers from one to the total number of payments in the loan. The number 78 equals the sum of integers 1 through 12 and thus serves as the denominator for rebate fractions on all 1-year, monthly payment loans. For example, a 1-year loan with 12 monthly payments that is prepaid after the seventh month produces a rebate percentage of $(1 + 2 + 3 + 4 + 5)/(1 + 2 + \ldots + 12) = 19.23$ percent. The lender would take 80.77 percent of the finance charge and rebate 19.23 percent to the borrower.

competition for commercial customers narrowed commercial loan yields so that returns fell relative to potential risks. As indicated earlier, consumer loans now provide some of the highest net yields for banks. Second, developing loan and deposit relationships with individuals presumably represents a strategic response to deregulation. The removal of interest rate ceilings substantially reduced banks' core deposits by making high-balance customers more price sensitive. Individuals, on average, hold small balances and move deposit accounts less frequently, providing a more stable deposit base. Thus, liquidity risk declines as a bank's retail deposit base increases.

Revenues from Consumer Loans

Banks earn significant revenues from interest on loans and associated fees. Since many usury ceilings have been eliminated or are no longer effective, banks can ration credit via price rather than by altering nonprice credit terms. This permits banks to quickly raise consumer loan rates as conditions require. When conditions permit, banks also delay lowering rates when their borrowing costs decline.

Consumer loan rates have been among the highest gross rates quoted at banks in recent years. Most consumer loans are made at fixed rates that banks do not change frequently. Exhibit 22.9 documents changes in the spread between various consumer loan rates and the prime rate in the 1980s. The federal funds rate indicates general movements in short-term market rates over the same period. During 1980 and 1981, the spread was negative, reflecting restrictive usury ceilings. After 1981 the spread widened evidencing banks' ability to raise consumer loan rates relative to prime. Notice the general pattern that the credit card rate spread widens when the level of rates declines and declines briefly when rates rise. This occurs because credit card rates do not change with any frequency. One interesting implication is that consumers are not sensitive to price such that credit card loan rates follow bank funding costs with a long lag.

Consumer groups routinely argue that consumer loan rates are too high, especially when the prime rate declines. They claim that lenders must be conspiring to fix prices. There are many reasons for large spreads, however. First, consumer loans are typically smaller in size and thus cost more to administer on a unit basis than commercial loans. Still, to eliminate "excess" profits that banks might earn when rates fall and the spread widens, noninterest costs from handling consumer loans would have to increase. There is no reason this would occur. Second, consumer loans are longer-term and often carry fixed rates. New car loans, for example, now average 4 years until maturity. Banks include a premium in longer-term, fixed-rate loans to compensate for the risks of inflation and volatile funding costs. Third, individuals are more likely to default than are businesses. The spread should be large enough to cover greater losses. Finally, many lenders still face state usury ceilings that may not be lifted when rates increase. These banks essentially make up for reduced profits during high-rate environments by keeping loan rates high when their financing costs fall.

The simple truth, however, is that competition should determine prices so that market rates reflect the cost of providing the service plus a normal profit. In reality, the market for consumer loans is not nearly as competitive as the market for commer-

**Exhibit 22.9 Consumer Loan Rates and Prime Rate:
Quarterly Averages, 1982–1990**

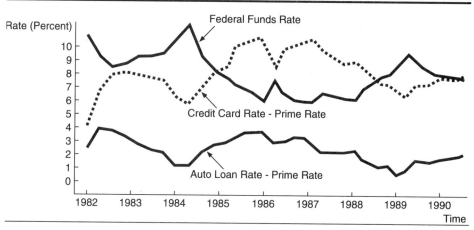

Source: Federal Reserve Bulletin.

cial loans. Banks have successfully forced individuals to be full-service customers of single institutions. They charge higher rates to customers who do not have an existing relationship with the bank and simultaneously discount selected prices to customers who purchase a wide range of products from their institution. Individuals would consequently have to move their entire banking relationship to take advantage of lower loan rates elsewhere or, alternatively, be able to afford several banking relationships.

More importantly, individuals as a group are not price sensitive. For example, the difference in monthly interest on a $6,000 loan for 4 years at 1 percent versus 1.5 percent monthly is only $18. This is too small for many borrowers to care about, especially after taxes. In addition, surveys indicate that consumers generally borrow via credit cards expecting to repay the loan in full before interest is due. Many are unable to do so consistently. This repayment illusion enhances bank returns.

Rate insensitivity is especially prevalent with credit cards. Using charge cards has become a way of life for many, with convenience and prestige valued more than financing costs.[9] Many analysts believe that consumer loan rates will not vary substantially until consumers learn to shop around for lower rates.[10] Still, the entrance of Sears with its Discover card and AT&T with its Universal card has shaken banks because of the cards' wide acceptance. Both are priced at a discount. Discover charges no annual

---

[9]This fact was borne out when American Express introduced its ultraprestigious Platinum Card. Membership cost $250 instead of $65 as for the Gold Card, yet the services offered were essentially the same except for greater insurance coverage and access to selected private clubs. American Express raised the costs to $300 and $75, respectively, in 1990 with virtually no reaction from cardholders. At what price prestige?

[10]Approximately one-half of the states impose ceilings on credit card interest rates. Many, however, are not effective because the ceilings are quite high, such as New Jersey's 30 percent. This has increased pressure for a federally mandated ceiling rate. The Federal Reserve Board is currently experimenting with a program to publish loan rates at competing banks, thrifts, credit unions, and finance companies in local markets to see if increased consumer awareness puts pressure on lenders to lower rates without more regulation.

fee and pays a 1 percent rebate on all purchases. AT&T introduced its card with a guarantee that the cardholder would never have to pay an annual fee. The card can also be used to charge telephone calls at a 10 percent discount. In 1991, various retailers challenged the fees paid American Express protesting that they were excessive at 3-4 percent. This started a chain reaction by AMEX to meet competitive pressures, because VISA and MasterCard fees averaged 1.5 percent.

In addition to interest income, banks generate substantial noninterest revenues from consumer loans. With traditional installment credit, banks often encourage borrowers to purchase credit life insurance on which the bank may earn premium income. Credit card operations also provide different types of fee income. Most banks now impose annual fees, ranging from $20 to $40 per customer, for the right to use the card and for access to related bank services. The customer essentially receives a line of credit with travel-related services, debit card privileges, and merchandise discounts also available. Banks bill cardholders monthly and expect the customer to repay the debt on a revolving credit basis with minimum payments equal to 5 percent of the outstanding balance. Historically, customers have had the option to repay the entire balance within a specified grace period, such as 25 days, and avoid any interest. Experience during the early 1980s demonstrated that approximately one-third of all customers took advantage of this interest-free period. Many banks have eliminated this option by charging interest on each transaction from the date of posting. Banks often impose other fees for late payments and cash advances.

Consumer Loan Losses

Losses on consumer loans are normally the highest among all categories of bank credit. This reflects highly cyclical patterns in personal income as well as extensive fraud. Losses are anticipated because of mass marketing efforts pursued by many lenders, particularly with credit cards. In 1989, consumer credit card losses amounted to an estimated $4.3 billion, of which 80 percent represented outright defaults and 20 percent fraud. By mid-1990, almost 4.5 percent of outstanding credit card balances were more than 30 days past due. Both losses and delinquent accounts rise during recessions and decline during high-growth periods. Many lenders simply factor losses into their pricing as a part of doing business.[11]

Credit card fraud arises out of the traditional lender/merchant relationship. In most cases, a bank gives merchants credit for sales long before it is reimbursed by cardholders. In 1989 the estimated time lag between the transaction date and reimbursement to the bank averaged 45 days. This allows fraudulent merchants to set up a temporary operation, bill card-issuing banks for bogus sales, and escape with the proceeds before cardholders recognize billing errors.

To perpetrate the fraud, thieves need access to a retail business and cardholder account information. Frequently, the business front is nothing more than a telephone-based mail-order operation. Callers tell cardholders that they have won prizes but must

---

[11]See Merwin (1985). Peterson (1985) provides a detailed analysis of issues related to pricing consumer loans and individual transaction accounts.

provide account numbers, expiration dates, and billing addresses to collect. Alternatively, thieves can obtain credit card information by stealing credit cards or by copying information from carbons of card charges at legitimate businesses. Thieves use the information to make purchases or receive cash advances during the 45-day lag period. Unsuspecting cardholders eventually discover that fraudulent charges appear on their monthly statements. By the time the card-issuing bank recognizes the fraud, the thief has closed down the business and moved on. Default rates at major card issuers across the United States ranged from 2.1 to 4.7 percent in 1989 (see Contemporary Issues: Variable-Rate Credit Cards).

Interest Rate and Liquidity Risk with Consumer Credit

The majority of consumer loans are priced at fixed rates. New auto loans typically carry 4-year maturities, and credit card loans exhibit an average 15- to 18-month maturity. In most cases, the borrower can prepay a loan without any penalty when rates decline. This creates difficult problems in trying to match-fund the consumer portfolio.

Bankers have responded in two ways. First, they price more consumer loans on a floating-rate basis. Such policies have been relatively successful in the mortgage market but require substantial discounts below fixed-rate loans to attract interest. Second, commercial and investment banks have created a secondary market in consumer loans that allows loan originators to sell a package of loans with longer-term holding periods to investors. The first efforts appeared in early 1985 when Marine Midland Bank, in conjunction with Salomon Brothers, sold automobile loans to secondary market investors. Salomon Brothers sold the loans in the form of collateralized securities, conveniently labeled *certificates of automobile receivables (CARs)*. As with mortgage banking operations, Marine Midland agreed to service the loans, for which it receives servicing income. Banks now routinely sell certificates supported by credit card receivables and other consumer credit as a means of moving assets off the balance sheet, reducing capital requirements, and increasing noninterest income.

SUMMARY

Commercial banks aggressively compete for consumer loans for a variety of reasons. In recent years, net yields on consumer loans have exceeded those on commercial loans. Default rates are above those on other loans, but the gross yield charged more than compensates for the higher losses. When rates decline, net profits on credit card and other fixed-rate loans rise sharply because consumer loan rates are relatively sticky. Individuals also typically maintain deposit accounts where they borrow. Retail deposits are relatively low cost and not nearly as interest rate sensitive as commercial deposits. Thus liquidity risk is reduced the greater is the volume of consumer deposits at a bank. Consumer loans, however, exhibit greater interest rate risk than commercial loans. Most are fixed-rate loans, and many carry 3- to 5-year maturities. If rates rise, the net interest earned declines.

CONTEMPORARY ISSUES

Variable-Rate Credit Cards

Politicians and some consumers routinely criticize banks for raising loan rates too quickly when interest rates increase in general, but not lowering loan rates when interest rates fall. This is particularly true with consumer credit. For example, regardless of movements in federal funds and the prime rate, credit card rates generally remain around 20 percent.

Banks respond by pointing out that both the cost of making consumer loans and consumer loan losses are high. Exhibit 22.2 demonstrates that credit card losses in 1989 represented 2 to 5 percent of outstanding loans. Nominal rates have to be high to compensate for the large losses.

Some banks have responded to the criticisms by introducing variable-rate credit cards. Rates generally change quarterly with changes in a bank's cost of funds. The most aggressive banks, however, have used variable-rate cards to attract affluent card users. These banks offer variable rates on premium cards that are set below the fixed rate on traditional credit cards. Loan losses on premium cards average under 1 percent, which justifies a lower rate. Premium card users tend to charge more with their cards and leave a larger unpaid balance. They are also considerably more price sensitive. Variable-rate premium cards thus reduce interest rate risk and help attract affluent customers.

Loan officers consider the same basic issues applicable to commercial loans when evaluating the riskiness of consumer loans: use of proceeds, size of loan, cash flow repayment sources, collateral, and the borrower's character. The fundamental difference is that personal financial statements are generally unaudited and it is more difficult to forecast net cash flow. Evaluation procedures may involve the subjective interpretation of financial information provided directly by an individual on a credit application and obtained indirectly from credit bureaus and references. Alternatively, banks may use credit scoring models based on a numerical assessment of a low-risk borrower's profile. This chapter introduces a basic credit scoring model and describes the risk and return features of various types of consumer loans, such as credit card transactions and the purchase of dealer paper.

Questions

Types of Loans

1. Give two reasons banks have switched their emphasis from commercial to consumer loans.

Installment Loans

2. Indicate whether each of the following would be a direct installment loan (D), an indirect installment loan (I), or neither (N). What institution is serving as the financial intermediary in each case?
   a. Borrowing from a bank to buy a TV
   b. Buying a car from a dealer who arranges financing through Citicorp

c. Buying a refrigerator from Sears who arranges its own financing
d. Buying new luggage using your MasterCard
e. Taking out a student loan
f. Buying a computer through your university and paying for it with monthly checks

3. From Exhibit 22.1, which size bank had the largest cost of making loans? How would you explain this?

4. Exhibits 22.1 and 22.4 provide data regarding consumer loan revenues and expenses in 1989. What are the major expenses associated with making consumer loans? Is there any pattern or relationship between loan losses, the business cycle, and a bank's cost of funds?

Revolving Credits

5. How does the risk differ for a revolving credit versus an installment loan?

6. Explain the differences among a credit card, debit card and smart card.

7. How does the default rate on credit cards, from Exhibit 22.2, compare with that of installment loans, from Exhibit 22.1? Which type of loan has proven more profitable after risk?

8. How does the profitability of credit cards compare to installment cards?

9. Overdraft loans are much more common in Europe than in the United States. What are they and why do Americans not need them?

10. What three uses do consumers usually make of home equity loans? Which is the most risky for the bank?

11. The Tax Reform Act of 1986 increased the appeal of home equity loans for many individuals. Explain why and describe how a bank ties home equity loans to a credit card.

12. Are premium credit cards worth the higher annual fee? What additional services do consumers get with a premium card?

Non-installment Loans

13. What use is the most commonly made of non-installment loans?

Credit Regulations

14. What are the key provision of the Equal Credit Opportunity Act? Why was such legislation necessary?

15. What is the goal of the Truth-in-Lending legislation and under what circumstances does it apply?

16. Calculate the effective annual rate on each of the following loans:
   a. a $5,000 loan for 2 years, with 10 percent simple annual interest and principal repayment at the end of the second year.
   b. a $5,000 loan for 2 years, with 10 percent add-on interest, paid in 24 equal monthly installments

c. $5,000 to be repaid at the end of 2 years, with a 10 percent discount rate

17. What is the goal of the Fair Credit Reporting Act?

18. What is the goal of the Community Reinvestment Act?

19. Explain the difference between a Chapter 7 and a Chapter 13 bankruptcy filing by an individual.

Credit Analysis

20. In addition to the 5 Cs of credit, bankers consider two additional Cs on consumer loans. What are they and why are they important?

21. Describe how a bank should apply an objective credit scoring model when evaluating consumer loan requests.

22. Discuss the difference between direct and indirect car loans. Is the bank's credit analysis the same?

23. What is the purpose of a dealer reserve in indirect lending? When is a bank at risk with indirect loans?

24. Dealer reserves in indirect lending serve to protect a bank against loan losses and prepayments. Suppose that a bank enters into an agreement with a used car dealer to buy dealer paper at a 6.5 percent add-on rate, and retain 30 percent of the interest differential relative to the rate the dealer charges the car buyer. Under the agreement, the bank charges losses and prepayments against the reserve, transferring any excess to the dealer periodically. Interest rebates on prepayments are computed according to the rule of 78s.

    Consider the case in which the dealer charges a customer a 9 percent add-on rate for the purchase of a $12,500 automobile to be financed over 36 months. Calculate the total interest expense to the customer, the bank's share, and the interest differential allocated to the dealer reserve. Suppose that the customer prepays the entire loan after 13 months. Determine how much interest the bank must rebate to the car buyer and any charge to the dealer reserve.

Activities

1. **Credit cards**

   Collect the following information on three currently advertised nationally advertised credit cards and three locally offered credit cards.
   a. the annual fee
   b. the interest rate and date effective
   c. any additional services

   Is there a pattern of differences between national and local cards? Which of the six cards appeals to you? Why? What combination of features suits your needs?

2. Consumer loans

Pick up three consumer loan applications at local banks. What variables are all three banks using in the loan decisions. Are there any variables that seem to be unique to a particular bank? How long does each bank suggest it would take to get a decision on a loan application?

FIRST FINANCIAL REVISITED:
THE IMPORTANCE OF CONSUMER LENDING

Analysis of First Financial's problems reveals that the bank had virtually no consumer business which is somewhat surprising in a branch banking environment. The bank had virtually no consumer deposits. These deposits are relatively low cost and interest-insensitive. Equally important is the fact that they represent a stable source of funds and thus reduce liquidity problems.

As indicated in the text, consumer loans also contribute strongly to bank profitability. Banks normally look to existing deposit customers to make consumer loans. The limited reliance on consumer deposits thus meant that First Financial had limited contact with consumer borrowers. One obvious policy change would be for First Financial to focus on the consumer in future years. It could use its branch system to compete for deposits and consumer loans. It might consider marketing a range of new consumer products, such as credit cards and senior citizens deposit accounts, to enhance its consumer contacts.

References

Alexander, Walter. "What's the Score?" *ABA Banking Journal* (August 1989).

Avery, Robert, et al. "Survey of Consumer Finances, 1983: A Second Report." *Federal Reserve Bulletin,* Board of Governors of the Federal Reserve System, Washington, D.C. (December 1984).

1989 Functional Cost Analysis, Board of Governors of the Federal Reserve System, Washington, D.C., 1990.

Garea, Raymond, and Gail Triner. "What's the Secret of Profitable Retail Banking?" *ABA Banking Journal* (April 1986).

Grablowsky, Bernie. "Credit Scoring: New Discriminant Methodology." *Journal of Consumer Credit Management* (Winter 1979).

Hilder, David, and Peter Pac. "Rivalry Rages among Big Credit Cards." *The Wall Street Journal* (May 3, 1991).

Kantrow, Yvette. "AT&T Card Judged Top 1990 Innovation." *American Banker* (December 17, 1990).

Maynor, James, and Paul Havemann. "Home Equity Loans: Does Everybody Win?" *Journal of Commercial Bank Lending* (November 1990).

Merwin, John. "How the Smart Cooks Use Plastic." *Forbes,* September 9, 1985.

Pavel, Christine, and Paula Binkley. "Costs and Competition in Bank Credit Cards." *Economic Perspectives* (March–April 1987).

Pearce, Douglas. "Rising Household Debt in Perspective." *Economic Review* (Federal Reserve Bank of Kansas City, July–August 1985).

Peterson, Richard. "Pricing Consumer Loans and Deposits." In *Handbook for Banking Strategy,* edited by Richard Aspinwall and Robert Eisenbeis, chapter 18. New York: John Wiley & Sons, 1985.

Saporito, Bill. "Melting Point in the Plastic War." *Fortune* (May 20, 1991).

White, Larry. "Credit Analysis: Two More Cs of Credit." *Journal of Commercial Bank Lending* (October 1990).

Chapter 23

Problem Loans and Loan Losses

How many times have you seen a bank report a substantial quarterly increase in provisions for loan losses that wipes out normal operating earnings? Management, often newly hired to replace previous managers who were in charge when the problems arose, announces that the loss provision represents a thorough "housecleaning" such that the loan portfolio is purged of all problems. Too frequently the bank underestimates the amount of problem loans and reports another large loss provision within 2 years. The net effect is that reported loan losses and earnings are highly volatile. Regulators and stock analysts, in turn, lose faith that management has control of the problems. Twice burned, market participants are generally skeptical about management pronouncements until future performance is consistently strong and the firm regains credibility.

How can credibility be restored? The answer is that bank managers have considerable flexibility in deciding when to recognize loan losses. Regulators routinely evaluate credit quality at banks through the examination process and may force minimum loss recognition. This typically happens after problem loans are apparent to the market, however, as regulatory exams occur at infrequent intervals. Historically, too many bankers have been overly optimistic about asset quality and thus systematically understated losses. A one-time increase in provisions for losses is essentially a recognition that earnings reported previously have been overstated. Unfortunately, dividend payouts have consequently been too large and the bank's capital position has worsened.

Net loan losses as a fraction of total loans at insured commercial banks increased from 0.1 percent to 1.2 percent from 1979 to 1990. These figures reflect many good loans made in inflationary times that converted to bad loans in a deflationary environment. They also include speculative loans that defaulted. As loan losses increased, bank regulators raised capital requirements, and the U.S. Congress eliminated special bad debt allowances for large institutions.

From 1969 to 1986 all commercial banks could use the reserve method when accounting for loan losses. This enabled banks with growing loan portfolios to take tax deductions for future loan losses in excess of actual current loss experience. However, deductions often exhibited no relationship to actual loss experience. The Tax Reform Act of 1986 forced all banks with more than $400 million in assets to base loan loss deductions on actual loss experience. Moreover, the Act required banks to recapture excess deductions taken in previous years, which continues to raise bank taxes.

The higher capital requirements and tax changes alter the way banks view problem loans and the cost of loan workouts because there is less incentive to enter a protracted workout situation. This chapter describes the tax and accounting treatment of loan losses, as well as indicators of problem loans and corrective actions and management issues associated with recognizing problem assets.

AN OVERVIEW OF LOAN LOSSES

Loans are classified as problem credits when they cannot be repaid according to the terms of the initial agreement or in an otherwise acceptable manner. Loans become problem credits as a result of many factors. The credit analysis may have been faulty because it was based on inadequate information or incomplete analytical procedures. Economic conditions may change adversely after the loan is granted so that the borrower cannot meet debt service requirements. Alternatively, a borrower may simply choose not to repay if circumstances permit. Problem loans and loan losses essentially reflect the default risk inherent in a borrower's willingness and ability to repay all obligations.

The lending process is, by its nature, imperfect. Credit analysis may be incomplete or based on faulty data, loan officers may ignore the true condition of a borrower with strong personal ties to the bank, and a borrower's ability to repay may simply change after a loan is granted. If management concentrates solely on minimizing losses, a bank will make virtually no loans, profits will shrink, and the legitimate credit needs of customers will not be met. Lenders cannot completely eliminate risk, so some loan losses are expected. The objective is to manage loss experience so that the bank can meet its risk and return targets.

The third stage of the credit process introduced in Chapter 20 is credit review. Review procedures help identify when loans start to deteriorate and how to institute corrective action. Most problem loans can be restructured to buy time until the borrower's financial condition improves. Problem loan analysis thus consists of detecting problem situations and modifying the initial terms to improve repayment prospects.

Loan officers constantly monitor each borrower's circumstances to detect loan problems before they become uncorrectable. Still, perceived loan quality often varies among those reviewers. Examiners from the regulatory agencies typically follow strict guidelines listed in review manuals. They appraise the quality of financial data, the borrower's credit history as outlined in the credit file, the completeness of loan documentation, and the value of collateral. If weaknesses exist, examiners may grade the loans as substandard, doubtful, loss, and "other specially mentioned." Banks then must allocate reserves against potential losses in varying percentages relative to the loan grading.

Many bankers feel that regulatory loan grading is too severe and ignores important information. Fully collateralized loans with the collateral in the bank's possession may be classified as substandard, for example, if the borrower's cash flow from operations is insufficient to meet debt service requirements. A bank may thus have to allocate additional reserves even when it controls a guaranteed source of repayment.

Measures of Loan Losses

When a loan ultimately proves to be uncollectable, a bank must charge it off. Such charge-offs reduce reserves for loan losses, lower reported profits, and decrease a bank's equity capital. The reduction in profits arises from adding to the reserve via provisions for loan losses. If these provisions are ordinary, and thus fully expected, earnings are not reduced unexpectedly. When the reserve is depleted by unanticipated losses, the profit decline is problematic. Such losses adversely affect liquidity by raising borrowing costs on purchased funds. To fully understand the data and implications, it is necessary to clarify terminology. The following terms are used to describe asset quality and loan losses.

Gross loan charge-offs: When a bank formally recognizes that a loan is uncollectable, it charges it off. In an accounting sense, it writes the loan off against its loss reserve by subtracting the dollar amount of the charge-off from the reserve. A loan is thus removed as an asset.

Recoveries: Recoveries represent actual cash receipts from loans that were previously charged off. Recoveries are added back to the loss reserve.

Net loan charge-offs: Gross loan charge-offs minus recoveries.

Provisions for loan losses: Provisions for loan losses is reported on the income statement as a deduction from income representing an allocation to the loan loss reserve. It is management's estimate of reported income that will not be received due to anticipated defaults. It is a noncash expense.

Loss reserve: The loan loss reserve is a contra-asset on the balance sheet and represents the cumulative provisions for loan losses minus net loan charge-offs. The loss reserve appearing on the balance sheet is formally labeled the valuation reserve. Regulators treat a portion of the loss reserve as capital for capital adequacy purposes.

Nonaccrual loans: With accrual accounting banks record interest and principal payments on loans as if they have been received regardless of whether any cash payment is actually made. Loans that banks have put on a cash basis are labeled nonaccrual loans, and payments are recorded only when actually received.

Past-due loans: Loans in which the borrower is delinquent at least 90 days in making obligated interest and principal payments.

Restructured loans: Loans in which the lender renegotiates terms and makes concessions to the borrower in the form of a lower rate, longer maturity, or reduced principal owed.

**Exhibit 23.1 Loan Loss, Loss Reserve, and Nonperforming
Loan Experience by Size of Bank: December 1990**

Bank Asset Size	Loss Provision Average Loans	Net Charge–offs Average Loans	Loss Reserve Average Loans	Loss Reserve Nonaccrual Loans
< $50 Million	0.45	0.39	1.48	2.05×
$50–$100 Million	0.55	0.41	1.41	2.07×
$100–$500 Million	0.69	0.53	1.51	1.53×
$500–$1,000 Million	0.76	0.61	1.55	1.43×
$1–$3 Billion	1.06	0.79	1.75	1.16×
$3–$10 Billion	1.65	1.08	2.22	1.05×
> $10 Billion	1.41	1.67	2.73	0.85×

Real estate owned: Real estate acquired by the lender in settlement of a loan default.

The above descriptions raise questions about how problem loans, evidenced by the last four categories, and loan losses are recognized. Foremost is the fact that provisions for loan losses is a subjective estimate. It can be manipulated at management's discretion within certain bounds. If provisions are understated, the loss reserve will be too low relative to expected losses. In addition, when is a loan truly past due? Suppose an interest payment is 80 days past due, so the bank lends the borrower the proceeds to make the payment. The bank reports the interest as income and does not recognize the loan as past due. Is this reasonable? A well-known saying is "A rolling loan gathers no loss." The lack of rigid criteria makes it difficult to evaluate asset quality and compare performance between banks over the short run.[1]

Exhibits 23.1 and 23.2 summarize recent loan loss experience at different size U.S. banks at year-end 1990 and by type of loan at all banks from 1982 to 1990. According to these figures, loss provisions generally increased as a fraction of total loans with size. Banks with assets over $3 billion charged off more than twice the proportions of loans of banks under $1 billion. Interestingly, the largest banks reported the highest loss reserves as a fraction of loans, but these reserves actually represented the smallest fraction of nonaccrual loans. The implication is that the largest banks appear to have the lowest-quality loan portfolios, on average. The figures for banks under $100 million similarly indicate more problems than larger banks.

Exhibit 23.2 further indicates that past-due loans were relatively stable from 1982 through 1990 for all but other loans to foreign governments and depository institutions, which rose sharply in 1987 and have remained high. Although not reported in the exhibit, past-due real estate loans increased sharply in 1991 to where they exceeded problem loans in any other category. Contemporary Issues: Troubled Real Estate Asset Rates by State indicates the extent of problem real estate loans at banks in 1990 by state.

---

[1] In a 1990 survey, Bailey noted that banks over $20 billion in assets accounted for nonaccrual loans, foreclosures, and adjustments in value or reserves for other real estate owned far differently than smaller banks.

Exhibit 23.2 Trends in Past-Due Loans and Net Charge-Offs by Type of Loan: 1982–1990

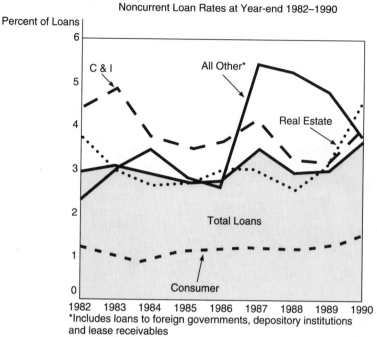

Noncurrent Loan Rates at Year-end 1982–1990

*Includes loans to foreign governments, depository institutions and lease receivables

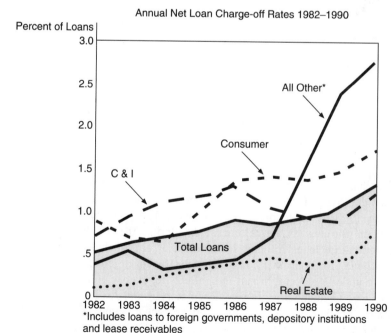

Annual Net Loan Charge-off Rates 1982–1990

*Includes loans to foreign governments, depository institutions and lease receivables

Troubled Real Estate Asset Rates by State, December 30, 1990[a]

The percentages indicate the value of past-due real estate loans plus other real estate owned (OREO) divided by total real estate loans plus OREO.

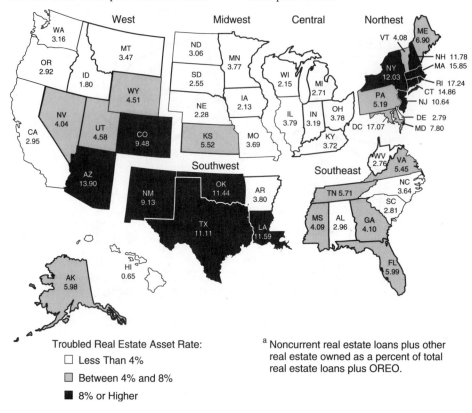

Troubled Real Estate Asset Rate:

☐ Less Than 4%

▦ Between 4% and 8%

■ 8% or Higher

[a] Noncurrent real estate loans plus other real estate owned as a percent of total real estate loans plus OREO.

Source: The FDIC Quarterly Banking Profile, FDIC, Fourth Quarter, 1990.

The bottom chart in Exhibit 23.2 demonstrates that net charge-offs generally followed the past-due loans. Except for commercial and industrial loans, net charge-offs rose through 1990 as economic growth slowed. The data do not isolate the dramatic change in fortunes at agriculture banks during the 1980s. In 1986 net charge-offs on agriculture loans reached 2.2 percent, or almost three times the next highest charge-off rate for consumer loans. By 1990 net charge-offs on agriculture loans had fallen to under 1 percent. In part this reflects regulatory policy to assist U.S. agriculture banks (see Contemporary Issues: Regulatory Relief for Farm Lenders).

The remainder of this chapter examines management strategies for handling problem loans and loan losses. It initially focuses on the financial reporting and tax

Regulatory Relief for Farm Lenders

Many of the nation's agriculture banks have experienced large loan losses with the decline in land values and farmers' inability to meet obligated debt payments. Roughly 40 percent of all failed banks from 1984 to 1986 were agriculture banks. This has created considerable uncertainty for the remaining agriculture banks and their borrowers regarding the availability of financing.

In March 1986 bank regulatory agencies announced a plan of capital forbearance. The purpose was to buy time until farmers and banks could strengthen their operations and loan portfolios. The plan consisted of two key provisions. First, banks experiencing difficulties would be allowed to operate with capital below the 6 percent regulatory minimum if they could demonstrate the capacity

to reach the minimum within 5 years. Second, regulators allowed banks to not charge off restructured loans if they could show that reduced interest payments or longer maturities produced a reasonable expectation of repayment.

Clearly, this plan has lowered the number of banks that would have been forced to cease operations and encouraged continued farm lending. The risk, however, is that problem banks will gamble by continuing to lend to high-risk farmers with limited repayment prospects. Bank failures may only be postponed, with greater long-term costs. This plan did represent the only short-term solution to preventing large-scale defaults and making credit available to farmers.

---

treatment of loan losses and the function of the loan loss reserves. It then outlines procedures for controlling loan losses through implementing loan policy guidelines, monitoring early detection signals, and collecting on problem loans.

TAX TREATMENT AND FINANCIAL REPORTING OF BANK LOAN LOSSES

Regulators have pressured many banks to increase their loss reserves in recent years because of the widespread growth in problem loans. This pressure results from a general perception that bank asset quality is lower than that suggested by historical loss experience and reported earnings. This increase in reserves results from greater loan loss provisions, which lowers reported net income. Increasing reserves carries a negative connotation because it lowers reported earnings. According to regulatory guidelines, a bank with low reserves and low capital cannot pay the amount of dividends they would prefer. Reserves are beneficial because they must be sufficient to cover net charge-offs, and a portion is included in the regulatory definition of capital.

When a bank reports high provisions for loan losses, high loss reserves and higher profits, it has the best of both worlds. It is improving its ability to absorb future losses, yet demonstrating improved performance over previous years. A substantial increase in reported losses, however, creates a perception that future losses will be extensive and the loss reserve might be inadequate. A bank's ability to pay dividends increases in the first situation and decreases in the second, with its share price following.

The Tax Treatment of Loan Losses

Historically, the size of a bank's loan loss reserve and allowable tax deductions have not necessarily reflected actual loss experience. The Tax Reform Act of 1986 changed the tax treatment of large banks' loss reserves to correct this.

From 1969 to 1986, banks could choose either the reserve method or the direct charge-off method for reporting losses. Virtually all banks used the reserve method because it allowed them to report greater tax deductions than the direct charge-off method and thus reduced their tax liability. The Tax Reform Act restricted this choice to banks with no more than $400 million in assets or those with problem loans equal to 75 percent or more of capital. Since 1987, all other banks must use the direct charge-off method. Moreover, banks that previously used the reserve method but were no longer eligible had to recapture excess deductions taken in prior years. They simultaneously lost a tax shelter and saw their tax liability increase with no corresponding increase in cash inflows.

Under the reserve method, banks establish a bad debt or loss reserve that meets Internal Revenue Service (IRS) specifications. Loans that are recognized as uncollectable during a taxable year are charged against the reserve. Recoveries from previously charged off loans are added back to the reserve. At the end of each reporting period, banks can take a tax deduction for additions to the reserve that would restore it to an appropriate level.

The size of the allowable tax reserve is determined as a percentage of qualifying loans. The percentage varies across banks and is based on each bank's historical loss experience. Under regulation, additions to the reserve are limited to the greater of an amount equal to the average ratio of net charge-offs to total loans over the most recent 6 years (the experience percentage) times year-end total loans, or an amount sufficient to bring the reserve to its base level at the beginning of the tax year.

Exhibit 23.3 demonstrates the tax computation. Under this procedure, the allowable loss reserve is determined by the size of the loan portfolio and actual loss experience. The base figure is total loans and the applicable reserve percentage equals the average ratio of net charge-offs to total loans outstanding at the end of each of the previous 6 tax years. At the end of 1990, the maximum loss reserve equaled $1,528,000 as determined by the loss ratio of 0.443 percent times $345 million in loans. During 1991 total loans increased by $65 million while the average loss ratio declined to 0.42 percent so that the allowable year-end reserve equals $1.722 million. The maximum transfer to the loss reserve, which represents the maximum tax deduction, is determined by subtracting loan losses of $1.27 million from the initial reserve, adding back $0.21 million in recoveries, and determining what addition is necessary to bring the reserve back up to its maximum allowable value of $1.722 million. In this case, net charge-offs reduce the reserve to $0.468 million, so the allowable transfer equals $1.254 million. As noted, this also represents the maximum allowable tax deduction. Note that it exceeds actual net charge-offs during the year ($1.06 million) because the loan portfolio grew at

Exhibit 23.3 Loan Loss Tax Treatment under the Experience Method for Reserves at Banks with $400 Million or Less in Total Assets[a]

	December 31, 1990		December 31, 1991
Total loans	$345.000		$410.000
Ratio of net charge-offs to total loans[b]	0.443%		0.420%
Maximum reserve	$ 1.528		$ 1.722
Loan charge-offs, 1991		1.270	
Recoveries, 1991		0.210	
Net charge-offs, 1991		$1.060	
Adjusted loss reserve	$ 0.468		
Maximum tax deduction $1.722 − $0.468 = $1.254			

[a] All figures are in millions of dollars.

[b] Average over the past 6 years.

a relatively high rate.[2] This method of determining tax deductions favors fast-growing banks with worsening loan losses.

Large Banks and Loan Losses. Banks with total assets of more than $400 million or smaller banks that are part of a holding company with at least $400 million in assets must use the direct charge-off method for reporting loan losses. Under this procedure, a bank can deduct only its actual net losses as incurred during the current reporting period. If the bank in Exhibit 23.3 reported losses in this manner, it would take a tax deduction of just $1.06 million, its net charge-offs for the year. Large banks can no longer use the loss reserve as a tax shelter.

Beginning in 1987 large banks were also required to add amounts in their loss reserves from prior years to taxable income when determining their tax liability. This represents a recapture of excess deductions for additions to the loss reserve in prior years. The total reserve must be recognized as income over 5 years but still represents a direct cost because tax obligations rise with no offsetting cash inflows. The aggregate effect on the banking industry is an estimated $4 billion increase in taxes.

Financial Reporting of Loan Losses

Tax law allows banks to take deductions for funds transferred to the loss reserve. Historically, the allowable reserve has been large enough so that funds transfers normally exceed losses. Not surprisingly, most banks transfer the maximum amount permitted in order to reduce taxes by the largest amount.

Notice, however, that no mention has been made of provisions for loan losses. Tax accounting differs from book accounting as banks can report different sets of reserve and loss figures to the IRS and to shareholders. According to generally accepted

[2] A deduction in excess of actual charge-offs represents a deduction for future loan losses. The Internal Revenue Service limits the amount of the excess in any given year. A portion of this excess deduction is also included as a tax preference item under the corporate minimum tax.

accounting principles, banks must report reserves for possible losses, labeled *valuation reserves,* as a contra-asset account representing a deduction from gross loans on the balance sheet. Actual loan losses are deducted from this reserve, and recoveries are credited to the reserve. If net charge-offs exceed the valuation reserve, a bank cannot use the full amount of losses in determining the allowable tax deduction. During each accounting period, banks report an expense item, *provisions for loan losses,* as a deduction from operating income on the income statement. The amount of provisions actually reported affects the size of the valuation reserve, which changes by the amount that provisions for loan losses exceed net charge-offs.

The accounting treatment is shown in Exhibit 23.4 using the data from the previous exhibit. In the example, the valuation reserve equals $1.4 million at the end of 1990. The bank reports provisions for loan losses of $1.2 million on its income statement, which is $54,000 less than it reported to the IRS. Thus $1.2 million of the total tax deduction is allocated to the valuation reserve which replenishes the reserve after the net charge-offs deplete the reserve to $340,000. The amount appearing on the bank's balance sheet as a contra-asset account rises from $1.4 million to $1.54 million, with the $0.14 difference equal to provisions minus net charge-offs.

The critical management decision is to determine what level of valuation reserve is appropriate. In practice, each bank subjectively evaluates the quality of its loan portfolio and assigns a value to the valuation reserve. Ideally, the amount in the reserve should be enough to cover potential loan losses over the entire life of the outstanding loans. It is difficult to determine the correct size of the valuation reserve because it is difficult to predict loan defaults accurately. At this juncture, regulators' views often clash with bank management's views. Regulators prefer that the banks err by overestimating potential losses. This guarantees that valuation reserves will exceed actual loss experience. Thus regulators often appear strict in classifying lower-quality loans and mandating reserve allocations. Banks, in contrast, often prefer to report the lowest possible reserve that still protects against losses because this provides the highest possible reported net income.

The size of the valuation reserve normally falls short of the total reserve for tax purposes because banks do not report the entire transfer to reserves allowed by the IRS. Accounting rules thus recognize three reserves for reporting purposes: the valuation reserve, the contingency reserve, and the deferred tax reserve. As described earlier, transfers to the valuation reserve must be reported on financial statements. Actual net losses can be charged only against this reserve. The contingency and deferred tax reserves represent transfers in excess of provisions for loan losses that reduce federal income taxes. The amount that represents a tax saving, equal to the bank's marginal tax rate times the excess deduction $(0.34 \times \$1.254 - \$1.2)$, is allocated to the deferred tax reserve. The residual amount that would have represented retained earnings if the tax deduction did not exceed reported provisions is allocated to the contingency reserve.

Analyzing the Adequacy of Valuation Reserves. As shown, banks report only the valuation portion of loan loss reserves on their balance sheets. The amount in this reserve is subjectively determined by estimating probable charge-offs as of the state-

Exhibit 23.4 Financial Reporting of Loan Losses Using Data from Exhibit 23.3

Changes in Valuation Reserve	Millions of Dollars
1. Balance reported on December 31, 1990	$1.400
2. Plus: Recoveries in 1991	+0.210
3. Minus: Gross loan charge-offs in 1991	−1.270
Adjusted loss reserve	$0.340
4. Plus: Provisions for loan losses	+1.200
5. Balance reported on December 31, 1991	$1.540
6. Change in valuation reserve	0.140

ment date. While regulators and accountants are also involved in the estimation process, bank management largely establishes the final reserve value. This judgmental assessment thus produces wide variances in reported reserves between institutions.

One analyst has developed a series of ratios to help evaluate the adequacy of a bank's valuation reserve.[3] The ratios include three summary measures and several supplementary measures. The most commonly cited ratio, valuation reserves divided by total loans, directly compares the size of the reserve as a percentage of loans. The ratio has two weaknesses. It ignores off-balance sheet loan risk, such as that inherent in financial guarantees, and it indicates nothing about the quality of the existing loan portfolio. An analyst should compare the reserve to net charge-offs and nonperforming loans as approximate measures of loan quality. Presumably, there is some substitution between charge-offs and nonperforming loans because management can often manipulate the timing of charge-offs. If so, nonperforming loans will likely be high when charge-offs are low, and vice versa.

The adequacy of individual bank reserves can be assessed by comparing specific bank reserve measures with industry norms. Exhibit 23.5 compares measures for Continental Illinois and Wachovia Corp. just prior to Continental's restructuring in 1984. It is well known that Wachovia manages a conservative credit portfolio. Every ratio suggests that Continental Illinois was underreserved in general, and relative to Wachovia. Valuation reserves were a smaller fraction of total loans, net charge-offs, and nonperforming loans by a considerable amount. Net charge-offs to total loans was 4.5 times greater. Implicitly, Continental Illinois systematically understated its provisions for loan losses and thus overstated periodic earnings. Wachovia, in contrast, reported a significantly greater valuation reserve but lower losses, fewer nonperforming loans, and greater recoveries. Wachovia's conservative management appears to have systematically understated earnings relative to actual losses. The quality of assets is better than prior provisions suggested.

The supplementary ratios further support the direct comparison and provide evidence of Continental Illinois' deteriorating performance. Both net charge-offs and nonperforming loans rose in 1983 relative to the prior 4 years, while recoveries fell. Loan growth was high, as were unfunded commitments on standby letters of credit.

---

[3]See Cates (1985).

Exhibit 23.5 Adequacy of Loan Loss Reserves for Two Bank Holding Companies

	Continental Illinois	Wachovia Corp.
Summary Ratios		
1983 Valuation reserve divided by:		
Year-end loans	1.2%	1.4%
Net charge-offs	1.0x[a]	13.5x[a]
Nonperforming loans	15.0	72.0
Supplementary Ratios		
Net charge-offs to loans, 1983	1.2	0.1
Net charge-offs to loans, 1980–1983	0.9	0.2
Recoveries to charge-offs, 1983	10.2	48.4
Recoveries to charge-offs, 1980–1983	12.9	29.9
Retail loans to total loans	7.0	39.0
Nonretail loan growth, 1980–1983	22.0	10.0
Standby letters of credit to loans	18.0	4.0
Nonperforming loans to total loans, 1983	8.0	2.0
Nonperforming loans to total loans, 1980–1983	5.9	1.4
Loans to earning assets	88.0	62.0
Earnings coverage of net charge-offs	1.3x[a]	31.5x[a]

[a] x signifies a "times" ratio.

Source: Cates Bancompare I reports; "What's An Adequate Loan-Loss Reserve?" *ABA Banking Journal,* March, 1985.

Finally, Continental operated with a higher percentage of loans to earning assets yet earned less relative to loan charge-offs.[4] Thus the adequacy of reserves is reflected over time by comparing actual reserves to average losses and observing whether a consistent buffer exists.

Substandard, Doubtful, Loss, and Other Specially Mentioned Loans

Examiners periodically evaluate bank asset quality by reviewing actual loans that are on a bank's books. They determine whether the borrower has capacity to borrow, whether the appropriate documents have been accurately recorded and filed, and whether the cash flow or repayment source supporting the loan is sufficient to meet debt service requirements. Based on their analysis, examiners classify loans into categories that reflect the likelihood of loss. The problem categories are substandard, doubtful, and loss with the probability of loss increasing from the first to third category. When assessing the adequacy of the valuation reserve and a bank's capital base, examiners calculate an estimated loan loss equal to fixed percentages times the loan amounts in each category. For example, using loss estimates of 20, 50, and 100 percent, respectively, examiners would compare

$$\text{estimated loss} = 0.2(\text{substandard loans}) + 0.5(\text{doubtful loans}) + 1.0(\text{loss loans})$$

[4] A complete analysis would also recognize the importance of foreign loans and regulatory loan classifications, if available.

with the sum of the period-ending valuation reserve and equity capital. If the estimated loss exceeds the base, the bank is clearly deficient in allocating reserves because it has understated provisions for loan losses. Regulators would thus mandate increased provisions and require the bank to obtain more equity capital.

It is extremely important to consider data over a long time interval when evaluating the adequacy of loss reserves and the treatment of problem assets. Data can be manipulated in the short run. A bank that reports high profits because it understates provisions for loan losses is simply deferring the time until it recognizes the losses and lower profits. A time series of reported provisions, nonperforming loans, the loss reserve, and net loan charge-offs relative to average loans will reveal whether management is relatively conservative in reporting loan problems. If it is conservative, there will be no extraordinary blips in the ratios because there are no surprises. Recoveries will also be a relatively large fraction of net charge-offs because management recognizes bad assets before they become too problematic.

CONTROLLING LOAN LOSSES THROUGH EARLY DETECTION

Loan losses are a natural by-product of extending credit. Bank management cannot forecast with perfect accuracy which loans will be paid in a timely manner. Otherwise, no bad loans would be made without some form of fraud. Still, management can pursue policies that limit problem loans. This section examines procedures for controlling loan losses. It describes the typical causes of problem loans, procedures to prevent making loans with high default risk, and signals of loans that are deteriorating in quality.

Causes of Problem Loans

Problem loans and loan losses are caused by a variety of factors, some controllable and some uncontrollable. Controllable factors are those that reflect overall bank credit policy as well as inadequate credit analysis, loan structuring, and loan documentation. Uncontrollable factors typically reflect adverse economic conditions, adverse changes in regulations, environmental changes surrounding the borrower's operations, and catastrophic events. While there is little that can be done to prevent uncontrollable problems, effective credit-granting procedures can significantly reduce other sources of losses.

Problem loans and loan losses vary with the composition of a bank's loan portfolio. Retail loan losses are much more predictable than commercial loan losses. An individual's ability to repay is directly related to his or her employment stability and income. As Chapter 22 suggests, these factors are consequently weighted most heavily when analyzing a loan request. In the aggregate, variations in employment and income follow the business cycle and local economic conditions, such that management can project losses from historical experience and incorporate the cost into its retail loan pricing. Commercial loan losses are less predictable because a broader range of factors adversely affect a firm's performance. The major contributing factors include poor management quality, inadequate initial capitalization, high financial and operating leverage resulting from high growth, strong competitors capturing market share, and a general economic downturn.

Management Quality. Most business failures result from management shortcomings. Typical problems include a lack of depth and diversity in management expertise, inadequate planning and accounting systems, outright fraud, and general incompetence. In many cases, the original founder of a company is unwilling to relinquish any responsibility to subordinates. As the company grows, the founder does not have sufficient expertise and time to handle all operational details. Because all key decisions are centralized, the firm does not react quickly to changing market conditions and does not generate new product ideas. Many companies simply outgrow their existing management skills, which are limited in the areas of accounting, finance, and marketing.

Inadequate Initial Capitalization. Small businesses often run into problems shortly after beginning operations because of inadequate capitalization. Owners underestimate the costs of opening the doors for business and overestimate the speed at which they can turn a profit. By the time they recognize the problems, their capital is depleted and lenders refuse to extend additional credit.

High Financial and Operating Leverage. If a company has a large amount of outstanding debt and a high percentage of its total costs are fixed, it operates with a high degree of financial and operating leverage. High financial leverage exposes the firm to large interest payments that must be met when sales decline. High operating leverage exposes the firm to substantial depreciation and maintenance expenses when sales decline. In both cases, the volatility of earnings is high relative to changes in sales.

High Sales Growth. A firm's operating problems are accentuated when it grows too fast. Inventory turnover slows with expanded purchasing requirements. The collection of receivables slows because sales are made to higher-risk customers. Operating overhead increases with the greater sales effort. Yet, with growth, more assets are needed to support the increased size of operation, and thus more financing is required. Returns, allowances, and, eventually, bad debts rise so that net margins decline. A bank must restrict the firm's asset growth by forcing the firm to collect on sales and monitor inventory. In such cases, additional short-term financing will not overextend the borrower's debt service capacity.

Strong Competition. To grow and remain profitable, companies must adapt to economic events. They should regularly improve existing operations and introduce new products to remain competitive. Frequently, new competitors move into a firm's market and disrupt normal operations. A company can react either offensively or defensively. Offensive responses normally focus on marketing efforts intended to differentiate the firm's products and segment the market. In many cases, the firm cuts prices to retain market share. The near-term response is declining or stable sales, rising costs, and reduced earnings. Defensive responses normally involve cost-cutting efforts to reduce personnel and overhead expenses and maintain earnings with declining sales. Companies that do not adapt eventually decay.

Economic Downturn. Many firms cannot operate profitably in a declining economic environment. Their costs may be fixed because of high financial and operating leverage, and their sales may deteriorate if they are not the market leader. The demand for their products is relatively price elastic and income elastic. They cannot generate sufficient cash flow when customers slow payments, and they do not have assets to sell or expenses to cut to reduce their break-even level of output. The resulting strain on cash flow forces firms to rely on increased bank borrowing until economic growth accelerates.

Preventing Problem Loans

It is virtually impossible to eliminate loan losses entirely. Adherence to sound credit analysis principles framed by a sound credit policy can, however, reduce the frequency and depth of loan problems. Two fundamental tenets of lending still hold: a bank should concentrate lending in fields where it possesses a demonstrated expertise, and a bank should not lend outside its trade area. Banks that emphasize loan growth do so at the expense of credit quality. Loan officers often meet growth targets by lending to increasingly marginal borrowers, lending for purposes in which the officer has limited expertise, and lending in geographic areas where the bank has no permanent market presence.

Lending difficulties can be reduced if management establishes and adheres to loan policy guidelines that restrict unacceptable activity. Such guidelines specify quantitative goals for loan production within loan quality guidelines and indicate procedures to attain these goals. The procedures document the format for obtaining loan applications, grading loans, approving loans, and systematically reviewing loan performance and quality. These guidelines comprise steps 1 and 2 of the credit process outlined in Exhibit 20.2.

Problem loans increase when credit policies break down and loan officers depart from detailed credit analysis. The following 25 red flags can help prevent such procedural breakdowns:[5]

Red Flags for Problem Loans

Borrower's History

1. Previous bankruptcy

2. Discrepancies in antecedent information (background facts, especially trade checks)

Borrower's Management Concerns

3. Borrower obtaining advice from professionals who rely on their relationship with the borrower for income

---

[5]See Benbow (1985).

4. Lack of forthrightness

5. Fighting within management, among partners, or among family members

6. Excessive deposit withdrawals by principals

7. Poor character

8. Borrower in a hurry for a loan tries to rush the credit approval process and to pressure the loan officer

9. Relaxation of character checks on prospective borrowers

Credit Facts

10. Borrower with bottlenecks or excessive dependencies on types of resources that could adversely affect business if interrupted (key raw materials, few customers for a majority of sales, dominant person in management, and so forth)

11. Industries or businesses with excess capacity that have developed unusual problems or that seem poised to experience such problems

12. Loans to wealthy or society people whose assets and liabilities are not clearly defined or easy to locate

Loan Structure

13. Borrower poorly understands the purpose of the loan for which he or she is applying

14. Borrower seeks a repayment program more generous than projected cash flow suggests

15. Loans that are structured so that cash flow for repayment is problematic, making the second source the only source of funds for repayment

16. Borrower who is a deal maker or entrepreneur and proposes a loan without having a material stake in the deal or the business

17. An inadequate or piecemeal financing request

18. Borrower who proposes loans against the value of the corporation's common stock and simultaneously seeks credit based on the corporation's assets

19. Loans based more on completing a business transaction successfully than on existing net worth

20. A loan that is beyond the reasonable capacity of the borrower to repay

Changes in Established Patterns

21. Change in established habits, especially delays in providing financial statements after transmitting them at regular intervals

22. Changes in the pattern of checking account balances, especially onset of overdrafts, whether rapid or over a period of time

23. Renegotiations of loan covenants, resetting of repayment plans, and renewal of loans

24. Material changes in a business's financial measures

25. Changes in accounting methods or auditors

Detecting Problem Loans

Once a loan is granted, the account officer is responsible for monitoring the borrower's performance. The purpose is to detect problems before they become too severe. This allows a bank to help the borrower take corrective action if necessary.

Most borrowers experience a severe cash crisis prior to defaulting on a loan. Unfortunately, banks that do not monitor borrower performance are often the last to know that such a crisis is pending. There are three distinct stages of cash problems.[6] During the first stage, liquidity becomes strained. Inventory starts to accumulate and receivables collection slows. Management reacts by slowing payment on trade credit and cutting expenses. In stage 2, cash management becomes the top priority. Caps are imposed on expenses, employees are let go, capital outlays are eliminated, and the company attempts to liquidate nonessential assets. The firm's relationship with the bank deteriorates as it attempts to obtain additional credit while it violates existing loan covenants. Frequently, the company omits dividends to shore up equity reduced by operating losses. During stage 3, the company teeters on the brink of bankruptcy. The company overdraws its deposit account, misses loan payments, and omits tax payments. The ultimate choice is to declare bankruptcy or find a merger/acquisition partner.

While failed companies exhibit different traits, the three cash stages suggest that obvious signals of problems, such as overdrafts and missed loan payments, occur long after corrective action is necessary. Early detection requires the account officer to understand the borrower's business, communicate regularly with the principals, and closely review the borrower's financial data. Exhibit 23.6 provides a checklist of early warning signals regarding different phases of a firm's operations.[7]

PROBLEM LOAN WORKOUT

Once a bank identifies a problem loan, it should initiate an action plan that leads to payout.[8] In most cases, the borrower is solvent but needs to modify the terms of the loan agreement to pay off the debt. This is often the situation when a firm grows too fast. It may have lost control of inventory growth and receivables collection while sales accelerate. The bank's action plan might involve limiting purchases from selected suppliers, tightening the terms on credit sales, and recognizing losses on uncollectable accounts. In other cases, the borrower is technically insolvent, with the value of assets below that of liabilities. It may still be advantageous for the bank to modify the loan agreement and give the borrower time to work out the difficulties. Alternatively, the bank may need to cut its losses and call in the loan.

---

[6]The three cash crisis stages are described in Robert Morris Associates' *Problem Loan Strategies* (McKinley, et al, 1985).

[7]Altman (1986) and Edminster (1972) developed empirical models to predict business failures that can be applied to detecting problem loans.

[8]The following discussion draws heavily from *Problem Loan Strategies* (McKinley, et al, 1985).

Exhibit 23.6 Early Warning Signals

Early Financial Warning Signals

Balance Sheet
- Failure to get statements in timely fashion
- Slowdown in receivables collection period
- Deterioration in customer's cash position
- Sharp increases in dollar amounts or percentage of accounts receivable
- Sharp increase in dollar amounts or percentage of inventory
- Slowdown in inventory turnover
- Decline in current assets as percentage of total assets
- Deterioration of liquidity working capital position
- Marked changes in mix of trading assets
- Rapidly changing concentrations in fixed assets
- Large increase in reserves
- Concentrations in noncurrent assets other than fixed assets
- High concentration of assets in intangibles
- Disproportionate increases in current debt
- Substantial increases in long-term debt
- Low equity relative to debt
- Significant changes in balance sheet structure
- Presence of debt due to/due from officer/stockholders

- Unqualified audit
- Change of accounts

Income Statement
- Declining sales
- Rapidly expanding sales
- Major gap between gross and net sales
- Rising cost percentages/narrowing margins
- Rising sales and falling profits
- Rising levels of bad debt losses
- Disproportionate increases in overhead, relative to sales
- Rising levels of total assets relative to sales/profits
- Operating losses

Receivables Aging
- Extended average age of receivables
- Changes in credit policies
- Extended terms
- Replacement of accounts receivable with notes receivable
- Concentrations of sales
- Compromise of accounts receivable
- Concentrations of seriously past due accounts
- Receivables from affiliated companies

Early Management Warning Signals

- Change in behavior/personal habits of key people
- Marital problems
- Change in attitude toward bank or banker, especially seeming lack of cooperation
- Recurrence of problems presumed to have been solved

- Failure to perform personal obligations
- Changes in management, ownership, or key personnel
- Illness or death of key personnel
- Inability to meet commitments on schedule
- Neglect or discontinuance of profitable standard lines

The Preliminary Investigation

Banks deal with problem loans in a variety of ways. The eventual path to payout depends on how early the problems are discovered, how strong the bank is capitalized relative to its total problem loan portfolio, and the peculiar features of each loan. Problems that are discovered early enough can frequently be corrected by restructuring the borrower's operations and repayment schedule. Typically, such loan workout arrangements reduce the size of a borrower's loan payments until cash flow is large enough to resume normal repayment. Occasionally, a problem borrower will move its

Early Management Warning Signals

- Inability to plan
- Poor financial reporting and controls
- Fragmented functions
- Venturing into acquisitions, new business, new geographic area, or new product line
- Desire and insistence to take business gambles and undue risk
- Unrealistic pricing of goods and services

- Delay in reacting to declining markets or economic conditions
- Lack of visible management succession
- One-man operations showing growth patterns that strain owner's capacity to manage and control
- Change in business, economy, or industry
- Labor problems

Early Operations Warning Signals

- Change in nature of company's business
- Poor financial records and operating controls
- Inefficient layout of plant and equipment
- Poor use of people
- Loss of key product lines, franchises, distribution rights, or sources of supply
- Loss of one or more major, financially sound customers
- Substantial jumps in size of single orders

or contracts that would strain existing productive capacity
- Speculative inventory purchases that are out of line with normal purchasing practices
- Poor maintenance of plant and equipment
- Deferred replacement of outmoded or inefficient plant and equipment
- Evidence of stale inventory, large levels of inventory, or inappropriate mix of inventory

Early Banking Warning Signals

- Declining bank balances
- Excessive note renewals or unanticipated note renewals
- Poor financial planning for fixed asset requirements or working capital requirements
- Heavy reliance on short-term debt
- Marked changes in timing of seasonal loan requests
- Sharp jumps in size/frequency of loan requests
- Loans where more than single source of

repayment cannot be easily or realistically identified
- Loans where purpose is "working capital"
- Calls from existing suppliers requesting information to evaluate requests for special terms or expanded credit information
- Calls from new suppliers requesting information to open new credit lines
- Appearance of other lenders in financial picture, especially collateral lenders
- Evidence of checks written against uncollected funds

Source: Jay M. McDonald and John I. McKinley, *Corporate Banking*, (Washington, D.C.: American Bankers Association), 1981. © American Bankers Association. Reprinted with permission. All rights reserved.

loan to another bank that miscalculates the credit quality, and the first bank escapes with full and immediate payment.

Whether or not a bank is willing to enter a protracted workout arrangement depends on the bank's financial strength. If the bank has a strong capital base and history of good earnings, it may be more willing to carry the borrower. If, instead, the bank has many problem loans, it is typically eager to clear its books by taking near-term losses. This often occurs when management changes hands and the new team wants to start with a clean slate. The bank's collateral position has the same effect. If a problem loan is adequately collateralized, a bank will allow a borrower to work out its problems over time rather than immediately liquidate its position.

Finally, many problem loans are simply ignored. A loan officer renews a note in the hope that the problem will correct itself. This has occurred with many foreign loans at large, multinational banking organizations. U.S. government officials in conjunction with International Monetary Fund and World Bank officers encourage U.S. banks to lend additional funds to third world borrowers so they can pay interest on outstanding debt. There is no real chance that these borrowers can repay the debts under existing circumstances.

The Possible Stages to Payout

Loan workout refers to the entire process of collecting on a problem loan. In its most common form, it involves a cooperative, nonlegal agreement between the bank and borrower to design a plan for debt repayment. At the other extreme, it involves complex litigation as the borrower petitions for bankruptcy. A bank's plan of action should consider every option and target the least-cost, highest-return alternative.

The possible stages to payout after identification of a problem loan are outlined in Exhibit 23.7. The first stage is typically the establishment of a cooperative workout agreement. Successive stages follow legal constraints and include collateral liquidation, reduction of a debt to judgment, collection of the judgment, and bankruptcy. Payout may occur at almost any stage, but the process usually involves the first two steps. If collateral is insufficient, steps 3 through 5 are followed. The process is not always sequential, however, as borrowers often jump into bankruptcy to limit creditors' options. The following discussion identifies the critical issues at each stage.[9]

Cooperative Workout Arrangements. Cooperative workouts are negotiated when they are in the best interests of both the bank and the borrower. The borrower benefits by maintaining long-term ownership and control of productive assets. A workout agreement provides time to correct temporary deficiencies and can take many forms. In many cases, a bank restricts borrower activities, such as investing in new equipment or expanding a plant. Expenses are normally reduced either through employee layoffs or the reduction of salaries and fringe benefits. In other cases, a bank may assist in managing the borrower's business. This may consist of placing bank officers on the board of directors, requiring bank personnel to handle the comptroller's function, or even replacing present management of the business. Borrowers accept such austerity plans to avoid foreclosure and with hope that cash flow will rise. In most cases, workout plans lead directly to payout without legal intervention. In other cases, such as with Farah Manufacturing, courts have ruled that certain workout plans may make the lender legally liable for damages (see Contemporary Issues: Lender Liability).

Banks also benefit from workouts in which the borrower's revised operating policies increase the likelihood of repayment. After all, once credit is granted, a

---

[9]The discussion does not address the fine points of law or consider all motives and options. *Problem Loan Strategies* (McKinley, et al, 1985) covers these issues in considerable detail.

Exhibit 23.7 Problem Loan Workout Schematic

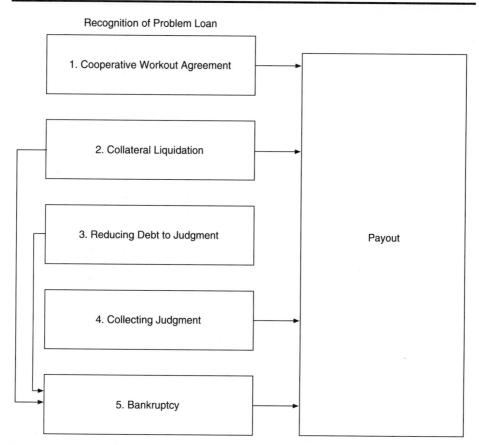

The diagram outlines possible steps before a bank collects a problem loan. While payout may occur at each stage, collections frequently follow the sequence from a cooperative workout agreement to collateral liquidation. If collateral is insufficient, collection reverts to obtaining and collecting a judgment against the borrower and, ultimately, bankruptcy. Borrowers may short-circuit the process by declaring bankruptcy at any time.

lender is effectively a partner with the borrower. Workouts also allow a bank to strengthen its position in case the borrower eventually defaults. If, for example, a bank discovers that its security interest in collateral is not perfected, it can correct existing errors before it is forced to liquidate collateral. It may similarly use the uncertainty regarding the borrower's future prospects to obtain additional collateral in support of the loan. In general, a bank can position itself for later court-determined payout procedures such as bankruptcy. Unfortunately, these actions tend to attract lender liability suits.

CONTEMPORARY ISSUES

Lender Liability

During the past several years, many disgruntled borrowers have filed lawsuits against banks claiming unfair treatment in handling their loans. Banks have had to move cautiously in enforcing loan covenants and collecting loans to avoid liability.

The first prominent case involved Farah Manufacturing Co. of El Paso, Texas, in the early 1970s. Willie Farah, chairman of the clothing manufacturer, had directed the firm's operations for almost 20 years. When the company's performance deteriorated during the recession of 1974 and 1975, Farah could not meet its scheduled debt service payments. As part of the loan workout agreement, State National Bank forced Willie Farah to step down and replaced the company's senior officers with its own management team. When Farah Manufacturing continued to experience problems, the bank's management team auctioned off some of the company's assets to service the debt.

In 1978 Willie Farah returned as chief executive officer and sued State National Bank for damages, claiming that the managers selected by the bank had interfered in Farah's business, accentuated losses, and generally mismanaged operations. Eventually Farah Manufacturing won an $18.6 million award through the litigation.

Since that action, borrowers have been more willing to claim that bank actions caused bankruptcy or losses. When are banks liable? Recent court rulings suggest that banks must act "in good faith." This means that if they intend to curtail financing, they must give reasonable notice. A bank cannot mislead a borrower into believing credit will be available. It must also make a reasonable effort to work out the loan and not immediately force bankruptcy. The catalyst underlying most litigation is often a sudden act to seize borrower collateral. Today, lender liability is a growth area for lawyers and a fearsome shadow for bankers.

Collateral Liquidation. If a workout agreement does not improve performance, a bank next looks to liquidate collateral. With secured loans, the lender has a claim on certain borrower assets in the case of default. Collateral liquidation refers to the process of converting these assets into cash to repay the bank loan. Banks normally liquidate collateral only after they realize that a workout agreement will not succeed. Borrowers often allow collateral to deteriorate after they know they will eventually lose it. Even when a bank quickly seizes collateral, it may realize only a fraction of its value at sale. In other cases, banks quickly seize collateral when the borrower commits fraud or declares bankruptcy. The very act of seizing collateral often induces a borrower to file for bankruptcy.

Before a bank attempts to liquidate collateral, it should determine that its interest is perfected. Perfection problems arise when a bank 1) fails to file the appropriate claims under local requirements or the Uniform Commercial Code, 2) files in the wrong locale, 3) files a financing statement on collateral in which the terms or conditions of the assets differ from those identified in the security agreement, and 4) allows the financing statement to expire. In such cases, a bank may lose its direct claim on collateral and become a general creditor.

While collateral liquidation may be the shortest path to payout, it often presents unforeseen difficulties, as banks that take possession of collateral must convert it to cash. This conversion may involve extensive marketing efforts or auctions to dispose of real estate, personal property, and other assets. Typically, a bank receives only a fraction of the asset's initial value in a distress sale. Oil rigs, for example, sold for $500,000 in 1985, compared to a lofty $4 million in 1980. Some foreclosures necessitate running a business until a potential buyer can be found. This often imposes considerable costs because the bank must hire knowledgeable management and pay maintenance expenses.[10] Contemporary Issues: Unusual Collateral from Failed Banks reveals several cases in which collateral was highly unusual and difficult to value and market.

Reducing Debt to Judgment. When a borrower defaults on a loan, a bank can demand payment. If the loan is unsecured or if collateral liquidation leaves a deficiency, the bank can then obtain a judgment against either the borrower or guarantors. A judgment is a legal document that confirms the obligations and claims of parties to the loan. It also indicates the remaining principal outstanding and interest owed.

From a creditor's perspective, it takes too long to reduce a debt to final judgment, and borrowers generally possess too many defenses in refuting or postponing verification of any claims. In many cases, borrowers use legal means to defer judgments with the intent of hiding assets or transferring them to third parties that are protected from a creditor's claims. Obtaining a judgment often precedes a borrower filing for bankruptcy. After the judgment, the bank often discovers that the borrower's assets have either disappeared or depreciated.

Collecting a Judgment. Once a bank obtains a judgment, it can take steps to collect on the defaulted loan. In some instances, a borrower promptly pays the judgment and the process ends. Typically, however, a bank must pursue postjudgment discovery, and attach borrower income or assets before it collects. Postjudgment discovery is a process by which a bank investigates what sources of income and types of assets are available from the borrower for debt service. After determining what resources exist, a bank can use various techniques to collect.

Four collection techniques are commonly used: levy, public sale, garnishment, and receivership. A levy is the outright seizure of property held by a debtor for the purpose of settling a debt. The seized assets are sold at a public auction, with the proceeds applied against the judgment. Any interested party, including the bank and borrower, may bid on the items. In many cases, banks bid on assets they feel are selling below market value at auction. The bid price offsets their judgment, and they later try to resell the items at higher prices. Garnishment permits a bank to have a third party withhold funds owed to a debtor to be applied against a judgment. The garnishment of wages, whereby an employer withholds a portion of an employee's pay to be allocated against a debt, is a common example. Of course, the law limits the extent to which wages can be seized so that the debtor can still conduct personal business. Finally, the court may appoint a receiver to take control of the debtor's assets. The purpose is to maintain the

---

[10]One well-known maxim states that a bank should never take possession of collateral that eats. The investment required to sustain the operation frequently exceeds the potential value of any sale, yet a creditor is prohibited from simply walking away from the collateral.

Unusual Collateral from Failed Banks

The FDIC, which closes failed banks, is charged with the responsibility of liquidating collateral taken in loan foreclosures. In some instances the collateral is highly liquid and can readily be sold at a predictable price. In many other cases, the collateral is illiquid because it is either obsolete or specific to a certain usage so that few buyers are interested. The onslaught of failed banks since 1985 has demonstrated that loan officers often accept peculiar forms of collateral as security. A few of the more unique examples include the following.

Personal collection of rare gold coins: some coins were over 400 years old, and the collection sold for $2.5 million at auction.

Interest in a thoroughbred stallion: the value of the collateral was based on the stallion's use in breeding. Unfortunately, the stallion had syphilis.

Automobile with six wheels: only two of these vehicles were built in 1977, but potential buyers are not sure why even one exists. The estimated value in 1988 ranged from $10,000 to $200,000.

Frozen bull semen: Ralph, a Red Brahman bull, contributed 5,591 units of frozen semen that were pledged as collateral. Statistically, a cow inseminated with semen from one unit has a 70 percent chance of giving birth to a calf. The estimated value of the collateral was initially set at $250,000.

Source: Richman, *Fortune*, April 25, 1988.

assets' value—for example, when a debtor owns a business—so that funds will be available for debt service.

Bankruptcy

An individual or business enters bankruptcy when the principals are unable to pay their debts. Debtors may voluntarily file for bankruptcy, seeking relief from debts, or creditors may file an involuntary petition against a debtor, requesting a settlement. The federal Bankruptcy Act and subsequent amendments set forth provisions for the distribution of assets and settlement of debts. Most bankruptcy petitions are filed under Chapter 7, Chapter 11, or Chapter 13 of the Act. Chapter 7 deals with liquidations, Chapter 11 with business reorganizations, and Chapter 13 with consumer reorganizations.

Once a bankruptcy petition is filed, an automatic stay takes effect. This stay restricts the use of virtually all legal remedies that creditors have against a debtor. In particular, a creditor cannot 1) pursue any lawsuit against the debtor that commenced before the bankruptcy, 2) enforce a judgment obtained before bankruptcy, 3) seize possession or exercise control of debtor property regarding a judgment obtained before bankruptcy, 4) take any action to establish, protect, or enforce a lien against the debtor, 5) take any action to collect a claim against a debtor that arose before bankruptcy, or 6) set off any debt owed to a debtor, such as funds on deposit at a bank.[11] In addition, a creditor must remove any garnishment of debtor funds or be in violation of the stay.

---

[11]The implications of each restriction and exceptions are discussed in *Problem Loan Strategies* (McKinley, et al, 1985).

The purpose of bankruptcy is to provide for the orderly repayment of debts without totally debilitating a debtor. Creditors have long argued that the Bankruptcy Act enables many debtors to abuse the system. After the 1978 reforms, for example, debtors could select which assets they wanted to exempt via federal and state statutes under Chapter 7 liquidations, often avoiding any substantial repayment. Banks and other creditors had virtually no recourse because the exemptions were extremely broad.

In 1984 Congress modified the existing bankruptcy statutes to eliminate many abuses. The new provisions effectively limited the conditions under which consumers eliminated their debts under Chapter 7 liquidations. Key provisions include:

1. Bankruptcy judges can now dismiss any consumer case that violates existing codes. Historically, certain individuals have temporarily distributed assets and filed for bankruptcy without genuinely needing relief.

2. Consumers must notify the court within 45 days of filing for bankruptcy which items they will exempt from liquidation, with the cumulative value limited to $4,000.

3. Consumers filing repayment plans under Chapter 13 must effect the terms of the plans within 30 days of court approval.

4. Debts of over $500 per creditor incurred within 20 days of filing will not be erased.

5. Individual loans taken out within 40 days of a bankruptcy filing will not be erased.

In Chapter 11 cases, the debtor continues to hold the assets in question and conduct business. The court appoints a committee representing unsecured creditors to make recommendations concerning the settlement of debts. This committee evaluates the debtor's operations and devises a plan that leads to relief of the debts. Such plans often provide for a restructuring of the borrower's line of business and certain revisions in outstanding debts. Creditors may even substitute equity claims in the business for debt they currently hold.

SUMMARY

Bank management generally expects to report some loan losses because officers cannot perfectly forecast borrowers' future performance. Recognized loan losses directly reduce earnings before taxes in the form of provisions for loan losses on a bank's income statement. The Tax Reform Act of 1986 forced large banks to use the direct charge-off method for tax purposes, whereby reported losses equal actual net charge-offs during the current period. Banks with $400 million or less in assets can use an experience method for handling loan losses. These banks establish loss reserves based on the size of their loan portfolio to absorb anticipated charge-offs. Analysts evaluating asset quality should compare a bank's loss experience and the size of its loss reserve on trend and relative to peer banks to assess whether the bank systematically overstates or understates losses.

Loans go bad for a variety of reasons: mismanagement, fraud, a decline in business activity, or personal unemployment. While problem loans tend to limit management's strategies and dominate its thoughts, they are largely correctable. Sound credit policies combined with comprehensive credit analysis procedures can eliminate many problem credits. Problems caused by economic conditions can be minimized through diversification. Management should not expect to eliminate loan losses totally. This can be done only by refusing to take credit risk, which reduces profitability.

Banks can, however, take certain steps to identify loans in trouble before the problems get too severe. Most borrowers having financial difficulties experience a serious cash crisis, evidenced by liquidity problems, expense cutbacks, and the violation of loan covenants. Corrective action may involve restructuring the loan terms to improve repayment prospects or, ultimately, calling the loan and forcing a liquidation of collateral or bankruptcy. If problems can be identified in the early stages, borrowers can be encouraged to move their business.

Questions

Loan losses

1. Name three reasons loans become problems.

2. Explain the difference between the phrases "provision for loan losses" and "loss reserve."

3. Explain the saying, "A rolling loan gathers no loss."

Financial Reporting of Loan Losses

4. What is capital forbearance? Why was it needed, and what two "breaks" does it give to banks?

5. Describe how the reserve method for loan loses potentially shelters income from taxes. What is the rationale for forcing large banks, but not small banks, to use direct charge-offs rather than the experience method?

6. What is the difference between a bank's valuation reserve, deferred tax reserve, and contingency reserve?

7. Prime State Bank uses the experience method for handling loan losses. During the year the bank experiences $515,000 in loan losses but is able to recover $233,000 from loans previously charged off. Its 6-year average of net loan losses to total loans ratio increased during the year from 0.32 percent to 0.34 percent. Calculate the bank's maximum allowable tax deduction if its total loan portfolio increased from $105 million to $111 million.

8. A large bank has collected the following information for the past year's operation.

Beginning of Year Balance Sheet (in millions)

Assets			
Investments	$300	Deposits	$700
Gross loans	600	Liabilities	100
Less: valuation reserve	10	Equity	200
Fixed assets	110		
Total assets	1,000		

Loan Information

Ratio of net charge-offs to total loans	0.5%
Loans charged-off during year	$2
Loan recoveries during the year	$0.4
New loans added to gross during the year	$100
Year-end ratio of net charge-offs to total loans	0.6%

a. What is the bank's maximum tax deduction for loan losses?

b. If the bank decides to take $2.1 provision for loan loss on its GAAP income statement what will be the year end balance in these accounts: valuation reserve, contingency reserves, and deferred tax reserve? Currently the bank is in the 40 percent tax bracket.

9. Exhibit 23.5 presents comparative loan loss and reserve figures for Wachovia and Continental Illinois. Explain why Wachovia's figures represent a more conservative approach to reporting loan losses. What would you expect the pattern of share prices to look like for the two banking organizations from 1980 to 1983?

10. Calculate the following three valuation reserve (VR) ratios for the bank in problem 8 to compare with the two banks reported in Exhibit 23.5: VR/ year-end loans; VR/net charge-offs; and VR/nonperforming loans. The bank's nonperforming loans were $25. How would you judge the quality of former loan decisions and the current risk of the bank in problem 8?

11. Discuss the costs and benefits of a bank selecting a high value for its valuation reserve. What is the importance of the valuation reserve in financial reporting?

Early Detection

12. Exhibit 23.6 lists early warning signals of future loan problems. Examine the section describing the financial signals and determine what impact each factor has on the firm's cash flow from operations and financial leverage.

13. Being an anachronism fan you have created the abbreviation HEMISH (rhymes with Flemish) to remember the causes of problem loans. Now you want to test yourself to see if it helps you remember the six causes of problem loans. What does each letter stand for?

14. There are three stages in a loan failure. What is a typical sign of each stage?

Loan Workouts

15. Two extremes of handling problem loans are workouts and seizure of collateral. When would a bank prefer each choice? Which choice indicates loan officers are doing a good job?

16. A popular banking saying is,"Never take collateral that eats." Why might this be good advice? Discuss the problems that often arise in taking possession of and liquidating collateral.

17. Define the following terms: judgment, levy, garnishment, and receivership.

Activity

Chapter 11 filings are becoming part of many corporations' standard financial strategies. Examine current financial publications for firms that filed Chapter 11 bankruptcy petitions. What are the motives for declaring Chapter 11, and what alternatives exist? How did the market respond to the filings?

References

Altman, Edward. "Financial Ratios, Discriminant Analysis and the Prediction of Corporate Bankruptcy." *Journal of Finance* (September 1968).

Bailey, John. "Accounting for Troubled Assets." *Bank Management* (September 1990).

Benbow, Robert F. "Preventing Problem Loans before They Happen: 25 Red Flags." *The Journal of Commercial Bank Lending* (April 1985).

Cates, David C. "What's an Adequate Loan-Loss Reserve?" *ABA Banking Journal* (March 1985).

Cocheo, Steve. "Anatomy of an Examination." *ABA Banking Journal* (February 1986).

Edminster, Robert O. "An Empirical Test of Financial Ratio Analysis for Small Business Failure Prediction." *Journal of Financial and Quantitative Analysis* (March 1972).

Hudgins, Tom. "Problem Loan Management: Be Forewarned." *Bank Management* (September 1990).

Kester, George, and Thomas Bixler. "Why 90-Day Working Capital Loans Are Not Repaid on Time." *Journal of Commercial Bank Lending* (August 1990).

Miller, Richard B. "Lawyers Who Cash in on Lender Liability." *Bankers Monthly* (October 1986).

McKinley, John E. III, et al. *Problem Loan Strategies.* Philadelphia, Pa.: Robert Morris Associates, 1985.

Richman, Louis. "Bizarre Booty from Bank Bailouts." *Fortune* (April 25, 1988).

Schweitzer, Stuart A. "Bank Loan Losses: A Fresh Perspective." *Business Review* (Federal Reserve Bank of Philadelphia, September 1975).

Sorenson, Richard. "Why Real Estate Projects Fail." *Journal of Commercial Bank Lending* (April 1990).

Strischek, Dev. "Assessing Creditworthiness: Importance of Evaluating Company Management." *Journal of Commercial Bank Lending* (March 1990).

Viscione, Jerry. "Assessing Financial Distress." *The Journal of Commercial Bank Lending* (July 1985).

Wetzel, Debra A. "Improving Loan Documentation Demands a Process." *ABA Banking Journal* (May 1986).

Chapter 24

Customer Profitability Analysis and Loan Pricing

From 1985 through 1989, fourteen of the best known U.S. commercial banks reported combined pretax profits of $25 billion. Over the same period these banks reported aggregate provisions for loan losses of $58 billion. Only 3 of the 14 banks generated positive net income over the 5 years. Clearly, loans were not priced adequately to compensate for default risk as well as other risks and the cost of operating the banks. Why? Is competition too great? Are banks unable to measure the cost of doing business accurately?

Bank managers are routinely confronted with many issues related to pricing. Should they make variable-rate loans or fixed-rate loans? Should they quote their own local bank prime rate or use a prime rate quoted by another bank? Is the bank willing to lose a customer's business by raising the rate charged on a loan? Is charging fees better than requiring a borrower to maintain a deposit account at the bank? How does a loan officer adjust the pricing of a borrower's credit relationship when the customer insists on reducing compensating balance requirements? These are key issues confronting commercial bankers in today's environment of deregulated interest rates and intense price competition for credit services.

Most banks use a customer profitability analysis framework as a guideline to address these issues. While loan pricing should not be based solely on a mechanical system, the framework does demonstrate the relationships between account revenues, expenses, and a bank's target return to shareholders. The examples in this chapter demonstrate why banks have underpriced loans and provide a basis for resolving each of the above questions and other related pricing problems.

For many years managers looked at their bank's aggregate profitability measures to determine whether strategies were appropriately conceived and implemented. Frequently, they did not know the cost of providing services and thus set prices artificially high or low. Deregulation changed this practice. Declining net interest margins forced banks to reassess their expenses and revenues in search of better cost control and more efficient pricing. Today most banks use formal customer profitability analysis procedures to meet these objectives.

Customer profitability analysis is a decision tool used to evaluate the profitability of a customer relationship. Historically, it has been used to determine the cost of deposit services and consequent balance requirements, along with how to price specific products such as loans. It is used here, instead, to evaluate all relevant expenses and revenues associated with a customer's total banking relationship. The analysis enables management to estimate the net profit from a given account and provides a framework for repricing specific products to meet profit objectives.

The analysis procedure compels banks to be aware of the full range of services purchased by each customer and to generate meaningful cost estimates for providing each service. It identifies the various sources of income and expense and dollar charges by category of service. If performed systematically, the analysis can help a bank identify when and why profitability declines and what steps must be taken to correct any deterioration in the relationship. A commercial customer may, for example, reduce deposit balances because it is unable to get trade credit or sales are declining. A corresponding decrease in revenues is easily recognizable. Alternatively, the procedure assists banks in negotiating terms. In many instances, bank officers antagonize credit customers by rejecting requests for repricing without fully comprehending the profit relationship. This analysis indicates what repricing flexibility exists.

The applicability of customer profitability analysis has been questioned in recent years with the move toward unbundling services. Bank customers often selectively purchase single products from different institutions and thus maintain relationships with several banks. It is important for banks to allocate their costs across different products and price each accordingly. As such, each product should stand alone in generating revenues to cover associated expenses and add to profits. A similar type of analysis, labeled segment profitability analysis, addresses whether specific lines of business generate acceptable risk-adjusted returns on equity. If specific products or services are underpriced, it will show up in this segment returns data. The effect will be to lower realized profits across similar accounts systematically.

This chapter examines the contributing factors in customer profitability and account analysis. The first part describes a general framework and important terminology. The next part provides an application, using data from a hypothetical commercial account. The final part shows extended applications of the framework to pricing new loan agreements and determining minimum acceptable balances and maturities on installment loan contracts. The loan pricing analysis involves forecasting expenses and customer borrowings. It provides a framework for projecting a required interest charge, emphasizing the role of base lending rates. Both applications reveal the format of and difficulties with segment profitability analysis.

ACCOUNT ANALYSIS FRAMEWORK

Customer profitability analysis is used to evaluate whether net revenue from an account meets a bank's profit objectives. It is performed ex post facto, usually monthly or quarterly, allowing for repricing when necessary. The procedure involves comparing revenues from all services provided a customer with the associated costs and the bank's target profit. It uses historical quantity data associated with the appropriate marginal prices. While the analysis applies particularly well to loan customers, it can easily be modified to evaluate noncredit activities. The appropriate comparison is:

$$\text{Account revenues} \gtreqless \text{Account expenses} + \text{Target profit} \qquad \textbf{(24.1)}$$

If revenues exceed the sum of expenses and the target profit, the account generates a return in excess of the minimum return required by the bank. If revenues equal expenses plus the target profit, the account just meets the required return objective. There are two other possible outcomes. If revenues fall short of expenses, the account is clearly unprofitable. When revenues exceed expenses but are less than the sum of expenses and target profit, the account is profitable but does not generate the minimum return acceptable to the bank. The following discussion summarizes the components to each element in (24.1).

Expense Components

The first step is to identify the full list of services used by a customer. The list normally includes transactions account activity, extension of credit, security safekeeping, and related items such as wire transfers, safety deposit boxes, and letters of credit. The next step is to assess the cost of providing each service. Unit costs can be determined from the bank's cost accounting system or approximated from Federal Reserve Functional Cost Analysis data. While the data quality is improving over time, specific figures vary substantially between banks because they allocate fixed costs and overhead differently. There is no best method for allocating fixed costs, so estimated unit expenses are, at best, an approximation.

Noncredit Services. Aggregate cost estimates for noncredit services are obtained by multiplying the unit cost of each service by the corresponding activity level. If, for example, it costs $5 to facilitate a wire transfer and the customer authorized eight such transfers, the total periodic wire transfer expense to the bank is $40 for that account. In general, check processing expenses are the major noncredit cost item for commercial customers. If priced separately, service charge income should at least equal this aggregate cost.

Cost estimates for credit services represent the largest expense and are typically related to the size of the loan. These costs include the interest cost of financing the loan, loan administration costs, and risk expense associated with potential default. The first two are actual cash expenses, while default risk expense is a noncash expense.

Cost of Funds. The cost of funds estimate may be a bank's weighted marginal cost of pooled debt or its weighted marginal cost of capital at the time the loan was made. Most banks distinguish between their cost of debt and cost of equity, which together comprise the cost of capital, by separately calculating a target return to shareholders representing the cost of equity. The cost of funds refers to the weighted marginal cost of pooled debt. This calculation follows that described in Chapter 13. A bank computes the effective marginal dollar cost of obtaining each source of debt funds and divides the estimate by the dollar amount of investable balances from that source. The weights then reflect the anticipated proportion of financing for each source from the bank's target capital structure. Because equity is excluded, the weights sum to 1 minus the targeted percentage financing from equity. Alternatively, banks can use the weighted marginal cost of capital, which incorporates the cost of both debt and equity. In this case, a separate target profit measure would count equity twice, and thus is excluded.

Loan Administration. Loan administration expense is the cost of a loan's credit analysis and execution. It includes personnel and overhead costs as well as direct costs for sending interest bills, processing payments, and maintaining collateral. The charge may be imposed on a per-item basis, determined by the unit cost of handling a loan times the number of notes outstanding, or as a fixed percentage of the loan amount.

Default Risk Expense. A formal risk expense measure represents one method of handling potential loan losses. Many banks categorize loans according to their risk characteristics at the time of issue. Low-risk loans, which typically have short-term maturities, are those extended to borrowers with strong financial statements, adequate cash flow and collateral, and sound management. High-risk loans, which generally have longer maturities, are extended to borrowers with weaker financial statements, low cash flow, and collateral that fluctuates in value. Management first ranks loans by these characteristics and historical default experience evidenced by borrowers, assigning each credit to a particular risk class. The actual risk expense measure equals the historical default percentage for loans in that risk class times the outstanding loan balance.[1]

Exhibit 24.1 shows a simplified classification using hypothetical data with only four loan categories. The historical default percentage serves as a proxy for the expected percentage of charge-offs on existing loans. A 1-year $300,000 loan assigned to the second risk class is charged a $2,070 risk expense, for example, because average loss experience on loans of this type equals 69 cents per $100. This risk estimate recognizes that the bank expects to charge off $2,070 on the average $300,000 loan of this type. The relationship should thus be priced to reflect this anticipated loss. If the

---

[1]When pricing loans, many banks levy risk charges that increase systematically with the presumed riskiness of loans. Thus loans in category 1 of Exhibit 24.1 might be charged 25 basis points for risk, loans in category 2 might be charged 50 basis points, and so forth to where loans in category 4 are charged 100 basis points. There are many problems with this, particularly the fact that average default losses are not linear. Loans in the highest risk class will normally exhibit default loss rates that are exponentially greater than default loss rates in the lowest risk class. The last section indicates how this technique leads to mispricing loans.

Exhibit 24.1 Commercial Loan Classification by Risk Category

Risk Class	Characteristics	Historical Default Percentage[a]
1	Short-term working capital loans secured with accounts receivable and inventory	0.24%
2	Short-term real estate loans secured by facility and borrower's cash flow from total operations	0.69
3	Term plant and equipment loans secured by physical plant and other real estate	1.25
4	Other loans	1.96

[a]Average of loan charge-offs divided by total loans in that risk class during the past 5 years.

loan were in risk category 4, the risk expense charge would equal $4,380 because average losses are greater.

Rather than charge directly for default risk, some banks formally recognize different default risks on different loans by allocating varying proportions of equity financing in the cost of funds estimate. Because equity costs more than debt, riskier loans are assigned a higher percentage of equity funding. For example, a bank might assume 7 percent equity financing for a loan in the lowest risk class and 10 percent equity financing for a loan in the highest risk class. This raises the cost of capital or target return requirement, and thus the minimum revenue necessary for an account to be profitable.

Target Profit

The recognition of a target return separate from the cost of debt funds forces management to allocate equity in support of each account relationship. The target profit is then based on a minimum required return to shareholders per account. Equity capital can readily be allocated to credit relationships on the basis of a bank's financial leverage. For an average-risk loan, the appropriate percentage equals the ratio of a bank's average equity to total assets.[2] A bank with a 7 percent equity-to-asset ratio, for example, implicitly finances 7 percent of every dollar loaned out with equity and 93 percent with debt. The dollar magnitude of the required pretax target profit equals the product of this equity-to-asset percentage, the percentage target return to shareholders, and the dollar amount of the borrower's outstanding loan. The general formula applicable to a credit relationship is:

$$\text{Target profit} = \left(\frac{\text{Equity}}{\text{Total assets}}\right)\left(\begin{array}{c}\text{Target return to}\\\text{shareholders}\end{array}\right)\left(\text{Loan amount}\right) \qquad \textbf{(24.2)}$$

[2]It is not appropriate to divide this percentage by the ratio of a bank's earning assets unless the marginal cost of funds and target return to shareholders calculations are not adjusted by the investable portion of bank assets. (See Chapter 13.)

The target return to shareholders can be determined from a dividend valuation model, capital asset pricing model framework, or cost of debt plus risk premium analysis. Each measure was discussed in Chapter 13, with sample calculations.

Revenue Components

Banks generate three types of revenue from customer accounts: investment income from the customer's deposit balances held at the bank, fee income from services, and interest income on loans. Account profitability analysis provides a pricing framework that compares aggregate revenues with expenses and the target profit.

Investment Income from Deposit Balances. Every deposit that customers hold generates investment income for the bank. In most cases, banks must set aside legal reserves as a percentage of deposits, but they can invest remaining balances that exceed customer float on the account. Many customers are net depositors: their balances exceed any loans the bank has extended them. Other customers are net borrowers: their outstanding loans are greater than their total deposits. This account analysis procedure treats investment income on balances separately from loan interest. A bank gives each depositor an earnings credit for interest it can earn on investable balances. Implicitly, customer deposits are viewed as part of a bank's total available funds. Thus the cost of financing a loan equals the weighted cost of debt times the full amount of the loan. Some procedures assume that a borrower's deposit balances at a bank directly fund the associated loan.[3] In this case, no separate earnings credit would apply.

Estimating investment income from balances involves four steps. First, a bank determines the average ledger (book) balances in the account during the reporting period. Second, the average transactions float—uncollected funds that still appear as part of the customer's ledger deposit—is subtracted from the ledger amount. This difference equals collected balances. Third, the bank deducts required reserves that must be maintained against collected balances to arrive at investable balances. Finally, management applies an earnings credit rate against investable balances to determine the average interest revenue earned on the customer's account.

This earnings credit rate is subjectively determined. Therefore, banks and their customers frequently debate what the appropriate rate should be. Banks argue that the rate should reflect the customer's opportunity cost of funds, measured as the best alternative rate available on a comparable investment. Many banks use a moving average of 3-month Treasury bill or CD rates. Customers, in contrast, argue that the rate should reflect a higher rate charged on the customer's loan or, at worst, the bank's average interest yield on earning assets. The ultimate rate used depends on each side's bargaining position and negotiation skills.

Exhibit 24.2 demonstrates the computation of investment income generated from a corporation's investable deposits during a single month. The firm's ledger balances of $210,000 were reduced by $82,500 in float and $15,300 in reserves at 12 percent to yield net investable balances of $112,200. The bank applied an earnings credit rate

---

[3]This assumes that interest is paid on the deposit at the same rate as interest earned on the loan.

Exhibit 24.2 Calculation of Investment Income from Demand Deposit Balances

Analysis of Demand Deposits: Corporation's Outstanding Balances for April
Average ledger balances = $210,000
Average float = $82,500
Collected balance = $210,000 − $82,500 = $127,500
Required reserves = (0.12)$127,500 = $15,300
Investable balance = $112,200

Earnings Credit Rate:
Average 90-day CD rate for April = 8.15%

Investment Income from Balances: April

Investment income = $0.0815 \dfrac{(30)}{(365)}$ ($112,200) = $751.58

---

of 8.15 percent to yield $751.58 in investment income over the 30-day period. If the corporation also held a CD at the bank, the net investable portion would simply be added to the $112,200.

Compensating Balances. In many commercial credit relationships borrowers must maintain compensating deposit balances with the bank as part of the loan agreement. Typically, the qualifying balances must be demand deposits, with the minimum amount stipulated as some percentage of the loan. The agreement indicates whether the minimum is specified in terms of ledger, collected, or investable balances.

Consider a $1 million credit line. A bank that does not know the magnitude and timing of the customer's draws against the line might negotiate compensating balance requirements equal to 5 percent of the available credit plus 5 percent of the actual amount borrowed (5 + 5 balances). A customer who borrowed an average of $800,000 against the line would be required to hold $90,000 ($50,000 + $40,000) in qualifying demand deposits. Suppose that float averages $35,000 during any month. If the balance requirement were stipulated in terms of ledger balances, a customer who maintained $90,000 in ledger balances would actually have only $55,000 in collected balances and $48,400 in investable balances with a 12 percent reserve ratio. In contrast, 5 + 5 collected balances is more restrictive because it necessitates $90,000 in ledger balances net of float ($125,000 ledger − $35,000 float), and investable balances would equal $79,200. Obviously, a bank could earn more interest with $90,000 in collected balances versus ledger balances. Finally, if the requirement were stipulated in terms of investable balances, the minimum investable funds would equal $90,000 and the corresponding ledger amount would rise to $137,273.[4]

A bank can raise the effective cost of balances in several ways. First, it can simply raise the percentages applied against the line. Instead of 5 + 5 balances, it could require 8 + 5 balances. Second, it can shift from ledger balance requirements to having only collected or investable balances qualify, keeping the same percentage requirement.

---

[4]$90,000/(1 − .12) + $35,000 = $137,273

Finally, it can encourage increased borrowing against the line. A customer that borrowed the full amount in the above example would see balance requirements increase to $100,000. Actual usage against a line can often be influenced by fees.

Compensating balances are fast becoming unpopular among corporate customers. Using sophisticated cash management techniques, financial officers can calculate and invest excess cash balances in earning assets rather than leave them in nonearning demand deposits at a bank. Many borrowers prefer to pay fixed fees that require no fine tuning and create an opportunity for increased income if the level of interest rates rises. The opportunity cost of compensating balances, in contrast, varies directly with the level of interest rates.

Both borrowers and the bank benefit from eliminating balance requirements when the bank lends the customer the deposits to meet balance requirements. This anomaly results from eliminating reserve requirements. Suppose, for example, that a bank charged 13 percent on actual borrowings in the above $1 million credit line and that the customer needed only a $675,000 loan for operating purposes. The remaining $125,000 loan went to meet balance requirements. The following data reveal the comparative return to the bank and cost to the borrower with and without balance requirements.

	$125,000 Ledger Balances	**No Balances Required**
Cost to borrower:	$\dfrac{.13(\$800,000)}{\$675,000} = 15.41\%$	$\dfrac{.1541(\$675,000)}{\$675,000} = 15.41\%$
Return to bank:	$\dfrac{.13(\$800,000)}{\$675,000 + \$10,800} = 15.16\%$	$\dfrac{.1541(\$675,000)}{\$675,000} = 15.41\%$

With balance requirements, the borrower paid $104,000 in interest during the year for an effective rate of 15.41 percent. The bank, in turn, allocated $675,000 for the loan but also had to increase its required reserves by 12 percent of $90,000, or $10,800. The bank earned $104,000 in interest on a net investment of $685,800, for a net yield of 15.16 percent. If, alternatively, the bank charged 15.41 percent with no balance requirements on a loan of $675,000, the cost to the borrower and return to the bank would equal 15.41 percent. Both the bank and borrower would have been better off if compensating balances were eliminated and the bank charged a rate between 15.16 and 15.41 percent on a $675,000 loan.

There are instances, however, when a borrower will move balances from another institution to the lending bank to meet balance requirements. In these cases, the lending bank has additional loanable funds equal to the new deposit less required reserves against the deposit. Over time firms tend to reduce their deposits to the minimum necessary to handle transactions requirements. Investment income from such transferred deposits is thus frequently short-lived.

Fee Income. Banks increasingly rely on fee income to supplement earnings. Competition among savings and loans, credit unions, brokerage houses, and other commercial banks has raised borrowing costs relative to yields available on loans. This pressure on net interest margins and growth constraints from capital restrictions make new products and fee income the most promising source of earnings growth. Many corporate customers in turn are so efficient in minimizing their deposit balances that fees represent a better source of income than interest income from compensating balances.

When analyzing a customer's account relationship, fee income from all services rendered is included in total revenue. Fees are frequently charged on a per-item basis, as with Federal Reserve wire transfers, or as a fixed periodic charge for a bundle of services, regardless of usage rates. Fees for servicing mortgage loans supported by pass-through securities and for providing letters of credit, financial guarantees, data processing, and cash management have recently risen at banks, which aggressively market these services.

With credit relationships banks often negotiate loan fees and compensating balance fees. Three such fees merit attention. Banks that extend formal loan commitments to corporate borrowers normally charge for the service. The loan commitment represents credit that is available at the borrower's discretion. If the customer chooses not to borrow, a bank earns no income from the service except for fees. The most common fee selected is a *facility fee*, which ranges from $1/8$ of 1 percent to $1/2$ of 1 percent of the total credit available. The fee applies regardless of actual borrowings because it is a charge for making funds available. Finance companies, for example, need back-up credit lines when their outstanding commercial paper matures, and a facility fee is the price for guaranteed bank financing.

A *commitment fee* serves the same purpose but is imposed against the unused portion of the line. Because it applies only to committed funds that are not actually borrowed, it represents a penalty charge for not borrowing. A customer that fully uses the available funds pays no commitment fee. The last fee is selectively applied to loan commitments that convert to a term loan after a specified period. Called a *conversion fee*, it equals as much as $1/2$ of 1 percent of the loan principal converted to a term loan and is paid at the time of conversion.

Determining the impact of these fees on revenues is straightforward. Suppose that each fee equals $1/4$ of 1 percent and applies to the $1 million credit line previously discussed. The customer borrows $800,000, which is converted to a term loan at the end of the year. The annual facility fee, commitment fee, and conversion fee amount to $2,500, $500, and $2,000, respectively.

Loan Interest and Base Lending Rates. Loans are the dominant asset in bank portfolios, and loan interest is the primary revenue source. The actual interest earned depends on the contractual loan rate and the outstanding principal. While banks quote many different loan rates to customers, several general features stand out. Most banks price commercial loans off of base rates, which serve as indexes of a bank's cost of funds. Common base rate alternatives include the federal funds rate, CD rate, commercial paper rate, the London Interbank Offer Rate (LIBOR), and a bank's own weighted cost of funds. The contractual loan rate is set at some mark-up over the base rate, so that interest income varies directly with movements in the level of borrowing costs. Such floating-rate loans are popular at banks because they increase the rate sensitivity of loans in line with the increased rate sensitivity of bank liabilities. Also, the magnitude of the mark-up reflects differences in perceived default risk associated with the borrower. The mark-up increases with loans in higher risk classes and with maturity as there is more time for the borrower's condition to deteriorate.[5] Finally, a substantial portion of commercial loans and virtually all consumer loans carry fixed rates. In each case, the contractual rates should reflect the estimated cost of bank funds, perceived default risk, and a term interest rate risk premium over the life of the agreement.

The use of several base rates masks the traditional role filled by the prime rate. Prior to the mid-1970s, banks tied most commercial loan rates to prime, which they described as the lowest loan rate available for the best commercial borrowers (see Contemporary Issues: The Prime Rate Controversy). Prime was an administered rate that banks changed in response to longer-term fundamental changes in money market rates. Prime rate changes thus occurred infrequently, but signaled relatively permanent movements in interest rate levels.

There are, in fact, many different prime rates. A national prime rate quoted by the money center banks receives most of the attention. These banks compete in the same national and international markets, so that when one bank changes its prime, the others quickly follow. Large regional banks and smaller banks typically quote their own local prime rates that reflect their own cost of funds. The money center banks serve as price leaders, but most other banks change their local prime with a lag, depending on local market conditions. If customers insist, they may tie their base rate to New York prime or the prime rate of a specific large regional bank. This creates problems, however, because other banks then control base rate changes and thus the yield on many loans. In this environment loan rates may not change coincidentally with the banks' cost of funds. Small banks have consequently moved to using their own prime rate where possible.

Since the mid-1970s, the prime rate has decreased in importance to the point that it now represents just another potential base rate. Large and financially strong corporations can issue commercial paper or obtain bank financing overseas at a small premium over Eurodollar deposit rates. Domestic banks that lend in these markets typically allow borrowers to select their own base rate from CDs, commercial paper, federal funds, and LIBOR. LIBOR pricing is particularly popular because the market is very liquid and many customers routinely deal in international markets. The federal funds rate is more volatile because it represents a target variable of the Federal Reserve's monetary policy and prime rates change too slowly at a bank's discretion. When borrowers choose among these alternatives, the bank's effective yield is invariably below its prime rate. Prime-rate pricing now applies almost exclusively to small businesses. Banks that use prime-rate pricing effectively segment borrowers in terms of their alternative credit sources. Borrowers with direct access to money markets pay subprime rates as banks act as price takers. Borrowers with no alternatives to bank credit pay higher rates set by banks.

The net result is that the prime rate no longer tracks money market rates as closely during periods of declining rates. When money market rates increase, borrowing costs also increase and banks raise prime with a short lag. When money market rates

---

[5]When a comprehensive customer profitability analysis is used, the markup reflects either default risk or required interest to cover expenses and meet profit targets. Many banks price loans independently from other account activity.

The Prime Rate Controversy

For many years banks described the prime rate as the rate they charged their best corporate customers. It was the lowest rate available to corporate borrowers, with most commercial loans carrying rates set at a mark-up over prime. This environment deterred price competition between the money center banks that administered the rate. When money market rates increased, a money center bank serving as a price leader would raise its prime. The others would follow closely. When market rates fell, another price leader would lead the group in lowering quoted prime.

Eventually, the money center banks broke with traditional prime rate pricing. In the mid-1970s, the best large corporate borrowers developed cheaper funding sources in the commercial paper market and with foreign banks that based loan rates at narrow margins over LIBOR. Rather than lower prime, and thus the effective yield on all

floating-rate loans, U.S. banks simply priced selected loans below prime when competition demanded it. The result was that prime-rate borrowers were not paying the lowest advertised rate available.

In 1980 Jackie Kleiner sued the First National Bank of Atlanta claiming that, by definition, the bank's prime rate was its lowest rate. Because other borrowers paid less than his prime rate loan, he argued that the prime rate was a fraud. First Atlanta settled the suit for an estimated $12 million. Other similar cases were quickly filed, most of which were settled out of court at considerable expense to banks. Most banks now substitute the generic term "base rate" for "prime rate" in their loan agreements. Those that still use "prime" explicitly define it as the bank's quoted commercial loan rate or add a disclaimer that it is not always the lowest rate.

---

decrease, banks are slow to lower prime. This behavior maintains interest spreads when rates increase and widens spreads when rates decrease. Exhibit 24.3 compares the prime rate with the secondary market rate on 90-day CDs. During periods when CD rates rose, the prime-minus CD spread was considerably less than during periods when CD rates declined. Implicitly, the lag in changing prime rates is shorter during a rising rate environment.[6]

CUSTOMER PROFITABILITY ANALYSIS: AN APPLICATION TO COMMERCIAL ACCOUNTS

The following analysis applies the customer profitability characteristics discussed previously. The bank's account manager has collected information regarding services used by Moeller Electronics, a large manufacturer of satellite dishes and specialty electronics equipment, for the first 3 months of the year. During this time the company borrowed $1.35 million of a $2 million credit line. Exhibit 24.4 lists pertinent infor-

---

[6]The interesting question is why would any borrower accept a floating-loan rate tied to prime? Each bank changes prime at its discretion, and changes may or may not reflect movements in actual interest rates. A loan rate tied to a specific money market rate at least varies with market conditions.

Exhibit 24.3 The Prime Rate versus 90-Day Certificate of Deposit (CD) Rates: Monthly Data, 1986–1990.

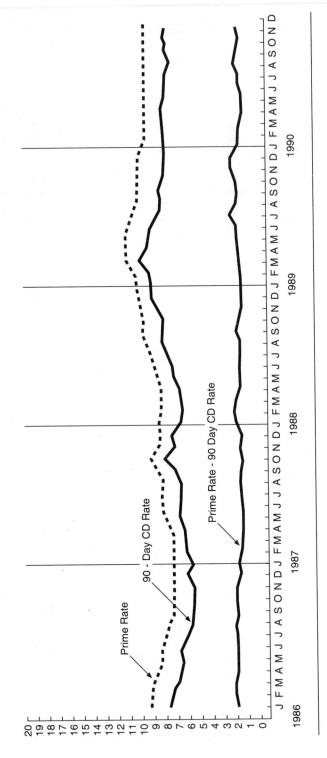

Source: *Federal Reserve Bulletin.*

Exhibit 24.4 Account Activity for Moeller Electronics, January through March

Loan Agreement
Revolver: $2 million commitment that converts to term loan after 3 years.
Interest rate: Bank's average 90-day CD rate + 2%
Fees: 0.5% facility fee; 0.25% conversion fee
Compensating balances: 5% of facility + 5% of actual borrowing; collected balances

Account Activity	Activity: (No. of Items)	Item Cost
Demand deposit activity		
Home debits	3,624	$0.17
Transit items	17,230	0.10
Deposits	106	0.33
Account maintenance	3	6.00
Returned items	24	2.50
Wire transfers	210	1.50
Security safekeeping	9	3.00
Payroll processing	3	1,000.00

Loan and Deposit Activity: January 1–March 31

Average borrowing	$1.35 million
Contractual interest rate	12.22%
Loan administration (annual)	0.61%
Risk expense (annual)	0.61%
Average ledger demand deposit balance	$271,627
Average float	$ 88,105
Required reserve ratio	12.00%
Earnings credit rate	9.25%
Weighted marginal cost of debt	10.06%[a]
Bank tax rate	40.00%

[a]Calculated assuming 93 percent of the loan financing is in the form of debt.

mation on the loan and other services provided. Exhibit 24.5 formally compares the bank's expenses and profit target with revenues from the total account relationship.

The loan is a revolving credit agreement in which Moeller Electronics has the option after 3 years of converting its outstanding loan to a term loan with fixed principal payments. It will pay a conversion fee only if it converts the line to a term loan. Compensating balances are set at 5 percent of the available credit, or facility, plus 5 percent of borrowings. Moeller Electronics used a variety of check-clearing services, wire transferred funds between banks, and had the bank hold securities for safekeeping in addition to borrowing funds. The bank also processed Moeller's payroll at a cost of $1,000 per month.

Expenses during the quarter totaled $43,110. Of this total, over 77 percent related to financing the loan, with the remainder attributable primarily to processing checks and Moeller's payroll. Check-handling expenses, while measurable, do not represent direct cash outlays. The cost of processing checks includes labor costs, processing equipment, repairs, overhead, and an allocation for fixed costs. Security safekeeping and loan handling add to personnel expenses. Risk expense on the loan is a noncash

**Exhibit 24.5 Customer Profitability Analysis for
                Moeller Electronics, January through March**

Expenses

Demand deposit expense

Home debits	3,624 @ $0.17	$ 616
Transit items	17,230 @ 0.10	1,723
Deposits	106 @ 0.33	35
Returned items	24 @ 2.50	60
Account maintenance	3 @ 6.00	18
Total		$ 2,452
Wire transfers	210 @ $1.50	315
Security safekeeping	9 @ $3.00	27
Payroll processing	3 @ $1,000.00	3,000

Loan expense

Loan administration: (0.0054)(90/365)($1.35 million)	1,798
Risk expense: (0.0061)(90/365)(1.35 million)	2,031
Interest expense on pooled debt financing: (0.1006)(90/365)($1.35 million)	33,487
Total expenses	$43,110

Target Profit

Target pretax return to shareholders = 18%
Relevant financing percentage: 7% equity, 93% debt

Target profit: (0.18)(90/365)(0.07)($1.35 million)	$4,194
Expenses + Target Profitl	$47,304

Revenues

Investment income from balances

Ledger balances	$271,627	
Minus float	88,105	
Collected balance	183,522	
Minus required reserves @ 12%	22,022	
Investable balances	$161,500	
Investment income: (0.0925)(90/365)($161,500)		$ 3,684
Fee income: (0.005)(90/365)($2 million)		2,466
Loan interest: (0.1222)(90/365)($1.35 million)		40,678
Total revenues		$46,828
Revenues − (Expenses + Target Profit)		−$ 476

charge based on historical loan loss experience. Interest expense on borrowed funds totals $33,487 and is obtained by multiplying the bank's weighted marginal cost of debt, assuming 93 percent of the loan is financed by debt.

The bank's target profit is expressed as a percentage of the loan. The percentage, derived from Equation 24.2, assumes an 18 percent pretax target return to shareholders determined by management, with 7 percent of the financing coming from equity. Based on $1.35 million borrowed, the target profit over 90 days equals $4,194. The sum of target profit and expenses—$47,304—represents the minimum revenue that must be generated for the bank to meet profit objectives. To provide a margin of error, or buffer, some banks include a markup over costs in their unit cost estimates. If so, this sum overstates the true revenue floor.

Revenues are separated into three components. Investment income from Moeller's demand deposit balances equals $3,684. This is obtained by multiplying the periodic earnings credit rate by investable balances of $161,500. Moeller Electronics actually held an average $183,522 in collected balances, while the 5 + 5 compensating balance requirement mandated only $167,500. Had the company just met its minimum balance requirement, investment income would have been $322 less. Facility fee income contributed $2,466, and loan interest, $40,678, for total revenue of $46,828. This fell short of expenses plus the target profit by just under $500. The Moeller Electronics account thus generated profits in excess of the bank's estimated expenses but did not meet its 18 percent targeted pretax return to shareholders.

PRICING NEW COMMERCIAL LOANS

The same framework can be used to price new loan agreements. The approach is the same, equating revenues with expenses plus target profit, only now the loan officer must forecast borrower behavior and bank expenses. Hence marginal analysis is appropriate using incremental data, not historical data. For loan commitments this involves projecting the magnitude and timing of actual borrowings, compensating balances held, and the volume of services consumed. For other loans the amount borrowed is known. Once projections are formalized, the officer can solve for the loan interest rate that equates expected revenues with expected costs. The analysis assumes that the contractual loan rate is set at a markup over the bank's weighted marginal cost of funds and thus varies coincidentally with borrowing costs.

Suppose that a bank is analyzing a request for a new 1-year $5 million working capital line of credit. The prospective borrower has no prior relationship with the bank. The officer handling the account forecasts that the customer will borrow an average $4 million during the year and that the annual cost of deposit services will equal $55,000. The bank will charge a commitment fee of ½ of 1 percent on the unused line, its weighted marginal cost of debt equals 11 percent, and its pretax target profit equals 20 percent. The loan is financed 6 percent by equity and 94 percent by debt. The combined risk and loan administration expense is projected at 1.5 percent of the loan. The issue is, what loan rate and compensating balance requirement will cover expected costs? For simplicity, the customer is required to hold a specified percentage of the loan in investable balances and will receive an 11.5 percent earnings credit rate.[7] The bank's weighted average marginal cost of debt over the year is expected to equal 11 percent.

Exhibit 24.6 summarizes two pricing alternatives. Estimated expenses and target profit based on 80 percent usage total $603,000 for the year. Option A requires 8 + 5 investable balances or $600,000 net of account float and required reserves. With

---

[7]If ledger or collected balances were required, the bank would also have to forecast float and required reserves.

Exhibit 24.6 Loan Pricing Analysis

Expenses

Deposit activity	$ 55,000
Loan administration and risk	60,000
Interest on borrowed funds	440,000
	$555,000

Target Profit	48,000
Total	$603,000

Revenues

Option A: Compensating balances set at 8 + 5 Investable balances ($600,000)
Option B: Compensating balances set at 5 + 0 Investable balances ($250,000)

	Option A	Option B
Fee income	$ 5,000	$ 5,000
Investment income from balances	69,000	28,750
Required loan interest	$529,000	$569,250
Total	$603,000	$603,000
Required loan rate[a]	13.225%	14.231%

[a]($529,000/$4,000,000) = 13.225%; ($569,250/$4,000,000) = 14.231%

$600,000 in investable balances, fee and investment income equal $74,000, leaving $529,000 in loan interest that must be earned for total revenues to equal $603,000. The required loan rate of 13.225 percent is calculated by dividing loan interest by the $4 million estimated loan. With these terms and the 11 percent weighted cost of funds serving as a base rate, the interest charge would be quoted at the bank's base rate plus 2.25 percent.

Many influential borrowers refuse to maintain substantial balances at a bank and instead prefer to pay explicit fees. Option B in this example assumes that the customer holds substantially lower balances of $250,000. In this environment the bank would need to increase the loan rate by 1 percent if fees were held constant. In essence, the bank expects to earn more than $40,000 less in investment income from balances, which is offset by $40,000 more in loan interest. In both cases, the required loan rate will vary directly with the bank's cost of funds.

The usefulness of the pricing procedure is that it provides a basis for understanding costs and revenues and negotiating terms. A bank is largely indifferent as to how revenues are obtained as long as the total covers expected costs. This example shows the quantitative relationship between compensating balances and the interest spread over the bank's base rate. A reduction in investable balances from 15 percent to 6.25 percent of the loan is equivalent to raising the interest rate by 1 percent.

Risk-Adjusted Returns on Loans

When deciding what rate to charge, loan officers attempt to forecast default losses over the life of a loan. Credit risk in turn can be divided into expected losses and unexpected losses. Expected losses might reasonably be based on mean historical loss rates, much like the summary ratios in Exhibit 24.1. Unexpected losses, in contrast, should be measured by computing the standard deviation of realized losses from the historical mean. Ideally, the interest rate on a loan will encompass both expected and unexpected losses.

Unfortunately, many banks ignore these risk components entirely. A common loan pricing scheme is for banks to classify loans into risk categories like that in Exhibit 24.1 based on mean historical loss rates. Low-risk loans have low default rates while default rates on higher-risk loans increase systematically. Risk expense, or the charge for potential default losses, is then levied in an approximate linear fashion with perceived riskiness. For example, the incremental risk charge might increase by 25 basis points per category from the lowest to the highest risk types.

There are two problems with this approach. First, expected losses do not normally vary in a linear fashion. Mean loss rates in each successive risk class typically increase by a greater amount from the lowest to highest risk categories. The loss rates in Exhibit 24.1 support this. A 25 basis point risk charge for risk class 1 loans exceeds the mean loss rate. A 50 basis point risk charge for risk class 2 loans is less than the mean loss rate because the default percentage increased by 45 basis points rather than just 25. The default percentage rises by an increased amount from risk class 2 to 3 and from risk class 3 to 4 as well. Any risk charge should thus increase nonlinearly. Second, even if expected losses vary linearly, unexpected losses typically do not. Suppose, for example, that the default percentages in the four risk classes varied at 25 basis point increments from .25 percent to 1 percent. The normal situation is that the highest-risk loans will exhibit the greatest volatility of loss rates such that the standard deviation of unexpected loss is greatest. These loans are thus riskier yet, and this risk should be priced.

Some banks now calculate a risk-adjusted return on equity on individual loans using the volatility in unexpected loan loss rates to allocate equity to each type of loan. Rose (1991) documents an application in which a bank allocates equity to each class of loans equal to one standard deviation of unexpected losses. The risk-adjusted return is then calculated as the net profit divided by allocated equity. The procedure adjusts for risk because loans with highly volatile unexpected losses are allocated large amounts of equity, while loans with little volatility in unexpected losses are allocated little equity. When the procedure was applied to historical loan performance, the results indicated that the highest-quality loans produced the highest risk-adjusted returns. Even though the dollar amount of net profit was small per loan, losses were so low that the equity allocation was similarly small.

The key point is that commercial loans have been underpriced at most banks in recent years because lenders appear to have systematically understated risk. The appropriate procedure is to identify both expected and unexpected losses and incorporate both in determining the appropriate risk charge. This does not appear to be the case with many other types of loans at banks. Witness the substantial profits banks have earned on consumer credit cards. Nonbank financial institutions similarly have had greater success in pricing loans. Consumer finance companies, for example, experience higher default rates but charge much higher loan rates than banks so that net profits and returns to stockholders exceed that at most banks. At the extreme are pawn shops. A recent study of pawn shops in five states determined that the effective APRs paid by consumers ranged from 36 percent to 240 percent in 1987 and 1988, high enough to cover default rates as high as 20 percent.[8]

Fixed Rates versus Floating Rates

When interest rates were relatively stable and the yield curve was upsloping, banks were willing to make loans at fixed rates above those being paid on shorter-term liabilities. Even though its funding GAP was negative, a bank could continually roll over deposits at relatively low rates and maintain a positive spread. In a volatile rate environment with an increased reliance on market rate liabilities, banks prefer floating-rate loans and short loan maturities. Floating-rate loans increase the rate sensitivity of bank assets, increase the GAP, and reduce potential net interest losses from rising interest rates. Because most banks operate with negative funding GAPs through 1-year maturities, floating-rate loans normally reduce a bank's interest rate risk.

As indicated in Exhibit 24.7, over 72 percent of commercial and industrial loans were made at fixed rates in 1985, while just under 28 percent carried floating rates. These figures are misleading, however, because most of the fixed-rate loans were short term, with an average maturity of just 23 days. Short-term floating-rate loans, in comparison, had an average maturity of 125 days. Loans with original maturities beyond 1 year were priced on a floating-rate basis by a margin of almost 2 to 1. Thus there appears to be a direct relationship between maturity and the frequency of floating-rate loans. A higher proportion of construction loans and agriculture loans carried fixed rates.

Floating-rate loans effectively transfer interest rate risk from the bank to the borrower. While this is normally desirable, it may eventually return to haunt the bank in the form of higher credit risk. Rising interest rates increase a borrower's interest expense. If corporate cash flow from operations or personal income do not increase accordingly, the borrower may be unable to meet debt service requirements.

This scenario became real in 1980 and 1981 for small businesses and again in 1985 for residential mortgages. When the prime rate rose above 20 percent in 1980 and 1981, small business's cash flow could not support the high interest payments and failures rose. During the late 1970s, housing prices rose by more than 10 percent annually. Many individuals, fearing that housing might not be affordable if they waited, stretched themselves to the limit financially to purchase a home. This often meant paying as little as 5 percent down and negotiating some form of adjustable-rate mortgage for the remainder of the purchase price. After 1980 the U.S. economy entered a deflationary environment, in which housing values increased at roughly the rate of inflation but personal income did not increase fast enough to meet rising mortgage payments. Home buyers, in turn, started defaulting on their mortgages. By 1985 payments on more than 6 percent of all mortgages were delinquent, and foreclosures

---

[8]Caskey and Zikmund (1990) document the performance of pawn shops in Indiana, New Jersey, Oklahoma, Oregon, and Pennsylvania.

Exhibit 24.7 Fixed-Rate versus Floating-Rate Loans, February 1985 (Millions of Dollars)

Loan Type and Rate	Amount	% of Total	Average Size[a]	Average Maturity[a]
Commercial and Industrial Loans				
Short-term	$33,766	87.8%	0.213	40 days
Fixed rate	26,114	67.9	0.257	23 days
Floating rate	7,652	19.9	0.134	125 days
Long-term	4,675	12.2	0.152	50 months
Fixed rate	1,632	4.3	0.084	42 months
Floating rate	3,043	7.9	0.272	54 months
Total	38,441	100.0		
Fixed rate	27,746	72.2		
Floating rate	10,695	27.8		
Construction and land development loans	1,535	100.0	0.092	8 months
Fixed rate	747	48.7	0.080	6 months
Floating rate	788	51.3	0.108	11 months
Agriculture loans	1,185	100.0	0.021	7 months
Fixed rate	723	61.0		
Floating rate	462	39.0		

[a]Average size and maturity are weighted by the dollar amount of loans.

Source: Survey of Loans Made, February 1985, *Federal Reserve Bulletin*, June 1985.

had reached almost 0.25 percent of outstanding mortgages. In subsequent years conditions improved but by 1990 the cycle had repeated itself, and mortgage delinquencies rose sharply to 6 to 7 percent. Banks effectively traded interest rate risk for default risk.

Given equivalent rates, most borrowers prefer fixed-rate loans in which the bank assumes all interest rate risk. Banks frequently offer two types of inducements to encourage floating-rate pricing. First, floating rates are initially set below fixed rates for borrowers with a choice. The discount may be as high as 3 percent, depending on the current level of rates. A bank essentially charges a term premium to cover the added interest rate risk on fixed-rate loans. The size of the discount is, of course, constrained by a bank's cost of funds and required return. Second, a bank may establish an interest rate cap on floating-rate loans to limit the possible increase in periodic payments. This cap represents the maximum interest rate that will be applied and may be fixed over the entire maturity or vary during successive periods. A borrower pays the negotiated floating rate until the cap is reached. While cap rate agreements improve a bank's ability to market floating-rate loans, they lower revenues when interest rates rise. Most lenders thus use caps sparingly.

While many commercial loans carry floating rates, it has been difficult for banks to market floating-rate consumer loans except for real estate. During 1989 adjustable-rate mortgages exceeded 50 percent of new mortgages. It also appears that floating-rate installment loan pricing will evolve slowly. Banks that market variable-rate consumer loans generally follow these guidelines:

1. Select an index or base rate that varies closely with the bank's cost of funds. The bank's weighted cost of funds is preferred, assuming the bank can adequately explain it to customers. Borrowers, however, may prefer a more visible, publicly quoted index.

2. Link variation in the floating rate with the timing of index changes. If the index on consumer credit lines changes monthly, for example, vary the floating rate monthly.

3. Offer both fixed-rate and floating-rate options. Price the fixed rate at a premium large enough to protect against possible increases in the cost of funds. Impose prepayment penalties on all fixed-rate contracts.

4. Use interest rate caps sparingly.

Matched Funding and Hedging. Some banks make fixed-rate loans and attempt to control interest rate risk by matched funding or financial futures. Matched funding involves negotiating loans and purchasing funds with identical maturities. If, for example, a customer requests a 1-year fixed-rate loan, a bank would issue 1-year CDs to fund it. If the loan is priced at a positive spread over the CDs and the timing of interest payments coincides, the bank assumes no additional interest rate risk. This strategy is limited to large banks with an extensive customer base that can generate different-maturity deposits on demand. Chapter 13 outlines the mechanics of transfer pricing systems, which are flexible enough to hedge interest rate risk via matched funding.

Chapters 9 and 10 covered hedging tools and strategies that banks can use to hedge interest rate risk. With financial futures it is possible to make fixed-rate loans and hedge against potential losses from higher borrowing costs later by selling futures contracts or buying put options on financial futures. It is also possible to enter into interest rate swaps by agreeing to make fixed-rate payments in return for floating-rate receipts. Hedging can be applied either to a bank's funding GAP, duration gap, or individual transactions. Details for the various hedging strategies are provided in these earlier chapters.

Both matched funding and the use of financial futures entail certain risks. A bank will lose in both instances if a borrower prepays a loan. Prepayments normally occur when interest rates fall. With matched funding, a bank will still pay interest on its liabilities at the original rates but must reinvest the proceeds at lower rates. Any "fixed" spread will decline and possibly even become negative. With interest rate futures, the bank will have a loss on its (short) futures position. This necessitates prohibiting prepayments or imposing substantial prepayment penalties.

Base Rate Alternatives

Contractual loan rates for commercial customers are determined through negotiation. As Exhibit 24.6 demonstrates, banks take into account projected expenses, compensating balances, fee income, and profit objectives. The two parties often negotiate the base rate as well in floating-rate loans. Large, multinational borrowers can virtually dictate terms. Frequently, a major customer will circulate a loan request among several financial institutions and accept bids on the loan terms. It is common for the borrower to retain the option to price the loan off of several potential base rates. The actual base rate is determined not when the agreement is signed, but when the borrower actually takes down the funds. Thus a borrower can wait until the funds are needed to determine which alternative will likely provide the lowest-cost alternative.

For example, a large bank has agreed to extend a 6-year $50 million revolver/term loan to a Fortune 500 member with domestic and overseas operations. The revolver portion extends 2 years with the 4-year term portion also divided into consecutive 2-year agreements. Because of its market power, the borrower is granted three base rate options: the bank's 3-month CD rate, 3-month LIBOR, or the bank's weighted cost of debt. Exhibit 24.8 indicates the size of premium over each base rate.

Chapter 13 describes the weighted cost of funds calculation. The CD base rate is normally the quoted nominal rate adjusted for required reserves and the cost of Federal Deposit Insurance Corp. insurance. LIBOR represents the quoted rate, as neither reserves nor insurance is required. The customer selects which alternative applies at the time funds are borrowed under the revolver. At the end of each following quarter, the customer can reset the base rate according to the scale. Obviously, the customer will select the base rate and premium that it forecasts will provide the lowest-cost alternative.

Smaller corporations do not possess the same financial flexibility and thus do not receive the same treatment. Banks are moving toward using their weighted marginal cost of debt as the preferred base rate for these customers. This rate represents the effective marginal cost of bank borrowing. Loans priced at a positive spread over this cost of funds lock in a return as long as the borrower does not default. Two issues continually arise, however. What is the best measure of the bank's cost of funds and subsequent base rate for pricing purposes? How can the bank readily communicate its base rate computation to customers?

The Weighted Cost of Funds and Base Rate. Chapter 13 introduced a procedure to estimate the weighted marginal cost of total bank funds, including debt and equity. In loan pricing, the cost of equity represents the bank's target profit. Base rate analysis focuses on the cost of debt plus target return.

The following calculation of a base rate is an attempt to ensure that loans are priced to cover bank costs. It rests on several assumptions that guarantee a base rate estimate above a bank's weighted marginal cost of total debt. First, core deposits are not available to fund loans. This is justified because loans presumably do not exceed deposits, and long-term funds should finance long-term bank assets. Second, deposits paying below-market rates will continue to decrease as a funding source. For these reasons, the cost-of-debt calculation excludes core deposits, such as demand deposits, NOW accounts, and savings deposits as funding sources for loans.

Exhibit 24.9 provides an estimate of a hypothetical bank's weighted cost of market-rate debt. The bank expects to operate with $88.5 million in MMDAs, time

Exhibit 24.8 Pricing Alternatives over Various Base Rates

| | 6-Year Revolver/Term Loan Pricing Options | | | |
	Years	CD +	LIBOR +	Weighted Cost of Debt +
Revolver	1–2	1	$7/8$	$1/4$
Term	3–4	$1 1/8$	1	$1/2$
Term	5–6	$1 3/8$	$1 1/4$	$3/4$

deposits, CDs, and federal funds purchased. The weighted cost of 9.25 percent is calculated as the sum of the proportionate financing from each source times the corresponding current market interest rate across components. Current interest rates are adjusted for reserves and FDIC insurance.

The base rate quotation uses this weighted cost as the primary input. A bank's target loan rate equals this composite cost plus a premium that reflects the bank's target net interest margin. This net interest margin includes coverage for anticipated expenses, taxes, and target profit. Finally, most borrowers resent paying too large of a premium over any base rate. This reflects the perception that loans priced at a bank's base rate are available only to the most creditworthy borrowers. The base rate quote is set at the target loan rate minus the maximum premium acceptable to normal-risk customers, 13.75 percent minus 2.50 percent in this example.

Communicating any base rate to customers can be confusing. Borrowers constantly hear references to the national prime rate and federal funds rates following the weekly money supply announcement. The natural tendency is to compare base rates, and normally the rate calculated from Exhibit 24.9 is above the national prime rate. A bank must clearly indicate why its cost of funds does not match a money center bank's and focus on the fact that the bank's own base rate tracks its cost of market rate funds. Most discussions eventually focus on the benefits from this bank's personal relationship and quality of service.

CUSTOMER PROFITABILITY ANALYSIS: CONSUMER INSTALLMENT LOANS

The previous applications focused on commercial accounts. In general, banks can use the same format in evaluating the profitability of individual accounts. There are, however, two significant differences that alter the analysis: consumer loans are much smaller than commercial loans, on average, and their processing costs per dollar of loan are much higher. In 1989, for example, the average installment loan at banks with $50 to $200 million in deposits equaled only $4,600, ranging from $1,640 for check credit plans to $21,250 for floor plan arrangements. Each consumer loan officer processed an average 528 applications at a cost of $118 per loan, and it cost almost $7 to collect each payment.[9] Loans will not generate enough interest to cover costs if

---

[9] The information is drawn from the *Federal Reserve's Functional Cost Analysis* data for banks with deposits from $50 million to $200 million.

Exhibit 24.9 Sample Base Rate Calculation: Weighted Cost of Debt, Core Deposits Excluded (Millions of Dollars)

Loanable Market-Rate Debt	Amount	%	Current Rates	Weighted Cost
Money market deposit accounts	$16.8	19%	8.00%	1.52%
Small time deposits (6-mo.)	19.5	22	9.15	2.01
Small time deposits (30-mo.)	8.0	9	10.70	0.96
Jumbo CDs	38.9	44	9.65	4.25
Federal funds purchased	5.3	6	8.45	0.51
Total	$88.5	100%		9.25%

Base Rate Calculation:

Weighted cost of market-rate debt	9.25%
Target net interest margin	4.50
Target loan rate	13.75
Maximum premium over base rate	−2.50
Base rate	11.25%

they are too small or the maturity is too short, even with high loan rates. Banks thus set pricing targets with regard to minimum loan size, maturity, and the contract interest rate.[10]

The profitability framework discussed below recognizes this trade-off between size, maturity, and rate. It establishes break-even values for each pricing element based on average unit costs associated with consumer installment loans, assuming values for the other pricing elements. The break-even relationship is based on the objective that loan interest revenues net of funding costs and losses equal loan costs:

$$\text{Net interest income} = \text{Interest expense} + \text{Loan losses} \qquad \textbf{(24.3)}$$
$$+ \text{Acquisition costs} + \text{Collection costs}$$

More generally, if:

r = annual percentage loan rate (%)
d = interest cost of debt (%)
l = average loan loss rate (%)
S = initial loan size
B = average loan balance outstanding (% of initial loan)
M = number of monthly payments
C_a = loan acquisition cost, and
C_c = collection cost per payment

then

$$(r - d - l)SB(M/12) = C_a + (C_c)(M) \qquad \textbf{(24.4)}$$

---

[10]Peterson (1985) provides a comprehensive analysis of consumer loan and deposit pricing issues.

Exhibit 24.10 Break-Even Analysis: Consumer Installment Loans

Average Costs: 1989 Functional Cost Analysis Data

Acquisition cost per loan	$C_a = \$118.00$
Collection cost per payment	$C_c = \$6.70$
Interest cost of debt	$d = 6.95\%$
Loan loss rate	$i = 0.53\%$

Break-Even Loan Size (S)

Assume:

No. of monthly payments	$M = 24$
Annual percentage loan rate	$r = 12\%$
Average loan balance outstanding (%)	$B = 55\%$

$$(0.12 - 0.0695 - 0.0053)S(0.55)(24/12) = \$118 + \$6.70(24)$$
$$S = \$5,607$$

Break-Even Loan Rate (r)

Assume:

$M = 24$

$S = \$3,000$

$B = 55\%$

$$(r - 0.0695 - 0.0053)(\$3,000)(0.55)2 = \$118 + \$6.70(24)$$
$$(r - .0748) = .084485$$
$$r = .1593$$
$$= 15.93\%$$

The left side of the equality represents total net interest revenue over the life of the loan. The right side represents the initial cost of making the loan plus the cost of collecting all payments.

Two applications of Equation (24.4) are provided in Exhibit 24.10, using 1989 Functional Cost data.[11] A 2-year loan with 24 monthly payments priced at a 12 percent annual percentage rate (APR) required a minimum $5,607 initial loan to cover costs. A similar $3,000 loan over 2 years requires a 15.93 percent APR for the bank to break even. The bank's realized return on equity depends on whether actual loan rates or loan sizes exceed these break even levels. Adding in a target dollar return with expenses produces the target ROE to pay shareholders.

While these examples are simplistic, they show the procedure to calculate break-even costs and returns. In practice, banks must include other expenses that the federal data omit, such as costs from overhead, credit reports, advertising, and repossession. They should also recognize income from late-payment charges, fractions of months interest, and the effect of rebates and then compare the difference between income and expenses with their target return.

---

[11]Equation (24.4) approximates the true relationship. In fact, the average loan outstanding varies with the true interest rate and maturity. A precise equation appears in *Functional Cost Analysis* (Board of Governors of the Federal Reserve System, 1989).

SEGMENT PROFITABILITY ANALYSIS

Many banks attempt to evaluate the profitability of specific products or lines of business. The intent is to determine whether shareholders earn a reasonable risk-adjusted return in line with a bank's strategic objectives regarding how resources are allocated. For example, the question is commonly asked whether commercial loans to Fortune 500 companies are profitable. How does trust department profitability compare with consumer lending?

Segment profitability analysis is the label assigned the evaluation process. The basic concept is to calculate a return on equity (ROE) associated with each line of business. A bank essentially creates an income statement for each segment by identifying the relevant revenues and expenses attributable to the underlying product or service. Management must, in turn, allocate equity capital to support each segment based on the presumed riskiness of the underlying revenues and expenses. Commercial real estate lending is more risky than residential mortgage lending, for example, so more equity is allocated to the real estate business.

First Manhattan Consulting Group has been active in performing this type of analysis. Exhibit 24.11 documents aggregate results from a recent study of theirs for 14 different lines of business. The second and final column of data indicate the value that was created or destroyed in 1989 and 1990. Note the volatility between the two years. Note also that branch delivery systems, trust services, credit card services, middle market (firms with sales under $10 million annually) lending, and cash management added significant value in both years. Most of these are associated with retail customers, not commercial customers.

SUMMARY

Customer profitability analysis is a procedure for analyzing the profitability of existing account relationships. It compares revenues generated from fees, investment income from a customer's deposit balances, and loan interest to expenses associated with extending credit and providing noncredit services plus a target return to shareholders. If revenues exceed or equal the sum of expenses and target profit, the account relationship at least meets the bank's minimum acceptable rate of return criteria. If revenues are less than expenses, the relationship is clearly unprofitable. If revenues exceed expenses but are less than expenses plus the target profit, the account covers costs but does not meet the minimum return objectives. These last two relationships consequently need to be repriced.

The same framework can be used to price commercial loans. It further demonstrates the trade-off between desired loan interest income, fee income, and compensating balance requirements in pricing decisions. In today's environment, fees are preferred to compensating balances because banks must hold reserves against balances, which lowers the net yield on the account relationship. Corporate treasurers are also quite sophisticated in minimizing balances such that they prefer explicit pricing via fees. In recent years, loan yields have been too low, on average, relative to the risk assumed

Exhibit 24.11 Shareholder Values in Commercial Banking:
Year-end 1989 vs. 11/30/90 ($ Billions)

Business (Ranked by Value Created as of 12/31/89)	12/31/89 Estimate of Market Capital Attributable to the Business	12/31/89 Shareholder Value Created/ (Destroyed)[a]	11/30/90 Estimate of Market Capital Attributable to the Business	11/30/90 Shareholder Value Created/ (Destroyed)[a]
1. Branch Delivery (consumer and small business)	$85 billion	$65 billion	$80 billion	$50 billion
2. Commercial Real Estate Lending	40	20	(18)	(38)
3. Trust (personal and institutional svcs.)	20	15	22	17
4. Credit Card	18	12	16	9
5. Middle Market	35	8	34	7
6. Cash Management	10	6	11	7
7. Corporate Finance	10	6	(3)	(10)
8. Other Fee-Based Services	−10	4	11	5
9. Swaps, FX, Securities Trading	6	2	6	2
10. Other Consumer Lending	15	(5)	16	(6)
11. International Banking	0	(15)	0	(13)
12. Residential Mortgages (on balance sheet)	0	(15)	0	(17)
13. Large Corporate (loans and lines)	0	(25)	0	(23)
14. Other (includes LDC)	(9)	(33)	(5)	(30)
Total U.S. Banks	**$240 billion**	**$35 billion**	**$170 billion**	**$(40) billion**

[a]Value Created = Market capital value less invested common equity; variability by banks is high, with some creating—and some destroying—value in virtually every category.

In terms of enhancing shareholder value, branch operations focusing on consumers and small businesses was the single most valuable business, according to First Manhattan Consulting Group estimates. In this analysis, the difference between market capital attributable to a line of business and the amount of equity invested in the business is the shareholder value either created or destroyed. For example, bank branch delivery operations at the end of 1989 generated an estimated $85 billion in market capital on $30 billion of invested equity, creating an estimated $55 billion in shareholder value.

Source: William Lowe, and Christopher Svare. "Restructuring Intensifies." *Bank Management* (January 1991).

on many commercial loans. This is evidenced by the extraordinary increases in provisions for loan losses that have swamped many banks' earnings. The problem is that banks have generally miscalculated default risk and consequently underpriced credit.

Consumer loan pricing is based on break-even analysis regarding the minimum acceptable size of loan or minimum acceptable rate of return. Because most loans are relatively small and do not generate significant fees or investment income from balances, consumer loan rates are relatively high. Alternatively, banks need to increase the minimum size of consumer installment loans before revenues cover the cost of making the loans and processing payments.

Finally, most banks prefer to make floating-rate loans that increase the rate sensitivity of assets. Banks now price floating-rate loans off of many different base rates, including money market rates, a money center bank's prime rate, and their own local bank prime rate. The latter alternative assures a bank that loan yields will vary with its marginal cost of funds. Banks can generally lock in a spread and transfer interest rate risk to borrowers.

Questions

Framework

1. What is the purpose of customer profitability analysis?

2. What are the three types of loan expenses, in order, from the most expensive to the least.

3. What are the two ways of accounting for the cost of default risk on a loan?

4. If a borrower requests a $100,000 working capital loan using inventory as collateral, what default risk expense would the bank charge to the loan if the bank's historical default experience matches Exhibit 24.1?

5. What are the three sources of revenue from a customer's account? Which is declining in use and why?

6. Explain how ledger deposit balances differ from collected balances and investable balances. Which is more restrictive to a borrower in meeting compensating balance requirements?

7. **a.** Suppose a business establishes a $200,000 credit line with 4 + 6 compensating balance requirements in the ledger account. The business draws down the line by $150,000 for a year and gets average float of $10,000. The bank must maintain 8 percent as required reserves. How large a ledger compensating balance would be required? What would the collected balance be? The investable balance?

   b. How large would each of these three balances be if the 4 + 6 requirement were in investable funds?

   c. If the bank can earn 10 percent return on investable funds, what would the revenue difference between the two accounts (ledger versus investable balances) be for the bank?

8. Suppose that a borrower needs $80,000. A bank gives the borrower a choice of two pricing schemes. The first is a $100,000 loan with 20 percent compensating balance requirements (funded from the loan) priced at 10 percent. The second is an $80,000 loan with no balance requirements priced at 12.5 percent. Calculate the effective cost to the borrower of each alternative. Assuming the bank must hold 12 percent required reserves against customer deposits, calculate the effective return to the bank of each alternative. Which pricing scheme is preferred for the bank?

9. Loan officers and borrowers negotiate the earnings credit rate applicable to the borrower's deposit balances. What rate is appropriate theoretically? Describe both the banker's and borrower's position.

10. If consumer loans tend to have longer maturities than commercial loans, why are fewer consumer loans tied to a base rate than commercial loans?

11. "Prime was an administered rate . . ." What does this statement mean, and has its truth promoted or curtailed the use of the prime rate?

12. The difference between the prime rate charged by money center banks and short-term money market rates can be quite volatile. What factors determine the differential and its volatility?

Profitability of Existing Loans

13. You are responsible for identifying customer accounts that are not meeting the bank's profit target of an 18 percent pretax return to shareholders. Applicable direct expenses and revenue factors are listed below for Crowe Labs Inc. for 1992.

    Actual borrowing: $550,000 of a $700,000 loan commitment
    Deposit activity expense: $20,470
    Loan risk expense: 0.75%
    Loan handling expense: 1.1%
    Pooled cost of debt financing the loan: 10.15%
    Bank commitment fee: 0.25%
    Crowe's investable deposit balances: $41,390
    Bank interest income: $81,500

    The bank pays taxes at the 34 percent rate, provides a 6.5 percentage earnings credit, and allocates 8 percent equity and 92 percent debt financing to all loans. The pooled cost of debt estimate incorporates the 92 percent debt financing assumption. Did this account generate enough revenue to cover bank expenses and pay shareholders an 18 percent pretax return? How much did the bank earn on the account?

14. What is the motivation for a bank to require a compensating balance requirement in lieu of fees when pricing a loan?

15. Explain why a bank might prefer to charge a commitment fee instead of a facility fee.

Pricing New Loans

16. In the marginal analysis necessary to price a new loan, the bank must estimate a cost for risk. Discuss the following two difficulties.
    a. Some banks ignore the risk and price as though risk were zero. If your bank were approached by a potential loan customer who had been shopping around for loans and who presented you with terms offered by a risk-ignoring competitor, what should you do?
    b. Categorizing loans by risk category can be deceiving if the bank prices each higher-risk category with a constant marginal premium. What is wrong with this approach?

17. A senior officer at your bank estimates that the annual expenses and target profit of a customer's account relationship will total $85,000 for the next year. The customer is expected to borrow $600,000 of a $900,000 credit line. The bank will charge no fees. The customer has a choice of two pricing schemes:

	A	B
Compensating balances:	5% + 0% ledger balances	5% + 5% investable balances
Loan interest:	prime rate + 1.5%	prime rate + 1%
Earnings credit:	8%	8%

   a. If the customer's average deposit float equals $15,000, the prime rate averages 12 percent, and the bank must hold 12 percent required reserves against collected balances, which alternative will produce the greatest revenue for the bank?

   b. Using the data for pricing scheme A, determine the interest rate the bank should charge for total revenues to equal expenses plus the target profit exactly.

18. What problems arise when a bank attempts to determine the appropriate interest rate on a fixed-rate term loan? Should it use the framework suggested in Exhibit 24.6?

19. The chief financial officer for Ferrell Imports just requested an increase in the firm's credit line to $4 million from the present $3 million. As the first step in the pricing analysis, you collected information concerning Ferrell's account relationship with the bank during the past year (Table 1). During the year, Ferrell Imports borrowed the full $3 million and maintained relatively small compensating balances that were set at 5 + 3 collected balances.

   a. Using the information in Table 1, determine whether bank revenues from the account covered expenses during the year and met the bank's profit target of a 16 percent pretax return on equity.

   b. Assume that Ferrell's noninterest expense increases by 10 percent during the next year and that all other items remain constant except the weighted cost of debt, which is expected to equal 9.5 percent. Determine the nominal loan rate the bank should charge to cover expenses plus meet the 16 percent pretax profit target.

Consumer Loan

20. George Smith comes into the bank to request a loan to buy a boat for $50,000. He will put up $10,000 and wants to borrow the rest over 3 years with monthly payments. With the following information and assuming George is an acceptable credit risk, what rate should you place on this loan?

Cost of processing boat loan applications	$200
Collection cost per payment	$7
Marginal cost of bank funds	8%
Loan loss rate on collateralized boat loans	0.5%

   Since this will be an installment loan, the principal will be gradually repaid over the 3 years. On average the outstanding loan will be 55 percent of the initial balance.

Table 1 Account Activity for Ferrell Imports; Previous 12 Months

	No. of Items	Item Cost
Account Activity		
Demand deposit activity		
Home debits	6,481	$ 0.21
Transit items	25,336	0.15
Deposits	273	0.47
Account maintenance	12	10.00
Wire transfers	1,727	2.25
Payroll processing	1	1,500

Loan and Deposit Activity
Average loan outstanding: $3 million
Average contract loan rate: 11.42%
Loan administration expense: 0.70%
Loan risk expense: 0.95%
Average ledger demand deposit balance: $128,622
Average account float: $24,900
Bank required reserve ratio: 12%
Weighted marginal cost of debt: 8.47%
Facility fee: 0.25%
Earnings credit rate: 8%
Bank marginal tax rate: 34%
Bank target capital structure: debt = 91%; equity = 9%

References

Board of Governors of the Federal Reserve System. *Functional Cost Analysis.* Washington, D.C.: Government Printing Office, 1989.

Brick, Jack. "Pricing Commercial Loans." *The Journal of Commercial Bank Lending* (January 1984).

Caskey, John, and Brian Zikmund. "Pawnshops: The Consumer's Lender of Last Resort." *Economic Review* (Economic Review, March/April 1990).

Cramer, Robert, and Peter Struck. "The Present Value Approach to Commercial Loan Pricing." *The Journal of Bank Research* (Winter 1982).

Crenshaw, Ari. "The Role of Deposits in Loan Pricing." *Journal of Commercial Bank Lending* (June 1989).

Fischer, Gerald. "The Prime Rate Controversy: There Is Light at the End of the Tunnel." *The Journal of Commercial Bank Lending* (November 1984).

James, Christopher. "Pricing Alternatives for Loan Commitments: A Note." *Journal of Bank Research* (Winter 1983).

James, Christopher. "An Analysis of Bank Loan Rate Indexation." *Journal of Finance* (June 1982).

Johnson, Bradford. "An Analysis of Modern Concepts of Loan Yields." *The Magazine of Bank Administration* (August 1977).

Knight, Robert. "Customer Profitability Analysis: Parts I–II." *Monthly Review* (Federal Reserve Bank of Kansas City, April 1975 and September–October 1985).

Lowe, William, and Christopher Svare. "Restructuring Intensifies." *Bank Management* (January 1991).

Nadler, Paul. "Balances and Buggy Whips in Loan Pricing." *Journal of Commercial Bank Lending* (February 1989).

Peterson, Richard. "Pricing Consumer Loans and Deposits." In *Handbook for Banking Strategy,* edited by Richard Aspinwall and Robert Eisenbeis. New York: John Wiley & Sons, 1985.

Rose, Sanford. "Higher Returns Possible from The Blue Chips." *American Banker* (January 30, 1991).

Santomero, Anthony M. "Pricing Business Credit." In *Handbook for Banking Strategy,* edited by Richard Aspinwall and Robert Eisenbeis. New York: John Wiley & Sons, 1985.

"Who Are Your Most Profitable Customers?" *ABA Banking Journal* (February 1991).

Part VI

Special Topics

Chapter 25

Off-Balance Sheet Activities
and Noninterest Income

Put yourself in the shoes of a chief executive officer whose bank is undercapitalized. Prior to risk-based capital standards, the minimum capital required by regulators was set at a fixed percentage of total assets. One strategy to improve profitability and help meet the capital requirement was to book new assets and move them off the balance sheet, yet retain some earnings power by servicing the assets. Alternatively, you could sell assets, use the proceeds to pay down debt, and thus shrink the size of the bank. If you again retained some claim on the assets' earning power, your overall capital position would improve dramatically.

Risk-based capital requirements obviously hamper this strategy because banks must now hold capital in support of on-balance sheet risk assets as well as certain types of off-balance sheet activities. Still, some off-balance sheet activities require no capital support. To be beneficial, off-balance sheet business must generate sufficient income to offset the additional capital needs. Banks that book such business presumably recognize the greater returns necessary and find that off-balance sheet activities add value to the firm.

This chapter describes the nature of bank off-balance sheet activities and their risk and return features. Particular attention is paid to asset securitization and available benefits from outright asset sales.

TYPES OF OFF-BALANCE SHEET ACTIVITIES

An off-balance sheet item is a contingent claim or contract that legally binds a bank to perform some action under prespecified circumstances. Until the circumstances are realized and the bank acts on the obligation, the claim does not show up on a bank's books. Hence it is an off-balance sheet item. Off-balance sheet activities are attractive because they generate fee income regardless of whether the contingency is ever realized. The primary reason that federal regulators impose capital requirements against certain off-balance sheet transactions is that they also entail risk. If banks were allowed to engage in off-balance sheet activities without constraint, they could end up with liabilities that swamp their ability to absorb potential losses. As indicated in the following discussion, the motivation underlying many off-balance sheet activities varies. Positions in some contracts actually reduce interest rate or exchange rate risk. Other activities are pursued primarily to generate income and enhance long-term customer credit relationships.

As the term indicates, off-balance sheet activities can take a variety of forms. Most involve little or no up-front cash outlay. The most common types are loan commitments, standby letters of credit, interest rate swaps, foreign exchange transactions, and positions in futures and forward contracts.

Loan Commitments

Loan commitments are used by businesses and individuals in the normal course of business activity. They represent legally binding commitments in which a bank agrees to lend a borrower a specified amount of funds over a fixed period of time. The agreement normally specifies appropriate uses of the proceeds, the interest rate to be charged, and the timing of maximum borrowing against the commitment. For example, a bank may agree to lend a builder $2 million over the next year. The builder agrees to pay interest at the bank's prime rate plus 3 percent against the amount actually borrowed. The proceeds are to be used for the construction of a strip shopping mall. The builder can borrow up to $2 million over the life of the loan, but must provide documentation of actual expenditures for the project to take down or draw against the loan.

Loan commitments are used for a variety of purposes. A firm that regularly issues commercial paper may request a backup or standby loan commitment under which a bank agrees to extend credit to back up maturing commercial paper. In normal circumstances the firm plans to simply issue new commercial paper to repay outstanding paper. If, however, market conditions are not attractive when the commercial paper issue comes due, the firm can draw against the commitment to pay off the commercial paper holders. Neither the bank nor the borrower anticipates that the commitment will be used, in general. Another firm that needs seasonal working capital financing may request a loan commitment to fund the temporary increase in inventory and receivables. In every instance, the borrower pays a facility fee and/or commitment fee for the service regardless of how much is actually borrowed. Interest is paid only on the amount actually borrowed.

Commitments essentially represent guaranteed financing for the borrower and thus serve as a form of insurance. The bank assumes the risk that the borrower will demand funds when credit is tight. As such, loan commitments entail liquidity risk. This risk may be substantial because in a credit crunch many borrowers will use their commitments simultaneously and the bank will have to borrow the supporting funds or sell assets. Both alternatives are costly because interest rates rise when credit is tight. In addition, the borrower's financial condition might deteriorate during the time between when the commitment is negotiated and final maturity. If the bank does not control the timing of take-downs, the borrower may draw down the commitment when in distress. Thus commitments also entail credit risk. For this reason, banks typically offer loan commitments only to high-quality borrowers.

Banks must have sufficient capital to support loan commitments. Specifically, loan commitments that will be outstanding beyond 1 year are effectively in the 50-percent risk class. Thus each commitment dollar requires 2 cents core capital and 4 cents of total capital. Shorter-term commitments do not raise bank capital requirements.

Note Issuance Facilities

Rather than lend funds directly, large banks often help corporations and foreign governments place their securities privately with foreign investors in the form of a note issuance facility. Participating banks agree to make funds available to the borrower for 2 to 7 years. The loan is financed by selling the borrower's short-term paper to investors on a revolving basis. If the borrower cannot obtain financing at any interval, the banks agree to buy the paper themselves. Thus a note issuance facility represents a loan commitment with a 2 to 7 year maturity. While the bank does not book any assets, it has a contingent liability for its share of the facility. The normal fee is 25 to 50 basis points.

Standby Letters of Credit

Banks also generate fee income by issuing standby letters of credit. These letters of credit are functionally equivalent to a surety bond in that the issuing bank guarantees the performance of another party in fulfilling the terms of a contract. The intent is to substitute the bank's credit standing for the buyer's. The issuer of a standby letter of credit only makes payment when nonperformance of a contract is proved, so many letters expire unused. Consider the example in Exhibit 25.1, in which a regional bank plans to sell part of its municipal bond portfolio with put options. The bank needs to sell the municipals because it has no use for tax-exempt interest due to negative earnings for the year. The put options enable the bank to sell the bonds without reporting securities losses. These put options give the buyer the right to sell the bonds back to the bank after a set period of time. The regional bank uses an underwriter to package the bonds, obtain legal opinions, and help negotiate a standby letter of credit with a money center bank. The bonds are then sold to a tax-exempt money market fund. The money center bank effectively guarantees that the money market fund will be paid in full when it puts the bonds back to the regional bank. If the regional bank defaults, the money center bank must make the obligated payments. The money market fund is more willing to buy the bonds because it knows that the money center bank's credit position is strong. The money center bank receives a fee from the regional bank

Exhibit 25.1 The Role of a Standby Letter of Credit in the Sale of Put Bonds

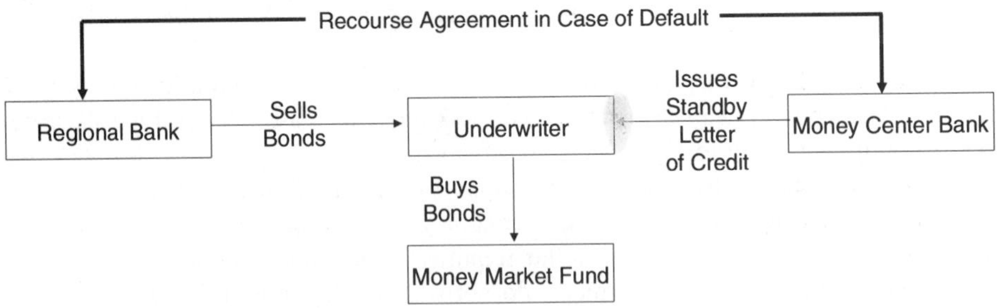

for its letter of credit and does not have to invest anything unless the regional bank goes under.

Most standby letters of credit are used as guarantees for commercial paper and municipal securities issues, as well as in construction financing. The advantage to the bank's customer is that a letter of credit enhances the credit quality of the underlying security. Thus the customer can borrow funds at a lower cost even after paying the guarantor a fee. The bank that provides the letter of credit analyzes the associated risks and charges a fee to cover transactions costs plus potential losses. Such losses can arise from defaults as well as from liquidity problems when outstanding letters of credit are activated. In most cases banks do not require collateral so that default losses can be extensive, especially in light of the small fee that is earned from the guarantee. Similarly, banks have to fund letters of credit only when they are activated. Because letters of credit are typically activated when the customer is distressed and economic conditions are poor, the money market may not readily accept additional bank borrowing without demanding a stiff interest premium on bank liabilities.

Exhibit 25.2 summarizes the growth in standby letters of credit and loan commitments issued by banks from 1980 to 1986. The top figure documents the sharp increase in dollar value of off-balance sheet activities for all U.S. banks, while the bottom figure indicates the fraction of total activity attributed to the 15 largest banks. As expected, the largest banks and those carrying the best quality ratings issue the majority of these guarantees. This reflects the high value the market places on financial strength and ability to tap the credit markets at relatively low cost. At year-end 1986, for example, the 15 largest banks issued 66 percent of the total outstanding letters of credit from U.S. banks and 53 percent of the loan commitments. Foreign banks, particularly Japanese banks with Aaa credit ratings, overtook all U.S. banks in providing letters of credit in support of municipal debt offerings to the point where they handled over 80 percent of all such letters in 1990.

Loan commitments and standby letters of credit do not appear on a bank's balance sheet and thus do not directly affect its capital ratios. Banks must, however, report their volume of commitments and letters of credit outstanding. Chapter 12 demon-

**Exhibit 25.2 Commercial Bank Issues of Standby Letters of Credit
and Loan Commitments: 1980–1986**

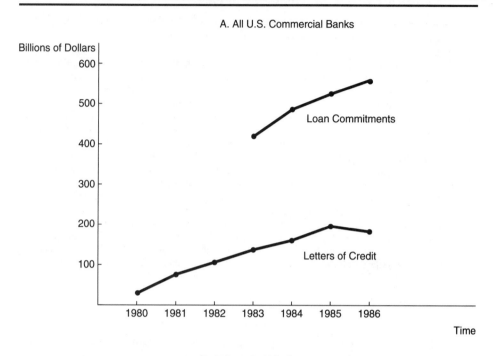

A. All U.S. Commercial Banks

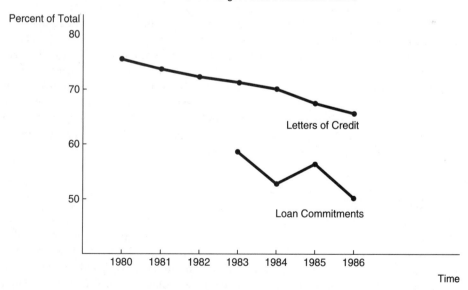

B. 15 Largest U.S. Commercial Banks

Source: Johnson and Murphy, *Economic Review*, Federal Reserve Bank of Atlanta, September/October 1987.

BankAmerica Corp.'s Mortgage Problems

There are times when banks are at risk even without direct financial guarantees. Take the case of BankAmerica Corp., which charged off $95 million in the fourth quarter of 1984 related to mortgage participations. In 1982 the bank was named trustee and escrow agent for mortgage-backed securities originated by the National Mortgage Equity Corp. In this capacity, the bank held the mortgage documents in trust for investors and administered the collection and disbursement of mortgage payments. One of its responsibilities was to review the documents and verify that the underlying properties and associated mortgages matched the description in the loan agreement. This process, labeled "pool certification," is necessary before securities can be issued against the mortgages. BankAmerica ultimately took its losses because it failed to perform these duties adequately.

In this case, National Mortgage Equity Corp. assembled mortgages to be paid off by West Pac Corp. All properties were appraised, and the mortgage payments were privately insured by two insurance companies. With BankAmerica as trustee, National Mortgage Equity sold mortgage-backed securities to 22 different thrift institutions. Eventually, West Pac Corp. defaulted on the loans, the insurance companies could not make the mortgage payments, and the thrift investors looked to BankAmerica for payment. BankAmerica paid the thrifts $133 million and wrote off $95 million after appraising the properties at $38 million. It later filed suit against West Pac Corp. claiming fraud because the original appraisals were inflated.

strates that banks are required to hold capital against these items according to a fixed schedule. In general, 8 percent capital must be held to support most of these off-balance sheet items. Regulators may impose additional capital requirements if deemed necessary, that is, if the overall perceived riskiness of the bank is greater than that suggested by balance sheet composition and off-balance sheet exposure. The bank's fee ranges from 10 to 75 basis points for each loan commitment and 25 to 125 basis points for each letter of credit, depending on the type of transaction and perceived risk. The most serious problem is that the potential liability is quite large relative to the return. Insurers of the Washington Public Power Supply municipal bonds that went into default in 1983, for example, will pay $76 million to bondholders through the year 2020. Contemporary Issues: BankAmerica's Mortgage Problems similarly demonstrates a large payout when a guarantee was not even provided.

Foreign Exchange

Many of the nation's largest banks operate foreign exchange trading desks in which traders make markets in foreign currencies and negotiate forward contracts.[1] The process involves buying and selling currencies trying to profit directly from increases or decreases in the value of a currency, or by trading for customers and charging a fee. If, for example, a trader anticipates a decline in the value of the U.S. dollar relative

---

[1] In strict terms, foreign exchange trading is not an off-balance sheet activity. Banks do report their trading accounts in periodic statements.

to the yen, he or she could buy yen and sell dollars. If the guess is correct, the trader will later reverse the transactions by selling yen and buying dollars and profit handsomely. Of course, if the dollar increases in value, the losses may be substantial. Such positions can be held for minutes or days depending on the market's move. Any trader who pursues this strategy is speculating on future price movements. In recent years, several banks have announced losses attributable to ill-advised speculation in foreign exchange trading. Speculative trading is risky indeed.

Futures, Forwards, and Interest Rate Swaps

Chapters 9 and 10 describe the nature of futures and forward contracts and interest rate swap agreements. Banks engage in futures and forwards as a means of hedging interest rate risk. Thus they may buy or sell futures and forward contracts to offset anticipated cash market transactions. Banks engage in interest rate swaps as a party to the swap with the intent of hedging interest rate risk, or they may act as intermediaries in arranging swap transactions. Even though they are designed to reduce interest rate risk, each of these off-balance sheet activities entails credit and liquidity risk. They may also generate additional income or losses if not used as hedging vehicles.

A forward contract is an agreement between two parties to exchange assets at a fixed point in time in the future. All terms of the agreement, including price and specific features of the asset, are negotiated at the time the agreement is signed so that the cash flows at maturity are predetermined. The price does not change between the time the contract is negotiated and maturity, and there are no interim cash flow responsibilities of either buyer or seller. A standby forward contract is a forward contract with an option in which the buyer (a put) or seller (a call) has the option, but not the obligation, to act on the contract.

A futures contract represents a commitment between a buyer and a seller regarding the price of a standardized asset or index at a set time in the future. Buyers agree to pay the price while sellers agree to deliver the underlying asset. Futures contracts are traded on organized exchanges so that prices fluctuate throughout each trading day. Futures participants must mark their positions to market by recognizing daily the change in value of the underlying contract. If the futures trader's position declines in value, the holder must post additional margin. If instead the position increases in value, the holder may take cash out. Thus there are potentially substantial interim cash flows prior to expiration of the contract. Because futures are widely traded, market participants can eliminate any commitment by offsetting their initial position with an opposite trade prior to expiration. Thus a trader who initially buys a futures contract can simply sell it to remove any commitment. While there is little default risk, a participant does assume liquidity risk with marking to market because margin requirements may drain cash reserves or force securities to be pledged as collateral.

In their simplest form, interest rate swaps are agreements between two parties that face different interest rate risk and want to reduce that risk. Under swap terms, one party agrees to exchange floating-rate payments for fixed receipts. The other party agrees to exchange fixed payments for floating-rate receipts. The payments are pegged to a base interest rate, such as LIBOR or a Treasury rate, so that the size of the payment exchanged varies depending on the level of the underlying base rate. For example, a firm may agree to pay a fixed 9 percent and receive LIBOR. If LIBOR is less than 9 percent, the firm pays the difference. If LIBOR exceeds 9 percent, the firm receives the difference. Banks can participate in this market either by being a fixed- or floating-rate payer, or by serving as the financial intermediary that arranges the transaction. Large banks essentially make a market in swaps in which they match participants and make a profit on the spread, or buy and sell "legs" representing one side of a swap transaction and effectively take the opposite side if they leave the position open.

Swaps entail both credit risk and liquidity risk depending on the nature of the position taken. Credit risk arises because the party on the other side may not make the obligated swap payment. Interest rate risk arises when a bank acts as intermediary in arranging swaps, and does not run a matched book by balancing the value of positions on both the fixed- and floating-rate sides. With a matched book the bank balances each fixed-rate exposure with an offsetting floating-rate exposure. Finally, when interest rates move against a hedged bank's swap position, the bank must make a cash payment, which requires access to additional liquid funds.

Note that forwards, futures, and interest rate swaps involve little if any up-front cash to take a position. Each position represents a commitment that does not have a direct balance sheet impact until effected. There is, however, risk involved with the commitments which varies with economic conditions. The data in Chapter 12 again indicate that 4 percent core capital and 8 percent total capital is required to support these items.

THE OFF-BALANCE SHEET EXPOSURE OF LARGE BANKS

Given the nature of off-balance sheet activities, it is not surprising that large banks make extensive use of the associated contracts and transactions. They are involved in a broad range of business activities, both domestically and outside the United States, that require the use of hedging strategies. They have reputations that allow them to provide letters of credit and serve as intermediaries in swap agreements. Small banks, in contrast, are generally not as well known and therefore do not have the capacity to rent their credit rating. They thus do not deal extensively in foreign currencies.

Exhibit 25.3 summarizes the off-balance sheet activities for Citicorp and J.P. Morgan in 1989 and provides an example of the magnitude of these activities. The first two lines of data indicate the outstanding volume of unused loan commitments and standby letters of credit. The size of loan commitments amounts to 5 or 7 times each bank's stockholders' equity. Standby letters of credit similarly exceed equity by more than two times. The bottom part of the exhibit lists the notional principal amounts of futures, forwards, options, and swap contracts that each bank has entered into. Note that these magnitudes may not be directly related to the riskiness of off-balance sheet activities because many of the positions in the instruments offset other positions. With interest swaps, for example, Citicorp and J.P. Morgan have both fixed-rate and floating-rate payment obligations. If interest rates rise or fall, one side of the swap agreement will increase in value while the other side declines in value. It is thus difficult to assess overall off-balance sheet risk without having detailed information on each position.

Exhibit 25.3 Off-Balance Sheet Activities of Citicorp and J.P. Morgan: 1989 (Billions of Dollars)

	Citicorp	J.P. Morgan
Off-Balance Sheet Activity		
Loan commitments	$51.8	$32.4
Guarantees & standby letters of credit	26.0	9.0
	$77.8	$41.4
Notional amounts of futures, forwards & options on foreign currencies & U.S. dollars[a]	$588.4[b]	$177.9
Interest rate swaps	187.5	118.1
Currency swaps		52.6
Interest rate futures, options, caps & floors	205.1	112.1
Total	$1,058.8	$502.1
Bank Stockholders' Equity	$10.1	$4.5
Total assets	$230.6	$89.0

[a]Notional amounts indicate the total volume of positions. They are not representative of the risk exposure because some positions offset others.

[b]Includes currency swap volume.

Source: Annual Reports.

It is informative, however, to recognize that the total volume of off-balance sheet exposure greatly exceeds the on-balance sheet assets of each bank as well as stockholders' equity. The important issue is for each bank and regulators to identify how much risk is associated with each type of activity. Regulators handle this indirectly by requiring capital in support of these activities. At the end of 1989, Citicorp's Tier 1 and total capital ratios were 4.04 percent and 8.08 percent, respectively. J.P. Morgan's respective ratios were 5.9 percent and 10.1 percent. Thus risk-based capital ratios at both banks exceeded the regulatory guidelines.

Unfortunately, little information is provided in financial statements regarding the contribution of off-balance sheet activities to aggregate bank profits. It is important to recognize that most of these activities generate revenues in the form of fees. Other activities, such as interest rate and currency swaps, are used primarily to reduce interest rate risk. The analytical focus should be on whether the profit potential balances the incremental risk to the bank's operations. Some activities, such as foreign exchange trading, exhibit substantial risk. Does management adequately control risk? Is the bank's capital base sufficient to absorb substantial losses? If the answer is no, a bank's involvement in off-balance sheet activities should be limited.

LOAN BROKERAGE

For many years banks have sold commercial loan participations among themselves and entered into syndications when a loan was too large for any single bank. Recently, large banks have concentrated on serving as commercial loan brokers. They negotiate large loans through their credit departments, then sell pieces to various investors, including thrifts, pension funds, and life insurance companies as well as other banks. The purpose is two-fold. First, the selling bank does not book the assets as long as the sale is without recourse. Second, the seller typically earns a fee for originating the loan and another fee for collecting and passing on interest and principal payments to the investors. The bank serves as an investment banker without any adverse impact on its required capital or interest rate risk position. As long as the sale is without recourse, the bank bears no credit risk and does not need new capital.

Several inherent risks are associated with this service. If the seller assumes any residual credit risk in the transaction, the transaction is not a sale and the bank must recognize the assets on its balance sheet. In addition, many commercial customers may not want their loans sold because it involves sharing the company's financial records with other institutions. Any subsequent loss of goodwill might preclude future business with the customer. Finally, banks may relax their credit standards when evaluating loans for sale. If these loans go sour, there is a real possibility that the selling bank may ultimately be forced to absorb the loss. Recent experience shows that the firm with the deepest pocket often takes the loss during a financial crisis, regardless of legal liability. Chase Manhattan Bank's experience with Drysdale securities losses in the RP market and BankAmerica's losses with mortgage-backed securities confirm this.

Loan sales resemble asset securitization in many ways because assets are moved off-balance sheet under similar conditions. The following section describes the securitization process and the use of special-purpose corporations as a strategy to enhance returns while holding capital requirements relatively unchanged.

SECURITIZATION

Securitization is the process of making loans, pooling them into a package, and selling securities backed by the cash flows of the loans in the package. Investors buy the securities because they can earn attractive yields relative to those on other debt instruments. As indicated in Chapter 17, banks are major investors in mortgage-backed securities. Banks also originate mortgage pools that they securitize. This latter function keeps the loans off-balance sheet as long as the transaction is completed without recourse to the bank. The process, however, does entail some contingent claims and thus additional risk.

The Securitization Process

Many groups are involved in securitizing assets: a loan originator, trust, third-party credit enhancer, rating agency, and security underwriter. An example best demonstrates the process and characterizes the risks and returns to all parties.[2] Consider the sequence of transactions in Exhibit 25.4.

---

[2]This example is based on Pavel (1989), who summarizes the process in detail.

Exhibit 25.4 The Securitization Process

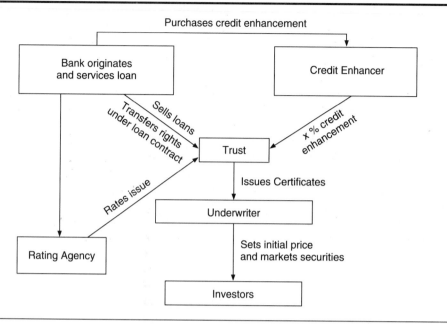

Source: Pavel, C. "Would You Buy a Car Loan from This Bank?" *Chicago Fed Letter* (Federal Reserve Bank of Chicago, May 1989).

1. The securitization process begins with a loan originator, potentially a bank, who makes loans and pools them into a package. In order to minimize costs associated with an investor trying to determine the quality and terms of individual loans, the originator typically pools loans that are very similar in use of proceeds, interest rate, and maturity. Suppose in this analysis that the loans are 5-year new domestic automobile loans that carry an annual percentage rate of 12 to 14 percent.

2. The originator sells the loans to a trust. If the trust has no recourse with the bank as originator in terms of requiring compensation for loan losses, the bank can move the assets off its balance sheet. Typically the originator will service the loans after the sale. Servicing involves collecting principal and interest payments from the borrowers. If car buyers in the above example miss payments, it is the servicer's responsibility to investigate and collect delinquent payments.

3. A trustee acts on behalf of the trust to monitor the performance of the originator and help issue securities backed by the loans through an underwriter. The trustee essentially represents investors by auditing the originator throughout the life of the loans. In particular, the trustee supervises a formal audit at least once each year and communicates important information and financial reports to investors. The

trustee sells securities or participation certificates to the underwriter. In actuality, the trustee works closely with the underwriter to determine the structure of the securities including maturity, market interest rate, and sequence of principal and interest payments. As asset-backed securities, interest and principal payments are secured by actual interest and principal payments on the underlying automobile loans.[3] In addition, the quality of the securities is typically enhanced by the guarantee of some third party.

4. Most asset-backed securities involve credit enhancement. As indicated in Exhibit 25.4, the originator may purchase the credit enhancement in the form of a letter of credit or an insurance bond. In this case, the bank or insurance company that provides the guarantee is renting its credit quality to the originating bank. For this service it charges up to 50 basis points. As Contemporary Issues: Credit Enhancement and Spread Accounts suggests, the credit enhancer is generally protected beyond the normal loss experience of the underlying loans. Such credit enhancement gives an investor in the underlying securities additional security in the case of loan defaults. Credit enhancement makes securities more attractive to investors because they have another party as a source of repayment in case of default.

5. Before the underwriter takes the securities to market, the trustee obtains a credit rating. Rating agencies, such as Moody's and Standard and Poor's (S&P), evaluate the quality of the loans, the capital strength of the credit enhancer, and the structure of the deal in case of default to determine the likelihood that investors will receive timely interest and principal payments. In the above example, the important factors are the cash flows generated by the automobile loans and the strength of the guarantor. Some deals are especially sound because the originator pledges collateral far in excess of the promised cash flows. In general, both Moody's and S&P assign ratings equal to that of the credit enhancer's quality rating. If the rating is not Baa or better, the deal typically falls through because most investors, such as pension funds and banks, can purchase only investment-grade instruments.

6. Underwriters serve to place the securities with final investors. In this capacity, they buy the securities from the trust, having determined the terms investors will require. Underwriters profit by selling the securities to investors at higher prices (lower yields) than what they pay for the securities.

7. The final stage is for borrowers on the automobile loans to make payments to the servicer. The servicer collects the payments and transfers them to the trustee after subtracting a servicing fee. The trustee, in turn, passes the payments on to investors. In general, a portion of the payments goes to a reserve to cover loan losses. If the payments are less than that promised investors, the trustee calls on the credit enhancer to pay the difference.

---

[3]These securities are structured after the Certificates for Automobile Receivables (CARS) issued by Marine Midland Bank through Salomon Brothers in 1987.

Credit Enhancement and Spread Accounts

Providing credit enhancements for 50 basis points doesn't appear to be a highly profitable business given the inherent risks. What makes it attractive is that the loan originator typically establishes a spread account to handle losses. Under this arrangement, the originating bank allocates a portion of loan payments to a special account until the balance reaches some predetermined amount. If the historical loss rate on automobile loans equals 3 percent, the amount might be set at twice historical losses or 6 percent. Losses on the underlying loans are first charged to this account. The credit enhancer is responsible for any additional losses. If losses are less than the 6 percent, the originating bank receives the difference.

The net effect is that the originating bank defers a portion of earnings until the loss reserve accumulates to the maximum and loan loss experience is realized. Using the previous data, the originating bank would not collect any revenues until the spread account equaled 6 percent of the outstanding loan balance. The bank or insurance company that provides the guarantee is insulated from normal losses plus some buffer, so its risk is reduced.

In some deals, investors are at risk beyond a predetermined loss rate. Suppose in the above example, the credit enhancer issued a letter of credit against losses up to 12 percent of outstanding securities. Here the originator would eat the first 6 percent of losses, the credit enhancer the next 6 percent, and investors would be liable for additional losses. Obviously, the greater the guarantor's risk, the higher the credit enhancement fee. Similarly, the greater the risk assumed by investors, the higher the required yield.

What Loans Can Be Securitized?

Some loans are easy to securitize while others present serious obstacles. What produces the difference? Consider mortgages, the most popular form of securitized loans. Most residential mortgages are long-term contracts with fixed 15-year or 30-year maturities. Fixed-rate mortgages have set monthly payments that vary only in number given prepayment risk. Many are FHA or VA guaranteed and all are collateralized by residences. In short, they are highly standardized contracts for which investors have little difficulty assessing default risk.

Consider instead commercial and industrial (C&I) loans. As a group, they are highly diverse contracts because they vary by borrower, use of proceeds, term to maturity, and whether the rate is fixed or floating. Their cash flows are unpredictable. An investor in securities backed by a general pool of C&I loans would have an extremely difficult time assessing default risk and the expected stream of loan payments. Not surprisingly, C&I loans have not yet been successfully securitized. Securitized Small Business Association (SBA) loans have been successful because they are somewhat standardized and, more importantly, 85 percent of the balances are federally insured.

Banks have been somewhat successful in securitizing loans that exhibit standard features. The list includes credit card receivables, automobile loans, lease receivables, and boat or mobile home loans. Still, the greater is the heterogeneity and default risk of the underlying loans, the more difficult it is to securitize them. This also raises the required yield to investors. For securitization to succeed, banks must be able to reduce the risk to investors.

LOAN SALES TO SPECIAL-PURPOSE CORPORATIONS

One of the difficulties in securitization and moving assets off balance sheet is how to handle recourse. If an asset is sold with recourse, the buyer has the right or option to return it to the seller or force the seller to cover any losses on the asset. When recourse exists, the seller is clearly at risk because it is liable for future losses. One way to circumvent recourse problems is to sell securities outright. Exhibit 25.4 showed a trust as the vehicle to which a bank sold securities. Alternatively, a bank can create a special-purpose corporation as a subsidiary and sell assets to that subsidiary.

A special-purpose corporation has the advantage of being able to borrow directly in the money and capital markets. Thus the strategy is for a highly rated bank to establish a special-purpose corporation that issues commercial paper and longer-term corporate debt and uses the proceeds to buy assets from the bank. The bank's rating is important because borrowing costs will reflect the perceived strength of the firm and the riskiness of operations. The net cost from setting up a special-purpose corporation is also less than the cost of securitization. The corporation earns a profit because its borrowing cost plus operating cost is less than the return on assets purchased from the bank. A bank can continue to sell loans to the corporation to move assets off balance sheet as part of an ongoing business rather than repeat the entire securitization process after each loan pool matures.

NONINTEREST INCOME

One of the attractive features of off-balance sheet activities is that they generate fee income. In general, banks that produce the highest noninterest income as a fraction of assets or relative to noninterest expense are among the most profitable. During the 1980s banks successfully increased their noninterest income by raising service charges on checking accounts and expanding the range of services offered in corporate cash management and in trust departments. Between 1985 and 1989, for example, noninterest income jumped from 30 percent of net interest income to 44 percent.

Most fee income in the area of service charges comes from monthly account maintenance fees and charges for writing insufficient funds checks. Still, a growing number of banks have expanded fee services to include such items as balance inquiries and ATM usage at other institutions' machines. Fee income from corporate customers derives largely from corporate cash management, corporate trusts, and letters of credit. With pressures on net interest earnings and problem loans, banks have been quite aggressive in raising prices for these items.

Exhibit 25.5 demonstrates, however, that the growth in fee income has slowed sharply since 1985, with the decline sharpest at the nation's largest banks. Given earnings and capital problems at many banks, this trend must be reversed. The most

Exhibit 25.5 Recent Trends in Bank Noninterest Income: 1985–1989

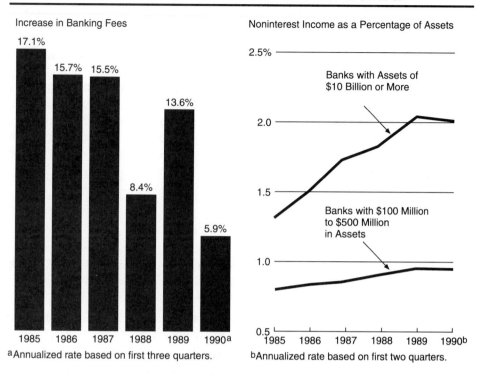

Increase in Banking Fees

Noninterest Income as a Percentage of Assets

Banks with Assets of $10 Billion or More

Banks with $100 Million to $500 Million in Assets

a Annualized rate based on first three quarters.

b Annualized rate based on first two quarters.

Source: Roosevelt, *American Banker*, 1991.

promising areas of generating additional fee income include personal trust services, as the average age of consumers rises, and fees associated with underwriting securities at the largest banks.[4] Banks will also benefit if they are allowed to offer an expanded array of insurance services and enter other lines of business currently off limits.

SUMMARY

Large commercial banks increasingly rely on off-balance sheet activities to generate earnings and control risk. Many of these activities, however, add to a bank's credit risk and liquidity risk exposure. Management is responsible for monitoring the riskiness of these activities relative to the potential returns. Under risk-based capital requirements, regulators require capital in support of selected off-balance sheet items. This increases the cost of engaging in these activities and has thus encouraged banks to move assets off balance sheet entirely via securitization or direct asset sales.

[4] Roosevelt (1991) summarizes the results of a recent survey and the implications of fee structures in 1989.

Off-balance sheet activities include loan commitments, guarantees and standby letters of credit, the use of futures, forwards, and options on currencies and interest rate instruments, and interest rate and currency swap agreements. At most large banks, the nominal volume of off-balance sheet business greatly exceeds the asset base and stockholders' equity. As part of the process, banks are increasingly securitizing assets by pooling them and selling securities collateralized by cash flows on the underlying assets. If a bank sells these assets without recourse, they are removed from the books and no longer subject to capital requirements. To be securitized, the loan terms must be fairly standard and easily recognized. Thus the most popular securitized assets are residential mortgages, credit card receivables, automobile loans, and certain types of leases. Many banks will look to securitize assets in future years as a source of income with limited risk.

Questions

Types of Off-Balance Sheet Activities

1. A bank grants some loan commitments it never expects to have to honor. Give one example, and explain why the customer is willing to pay for a service he doesn't expect to use.

2. Would participants in the commercial paper market be more interested in a loan commitment or in a standby letter of credit. Why?

3. A bank offering a note-issuance facility might be explained as creating an *international* commercial paper *market* with an automatic *commitment*. Explain the role of each italicized phrase in this definition.

4. Banks create off-balance sheet income by using:
   stand-by commitments
   note-issuance facilities
   letters of credit
   foreign exchange
   futures, forwards, and swap

   Given the way they are commonly used by banks, rank these from highest to lowest risk.

Large Banks

5. Explain the meaning of the following statement: "Small banks . . . do not have the capacity to rent their credit rating."

Brokerage and Securitization

6. Explain the difference between loan brokerage and securitization.

7. There are four major participants involved in taking car loans through securitization to ultimate investors. Who are each of these participants and what functions do they serve?

8. What differentiates a loan suitable for securitization from one that is not?

9. Name four current sources of high-fee income for banks and create four potential new sources. Do highly profitable banks generate large- or small-fee income?

Activity

Obtain a copy of a large regional bank's annual report. Examine the text and footnotes of the financial statements to determine the type and magnitude of off-balance sheet activities at the bank. Compare the dollar magnitude of the bank's total assets and stockholders' equity. What risks do these figures suggest?

References

Bennett, Barbara. "Off Balance Sheet Risk in Banking: The Case of Standby Letters of Credit." *Economic Review* (Federal Reserve Bank of San Francisco, Spring 1986).

Berlin, Mitchell. "Loan Commitments: Insurance Contracts in a Risky World." *Business Review* (Federal Reserve Bank of Philadelphia, May/June 1986).

Bisky, Tom. "Securitization Gives New Meaning to 'Car Pools'." *ABA Banking Journal* (August 1986).

Caouette, John. "Asset-Backeds." *Bank Management* (June 1990).

Goldberg, Michael, and Peter R. Lloyd-Davies. "Standby Letters of Credit: Are Banks Overextending Themselves?" *The Journal of Bank Research* (Spring 1985).

Hirtle, Beverly. "The Growth of the Financial Guarantee Market." *Quarterly Review* (Federal Reserve Bank of New York, Spring 1987).

Holland, Kelley. "Banks Rushing to Securitize Assets, But Analysts Fear Long-Term Harm." *American Banker* (July 11, 1990).

Holland, Kelley. "Banks Mull Special-Purpose Corporations." *American Banker* (September 28, 1990).

Johnson, Sylvester, and Amelia Murphy. "Going Off the Balance Sheet." *Economic Review* (Federal Reserve Bank of Atlanta, September/October 1987).

Pavel, Christine. "Securitization." *Economic Perspectives* (Federal Reserve Bank of Chicago, July/August 1986).

Pavel, Christine. "Would You Buy a Car Loan from This Bank?" *Chicago Fed Letter* (Federal Reserve Bank of Chicago, May 1989).

Rogowski, Robert. "The Role of Commercial Banks in a Securitized World." *The Bankers Magazine* (July–August 1988).

Roosevelt, Phil. "Fee-Income Boom of the Eighties Cools Off." *American Banker* (January 7, 1991).

Simpson, Thomas. "Developments in the U.S. Financial System Since the Mid-1970s." *Federal Reserve Bulletin* (January 1988).

Chapter 26

Global Banking Activities

Capital is king. This fact is especially true in global banking activities where competition is fierce and business flows to multinational firms with the lowest prices. In 1992 all banks in industrialized nations must have capital equal to at least 8 percent of risk based assets. While this will be relatively easy for many banks, the largest U.S. banks are relatively undercapitalized compared with foreign banks. In 1990, Sumitomo Bank of Osaka, Japan, a bank with more than $350 billion in assets, had sufficient capital to grow an additional 20 percent. In contrast, loan losses to less-developed countries wiped out most of the earnings reported by the largest U.S. money center banks during the 1980s. Citicorp, for example, allocated $3 billion to its loan loss reserve in late 1987 to cover loans to Latin American borrowers that were not going to be repaid. Real estate loan problems produced the same result during the early 1990s. U.S. banks have thus found it extremely difficult and expensive to issue stock to improve their capital, yet cannot generate earnings fast enough to offset asset quality problems. The net effect is that the cost of capital at U.S. banks far exceeds that of foreign competitors and U.S. banks are frequently priced out of international business. Not surprisingly, all but a few U.S. banks are withdrawing from international banking activities while banks in Japan and Europe are expanding their activities.

This comes at a time when more firms are expanding operations outside their home country. The European Community, essentially a confederation of 12 countries, will remove barriers to trade by 1992 which should expand business and banking opportunities. Finally, the unification of Germany has created an economic powerhouse with a strong banking system that should get even stronger. How should U.S. and foreign banks best position themselves to compete as equals?

CONTEMPORARY ISSUES

True Multinational Businesses

What do the following U.S. companies have in common?

1. IBM
2. Gillette
3. Colgate
4. Coca-Cola
5. Hewlett-Packard
6. Xerox
7. Dow Chemical
8. CPC International

Answer: They all generate more than 50 percent of their sales outside the United States.

What do the following non-U.S. companies have in common?

1. Nestle
2. Hoffmann-LaRoche
3. SmithKline Beecham
4. Unilever
5. Volvo
6. Philips
7. SKF
8. Michelin

Answer: They all generate more than 75 percent of their sales outside their home country.

One of the most significant trends of this century is the cross-border expansion of corporations throughout the world. Such firms have developed the capacity to produce products in plants located in different countries and alter production to meet changes in technology and demand. As corporations expand, their banking needs can and must be met by a variety of institutions. Banks must thus be able to provide trade financing, hedge exchange rate risk, and offer legal advice in a variety of countries to attract and retain business.

GLOBAL BANKING ACTIVITIES

One clear trend in the evolution of financial institutions and markets is the expansion of activities across national boundaries. Technology has made it possible to conduct business around the world with relative ease and minimal cost. Producers recognize that export markets are as important as domestic markets and that the range of competitors includes both domestic and foreign operatives. This is increasingly apparent in agriculture, textiles, steel, and microelectronics. Contemporary Issues: True Multinational Business documents the global nature of many well-known corporations. Many financial institutions have similarly expanded their activities internationally while developing financial instruments to facilitate trade and funds flows.

Global banking activities involve both traditional commercial banking and investment banking products. Large commercial banks accept deposits, make loans, provide letters of credit, trade bonds and foreign exchange, and underwrite debt and equity securities in dollars and other currencies. With the globalization of financial markets, all firms compete directly with other major commercial and investment banks throughout the world.

Those who view the United States as the dominant player in world markets might be surprised. Exhibit 26.1 compares the dollar amount and market share of international assets controlled by banks in the United States, Japan, and Europe from 1983 through 1988. Note the more than 200 percent increase in Japan's bank assets after 1984 reflecting Japan's strong economy and competitiveness, and the virtual doubling of market share to 40 percent. The growth in European bank assets exceeded 100 percent so that market share remained stable at 30 percent. Finally, U.S. bank assets increased just 10 percent so that market share fell to 15 percent.

Exhibit 26.1 The Growth in International Assets at Commercial Banks in the United States, Japan, and Europe.

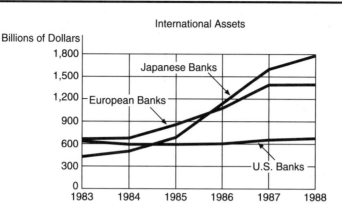

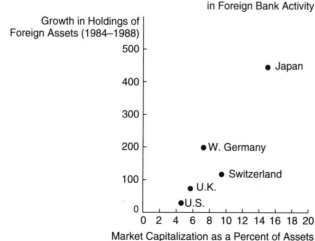

Source: Baer, H., "Foreign Competition in U.S. Banking Markets." *Economic Perspectives* (Federal Reserve Bank of Chicago, May/June 1990).

Exhibit 26.2 The Largest Commercial Banks in the World: December 31, 1989

Rank	Commercial Bank	Total Assets[a]	Equity Capital[b] Total Assets
1	Dai-Ichi Kangyo, Ltd., Japan	$403.4	2.91%
2	Sumitomo Bank, Ltd., Japan	368.2	3.49
3	Fuji Bank, Ltd., Japan	362.6	3.12
4	Mitsubishi Bank, Ltd., Japan	360.0	2.89
5	Sanwa Bank, Ltd., Japan	353.7	3.11
6	Industrial Bank of Japan, Japan	256.9	3.17
7	Credit Agricole Mutual, France	243.3	4.88
8	Banque Nationale de Paris, France	231.8	2.67
9	Tokai Bank, Ltd., Japan	227.7	2.85
10	Norinchukin Bank, Japan	219.8	2.85
11	Mitsubishi Trust & Bank, Japan	213.5	2.97
12	Credit Lyonnais, France	211.0	3.18
13	Barclays Bank Pfc., United Kingdom	205.5	5.12
14	Mitsui Bank, Ltd., Japan	203.3	2.69
15	Deutsche Bank, Germany	202.6	4.18
U.S. Banks			
24	Citibank	157.8	4.44
50	BankAmerica	85.3	5.69
54	Chase Manhattan	82.1	4.65
72	Morgan Guaranty Trust Co.	63.5	5.13
81	Manufacturers Hanover Trust	53.6	5.68
82	Security Pacific	53.6	5.58
87	Bankers Trust Co.	49.9	4.39
96	Wells Fargo Bank	45.3	5.90
98	Bank of New York	45.0	5.82

[a]Billions of dollars

[b]Ratio is for the holding company.

Source: Top Numbers: Part Two, *American Banker*, 1990.

Exhibit 26.2 reports the rankings of the world's 15 largest institutions according to asset size at the end of 1989, plus the U.S. banks in the top 100. The final column lists each bank's equity-to-asset ratio at the end of 1989. This approximately equals the Tier 1 (core) capital ratio, but excludes Tier 2 capital.[1] Ten of the 15 largest commercial banks have their main offices in Japan with the other five based in Europe. The exhibit actually understates the size discrepancies because two large Japanese banks, Mitsui and Taiyo Kobe, ranked 14th and 22nd, respectively, announced a merger in 1989 that would make them the second largest bank in the world with $380 billion in assets. Citicorp is the largest U.S. bank, ranked number 24 with $158 billion in assets. The equity-to-asset ratios appear to indicate that U.S. banks rank higher than

[1]Chapter 12 introduces the international risk-based capital requirements that were agreed upon in 1988 and implemented in 1992. While Tier 1, or core capital, is generally comparable across national boundaries, Tier 2 capital may differ substantially based on each country's accounting conventions and standards. Japanese banks, for example, can include the market value of stocks owned in calculating Tier 2 capital. U.S. banks cannot own stock for investment purposes.

most other large banks.[2] These ratios are misleading, however, because many of the largest U.S. banks suffered large losses in 1990 to 1991 and were unable to obtain capital externally. Japanese and European banks were generally able to issue equity over the same period at high price/earnings multiples. The bottom part of Exhibit 26.1 demonstrates that a higher market value of bank equity is associated with a greater growth in foreign assets through much of the 1980s.

These figures suggest that U.S. banks are generally withdrawing from global banking activities, at least relative to the growth of foreign competitors. The rationale is that profits are negligible and the capital necessary to support global business is too expensive. Many analysts and regulators believe that only Citicorp, Bankers Trust, J.P. Morgan, and Chase Manhattan among U.S. banks intend to compete globally in most lines of lending and investment banking activities over the long term.

While the largest money center banks attract most of the attention with their international business, many community banks located along the nation's borders also rely heavily on businesses and individuals outside the United States as large depositors and large borrowers. These banks, especially those near Mexico, face additional risks with the devaluation of foreign currencies if foreign business slows.[3]

Exhibit 26.3 documents U.S. banks' international activities according to the type of office involved.[4] At the end of 1983, U.S. banks reported $521 billion in total claims on unrelated foreign residents, originating from 2,348 separate offices. Exhibit 26.4 provides similar figures for the loans owed U.S. banks by foreign borrowers according to the country of origin. At the end of 1983, the total outstanding credit equaled $359 billion, of which the largest shares of $164 billion and $109 billion were owed by borrowers in the G-10 countries representing Western Europe, the United Kingdom, and the non-oil-exporting developing countries.

Foreign banks operating through their U.S. banking offices have also aggressively pursued U.S. business. At mid-year 1989 these bank offices held almost $180 billion in commercial and industrial loans in the United States (Exhibit 26.5), which amounted to almost 29 percent of total U.S. commercial loans. This represented the fifth straight year of increased market share, up from just 20.5 percent in 1984. In comparison, foreign loans at U.S. banks actually decreased in dollar terms over the same period evidencing a larger decline in market share. Clearly, the structure of lending within the United States is shifting toward more aggressive activity by foreign institutions, while U.S. banks are retrenching outside the United States. Foreign banks' deposit growth within the United States has similarly jumped to where they controlled over 17 percent of total U.S. bank deposits in 1989. U.S. banks are not as competitive as foreign banks in conducting international business either due to management strength and direction or legal and regulatory restrictions that vary across national boundaries.

---

[2]Exhibits 26.1 and 26.2 convert foreign assets and equity into dollars. When the value of the dollar declines or rises relative to a foreign currency the dollar-valued magnitude of foreign assets and equity rises or declines. Thus comparisons between countries incorporate fluctuations in the relative prices of currencies.

[3]The term *devaluation* refers to the situation in which a government administratively resets the value of its currency to a lower level relative to other currencies.

[4]Sydney Key (1985) presents Exhibits 26.3 and 26.4 and interprets the figures in detail.

**Exhibit 26.3 Structure of International Activities of Multinational
U.S.-Chartered Banks, December 1983**

Banks	No. of Offices	Claims on Unrelated Parties (Billions of Dollars)[e]	Share of Total Claims on Unrelated Parties (%)[f]
Domestic offices, including IBFs[a]	196	$146	28.0%
Foreign branches[b]	924	296	56.7
Shell	185	66	12.6
Other	739	230	44.1
Foreign subsidiaries[c]	1,025	68	13.1
Edge corporations[d]	203	11	2.2
Total	2,348	$521	100.0%

[a]Includes only multinational U.S.-chartered banks, or U.S.-chartered banks with foreign offices. U.S.-chartered banks owned by foreign banks are included in these data. IBF indicates international banking facility.

[b]Includes foreign branches of banking Edge and Agreement corporations, which had 11 foreign branches, mainly shell branches in the Caribbean, with total claims on unrelated parties of less than $1 billion. Excludes branches in U.S. territories and possessions. Figures for claims on unrelated parties are for shell branches with total assets of at least $50 million and for all other branches with total assets of at least $150 million.

[c]Includes majority-owned subsidiaries and non-majority-owned subsidiaries that are considered by the Federal Reserve Board to be controlled by U.S. banking organizations. December 1983 figures for claims on unrelated parties are estimated.

[d]Includes domestic offices (including IBFs) of banking Edge and Agreement corporations only.

[e]Figures for domestic offices (including IBFs) are for claims on unrelated foreign residents plus customers' liabilities on acceptances outstanding. All figures in this column include claims on foreign offices of other U.S. banks.

[f]Shares were computed using unrounded numbers.

Source: Board of Governors of the Federal Reserve System, Sydney Key, "The Internationalization of U.S. Banking," in *Handbook for Banking Strategy*, edited by Richard Aspinwall and Robert Eisenbeis, John Wiley & Sons, 1985. Reprinted with permission.

Exhibit 26.6 indicates which countries are most active in the United States and where they conduct most of their business. At the top of the list are Japanese banks. By mid-year 1989 Japanese firms controlled 56 percent of foreign bank loans in the United States or 16 percent of U.S. commercial loans. British, Canadian, and Italian banks have the next highest exposure. This figures reflect several important developments. First, foreign banks regularly price short-term commercial loans below their U.S. counterparts. This is possible because the cost of capital at foreign banks is below that of U.S. banks. Foreign banks pay relatively low deposit rates and operate with higher capital ratios. Second, foreign banks are willing to take silent participations in deals originated by U.S. banks. Domestic borrowers that might object to negotiating a credit agreement with a foreign bank are often unaware that the originating U.S. bank sells part of the loan. Finally, foreign banks are extremely aggressive in underwriting Eurobonds and engaging in off-balance sheet activities, including interest rate swaps, standby letters of credit, and municipal bond guarantees. This provides them instant credibility and a foothold when negotiating loans later.

**Exhibit 26.4 Amounts Owed to U.S.-Chartered Banks
by Foreign Borrowers, December 1983**

Country of Borrower	Amounts Owed to U.S. Banks (Billions of Dollars)[a]	Share of Total Amount Owed (%)[b]
G-10 countries[c]	$164	45.7%
Non-G-10 developed countries[d]	41	11.5
Eastern European countries	5	1.4
OPEC members[a]	25	7.0
Non-oil-exporting and developing countries:	109	30.2
Latin America and Caribbean	72	19.8
Asia	33	9.3
Africa	4	1.1
Offshore banking centers	14	3.9
International and regional organizations	1	0.3
Total	$359	100.0%

[a]Figures includes all amounts owed to domestic and foreign offices of U.S.-chartered banks that have foreign offices, Edge and Agreement corporations, or international banking facilities and have total outstanding claims on foreign residents of more than $30 million. The figures do not include local lending in local currencies by foreign offices of U.S. banks. Amounts have been adjusted so that claims on borrowers in one country with a head office or guarantor in another country are reallocated from the first country to the second country.

[b]Shares were computed using unrounded numbers.

[c]Excluding the United States. G-10 (Group of Ten) countries are the 11 participants in the General Arrangements to Borrow of the International Monetary Fund: Belgium-Luxembourg, Canada, France, Germany, Italy, Japan, the Netherlands, Sweden, Switzerland, the United Kingdom, and the United States. Switzerland officially became a participant in 1984, but the countries are still referred to as the G-10.

[d]Includes Australia, Austria, Denmark, Finland, Greece, Iceland, Ireland, New Zealand, Norway, Portugal, South Africa, Spain, and Turkey.

Source: Federal Financial Institutions Examination Council, *Statistical Release E.16*, May 24, 1984. Sydney Key, "The Internationalization of U.S. Banking," in *Handbook for Banking Strategy*, edited by Richard Aspinwall and Robert Eisenbeis, John Wiley & Sons, 1985. Reprinted by permission.

The European Community

In 1985 the countries of Western Europe started a process to design a plan for economic stability and growth. The result, labeled the European Community or EC, is a confederation of countries that are negotiating the removal of trade barriers that restrict competition. The objective is to increase national output and employment by creating a unified economic engine that can better compete with Japan, the United States, and Eastern Europe.

The 12 countries in the EC—Belgium, Denmark, France, Germany, Greece, Ireland, Italy, Luxembourg, the Netherlands, Portugal, Spain, and the United Kingdom—have generally agreed on rules that allow the

- free flow of capital across borders
- elimination of customs formalities, and
- establishment of a central bank which creates the potential for a single currency.

Exhibit 26.5 Foreign Bank Activity in the United States, 1982–1989

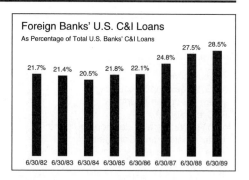

C&I Loans, Deposits, and Assets at U.S. Offices of Foreign Banks

Dollar Amounts in Billions

	Number of Offices	C&I Loans	Deposits	Assets
(1) Agencies and branches	565	$129.9	$247.1	$527.5
(1a) Agencies	201	$ 27.8	$ 22.4	$ 83.9
(1b) Branches	364	$102.1	$224.7	$443.5
(2) Commercial banks	100	$ 46.6	$121.3	$161.3
(3) Edge Act banks	26	$ 0.26	$ 1.6	$ 2.0
(4) Investment companies	11	$ 2.2	$ 0.4	$ 4.9
Totals for U.S. offices of foreign banks	697	$178.9	$370.4	$695.6
Totals for all U.S. banks	13,639	628.3	2,138.2	3,073.6
Ratio of foreign to all U.S. banks	5.1%	28.5%	17.3%	22.6%

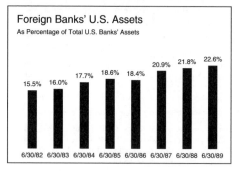

Foreign Banks' U.S. C&I Loans

As Percentage of Total U.S. Banks' C&I Loans

21.7% 21.4% 20.5% 21.8% 22.1% 24.8% 27.5% 28.5%

6/30/82 6/30/83 6/30/84 6/30/85 6/30/86 6/30/87 6/30/88 6/30/89

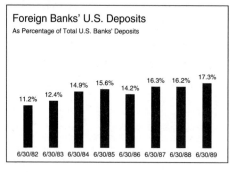

Foreign Banks' U.S. Deposits

As Percentage of Total U.S. Banks' Deposits

11.2% 12.4% 14.9% 15.6% 14.2% 16.3% 16.2% 17.3%

6/30/82 6/30/83 6/30/84 6/30/85 6/30/86 6/30/87 6/30/88 6/30/89

Foreign Banks' U.S. Assets

As Percentage of Total U.S. Banks' Assets

15.5% 16.0% 17.7% 18.6% 18.4% 20.9% 21.8% 22.6%

6/30/82 6/30/83 6/30/84 6/30/85 6/30/86 6/30/87 6/30/88 6/30/89

Source: Federal Reserve Board for Edge bank, branch, and agency data and the Federal Deposit Insurance Corp. for national bank, state member (Federal Reserve System) banks and state nonmember (FDIC insured) banks. In Baer, 1990.

[d]Revised.

The expected result is an environment in which trade quotas will no longer exist, the removal of tariffs and license restrictions will lower production costs and ultimately prices to consumers, and national output will soar.

The implications for the banking industry are wide ranging. First, trade restrictions have generally protected European banks from outside competition. Banks in France, for example, reported noninterest expense to total operating ratios of 60 to 70 percent during the 1980s, while U.S. banks reported similar ratios closer to 55 percent. In order to improve their competitive opportunities, many banks have merged with banks in other countries. Some analysts forecast that by the year 2000, there will be as few as 15 distinct European banks. U.S. banks similarly view the EC has an opportunity to expand their market presence. Many are forming joint ventures with European banks. In addition, any benefits to consumers in the form of lower prices or enhanced output will benefit all lenders, regardless of where the home office is located.

The remainder of this chapter examines the basic features of international banking. The analysis begins with a description of the different types of organizational units that engage in international activities. The following sections analyze the Eurocurrency

**Exhibit 26.6 Foreign Bank Activity by Country and Location
of U.S. Offices: June 30, 1989**

*Top 10 Countries in C&I Loans Held by Banks' U.S. Offices (Dollar Amounts in Billions)
(Growth from 1988 in parentheses)*

	Number of Banks with U.S. Offices	Number of U.S. Offices	C&I Loans	Ratio	Deposits	Assets
Japan	39	120	$100.3	56.1%	$195.6	$372.5
United Kingdom	(+6) 12	(+4) 45	(+20.7%) 13.4	7.5%	(+20.7%) 26.7	(+13.3%) 40.2
Canada	(+1) 6	(−1) 50	(−11.3%) 11.2	6.3%	(−11.0%) 19.3	(−11.5%) 42.4
Italy	13	(+4) 27	(−14.5%) 10.5	5.9%	(−11.9%) 13.0	(−8.4%) 45.1
Hong Kong	(+1) 10	(+2) 30	(+15.4%) 6.6	3.7%	(−3.7%) 19.3	(+19.3%) 26.4
France	15	(−2) 39	(−8.3%) 5.1	2.9%	(−2.5%) 16.5	(−4.0%) 30.3
Switzerland	(+1) 7	(−1) 18	(+2.0%) 4.9	2.7%	(+9.3%) 10.6	(+11.0%) 20.5
Netherlands	(+1) 4	(+1) 22	(−31.9%) 3.3	1.8%	(−10.2%) 6.0	(−9.3%) 11.6
Israel	4	(+5) 27	(+10.0%) 3.2	1.8%	(+36.4%) 10.7	(+14.9%) 12.2
Spain	9	(+1) 28	2.8	1.6%	(+16.3%) 7.9	(+15.1%) 11.2
Total for Top 10	(−1) 119	(−1) 406	(+21.7%) 161.3	90.2%	(23.4%) 325.6	(+21.7%) 612.4
Total for All Foreign in the U.S.	(+6) 281 (+15)	(+19) 697 (+31)	(+8.5%) 178.9 (+8.9%)		(+10.5%) 370.4 (+11.8%)	(+7.5%) 695.6 (+8.9%)

Number of U.S. Offices: includes foreign banks' U.S. branches, agencies, Edge banks, commercial banks, and New York State investment companies. The number of U.S. offices reported for each country in the top 10 is the number for which June 30 data were available. Ratio: commercial and industrial loans outstanding at the U.S. offices of a country's banks to C&I loans outstanding at all U.S. offices of foreign banks.

and Eurobond markets, international lending activities, fee-based services, and foreign exchange operations. Improved communications systems and the development of innovative securities permit market participants to look globally before making investment

Exhibit 26.6 *(Continued)*

Location of Foreign Banks' U.S. Offices: The Top 10 Cities (Excludes Offices Opened since Mid-1989)

	Total Offices[a]	Agencies	Branches	Commercial Bank Subs.	Edge Act Banks	Represent. Offices	Invest Co.
New York	480	36	233	33	6	162	11
Los Angeles	127	60	30	13	0	24	0
Chicago	89	0	53	5	2	29	0
Houston	74	14	0	0	6	54	0
San Francisco	63	28	7	7	2	19	0
Miami	54	35	0	3	9	7	0
Atlanta	27	15	0	0	0	12	0
Washington, D.C.	15	0	3	0	1	11	0
Dallas	14	1	0	0	0	13	0
Seattle	14	0	9	0	0	5	0
Total for 10 Largest	957	188	335	61	26	336	11
Total for all U.S. Offices	1,081	201	364	101	27	377	11
Total Number of Cities[b]	81	15	20	41	7	37	1

---

[a]Total offices is the sum of agencies, branches, commercial bank subsidiaries, Edge banks, representative offices, and investment companies.

[b]The first number in this row shows the total number of different U.S. cities that have foreign banking offices. If office in one city included in data of office in another city, it is still included in city total. Each of the six other numbers in that row indicate the number of U.S. cities that have banking offices of the six different types listed (agencies, branches, commercial bank subsidiaries, Edge Act banks, representative offices, and investment companies).

Source: *Top Numbers: Part Two, American Banker*, 1990.

or borrowing decisions. Participants benefit greatly from the increased liquidity and lower interest rates that would otherwise not exist.

ORGANIZATIONAL STRUCTURE

U.S. commercial banks conduct their international activities through a variety of units. Small- and medium-sized banks typically do business strictly through the bank's head office. Large banks and multibank holding companies typically operate a variety of representative offices, foreign branches, foreign subsidiaries, Edge Act and Agreement corporations, and export trading companies. These units differ in terms of where they are located, what products they can offer, who they can conduct business with, and how they are regulated. The top part of Exhibit 26.5 indicates the volume of business generated in the United States by type of organization.

Head Office. U.S. banks involved in international activities normally have an international division or department as part of the home office's organizational structure. Division managers supervise all international activities, with the possible exception of funding responsibilities if a bank has a funds management division. These activities include direct commercial and retail lending, lease financing, and securities operations. Other international units report to senior management through this division.

Representative Office. A representative office is usually the first type of international office that a bank forms. The term "representative" indicates that the office does not conduct normal banking business but simply represents the corporation. Employees cannot accept deposits or make loans. The purpose is to promote the corporation's name and develop business that can be funneled to the home office. Banks that establish these offices are trying to assess whether it is feasible to pursue normal banking activities in that location. Because they are exploratory in nature, representative offices have few employees until their transition to full-service banking units.

Foreign Branch. As indicated in Exhibit 26.3, U.S. banks conduct almost 60 percent of their international business through foreign branches. Branch offices are legally part of the home bank but are subject to the laws and regulations of the host nation. Foreign branches are either shell offices or full-service banks. Shell branches normally do not solicit business from local individuals, companies, or governments. Instead, they serve as conduits for Eurodollar activities that originate in the head office. Since December 1981 banks have been allowed to engage in the same activities as shell branches via International Banking Facilities (IBFs). IBFs provide cheaper access to the Eurodollar market, reducing the value of pure shell branches. Full-service branches operate much like domestic banks. They accept deposits, make loans, trade securities, and provide fee-based services. Most large U.S. banks have a branch located in London, the center of Eurodollar activity.

Foreign Subsidiary. Domestic commercial banks can acquire an ownership interest in foreign banks. A bank holding company or Edge Act corporation can acquire both foreign banks and qualifying nonbank subsidiaries. At the end of 1983 these subsidiaries generated over 13 percent of U.S. banks' foreign business. Unlike branches, subsidiaries are organizations distinct from the parent bank with their own sets of books.

Most nonbank subsidiaries serve the same functions as their domestic counterparts: commercial and consumer financing, data processing, and leasing. The largest U.S. bank holding companies have also formed investment banking subsidiaries (merchant banks) that underwrite a broad range of stocks and bonds in full competition with foreign investment banks. Foreign bank subsidiaries operate much like foreign branches, concentrating on loans and deposits.[5]

Edge Act and Agreement Corporations. Edge Act corporations are domestic subsidiaries of banking organizations chartered by the Federal Reserve. All "Edges" are located in the United States but may be established by U.S. or foreign banks and bank holding companies.[6] Agreement corporations are the state-chartered equivalents of an Edge. Both types of firms are limited to activities involving foreign customers. These include accepting demand and time deposits, extending credit, and other activities incidental to international business.[7] The primary advantage of Edge Act corporations is that they can locate anywhere in the United States, independently of McFadden Act (interstate branching) restrictions. They can establish overseas branches and IBFs and own foreign subsidiaries. Domestic and foreign banking organizations can consequently conduct international business near their sources.

Exhibit 26.3 demonstrates that Edge Act corporations account for a very small share of total claims on foreign entities. Most of this activity involves firms in New York and Miami, where many international businesses set up offices. At year-end 1989, 75 percent of total Edge assets originated at either Miami or New York firms. Still, Edge Act corporations primarily represent deposit gatherers as they do not keep many commercial loans on their books.

International Banking Facilities. Many international banking units were formed expressly to circumvent U.S. regulations. Shell branches are a prime example. By channeling Eurodollar transactions through shell branches, domestic banks could avoid legal reserve requirements, Regulation Q interest ceilings where applicable, and FDIC insurance payments. IBFs were created to make it easier for U.S. banks to conduct international business without the cost and effort of avoiding regulatory requirements through shell units. IBFs are not required to have legal reserves or pay FDIC insurance.[8]

Much like Edge Act corporations, IBFs accept deposits from and extend credit to foreign entities. They also engage in numerous transactions with Edge Act corporations, foreign banks, and other IBFs. IBFs, in fact, are part of other banking organizations because they exist simply as a set of accounting entries. The organizing unit—a domestic commercial bank or savings and loan, a U.S. branch or agency of a foreign

---

[5]U.S. banks are also involved in joint ventures with foreign organizations, including consortium banks that are jointly owned by several foreign banks. The primary purpose is to share credit expertise in loan syndications.

[6]At the end of 1990, three nonbank banks—Merrill Lynch & Co., American Express Bank Ltd, and Prudential-Bache Securities Inc. —also owned Edge corporations.

[7]In October 1985 the Federal Reserve allowed Edge corporations to provide full banking services to international businesses. Previously, Edges had to verify that all deposits from a foreign firm and credit granted were for the sole purpose of carrying out international transactions.

[8]A parent company of an IBF must hold reserves against any borrowings from the IBF.

bank, or an Edge Act corporation—makes all the financial decisions, as it does with a shell branch.

Four basic restrictions on IBF activities are intended to distinguish IBF transactions from domestic money market operations.[9] First, IBFs cannot offer transaction accounts to nonbank customers. Deposit maturities must thus be a minimum of 2 business days. Second, IBFs cannot issue large, negotiable CDs that would be competitive with CDs offered by domestic depository institutions. Third, $100,000 is the minimum acceptable transactions amount. This limits IBF customers to major wholesale participants, including corporations and governments. Finally, loans and deposits must be directly tied to a customer's foreign activity so that direct competitors are those involved in international trade.

Export Trading Companies. Under federal legislation an export trading company is "exclusively engaged in activities related to international trade and is organized and operated principally for purposes of exporting goods and services produced in the United States by unaffiliated persons."[10] Bank holding companies can acquire export trading companies as part of their international business efforts and extend them credit within limits. These subsidiaries enable banks to expand the range of services offered companies, including handling transportation and shipping documentation, field warehousing, and insurance coverage. Export trading companies can also take title to trade items, which a bank is not permitted to do directly.

Agencies of Foreign Banks. Foreign banks compete in the United States through their head offices, U.S. branches, subsidiaries, Edge Act and Agreement corporations, agencies, and investment companies. The first four types of facilities are structured and operate much like U.S. facilities. Agencies and investment companies, in contrast, can offer only a limited range of banking services.[11] They cannot accept transactions deposits from U.S. residents or issue CDs, but must deal exclusively with commercial customers. Their primary purpose is to finance trade originating from firms in their own country. Agencies also actively participate in interbank credit markets and in lending to U.S. corporations. Agencies and investment companies can accept credit deposit balances, much like correspondent balances from commercial customers, if the account is directly tied to the commercial services provided. The bottom part of Exhibits 26.5 and 26.6 indicate the volume of business by type of foreign organization and location in 1989.

---

[9]See Chrystal, "International Banking Facilities" (1984).

[10]Edge Act and Agreement subsidiaries of bank holding companies as well as bankers banks can similarly purchase export trading companies. Park and Zwick (1985) describe the legislation that authorized this investment.

[11]New York State charters foreign agencies as investment companies. These companies are granted powers similar to federally chartered agencies of foreign banks.

INTERNATIONAL FINANCIAL MARKETS

International banking activities have grown along with the growth in international trade. The development of international financial instruments and markets has necessarily followed. Firms that export or import goods and services and banks that finance these activities transact business in many different currencies under different sets of regulations. International financial markets have evolved to facilitate these funds flows and reduce the risk of doing business outside the home country.

International banks are active in soliciting deposits and lending funds outside their domestic borders. The market in which banks and their international facilities obtain international deposits is labeled the *Eurocurrency market*. The market for long-term international securities is the *Eurobond market*. Term lending activities tied to Eurocurrency operations occur in the *Eurocredit market*.

The Eurocurrency Market

A *Eurocurrency* is a deposit liability denominated in any currency except that of the country in which the bank is located. Two features identify qualifying Eurocurrencies. First, a bank or one of its international facilities must accept the deposit. Second, the accepting bank must be located outside the country that issues the currency. Thus a BankAmerica branch located in London that accepts U.S. dollar deposits is dealing in Eurodollars, one type of Eurocurrency. If the same bank accepts a sterling deposit, it is not operating in the Eurocurrency market. Banks that issue Eurocurrency claims are called *Eurobanks*.

Eurodollar deposits are the dominant type of Eurocurrency. Eurodollars are dollar-denominated deposits at banks located outside the United States. Functionally, deposits at IBFs are equivalent and are often included as Eurodollars. Chapter 11 introduces Eurodollars and Exhibit 11.7 describes how Eurodollars originate. Briefly, they arise when the owner of a dollar deposit at a U.S. bank moves the deposit outside the United States. The Eurobank accepting the deposit receives a dollar claim on the U.S. bank from which the funds were transferred. The Eurodollar and Eurocurrency markets consist of a series of transactions leading to the eventual extension of a loan.

Eurodollar deposits are equivalent to domestic CDs from the depositor's perspective. They are issued in large denominations, typically some multiple of $1 million, have fixed maturities, and pay interest at rates slightly above rates on comparable-maturity CDs issued by U.S. banks. The deposits take the form of both nonnegotiable time deposits and negotiable CDs.[12] Issuing banks do not hold reserves against Eurodollar liabilities and do not pay deposit insurance, which justifies the higher interest rates.

Because Eurobanks that issue Eurodollars pay interest but receive a nonearning U.S. demand deposit, they are eager to reinvest the funds. Eurobanks without immediate credit demand for U.S. dollars simply redeposit the Eurodollar proceeds in another Eurobank. Normally, this deposit is made at a small spread over the initial Eurodollar rate paid. The second Eurobank that accepts the deposit either lends dollars

---

[12]A small amount of Eurodollars is callable on demand by the depositor. Because the funds have an effective 24-hour maturity, they earn much lower rates than time deposits or CDs.

to a commercial or government unit or also redeposits the proceeds. Such pyramiding of deposits continues until a loan is granted. The initial or base rate at which a Eurodollar deposit is accepted is called the *London Interbank Offer Rate (LIBOR)*. Each redeposit is priced at a markup over LIBOR, as is the final loan. Many U.S. banks also price loans to domestic firms at a premium over LIBOR, in recognition of the fact that dollars obtained outside the country are identical to dollars obtained domestically.

The markets for other types of Eurocurrencies are similarly structured. Eurosterling represents claims on deposits denominated in pounds sterling at banks located outside the United Kingdom. A nonfinancial firm or bank that needs sterling can borrow in either the Eurosterling market or from Great Britain's domestic banks at a markup over LIBOR. The size of each Eurocurrency market reflects the underlying demand for that currency. The Eurodollar market dominates because U.S. dollars are accepted as a means of payment throughout the world.

The Eurobond Market

Many international banks are active in the Eurobond market. Traditional corporate bonds are long-term instruments, underwritten by well-known investment banks, that are subject to the securities laws of the country in which they are issued. The U.S. Securities and Exchange Commission, for example, requires extensive disclosure regarding the terms of the offering before it will approve a bond issue. Eurobonds are similar in form but subject to virtually no regulation. They can be denominated in any currency or international currency units. As Park and Zwick state, "Eurobonds are issued in the international Euromarket, underwritten by an international banking syndicate not subject to any one country's securities laws, and denominated in any major national currency or even in an artificial currency unit such as the Special Drawing Right, Eurco, the European Unit of Account, and the European Currency Unit."[13]

The primary issuers of Eurobonds are nonfinancial corporations that view them as alternatives to traditional corporate bonds and direct international loans from banks. International banks with investment banking subsidiaries underwrite the bond offerings and often engage in secondary market trading activities. Borrowers issued almost $170 billion in Eurobonds during 1989, which exceeded the volume of corporate bond issues in the United States.

Some international banks issue a hybrid form of Eurobonds structured as a floating-rate note. Floating-rate notes are issued in denominations as low as $5,000, with maturities ranging from 2 to 5 years, and carry interest rates that vary with LIBOR. Typically, the interest rate floats every 6 months at a fixed spread over the 6-month LIBOR. Through floating-rate notes an issuing bank can obtain long-term financing by paying short-term rates. These markets should continue to grow with the move toward syndications among financial institutions and the gradual removal of regulatory restrictions. In recent years, Japanese institutions have significantly increased their international banking activity (see Contemporary Issues: Japan's Finan-

---

[13]See Park and Zwick (1985).

cial Presence Is Growing). Borrowers benefit because interest rates are generally lower than they would be without Euromarket opportunities.

Eurocredits

Banks that accept Eurocurrency deposits face the same asset and liability management decisions that derive from other funding sources. The fundamental difficulty is in managing interest rate risk. This problem disappears when a bank redeposits Eurodollars because it matches the asset maturity with that of the initial deposit. When a bank makes a commercial loan, however, it often mismatches the loan maturity with the deposit maturity.

This risk was especially evident during the credit crunches of the 1960s. U.S. banks that could not issue domestic CDs were forced to go to the Eurodollar market for funding. During these periods, Eurodollar rates rose above ceiling rates on new-issue domestic CDs with the competition for funds and the credit-tightening efforts of the Federal Reserve. Eurobanks consequently faced a dilemma. While dollar borrowers generally required term loan financing, Eurobanks did not want to make fixed-rate term loans funded by short-term deposits representing "hot" money. Borrowing costs could potentially rise above the fixed loan rate if depositors moved their funds.

One solution was the development of *Eurocredits,* term loans priced at a premium over LIBOR. In most cases, the loan rate floats every 3 or 6 months, thereby reducing the mismatch between asset and liability maturities. For large loans, banks form a syndicate of international banks in which each member takes a share of the loan and participates in the negotiation of terms. Because both credit and interest rate risk are reduced, Eurocredits are generally priced at spreads as low as 12.5 basis points over LIBOR.

INTERNATIONAL LENDING

International loans exhibit many of the same characteristics as domestic loans. Individuals, multinational businesses with offices in the United States and overseas, domestic export/import companies, foreign businesses, and foreign governments constitute the basic borrowing groups. The use of proceeds ranges from working capital lines to production loans that facilitate a country's long-term economic development. The difference with international loans is that they entail unique risks. Historically, many large banks have found these risks attractive because of high promised yields. During the early 1980s, several U.S. money center banks generated over 50 percent of their earnings from international operations. In 1987 and again in 1989, most of the largest banks charged off significant portions (up to 25 percent) of their loans to Latin American and other foreign borrowers, and consequently reported net losses. After the fact, many bankers realized that foreign loans effectively produced little profit because the losses offset earlier earnings. In response, many U.S. banks no longer pursue international loans. Since 1987 banks such as First Chicago, BankAmerica, Chemical,

Japan's Financial Presence is Growing

During the past few years, Japanese banks and brokerage houses have made tremendous inroads in global financial markets. In 1989 Japanese banks held 28.5 percent of commercial loans to U.S. borrowers, underwrote 30 percent of total Eurobond offerings, and provided an estimated 50 percent of municipal bond guarantees in the United States. On the investment banking side, four of the ten largest firms in the world are Japanese. The Federal Reserve System approved four Japanese firms as primary dealers in U.S. government securities and allowed various Japanese investors to acquire a significant equity interest in leading U.S. investment banks, such as Goldman Sachs, Shearson Lehman, and PaineWeber.

Japanese firms operate with several inherent advantages. With the country's huge foreign trade surpluses, financial institutions are loaded with funds to reinvest. Japan's government limits rates that banks can pay depositors to less than 4 percent, and banks operate with equity-to-asset ratios close to 2 percent. Banks can thus compete aggressively for business by offering reduced interest rates on loans and lower fees on underwriting activities and financial guarantees. If the trend toward fewer and larger financial institutions continues, Japanese firms expect to be major players.

Consumers and borrowers benefit from the increased competition. More services are available and interest rates are lower because spreads are smaller. Some critics claim, however, that foreign institutions compete in the United States without the same opportunities being available to U.S. firms abroad. Discrepancies in different nations' regulations create inequities, but are slowly disappearing.

The Major Investments from Japan

U.S. Investment Banking Firm	Japanese Investor	Investment	
		Amount (Millions)	Percent of Equity
Shearson Lehman	Nippon Life	$508.0	13.0%
Goldman Sachs	Sumitomo Bank	500.0	12.5
PaineWebber	Yasuda Mutual Life	300.0	20.0
Blackstone	Nikko Securities	100.0	20.0
Wasserstein	Nomura Securities	100.0	20.0
Wolfensohn	Fuji Bank	52.5	0.0[a]
Mitsui Bank	Carlyle Group	25.0	0.0[b]

[a] Each owns 50% of a joint venture.

[b] Mitsui committed at least $25 million to a Carlyle fund.

Data Source: Nathans and Glassgall, 1990.

---

and Manufacturers Hanover have permanently reduced their foreign loan exposure and foreign presence, selling off branches and offices as well. Banks that continue to be aggressive are those that follow U.S. customers as they expand outside the United States.

The previous section introduced Eurocredits. U.S. banks are also heavily involved in financing foreign trade and making direct loans to major commercial customers. The characteristics of these loans are described below.

Short-Term Foreign Trade Financing

International trade and international trade financing are considerably more complex than simply dealing with trading partners within the same country. Not only is the importer located far from the exporter, but the two parties usually operate under different rules and regulations and may be totally unfamiliar with each other's financial stability and credit rating. Frequently, they transact business in different currencies. To facilitate trade, someone must enter the transaction and assume the risk that the importer may not pay. Commercial banks fulfill this role through bankers' acceptance financing.[14] Trading partners must also have the opportunity to convert one currency into another, which creates a demand for foreign exchange services as well.

A *banker's acceptance* is a time draft that represents an order to pay a specified amount of money at a designated future date. A bank accepts the draft when it stamps the word "accepted" across the document. This approval represents a guarantee under which the accepting bank agrees to remit the face value of the draft at maturity. Acceptances are attractive because a bank substitutes its credit rating for that of the importer. The maturity date is far enough forward to allow the goods being financed to be shipped and inspected before the draft matures. Bankers' acceptances are negotiable instruments, with maturities ranging from 1 to 6 months. Most bankers' acceptance transactions are associated with letters of credit, documents that stipulate the contract terms and duties of all parties and authorize an exporter to draw a time draft on a participating bank. The draft is then converted to a negotiable instrument when it is accepted.

Exhibit 26.7 illustrates the mechanics of how a bankers' acceptance is created and used to finance trade.[15] Drafts accepted by U.S. banks are used almost exclusively to finance either U.S. imports or U.S. exports. A small portion finances the warehousing of goods in transit. The trade activity outlined in the exhibit involves a U.S. importer, but the sequence of events is similar for all types of transactions. After agreeing to terms with the exporter (stage 1), the U.S. importer applies for a letter of credit (L/C) from a U.S. bank (stage 2). Upon approving the request, the U.S. bank issues an L/C, which authorizes the exporter to draw a time draft against the U.S. bank, and delivers it to the exporter's bank (stage 3). The foreign bank then notifies the exporter, who ships the goods and submits the L/C, time draft, and shipping documents, which the foreign bank forwards to the U.S. bank. When the U.S. bank accepts the draft, it creates a bankers' acceptance (stage 8).

The bankers' acceptance has a face value and fixed maturity. The exporter discounts the draft with the issuing bank and receives immediate payment (stage 9). If, for example, the bankers' acceptance carried a face value of $1 million and 90-day maturity, the discounted price would equal $980,000 at an 8 percent discount rate.[16] This covers the purchase price of the goods, although the importer will

---

[14]Exporters who are familiar with an importer often extend credit on open account and receive payment after the goods have been delivered. In other cases, an exporter may demand payment from the importer before shipping the goods.

[15]Exhibit 26.7 is taken from Duffield and Summers (1981). The following discussion is based on their explanation of the transactions underlying the exhibit.

[16]Price = [1 − (90/360)(0.08)] ($1 million) = $980,000.

Exhibit 26.7 Bankers' Acceptance Financing of U.S. Imports: A Banker's Acceptance Is Created, Discounted, Sold, and Paid at Maturity

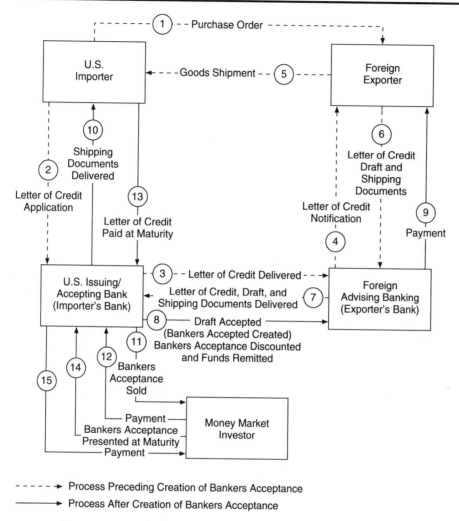

----→ Process Preceding Creation of Bankers Acceptance

——→ Process After Creation of Bankers Acceptance

Source: J. Duffield and B. Summers, "Bankers Acceptances," in *Instruments of the Money Market*, T. Cook and B. Summers, editors, Federal Reserve Bank of Richmond, 1981.

remit the full face value at maturity. The accepting bank delivers the shipping documents to the importer (stage 10), who can then legally obtain the goods.

Use of the acceptance enables the exporter to be paid before the importer receives the goods, and the importer to effectively borrow the purchase price. If the issuing bank keeps possession of the bankers' acceptance, it essentially finances the importer's purchase, much like a direct loan. In most cases, the issuing bank will sell the acceptance to a third-party investor in the money market (stage 11). If the bank receives the same discount value, $980,000 in this example, it has no funds committed to the financing. It must, however, pay off the acceptance at maturity (stages 13 to 15), when it presumably receives payment from the importer.

The issuing bank makes a profit in several ways. First, it levies a fee on the importer for accepting the draft and providing its guarantee. Second, it earns the discounted value of the draft, $20,000 in this example, if it simply keeps the acceptance in its portfolio. Finally, it can earn additional profits if it sells the acceptance prior to maturity at a price below the original discounted value ($980,000). Of course, the sale eliminates any interest income.

Historically, exporters and importers originated most of the time drafts that evolved into bankers' acceptances. Since the early 1970s, however, many bankers' acceptances have refinanced credits of foreign banks that wanted to liquidate their direct financing of foreign trade. These bank-drawn drafts are known as *refinancing acceptances* or *accommodations*.

Direct International Loans

International loans originate from international departments of domestic banks, Edge Act corporations, and the credit offices of foreign branches and subsidiaries. Eurodollar loans to foreign governments and well-established multinational corporations are generally low risk. Defaults are extremely rare, so that the loans are priced at a small markup over LIBOR. Some loans are extended to private corporations but carry an explicit guarantee from the source country's government. These loans carry higher risk because some governments have reneged on their guarantees. Loans that have received the greatest attention recently are made within less-developed countries (LDCs). LDC credit extended to both private borrowers and government units has generally shown a poor repayment history over the long term. With increasing frequency, regulators and bank shareholders express concern about U.S. banks' exposure to potential foreign loan losses. International loans to LDCs, in fact, clearly contributed to regulators' demand that U.S. money center banks increase their capital-to-asset ratios.

U.S. money center banks as a group are especially exposed to the financially troubled countries in Latin America. Exhibit 26.8 documents the largest banks' lending activity to borrowers in the five countries with the highest debt exposure to U.S. banks. Citicorp, BankAmerica and Chase Manhattan had the highest ratios of nonperforming loans to exposure in 1985 at 5.4 percent, 7.3 percent, and 7.3 percent, respectively. Most of the others reported ratios closer to 3 percent. Loans to Argentina and Venezuela, where 11.1 percent and 15.1 percent of total loans were classified as nonperforming, were the worst performers. This reflected extremely weak exports from these countries because of worldwide agriculture and energy gluts.

Unfortunately, nonperforming loans do not completely reflect potential losses. Many loans are not classified as nonperforming because U.S. banks have lent the borrowers funds to make interest and principal payments on existing loans to keep the loans current. Several Latin American governments, including those of Peru and Mexico, have also called for a moratorium on debt service to U.S. banks. Unilaterally,

Exhibit 26.8 Loan Exposure of U.S. Money Center Banks to Latin America: December 31, 1985 (Millions of Dollars)

Bank	Argentina	Brazil	Chile	Mexico
Citicorp				
Exposure	$1,400	$ 4,700	$ 500	$ 2,800
Nonperforming	116	99	13	52
BankAmerica				
Exposure	a	2,799	a	2,709
Nonperforming	a	11	a	94
Chase Manhattan				
Exposure	920	2,820	a	1,680
Nonperforming	155	7	a	123
Manufacturers Hanover				
Exposure	1,400	2,200	791	1,800
Nonperforming	131	4	14	34
J.P. Morgan				
Exposure	822	1,862	a	1,152
Nonperforming	96	10	a	12
Chemical				
Exposure	402	1,434	369	1,471
Nonperforming	67	6	4	18
Security Pacific				
Exposure	a	590	a	520
Nonperforming	a	13	a	23
Bankers Trust				
Exposure	383	864	a	1,277
Nonperforming	10	30	a	4
First Chicago				
Exposure	a	806	a	912
Nonperforming	a	8	a	12
Wells Fargo				
Exposure	133	603	104	606
Nonperforming	32	15	a	16
Totals[b]				
Exposure	$5,460	$18,678	$1,764	$14,927
Nonperforming	607	203	31	389

these countries may determine that borrowers, including governments, should suspend interest and principal payments until their revenues increase sufficiently. The key ratio is thus each bank's total exposure as a percentage of stockholders' equity. This ratio, reported in the final column of Exhibit 26.8, exceeds 100 percent for six of the ten banks analyzed. It ranges from a low of 45 percent for Security Pacific to 205 percent for Manufacturers Hanover.

What, then, is the true foreign loan risk position of U.S. money center banks? The Latin American debt crisis officially began in 1982. Why did many of the largest banks increase their exposure to these same countries after 1982 with full knowledge of the problems? Why have these same banks largely withdrawn from international commercial lending since 1988?

Exhibit 26.8 *(Continued)*

Venezuela	Total	Nonperforming/Exposure	Exposure/Stockholders' Equity
$1,200 295	$10,600 575	5.4%	130%
1,450 405	6,958 510	7.3	153
1,250 200	6,670 485	7.3	175
1,100 16	7,291 199	2.7	205
a a	3,836 118	3.0	87
714 47	4,390 142	3.2	143
a a	1,110 36	3.2	45
419 44	2,943 88	3.0	85
425 11	2,143 32	1.5	82
259 13	1,705 76	4.5	117
$6,817 1,031	$47,646 2,261	4.7%[c]	122%[c]

[a]The exposure is generally less than 1 percent of total loans and investments and thus is not significant.

[b]Total nonperforming loans as a percentage of the total exposure to each country for all banks is: Argentina, 11.1; Brazil, 1.1; Chile, 1.8; Mexico, 2.6; and Venezuela, 15.1.

[c]Average.

Source: *American Banker*, March 31, 1986. Reprinted with permission of *American Banker*.

To assess risk, the analyst must understand the relationship between large financial institutions and the U.S. government. International loans are part of the price banks pay for the U.S. government's implied guarantee that they will not be allowed to fail. If the banks were to demand payment on defaulted foreign loans or charge off loans as uncollectible and refuse to extend additional credit, economic conditions in LDCs would worsen. Not wanting to bring about a collapse of world trade and financial markets, the government encouraged the largest banks to renegotiate existing agreements and continue lending.

Through 1986 U.S. banks generally acceded to the government's request and continued lending to LDCs. In May 1987, however, Citicorp reversed the trend by allocating $3 billion to its loan loss reserve for possible loan charge-offs with Latin American borrowers. The transfer produced a quarterly loss near $2.5 billion. Other money center banks quickly increased their associated loss reserves. The reserve allocations enabled the banks to recognize discounts on the loans so that they could sell the loans in the secondary market and engage in debt-for-equity swaps with foreign borrowers. In essence, U.S. banks acknowledged that the financial markets realized LDC debts would not be paid in a timely fashion. In many cases, bank stock prices rose as market participants interpreted the action to mean that balance sheets would be healthier and future profitability would improve. Banks prefer foreign exposure in the form of equity investments to long-term, constantly renegotiated loans to foreign central banks.

Credit Analysis. It is difficult to evaluate international loans from a traditional credit analysis viewpoint. Many foreign governments rely heavily on single industries or products as a source of reserves to pay off their debt. Mexico, with its reliance on oil revenues, is a prime example. When oil prices were rising in the late 1970s and early 1980s, Mexico increased its foreign borrowing to finance internal economic development. The subsequent steep drop in oil prices eliminated its source of foreign currency and forced a total restructuring of the country's international debt obligations.

Credit analysis for international loans generally follows the same systematic procedures outlined previously for domestic loans. Analysts evaluate the required loan amount, use of the proceeds, source and timing of expected repayment, and availability of secondary collateral sources. What makes international lending different is a series of additional risks associated with debt repayment prospects and constraints. If, for example, a bank accepts payment in a currency other than its own country's monetary unit and does not hedge, it assumes foreign exchange risk. If the value of the foreign currency declines relative to the domestic currency, the value of the debt service declines, even though all payments might be received on a timely basis. Other potential problems are usually classified under the heading of "country risk," which includes economic and political risks. Economic risks are readily quantifiable, reflecting the considerations discussed above. Political risks are much more difficult to assess. Bankers frequently analyze sovereign risk, which refers to the likelihood that foreign governments will unilaterally alter their debt service payments, regardless of the formal repayment schedule. In 1985, for example, governments in Nigeria and Peru both capped the amount of interest their countries would pay toward international debt obligations.

Many banks have developed credit scoring systems for assessing country risk. One bank's system measures country risk by using discriminant analysis to quantify economic risks and subjective checklists to quantify political risks.[17] The evaluation

---

[17]Morgan (1985) describes the inputs and evaluation procedures in detail.

produces an index that ranks different countries according to their riskiness in re-scheduling debt payments. In this application, economic risk is measured by debt management factors and economic indexes. The best indicators of risk are a country's current debt service ratio, defined as the sum of debt service and short-term debt outstanding divided by total exports; total debt divided by exports; and basic economic measures such as per capita income, real growth in a gross domestic product, and the inflation rate. Political risk is measured according to a subjective political rating model and structural factors. The political model assesses both political stability and general government characteristics (see Exhibit 26.9). Each country receives a weighted score representing its cumulative risk profile. The bank determines appropriate loan limits or concentrations in different countries according to these rankings.

FOREIGN INCOME AND FEE-BASED SERVICES

Many large U.S. commercial banks earn a substantial portion of their net income from foreign operations. Traditionally, these earnings have come from loans. More recently, noncredit services have contributed an increasing share. Exhibit 26.10 presents summary data for J.P. Morgan from 1988 to 1990. J.P Morgan assigns income and expenses according to the geographic region in which they arise. Note the large loss on foreign business in 1989 that helped produce at net loss for the bank that year. In general, J.P. Morgan is slowly reducing its foreign exposure as the company generated just 45 percent of its total operating income from foreign activities in 1990, 4 percent below that in 1988. In 1990, however, foreign activities accounted for 70 percent of net income up from 54 percent in 1988. Figures and trends for other money center banks are comparable, suggesting that global activities already dominate domestic activities for the largest banks.

In the current environment, U.S. banks view international investment banking activities as the primary source of earnings growth. Other than underwriting corporate bonds and equities in the United States, large commercial banks offer the same investment banking services as Salomon Brothers and Japan's Nomura Securities. During 1989, for example, J.P. Morgan and Bankers Trust ranked second and twelfth, respectively, in underwriting securities outside the United States.

International banks offer a wide range of fee-based services, with letters of credit, interest rate and currency swaps, and security underwriting contributing the most to earnings. These same banks also trade bonds and foreign exchange for their own accounts. There are brokers, dealers, and underwriters of all types of securities on virtually every exchange in the world.[18]

FOREIGN EXCHANGE ACTIVITIES

Because different countries use different monetary units, traders must be able to convert one unit into another. Foreign exchange markets are the markets in which these

---

[18]The Glass-Steagall Act passed during the Depression is clearly a relic of the past. The largest U.S. commercial banks currently offer full-scale investment banking services internationally but are prohibited from doing so domestically unless the Federal Reserve directly authorizes such activity. Such restrictions create an artificial barrier between institutions and a false perception of the nature of money center bank operations.

Exhibit 26.9 Political Rating Models

Government Characteristics, Country *ABC*	
What classification best describes the current government?	
Government type (0 to 10)	6
0 Despot, dictator	
2 Military dictator	
4 Monarchy, family rule	
6 One-party democracy or nonviable multiparty democracy	
8 Multiparty (coalition) democracy	
10 Viable two-party democracy	
Latest change in government (0 to 10)	8
0 Bloody and violent coup d'etat	
2 Bloodless coup d'etat	
4 Peaceful dictator change	
6 Monarch change, change in colonial status	
8 Elections, one candidate only	
10 Peaceful elections, two or more candidates	
Relations with United States (0 to 10)	4
0 Considered a threat to U.S. security	
2 Anti-American policies	
4 Nonaligned but leaning to the East	
5 Nonaligned	
6 Nonaligned but leaning to the West	
8 Supports most U.S. foreign policies	
10 Strongly pro-American, supports all U.S. policies	
Government's role in economy (0 to 10)	6
0 Government controls all aspects of economy (communism)	
2 Government influences all aspects of economy	
4 Socialist type of economy	
6 General agreement between capitalists and government	
8 Capitalism with minor government intervention	
10 Strongly capitalistic, free enterprise	
Stability of present government (0 to 10)	6
0 Violent coup d'etat imminent	
2 Overthrow of government likely	

Government Characteristics, Country *ABC*

4 Unexpected change in government possible (i.e., death of leader)	
6 Government could lose in next election	
8 Likely change in government, political power remains intact	
10 Government unlikely to lose in next elections	

Political Stability, Country *ABC*

What are the chances of the following events in the short term and medium term?[a]

	Short Term	Medium Term
Destabilizing riots, civil unrest	3	2
Increased terrorist activities	3	2
Guerilla activity, armed rebels	3	2
Civil war	4	4
Government overthrow, coup d'etat	4	3
Foreign war, border skirmishes	4	4
Political moratorium of debt	4	4
Nationalization of major industries	3	3
Socialistic party comes to power	3	3
Communist party comes to power	4	4
Total	35	31

Probabilities

5	Extremely unlikely
4	Unlikely
3	Neutral
2	Likely
1	Extremely likely
0	Present situation

Government characteristics	30
Political stability (short term/medium term)	35/31
Total political rating	65/61

[a]Short term is within 1 year; long term is between 1 and 5 years.

**Exhibit 26.10 U.S. and Foreign-Related Income for
J.P. Morgan & Co. Inc., 1987–90 (Millions of Dollars)**

	1988	%	1989	%	1990	%
Foreign Country-Related Operations						
Total operating income	$4,189	49.0	$4,888	47.0	$4,752.0	45.4
Income before taxes	888	67.5	(1,500)	na	762.0	72.3
Net income[a]	545	54.4	(1,693)	na	692.0	68.9
U.S.-Related Operations						
Total operating income	4,367	51.0	5,506	53.0	5,713.0	54.5
Income before taxes	427	32.5	400	na	292.0	27.7
Net income	457	45.6	418	na	313.0	31.1
Consolidated						
Total operating income	8,556	100.0	10,394	100.0	10,465.0	100.0
Income before taxes	1,315	100.0	(1,100)	100.0	1,054.0	100.0
Net income	1,002	100.0	(1,275)	100.0	1,005.0	100.0
Foreign Exchange Trading Income/Total Operating Income		2.19%		1.84%		2.95%
Foreign-Related Assets/Total Assets		42%		43%		43%

[a]After income tax expense or benefit.

Source: Annual Reports

monetary units are traded. Foreign exchange refers to currency other than the monetary unit of the home country, and an exchange rate is the price of one currency in terms of another currency. For example, Japanese yen represent foreign exchange in the United States, such that 1 U.S. dollar may be worth 153 yen if exchanged today. Banks participate in foreign exchange markets by buying and selling currencies from participants who use different currencies in their business or travels. They also coordinate foreign exchange hedges for bank customers, enter arbitrage transactions, and speculate on currency price movements for their own account by taking unhedged positions.

A fundamental responsibility of international banks is to facilitate funds transfers between trading partners who deal in different currencies. Most transactions are settled by exchanging deposits, so that banks must either maintain correspondent bank relationships or operate their own foreign bank offices to have access to Eurocurrencies. Each funds transfer may require a conversion of deposits to another currency and thus may affect exchange rates if banks choose to realign their inventories.

Suppose, for example, that a U.S. retail outlet negotiates the purchase of video recording equipment for $500,000 from a Japanese manufacturer. If the purchase is invoiced in yen, the buyer will convert U.S. dollars to yen at $1 to 153 yen and exchange 76.5 million yen for the goods. The hypothetical transaction is summarized in Exhibit 26.11, assuming that the traders deal with Security Pacific and Fuji Bank Ltd. After the purchase, Security Pacific's inventory of currencies has changed because

Exhibit 26.11 Facilitating Funds Transfers of Different Currency-Denominated Deposits

U.S. retailer imports $500,000 in video equipment from Japanese manufacturer. Spot exchange rate is $1 = 153 yen.

Security Pacific		Fuji Bank Ltd	
ΔASSETS	ΔLIABILITIES	ΔASSETS	ΔLIABILITIES
1. Deposit at Fuji Bank	Deposit—U.S. retailer		1. Deposit—U.S. retailer
−76.5 million yen	−$500,000		+76.5 million yen
			Deposit—Security Pacific
			−76.5 million yen
			2. Deposit—U.S. retailer
			−76.5 million yen
			Deposit—Japanese manufacturer
			+76.5 million yen

1. U.S. retailer buys yen from Security Pacific and deposits balance at Fuji Bank in Tokyo.
2. U.S. retailer pays Japanese manufacturer for goods.

---

it holds 76.5 million fewer yen than previously. The bank will have to buy yen to bring its foreign exchange holdings back to the initial position. If the transaction was denominated in dollars, Fuji Bank would hold $500,000 more and would need to sell dollars to reach its initial foreign exchange position. Both the purchase of yen by Security Pacific and sale of dollars by Fuji Bank would put pressure on the dollar to decrease in value (increased supply of dollars) and the yen to increase in value (increased demand for yen). Current exchange rates will thus be affected when transactions force a realignment of foreign exchange holdings.

In actuality, there is a spot market, forward market, futures market, and market for options on futures for foreign exchange. The spot market is the exchange of currencies for immediate delivery. The forward market comprises transactions that represent a commitment to exchange currencies at a specified time in the future at an exchange rate determined at the time the contract is signed. For example, a bank might commit to buy 1 million yen 90 days forward for $6,579. After 90 days the bank pays $6,579 and receives 1 million yen, regardless of movements in exchange rates during the 90-day period. The 90-day forward rate in this case is different from the spot rate quoted earlier because $1 equals 152 yen. Foreign exchange trading also occurs in organized markets for futures and options on futures, which enables traders to hedge spot transactions or speculate on future exchange rate changes.[19]

---

[19]Chrystal (1984) describes the rudiments of foreign exchange futures and options in "A Guide to Foreign Exchange Markets."

Banks that buy or sell currencies for customers normally charge a commission. Alternatively, they may enter into forward contracts with customers and speculatively trade for their own account. For example, suppose that the current dollar-to-yen spot rate is $1 equals 153 yen, and the 90-day forward rate is $1 equals 152 yen. If a bank buys 100 million yen with dollars 90 days forward, it agrees to pay $657,895 for the yen when the forward contract comes due, even though the current exchange rate sets the value at $653,595. If the position is unhedged, the bank assumes the risk that dollars will increase in value relative to yen during the 90-day interval. It will gain if dollars fall more in value than that suggested by the forward-to-spot rate differential (153 yen versus 152 yen).

A spot rate of $1 to 155 yen at the time of delivery of the forward contract would indicate that the dollar rose in value and the bank could have purchased 100 million yen for only $645,161. A spot rate of $1 to 150 yen at delivery would require a price of $666,667, which exceeds the contracted price by almost $10,000. When the forward price of a foreign currency is higher than its spot price, the foreign currency is priced at a forward premium. When the forward price is lower, the foreign currency is priced at a forward discount. In the above case, the yen is priced at a forward premium against the dollar.

The Relationship between Foreign Exchange Rates and Interest Rates

The relationship between spot rates and forward rates is determined by the same factors that influence relative interest rates between countries. Arbitrage transactions essentially guarantee that interest rate changes produce changes in foreign exchange rates, and vice versa. Suppose that a trader can borrow U.S. dollars for 1 year at 9 percent at the same time that 1-year maturity, risk-free, Swiss franc-denominated securities yield 10 percent. The trader can convert dollars to francs at the spot rate of $1 for 1.7 francs and sell francs for dollars 1-year forward at $1 = 1.667 francs.

This series of transactions is demonstrated in Exhibit 26.12. A trader borrows $1 million and agrees to repay $1.09 million 1 year later. Simultaneously, the trader sells the dollars for francs, buys a Swiss security, and sells the expected amount of francs at maturity for dollars 1 year forward. As indicated, the trader can earn a riskless profit of $31,776 for each $1 million borrowed. The profit is riskless because the trader has borrowed in one currency yet covered the transaction by selling the expected foreign exchange after investment for the original currency in the forward market. A profit is available because the interest rate differential between securities in the two countries is out of line with the spot-to-forward exchange rate differential. This series of trades is called *covered interest arbitrage.*[20]

If the exchange rates and interest rates were this far out of line and the large profit was available, arbitragers would quickly negotiate the same series of transactions until prices moved back in line to eliminate (net of transactions costs) the riskless return.

---

[20]If the calculation showed a loss, a profit could be made by reversing the direction of transactions by borrowing in the opposite currency and converting it in a similar fashion.

Exhibit 26.12 Covered Interest Arbitrage

2. Convert dollars to francs at $1 = 1.7 francs   3. Invest in Swiss securities yielding 10%

$$\frac{\$1,090,000}{1+0.09}(1.7) = 1.7 \text{ million francs} \qquad \frac{\$1,090,000}{1+0.09}(1.7)(1.10) = 1.87 \text{ million francs}$$

$$\frac{\$1,090,000}{1+0.09} = \$1,000,000 \qquad \frac{\$1,090,000}{(1+0.09)}\frac{(1.7)(1.10)}{(1.667)} = \$1,121,776$$

1. Borrow dollars at 9%   4. Sell francs for dollars 1 year forward at $1 = 1.667 francs

Sample Transaction: Borrow $1,000,000

1. Borrow $1,000,000 at 9%; agree to repay $1,090,000 in one year.
2. Convert $1,000,000 to 1.7 million francs in spot market at $1 = 1.7 francs.
3. Invest 1.7 million francs in 1-year security yielding 10%; will receive 1.87 million francs after 1 year.
4. Sell 1.87 million francs 1 year forward for $1,121,776 at $1 = 1.667 francs
Net profit = $1,121,776 − $1,090,000 = $31,776

Interest rate parity exists when covered interest arbitrage profit potential is eliminated. Letting

i_1 = annual interest rate in Country 1
i_2 = annual interest rate in Country 2
$s_{1,2}$ = spot exchange rate equal to the number of units of Country 2's currency for one unit of Country 1's currency
$f_{1,2}$ = 1-year forward exchange rate equal to the number of units of Country 2's currency for one unit of Country 1's currency

interest rate parity implies: $\dfrac{1+i_2}{1+i_1}\left(\dfrac{s_{1,2}}{f_{1,2}}\right) = 1$, or   **(26.1)**

$$\frac{i_2 - i_1}{1+i_1} = \frac{f_{1,2} - s_{1,2}}{s_{1,2}} \qquad \textbf{(26.2)}$$

The equilibrium condition, expressed in Equation (26.2), suggests that the forward exchange rate differential as a fraction of the spot rate should equal the interest rate differential relative to 1 plus an interest factor to eliminate arbitrage profits. If i_1 is 9 percent, i_2 is 10 percent, and $s_{1,2}$ is 1.7 in the previous example, then $f_{1,2}$ should equal 1.7156:

$$\frac{0.10 - 0.09}{1 + 0.09} = \frac{f_{1,2} - 1.7}{1.7}, \text{ or}$$

$$f_{1,2} = 1.7156$$

Conceptually, if interest rates are relatively low in one country, that country's currency should sell at a forward premium. Any gain from borrowing at low rates and investing at higher rates (0.01/1.09) is exactly offset (0.0156/1.7) when the borrower attempts to sell the investment proceeds forward at a premium price.

International banks actively trade most foreign currencies. They buy and sell foreign exchange for customers by request, to hedge transactions for customers and themselves, to earn arbitrage profits by taking advantage of temporary price discrepancies, and to trade speculatively for their own account. Foreign exchange gains often supplement normal operating earnings, as Exhibit 26.10 shows for J.P. Morgan, whose foreign exchange trading contributed $191 million in 1989, almost 2 percent of the bank's operating income.

SUMMARY

Large international banks effectively operate as commercial banks and investment banks. They accept foreign deposits and make loans to foreign borrowers. They act as brokers, dealers, and underwriters in negotiating Eurobond issues, floating-rate note issues, interest rate and currency swaps, and foreign equity issues. Banks located outside the United States are more heavily capitalized and thus better able to compete globally. These banks have consequently captured a bigger market share of business activity both within and outside the United States.

Because of large losses on international loans, many large U.S. money center banks have substantially reduced their international commercial loan exposure. With this slow growth, they have aggressively courted overseas investment banking business in search of fee income. Many of the largest domestic banks generate 30 to 50 percent of their income from foreign activities.

International banks operate a wide range of offices to conduct foreign banking business. These offices generally provide access to the Eurocurrency markets and Eurocredits. Loans to foreign governments and businesses entail two additional risks compared with loans to domestic borrowers. Country risk involves both economic risk that the borrower's ability to repay may deteriorate, and political risk that the country's government may simply renege on contracted debt service payments. International loans may also involve foreign exchange risk when lenders receive payment in a currency other than their own. At the end of 1985, six of the ten largest U.S. commercial banks had loans outstanding to Latin American countries in excess of stockholders' equity. The other four had loan exposures from 40 to 80 percent of equity. U.S. banks are generally trying to reduce their international credit exposure and increase their investment banking activities.

Questions

Global Activities

1. To determine how the United States stacks up in global banking operations, indicate which country is the largest according to the following criteria.
   a. Biggest bank by asset size

  b.   Fastest growing in last five years
  c.   Highest capitalization

2.   What seems to be the main competitive advantage of Japanese banks? What does this indicate about the efficiency of financial markets?

3.   Describe the types of international investment banking activities that U.S. commercial banks can offer.

4.   What foreign institutions are major lenders in the United States? Do any operate with advantages over U.S. firms?

Organizational Structure

5.   Why were international banking facilities created? How do they differ from Edge Act and Agreement corporations?

6.   Which of the following types of foreign banking operations would be most suitable in these circumstances?

Type of operations:
  Head office
  Representative office
  Foreign branch
  Foreign subsidiary
  Export trading company

  a.   A major bank customer requests a loan to support a new export operation to Canada. The customer has never exported before and needs help.

  b.   The bank notices a continually-increasing trend among its business customers to establish offices in Mexico. Although the bank can not yet justify its own Mexican office, it does want to provide loans to the customer's offices and help with currency exchange.

  c.   The bank above finds that its Mexico business is booming and that Mexican firms have heard of their lending policies and have contacted them for loans. The bank thinks Mexico City may provide enough business to warrant an exploratory staff of two people.

  d.   Indonesia has just announced the privatization of numerous small banks. Your bank is going to buy one of these banks to establish a lending-deposit base in the booming S.E. Asia market.

  e.   The bank wants to establish a full service office in the USSR. However, the possibility of government seizure of foreign assets still exists, so the unit should be structured to be financially independent of the parent.

Markets and Loans

7.   Discuss the differences between Eurocurrency, Eurobonds, and Eurocredits.

8.   "Bankers' acceptances are really only checks guaranteed by the check writer's bank to be 'good.'" In what ways is this analogy not precisely correct?

9. What is the relationship of loans to less-developed countries and stockholders' equity at the largest U.S. commercial banks? What actions should regulators take to reduce risk associated with international loans?

10. Should bank regulators force large U.S. money center banks to value foreign loans at market value? What would the impact be? Is regulatory policy discriminatory in favor of multinational banks? Why are small banks allowed to fail and not large banks?

11. Explain how you would measure country risk in international lending. Is it quantifiable?

12. U.S. banks cannot underwrite corporate stocks and bonds in the United States because it is too risky, but they can do so outside the United States. Do they utilize this overseas opportunity, and what is the effect?

Foreign Exchange

13. Explain how the forward market for foreign exchange differs from the spot market. When will forward exchange rates be at a premium or discount to spot exchange rates?

14. Suppose that the following exchange rates and interest rates prevail:

    Spot exchange rate: $1 = 148 yen

    1-year forward rate: $1 = 146 yen

    1-year interest rates: U.S. = 8.4 percent, Japan = 7.3 percent

    Can a trader earn covered interest arbitrage profits? If not, explain. If possible, determine what the likely directional impact on each rate would be if arbitragers took advantage of the profit potential.

15. Assume that the forward exchange rate in Question 14 is for 90 days forward and the interest rates are annualized 90-day rates. Can a trader earn covered interest arbitrage profits? If the investor trades $1 million, how many dollars of profits will he make?

References

Baer, Herbert. "Foreign Competition in U.S. Banking Markets." *Economic Perspectives* (Federal Reserve Bank of Chicago, May/June 1990).

Chrystal, K. Alec. "A Guide to Foreign Exchange Markets." *Review* (Federal Reserve Bank of St. Louis, March 1984).

Chrystal, K. Alec. "International Banking Facilities." *Review* (Federal Reserve Bank of St. Louis, April 1984).

Duffield, J.G., and B.J. Summers. "Bankers' Acceptances." In *Instruments of the Money Market,* edited by Timothy Cook and Bruce Summers. Richmond, Va.: Federal Reserve Bank of Richmond, 1981.

Gasser, William, and David Roberts. "Bank Lending to Developing Countries: Problems and Prospects." *Quarterly Review* (Federal Reserve Bank of New York, Autumn 1982).

Hector, Gary. "Why U.S. Banks Are in Retreat." *Fortune* (May 7, 1990).

Hervey, Jack. "Bankers' Acceptances Revisited." *Economic Perspectives* (Federal Reserve Bank of Chicago, May–June 1985).

Holstein, William, et al. "The Stateless Corporation." *Business Week* (May 14, 1990).

Jensen, Frederick, and Patrick Parkinson. "Recent Developments in the Bankers Acceptance Market." *Federal Reserve Bulletin* (Board of Governors of the Federal Reserve System, January 1986).

Key, Sydney. "The Internationalization of U.S. Banking" In *Handbook for Banking Strategy,* edited by Richard Aspinwall and Robert Eisenbeis. New York: John Wiley & Sons, 1985.

MacPhee, William. "Bankers' Acceptance Finance." *The Journal of Commercial Bank Lending* (February 1978).

Mills, Rodney. "Foreign Lending by Banks: A Guide to International and U.S. Statistics." *Federal Reserve Bulletin* (Board of Governors of the Federal Reserve System, October 1986).

Morgan, John. "Assessing Country Risk at Texas Commerce." *The Bankers Magazine* (May–June 1985).

Nathans, Leah, and William Glasgall. "Japan's Waiting Game on Wall Street." *Business Week* (February 19, 1990).

Park, Yoon, and Jack Zwick. *International Banking in Theory and Practice.* Reading, Mass.: Addison-Wesley Publishing, 1985.

Pavel, Christine, and John McElravey. "Globalization in the Financial Services Industry." *Economic Perspectives* (Federal Reserve Bank of Chicago, May/June 1990).

Rodriguez, Rita, and E. Eugene Carter. *International Financial Management.* Englewood Cliffs, N.J.: Prentice-Hall, 1984.

Sarver, Eugene. *The Eurocurrency Market Handbook.* New York Institute of Finance, 1988.

Seth, Rama, and Alicia Quijano. "Japanese Banks' Customers in the United States." *Quarterly Review* (Federal Reserve Bank of New York, Spring 1991).

Steckler, Lois. "U.S. International Transactions in 1990." *Federal Reserve Bulletin* (Board of Governors of the Federal Reserve System, May 1991).

Chapter 27

Trust and Personal Banking

Recent studies of trust department performance at commercial banks indicate that trust activities add from 5 to 10 basis points to the average bank's return on assets. Many banks expect to have their trust departments spearhead the provision of comprehensive personal banking services. Security Pacific Corp., for example, claims that it no longer is in just the trust business, but the personal asset management business. Only one in five banks, however, even offers trust services because the break-even level of trust assets required is too high to justify the investment in trust personnel.

In recent years banks with trust departments have become more aggressive in advertising and promoting their trust services. They have expanded the range of customers who qualify in hopes of attracting younger individuals with early wealth. Banks have also altered investment strategies to improve their competitiveness with other vendors such as mutual funds and investment advisors.

This chapter describes the basic trust services offered through bank trust departments. It shows why trust officers' decisions are kept separate from traditional credit, investment, and operations decisions for a bank's benefit. It examines trust department profitability and the recent trend to extend the market presence of trust operations.

B anks with trust departments are trying to integrate trust services with other retail services to compete with insurance companies, brokerage houses, and investment advisory companies. Management of banks without trust departments must address whether the bank should offer trust services, add financial planning, tax preparation, insurance, and related brokerage services, or enter into a referral relationship with a trust bank. Banks operating trust departments need to examine whether they should integrate trust services with other services and how to design the best delivery system. Many bankers view the trust department as part of a different world. Management often locates trust personnel in a remote part of the bank to differentiate trust services from normal banking business. Trust officers are typically lawyers or investment specialists who have little lending or operations experience. Their language sounds legalistic, and few bankers believe that trust departments add much to bottom-line profits.

The separation results largely from a distinction between trust decisions and traditional banking decisions imposed by regulators. Trust personnel act on behalf of individuals or corporations, so their decisions presumably focus on the client's interests, not the bank's. Because the two might differ in some cases, bank lending and investment activities are kept separate from trust activities. This division, labeled the "Chinese Wall," has made trusts somewhat mysterious.

The Chinese Wall is necessary because of the potential conflict of interest inherent in many trust activities. Banks must manage trust assets for the benefit of the trust beneficiaries and not the bank. The distinction raises many interesting issues. What amount of bank deposits should a trust department have individual trust accounts hold for transactions purposes? The greater the amount, the lower the income earned by the trust and the greater is overall bank profitability. If a bank holding company offers discount brokerage services through a subsidiary, should management use the discount broker for trust stock transactions? There are no specific requirements in these cases other than that, as a fiduciary, the bank warrants that its services are competitive with other sources.

With the changing economic and regulatory environment, however, many banks are integrating trust activities with traditional services. For example, trust services are now part of a broader package of personal banking services directed at affluent customers. The goal is better cross-selling of services and greater fee income.

This chapter describes trust activities offered by banks. The first section introduces terminology and examines a hypothetical trust. The remaining sections describe the types and functions of trusts, management of trust assets, trust department profitability, and potential links between trusts and total personal banking services.

AN OVERVIEW OF TRUSTS AND TRUST TERMINOLOGY

Trust banking includes a wide array of services offered by commercial banks to customers in a fiduciary relationship. A fiduciary is an individual or institution, such as a bank, charged with acting for the benefit of another. The charge frequently takes the form of a trust agreement that stipulates the nature of responsibilities and imposes constraints on the fiduciary's decisions. In most instances, the underlying trust service involves the management of customer assets.

Consider a trust established as part of a married couple's estate planning. Both spouses would like to transfer assets to the other spouse and the couple's two children if they die, yet minimize the estate's tax liability. If they do not create a trust, the distribution of assets will be taxed twice—once when one spouse dies and again when the other spouse dies. Exhibit 27.1 outlines the structure of a trust the couple might establish with a bank as fiduciary to circumvent the double taxation of an estate. The

Exhibit 27.1 Establishing Trusts to Assist in the Settlement of an Estate

Upon Husband's Death—Wife Surviving

Wife's Property

Wife may retain her half-interest in community property and her separate property, if any, or she may place all or any part in her trust below.

Husband's Estate

Executors: Wife and Bank

Half-interest in community property and his separate property, if any.

Wife receives his interest in home, furnishings, auto, jewelry, and all other personal effects.

Wife's Trust

Trustee: Wife and Bank

- Wife will receive all trust income.
- She can withdraw principal for her health, support, maintenance, and gifts to her children. Trustee may use principal for wife's health, support, and maintenance.
- Wife has right to remove bank as co-trustee.
- Wife has general power of appointment (exercisable by will) to pass trust property to whomever she chooses. If she fails to exercise the power, trust property passes to children's trust on her death.

Husband's Trust

Trustee: Wife and Bank

- Wife will be primary beneficiary of trust; children will be secondary beneficiaries.
- Each beneficiary will receive income and principal as trustees deem necessary to provide for his health, support, education, and standard of living.
- Wife has right to remove bank as co-trustee and appoint another corporate fiduciary.

Upon Wife's Subsequent Death

Property in husband's trust will not be taxed in wife's estate, upon her subsequent death.

Children's Trust

- Income and principal in trustee's discretion to or for benefit of children according to respective needs, with particular attention to minors and those in school.
- When youngest child attains age 22, trust will terminate and all trust assets will be delivered to children in equal shares.

[a] Testamentary trusts that would be incorporated in a husband's will.

[b] Distributions to wife will be made at bank at trustee's sole discretion.

analysis traces the control of assets, assuming the husband dies first. Exhibit 27.2 defines important terminology.

The trust agreement creates separate trusts for the husband, wife, and children. Each trust represents a portfolio of assets. At the husband's death, the wife immediately retains one-half of the estate tax free. She can allocate all or part of the assets to a trust (wife's trust), for which she and the bank serve as trustees. The bank is responsible for professionally investing the assets while the wife receives all the income. The wife must be able to determine who gets the assets when she dies to keep the tax exemption.

The other half of the couple's estate, net of estate taxes, is allocated to the husband's trust. The trust agreement provides that the bank should invest the proceeds and distribute trust income to the wife as needed. In most cases, the bank can distribute part of the principal in an emergency. The wife does not have free access to the principal and cannot bequeath the assets to her estate or selected beneficiaries. The assets will ultimately be distributed to a children's trust when the wife dies. This tax-free transfer represents the fundamental attraction of the trust plan. The assets are professionally managed, the wife receives the income during her lifetime, and estate taxes do not apply to the husband's original property when distributed to the children.

While the example describes only one type of trust, it demonstrates the relationship between a fiduciary and the individual who creates the trust (trustor). A bank that serves as a trustee manages assets that the trustor intends to pass on to beneficiaries. The trust agreement may stipulate what investments are acceptable or leave the decision to trust department personnel. Bank trust officers advise the lawyers who draw up the legal documents, provide safekeeping for valuable papers and assets, invest the assets, handle transactions activity, offer accounting services, and maintain records. These duties are similar to services a bank engages in for its direct benefit. With a trust, however, trust officers make decisions for the customer's benefit, aside from the bank's best interest.

Benefits of a Corporate Trustee

Serving as a trustee requires a high degree of integrity. Most individuals, business owners, and managers choose their fiduciaries carefully. Individuals who have accumulated substantial wealth delegate the authority to manage that wealth expecting legal assistance and professional investment expertise. Corporate trustees are ideally situated to handle a wide range of duties. They have legal stature, a permanence extending beyond the lives of specific individuals, and the resources to employ a staff of experts in different fields. Banks have the additional advantage of being able to tie trust services into other banking products. Affluent customers who need trust services can generally use a full range of personal financial planning assistance, including tax planning, investment advice, and retirement counseling. Trust services can be cross-sold as part of a package and priced appropriately.

Most large banks have trust departments with extensive legal and investment expertise. At year-end 1990, for example, Bankers Trust managed well over $100 billion in trust assets with a large staff of portfolio managers and legal experts. Most

Exhibit 27.2 Important Terminology

Agent: An individual who performs duties for another under the authority of the latter. An agent does not have legal title to trust assets.

Executor: The individual or trust institution named in a will and charged with settling the estate of the deceased.

Fiduciary: An individual or institution who acts on behalf of another party for the benefit of that party.

Irrevocable trust: A trust that cannot be canceled by the trustor after it is established.

Letters testamentary: A certificate of authorization provided by a court that provides the legal basis for an executor to settle an estate.

Living (inter vivos) trust: A trust established and effective during the lifetime of the trustor.

Principal: The individual (or institution) who authorizes an agent to perform specific duties on his or her behalf.

Probate: The process of submitting a will before a court to establish the document as the final will and testament of the deceased.

Testamentary trust: A trust established by a will that becomes effective after death.

Trust: A property interest, distinct from ownership, held by one party for the benefit of another.

Trust agreement: The document that provides for the distribution of assets in a trust.

Trustee: The individual or party responsible for administering trust assets as indicated by the trustor. A trustee retains legal title to trust assets.

Trustor: The individual who creates a trust.

---

small banks do not have a large enough customer base to justify hiring trust experts. They can, however, enter into agreements with larger correspondent banks to provide trust services to their local customers. They also can contract with outside vendors, such as mutual funds, to offer their funds to the banks' customers, for which they receive a fee.

TRUST SERVICES

Bank trust departments serve as trustees and agents in their fiduciary relationships. As a trustee, a bank obtains legal title to assets and the responsibility of managing the property. As an agent, legal title to assets remains in the possession of trustors, and the bank manages the assets as directed. Trustors can generally terminate agency relationships but not a trustee's responsibilities.

Trust departments typically segment their activities into personal banking and institutional services. Personal banking services focus on tax, retirement, and estate planning for individuals. Institutional banking services generally concentrate on pension and profit-sharing plans and agency services related to stock distributions or bond issues.

Personal Trust Services

In its fiduciary capacity, a bank trust department provides four basic services to individuals: administering personal trusts, settling estates, acting as guardian or conservator of an estate, and handling personal agency accounts.[1]

---

[1]This section draws on the description of trusts presented in Chapter 18 of Reed, Cotter, Gill, and Smith (1984).

Administering Personal Trusts. A bank trust department generally serves as trustee for a variety of personal trusts established for different reasons. A trust established by a will is a *testamentary trust.* Such trusts, such as those in Exhibit 27.1, go into effect only after one spouse dies. Individuals can also establish *living trusts* that are effective during the lifetime of the creator. Testamentary trusts are generally established by a trustor who wishes to distribute assets to beneficiaries in the form of a trust. If the trust is irrevocable, that is, the trustor cannot cancel it after creation, the distribution of assets is tax sheltered. Living trusts are created to transfer title to assets so that the creator can avoid taxes or the daily investment decisions associated with managing wealth. Living trusts also circumvent probate so that the assets are distributed privately when the trustor dies.

Living trusts offer significant advantages over wills. With a will, an individual's estate must be handled in probate court where the proceedings can be easily delayed, are a matter of public record, and often require huge legal fees.[2] Living trusts circumvent these problems because the court is not involved. The trustee distributes the assets per the trust document, with the entire process handled privately. Settlement is quicker and cheaper. Since the early 1980s living trusts have been one of the fastest-growing financial products nationally.

Both types of trusts are administered by banks according to the terms of a trust agreement. The creator may stipulate strict investment guidelines or give trust officers considerable flexibility in making portfolio decisions. Unlike a bank making investments for its own portfolio, trusts can accumulate common stocks, real property, and other assets generally prohibited to banks. The fundamental trust management objective is to balance the demand for current income with the preservation of principal consistent with the customer's risk preferences.

Settling Estates. Because trust officers have a broad experience base, bank trust departments make excellent executors or administrators of estates. When an individual dies, his or her property must be distributed to beneficiaries. Many people write a will that indicates how the assets are to be distributed and who should supervise the process. The individual or trust institution so designated is an *executor.* If no will exists, the court appoints an *administrator* to settle the estate.

As executor or administrator, a trust department is responsible for collecting and preserving the estate's assets, settling all claims against the estate, including paying off debts and tax liabilities, and distributing the net proceeds to the appropriate beneficiaries. The first step is normally to verify that the executor has legal authority to administer the estate. An executor does this by offering a will for probate in court and securing letters testamentary from the court authorizing it to act. The second step is to take possession of all property, keeping records of all assets and debts. Throughout the entire process, the executor manages the estate by collecting interest and dividends on investments, obtaining real property appraisals, arranging the supervision of busi-

---

[2]Probate fees vary state by state, ranging from under 4 percent of the gross value of an estate in Utah to 11 percent in Alaska. These fees do not include special charges for tax preparation, asset sales, and handling litigation.

ness interests, and collecting insurance payments where applicable. If necessary, an executor can sell certain assets such as a business or real property. Once all assets are assembled and the deceased's specific bequests are identified, the executor advertises for all interested parties to present claims against the estate. After legitimate claims are verified, the executor files the appropriate income and estate tax returns and a statement listing the estate's assets, liabilities, and administration expenses. The final step involves paying all debts and taxes and distributing the assets to beneficiaries.

Depending on the size of the estate and the complexity of the will, the entire process may take as long as 6 years; the normal length is around 2 years. Bank trust departments have settled many estates, so they know the responsibilities and have the appropriate business contacts and access to information to obtain fair assessments within a reasonable time frame. They also offer third-party objectivity, which a member of the deceased's family may not have.

Acting as a Guardian or Conservator. The U.S. legal system occasionally calls upon bank trust departments to serve as court-appointed guardians or conservators. As a guardian, a trust department manages assets for a minor who does not have the legal capacity to control certain assets or make business decisions. As a conservator, a trust department manages assets for an individual who is physically incapacitated or deemed mentally incompetent. The duties are similar to those associated with administering personal trusts, except that the trust department administers the estate under direct court jurisdiction rather than a trust agreement.

Handling Personal Agency Accounts. In a personal agency account, a bank trust department provides the same services as with personal trusts, except that the bank does not obtain title to the assets. A principal, either an individual or institution, enters into a contract with an agent to provide services for the benefit of the principal. The principal continues to own and control the property and can revoke the agreement. The types of services contracted for generally include investment or custodial expertise.

Consider, for example, the president of a major corporation who is too busy to handle his or her personal financial affairs. The president can contract with a bank trust department to manage key assets and pay routine expenses. As a principal, the president authorizes the bank, as an agent, to collect salary, interest, principal, dividend, and rent payments, make debt payments, and pay personal expenses as they arise. The contract may also grant the trust department the authority to buy and sell securities and to make other investment decisions at its discretion. The contract includes prearranged guidelines regarding what investments are acceptable and the specific services to be provided.

If trust officers have discretionary powers, the relationship is called a *managing agency account.* If they do not have discretionary authority, as with an *advisory agency account,* officers simply make recommendations and the principal authorizes each transaction. In both cases, the bank regularly informs the principal of all transactions undertaken by providing a periodic statement of income earned, expenses paid, and outstanding investment and deposit balances. Exhibit 27.3 summarizes the range of

Exhibit 27.3 Service Matrix for Individuals

Nature of Need	Type of Service			
	Estate Settlement	Trusts	Agencies	Guardianship (Conservatorship)
Protection of minor children		Educational trust Testamentary trust		Yes—when no other arrangements have been made.
Protection from financial incapacity		Living trust Standby trust	Power of attorney	Yes—when no other arrangements have been made.
Family protection from untimely death	A will at least avoids intestate succession.	Testamentary trust Living trust Standby trust		
Investment management		Living trust	Management agency	
Tax minimization		Charitable trusts Living trust Standby trust Testamentary trust Other specialized trusts	Management agency for tax-exempt securities.	
Controlled distribution of wealth at death	A will is always an essential ingredient to control property distribution.	Living trust Standby trust		
Charitable giving		Charitable trusts Testamentary trusts		
Recordkeeping and asset control			Safekeeping accounts Custodial accounts Escrow accounts	

Source: John Clarke, Jack Zalaha and August Zinsser. *The Trust Business.* 1988.

services offered to individuals in light of their family situations and needs. Note the variety of uses of trusts.

Institutional Trust Services

The passage of the Employee Retirement Income Security Act (ERISA) spurred the growth in trust services to corporations. The primary objective of ERISA was to protect the pension and profit-sharing benefits that qualifying employees were promised as part of employment contracts. There are many examples of firms that invest pension assets inappropriately, such as by making loans to owners of the company at below-market rates, or go bankrupt and leave the pension plan broke. Under ERISA corporations are held to a high level of accountability. Many consequently use trust departments to manage employee benefits programs.

Bank trust departments provide trust services for private corporations and nonprofit institutions that fall into three general categories: employee benefits, charitable and institutional services, and stock or bond services. In some situations, the bank serves as a trustee, while in others it acts only as an agent.

Employee Benefits. Competition in trust services is greatest for the management of institutional employee benefit plans. Benefit plans take the form of pension plans, profit-sharing plans, stock bonuses, and stock options. Employers establish employee benefit programs to provide retirement benefits and/or forced savings for loyal employees. The plans are funded by employer and employee contributions and represent a means of rewarding long-term service and loyalty to the institution. In general, employees do not pay taxes on their share of plan assets until they withdraw funds.

A trust department's specific responsibilities vary with the needs of the institution and terms of the trust agreement. A trust department may 1) have sole investment authority over plan assets or share the duties with other investment managers, 2) simply provide investment advice to plan supervisors, who make the actual decisions, or 3) serve as an agent that receives investment decisions and executes transactions. In virtually all cases, a bank trust department handles the accounting regarding how funds are invested and what each employee's claim on assets is. It also prepares periodic statements and distributes plan benefits to employees upon retirement or disability, as stipulated by the trust agreement.

Benefit plans take the form of pension plans, profit-sharing plans, stock bonuses, and stock options and thus represent trust accounts for employees' retirement benefits and supplementary compensation. An employer that establishes an employee benefit trust is referred to as a sponsor, and the sponsor contributes funds to the plan on a regular basis. Depending on the nature of their employment contract, employees may also contribute. Employees are referred to as plan participants. Trust officers invest the proceeds for the employees' benefit, but the employees do not pay taxes on contributions or earnings with qualifying plans until they withdraw their share of the funds, typically at retirement.

Pension Plans. Employers contribute to pension plans to fund retirement benefits. The amount of contributions necessary is based on the ages of employees and their life expectancies. Under a defined-contribution plan, an employer makes a fixed payment each period for each employee. Under a defined-benefit plan, the amount of each participants' retirement benefit is predetermined, and an employer makes whatever contribution is necessary to meet the fixed benefit.

Profit-Sharing Plans. Employers often establish trusts in order to share periodic profits with employees. Each year the employer contributes a predetermined portion of its profits to the trust to be distributed along with accumulated earnings to employees.

401(k) Plans. Some employers establish 401(k) plans in which employees contribute to separate individual retirement accounts, but the contributions are made from before-tax income. Payments are typically made in the form of salary reductions that may be matched by the employer. They are structured like pension plans or profit-sharing plans in the scheduled distributions and there are maximums that individuals can allocate each year. Withdrawal must be after age 59½ to avoid tax penalties.

Employee Stock Ownership Plans (ESOPs). An employer that establishes an ESOP allows employees to purchase the firm's common stock with contributions from the employer. An employer can contribute cash for the purchase of stock in the open market or directly contribute stock. Alternatively, an employer can borrow and use the proceeds to buy stock. ESOPs benefit employees because the participants have a claim on the contributed stock and any dividends received over time. Many firms have used ESOPs to make it more difficult for competitors to acquire them in a hostile takeover. ESOP plans have the disadvantage that they concentrate trust assets in one security and thus are not diversified. If the employer goes bankrupt, ESOP stock is worth little.

Keogh Plans. Self-employed individuals, such as doctors, lawyers, and qualifying small business owners, can establish Keogh plans that are the functional equivalent of pension plans. The employer, or individual, regularly contributes to the Keogh to fund retirement benefits for the owner and/or employees.

Banks find employee benefit plans attractive because they can earn fees based on the amount of assets managed if they serve as investment managers. When they act in an advisory or agency capacity without discretionary authority to invest funds, flat-rate fees often apply. Employers often separate the responsibility of the trustee to the plan from the duties of the investment manager, with a bank holding one role but not the other. In recent years, many employers with heavily funded pension plans have invited bids from interested investment managers, interviewed finalists regarding their investment strategies and past performance, then apportioned a share of plan assets to different groups. In 1986 the state of California used this process to select seven final managers for $3 billion in Public Employees' Retirement System assets.[3] To win such competitive bids, bank trust departments must show that past investment performance is at least comparable to that of insurance companies, mutual funds, and private investment advisory firms.

Charitable and Institutional Services. Bank trust departments handle trust accounts for a variety of nonprofit organizations. Charities, universities, and some hospitals and charitable foundations, for example, receive contributions for their use, but do not operate to earn a profit. Trust departments act as trustees through which these institutions collect, hold, and manage assets, collect interest and dividends, and make

---

[3]The California Public Employees' Retirement System selected the seven investment managers from 87 applicants. To be eligible, a manager had to already have $1 billion under management. Each applicant submitted a model portfolio and management proposal designed for the state employees' fund. After screening the 87 applicants to 14 finalists, the fund's directors selected the seven winners by interviewing each portfolio manager and evaluating the firm's recommended investment strategy and past performance.

payments as necessary. In addition, the trust departments are often required to prepare a formal accounting of the transactions.

Stock and Bond Services. Bank trust departments play an important role in the placement and transfer of corporate securities. Corporate bonds, for example, are typically issued under the terms of an indenture agreement, which protects bondholders from default by the issuer and mandates certain performance criteria that are comparable to loan covenants. The issuing corporation names a bank as a trustee, which legally owns all collateral backing the bonds and monitors the issuer to verify that it lives up to all terms of the indenture. Rather than pursue claims separately, bondholders look to the trustee to protect their interests.

Trust departments also serve as a registrar, transfer agent, and dividend agent for bond and stock issues. A registrar is responsible for registering who owns debt securities and certifying that the securities represent authentic obligations of the issuing firm. The registrar also processes interest payments by distributing interest checks for registered bonds and making coupon payments to holders of bearer bonds. A transfer agent records changes in stock ownership and processes the transfer of stock between investors. A bank may also be responsible for collecting stock dividends from a corporation and disbursing them to stockholders, for which it serves as a dividend agent. In each of these roles, a trust department performs an agency function and thus serves under contract with the issuing corporation.

TRUST DEPARTMENT OBJECTIVES AND PERFORMANCE

In their fiduciary capacity, trust departments must meet high standards of performance. They act on behalf of trustors or principals in agency agreements and are expected to adhere to the terms of all agreements. When settling an estate, for example, it is inappropriate to ignore the wishes of the will's creator and impose alternative provisions. In addition, a trust department must demonstrate prudence in managing the assets of its customers. Prudence involves operating within the law and exercising good judgment when buying or selling assets. Virtually all states have instituted a "prudent man rule" that limits investments to assets that will generate a reasonable rate of return while preserving principal. It is inappropriate to speculate with trust assets, thereby placing the principal at extraordinary risk, or to take no risk by exclusively holding cash assets or default-risk-free securities. Most trust managers interpret prudence to mean that they should broadly diversify a trust's investments.

Over time, however, the prudent man rule has been interpreted in contradictory ways by the courts. At various times, court rulings have stipulated that a prudent man would not buy real estate, not invest in partnerships, not sell assets unless there were some overriding reason, and alternatively sell assets immediately when potential problems arose. In 1987, the Alabama Supreme Court ruled that a bank's trust managers were liable because they did not adequately diversify a client's trust assets. The individual who formed the trust had stipulated that 70 to 75 percent of the assets were to be invested in the stock of the bank where he had served as chairman. After his death, his heirs argued that the trust would have increased more in value if managers had diversified with a wide range of stocks and bonds. Overall the trust grew 12 percent annually, but it failed a court-imposed prudence guideline even though the investment conformed to the trust grantor's wishes. The point is that the concept of prudence has varied over time and between court jurisdictions. It may even violate the terms of a trust as drawn up by whoever establishes the trust.

ERISA formally states that for employee benefit plans the prudent man rule recognizes that an asset's risk does not, in itself, render its purchase prudent or imprudent. Individual assets must be viewed within the context of a total portfolio. Thus the volatility of returns for a portfolio is more important than the volatility of returns for any single asset. This is consistent with finance theory. Prudence should be determined by the degree of diversification and liquidity in a portfolio relative to the expected return.

To implement decisions prudently, large bank trust departments employ officers with diverse backgrounds ranging from portfolio managers specializing in bonds or equities to real estate experts and legal counsel. Legal counsel verifies that trust decisions conform to prudent man rules and thus meet the bank's fiduciary responsibility. Portfolio specialists select specific securities for inclusion in trust accounts. Real estate and other analysts provide specialized valuation and investment expertise in their fields.

Investment Performance

Trust departments can invest in all types of assets, as determined by trust agreements. Trust investments generally include interest-bearing bank deposits, U.S. Treasury and agency securities, municipal and corporate bonds, mortgage-backed securities, preferred and common stock, and real estate. Under the prudent man requirement, portfolio managers attempt to diversify discretionary trust assets by investing in securities with different risk and return features. While this can readily be accomplished with trusts containing significant assets, it is difficult to diversify small trust portfolios.

Banks circumvent this problem in a variety of ways. First, they may diversify through the use of common trust funds. Second, they may offer mutual funds through a separate bank subsidiary and allocate trust assets to these mutual funds. Third, they may offer mutual funds managed by outside vendors and thus buy mutual fund shares with trust assets.

Common Trust Funds. A common trust fund is maintained for the collective investment of trust assets and operates like a mutual fund. Rather than buy specific assets for each trust, a bank pools the funds of small trusts and buys securities that are consistent with the trusts' objectives. Each trust owns a portion of the common fund that reflects its proportionate contribution to fund value. As the fund value increases due to price appreciation in the underlying securities or interest and dividend receipts, the net value of each trust's units (or the number of units obtained) increases. When a trust is terminated, the estate receives the prevailing net asset value for each unit.

Common trust funds thus extend diversification and liquidity benefits to smaller trusts. By pooling investments, a bank can acquire more distinct securities with different return and risk characteristics. Each common trust fund unit represents a claim on the total portfolio, not a specific security. When a trust redeems units, the fund can meet its obligations out of new contributions, maturing securities, or the sale of part of its portfolio. A trust manager has greater flexibility in making portfolio decisions yet can still meet each trust's objectives.

Common trust funds have been so popular that large trust departments offer specialized funds that purchase only certain types of securities. J.P. Morgan's trust department, for example, offers over 35 different types of common funds that operate similarly to a family of mutual funds. Distinct funds invest only in high-dividend stocks, foreign stocks, taxable fixed-income securities, municipal bonds, stock index funds, and short-term money market instruments and can be used to meet different trust objectives.

Mutual Funds Via Outside Vendors. The Glass-Steagall Act prevents banks from directly offering mutual funds to customers. This means that while banks can manage funds through subsidiaries, they cannot distribute the fund shares. As an alternative, banks can contract with an outside vendor, such as a mutual fund, to distribute and manage the funds under the bank's name. Small banks are particularly attracted to this strategy because they do not have the outside vendor's expertise in asset management, yet they profit from the business. They can direct their efforts at marketing trust services rather than providing the investment expertise. A 1989 survey by BEI Golembe found that two-thirds of surveyed banks under $2.5 billion in assets offered mutual funds through their own trust departments, while 57 percent used some outside vendors. As might be expected, 83 percent of larger banks offered their own mutual funds, while just 42 percent used other vendors.[4]

Comparative Performance of Bank Trusts. As indicated earlier, investment management of pension and trust funds is an extremely competitive business. At one time, bank trust departments managed the bulk of pension assets. After the early 1970s, however, banks lost an estimated 15 percent of their total market share to private investment companies. Other fund managers criticized banks for their lack of innovative strategies and an inability to retain top-quality portfolio managers. Too often investment decisions could be made only by committee. Banks also refused to compensate funds managers like their investment company counterparts. As a consequence, other portfolio managers outperformed bank trust department portfolio managers during the latter half of the 1970s.

This poor performance and general lack of competitiveness with other money managers created the perception that bank trust departments were poor investment managers. However, studies show that bank investment managers have performed on par with other portfolio managers during the 1980s. The top part of Exhibit 27.4

---

[4]Some banks allow the choice of bank-managed funds or those managed by other institutions. Leander (1989) provides details of the survey.

Exhibit 27.4 Comparative Performance of Funds Managed by Selected Institutions

A. Equities: 1979–1988

Annualized Rates of Return

	1986–1988	1984–1988	1979–1988
Banks	12.6%	14.5%	15.9%
Insurance companies	13.2	14.5	16.1
Investment counselors	12.3	13.6	16.5
Mutual funds	11.0	12.0	15.1
Standard & Poor's 500	13.3	15.2	16.3

Universe

315	Bank collective funds
90	Insurance company separate and variable accounts
484	Mutual funds
456	Investment counselors

B. Equities

	1987–1989
Banks	16.1%
Insurance companies	15.9
Investment counselors	16.0
Mutual funds	13.8

C. Fixed Income

Banks	7.7%
Insurance companies	8.2
Investment counselors	7.0
Mutual funds	5.9

Source: CDA Investment Technologies.

compares annualized rates of return on equity funds managed by a sample of banks, insurance companies, mutual funds, and investment companies. Median returns indicate that banks and insurance companies outperformed others from 1984 to 1988, while investment advisors ranked first over the 10 years from 1979 to 1988. The bottom part of the exhibit examines equity and fixed-income security performance from 1987 to 1989. As noted, banks reported the highest average return on equities and ranked behind insurance companies in their bond returns. The net result is that banks are competitive with other institutions. Banks with large trust operations have generally improved performance by retaining their best managers via incentive compensation programs. They recognize that they no longer hold a monopoly on managing pension assets and must operate like investment companies to compete for the best money managers and trust business.

TRUST DEPARTMENT PROFITABILITY

Bank managers are looking increasingly to trust departments for additional noninterest income. Trust departments and related personal or private banking activities cater to affluent customers who are willing to pay for quality service. However, competition is driving trust fees lower and making it more difficult to generate profits. Unfortunately, many bank presidents do not believe that they can accurately measure trust department expenses and revenues to establish a pricing schedule that covers costs and generates a reasonable return to bank shareholders.

Trust Expenses

Trust department expenses can be categorized as direct expenses and indirect overhead expenses. One practical difficulty in measuring overall profitability is the fact that overhead allocations are extremely subjective. Exhibit 27.5 summarizes expense and revenue components of trust profitability in 1989 for different-sized banks. The expense and aggregate revenue figures are measured as a percentage of total trust expenses in the middle of the exhibit. Direct expenses include salaries and fringe benefits paid to trust employees and data processing services if purchased from an outside supplier. Other operating expenses includes legal fees and payments for investment research so that a large portion constitutes a direct expense. Indirect overhead costs include occupancy, fixed assets, and advertising. If the trust department shares bank computer facilities with lending and operations, data services represent an indirect allocation of overhead. Measurement problems are especially acute at smaller banks, where loan and operations officers also administer trust activities. Exhibit 27.5 indicates that direct expenses compose a minimum of two-thirds of all expenses, while overhead allocations contribute as much as one-third.

Trust Revenues

Trust department revenues can also be classified as direct or indirect receipts. Only fees and commissions are directly quantifiable.[5] Trust departments charge for their services by imposing fixed dollar charges, flat-rate percentage fees, or variable-rate fees and commissions based on trust income or a trust's aggregate asset value. In many states, maximum fees on personal trusts are set by statute. Other fees are completely negotiable. When a large portion of trust fees is based on the value of trust assets, including equities, trust revenues and overall profitability vary directly with market fluctuations in common stock prices.

Exhibit 27.5 shows that banks over $50 million in deposits generate just under 50 percent of their direct revenues from managing personal trusts. Smaller banks generate a higher fraction of revenues from personal trusts. Estate settlements, employee benefit plans, and personal agencies contribute the remainder.[6] The major problem, however,

---

[5]Miscellaneous income, consisting of specific charges for transactions-related services, is negligible.

[6]More detailed bank comparisons suggest that fees from employee benefit plans increase with bank size, such that money center banks with the largest trust departments obtain approximately 20 percent of their trust revenues from these plans.

Exhibit 27.5 Trust Department Revenues and Expenses, 1989[a]

	Commercial Bank Deposit Size		
	≤ $50 Million	$50–$200 Million	> $200 Million
Composition of Commissions and Fees			
Estates	12.3%	11.3%	10.8%
Personal trust	74.0	48.5	47.3
Employee benefits	2.0	14.4	18.0
Personal agencies	4.3	14.0	13.8
Corporate trusts	2.6	3.8	2.9
Corporate agencies	—	1.7	1.2
Other trusts[b]	4.8	6.4	6.0
Total	100.0%	100.0%	100.0%
Income and Expense Components			
Commissions and fees	37.4%	92.5%	108.2%
Other income	0.5	0.4	0.7
Total income	37.9%	92.9%	108.9%
Officer salaries	41.7%	34.1%	34.1%
Employee salaries	8.7	15.6	15.1
Fringe benefits	13.3	11.6	12.8
Total salaries and fringe benefits	63.7%	61.3%	62.0%
Data services	3.3%	6.7%	5.3%
Furniture and equipment	5.1	4.0	3.4
Occupancy	6.5	7.7	7.1
Publicity and advertising	2.1	2.1	1.8
Other operating	19.3	18.2	20.4
Subtotal	36.3%	38.7%	38.0%
Total Expense	100.0%	100.0%	100.0%
Net profit without balance credit (Income – Expense)	−62.1%	−7.1%	8.9%
Theoretical earnings on deposit balances	13.5	19.0	18.7
Net profit with balance credit	−48.6%	11.9%	26.6%
Total average trust assets	$4,988,000	$94,070,000	$303,133,000
No. of Banks	15	82	31

[a]Figures expressed as a percentage of total for each category.

[b]Data for banks unable to separate income by source.

Source: *Functional Cost Analysis*, Federal Reserve System, 1989.

is that direct revenues, on average, do not cover total expenses. The shortfall is greatest for banks with less than $50 million in deposits, where direct revenues averaged just under 40 percent of expenses in 1989. Thus the net loss before other income equals over 62 percent of expenses. Profitability improves at larger institutions. Fees and commissions at banks with deposits between $50 and $200 million averaged almost 93 percent of expenses, producing a loss of just 7 percent of expenses. Only banks with more than $200 million in deposits were able to generate more direct revenues than expenses.

This analysis suggests two significant conclusions. First, small banks must rely on indirect revenues to cover trust expenses and earn a profit. Second, trust departments at large banks are better able to generate fee income than those at small banks. This is consistent with the generally accepted fact that trust departments must achieve a relatively large size before they are profitable on their own. Many expenses are fixed, including overhead, and investment expertise is often expensive. To minimize unit costs, trust departments must generate a large volume of trust business.

In addition to fees and commissions, trust activities generate deposits that can be invested in interest-bearing securities. Deposits arise from normal transactions associated with managing trust and agency accounts. At any time, some accounts have received cash inflows from asset sales, maturing securities, employer contributions for a pension plan, and other transactions. Until the trust department invests the deposits or distributes them to beneficiaries, they sit idly in demand accounts at the bank. Obviously the prudent man rule does not permit a bank to keep these funds idle for long. Even though nonearning deposit balances in any single trust or agency account appear only temporarily, the cumulative total from all accounts can be quite large.

The figures in Exhibit 27.5 show that the average trust department at banks under $200 million is unprofitable if no earnings credit is allocated to trust-generated deposit balances. After applying an earnings credit, the smallest banks still showed losses equal to almost 49 percent of expenses. The two largest groups of banks, in contrast, showed profits of 11.9 percent and 26.6 percent of total expenses, respectively.[7]

Trust profits can be substantial at many banks even though the average performer is moderately profitable or suffers losses. Cates Consulting Analysts Inc. conducts an annual survey of trust department profitability that is far more comprehensive than the *Functional Cost Analysis* data. Recent surveys indicate that trust activities add 5 to 10 basis points to the average bank's return on assets and 8 to 12 basis points to return on equity for banks with more than $15 million in annual trust revenues. Again, trust profitability appears to vary directly with the volume of assets managed.

INTEGRATING TRUST AND PERSONAL BANKING SERVICES

Events of the last decade have brought about dramatic changes in the structure of commercial banking. Congress and regulators removed interest rate ceilings on deposits and expanded the list of products that banks can offer. Most states allow some form of interstate banking, and limited-service banks offer banking products throughout the nation. Banks with trust departments have used their expertise to counteract the increased competition for retail customers and the overall decline in loan profitability by integrating trust services with traditional banking services. The package is then marketed under personal banking services labels.

---

[7]Many bankers and analysts feel that it is inappropriate to give any earnings credit against balances generated by trust departments. As a fiduciary, trust departments should minimize nonearning assets in all accounts. Giving credit for balances may create an incentive to let deposits sit idle.

Integrating trust services with other bank services is a response to four related factors. First, with deregulation, banks recognize that they need to obtain more noninterest revenue, which is what trust departments have generated for years. For most banks, retail customers represent the greatest potential source of fee income. This leads to the second factor, the focus on relationship banking. Traditionally, banks focused on specific transactions and whether they were earning a profitable spread on each item across all purchasers. Relationship banking, in contrast, views a customer's entire relationship with a bank as a product. Banks thus concentrate on packaging services that a customer will need over different stages of his or her personal life cycle. While trust departments have generally supplied estate planning services, they can use the same expertise to provide personal financial planning, discount brokerage, and many other related services. Third, offering a package of financial services is the best way banks can compete with nonbank banks for retail business. Once bank customers begin to accumulate wealth, they change focus to tax, retirement, and estate planning. If banks cannot provide these services, customers will move their business to brokerage houses, insurance companies, or investment advisors. Finally, high-volume trust departments exhibit the highest profitability, on average. Integrating trust services allows a bank to cross-sell services and to take better advantage of economies of scale.

Personal Banking Services

Organized efforts to package personal financial services have inspired banks to establish personal, or private, banking departments. As the name suggests, personal banking refers to the development of products and services that are targeted to individuals at all stages of the personal banking relationship. One author describes personal banking as:

> targeting specialized banking products and services to the groups of people who provide high-value relationships. A high-value relationship is one that is measurably more profitable than average, either directly (high-balances, fees and/or loans) or by extension (officer of commercial banking client, source of referrals, etc.).[8]

The success of a personal banking strategy depends on management's ability to segment groups of individuals who are at different stages in the financial life cycle. Once these groups are identified, the bank should design specific products and services to meet their special needs. Trust department services are integrated with transactions services, savings instruments, investment alternatives, and overall financial planning.

Some banks direct their private banking activity strictly at high-net-worth or high-income customers. To be eligible, individuals must have an annual income in six figures and a net worth of at least $1 million exclusive of their primary home. Typically they have $500,000 or more in investible assets and have large transactions account balances or CDs with the bank. Obviously, these criteria prevent many individuals from qualifying and free up private bankers to deal closely with a small number of customers on a personal basis.

---

[8]See Hile (1986).

Other banks target personal banking services at a broader spectrum of customers. There are two general types of individuals at different stages in their financial life cycle.[9] Wealth creators are individuals in the early stages of financial development who are accumulating a stock of assets to increase future purchasing power. They have a high degree of risk tolerance and are generally transactions oriented. Wealth preservers, as the name suggests, are in the later stage of their financial development and thus focus on preserving what they have accumulated to assure financial stability. They are less willing to take risks and more concerned about current income. While these broad distinctions do not apply to all individuals, they do demonstrate the application of targeting specific banking products to interested individuals.

Exhibit 27.6 associates bank products and services with each class of individuals. Because wealth creators are most interested in credit availability and transactions convenience, banks have designed credit terms and delivery services to meet these needs. Each customer deals with a personal banker who handles all facets of the credit and deposit relationship. Credit terms are structured to give the customer discretion regarding when to borrow. Credit lines are popular, especially home equity lines and credit cards, as well as separate loans for specific transactions. As the customer begins to accumulate wealth, the personal banker encourages the use of discount brokerage and general financial planning services, along with insurance and pension products. It is important that banks offer brokerage services to these clients or they will lose them to nonbank banks when potential fee income is greatest.

Trust services apply directly to wealth preservers, who are more interested in financial security and eventually distributing their estate to beneficiaries. Qualifying individuals often maintain substantial balances at the bank and want to maximize current investment income. These customers are especially concerned about discussing their wealth with others and want to deal with someone whom they perceive to be experienced and discreet. Banking products focus on savings vehicles, convenience credit, and trust services.

The primary roadblock to successful personal banking is finding qualified personnel. Few bankers have the experience to understand and meet a customer's credit and investment needs. If banks are to be competitive with insurance companies and brokerage houses, they need to hire, train, and retain specialists in both areas. Customers dislike banker turnover because each time they have to educate the new account officer regarding their situation. A staff of stable, experienced personal bankers is a major strength. Banks must also concentrate more on marketing and cross-selling services. Management should educate credit and operations employees about services offered by the personal banking group so they can refer potential customers to the personal bankers.

Referral Services

Unfortunately, many small banks do not face the demand or have the in-house expertise to offer trust services profitably. Customers who desire these services look to other

---

[9]The following discussion is based on Hile (1986).

Exhibit 27.6 Specialized Products and Services for Personal Banking Market Segments

Wealth Creators	Wealth Preservers
Products:	***Products:***
Personal lines of credit	Certificates of deposit
Convenience credit	Municipal bonds
Transaction loans	Money market accounts
Mortgage and installment loans	Convenience credit
Transaction and money market accounts	Trust services: estate planning, custodial accounts, investment management, living trusts
Pension accounts	Pension accounts
Services:	***Services:***
Personal banker	Personal banker
Personal teller	Personal teller
Discount brokerage	Personal financial planning (broad)
Personal financial planning (limited)	

Source: Douglas Hile, "Marketing Focus in Personal Banking: Wealth Creators vs. Wealth Preservers," *The Magazine of Bank Administration*, January 1986.

banks or investment advisors and may move their entire banking business. To overcome this problem, a growing number of banks have entered into formal service contracts with larger institutions located outside their basic trade area to provide trust services to local customers. Typically, the community bank enrolls a customer as a client, but the large bank acts as a trustee or agent. The large bank's trust officers periodically schedule visits to the community bank to meet with customers.

The small bank's objective is to provide trust services to its customers and to eliminate any incentive to move their business. Both banks share in the fees, with the trust bank retaining the bigger share. The service is profitable for the small bank because its costs are negligible. Large banks benefit because they can increase their volume of trust services and thus distribute their fixed costs across a broader base.

The future of trust banking likely entails greater integration of trust services with traditional banking services, restructuring the delivery of retail products along personal banking lines, increased use of referral agreements between small and large banks, and greater profitability from increased fee income. Trust bankers will attempt to identify and serve potential customers long before their primary interest is estate planning.

SUMMARY

Bank trust departments act as fiduciaries for customers, providing services that differ widely from banking's traditional loan and deposit business. They serve as executors of wills, trustees and agents in managing customer assets, investment advisors, and administrators in corporate employee benefit plans and bond or stock issues. With each type of activity, trust officers must demonstrate a high degree of integrity. They must also be discreet and put the customer's interests ahead of the bank's.

Trust departments generally charge fees or commissions tied to the income from a trust or the value of trust assets. *Functional Cost Analysis* data suggest that trust fees and commissions do not even cover trust expenses for the average bank. Trust departments are profitable as a separate profit center only if they generate sufficient deposit balances that can be invested in earning assets. In 1989 the average bank with under $50 million in deposits that operated a trust department lost money, even after accounting for investment income from balances. Larger banks earned relatively large profits on their trust operations.

Many banks are using their trust personnel to lead the move toward relationship banking. They now integrate trust services with traditional loan, investment, and transaction services as part of personal banking systems that concentrate on a customer's total account relationship over his or her financial life cycle. This leads to better cross-selling of services and helps retain individuals as customers rather than lose them to competitors.

Questions

Overview

1. What is a fiduciary?

2. What is one motivation for a wealthy individual to set up a trust? Why use a bank?

3. Assume that the trust department of Sunrise Bank has acquired common stock in American Bank for its trust accounts. Sunrise Bank's holding company has submitted a bid to buy American Bank in a hostile takeover attempt. Under what conditions should the trust management vote the trusts' shares in support of the merger? Under what conditions should it vote against the merger?

Trust Services

4. What is the difference between a bank trust department and an agent serving as trustee in managing a customer's assets?

5. What are the advantages of a living trust over a testamentary trust?

6. Normally how long does it take to settle an estate? Describe the 4-step settlement process.

7. What is the difference between a bank acting as 1) a guardian, 2) a conservator, and 3) a trustee.

8. What are the two key differences between a personal trust and a personal agency account?

9. Why do firms use bank trust departments to manage employee benefits? What three kinds of benefits do they manage?

10. What institutions compete with banks in offering these services?

11. Do banks possess any inherent advantages or disadvantages when competing with other money managers for the opportunity to serve as investment manager of employee benefit plans? Explain.

12. Banks serve the stock and bond markets by serving as trustees to an indenture, registrar, transfer agent, and dividend agent. What are these duties?

Trust Objectives

13. Assume that a bank trust department is named as guardian in managing the substantial assets of a 14-year-old boy whose parents died unexpectedly. What types of investments might be reasonable according to the prudent man rule?

14. Explain how common trust funds serve the same purpose as mutual funds. Explain how it is possible for a trust to invest in common trust units and still meet the prudent man requirement.

15. The Federal Reserve's *Functional Cost Analysis* data suggest that trust profitability is highly dependent on the generation of deposit balances. Why might it be inappropriate to include investment income from balances when measuring trust profits?

16. Explain why size is an important determinant of trust department profitability. Do trust departments provide nonquantifiable benefits to a bank indirectly?

Trusts and Personal Banking

17. Describe the factors that have encouraged banks to integrate trust and traditional services under personal banking departments.

18. What is the advantage of segmenting retail customers into wealth creators and wealth preservers? Who are banks' major competitors in providing services directed at wealth preservers?

19. What are the risks a small bank faces if it enters into a referral service contract with a large bank's trust department? What are the benefits?

Activity

Talk to a trust department representative at your bank and discover what criteria you would have to meet to open a trust account. If they don't offer trusts, approach a bank that does. Identify 5 situations in which establishing a trust is beneficial to an individual or corporation. What would be the fee for managing a living trust?

References

Abney, David, and Mark Nadeau. "National Banks, the Impassable 'Chinese Wall,'" and "Breach of Trust: Shaping a Solution." *The Banking Law Journal* (May–June 1990).

Anthony, Warner, et al. *Bankers' Guide to Establishing, Managing, and Operating Common Trust Funds.* Washington, D.C.: American Bankers Association, 1986.

Bisky, Tom. "Sales Gurus Lead Cultural Revolution in Trust." *ABA Banking Journal* (November 1986).

Cacace, Michael. "Citicorp Tops Morgan in Managed Trust Assets." *American Banker* (June 30, 1986).

Cartnell, Michael. "Trust Services for the Private Bank." *Bank Management* (November 1990).

Chapman, Daniel. "Private Banking Broadens Relationships with Affluent Customers." *Bank Marketing* (November 1986).

Clark, Danial. "Banks as Investment Advisors: How Good Are They?" *ABA Banking Journal* (January 1986).

Clarke, John, Jack Zalaha, and August Zinsser. *The Trust Business* Washington, D.C.: American Bankers Association, 1988.

DeCotiis, Allen, and John DeMarco. "Does Financial Counseling Suit Your Bank?" *ABA Banking Journal* (April 1984).

Galt, Martin. "Retail and Trust Can Work Together." *ABA Banking Journal* (February 1991).

Gjoraag, G.R. "How to Play Matchmaker for Trust and Retail." *ABA Banking Journal* (April 1984).

Grody, Allan. "Should Trust Departments Offer Discount Brokerage Services?" *Trusts & Estates* (May 1986).

Hile, Douglas. "Marketing Focus in Personal Banking: Wealth Creators vs. Wealth Preservers." *The Magazine of Bank Administration* (January 1986).

Jessup, Paul. *Modern Bank Management.* St. Paul, Minn.: West Publishing Co., 1980.

Layne, Richard. "Trust Areas Gained Some Glitter in '89." *American Banker* (July 19,1990).

Leander, Tom. "Outside Vendors Are Changing the Playing Field in Trust Banking." *American Banker* (July 12, 1989).

Reed, Edward, Richard Cotter, Edward Gill, and Richard Smith. *Commercial Banking.* Englewood Cliffs, N.J.: Prentice-Hall, 1984.

Chapter 28

Bank Mergers and Acquisitions

The most fundamental issue faced by a bank's Board of Directors and senior managers is how to maximize shareholder value. One important facet of the associated strategic plan is whether the bank should buy other banks, remain independent, or position itself for sale. Each alternative has dramatically different implications regarding future growth in earnings, the security of employees' jobs, and the nature of services provided the bank's customers.

During the 1970s and early 1980s, many individuals chartered banks or purchased groups of community banks in anticipation of selling the package to a large multibank holding company. Because of restrictions against interstate banking and branching, it was a seller's market and those willing to part with the franchise could often extract large premiums. The latter part of the 1980s brought about a reevaluation of acquisition strategies. With the increased number of bank and thrift failures, acquirers had several options to enter new markets. They could buy a failed institution outright or simply purchase its deposits, purchase a healthy firm, or enter via a new charter. More restrictive regulatory capital requirements in turn raised the cost of doing business. Many banks with problem assets and especially smaller banks with limited access to new capital discovered that becoming part of a financial conglomerate offered an attractive alternative to remaining independent. In many cases, it was their only alternative. By 1991 it was a buyer's market in which banks with adequate capital could dictate terms. Premiums subsequently declined as acquirers cherry-picked the best deals.

This chapter examines the merger and acquisition phenomenon in recent years. It focuses on three key issues. Why are mergers increasingly common and how do mergers add value? How do you value a bank for acquisition or sale? What nonmonetary considerations affect the valuation and post-merger success of the new firm?

RECENT TRENDS IN MERGERS AND ACQUISITIONS

Bankers are generally sensitive to the issue of size. Community bank employees typically take pride in annual asset growth and working for the biggest bank in town. Size connotes market power and influence. Why else do bankers continually build larger and taller buildings than competitors? Regional banks similarly put a premium on being the biggest bank in a state or region, and ultimately reaching the top 100 or 50 banks in the country. In the old days, banks would try to bulk up their balance sheets just prior to the end of each quarter when they filed financial reports so that assets would be as large as possible. Money center banks in turn compare their size and growth to other money center banks and multinational banks throughout the world.

Why is size so important? Historically, managers of the largest banks in a market had considerable influence and received extraordinary attention. They were compensated well, to some degree based on the size of the empire they controlled rather than bank profitability. They served on community, state, and national boards that set policy and lobbied legislators. Many believed that economies of scale or scope existed such that increased size lowered unit operating costs. The evidence, however, suggests that average unit costs are flat across different sized banks.[1] Size essentially represented prestige and financial power.

In recent years, bankers have paid less attention to size. This is due largely to poor operating performance and the need to improve their firms' financial strength. Thus many money center banks as well as smaller banks have consciously downsized. Risk-based capital requirements obviously contributed to this reassessment because capital is expensive and difficult to obtain. The larger a bank, the greater the pressure to generate earnings and/or issue common or preferred stock.

Bank mergers and acquisitions have followed this change in philosophy. Formally, a merger is a combination of two or more separate enterprises typically involving the issuance of new securities. An acquisition occurs when one firm purchases the stock of another firm. There is a clear buyer and seller in terms of the transaction terms and the structure of the surviving entity. Prior to the early 1980s, geographic restrictions largely limited where and how banks could compete. Interstate branching was prohibited. Many states further restricted in-state branching, either limiting it to local counties or cities, or prohibiting it altogether. Mergers and acquisitions were a natural response to penetrate new markets, particularly in states with no branching. Without branching, the only way that banks could expand was via multibank holding companies which were formed to acquire banks in different markets. During this period, the demand for acquisitions raised serious concerns that the seller's market would be controlled by monopolistic competitors. Regulators evaluated all transactions closely to ensure that the acquiring firm did not gain too large a market share. (See Contemporary Issues: Merger Antitrust Analysis.) That problem has virtually disappeared in today's environment, where the key question is whether a buyer can be found.

---

[1]There is little evidence that scale economies exist beyond very small banks. Humphrey (1990) documents the results of recent studies and concludes that "the average cost curve in banking reflects a relatively flat U-shape at the firm level, with significant economies at small banks, but small and significant diseconomies at the largest (banks)."

Merger Antitrust Analysis

There once was a great concern that mergers might violate antitrust provisions which stipulated that firms should not gain control of a market whereby they could pursue monopolistic pricing and output policies. The decision as to whether a proposed acquisition would be approved was largely based on a simple calculation.

The first step was to define the trade area of the target bank, such as the metropolitan area or county where the bank was located. The second step was to identify the number of competing firms within the area. Regulators then calculated a Herfindahl-Hirschmann Index (HHI) based on the fractional share of deposits controlled by each competitor as a measure of the degree of market concentration. They would determine whether the transaction violated anticompetitive guidelines by comparing the index before and after the proposed acquisition. The standard was the 1800/200 rule. If the post-acquisition HHI was less than 1800 and increased by less than 200, the transaction would generally be approved.

The HHI is calculated by summing the squares of the market shares of each distinct competitor. Suppose, for example, that there are eight competing institutions in a market. The two largest control 25 and 15 percent of deposits. The remaining six control 10 per-

cent each. The HHI would equal 625 + 225 + 600, or 1450. If the largest and smallest banks were to merge, the post-merger HHI would equal 1950 (1225 + 225 + 500). According to the rule, the post-merger HHI would exceed 1800 and the increase would equal 500, thereby violating both conditions. Thus the transaction would be deemed anticompetitive and denied.

Of course, even if the rule were not violated, regulators could deny the transaction if competition would be better enhanced in other ways. It was often argued that the buyer would enter by new charter if it was not allowed to buy an existing firm. Because this would increase competition even more, the original acquisition would be denied.

In today's environment, regulators are considerably less aggressive in denying mergers and acquisitions. This can be accomplished in line with the numerical formula by lowering the existing market share figures. To do this one need only expand the geographic area used to identify competitors. Alternatively, one could expand the types of firms viewed as competitors by including thrift and credit union deposits in the base deposit figure. Both of these adjustments have been made and the HHI standard has effectively been ignored so that fewer transactions are now denied.

Exhibit 28.1 documents the increase in number of large merger and acquisition transactions through 1986, followed by a sharp decrease following the stock market crash of 1987. The decline in bank mergers and acquisitions reflects several important trends. First, many banks saw their stock prices plummet with the market crash and subsequent asset quality and earnings problems. It is extremely difficult for a bank with a low stock price to be an acquirer. Second, with risk-based capital requirements banks are forced to conserve capital. Third, this list includes private transactions, but omits government-assisted acquisitions. Given the large number of bank and thrift failures, many banks preferred to purchase failed institutions or buy the deposits of failed firms. During 1990 many planned private acquisitions were canceled because the seller's financial condition was worse than that anticipated, and buyers exercised clauses that allowed them to withdraw their offers. In 1991, merger activity accelerated, particularly among the largest banks, as firms tried to position themselves

Exhibit 28.1 Number of Bank Mergers & Acquisitions:
Transactions Valued Over $25 Million

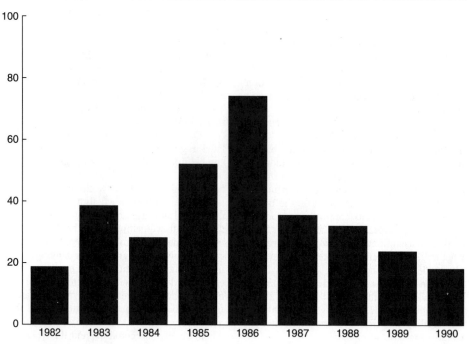

Source: Svare, 1990, *Bank Management* for data through 1989; updated.

for future growth and took advantage of cost cutting by eliminating duplicate services. The merger of Chemical Bank and Manufacturers Hanover to form a $135 billion bank represents such a transaction.

Consistent with the shift from a seller's to a buyer's market, the premiums paid for banks have followed the same pattern as the number of successful acquisitions. As indicated in Exhibit 28.2, the premium, measured by the average price-to-earnings multiple and price-to-book-value multiple, rose through 1986 then dropped sharply. The decline is actually understated because book values after 1986 more closely reflected true economic value due to more precise recognition of loan problems. The significance of these ratios is discussed in detail as part of the valuation process.

HOW DO MERGERS ADD VALUE?

It is not uncommon for two banks to announce a merger and stock analysts immediately praise the transaction as enhancing value or criticize it for making little sense for

**Exhibit 28.2 Average Premiums Paid in Bank Acquisitions:
Transactions Valued Over $25 Million**

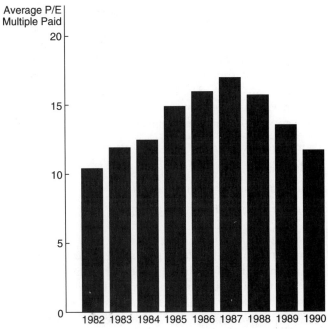

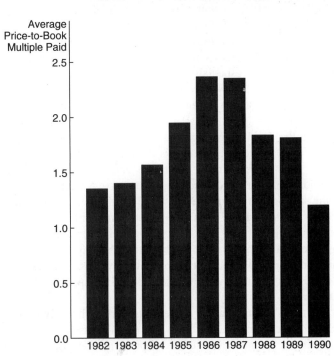

Source: Svare, 1990, *Bank Management*; updated.

shareholders. Why the difference? Is it possible to get a quick sense of whether a transaction is inherently good or bad? The following discussion outlines various factors that both enhance value and diminish value.

It is easy to specify in abstract terms when a merger is beneficial. Simply compare the market value of the combined firm after the transaction with the sum of the market values of the independent firms prior to the transaction. If the combined value exceeds the pre-merger value, the merger is value enhancing. Otherwise, value declines. The obvious question is, how does an acquisition increase the combined value?

Value is created in two ways. The first way is that the combined bank might be able to generate increased earnings compared to historical norms. The sources of these potential earnings are wide-ranging and include:

- entry into attractive new markets
- stronger product lines
- improved marketing/distribution of products
- improved managerial capabilities, and
- cost cutting

The first four sources are difficult to quantify because of uncertainties about the structure of the combined firm. To enhance value the acquirer would like to retain the best employees of the target bank, retain the target's best customers, and preserve the best parts of the target's culture. In many cases, however, employees and directors of an acquired bank often leave because they perceive either that they will not have the same opportunities as before or that they will eventually be let go. Customers also often move their relationships. They may be frustrated at the buyer being out of state and prefer to conduct business with a locally owned bank. They may also follow the officer with whom they previously conducted business. With this uncertainty, earnings forecasts are highly suspect, especially near term.

Cost cutting typically receives considerable attention because the acquirer has some direct control of noninterest expense. Banks with excess data processing capacity, for example, often view acquisitions as a way of generating activity that lowers unit costs by spreading the fixed technology cost across more items. As mentioned earlier, however, there is mixed evidence that banks realize significant economies of scale by expanding. True cost cutting arises when the acquirer and target have duplicate facilities, operations, and staff and general overcapacity. A merger allows the combined firm to offer the same quality and level of service with fewer people and fewer capital assets than two separate banks. For this reason, the mergers that make the most sense are in-market transactions. One bank's excess systems capacity and employees can serve the customers of both merger parties so that the duplicate noninterest expense can be eliminated. This cost reduction goes directly to the bottom line and, more importantly, represents an annuity. How else can banks, especially large money center banks, increase profits so quickly?

Value is created a second way by increasing market share. Even if earnings rates remain unchanged after a merger, a bank can position itself as a future acquisition target by capturing a greater share of its deposit market. Buyers value a target's customer base and will pay a premium to obtain core deposits. Thus a bank's deposit market share is an important determinant of value in an acquisition.

Problem Mergers

What makes a merger unattractive? In financial terms, mergers are problematic when the buyer does not earn the expected return on investment in a reasonable period of time. The first evaluative hurdle is that the transaction should not dilute earnings. One broad standard of performance is that a merger should not produce any dilution in earnings per share (EPS) for the acquiring bank greater than 5 percent. Formally, EPS dilution is measured as

$$\text{EPS dilution} = \frac{\left(\begin{array}{c} \text{Current EPS of acquiring bank} - \text{pro forma} \\ \text{EPS of consolidated entity} \end{array}\right)}{\text{Current EPS of acquiring bank}} \quad (28.1)$$

The pro forma consolidated EPS is a forecast value for the upcoming period. The standard suggests that some dilution is acceptable because most transactions are financed by an exchange of stock and the EPS's of the target and acquirer are not the same. Many mergers, however, dilute the acquirer's EPS and the question is how long it will take to overcome the dilution.

A second hurdle is whether the acquisition, when treated as an investment, earns the expected rate of return over time. EPS dilution analysis concentrates on short-run performance. Many firms also perform a workout time analysis that focuses on long-run results. The analysis essentially computes the time necessary for the acquirer to earn enough to pay for the initial investment and meet the cumulative target return objective. Obviously, the less the acquirer pays and the greater the earnings growth, the shorter is the time required to generate the target return.

Exhibit 28.3 documents the average workout time for bank mergers from 1986 through 1990.[2] Over this period, the average workout time was 22 years, hardly a quick return on investment. The trend, however, is that average workout time has slowly shortened. This is consistent with the lower premiums paid after the 1987 stock market crash. Banks may also be improving their ability to grow earnings from target banks. For example, the average workout period for Banc One, an extremely aggressive acquirer, is under 10 years. This reflects both the relatively low prices paid for acquisitions and the quick profit improvement shown by Banc One's targets. In general, problems arise when the estimated workout time exceeds 20 years. Beyond this point acquirers overpay according to financial performance.

Value Added by Buying Failed Thrifts

Several of the largest banks in the country have pursued an aggressive strategy of buying failed thrifts. Rather than assume all the thrift's assets, most transactions are

---

[2]Sanchez (1990) analyzes trends in the pattern of premiums and expected workout time as described by SNL Securities.

Exhibit 28.3 Average Workout Periods for Bank Mergers

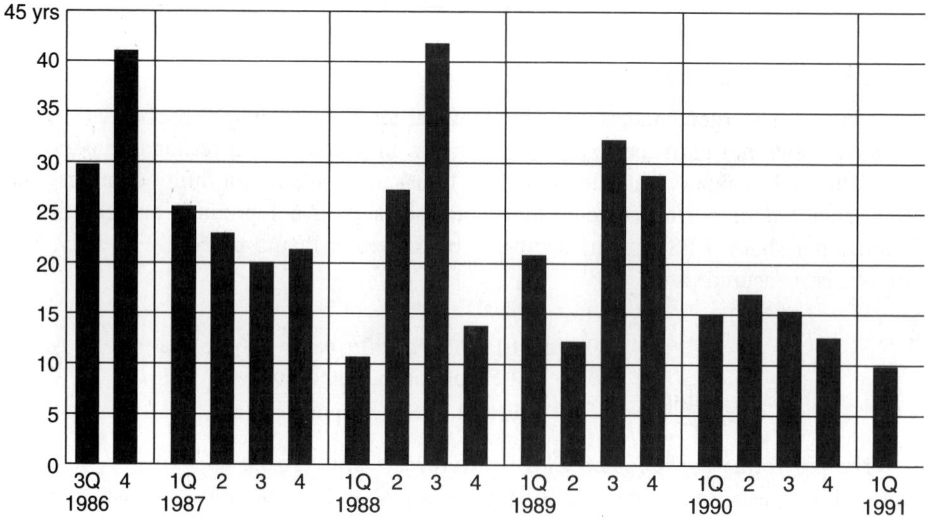

Averages (in years) are based on assumption that buyer would sustain a 10% rate of income growth over the long term.

Source: Sanchez, "Workout Time Proves Key Measure," *American Banker,* November 14, 1990.

structured so that the buyer gets to screen the loans and buy only ones that meet its standards. For example, in 1989 NCNB Texas acquired University Savings Association and got $3.5 billion in deposits. As part of the deal, it agreed to buy just 15 percent of the savings and loan's assets. From January 1989 through June 1990, NCNB bought 18 failed savings banks in Texas. It obtained almost $7 billion in core deposits, but never bought more that 15 percent of the failed thrift's assets. The Resolution Trust Corp. as seller keeps the remaining assets, which have the lowest prospects for collection.

Clearly, the failed institution's core deposit base makes the deals attractive. Buyers know that the government wants to move its inventory and thus they often get the deposits cheap. A study of 287 failed thrift purchases through October 1990 revealed that the average premium paid on deposits equaled 2.1 percent.[3] As might be expected, the average premium varied substantially state by state from a low of 0.43 percent in Colorado to 4.53 percent in Illinois. In general, states with strong economies, such as California and Illinois, garnered the highest premiums while states with weak economies or limited demand for the deposits produced low premiums.

---

[3]See Rehm, 1990. When buying deposits the acquirer assumes the liability to each deposit owner. What then does the buyer actually pay? If the premium is 2 percent, the buyer effectively pays $2 cash for each $100 in deposits assumed. In actuality, the RTC gives the bank $98 per $100 in liabilities assumed. If the bank buys assets, it receives even less.

Purchasing deposits adds value for the same reasons that buying a healthy bank adds value. The deposits can be used to increase earnings and they increase the buyer's market share. These deposits are core deposits in the sense that they are noninterest-bearing demand balances and small time and savings balances that are relatively stable. They also carry the lowest interest rates. An acquirer must be able to reinvest these funds at a positive spread to increase earnings. In recent deposit transactions, buyers have simply used the proceeds to buy securities rather than make new loans.

VALUATION PROCEDURES

A merger or acquisition involving financially sound banks is successful if it maximizes shareholder wealth for stockholders of both banks. Transaction terms should reflect a combined firm value that exceeds the sum of firm values when viewed independently. This greater value is derived from improved profitability attributable to an improved earning asset mix, improved pricing, reductions in unit operating costs, opportunities to enter new markets and offer new products, and access to core deposits. All these factors should be incorporated in the analysis of what price an acquirer should pay for a target, or what minimum price a seller will accept.

Before calculating a purchase price, both buyer and seller should evaluate the other's risk and return profile using historical financial data. The common approach is the ROE framework outlined in Chapter 4 along with the analysis of the bank's credit, liquidity, interest rate, capital, operational, and solvency risk position. While the ratios simply reflect historical performance, they are important indicators of the bank's financial strengths and weaknesses and help determine the economic value of the firm.

Stockholders in the target bank focus on the premium offered relative to the price of the stock prior to the announcement. In a cash transaction, the premium represents the realized increase in value from the transaction. If instead the acquirer proposes to exchange stock in the acquiring firm for stock in the target, target stockholders gain if the value of the new stock exceeds the value of stock in only the target. This represents an increase in value if the stock can be immediately liquidated for more than the value of the target's stock, or if expected cash flows from holding the new stock exceed that from holding just the target's stock. In this case, the correct valuation depends on the expected dividend payments and price of the stock when it is eventually sold.

As discussed above, any merger or acquisition should be treated as an investment and evaluated accordingly. Thus the theoretically correct procedure for determining value is to discount expected cash flows from the new entity at the appropriate discount rate. Because this approach involves estimating many key components of the present value model, market participants typically use a variety of less rigorous techniques to obtain a range of fair price estimates. This range of potential prices is then used in negotiations with the other party. The final result will reflect these prices plus each party's bargaining strength and the nonpecuniary benefits that the negotiators include in the price, such as public recognition, ego, etc. Different valuation procedures produce different benchmark price estimates as described below. Each assumes an exchange of stock.[4]

Premium to Book Value

Most bankers and market analysts discuss merger prices in terms of book values. Formally, the book value of a share of stock equals the book value of a firm's stockholders' equity divided by the number of shares outstanding. The book value of stockholders' equity is based on reported balance sheet values and equals the dollar amount of assets minus the dollar amount of liabilities. The premium to book value in a transaction compares the per share price offered to target bank stockholders with the book value of the target's stock. Letting

MP_t = per-share market price offered for target's stock, and
BV_t = per-share book value of target's stock,

the premium to book value is

$$\text{Premium to book value} = \frac{(MP_t - BV_t)}{BV_t} \qquad (28.2)$$

Thus if the target bank's book value per share is $20 and an acquirer offers $26 per share, the premium to book value equals 30 percent.

In order to use this concept in valuing a bank, participants simply calculate the average premium offered on recent successful transactions of comparable institutions and extrapolate what the equivalent price would be for the target if the same premium applied. Formally, the transactions price per share of target stock under this approach (P_{bv}) is determined by

$$P_{bv} = \left[\frac{MP_t}{BV_t}\right]_{avg} \times BV_t \qquad (28.3)$$

Thus if the average premium on comparable transactions is 80 percent, the average purchase price-to-book value multiple will equal 1.8 and the transactions price for the target bank's stock should equal $36 (1.8 × $20) in the above example.

Merger terms are also described in terms of exchange ratios, or the number of shares of the acquiring bank's stock that target bank stockholders receive for each share in the target bank. Letting

e = exchange ratio, and
MP_a = per-share market price of the acquirer's stock

---

[4]This discussion follows Bullington, 1981, and Cates, 1985. Many tax and accounting issues are ignored. Issues, such as the costs and benefits of purchase accounting versus pooling-of-interests accounting, are critical to the evaluation and success of mergers. See Koch and Baker, 1983, for a discussion of these issues.

then

$$e = \frac{P_{bv}}{MP_a} = \frac{BV_t(1 + \text{Premium})}{MP_a} \qquad (28.4)$$

This procedure has many weaknesses. The most obvious is that book value may not even closely resemble a bank's true economic value. Suppose that a bank systematically understates problem loans. Reported loan values will overstate true values and book value will be artificially large. Suppose also that the bank has a severe interest rate mismatch between rate-sensitive assets and liabilities in a volatile interest rate environment. Book values do not reflect this risk. Alternatively, book value may understate true value. Consider a bank that operates a large mortgage servicing portfolio. This value does not appear on balance sheet and thus book value understates economic value. The essential point is that book values can be misleading because the market value of assets and liabilities may differ widely from that reported in periodic financial statements, and off-balance sheet items are ignored.

Another weakness is that premiums paid on other bank acquisitions have no relation to the rate of return that an acquirer can potentially earn on the investment, and completely ignore risk. Market prices incorporate nonpecuniary values that both acquiring and target bank managers place on doing the deal. These values may not be those of other participants in the proposed deal. In general, a premium over book value is justified when expected returns are high relative to the associated risk or when the acquisition provides benefits that are not directly measurable.

Premium to Adjusted Book Value

Because reported book value may differ substantially from true economic value, it is appropriate to compute an adjusted book value of equity for the target bank that recognizes the measurement error. A comparison of the market price to adjusted book value then provides a better measure of the premium paid.

Adjusted book value may be greater or less than book value. It can be obtained by adding or subtracting from stated book value the following items:

Change in loan loss reserve: If asset quality is lower than that reported, the loan loss reserve should be restated higher such that net loans is lower than that reported. If asset quality is higher than that reported, the loss reserve should be adjusted downward such that net loans is higher.

Change in market value of investments: The investment portfolio is listed at cost. If market values of securities differ sharply from cost because interest rates have either risen or fallen, any difference between market and book values should be added to book value.

Change in other asset appraisals: Occasionally banks own real estate and other assets that have market values far different from the cost that appears on the balance sheet. A bank may own stock acquired in a foreclosure that has risen in value or land with proven oil reserves that is not currently in production. If the market value is above book value, the difference should be added to the book value of equity.

Value of off-balance sheet activities: The earning power of off-balance sheet items is generally not reflected in the balance sheet. The value of mortgage servicing from bank-originated mortgages is such an item. If these activities are valuable, an estimate of the market value should be added to the book value of equity.

Value of core deposits: Core deposits are attractive because they are relatively stable. An acquirer can leverage them by selling additional services to existing deposit holders. This value also incorporates the franchise value of the bank, or its value as an ongoing concern. Unfortunately, the value is difficult to estimate.

Letting ABV_t equal the adjusted book value of stock per share, the premium is

$$\text{Premium to adjusted book value} = \frac{(MP_t - ABV_t)}{ABV_t} \qquad (28.5)$$

To apply this concept to new acquisitions, an analyst must be able to estimate the adjusted book values of targets in previously successful transactions. The average premium is then applied to an estimate of the adjusted book value of the target under consideration. Formally, the transactions price under the adjusted book value approach (P_{abv}) is determined from

$$P_{abv} = \left[\frac{MP_t}{ABV_t} \right]_{avg} \times ABV_t \qquad (28.6)$$

The exchange ratio takes a similar form:

$$e = \frac{P_{abv}}{MP_a} = \frac{ABV_t\,(1 + \text{Premium})}{MP_a} \qquad (28.7)$$

Price to Earnings Per Share

Many analysts prefer to focus on earnings rather than balance sheet values when estimating a market price to pay for a target bank. In this case, the key variable is earnings per share of the target. The valuation approach involves computing the average purchase price-to-EPS ratio for successful acquisitions of similar type, and multiplying this mean ratio by the target bank's earnings per share (EPS_t). The transactions price per share under this approach (P_{eps}) is determined from

$$P_{eps} = \left[\frac{MP_t}{EPS} \right]_{avg} \times EPS_t \qquad (28.8)$$

In this case the premium equals

$$\text{Premium to EPS} = \frac{(MP_t - EPS_t)}{EPS_t} \qquad (28.9)$$

and the exchange ratio equals

$$e = \frac{P_{eps}}{MP_a} = \frac{EPS_t\,(1 + \text{Premium})}{MP_a} \qquad (28.10)$$

The use of a flow earnings measure as a base has numerous weaknesses. First, an appropriate earnings measure would reflect the volatility of earnings, which gives some indication of the riskiness of the bank's operations. Second, it is not clear what time interval is appropriate. The current year's EPS may be dramatically different from EPS over the past few years, and different also from expected EPS. Analysts get around these problems by using a weighted average of historical earnings per share figures, and then using a forecast average value of EPS over the near future.

Price to Prevailing Stock Price

This approach simply compares the offered purchase price for a share of the target bank's stock with its prevailing price (SP_t). The same formulas (28.2) through (28.4) apply after substituting SP_t for BV_t. The transactions price for the target's stock (P_{sp}) thus equals the average offered price-to-prevailing price multiple for comparable transactions times the target's prevailing stock price.

$$P_{sp} = \left[\frac{MP_t}{SP_t} \right]_{avg} \times SP_t \qquad (28.11)$$

This estimate is potentially biased because it assumes that the current stock price accurately reflects current market conditions. There are in fact many instances when this is not true. If a bank's stock is not widely traded, the current price may be stale and not reflect current market value at sale. Similarly, the price may not reflect the fact that a single stockholder controls voting interest in the bank, as is the case with many community banks. Here the owner effectively makes the market in the bank's stock and determines the price at which ownership control will change hands. Finally, even for widely held stock the most recent price quote may not incorporate a bank's franchise value or the value of intangibles. The essential point is that a bank's stock price may not reflect the market price at which a change of ownership might occur.

EPS Dilution Constraints

Most bank acquisitions have a negative short-term effect on earnings largely because the acquiring bank pays a premium for the target. This decline in EPS should be of negligible size and short-lived for a merger to be attractive to the purchaser. The earlier discussion of problem mergers noted that banks have historically been unwilling to close deals in which EPS dilution exceeds 5 percent. Cates in fact notes that such acquisitions are termed "dilutions of grandeur."[5] The difficulty with excessive EPS dilution is that the purchase price is so high that it takes forever for the acquiring bank to improve performance to where it earns a reasonable risk-adjusted return on investment.

Consider the case summarized in Exhibit 28.4 where Bank B has proposed buying Bank S in a 2 for 1 stock exchange. The top panel indicates that prior to the acquisition, Bank B reports an EPS of $5 while Bank S has an EPS of $3.50 on net income of $14 million with 4 million shares outstanding. Bank S is less than 10 percent of the size

---

[5]Cates (1985).

Exhibit 28.4 Analysis of Earnings Per Share Dilution

A. Pre-acquisition: December 31, 1991	Bank B	Bank S
Net income	$160 million	$14 million
Number of shares outstanding	32 million	4 million
Earnings per share	$5.00	$3.50
Total assets	$22.2 billion	$1.5 billion

B. Forecast for 1992

Assume: i) Net income for both banks increases by 10%
    ii) Bank B offers a 2 for 1 stock exchange whereby Bank S stockholders receive 2
       shares in Bank B for every share of Bank S

	Bank B	Bank S	Consolidated
Net income	$176 million	$15.4 million	$191.4 million
Number of shares outstanding	32 million	8 million	40 million
Earnings per share	$5.00	$1.925	$4.785
EPS dilution	$\dfrac{\$5.00 - \$4.785}{\$5.00} = 4.3\%$		

Summary
1. With no acquisition, Bank B's EPS would increase to $8.05 by 1996.
2. Earnings at Bank S would have to increase to $64.4 million in 1996 to increase its EPS to
   the same $8.05 by 1996. Thus earnings would have to grow at a 35.7% annual rate for dilu-
   tion to be recovered within 5 years.

of Bank B, but has a higher return on assets. The bottom panel demonstrates the
EPS dilution when net income for each bank is forecast to grow by 10 percent in
the upcoming year and the acquisition goes through as planned. Without any
transaction, Bank B's EPS would have increased by the same 10 percent to $5.50.
The consolidated firm, however, is expected to report $191.4 million in net income
on 40 million shares, for an EPS of $4.785. This dilutes Bank B's EPS by 4.3
percent, which is just under the 5 percent threshold viewed as maximum acceptable
dilution.

Cates introduced a micro-dilution framework that provides even clearer evidence
of problem acquisitions. The term *micro-dilution* refers to EPS dilution of the target.
In the bottom panel this amounts to computing the earnings per issued share for Bank
S of $1.925 from a projected $15.4 million net income with 8 million shares outstanding. This contrasts with Bank B's projected EPS of $5.50. Suppose that no acquisition
occurred. If Bank B's earning grew 10 percent annually for 5 years, its EPS would
grow to $8.05. In order for the dilution in the above example to be temporary, Bank
S's EPS must also grow to $8.05 by the fifth year. This means that after the acquisition
Bank S's net income would have to increase at a 35.7 percent annual rate. It is highly
unlikely that any bank's earnings will increase at such a rate under normal circumstances. This transaction is of highly questionable value because dilution is permanent,
unless there is some strategic value to the purchase that is not revealed by the earnings
data.

Return on Investment

This approach views the purchase of a bank's stock as an investment and compares the present value of expected stockholders' equity discounted at some target rate of return with the current equity value. If the discounted value exceeds the current equity value, the net present value of the stock purchase is positive and the investment meets the minimum required return. Expected stockholders' equity is determined by forecasting return on equity through at least 10 years.

The real value of this procedure is that it provides an estimate of economic value. The estimated value or premium to be paid for the target bank's stock is typically lower than with other approaches, however, because only earnings are incorporated in the analysis. Thus sellers largely ignore this analysis when they have any market power. Buyers can use it to assess the true economic premium that can be justified in terms of the required return on investment.

AN APPLICATION

The following analysis demonstrates the application of the valuation procedures just described. Each procedure is addressed using the balance sheet and income statement data for Sterling National Bank and Target Bank that appear in Exhibits 28.5 through 28.8. Exhibit 28.9 provides information on each bank's earnings per share and dividends per share in the two most recent years, as well as average price-to-book-value and earnings multiples for completed acquisitions in 1990. Finally, for comparative purposes, key performance ratios for peer banks are listed in Exhibit 28.10. The nonquantitative aspects of the analysis are ignored.

Sterling National Bank (SNB) is considering buying 100 percent of Target Bank's stock. SNB's stock price is currently $46 and Target Bank's stock price is $32. Book values for each bank can be obtained from the balance sheet. SNB's management has determined, however, that these book values overstate each bank's true economic value, and has made the following adjustments in millions of dollars.

	SNB	Target Bank
Additional provisions for losses	$32	$15
Securities depreciation	6	5
Franchise value (1.5% of core deposits)	23	14

SNB's management is also unwilling to accept EPS dilution beyond 5 percent. Net income for SNB is forecast to be $17 million in 1991, while net income for Target Bank is forecast at $8 million.

The problem is to determine a range of acquisition prices for Target Bank by applying each of the valuation procedures described earlier. When evaluating EPS dilution, assume that SNB is considering a 1 for 1 stock exchange whereby Target Bank stockholders will get 1 share of SNB stock for each share of Target Bank stock. When using the return-on-investment approach, SNB uses reported book value (unadjusted) and assumes that Target Bank's return on equity will equal the following values

Exhibit 28.5 Balance Sheet for Sterling National Bank (Dollars in Millions)

	December 31	
Assets	1989	1990
Cash and due from banks	$ 107	$ 111
Interest-bearing deposits with banks	46	63
Investment securities:		
Treasury & U.S. agency	152	171
Corporate & mortgage-backed	60	74
Municipals	71	61
Total loans and leases	993	1,028
Less reserve for losses	14	17
Net loans and leases	$ 979	$1,011
Real estate owned	22	27
Premises and equipment	27	28
Other assets	62	64
Total assets	$1,526	$1,610
Liabilities		
Demand deposits	$ 235	$ 240
Savings deposits	358	369
Time deposits	504	549
Total deposits	$1,097	$1,158
Borrowed funds:		
Federal funds purchased & RPs	$ 171	$ 163
Other borrowed funds	123	138
Acceptances and other liabilities	48	52
Total liabilities	$1,439	$1,511
Stockholders' Equity		
Common stock	$ 7	$ 7
Paid-in capital	40	40
Retained earnings	40	52
Total stockholders' equity	$ 87	$ 99
Total liabilities and equity	$1,526	$1,610

from 1991 through the year 2000. SNB has a minimum acceptable rate of return of 15 percent per year.

	Forecast ROE
1991:	14%
1992:	15%
1993–1995:	16%
1996–2000:	18%

Historical Performance Analysis

The first stage of the valuation process involves familiarizing oneself with the historical profitability and risk profile of the prospective parties to the transaction. Exhibit

Exhibit 28.6 Income Statement for Sterling National Bank (Dollars in Millions)

Interest Income	1989	1990
Loans and losses (includes fees)	$123.2	$128.8
Interest-bearing deposits	3.1	4.9
Treasury & U.S. agency securities	12.2	13.3
Corporate & mortgage-backed securities	5.9	7.5
Municipals	4.7	3.8
Total interest income	$149.1	$158.3
Interest Expense		
Deposits	$ 66.2	$ 71.8
Federal funds purchased & RPs	12.0	11.6
Other borrowed funds	10.2	10.9
Total interest expense	$ 88.4	$ 94.3
Net Interest Income	$ 60.7	$ 64.0
Provisions for loan losses	5.3	6.1
Net interest for income after provisions	$ 55.4	$ 57.9
Noninterest Income	$ 38.6	$ 41.7
Noninterest Expense		
Salaries & benefits	$ 36.3	$ 38.0
Other expense	40.2	41.8
Total noninterest expense	$ 76.5	$ 79.8
Income before taxes	$ 17.5	$ 19.8
Provision for income taxes	4.0	4.9
Net income	$ 13.5	$ 14.9

28.11 summarizes the basic components to the ROE model for 1990 using average balance sheet data for both banks. Several brief conclusions are offered. First, SNB was comparatively more profitable than Target Bank in 1990 and above peers in terms of ROE. SNB reported a lower ROA than peers, indicating its ROE was higher because it used greater financial leverage. SNB's profit margin and asset utilization both exceeded Target Bank's by a substantial amount. Peer banks, however, exhibited greater expense control than SNB, but SNB reported a higher gross yield on assets. Both SNB and Target Bank have high noninterest expense, but low interest expense relative to peers. Provisions for loan losses at SNB are in line with peers', while Target Bank's loss ratio is substantially higher than peers' indicating a potential source of problems. On the asset side, SNB earns more in interest and noninterest income than both the Target Bank and peers. Target Bank, in contrast, earns substantially lower interest income, but reported substantial noninterest income. Thus SNB's net interest margin was higher than average, while Target Bank's was lower.

Key risk ratios are not available so it is difficult to get a clear picture of the banks' overall risk and return profile. Still, several potential sources of difficulty for Target

Exhibit 28.7 Balance Sheet for Target Bank (Dollars in Millions)

	December 31	
Assets	1989	1990
Cash and due from banks	$ 74	$ 77
Interest-bearing deposits with banks	57	60
Investment securities:		
Treasury & U.S. agency	124	133
Corporate & mortgage-backed	43	59
Municipals	84	76
Total loans and leases	602	619
Less reserve for losses	10	12
Net loans and leases	$ 592	$ 607
Real estate owned	10	12
Premises and equipment	21	22
Other assets	46	47
Total assets	$1,051	$1,093
Liabilities		
Demand deposits	$ 217	$ 228
Savings deposits	324	329
Time deposits	320	357
Total deposits	$ 861	$ 914
Borrowed funds:		
Federal funds purchased & RPs	$ 102	$ 73
Other borrowed funds	10	14
Acceptances and other liabilities	30	39
Total liabilities	$1,003	$1,040
Stockholders' Equity		
Common stock	$ 5	$ 5
Paid-in capital	25	25
Retained earnings	18	23
Total stockholders' equity	$ 48	$ 53
Total liability and equity	$1,051	$1,093

Bank appear to be its relatively low stockholders' equity, its weakness in controlling noninterest expense, relatively poor asset quality, and poor interest earnings with a larger earning asset base. Target Bank's assets do not appear to be accruing interest as they should, which could be attributed to poor loan quality, an investment portfolio earning below market coupon interest, and other problems.

Valuation Based on Alternative Procedures

The first step is to calculate the book value of Target Bank's stock both with and without adjustment for valuation biases. According to Exhibit 28.5, stockholders' equity at Target Bank at the end of 1990 is $53 million or $33.125 per share. The

Exhibit 28.8 Income Statement for Target Bank (Dollars in Millions)

Interest Income	**1988**	**1989**
Loans and losses (includes fees)	$69.8	$70.7
Interest-bearing deposits	3.9	3.8
Treasury & U.S. agency securities	10.4	10.3
Corporate & mortgage-backed securities	4.1	6.0
Municipals	5.7	4.8
Total interest income	$93.9	$95.6
Interest Expense		
Deposits	$47.2	$51.0
Federal funds purchased & RPs	7.5	5.2
Other borrowed funds	3.4	1.3
Total interest expense	$58.1	$57.5
Net Interest Income	$35.8	$38.1
Provisions for loan losses	4.6	4.6
Net interest income after provisions	$31.2	$33.5
Noninterest Income	$25.2	$28.0
Noninterest Expense		
Salaries & benefits	$25.1	$27.4
Other expense	25.2	26.1
Total noninterest expense	$50.3	$53.5
Income before taxes	$ 6.1	$ 8.0
Provision for income taxes	0.1	1.1
Net Income	$ 6.0	$ 6.9

adjustments to book value reduce this by $6 million to $47 million. For comparative purposes SNB's book value per share equals $49.5, while its adjusted book value equals $42.[6]

Estimated per-share offering prices can be obtained using the average multiples for recently completed transactions appearing at the bottom of Exhibit 28.9.

	Premium
$P_{bv} = [1.5] \times \$33.125 = \$49.69$	55.3%
$P_{abv} = [1.9] \times \$29.375 = \$55.81$	74.4
$P_{eps} = [13.6] \times \$3.75 = \$51.00$	59.4
$P_{sp} = [1.8] \times \$32.00 = \$57.60$	80.0

According to these procedures, the prospective offering price for a share of Target Bank's stock ranges from just under $50 with the premium-to-book value approach

---

[6]At Target Bank the $15 million understatement of provisions for loan losses and $5 million in securities depreciation reduce total book equity by $20 million, which is partially offset by the estimated $14 million in franchise value. The net reduction per share is $3.75. For SNB book equity falls by $15 million in the aggregate or $7.50 per share due to a $38 million reduction in value due to loan loss provisions and securities depreciation, which is partially offset by a $23 million estimated franchise value.

Exhibit 28.9 Data Related to SNB Acquisition of Target Bank

A. Summary Profit and Dividend Figures	SNB		Target Bank	
	1989	1990	1989	1990
Net income	$13,500,000	$14,900,000	$6,000,000	$6,900,000
Number of shares outstanding	2,000,000	2,000,000	1,600,000	1,600,000
Earnings per share	$6.75	$7.45	$3.75	$4.31
Dividends	$ 2,900,000	$ 2,900,000	$1,950,000	$1,950,000
Dividends per share	$1.45	$1.45	$1.22	$1.22

B. 1990 Average Multiples for Completed Bank Acquisitions	Multiples
Actual purchase price per share/Book value of seller per share	1.5×
Actual purchase price per share/Adjusted book value of seller per share	1.9×
Actual purchase price per share/Earnings per share of seller	13.6×
Actual purchase price per share/Stock price of seller per share	1.8×

to almost $58 based on Target Bank's prevailing stock price. The column of data under *Premium* indicates the fractional premium that each share price represents relative to the Target Bank's current $32 share price. These estimates actually provide a fairly tight range of values. The fact that the figure is highest with the current stock price might indicate that there is a merger premium built into the price to reflect Target Bank's status as a merger candidate. Alternatively, it may simply reflect information not captured by the other procedures, such as the value of off-balance sheet activities.

EPS Dilution. SNB's management has stipulated that dilution will not be allowed to exceed 5 percent. This constraint means that EPS of the consolidated bank after acquisition cannot fall below $7.08. From equation (28.1)

$$\frac{(\$7.45 - \text{consolidated EPS})}{\$7.45} = .05$$

or

$$\text{consolidated EPS} = \$7.08$$

The exchange ratios consistent with the four valuation procedures range from 1 to 1 up to 5 to 4.

$$\frac{P_{bv}}{MP_a} = \frac{\$49.69}{\$46} = 1.02$$

$$\frac{P_{abv}}{MP_a} = \frac{\$55.81}{46} = 1.21$$

$$\frac{P_{eps}}{MP_a} = \frac{\$51}{\$46} = 1.11$$

$$\frac{P_{sp}}{MP_a} = \frac{\$57.60}{\$46} = 1.25$$

**Exhibit 28.10 Performance Ratios for Peer Banks:
Banks with Assets from $1 Billion to $3 Billion in 1990**

Percentage of Average Assets	Percent
Cash and due from banks	6.73%
Interest-bearing deposits	0.60
Taxable securities	14.03
Municipals	3.65
Federal funds sold & RPs	3.01
Net loans & leases	63.64
Other assets	8.34
Total assets	100.00%
Deposits	66.36%
Borrowed funding	14.69
Federal funds purchased & RPs	8.82
Other liabilities	3.48
Total liabilities	93.35%
Stockholders' equity	6.65%

Profitability Ratios	Percent
ROE	15.79%
ROA	1.05
Equity multiplier	15.04×
Profit margin (Net income/Operating income)	9.79%
Asset utilization (Operating income/Total assets)	10.72
Interest expense/Operating income	52.71
Noninterest expense/Operating income	32.28
Provisions for loan losses/Operating income	3.17
Taxes/Operating income	2.05
Interest income/Total assets	9.44
Noninterest income/Total assets	1.28
Net interest margin	4.56
Earning assets/Total assets	88.9

Assuming a 1 for 1 stock exchange whereby holders of Target Bank stock get one share of SNB stock for each share of Target Bank stock, the number of shares outstanding in the combined firm would total 3.6 million. Given forecast net income of $17 million and $8 million for the two banks, the combined EPS would equal $6.94 for 1991. This is well below the $7.08 minimum established by SNB's management and actually represents 6.85 percent dilution. If management sticks to this restriction, it must offer a less than 1 for 1 stock exchange. In fact, the maximum stock exchange to keep EPS dilution at 5 percent is 96 shares of SNB's stock for each 100 shares in Target Bank. This is obtained by solving for the maximum number of shares that can be outstanding (n) if projected income is $25 million for the combined firm.

$$\frac{(\$7.45 - \$25/n)}{\$7.45} = .05$$

Exhibit 28.11 Profitability Ratios Comparison for 1990 Data
(Percent unless otherwise noted.)

	Sterling National Bank	Target Bank	Peer Bank
Return on equity	16.02%	$13.66%	15.79%
Return on assets	.95	.64	1.05
Equity multiplier	16.86×	21.34×	15.04×
Profit margin	7.45%	5.58%	9.79%
Asset utilization	12.76	11.53	10.72
Interest expense/Operating income	47.15	46.52	52.71
Noninterest expense/Operating income	39.90	43.28	32.28
Provisions for loan losses/Operating income	3.05	3.72	3.17
Taxes/Operating income	2.45	.89	2.05
Interest income/Total assets	10.10	8.92	9.44
Noninterest income/Total assets	2.66	2.61	1.28
Net interest margin	4.71	4.10	4.46
Earning assets/Total assets	86.70	86.61	84.90

or

$$n = 3.53 \text{ million}$$

Thus Target Bank stockholders can receive no more than 1.53 million shares in SNB, or 96 percent of the 1.6 million they currently hold. Whether this will be acceptable or not depends on the increase in value this provides Target Bank's stockholders. If Target Bank's current stock price is $32, the value of a share in SNB after the acquisition would have to be at least $33.33 for stockholders to be indifferent on strictly a cash basis. This price represents a steep discount to SNB's current $46 stock price.

Return on Investment. SNB applies this model against a prospective seller's book value. In this case, Target Bank's book value equals $53 million. The earlier discussion presents SNB's forecast of Target Bank's ROE from 1991 through the year 2000. Note that the projected ROE exceeds SNB's 15 percent minimum acceptable rate of return only for the last 8 years. At the end of the year 2000, Target Bank's stockholders' equity will increase to $248.12 million based on these forecasts. When discounted at 15 percent, this produces a present value of future book value equity of $61.33.

$$\text{PV target equity} = \frac{\$53 \, (1.14)(1.15)(1.16)(1.18)}{(1.15)^{10}} = \frac{\$248.12}{4.046}$$

$$= \$61.33$$

The associated premium to the current book value of $53 is just 15.7 percent.

$$\frac{\$61.33}{\$53} = 1.157$$

Think back to the basic assumptions here. For the first 2 years, Target Bank's ROE will be less than SNB's target return. The primary determinant of the premium is thus how much higher Target Bank's ROE will be compared with the acquirer's minimum acceptable rate of return. To justify a substantial premium, the acquirer must be able to increase earnings very sharply. But this is obvious. The basic issue is to accurately assess how fast and to what level earnings of the acquired bank will grow.

In this example, the premium is well below the premiums suggested by the other valuation procedures. Of course, this approach only accounts for any directly measurable improvement in earnings.

Implications

The previous analysis suggests a wide range of potential prices for Target Bank stock. The final resolution will depend on the negotiating strength of each party as well as nonfinancial considerations that have not been addressed. The relationships observed among the various procedures is representative of results in many applications. From an economic perspective, the present value approach often produces the lowest price estimate. If a transaction can be negotiated close to this price, the acquirer will experience the smallest EPS dilution and will be able to reach its earnings objectives soonest. Not surprisingly, sellers prefer to focus on historical premium-to-book value and premium-to-earnings valuation approaches.

NONFINANCIAL CONSIDERATIONS THAT AFFECT MERGERS AND ACQUISITIONS

The previous discussion focused on financial aspects of analyzing a prospective merger or acquisition. In every transaction, there are nonfinancial considerations that are even more important. Managers of buyers and sellers have fundamental objectives, opportunities, and fears that can be beneficially served or seriously harmed by such deals. At the forefront are the egos of the senior managers for both acquirer and target. Even in the case in which there is a presumed *merger of equals* where the two institutions are comparable in size, one group generally gains at the expense of the other and egos must be accommodated accordingly. It is difficult for a bank CEO or president to willingly give up control of an organization that he or she once dominated, even if it is best for shareholders. Thus friendly transactions are difficult to complete unless serious personnel issues are successfully resolved. Of course, in a hostile takeover the seller's most senior management team is generally removed.

While price is the most important consideration in most transactions, buyers and sellers have important nonprice objectives. Buyers typically want to

- avoid postmerger financial and operational complications
- retain the best employees of the acquired bank

- keep the acquired bank's best customers

- maintain the beneficial aspects of the acquired bank's culture

In many cases, the banks have different computer systems and software, but the acquirer wants to convert the target bank to its system to cut costs. If there are operational snags, customers are relatively impatient and will move their relationships.

Key employees are also difficult to retain. Those who are exceptional will have alternatives to move, often at a substantial increase in pay. These same employees may be able to move profitable accounts with them. This routinely occurs when bankers at acquired institutions charter a new community bank. They criticize the previous organization for forgetting the individual and commit to serving customers again on a personal basis. Any loss of key personnel and accounts makes it difficult to increase earnings and can damage the bank's public image. Of course, the seller's lower-level employees are often frightened by loss of job security. Many acquisitions are motivated in large part by perceived cost savings. These savings are typically derived from shrinking personnel expense. Thus even if employees keep their jobs, the potential increase in salary is unknown and the benefits package may worsen. Uncertainty creates tremendous anxiety.

Sellers in a friendly transaction typically want to walk away from the deal without any residual risk. This means they want to be indemnified against yet-unrevealed liabilities or losses that might arise from decisions under their tenure. They are primarily concerned, however, with the size of the premium offered. In a cash transaction, the subsequent issue is when the cash payment will be made. In a securities transaction, the key issue is the value and marketability of the securities. Sellers of community banks are also concerned about whether a deal will adversely affect the local community. Many will try to exact concessions from acquirers to keep employees, not move data processing facilities out of the community, and keep supporting local community projects.

SUMMARY

Recent earnings and capital problems at banks have lead to the consolidation of once-separate banking organizations. Banks with strong equity capital positions now find that it is a buyer's market. There are many failed institutions as well as profitable organizations that need a buyer. As a consequence, buyers can be more selective in their expansion plans.

Buyers and sellers must examine a variety of financial and nonfinancial considerations when deciding whether to negotiate a deal, and if so, at what price. Participants generally use several different procedures for establishing a value for the acquired bank. The most appropriate procedure views the purchase of bank stock as an investment. The buyer projects future earnings (cash flows) which are discounted at the minimum required rate of return to determine the true economic value. Other procedures focus on recently completed transactions and average premium-to-book value or earnings ratios. These historical averages are then applied to a target bank's financial measures to estimate a range of prices. In general, these latter procedures produce higher price estimates than discounting future cash flows.

Participants also consider nonfinancial issues when negotiating a merger or acquisition. The most important concern in a friendly transaction is whether the two cultures match and whether senior officers can work together. It is also important to recognize what impact efforts to cut noninterest expense will have on employee attitudes and opportunities. Mergers generally have both beneficial and harmful aspects depending on whether stockholders, bank employees, or bank customers are viewing the transaction.

Questions

Trends in Mergers

1. At a recent job-fair luncheon two bank managers were boasting about their respective banks. The first was stressing that his was the biggest bank in the region and very proud to have maintained that position for the past 20 years, despite mergers and acquisitions by other local banks. The second indicated that not only was his bank NOT the biggest, but that it was making an effort to downsize. What might be the advantages and disadvantages of working for each of these banks?

2. What is the difference between a bank merger and a bank acquisition?

3. When did merger and acquisition activity peak, why has it apparently dwindled since then, and what events might lead to another increase in mergers?

Source of Value

4. The value of the expansion opportunities of combined banks is often speculative. What can happen to an acquired bank upon announcement of the acquisition to diminish its prospects?

5. What types of cost savings might result from a merger?

Valuation Procedures

6. What five areas of a bank's organization may provide synergistic value?

7. What types of bank risk should be considered when evaluating a merger?

Book Value

8. Aggressive Bank Inc. is considering buying Specialized Bank Inc. Aggressive Bank has acquired many banks in the last few years. These purchases have shown, on average, the following relationships:
   1. Bid price per share/book value per share = 1.8×
   2. Bid price per share/adjusted book value per share = 2.0×
   3. Bid price per share/EPS = 15×
   4. Bid price per share/pre-announcement price per share = 1.9×

The following information has been collected on the potential new acquisition:

Total assets = $800 million
Total debt = $750 million
Number of shares = 5 million
Book value of investments = $30 million
Market value of investments = $45 million
Market value of off-balance-sheet activities = $3 million
Anticipated loan losses not reflected on balance sheet = $20 million
Market price of stock = $12
Net income = $8 million

What range of stock prices could Aggressive Bank offer in a tender offer, according to the various procedures?

9. A takeover attempt is being received by the bank for which you are a stockholder. Currently you have two offers. One is a tender offer for $40 a share if tendered by Friday. The other is a 3 for 2 stock swap. The acquiring bank's stock is currently selling for $60 a share and you would get 2 shares for every 3 you turn in. Before all this actively started your stock was selling for $33 a share. What is your stock selling for now? Which of these is the better offer and why?

EPS Dilution

10. Interstate Bank (IB) is considering buying Community Bank (CB). Community stockholders receive 2 shares in IB for every 1 of CB. IB, whose revenues and expenses are growing at 10 percent a year, is interested in CB because its revenues are growing at 11 percent a year while its expenses are only growing at 10 percent. The current financial data for the two firms is shown below.

	IB	CB
Revenues	$800 million	$250 million
Expenses	$720 million	$220 million
Number of shares	20 million	5 million
Total assets	$5 billion	$1 billion

What current EPS dilution and dilution in one year will occur with this merger if the combined firm is able to grow at 10.2 percent a year? Calculate the microdilution EPS. Will EPS be restored for IB stockholders within 5 years?

11. A bank has a target required return of 14 percent on all S&L acquisitions. It has two potential S&Ls it can buy and it has sufficient funding for both. What should it do given the following forecasts?

	East S&L	West S&L
Current book value	$30	$70
ROE forecasts		
19X1	10%	10%
19X2	12%	10%
19X3	13%	16%
19X4	14%	16%
19X5	15%	16%

12. Growth Bank is looking at a potential acquisition on which it will require a return of 18 percent. ROE forecasts for the next 2 years are for 12 percent and 14 percent. Growth Bank's management feels there is little they can do to improve these returns, but they think they can have a dramatic subsequent effect on performance. If they allow themselves 5 years after the acquisition to achieve their target return, what annual performance will they have to achieve during the last 3 years?

Application

13. Bigtime Bank (BB) is considering making an offer on Local Lender (LL), a small community bank. BB has collected the following information:

Balance Sheet (in million)

Assets	BB 19X1	BB 19X2	LL 19X1	LL 19X2
Cash and near cash	$100	110	$40	50
Investments	200	200	10	15
Gross loans	1,000	1,100	400	400
Less: reserves	50	55	40	50
Net loans	950	1,045	360	350
Other assets	50	50	10	10
Total	$1,300	1,405	$420	425
Liabilities				
Deposits	1,000	1,100	300	350
Borrowed funds	100	85	65	20
Equity	200	220	55	55

Other Balance Sheet Considerations	BB	LL
Additional provisions for losses	60	—
Securities depreciation	20	—
Franchise value (2% of core deposits)	4	4
Number of shares	5	3

Income Statement (in millions)

	BB 19X1	BB 19X2	LL 19X1	LL 19X2
Interest income	150	160	60	50
Interest expense	70	75	20	18
Non-interest income	30	40	5	5
Non-interest expense	60	65	45	40
Taxes	20	20	—	—
Net income	30	40	0	(3)

	BB	LL
Net income forecast for 19X3	45	0
Net income forecast if merger succeeds	44	8

BB management has already made these decisions:

Two LL shares (currently at $20/share) will trade for 1 BB share (currently at $34/share);

EPS dilution must be restricted to 4%;

Required return on investments of this risk is 14%;

a. With the following additional information perform a historical analysis of both BB and LL. Start by completing the following table.

	BB	LL	Peer
ROE			15%
ROA			1%
Total assets/equity			15×
Total assets/interest income			10×
Interest expense/interest income			50%
Non-interest expense/total assets			1%

b. Calculate the book value per share and the adjusted book value per share for both banks. Use the Other Balance Sheet Considerations section of data to do the adjusting.

c. Using the following ratios taken from recent mergers and acquisitions, what range of prices is reasonable for LL?

i.	bid price per share/book value per share	1.5×
ii.	bid price per share/adjusted book value	1.9×
iii.	bid price per share/EPS	14×
iv.	bid price per share/pre-announcement stock price	1.8×

d. Since management has specified that earnings dilution be limited to 4 percent, what is the minimum EPS acceptable to BB after a merger?

e. What exchange ratios would be fair if BB stock is worth $45 and LL's stock is worth the following "true" values?

$20

$25

$30

$35

Which of these exchange ratios would be best for BB stockholders? Would the same be the best for LL stockholders? At the proposed rate of two LL for one BB, would you expect the merger to receive approval?

f. If the merger is consummated at two for one and projected earnings materialize, will BB receive an acceptable EPS after dilution?

g. Why might the earnings forecast differ with a merger rather than without a merger?

Nonfinancial Considerations

14. What is a seller's most important non-financial consideration? What is a buyer's? What is an employer's? Who else would have a non-financial consideration?

Activity

Identify a recent merger of banks summarized in the financial press. Determine the terms of the transaction, including the EPS dilution. Make a list of the beneficial and harmful effects of the merger.

References

Bullington, Robert, and Arnold Jensen. "Pricing a Bank." *The Bankers Magazine* (May–June 1981).

Buying and Selling Banks: A Guide to Making It Work. Arthur Anderson & Co. (August 1989).

Cates, David. "Prices Paid for Banks." *Economic Review* (Federal Reserve Bank of Atlanta, January 1985).

Cates, David. "Bank Analysis for a Takeover Era." *Bank Administration* (December 1988).

Heggestad, Arnold. "Fundamentals of Mergers and Acquisitions." In *Handbook for Banking Strategy,* Richard Aspinwall and Robert Eisenbeis, editors. New York: John Wiley & Sons, Inc., 1985.

Humphrey, David. "Why Do Estimates of Bank Scale Economies Differ?" *Economic Review* (Federal Reserve Bank of Richmond, September/October 1990).

Koch, Donald, and Robert Baker. "Purchase Accounting and the Quality of Bank Earnings." *Economic Review* (Federal Reserve Bank of Atlanta, April 1983).

Matthews, Gordon. "In Mergers, Buyers May Soon Hold the Cards." *American Banker* (January 8, 1991).

Neely, Walter. "Banking Acquisitions: Acquirer and Target Shareholder Returns." *Financial Management* (Winter 1987).

Rehm, Barbara. "Paltry 2.1% Is Average Premium On Sales of Seized Thrift Deposits." *American Banker* (November 19, 1990).

Sanchez, Joseph. "Workout Time Proves Key Measure." *American Banker* (November 14, 1990).

Svare, J. Christopher. "The New M&A Market." *Bank Management* (February 1990).

Varian, Hal. "Symposium on Mergers." *Journal of Economic Perspectives* (Winter 1988).

Cases

CASE 1

Hamilton National Bank: Performance Evaluation

Dennis Thompson was trying to compose himself before his meeting with the board of directors the following day. As president and CEO of Hamilton National Bank (HNB), he was about to propose a wholesale housecleaning of the bank's senior credit officers. It was February 23, 1991, and the regional and national economies were in the midst of a recession. The previous day, federal bank examiners had completed their evaluation of the bank's books and found evidence of self-dealing and mismanagement of the bank's credit portfolio. At the end of the first quarter, the bank would be forced to announce a large increase in nonperforming loans and in loan losses such that the quarterly net loss would exceed $15 million. Thompson, or D.T. as his friends call him, realized that he had failed to monitor the bank's risk profile. Over the years he had become increasingly involved in civic affairs and taken additional time for travel and recreational opportunities. In retrospect, he had delegated too much authority to individuals who abused it.

D.T. had been with HNB for twenty years, serving as president and CEO for the past eight. At 56, he expected to work in the bank until retirement at age 65. One fear was that the board would hold him accountable for the recent problems and terminate his employment. What does a fired CEO of a problem bank do when banks are closing throughout the country and there are few job opportunities?

The examiners had asked D.T. to set up a meeting with the board of directors, at which time they would report their findings. D.T. leaked some of the bad news to his two strongest supporters on the board, because he wanted to position himself to maintain control of the situation. He subsequently collected HNB's financial data to review with board members and prepared a brief memorandum summarizing the alleged self-dealing and credit mismanagement. This information appears as Exhibits 1–8.

From 1980 to 1989, HNB was the region's largest and most prestigious bank. It was dominant in the areas of consumer and business lending, and it banked most of the region's large corporations and their executives. In many ways, HNB had grown too fast. During the early 1980s, it acquired the fifth largest bank in the state along with a small, failed savings and loan. With the growth in assets, HNB's management team was spread quite thin. D.T. once required that the bank's senior loan committee review all loans over $100,000. With expansion, this minimum was raised to $1 million. In actuality, only loans in excess of $5 million were reviewed carefully, because of the senior staff members' other responsibilities and the time constraints faced by them.

The difficulty, of course, is to know precisely what risks the bank faced. Did it have sufficient earning power and capital to absorb future losses? If depositors withdraw their funds, could HNB meet the payment obligations? Were there other risks that the board should be made aware of? Finally, if the credit risk is so large, did HNB earned above-average profits earlier to compensate for the anticipated losses?

Problems

1. By means of a return-on-equity analysis using the data for 1988–1990 given in the tables, examine HNB's profitability over time compared to that of its peers in 1990. Determine where HNB's performance deviates from that of its peers and explain why it does so. Identify the key trends from 1988 to 1990. Indicate how the adverse trends might be corrected.

2. Using data for 1988–1990, examine the trends in HNB's risk position in terms of (a) asset quality, (b) liquidity (both asset and liability), (c) capital adequacy/solvency, (d) interest rate risk, and (e) operational risk. Using the UBPR comparisons, compare HNB's risk profile in 1990 with that of its peers.

3. Prepare a list of strategic recommendations for D.T. Explain how each is linked to a prior problem or opportunity, and indicate how each will improve the bank's performance.

Exhibit 1 Memorandum to the Board of Directors of Hamilton National Bank

To: Board of Directors
From: Dennis Thompson
Subject: Asset Quality Problems
Date: February 24, 1991

From 1988 to 1990, the quality of Hamilton National Bank's business loan portfolio deteriorated substantially. The extent of the problem is more severe than that suggested by the reported financial data. James Clyburn, EVP in charge of commercial lending, and Scott Frederick, the bank's real estate specialist, have made questionable loans that HNB will eventually charge off. Included are:

1. A $9.5 million loan to CRV Corp. for plant expansion. Clyburn is one of 6 principal owners of CRV, a fact not disclosed until last week. The original loan was for $7.5 million but was renewed twice, adding a $1 million increment to the outstanding principal at each renewal.

2. A $2.2 receivables loan to Parsons Piping. Frederick's wife is a minority stockholder in Parsons.

3. A $4 million loan to Thacker Construction. There is conflicting evidence that Clyburn and Frederick personally received $50,000 each from Thacker following HNB's loan negotiations with the firm. The loan was nonperforming 180 days after origination.

In addition, both Clyburn and Frederick are significant borrowers from Midlands County Bank (MCB), a major provider of correspondent banking services to HNB. Both men were instrumental in moving the bulk of HNB's correspondent business to MCB in 1988.

It is the board's responsibility to take appropriate action regarding these loan officers. The loans described above violate HNB's credit policy. In addition, material information was withheld regarding the officers' ownership interest and the true financial performance and condition of certain borrowers.

Exhibit 2 Balance Sheet Data for Hamilton National Bank
(Daily Averages in Thousands of Dollars)

	1988	1989	1990
Assets			
Cash and due from banks (noninterest-bearing)	$ 61,118	$ 63,844	$ 63,627
Due from banks (interest-bearing)	111,014	116,152	30,655
State and local government obligations	24,903	27,860	22,095
Other securities	94,432	106,772	97,721
Federal funds sold and RPs	32,820	12,500	7,882
Loans			
C&I	297,306	302,624	290,336
Consumer	139,977	149,819	155,222
Real estate	82,239	125,358	148,538
Other	4,443	4,872	5,429
Total	$523,965	$582,673	$599,525
Less reserve for loan losses	17,488	17,760	18,149
Net loans	$506,477	$564,913	$581,376
Premises and equipment	$ 23,447	$ 23,951	$ 24,807
Other assets	16,581	16,873	16,022
Total assets	$876,792	$932,865	$844,185
Liabilities and Equity			
Demand deposits	$161,365	$172,890	$141,755
Interest checking	90,974	104,623	91,090
Money market accounts	161,370	165,088	151,232
Savings and small time deposits	271,418	266,682	257,312
Large CDs ≥ $100,000	107,620	128,341	92,246
Total deposits	$792,697	$837,624	$733,635
Federal funds purchased and RPs	$ 124	$ 2,187	$ 14,864
Other liabilities	35,046	39,726	42,145
Total liabilities	$827,867	$879,537	$790,644
Common stock	$ 10,000	$ 10,000	$ 10,000
Surplus	10,000	10,000	10,000
Retained earnings	28,925	33,328	33,541
Total stockholders' equity	$ 48,925	$ 53,328	$ 53,541
Total liabilities and equity	$876,792	$932,865	$844,185

Exhibit 3 Income Statement Data for Hamilton National Bank
(Thousands of Dollars)

	1988	1989	1990
Interest Income			
Loans	$59,296	$70,179	$68,518
Due from banks	7,560	7,241	1,841
Federal funds sold	3,009	903	515
State and local government obligations[a]	1,627	1,704	1,301
Other securities	8,593	9,291	7,937
Total	$80,085	$89,318	$80,112
Interest Expense			
Checking deposits	$ 4,363	$ 5,850	$ 5,122
Money market accounts	9,634	11,079	9,255
Savings and small time deposits	19,047	21,126	18,755
Large CDs	9,440	11,939	8,238
Federal funds purchased	11	166	1,093
Total	$42,495	$50,160	$48,471
Net Interest Income	$37,590	$39,158	$37,649
Provisions for loan losses	8,652	7,956	12,382
Net Interest Income after Provisions	$28,938	$31,202	$25,267
Noninterest Income			
Fees and service charges	$ 4,705	$ 5,163	$ 5,498
Trust department income	1,371	1,387	1,861
Securities gains (losses)	1,345	(109)	244
Other income[b]	2,492	1,077	1,489
Total	$ 9,913	$ 7,518	$ 9,092
Noninterest Expense			
Salaries and employee benefits	$11,827	$13,562	$13,890
Occupancy (premises)	2,942	3,051	3,253
Occupancy (furniture and equipment)	1,207	1,471	1,410
Other operating expense	10,283	10,994	10,908
Total	$26,259	$29,078	$30,461
Income before taxes	$12,592	$ 9,642	$3,898
Income taxes	3,870	2,373	614
Net income	$ 8,722	$ 7,269	$3,284

[a]Tax-equivalent income: 1988: $2,465; 1989: $2,582; 1990: $1,971.

[b]HNB sold property for a $1.5 million pre-tax gain in 1988.

Exhibit 4 Supplementary Risk Measures for Hamilton National Bank

	1988	1989	1990
Credit Risk			
Net charge-offs/Net income	1.57%	1.36%	1.84%
Provisions for loan losses/Net loans	1.71	1.41	2.13
Nonperforming loans/Net loans	1.54	2.29	3.88
Nonperforming loans/Loss reserves	44.60	72.84	123.29
Classified loans/Net loans	0.85	0.89	1.28
Liquidity Risk			
Core deposits/Total assets	56.88%	57.05%	59.21%
Short-term securities – Purchased liabilities/Equity	−121.44	−127.58	−145.06
Market value/Book value of securities	98.95	99.73	100.56
Pledged assets/Securities	55.96	61.52	64.71
Liquid assets/Total assets	2.91	2.63	1.35
Capital/Solvency Risk			
Tier 1 capital ratio	7.51%	7.16%	7.01%
Total capital ratio	8.59	8.30	8.06
Interest Rate Risk			
GAP/Total assets[a]:			
≤ 90 days	−8.57%	−8.96%	−10.11%
91 days–180 days	−2.13	−3.07	−3.85
181 days–1 year	−4.09	−4.64	−5.22
Operational Risk			
Total assets/Number of employees	$ 1,356	$ 1,481	$ 1,309
Salaries and benefits/Number of employees	26,507	29,273	34,538

[a]GAP = Rate-sensitive assets − Rate-sensitive liabilities within each time interval.

Exhibit 5 Peer Bank Averages: Profit Ratios[a]

Return on equity	17.38%
Return on assets	1.01
Equity multiplier	17.21×
Profit margin	9.38
Asset utilization	10.77
Interest expense/Operating income	49.58
Noninterest expense/Operating income	30.65
Provision for loan losses/Operating income	8.53
Income taxes/Operating income	1.86
Interest income/Assets	9.34
Noninterest income/Assets	1.43
Average gross yields on assets:	
Due from banks: interest-bearing	5.96
State and local government obligations (te)[b]	9.54
Other securities	8.03
Gross loans	12.97
Federal funds sold	6.73
Average interest cost of liabilities:	
Interest checking	5.01
Money market accounts	5.78
Small time deposits	7.01
Jumbo CDs	8.56
Federal funds purchased	7.00
Subordinated notes and debentures	9.08
Percentage of noninterest income:	
Fees and service charges	56.03
Trust department revenues	14.52
Securities gains (losses)	2.06
Other income	27.39
Percentage of noninterest expense:	
Salaries and benefits	43.74
Occupancy	20.04
Other operating expense	36.22
Net interest margin	4.59
Earning assets/Total assets	93.30
Burden/Total assets	−1.87
Spread	4.28

[a]Percentages unless otherwise noted.

[b]Tax-equivalent.

Exhibit 6 Peer Bank Averages: Balance Sheet Data

	UBPR Sample Percentage of Total Assets (1990)
Assets	
Cash and due from banks (noninterest-bearing)	8.26%
Due from banks (interest-bearing)	6.31
Securities	28.34
Federal funds sold	2.35
Loans and lease financing	51.27
Less allowance for losses	2.01
Net loans and leases	49.26
Premises and fixed assets	2.06
Other real estate owned	1.82
Other assets	1.78
Total	100.00%
Liabilities	
Total deposits	88.56%
Noninterest-bearing	15.20
Interest-bearing	73.36
Federal funds purchased	3.44
Subordinated notes and debentures	0.10
Other liabilities	2.09
Total liabilities	94.19%
Equity Capital	
Preferred stock	0.01%
Common stock	1.33
Surplus	3.29
Retained earnings	1.18
Total equity capital	5.81%

Exhibit 7 Income Statement Data for Peer Bank

	UBPR Sample Percentage of Total Assets (1990)
Interest and fees on loans	6.65%
Interest on bank balances	0.32
Income on securities	2.21
Interest on federal funds sold	0.16
Total interest income	9.34%
Interest expense on deposits	5.09%
Interest on federal funds purchased	0.24
Interest on subordinated notes and debentures	0.01
Total interest expense	5.34%
Net interest income	4.00
Provision for loan losses	0.91
Net interest income after provisions	3.09%
Service charges on deposits	0.80%
Other noninterest income	0.60
Securities gains (losses)	0.03
Total noninterest income	1.43%
Salaries and employee benefits	1.44%
Premises and fixed assets expense	0.65
Other noninterest expense	1.21
Total noninterest expense	3.30%
Income before taxes	1.22%
Applicable income taxes	0.21
Net income	1.01%

Exhibit 8 Peer Bank Averages: Risk Measures

	Average Ratios for Banks in the State (1990)
Asset Quality	
Loss reserve/Gross loans	3.92%
Net charge-offs/Gross loans	2.00
Provision/Gross loans	1.77
Nonperforming loans/Gross loans	4.12
Loan mix: Percentage of total loans	
Real estate loans	46.22
Commercial and industrial loans	27.83
Loans to individuals	15.09
Market value/Book value of securities	99.81
Investments: Percentage of total securities	
U.S. Treasuries and government agencies	57.92
Municipal securities	20.15
Mortgage-backed securities	17.21
Short-term investments/Total assets	4.72
Cash/Total assets	8.26
Earning assets/Total assets	88.14
Loan growth rate	5.23
Liquidity	
Cash/Total deposits	9.33%
Purchased funds/Earning assets	19.44
Gross loans/Total deposits	57.89
Short-term investments/Total assets	6.90
Market value/Book value of securities	99.05
Pledged assets/Total securities	46.22
Interest Rate Risk	
Yield on earning assets	10.60%
Average cost of funds	6.76
Net interest spread	3.84
Net interest margin	4.54
Rate-sensitive assets/Total assets: 90 days	18.56
Rate-sensitive liabilities/Total assets: 90 days	24.66
GAP/Assets: 90 days	−6.10
Capital Risk/Solvency	
Tier 1 capital	5.19%
Total capital	10.07
Operational Risk	
Assets/Number of employees	$ 1,986
Salaries and benefits/Number of employees	$27,288

CASE 2

Liberty National Bank: Liquidity Planning

On January 10, 1991, Paul Gonzalez was reviewing selected balance sheet data for Liberty National Bank (LNB). As executive vice president in charge of investments and funding, he was responsible for analyzing the bank's securities portfolio and deposit sources to ensure that liquidity needs were met. The bank's normal policy was to establish the budget and target portfolio in September of each year. Gonzalez needed to revise his earlier estimates of LNB's liquidity position, however, because deposit flows and loan demand during the last three months of 1990 had deviated significantly from the plan.

Background Information

Liberty National Bank was the second largest bank in Harlingen, the primary trade center for economic activity throughout the valley. Because of its location only 30 miles from Mexico and 40 miles from South Padre Island, a popular resort area on the Gulf of Mexico, much of the business activity centered around trade with Mexico and tourism. Agriculture also contributed heavily as valley farmers produced a significant portion of the nation's citrus and vegetable crop each year.

The three-pronged economic base generally served to insulate the area from wide cyclical swings in employment and retail sales. In recent years, however, the valley had suffered from the continued depreciation in the peso relative to the dollar and a late season freeze that killed many fruit-bearing trees. Tourism was also off due to farm problems in the Midwest. Traditionally, the valley represented a popular winter haven for the "snowbirds" from Iowa, Minnesota, and Missouri. Snowbirds was the local name for the vacationers who came to the valley in campers or to stay in mobile home parks from November through February to avoid northern winters. During these months, population and retail sales each increased by 10 to 20 percent in Harlingen and the surrounding communities.

Liberty National Bank was a highly capitalized bank with conservative manage-ment. Its loan-to-asset ratio was one of the lowest among its peer banks and it had successfully accumulated a broad base of retail deposits that allowed it to rely less on purchased funds. This enabled it to easily avoid the recent economic problems faced by many of its competitors that had to cut back their operations. LNB had continued its growth and thus was able to increase its market share.

Factors Affecting LNB's Liquidity

Gonzalez felt that LNB's liquidity needs were influenced by the same factors affecting all banks, except that its seasonal trends were more pronounced. LNB had an excellent reputation with local businesses and was able to capture a major portion of the tourist dollar. Most of the snowbirds came back to the valley every year and used LNB to handle their transactions accounts. This produced large deposit inflows in November upon the tourists' arrival and subsequent outflows in February and March when they left. Unfortunately, the peaks and troughs in LNB's loan demand appeared at opposite times. The bank's loans were concentrated in agriculture, both to farmers and agriculture-related businesses, so that loan demand typically peaked in May and bottomed out in December.

Senior management purposefully kept LNB's loan-to-asset ratio low and investment portfolio large to handle the mismatch in deposit inflows and high loan demand. Gonzalez managed the investments and made periodic forecasts that management used to evaluate liquidity. Exhibits 1 and 2 provide summary balance sheet information and the composition of investments for LNB in 1989 and 1990. Exhibit 3 presents yield information related to investments and prevailing interest rates.

Finally, Exhibit 4 represents Gonzalez's best forecast of monthly trend, seasonal, and cyclical components of deposits (excluding CDs) and loans. The seasonal indexes equal the average monthly balance divided by the preceding December figure, for 1987 to 1990. Cyclical deposits and loans are measured as monthly deviations in actual balances for 1990 from the coincident trend plus seasonal component estimate.

It was the cyclical components in 1990 that concerned Gonzalez. Tourism in the winter months had been well below historical norms, making deposit growth considerably below average. At the same time, loan demand had been much higher than normal in March and April, which forced LNB to come up with $3 million to $7 million more in liquid funds than expected.

Exhibit 1 Balance Sheet Data (Thousands of Dollars)

	December 31, 1989	December 31, 1990
Assets		
Cash and due from banks (noninterest bearing)	$ 8,936	$ 9,667
Due from banks (interest bearing)	2,730	5,218
Federal funds sold	4,255	3,002
Loans	54,964	61,097
Investment securities	26,583	26,401
Other assets	7,842	8,351
Total assets	$105,310	$113,736
Liabilities and Equity		
Transaction deposits	$ 29,165	$ 31,411
Nonnegotiable deposits under $100,000	41,921	43,852
Total	$ 71,086	$ 75,263
Certificates of deposit: $100,000 or more	17,491	19,895
Other short-term borrowings	4,270	5,003
Other liabilities	3,031	3,408
Total liabilities	$ 95,878	$103,569
Stockholders' equity	9,432	10,167
Total liabilities and equity	$105,310	$113,736

Exhibit 2 Composition of Investment Securities (Thousands of Dollars)

	December 31, 1989	December 31, 1990
Investment Securities		
U.S. Treasury securities		
Treasury bills	$ 2,798	$ 2,585
Treasury bonds	5,125	5,650
Total	$ 7,923	$ 8,235
U.S. agency & CMO securities	$10,750	$10,600
Municipal securities		
Tax warrants and housing notes	$ 1,000	$ 1,000
In-state bonds	5,465	5,256
Out-of-state bonds	1,445	1,310
Total municipals	$ 7,910	$ 7,566
Total investment securities	$26,583	$26,401
Amount pledged[a]	$ 6,100	$ 4,950
Maturities		
One year or less		
Treasury bills	$ 2,798	$ 2,585
Tax warrants and housing notes	1,000	1,000
Treasury bonds	300	500
Agency bonds	1,000	500
Municipal bonds	560	716
Total	$ 5,658	$ 5,301
One to five years		
Treasury bonds	$ 2,025	$ 2,300
Agency bonds	2,750	2,100
Municipal bonds	2,600	1,950
Total	$ 7,375	$ 6,350
Five to ten years		
Treasury bonds	$ 2,400	$ 2,200
Agency bonds	3,650	3,750
Municipal bonds	2,800	2,700
Total	$ 8,850	$ 8,650
Over ten years		
Treasury bonds	$ 400	$ 650
Agency bonds	3,350	4,250
Municipal bonds	950	1,200
Total	$ 4,700	$ 6,100

[a]Of the pledged securities, 75 percent are long-term municipals and 25 percent are Treasury bonds.

Because it was a relatively small bank and not a regular participant in the national money markets, LNB did not rely heavily on purchased funds to meet liquidity requirements. Last year LBN obtained almost $20 million in large CDs, but borrowed significant amounts in federal funds and security repurchase agreements only during April and May. Gonzalez complained at the time about the 15 to 25 basis point premium LNB had to offer to attract funds. He did not want to subject the bank to that

Exhibit 3 Investment Portfolio Yields and Market Interest Rates

	1989	1990
Investment Portfolio Yields		
Treasury bills	7.93%	6.41%
Treasury bonds	11.08	10.95
Agency & CMO bonds	11.32	11.18
Tax warrants and housing notes (tax-exempt)	5.47	5.16
Municipal bonds (tax-exempt)	8.23	8.52
Market Interest Rates		
Treasury bills	7.48%	5.98%
Treasury bonds (10-year)	10.62	7.68
Agency & CMO bonds (10-year)	10.81	7.85
Tax warrants and housing notes (tax-exempt)	5.41	5.01
Municipal bonds (Moody's Aaa) (tax-exempt)	8.60	6.95
Market Value/Book Value (December 31)		
Treasury bills	102%	103%
Treasury bonds	100	102
Agency & CMO bonds	102	104
Tax warrant and housing notes	100	101
Municipal bonds	101	103

Exhibit 4 Forecast Factors for Trend, Seasonal, and Cyclical Components of Liberty National Bank's Loans and Deposits in 1991

Trend Components

1. Deposits excluding CDs: December-to-December growth trend should equal 7.7 percent (0.62 percent monthly).
2. Loans: December-to-December growth trend should equal 10.0 percent (0.8 percent monthly).

Seasonal and Cyclical Components (Thousands of Dollars)

	Seasonal Deposit Index	Seasonal Loan Index	Cyclical Deposits	Cyclical Loans
January	105	93	$ 836	$ −127
February	103	95	−3,744	−2,066
March	101	100	−1,502	5,206
April	98	103	−185	2,930
May	96	109	361	−755
June	93	107	493	−514
July	95	106	659	239
August	97	103	−206	−348
September	100	101	773	−553
October	101	98	1,182	169
November	104	93	620	20
December	107	92	−1,989	642

again in 1991. As a precaution, however, Gonzalez did arrange federal funds lines at two correspondent banks for $3 million each. He also estimated that LNB could obtain an additional $15 million in CDs without using a broker if it aggressively marketed its deposits and paid a 15 basis point premium.

One source of funds that Gonzalez avoided was discount window credit from the Federal Reserve. He felt that borrowing from the Fed would be interpreted as a sign of weakness and could potentially frighten depositors. Even though the discount rate was cheap relative to money market rates, LNB had not borrowed from the Fed since 1980.

Liquidity Projections for 1991

Gonzalez intended to revise his forecasts because he expected a liquidity crunch in 1991 like that in 1990. He wanted to justify a bigger investment portfolio and acquire more Treasury bills. Tourism was level with last year, but total retail sales were down. If loan demand picked up, LNB would need to sell securities or borrow additional funds to meet the credit requests. Gonzalez believed that interest rates were as low as they would go and that, in all likelihood, they would rise as economic activity increased. This would make it difficult to sell securities and would increase interest expense when profit pressures were strong enough already.

Problems

1. Determine Liberty National Bank's liquidity needs on a monthly basis for 1991. Use Gonzalez's forecast of deposit and loan components and the coincident change in required reserves to estimate a monthly surplus or deficit relative to December 1990 figures. Assume that required reserves equal 12 percent of deposits.

2. Discuss how Gonzalez might restructure the bank's investment portfolio or invest any surplus funds to best position the bank in terms of anticipated funds needs and interest rate movements.

3. Identify potential liability sources of funds and compare the costs and benefits of each.

4. What portfolio alternatives should the bank pursue to improve its long-run liquidity position?

CASE 3

Promenade State Bank: Investments and Funding

Overview

Promenade State Bank (PSB) is a community bank headquartered in Cincinnati, Ohio. From 1985 to 1990, the bank grew 10 percent annually from $400 million in assets to $644 million. Most of the growth reflects a concentrated effort to extend credit to middle-market (less than $10 million in sales) commercial customers. By year-end 1990, loans represented almost 66 percent of assets, up from just 47 percent in 1985. This loan growth came largely at the expense of the securities portfolio. Consumer loans were a stable fraction of total assets, but the investment portfolio fell from over 33 percent of assets in 1985 to under 20 percent by 1990.

Throughout the 1980s, PSB operated under the management of Oscar Swift, who served as president and CEO. Swift's strengths were his openness, engaging personality, and work ethic. His primary weakness was an inability to delegate decision-making authority to associates. As the bank's growth accelerated, Swift found it increasingly difficult to manage the entire bank. He customarily reviewed and approved all loans over $50,000 and made every investment decision. With the removal of ceilings on deposit rates, he also found that he was constantly forced to reprice money market accounts, time deposits, and jumbo CDs for PSB to be competitive. But he had little time to evaluate and understand current market conditions.

Not surprisingly, PSB's profitability suffered during the late 1980s. The bank lost money in 1988 and reported only $1.9 million in net income in 1989. The basic problem was nonperforming loans reflecting deteriorating economic conditions and the loss of asset quality control in the credit process. Despite these problems, however, PSB continued to pay annual stock dividends of $2,240,000.

Management Change

Concerned about PSB's deteriorating financial condition, the bank's board of directors authorized Swift to hire a strong individual to be second in command and thus Swift's eventual replacement. Swift reluctantly hired Susan Brewer early in 1990 as president, keeping the title of CEO for himself. Brewer moved to PSB from a large superregional bank, where she had served as chief financial officer for 10 years. She was particularly attracted to the opportunity to run the show, which was promised to her after a brief transition period of no more than 18 months.

Swift and Brewer clashed from the beginning. Swift resented sharing control and tried to circumvent Brewer by conducting business as usual without advising her. Brewer quickly realized that unless she asserted her authority, she would lose it. By November 1990 the turmoil within PSB was undermining employee morale. The board subsequently persuaded Swift to retire and give Brewer the additional title of CEO, along with full responsibility for the bank.

Critical Decisions

In December 1990, Brewer assembled a small staff to review the bank's recent financial condition, strategic profile, and market image. The following information summarizes the issues and problems that were studied. This information will be distributed to key officers preparatory to a brainstorming session dealing with PSB's strengths, weaknesses, opportunities, and threats for 1991 and beyond.

Credit. Due to earnings pressures, PSB has concentrated on acquiring assets that promise high yields. These same assets entail considerable risk. Loan growth accelerated, particularly in 1989 and in the first 6 months of 1990. In addition to middle-market lending, PSB aggressively entered the real estate business by lending to shopping mall developers. Loan demand is currently strong, with over $30 million in real estate loan requests under consideration. Most of the construction loans are priced at PSB's prime rate plus 3 percent. Longer-term mortgage business is priced at prevailing fixed rates. The bank's regulators, however, have strongly encouraged the bank to reduce its real estate exposure. In fact, problem real estate loans throughout the United States have led to bank failures and to a significant increase in loan losses during the early 1990s.

Funding. Starting in 1989, several large, superregional banks began pricing retail deposits quite aggressively. PSB reacted slowly and thus saw its money market deposits shrink. It countered by offering interest-bearing checking accounts with no monthly maintenance fee or minimum-balance requirement. The bank expected to cover its costs with a $20 charge for each check written with insufficient funds in the account. Because of the large growth in assets during 1990, PSB was forced to pay above-market rates on small time deposits and jumbo CDs. For the first time, PSB was also a large purchaser of federal funds.

Investments. Oscar Swift traditionally made all investment decisions. In order to compensate for the loan losses in 1988–1989, Swift improved coupon income from the investment portfolio by extending maturities. The bulk of the securities portfolio was thus either short-term or had maturities beyond 3 years. Swift also allocated most new taxable investments to mortgage-backed securities, including CMOs. He argued that they were government-guaranteed and thus carried little risk. When available, PSB added to its holdings of bank-qualified municipals (state and local government obligations), which still carried the 80 percent deductibility of bank carrying costs.

Issues

PSB's regulators are concerned that the bank has not accurately measured or monitored its risk profile. In particular, real estate loans now represent a large fraction of new credit extended. Security maturities have lengthened such that the bank might lose if interest rates increase over time. This is particularly troublesome because regulators would like to require that banks mark the securities portfolio to market, especially when bonds are held for sale prior to final maturity. The bank's core funding base is also eroding. PSB increasingly relies on highly rate-sensitive liabilities in lieu of core retail deposits. Finally, in previous years, PSB has sold securities at a gain whenever it needed to supplement reported earnings. Regulators believed that such sales and swaps into new securities hurt rather than helped the bank.

Problems

A. Balance sheet and income statement data are provided for Promenade State Bank (PSB) in Exhibits 1 and 2. Exhibits 3 and 4 list GAP data and maturities of the investment portfolio, respectively. Use this information and the discussion above to answer the questions below.

    1. What are the primary objectives in managing a bank's investment portfolio? How well is PSB's portfolio meeting these objectives?

    2. What are your reactions to (a) shrinking the size of PSB's investment portfolio, (b) the bond maturities chosen, and (c) the shift into mortgage-backed bonds?

    3. What is the impact of the shift in funding sources at PSB?

    4. What considerations exist concerning the relationship between the *nature of funding sources* and the *types of assets* into which the funds are deployed? Are you comfortable with the bank's position?

    5. Assume that you will be called on to make some immediate decisions before having had time to assess the bank's position fully. What would be your decision on the following and why?

        a. The outstanding loan requests mentioned by the credit officer.

        b. Borrowing in the federal funds market and security swaps.

        c. Taking securities gains.

    6. If interest rates should continue to rise, what impact would you expect this to have on PSB?

    7. At year-end 1990, PSB reported owning $39.6 million (book value) in municipal securities. These securities earned an average after-tax yield of 6.5 percent. Tax-exempt interest for 1990 amounted to $2.6 million. Would you recommend buying or selling municipals? (What is the optimal amount of municipals that PSB should own?)

    8. The examiners used the term "marking to market." What were they talking about? Why would this activity be of concern to them and to the bank?

B. Address the issue of whether PSB should sell securities for a gain. Exhibit 5 lists information for three securities that the bank owns as of March 31, 1991. Assume that the bank sells each (viewed separately) and reinvests the proceeds in a comparable-maturity, taxable security paying the rate indicated under reinvestment rate. Calculate the present value of the net benefit or cost to the bank of the incremental cash flow associated with each swap. Discuss the effect each security swap would have on PSB's reported net income. Finally, do the same calculations

**Exhibit 1 Year-End Balance Sheet for Promenade State Bank
(Thousands of Dollars**

	1989	1990
Assets		
Cash and due from banks	$ 56,020	$ 58,050
Federal funds sold	36,490	3,910
Investment securities		
Money market securities	$ 14,080	$ 16,670
Government and agency securities	70,720	21,330
State and local government obligations	44,650	39,620
Mortgage-backed securities	9,590	48,740
Total securities	$139,040	$126,360
Loans (net of reserves)	$327,740	$422,600
Premises and equipment	12,110	16,950
Other assets	15,830	15,360
Total assets	$587,230	$643,230
Liabilities		
Deposits		
Noninterest-bearing checking	$ 61,300	$ 60,550
Interest-bearing checking	164,790	175,360
Savings and time deposits	210,840	231,430
Money market accounts	73,200	62,120
Total deposits	$510,130	$529,460
Federal funds purchased and repos		40,000
Other liabilities	25,650	20,080
Total liabilities	$535,780	$589,540
Stockholders' Equity		
Common stock	$ 8,000	$ 8,000
Surplus	12,000	12,000
Undivided profits	31,450	33,690
Total stockholders' equity	$ 51,450	$ 53,690
Total liabilities and equity	$587,230	$643,230

assuming PSB sells the mortgage-backed security and municipal bond at the same time and with the same reinvestment of proceeds described above.

Exhibit 2 Income Statement for Promenade State Bank (Thousands of Dollars)

	1989	1990
Interest income		
Federal funds sold	$ 2,500	$ 250
Loans	37,590	45,010
Securities	11,370	10,390
Total	$51,460	$55,650
Interest expense		
Deposits	$30,730	$31,510
Federal funds purchased		1,950
Total	$30,730	$33,460
Net interest income	$20,730	$22,190
Provision for loan losses	9,600	6,730
Net interest income after provisions	$11,130	$15,460
Noninterest income	$ 7,040	$ 7,500
Noninterest expense	$16,270	$16,760
Net income before taxes	$ 1,900	$ 6,200
Applicable taxes	—	1,240
Net income	$ 1,900	$ 4,960

Exhibit 3 GAP Analysis for Promenade State Bank, March 31, 1991 (Thousands of Dollars)

	0–30 Days	31–90 Days	90 Days–1 Year
Rate-Sensitive Assets			
Investments	$ 4,300	$12,650	$17,800
Loans			
Maturities/Amortized payments	$ 7,660	$18,480	$56,190
Floating rate	62,700	—	—
Total loans	$70,360	$18,480	$56,190
Federal funds sold	3,910	—	—
Total	$74,270	$31,130	$73,990
Liabilities			
Deposits			
Money market accounts	$ 62,120	—	—
CDs over $100,000	42,400	$24,810	$20,200
Time deposits under $100,000	12,990	13,060	29,240
Floating rate	6,050	—	—
Total	$127,560	$37,870	$49,440
Federal funds purchased	$ 40,000	—	—
Total	$167,560	$37,870	$49,440
GAP	($93,290)	($19,390)	$24,550
Ratio: $\frac{\text{Rate-sensitive assets}}{\text{Rate-sensitive liabilities}}$	44.3%	82.2%	149.7%
GAP/Total assets[a]	(14.5%)	(3.0%)	3.8%

[a]Total assets are $644 million on March 31, 1991.

Exhibit 4 Investment Portfolio for Promenade State Bank, March 31, 1991
      (Thousands of Dollars)

Maturity[a]	MMIs[b]	Government and Agency Securities	MBS[b]	STLs[b]	Total
0–3 mos.	$ 3,200	$ 5,000		$ 6,500	$ 14,700
3–6 mos.	10,470	2,330		2,120	14,920
6–12 mos.	3,000	3,000		2,000	8,000
1–2 yrs.		2,500	$ 1,500	1,000	5,000
2–3 yrs.			14,000	2,000	16,000
3–5 yrs.		2,500	20,740	11,000	34,240
5–10 yrs.		4,000	11,500	5,000	20,500
Over 10 yrs.		2,000		10,000	12,000
Book Value	$16,670	$21,330	$48,740	$39,620	$126,360
Market Value	$17,118	$20,875	$47,020	$41,110	$123,423
Gain (loss)	$448	($455)	($1,720)	$1,490	($2,937)

[a]Final maturity except for mortgage-backed securities in which time designates the estimated payout term with forecast prepayments at 6% constant prepayment rate.

[b]MMI: money market investments; MBS: mortgage-backed securities; STLs: state and local government obligations.

Exhibit 5 Securities Considered for a Swap

	Par Value	Annual Coupon Rate[a]	Market Value[b]	Maturity	Reinvestment Rate
A. Treasury bond	$5,000,000	9.0%	$5,209,875	7 yrs.	8.4%
B. Mortgage-backed security	6,000,000	7.4	5,936,892	3 yrs.	7.8
C. Municipal bond	6,000,000	7.0	6,252,594	5 yrs.	7.6

[a]Coupon payments are semiannual on September 30 and March 31.

[b]Current market rates are: Treasury bond: 8.2%; Mortgage-backed security 7.8%; and municipal bond 6.6%.

[c]The reinvestment rate represents the annual coupon rate on a par taxable bond of maturity comparable to the swapped bond for the alternative reinvestment vehicle.

CASE 4

Classic Touch Inc.: Short-Term Commercial Lending

Classic Touch Inc. is a relatively small but nationally known manufacturer of women's sportswear. Its primary product is a line of swimwear that is featured annually in a major sports magazine. Other products include knit shirts, sports slacks, and sweat-shirts. The firm employs 130 people, including a young designer who develops all products sold exclusively under the Classic Touch label.

Early in September 1989, Elisa Barringer, founder and president of Classic Touch, approached your bank with a loan request for $300,000 to purchase a new type of fabric. The firm's designer had created a lightweight jogging suit that Barringer felt represented a major innovation in casual sportswear. The line was shown recently at a trade show, where the volume of advance orders indicated that the jogging suit would be extremely well received and thus highly profitable. It would be marketed year-round because it would be popular as casual wear.

Barringer came to you because she felt that her current bank was too small to handle the potential business that Classic Touch could generate. She was also disappointed because her bank had just assigned a new loan officer, the fourth one in three years, to handle the account. Classic Touch currently needs $300,000 to purchase a year's supply of fabrics for production of the jogging suit. If the line sells as well as Barringer anticipates, the firm will need additional financing on short notice to continue production. The request represents a major coup. You have called on Barringer six times during the past two years; this is the first business that Classic Touch has presented. In all likelihood, the bank can sell Classic Touch additional services once the working capital financing is in place.

Management

Barringer is an arts department graduate of Northwestern University. After college, she worked for a major retailer as a buyer while she developed her own clothing designs. At the age of 27, she left the retailer and founded Classic Touch with the financial backing of her parents. Performance was sluggish until 5 years ago, when she hired a young designer whose work she had admired as a buyer. The designer was immediately successful with a line of swimwear that featured bright colors and a light but sturdy fabric. Classic Touch was profitable, and sales increased during each of the last 5 years.

Barringer employs a small management team, including a financial vice president, a marketing vice president and two production supervisors. A fifth member handles distribution throughout the United States. Except for one production supervisor, all officers are under the age of 40. The designer is under a contract that grants Classic Touch exclusive rights to market her designs.

Financial Information

Classic Touch's production process and sales are highly seasonal. Customarily, Barringer authorizes large material purchases for October and November and again in March and April. Approximately two-thirds of total sales occur from March through July, which can be attributed to the swimwear's popularity. Sales in November and December are also substantially above those in other months. One benefit of the jogging suit line is that it will level off the firm's seasonal sales cycle. Exhibit 1 indicates the pattern of monthly sales and material purchases for the last fiscal year. A receivables aging schedule for February and August (Exhibit 2) indicates recent collection activity.

Barringer has provided you with 3 years of unaudited balance sheet and income statement data (Exhibits 3 and 4). According to Barringer, net income dropped by almost two-thirds in 1989 because production problems delayed shipment of fall

Exhibit 1 Classic Touch: Monthly Pattern of Sales and Purchases, Fiscal Year

Month	Sales	Purchases
September 1988	$ 157,000	$ 78,000
October	294,000	255,000
November	418,000	338,000
December	494,000	317,000
January	285,000	196,000
February	220,000	148,000
March	562,000	501,000
April	891,000	529,000
May	1,013,000	404,000
June	911,000	369,000
July	605,000	136,000
August 1989	223,000	97,000
Total	$6,073,000	$3,368,000

merchandise. Fortunately, summer sales of swimwear were the best in the firm's history.

During 1989 Classic Touch sold its plant and land and negotiated a 20-year lease with the buyer, with quarterly payments of $36,000 each March, June, September, and December. It used the proceeds to pay down the outstanding mortgage on the building and help finance its working capital needs. Barringer noted that Classic Touch had a

Exhibit 2 Accounts Receivable Aging Summary

Customer	Current	1–30 Days	31–60 Days	61–90 Days	Over 90 Days
February 1989					
Bozeman Department Stores	$ 63				
Crown Distributors	48	$ 33			
Marilyn's Inc.	72				
Olathe Distributors	57				
Prime Department Stores	53	40	$ 42		
Solo Distribution	36	25	28		
Miscellaneous department stores	120	41	56	$ 70	$18
Total ($802)	$449	$139	$126	$ 70	$18
August 1989					
Bozeman Department Stores	$ 68				
Crown Distributors	45	$ 47			
Marilyn's Inc.	49				
Olathe Distributors	56				
Prime Department Stores	42	51	$ 46		
Solo Distribution	39	14	23	$ 38	$36
Miscellaneous department stores	114	36	62	64	19
Total ($849)	$413	$148	$131	$102	$55

Exhibit 3 Classic Touch: Income Statement: Fiscal Year Ending August 31
Thousands of Dollars

Item	1987	1988	1989
Net sales	$6,128	$6,814	$6,073
Cost of goods sold[a]	3,316	3,667	3,398
Margin	$2,812	$3,147	$2,675
General and administrative expenses	$ 849	$ 927	$ 889
Delivery and selling expenses	1,462	1,603	1,492
Depreciation	129	124	70
Operating expenses	$2,440	$2,654	$2,451
Operating income	$ 372	$ 493	$ 224
Interest expense	79	62	87
Other expense[b]	15	13	(18)
Income before taxes	$ 278	$ 418	$ 155
Applicable income taxes	95	146	58
Net income[c]	$ 183	$ 272	$ 97

[a]Includes labor costs.

[b]In 1989 Classic Touch sold and leased back its building and land. It reported a profit of $32,000 after taxes and agreed to make a fixed lease payment of $144,000 for 20 years for use of the property.

$200,000 credit line with its current bank and had borrowed the full $200,000 at one point in 1989. It had not reduced its borrowings to zero since September, 1987, however, even though the loan required an annual clean-up period.

Credit History. Credit checks with Classic Touch's suppliers showed that the firm generally paid its bills promptly. Still, the company's payments were occasionally slow beyond 30 days in 1989, and the firm never took available discounts of 2/10 net 30. Interest and principal payments on all long-term debt were promptly paid. You have not yet contacted the loan officer at Classic Touch's current bank for a review of the credit relationship.

Projected Operating Activity. Barringer believes that a $300,000 working capital loan will enable Classic Touch to offer its new products and phase out slower-selling lines of sportswear. If sales are as strong as expected, the firm should be able to repay the loan within 6 months. Sales for fiscal year 1990 are projected to increase by 8 percent over the previous year and to rise by an additional 15 percent in 1991. All sales are on credit. While buyers often ride the company in delaying payments, Classic Touch generates cash from sales, on average, according to the following schedule: current month's sales, 25 percent; 1 to 30 days, 50 percent; 31 to 60 days, 15 percent; 61 to 90 days, 6 percent; and over 90 days, 2 percent. Of raw materials purchased, 20 percent are for cash and 80 percent are on credit. Classic Touch typically pays down its outstanding payables during the following month. Operating expenses arise evenly

Exhibit 4 Classic Touch: Balance Sheet, Fiscal Year Ending August 31 (Thousands of Dollars)

	1987	1988	1989
Assets			
Cash	$ 51	$ 68	$ 36
Accounts receivable	$ 654	$ 790	$ 849
Inventory			
Raw materials	$ 289	$ 325	$ 364
Goods in process	170	202	150
Finished goods	313	366	269
Total inventory	$ 772	$ 893	$ 783
Prepaid expenses	$ 73	$ 88	$ 65
Current assets	$1,550	$1,839	$1,733
Building and land	$1,078	$1,078	—
Equipment	319	336	412
Leasehold improvements	—	—	18
Less: Accumulated depreciation	342	357	104
Net fixed assets	$1,055	$1,057	$ 326
Other assets	$ 27	$ 31	$ 97
Total assets	$2,632	$2,927	$2,156
Liabilities and Equity			
Accounts payable	$ 496	$ 594	$ 543
Accruals	60	89	77
Notes payable (bank)	52	101	174
CMLTD	120	120	18
Income tax payable	53	105	44
Current liabilities	$ 781	$1,009	$ 856
Long-term debt	$ 769	$ 649	$ 19
Total liabilities	$1,550	$1,658	$ 875
Common stock	$ 200	$ 200	$ 200
Capital surplus	254	254	254
Retained earnings	628	815	827
Total equity	$1,082	$1,269	$1,281
Total liabilities and equity	$2,632	$2,927	$2,156

during the year except for advertising, which is directed solely at distributors during the months of September, October, April, and May. During 1990 Barringer expects to spend $250,000 on advertising, of which $220,000 will be spent evenly during the four months noted. Interest payments on bank loans and other debts will be made at the end of March, June, September, and December. The relevant income tax rate is 35 percent. Other items will equal industry norms.

Problems

1. Spread Classic Touch's financial statements and generate a statement of changes reconciled to cash for fiscal years 1988 and 1989. Interpret the key figures by comparing them with industry norms.

2. Calculate the firm's working capital loan needs determined by the cash-to-cash cycle comparison of current assets and current liabilities.

3. Prepare a detailed monthly cash budget for 1990. Make appropriate assumptions where necessary.

4. Determine the maximum loan need for Classic Touch in 1990. What risk does the bank face if it extends this loan? How and when will the bank be repaid?

5. Provide a list of questions that a loan officer should obtain answers to before extending credit. Would you make the loan? If so, under what terms?

CASE 5

HiFi Sounds: Term Commercial Lending

Southwest National Bank in Houston, Texas, has been approached to fund a $2.5 million term loan and provide $2 million in working capital financing for HiFi Sounds. Vivian Belmont, vice president for commercial lending, has received from Jim Howard, president of HiFi Sounds, the letter and enclosures shown in Exhibits 1, 3, 4, and 5. She has asked you to conduct an analysis of HiFi Sounds' financial condition and to examine other key issues relating to the firm, the electronics industry, and the loan request.

HiFi Sounds is a manufacturer and wholesale distributor of stereo equipment and VCRs. Its manufacturing facilities are located in South Korea, where costs of labor and materials are low. Finished equipment is sold under various brand names throughout the world, with 85 percent of sales occurring in the United States.

The manufacture and distribution of stereo equipment is an extremely competitive business. HiFi Sounds currently has the second-best-selling midprice unit in the United States, for which sales represent 30 percent of its business. Other equipment is priced at the low end of the market and is generally sold through warehouses and discount stores. In recent years, the industry has undergone extensive consolidation, and as a result pricing is expected to stabilize within a few years. As noted in the *U.S. Industrial Outlook* report in Exhibit 2, changes in technology have been substantial and may sharply alter the competitive environment.

Jim Howard is interested in expanding the company's warehouse facilities within the Houston area, and he projects a $7 million building program over the next six years. The working capital financing thus represents an expected permanent increase in HiFi's inventory and receivables.

HiFi was founded in 1981 by Jim Howard. He had previously worked for another stereo manufacturer as production manager. Howard started the firm with his life savings and stock sold to friends and associates. The firm experienced losses during the first two years of operations and then small but continuous profits through 1986. During 1987, HiFi manufactured and marketed a compact disc system that quickly became outdated. Two competitors offered superior units at a comparable price, with the result that HiFi's sales were much less than expected and inventory accumulated. The firm's basic stereo system also suffered its lowest sales totals ever, causing HiFi to lose $1.7 million. The firm returned to profitability in 1988.

You are expected to prepare a report on HiFi Sounds and its loan request. Following is a list of points that must be addressed. Focus on the pro forma analysis. Use whatever assumptions are relevant in a "most likely" environment. Specify each assumption and its impact.

Problems

Following is a list of specific tasks relating to the HiFi Sounds loan that you should address. Incorporate all of your findings in a report to be submitted to the commercial lending department of Southwest National Bank.

1. Spread HiFi Sounds' financial statements; i.e., compute common-size balance sheets and income statements and key performance ratios.

2. Generate a statement of changes reconciled to cash for each year.

3. Interpret the key financial ratios and draw inferences from the statement of changes regarding the firm's operating strengths and weaknesses.

4. Project HiFi Sounds' balance sheet, income statement, and cash flow annually for 1990–1992. Do this by making assumptions about sales, inventory turnover, and other key variables. Be sure you outline your assumptions and obey the primary rule: Keep it simple.

5. Realistically determine the primary source(s) of repayment. Using the 1990–1992 balance sheets, determine the probable changes in working capital needs.

6. Review the receivables aging schedule. What would be acceptable collateral for the bank? What receivables would you exclude? How would you margin the acceptable receivables?

7. Determine the projected value of inventory as collateral.

8. What further questions would you have regarding the credit before arriving at an accept/reject decision?

9. Exactly how will the loan proceeds be used?

10. What is your recommendation on granting the loan? How would you structure the loan if it were granted?

11. Provide a list of questions that you would ask key personnel at HiFi Sounds. Be as specific as possible.

Exhibit 1 Request for Term Loan from Southwest National Bank

HiFi Sounds
283 Melody Lane
Houston, Texas 77001

February 6, 1990

Ms. Vivian Belmont
Vice President
Southwest National Bank

Dear Ms. Belmont,

The purpose of this letter is to request a $2.5 million term loan to support our warehouse expansion and a $2 million revolving credit agreement secured by the firm's accounts receivable and inventory. The funds will be used as working capital to finance our expansion. We intend to repay the loan on a quarterly basis as the receivables are collected over the next three years.

As you know, the firm is a wholesale distributor and manufacturer of stereo equipment. We design our own stereo equipment, build most of it in the Orient, then sell our own brand and private labels to retail distributors throughout the United States and Canada.

We have been able to expand rapidly because we offer favorable credit terms to the retail distributors. We recently began offering credit terms to dealers. These dealers have 30 days to pay for their purchase. This has allowed us to grow substantially over the last year, as we have added many new dealers to handle our lines. Currently we have 1,241 retail distributors, up from 158 when we began operations. Our goal is to reach 1,500 by year end.

Since we began operation in Houston, we have maintained our payroll account at Southwest National Bank, but we have never borrowed money from your institution. Now we are consolidating our banking relationships, which is why we are giving you the opportunity to grow with us.

For your information, I have enclosed audited financial statements for the last three years, and a summary of our aging of accounts receivable schedule.

I would like to meet with you on February 21, 1990, to discuss the loan. Please let me know what time will be convenient for you.

I look forward to hearing from you.

Sincerely,

Jim Howard
President

JH/mi
Enclosures

Exhibit 2 U.S. Industry Outlook for VCRs and Stereo Equipment

VCR Market

The VCR market's first downturn ever, which occurred in 1987, brought to an end the explosive growth in sales of those products between 1982 and 1986. Figures for 1989 indicate a continuation of the downward trend in sales, at about 11.2 million units for the year. Several serious problems face VCR producers, none of whom are U.S. companies. Attempts to bring assembly of these machines to the United States, widely heralded in 1987, proved to be impractical, and efforts to do so were largely discontinued in 1988. Never having produced significant numbers of consumer VCRs, American companies are unable to supply most of the internal workings necessary to manufacture such items efficiently in the United States. Japan remains the largest global source of VCRs, yet the skyrocketing value of the yen beginning in 1985, in the face of falling retail prices in the U.S. market, has had a severe effect on producers. South Korean companies, the only important non-Japanese sources of these products, have increased their share of the world market to nearly 10 percent, though the rising cost of components imported from Japan has forced them to restrict production. A survey by the Roper Corporation estimated that 57 percent of American households had VCRs in 1988, and penetration was even higher among those homes with two incomes and those with incomes higher than $35,000 a year. Figures suggest that the saturation point for VCRs is close to being reached, and sales trends are beginning to mirror those of television sets, wherein upgrading and extra units are driving the market. Among the several video recording formats available, VHS achieved its final victory over Beta in 1988, as Sony, the longtime promoter of the latter format, finally introduced its first VHS machines. As video recording advances technologically, super-VHS (S-VHS) will thus likely predominate over extended-definition Beta (ED-BETA).

The introduction of one-piece camera-recorder combinations, or camcorders, during the mid 1980s has taken up some of the slack in VCR sales. In fact, when camcorders and VCRs are taken together, as they are in some industry statistics, total sales, in both units and dollar value, are still breaking records. In 1989 about 3 million camcorders were sold, up 30 percent from 1988. While the saturation point for the camcorder will probably be reached at a lower level than that of the VCR, there is still substantial room for growth in the coming years. Camcorders, in fact, may breathe new life into VCR sales, because with the camcorder consumers can record events such as birthdays, weddings, vacations, and the like. Use of the VCR to view materials recorded off the air decreased substantially during 1989 and 1988, as the novelty of time shifting began to wear off. When retail prices for camcorders come within the means of middle-income consumers, sales are certain to rise even further.

Audio Market

The audio market was characterized more by lack of movement than by innovation and change in 1989. AM stereo receivers still continue to struggle to live, since the market has not yet yielded victory to any one broadcasting format. The Commerce Department's recommendation in 1988 that the C-Quam format be favored in any decision of the Federal Communications Commission has not led to a significant change in the stagnant AM stereo situation.

Exhibit 2 *(Continued)*

Digital audio tape recorders (DATs) faced much the same sluggishness in 1988 and 1989, because Congress failed to enact any prohibitive legislation and Japanese producers continued their self-imposed export ban. Available only in limited areas of the country, DAT recorders, with the ability to make virtually exact copies, generation after generation, of audio material, have given rise to two opposing factions: the Recording Industry Association of America (RIAA), which opposed their unrestricted introduction into the country, and the Home Recording Rights Coalition (HRRC), which is promoting the unregulated sale of DATs. With the retail price of a DAT recorder at around $2,000, well out of the range of casual consumers, DAT sales in the United States are not predicted to rise in 1989, especially without a clear signal from producers and marketers that conflicts over possible copyright infringements have been resolved.

Sales of CD (compact disc) players increased spectacularly during 1988–1989, up more than 60 percent from the previous year, with an increasing number of CD recordings available at moderating prices, along with lower retail prices for the players. Sales of traditional long-playing phonographs are down, and CD players are gaining wider use in portable and automotive applications.

The Tandy Corporation announced in 1988 that it had developed a recordable, erasable compact disc with possible applications in both computers and audio equipment. Although no audio CD recorder-player is yet available, it is likely that such a medium would encounter the same proponents and foes as has DAT. While the race to produce a viable prototype is under way, analysts are interested to see whether this technology, pioneered in the United States, will find its way to manufacture and sale by foreign companies rather than domestic.

Legislative Initiatives

Legislation considered by Congress in 1987 to prohibit the sale and manufacture of DAT cassettes and recorders not containing a copycode chip to prevent unauthorized recording was not enacted by 1989, largely because a report released by the National Bureau of Standards that year claimed that the chip would damage the sound quality even of legitimately obtained audio material. It is likely that the hardware and software industries will somehow work out their differences in 1990 without the intervention of legislation.

Outlook for 1990

Demand for all consumer electronic products will continue to rise in 1990, but the domestic industry will show only sluggish growth. Much of that movement will be influenced by the decision of foreign-owned companies whether to manufacture at their plants here, in Mexico, or in Asia. The constant dollar value of U.S. product shipments is expected to rise about 8 percent in 1990, although retail prices that producers are able to command in the market will continue to be depressed. Sales will grow faster in volume than in value, and industry projects show an increase in value of less than 5 percent. Technological improvements in consumer electronic products will continue to fuel consumers' expenditures, although manufacturers' attempts to raise retail prices may have a negative effect on demand. Imports and exports alike will grow in 1990. Japanese-owned brands will

Exhibit 2 *(Continued)*

continue to dominate sales, but a growing number of products will bear labels of origin from Taiwan, Mexico, Hong Kong, and the United States. Maquiladora plants will increase demand for exports to Mexico, more of which will in turn be shipped back to the United States than in 1989.

Long-Term Prospects

Shipments of consumer electronics are expected to decline at an estimated annual rate of 0.2 percent from 1990 to 1993. For U.S. companies in this field, the outlook is not promising, except in niche areas such as large-screen television sets and high-quality loudspeakers. Import, export, and domestic production decisions in the consumer electronics field will be made more and more by foreign owned companies during the next 5 years, unless new forces enter the market in such areas of advanced technology as high-definition television and recordable compact discs. Yet prospects are dim that any such advances will be transformed into domestically designed and produced goods, since the United States is no longer a supplier of many components vital to the production of electronics items. Research and development may also be constrained now that the largest forces in the market are controlled by interests outside the United States. In a market dominated by imports, investors and manufacturers alike are wary of attempting to operate. Capital flight from this industry during the 1980s has been mirrored in loss of engineering and skilled manufacturing jobs, which has in turn then limited the ability of companies to innovate and compete to succeed.

Source: *U.S. Industrial Outlook—Household Consumer Durables.*

Exhibit 3 HiFi Sounds: Year-End Balance Sheet (Thousands of Dollars)

	1987	Percent of Total	1988	Percent of Total	1989	Percent of Total
Assets						
Cash	$ 680	11.6%	$ 411	4.1%	$ 794	3.3%
Marketable securities	0	0.0	0	0.0	0	0.0
Accounts receivable	550	9.4	1,479	14.7	5,776	24.3
Inventory	1,262	21.5	2,629	26.2	6,073	25.6
Prepaid expenses	180	3.1	114	1.1	415	1.7
Other current assets	0	0.0	0	0.0	173	0.7
Current assets	$2,672	45.6	$ 4,633	46.1	$13,231	55.7
Gross fixed assets	$3,185	54.3	$ 5,886	58.6	$11,162	47.0
Less accumulated depreciation	0	0.0	651	6.5	992	4.2
Net fixed assets	$3,185	54.3	$ 5,235	52.1	$10,170	42.8
Long-term investments	$ 0	0.0	$ 0	0.0	$ 0	0.0
Intangible assets	0	0.0	0	0.0	0	0.0
Other noncurrent assets	6	0.1	177	1.8	336	1.4
Total assets	$5,863	100.0%	$10,045	100.0%	$23,737	100.0%
Liabilities and Equity						
Notes payable—bank	$ 782	13.3	$ 901	9.0	$ 2,114	8.9
Accounts payable	3,078	52.5	3,555	35.4	7,688	32.4
Accruals	438	7.5	1,173	11.7	1,959	8.3
Income tax payable	0	0.0	0	0.0	87	0.4
Current maturity—term notes	0	0.0	0	0.0	0	0.0
Current maturity—long-term debt	479	8.2	525	5.2	474	2.0
Other current liabilities	0	0.0	0	0.0	0	0.0
Current liabilities	$4,777	81.5	$ 6,154	61.3	$12,322	51.9
Deferred tax liability	$ 0	0.0	$ 0	0.0	$ 173	0.7
Term notes	0	0.0	0	0.0	0	0.0
Long-term debt	219	3.7	2,679	26.7	3,015	12.7
Other noncurrent liabilities	475	8.1	250	2.5	224	0.9
Total liabilities	$5,471	93.3	$ 9,083	90.4	$15,734	66.3
Common stock—par	$ 75	1.3	$ 75	0.7	$ 93	0.4
Paid-in surplus	3,348	57.1	3,349	33.3	6,985	29.4
Retained earnings	(3,031)	−51.7	(2,462)	−24.5	925	3.9
Stockholders' equity	392	6.7	962	9.6	8,003	33.7
Total liabilities and equity	$5,863	100.0%	$10,045	100.0%	$23,737	100.0%

Exhibit 4 HiFi Sounds: Annual Income Statement (Thousands of Dollars)

	1987	Percent of Total	1988	Percent of Total	1989	Percent of Total
Net sales	$12,950	100.0%	$22,367	100.0%	$54,120	100.0%
Cost of goods sold	11,190	86.4	14,581	65.2	38,101	70.4
Gross profit	$ 1,760	13.6	$ 7,786	34.8	$16,019	29.6
Selling expenses	$ 2,117	16.3	$ 3,818	17.1	$ 7,732	14.3
General and administrative expenses	822	6.3	1,512	6.8	2,944	5.4
Depreciation and amortization	0	0.0	672	3.0	1,004	1.9
Other operating expenses	724	5.6	1,192	5.3	1,351	2.5
Total operating expenses	$ 3,663	28.3	$ 7,194	32.2	$13,031	24.1
Operating profit	($ 1,903)	−14.7	$ 592	2.6	$ 2,988	5.5
Interest on marketable securities	$ 0	0.0%	$ 0	0.0	$ 0	0.0
Other income (including LT investments)	314	2.7	232	1.0	2,224	4.1
Interest expense—term notes	0	0.0	0	0.0	0	0.0
Interest expense—notes payable	114	0.9	151	0.7	239	0.4
Interest expense—long-term debt	41	0.3	44	0.2	41	0.1
Other noninterest expense	0	0.0	0	0.0	0	0.0
Profit before taxes	($1,714)	−13.2	$629	2.8	$4,932	9.1
Income taxes	0	0.0	$ 60	0.3	$1,545	2.9
Net profit	($1,714)	−13.2	$569	2.5	$3,387	6.3
Dividends	0	0.0	0	0.0	0	0.0
Retained earnings	($1,714)	−13.2	$569	2.5	$3,387	6.3

Exhibit 5 Summary of Aging of HiFi Sounds' Accounts Receivables for 1989 (Month-end Percentage of Outstanding Receivables)

	Days Outstanding			
Month	≤30	31–60	61–90	>90
January	15%	57%	23%	5%
February	58	11	20	11
March	61	19	14	6
April	63	22	10	5
May	64	27	8	1
June	75	20	3	2
July	63	25	10	2
August	48	33	16	3
September	50	28	13	9
October	55	21	14	10
November	70	13	10	7
December	74	18	5	3

CASE 6

Glass Works Inc.: Term Commercial Lending

Overview

Walter Busby, senior vice president in charge of corporate lending for American National Bank (ANB), was ecstatic. It was February 1990, and it appeared that he had a chance to capture a major corporate client from several competing banks. Carmilla Lopez, chief financial officer for Glass Works Inc., has just brought him a loan request for a major capital expenditure program. Busby has been calling on Lopez and Glass Works' other officers since 1986 and this was the first significant borrowing request from the firm, over three years after his initial contact. While he did not feel comfortable with all aspects of the loan request, Busby knew that Glass Works had an excellent reputation for financial stability and professional management.

Background of the Company

Glass Works Inc. is a major producer of glass and plastic containers. It was founded in 1912 and by 1960 was the largest glass producer in the United States. The company sells on and receives terms of 2/10, net 30 days. Sales are made to food, beverage, and pharmaceutical companies. Among its major customers are Nabisco, Pepsico, and Eli Lilly. Sales are cyclical, reaching peaks during the fall canning season and the summer bottling period. Firms in this segment of the manufacturing industry are currently consolidating. Glass Works' major competitors are Maxim Glass and Glass Industries, respectively ranked first and second in U.S. sales in 1989; both companies grew by acquiring smaller firms during the past 5 years. In 1989 Glass Works acquired Frothy Bottlers Inc., a soft-drink bottle manufacturer.

Carmilla Lopez has provided detailed financial statements for the past 3 years. Balance sheet data appear in Exhibit 1 and income statement data appear in Exhibit 2. Key figures and financial ratios for Glass Works and its two major competitors appear in Exhibit 3.

Proposed Loan

Carmilla Lopez specifically requested a $30 million revolving credit facility for 3 years for the purpose of expanding Glass Works' manufacturing facilities. Of the total, $20 million will be needed during the first 2 years and the remaining $10 million at the start of the third year. Expenditures would be for construction of the physical plant and remodeling of existing facilities to handle a new production process. The need for these outlays arose from a new technological breakthrough. At the end of the 3-year period, Lopez requested that the outstanding balances be converted to a 3-year term loan repayable in equal annual installments. Thus the total loan commitment would be for 6 years.

Because of Glass Works' financial strength and stability, Lopez asked that the loan be unsecured and that the interest rate be set at ANB's prime rate throughout the 6 years. Due to the size of the loan and ANB's diversification strategy, Busby and Lopez agreed that ANB might put together a consortium of banks to fund the loan with ANB as agent.

Bank Relationships

Glass Works maintained deposit relationships at three banks, of which ANB held the lowest balances. ANB was, however, the biggest bank, which was why Lopez approached Busby. In prior years, Glass Works had borrowed up to $1.2 million annually for working capital from one of the other banks under a $5 million credit line. The $30 million loan request thus represented a significant increase in its traditional bank borrowing. In addition to its deposit relationships, Glass Works used ANB as transfer agent for its common stock, which is traded over the counter.

ANB has another link through Franklin Edmond, who serves on the board of directors of Glass Works. Until 2 years ago, Edmond was an executive vice president in charge of the bank's Treasury function.

General Issues

You are now confronted with the decision whether to grant Glass Works' loan request. If you make the loan, you must determine the specific terms. If you deny the request, you must assess why. In either case, you will be expected to justify your conclusion to ANB's loan review committee. Some of the more substantive issues involved are:

1. What do you need to know about the new technology necessitating the capital expenditures?
2. What would you do if your bank's legal lending limit were $10 million?
3. When you are making your basic credit decision about whether to go forward and at what rate, what consideration should you give to:
   a. The potential for large deposit balances from Glass Works?
   b. Franklin Edmond's relationship with Glass Works?
4. Would your answers to Question 3 be different if Edmond were the current senior lending officer of your bank?
5. Is a revolving-credit term loan an appropriate vehicle for this financing? If not, what would you recommend? Why?
6. If a revolving-credit term loan is appropriate, what covenants should be included in a loan document? Would you include requirements relating to working capital, debt-to-worth ratios, capital expenditures, cash dividends, limitations on additional borrowings, guarantees of the debts of other companies, loans or investments in other companies, rental obligations, sale-leasebacks, and encumbrances or liens?

Exhibit 1 Glass Works Inc.: Consolidated Balance Sheet, December 31 (Thousands of Dollars)

	1987	1988	1989
Assets			
Cash	$ 4,950	$ 5,233	$ 6,805
Marketable securities	10,027	10,297	11,284
Accounts receivable	28,261	30,188	39,963
Inventory	34,437	39,438	49,557
Prepaid expenses	563	601	829
Current assets	$ 78.238	$ 85,757	$108,438
Gross fixed assets	$169,004	$175,439	$226,208
Accumulated depreciation	77,655	79,365	100,047
Net fixed assets	$ 91,349	$ 96,074	$126,161
Other assets	10,864	11,527	14,881
Total	$180,451	$193,358	$249,480
Liabilities			
Accounts payable	$10,292	$11,810	$16,061
Accrued expenses	12,664	14,221	17,518
Current maturity—long-term debt	290	315	1,680
Current liabilities	$23,246	$26,346	$35,259
Long-term debt	$ 2,591	$ 2,276	$20,800
Deferred taxes	6,011	6,985	9,095
Other liabilities	10,370	9,239	8,163
Total	$42,218	$41,846	$73,317
Equity			
Preferred stock	—	—	$ 8,394
Common stock	$ 12,640	$ 12,640	15,180
Retained earnings	125,593	138,872	152,589
Total	$138,233	$148,512	$176,163
Liabilities and equity	$180,451	$193,358	$249,480

Problems

Determine whether you would loan Glass Works Inc. the $30 million as requested. If not, would you modify the terms and offer a different loan, or would you reject the loan outright? To address the issues, perform the following tasks:

1. Spread the financial statements. Calculate common size balance sheet and income statement ratios for 1987–1989, and calculate key profitability, liquidity, activity, and leverage ratios. Interpret the ratios by analyzing significant trends and identifying differences with peer ratios.

2. Construct a statement of changes reconciled to cash for 1987–1989 data. Assess Glass Works' financial condition and trends according to key figures.

Exhibit 2 Glass Works Inc.: Income Statement (Thousands of Dollars)

	1987	1988	1989
Net sales	$186,726	$213,712	$311,580
Cost of goods sold	153,975	174,702	262,350
Gross profit	$ 32,751	$ 39,010	$ 49,230
Selling and administrative expense	$ 9,794	$ 10,743	$ 11,339
Depreciation	1,857	2,148	11,182
Other operating expense	3,361	4,179	2,516
Operating profit	$ 17,739	$ 21,940	$ 24,193
Other income	20	29	175
Other expense	—	—	—
Income before interest expense	$ 17,759	$ 21,969	$ 24,368
Interest expense	1,022	958	2,139
Income before taxes	$ 16,737	$ 21,011	$ 22,229
Income taxes	4,766	4,853	5,963
Net income	$ 11,971	$ 16,158	$ 16,266

Exhibit 3 Comparative Industry Figures (Thousands of Dollars)

	Glass Works	Maxim Glass	Glass Industries
Net Sales			
1987	$187,726	$644,700	$419,500
1988	213,712	900,100	503,750
1989	311,580	937,200	529,800
Gross Profit Margin			
1987	17.5%	20.2%	17.5%
1988	18.3	18.6	17.7
1989	15.8	19.5	18.9
Net Profit Margin			
1987	6.4%	5.3%	4.3%
1988	7.6	5.2	4.7
1989	5.2	5.8	4.7
Total Assets			
1987	$180,451	$441,335	$398,702
1988	193,358	562,852	450,213
1989	249,480	603,716	474,680
Return on Equity			
1987	8.7%	11.4%	9.1%
1988	10.9	8.9	9.8
1989	9.2	10.7	10.6

3. Provide forecasts of Glass Works' financial condition for the years 1990–1995, assuming that the capital expenditures are made as Lopez requests. Forecast all balance sheet and income statement items. Estimated loan needs can be obtained from pro forma balance sheets and income statements. As part of your initial forecast, assume that Busby uses the following assumptions:

   a. Annual sales growth: 8 percent.
   b. Capital expenditures: 1990—$12 million, 1991—$8 million, 1992—$10 million.
   c. Depreciation expense/Gross fixed assets: 9 percent.
   d. Debt repayment on the term note: year end 1993—$10 million, 1994—$10 million, 1995—$10 million.
   e. Dividends will increase by 10 percent annually.
   f. Glass Works will make its regular committed payments on existing debt (outstanding at year-end 1989) at the rate of $325,000 annually until retirement.
   g. An additional $3 million in annual capital expenditures will be made for normal replacement of equipment and other fixed assets.
   h. All other balance sheet and income statement items will conform to industry norms for peers.

4. Conduct a worst-case forecast in which Glass Works' performance is at its weakest. Document the assumptions used.

5. Provide a list of questions that you would ask Lopez and other interested parties that might clarify the issues raised.

Glossary

Accelerated depreciation
A method of computing depreciation deductions for income taxes that permits deductions in early years greater than those under straight line depreciation.

Account activity Transactions associated with a deposit account, including home debits, transit checks, deposits, and account maintenance.

Account analysis An analytical procedure for determining whether a customer's deposit account or entire credit-deposit relationship with a bank is profitable. The procedure compares revenues from the account with the cost of providing services.

Account maintenance
The overhead cost associated with collecting information and mailing periodic statements to depositors.

Accrual The accumulation of income earned or expense incurred, regardless of when the underlying cash flow is actually received or paid.

Accrued interest Interest income that is earned but not yet received.

Acid-test ratio A measure of liquidity from reported

balance sheet figures with a targeted minimum value of 1. Calculated as the sum of cash and marketable securities divided by current liabilities.

Activity charge A service charge based on the number of checks written by a depositor.

Add-on rate A method of calculating interest charges by applying the quoted rate to the entire amount advanced to a borrower times the number of financing periods. An 8 percent add-on rate indicates $80 interest per $1,000 for 1 year, $160 for 2 years, and so forth. The effective interest rate is higher than the add-on rate because the borrower makes installment payments and cannot use the entire loan proceeds for the full maturity.

Adjustable rate mortgage A mortgage with an interest rate that can be adjusted with changes in a base rate or reference index. The index generally varies with market interest rates.

Affiliate Any organization owned or controlled by a bank or bank holding company, the stockholders, or executive officers.

Agency A trust account in which title to property remains in the owner's name.

Agency securities Fixed-income securities issued by agencies owned or sponsored by the federal government. The most common securities are issued by the Federal Home Loan Bank, Federal National Mortgage Association, Government National Mortgage Association, and Farm Credit System.

Aging accounts receivable A procedure for analyzing a firm's accounts receivable by dividing them into groups according to whether they are current or 30, 60, or over 90 days past due.

Amortize To reduce a debt gradually by making equal periodic payments that cover interest and principal owed.

Anticipated income theory A theory that the timing of loan payments should be tied to the timing of a borrower's expected income.

Appreciation An increase in the market value of an asset.

Arbitrage The simultaneous trading (purchase

and sale) of assets to take advantage of price differentials.

ARM Adjustable rate mortgage—a mortgage in which the contractual interest rate is tied to some index of interest rates and changes when supply and demand conditions change the underlying index.

Ask price The price at which an asset is offered for sale.

Asset-liability management The management of a bank's entire balance sheet to achieve desired risk-return objectives and to maximize the market value of stockholders' equity.

Asset utilization Ratio of total operating income to total assets; a measure of the gross yield earned on assets.

Assignment The transfer of the legal right or interest on an asset to another party.

Automated teller machine A machine that serves as a computer terminal and allows a customer to access account balances and information at a bank.

Bed debts Loans that are due but are uncollectable.

Balance sheet A financial statement that indicates the type and amount of assets, liabilities, and net worth of a firm or individual at a point in time.

Balloon loan A loan that requires small payments that are insufficient to pay off the entire loan so that a large final payment is necessary at termination.

Bank acceptance A draft drawn on a bank and accepted, wich makes it a negotiable instrument.

Bank holding company Any firm that owns or controls at least one commercial bank.

Bankers bank A firm that provides correspondent banking services to commercial banks and not to commercial or retail deposit and loan customers.

Bankrupt The situation in which a borrower is unable to pay obligated debts.

Base rate An interest rate used as an index to price loans; typically associated with a bank's weighted marginal cost of funds.

Basis With financial futures contracts, the futures rate minus the cash rate.

Basis point 1/100th of 1 percent, or 0.001; 100 basis points equals 1 percent.

Basis risk The uncertainty that the futures rate minus the cash rate will vary from that expected.

Beneficiary The recipient of the balance in a trust account upon termination of the trust.

Bid price The price at which someone has offered to buy an asset.

BIF Bank Insurance Fund which insures deposits at commercial banks.

Board of directors Individuals elected by stockholders to manage and oversee a firm's operations.

Bond An interest-bearing security representing a debt obligation of the issuer.

Bond rating The subjective assessment of the likelihood that a borrower will make timely interest and principal payments as scheduled. Letters are assigned to a security by rating agencies to reflect estimated creditworthiness.

Book value Accounting value typically measured as historical cost minus depreciation.

Branch banking An organizational structure in which a bank maintains facilities that are part of the bank in offices different from its home office. Some states allow banks to set up branches through the state, county, or city. Others prohibit branches.

Call loan A loan that is callable on 24 hours' notice.

Call option An agreement in which the buyer has the right to buy a fixed amount of the underlying asset at a set price for a specified period of time.

Call provision A provision in a bond that allows the issuer to redeem the bond, typically at a premium over par, prior to maturity.

Cap   Use of options to place a ceiling on a firm's borrowing costs.

Capital   Funds subscribed and paid by stockholders representing ownership in a bank. Regulatory capital also includes debt components and loss reserves.

Capital gain (loss)   Profit (loss) resulting from the sale of an asset for more (less) than its purchase price.

Card bank   Bank that administers its own credit card plan or serves as a primary regional agent of a national credit card operation.

Cash basis   The accounting procedure that recognizes revenues when cash is actually received and expenses when cash is actually paid.

Cash budget   A comparison of cash receipts and cash expenditures over a period of time.

Cash letter   Transit letter on tape that lists items submitted between banks for collection.

Cash market   The spot market for the immediate exchange of goods and services for immediate payment.

Cash-to-cash asset cycle
The time it takes to accumulate cash, purchase inventory, produce a finished

good, sell it, and collect on the sale.

Cash-to-cash liability cycle   The length of time to obtain interest-free financing from suppliers in the form of accounts payable and accrued expenses.

Cash-to-cash working capital cycle   The timing difference between the cash-to-cash asset cycle and the cash-to-cash liability cycle.

Certificate of deposit (CD)   A large-denomination time deposit representing the receipt of funds for deposit at a bank.

Charge-off   The act of writing off a loan to its present value in recognition that the asset has decreased in value.

Charter   A document that authorizes a bank to conduct business.

Check kiting   The process of writing checks against uncollected deposits while checks are in the process of collection, thereby using funds (float) not actually available.

Chinese wall   The imaginary barrier that ensures a trust department will manage trust assets for the benefit of the trust beneficiaries, not for other departments in the bank.

Clearinghouse association   A voluntary association of banks formed to assist the daily exchange of checks among member institutions.

CMO   Collateralized mortgage obligation—a security backed by a pool of mortgages, which is structured to fall within an estimated maturity range (tranche) based on the timing of allocated interest and principal payments on the underlying mortgages.

Collar   Use of options to place a cap and floor on a firm's borrowing costs.

Collateral   Property a borrower pledges as security against a loan for repayment if the borrower defaults.

Collected balances
Ledger balances minus float.

Commercial loan theory
A theory suggesting that banks make only short-term, self-liquidating loans that match the maturity of bank deposits.

Commercial paper   A short-term unsecured promissory note of a prime corporation.

Commitment fee   Fee charged for making a line of credit available to a borrower.

Compensating balance   A deposit balance required as compensation for services provided by a lender or correspondent bank.

Conservator   An individual or trust department appointed by a court to manage the property of an incapacitated individual.

Consolidated balance sheet A balance sheet showing the aggregate financial condition of a firm and its subsidiaries, netting out all intracompany transactions.

Consumer bank A bank that does not make commercial loans.

Contingent liabilities Items, such as guarantees or related contracts, that may become liabilities if certain developments arise in the future.

Conventional mortgage A mortgage or deed of trust that is not obtained under a government-insured program.

Conversion fee Fee charged for converting a loan commitment to a term loan.

Convertible debt A bond that may be exchanged for common stock in the same firm.

Core capital Tier 1 capital consisting primarily of stockholders' equity.

Core deposits A base level of deposits a bank expects to remain on deposit, regardless of the economic environment.

Correspondent bank A bank that provides services, typically check clearing, to other banks.

Country risk The credit risk that government or private borrowers in a specific country will refuse to repay their debts as obligated for other than pure economic reasons.

Coupon rate The ratio of the dollar-valued coupon payment to a security's par value.

Covenant An element of a loan agreement whereby the borrower agrees to meet specific performance requirements or refrain from certain behavior.

Credit bureau An association that collects and provides information on the credit (payment) histories of borrowers.

Credit department The bank department where credit information is collected and analyzed to make credit decisions.

Credit file Information related to a borrower's loan request, including application, record of past performance, loan documentation and analyst opinions.

Credit risk Potential variation in net income and market value of equity resulting from the nonpayment of interest and principal.

Cross hedge Use of a futures contract for a specific asset that differs from the cash asset being hedged.

Current ratio The ratio of current assets to current liabilities that indicates a firm's ability to pay current debts when they come due.

Customer profitability analysis A procedure that compares revenues with expenses and the bank's target profit from a customer's total account relationship.

Cyclical liquidity needs An estimate of liquid funds needed to cover deposit outflows or loan demand in excess of trend or seasonal factors.

Daylight overdrafts Bank payments from deposits held at a Federal Reserve bank or correspondent bank in excess of actual collected balances during a day.

Debenture A long-term bond that is secured by the general performance of the issuer.

Debit card A plastic card that, when used, immediately reduces the balance in a customer's transactions deposit.

Defalcation The misappropriation of funds or property by an individual.

Default The failure to make obligated interest and principal payments on a loan.

Deferred availability credit items Checks received for collection for which a bank has not provided credit to the depositor.

Delivery date Specific day that a futures contract expires.

Demand deposit Transactions account, payable on demand, that pays no interest to the depositor.

Depreciation Writing down the value of a capital asset, reported as an expense. Also, a decrease in the market value of a financial asset.

Direct loan Loan with terms negotiated directly between the lender and actual user of the funds.

Discount rate Interest rate charged by Federal Reserve banks for borrowing from the discount window.

Discount window The process of Federal Reserve banks lending to member institutions.

Draft A written order requesting one party to make payment to another party at a specified point in time.

Duration gap The weighted duration of assets minus the product of the weighted duration of liabilities and the ratio of total liabilities to total assets.

Early withdrawal penalty An interest penalty a depositor pays for withdrawing funds from a deposit account prior to maturity.

Earning assets Income-earning assets held by a bank.

Earnings credit Interest rate applied to investable balances.

Earnings dilution A decrease in earnings per share after one bank acquires another.

Economies of scale Cost efficiencies evidenced by low operating costs per unit of output.

Edge corporation A bank subsidiary that engages in international banking activities.

Elasticity A measure of the relative quantity response to a change in price, income, interest rate, or other variable.

Equity Ownership interest in a firm represented by common and preferred stockholders.

Equity multiplier Ratio of total assets to equity; a measure of financial leverage.

Eurocurrency A financial claim denominated in a currency other than the one where the issuing institution is located.

Eurodollars Dollar-denominated deposits at banks located outside the United States.

Exchange rate Price of one currency in terms of another.

Executor An individual or trust department responsible for handling settlement.

Facility fee Fee imposed for making a line of credit available.

Factoring An advance of credit whereby one party purchases the accounts receivable of another party at a discount, without recourse.

Fannie Mae Name referring to the Federal National Mortgage Association.

Federal funds Unsecured short-term loans that are settled in immediately available funds.

FHA Federal Housing Administration—a federal agency that insures mortgages.

FHLMC Federal Home Loan Mortgage Corporation (Freddie Mac)—a private corporation operating with an implicit federal guarantee that buys mortgages financed largely by mortgage-backed securities.

Fiduciary An individual or trust department responsible for acting in the best interests of a designated third party.

Finance charge The aggregate dollar amount of funds paid to obtain credit.

Financial futures contract A commitment between two parties to exchange a standardized financial asset through an organized exchange at a specified price for future delivery. The price of futures contracts changes prior to delivery, and participants must settle daily changes in contract value.

Financial leverage Relationship between the amount of debt versus equity financing.

Financial risk Potential variation in income before interest and taxes associated with fixed interest payments on debt and lease payments.

Financial services holding company A parent company owns a bank holding company plus other subsidiaries such as a thrift holding company and insurance subsidiary.

Fixed rate An interest rate that does not change during a specified period of time.

Float Dollar amount of checks in process of collection, net of deferred availability amounts, to depositors.

Floating rate An interest rate tied to a base rate that changes over time as market conditions dictate.

Floor Use of options to establish a minimum borrowing cost.

FNMA Federal National Mortgage Association (Fannie Mae)—a private corporation operating with an implicit federal guarantee that buys mortgages financed by mortgage-backed securities.

Foreclosure Selling property in order to apply the proceeds in payment of a debt.

Foreign exchange Currency of a foreign country acceptable as a medium of exchange.

Foreign tax credit Income taxes paid to a foreign country that can be claimed as a tax credit against a domestic tax liability.

Forward contract A commitment between two parties to exchange a nonstandardized asset at a fixed price for future delivery. The price of the contract does not change prior to delivery, and no interim payments are required.

Forward rate Yield on a forward contract. Also, break even yield calculated under pure expectations theory according to prevailing interest rates.

Funding GAP Dollar value of rate-sensitive assets minus the dollar value of rate-sensitive liabilities.

Garnishment A court directive authorizing a bank to withhold funds from a borrower.

General obligation bonds Municipal bonds secured by the full faith, credit, and taxing power of the issuing state or local government.

Ginnie Mae Name referring to the Government National Mortgage Association.

GNMA Government National Mortgage Association (Ginnie Mae)—a government entity that buys mortgages for low-income

housing and guarantees mortgage-backed securities issued by private lenders.

Goodwill An intangible asset representing the difference between the book value of an asset or firm and the actual sales price.

Grandfather clause A legislative provision that exempts parties previously engaged in activities prohibited by new legislation.

Guarantee Make oneself liable for the debts of another.

Guardian An individual or trust department appointed by a court to manage a minor's property or personal affairs.

Hedge Take a position in the forward or futures market to offset risk associated with cash market activity.

Highly leveraged transaction (HLT) Transaction in which borrower's debt increases sharply after the asset exchange, such as an LBO.

Home debit A check drawn on a bank that is presented to the same bank for deposit or payment.

Home equity loan Loan secured by an individual's equity in a home.

Hot money Funds that move between institutions quickly in search of higher yields or greater safety.

Immediately available funds Collected deposits held at Federal Reserve banks or certain collected liabilities of private financial institutions.

Independent bank A bank operating in one locality that is not part of a large multibank holding company or group of banks.

Indirect loan Loan in which a retailer takes the credit application and negotiates terms with the actual borrower. The lender then purchases the loan from the retailer under prearranged terms.

Individual retirement account A retirement account available to individuals to defer income taxes.

Insolvency The inability to pay obligated debts as they come due.

Installment loan A loan that is payable in periodic, partial installments.

Interest rate risk Potential variability in a bank's net interest income and market value of equity caused by changes in the level of interest rates.

Internal audit Routine examination of a bank's accounting records.

Inter vivos Phrase referring to "between living persons."

Inverted yield curve Yield curve with long-term rates below short-term rates.

Investable balances Ledger balances minus float minus required reserves against associated deposit balances.

Investment banking Activity involving securities underwriting, making a market in securities, and arranging mergers and acquisitions.

IO Interest-only security representing the interest portion of a stripped Treasury or stripped mortgage-backed security.

Judgment Legal ruling regarding the final payment of a court-determined transfer of assets.

Judgmental credit analysis Subjective assessment of a borrower's ability and willingness to repay debts.

Kite Writing checks against uncollected deposits in the process of clearing through the banking system.

Lagged reserve accounting System of reserve requirements based on deposits outstanding prior to the reserve maintenance period.

LBO Leveraged buyout.

Lease A contract in which the owner of a property allows another party to use the property if certain terms are met and lease payments (rent) are made.

Ledger balances Dollar value of deposit balances appearing on a bank's books.

Lender liability Circumstances in which the courts have found lenders liable to their borrowers for fraud, deception, breached fiduciary activities, broken promises, and good faith negotiations.

Letter of credit A bank's guarantee of payment, indicated by a document that describes the handling of a specific transaction.

Liability management theory A theory that focuses on banks issuing liabilities to meet liquidity needs.

Lien Legal right granted by the court to attach property until a legal claim is paid.

Limited branching Provisions that restrict branching to a geographic area smaller than an entire state.

Line of credit A lending agreement between a bank and borrower in which the bank makes a fixed amount of funds available to the borrower for a specified period of time. The customer determines the timing of actual borrowing.

Liquidity risk The variation in net income and market value of bank equity caused by a bank's difficulty in obtaining immediately available funds, either by borrowing or selling assets.

Loan commitment Formal agreement between a bank and borrower to provide a fixed amount of credit for a specified period.

Loan participation Credit extended to a borrower in which members of a group of lenders each provide a fraction of the total financing; typically arises because individual banks are limited in the amount of credit they can extend to a single customer.

Loan-to-value ratio The loan amount divided by the appraised value of the underlying collateral.

London interbank offer rate Interest rate at which banks deposit Eurodollars with other banks outside the United States.

Long hedge The purchase of a futures contract to reduce the risk of an increase in the price of a cash asset.

Long position Market position in which an investor actually owns an asset.

Long-term securities Securities with maturities in excess of 1 year.

Make a market Stand ready to buy or sell particular assets.

Margin Deposit with a broker that protects the broker from losses arising from customer transactions.

Marginal cost of funds The incremental cost of additional funds to finance firm operations.

Marginal tax rate Tax rate applied to the last increment of taxable income.

Mark to market Requirement that futures traders must deposit additional cash with a broker to cover a decline in the current value of margin.

Market value The actual value indicating what an asset can be currently sold for.

Maturity The date at which the principal of a note, draft, or bond becomes due and payable.

MBS Mortgage-backed security—a security that evidences an undivided interest in the ownership of a pool of mortgages.

Money market deposit account Small time deposit whose holder is limited to three written checks per month.

Money market mutual fund Mutual fund that accepts customer funds and purchases short-term marketable securities.

Mortgage A contract whereby a borrower provides a lender with a lien on real property as security against a loan.

Multibank holding company A bank holding company that owns controlling interest in at least two commercial banks.

Municipals Securities issued by states, local governments, and their political subdivisions.

Mutual savings banks Firms without capital stock that accept deposits and make loans.

Negotiable order of withdrawal Interest-bearing transactions account offered by banks.

Net interest margin Ratio of net interest income to total earning assets.

Net overhead burden Difference between noninterest expense and noninterest income as a fraction of total bank assets.

Net worth Owners' (stockholders') equity in a firm.

Nominal interest rate Market interest rate stated in current, not real, dollars.

Nonperforming loan Loan for which an obligated interest payment is past due.

Nonrate gap Noninterest-bearing liabilities plus equity minus nonearning assets as a fraction of earning assets.

Nonrecourse Holder of an obligation has no legal right to force payment on a claim.

Off-balance sheet activities Commitments, such as loan guarantees, that do not appear on a bank's balance sheet but represent actual contractual obligations.

One bank holding company A holding company that owns or controls only one commercial bank.

Open account Credit not supported by a note or other written record.

Open interest Total number of outstanding unfilled futures positions measured on one side of the transaction.

Operating income Sum of interest income and non-interest income.

Operating leverage Ratio of fixed costs to total costs; measure of business risk that indicates the relative change in operating income that arises from a change in sales.

Option Right to buy or sell a specific asset at a fixed price during a specified interval of time.

Other real estate owned Real estate owned by a bank that is acquired in settlement of debts.

Overdraft Depositor writing a check for an amount greater than the deposit balance.

Overhead Expenses that generally do not vary with the level of output.

PAC Planned amortization class CMO—a security that is retired according to a planned amortization schedule, while payments to other classes of securities are slowed or accelerated. The objective is to ensure that PACs exhibit highly predictable maturities and cash flows.

Par value Dollar value of a bond's principal payment at maturity; face value printed on a security.

Passbook savings Nonnegotiable, small savings account evidenced by a passbook listing the account terms.

Pass-through security Instrument secured by mortgages in which the mortgage banker passes mortgage interest and principal payments to the holder of the security minus a servicing charge.

Peer group Sample firms used to generate average reference data for comparison with an individual firm's performance data.

Permanent working capital Minimum level of current assets minus minimum level of current liabilities net of short-term bank credit and current maturity of long-term debt; represents the amount of long-term financing required for current assets.

Perpetual preferred stock Nonmaturing preferred stock.

Personal banker Individual assigned to a bank customer to handle a broad range of financial services.

Pledged securities Bank securities pledged as collateral against public deposit, borrowings from Federal Reserve banks, and securities sold under agreement to repurchase.

PO Principal-only security representing the principal portion of a stripped Treasury or stripped mortgage-backed security.

Point of sale Electronic terminals that enable customers to directly access deposit accounts.

Preferred stock Class of stock representing ownership with a claim on firm income senior to common stock.

Premium Difference between the price of a bond and its par value when the price is higher.

Primary capital The sum of common stock, perpetual preferred stock, surplus, undivided profits, contingency and other capital reserves, valuation reserves, mandatory convertible securities, and minority interest in consolidated subsidiaries at a bank.

Prime rate One of several base interest rates used as an index to price commercial loans.

Pro forma financial statements Projected or forecast balance sheet and income statements.

Probate Legal act of submitting a will before a court to verify authenticity of the document.

Problem loans Loans currently in default or expected to obtain default status.

Prudent man rule Requirement that a fiduciary exercise discretion, prudence, and sound judgment in managing the assets of a third party.

Put Option to sell an asset (security) for a fixed price during a specific interval of time.

Quality spread Difference in the yield differential representing fixed rate and floating rate borrowing costs for participants in an interest rate swap.

Rate sensitive Classification of assets and liabilities that can be repriced within a specific time frame, either because they mature or carry floating or variable rates.

Rating System of assigning letters to security issues indicating the perceived default risk associated with that class of issues.

Real interest rate Interest rate after inflation expectations are netted from a nominal interest rate.

Rebate The return of a portion of unearned interest to a borrower.

Recourse Legal right to enforce a claim against another party.

Repurchase agreement (RP) Short-term loans secured by government

securities and settled in immediately available funds.

Reserve for bank debts Amount appearing on a bank's balance sheet that represents the estimated value of uncollectable loans.

Reserve requirement ratios Percentages applied to transactions accounts and time deposits to determine the dollar amount of required reserve assets.

Reserves Qualifying assets to meet reserve requirements, including vault cash and deposit balances held at Federal Reserve banks.

Respondent bank Bank that purchases services from a correspondent bank.

Return on assets Net income divided by average total assets.

Return on equity Net income divided by average stockholders' equity.

Revenue bond Municipal bond issued to finance a project in which debt service payments are secured by specific revenues from the project.

Reverse repurchase agreement Securities purchased under an agreement to resell them at a later date.

Revolver Loan commitment or line of credit that converts to a term loan.

Risk assets Total assets minus cash and due from balances minus U.S. government securities.

Run on a bank Situation in which a large number of depositors lose confidence in the safety of their deposits and attempt to withdraw their funds.

Safe deposit box Privacy boxes for storage located in a bank vault under lock and key.

SAIF Savings Association Insurance Fund which insures deposits at thrift institutions.

Sale and lease back Transaction in which an asset is sold, with title exchanged to a lessor, that leases the asset to the original owner.

Seasonal liquidity needs Cash flow needs that arise from predictable seasonal loan demands and deposit outflows.

Secondary capital Limited life preferred stock, subordinated debt, and mandatory convertible securities not included as primary capital.

Security Collateral a borrower pledges against a loan or secondary source of repayment in case of default.

Security interest The legal claim on property that secures a debt or the performance of an obligation.

Service charges Fees imposed for bank services.

Short hedge Sale of a futures contract to protect against a price decline.

Short position The sale of an asset not owned.

Short-term securities Securities that mature in 1 year or less.

Sight draft A draft payable "on sight."

Simple interest Interest applied against principal only.

Speculator Trader who takes a position to increase risk in hope of earning extraordinary returns.

Spot market Market for immediate delivery of assets.

Statewide branching Allowing banks to establish branches throughout an entire state.

Stop payment Request by a depositor to stop payment on a previously issued check that has not yet cleared.

Strategic planning The process through which managers formulate the firm's mission and goals, and identify strengths, weaknesses, opportunities, and threats.

Strike price Fixed price at which an asset may be purchased in a call option or sold under a put option.

Swap Simultaneous purchase and sale of like securities to alter the portfolio composition and characteristics.

Syndicate Group of banks that jointly negotiate a contract to sell securities or make loans.

Takedown Actual borrowing against a line of credit or loan commitment.

Tax anticipation note Short-term municipal security issued in anticipation of future tax receipts and repaid from same.

Tax credit Direct reduction in tax liability arising from qualifying expenditures.

Tax-equivalent yield Tax-exempt interest yield converted to a pretax taxable equivalent by dividing the nominal rate by 1 minus the investor's marginal income tax rate.

Term loan Loan with a maturity beyond 1 year, typically repaid from the borrower's future cash flow.

Thrifts Savings and loan associations, savings banks, and mutual savings banks.

Trading account Inventory of securities held by a bank making a market for sale and purchase.

Tranche The principal amount related to a specific class of stated maturities on a collateralized mortgage obligation.

Transactions account Deposit account on which a customer can write checks.

Transit item Checks drawn on banks located outside the community of the bank in which they are deposited.

Transfer pricing The pricing of funds transferred between organizational units of a bank, such as determining the cost of collecting deposits and borrowed funds to finance a loan.

Trust A property interest held by one party for the benefit of another.

Trustee Individual or firm charged with managing trust assets.

Underwrite Purchase securities from the initial issuer and distribute them to investors.

Undivided profits Retained earnings or cumulative net income not paid out as dividends.

Unearned interest Interest received prior to completion of the underlying contract.

Unit bank Single, independent bank with one home office.

Usury Interest charges in excess of that legally allowed for that specific instrument.

VA Veterans Administration—a federal agency that insures mortgages.

Valuation reserve Loan-loss reserve reported on the balance sheet; losses can be charged only against this reserve.

Variable rate Automatic repricing, usually by changing the interest rate, at regular intervals.

Volatile deposits Difference between actual outstanding deposits and core deposits; represents balances with a high probability of being withdrawn.

Weighted marginal cost of funds Marginal cost of pooled debt funds used in pricing decisions.

Yield curve Diagram relating market interest rates to term-to-maturity on securities that differ only in terms of maturity.

Yield rate Tax-equivalent interest income divided by earning assets.

Zero GAP Rate-sensitive assets equal rate-sensitive liabilities.

Z-tranche The final class of securities in a CMO exhibiting the longest maturity and greatest price volatility. These securities often accrue interest until all other classes are retired.

Name Index

Subject Index